Lecture Notes in Computer Science   11272

Commenced Publication in 1973
Founding and Former Series Editors:
Gerhard Goos, Juris Hartmanis, and Jan van Leeuwen

More information about this series at http://www.springer.com/series/7410

Thomas Peyrin · Steven Galbraith (Eds.)

Advances in Cryptology – ASIACRYPT 2018

24th International Conference on the Theory
and Application of Cryptology and Information Security
Brisbane, QLD, Australia, December 2–6, 2018
Proceedings, Part I

 Springer

Editors
Thomas Peyrin (iD)
Nanyang Technological University
Singapore, Singapore

Steven Galbraith
University of Auckland
Auckland, New Zealand

ISSN 0302-9743   ISSN 1611-3349   (electronic)
Lecture Notes in Computer Science
ISBN 978-3-030-03325-5   ISBN 978-3-030-03326-2   (eBook)
https://doi.org/10.1007/978-3-030-03326-2

Library of Congress Control Number: 2018959424

LNCS Sublibrary: SL4 – Security and Cryptology

This Springer imprint is published by the registered company Springer Nature Switzerland AG
The registered company address is: Gewerbestrasse 11, 6330 Cham, Switzerland

Preface

ASIACRYPT 2018, the 24th Annual International Conference on Theory and Application of Cryptology and Information Security, was held in Brisbane, Australia, during December 2–6, 2018.

The conference focused on all technical aspects of cryptology, and was sponsored by the International Association for Cryptologic Research (IACR).

Asiacrypt 2018 received a total of 234 submissions from all over the world. The Program Committee selected 65 papers for publication in the proceedings of this conference. The review process was made by the usual double-blind peer review by the Program Committee, which consisted of 47 leading experts of the field. Each submission was reviewed by at least three reviewers and five reviewers were assigned to submissions co-authored by Program Committee members. This year, the conference operated a two-round review system with rebuttal phase. In the first-round review the Program Committee selected the 145 submissions that were considered of value for proceeding to the second round. In the second-round phase the Program Committee further reviewed the submissions by taking into account their rebuttal letter from the authors. The selection process was assisted by a total of 347 external reviewers. These three-volume proceedings contain the revised versions of the papers that were selected. The revised versions were not reviewed again and the authors are responsible for their contents.

The program of Asiacrypt 2018 featured three excellent invited talks by Mitsuru Matsui, Melissa Chase, and Vanessa Teague. The conference also featured a traditional rump session that contained short presentations on the latest research results of the field. The Program Committee selected the work "Block Cipher Invariants as Eigenvectors of Correlation Matrices" by Tim Beyne for the Best Paper Award of Asiacrypt 2018. Two more papers, "Learning Strikes Again: the Case of the DRS Signature Scheme" by Yang Yu and Léo Ducas, and "Tighter Security Proofs for GPV-IBE in the Quantum Random Oracle Model" by Shuichi Katsumata, Shota Yamada, and Takashi Yamakawa, were solicited to submit the full versions to the *Journal of Cryptology*. The program chairs selected Chris Brzuska and Bart Mennink for the Best PC Member Award.

Many people contributed to the success of Asiacrypt 2018. We would like to thank the authors for submitting their research results to the conference. We are very grateful to all of the PC members as well as the external reviewers for their fruitful comments and discussions on their areas of expertise. We are greatly indebted to Josef Pieprzyk, the general chair, for his efforts and overall organization. We would also like to thank Waleed Alkalabi, Niluka Arasinghe, Mir Ali Rezazadeh Baee, Lynn Batten, Xavier Boyen, Ed Dawson, Ernest Foo, Mukhtar Hassan, Udyani Herath, Qingyi Li, Georg Lippold, Matthew McKague, Basker Palaniswamy, Anisur Rahman, Leonie Simpson, Shriparen Sriskandarajah, Gabrielle Stephens, and Chathurika Don Wickramage, the local Organizing Committee for their continuous support. We thank Craig Costello, Léo Ducas, and Pierre Karpman for expertly organizing and chairing the rump session.

Finally we thank Shai Halevi for letting us use his nice software for the paper submission and review process. We also thank Alfred Hofmann, Anna Kramer, and their colleagues for handling the editorial process of the proceedings published in Springer's LNCS series.

December 2018   Thomas Peyrin
                                                 Steven Galbraith

ASIACRYPT 2018

**The 24th Annual International Conference on Theory
and Application of Cryptology and Information Security**

Sponsored by the International Association for Cryptologic Research (IACR)

December 2–6, 2018, Brisbane, Australia

General Chair

Josef Pieprzyk   CSIRO, Data61, Australia

Program Co-chairs

Thomas Peyrin   Nanyang Technological University, Singapore
Steven Galbraith   University of Auckland, New Zealand

Program Committee

Martin Albrecht	Royal Holloway University of London, UK
Prabhanjan Ananth	MIT, USA
Lejla Batina	Radboud University, The Netherlands
Sonia Belaïd	CryptoExperts, France
Daniel J. Bernstein	University of Illinois at Chicago, USA
Chris Brzuska	Aalto University, Finland
Bernardo David	Tokyo Institute of Technology, Japan
Nico Döttling	Friedrich-Alexander University Erlangen-Nürnberg, Germany
Léo Ducas	CWI, The Netherlands
Jens Groth	University College London, UK
Dawu Gu	Shanghai Jiao Tong University, China
Goichiro Hanaoka	AIST, Japan
Viet Tung Hoang	Florida State University, USA
Takanori Isobe	University of Hyogo, Japan
Jérémy Jean	ANSSI, France
Stefan Kölbl	Technical University of Denmark, Denmark
Ilan Komargodski	Cornell Tech, USA
Kaoru Kurosawa	Ibaraki University, Japan
Virginie Lallemand	Ruhr-Universität Bochum, Germany
Gaëtan Leurent	Inria, France
Benoît Libert	CNRS and ENS de Lyon, France
Helger Lipmaa	University of Tartu, Estonia

Atul Luykx	Visa Research, USA
Stefan Mangard	TU Graz, Austria
Bart Mennink	Radboud University, The Netherlands
Brice Minaud	Royal Holloway University of London, UK
Mridul Nandi	Indian Statistical Institute, India
Khoa Nguyen	Nanyang Technological University, Singapore
Svetla Nikova	KU Leuven, Belgium
Elisabeth Oswald	University of Bristol, UK
Arpita Patra	Indian Institute of Science, India
Giuseppe Persiano	Università di Salerno, Italy and Google, USA
Carla Ràfols	Universitat Pompeu Fabra, Spain
Amin Sakzad	Monash University, Australia
Jae Hong Seo	Hanyang University, Korea
Ling Song	Institute of Information Engineering, Chinese Academy of Sciences, China
	Nanyang Technological University, Singapore
Douglas Stebila	University of Waterloo, Canada
Marc Stevens	CWI, The Netherlands
Qiang Tang	New Jersey Institute of Technology, USA
Mehdi Tibouchi	NTT laboratories, Japan
Yosuke Todo	NTT Secure Platform Laboratories, Japan
Dominique Unruh	University of Tartu, Estonia
Gilles Van Assche	STMicroelectronics, Belgium
Frederik Vercauteren	KU Leuven, Belgium
Bo-Yin Yang	Academia Sinica, Taiwan
Yu Yu	Shanghai Jiao Tong University, China
Aaram Yun	UNIST, Korea

External Reviewers

Behzad Abdolmaleki
Aysajan Abidin
Shweta Agrawal
Estuardo Alpirez Bock
Joël Alwen
Abdelrahaman Aly
Andris Ambainis
Elena Andreeva
Jan-Pieter d'Anvers
Kazumaro Aoki
Nuttapong Attrapadung
Karim Baghery
Shi Bai
Gustavo Banegas
Subhadeep Banik

Paulo Barreto
Gilles Barthe
Hridam Basu
Aurélie Bauer
Carsten Baum
Christof Beierle
Adi Ben-Zvi
Ela Berners-Lee
David Bernhard
Pauline Bert
Ward Beullens
Rishiraj Bhattacharyya
Jean-Francois Biasse
Nina Bindel
Bruno Blanchet

Olivier Blazy
Xavier Bonnetain
Charlotte Bonte
Carl Bootland
Jonathan Bootle
Cecilia Boschini
Raphael Bost
Christina Boura
Florian Bourse
Dusan Bozilov
Andreas Brasen Kidmose
Jacqueline Brendel
Ignacio Cascudo
Dario Catalano
Andrea Cerulli
Avik Chakraborty
Debrup Chakraborty
Long Chen
Yu Chen
Yu Long Chen
Wonhee Cho
Ashish Choudhury
Chitchanok Chuengsatiansup
Michele Ciampi
Sandro Coretti
Alain Couvreur
Ben Curtis
Dana Dachman-Soled
Joan Daemen
Nilanjan Datta
Pratish Datta
Alex Davidson
Thomas De Cnudde
Luca De Feo
Lauren De Meyer
Gabrielle de Micheli
Fabrizio De Santis
Rafael Del Pino
Cyprien Delpech de Saint Guilhem
Yi Deng
Amit Deo
David Derler
Apoorvaa Deshpande
Lin Ding
Ning Ding
Christoph Dobraunig

Rafael Dowsley
Alexandre Duc
Avijit Dutta
Ratna Dutta
Sébastien Duval
Edward Eaton
Maria Eichlseder
Ali El Kaafarani
Keita Emura
Naomi Ephraim
Muhammed Esgin
Thomas Espitau
Martianus Frederic Ezerman
Leo (Xiong) Fan
Antonio Faonio
Oriol Farràs
Prastudy Fauzi
Serge Fehr
Dario Fiore
Tore Frederiksen
Thomas Fuhr
Eiichiro Fujisaki
Benjamin Fuller
Philippe Gaborit
Clemente Galdi
Nicolas Gama
Chaya Ganesh
Si Gao
Luke Garratt
Romain Gay
Nicholas Genise
Rosario Gennaro
Essam Ghadafi
Anirban Ghatak
Satrajit Ghosh
Junqing Gong
Alonso González
Hannes Gross
Paul Grubbs
Charles Guillemet
Siyao Guo
Qian Guo
Kyoohyung Han
Javier Herranz
Julia Hesse
Harunaga Hiwatari

Thang Hoang
Dennis Hofheinz
Seungwan Hong
Akinori Hosoyamada
Kathrin Hövelmanns
James Howe
Andreas Huelsing
Ilia Iliashenko
Ai Ishida
Masahito Ishizaka
Mitsugu Iwamoto
Tetsu Iwata
Håkon Jacobsen
Christian Janson
Dirmanto Jap
Jinhyuck Jeong
Ashwin Jha
Luke Johnson
Antoine Joux
Pierre Karpman
Shuichi Katsumata
Andrey Kim
Dongwoo Kim
Duhyeong Kim
Jeongsu Kim
Jihye Kim
Jiseung Kim
Myungsun Kim
Elena Kirshanova
Fuyuki Kitagawa
Susumu Kiyoshima
Yashvanth Kondi
Ben Kreuter
Toomas Krips
Veronika Kuchta
Marie-Sarah Lacharite
Junzuo Lai
Esteban Landerreche
Tanja Lange
Joohee Lee
Iraklis Leontiadis
Tancrède Lepoint
Jie Li
Qinyi Li
Shun Li
Wei Li

Xiangyu Li
Fuchun Lin
Donxi Liu
Fukang Liu
Hanlin Liu
Junrong Liu
Shengli Liu
Ya Liu
Zhen Liu
Zhiqiang Liu
Victor Lomne
Yu Long
Xianhui Lu
Yuan Lu
Chen Lv
Shunli Ma
Xuecheng Ma
Rusydi Makarim
Giulio Malavolta
Mary Maller
Alex Malozemoff
Yoshifumi Manabe
Avradip Mandal
Mark Manulis
Marco Martinoli
Daniel Masny
Pedro Maat Costa Massolino
Takahiro Matsuda
Alexander May
Sogol Mazaheri
Patrick McCorry
Florian Mendel
Peihan Miao
Vincent Migliore
Kazuhiko Minematsu
Matthias Minihold
Takaaki Mizuki
Andrew Morgan
Paz Morillo
Fabrice Mouhartem
Pratyay Mukherjee
Alireza Naghipour
Yusuke Naito
Maria Naya-Plasencia
Ryo Nishimaki
Ariel Nof

Wakaha Ogata
Emmanuela Orsini
Rafail Ostrovsky
Carles Padró
Tapas Pandit
Louiza Papachristodoulou
Alain Passelègue
Kenny Paterson
Goutam Paul
Michaël Peeters
Chris Peikert
Massimo Perillo
Léo Perrin
Edoardo Persichetti
Peter Pessl
Thomas Peters
Christophe Petit
Stjepan Picek
Zaira Pindado
Bertram Poettering
Eamonn Postlethwaite
Thomas Prest
Emmanuel Prouff
Elizabeth Quaglia
Adrián Ranea
Shahram Rasoolzadeh
Divya Ravi
Ling Ren
Guénaël Renault
Joost Renes
Joost Rijneveld
Thomas Roche
Paul Rösler
Mélissa Rossi
Dragos Rotaru
Yann Rotella
Arnab Roy
Sujoy Sinha Roy
Sylvain Ruhault
Mohammad Sabt
Mohammad Reza Sadeghi
Yusuke Sakai
Simona Samardzijska
Olivier Sanders
John Schanck
Peter Scholl

André Schrottenloher
Jacob Schuldt
Peter Schwabe
Danping Shi
Kyoji Shibutani
SeongHan Shin
Ferdinand Sibleyras
Janno Siim
Javier Silva
Thierry Simon
Luisa Siniscalchi
Kit Smeets
Yongha Son
Gabriele Spini
Christoph Sprenger
Martijn Stam
Damien Stehle
Ron Steinfeld
Joshua Stock
Ko Stoffelen
Shifeng Sun
Siwei Sun
Moon Sung Lee
Koutarou Suzuki
Alan Szepieniec
Akira Takahashi
Katsuyuki Takashima
Benjamin Tan
Adrian Thillard
Jean-Pierre Tillich
Elmar Tischhauser
Radu Titiu
Junichi Tomida
Ni Trieu
Boaz Tsaban
Thomas Unterluggauer
Christine Van Vredendaal
Prashant Vasudevan
Serge Vaudenay
Philip Vejre
Muthuramakrishnan
    Venkitasubramaniam
Daniele Venturi
Benoît Viguier
Jorge L. Villar
Srinivas Vivek

Antonia Wachter-Zeh
Alexandre Wallet
Michael Walter
Peng Wang
Ping Wang
Yuyu Wang
Man Wei
Zihao Wei
Friedrich Wiemer
Tim Wood
Joanne Woodage
Thomas Wunderer
Keita Xagawa
Haiyang Xue
Shota Yamada
Takashi Yamakawa
Avishay Yanai
Kang Yang
Qianqian Yang
Kan Yasuda
Kevin Yeo

Scott Yilek
Kazuki Yoneyama
Jingyue Yu
Yang Yu
Xingliang Yuan
Thomas Zacharias
Michal Zajac
Rina Zeitoun
Mark Zhandry
Bin Zhang
Cong Zhang
Fan Zhang
Jiang Zhang
Juanyang Zhang
Ren Zhang
Yingjie Zhang
Raymond K. Zhao
Shuoyao Zhao
Linfeng Zhou
Vincent Zucca

Local Organizing Committee

General Chair

| Josef Pieprzyk | CSIRO, Data61, Australia |

Advisors

| Lynn Batten | Deakin University, Australia |
| Ed Dawson | QUT, Australia |

Members

Waleed Alkalabi	QUT, Australia
Niluka Arasinghe	QUT, Australia
Mir Ali Rezazadeh Baee	QUT, Australia
Xavier Boyen	QUT, Australia
Ernest Foo	QUT, Australia
Mukhtar Hassan	QUT, Australia
Udyani Herath	QUT, Australia
Qingyi Li	QUT, Australia
Georg Lippold	Mastercard, Australia
Matthew McKague	QUT, Australia
Basker Palaniswamy	QUT, Australia
Anisur Rahman	QUT, Australia

Leonie Simpson	QUT, Australia
Shriparen Sriskandarajah	QUT, Australia
Gabrielle Stephens	QUT, Australia
Chathurika Don Wickramage	QUT, Australia

Contents – Part I

Lattice-Based Cryptography

Quantum Symmetric Cryptanalysis

Zero-Knowledge

Contents – Part II

Contents – Part III

Asiacrypt 2018 Best Paper

Block Cipher Invariants as Eigenvectors of Correlation Matrices

Tim Beyne[(✉)]

imec-COSIC, KU Leuven, Leuven, Belgium
tim.beyne@esat.kuleuven.be

Abstract. A new approach to invariant subspaces and nonlinear invariants is developed. This results in both theoretical insights and practical attacks on block ciphers. It is shown that, with minor modifications to some of the round constants, Midori-64 has a nonlinear invariant with 2^{96} corresponding weak keys. Furthermore, this invariant corresponds to a linear hull with maximal correlation. By combining the new invariant with integral cryptanalysis, a practical key-recovery attack on 10 rounds of unmodified Midori-64 is obtained. The attack works for 2^{96} weak keys and irrespective of the choice of round constants. The data complexity is $1.25 \cdot 2^{21}$ chosen plaintexts and the computational cost is dominated by 2^{56} block cipher calls. Finally, it is shown that similar techniques lead to a practical key-recovery attack on MANTIS-4. The full key is recovered using 640 chosen plaintexts and the attack requires about 2^{56} block cipher calls.

Keywords: Invariant subspace attack · Nonlinear invariant attack
Linear cryptanalysis · Integral cryptanalysis · Correlation matrices
Midori-64 · MANTIS

1 Introduction

Block ciphers are an essential primitive for the construction of many cryptosystems. This leads to a natural desire to optimize them with respect to various application-dependent criteria. Examples include low-latency block ciphers such as PRINCE [6] and MANTIS [4], and the low-power design Midori-64 [2]. Biryukov and Perrin [5] give a broad overview of such *lightweight* primitives.

One requirement is shared by all applications: the block cipher must be secure – at the very least it must approximate a pseudorandom permutation. A common design decision that often helps to reduce latency, energy consumption and other cost measures is the simplification of the key-schedule. This, along with other aspects of lightweight designs, has led to the development of new cryptanalytic tools such as *invariant subspaces* [17] and *nonlinear invariants* [22]. These attacks are the subject of this paper.

This work was supported by the Research Council KU Leuven: C16/18/004.

T. Peyrin and S. Galbraith (Eds.): ASIACRYPT 2018, LNCS 11272, pp. 3–31, 2018.
https://doi.org/10.1007/978-3-030-03326-2_1

At CRYPTO 2017, it was shown by Beierle, Canteaut, Leander and Rotella that invariant attacks can often be averted by a careful choice of the round constants [3]. Their work, as well as the earlier work by Todo, Leander and Sasaki on nonlinear invariants [22], invites several questions. This paper will be concerned with three related problems that arise in this context.

1. In their future work sections, Todo *et al.* [22] and Beierle *et al.* [3] both express the desire to generalize the nonlinear invariant attack. One can argue that a deeper theoretical understanding of block cipher invariants is helpful, if not essential, to achieve this goal.
2. One potential generalization is the existence of block cipher invariants which are not invariants under all of the round transformations. It is important to investigate this possibility, because such cases are not covered by the techniques introduced by Beierle *et al.* for choosing the round constants.
3. The previous problem leads to a third question: do such (generalized) invariants *only* impact the security of the cipher for a specific choice of the round constants? The results in this paper suggest otherwise.

Contribution. The first of the problems listed above is addressed in Sect. 4, where the main contribution is Definition 2 and the discussion following it. It is shown that block cipher invariants have an effective description in terms of eigenvectors of *correlation matrices*. These matrices were first introduced by Daemen, Govaerts and Vandewalle [8] in the context of linear cryptanalysis [20]. As a side result, more insight into the relation between invariants and linear cryptanalysis is obtained.

Section 5 takes a closer look at the invariants of Midori-64, leading up to an example of an invariant of the type described in the second problem above. It will be shown in Sect. 5.3 that, with minor changes to the round constants, Midori-64 has an invariant which is not invariant under the round function. It applies to 2^{96} weak keys. Note that this is a significantly larger class of weak keys compared to previous work, *i.e.* 2^{32} for the invariant subspace attack of Guo *et al.* and 2^{64} for the nonlinear invariant attack of Todo *et al.* [22]. In fact, it will be demonstrated that the invariant discussed in Sect. 5.3 corresponds to a linear hull with maximal correlation. This observation is of independent interest and will be briefly discussed in Sect. 5.4.

Finally, Sects. 6 and 7 address the third question listed above. That is, two cryptanalytic results are given to demonstrate that block cipher invariants may impact the security of a block cipher regardless of the choice of round constants.

In Sect. 6, a practical attack on 10 rounds of Midori-64 – for any choice of round constants – will be given. The attack applies to 2^{96} weak keys and requires roughly $1.25 \cdot 2^{21}$ chosen plaintexts. The computational cost is dominated by 2^{56} block cipher calls. Note that the data complexity and especially the computational cost to determine whether a weak key is used, are significantly lower. As discussed by Luykx, Mennink and Paterson [19] in ASIACRYPT 2017, this has a significant impact on the multi-key security of the block cipher.

Section 7 shows that the full key of MANTIS-4 [4] can be recovered given 640 chosen plaintexts. This attack works for all keys provided that a weak tweak is used. The number of weak tweaks is 2^{32} (out of 2^{64}). The computational cost of this attack is dominated by 2^{56} block cipher calls.

2   Preliminaries and Related Work

Most of the notation used in this paper is standard, for instance $(\mathbb{F}_2, +, \cdot)$ denotes the field with two elements. Random variables are denoted in boldface.

Many of the results in this work can be compactly described by means of tensor products of real vector spaces. Let $V_1, \ldots, V_n$ be vector spaces over $\mathbb{R}$. Their tensor product is a real vector space $V_1 \otimes \cdots \otimes V_n$. Elements of $V_1 \otimes \cdots \otimes V_n$ will be called tensors. For $V = V_1 = \cdots = V_n$, the tensor product $V_1 \otimes \cdots \otimes V_n$ will be denoted by $V^{\otimes n}$. Knowledge of tensor products is not essential to understand this work.

The invariant subspace attack was introduced by Leander, Abdelraheem, AlKhzaimi and Zenner in the context of PRINTCIPHER [17]. Let $E_k : \mathbb{F}_2^n \to \mathbb{F}_2^n$ be a block cipher. An affine subspace $a + V$ of $\mathbb{F}_2^n$ such that

$$E_k(a + V) = a + V, \tag{1}$$

is called an invariant subspace for E_k. The keys k for which (1) holds, will be called weak keys. At ASIACRYPT 2016, Todo et al. introduced the *nonlinear invariant attack* as an extension of this attack [22]. A Boolean function $f : \mathbb{F}_2^n \to \mathbb{F}_2$ is called a nonlinear invariant for E_k iff there exists a constant $c \in \mathbb{F}_2$ such that for all $x \in \mathbb{F}_2^n$,

$$f(x) + f(E_k(x)) = c.$$

Importantly, the constant c may depend on the key k, but not on x.

The description of block cipher invariants in this paper is based on *correlation matrices*, which were first introduced by Daemen et al. [8]. The definition of these matrices has been postponed to Sect. 3, as they will be introduced from a novel point of view.

Finally, a brief description of Midori-64 is given here. This information will be used extensively in Sects. 5 and 6. Midori-64 is an iterated block cipher with a block size of 64 bits and a key length of 128 bits [2]. It operates on a 64-bit state, which can be represented as a 4×4 array of 4-bit *cells*. The round function consists of the operations SubCell ($\mathfrak{S}$), ShuffleCell (P), MixColumn ($\mathfrak{M}$) and a key addition layer. This structure is shown in Fig. 1.

The SubCell ($\mathfrak{S}$) mapping applies a 4-bit S-box S to each cell of the state. The fact that the S-box is an involution will be used in Sect. 5. The algebraic normal form of $S(x) = (S_1(x), S_2(x), S_3(x), S_4(x))$ is provided below. These expressions will not be used explicitly, but they can be helpful to verify the calculations in Sects. 6 and 7.

$$S_1(x_1, x_2, x_3, x_4) = x_1 x_2 x_3 + x_1 x_3 x_4 + x_1 x_2 + x_1 x_3 + x_3 x_4 + 1$$
$$S_2(x_1, x_2, x_3, x_4) = x_1 x_2 x_3 + x_1 x_3 x_4 + x_2 x_3 x_4 + x_1 x_4 + x_1 + x_4 + 1$$
$$S_3(x_1, x_2, x_3, x_4) = x_1 x_2 + x_1 x_4 + x_2 x_4 + x_2 + x_4$$
$$S_4(x_1, x_2, x_3, x_4) = x_1 x_2 x_3 + x_1 x_3 x_4 + x_2 x_3 x_4 + x_1 x_4 + x_2 x_4 + x_3.$$

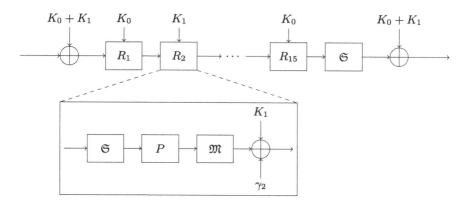

Fig. 1. The overall structure and round function of Midori-64.

The permutation ShuffleCell (P) interchanges the cells of the state. It operates on the state as follows:

$$
\begin{array}{|c|c|c|c|}
\hline
s_1 & s_5 & s_9 & s_{13} \\
\hline
s_2 & s_6 & s_{10} & s_{14} \\
\hline
s_3 & s_7 & s_{11} & s_{15} \\
\hline
s_4 & s_8 & s_{12} & s_{16} \\
\hline
\end{array}
\xrightarrow{P}
\begin{array}{|c|c|c|c|}
\hline
s_1 & s_{15} & s_{10} & s_8 \\
\hline
s_{11} & s_5 & s_4 & s_{14} \\
\hline
s_6 & s_{12} & s_{13} & s_3 \\
\hline
s_{16} & s_2 & s_7 & s_9 \\
\hline
\end{array}
$$

The MixColumn $(\mathfrak{M})$ transformation acts on each state column independently by the following matrix over $\mathbb{F}_{2^4}$:

$$
M = \begin{pmatrix} 0\ 1\ 1\ 1 \\ 1\ 0\ 1\ 1 \\ 1\ 1\ 0\ 1 \\ 1\ 1\ 1\ 0 \end{pmatrix}.
$$

That is, each cell of a column of the state is replaced by the exclusive or of the other elements in the same column. Finally, the round key in round i is alternatingly taken to be $K_0 + \gamma_i$ or $K_1 + \gamma_i$, where γ_i is a round constant. Importantly, round constants are only added to the least significant (rightmost) bit of each cell, *i.e.* $\gamma_i \in \{0,1\}^{16}$.

The tweakable block cipher MANTIS [4] is quite similar to Midori-64, having nearly the same round function. Details will be given in Sect. 7.

3   Correlation Matrices

The cryptanalysis of symmetric-key primitives is generally based on properties of the plaintext that are reflected by the corresponding ciphertext. To every such property, one could associate a set of values satisfying it. A convenient way to work with sets of plaintexts, or more generally multisets, is to associate a probability space with the set of block cipher inputs. Let x be a random variable on $\mathbb{F}_2^n$ with probability mass function p_x. The Fourier transform $\widehat{p}_x$ of p_x is defined by

$$\widehat{p}_x(\chi_u) = \sum_{x \in \mathbb{F}_2^n} p_x(x)\chi_u(x),$$

where $\chi_u : x \mapsto (-1)^{u^T x}$ is a character of $\mathbb{F}_2^n$. That is, the function p_x is expressed in the character basis of the algebra $\mathbb{C}[\mathbb{F}_2^n]$ of functions $\mathbb{F}_2^n \to \mathbb{C}$. Since the character group of $\mathbb{F}_2^n$ is isomorphic to $\mathbb{F}_2^n$, we may consider $\widehat{p}_x$ to be a function on $\mathbb{F}_2^n$ instead. That is,

$$\widehat{p}_x(u) = \mathbf{E}\left[(-1)^{u^T x}\right],$$

where $\mathbf{E}[\,\cdot\,]$ denotes the expected value. Additional information regarding the use of characters and, more generally, representations in the context of probability theory can be found in the references [7,10].

Example 1. The Fourier transform of the uniform distribution on $\mathbb{F}_2^n$ is zero everywhere except at $u = 0$, *i.e.* it has coordinates $(1, 0, \ldots, 0)^T$. Let $p(x) = 0$ for all $x \neq c$ and $p(c) = 1$, then $\widehat{p}(u) = (-1)^{u^T c}$. To stress that $\widehat{p}$ is a vector, we will regularly use the notation $\widehat{p}_u = \widehat{p}(u)$.   ▷

The following result is essential to the discussion of the invariants of Midori-64 in Sect. 5. Note that here, and further on, the vector spaces $\mathbb{F}_2^{mn}$ and $(\mathbb{F}_2^n)^m$ are treated as essentially the same. Recall that the symbol "$\otimes$" denotes the tensor product, which in this case coincides with the Kronecker product.

Theorem 1 (Independence). *Let $x_1, \ldots, x_m$ be independent random variables on $\mathbb{F}_2^n$. The Fourier transform of the joint probability mass function of $x_1, \ldots, x_m$ is given by*

$$\widehat{p}_{x_1,\ldots,x_m} = \bigotimes_{i=1}^m \widehat{p}_{x_i},$$

where $\widehat{p}_{x_i}$ is the Fourier transform of the probability mass function of x_i.

Proof. By the independence of $x_1, \ldots, x_m$, we have

$$\widehat{p}_{x_1,\ldots,x_m}(u_1, \ldots, u_m) = \mathbf{E}\left[(-1)^{\sum_{i=1}^m u_i^T x_i}\right] = \prod_{i=1}^m \mathbf{E}\left[(-1)^{u_i^T x_i}\right].$$

□

In fact, Theorem 1 generalizes to arbitrary functions $f : (\mathbb{F}_2^n)^m \to \mathbb{C}$ such that $f(x_1, \ldots x_m) = \prod_{i=1}^m f_i(x_i)$ with $f_i \in \mathbb{C}[\mathbb{F}_2^n]$.

The reader who is familiar with tensors may find it intuitive to consider $\widehat{p}_{x_1,\ldots,x_m}$ in Theorem 1 to be a simple (*i.e.* rank one) tensor in $[\mathbb{R}^{2^n}]^{\otimes m}$. This fact is not essential to the remainder of the paper.

The discussion so far has been limited to probability distributions. The remainder of this section deals with transformations of these distributions. The relation between the probability distribution of x and $F(x)$ is in general given by a transition matrix. When represented in the basis of characters, such a matrix may be called a correlation matrix (not to be confused with a matrix of second moments).

Definition 1 (Correlation matrix over $\mathbb{F}_2^n$). *Let $F : \mathbb{F}_2^n \to \mathbb{F}_2^m$ be a vectorial Boolean function. The correlation matrix $C^F \in \mathbb{R}^{2^m \times 2^n}$ of F is the representation of the transition matrix of F with respect to the character basis of $\mathbb{C}[\mathbb{F}_2^n]$ and $\mathbb{C}[\mathbb{F}_2^m]$.*

Theorem 2. *Let $F : \mathbb{F}_2^n \to \mathbb{F}_2^m$ be a vectorial Boolean function with correlation matrix C^F. Let x be a random variable on $\mathbb{F}_2^n$ with probability mass function p_x, then*

$$\widehat{p}_{F(x)} = C^F \widehat{p}_x.$$

Proof. This result is essentially a restatement of Definition 1. □

It is instructive to consider the coordinates of C^F. By the Fourier inversion formula, we have

$$p_x(x) = \frac{1}{2^n} \sum_{u \in \mathbb{F}_2^n} (-1)^{u^T x} \widehat{p}_x(u).$$

By substituting the above into the definition of $\widehat{p}_{F(x)}$, and from Theorem 2, one obtains

$$\widehat{p}_{F(x)}(u) = \sum_{v \in \mathbb{F}_2^n} \left[\frac{1}{2^n} \sum_{x \in \mathbb{F}_2^n} (-1)^{u^T F(x) + v^T x} \right] \widehat{p}_x(v) = \sum_{v \in \mathbb{F}_2^n} C_{u,v}^F \, \widehat{p}_x(v).$$

Since this holds for all functions $\widehat{p}_x$, the coordinates of C^F are

$$C_{u,v}^F = \frac{1}{2^n} \sum_{x \in \mathbb{F}_2^n} (-1)^{u^T F(x) + v^T x}. \tag{2}$$

This establishes the equivalence of Definition 1 and the definition due to Daemen *et al.* [8], which originates in the notion of *correlation* between Boolean functions. Note that (2) coincides with the Walsh-Hadamard transformation of F, but since the result of this transformation is not typically interpreted as a linear operator, we will avoid this term.

To conclude this section, a few useful properties of correlation matrices will be listed. These results can also be found (some in a slightly different form) in [8]. In Theorem 5, δ denotes the Kronecker delta function.

Theorem 3 (Composition). *Let $F : \mathbb{F}_2^l \to \mathbb{F}_2^m$ and $G : \mathbb{F}_2^m \to \mathbb{F}_2^n$, then $C^{G \circ F} = C^G C^F$.*

Theorem 4 (Orthogonality). *Let $F : \mathbb{F}_2^n \to \mathbb{F}_2^n$. If F is a bijection, then its correlation matrix C^F is orthogonal.*

Theorem 5 (Linear maps). *Let $L : \mathbb{F}_2^n \to \mathbb{F}_2^m$ be a linear map, then $C_{u,v}^L = \delta(v + L^T u)$. Furthermore, if L is bijective, C^L is a permutation matrix.*

Theorem 6 (Boxed maps). *Let $F : \mathbb{F}_2^{sn} \to \mathbb{F}_2^{sm}$ be a vectorial Boolean function such that there exist functions $F_i : \mathbb{F}_2^n \to \mathbb{F}_2^m$, $i = 1, \ldots, s$ with the property that $F = (F_1, \ldots, F_s)$. Then*

$$C^F = \bigotimes_{i=1}^{s} C^{F_i}.$$

In light of Theorem 1, the property expressed by Theorem 6 is intuitively clear: a function satisfying the conditions of Theorem 6 preserves the independence of its inputs.

Example 2. Let C^K denote the correlation matrix corresponding to the function $x \mapsto x + K$ with $x, K \in \mathbb{F}_2^2$. Let $K = (\kappa_1, \kappa_2)$. By Theorem 6, $C^K = C^{\kappa_1} \otimes C^{\kappa_2}$. It follows that C^K is given by

$$C^K = \begin{pmatrix} 1 & 0 \\ 0 & (-1)^{\kappa_1} \end{pmatrix} \otimes \begin{pmatrix} 1 & 0 \\ 0 & (-1)^{\kappa_2} \end{pmatrix} = \begin{pmatrix} 1 & 0 & 0 & 0 \\ 0 & (-1)^{\kappa_1} & 0 & 0 \\ 0 & 0 & (-1)^{\kappa_2} & 0 \\ 0 & 0 & 0 & (-1)^{\kappa_1 + \kappa_2} \end{pmatrix}.$$

The fact that the correlation matrix of a constant addition is diagonal will be essential to motivate our definition of block cipher invariants in Sect. 4.   ▷

4   Block Cipher Invariants

The invariant subspace attack is based on the existence of an affine space which is mapped to itself by a block cipher. A nonlinear invariant is a set which is encrypted to itself or its complement. The purpose of this section is to define what it means for a "cryptanalytic property" to be invariant under a block cipher, and then to show that this definition includes the nonlinear invariant and invariant subspace attacks as special cases.

Let $F : \mathbb{F}_2^n \to \mathbb{F}_2^n$ be an arbitrary function – in particular, F need not be bijective. With invariant subspace attacks in mind, it is reasonable to ask which probability distributions are invariant under F. This is equivalent to determining all multisets which are mapped to themselves by F. The solutions to this problem are precisely the eigenvectors of the transition matrix of F which are also probability distributions. The main issue with this formulation is that, even for a simple function such as the addition of a constant, computing the eigenvectors of the transition matrix is not as trivial as one might hope.

To simplify matters, we will make a change of basis to the character basis of $\mathbb{C}[\mathbb{F}_2^n]$, which was introduced in Sect. 3. That is, we consider the eigenvectors of correlation matrices instead of transition matrices. This has the important advantage that the correlation matrix of a constant addition is a diagonal matrix. This is helpful, because the columns of a diagonal matrix also form a basis of eigenvectors.

One final simplification can be made before stating Definition 2: there is no good reason to consider only probability distributions – one can simply allow all eigenvectors. It will be shown in Sect. 4.1 that nonlinear invariants are examples of eigenvectors that are not Fourier transformations of probability distributions.

Definition 2 (Block cipher invariant). *A vector $v \in \mathbb{C}^{2^n}$ is an invariant for a block cipher $E_k : \mathbb{F}_2^n \to \mathbb{F}_2^n$ iff it is an eigenvector of the correlation matrix C^{E_k}. If v is a multiple of $(1, 0, \ldots, 0)^T$, it will be called a trivial invariant.*

This paper is only concerned with eigenvectors which correspond to real eigenvalues, *i.e.* ± 1 due to Theorem 4. More generally, one could also have eigenvalues which are complex roots of unity. This will be discussed briefly in Sect. 8, which covers future work.

Not all vectors satisfying Definition 2 can be used in cryptanalysis. A sufficient condition for an invariant to be useful is that it depends only on part of the key, and that it comes with an efficient way of testing whether it holds for a given set of plaintext/ciphertext pairs. Section 4.1 shows that the latter requirement is usually not a problem.

Finally, note that some work related to Definition 2 can be found in the literature. Abdelraheem *et al.* [1] have observed that invariant subspaces correspond to eigenvectors of a submatrix of C^{E_k}. This can be seen to be a special case of Definition 2. Dravie *et al.* [12] give several results related to the spectrum of correlation matrices (not in the context of invariant attacks).

4.1 Nonlinear Invariants

The goal of this section is to establish the relation between Definition 2 and nonlinear invariants. Theorem 7 provides a general result to this end, but the simpler Corollary 1 is sufficient to obtain the desired relation. For the following results, the notation $e_0 = (1, 0, \ldots, 0)^T$ will be used.

Theorem 7 (Nonlinear invariant). *Let $E_k : \mathbb{F}_2^n \to \mathbb{F}_2^n$ be a block cipher with correlation matrix C^{E_k} and $f : \mathbb{F}_2^n \to \mathbb{F}_2$ a Boolean function with correlation matrix $(e_0\ v)^T$. If v is an eigenvector of C^{E_k} with eigenvalue $\lambda = \pm 1$, then for any random variable x on $\mathbb{F}_2^n$, it holds that*

$$\Pr\left[f(E_k(x)) = 0\right] - \frac{1}{2} = \lambda \left(\Pr\left[f(x) = 0\right] - \frac{1}{2}\right). \tag{3}$$

Conversely, suppose (3) holds for a set of random variables $x_1, \ldots, x_m$ with probability distributions $p_{x_1}, \ldots, p_{x_m}$ such that $\mathrm{Span}\,\{p_{x_1}, \ldots, p_{x_m}\} = \mathbb{R}^{2^n}$. Then v is an eigenvector of C^{E_k} with eigenvalue λ.

Proof. By the orthogonality of C^{E_k}, it holds that $\left[C^{E_k}v\right]^T\left[C^{E_k}w\right] = v^Tw$. Since $C^{E_k}v = \lambda v$ with $\lambda = \pm 1$, it follows that $\lambda v^T\left[C^{E_k}w\right] = v^Tw$ and hence $v^T\left[C^{E_k}w\right] = \lambda v^Tw$.

For any x, choose w as the Fourier transform of the probability mass function of x. Since $v^T\left[C^{E_k}w\right] = \lambda v^Tw$, the correlations of $f(x)$ and $f(E_k(x))$ are equal if $\lambda = 1$ and opposite if $\lambda = -1$. To show the converse, extract a basis $\{w_1, \ldots, w_{2^n}\}$ for $\mathbb{R}^{2^n}$ from the vectors $\widehat{p}_{x_1}, \ldots, \widehat{p}_{x_m}$. From $v^T[C^{E_k}w_i] = \lambda v^Tw_i$, $i = 1, \ldots, 2^n$ it follows that $v^TC^{E_k} = \lambda v^T$. The result follows from the orthogonality of C^{E_k}. □

Theorem 7 has the following corollary, which gives the precise relation between the eigenvectors of C^{E_k} and the nonlinear invariants of E_k as defined by Todo, Leander and Sasaki [22].

Corollary 1. *Let $E_k : \mathbb{F}_2^n \to \mathbb{F}_2^n$ be a block cipher with correlation matrix C^{E_k} and $f : \mathbb{F}_2^n \to \mathbb{F}_2$ a Boolean function with correlation matrix $(e_0\ v)^T$. v is an eigenvector of C^{E_k} with eigenvalue $(-1)^c$, $c \in \mathbb{F}_2$ if and only if for all $x \in \mathbb{F}_2^n$, it holds that*

$$f(x) + f(E_k(x)) = c.$$

Proof. For any x, apply Theorem 7 to a random variable x with probability distribution concentrated on x. For the converse, it suffices to note that the Fourier transforms of these probability distributions form a basis for $\mathbb{R}^{2^n}$. □

Finally, the following is a simple result that is useful to obtain the nonlinear invariant corresponding to an eigenvector v. Note that $\mathbf{1}_S$ denotes the indicator function of a set S.

Theorem 8. *Let S be any subset of $\mathbb{F}_2^n$ and let p_1, p_2 be functions[1] defined by $p_1(x) = 2^{-n}\mathbf{1}_S$ and $p_2(x) = 2^{-n}\mathbf{1}_{\mathbb{F}_2^n\setminus S}$ respectively. If $v \in \mathbb{F}_2^n$ is the difference of the Fourier transforms of p_1 and p_2, i.e., $v = \widehat{p}_2 - \widehat{p}_1$ then $\mathbf{1}_S$ has correlation matrix $(e_0\ v)^T$.*

Proof. The (scaled) Walsh-Hadamard transform of $\mathbf{1}_S$ is given by

$$\frac{1}{2^n}\sum_{x\in\mathbb{F}_2^n}(-1)^{\mathbf{1}_S(x)+u^Tx} = \frac{1}{2^n}\left[\sum_{x\notin S}(-1)^{u^Tx} - \sum_{x\in S}(-1)^{u^Tx}\right] = \widehat{p}_2(u) - \widehat{p}_1(u).$$

□

Example 3. Consider the function $F : (x_1, x_2) \mapsto (x_2, x_1)$. It has correlation matrix

$$C^F = \begin{pmatrix} 1 & 0 & 0 & 0 \\ 0 & 0 & 1 & 0 \\ 0 & 1 & 0 & 0 \\ 0 & 0 & 0 & 1. \end{pmatrix}.$$

The vector $2^{-1}(1,1,1,-1)^T = 2^{-2}[(3,1,1,-1)^T - (1,-1,-1,1)^T]$ is an eigenvector of C^F. The corresponding nonlinear invariant is $f(x_1, x_2) = x_1x_2$. ▷

---

[1] Such functions may be called *defective* probability mass functions [14].

4.2 Computing Invariants

In general, it is nontrivial to compute the invariants of a block cipher. This is in part due to large block sizes, and in part due to the key-dependence of the invariants. To avoid dependencies on the key, one could attempt to find invariants for parts of the block cipher that do not involve the key. The influence of the key addition can easily be checked afterwards. In fact, when working in the character basis, it only depends on the nonzero pattern of the invariant.

The problem is then reduced to computing the invariants of an unkeyed permutation $F : \mathbb{F}_2^n \to \mathbb{F}_2^n$. With Definition 2 in mind, one might consider using a standard numerical procedure to compute the eigenvectors of C^F. This is not a particularly efficient approach: the computational cost is $\mathcal{O}(2^{3n})$, which is of the same order as the ANF-based algorithm proposed by Todo $et\ al.$ [22] to find nonlinear invariants.

In fact, due to the structure of the matrix C^F, its eigendecomposition can be computed using at most $\mathcal{O}(n2^{2n})$ operations. The following algorithm generalizes the cycle structure approach which is mentioned by Todo $et\ al.$ [22] as "potentially applicable". One computes the cycle-decomposition of F. Then, for each cycle $(x_0, \ldots, x_{l-1})$ and for each $0 \le j < l$, let $v^{(j)}$ be the Fourier transform of the uniform distribution on the singleton $\{x_j\}$. Let $\zeta = e^{2\pi\sqrt{-1}/l}$. For every $0 \le k < l$, one obtains an eigenvector[2] $w = \sum_{j=0}^{l-1} \zeta^{-kj} v^{(j)}$ corresponding to the eigenvalue ζ^k:

$$C^F w = \sum_{j=0}^{l-1} \zeta^{-kj} C^F v^{(j)} = \sum_{j=0}^{l-1} \zeta^{-k(j-1)} v^{(j)} = \zeta^k w.$$

This method obtains a complete eigenvector basis, since the sum of all cycle lengths is 2^n.

Unfortunately, even the algorithm above is impractical for $n = 64$. To obtain invariants, it is thus necessary to exploit structural properties of the block cipher. Here, Definition 2 will be of use by facilitating a convenient description of invariants. Theorem 9 in Sect. 5 provides an example in the context of Midori-64.

The main structural property that has been exploited in previous work such as [15, 17, 22] is the existence of non-trivial $simultaneous$ invariants for the linear layer and the nonlinear layer of a block cipher. In the first part of Sect. 5, this approach is briefly revisited from the point of view of Definition 2. Then, more general ($i.e.$ not requiring simultaneous eigenvectors) invariants will be discussed. Note that the discussion in Sect. 5 will be tailored to the block cipher Midori-64.

5   Invariants for Midori-64

In this section, the invariants of Midori-64 are discussed in the correlation matrix framework. As an example, in Sect. 5.2 we recover the invariant subspace attack of Guo $et\ al.$ [15] and the nonlinear invariant from Todo $et\ al.$ [22]. Then, in

---

[2] It is not hard to see that it will be linearly independent from any previously computed eigenvectors.

Sect. 5.3, a more general invariant will be obtained. This invariant will be used in Sects. 6 and 7 to obtain practical attacks on (round reduced) Midori-64 and MANTIS.

Before proceeding with the computation of the invariants, it is necessary to analyze the structure of Midori-64 in more detail. Section 5.1 provides the necessary preliminaries.

5.1 State Representation and Round Transformations

In its most general form, the Fourier-domain representation of the Midori-64 state is a vector $v \in \mathbb{C}^{2^{64}}$. Recall from Sect. 2 that it is convenient to represent the Midori-64 state as a 4×4 array of 4-bit cells. For this reason, we will denote coordinate $u = (u_1, \ldots, u_{16})$ with $u_i \in \mathbb{F}_2^4$ of v by $v_u = v_{u_1,\ldots,u_{16}}$. This notation reflects the fact that we can think of v as a tensor of order 16, i.e. $v \in [\mathbb{C}^{2^4}]^{\otimes 16}$.

From Fig. 1, and by using Theorem 3, the correlation matrix of the Midori-64 round function is given by

$$C^{R_i} = C^{\kappa_i + \gamma_i} C^{\mathfrak{M}} C^P C^{\mathfrak{S}},$$

where $\kappa_i = K_0$ when i is odd and K_1 when i is even. Recall that $C^{\kappa_i + \gamma_i}$ is a diagonal matrix. It follows from Theorem 6 that $C^{\mathfrak{S}} = [C^S]^{\otimes 16}$ and $C^{\mathfrak{M}} = [C^M]^{\otimes 4}$. The matrix $C^S \in \mathbb{R}^{16 \times 16}$ is a symmetric orthogonal matrix and $C^M \in \mathbb{R}^{2^{16} \times 2^{16}}$ is a symmetric permutation matrix. Specifically, we have $C_{u,v}^M = \delta(u + Mv)$ by Theorem 5. Finally, C^P is a permutation matrix such that $C^P v_{u_1,\ldots,u_{16}} = v_{u_{\pi^{-1}(1)},\ldots,u_{\pi^{-1}(16)}}$ with π the ShuffleCell permutation.[3]

It is convenient to look only for invariants with *independent cells* in the sense of Theorem 1 – but the reader should be reminded that the invariants need not be Fourier transforms of probability distributions. That is, we will assume that there exist vectors $v^{(1)}, \ldots, v^{(16)}$ such that

$$v_{u_1,\ldots,u_{16}} = \prod_{i=1}^{16} v_{u_i}^{(i)}. \tag{4}$$

Equivalently, $v = \otimes_{i=1}^{16} v^{(i)}$. Of course, this assumption imposes a serious restriction. However, assuming (4) greatly simplifies the theory and is sufficiently general to recover the invariant attacks of Guo et al. [15] and Todo et al. [22]. Furthermore, more general assumptions are not necessary to obtain the invariant that will be presented in Sect. 5.3.

The invariants considered in Sect. 5.2 will be required to be invariant under $\mathfrak{S}$, $\mathfrak{M}$ and P. Consider the last requirement, i.e. v is an eigenvector of C^P. Recall that C^P is a permutation matrix such that

$$C^P \bigotimes_{i=1}^{16} v^{(i)} = \bigotimes_{i=1}^{16} v^{(\pi^{-1}(i))}.$$

---

[3] A transformation such as C^P may be called a *braiding map*.

If v is symmetric, that is, $v^{(1)} = \cdots = v^{(16)} = \tilde{v}$, then $\otimes_{i=1}^{16} v^{(i)} = \tilde{v}^{\otimes 16}$ is clearly invariant under C^P. It turns out that for the purpose of this paper, it suffices to consider only invariants v such that there exists some $\tilde{v} \in \mathbb{C}^{16}$ such that

$$v_{u_1,\ldots,u_{16}} = \prod_{i=1}^{16} \tilde{v}_{u_i}. \tag{5}$$

That is, $v = \tilde{v}^{\otimes 16}$ and v will be called symmetric, in line with standard terminology for such tensors. Note that assumption (5), is less restrictive than (4). Indeed, for any realistic choice of round constants, an asymmetric invariant tends to lead to conflicting requirements on the key after a sufficient number of rounds. Slightly more general invariants can be obtained by requiring that $v^{(i)}$ is constant on the cycles of π.

Computing an eigenvector basis for $C^{\mathfrak{S}}$ is not difficult. In the remainder of this section, the eigenvectors of $C^{\mathfrak{M}}$ satisfying (4) and (5) will be listed. In particular, it is not necessary to compute these eigenvectors numerically. We begin with the straightforward result in Lemma 1. The main result is stated in Theorem 9.

Lemma 1. *If $v^{\otimes 4}$ is a real eigenvector of C^M, then there exists a scalar $\alpha \in \mathbb{R}_0$ such that all coordinates of v in the standard basis are equal to 0 or $\pm \alpha$.*

Proof. The condition that $v^{\otimes 4}$ is an eigenvector of C^M is equivalent to

$$v^{\otimes 4}_{u_1,u_2,u_3,u_4} = \lambda v^{\otimes 4}_{M(u_1,u_2,u_3,u_4)^T}.$$

Hence, we have for all $u_1, \ldots, u_4 \in \mathbb{F}_2^4$ that

$$\prod_{i=1}^{4} v_{u_i} = \lambda \prod_{i=1}^{4} v_{\Sigma_{j \neq i} u_j}. \tag{6}$$

Note that no vector of the form $v^{\otimes 4}$ can correspond to $\lambda = -1$, since it follows from (6) that $v_u^4 = \lambda v_u^4$. Suppose that at least one coordinate of v is nonzero, i.e. $v_u = \alpha$ for some u. By (6), this implies $\alpha v_{u'}^3 = \alpha^3 v_{u'}$ for any $u' \in \mathbb{F}_2^4$. Consequently, $v_{u'} \in \{0, \pm\alpha\}$. □

Theorem 9. *If $v^{\otimes 4}$ is a real eigenvector of C^M, then $\mathcal{A} = \{u \mid v_u \neq 0\}$ is an affine subspace of $\mathbb{F}_2^4$ and there exists a scalar $\alpha \in \mathbb{R}_0$ such that $v_u = \pm\alpha$ for all $u \in \mathcal{A}$. The converse is also true in the following cases:*

- *For $\dim \mathcal{A} = 0$, $\dim \mathcal{A} = 1$ and $\dim \mathcal{A} = 2$.*
- *For $\dim \mathcal{A} = 3$, provided that the number of negative coordinates of v is even.*

The condition for $\dim \mathcal{A} = 3$ is also necessary.

Proof. Suppose $v^{\otimes 4}$ is a real eigenvector of C^M. Let $a, u, u' \in \mathbb{F}_2^4$ such that $v_a \neq 0$, $v_{a+u} \neq 0$ and $v_{a+u'} \neq 0$. By (6), we have

$$v_{a+u+u'}^2 v_{a+u'} v_{a+u} = v_a^2 v_{a+u} v_{a+u'} \neq 0.$$

Hence, $v_{a+u+u'} \neq 0$. It follows that $\mathcal{A}$ is an affine space. Lemma 1 completes the argument.

To show the converse, first consider the case $\dim \mathcal{A} \in \{0, 1, 2\}$. It suffices to demonstrate that if $u_1, \ldots, u_4 \in \mathcal{A}$, then $\prod_{i=1}^{4} v_{u_i} = \prod_{i=1}^{4} v_{\Sigma_{j \neq i} u_j}$. Note that $\{u_1, \ldots, u_4\}$ and $\{\Sigma_{i \neq 1} u_i, \ldots, \Sigma_{i \neq 4} u_i\}$ generate the same affine space. Since the dimension of this space is at most two, it contains at most four elements. Hence, both products contain the same factors.

For $\dim \mathcal{A} = 3$, the previous argument no longer applies when $u_1, \ldots, u_4$ are linearly independent. In this case the left and right hand side of $\prod_{i=1}^{4} v_{u_i} = \prod_{i=1}^{4} v_{\Sigma_{j \neq i} u_j}$ involve different variables. Hence, since $\mathcal{A}$ contains eight elements, the products of these elements must be positive. $\qquad \square$

The only symmetric rank one invariants which are not covered by Theorem 9 are those containing only nonzero entries. It would be possible to extend the result to cover this case as well, but this would have little practical value since such eigenvectors can never lead to a significant class of weak keys. This will become clear in Sect. 5.2.

5.2   Simultaneous Eigenvectors

As discussed in Sect. 4.2, it is not possible to find the eigenvectors of C^{E_k} directly and to subsequently identify those vectors that depend only on a limited portion of the key. A more realistic approach is to find joint eigenvectors for all of the transformations in the round function. This corresponds to the strategy that is commonly used, and it is the strategy that will be applied in this section.

The problem considered in this section is thus to find vectors $v \in \mathbb{R}^{2^{64}}$ such that $[C^S]^{\otimes 16} v = \lambda v$ and $[C^M]^{\otimes 4} v = \mu v$ with $\lambda, \mu \in \{-1, 1\}$. Furthermore, v must be an eigenvector of C^P, but if v is symmetric, we need not separately consider this requirement. For each of these vectors v, we additionally require that they are eigenvectors of $C^{K+\gamma_i}$ for $i = 1, \ldots, 16$. In general, this is not possible without making some assumptions on the key K.

If $\{v_1, \ldots, v_{16}\}$ is a basis of eigenvectors of C^S, then the set of all vectors of the form $\otimes_{i=1}^{16} v_{\ell_i}$ with $\ell_i \in \{1, \ldots, 16\}$ is a basis of eigenvectors of $[C^S]^{\otimes 16}$. Suppose that E_{+1}^S is the eigenspace of C^S corresponding to eigenvalue 1, and E_{-1}^S likewise for eigenvalue -1. Any useful invariant must be an eigenvector of the diagonal matrices $C^{\kappa_i + \gamma_i}$ as well. That is, the invariants must be an element of one of the vector spaces listed in Table 1.

The vectors $v^{\otimes 4}$ should additionally be eigenvectors of C^M. A necessary condition to this end is given by Theorem 9 (in fact, Lemma 1 is sufficient here). Using this result, only four nontrivial invariants of the form $v^{\otimes 16}$ remain. These are listed in Table 2. The first of these invariants satisfies the conditions of Theorem 8. It corresponds to the nonlinear invariant discovered by Todo, Leander and Sasaki [22].

Table 1. Bases for the intersection of the eigenspaces of C^S and C^{γ_i}.

$\cap$	Span$\{e_1, e_3, \ldots, e_{15}\}$	Span$\{e_0, e_2, \ldots, e_{16}\}$
E_{+1}^S	$(1,0,0,0,0,0,0,0,0,0,0,0,0,0,0,0)^T$ $(0,0,1,0,1,0,1,0,-1,0,-1,0,-1,0,-1,0)^T$	$(1,0,0,0,0,0,0,0,0,0,0,0,0,0,0,0)^T$
E_{-1}^S	$(0,1,0,0,0,1,0,0,0,-1,0,0,0,-1,0,-2)^T$ $(0,0,0,1,0,0,0,1,0,0,0,-1,0,0,0,1)^T$	$(0,0,0,0,0,0,0,0,0,0,0,0,0,0,0,0)^T$

Table 2. Invariants for Midori-64. Note that the last invariant is simply the nonlinear invariant corresponding to the second invariant (which is an invariant subspace).

Eigenvector (v for $v^{\otimes 16}$)	Weak-key class	Number of weak-keys
$(0,0,0,1,0,0,0,1,0,0,0,-1,0,0,0,1)^T$	$\kappa_1 = \kappa_2 = 0$	2^{64}
$(1,0,1,0,1,0,1,0,-1,0,-1,0,-1,0,-1,0)^T$	$\kappa_1 = \kappa_2 = \kappa_3 = 0$	2^{32}
$(1,0,-1,0,-1,0,-1,0,1,0,1,0,1,0,1,0)^T$	$\kappa_1 = \kappa_2 = \kappa_3 = 0$	2^{32}
$(0,1,0,1,0,1,0,1,0,-1,0,-1,0,-1,0,-1)^T$	$\kappa_1 = \kappa_2 = \kappa_3 = 0$	2^{32}

Note that the weak-key class corresponding to a given invariant (the second column in Table 2), is readily determined from the vector v. For instance, consider the vector $C^\kappa v$, with $\kappa = (\kappa_1, \ldots, \kappa_4)^T \in \mathbb{F}_2^4$ a single nibble of the round key:

$$v = (0,0,0,1,0,0,0,1,0,0,0,-1,0,0,0,1)^T,$$
$$C^\kappa v = (-1)^{\kappa_3 + \kappa_4}(0,0,0,1,0,0,0,(-1)^{\kappa_2},0,0,0,(-1)^{1+\kappa_1},0,0,0,(-1)^{\kappa_1 + \kappa_2})^T.$$

Hence, v is invariant under C^κ provided that $\kappa_1 = \kappa_2 = 0$. Note that v is also invariant under the addition of the round constants – which has the same effect as modifying κ_4.

An alternative approach to finding invariants starts from the eigenvectors of C^M. Theorem 9 makes this method efficient. This will be the starting point to obtain more general invariants in Sect. 5.3.

5.3 Nonlinear Invariant for "Almost Midori-64"

In the previous section, a few eigenvectors of C^{R_i} were obtained by intersecting the eigenspaces of $C^{\mathfrak{M}}$, $C^{\mathfrak{S}}$ and $C^{K+\gamma_i}$. In general the eigenvectors of C^{R_i} are not eigenvectors of $C^{\mathfrak{M}}$ or $C^{\mathfrak{S}}$. Furthermore, the eigenvectors of C^{E_k} need not be eigenvectors of the round functions C^{R_i}. In order to find all invariants, then, it would be necessary to solve the eigenvalue problem of Definition 2 directly. As discussed before, tackling this problem is out of the scope of this paper, but a slightly more general type of invariant for Midori-64 is presented in this section.

Figure 2 shows the general idea: it may be possible to find a vector $u^{\otimes 16}$ which is mapped to a vector $v^{\otimes 16}$ by C^{R_i}, such that $C^{R_{i+1}}v^{\otimes 16} = u^{\otimes 16}$. Such a vector $u^{\otimes 16}$ would be an eigenvector of $C^{R_{i+1}}C^{R_i}$, but not of C^{R_i}.

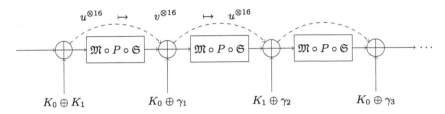

Fig. 2. If $u \neq v$, this figure depicts an invariant for two rounds which is not invariant under one round.

To find such an invariant, it suffices to obtain vectors u and $v = C^S u$ such that $C^M u^{\otimes 4} = u^{\otimes 4}$ and $C^M v^{\otimes 4} = v^{\otimes 4}$. Theorem 9 provides a complete list of possible choices for u and v. This approach is formalized in Algorithm 1. This algorithm requires a negligible amount of time, as the inner loop is only executed 5216 times – once for each symmetric rank one invariant of $C^{\mathfrak{M}}$. Note that it also returns invariants of the conventional type.

A list of invariants produced by Algorithm 1 is given in Appendix A. The most interesting pair of vectors u, v is given by

$$u = (0,0,0,0,0,1,0,0,0,0,0,0,0,0,0,0)^T$$
$$v = (0,0,0,0,0,0,0,0,0,0,-1/2,-1/2,0,0,1/2,-1/2)^T.$$

Clearly, u is invariant under the addition of any constant. For v, it holds that

$$C^\kappa v = (-1)^{\kappa_1+\kappa_3}/2 \cdot (0,0,0,0,0,0,0,0,0,0,-1,(-1)^{1+\kappa_4},0,0,(-1)^{\kappa_2},(-1)^{1+\kappa_2+\kappa_4})^T,$$

which is a multiple of v provided that $\kappa_2 = \kappa_4 = 0$. For the usual choice of round constants of Midori-64, v is not invariant under the addition of the constants. However, had the round constants been chosen as $\gamma_i \in \{0,2,8,\mathtt{A}\}^{16}$ rather than $\gamma_i \in \{0,1\}^{16}$, the attack would apply. Moreover, such a restriction only applies to half of the rounds – the round constants of other rounds may be chosen arbitrarily.

The restriction $\kappa_2 = \kappa_4 = 0$ (which applies to K_0 or K_1, but not both) corresponds to a class of 2^{96} weak keys. By Theorem 8, v corresponds to the following nonlinear invariant:

$$f(x_1,\ldots,x_{64}) = \sum_{i=1}^{16} [x_{4i}x_{4i-2} + x_{4i} + x_{4i-1} + x_{4i-3}] \tag{7}$$

Algorithm 1. Finding symmetric rank-one invariants for two rounds of Midori-64.

1: **for** each affine subspace $\mathcal{A} \subseteq \mathbb{F}_2^4$ with $d := \dim \mathcal{A} \in \{0, 1, 2, 3\}$ **do**
2:     $S \leftarrow \{1\} \times \{1, -1\}^{2^d - 2}$
3:     **if** $d = 3$ **then**
4:         $S \leftarrow \{(s_1, \ldots, s_{2^d - 1}, \prod_i s_i) \mid (s_1, \ldots, s_{2^d - 1}) \in S\}$
5:     **else**
6:         $S \leftarrow S \times \{1, -1\}$
7:     **end if**
8:     **for** $(v_u)_{u \in \mathcal{A}} \in S$ **do**
9:         $w \leftarrow C^S v$
10:         $\mathcal{A}' \leftarrow \{u \in \mathbb{F}_2^4 \mid w_u \neq 0\}$
11:         **if** $\mathcal{A}'$ is affine **and** $(\dim \mathcal{A}' \neq 3$ **or** $|\{u \in \mathcal{A}' \mid w_u < 0\}|$ is even) **then**
12:             **yield** v ▷ $v^{\otimes 16}$ is invariant for some choice of round constants
13:         **end if**
14:     **end for**
15: **end for**

That is, there exists a constant $c \in \mathbb{F}_2$ such that $f(E_k(x)) + f(x) = c$ for all x and for any even number of rounds. By Theorem 8, u corresponds to the following "nonlinear" invariant:

$$g(x_1, \ldots, x_{64}) = \sum_{i=1}^{16} [x_{4i} + x_{4i-2}] . \tag{8}$$

Hence, for an even number of rounds, $g(E_k(x)) + g(x)$ is constant. Note that if the number of rounds is odd, the value $f(E_k(x)) + g(x)$ is constant instead. Appendix B provides test code for this property.

5.4   Trail Clustering in Midori-64

It is worthwhile to take a closer look at the invariant g given by (8) in Sect. 5.3. Since g is a linear function, it corresponds to a linear hull with correlation ± 1 (where the sign depends on the key). Considering the fact that Midori-64 has been designed with resistance to linear cryptanalysis in mind, this is remarkable.

Remark 1. *The correlation of any trail in "almost Midori-64" is (much) smaller than 2^{-32}, yet there is a linear hull with correlation ± 1 for 2^{96} keys.*

The correlation of a linear hull is equal to the sum of the correlations of all trails within the hull. It is well-established that, in theory, this sum could become large even if all terms are small. Such ideas go back to Nyberg [21]. Daemen and Rijmen [9] refer to this effect as *trail clustering*.

Remark 1 demonstrates an extreme case of trail clustering: the absolute correlation of the hull is not just large, it is maximal. This appears to be the first real-world observation of such behavior.

6   Practical Attack on 10 Rounds of Midori-64

The purpose of this section is to demonstrate that the invariant for "almost Midori-64" can be used even when the round constants are not modified. In fact, the attack in this section is valid for any choice of round constants.

Specifically, it will be shown that 10 rounds of Midori-64 are subject to a key-recovery attack that requires $1.25 \cdot 2^{21}$ chosen plaintexts and has a computational cost of 2^{56} block cipher calls. The downside of this attack is that it is limited to 2^{96} out of 2^{128} keys. Note that Midori-64 has been analyzed in several prior works. Lin and Wu [18] demonstrate meet-in-the-middle attacks on 10, 11 and 12 rounds of Midori-64. Chen and Wang [23] give a 10 round impossible differential cryptanalysis. The downside of those attacks is that they can not be executed in practice. Table 3 provides an overview of attacks on Midori-64.

Table 3. Overview of key-recovery attacks on Midori-64. Time is measured by the number of encryption operations. Memory is expressed in number of bytes.

Attack	Rounds	Time	Memory	Data	Weak keys	Reference
Meet-in-the-middle	10	$2^{99.5}$	$2^{95.7}$	$2^{59.5}$	N/A	Lin and Wu [18]
Meet-in-the-middle	11	2^{122}	$2^{92.2}$	2^{53}	N/A	Lin and Wu [18]
Meet-in-the-middle	12	$2^{125.5}$	2^{109}	$2^{55.5}$	N/A	Lin and Wu [18]
Impossible differential	10	$2^{80.81}$	$2^{68.13}$	$2^{62.4}$	N/A	Chen and Wang [23]
Invariant subspace	16	2^{16}	–	2	2^{32}	Leander *et al.* [17]
Nonlinear invariant[a]	16	$2^{15}h$	–	$33h$	2^{64}	Todo *et al.* [22]
Attack in this section	10	2^{56}	–	$2^{21.32}$	2^{96}	–

[a]This is an attack on a mode of operation. It recovers $32h$ bits of h encrypted blocks.

The attack presented below is based on the observation that integral properties [16] and invariants can often be combined. However, since we allow arbitrary round constants in this section, the invariant can only be used once. In this regard the nonlinear invariant that was introduced in Sect. 5.3 has an important advantage: with one assumption on the key, it covers two rounds.

6.1   Nonlinear Property for 6 Rounds of Midori-64

This section shows that the two-round nonlinear invariant for Midori-64 can be extended to a six round nonlinear property. When a key which does not belong to the weak key class is added to the state, the vector corresponding to a nonlinear invariant will be mapped to another vector which only depends (up to a scale factor) on key bits that are already "known", *i.e.* that had to be fixed to obtain the invariant in the first place. This holds in both the forward and backward direction, leading to a 6-round nonlinear property. This is illustrated in Fig. 3.

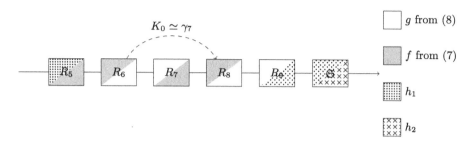

Fig. 3. Nonlinear property over six rounds of Midori-64. The notation "$\simeq$" is used to indicate equality in the second and fourth bits of every nibble of each of its arguments.

The functions h_1 and h_2 in Fig. 3 depend on the choice of the round constants. Specifically, h_1 depends on $P^{-1}(\mathfrak{M}(\gamma_5 + \gamma_7))$ and h_2 depends on $\gamma_7 + \gamma_9$. For the purposes of this paper, a detailed description of h_1 is not necessary. For h_2, it holds that

$$h_2(x_1, \ldots, x_{64}) = \sum_{i=1}^{16} f(S(x_{4i-3}, x_{4i-2}, x_{4i-1}, x_{4i}) + \gamma_{7,i} + \gamma_{9,i}).$$

In general, h_j can be written in the form

$$h_j(x_1, \ldots, x_{64}) = \sum_{i=1}^{16} h^{(\beta_{j,2i}, \beta_{j,2i+1})}(x_{4i}, x_{4i+1}, x_{4i+2}, x_{4i+3}), \qquad (9)$$

where $\beta_j \in \mathbb{F}_2^{32}$ is a constant depending on the round constants. In particular, β_2 consists of the second and fourth bits of every nibble of $\gamma_7 + \gamma_9$. For the default choice of round constants of Midori-64, $\beta_{j,2i} = 0$. Hence, only two different Boolean functions can occur as terms in (9):

$$h^{(00)}(x_1, x_2, x_3, x_4) = x_2 + x_4$$
$$h^{(01)}(x_1, x_2, x_3, x_4) = x_2 x_3 x_4 + x_1 x_3 x_4 + x_1 x_2 x_3 + x_1 x_4 + x_1 + x_2.$$

Since the functions h_1 and h_2 are balanced *on every cell* of the state, it holds that $\sum_{x \in S} h_i(x) = 0$ with S a set of state values such that every cell takes all values exactly once. This makes it possible to combine integral cryptanalysis with the 6-round nonlinear property described above.

6.2   Integral Property for 4 Rounds of Midori-64

An integral attack on Midori-64 that is suitable for our purposes will now be given. The following notation will be used: cells taking all values an equal number of times are denoted using the label "A", constant cells will be labeled by "C". Subscripts are used to denote groups of values which jointly satisfy the "A" property. Note that cells can be part of several groups, *e.g.* a cell marked "$A_{i,j}$" is contained in groups i and j. The Midori-64 designers discuss the existence of a 3.5 round integral distinguisher. In fact, one can see that a 4-round integral property[4] exists. Note that the property is nearly identical to the Rijndael distinguisher discussed by Knudsen and Wagner [16], the difference being that the property works better than expected for Midori-64.

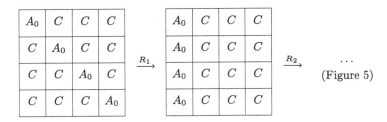

Fig. 4. First two rounds of the integral property for four rounds of Midori-64.

The integral property is based on a set of chosen ciphertexts such that the diagonal cells take all possible values exactly once and all other cells are constant. After one round, the same property then holds for the first column whereas all other cells are constant. This is shown in Fig. 4.

The effect of the remaining rounds is shown in Fig. 5. Figure 5 shows that, before the last application of $\mathfrak{M}$, any four distinct cells in a column jointly satisfy the "A" property. This implies that all cells can be labeled "A" after four rounds.

The derivation in Fig. 5 starts by forming appropriate groups of cells which are independent before the third round. Four (sometimes overlapping) groups of such cells are indicated using "A_i", $i = 0, \ldots, 3$ in Fig. 5. The maps $\mathfrak{S}$ and P preserve the groups. Furthermore, one can see that four new groups can be obtained after the application of $\mathfrak{M}$. These groups can be chosen in such a way that they are aligned in different columns of the state after P has been applied. The four round property then follows.

---

[4] If the zero-sum property can be used, this actually yields a 5-round property.

C	A_1	A	$A_{2,3}$
A_0	A_2	C	A_1
$A_{2,3}$	A_0	A_3	C
A_1	C	A	A_0

C	A_1	A_1	A_2
A_2	A_0	C	A_0
A_3	A_3	A_2	C
A_0	C	A_3	A_1

C	A_2	A_1	A_2
A_0	A_1	C	A_0
A_2	A_3	A_0	C
A_1	C	A_3	A_3

C	A_2	A_3	A_1
A_0	A_1	C	A_0
A_2	A_0	A_2	C
A_3	C	A_1	A_3

$\downarrow P \circ \mathfrak{S}$

C	C	C	C
A_3	A_1	A_1	A_1
A_2	A	$A_{2,3}$	$A_{2,3}$
A_0	A_0	A_0	A

C	C	C	C
A_2	A_1	A_0	A_0
A_0	A_3	A_2	A_3
A_1	A_2	A_3	A_1

C	C	C	C
A_0	A_2	A_1	A_0
A_1	A_3	A_2	A_2
A_3	A_0	A_3	A_1

C	C	C	C
A_2	A_2	A_3	A_0
A_1	A_1	A_1	A_2
A_3	A_0	A_0	A_3

$\downarrow \mathfrak{M}$

A_0	A_1	A	A_2
A	A_0	A_2	A_3
A_3	A	A_0	A_1
A_2	A_3	A_1	A

A_0	A_1	A_3	A
A_1	A	A_2	A_3
A	A_2	A_0	A_1
A_2	A_3	A	A_0

A_0	A	A_3	A_2
A_1	A_0	A_2	A
A_3	A_2	A	A_1
A	A_3	A_1	A_0

A	A_1	A_3	A_2
A_1	A_0	A	A_3
A_3	A_2	A_0	A
A_2	A	A_1	A_0

$\downarrow P \circ \mathfrak{S}$

A_0	A_1	A_2	A_3
A_0	A_1	A_2	A_3
A_0	A_1	A_2	A_3
A	A	A	A

A_0	A_1	A_2	A_3
A_0	A_1	A_2	A_3
A	A	A	A
A_0	A_1	A_2	A_3

A_0	A_1	A_2	A_3
A	A	A	A
A_0	A_1	A_2	A_3
A_0	A_1	A_2	A_3

A	A	A	A
A_0	A_1	A_2	A_3
A_0	A_1	A_2	A_3
A_0	A_1	A_2	A_3

$\downarrow \mathfrak{M}$

A	A	A	A
A	A	A	A
A	A	A	A
A	A	A	A

Fig. 5. Last two rounds of the integral property for four rounds of Midori-64.

6.3 Combination of the Nonlinear and Integral Properties

The final attack can now be described. Figure 6 provides an overview. Let $\mathcal{I}$ denote a set of plaintext/ciphertext pairs with the structure required by the integral property from Fig. 4. Then, due to the nonlinear property from Fig. 3, the following holds:

$$\sum_{(P,C)\in\mathcal{I}} h_2(C + K_0 + K_1) = \sum_{(P,C)\in\mathcal{I}} h_1((R_4 \circ \cdots \circ R_1)(P + K_0 + K_1)) = 0.$$

Hence, every set $\mathcal{I}$ defines a low-degree nonlinear polynomial equation in (part of) $K_0 + K_1$. Given enough such equations, one observes that a Gröbner basis for the ideal generated by these polynomials can be efficiently (within a second on a regular computer) computed. Although computing Gröbner bases is hard in general, it is easy in this case due to the fact that key bits from different cells are never multiplied together.

Note that only those key bits which are involved in h_2 in a nonlinear way can be recovered by solving the system of polynomial equations. That is, the number of key bits recovered is four times the number of nonlinear terms in (9). For the default Midori-64 round constants, 40 key bits can be recovered. This requires $40 \cdot 2^{16} = 1.25 \cdot 2^{21}$ chosen plaintexts.

The remaining 24 bits of $K_0 + K_1$ can be guessed, along with the 32 unknown bits in K_0. This requires 2^{56} block cipher calls. Note that this additional work is only necessary after it has been established that a weak key is used. Hence, an attacker in the multi-key setting has a very efficient method to identify potential targets.

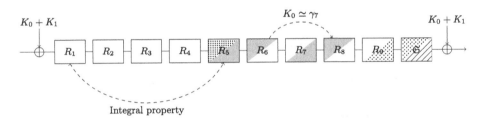

Fig. 6. Overview of the attack on 10 rounds of Midori-64.

7   Practical Attack on MANTIS-4

This section presents an attack on the block cipher MANTIS [4], which is closely related to Midori-64. Dobraunig, Eichlseder, Kales and Mendel give a practical attack against MANTIS-5 in the chosen tweak setting [11]. This attack has been extended to six rounds by Eichlseder and Kales [13]. The attack presented in this section is limited to MANTIS-4, but the assumptions about the capabilities of the attacker are different. The attacker is not allowed to choose the tweak,

24   T. Beyne

but it is assumed that a *weak tweak* is used. It will be shown that for every choice of the key, there are 2^{32} (out of 2^{64}) weak tweaks. When a weak tweak is used, the full key can be recovered from (on average) 640 chosen plaintexts and with a computational cost of approximately 2^{56} block cipher calls.

Figure 7 illustrates the overall structure of MANTIS-4. Unlike in Midori-64, the round key K_1 is the same in all rounds. Additional whitening keys K_0 and $K_0' = (K_0 \ggg 1) + (K_0 \gg 63)$ are added before the first round and after the last round. The round function is nearly identical to the Midori-64 round function, the difference being that the round keys and constants are added before rather than after the application of $\mathfrak{M}$. Hence, the 2-round nonlinear invariant for Midori-64 also applies to MANTIS-4. Note that the values of the round constants $RC_1, \dots, RC_4$ are not essential to the attack described here.

Structurally, MANTIS differs from Midori-64 in two major aspects: it takes an additional tweak as an input, and it is a reflection cipher. In every round, the tweak is permuted cellwise by a permutation σ. In all other aspects, the tweak is treated in the same way as the round key K_1. The reflection property will make it be possible to extend the 6-round nonlinear property of Midori-64 to eight rounds. The presence of a tweak allows mounting a weak tweak rather than a weak key attack, which corresponds to a significantly weaker adversarial model.

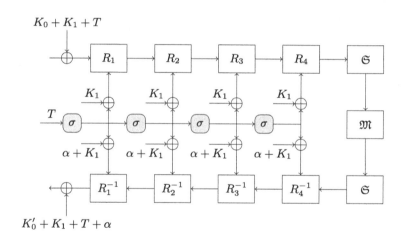

Fig. 7. Overview of MANTIS-4.

An overview of the attack is shown in Fig. 8. As in the attack on Midori-64 from Sect. 6, a few initial rounds are covered by an integral property. Since the nonlinear property extends over eight rounds for MANTIS, it suffices to use a weaker integral property. Figure 9 shows the property that will be used. It requires 16 chosen plaintexts.

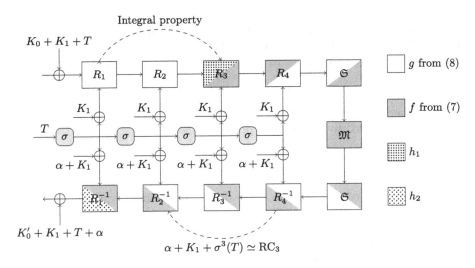

Fig. 8. Nonlinear property over eight rounds of MANTIS-4. The notation "$\simeq$" is used to indicate equality in the second and fourth bits of every nibble of each of its arguments.

The nonlinear property is similar to the property that was discussed in Sect. 6, but slightly more complicated. Specifically, due to the tweak-key schedule, the functions h_1 and h_2 can depend on the tweak. As for Midori-64, h_1 and h_2 can be written in the form

$$h_j(x_1,\ldots,x_{64}) = \sum_{i=1}^{16} h^{(\beta_{j,2i},\beta_{j,2i+1})}(x_{4i},x_{4i+1},x_{4i+2},x_{4i+3}), \tag{10}$$

where $\beta_j = (\beta_{j,1},\ldots,\beta_{j,32}) \in \mathbb{F}_2^{32}$ is a constant that possibly depends on the tweak and the functions $h^{(\beta_{j,2i},\beta_{j,2i+1})}$ are given by

$$h^{(00)}(x_1,x_2,x_3,x_4) = x_1 + x_2$$
$$h^{(11)}(x_1,x_2,x_3,x_4) = x_1x_3 + x_2 + x_3 + x_4$$
$$h^{(01)}(x_1,x_2,x_3,x_4) = x_1x_2x_3 + x_1x_2x_4 + x_2x_3x_4 + x_1x_4 + x_3 + x_4$$
$$h^{(10)}(x_1,x_2,x_3,x_4) = x_1x_2x_3 + x_1x_2x_4 + x_2x_3x_4 + x_1x_4 + x_1x_3 + x_1 + x_2 + x_3.$$

A	C	C	C
C	C	C	C
C	C	C	C
C	C	C	C

$\xrightarrow{R_1}$

C	C	C	C
A	C	C	C
A	C	C	C
A	C	C	C

$\xrightarrow{R_2}$

C	A	A	A
C	A	C	A
C	A	A	C
C	C	A	A

Fig. 9. Integral property for two rounds of MANTIS.

Note that all of these functions are balanced. The constant β_1 consists of the second and fourth bits of every nibble of α. For convenience, this will be denoted by $\beta_1 \simeq \alpha$. For β_2, we have $\beta_2 \simeq \mathrm{RC}_1 + \alpha + K_1 + \sigma(T)$. This implies that

$$\beta_2 \simeq \mathrm{RC}_1 + \mathrm{RC}_3 + \sigma(T) + \sigma^3(T).$$

Let $\mathcal{I}$ denote a set of plaintext/ciphertext pairs such that the plaintexts have the structure required by the integral property, then

$$\sum_{(P,C)\in\mathcal{I}} h_2(C + K_0' + K_1 + T + \alpha) = \sum_{(P,C)\in\mathcal{I}} h_1(R_1(R_2(P + K_0 + K_1 + T))) = 0.$$

Hence, each set $\mathcal{I}$ corresponds to a low-degree polynomial equation in (part of) the key. As in Sect. 6, a Gröbner basis for the ideal generated by these polynomials can be efficiently computed.

As in the attack on Midori-64, only those key bits which are involved in h_2 in a nonlinear way can be recovered by solving the system of polynomial equations. For simplicity, assume that the functions $h^{(00)}$, $h^{(01)}$, $h^{(10)}$ and $h^{(11)}$ all occur as terms in (10) in the same proportion. Then the expected number of key bits that can be recovered by solving the system of polynomial equations is equal to $40.^5$ For obtaining 40 key bits, it was observed that 40 equations are sufficient. This requires $2^4 \cdot 40 = 640$ chosen plaintexts.

The remaining bits of the whitening key $K_0' + K_1$ (24 bits on average) can then be guessed, along with the 32 unknown bits of K_1. For each such guess, it is possible to compute K_0' (since $K_0' + K_1$ is already known) and hence K_0. No additional plaintext/ciphertext pairs are necessary to carry out this process. Hence, the work required for the entire key-recovery attack is then roughly 2^{56} block cipher calls.

8   Future Work

Returning to Definition 2, one potentially interesting direction for future work is the use of complex eigenvalues. The corresponding eigenvectors are related to real invariants of $[C^{E_k}]^l$ with l the order of the corresponding eigenvalue. If l is not too large, then such invariants might lead to additional attacks.

Another topic that deserves more attention is the development of practical methods to compute an eigenvector basis for the correlation matrix of the entire round function. Even if this does not lead to new attacks, it could be a tool for designers to demonstrate security with respect to attacks based on invariants.

Yet another direction for future work is to improve and extend the attack on 10 rounds of Midori-64 from Sect. 6 and the attack on MANTIS-4 from Sect. 7.

---

[5] For some tweaks, many more key bits can be recovered, and for others only a small number of key bits can be recovered. For instance, one finds that (for the default round constants) for 10% of the weak tweaks less than 32 bits can be recovered. Although this is a small fraction of tweaks, in such cases it may be worthwhile to obtain more key bits by performing the attack in the reverse direction (*i.e.* as a chosen ciphertext attack).

9   Conclusion

The three problems mentioned in the introduction have been addressed. In Sect. 4, a new theory of block cipher invariants was developed. Beside providing the foundation for the remainder of the paper, Definition 2 provides insight and uncovers several directions for future research. Section 5 provides a detailed analysis of invariants in Midori-64, leading to a new class of 2^{96} weak keys when minor modifications to the round constants are made. It was shown that this invariant is equivalent to a linear hull with maximal correlation. Finally, Sects. 6 and 7 illustrate the importance of invariants, even when round constants initially seem to limit their applicability. Two practical attacks were described: (1) a key-recovery attack on 10-round Midori-64 for 2^{96} weak keys, requiring $1.25 \cdot 2^{21}$ chosen plaintexts (2) a key-recovery attack on MANTIS-4 with an average data complexity of 640 chosen plaintexts.

Acknowledgments. I acknowledge the anonymous referees for their comments and corrections. In addition, I thank Tomer Ashur and Yunwen Liu for discussions related to this work. Finally, I am especially grateful to Vincent Rijmen for his comments on a draft version of this paper, and for his support.

A   List of Invariants Produced by Algorithm 1

See Table 4.

Table 4. Invariants for two rounds of (modified) Midori-64, as obtained using Algorithm 1. Only invariants with at least 2^{64} weak keys are listed. Note that these invariants are not valid for all choices of the round constants. The label "type I" refers to invariants with $u = v$, whereas "type II" indicates that $u \neq v$. Note that not all of these invariants are linearly independent.

Correlation vector (v for $v^{\otimes 16}$)	Amount of weak-keys	Type
$(1, 0, 0, 0, 0, 0, 0, 0, 0, 0, 0, 0, 0, 0, 0, 0)^T$	2^{128}	Trivial
$(0, 0, 0, 0, 0, 0, 0, 0, 0, 0, 1, 1, 0, 0, -1, 1)^T$	2^{96}	Type II
$(0, 1, 0, 0, 1, 0, 0, 0, -1, 0, 0, 0, 0, 1, 0, 0)^T$	2^{80}	Type II
$(0, 0, 0, 1, 0, 0, -1, 0, 0, 0, 0, -1, 0, 0, -1, 0)^T$	2^{80}	Type II
$(1, -1, 0, 0, 0, 0, 0, 0, -1, -1, 0, 0, 0, 0, 0, 0)^T$	2^{64}	Type II
$(1, 0, 0, 0, -1, 0, 0, 0, -1, 0, 0, 0, 1, 0, 0, 0)^T$	2^{64}	Type II
$(1, 0, 0, 0, 1, 0, 0, 0, 1, 0, 0, 0, -1, 0, 0, 0)^T$	2^{64}	Type II
$(1, 1, 0, 0, 0, 0, 0, 0, 1, 1, 0, 0, 0, 0, 0, 0)^T$	2^{64}	Type II
$(0, 0, 0, 0, 0, 0, 0, 0, 0, 0, 1, -1, 0, 0, 1, 1)^T$	2^{64}	Type I
$(0, 0, 0, 0, 0, 0, 1, -1, 0, 0, 0, 0, 0, 0, 1, 1)^T$	2^{64}	Type I
$(0, 0, 0, 1, 0, 0, 0, 1, 0, 0, 0, -1, 0, 0, 0, 1)^T$	2^{64}	Type I

B   Test Code for Nonlinear Invariant from Sect. 5.3

The following code was tested using SAGE 8.1.

```
1   import random
2   from operator import xor
3   from sage.crypto.sboxes import Midori_Sb0 as Sb0
4   from sage.crypto.boolean_function import BooleanFunction
5
6   def xor3(a, b, c):
7       return xor(a, xor(b, c))
8
9   def mixColumn(nibbles):
10      return [
11          xor3(nibbles[1], nibbles[2], nibbles[3]),
12          xor3(nibbles[0], nibbles[2], nibbles[3]),
13          xor3(nibbles[0], nibbles[1], nibbles[3]),
14          xor3(nibbles[0], nibbles[1], nibbles[2])
15      ]
16
17  def subCell(nibbles):
18      for i in range(16):
19          nibbles[i] = Sb0(nibbles[i])
20
21  def addKey(nibbles, key):
22      for i in range(16):
23          nibbles[i] = xor(nibbles[i], key[i])
24
25  RC = [
26      [0,0,0,1,0,1,0,1,1,0,1,1,0,0,1,1], [0,1,1,1,1,0,0,0,1,1,0,0,0,0,0,0],
27      [1,0,1,0,0,1,0,0,0,0,1,1,0,1,0,1], [0,1,1,0,0,0,1,0,0,0,0,1,0,0,1,1],
28      [0,0,0,1,0,0,0,0,0,1,0,0,1,1,1,1], [1,1,0,1,0,0,0,1,0,1,1,1,0,0,0,0],
29      [0,0,0,0,0,0,1,0,0,1,1,0,0,1,1,0], [0,0,0,0,1,0,1,1,1,1,0,0,1,1,0,0],
30      [1,0,0,1,0,1,0,0,1,0,0,0,0,0,0,1], [0,1,0,0,0,0,0,0,0,1,0,1,1,1,0,0,0],
31      [0,1,1,1,0,0,0,1,1,0,0,1,0,1,1,1], [0,0,1,0,0,0,1,0,1,0,0,0,1,1,1,0],
32      [0,1,0,1,0,0,0,1,0,0,1,1,0,0,0,0], [1,1,1,1,1,0,0,0,1,1,0,0,1,0,1,0],
33      [1,1,0,1,1,1,1,1,1,0,0,1,0,0,0,0]
34  ]
35
36  def addRoundConstants(nibbles, r, b):
37      for i in range(16):
38          nibbles[i] = xor(nibbles[i], RC[r][i] << b)
39
40  ShuffleCell = [0, 10, 5, 15, 14, 4, 11, 1, 9, 3, 12, 6, 7, 13, 2, 8]
41  def shuffleCells(nibbles):
42      result = [0] * 16
43      for i in range(16):
44          result[i] = nibbles[ShuffleCell[i]]
45      return result
46
47  def midori64(nibbles, rounds, key, b = 0):
48      whitening_key = [xor(key[0][i], key[1][i]) for i in range(16)]
49      addKey(nibbles, whitening_key)
50      for i in range(rounds - 1):
```

```
51          subCell(nibbles)
52          nibbles = shuffleCells(nibbles)
53          for j in range(4):
54              result = mixColumn(nibbles[4*j:4*j+4])
55              for k in range(4):
56                  nibbles[4*j + k] = result[k]
57          addRoundConstants(nibbles, i, b)
58          addKey(nibbles, key[i % 2])
59      subCell(nibbles)
60      addKey(nibbles, whitening_key)
61      return nibbles
62
63
64  R.<x0, x1, x2, x3> = BooleanPolynomialRing(4)
65  f = BooleanFunction(x0*x2 + x0 + x1 + x3)
66  g = BooleanFunction(x0 + x2)
67
68  key = [[0] * 16, [0] * 16]
69
70  # Test vector
71  assert midori64([0] * 16, 16, key) == \
72      [3, 12, 9, 12, 12, 14, 13, 10, 2, 11, 11, 13, 4, 4, 9, 10]
73
74  nb_tests = 100
75  b = 1 # Add RC to bit b
76
77  counts = [0, 0]
78  for i in range(nb_tests):
79      input_value = [random.randint(0, 15) for i in range(16)]
80      input_projection = reduce(xor, map(g, input_value))
81      output_value = midori64(input_value, 16, key, b)
82      output_projection = reduce(xor, map(g, output_value))
83      counts[xor(input_projection, output_projection)] += 1
84
85  print ''Correlation: '', 2 * counts[1] / sum(counts) - 1
```

References

1. Abdelraheem, M.A., Ågren, M., Beelen, P., Leander, G.: On the distribution of linear biases: three instructive examples. In: Safavi-Naini, R., Canetti, R. (eds.) CRYPTO 2012. LNCS, vol. 7417, pp. 50–67. Springer, Heidelberg (2012). https://doi.org/10.1007/978-3-642-32009-5_4
2. Banik, S.: Midori: a block cipher for low energy. In: Iwata, T., Cheon, J.H. (eds.) ASIACRYPT 2015, part II. LNCS, vol. 9453, pp. 411–436. Springer, Heidelberg (2015). https://doi.org/10.1007/978-3-662-48800-3_17
3. Beierle, C., Canteaut, A., Leander, G., Rotella, Y.: Proving resistance against invariant attacks: how to choose the round constants. In: Katz, J., Shacham, H. (eds.) CRYPTO 2017, part II. LNCS, vol. 10402, pp. 647–678. Springer, Cham (2017). https://doi.org/10.1007/978-3-319-63715-0_22
4. Beierle, C.: The SKINNY family of block ciphers and its low-latency variant MANTIS. In: Robshaw, M., Katz, J. (eds.) CRYPTO 2016, part II. LNCS, vol. 9815, pp. 123–153. Springer, Heidelberg (2016). https://doi.org/10.1007/978-3-662-53008-5_5
5. Biryukov, A., Perrin, L.: State of the art in lightweight symmetric cryptography. Cryptology ePrint Archive, Report 2017/511 (2017). http://eprint.iacr.org/2017/511
6. Borghoff, J.: PRINCE – a low-latency block cipher for pervasive computing applications - extended abstract. In: Wang, X., Sako, K. (eds.) ASIACRYPT 2012. LNCS, vol. 7658, pp. 208–225. Springer, Heidelberg (2012). https://doi.org/10.1007/978-3-642-34961-4_14
7. Ceccherini-Silberstein, T., Scarabotti, F., Tolli, F.: Harmonic Analysis on Finite Groups. Cambridge University Press, Cambridge (2008)
8. Daemen, J., Govaerts, R., Vandewalle, J.: Correlation matrices. In: Preneel, B. (ed.) FSE 1994. LNCS, vol. 1008, pp. 275–285. Springer, Heidelberg (1995). https://doi.org/10.1007/3-540-60590-8_21
9. Daemen, J., Rijmen, V.: The wide trail design strategy. In: Honary, B. (ed.) Cryptography and Coding 2001. LNCS, vol. 2260, pp. 222–238. Springer, Heidelberg (2001). https://doi.org/10.1007/3-540-45325-3_20
10. Diaconis, P.: Group Representations in Probability and Statistics. Lecture Notes-Monograph Series, vol. 11. Institute of Mathematical Statistics, Hayward, CA (1988). https://doi.org/10.1214/lnms/1215467418
11. Dobraunig, C., Eichlseder, M., Kales, D., Mendel, F.: Practical key-recovery attack on MANTIS5. IACR Trans. Symm. Cryptol. 2016(2), 248–260 (2016). https://doi.org/10.13154/tosc.v2016.i2.248-260. http://tosc.iacr.org/index.php/ToSC/article/view/573
12. Dravie, B., Parriaux, J., Guillot, P., Millérioux, G.: Matrix representations of vectorial Boolean functions and eigenanalysis. Cryptogr. Commun. Discret. Struct. Boolean Funct. Seq. 8(4), 555–577 (2016). https://doi.org/10.1007/s12095-015-0160-7. https://hal.archives-ouvertes.fr/hal-01259921
13. Eichlseder, M., Kales, D.: Clustering related-tweak characteristics: application to MANTIS-6. IACR Trans. Symm. Cryptol. 2018(2), 111–132 (2018). https://doi.org/10.13154/tosc.v2018.i2.111-132
14. Feller, W.: An Introduction to Probability Theory and Its Applications, vol. 2. Wiley, New York (1971)

15. Guo, J., Jean, J., Nikolic, I., Qiao, K., Sasaki, Y., Sim, S.M.: Invariant subspace attack against Midori64 and the resistance criteria for S-box designs. IACR Trans. Symm. Cryptol. **2016**(1), 33–56 (2016). https://doi.org/10.13154/tosc.v2016.i1. 33-56. http://tosc.iacr.org/index.php/ToSC/article/view/534
16. Knudsen, L.R., Wagner, D.: Integral cryptanalysis. In: Daemen, J., Rijmen, V. (eds.) FSE 2002. LNCS, vol. 2365, pp. 112–127. Springer, Heidelberg (2002). https://doi.org/10.1007/3-540-45661-9_9
17. Leander, G., Abdelraheem, M.A., AlKhzaimi, H., Zenner, E.: A cryptanalysis of PRINTCIPHER: the invariant subspace attack. In: Rogaway, P. (ed.) CRYPTO 2011. LNCS, vol. 6841, pp. 206–221. Springer, Heidelberg (2011). https://doi.org/10.1007/978-3-642-22792-9_12
18. Lin, L., Wu, W.: Meet-in-the-middle attacks on reduced-round Midori64. IACR Trans. Symm. Cryptol. **2017**(1), 215–239 (2017). https://doi.org/10.13154/tosc.v2017.i1.215-239
19. Luykx, A., Mennink, B., Paterson, K.G.: Analyzing multi-key security degradation. In: Takagi, T., Peyrin, T. (eds.) ASIACRYPT 2017, part II. LNCS, vol. 10625, pp. 575–605. Springer, Cham (2017). https://doi.org/10.1007/978-3-319-70697-9_20
20. Matsui, M.: Linear cryptanalysis method for DES cipher. In: Helleseth, T. (ed.) EUROCRYPT 1993. LNCS, vol. 765, pp. 386–397. Springer, Heidelberg (1994). https://doi.org/10.1007/3-540-48285-7_33
21. Nyberg, K.: Linear approximation of block ciphers. In: De Santis, A. (ed.) EUROCRYPT 1994. LNCS, vol. 950, pp. 439–444. Springer, Heidelberg (1995). https://doi.org/10.1007/BFb0053460
22. Todo, Y., Leander, G., Sasaki, Y.: Nonlinear invariant attack - practical attack on full SCREAM, iSCREAM, and Midori64. In: Cheon, J.H., Takagi, T. (eds.) ASIACRYPT 2016, part II. LNCS, vol. 10032, pp. 3–33. Springer, Heidelberg (2016). https://doi.org/10.1007/978-3-662-53890-6_1
23. Zhan, C., Xiaoyun, W.: Impossible differential cryptanalysis of Midori. Cryptology ePrint Archive, Report 2016/535 (2016). http://eprint.iacr.org/2016/535

Post-Quantum Cryptanalysis

Practical Attacks Against the Walnut Digital Signature Scheme

Ward Beullens[1]([⊠]) and Simon R. Blackburn[2]

[1] imec-COSIC KU Leuven, Kasteelpark Arenberg 10 - bus 2452,
3001 Heverlee, Belgium
Ward.Beullens@esat.kuleuven.be
[2] Department of Mathematics, Royal Holloway, University of London,
Egham, Surrey TW20 0EX, UK
S.Blackburn@rhul.ac.uk

Abstract. Recently, NIST started the process of standardizing quantum-resistant public-key cryptographic algorithms. WalnutDSA, the subject of this paper, is one of the 20 proposed signature schemes that are being considered for standardization. Walnut relies on a one-way function called E-Multiplication, which has a rich algebraic structure. This paper shows that this structure can be exploited to launch several practical attacks against the Walnut cryptosystem. The attacks work very well in practice; it is possible to forge signatures and compute equivalent secret keys for the 128-bit and 256-bit security parameters submitted to NIST in less than a second and in less than a minute respectively.

Keywords: WalnutDSA · NIST PQC
Post-quantum digital signatures · Cryptanalysis
Group based cryptography

1 Introduction

As more and more progress is being made towards building large scale quantum computers, the need for cryptography that can withstand cryptanalysis from these machines has become increasingly urgent. In recognition of this fact, NIST has started the Post-Quantum Cryptography standardization project [20] and made a call for quantum-resistant public-key cryptographic algorithms for standardization. The community has answered this call by submitting 20 proposals for signature schemes and 49 proposals for encryption schemes. One of the submitted signature schemes is the Walnut digital signature algorithm [5,8], submitted by D. Atkins and owned by SecureRF. SecureRF is a corporation founded in 2004 that develops and licenses public-key security tools for the low-resource processors powering the Internet of Things (IoT) [1]. SecureRF received the ARM Techcon 2017 "Best contribution to IoT security" award for the Walnut signature scheme and their "Key Agreement Protocol". SecureRF wants to achieve widespread usage of the Walnut signature scheme in the booming IoT

© International Association for Cryptologic Research 2018
T. Peyrin and S. Galbraith (Eds.): ASIACRYPT 2018, LNCS 11272, pp. 35–61, 2018.
https://doi.org/10.1007/978-3-030-03326-2_2

market through standardization, partnerships with manufactures like Intel and STMicroelectronics and by providing free toolkits for popular low end platforms. Because of this potential for widespread use, it is crucial to analyze the Walnut scheme for potential weaknesses.

Related Work. For its security, Walnut relies on problems taken from the theory of infinite non-commutative groups (more precisely, problems based on an action of a braid group on a finite set via the coloured Burau representation). The idea of using infinite groups in cryptography goes back at least as far as Wagner and Magyarik [26] in 1985; see González Vasco and Steinwandt [25] for an attack on this proposal. Problems in braid groups have been proposed as hard problems for cryptographic primitives for about 20 years now: key agreement protocols due to Ko et al. [18] and Anshel, Anshel and Goldfeld [3] (which is in a more general setting) are the best known examples. The Algebraic Eraser [4] is a more recent proposal, also promoted by SecureRF, which uses many of the same algebraic techniques as Walnut. Early cryptanalyses of these schemes used length-based attacks [15,16], but the most convincing attacks [10–12,17,23] have generally been based on representation theory (where 'linearisation' techniques reduce the underlying security to a problem in linear algebra). Walnut is interesting because these linearisation techniques do not seem to apply.

The first attack on (an earlier version of) Walnut [6] is due to Hart et al. [14]. The attack forges signatures in minutes for the suggested parameters, but the resulting signatures are significantly longer than legitimately produced signatures. So the Hart et al. attack can be blocked by imposing a length limit on valid signatures. In their submission to NIST, the designers of Walnut impose such a length limit in order to block the Hart et al. attack, but also modify the scheme in a significant way (in particular changing the form of the public and private keys) in an attempt to block the attack altogether.

Contributions. In this paper we present three independent practical attacks on the Walnut signature scheme. The first attack is a modification of the attack of [14] that applies to the adapted version of Walnut that was supposed to resist this attack. This first attack is practical, but has the same limitation as the original attack by Hart et al.: the forged signatures are very long. This attack demonstrates that the modifications intended to completely block the Hart et al. attack are not effective, but the attack can be blocked (as before) by imposing a length limit on signatures. The other two attacks presented in this paper produce forgeries whose lengths are the same or even shorter than those of legitimate signatures. The second attack in this paper constructs pairs of messages with the same signature; the attacker can choose a large amount of the structure of these messages. Our third attack directly constructs equivalent secret keys. We are able to forge signatures and compute equivalent secret keys in under one second for 128-bit security parameters, and in less than a minute for 256-bit security parameters. This shows that the parameter sets submitted to the NIST PQC standardization project are totally insecure, and that the corresponding implementation (which was freely available on the SecureRF website before we notified them of our attacks) should not be used. Our attacks exploit various algebraic properties of the one-way function called E-Multiplication, which is fundamental for the Walnut scheme (and other SecureRF methods). In fact, we give a practical algorithm to break the one-wayness of this function for the parameters submitted to NIST. In order to avoid the attacks given here, the parameters of Walnut need to be increased significantly (see the conclusion at the end of the paper for details). However, with these increased parameter sizes, it seems that Walnut loses its performance advantage over other post-quantum signature schemes such as lattice-based, code-based, multivariate and hash-based signatures.

Outline. In Sect. 2 we explain some necessary preliminaries such as distinguished point collision finding, a very short introduction to braid groups, and an explanation of E-Multiplication and the workings of the Walnut signature scheme. The following Sects. 3, 4 and 5, each introduce a practical attack against the Walnut scheme and discusses the feasibility of countermeasures. Section 3 contains an adaptation of the factorization attack of [14] that applies to the updated version of Walnut that was submitted to NIST. Section 4 describes an attack where we use a generic distinguished point collision finding method to find two documents d_1 and d_2 such that a signature that is valid for d_1 is automatically valid for d_2 and vice versa. In Sect. 5 we give an algorithm that breaks the one-wayness of the E-Multiplication map. This algorithm can be used to forge signatures and compute equivalent secret keys, even for the 256 bits of security parameters. The last section presents the conclusions of the paper.

2   Preliminaries

2.1   Distinguished Point Collision Finding

The attacks introduced in this paper rely on a collision finding algorithm that is able to find a collision in any function $f : D \to D$ which maps a domain D to itself. Our algorithm of choice is the distinguished point method of van Oorschot and Wiener [24]. Finding a single collision with this method has the same $O(\sqrt{|D|})$ time complexity as Pollard's rho method with cycle finding [21, 22], but it can be parallelized more efficiently. Moreover, the method of van Oorschot and Wiener is much more efficient for finding multiple collisions; the number of collisions found grows quadratically with the time spent.

The algorithm repeatedly chooses a random starting point $x_1 \in D$ and iteratively applies the function f to obtain a chain of values $x_1, x_2, \cdots$, where $x_i = f(x_{i-1})$ for all $i > 1$. This process continues until a *distinguished* value x_k is reached. This is a value which satisfies some easily verified property, such as having a fixed number of leading zero bits. This property is chosen such that it is satisfied by a fraction ϑ of the elements of D. When the distinguished point is reached the starting point x_1, the distinguished point x_k and the length k of the chain is stored in a table. Assuming f behaves like a random function, after an expected number of $O(\sqrt{|D|})$ function calls the current chain will collide with one of the previously computed chains. From this point on we will follow the same chain and we will end up at the same distinguished point. We read the starting poins x_1, x_1' and the corresponding chain lengths k, k' from the table. Without loss of generality, we assume that $k \geq k'$. We then know that for some $i < k'$

$$x_{k-k'+i} \neq x_i' \qquad \text{and} \qquad f(x_{k-k'+i}) = f(x_i'),$$

unless the starting point x_0' appears in the chain starting at x_0 (which only happens with a very small probability). This collision can be extracted with $k - k' + 2i$ function calls. If we require more than one collision we can continue the process, maintaining the contents of the table. Since over time the table will contain more and more chains, the rate at which collisions are found will also increase.

2.2   Braid Groups

Informally, the braid group on N strands is a group whose elements are represented by a configuration of N non-intersecting vertical strands in three dimensional space, where 2 configurations are considered equal if one can be transformed continuously into the other configuration without intersecting the strands. The group multiplication is defined as the concatenation of the strands. Artin [9] showed that there is an equivalent definition of braid groups, given by the presentation

$$\left\langle b_1, \cdots, b_{N-1} \,\middle|\, \begin{array}{ll} b_i b_j = b_j b_i & \text{for } 1 \leq i < j < N \text{ and } j - i \geq 2 \\ b_i b_{i+1} b_i = b_{i+1} b_i b_{i+1} & \text{for } 1 \leq i < N - 1 \end{array} \right\rangle.$$

Here, the *Artin generator* b_i represents the braid where the i-th strand crosses over the $(i+1)$-th strand. The relations $b_i b_j = b_j b_i$ for $|i - j| \geq 2$ correspond to the fact that crossings that involve different strands are free to move past each other. The relations $b_i b_{i+1} b_i = b_{i+1} b_i b_{i+1}$ correspond to moving one strand over the crossing of two other strands. The Artin generators and their relations are graphically represented in Figs. 1, 2 and 3.

There is a natural homomorphism $\sigma : B_N \to S_N$ from the braid group on N strands to the symmetric group of order N that maps each braid to the permutation obtained by following the strands. This map sends an Artin generator b_i to the transposition $\sigma(b_i) = (i \ \ i+1)$. Elements in the kernel of this homomorphism are called *pure braids*, the kernel itself is called the *pure braid group on N strands* and is denoted by P_N.

The braid group B_2 on two strands is the infinite cyclic group, so this group is its own center. For $N > 2$ the center of the braid group on N strands is generated by the full-twist braid which is obtained by grabbing the ends of the strands of the identity braid and rotating them by $360°$ [13]. This braid is commonly denoted by Δ^2 and is depicted in Fig. 4.

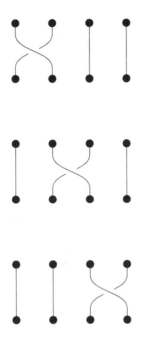

Fig. 1. The three Artin generators b_1, b_2 and b_3 that generate B_4.

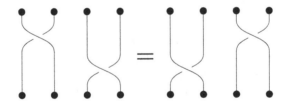

Fig. 2. Crossings that do not share strands commute, i.e. $b_1 b_3 = b_3 b_1$

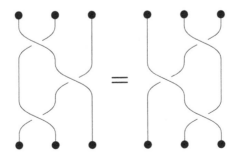

Fig. 3. The first strand moves over the crossing of strand 2 and 3, i.e. $b_1 b_2 b_1 = b_2 b_1 b_2$.

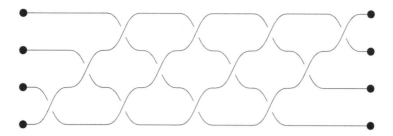

Fig. 4. The full-twist braid Δ^2 in the braid group on 4 strands.

2.3   The Colored Burau Representation and E-Multiplication

The Walnut digital signature algorithm relies heavily on a group action called *E-Multiplication*. To define this group action we need the colored Burau Representation (see, for example, Anshel et al. [2]) which is a homomorphism from the braid group B_N to the *colored Burau group* $GL_N(\mathbb{Z}[t_1^{\pm 1}, \cdots, t_N^{\pm 1}]) \rtimes S_N$. This group is defined as a semidirect product, by letting the symmetric group S_N act on $GL_N(\mathbb{Z}[t_1^{\pm 1}, \cdots, t_N^{\pm 1}])$ by permuting the variables t_i. More concretely, the elements of the colored Burau group are pairs $(\mathbf{A}(t_1, \cdots, t_N), \pi)$ where $\pi \in S_N$ is a permutation and where $\mathbf{A}(t_1, \cdots, t_N)$ is an invertible $N \times N$ matrix whose entries lie in $\mathbb{Z}[t_1^{\pm 1}, \cdots, t_N^{\pm 1}]$. Multiplication in the colored Burau group is defined by

$$(\mathbf{A}(t_1, \cdots, t_N), \pi) \cdot (\mathbf{B}(t_1, \cdots, t_N), \tau) := (\mathbf{A}(t_1, \cdots, t_N) \cdot \pi(\mathbf{B}(t_1, \cdots, t_N)), \pi\tau)$$
$$= (\mathbf{A}(t_1, \cdots, t_N) \cdot \mathbf{B}(t_{\pi(1)}, \cdots, t_{\pi(N)}), \pi\tau).$$

The *colored Burau representation* $CB : B_N \to GL_N(\mathbb{Z}[t_1^{\pm 1}, \cdots, t_N^{\pm 1}]) \rtimes S_N$ is defined at each Artin generator as $CB(b_i) = (CBM(i), \sigma(b_i))$, where $CBM(i)$ is a matrix and $\sigma(b_i)$ is a permutation, defined as follows. The permutation $\sigma(b_i)$ is the transposition $(i\ i+1)$. We define $CBM(b_1)$, the colored Burau matrix of b_1, as

$$CBM(b_1) = \left(\begin{array}{cc|c} -t_1 & 1 & 0 \\ 0 & 1 & 0 \\ \hline 0 & 0 & \mathbb{1}_{N-2} \end{array} \right),$$

where $\mathbb{1}_{N-2}$ is the $(N-2) \times (N-2)$ identity matrix. For $i > 1$ the colored Burau matrix of b_i is defined as

$$CBM(b_i) = \left(\begin{array}{c|ccc|c} \mathbb{1}_{i-2} & 0 & 0 & 0 & 0 \\ \hline 0 & 1 & 0 & 0 & 0 \\ 0 & t_i & -t_i & 1 & 0 \\ 0 & 0 & 0 & 1 & 0 \\ \hline 0 & 0 & 0 & 0 & \mathbb{1}_{N-i-1} \end{array} \right).$$

This definition of $CB(b_i)$ is compatible with the relations of the braid group, so it can be extended to define a homomorphism on the entire group B_N. For a braid b, the matrix component of $CB(b)$ is called the *colored Burau matrix* of b and is denoted by $CBM(b)$, the permutation component of $CB(b)$ is simply equal to $\sigma(b)$. This implies that pure braids are mapped into the subgroup $GL_N(\mathbb{Z}[t_1^{\pm 1}, \cdots, t_N^{\pm 1}]) \subset GL_N(\mathbb{Z}[t_1^{\pm 1}, \cdots, t_N^{\pm 1}]) \rtimes S_N$.

Now we fix a finite field $\mathbb{F}_q$, and for any integer k with $1 < k \leq N$ we define A_k to be the group of invertible N-by-N matrices of the form

$$A_k = \left\{ \begin{pmatrix} X & Y & 0 \\ 0 & 1 & 0 \\ 0 & 0 & \mathbb{1}_{N-k} \end{pmatrix} \,|\, X \in GL_{k-1}(\mathbb{F}_q), Y \in \mathbb{F}_q^{k-1} \right\}.$$

Let $T = [\tau_1, \cdots, \tau_N]$ be a list of N non-zero values in a finite field $\mathbb{F}_q$. The *evaluation* $M \downarrow_T$ of a matrix $\mathbf{M}(t_1, \cdots, t_n)$ at T is computed by replacing each occurence of variable t_i by τ:

$$M \downarrow_T := M(\tau_1, \cdots, \tau_N).$$

This map is a well-defined homomorphism on the image $\mathrm{im}(CB)$ of CB. For a list T containing N non-zero finite field elements, we can now define a right group action, called E-Multiplication and denoted by $\star$, of the braid group B_N on the set $A_N \times S_N$. A braid b acts on the first component of the pair (M, π) by multiplying from the right with a matrix obtained from the colored Burau matrix of b by permuting the variables t_i using π and then evaluating at T. The second component of the action is obtained by multiplying on the right by $\sigma(b)$. Written out symbolically, this is

$$(M, \pi) \star b := (M \cdot \pi(CBM(b)) \downarrow_T, \pi\sigma(b)).$$

The fact that this defines a group action follows from the fact that the colored Burau representation is a homomorphism of groups. In practice, when calculating $(M, \pi) \star b$, the action is calculated one Artin generator at a time (see Algorithm 1). Given the sparsity of the colored Burau matrices $CBM(b_i)$, acting with an Artin generator requires only a few column operations on M and one swap on π, so this is very efficient. This action was first introduced in [4], where it was used to build a key agreement protocol. More recently, E-Multiplication has been used as the basic building block for a cryptographic hash function [7] and the Walnut digital signature scheme [5].

By letting B_N act on $(\mathbb{1}_N, e) \in A_N \times S_N$ we define a map $\mathcal{P}$

$$\mathcal{P} : B_N \to A_N \times S_N : s \mapsto (\mathbb{1}_N, e) \star s.$$

When restricted to the subgroup of pure braids P_N, the second component of $\mathcal{P}$ always maps to the identity permutation, so we can think of it as a map $\mathcal{P}|_{P_N} : P_N \to A_N$. The map $\mathcal{P}|_{P_N}$ is actually a homomorphism because it is the composition of the colored Burau representation $CB : P_N \to GL_N(\mathbb{Z}[t_1^{\pm 1}, \cdots, t_N^{\pm 1}])$ and the evaluation homomorphism $\downarrow_T : \mathrm{im}(CB) \to A_N$. Moreover, if we further restrict $\mathcal{P}$ to the subgroup P_k of pure braids where only the first k strands cross over each other, i.e. the intersection of P_N with the subgroup generated by $b_1, \cdots, b_{k-1}$, the homomorphism $\mathcal{P}|_{P_k} : P_k \to A_k$ maps into the subgroup A_k. This fact will be exploited in the attack of Sect. 5.

Algorithm E-Multiplication   ————

input: (M, π) — a pair in $A_N \times S_N$ to act on
        s — a braid to act with
        $T = \{\tau_1, \cdots, \tau_N\}$ — a list of T-values
output: (M, π) — the resulting pair

1: **while** $|s| > 0$ **do**
2:     $b_i^{\pm 1} \| s \leftarrow s$ ▷ split the first generator $b_i^{\pm 1}$ from the rest of s
3:     $N \leftarrow CBM(b_i)^{\pm 1}$ ▷ The CB Matrix of b_i, inverted if necessary.
4:     $N \leftarrow N(\tau_{\pi(i)})$ ▷ Evaluate in $\tau_{\pi(i)}$
5:     $M \leftarrow M \cdot N$
6:     $\pi \leftarrow \pi \circ \sigma(b_i)$
7: **end while**
8: **return** (M, π)

Algorithm 1. The algorithm for computing the E-Multiplication action.

2.4 The Walnut Signature Scheme

We now introduce the Walnut signature scheme, which is the subject of our cryptanalysis. Before we describe the key generation, signing and verification algorithms (Algorithms 2, 4 and 5) in detail we will summarize the scheme very briefly: the secret key consists of two braids s_1, s_2 and the public key is $(M_1, \pi_1) = \mathcal{P}(s_1)$ and $M_2 = \mathsf{mat}(\mathcal{P}(s_2))$, the matrix component of $\mathcal{P}(s_2)$. To sign or verify a document d it is hashed and encoded as a pure braid $E(d)$ with an encoding mechanism E. The Walnut design [5] defines a braid sig to be a valid signature for the document d if and only if the verification equation

$$\mathsf{mat}(\mathcal{P}(s_1) \star \mathsf{sig}) = \mathsf{mat}(\mathcal{P}(E(d))) \cdot M_2 \tag{1}$$

is satisfied. However, this equation is equal to the matrix component of

$$\mathcal{P}(s_1) \star \mathsf{sig} = \mathcal{P}(E(d)) \star s_2, \tag{2}$$

and the permutation component of Eq. (2) is also satisfied by all the legitimately produced signatures. In this document we define a valid signature as a braid sig that satisfies the stronger verification Eq. (2). It is clear that $\mathsf{sig} = s_1^{-1} E(d) s_2$ would be a valid signature. In order to prevent length-based attacks [16,19] *cloaking elements*, namely braids that do not affect E-Multiplication, are inserted into the signature and the braids are put through a rewriting algorithm so that (it is hoped) s_1 and s_2 cannot easily be extracted from the signature (Table 1).

Parameters. The scheme is parametrized by:

– The number N of strands of the braid group that is being used (which is equal to the dimension of the associated square matrices).

- The size q of a finite field $\mathbb{F}_q$.
- A rewriting algorithm $\mathcal{R} : B_N \to B_N$.
- L and l, the length of certain random braid words.
- A hash function $\mathcal{H}$.

Table 1. The Walnut parameter sets submitted to the NIST Post Quantum Cryptography project, and the corresponding public key and signature sizes.

Claimed security level	128-bit	256-bit
N	8	8
q	2^5	2^8
L	15	30
l	132	287
$\mathcal{H}$	SHA2-256	SHA2-512
Public key length	83 Bytes	128 Bytes
Signature length[a]	$\approx$646 Bytes	$\approx$ 1248 Bytes

[a]Signatures have variable length. The reported signature size is an average, using the BKL + Dehornoy rewriting method.

Key Generation. The private key consists of two randomly chosen braids $s_1, s_2 \in B_N$ of length l. The braids are chosen such that their underlying permutations $\sigma(s_1)$ and $\sigma(s_2)$ are distinct and not equal to the identity permutation e. The public key contains a list $T = \{\tau_1 = 1, \tau_2 = 1, \tau_3, \cdots, \tau_n\} \in \mathbb{F}_q^N$ of N elements of the finite field $\mathbb{F}_q$ such that the first two elements are equal to 1, and such that the remaining values are non-zero and different from 1. The public key also contains $\mathcal{P}(s_1)$ and the matrix component of $\mathcal{P}(s_2)$.

Encoding a Document. In order to sign a document d or verify a signature the document is converted to a pure braid $E(d) \in P_N$. This conversion consists of two stages. First, a hash digest of d is computed with a standard hash function (SHA2-256 or SHA2-512), then this hash is converted to a braid. To make the second conversion 4 pure braids g_1, g_2, g_3, g_4 are fixed such that they generate a free subgroup of P_N. The Walnut specification document [8] defines

$$g_1 = b_N b_{N-1} \cdots b_2 \cdot b_1^2 \cdot b_2^{-1} \cdots b_{N-1}^{-1} b_N^{-1}$$
$$g_2 = b_N b_{N-1} \cdots b_4 \cdot b_3^2 \cdot b_4^{-1} \cdots b_{N-1}^{-1} b_N^{-1}$$
$$g_3 = b_N b_{N-1} \cdots b_6 \cdot b_5^2 \cdot b_6^{-1} \cdots b_{N-1}^{-1} b_N^{-1}$$
$$g_4 = b_N b_{N-1} \cdots b_8 \cdot b_7^2 \cdot b_8^{-1} \cdots b_{N-1}^{-1} b_N^{-1} .$$

```
┌─────── Algorithm GenerateKeys ──────────────────────────────┐
│  input: random bits to generate s₁, s₂ and τᵢ               │
│  output: pk — a public key                                   │
│          sk — a corresponding secret key                     │
│  1: s₁, s₂ ← a randomly chosen braid words of length l.      │
│  2: τ₁, τ₂ ← 1                                               │
│  3: for i from 3 to N do                                     │
│  4: │  τᵢ ← a randomly chosen field element, not equal to 0 or 1 │
│  5: end for                                                  │
│  6: T ← {τ₁, ⋯ , τ_N}                                       │
│  7: (M₁, π₁) ← P(s₁)                                        │
│  8: (M₂, π₂) ← P(s₂)                                        │
│  9: return pk = (T, M₁, M₂, π₁) and sk = (s₁, s₂)            │
└──────────────────────────────────────────────────────────────┘
```

Algorithm 2. The Walnut key pair generation algorithm

The encoding process starts from the trivial braid. Two bits are taken from the hash digest to choose one g_i of the 4 generators, and the next two bits of the digest define an exponent $e \in \{1, 2, 3, 4\}$. Then g_i^e is appended to the braid, and four bits are removed from the digest. This is repeated until the entire hash output is consumed.

```
┌─────── Algorithm EncodeDocument ─────────────────────────────┐
│  input: A document d                                         │
│  output: b — a pure braid                                    │
│  1: h ← H(d)                                                 │
│  2: b ← e                                                    │
│  3: for a from 0 to |h|/4 − 1 do                            │
│  4: │  i ← h[4a : 4a + 1]              ▷ Select index        │
│  5: │  e ← h[4a + 2 : 4a + 3]+1        ▷ Select exponent     │
│  6: │  b ← b · gᵢᵉ                                          │
│  7: end for                                                  │
│  8: return b                                                 │
└──────────────────────────────────────────────────────────────┘
```

Algorithm 3. The document encoding mechanism.

Signing Algorithm. The signing algorithm produces a signature which is a braid word of the form

$$\mathsf{sig}' = v_1 \cdot s_1^{-1} \cdot v \cdot E(d) \cdot s_2 \cdot v_2 ,$$

where v_1, v and v_2 are so called cloaking elements, which are braids in the stabilizer of $\mathcal{P}(s_1), (\mathbb{1}_N, e)$ and $\mathcal{P}(E(d)s_2)$ respectively. Therefore we have

$$\begin{aligned}
(\mathbb{1}_N, e) \star s_1 \cdot \mathsf{sig}' &= \mathcal{P}(s_1) \star s_1^{-1} \cdot v \cdot E(d) \cdot s_2 \cdot v_2 \\
&= (\mathbb{1}_N, e) \star v \cdot E(d) \cdot s_2 \cdot v_2 \\
&= \mathcal{P}(E(d)s_2) \cdot v_2 \\
&= (\mathbb{1}_N, e) \star E(d) \cdot s_2\,,
\end{aligned}$$

so sig' is a valid signature. To hide the secret key s_1 and s_2 which are substrings of sig' one of three proposed rewriting algorithms (BKL + Dehornoy, Stochastic + Dehornoy or Stochastic) is used to produce a different braid word sig which represents the same braid as sig'. The various rewriting algorithms differ in performance and in the length of the signatures that are produced.

The cloaking elements are generated using the following lemma.

Lemma 1. *Suppose that* $\tau_1 = \tau_2 = 1$. *Take any pair* $(M, \pi) \in A_N \times S_N$, *an Artin generator* b_i, *and any braid* w *such that*

$$\pi \circ \sigma(w)(i) = 1 \qquad \text{and} \qquad \pi \circ \sigma(w)(i+1) = 2\,.$$

Then the braid $v = w \cdot b_i^2 \cdot w^{-1}$ *is in the stabilizer of* (M, π).

To produce a cloaking element for $\mathcal{P}(s_1), (\mathbb{1}_N, e)$ or $\mathcal{P}(E(d)s_2)$ we first pick a random integer i such that $1 < i < N$, then we choose a random braid w satisfying the conditions of Lemma 1 and we set $v = wb_i^2w^{-1}$. For the details of how w is chosen (which depends on the parameter L) and the details on how the various rewriting algorithms work we refer to the WalnutDSA NIST submission [8].

Algorithm Sign ─────────

input: d — a document to sign
            $\mathsf{sk} = (s_1, s_2)$ — a secret key
output: sig — a signature for document d
1: $v_1 \leftarrow \text{GetCloakingElement}(\sigma(s_1))$
2: $v \leftarrow \text{GetCloakingElement}(e)$
3: $v_2 \leftarrow \text{GetCloakingElement}(\sigma(s_2))$
4: $E_d \leftarrow \text{EncodeDocument}(d)$
5: $\mathsf{sig}' \leftarrow v_1 \cdot s_1^{-1} \cdot v \cdot E_d \cdot s_2 \cdot v_2$
6: $\mathsf{sig} \leftarrow \mathcal{R}(\mathsf{sig}')$
7: **return** sig

Algorithm 4.   The Walnut signature generation algorithm

Verification Algorithm. Given a document d, a public key $\mathsf{pk} = (T, M_1, M_2, \pi_1)$ and a signature sig. The verification algorithm simply calculates the encoding of the message $E(d)$ and the matrix components of $(M_1, \pi_1) \star \mathsf{sig}$ and $\mathcal{P}(E(d))$. It then accepts the signature if the computed matrices satisfy the equation

$$\mathsf{mat}((M_1, \pi_1) \star \mathsf{sig}) = \mathsf{mat}(\mathcal{P}(E(d))) \cdot M_2 \, .$$

Algorithm Verify

---

input: d — a document
$\quad\quad\quad$ $\mathsf{pk} = (T, M_1, M_2, \pi_1)$ — a secret key
$\quad\quad\quad$ sig — a signature
output: **True** if sig is a valid signature for d, **False** otherwise

1: $E_d \leftarrow \mathrm{EncodeDocument}(d)$
2: LHS $\leftarrow \mathsf{mat}(\ \mathrm{E\text{-}Multiplication}((M_1, \pi_1), \mathsf{sig}, T))$
3: RHS $\leftarrow \mathsf{mat}(\ \mathrm{E\text{-}Multiplication}((\mathbb{1}_N, e), E_d, T)) \cdot M_2$
4: **if** LHS equals RHS **then**
5: $\quad$| **return True**
6: **end if**
7: **return False**

Algorithm 5. The Walnut signature verification algorithm

3   A Factorization Attack

This section describes an adaptation of the factorization attack of Hart et al. [14] on an earlier version of Walnut [6]. This earlier version is a special case of the newer construction where the two secret braids s_1 and s_2 are equal. This means that the secret key essentially consists of only a single braid s, and that the public key is a single matrix-permutation pair $(M, \pi) = \mathcal{P}(s)$. The signing and verification algorithms of the earlier version are the same as the algorithms described in the previous section after substituting s for s_1 and s_2, and substituting M for M_1 and M_2. The attack of Hart et al. exploits the following malleability property:

Theorem 1 (for the earlier version of Walnut with $s_1 = s_2$). *Suppose* d, d_1, d_2 *are three documents. Let* h, h_1, h_2 *be the matrix part of* $\mathcal{P}(E(d))$, $\mathcal{P}(E(d_1))$ *and* $\mathcal{P}(E(d_2))$ *respectively. Then we have*

1. *If* $h = h_1^{-1}$ *and* sig_1 *is a valid signature for* d_1, *then* sig_1^{-1} *is a valid signature for* d.
2. *If* $h = h_1 \cdot h_2$ *and* $\mathsf{sig}_1, \mathsf{sig}_2$ *are valid signatures for* d_1 *and* d_2 *respectively, then* $\mathsf{sig}_1\mathsf{sig}_2$ *is a valid signature for* d.

This opens up the following strategy to attack the signature scheme. First we collect a set of valid document-signature pairs (d_i, sig_i) and we let $h_i = \mathsf{mat}(\mathcal{P}(E(d_i)))$. Then, if we want to forge a signature for a document d with $h = \mathsf{mat}(\mathcal{P}(E(d)))$ it suffices to write h as a product $\prod_{j=1}^{k} h_{i_j}^{e_j}$ of the h_i. Once we have this, a valid signature for d is given by $\prod_{j=1}^{k} \mathsf{sig}_{i_j}^{e_j}$. This reduces breaking the signature scheme to breaking the factorization problem in A_N:

Factorization Problem in a Group G. Given a list of elements $g_1, \cdots, g_k$ that generate the group G and a target element g, write the target g as a (preferably short) product of the g_i and their inverses.

The paper of Hart et al. [14] proposes an algorithm to solve the factorization problem in A_N, exploiting a chain of subgroups. This allows them to forge signatures in minutes, but the factorizations that are found by the algorithm are very long, so this results in very long signatures. The forged signatures are many orders of magnitude longer than legitimate signatures, so the Walnut scheme can be saved by imposing an upper limit to the length of the signatures.

The Walnut signature scheme was adapted to destroy the malleability property of Theorem 1. In the remainder of this section we prove that an adapted version of the maleability property still holds for the new WalnutDSA scheme and we show how the property can be used to reduce breaking Walnut to solving the factorization problem in A_N, which can be solved with the techniques of [14].

3.1 Signature Malleability of Walnut

Walnut has the following malleability property, which is a generalization of the property discovered by Hart et al. (Theorem 1).

Theorem 2. *Suppose* d, d_1, d_2 *are three documents. Let* h, h_1, h_2 *be the matrix part of* $\mathcal{P}(E(d)), \mathcal{P}(E(d_1))$ *and* $\mathcal{P}(E(d_2))$ *respectively. Let* $s_1, s_2, s_3 \in B_N$ *be three braids. Then*

1. *If* $h = h_1^{-1}$ *and* sig_1 *is a valid signature for* d_1 *under the public key* $(\mathcal{P}(s_1), \mathcal{P}(s_2))$, *then* sig_1^{-1} *is a valid signature for* d *under the public key* $(\mathcal{P}(s_2), \mathcal{P}(s_1))$.
2. *If* $h = h_1 \cdot h_2$ *and* $\mathsf{sig}_1, \mathsf{sig}_2$ *are valid signatures for* d_1 *and* d_2 *under the public keys* $(\mathcal{P}(s_1), \mathcal{P}(s_2))$ *and* $(\mathcal{P}(s_2), \mathcal{P}(s_3))$ *respectively, then* $\mathsf{sig}_1 \cdot \mathsf{sig}_2$ *is a valid signature for* d *under the public key* $(\mathcal{P}(s_1), \mathcal{P}(s_3))$.

Proof. We start by proving 1. Since sig_1 is a valid signature for d_1 we have

$$\mathcal{P}(s_1) \star \mathsf{sig}_1 = \mathcal{P}(E(d_1)) \star s_2.$$

Acting on this by sig_1^{-1} and using the definition of $\mathcal{P}$ we get

$$(\mathbb{1}_N, e) \star s_1 = (h_1, e) \star s_2 \cdot \mathsf{sig}_1^{-1},$$

where we have used the fact that $E(d_1)$ is a pure braid. Multiplying the matrix part of this equality by h_1^{-1} from the left (multiplying on the left by a matrix commutes with $\star$), we get

$$(h_1^{-1}, e) \star s_1 = (\mathbb{1}_N, e) \star s_2 \cdot \mathsf{sig}_1^{-1},$$

or equivalently

$$\mathcal{P}(E(d)) \star s_1 = \mathcal{P}(s_2) \star \mathsf{sig}_1^{-1},$$

which shows that sig_1^{-1} is a valid signature for d for the public key $(\mathcal{P}(s_2), \mathcal{P}(s_1))$.

To prove 2 we start by acting with sig_2 on the verification equation for sig_1 to get

$$\mathcal{P}(s_1) \star \mathsf{sig}_1 \cdot \mathsf{sig}_2 = \mathcal{P}(E(d_1)) \star s_2 \cdot \mathsf{sig}_2$$
$$= (h_1 \cdot CBM(s_2)_{\downarrow T} \cdot {}^{\sigma(s_2)} (CBM(\mathsf{sig}_2))_{\downarrow T}, \sigma(s_2) \circ \sigma(\mathsf{sig}_2)).$$

Using the fact that sig_2 is a valid signature for d_2 under the public key $(\mathcal{P}(s_2), \mathcal{P}(s_3))$, we see that

$$\mathcal{P}(s_1) \star \mathsf{sig}_1 \cdot \mathsf{sig}_2 = (h_1 \cdot h_2 \cdot CBM(s_3)_{\downarrow T}, \sigma(s_3))$$
$$= (h_1 \cdot h_2, e) \star s_3$$
$$= \mathcal{P}(E(d)) \star s_3,$$

which shows that $\mathsf{sig}_1 \cdot \mathsf{sig}_2$ is a valid signature for d under the public key $(\mathcal{P}(s_1), \mathcal{P}(s_3))$.

3.2   The Factorization Attack

Given an oracle $\mathcal{O}_f$ (which can be instantiated by the algorithm of [14]) that solves the factorization for the group A_N, we can now break Walnut as follows. Suppose we want to forge a signature for a document d under the public key $(\mathcal{P}(s_1), \mathcal{P}(s_2))$. Let h be the matrix part of $\mathcal{P}(E(d))$. We start by collecting a number of document-signature pairs $(d_1, \mathsf{sig}_1), \cdots, (d_k, \mathsf{sig}_k)$ that are valid under the same public key, and we compute the matrix part h_i of each pair $\mathcal{P}(E(d_i))$. Now it suffices to find a factorization $h = h_{i_1} \cdot h_{i_2}^{-1} \cdot h_{i_3} \cdots h_{i_{m-1}}^{-1} \cdot h_{i_m}$ whose factors have powers that alternate between 1 and -1. Indeed, combining properties of Theorem 2 we see that $\mathsf{sig}_{i_1} \cdot \mathsf{sig}_{i_2}^{-1}$ is a valid signature for any document d' such that $\mathsf{mat}(\mathcal{P}(E(d'))) = h_{i_1} \cdot h_{i_2}^{-1}$ under the public key $(\mathcal{P}(s_1), \mathcal{P}(s_1))$. Adding an extra factor, we get that $\mathsf{sig}_{i_1} \cdot \mathsf{sig}_{i_2}^{-1} \cdot \mathsf{sig}_{i_3}$ is a valid signature for an appropriate document under the public key $(\mathcal{P}(s_1), \mathcal{P}(s_2))$. Continuing the same argument for the odd number m of factors of the product we get that $\mathsf{sig}_{i_1} \cdot \mathsf{sig}_{i_2}^{-1} \cdot \mathsf{sig}_{i_3} \cdots \mathsf{sig}_{i_{m-1}}^{-1} \cdot \mathsf{sig}_{i_m}$ is a valid document for d under the desired public key $(\mathcal{P}(s_1), \mathcal{P}(s_2))$.

We can use the oracle $\mathcal{O}_f$ to find the factorization $h = h_{i_1} \cdot h_{i_2}^{-1} \cdot h_{i_3} \cdots h_{i_{m-1}}^{-1} \cdot h_{i_m}$. We construct the list of generators

$$\mathsf{gens} = \{h_i \cdot h_j^{-1} \mid i \neq j \in \{1, \cdots, k\}\}$$

and call the oracle $\mathcal{O}_f$ to obtain a factorization for $h \cdot h_1^{-1}$ with factors in this set of generators. Appending the factor h_1 to the resulting factorization we then get a factorization of h of the desired form.

3.3 Implications and Countermeasures

The factorization algorithm of [14] has a time complexity of $O\left(q^{\frac{N-1}{2}}\right)$ and for the 128 bit security parameters of Walnut (i.e. $N = 8$, $q = 2^5$) the algorithm finds a factorization in minutes. However, these factorizations contain roughly 2^{25} factors, so the forged signatures are the concatenation of roughly 2^{25} legitimate signatures. This implies that the forged signatures are many orders of magnitude longer than legitimate signatures and so they can be detected easily by the verifier. To protect against this attack it suffices to impose a limit on the length of signatures. Interestingly, when the WalnutDSA scheme was updated to counter the attack of [14], no such upper limit was included in the design. Our adaptation of the attack shows that this limit is necessary for the security of the scheme, because long forgeries can be produced in a matter of minutes.

The implementation submitted to the NIST PQC standardization project implicitly imposes such an upper limit by specifying that the length of the signature (measured by the number of Artin generators) be encoded by two bytes. This effectively limits the signature braids to be at most 2^{16} Artin generators long. Therefore the attack cannot be used to break the NIST implementation of WalnutDSA.

4 A Collision Search Attack

From the verification equation

$$\mathcal{P}(s_1) \star \mathsf{sig} = \mathcal{P}(E(d)) \star s_2$$

it is clear that the only dependence on the document d is through the encoding mechanism E and the mapping $\mathcal{P}$. This implies that if d_1 and d_2 are two documents such that $\mathcal{P}(E(d_1)) = \mathcal{P}(E(d_2))$, then any signature that is valid for d_1 is automatically valid for d_2 and vice versa. Therefore breaking EUF-CMA security reduces to finding such a pair of documents. Once an attacker has found two such documents he can ask the signing oracle to produce a signature sig for d_1, and return (sig, d_2) to win the EUF-CMA game. Since the first step of the encoding function E is the application of a cryptographically secure hash function to the document d we cannot reasonably expect to have a more efficient way of finding collisions than with a generic collision search. A generic collision search requires roughly $|\mathcal{P}(E(\{0,1\}^*))|^{1/2}$ evaluations of $\mathcal{P} \circ E$. In the rest of this section we give an upper bound for this quantity and we demonstrate with computer experiments that a collision attack is practical.

4.1   Sizes of Orbits of E-Multiplication

To estimate the time complexity of the collision search attack we need to find the size of $\mathcal{P}(E(\{0,1\}^*))$. Without much motivation the designers of WalnutDSA claim that $q^{N(N-3)}N!$ is a conservative lower bound on the number values that $\mathcal{P}$ can take [5]. For 128-bit and 256-bit security parameters this number is roughly 2^{216} and 2^{336} respectively, which means that finding a collision should require roughly 2^{108} and 2^{168} evaluations of $\mathcal{P} \circ E$. Note that this is already significantly less than the claimed security levels. Moreover, an elementary analysis will reveal that this "conservative lower bound" is actually much larger than the true value of $|\mathcal{P}(B_N)|$. Even worse, when $\mathcal{P}$ is restricted to the set of braids that can be produced by the encoding mechanism E, the number of values that can be reached is much smaller still.

We know that $\mathcal{P}$, when restricted to the subgroup of pure braids, is a homomorphism from P_N to A_N. This implies that the full twist braid Δ^2 (see Sect. 2.2) which generates the center of P_N is mapped to a matrix in the center of $\mathcal{P}(P_N)$. It can be verified that the only matrix in the center of A_N is the identity matrix, but for a randomly chosen set of T-values $\mathcal{P}(\Delta^2)$ is typically not the identity matrix. This means that $\mathcal{P}(A_N)$ sits inside the centralizer of $\mathcal{P}(\Delta^2)$, which is typically a proper subspace of $\langle A_N \rangle$. This begs the question of what the dimension of $\langle \mathcal{P}(P_N) \rangle$ is. From computer experiments we can conclude that for randomly chosen T-values this is equal to the dimension of the centralizer of $\mathcal{P}(\Delta^2)$, which is equal to $(N-1)^2 + 1$ (since $\mathcal{P}(\Delta^2)$ has one eigenspace of dimension $N-1$ and one of dimension 1). However, if we impose the extra condition that the first two T-values are equal to one, $\mathcal{P}(P_N)$ is contained in an affine subspace of dimension $(N-2)^2 + 1$, so $|\mathcal{P}(P_N)|$ is at most $q^{(N-2)^2+1}$. Our computer experiments suggest that this upper bound is reasonably tight, and so we estimate $|\mathcal{P}(P_N)| \approx q^{(N-2)^2+1}$. Since P_N is a subgroup of B_N of index $N!$ we have $|\mathcal{P}(B_N)| < q^{(N-2)^2+1}N!$. Note that this upper bound is strictly lower than the lower bound which was claimed by the designers of Walnut.

Any braid output by the encoding mechanism E is a product of the generators g_1, g_2, g_3, g_4. From computer experiments we conclude that when applying $\mathcal{P}$ to braids of this form we end up with matrices in an affine subspace of surprisingly low dimension. We found that they live in a subspace of dimension 13, independent of the values of q or N (provided that $N^2 > 13$). This means that $|\mathcal{P}(E(\{0,1\}^*))|$ is at most q^{13}, and that finding a collision cannot take much more than $q^{13/2}$ evaluations of $\mathcal{P} \circ E$. For 128-bit security parameters this number is as low as $2^{32.5}$, and for 256-bit security parameters this is 2^{52}.

4.2   Implementation

We implemented the generic collision finding algorithm of van Oorschot and Wiener [24] (briefly explained in Sect. 2.1) and used it to find collisions for the function $g \circ \mathcal{P} \circ E$, where g is a function that takes the ouput of $\mathcal{P}$, and converts it to some plausible document d. Even though the method is completely generic, it is still efficient enough to find colliding documents in practice. It took approximately $2^{32.2}$ evaluations of f (which agrees very well with the expected value of $2^{32.5}$) or one hour on a standard desktop PC to find the following pair of colliding documents.

$d_1 =$ "I would like to receive 9156659270109667494 free samples

of chocolate chip cookies."

$d_2 =$ "I would like to receive 10213941738370235726 free samples

of gluten $-$ free raisin cookies."

The documents can be cunningly crafted such that a victim would be eager to sign the first document with his/her secret key. However, by producing a signature for this document, the victim would unknowingly also sign the second document, which might lead to unsavory consequences.

4.3   Implications and Countermeasures

This practical attack shows that the Walnut signature scheme should not be used with the parameters that are submitted to the NIST PQC project.

Increasing q to raise $q^{13/2}$ to the required security level would lead to $q = 2^{20}$ and $q = 2^{40}$ for 128-bit and 256-bit security parameters respectively. For 256-bit security parameters this would increase the size of the public key by a factor of 5 and we estimate that this would slow down the verification algorithm by a factor of 25. A better approach would be to change the encoding algorithm to output pure braids that are not restricted to the subgroup generated by g_1, g_2, g_3, g_4 (or any other proper subgroup). Since $\mathcal{P}(P_N)$ is contained in an affine subspace of dimension $(N-2)^2 + 1$, this would lead to an upper bound on the complexity of the attack of $\sqrt{q^{(N-2)^2+1}}$ evaluations of $\mathcal{P} \circ E$. We would then only need a slight increase in the parameters. For example, 256 bits of security would be achieved (against this attack) by the parameters $q = 2^8$ and $N = 10$, leading to an increase of the key size of roughly 50% and the signature size by at least 25%.

5   Reversing E-Multiplication

A fundamental hard problem underlying the Walnut signature scheme is the "Reversing E-Multiplication" (REM) problem. This problem asks, given a pair $(M, \sigma) \in A_N \times S_N$, such that $(M, \sigma) = (\mathbb{1}_N, e) \star s$ for some braid $s \in B_N$, to find a braid $s' \in B_N$ such that $(\mathbb{1}_N, e) \star s' = (M, \sigma)$. In other words, the problem is to break the one-wayness of the function

$$\mathcal{P} : B_N \to A_N \times S_N : s \mapsto (\mathbb{1}_N, e) \star s.$$

The secret key in Walnut consists of two braids $s_1, s_2 \in B_N$. The corresponding public key is $\mathcal{P}(s_1)$ and the matrix part of $\mathcal{P}(s_2)$. The fact that the permutation part of $\mathcal{P}(s_2)$ is not available to the attacker is not a problem, because given a single signature sig which is valid for any message (which might be unknown to the attacker), the attacker can deduce the permutation of s_2 from the permutation component of the verification Eq. (2)

$$\sigma(s_1) \circ \sigma(\mathsf{sig}) = \sigma(s_2).$$

After solving the REM problem to get s_1', s_2' such that $\mathcal{P}(s_1) = \mathcal{P}(s_1')$ and $\mathcal{P}(s_2) = \mathcal{P}(s_2')$, an attacker can use the pair (s_1', s_2') as a secret key to sign any message. Alternatively, instead of solving two instances of the REM problem to obtain an equivalent secret key, it is also possible to solve a single instance of the REM problem to obtain a signature for a document which can be chosen freely.

In this section we give an algorithm that solves the REM problem in practice for the parameters that are proposed for Walnut. First, we describe a generic birthday attack that can reverse any group action. Then, we introduce an algorithm that exploits the subgroup structure of B_N and is much more efficient.

5.1   Birthday Attack

A brute force attack would repeatedly pick a random $s \in B_N$, compute $(\mathbb{1}_N, e) \star s$ and check if this is equal to the target (M, σ). This attack would take $O(|\mathcal{P}(B_N)|)$ attempts, where $|\mathcal{P}(B_N)|$ is the size of the orbit of $(\mathbb{1}_N, e)$. A more efficient approach is to look for $s_1, s_2 \in B_N$ such that

$$(M, \sigma) \star s_1 = (\mathbb{1}_N, e) \star s_2.$$

If such s_1 and s_2 are found, the solution to the REM problem is given by $s_2 s_1^{-1}$. A naive way of finding s_1 and s_2 is to compute a large table containing $\sqrt{|\mathcal{P}(B_N)|}$ values of s_1 and the corresponding values of $(M, \sigma) \star s_1$ and check for random values of s_2 whether $(\mathbb{1}_N, e) \star s_2$ lies in this table. This method takes $O(\sqrt{|\mathcal{P}(B_N)|})$ E-Multiplications, but requires a lot of memory. The problem can be reduced to collision finding for a function $f : \mathcal{P}(B_N) \rightarrow \mathcal{P}(B_N)$. Then, distinguished point methods (see Sect. 2.1) can solve the REM problem with the same time complexity as the naive approach but with constant memory complexity. Concretely, suppose $\mathsf{b} : \mathcal{P}(B_N) \rightarrow \{0, 1\}$ and $\mathsf{s} : \mathcal{P}(B_N) \rightarrow B_N$ are hash functions that take a matrix and a permutation from the orbit of $(\mathbb{1}_N, e)$ as input, and output a bit or a braid respectively. Then we can define

$$f(x) = \begin{cases} (\mathbb{1}_N, e) \star \mathsf{s}(x) & \text{if } \mathsf{b}(x) = 0, \\ (M, \sigma) \star \mathsf{s}(x) & \text{if } \mathsf{b}(x) = 1. \end{cases}$$

If s outputs sufficiently long braids such that $\mathcal{P}(\mathsf{s}(x))$ is distributed uniformly in the orbit of $(\mathbb{1}_N, e)$, then the distinguished point method will yield collisions $f(x_1) = f(x_2)$ such that $\mathsf{b}(x_1) \neq \mathsf{b}(x_2)$ with probability $1/2$. Once such a collision is found, a solution to the REM problem is given by $\mathsf{s}(x_1)\mathsf{s}(x_2)^{-1}$ or $\mathsf{s}(x_2)\mathsf{s}(x_1)^{-1}$ when $\mathsf{b}(x_1)$ is 0 or 1 respectively. For the security parameters aiming for 128 bits of security, the size of the orbit $\mathcal{P}(B_N)$ is bounded by 2^{200}

(see Sect. 4.1), so the number of E-multiplications required to solve REM is not much more than 2^{100}, considerably less than 2^{128} but still far from practical. For the 256 bit security parameters the number of E-multiplications is not much more than 2^{157}.

5.2 Subgroup Chain Attack

We next propose a practical method for solving the REM problem that improves the attack above by exploiting the following chain of subgroups of B_N:

$$\{e\} = P_1 \subset P_2 \subset \cdots \subset P_N \subset B_N.$$

The map $\mathcal{P}$ sends a braid to an element of $A_N \times S_N$ and, when restricted to P_i it is a homomorphism to A_i (see Sect. 2.3). Therefore we have the following commuting diagram:

$$
\begin{array}{ccccccc}
\{e\} & \hookrightarrow & P_2 & \hookrightarrow & \cdots \hookrightarrow & P_N & \hookrightarrow & B_N \\
\downarrow{\scriptstyle\mathcal{P}} & & \downarrow{\scriptstyle\mathcal{P}} & & & \downarrow{\scriptstyle\mathcal{P}} & & \downarrow{\scriptstyle\mathcal{P}} \\
\{(\mathbb{1}_N, e)\} & \hookrightarrow & A_2 & \hookrightarrow & \cdots \hookrightarrow & A_N & \hookrightarrow & A_N \times S_N
\end{array}
$$

The meet-in-the-middle attacks in the previous subsection attempt to find a braid s such that $(M, \sigma) \star s = (\mathbb{1}_N, e)$ in one step. Given this subgroup structure, it is more efficient to solve REM in several steps. The first step is to find a braid $s' \in B_N$ such that $(M, \sigma) \star s' = (M', e) \in A_N$. This is trivial because any $s' \in B_N$ whose underlying permutation is σ^{-1} will do the job. The next step is to find a pure braid $s_N \in P_N$ such that $(M', e) \star s_N \in A_{N-1}$. Then, one continues iteratively to find $s_i \in P_i$ such that $(M, \sigma) \star s' s_N \cdots s_i \in A_{i-1}$. After the last step we have found $s' s_N \cdots s_2$ such that $(M, \sigma) \star s' s_N \cdots s_2 = (\mathbb{1}_N, e)$, so $(s' s_n \cdots s_2)^{-1}$ is a solution to the REM problem.

One caveat when using this method is that, a priori, it is possible to get stuck. After each step, we get a new target $(M, \sigma) \star s' s_N \cdots s_i$ which is sampled randomly from $\mathcal{P}(P_i) \cap A_{i-1}$. However, from that point on, we will only act on this target with pure braids from P_{i-1}. This means that if the new target is not in $\mathcal{P}(P_{i-1})$ we will not be able to complete the attack. If we assume for each i that

$$\mathcal{P}(P_i) \cap A_{i-1} = \mathcal{P}(P_{i-1}),$$

then the attack is guaranteed to work. In practice, this assumption seems to hold with large probability for the parameter sets that are proposed, because the algorithm works without having to backtrack. We encounter this problem when instantiating the Walnut scheme with a smaller finite field such as $\mathbb{F}_5$. Then, it occurs for a small but noticeable fraction of the choices of T-values that for some small i all the generators of $\mathcal{P}(P_{i-1})$ have determinant 1 or -1, while the subgroup $\mathcal{P}(P_i) \cap A_{i-1}$ contains matrices with any determinant. This problem is unlikely to occur in large finite fields and with large i, because then there are many generators of $\mathcal{P}(P_{i-1})$ that all have to map to a matrix with determinant ± 1.

Each step can be solved with a collision search in the space $A_{i-1}\mathcal{P}(P_i)\backslash A_{i-1}$ of cosets of A_{i-1} in $A_{i-1}\mathcal{P}(P_i)$. Let b : $A_{i-1}\mathcal{P}(P_i)\backslash A_{i-1} \rightarrow \{0,1\}$ and s : $A_{i-1}\mathcal{P}(P_i)\backslash A_{i-1} \rightarrow P_i$ be hash functions that take a right coset and output a bit or a pure braid respectively. Then we can define $f : A_{i-1}\mathcal{P}(P_i)\backslash A_{i-1} \rightarrow A_{i-1}\mathcal{P}(P_i)\backslash A_{i-1}$ as

$$f(x) = \begin{cases} A_{i-1}\mathcal{P}(\mathsf{s}(x)) & \text{if } \mathsf{b}(x) = 0, \\ A_{i-1}M'\mathcal{P}(s_N \cdots s_{i+1}\mathsf{s}(x)) & \text{if } \mathsf{b}(x) = 1. \end{cases}$$

The distinguished point method can find collisions $f(x_1) = f(x_2)$ at a cost of roughly $\sqrt{|A_{i-1}\mathcal{P}(P_i)\backslash A_{i-1}|}$ E-Multiplications. Under the assumption we made earlier that $\mathcal{P}(P_i) \cap A_{i-1} = \mathcal{P}(P_{i-1})$ this is equal to $\sqrt{|\mathcal{P}(P_i)|/|\mathcal{P}(P_{i-1})|}$ E-Multiplications.

If we plug the estimate of $|\mathcal{P}(P_i)| \approx q^{(i-2)^2+1}$ from Sect. 4.1 into this formula, we get an estimate of $\sqrt{\frac{q^{(i-2)^2+1}}{q^{(i-3)^2+1}}} = q^{i-5/2}$ E-Multiplications to find s_i. The runtime of the algorithm is dominated by the step that searches for s_N, which is estimated to require $q^{N-5/2}$ E-Multiplications. For 128-bit security parameters this number is $2^{27.5}$ and this agrees very well with our computer experiments. For 256-bit security parameters, the required number of E-Multiplications is estimated to be 2^{44}.

5.3   Representing and Manipulating Cosets of A_k

In order to implement the hash functions b and s we need to be able to uniquely represent right cosets with respect to A_k. We give a method to do this efficiently in this subsection. Suppose, $\mathbf{X}, \mathbf{Y}$ are two matrices in A_N, that are in the same right coset of A_{N-1}. That is, there exists a matrix $\mathbf{A} \in A_{N-1}$ such that $\mathbf{AX} = \mathbf{Y}$. If we split up the matrices to make their structure visible we get:

$$\begin{pmatrix} \mathbf{A}_1 & \mathbf{A}_2 & \mathbf{0} \\ \mathbf{0} & 1 & 0 \\ \mathbf{0} & 0 & 1 \end{pmatrix} \begin{pmatrix} \mathbf{X}_1 & \mathbf{X}_2 \\ \mathbf{X}_3 & \mathbf{X}_4 \\ \mathbf{0} & 1 \end{pmatrix} = \begin{pmatrix} \mathbf{Y}_1 & \mathbf{Y}_2 \\ \mathbf{Y}_3 & \mathbf{Y}_4 \\ \mathbf{0} & 1 \end{pmatrix} .$$

From this it is obvious that the $(N-1)$-th row of $\mathbf{X}$ and $\mathbf{Y}$ are identical, and that the first $(N-1)$ rows of $\mathbf{X}$ and $\mathbf{Y}$ span the same $(N-1)$-dimensional subspace. It is easily checked that the converse also holds, which implies that the right coset of A_{N-1} that contains a matrix $\mathbf{X} \in A_N$ is completely determined by the $(N-1)$-th row of $\mathbf{X}$ and the subspace spanned by the first $N-1$ rows of $\mathbf{X}$. In turn, this subspace is uniquely represented by the row reduced echelon form of the upper $(N-1)$-by-N submatrix of $\mathbf{X}$, which will be of the form

$$\begin{pmatrix} \mathbb{I}_{N-1} & \mathbf{v} \end{pmatrix}$$

for some $\mathbf{v} \in \mathbb{F}^{N-1}$. Therefore, the coset containing $\mathbf{X}$ is completely determined by the $(N-1)$-th row of $\mathbf{X}$, and the last column of the first $N-1$ rows of X after putting it in row reduced echelon form. More generally, we have the following lemma.

Lemma 2. *A right coset of $A_k \backslash A_{k-1}$ with representative $\mathbf{X} \in A_k$ is completely determined by the pair of vectors $(\mathbf{v}_1, \mathbf{v}_2) \in \mathbb{F}_q^N \times \mathbb{F}_q^{k-1}$, where $\mathbf{v}_1$ is the $(k-1)$-th row of $\mathbf{X}$ and $\mathbf{v}_2$ is the k-th column of the matrix $\mathbf{X}'$, which is obtained from $\mathbf{X}$ by taking the first $k-1$ rows and putting them in row reduced echelon form.*

This lemma gives a method for deciding whether two matrices $\mathbf{X}$ and $\mathbf{Y}$ are in the same coset. One simply computes the pair of vectors for both matrices $\mathbf{X}$ and $\mathbf{Y}$ and checks whether they are equal. To run the algorithm we also need a way to act on cosets by multiplying on the right by matrices. One way to do this is to work with a representative from the coset and carry out a matrix multiplication to get a representative from the next coset. It is more efficient to compute directly with the two-vector representation of the coset. The following lemma gives a way to do this.

Lemma 3. *Suppose $\mathbf{M}$ is a matrix in A_k for some k with $1 < k \leq N$. Let $\mathbf{A} \in GL_{k-1}(\mathbb{F}_q)$ and $\mathbf{b} \in \mathbb{F}_q^{k-1}$ be submatrices of $\mathbf{M}$ such that*

$$\mathbf{M} = \begin{pmatrix} \mathbf{A} & \mathbf{b} & \mathbf{0} \\ \mathbf{0} & 1 & \mathbf{0} \\ \mathbf{0} & \mathbf{0} & \mathbb{1}_{N-k} \end{pmatrix}.$$

If $(\mathbf{v}_1, \mathbf{v}_2)$ is the representation of a coset S as in Lemma 2, then the representation of the coset $S\mathbf{M}$ is given by $(\mathbf{v}_1 \mathbf{M}, \mathbf{A}^{-1}(\mathbf{b} + \mathbf{v}_2))$.

Proof. It is clear that if $\mathbf{v}_1$ is the $(k-1)$-th row of a representative of S, then $\mathbf{v}_1 \mathbf{M}$ is the $(k-1)$-th row of a representative $S\mathbf{M}$. For the second vector, suppose that the subspace spanned by the first $k-1$ rows of a representative of S is the row subspace of

$$\begin{pmatrix} \mathbb{1} & \mathbf{v}_2 & \mathbf{0} \end{pmatrix}.$$

Then there is a representative of $S\mathbf{M}$ whose first $k-1$ rows span the rowspace of

$$\begin{pmatrix} \mathbb{1} & \mathbf{v}_2 & \mathbf{0} \end{pmatrix} \mathbf{M} = \begin{pmatrix} \mathbf{A} & \mathbf{b} + \mathbf{v}_2 & \mathbf{0} \end{pmatrix}.$$

Putting this in row reduced echelon form we get

$$\begin{pmatrix} \mathbb{1} & \mathbf{A}^{-1}(\mathbf{b} + \mathbf{v}_2) & \mathbf{0} \end{pmatrix},$$

which shows that the second vector in the representation of $S\mathbf{M}$ is equal to $\mathbf{A}^{-1}(\mathbf{b} + \mathbf{v}_2)$.

5.4   Permuting T-Values to Improve the Attack

From Sect. 4.1 we know that the size of $\mathcal{P}(P_N)$ is influenced by the fact that the first two T-values are chosen to be equal to 1. This also impacts the performance of the subgroup chain attack, since at each step we carry out a search in the space of cosets $\mathcal{P}(P_k)\backslash\mathcal{P}(P_k+1)$. In the first column of Table 2 we see that if the T-Values would have been chosen randomly, the most expensive step would have been the first step, where we would have to perform a collision search in a set of at most q^{13} elements. However, Walnut fixes the two first T-values to be 1, so the most expensive step consists of a collision search in a space of at most q^{11} elements. In the last column of Table 2 we see that if the designers had chosen to fix the last two T-values to one instead, the complexity of the subgroup chain attack would have been reduced: the most expensive step would have been a collision search in a space with only at most q^9 elements. It turns out that we can first apply a transformation to the REM instance to reduce it to an instance of the REM problem where the final two T-values are set to one. Solving this REM instance then only takes $\sqrt{q^9}$ E-Multiplications, so this approach reduces the amount of work by a factor of q. For general values of N, the new method requires approximately $q^{N-7/2}$ E-Multiplications. The reduction relies on the following lemma.

Lemma 4. *Let s_1, s_2 be braids, let (M, π) be a matrix-permutation pair and let T be a set of T-values. Then $s_1 s_2$ is a solution for the REM problem for the pair (M, π) with respect to the list of T-values T if and only if s_2 is a solution for the REM problem for the pair $((CBM(s_1)\downarrow_T)^{-1}M, \sigma(s_1)^{-1}\pi)$ with respect to the permuted list of T-values $\sigma(s_1)(T)$.*

Proof. By applying the definition of E-Multiplication we find that

$$(\mathbb{1}_N, e) \star_T s_1 s_2 = (CBM(s_1)\downarrow_T \cdot \sigma(s_1)(CBM(s_2)\downarrow_T), \sigma(s_1 s_2)).$$

By multiplying from the left by $CBM(s_1)\downarrow_T^{-1}$ and $\sigma(s_1)^{-1}$ we see that the value above is equal to (M, π) if and only if

$$(\sigma(s_1)(CBM(s_2)\downarrow_T), \sigma(b_2)) = ((CBM(s_1)\downarrow_T)^{-1}M, \sigma(s_1)^{-1}\pi).$$

The main insight is that permuting the variables $t_i \mapsto t_{\sigma(b_1)(i)}$ and then evaluating at the values of T leads to the same result as evaluating at the set of permuted values $\sigma(s_1)(T)$. Therefore the left hand side is equal to

$$(CBM(s_2)\downarrow_{\sigma(b_1)(T)}, \sigma(s_2)) = (\mathbb{1}_N, e) \star_{\sigma(s_1)(T)} s_2.$$

Given this lemma, the reduction is straightforward. In order to solve the REM problem for (M, π) we fix a "transport braid" $s_1 = b_2 b_3 \cdots b_{N-1} b_1 b_2 \cdots b_{N-2}$ whose underlying permutation transports the first two entries to the back of the list. Then we calculate the pair $((CBM(s_1)\downarrow_T)^{-1}M, \sigma(s_1)^{-1}\pi)$ and use our REM solving algorithm with respect to the permuted T-values $\sigma(s_1)(T)$ on this pair to find s_2. This is now faster by a factor q because the last two T-values are equal to one. Then $s_1 s_2$ is a solution to the original REM problem.

Table 2. The dimension of the subspaces containing various subgroups, depending on the T-Values

	Generic T-values		First two T-values are equal to 1		Last two T-valuesare equal to 1	
	dim	Δ	dim	Δ	dim	Δ
$\mathcal{P}(P_2)$	1	1	0	0	1	1
$\mathcal{P}(P_3)$	4	3	2	2	4	3
$\mathcal{P}(P_4)$	9	5	5	3	9	5
$\mathcal{P}(P_5)$	16	7	10	5	16	7
$\mathcal{P}(P_6)$	25	9	17	7	25	<u>9</u>
$\mathcal{P}(P_7)$	36	11	26	9	31	6
$\mathcal{P}(P_8)$	49	<u>13</u>	37	<u>11</u>	37	6

5.5 Using a Finer Chain of Subgroups

With a complexity of $O(q^{N/2})$, the factorization algorithm of Hart et al. is more efficient (asymptotically) than the REM solving algorithm that we have described so far. This is due to the fact that Hart et al. use a finer chain of subgroups, which leads to smaller spaces of cosets to search in. In the next paragraph we describe a faster variant of our REM solving algorithm that uses a finer chain of subgroups, similar to the chain used by Hart et al. This variant is much faster than the previous REM solver, but yields solution braids that are longer.

In each step of our REM solving algorithm we have a matrix $M \in A_i$ and we are looking for a braid $s_i \in P_i$ such that $\mathsf{mat}((M,e) \star s_i)$ lies in A_{i-1}. To speed this process up, we can split each step in two substeps. Let C_{i-1} be the subgroup of invertible N-by-N matrices that only differ from the identity matrix in the upper left $(i-1)$-by-$(i-1)$ submatrix. This is a proper subgroup of A_i, which itself contains A_{i-1} as a proper subgroup. To solve the step of the REM solving algorithm we can first search for an $s_i' \in P_i$ such that $\mathsf{mat}((M,e) \star s_i')$ lies in the intermediate group C_{i-1}, then we search for a braid s_i'' such that $\mathsf{mat}((M,e) \star s_i' s_i'')$ lies in A_{i-1}. The first substep of finding s_i' can be carried out with a meet in the middle search. In order to be able to complete the second substep we start by searching for a list of braids $c_1, c_2, \cdots, c_k$ such that $\mathsf{mat}(\mathcal{P}(c_i)) \in C_1$. Then, to solve the second substep, we search for a braid s_i'' in the subgroup generated by the braids c_i such that $\mathsf{mat}((M,e) \star s_i' s_i'')$ lies in A_{i-1}.

5.6 Implications and Countermeasures

With this method we split each step into two much easier substeps, which greatly improves the efficiency of the algorithm. The downside is that the solutions to the REM problem that are produced are longer than those produced by the original algorithm. This is because the solution now contains braids s_i'' which are themselves a concatenation of several slightly longer braids c_i. To avoid inflating the size of the output signature needlessly, it is best to only use this technique for solving the most expensive steps. For 128-bit security parameters the signatures output are longer than legitimately produced signatures, but still small enough to be accepted by the NIST implementation. For 256-bit security parameters, the forged signatures are smaller than some legitimately produced signatures, depending on which variant of the signing algorithm is used. Hence, we cannot defend Walnut against this attack by imposing an upper limit on the length of the signatures. Note that it is trivial to convert a short signature into a longer signature, so imposing a lower bound does not help either.

With this method the most expensive step of the algorithm requires only $q^{N/2-1}$ E-Multiplications. The attack is very efficient in practice. We can produce a forgery for 128-bit security parameters in less than one second. Even for 256-bit security parameters we can forge signatures for any document in less than a minute.

The attack benefits from the fact that two of the T-values are equal to one (see Sect. 5.4), so the attack would be slightly less efficient if the Walnut scheme can be adapted to avoid this. If all T-values are chosen randomly the complexity of the attack becomes dominated by the first step, which requires now roughly $\sqrt{k}q^{(N-1)/2}$ E-multiplications (k, the number of braids produced in the first step is chosen to be 60 in our implementation). Other than this there does not seem to be a better way to block the attack other than just increasing the parameters to ensure that $q^{N/2-1}$ is higher than the desired security level. One way to do this is to take $N = 10, q = 2^{32}$ to achieve 128 bits of security, and $N = 10, q = 2^{64}$ for 256 bits of security.

6   Conclusion

In this paper we presented three different practical methods to break the Walnut digital signature scheme (See Table 3). All three attacks are made possible because of the rich algebraic structure of the E-Multiplication map, which is central to the Walnut scheme (and other protocols developped by SecureRF). The first method exploits a signature malleability property of Walnut, and expands on the work of [14] which attacks an earlier version of the Walnut scheme. The second attack is purely generic. It is much more efficient that expected because E-Multiplication maps a certain subgroup of P_N into a subspace of very low dimension. The last attack exploits the fact that E-Multiplication, when restricted to pure braids, is a homomorphism of groups and that this homomorphism maps the chain of subgroups $P_2 \subset P_3 \subset \cdots \subset P_N$ to a nice chain of subgroups of $GL_N(\mathbf{F}_q)$. Some poor design choices such as adopting an encoding mechanism that produces matrices in a low dimensional subspace and a failed attempt to block the attack of Hart et al. [14] seem to be symptomatic of a lack of understanding of the algebraic structure of E-Multiplication. It is the opinion of the authors that E-Multiplication can not be credibly used as a basis for cryptography until this structure and its implications for cryptography are better understood.

The security of the parameter sets submitted to the NIST PQC project is completely broken by the attacks (see Table 3). It is possible to forge signatures or compute equivalent secret keys in under a second for 128-bit security parameters. Even for 256-bit security parameters this takes less than a minute.

Table 3. An overview of the attacks introduced in this paper, compared with the legitimate signing algorithms.

	Complexity (in number of E-Mults or Mat mults)	128 bits of security		256 bits of security	
		Time	Length of signature (Artin generators)	Time	Length of signature (Artin generators)
Legitimate signing:					
BKL		<1 s	≈1480	<1 s	≈2661
Stoch. w/o Dehornoy		<1 s	≈2788	<1 s	≈5260
Attacks:					
Factorization	$q^{(N-1)/2}$	5 min	$>2^{32}$	—	—
Collision [a]	$q^{13/2}$	68 min	≈1480	—	—
Subgroup chain	$q^{N-7/2}$	4 s	899	58 h	1374
Fine subgroup chain	$q^{N/2-1}$	<1 s	4534	39 s	4525

[a] Has exactly the same length distribution as legitimately produced signatures

In response to the various attacks, the designers have announced a number of changes to Walnut and increased the parameters (see Table 4) to resist all known attacks. An upper bound of 2^{14} on the number of Artin generators of a signature is imposed, the encoding mechanism is changed so that it outputs braids that map into a larger subspace and the method of producing cloaking elements is changed such that two of the T-values are no longer required to be equal to 1.

Table 4. Comparison of the original parameter choices with the new parameter that resist the attacks introduced in this paper. Our timing experiments use the implementations that were submitted to NIST, and were run on a Dell OptiPlex 3050 Micro desktop machine.

		Original parameters	New parameters	Increase
128-bit	N	8	10	
	q	2^5	$2^{31} - 1$	
	Public key length	83 Bytes	780 Bytes	×9.4
	Signature length[a]	713 Bytes	1308 Bytes	+83%
	Signing time	39.5 ms	59.2 ms	+50%
	Verification time	0.05 ms	0.09 ms	+80%
256-bit	N	8	10	
	q	2^8	$2^{61} - 1$	
	Public key length	128 Bytes	1552 Bytes	×12.1
	Signature length[a]	1296 Bytes	2409 Bytes	+86%
	Signing time	155.2 ms	223.1 ms	+44%
	Verification time	0.07 ms	0.20 ms	×2.7

[a] Average signature length, computed over 1000 signatures generated with the BKL signing method.

Increasing the parameters to resist the attacks introduced in this paper increases the public key by a factor of 10 and the signature sizes by roughly 80%. The updated scheme uses arithmetic in much larger finite fields (e.g. $\mathbb{F}_{2^{61}-1}$ instead of $\mathbb{F}_{2^8}$). This has a relatively small impact on the efficiency of the implementation for high-end processors submitted to NIST (roughly 50% slower signing and 80% slower verification). However, the large finite fields make the scheme more difficult to implement on the low-resource processors that SecureRF is targeting. With the new parameter choices Walnut no longer stands out for its small key and signature sizes relative to other post-quantum signature schemes such as lattice-based, hash-based and multivariate signature schemes. For example, Walnut used to be the signature scheme with the smallest combined size of a public key and a signature out of all the 19 signature schemes submitted to NIST, but this is no longer the case with the new parameters.

Acknowledgements. This work was supported in part by the Research Council KU Leuven: C16/15/058. In addition, this work was supported by the European Commission through the Horizon 2020 research and innovation programme under grant agreement No.H2020-ICT-2014-645622 PQCRYPTO. This project was partially supported by the FWO through the WOG Coding Theory and Cryptography. Ward Beullens is funded by an FWO fellowship.

References

1. About SecureRF. https://www.securerf.com/about-us/. Accessed 08 Mar 2018
2. Anshel, I., Anshel, M., Fisher, B., Goldfeld, D.: New key agreement protocols in braid group cryptography. In: Naccache, D. (ed.) CT-RSA 2001. LNCS, vol. 2020, pp. 13–27. Springer, Heidelberg (2001). https://doi.org/10.1007/3-540-45353-9_2
3. Anshel, I., Anshel, M., Goldfeld, D.: An algebraic method for public-key cryptography. Math. Res. Lett. **6**, 287–292 (1999)
4. Anshel, I., Anshel, M., Goldfeld, D., Lemieux, S.: Key agreement, the Algebraic Eraser^{TM}, and lightweight cryptography. Contemp. Math. **418**, 1–34 (2007)
5. Anshel, I., Atkins, D., Goldfeld, D., Gunnells, P.E.: WalnutDSA^{TM}: a quantum-resistant digital signature algorithm. IACR eprint 2017/058 (version: 30-Nov-2017)
6. Anshel, I., Atkins, D., Goldfeld, D., Gunnells, P.E.: WalnutDSA^{TM}: a quantum-resistant digital signature algorithm. IACR eprint 2017/058 (version: 18-Sept-2017)
7. Anshel, I., Atkins, D., Goldfeld, D., Gunnells, P.E.: A class of hash functions based on the Algebraic Eraser^{TM}. Groups Complex. Cryptol. **8**(1), 1–7 (2016)
8. Anshel, I., Atkins, D., Goldfeld, D., Gunnells, P.E.: The Walnut digital signature algorithm^{TM} specifcation. Submitted to NIST PQC project (2017)
9. Artin, E.: Theory of braids. Ann. Math. **48**, 101–126 (1947)
10. Ben-Zvi, A., Blackburn, S.R., Tsaban, B.: A practical cryptanalysis of the algebraic eraser. In: Robshaw, M., Katz, J. (eds.) CRYPTO 2016. LNCS, vol. 9814, pp. 179–189. Springer, Heidelberg (2016). https://doi.org/10.1007/978-3-662-53018-4_7
11. Ben-Zvi, A., Kalka, A., Tsaban, B.: Cryptanalysis via algebraic spans. IACR eprint 41 (2014)
12. Cheon, J.H., Jun, B.: A polynomial time algorithm for the braid Diffie-Hellman conjugacy problem. In: Boneh, D. (ed.) CRYPTO 2003. LNCS, vol. 2729, pp. 212–225. Springer, Heidelberg (2003). https://doi.org/10.1007/978-3-540-45146-4_13

13. Garside, F.A.: The braid group and other groups. Q. J. Math. **20**(1), 235–254 (1969)
14. Hart, D., Kim, D.H., Micheli, G., Pascual-Perez, G., Petit, C., Quek, Y.: A practical cryptanalysis of WalnutDSA^{TM}. In: Abdalla, M., Dahab, R. (eds.) PKC 2018. LNCS, vol. 10769, pp. 381–406. Springer, Cham (2018). https://doi.org/10.1007/978-3-319-76578-5_13
15. Hughes, J.: A linear algebraic attack on the AAFG1 braid group cryptosystem. In: Batten, L., Seberry, J. (eds.) ACISP 2002. LNCS, vol. 2384, pp. 176–189. Springer, Heidelberg (2002). https://doi.org/10.1007/3-540-45450-0_15
16. Hughes, J., Tannenbaum, A.: Length-based attacks for certain group based encryption rewriting systems. arXiv preprint cs/0306032 (2003)
17. Kalka, A., Teicher, M., Tsaban, B.: Cryptanalysis of the Algebraic Eraser and short expressions of permutations as products. Arxiv preprint (2008)
18. Ko, K.H., Lee, S.J., Cheon, J.H., Han, J.W., Kang, J., Park, C.: New public-key cryptosystem using braid groups. In: Bellare, M. (ed.) CRYPTO 2000. LNCS, vol. 1880, pp. 166–183. Springer, Heidelberg (2000). https://doi.org/10.1007/3-540-44598-6_10
19. Myasnikov, A.D., Ushakov, A.: Length based attack and braid groups: cryptanalysis of Anshel-Anshel-Goldfeld key exchange protocol. In: Okamoto, T., Wang, X. (eds.) PKC 2007. LNCS, vol. 4450, pp. 76–88. Springer, Heidelberg (2007). https://doi.org/10.1007/978-3-540-71677-8_6
20. National Institute for Standards and Technology (NIST): Post-quantum crypto standardization (2016). http://csrc.nist.gov/groups/ST/post-quantum-crypto/
21. Pollard, J.M.: A Monte Carlo method for factorization. BIT Numer. Math. **15**(3), 331–334 (1975)
22. Sedgewick, R., Szymanski, T.G., Yao, A.C.: The complexity of finding cycles in periodic functions. SIAM J. Comput. **11**(2), 376–390 (1982)
23. Tsaban, B.: Polynomial-time solutions of computational problems in noncommutative-algebraic cryptography. J. Cryptol. **28**(3), 601–622 (2015)
24. Van Oorschot, P.C., Wiener, M.J.: Parallel collision search with cryptanalytic applications. J. Cryptol. **12**(1), 1–28 (1999)
25. Vasco, M.I.G., Steinwandt, R.: A reaction attack on a public key cryptosystem based on the word problem. Appl. Algebr. Eng. Commun. Comput. **14**(5), 335–340 (2004)
26. Wagner, N.R., Magyarik, M.R.: A public-key cryptosystem based on the word problem. In: Blakley, G.R., Chaum, D. (eds.) CRYPTO 1984. LNCS, vol. 196, pp. 19–36. Springer, Heidelberg (1985). https://doi.org/10.1007/3-540-39568-7_3

Two Attacks on Rank Metric Code-Based Schemes: RankSign and an IBE Scheme

Thomas Debris-Alazard[1,2(✉)] and Jean-Pierre Tillich[2]

[1] Sorbonne Universités, UPMC Univ, Paris 06, France
[2] Inria, Paris, France
{thomas.debris18,jean-pierre.tillich}@inria.fr

Abstract. RankSign [30] is a code-based signature scheme proposed to the NIST competition for quantum-safe cryptography [5] and, moreover, is a fundamental building block of a new Identity-Based-Encryption (IBE) [26]. This signature scheme is based on the rank metric and enjoys remarkably small key sizes, about 10KBytes for an intended level of security of 128 bits. Unfortunately we will show that all the parameters proposed for this scheme in [5] can be broken by an algebraic attack that exploits the fact that the augmented LRPC codes used in this scheme have very low weight codewords. Therefore, without RankSign the IBE cannot be instantiated at this time. As a second contribution we will show that the problem is deeper than finding a new signature in rank-based cryptography, we also found an attack on the generic problem upon which its security reduction relies. However, contrarily to the RankSign scheme, it seems that the parameters of the IBE scheme could be chosen in order to avoid our attack. Finally, we have also shown that if one replaces the rank metric in the [26] IBE scheme by the Hamming metric, then a devastating attack can be found.

Keywords: Code-based cryptography · Cryptanalysis · Rank metric
Signature scheme · Identity based encryption

1 Introduction

1.1 An Efficient Code-Based Signature Scheme: RankSign and a Code-Based Identity-Based-Encryption Scheme

Code-Based Signature Schemes. It is a long standing open problem to build an efficient and secure signature scheme based on the hardness of decoding a linear code which could compete in all respects with DSA or RSA. Such schemes could indeed give a quantum resistant signature for replacing in practice the aforementioned signature schemes that are well known to be broken by quantum computers. A first partial answer to this question was given in [13]. It consisted in adapting the Niederreiter scheme [39] for this purpose. This requires a linear code for which there exists an efficient decoding algorithm for a non-negligible set of inputs. This means that if $\mathbf{H}$ is an $r \times n$ parity-check matrix of the code,

© International Association for Cryptologic Research 2018
T. Peyrin and S. Galbraith (Eds.): ASIACRYPT 2018, LNCS 11272, pp. 62–92, 2018.
https://doi.org/10.1007/978-3-030-03326-2_3

there exists for a non-negligible set of elements $\mathbf{s}$ in $\{0,1\}^r$ an efficient way to find a word $\mathbf{e}$ in $\{0,1\}^n$ of smallest Hamming weight such that $\mathbf{He}^\mathsf{T} = \mathbf{s}^\mathsf{T}$.

The authors of [13] noticed that very high rate Goppa codes are able to fulfill this task, and their scheme can indeed be considered as the first step towards a solution of the aforementioned problem. However, the poor scaling of the key size when security has to be increased prevents this scheme to be a completely satisfying answer to this issue.

The Rank Metric. There has been some exciting progress in this area for another metric, namely the rank metric [31]. A code-based signature scheme whose security relies on decoding codes with respect to the rank metric has been proposed there. It is called RankSign. Strictly speaking, the rank metric consists in viewing an element in $\mathbb{F}_q^N$ (when N is a product $N = m \times n$) as an $m \times n$ matrix over $\mathbb{F}_q$ and the rank distance between two elements $\mathbf{x}$ and $\mathbf{y}$ is defined as the rank of the matrix $\mathbf{x} - \mathbf{y}$. This depends of course on how N is viewed as a product of two elements. Decoding in this metric is known to be an NP hard problem [11,12]. In the particular case of [31], the codes which are considered are not $\mathbb{F}_q$-linear but, as is customary in the setting of rank metric based cryptography, $\mathbb{F}_{q^m}$-linear: the codes are here subspaces of $\mathbb{F}_{q^m}^n$. Here the elements $\mathbf{x} = (x_1, \ldots, x_n)$ of $\mathbb{F}_{q^m}^n$ are viewed as $m \times n$ matrices by expressing each coordinate x_i in a certain fixed $\mathbb{F}_q$-basis of $\mathbb{F}_{q^m}$. This yields a column vector $\mathbf{x}^i$ in $\mathbb{F}_q^m$ and the concatenation of these column vectors yields an $m \times n$ matrix $\mathbf{Mat}(\mathbf{x}) = \left(\mathbf{x}^1 \ldots \mathbf{x}^n\right)$ that allows to put a rank metric over $\mathbb{F}_{q^m}^n$. This allows to reduce the key size by a factor of m when compared to the $\mathbb{F}_q$-linear setting (for more details see the paragraph at the end of Sect. 2).

Decoding such codes for the rank metric is not known to be NP-hard anymore. There is however a randomized reduction of this problem to decode an $\mathbb{F}_q$-linear code for the Hamming metric [32] when the degree m of the extension field is sufficiently big. This situation is in some sense reminiscent to the current thread in cryptography based on codes or on lattices where structured codes (for instance quasi-cyclic codes) or structured lattices (corresponding to an additional ring structure) are taken. However the $\mathbb{F}_{q^m}$-linear case has an advantage over the other structured proposals, in the sense that it has a randomized reduction to an NP-complete problem. This is not the case for the other structured proposals. Relying on $\mathbb{F}_{q^m}$-linear codes is one of the main reason why RankSign enjoys noticeably small public key sizes: it is about 10KBytes for 128 bits of security for the parameters proposed in the NIST submission [5]. Furthermore, RankSign comes with a security proof showing that there is no leakage coming from signing many times. It also proved to be a fundamental building block in the Identity-Based-Encryption (IBE) scheme based on the rank metric suggested in [26].

A New IBE Scheme Based on Codes. The concept of IBE was introduced by Shamir in 1984 [42]. It gives an alternative to the standard notion of public-key encryption. In an IBE scheme, the public key associated with a user can be an arbitrary identity string, such as his e-mail address, and others can send encrypted messages to a user using his identity without having to rely on a public-key infrastructure, given short public parameters. The main technical difference between a Public Key Encryption (PKE) and IBE is the way the public and private keys are bound and the way of verifying those keys. In a PKE scheme, verification is achieved through the use of a certificate which relies on a public-key infrastructure. In an IBE, there is no need of verification of the public key but the private key is managed by a Trusted Authority (TA).

There are two issues that makes the design of IBE extremely hard: the requirement that public keys are arbitrary strings and the ability to extract decryption keys from the public keys. In fact, it took nearly twenty years for the problem of designing an efficient method to implement an IBE to be solved. The known methods of designing IBE are based on different tools: from elliptic curve pairings [9,41]; from the quadratic residue problem [12]; from the Learning-With-Error (LWE) problem [33]; from the computational Diffie-Hellman assumption [17] and finally from the Rank Support Learning (RSL) problem [26]. The last scheme based on codes is an adaptation of the [33] technique, but instead of relying on the Hamming metric it relies on the rank metric. It has to be noted that there has been some recent and exciting progress in the design of IBE. In [16] it has been shown how to generalize the work of [17] by introducing a new primitive, One-Time Signatures with Encryption (OTSE), that enables to construct fully secure IBE schemes. Furthermore it was shown in [18] how to instantiate OTSE primitives from LWE and the Low Parity Noise problems (LPN). This gave after the IBE's [26,33] the third scheme which may hope to resist to a quantum computer.

1.2   Our Contribution

An Efficient Attack on RankSign. Our first contribution is that despite the fact that the security of RankSign might very well be founded on a hard problem (namely distinguishing an augmented LRPC code from a random linear code), we show here that all the parameters proposed for RankSign in [5] can be broken by a suitable algebraic attack. The problem is actually deeper than that, because the attack is actually polynomial in nature and can not really be thwarted by changing the parameters. The attack builds upon the following observations

- The RankSign scheme is based on augmented LRPC codes;
- To have an efficient signature scheme, the parameters of the augmented LRPC codes have to be chosen very carefully;
- For the whole range of admissible parameters, it turns out rather unexpectedly that these augmented LRPC codes have very low-weight codewords. This can be proved by subspace product considerations;
- These low-weight codewords can be recovered by algebraic techniques and reveal enough of the secret trapdoor used in the scheme to be able to sign like a legitimate user.

This attack has also a significant impact on the IBE proposal [26] whose security is based on the security of RankSign. Right now, there is no backup solution for instantiating this IBE scheme, since RankSign was the only rank-metric code based signature scheme following the hash and sign paradigm that is needed in the IBE scheme.

An Efficient Attack on the IBE [26]. Our second contribution is to show that the problem is deeper than finding a new hash and sign signature scheme in rank-based cryptography to instantiate the IBE proposed in [26]. Actually the security of this IBE scheme does not solely rely on the rank metric code-based signature scheme and the rank syndrome decoding, it also relies on the Rank Support Learning (RSL) problem. We show here that the RSL problem is much easier for the parameters proposed in the IBE scheme [26] and can be broken by a suitable algebraic attack. Interestingly enough, the approach for breaking the RSL problem is similar to what we did for RankSign:

- we exhibit a matrix code that can be deduced from the public data that contains many low-weight codewords and whose support reveals the secret support of the RSL problem;
- we find such low weight codewords efficiently by solving a largely overdetermined bilinear system.

However in this case, contrarily to the RankSign scheme, even if the set of parameters that could defeat our attack is small, it is non empty and our attack could be thwarted by choosing the parameters appropriately and if an appropriate signature scheme were found.

We have also explored whether it is possible to change in the IBE scheme of [26] the rank metric by the Hamming metric. It turns out that the problem is much worse for the Hamming case. Indeed by adapting the IBE [26] to the Hamming metric, based on the remark that signatures must have a small weight, we show that even the simplest generic attack, namely the Prange algorithm [40], breaks the IBE in the Hamming setting in polynomial time, and this irrespective of the way the parameters are chosen.

2   Generalities on Rank Metric and $\mathbb{F}_{q^m}$-linear Codes

2.1   Definitions and Notation

We provide here notation and definitions that are used throughout the paper.

Big O Notation. We will use the family of Bachmann-Landau notations, $f(n) = o(g(n))$, $f(n) = O(g(n))$, $f(n) = \Omega(g(n))$, $f(n) = \Theta(g(n))$, $f(n) = \omega(g(n))$ meaning respectively that $\lim_{n\to\infty} \frac{f(n)}{g(n)} = 0$, $\limsup_{n\to\infty} \frac{|f(n)|}{g(n)} < \infty$, $\liminf_{n\to\infty} \frac{f(n)}{g(n)} > 0$, $f(n) = O(g(n))$ and $f(n) = \Omega(g(n))$, $\lim_{n\to\infty} \frac{|f(n)|}{|g(n)|} = \infty$.

Vector Notation. Vectors will be written using bold lower-case letters, e.g. $\mathbf{x}$. The ith component of $\mathbf{x}$ is denoted by x_i. Vectors are in row notation. Matrices will be written as bold capital letters, e.g. $\mathbf{X}$, and the i-th column of a matrix $\mathbf{X}$ is denoted $\mathbf{X}_i$. The rank of a matrix $\mathbf{X}$ will be simply denoted by $|\mathbf{X}|$.

Field Notation. We will denote by $\mathbb{F}_q$ the finite field of cardinality q.

Coding Theory Notation. A linear code $\mathcal{C}$ over a finite field $\mathbb{F}_q$ of length n and dimension k is a subspace of the vector space $\mathbb{F}_q^n$ of dimension k. We say that it has parameters $[n, k]$ or that it is an $[n, k]$-code. A generator matrix $\mathbf{G}$ for it is a full rank $k \times n$ matrix over $\mathbb{F}_q$ which is such that

$$\mathcal{C} = \{\mathbf{uG} : \mathbf{u} \in \mathbb{F}_q^k\}.$$

In other words, the rows of $\mathbf{G}$ form a basis of $\mathcal{C}$. A parity-check matrix $\mathbf{H}$ for it is a full-rank $(n - k) \times n$ matrix over $\mathbb{F}_q$ such that

$$\mathcal{C} = \{\mathbf{c} \in \mathbb{F}_q^n : \mathbf{Hc}^\mathsf{T} = 0\}.$$

In other words, $\mathcal{C}$ is the null space of $\mathbf{H}$.

Rank metric codes basically consist in viewing codewords as matrices. More precisely, when N is the product of two numbers m and n, $N = mn$ we will equip the vector space $\mathbb{F}_q^N$ with the rank metric by viewing its elements as matrices over $\mathbb{F}_q^{m \times n}$, i.e.

$$d(\mathbf{X}, \mathbf{Y}) = |\mathbf{X} - \mathbf{Y}|.$$

An $[m \times n, K]$ *matrix code* of dimension K over $\mathbb{F}_q^{m \times n}$ is a subspace of $\mathbb{F}_q^{m \times n}$ of dimension K. Such a code is equipped in a natural way with the rank metric. There is a particular subclass of matrix codes that has the nice property to be specified much more compactly than a generic matrix code. It consists in taking a linear code over an extension field $\mathbb{F}_{q^m}$ of $\mathbb{F}_q$ of length n. Such a code can be viewed as a matrix code consisting of matrices in $\mathbb{F}_q^{m \times n}$ by expressing each coordinate c_i of a codeword $\mathbf{c} = (c_i)_{1 \leq i \leq n}$ in a fixed $\mathbb{F}_q$ basis of $\mathbb{F}_{q^m}$. When the $\mathbb{F}_{q^m}$-linear code is of dimension k the dimension of the matrix code viewed as an $\mathbb{F}_q$-subspace of $\mathbb{F}_q^{m \times n}$ is $K = k.m$. More precisely we bring in the following definition.

Definition 1 (Matrix code associated to an $\mathbb{F}_{q^m}$ linear code). *Let $\mathcal{C}$ be an $[n, k]$-linear code over $\mathbb{F}_{q^m}$, that is a subspace of $\mathbb{F}_{q^m}^n$ of dimension k over $\mathbb{F}_{q^m}$, and let $(\beta_1 \ldots \beta_m)$ be a basis of $\mathbb{F}_{q^m}$ over $\mathbb{F}_q$. Each word $\mathbf{c} \in \mathcal{C}$ can be represented by an $m \times n$ matrix $\mathbf{Mat}(\mathbf{c}) = (M_{ij})_{\substack{1 \leq i \leq m \\ 1 \leq j \leq n}}$ over $\mathbb{F}_q$, with $c_j = \sum_{i=1}^m M_{ij}\beta_i$. The set $\{\mathbf{Mat}(\mathbf{c}), \mathbf{c} \in \mathcal{C}\}$ is the $[m \times n, k.m]$ matrix code over $\mathbb{F}_q$ associated to the $\mathbb{F}_{q^m}$ linear code $\mathcal{C}$. The (rank) weight of $\mathbf{c}$ is defined as the rank of the associated matrix, that is $|\mathbf{c}| \stackrel{\triangle}{=} |\mathbf{Mat}(\mathbf{c})|$.*

This definition depends of course on the basis chosen for $\mathbb{F}_{q^m}$. However changing the basis does not change the distance between codewords. The point of defining matrix codes in this way is that they have a more compact description. It is readily seen that an $[m \times n, k.m]$ matrix code over $\mathbb{F}_q$ can be specified from a systematic generator matrix (i.e. a matrix of the form $[\mathbf{1}_{k.m}|\mathbf{P}]$ with $\mathbf{1}_{k.m}$ being the identity matrix of size $k.m$) by $k(n - k)m^2 \log_2 q$ bits whereas an $\mathbb{F}_{q^m}$-linear code uses only $k(n - k)\log_2 q^m = k(n - k)m \log_2 q$ bits. This is particularly interesting for cryptographic applications where this notion is directly related to the public key size. This is basically what explains why in general McEliece cryptosystems based on rank metric matrix codes have a smaller keysize than McEliece cryptosystems based on the Hamming metric. All of these proposals (see for instance [1,4,23–25,27,31]) are actually built from matrix codes over $\mathbb{F}_q$ obtained from $\mathbb{F}_{q^m}$-linear codes. In a sense, they can be viewed as structured matrix codes, much in the same way as quasi-cyclic linear codes can be viewed as structured versions of linear codes. In the latter case, the code is globally invariant by a linear isometric transform on the codewords corresponding to shifts of a certain length. In the $\mathbb{F}_{q^m}$-linear case the code is globally invariant by an isometric linear transformation that corresponds to multiplication in $\mathbb{F}_{q^m}$.

2.2 Rank Code-Based Cryptography

Rank-based cryptography relies on the hardness of decoding for the rank metric. This problem is the rank metric analogue of the well known decoding problem in the Hamming metric [7]. We give it here its syndrome formulation:

Problem 1 (Rank (Metric) Syndrome Decoding Problem)

> *Instance:* A full-rank $(n - k) \times n$ matrix $\mathbf{H}$ over $\mathbb{F}_{q^m}$ with $k \leq n$, a syndrome $\mathbf{s} \in \mathbb{F}_{q^m}^{n-k}$ and w an integer.
> *Output:* An error $\mathbf{e} \in \mathbb{F}_{q^m}^n$ such that $|\mathbf{e}| = w$ and $\mathbf{H}\mathbf{e}^\mathsf{T} = \mathbf{s}^\mathsf{T}$.

This problem has recently been proven hard in [32] by a probabilistic reduction to the decoding problem in the Hamming metric which is known to be NP-complete [7]. This problem has typically a unique solution when w is below the Varshamov-Gilbert distance $w_{\mathrm{rVG}}(q, m, n, k)$ for the rank metric which is defined as

Definition 2 (Varshamov-Gilbert distance for the rank metric). *The Varshamov-Gilbert distance $w_{rVG}(q, m, n, k)$ for $\mathbb{F}_{q^m}$-linear codes of dimension k in the rank metric is defined as the smallest t for which $q^{m(n-k)} \leq B_t$ where B_t is the size of the ball of radius t in the rank metric.*

Remark 1. 1. $q^{m(n-k)}$ can be viewed as the number of different syndromes $\mathbf{s} \in \mathbb{F}_{q^m}^{n-k}$.
2. From [36] we have when either m or n tends to infinity

$$w_{\mathrm{rVG}}(q, m, n, k) = \frac{m + n - \sqrt{(m - n)^2 + 4km}}{2}(1 + o(1)). \qquad (1)$$

The best algorithms for solving the decoding problem in the rank metric are exponential in n^2 as long as $m = \Theta(n)$, $w = \Theta(n)$ but w stays below the Singleton bound which is defined by

Definition 3 (Singleton distance in the rank metric). *The rank Singleton distance $w_{rS}(q, m, n, k)$ for $\mathbb{F}_{q^m}$-linear codes of dimension k is defined as*
$$w_{rS}(q, m, n, k) \triangleq \left\lfloor \frac{(n-k)m}{\max(m,n)} \right\rfloor + 1.$$

The usual notion of the support of a vector is generally relevant to decoding in the Hamming metric and corresponds for a vector $\mathbf{x} = (x_i)_{1 \leq i \leq n}$ to the set of positions i in $\{1, \ldots, n\}$ such that $x_i \neq 0$. Various decoding algorithms for the Hamming metric [6,8,10,14,19,22,35,37,38,40,44] use this notion in a rather fundamental way. The definition of the support of a vector has to be changed a little bit to be relevant to the rank metric. This notion was first put forward in [28,29] to obtain an analogue of the Prange decoder [40] for the rank metric.

Definition 4 (Support). *Let* $\mathbf{x} = (x_i)_{1 \leq i \leq n} \in \mathbb{F}_{q^m}^n$, *its support is defined as:*

$$\mathrm{Supp}(\mathbf{x}) \overset{\triangle}{=} \langle x_1, \cdots, x_n \rangle_{\mathbb{F}_q}.$$

This notion of support is among other things relied to the rank metric as it is easily verified that for any vector $\mathbf{x}$ of $\mathbb{F}_{q^m}^n$ we have $|\mathbf{x}| = \dim(\mathrm{Supp}(\mathbf{x}))$.

3   The RankSign Scheme

We recall in this section basic facts about RankSign [31]. It is based on augmented LRPC codes. Roughly speaking it is a hash and sign signature scheme: the message $\mathbf{m}$ that has to be signed is hashed by a hash function $\mathcal{H}$ and the signature is equal to $f^{-1}(\mathcal{H}(\mathbf{m}))$ where f is a trapdoor one-way function. In this way the pair $(\mathbf{m}, f^{-1}(\mathcal{H}(\mathbf{m})))$ forms a valid signature. Recall now that code-based cryptography relies on Problem 1 (rank syndrome decoding) which amounts to consider here the following one way-function to build a signature primitive:

$$f_{\mathbf{H}} : \mathbf{e} \in S_w \longrightarrow \mathbf{e}\mathbf{H}^{\mathsf{T}} \in \mathbb{F}_{q^m}^{n-k}$$

where S_w denotes the words of $\mathbb{F}_{q^m}^n$ of rank weight w, $\mathbf{H}$ a parity-check matrix of size $(n-k) \times n$. To introduce a trapdoor in $f_{\mathbf{H}}$ authors of [27] proposed to use parity-check matrices of the family of augmented LRPC codes. Indeed, when the underlying LRPC structure is known (roughly speaking, this is the trapdoor), there is a decoding algorithm based on the LRPC structure that computes for any (or for a good fraction) $\mathbf{s} \in \mathbb{F}_{q^m}^{n-k}$ an $\mathbf{e} \in \mathbb{F}_{q^m}^n$ of weight w such that $\mathbf{H}\mathbf{e}^{\mathsf{T}} = \mathbf{s}^{\mathsf{T}}$. This decoding algorithm is probabilistic and the parameters of the code have to be chosen in a very specific fashion in order to have a probability of success very close to 1 (see Fact 1 at the end of this section).

The following definition will be useful for our discussion.

Definition 5 (Homogeneous Matrix). *A matrix* $\mathbf{H} = (H_{ij})_{\substack{1 \leq i \leq n-k \\ 1 \leq j \leq n}}$ *over* $\mathbb{F}_{q^m}$ *is homogeneous of weight* d *if all its coefficients generate an* $\mathbb{F}_q$-*vector space of dimension* d:

$$\dim\left(\langle H_{ij} : 1 \leq i \leq n-k, \; 1 \leq j \leq n \rangle_{\mathbb{F}_q} \right) = d$$

LRPC (Low Rank Parity Check) codes of weight d and augmented LRPC codes of type (d, t) are defined from homogeneous matrices of weight d as

Definition 6 (LRPC and augmented LRPC code). *An LRPC code over* $\mathbb{F}_{q^m}$ *of weight* d *is a code that admits a parity-check matrix* $\mathbf{H}$ *with entries in* $\mathbb{F}_{q^m}$ *that is homogeneous of weight* d *whereas an augmented LRPC code of type* (d,t) *over* $\mathbb{F}_{q^m}$ *is a code that admits a parity-check matrix* $\mathbf{H}' = \begin{bmatrix} \mathbf{H}|\mathbf{R} \end{bmatrix} \mathbf{P}$ *where* $\mathbf{H}$ *is a homogeneous matrix of rank* d *over* $\mathbb{F}_{q^m}$, $\mathbf{R}$ *is a matrix with* t *columns that has its entries in* $\mathbb{F}_{q^m}$ *and* $\mathbf{P}$ *is a square and invertible matrix with entries in* $\mathbb{F}_q$ *that has the same number of columns as* $\mathbf{H}'$.

Remark 2. Note that any invertible $\mathbf{P} \in \mathbb{F}_q^{n \times n}$ is an isometry for the rank metric, since for any $\mathbf{x} \in \mathbb{F}_{q^m}^n$ we have $\mathrm{Supp}(\mathbf{x}) = \mathrm{Supp}(\mathbf{xP})$ and therefore $|\mathbf{x}| = |\mathbf{xP}|$.

The public key and the secret key for RankSign are given by:

Public Key: $\mathbf{H}_{\mathrm{pub}}$ which is a random $(n-k) \times n$ parity-check matrix of an augmented LRPC code of type (d,t). It is of the form

$$\mathbf{H}_{\mathrm{pub}} = \mathbf{QH}'$$

with $\mathbf{H}' = \begin{bmatrix} \mathbf{H}|\mathbf{R} \end{bmatrix} \mathbf{P}$ where $\mathbf{Q}$ is an invertible $(n-k) \times (n-k)$ matrix over $\mathbb{F}_{q^m}$, $\mathbf{H}$ is a homogeneous matrix of rank d over $\mathbb{F}_{q^m}$, $\mathbf{R}$ is a matrix with t columns that has its entries in $\mathbb{F}_{q^m}$ and $\mathbf{P}$ is a square and invertible matrix with entries in $\mathbb{F}_q$ that has the same number of columns as $\mathbf{H}'$.

Secret Key: The matrix $\mathbf{H}_{\mathrm{sec}} \overset{\triangle}{=} \begin{bmatrix} \mathbf{H}|\mathbf{R} \end{bmatrix}$.

From the knowledge of this last matrix a signature is computed by using a decoding algorithm devised for LRPC codes. Recall that LRPC codes can be viewed as analogues of LDPC codes for the rank metric. In particular, they enjoy an efficient decoding algorithm based on their low rank parity-check matrix. Roughly speaking, Algorithm 1 of [27] decodes up to w errors when $dw \leq n-k$ in polynomial time (see [27, Theorem 1]). It uses in a crucial way the notion of the linear span of a product of subspaces of $\mathbb{F}_{q^m}$:

Definition 7. *Let U and V be two subspaces of* $\mathbb{F}_{q^m}$, *then*

$$U \cdot V \overset{\triangle}{=} \langle uv : u \in U, \ v \in V \rangle_{\mathbb{F}_q}.$$

Roughly speaking, Algorithm 1 of [27] works as follows when we have to recover an error $\mathbf{e}$ of weight w from the knowledge of its syndrome $\mathbf{s}$ with respect to a parity-check matrix $\mathbf{H} = (H_{ij})_{\substack{1 \leq i \leq n-k \\ 1 \leq j \leq n}}$ over $\mathbb{F}_{q^m}$ that is homogeneous of weight d, that is

$$\mathbf{s}^{\mathsf{T}} = \mathbf{He}^{\mathsf{T}}. \tag{2}$$

1. Let $U \overset{\triangle}{=} \langle H_{ij} : 1 \leq i \leq n-k, \ 1 \leq j \leq n \rangle_{\mathbb{F}_q}$, $V \overset{\triangle}{=} \mathrm{Supp}(\mathbf{e})$ and $W \overset{\triangle}{=} \mathrm{Supp}(\mathbf{s})$. U and W are known, whereas V is unknown to the decoder. By definition U is of dimension d and it is convenient to bring in a basis $\{f_1, \ldots, f_d\}$ for it.
2. It turns out that we typically have $W = U \cdot V$. Moreover it is clear that in such a case $V \subset f_1^{-1}W \cap f_2^{-1}W \cdots f_d^{-1}W$. It also turns out that we typically have

$$V = f_1^{-1}W \cap f_2^{-1}W \cdots f_d^{-1}W.$$

V is therefore computed by taking the intersection of all the $f_i^{-1}W$'s.

3. Once we have the support of $\mathbf{e}$ ($V = \mathrm{Supp}(\mathbf{e})$), the error $\mathbf{e} = (e_1, \ldots, e_n)$ can be recovered by solving the linear equation $\mathbf{He}^{\mathsf{T}} = \mathbf{s}^{\mathsf{T}}$ with the additional constraints $e_i \in \mathrm{Supp}(\mathbf{e})$ for $i \in \{1, \ldots, n\}$. There are in this case enough linear constraints to recover a unique $\mathbf{e}$.

The last algorithm seems to apply when there is a unique solution to (2). It can also be used with a slight modification (by adding "erasures" [31]) for weights for which there are many solutions to it (this is typically the regime which is used for the RankSign scheme). It namely turns out, see [31], that this decoder can for a certain range of parameters be used for a large fraction of possible syndromes $\mathbf{s} \in \mathbb{F}_{q^m}^{n-k}$ to produce an error $\mathbf{e}$ of weight w that satisfies (2). It can even be required that $\mathrm{Supp}(\mathbf{e})$ contains a subspace T of some dimension t. Furthermore this procedure can also be generalized to a parity-check matrix of an augmented LRPC code. More precisely to summarize the discussion that can be found in [5, 31]

Fact 1. *Let $\mathbf{H}$ be a random homogeneous matrix of weight d in $\mathbb{F}_{q^m}^{(n-k) \times n}$, $\mathbf{H}' = \left[\mathbf{H} | \mathbf{R}\right] \mathbf{P}$ where $\mathbf{R}$ is a matrix with t columns that has its entries in $\mathbb{F}_{q^m}$ and $\mathbf{P}$ is a square and invertible matrix with entries in $\mathbb{F}_q$ that has the same number of columns as $\mathbf{H}'$. There is a probabilistic polynomial time algorithm that outputs for a large fraction of syndromes $\mathbf{s} \in \mathbb{F}_{q^m}^{n-k}$, subspaces T of $\mathbb{F}_{q^m}$ of $\mathbb{F}_q$–dimension t', an error $\mathbf{e}$ of weight w whose support contains the subspace T that satisfies $\mathbf{H}'\mathbf{e}^{\mathsf{T}} = \mathbf{s}^{\mathsf{T}}$ as soon as the parameters n, k, t, t', d, w satisfy*

$$m = (w - t')(d + 1) \tag{3}$$
$$n - k = d(w - t - t') \tag{4}$$
$$n = (n - k)d. \tag{5}$$

4 Identity-Based-Encryption in Code-Based Cryptography

We recall in this section the [26] approach for obtaining an IBE scheme whose security relies on code-based assumptions. In some sense, this scheme can be viewed as an adaptation of the first quantum-safe IBE which was introduced by [33] in the paradigm of lattice-based cryptography. The adaptation relies on two building blocks: (i) a signature scheme, RankSign whose security relies on code-based assumptions for the rank metric, (ii) a new encryption scheme, namely RankPKE [26], based on the Rank Support Leaning (RSL) problem. [26] gives a security proof of the IBE scheme that relies on two assumptions: (i) the key security of RankSign and (ii) the difficulty of RSL. Furthermore, the work of [26] can be easily generalized to the more common Hamming metric. It is why we present in what follows the [26] IBE scheme with codes independently of the metric.

Roughly speaking, an IBE is a specific public-key encryption scheme that allows senders to encrypt messages thanks to the receiver's identity (such as its

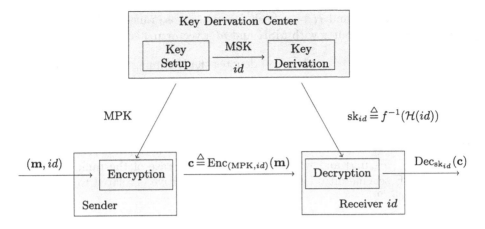

Fig. 1. IBE in the GPV context

email address). To permit this protocol there is a third party, say a Key Derivation Center, which owns a master secret-key MSK and an associated public-key MPK that allows to compute from *any* identity id a related secret quantity sk_{id} that will be used in a public-key encryption scheme involving an arbitrary sender and the receiver of identity id, with the pair of public/secret key $((id, \text{MPK}), sk_{id})$. In this paradigm any identity id needs to be matched with a secret key sk_{id} and to achieve this goal it was proposed in [33] to use a hash and sign primitive. Roughly speaking, for a trapdoor function f and a hash function $\mathcal{H}$ the Key Derivation Center will compute from id the quantity $f^{-1}(\mathcal{H}(id))$ which will be used as sk_{id}. We summarize in Fig. 1 how this IBE works.

IBE in Code-Based Cryptography. We give now the general framework of [26] for obtaining a code-based IBE scheme. It is only given in the rank metric case in [26], but the approach is really more general than this and can be given for the Hamming metric too. We will detail what happens for both metrics here. We will denote by $\mathbb{F}$ the finite field $\mathbb{F}_2$ or $\mathbb{F}_{q^m}$ depending on the Hamming or rank metric. As explained above, this scheme builds upon a hash and sign primitive and the authors of [26] proposed RankSign there but in our description the signature scheme is just a black-box.

Let $\mathcal{C}_{sgn}$ be a code of length n_{sgn} and dimension k_{sgn} for which there is a trapdoor that enables to compute for any $\mathbf{y} \in \mathbb{F}$ a codeword $\mathbf{c_y} \in \mathcal{C}_{sgn}$ at distance w_{sgn}. Let w_{dec} be an integer, $\mathcal{C}_{dec}$ be a code of length n_{dec} and dimension k_{dec} such that it exists a polynomial algorithm to decode a linear (in the length) error weight. Let $\mathbf{G}_{\mathcal{C}_{sgn}}$ and $\mathbf{G}_{\mathcal{C}_{dec}}$ be generator matrices of the codes $\mathcal{C}_{sgn}$ and $\mathcal{C}_{dec}$ respectively. Then it is proposed in [26] to set master secret and public keys as:

- MSK be the trapdoor which enables to decode at distance w_{sgn} in $\mathcal{C}_{sgn}$;
- MPK $\overset{\triangle}{=} (\mathcal{C}_{sgn}, \mathcal{C}_{dec})$.

Let id be an identity and $\mathcal{H}$ be a hash function whose range is $\mathbb{F}^{n_{\mathrm{sgn}}}$. The key derivation center computes with MSK and id a vector $\mathbf{u}_{id}$ such that:

$$|\mathbf{u}_{id}\mathbf{G}_{\mathcal{C}_{\mathrm{sgn}}} - \mathcal{H}(id)| = w_{\mathrm{sgn}} \text{ where } |\cdot| \text{ denotes the Hamming or rank metric} \quad (6)$$

This is used as the secret key associated to the identity id:

$$-\ \mathrm{sk}_{id} \stackrel{\triangle}{=} \mathbf{u}_{id}.$$

We are now ready to present the encryption scheme whose public/secret key is $((\mathbf{G}_{\mathcal{C}_{\mathrm{sgn}}}, \mathbf{G}_{\mathcal{C}_{\mathrm{dec}}}, id), \mathbf{u}_{id})$ and which in the particular case of the rank metric is the RankPKE scheme introduced in [26]. This primitive is related to the work of Alekhnovich [2].

- **Encryption.** Let $\mathbf{m}$ be the message that will be encrypted. The authors of [26] introduced the trapdoor function:

$$g_{\mathbf{G}_{\mathcal{C}_{\mathrm{sgn}}},\mathbf{G}_{\mathcal{C}_{\mathrm{dec}}},id} : \mathbb{F}^{k_{\mathrm{dec}}} \longrightarrow \mathbb{F}^{(k_{\mathrm{sgn}}+1)\times n_{\mathrm{dec}}}$$

$$\mathbf{m} \longmapsto \begin{bmatrix} \mathbf{G}_{\mathcal{C}_{\mathrm{sgn}}}\mathbf{E} \\ \mathcal{H}(id)\mathbf{E} + \mathbf{m}\mathbf{G}_{\mathcal{C}_{\mathrm{dec}}} \end{bmatrix}$$

where $\mathbf{E}$ has a size $n_{\mathrm{sgn}} \times n_{\mathrm{dec}}$. In the case of the rank metric $\mathbf{E}$ is a matrix uniformly picked at random among the homogeneous matrices of weight w_{dec} and in the case of the Hamming metric, $\mathbf{E}$ is picked uniformly at random among the matrices whose columns have all weight w_{dec}.

- **Decryption.** The secret key $\mathbf{u}_{id}$ is used as

$$(\mathbf{u}_{id}, -1)g_{\mathbf{G}_{\mathcal{C}_{\mathrm{sgn}}},\mathbf{G}_{\mathcal{C}_{\mathrm{dec}}},id}(\mathbf{m}) = (\mathbf{u}_{id}, -1)\begin{bmatrix} \mathbf{G}_{\mathcal{C}_{\mathrm{sgn}}}\mathbf{E} \\ \mathcal{H}(id)\mathbf{E} + \mathbf{m}\mathbf{G}_{\mathcal{C}_{\mathrm{dec}}} \end{bmatrix}$$

$$= \left(\mathbf{u}_{id}\mathbf{G}_{\mathcal{C}_{\mathrm{sgn}}} - \mathcal{H}(id)\right)\mathbf{E} - \mathbf{m}\mathbf{G}_{\mathcal{C}_{\mathrm{dec}}}$$

It can be verified that under certain restrictions on w_{sgn} and w_{dec}, the weight of the vector $\left(\mathbf{u}_{id}\mathbf{G}_{\mathcal{C}_{\mathrm{sgn}}} - \mathcal{H}(id)\right)\mathbf{E}$ is low enough, so that a decoding algorithm for $\mathcal{C}_{\mathrm{dec}}$ will recover $\mathbf{m}$. The following proposition gives a constraint on these parameters so that decoding is possible in principle.

Proposition 1. *In order to be able to decode asymptotically at constant rate R, there should exist an $\varepsilon(R) > 0$ such that all the parameters n_{sgn}, w_{sgn} and w_{dec} have to verify*

- *in the rank metric case*

$$w_{sgn}w_{dec} = (1 - \varepsilon(R))\min(m, n_{dec}) \quad (7)$$

- *in the Hamming metric case*

$$w_{sgn}w_{dec} = O(n_{sgn}). \quad (8)$$

The proof of this proposition can be found in the long version of the paper [15].

The constraint set on the parameters by this proposition is crucial to instantiate the IBE in code-based cryptography. Unfortunately, this constraint implies a fatal weakness for the Hamming based scheme and a hard to meet condition for the rank metric in order to have a secure scheme as we will see in what follows.

The RSL Problem. We recall here the assumption upon which the security of RankPKE relies (the previous encryption scheme in rank metric), namely the Rank Support Leaning (RSL) problem introduced in [26]. This problem is a rank syndrome decoding problem with syndromes that are associated to errors that all share the same support which is the secret.

Problem 2 (RSL - Rank Support Learning)

Parameters: n, k, N, w
Instance: $(\mathbf{A}, \mathbf{AE})$ where $\mathbf{A}$ is a full rank matrix of size $(n - k) \times n$, $\mathbf{E}$ a matrix of size $n \times N$ where all its coefficients belong to a same subspace F of $\mathbb{F}_{q^m}$ of dimension w
Output: the subspace F.

Remark 3. Let $(\mathbf{A}, \mathbf{AE})$ be an instance of RSL. The matrix $\mathbf{A}$ is of full-rank of size $(n - k) \times n$ and we can perform Gaussian elimination on its rows to get a matrix $\mathbf{S}$ such that $\mathbf{SA} = [\mathbf{1}_{n-k}|\mathbf{A}']$. The pair $(\mathbf{SA}, \mathbf{SAE})$ is still an instance of RSL with the same parameters and secret subspace F, it is why we can always assume that for any instance of RSL the matrix $\mathbf{A}$ is in systematic form.

5   Attack on RankSign

5.1   The Problem with RankSign: Low Rank Codewords in the Augmented LRPC Code

A natural way to attack RankSign is to find low weight codewords in the dual of the augmented LRPC code. Recall that the public parity-check matrix used in the scheme is a matrix $\mathbf{H}_{\mathrm{pub}}$ where

$$\mathbf{H}_{\mathrm{pub}} = \mathbf{QH}'$$

with $\mathbf{H}' = [\mathbf{H}|\mathbf{R}]\,\mathbf{P}$ where $\mathbf{H}$ is a homogeneous matrix of rank d over $\mathbb{F}_{q^m}$, $\mathbf{R}$ is a matrix with t columns that has its entries in $\mathbb{F}_{q^m}$, $\mathbf{P}$ is a square and invertible matrix with entries in $\mathbb{F}_q$ that has the same number of columns as $\mathbf{H}'$ and $\mathbf{Q}$ is a square and invertible matrix over $\mathbb{F}_{q^m}$ which has the same number of rows as $\mathbf{H}'$. If we call $\mathcal{C}_{\mathrm{pub}}$ the "public code" with parity-check matrix $\mathbf{H}_{\mathrm{pub}}$, then the dual code $\mathcal{C}_{\mathrm{pub}}^{\perp}$ that has for generator matrix $\mathbf{H}_{\mathrm{pub}}$ has codewords of weight $\leq d+t$ since rows of $\mathbf{H}'\mathbf{P}$ belong to this code, and all of its rows have rank weight $\leq d+t$ since the rows of $\mathbf{H}'$ have weight at most $d+t$ and $\mathbf{P}$ is an isometry for the rank metric. The authors have chosen the parameters of the RankSign scheme so that finding codewords of weight $t+d$ in $\mathcal{C}_{\text{pub}}^{\perp}$ is above the security level of the scheme. However, it turns out that due to the peculiar parameters chosen in the RankSign scheme (see Fact 1), $\mathcal{C}_{\text{pub}}$ has many very low weight codewords. This is the main problem in RankSign. Before we give a precise statement together with its proof, we will give a general result showing that LRPC codes may have under certain circumstances low weight codewords.

Lemma 1. *Let $\mathcal{C}$ be an LRPC code of length n and dimension k over $\mathbb{F}_{q^m}$ that is associated to an homogeneous matrix $\mathbf{H}$ that has all its entries in a subspace F of $\mathbb{F}_{q^m}$. Furthermore we suppose there exists a subspace F' of $\mathbb{F}_{q^m}$ such that*

$$(n - k)\dim(F \cdot F') < n \dim F'.$$

Then there exist non-zero codewords in the LRPC code whose support is included in F'. They are therefore of rank weight at most $\dim F'$. Furthermore this set of codewords, that is

$$\mathcal{C}' \overset{\triangle}{=} \{\mathbf{c} \in \mathcal{C} : c_i \in F', \ \forall i \in [\![1, n]\!]\}$$

forms an $\mathbb{F}_q$ subspace of $\mathbb{F}_{q^m}^n$ that is of dimension $\geq n \dim F' - (n-k)\dim(F \cdot F')$.

Proof. Denote the entry in row i and column j of $\mathbf{H}$ by $H_{i,j}$. A codeword $\mathbf{c}$ of the LRPC code satisfies

$$\forall i \in [\![1, n - k]\!], \quad \sum_{j=1}^{n} H_{i,j} c_j = 0. \tag{9}$$

Looking in addition for a codeword $\mathbf{c}$ that has all its entries in F' and expressing these $n - k$ linear equations over $\mathbb{F}_{q^m}$ in a basis of $F \cdot F'$ (since $\sum_{j=1}^{n} H_{i,j} c_j$ belongs by definition to $F \cdot F'$) and expressing each c_j in a $\mathbb{F}_q$ basis $\{f_1', \ldots, f_{d'}'\}$ of F' as $c_j = \sum_{\ell=1}^{d'} c_{j,\ell} f_\ell'$ we obtain $(n - k)\dim(F \cdot F')$ linear equations over $\mathbb{F}_q$ involving $n \dim F'$ unknowns (the $c_{j,\ell}$'s) in $\mathbb{F}_q$. The solution space is therefore of dimension greater $\geq n \dim F' - (n - k)\dim(F \cdot F')$.

Remark 4. This theorem proves the existence of low rank codewords in an LRPC-code under some conditions but it does not give any efficient way to find them.

By using this lemma, we will prove the following corollary that explains that the augmented LRPC codes that are used in the RankSign signature necessarily contain many rank weight 2 codewords. This is in a sense a consequence of the constraint (5) on the parameters of RankSign.

Corollary 1. *Let $\mathcal{C}_{pub}$ be an $[n+t, k+t]$ public code of RankSign over $\mathbb{F}_{q^m}$ which has been obtained from an $[n, k]$ LRPC-code that is associated to a homogeneous matrix $\mathbf{H}$ that has all its entries in an $\mathbb{F}_q$ subspace F of $\mathbb{F}_{q^m}$. Consider a subspace F' of F of dimension 2 and let*

$$\mathcal{C}'_{pub} \overset{\triangle}{=} \{\mathbf{c} \in \mathcal{C}_{pub} : c_i \in F', \ \forall i \in [\![1, n + t]\!]\}.$$

$\mathcal{C}'_{pub}$ is an $\mathbb{F}_q$ subspace of $\mathbb{F}_{q^m}^{n+t}$. If (5) holds, that is $n = (n-k)d$, then

$$\dim_{\mathbb{F}_q} \mathcal{C}'_{pub} \geq n/d.$$

Proof. Let $\mathbf{H}_{pub} \in \mathbb{F}_{q^m}^{(n-k)\times(n+t)}$ be the public parity-check matrix for the RankSign public code $\mathcal{C}_{pub}$. Recall that $\mathbf{H}_{pub}$ has been obtained as $\mathbf{H}_{pub} = \mathbf{Q}[\mathbf{H}|\mathbf{R}]\mathbf{P}$ where:

- $\mathbf{P}$ is a non-singular matrix with entries in $\mathbb{F}_q$ of size $(n+t) \times (n+t)$,
- $\mathbf{Q}$ is an invertible matrix of $\mathbb{F}_{q^m}$ of size $(n-k) \times (n-k)$,
- $\mathbf{R}$ is a random matrix of $\mathbb{F}_{q^m}$ of size $(n-k) \times t$,
- $\mathbf{H}$ is a homogeneous $(n-k) \times n$ matrix of weight d with all its entries in F.

Choose a basis $\{x_1, x_2, \ldots, x_d\}$ of F such that $\{x_1, x_2\}$ is a basis of F'. We observe now that

$$F \cdot F' = \langle x_i x_j : i \in [\![1, d]\!],\ j \in [\![1, 2]\!]\rangle_{\mathbb{F}_q}.$$

The cardinality of the set $\{x_i x_j : i \in [\![1, d]\!],\ j \in [\![1, 2]\!]\}$ is actually $2d - 1$ because $x_1 x_2 = x_2 x_1$. This implies that $\dim(F \cdot F') \leq 2d - 1$. Which leads to the following inequalities,

$$\begin{aligned}
n \dim(F') - (n-k)\dim(F \cdot F') &\geq 2n - (n-k)(2d-1) \\
&= 2d(n-k) - (n-k)(2d-1) \text{ (since } n = (n-k)d) \\
&= \frac{n}{d} \quad \text{(since } n = (n-k)d).
\end{aligned}$$

Let $\mathcal{C}_{\mathrm{LRPC}}$ be the LRPC code of weight d associated to the parity-check matrix $\mathbf{H}$ and let $\mathcal{C}'_{\mathrm{LRPC}}$ be an $\mathbb{F}_q$ subspace of it that is defined by

$$\mathcal{C}'_{\mathrm{LRPC}} \overset{\triangle}{=} \{\mathbf{c} \in \mathcal{C}_{\mathrm{LRPC}} : c_i \in F',\ \forall i \in [\![1, n]\!]\}.$$

By applying Lemma 1 we know that

$$\dim_{\mathbb{F}_q} \mathcal{C}'_{\mathrm{LRPC}} \geq \frac{n}{d}. \tag{10}$$

Consider now

$$\mathcal{C}'_{pub} \overset{\triangle}{=} \{(\mathbf{c}_{\mathrm{LRPC}}, \mathbf{0}_t)(\mathbf{P}^{-1})^{\mathsf{T}} : \mathbf{c}_{\mathrm{LRPC}} \in \mathcal{C}'_{\mathrm{LRPC}}\},$$

where $\mathbf{0}_t$ denotes the vector with t zeros. From (10) we deduce that $\dim_{\mathbb{F}_q} \mathcal{C}'_{pub} \geq \frac{n}{d}$. Moreover the entries of any element $\mathbf{c}'$ in $\mathcal{C}'_{pub}$ belong to F' because the entries of $\mathbf{P}$ are in $\mathbb{F}_q$. Let us now prove that $\mathcal{C}'_{pub}$ is contained in $\mathcal{C}_{pub}$. To verify this, consider $\mathbf{c}' = (\mathbf{c}_{\mathrm{LRPC}}, \mathbf{0}_t)(\mathbf{P}^{-1})^{\mathsf{T}} \in \mathcal{C}'_{pub}$. We observe now that

$$\begin{aligned}
\mathbf{H}_{pub}\mathbf{c}'^{\mathsf{T}} &= \mathbf{H}_{pub}\mathbf{P}^{-1}(\mathbf{c}_{\mathrm{LRPC}}, \mathbf{0}_t)^{\mathsf{T}} \\
&= \mathbf{Q}[\mathbf{H}|\mathbf{R}]\,\mathbf{P}\mathbf{P}^{-1}(\mathbf{c}_{\mathrm{LRPC}}, \mathbf{0}_t)^{\mathsf{T}} \\
&= \mathbf{Q}[\mathbf{H}|\mathbf{R}]\,(\mathbf{c}_{\mathrm{LRPC}}, \mathbf{0}_t)^{\mathsf{T}} \\
&= \mathbf{Q}\mathbf{H}\mathbf{c}_{\mathrm{LRPC}}^{\mathsf{T}} \quad (\mathbf{R} \in \mathbb{F}_{q^m}^{(n-k)\times t}) \\
&= \mathbf{0} \quad (\mathbf{c}_{\mathrm{LRPC}} \text{ belongs to the code of parity-check matrix } \mathbf{H})
\end{aligned}$$

This proves that $\mathcal{C}'_{pub} \subset \mathcal{C}_{pub}$ which concludes the proof.

5.2   Weight 1 Codewords in a Projected Code

Corollary 1 shows that there are many weight 2 codewords in $\mathcal{C}_{\text{pub}}$. We can even restrict our search further by noticing that without loss of generality we may assume that the space F in which the entries of the secret parity-check matrix $\mathbf{H}$ of the LRPC code are taken contains 1. Indeed, for any α in $\mathbb{F}_{q^m}^{\times}$, $\alpha\mathbf{H}$ is also a parity-check matrix of the LRPC code and has its entries in αF. By choosing α such that αF contains 1 we get our claim.

Consider now a supplementary space V of $\langle 1 \rangle_{\mathbb{F}_q} = \mathbb{F}_q$ with respect to $\mathbb{F}_{q^m}$, that is an $\mathbb{F}_q$-space of dimension $m-1$ such that $\mathbb{F}_{q^m} = V \oplus \mathbb{F}_q$. The previous discussion implies that there is a matrix-code in $\mathbb{F}_q^{(m-1)\times(n+t)}$, deduced from $\mathcal{C}_{\text{pub}}$ by projecting the entries onto V, that contains codewords of weight 1. More specifically, consider an $\mathbb{F}_q$ basis $\{\beta_1, \beta_2, \cdots, \beta_m\}$ of $\mathbb{F}_{q^m}$ such that $\beta_m = 1$ and for $\mathbf{c} = (c_i)_{1\le i\le n+t} \in \mathbb{F}_{q^m}^{n+t}$ consider

$$\mathbf{Mat}^{\text{proj}}(\mathbf{c}) = (M_{ij})_{\substack{1\le i\le m-1 \\ 1\le j\le n+t}} \in \mathbb{F}_q^{(m-1)\times(n+t)}$$

where $c_j = \sum_{i=1}^m M_{ij}\beta_i$. Now let $\mathcal{C}_{\text{pub}}^{\text{proj}}$ be the matrix-code in $\mathbb{F}_q^{(m-1)\times(n+t)}$ defined by

$$\mathcal{C}_{\text{pub}}^{\text{proj}} \triangleq \{\mathbf{Mat}^{\text{proj}}(\mathbf{c}) : \mathbf{c} \in \mathcal{C}_{\text{pub}}\}.$$

It is clear that

Fact 2. $\mathcal{C}_{pub}^{proj}$ contains codewords of rank weight 1.

These are just the codewords $\mathbf{c}'$ which are of the form $\mathbf{Mat}^{\text{proj}}(\mathbf{c})$ where $\mathbf{c} \in \mathcal{C}_{\text{pub}}'$ with $\mathcal{C}_{\text{pub}}'$ being defined from a subspace F' of F that contains 1 (we can make this assumption since we can assume that F contains 1).

$\mathcal{C}_{\text{pub}}^{\text{proj}}$ has the structure of an $\mathbb{F}_q$-subspace of $\mathbb{F}_q^{(m-1)\times(n+t)}$. It is typically of dimension $(k+t)m$ (i.e. the same as the $\mathbb{F}_q$ dimension of $\mathcal{C}_{\text{pub}}$). Moreover once we have these rank weight 1 codewords in $\mathcal{C}_{\text{pub}}^{\text{proj}}$ we can lift them to obtain rank weight ≤ 2 codewords in $\mathcal{C}_{\text{pub}}$ because for any $\mathbf{c} \in \mathcal{C}_{\text{pub}}$ the last row of $\mathbf{Mat}(\mathbf{c})$ can be uniquely recovered from $\mathbf{Mat}^{\text{proj}}(\mathbf{c})$ by performing linear combinations of the entries of $\mathbf{Mat}^{\text{proj}}(\mathbf{c})$. We call this operation deducing $\mathbf{c}$ from $\mathbf{Mat}^{\text{proj}}(\mathbf{c})$ *lifting* from $\mathcal{C}_{\text{pub}}^{\text{proj}}$ to $\mathcal{C}_{\text{pub}}$.

5.3   Outline of the Attack

Finding codewords of rank 1 in $\mathcal{C}_{\text{pub}}^{\text{proj}}$ obviously reveals much of the secret LRPC structure. Lifting elements in $\mathcal{C}_{\text{pub}}^{\text{proj}}$ that are of rank 1 to $\mathcal{C}_{\text{pub}}$ as explained at the end of Subsect. 5.2 yields codewords of $\mathcal{C}_{\text{pub}}$ that have typically rank weight 2. This can be used to reveal F' and actually the whole subspace F by finding enough rank 1 codewords in $\mathcal{C}_{\text{pub}}^{\text{proj}}$. Once F is recovered a suitable form for a parity-check matrix of $\mathcal{C}_{\text{pub}}$ can be found that allows signing like a legitimate user. For the case of the parameters of RankSign proposed in [5,31] for which we always have $d = 2$ we will proceed slightly differently here. Roughly speaking, our attack can be decomposed as follows

1. We find a particular element $\mathbf{M}$ in $\mathcal{C}_{\mathrm{pub}}^{\mathrm{proj}}$ of rank weight 1 by solving a certain bilinear system with Gröbner bases techniques.
2. We lift $\mathbf{M} \in \mathcal{C}_{\mathrm{pub}}^{\mathrm{proj}}$ to $\mathbf{c} \in \mathcal{C}_{\mathrm{pub}}$ and compute $F' \stackrel{\triangle}{=} \mathrm{Supp}(\mathbf{c})$.
3. We compute from F' the $\mathbb{F}_q$-subspace

$$\mathcal{C}_{\mathrm{pub}}' \stackrel{\triangle}{=} \left\{ \mathbf{c} = (c_i)_{1 \le i \le n+t} \in \mathcal{C}_{\mathrm{pub}} : c_i \in F' \ \forall i \in [\![1, n+t]\!] \right\}.$$

When $d = 2$ this set has typically dimension k.
4. We use this subspace of $\mathcal{C}_{\mathrm{pub}}$ to find a suitable parity-check matrix for $\mathcal{C}_{\mathrm{pub}}$ which allows us to sign like a legitimate user.

Steps 2 and 3 are straightforward. We just give details for Steps 1 and 4 in what follows.

5.4 Finding Rank 1 Matrices in $\mathcal{C}_{\mathrm{pub}}^{\mathrm{proj}}$ by Solving a Bilinear System

The Basic Bilinear System. Finding rank 1 matrices in $\mathcal{C}_{\mathrm{pub}}^{\mathrm{proj}}$ can be formulated as an instance of the MinRank problem [11,12]. We could use standard techniques for solving this problem [20,21,34,43] but we found that it is better here to use the algebraic modelling suggested in [5]. It basically consists in setting up an algebraic system with unknowns $\mathbf{x} = (x_1, \ldots, x_{m-1}) \in \mathbb{F}_q^{m-1}$ and $\mathbf{y} \in \mathbb{F}_q^{n+t}$ where the unknown matrix $\mathbf{M}$ in $\mathcal{C}_{\mathrm{pub}}^{\mathrm{proj}}$ that should be of rank 1 has the form

$$\mathbf{M} = \begin{pmatrix} x_1 y_1 & x_1 y_2 & \cdots & x_1 y_{n+t} \\ x_2 y_1 & x_2 y_2 & \cdots & x_2 y_{n+t} \\ \vdots & \vdots & \vdots & \vdots \\ x_{m-1} y_1 & x_{m-1} y_2 & \cdots & x_{m-1} y_{n+t} \end{pmatrix}.$$

Recall that $\mathcal{C}_{\mathrm{pub}}^{\mathrm{proj}}$ has the structure of an $\mathbb{F}_q$ subspace of $\mathbb{F}_q^{(m-1) \times (n+t)}$ of dimension $(k+t)m$. By viewing the elements of $\mathcal{C}_{\mathrm{pub}}^{\mathrm{proj}}$ as vectors of $\mathbb{F}_q^{(m-1)(n+t)}$, i.e. the matrix $\mathbf{M} = (M_{ij})_{\substack{1 \le i \le m-1 \\ 1 \le j \le n+t}}$ is viewed as the vector $\mathbf{m} = (m_\ell)_{1 \le \ell \le (m-1)(n+t)}$ where $m_{(i-1)(n+t)+j} = M_{i,j}$, we can compute a parity-check matrix $\mathbf{H}_{\mathrm{pub}}^{\mathrm{proj}}$ for it. It is an $((m-1)(n+t) - (k+t)m) \times (m-1)(n+t)$ matrix that we denote by $\mathbf{H}_{\mathrm{pub}}^{\mathrm{proj}} = (H_{ij}^{\mathrm{proj}})_{\substack{1 \le i \le (m-1)(n+t)-(k+t)m \\ 1 \le j \le (m-1)(n+t)}}$. This matrix gives $(m-1)(n+t) - (k+t)m$ bilinear equations that have to be satisfied by the x_i's and the y_j's:

$$\begin{cases} \sum\limits_{j=1}^{n+t} \sum\limits_{i=1}^{m-1} H_{1,(i-1)(n+t)+j}^{\mathrm{proj}} x_i y_j = 0 \\ \quad \vdots \\ \sum\limits_{j=1}^{n+t} \sum\limits_{i=1}^{m-1} H_{(n+t)(m-1)-(k+t)m,(i-1)(n+t)+j}^{\mathrm{proj}} x_i y_j = 0 \end{cases} \tag{11}$$

Restricting the Number of Solutions. We have solved the bilinear system (11) with standard Gröbner bases techniques that are implemented in Magma.

To speed-up the resolution of the bilinear system with Gröbner bases techniques (especially the change of order that is performed after a first computation of a Gröbner basis for a suitable order to deduce a basis for the lexicographic order which is more suited for outputting a solution) it is helpful to use additional equations that restrict the solution space which is otherwise really huge in this case. The purpose of the following discussion is to show where these solutions come from and how to restrict them. By bilinearity of System (11) we may fix

$$x_1 = 1 \tag{12}$$

when there is a solution $\mathbf{x}$ such that $x_1 \neq 0$). Furthermore, the fact that $\mathcal{C}'_{\text{pub}}$ is an $\mathbb{F}_q$ vector space of dimension n/d induces that for a given $\mathbf{x}$ solution to (11) the set of corresponding $\mathbf{y}$'s also forms a vector space of dimension n/d. We may therefore rather safely assume that we can choose

$$\forall i \in [\![1, \frac{n}{d} - 1]\!], \ y_i = 0 \quad \text{and} \quad y_{n/d} = 1. \tag{13}$$

There is an additional degree of freedom on $\mathbf{x}$ coming from the fact that even if $d = 2$ there are several spaces αF for which $1 \in \alpha F$. To verify this, let us study in more detail the case when F is of dimension 2, say $F = \langle a, b \rangle_{\mathbb{F}_q}$. We wish to understand what are the possible values for $z \in \mathbb{F}_{q^m}$ such that there exists $c \neq 0$ for which $\langle a, b \rangle_{\mathbb{F}_q} = c \langle 1, z \rangle_{\mathbb{F}_q}$. The possible values for $\mathbf{x}$ will then be the projection of those z to the $\mathbb{F}_q$ space $\langle \beta_1, \ldots, \beta_{m-1} \rangle_{\mathbb{F}_q}$. The possible values for z are then obtained from studying the possible values for c. There are two cases to consider:

- **Case 1:** $c = \frac{a+b\nu}{\mu}$ for $\mu \in \mathbb{F}_q^\times$ and $\nu \in \mathbb{F}_q$. In such a case $z = \frac{\beta b}{a+b\nu} + \delta$ for $\beta \in \mathbb{F}_q^\times$, $\delta \in \mathbb{F}_q$.
- **Case 2:** $c = \frac{b}{\mu}$ for $\mu \in \mathbb{F}_q^\times$. Here $z = \alpha \frac{a}{b} + \delta$ for $\alpha \in \mathbb{F}_q^\times$, $\delta \in \mathbb{F}_q$.

Since the δ term vanishes after projecting x onto $\langle \beta_1, \ldots, \beta_{m-1} \rangle_{\mathbb{F}_q}$ we have essentially two degrees of freedom over $\mathbb{F}_q$ for x. One has already been taken into account when setting $x_1 = 1$. We can add a second one $x_2 = \alpha$ where α is arbitrary in $\mathbb{F}_q$. We have actually chosen in our experiments that

$$(x_2 - \alpha)(x_2 - \beta) = 0 \tag{14}$$

for some random α and β in $\mathbb{F}_q$. This has resulted in some gain in the computation of the solution space. Finally the following proposition summarizes the system we have solved.

Proposition 2. *By eliminating variables using Eqs. (12), (13) and (14) in (11) we have*

- *$nm - k(m+1) - t + 2$ equations;*
- *$m - 1 + n + t$ unknowns.*

In the "typical regime" where $m \approx n$, $k \approx \frac{n}{2}$ and $t \ll n$ we have a number of equations of order n^2 and a number of unknowns of order n, therefore typically the regime where we expect that the Gröbner basis techniques take polynomial time.

5.5   Numerical Results

We give in Table 1 our numerical results to find a codeword of rank 2 in any public code of the RankSign scheme for parameters chosen according to [5]. These results have been obtained with an Intel Core i5 processor, clocked at 1.6 GHz using a single core, with 8 Go of RAM.

Table 1. Attack on NIST's parameters of RankSign with 100 random public keys.

Intended security [5]	(n, k, m, d, t, q)	Average time	Maximum memory usage
128 bits	$(20, 10, 21, 2, 2, 2^{32})$	23.66 s	49 MB
128 bits	$(24, 12, 24, 2, 2, 2^{24})$	36.92 s	65 MB
192 bits	$(24, 12, 27, 2, 3, 2^{32})$	150.02 s	97 MB
256 bits	$(28, 14, 30, 2, 3, 2^{32})$	289.62 s	137 MB

5.6   Finishing the Attack

We present in this subsection the end of our attack which consists in being able to sign with only the knowledge of the public key. The proofs of the lemmas can be found in the long version of the paper [15]. It holds for the parameters chosen for the NIST competition [5] for which $d = 2$. Observe that (5) implies that we have $k = n - k = n/2$.

We have at that point obtained the code $\mathcal{C}'_{\text{pub}}$ (see Sect. 5.3, Point 3.) that has dimension (over $\mathbb{F}_q$) $\geq n/d = n/2 = k$. This code is just $\mathbb{F}_q$-linear, but it will be convenient to extend it by considering its $\mathbb{F}_{q^m}$-linear extension, that we denote $\mathbb{F}_{q^m} \otimes \mathcal{C}'_{\text{pub}}$ that is defined by the $\mathbb{F}_{q^m}$-linear subspace of $\mathbb{F}_{q^m}^{n+t}$ obtained from linear combinations over $\mathbb{F}_{q^m}$ of codewords in $\mathcal{C}'_{\text{pub}}$. In other words if we denote by $\{\mathbf{c}'_1, \ldots, \mathbf{c}'_{k'}\}$ an $\mathbb{F}_q$-basis of $\mathcal{C}'_{\text{pub}}$, then $\mathbb{F}_{q^m} \otimes \mathcal{C}'_{\text{pub}} \overset{\triangle}{=} \langle \mathbf{c}'_1, \ldots, \mathbf{c}'_{k'} \rangle_{\mathbb{F}_{q^m}}$.

To simplify the discussion we make now the following assumption (which was corroborated by our experiments).

Assumption 1
$$\dim \mathbb{F}_{q^m} \otimes \mathcal{C}'_{pub} = k.$$

The rationale behind this assumption is that (i) the dimension of $\mathcal{C}'_{\text{pub}}$ is very likely to be n/d which is equal to k and (ii) an $\mathbb{F}_q$ basis of $\mathcal{C}'_{\text{pub}}$ is very likely to be an $\mathbb{F}_{q^m}$ basis too.

Lemma 2. *Under Assumption 1 the code* $\left(\mathbb{F}_{q^m} \otimes \mathcal{C}'_{pub} \right)^{\perp}$ *has length* $n + t$, *dimension* $n + t - k$ *and is an LRPC-code that is associated to a homogeneous matrix that has all its entries in an $\mathbb{F}_q$ subspace F of $\mathbb{F}_{q^m}$ of dimension 2 which contains 1. Furthermore, the sets*

$$\mathcal{D} \overset{\triangle}{=} \{\mathbf{c} \in \left(\mathbb{F}_{q^m} \otimes \mathcal{C}'_{pub} \right)^{\perp} : \text{Supp}(\mathbf{c}) \subseteq \mathbb{F}_q\} \text{ and } \mathcal{D}' \overset{\triangle}{=} \{\mathbf{c} \in \left(\mathbb{F}_{q^m} \otimes \mathcal{C}'_{pub} \right)^{\perp} : \text{Supp}(\mathbf{c}) \subseteq F\}$$

are $\mathbb{F}_q$-subspaces of dimension $\geq t$ and $\geq n - k + 2t$ respectively.

To end our attack we make now the following assumption that was again corroborated in our experiments.

Assumption 2. *We can extract from sets $\mathcal{D}$ and $\mathcal{D}'$ a basis of $\left(\mathbb{F}_{q^m} \otimes \mathcal{C}'_{pub}\right)^{\perp}$
with*

1. *t codewords of support $\mathbb{F}_q$,*
2. *$n - k$ codewords of a same support of rank 2 which contains 1.*

Lemma 3. *Under Assumptions 1 and 2 there exists a parity-check matrix $\mathbf{H}' \in
\mathbb{F}_{q^m}^{(n+t-k)\times(n+t)}$ of $\mathbb{F}_{q^m} \otimes \mathcal{C}'_{pub}$, an invertible matrix $\mathbf{P}$ of size $n + t$ with entries
in the small field $\mathbb{F}_q$ and an invertible matrix $\mathbf{S}$ of size $n + t - k$ with entries in
$\mathbb{F}_{q^m}$ such that*

$$\mathbf{SH}'\mathbf{P} = \begin{pmatrix} I_t & \mathbf{0} \\ \mathbf{0} & \mathbf{R} \end{pmatrix}$$

where $\mathbf{R}$ is homogeneous of degree 2 and of size $(n - k) \times n$.

The idea now to sign as a legitimate user will be to use the matrix $\mathbf{R}$ and the
decoder of Fact 1 (see Sect. 3). Recall that to make a signature for the matrix
$\mathbf{H}_{pub}$ (which defines the public code $\mathcal{C}_{pub}$) and a message $\mathbf{m}$, we look for an error
$\mathbf{e}$ of rank w satisfying $n - k = d(w - t - t')$ (see Eq. (4) of Fact 1), such that
$\mathbf{H}_{pub}\mathbf{e}^{\mathsf{T}} = \mathbf{s}^{\mathsf{T}}$ with $\mathbf{s} = \mathcal{H}(\mathbf{m})$ (the hash of the message). The algorithm that
follows performs this task:

---

1. We compute $\mathbf{y} \in \mathbb{F}_{q^m}^{n+t}$ such that $\mathbf{H}_{pub}\mathbf{y}^{\mathsf{T}} = \mathbf{s}^{\mathsf{T}}$.
2. Let $\mathbf{y}' = \mathbf{y}(\mathbf{P}^{-1})^{\mathsf{T}}$ and we compute $\mathbf{s}' = (\mathbf{SH}'\mathbf{P})\mathbf{y}'^{\mathsf{T}}$.
1. Let $\mathbf{s}'_1$ be the first t coordinates of $\mathbf{s}'$, $\mathbf{s}'_2$ its last $n - k$ ones. We apply
   the decoder of Sect. 3 with:
       - The subspace $T \overset{\triangle}{=} \text{Supp}(\mathbf{s}'_1) + T'$ where T' is a random subspace
         of $\mathbb{F}_{q^m}$ of dimension t'.
       - The parity-check matrix $\mathbf{R}$ and the syndrome $\mathbf{s}'_2$.
   Then we get a vector $\mathbf{e}'$ such that $T \subseteq \text{Supp}(\mathbf{e}')$ and $\mathbf{Re}'^{\mathsf{T}} = \mathbf{s}'_2{}^{\mathsf{T}}$.
4. We compute $\mathbf{e} = (\mathbf{s}'_1, \mathbf{e}')\mathbf{P}^{\mathsf{T}}$.

The correctness of this algorithm is proved in the long version of the paper [15].

6   Attack on the IBE in the Rank Metric

In the previous section we showed that RankSign is not a secure signature
scheme. This also shows the insecurity of the IBE proposal made in [26] since it
is partly based on it. It could be thought that it just suffices to replace in the
IBE scheme [26] RankSign by another signature scheme in the rank metric. This
is already problematic, since RankSign was the only known rank metric code-
based signature scheme up to now. We will actually show here that the problem
is deeper than this. We namely show that the parameters proposed in [26] can

be broken by an algebraic attack that attacks the RSL problem directly and not the underlying signature scheme. We will however show that the constraints on the parameters of the scheme coming from Proposition 1 together with the new constraint for avoiding the algebraic attack exposed here can in theory be met. In the IBE [26] we are given a matrix $\mathbf{G}_{\mathcal{C}_{\mathrm{sgn}}}$ of size $k_{\mathrm{sgn}} \times n_{\mathrm{sgn}}$ whose coefficients live in $\mathbb{F}_{q^m}$ and the matrix $\mathbf{G}_{\mathcal{C}_{\mathrm{sgn}}}\mathbf{E}$ where $\mathbf{E}$ has size $n_{\mathrm{sgn}} \times n_{\mathrm{dec}}$ with all its coefficients which live in a same secret subspace F of dimension w_{dec} and an attacker wants to recover F. We show in Sect. 6.1 that under the condition $n_{\mathrm{dec}} > w_{\mathrm{dec}}(n_{\mathrm{sgn}} - k_{\mathrm{sgn}})$ (which is verified in [26]) the code $\mathcal{C}$ defined by

$$\mathcal{C} = \{\mathbf{e}(\mathbf{G}_{\mathrm{sgn}}\mathbf{E})^{\mathsf{T}} : \mathbf{e} \in \mathbb{F}_q^{n_{\mathrm{dec}}}\} \subseteq \mathbb{F}_{q^m}^{k_{\mathrm{sgn}}}. \tag{15}$$

is an $\mathbb{F}_q$-subspace which contains words of weight $\leq w_{\mathrm{dec}}$ which reveal F. It turns out that the subspace $\mathcal{C}' \stackrel{\triangle}{=} \mathcal{C} \cap F^{k_{\mathrm{sgn}}}$ of words of $\mathcal{C}$ whose coordinates all live in F is of dimension $\geq n_{\mathrm{dec}} - w_{\mathrm{dec}}(n_{\mathrm{sgn}} - k_{\mathrm{sgn}})$. We then apply standard algebraic techniques in Subsect. 6.2 to recover $\mathcal{C}'$ and therefore F from it. This breaks all the parameters proposed in [26]. We conclude this section by showing that there is in principle a way to choose the parameters of the IBE scheme to possibly avoid this attack.

6.1 Low Rank Codewords from Instances of the RSL Problem

We prove here that a certain $\mathbb{F}_q$-linear code that contains many low-weight codewords can be computed by the attacker. This is explained by

Theorem 1. *Let* $(\mathbf{A}, \mathbf{A}\mathbf{E})$ *be an instance of RSL for parameters* n, k, N, w *with* $\mathbf{A} \in \mathbb{F}_{q^m}^{(n-k) \times n}$ *in systematic form and* $\mathbf{E} \in \mathbb{F}_{q^m}^{n \times N}$ *where all its coefficients belong to a same subspace* F *of dimension* w. *Furthermore, we suppose that*

$$N > wk. \tag{16}$$

Let

$$\mathcal{C} \stackrel{\triangle}{=} \{\mathbf{e}(\mathbf{A}\mathbf{E})^{\mathsf{T}} : \mathbf{e} \in \mathbb{F}_q^N\} \quad ; \quad \mathcal{C}' \stackrel{\triangle}{=} \mathcal{C} \cap F^{n-k}.$$

$\mathcal{C}'$ *is an* $\mathbb{F}_q$-*subspace of* $\mathcal{C}$ *of dimension* $\geq N - wk$.

Proof. Let us first decompose $\mathbf{E}$ in two parts $\begin{bmatrix} \mathbf{E}_1 \\ \mathbf{E}_2 \end{bmatrix}$ where $\mathbf{E}_1$ is formed by the first $n - k$ rows of $\mathbf{E}$ and $\mathbf{E}_2$ by the last k ones. The matrix $\mathbf{A}$ is in systematic form, namely $(I_{n-k}|\mathbf{A}')$ where $\mathbf{A}' \in \mathbb{F}_{q^m}^{(n-k) \times k}$, which gives: $\mathbf{A}\mathbf{E} = \mathbf{E}_1 + \mathbf{A}'\mathbf{E}_2$. Therefore, to prove our theorem we just need to show that

$$\mathcal{S} \stackrel{\triangle}{=} \{\mathbf{e} \in \mathbb{F}_q^N : \mathbf{E}_2\mathbf{e}^{\mathsf{T}} = 0\}$$

is an $\mathbb{F}_q$-subspace of dimension greater than $N - wk$. Indeed, for each error $\mathbf{e}$ of $\mathcal{S}$ we have $(\mathbf{A}\mathbf{E})\mathbf{e}^{\mathsf{T}} = \mathbf{E}_1\mathbf{e}^{\mathsf{T}}$ which belongs to F^{n-k} as coefficients of $\mathbf{E}_1$ are in the $\mathbb{F}_q$-subspace F and those of $\mathbf{e}$ are in $\mathbb{F}_q$.

Denote the entry in row i and column j of $\mathbf{E}_2$ by $E_{i,j}$. A word of $\mathcal{S}$ satisfies

$$\forall i \in [\![1, k]\!], \quad \sum_{j=1}^{N} E_{i,j} e_j = 0.$$

Looking in addition for $\mathbf{e}$ that has all its entries in $\mathbb{F}_q$ and expressing these k linear equations over $\mathbb{F}_{q^m}$ in a basis of F (since $\sum_{j=1}^{N} E_{i,j} e_j$ belongs by definition to $F \cdot \mathbb{F}_q = F$) we obtain $k \dim(F) = kw$ linear equations over $\mathbb{F}_q$ involving N unknowns (the e_j's) in $\mathbb{F}_q$. The solution space is therefore of dimension greater than $N - wk$ which concludes the proof of the theorem.

6.2   How to Find Low Rank Codewords in Instances of the RSL Problem

Theorem 1 showed that there are many codewords of weight $\leq w_{\mathrm{dec}}$ in the code $\mathcal{C}$ defined in (15). Let us show now how these codewords can be recovered by an algebraic attack. The sufficient condition $n_{\mathrm{dec}} > w_{\mathrm{dec}}(n_{\mathrm{sgn}} - k_{\mathrm{sgn}})$ ensuring the existence of such codewords is met for the parameters proposed in [26].

    To explain our algebraic modeling of the problem, let us first recall that for a fixed basis $(\beta_1, \cdots, \beta_m)$ of $\mathbb{F}_{q^m}$ over $\mathbb{F}_q$ we can view elements of $\mathbb{F}_{q^m}^{k_{\mathrm{sgn}}}$ as matrices of size $m \times k_{\mathrm{sgn}}$:

$$\forall \mathbf{x} \in \mathbb{F}_{q^m}^{k_{\mathrm{sgn}}}, \quad \mathbf{Mat}(\mathbf{x}) = (X_{i,j}) \in \mathbb{F}_q^{m \times k_{\mathrm{sgn}}} \text{ where } x_j = \sum_{i=1}^{m} \beta_i X_{i,j}.$$

The associated matrix code $\mathcal{C}^{\mathrm{Mat}}$ is defined as:

$$\mathcal{C}^{\mathrm{Mat}} \overset{\triangle}{=} \{\mathbf{Mat}(\mathbf{c}) : \mathbf{c} \in \mathcal{C}\} \subseteq \mathbb{F}_q^{m \times k_{\mathrm{sgn}}}.$$

It is easily verified that this matrix-code has dimension n_{dec}. It is clear now by applying Theorem 1 that:

Fact 3. $\mathcal{C}^{Mat}$ *contains codewords of rank* $\leq \dim(F)$ *which form a* $\mathbb{F}_q$*-subspace of dimension* $\geq n_{dec} - w_{dec}(n_{sgn} - k_{sgn})$.

    These are just the codewords $\mathbf{c}'$ which are of the form $\mathbf{Mat}(\mathbf{c})$ where $\mathbf{c} \in \mathcal{C}$ with $\mathrm{Supp}(\mathbf{c}) \subseteq F$. We do not expect other codewords of this rank in $\mathcal{C}^{\mathrm{Mat}}$ since w_{dec} is much smaller than the Varshamov-Gilbert bound in the case of the parameters proposed in [26].

The Basic Bilinear System. Finding codewords of rank w_{dec} in $\mathcal{C}^{\mathrm{Mat}}$ can be expressed as an instance of the MinRank problem [11,12]. Once again we propose the algebraic modeling which was suggested in [5]. It consists here in setting up the algebraic system with unknowns $\mathbf{x}^i = (x_1^i, \cdots, x_m^i) \in \mathbb{F}_q^m$ and $\mathbf{y}_j^i \in \mathbb{F}_q^{k_{\mathrm{sgn}}}$ for $1 \leq i \leq w_{\mathrm{dec}}$ and $1 \leq j \leq k_{\mathrm{sgn}}$ where the $\mathbf{x}^i$'s can be thought as a basis of the unknown subspace F and the y_j^i's as coordinates of the codeword in this basis. In that case the codeword $\mathbf{M}$ of $\mathcal{C}^{\mathrm{Mat}}$ of rank w_{dec} has the following form:

$$\mathbf{M} = \begin{pmatrix} \sum_{i=1}^{w_{\mathrm{dec}}} x_1^i y_1^i & \sum_{i=1}^{w_{\mathrm{dec}}} x_1^i y_2^i & \cdots & \sum_{i=1}^{w_{\mathrm{dec}}} x_1^i y_{k_{\mathrm{sgn}}}^i \\ \sum_{i=1}^{w_{\mathrm{dec}}} x_2^i y_1^i & \sum_{i=1}^{w_{\mathrm{dec}}} x_2^i y_2^i & \cdots & \sum_{i=1}^{w_{\mathrm{dec}}} x_2^i y_{k_{\mathrm{sgn}}}^i \\ \vdots & \vdots & \vdots & \vdots \\ \sum_{i=1}^{w_{\mathrm{dec}}} x_m^i y_1^i & \sum_{i=1}^{w_{\mathrm{dec}}} x_m^i y_2^i & \cdots & \sum_{i=1}^{w_{\mathrm{dec}}} x_m^i y_{k_{\mathrm{sgn}}}^i \end{pmatrix}.$$

Recall now that $\mathcal{C}^{\mathrm{Mat}}$ has the structure of an $\mathbb{F}_q$-subspace of $\mathbb{F}_q^{m \times k_{\mathrm{sgn}}}$ of dimension n_{dec}. By viewing the elements of $\mathcal{C}^{\mathrm{Mat}}$ as vectors of $\mathbb{F}_q^{mk_{\mathrm{sgn}}}$, i.e. the matrix $\mathbf{M} = (M_{ij})_{\substack{1 \le i \le m \\ 1 \le j \le k_{\mathrm{sgn}}}}$ is viewed as the vector $\mathbf{m} = (m_\ell)_{1 \le \ell \le mk_{\mathrm{sgn}}}$ where $m_{(i-1)k_{\mathrm{sgn}}+j} = M_{i,j}$, we can compute a parity-check matrix $\mathbf{H}^{\mathrm{Mat}}$ for it. It is an $(mk_{\mathrm{sgn}} - n_{\mathrm{dec}}) \times mk_{\mathrm{sgn}}$ matrix that we denote by $\mathbf{H}^{\mathrm{Mat}} = (H_{ij}^{\mathrm{Mat}})_{\substack{1 \le i \le mk_{\mathrm{sgn}}-n_{\mathrm{dec}} \\ 1 \le j \le mk_{\mathrm{sgn}}}}$. This matrix gives $mk_{\mathrm{sgn}} - n_{\mathrm{dec}}$ bilinear equations that have to be satisfied by the x_i^l's and the y_j^l's:

$$\begin{cases} \displaystyle\sum_{l=1}^{w_{\mathrm{dec}}} \sum_{j=1}^{k_{\mathrm{sgn}}} \sum_{i=1}^{m} H_{1,(i-1)k_{\mathrm{sgn}}+j}^{\mathrm{Mat}} x_i^l y_j^l = 0 \\ \quad\vdots \\ \displaystyle\sum_{l=1}^{w_{\mathrm{dec}}} \sum_{j=1}^{k_{\mathrm{sgn}}} \sum_{i=1}^{m} H_{mk_{\mathrm{sgn}}-n_{\mathrm{dec}},(i-1)k_{\mathrm{sgn}}+j}^{\mathrm{Mat}} x_i^l y_j^l = 0 \end{cases} \tag{17}$$

Restricting the Number of Solutions. We have solved the bilinear system (17) with Gröbner basis techniques that are implemented in Magma. To speed-up the resolution, as in the case of the attack on RankSign, we add new equations to (17) which come from the vectorial structure of F and the set of solutions.

With our notation we can view F as an $\mathbb{F}_q$ subspace of $\mathbb{F}_q^m$ of dimension w_{dec} generated by the rows of the matrix:

$$\begin{pmatrix} x_1^1 & \cdots & x_m^1 \\ x_1^2 & \cdots & x_m^2 \\ \vdots & & \vdots \\ x_1^{w_{\mathrm{dec}}} & \cdots & x_m^{w_{\mathrm{dec}}} \end{pmatrix}$$

In this way, we can put this matrix into systematic form, it will generate the same subspace. Therefore we can add equations

$$\forall (i,j) \in [\![1, w_{\mathrm{dec}}]\!]^2, \ j \ne i, \quad x_i^j = 0 \text{ and } x_i^i = 1 \tag{18}$$

without modifying the set of codewords of rank w_{dec}. Furthermore, this set is an $\mathbb{F}_q$-subspace of dimension greater than $n_{\mathrm{dec}} - (n_{\mathrm{sgn}} - k_{\mathrm{sgn}})w_{\mathrm{dec}}$ and as in the case of the attack on RankSign we may assume that for a random subset

$I \subseteq [\![1, k_{\text{sgn}}]\!] \times [\![1, w_{\text{dec}}]\!]$ of size $n_{\text{dec}} - (n_{\text{sgn}} - k_{\text{sgn}}) - 1$ there is an element in this set for which:

$$\forall (j, i) \in I, \; y_j^i = 0 \text{ and } y_{j_0}^{i_0} = 1 \text{ for } (i_0, j_0) \notin I. \tag{19}$$

Equations (18) and (19) enable us to reduce the number of variables of the previous bilinear system. The following proposition summarizes the number of equations and variables that we finally get.

Proposition 3. *By eliminating variables using Eqs.* (18) *and* (19) *in* (17) *we obtain*

- *$mk_{sgn} + w_{dec}^2 + (n_{sgn} - k_{sgn})$ equations;*
- *$m w_{dec} + k_{sgn} w_{dec}$ unknowns.*

In the "typical regime" where $m \approx n_{\text{sgn}} \approx k_{\text{sgn}}$ and $w_{\text{dec}} \approx n_{\text{sgn}}^\varepsilon$ for some ε in $(0, 1)$ we have a number of equations of order n_{sgn}^2 and a number of unknowns of order $n_{\text{sgn}}^{1+\varepsilon}$, therefore typically the regime where we expect that the Gröbner basis techniques take subexponential time.

6.3 Numerical Results

We give in Table 2 our numerical results to find codewords of rank w_{dec} in instances of the RSL problem for the parameters chosen according to [26]. These results have been obtained with an Intel Core i5 processor, clocked at 1.6 GHz using a single core, with 8 Go of RAM. In our implementation, we verified that when we generated an instance whose associated secret is the subspace F we only got codewords whose coordinates live in this subspace and therefore revealed it.

Table 2. Attack on parameters of the rank-based IBE [26] for 10 random instances of RSL.

Intended security	$(n_{\text{sgn}}, k_{\text{sgn}}, m, w_{\text{dec}}, n_{\text{dec}}, k_{\text{dec}}, q)$	Average time	Max. memory usage
128 bits	$(100, 80, 96, 4, 96, 9, 2^{192})$	603 s	1.7 GB

6.4 Avoiding the Attack

Although our attack breaks the parameters proposed in [26], there might in principle be a way to instantiate the IBE with a new signature scheme. Recall that the constraints that have to be satisfied are given by

$$w_{\text{rVG}}(q, m, n_{\text{sgn}}, k_{\text{sgn}}) \leq w_{\text{sgn}} \leq \frac{m(n_{\text{sgn}} - k_{\text{sgn}})}{\max(m, n_{\text{sgn}})} \quad \text{(signature constraint)} \tag{20}$$

$$w_{\text{sgn}} w_{\text{dec}} \quad \leq \quad w_{\text{rVG}}(q, m, n_{\text{dec}}, k_{\text{dec}}) \quad \text{(decoding works)} \tag{21}$$

$$w_{\text{dec}}(n_{\text{sgn}} - k_{\text{sgn}}) \quad \geq \quad n_{\text{dec}} \quad \text{(for avoiding our attack)}. \tag{22}$$

The lower-bound in (20) ensures that we can find a signature whereas the role of the upper-bound is to ensure that the problem of finding a signature does not become easy. The constraint (21) is here to ensure that the decoding procedure used for recovering the plaintext works and the last constraint is here to avoid our attack. This set of parameters is non-empty under the condition to find an efficient hash and sign signature scheme. For instance, if we have a signature scheme which achieves the lower bound (20), namely $w_{\mathrm{sgn}} = w_{\mathrm{rVG}}(q, m, n_{\mathrm{sgn}}, k_{\mathrm{sgn}})$ we can choose:

$$n_{\mathrm{sgn}} = 100 \quad ; \quad k_{\mathrm{sgn}} = 75 \quad ; \quad n_{\mathrm{dec}} = 96 \quad ; \quad k_{\mathrm{dec}} = 4 \quad ; \quad w_{\mathrm{dec}} = 4.$$

More generally, if one wants to set parameters of the IBE [26] we propose to proceed in the following way. We first propose to choose $m = n_{\mathrm{sgn}}$ and a signature code for which the ratio $\frac{w_{\mathrm{rVG}}(q, m, n_{\mathrm{sgn}}, k_{\mathrm{sgn}})}{n_{\mathrm{sgn}} - k_{\mathrm{sgn}}}$ is sufficiently small (it can even approach $\frac{1}{2}$) and we choose

$$w_{\mathrm{sgn}} = (1 - \varepsilon)(n_{\mathrm{sgn}} - k_{\mathrm{sgn}}) \tag{23}$$

for some appropriate ε. We then choose an $\mathbb{F}_{q^m}$-linear code of parameters $[n_{\mathrm{dec}}, k_{\mathrm{dec}}]$ of sufficiently small dimension such that

$$w_{\mathrm{rVG}}(q, m, n_{\mathrm{dec}}, k_{\mathrm{dec}}) \geq (1 - \varepsilon)n_{\mathrm{dec}}.$$

This is possible in principle. Therefore we can choose w_{dec} such that $w_{\mathrm{sgn}}w_{\mathrm{dec}} \geq (1 - \varepsilon)n_{\mathrm{dec}}$ and for which (21) holds. By satisfying the two first constraints (20) and (21) in this way, we also satisfy the last one, namely Eq. (22). This can be verified by arguing that

$$
\begin{aligned}
w_{\mathrm{dec}}(n_{\mathrm{sgn}} - k_{\mathrm{sgn}}) &= \frac{w_{\mathrm{sgn}}w_{\mathrm{dec}}}{1 - \varepsilon} \quad \text{(we use 23)} \\
&\geq \frac{n_{\mathrm{dec}}(1 - \varepsilon)}{1 - \varepsilon} \quad \text{(we use the particular choice of } w_{\mathrm{dec}}\text{)} \\
&= n_{\mathrm{dec}}
\end{aligned}
$$

6.5 Comparison with Previous Attacks Against RSL

Recall here that the Rank Support Learning (RSL) problem for parameters n, k, N, w can also be expressed as follows: we have access to a matrix of full rank $\mathbf{A} \in \mathbb{F}_{q^m}^{(n-k) \times n}$ and to N syndromes $\mathbf{A}\mathbf{e}^{\mathsf{T}}$ for $\mathbf{e}$ chosen uniformly at random in F^n where F is some fixed subspace of $\mathbb{F}_{q^m}$ of dimension w. The problem is then to recover F. When $N = 1$ this is just the Rank Syndrome Decoding (RSD) problem (see Problem 1 in Subsect. 2.2). It is readily verified that the difficulty of RSL decreases when N grows, however the question for cryptographic purposes is: "how large N can be while RSL remains hard?" In [26, Sect. 4, p. 14] a first answer was given by showing that N has to verify

$$N < wn \tag{24}$$

otherwise a polynomial attack can easily be mounted. Here, we strengthen this condition on N, we require namely that in order to avoid our new attack we should have

$$N \leq wk \quad (k < n). \tag{25}$$

where k is the dimension of the code of parity-check matrix $\mathbf{A} \in \mathbb{F}_{q^m}^{(n-k) \times n}$ used in the instance of RSL. This condition is clearly stronger since we always have $k < n$ at the cost of trading a polynomial attack in the case where (24) is met with a subexponential attack when (25) is not met.

In the context of the IBE it is actually *significantly stronger*. This comes from the fact that in this context we really expect that under reasonable assumptions that $k \ll n$. This can be explained as follows. In this case (25) translates into $n_{\text{dec}} \leq w_{\text{dec}}(n_{\text{sgn}} - k_{\text{sgn}})$. The point is that in the typical regime which is needed for the IBE, we have $n_{\text{sgn}} - k_{\text{sgn}} \ll n_{\text{sgn}}$. By typical regime we mean here that we can assume that for the IBE [26] we have

Assumption 3

$$\frac{k_{sgn}}{n_{sgn}} = \Omega(1); \tag{26}$$

$$m = \Theta(n_{sgn}); \tag{27}$$

$$w_{dec} = \omega(1) \tag{28}$$

This assumption is minimal in the special case of the IBE [26] as we are going to explain.

Equations (26) and (27) ensure that we are in the regime where the Gilbert-Varshamov and the Singleton bounds do not collapse which is essential as explained in the previous subsection to obtain parameters avoiding our attack on RSL.

Equation (28) permits to avoid a polynomial attack against the RSL problem. Indeed, suppose that w_{dec} is bounded, which is $w_{\text{dec}} = O(1)$. Recall that in the IBE, instances of RSL have the following form $(\mathbf{G}_{\mathcal{C}_{\text{sgn}}}, \mathbf{G}_{\text{sgn}}\mathbf{E})$ where $\mathbf{G}_{\mathcal{C}_{\text{sgn}}} \in \mathbb{F}_{q^m}^{k_{\text{sgn}} \times n_{\text{sgn}}}$ and $\mathbf{E}$ is homogeneous with underlying subspace F of dimension w_{dec}. Solving here the Rank Syndrome Decoding for $\mathbf{G}_{\mathcal{C}_{\text{sgn}}}$, a weight w_{dec} and the first column of $\mathbf{E}$ as syndrome will give with high probability F as w_{dec} is smaller than the Varshamov-Gilbert bound. By using Gröbner basis techniques for this and writing equations in the small field $\mathbb{F}_q$ this gives:

1. $n_{\text{sgn}}w_{\text{dec}}$ unknowns;
2. mk_{sgn} bilinear equations.

Under Assumptions (26), (27) and the fact that $k_{\text{sgn}} \leq n_{\text{sgn}}$, we have $mk_{\text{sgn}} = \Theta(n_{\text{sgn}}k_{\text{sgn}}) = \Theta(n_{\text{sgn}}^2)$. On the other hand, the number of unknowns is $O(n_{\text{sgn}})$ as $w_{\text{dec}} = O(1)$. This is the regime where we expect to solve the corresponding bilinear system in polynomial time. Therefore we can safely assume that w_{dec} tends to infinity to avoid such a polynomial attack.

Assumption 3 leads in this case to the following proposition.

Proposition 4. *Under Assumption 3, we have when n_{sgn} tends to infinity:*

$$n_{sgn} - k_{sgn} = o(n_{sgn}).$$

Proof. From Proposition 1 we have: $w_{sgn}w_{dec} \leq \min(n_{dec}, m)$ and thus from Assumption 3 $w_{sgn}w_{dec} = O(n_{sgn})$ which gives $\frac{w_{sgn}}{n_{sgn}} = O\left(\frac{1}{w_{dec}}\right)$. Under Assumption 3 we have that w_{dec} tends to infinity. Therefore we get

$$w_{sgn} = o(n_{sgn}). \tag{29}$$

Now under the signature constraint (see (20)) we have that $w_{sgn} \geq w_{rVG}(q, m, n_{sgn}, k_{sgn})$. From Eq. (1) and Assumption 3, particularly (27), it is easily verified that the last inequality and (29) imply $n_{sgn} - k_{sgn} = o(n_{sgn})$ which concludes the proof of the proposition.

7   Attack on the IBE in the Hamming Metric

The purpose of this section is to show that there is an even more fundamental problem with the general IBE scheme given in Sect. 4 in the Hamming metric. We will namely prove here that due to the constraint on the parameters coming from Proposition 1, we can not find a set of parameters which would avoid an attack based on using generic decoding techniques. Even the simplest of those techniques, namely the Prange algorithm [40], breaks the IBE in the Hamming metric in polynomial time. We refer the reader to Sect. 4 where we introduced all the notations that we are going to use.

   To show that the IBE can be attacked in the Hamming metric we proceed as follows. The attacker knows $\mathbf{G}_{\mathcal{C}_{sgn}}\mathbf{E}$ and that the columns of $\mathbf{E}$ have weight w_{dec}. We will show that we can solve efficiently for the range of parameters admissible for the IBE the following syndrome decoding problem: given a matrix $\mathbf{G}_{\mathcal{C}_{sgn}} \in \mathbb{F}_2^{k_{sgn} \times n_{sgn}}$ and $\mathbf{s} \in \mathbb{F}_2^{k_{sgn}}$ such that there exists $\mathbf{e} \in \mathbb{F}_2^{n_{sgn}}$ of weight w_{dec} for which $\mathbf{G}_{\mathcal{C}_{sgn}}\mathbf{e}^\mathsf{T} = \mathbf{s}^\mathsf{T}$, we want to recover $\mathbf{e}$. This allows to recover the columns of $\mathbf{E}$ and therefore $\mathbf{E}$. The scheme is broken with this knowledge, since the attacker also knows $\mathcal{H}(id)\mathbf{E} + \mathbf{m}\mathbf{G}_{\mathcal{C}_{dec}}$, $\mathcal{H}(id)$ and $\mathbf{G}_{\mathcal{C}_{dec}}$. This is used to derive $\mathbf{m}\mathbf{G}_{\mathcal{C}_{dec}}$ and finally $\mathbf{m}$.

   To solve this decoding problem, we use the Prange algorithm (see [40]) whose complexity is, up to a polynomial factor in n_{sgn}, equal to $\frac{\binom{n_{sgn}}{w_{dec}}}{\binom{k_{sgn}}{w_{dec}}}$. In the special case of the IBE we proved in Proposition 1 that the parameters have to verify the following constraint:

$$w_{sgn}w_{dec} = O(n_{sgn}).$$

Now the parameter w_{sgn} can not be too small either, since for fixed w_{sgn} the algorithms for decoding linear codes also solve the signature forgery in polynomial time. This problem amounts in the case of the IBE to find a $\mathbf{u}_{id}$ such that

$$|\mathbf{u}_{id}\mathbf{G}_{\mathcal{C}_{sgn}} - \mathcal{H}(id)| = w_{sgn}.$$

We will therefore make a minimal assumption that ensures that the decoding algorithms for solving this problem have at least some (small) subexponential complexity. We also make the same assumption for the aforementioned recovery of **e**. This is obtained by assuming that

Assumption 4. *For some* $\varepsilon, \varepsilon' > 0$,

$$w_{dec} = \Omega(n^{\varepsilon}) \quad ; \quad w_{sgn} = \Omega(n^{\varepsilon'})$$

The proof of this proposition is given in the long version of the paper [15].

Proposition 5. *Under Assumption 4, the Prange algorithm breaks the IBE scheme in Hamming metric in polynomial time in* n_{sgn}.

8   Concluding Remarks

We have presented here our attacks against the rank-based signature scheme RankSign and the IBE scheme proposed in [26]. Several comments can be made.

Attack on RankSign. We actually showed that in the case of RankSign, the complexity is polynomial for all possible strategies for choosing the parameters. Repairing the RankSign scheme seems to require to modify the scheme itself, not just adjust the parameters. It might be tempting to conjecture that the approach against RankSign could also be used to mount an attack on the NIST submissions based on LRPC codes such as [3,4]. Roughly speaking our approach consists in looking for low weight codewords in the LRPC code instead of looking for low weight codewords in the usual suspect, that is the dual of the LRPC code, that has in this case low weight codewords by definition of the LRPC code. This approach does not seem to carry over to the LRPC codes considered in those submissions. The point is that our approach was successful for RankSign because of the way the parameters of the LRPC code had to be chosen. In particular the length n, the dimension k and the weight of the LRPC code have to satisfy

$$n = (n - k)d.$$

It is precisely this equality that is responsible for the weight 2 codewords in the LRPC code. If d is not too small (say > 3) and $(n - k)d$ is sufficiently above n, then the whole approach considered here fails at the very beginning.

Attack on the IBE [26]. The attack on RankSign also breaks the IBE proposal of [26] since it is based partly on the RankSign primitive. We have shown here that the problem is actually deeper than this by showing that even if a secure signature scheme replaces in the IBE, RankSign, then an attack that breaks directly the RSL problem which is the other problem on which the IBE is based, can be mounted for the parameters proposed in [26]. Again, as in the case of RankSign, the reason why this attack was successful comes from the fact that the constraints on the parameters that are necessary for the scheme to work properly work in favor of ensuring that a certain code that can be computed from the public data has low weight codewords. These low codewords are then found by an algebraic attack. However, contrarily to the RankSign case, where the conditions on the parameters force a certain code to have codewords of low weight, this phenomenon can be avoided by a very careful choice of the parameters in the IBE. This opens the way for repairing the scheme of [26] if a secure signature scheme is found for the rank metric.

We have also studied whether the [26] approach for obtaining an IBE scheme based on coding assumptions could work in the Hamming metric. However in this case, and contrarily to what happens in the rank metric, we have given a devastating polynomial attack in the Hamming metric relying on using the simplest generic decoding algorithm [40] that can not be avoided by any reasonable choice of parameters. It seems that following the GPV [33]/[26] approach for obtaining an IBE scheme is a dead end in the case of the Hamming metric.

To conclude this discussion on [26], we would like to stress that our result in the Hamming case does not imply the impossibility of designing an IBE based on coding theory. It only suggests to investigate other paradigms rather than trying to adapt the GPV strategy. For instance, the recent progress of [16–18] made on the design of IBE's, particularly with the concept of one-time signatures with encryption, might be applied to cryptography based on decoding assumptions.

Acknowledgments. This work was supported by the ANR CBCRYPT project, grant ANR-17-CE39-0007 of the French Agence Nationale de la Recherche.

References

1. Melchor, C.A., et al.: Rank Quasi Cyclic (RQC). First round submission to the NIST post-quantum cryptography call, November 2017
2. Alekhnovich, M.: More on average case vs approximation complexity. Comput. Complex. **20**(4), 755–786 (2011)
3. Aragon, N., et al.: LAKE- Low rAnk parity check codes Key Exchange –. First round submission to the NIST post-quantum cryptography call, November 2017
4. Aragon, N., et al.: LOCKER-LOw rank parity ChecK codes EncRyption -. First round submission to the NIST post-quantum cryptography call, November 2017
5. Aragon, N., Gaborit, P., Hauteville, A., Ruatta, O., Zémor, G.: RankSign - a signature proposal for the NIST's call-. First round submission to the NIST post-quantum cryptography call, November 2017. NIST Round 1 submission for Post-Quantum Cryptography
6. Becker, A., Joux, A., May, A., Meurer, A.: Decoding random binary linear codes in $2^{n/20}$: how $1 + 1 = 0$ improves information set decoding. In: Pointcheval, D., Johansson, T. (eds.) EUROCRYPT 2012. LNCS, vol. 7237, pp. 520–536. Springer, Heidelberg (2012). https://doi.org/10.1007/978-3-642-29011-4_31
7. Berlekamp, E., McEliece, R., van Tilborg, H.: On the inherent intractability of certain coding problems. IEEE Trans. Inform. Theory **24**(3), 384–386 (1978)
8. Bernstein, D.J., Lange, T., Peters, C.: Smaller decoding exponents: ball-collision decoding. In: Rogaway, P. (ed.) CRYPTO 2011. LNCS, vol. 6841, pp. 743–760. Springer, Heidelberg (2011). https://doi.org/10.1007/978-3-642-22792-9_42

9. Boneh, D., Franklin, M.: Identity-based encryption from the weil pairing. In: Kilian, J. (ed.) CRYPTO 2001. LNCS, vol. 2139, pp. 213–229. Springer, Heidelberg (2001). https://doi.org/10.1007/3-540-44647-8_13

10. Both, L., May, A.: Optimizing BJMM with nearest neighbors: full decoding in $2^{2/21n}$ and McEliece security. In: WCC Workshop on Coding and Cryptography, September 2017. On line Proceedings. http://wcc2017.suai.ru/Proceedings_WCC2017.zip

11. Buss, J.F., Frandsen, G.S., Shallit, J.O.: The computational complexity of some problems of linear algebra. J. Comput. Syst. Sci. **58**(3), 572–596 (1999)

12. Courtois, N.T.: Efficient zero-knowledge authentication based on a linear algebra problem MinRank. In: Boyd, C. (ed.) ASIACRYPT 2001. LNCS, vol. 2248, pp. 402–421. Springer, Heidelberg (2001). https://doi.org/10.1007/3-540-45682-1_24

13. Courtois, N.T., Finiasz, M., Sendrier, N.: How to achieve a McEliece-based digital signature scheme. In: Boyd, C. (ed.) ASIACRYPT 2001. LNCS, vol. 2248, pp. 157–174. Springer, Heidelberg (2001). https://doi.org/10.1007/3-540-45682-1_10

14. Debris-Alazard, T., Tillich, J.-P.: Statistical decoding. Preprint, January 2017. arXiv:1701.07416

15. Debris-Alazard, T., Tillich, J.-P.: Two attacks on rank metric code-based schemes: RankSign and an identity-based-encryption scheme. Preprint, June 2018. arXiv:1701.07416

16. Döttling, N., Garg, S.: From selective IBE to Full IBE and selective HIBE. In: Kalai, Y., Reyzin, L. (eds.) TCC 2017. LNCS, vol. 10677, pp. 372–408. Springer, Cham (2017). https://doi.org/10.1007/978-3-319-70500-2_13

17. Döttling, N., Garg, S.: Identity-based encryption from the Diffie-Hellman assumption. In: Katz, J., Shacham, H. (eds.) CRYPTO 2017. LNCS, vol. 10401, pp. 537–569. Springer, Cham (2017). https://doi.org/10.1007/978-3-319-63688-7_18

18. Döttling, N., Garg, S., Hajiabadi, M., Masny, D.: New constructions of identity-based and key-dependent message secure encryption schemes. In: Abdalla, M., Dahab, R. (eds.) PKC 2018. LNCS, vol. 10769, pp. 3–31. Springer, Cham (2018). https://doi.org/10.1007/978-3-319-76578-5_1

19. Dumer, I.: On minimum distance decoding of linear codes. In: Proceedings of 5th Joint Soviet-Swedish International Workshop Information Theory, Moscow, pp. 50–52 (1991)

20. Faugère, J.-C., El Din, M.S., Spaenlehauer, P.-J.: Computing loci of rank defects of linear matrices using Gröbner bases and applications to cryptology. In: Proceedings of Symbolic and Algebraic Computation, International Symposium, ISSAC 2010, Munich, Germany, 25–28 July 2010, pp. 257–264 (2010)

21. Faugère, J.-C., Levy-dit-Vehel, F., Perret, L.: Cryptanalysis of MinRank. In: Wagner, D. (ed.) CRYPTO 2008. LNCS, vol. 5157, pp. 280–296. Springer, Heidelberg (2008). https://doi.org/10.1007/978-3-540-85174-5_16

22. Finiasz, M., Sendrier, N.: Security bounds for the design of code-based cryptosystems. In: Matsui, M. (ed.) ASIACRYPT 2009. LNCS, vol. 5912, pp. 88–105. Springer, Heidelberg (2009). https://doi.org/10.1007/978-3-642-10366-7_6

23. Gabidulin, E.M.: Attacks and counter-attacks on the GPT public key cryptosystem. Des. Codes Cryptogr. **48**(2), 171–177 (2008)

24. Gabidulin, E.M., Ourivski, A.V.: Modified GPT PKC with right scrambler. Electron. Notes Discrete Math. **6**, 168–177 (2001)

25. Gabidulin, E.M., Paramonov, A.V., Tretjakov, O.V.: Ideals over a non-commutative ring and their application in cryptology. In: Davies, D.W. (ed.) EUROCRYPT 1991. LNCS, vol. 547, pp. 482–489. Springer, Heidelberg (1991). https://doi.org/10.1007/3-540-46416-6_41

26. Gaborit, P., Hauteville, A., Phan, D.H., Tillich, J.-P.: Identity-based encryption from codes with rank metric. In: Katz, J., Shacham, H. (eds.) CRYPTO 2017. LNCS, vol. 10403, pp. 194–224. Springer, Cham (2017). https://doi.org/10.1007/978-3-319-63697-9_7

27. Gaborit, P., Murat, G., Ruatta, O., Zémor, G.: Low rank parity check codes and their application to cryptography. In: Proceedings of the Workshop on Coding and Cryptography WCC 2013, Bergen, Norway (2013). www.selmer.uib.no/WCC2013/pdfs/Gaborit.pdf

28. Gaborit, P., Ruatta, O., Schrek, J.: On the complexity of the rank syndrome decoding problem. CoRR, abs/1301.1026 (2013)

29. Gaborit, P., Ruatta, O., Schrek, J.: On the complexity of the rank syndrome decoding problem. IEEE Trans. Inf. Theory **62**(2), 1006–1019 (2016)

30. Gaborit, P., Ruatta, O., Schrek, J., Zémor, G.: New results for rank-based cryptography. In: Pointcheval, D., Vergnaud, D. (eds.) AFRICACRYPT 2014. LNCS, vol. 8469, pp. 1–12. Springer, Cham (2014). https://doi.org/10.1007/978-3-319-06734-6_1

31. Gaborit, P., Ruatta, O., Schrek, J., Zémor, G.: RankSign: an efficient signature algorithm based on the rank metric. In: Mosca, M. (ed.) PQCrypto 2014. LNCS, vol. 8772, pp. 88–107. Springer, Cham (2014). https://doi.org/10.1007/978-3-319-11659-4_6

32. Gaborit, P., Zémor, G.: On the hardness of the decoding and the minimum distance problems for rank codes. IEEE Trans. Inf. Theory **62**(12), 7245–7252 (2016)

33. Gentry, C., Peikert, C., Vaikuntanathan, V.: Trapdoors for hard lattices and new cryptographic constructions. In: Proceedings of the Fortieth Annual ACM Symposium on Theory of Computing, pp. 197–206. ACM (2008)

34. Kipnis, A., Shamir, A.: Cryptanalysis of the HFE public key cryptosystem by relinearization. In: Wiener, M. (ed.) CRYPTO 1999. LNCS, vol. 1666, pp. 19–30. Springer, Heidelberg (1999). https://doi.org/10.1007/3-540-48405-1_2

35. Lee, P.J., Brickell, E.F.: An observation on the security of McEliece's public-key cryptosystem. In: Barstow, D., et al. (eds.) EUROCRYPT 1988. LNCS, vol. 330, pp. 275–280. Springer, Heidelberg (1988). https://doi.org/10.1007/3-540-45961-8_25

36. Loidreau, P.: Asymptotic behaviour of codes in rank metric over finite fields. Des. Codes Cryptogr. **71**(1), 105–118 (2014)

37. May, A., Meurer, A., Thomae, E.: Decoding random linear codes in $\tilde{\mathcal{O}}(2^{0.054n})$. In: Lee, D.H., Wang, X. (eds.) ASIACRYPT 2011. LNCS, vol. 7073, pp. 107–124. Springer, Heidelberg (2011). https://doi.org/10.1007/978-3-642-25385-0_6

38. May, A., Ozerov, I.: On computing nearest neighbors with applications to decoding of binary linear codes. In: Oswald, E., Fischlin, M. (eds.) EUROCRYPT 2015. LNCS, vol. 9056, pp. 203–228. Springer, Heidelberg (2015). https://doi.org/10.1007/978-3-662-46800-5_9

39. Niederreiter, H.: Knapsack-type cryptosystems and algebraic coding theory. Probl. Control Inf. Theory **15**(2), 159–166 (1986)

40. Prange, E.: The use of information sets in decoding cyclic codes. IRE Trans. Inf. Theory **8**(5), 5–9 (1962)

41. Sakai, R., Ohgishi, K., Kasahara, M.: Cryptosystems based on pairing. In: SCIS 2000, Okinawa, Japan, January 2000

42. Shamir, A.: Identity-based cryptosystems and signature schemes. In: Blakley, G.R., Chaum, D. (eds.) CRYPTO 1984. LNCS, vol. 196, pp. 47–53. Springer, Heidelberg (1985). https://doi.org/10.1007/3-540-39568-7_5

43. Spaenlenhauer, P.-J.: Résolution de systèmes multi-homogènes et determinantiels. Ph.D. thesis, Univ. Pierre et Marie Curie- Paris 6, October 2012

44. Stern, J.: A method for finding codewords of small weight. In: Cohen, G., Wolfmann, J. (eds.) Coding Theory 1988. LNCS, vol. 388, pp. 106–113. Springer, Heidelberg (1989). https://doi.org/10.1007/BFb0019850

An Efficient Structural Attack on NIST Submission DAGS

Élise Barelli and Alain Couvreur[(✉)]

INRIA & LIX, CNRS UMR 7161, École polytechnique, 91128 Palaiseau Cedex,
France
elise.barelli@inria.fr, alain.couvreur@lix.polytechnique.fr

Abstract. We present an efficient key recovery attack on code based encryption schemes using some quasi-dyadic alternant codes with extension degree 2. This attack permits to break the proposal DAGS recently submitted to NIST.

Keywords: Code-based cryptography
McEliece encryption scheme · Key recovery attack
Alternant codes · Quasi-dyadic codes · Schur product of codes

1 Introduction

In 1978, in the seminal article [21], McEliece designed a public key encryption scheme relying on the hardness of the bounded decoding problem [7], *i.e.* on the hardness of decoding an arbitrary code. For a long time, this scheme was considered as unpractical because of the huge size of the public keys compared to public key encryption schemes relying on algorithmic number theoretic problems. The trend changed in the last decade because of the progress of quantum computing and the increasing threat of the existence in a near future of a quantum computer able to break usual cryptography primitives based on number theoretic problems. An evidence for this change of trend is the recent call of the National Institute for Standards and Technology (NIST) for post quantum cryptography. The majority of the submissions to this call are based either on codes or on lattices.

After forty years of research on code based cryptography, one can identify two general trends for instantiating McEliece's scheme. The first one consists in using codes from probabilistic constructions such as MDPC codes [1,23]. The other one consists in using algebraic codes such as Goppa codes or more generally alternant codes. A major difference between these two families of proposals is that the first one, based on MDPC codes benefits in some cases from clean security reductions to the decoding problem.

Concerning McEliece instantiations based on algebraic codes, which include McEliece's original proposal based on binary Goppa codes, two approaches have been considered in order to address the drawback of the large of pubic key sizes.

T. Peyrin and S. Galbraith (Eds.): ASIACRYPT 2018, LNCS 11272, pp. 93–118, 2018.
https://doi.org/10.1007/978-3-030-03326-2_4

On the one hand, some proposals suggested to replace Goppa or alternant codes by more structured codes such as generalised Reed-Solomon (GRS) codes [24], their low dimensional subcodes [6], or GRS codes to which various transformations have been applied [2,29,30]. It turns out that most of these proposals have been subject to polynomial time key-recovery attacks [9,13,28,31]. In addition, proposals based on Goppa codes which are *close* to GRS codes, namely Goppa code with a low extension degree m have been the target of some structural attacks [12,17]. On the other hand, many proposals suggest the use of codes with a non trivial automorphism group [5,18,22,26]. A part of these proposals has been either partially or completely broken [15,16,25]. In particular, in the design of such proposals, precautions should be taken since the knowledge of a non trivial automorphism group of the public code facilitates algebraic attacks by significantly reducing the degrees and number of variables of the algebraic system to solve in order to recover the secret key.

Among the recent submissions to NIST call for post quantum cryptography, a proposal called DAGS [3] is based on the use of quasi-dyadic (QD) generalised Srivastava codes with extension degree $m = 2$. By *quasi-dyadic* we mean that the permutation group of the code is of the form $(\mathbb{Z}/2\mathbb{Z})^\gamma$ for some positive integer γ. Moreover, generalised Srivastava codes form a proper subclass of alternant codes. DAGS proposal takes advantage of both usual techniques to reduce the size of the keys. First, by using alternant codes which are close to generalised Reed Solomon codes *i.e.* with an extension degree 2. Second, by using codes with a large permutation group. In terms of security with respect to key recovery attacks, DAGS parameters are chosen to be out of reach of the algebraic attacks [15,16]. In addition, it should be emphasised that the choice of alternant codes which are not Goppa codes permits to be out of reach of the distinguisher by shortening and squaring used in [12].

Our Contribution. In this article, we present an attack breaking McEliece instantiations based on alternant codes with extension degree 2 and a large permutation group. This attack permits to recover the secret key in $O\left(n^{3+\frac{2q}{|\mathcal{G}|}}\right)$ operations in $\mathbb{F}_q$, where $\mathcal{G}$ denotes the permutation group, n the code length and $\mathbb{F}_q$ is the base field of the public code. The key step of the attack consists in finding some subcode of the public code referred to as $\mathscr{D}$. From this code $\mathscr{D}$ and using an operation we called *conductor*, the secret key can easily be recovered. For this main step, we present two ways to proceed, the first approach is based on a partial brute force search while the second one is based on the resolution of a polynomial system of degree 2. An analysis of the work factor of this attack using the first approach shows that DAGS keys with respective estimated security levels 128, 192 and 256 bits can be broken with respective approximate work factors $2^{70}, 2^{80}$ and 2^{58}. For the second approach, we were not able to provide a complexity analysis. However, its practical implementation using Magma [8] is impressively efficient on some DAGS parameters. In particular, it permits to break claimed 256 bits security keys in less than one minute!

This attack is a novel and original manner to recover the structure of alternant codes by jointly taking advantage of the permutation group and the small size of the extension degree. Even if some variant of the attack reposes on the resolution of a polynomial system, this system has nothing to do with those of algebraic attacks of [15–17]. On the other hand, despite this attack shares some common points with that of [12] where the Schur product of codes (See Sect. 3 for a definition) plays a crucial role, the keys we break in the present article are out of reach of a distinguisher by shortening and squaring and hence our attack differs from filtration attacks as in [10,12].

It is worth noting that reparing DAGS scheme in order to resist to the present attack is possible. Recently, the authors presented new parameter sets which are out of reach of the first version of the attack. These new parameters are available on the current version of the proposal[1].

2 Notation and Prerequisites

2.1 Subfield Subcodes and Trace Codes

Definition 1. *Given a code $\mathscr{C}$ of length n over $\mathbb{F}_{q^m}$, its* subfield subcode *is the subcode of vectors whose entries all lie in $\mathbb{F}_q$, that is the code:*

$$\mathscr{C} \cap \mathbb{F}_q^n.$$

The trace code *is the image of the code by the component wise trace map*

$$Tr_{\mathbb{F}_{q^m}/\mathbb{F}_q}(\mathscr{C}) \overset{def}{=} \left\{ Tr_{\mathbb{F}_{q^m}/\mathbb{F}_q}(\boldsymbol{c}) \mid \boldsymbol{c} \in \mathscr{C} \right\}.$$

Let us recall a classical and well-known result on subfield subcodes and trace codes.

Theorem 1 (Delsarte Theorem [14]). *Let $\mathscr{C} \subseteq \mathbb{F}_{q^m}^n$ be a code. Then*

$$(\mathscr{C} \cap \mathbb{F}_q^n)^{\perp} = Tr_{\mathbb{F}_{q^m}/\mathbb{F}_q}(\mathscr{C}^{\perp}).$$

2.2 Generalised Reed-Solomon Codes and Alternant Codes

Notation 1. Let q be a power of prime and k a positive integer. We denote by $\mathbb{F}_q[z]_{<k}$ the vector space of polynomials over $\mathbb{F}_q$ whose degree is bounded from above by k. Let m be a positive integer, we will consider codes over $\mathbb{F}_{q^m}$ with their subfield subcodes over $\mathbb{F}_q$. In Sect. 3 and further, we will focus particularly on the case $m = 2$.

Definition 2 (Supports and multipliers). *A vector $\boldsymbol{x} \in \mathbb{F}_{q^m}^n$ whose entries are pairwise distinct is called a* support. *A vector $\boldsymbol{y} \in \mathbb{F}_{q^m}^n$ whose entries are all nonzero is referred to as a* multiplier.

---

[1] https://dags-project.org/pdf/DAGS_spec.pdf.

Definition 3 (Generalised Reed-Solomon codes). *Let n be a positive integer, $\boldsymbol{x} \in \mathbb{F}_{q^m}^n$ be a support and $\boldsymbol{y} \in \mathbb{F}_{q^m}^n$ be a multiplier. The generalised Reed-Solomon (GRS) code with support $\boldsymbol{x}$ and multiplier $\boldsymbol{y}$ of dimension k is defined as*

$$\mathbf{GRS}_k(\boldsymbol{x}, \boldsymbol{y}) \stackrel{\text{def}}{=} \{(y_1 f(x_1), \ldots, y_n f(x_n)) \mid f \in \mathbb{F}_{q^m}[z]_{<k}\}.$$

When $\boldsymbol{y} = \mathbf{1}$, the code is a Reed-Solomon code *and is denoted as* $\mathbf{RS}_k(\boldsymbol{x})$.

The dual of a GRS code is a GRS code too. This is made explicit in Lemma 1 below. Let us first introduce an additional notation.

Notation 2. *Let $\boldsymbol{x} \subseteq \mathbb{F}_{q^m}^n$ be a support, we define the polynomial $\pi_{\boldsymbol{x}} \in \mathbb{F}_{q^m}[z]$ as*

$$\pi_{\boldsymbol{x}}(z) \stackrel{\text{def}}{=} \prod_{i=1}^{n} (z - x_i).$$

Lemma 1. *Let $\boldsymbol{x}, \boldsymbol{y} \in \mathbb{F}_{q^m}^n$ be a support and a multiplier of length n and $k \leqslant n$. Then*

$$\mathbf{GRS}_k(\boldsymbol{x}, \boldsymbol{y})^{\perp} = \mathbf{GRS}_{n-k}(\boldsymbol{x}, \boldsymbol{y}^{\perp}),$$

where

$$\boldsymbol{y}^{\perp} \stackrel{\text{def}}{=} \left(\frac{1}{\pi_{\boldsymbol{x}}'(x_1) y_1}, \ldots, \frac{1}{\pi_{\boldsymbol{x}}'(x_n) y_n} \right),$$

and $\pi_{\boldsymbol{x}}'$ denotes the derivative of the polynomial $\pi_{\boldsymbol{x}}$.

Definition 4 (Alternant code). *Let m, n be positive integers such that $n \leqslant q^m$. Let $\boldsymbol{x} \in \mathbb{F}_{q^m}^n$ be a support, $\boldsymbol{y} \in \mathbb{F}_{q^m}^n$ be a multiplier and r be a positive integer. The* alternant code *of support $\boldsymbol{x}$, multiplier $\boldsymbol{y}$ and degree r over $\mathbb{F}_q$ is defined as*

$$\mathscr{A}_r(\boldsymbol{x}, \boldsymbol{y}) \stackrel{\text{def}}{=} \mathbf{GRS}_r(\boldsymbol{x}, \boldsymbol{y})^{\perp} \cap \mathbb{F}_q^n.$$

The integer m is referred to as the extension degree *of the alternant code.*

As a direct consequence of Lemma 1 and Definition 4, we get the following explicit description of an alternant code.

$$\mathscr{A}_r(\boldsymbol{x}, \boldsymbol{y}) = \left\{ \left(\frac{1}{\pi_{\boldsymbol{x}}'(x_i) y_i} f(x_i) \right)_{i=1,\ldots,n} \ \middle| \ f \in \mathbb{F}_{q^m}[z]_{<n-r} \right\} \cap \mathbb{F}_q^n. \qquad (1)$$

Next, by duality and using Delsarte's Theorem (Theorem 1), we have

$$\mathscr{A}_r(\boldsymbol{x}, \boldsymbol{y})^{\perp} = \mathrm{Tr}_{\mathbb{F}_{q^m}/\mathbb{F}_q} \left(\left\{ (y_i g(x_i))_{i=1,\ldots,n} \ \middle| \ g \in \mathbb{F}_{q^m}[z]_{<r} \right\} \right). \qquad (2)$$

We refer the reader to [20, Chap. 12] for further properties of alternant codes. Recall that the code $\mathscr{A}_r(\boldsymbol{x}, \boldsymbol{y})$ defined in Definition 4 has dimension $k \geqslant n - mr$ and equality holds in general. Moreover, these codes benefit from efficient decoding algorithms correcting up to $\lfloor \frac{r}{2} \rfloor$ errors (see [20, Chap. 12 Sect. 9]).

Fully Non Degenerate Alternant Codes. We conclude this subsection on alternant codes by a definition which is useful in the sequel.

Definition 5. *An alternant code $\mathscr{A}_r(\boldsymbol{x}, \boldsymbol{y})$ is said to be* fully non degenerate *if it satisfies the two following conditions.*

(i) A generator matrix of $\mathscr{A}_r(\boldsymbol{x}, \boldsymbol{y})$ has no zero column.
(ii) $\mathscr{A}_r(\boldsymbol{x}, \boldsymbol{y}) \neq \mathscr{A}_{r+1}(\boldsymbol{x}, \boldsymbol{y})$.

Most of the time, an alternant code is fully non degenerate.

2.3 Punctured and Shortened Codes

The notions of *puncturing* and *shortening* are classical ways to build new codes from existing ones. We recall here their definition.

Definition 6. *Let $\mathscr{C}$ be a code of length n and $\mathcal{I} \subseteq \{1, \ldots, n\}$. The* puncturing *and the* shortening *of $\mathscr{C}$ at $\mathcal{I}$ are respectively defined as the codes*

$$\mathcal{P}_{\mathcal{I}}(\mathscr{C}) \stackrel{def}{=} \{(c_i)_{i \in \{1,\ldots,n\} \setminus \mathcal{I}} \mid \boldsymbol{c} \in \mathscr{C}\},$$
$$\mathcal{S}_{\mathcal{I}}(\mathscr{C}) \stackrel{def}{=} \{(c_i)_{i \in \{1,\ldots,n\} \setminus \mathcal{I}} \mid \boldsymbol{c} \in \mathscr{C} \text{ such that } \forall i \in \mathcal{I}, \ c_i = 0\}.$$

Let us finish by recalling the following classical result.

Notation 3. Let $\boldsymbol{x} \in \mathbb{F}_{q^m}^n$ be a vector and $\mathcal{I} \subseteq \{1, \ldots, n\}$. Then, the vector $\boldsymbol{x}_{\mathcal{I}}$ denotes the vector obtained from $\boldsymbol{x}$ be removing the entries whose indexes are in $\mathcal{I}$.

Proposition 1. *Let m, r be positive integers. Let $\boldsymbol{x}, \boldsymbol{y} \in \mathbb{F}_{q^m}^n$ be as in Definition 4. Let $\mathcal{I} \subseteq \{1, \ldots, n\}$. Then*

$$\mathcal{S}_{\mathcal{I}}(\mathscr{A}_r(\boldsymbol{x}, \boldsymbol{y})) = \mathscr{A}_r(\boldsymbol{x}_{\mathcal{I}}, \boldsymbol{y}_{\mathcal{I}}).$$

Proof. See for instance [12, Proposition 9]. □

2.4 Quasi-dyadic Codes, Quasi-dyadic Alternant Codes

Quasi-dyadic (QD) codes are codes with a nontrivial permutation group isomorphic to $(\mathbb{Z}/2\mathbb{Z})^\gamma$ for some positive integer γ. Such a code has length $n = 2^\gamma n_0$. The permutation group of the code is composed of permutations, each one being a product of transpositions with disjoint supports. The example of interest in the present article is the case of QD-alternant codes. In what follows, we explain how to create them.

Notation 4. From now on, q denotes a power of 2 and ℓ denotes the positive integer such that $q = 2^\ell$.

- Let $\mathcal{G} \subset \mathbb{F}_{q^m}$ be an additive subgroup with γ generators, i.e. $\mathcal{G}$ is an $\mathbb{F}_2$-vector subspace of $\mathbb{F}_{q^m}$ of dimension γ with an $\mathbb{F}_2$-basis $a_1, \ldots, a_\gamma$. Clearly, as an additive group, $\mathcal{G}$ is isomorphic to $(\mathbb{Z}/2\mathbb{Z})^\gamma$. The group $\mathcal{G}$ acts on $\mathbb{F}_{q^m}$ by translation: for any $a \in \mathcal{G}$, we denote by τ_a the translation

$$\tau_a : \begin{cases} \mathbb{F}_{q^m} \longrightarrow \mathbb{F}_{q^m} \\ x \longmapsto x + a \end{cases}.$$

- Using the basis $(a_1, \ldots, a_\gamma)$, we fix an ordering in $\mathcal{G}$ as follows. Any element $u_1 a_1 + \cdots + u_\gamma a_\gamma \in \mathcal{G}$ can be regarded as an element $(u_1, \ldots, u_\gamma) \in (\mathbb{Z}/2\mathbb{Z})^\gamma$ and we sort them by lexicographic order. For instance, if $\gamma = 3$:

$$0 < a_1 < a_2 < a_1 + a_2 < a_3 < a_1 + a_3 < a_2 + a_3 < a_1 + a_2 + a_3.$$

- Let $n = 2^\gamma n_0$ for some positive n_0 and such that $n \leqslant q^m$. Let $\boldsymbol{x} \in \mathbb{F}_{q^m}^n$ be a support which splits into n_0 blocks of 2^γ elements of $\mathbb{F}_{q^m}$, each block being an orbit under the action of $\mathcal{G}$ by translation on $\mathbb{F}_{q^m}$ sorted using the previously described ordering. For instance, suppose $\gamma = 2$, then such an $\boldsymbol{x}$ is of the form,

$$\begin{aligned} \boldsymbol{x} = (t_1, t_1 + a_1, t_1 + a_2, t_1 + a_1 + a_2, \ldots, \\ \ldots, t_{n_0}, t_{n_0} + a_1, t_{n_0} + a_2, t_{n_0} + a_1 + a_2), \end{aligned} \quad (3)$$

where the t_i's are chosen to have disjoint orbits under the action of $\mathcal{G}$ by translation on $\mathbb{F}_{q^m}$.
- Let $\boldsymbol{y} \in \mathbb{F}_{q^m}^n$ be a multiplier which also splits into n_0 blocks of length 2^γ whose entries are equal.
- Let r be a positive integer and consider the code $\mathscr{A}_r(\boldsymbol{x}, \boldsymbol{y})$.
- The set of entries of $\boldsymbol{x}$ is globally invariant under the action of $\mathcal{G}$ by translation. In particular, for any $a \in \mathcal{G}$, the translation τ_a induces a permutation of the code $\mathscr{A}_r(\boldsymbol{x}, \boldsymbol{y})$. We refer this permutation to as σ_a. For instance, reconsidering Example (3), the permutations σ_{a_1} and $\sigma_{a_1 + a_2}$ are respectively of the form

$$\sigma_{a_1} = (1, 2)(3, 4) \cdots (n - 3, n - 2)(n - 1, n)$$
$$\sigma_{a_1 + a_2} = (1, 4)(2, 3) \cdots (n - 3, n)(n - 2, n - 1).$$

The group of permutations $\{\sigma_a \mid a \in \mathcal{G}\}$ is isomorphic to $\mathcal{G}$ and hence to $(\mathbb{Z}/2\mathbb{Z})^\gamma$. For convenience, we also denote this group of permutations by $\mathcal{G}$.

Proposition 2. *For any $r > 0$, the code $\mathscr{A}_r(\boldsymbol{x}, \boldsymbol{y})$ is quasi-dyadic.*

Proof. See for instance [27, Chap. 5]. □

2.5 Invariant Subcode of a Quasi-dyadic Code

Definition 7. *Given a code $\mathscr{C}$ with a non-trivial permutation group $\mathcal{G}$, we define the code $\mathscr{C}^\mathcal{G}$ as the subcode of $\mathscr{C}$:*

$$\mathscr{C}^\mathcal{G} \overset{\text{def}}{=} \{\boldsymbol{c} \in \mathscr{C} \mid \forall \sigma \in \mathcal{G}, \ \sigma(\boldsymbol{c}) = \boldsymbol{c}\}.$$

The invariant subcode has repeated entries since on any orbit of the support under the action of $\mathcal{G}$, the entries of a codeword are equal. This motivates an alternative definition of the invariant code where repetitions have been removed.

Definition 8. *In the context of Definition 7, let $\boldsymbol{c} \in \mathbb{F}_{q^m}^n$ be a vector such that for any $\sigma \in \mathcal{G}$, $\sigma(\boldsymbol{c}) = \boldsymbol{c}$. We denote by $\overline{\boldsymbol{c}}$ the vector obtained by keeping only one entry per orbit under the action of $\mathcal{G}$ on the support. We define the* invariant code with non repeated entries *as*

$$\overline{\mathscr{C}}^{\mathcal{G}} \stackrel{def}{=} \left\{ \overline{\boldsymbol{c}} \mid \boldsymbol{c} \in \mathscr{C}^{\mathcal{G}} \right\}.$$

We are interested in the structure of invariant of QD alternant codes. To study this structure, we first need to recall some basic notions of additive polynomials.

Additive polynomials

Definition 9. *An* additive polynomial *$P \in \mathbb{F}_{q^m}[z]$ is a polynomial whose monomials are all of the form z^{2^i} for $i \geqslant 0$. Such a polynomial satisfies $P(a + b) = P(a) + P(b)$ for any $a, b \in \mathbb{F}_{q^m}$.*

The zero locus of an additive polynomial in $\mathbb{F}_{q^m}$ is an additive subgroup of $\mathbb{F}_{q^m}$ and such polynomials satisfy some interpolation properties.

Proposition 3. *Let $\mathcal{G} \subset \mathbb{F}_{q^m}$ be an additive group of cardinality 2^γ. There exists a unique additive polynomial $\psi_{\mathcal{G}} \in \mathbb{F}_{q^m}[z]$ which is monic of degree 2^γ and vanishes at any element of $\mathcal{G}$.*

Proof. See [19, Proposition 1.3.5 & Lemma 1.3.6]. □

Notation 5. From now on, given an additive subgroup $\mathcal{G} \subseteq \mathbb{F}_{q^m}$, we always denote by $\psi_{\mathcal{G}}$ the unique monic additive polynomial of degree $|\mathcal{G}|$ in $\mathbb{F}_{q^m}[z]$ that vanishes on $\mathcal{G}$.

Invariant of a Quasi-dyadic Alternant Code. It turns out that the invariant code with non repeated entries of a QD alternant code is an alternant code too. This relies on the following classical result of invariant theory for which a simple proof can be found in [15].

Theorem 2. *Let $f \in \mathbb{F}_{q^m}[z]$ and $\mathcal{G} \subset \mathbb{F}_{q^m}$ be an additive subgroup. Suppose that for any $a \in \mathcal{G}$, $f(z) = f(z + a)$. Then, there exists $h \in \mathbb{F}_{q^m}[z]$ such that $f(z) = h(\psi_{\mathcal{G}}(z))$, where $\psi_{\mathcal{G}}$ is the monic additive polynomial of degree $|\mathcal{G}|$ vanishing at any element of $\mathcal{G}$.*

This entails the following result on the structure of the invariant code of an alternant code. We refer to Definition 8 for the notation in the following statement.

Theorem 3. *Let $\mathscr{C} = \mathscr{A}_r(\boldsymbol{x}, \boldsymbol{y})$ be a QD-alternant code with permutation group $\mathcal{G}$ of order 2^γ. Set $r' = \left\lfloor \frac{r}{2^\gamma} \right\rfloor$. Then,*

$$\overline{\mathscr{C}}^{\mathcal{G}} = \mathscr{A}_{r'}(\overline{\psi_{\mathcal{G}}(\boldsymbol{x})}, \overline{\boldsymbol{y}}),$$

Proof. See [4]. □

2.6   DAGS

Among the schemes recently submitted to NIST, the submission DAGS [3] uses as a primitive a McEliece encryption scheme based on QD generalised Srivastava codes. It is well known that generalised Srivastava codes form a subclass of alternant codes [20, Chap. 12]. Therefore, this proposal lies in the scope of the attack presented in what follows.

Parameters proposed in DAGS submission are listed in Table 1.

Table 1. Parameters proposed in DAGS.

Name	q	m	n	n_0	k	k_0	γ	r_0
DAGS_1	2^5	2	832	52	416	26	4	13
DAGS_3	2^6	2	1216	38	512	16	5	11
DAGS_5	2^6	2	2112	33	704	11	6	11

Let us recall what do the parameters $q, m, n, n_0, k, k_0, \gamma, r_0$ stand for:

- q denotes the size of the base field of the alternant code;
- m denotes the extension degree. Hence the GRS code above the alternant code is defined over $\mathbb{F}_{q^m}$;
- n denotes the length of the QD alternant code;
- n_0 denotes the length of the invariant code with non repeated entries $\overline{\mathscr{A}_r(\boldsymbol{x}, \boldsymbol{y})}^{\mathcal{G}}$, where $\mathcal{G}$ denotes the permutation group;
- k denotes the dimension of the QD alternant code;
- k_0 denotes the dimension of the invariant code;
- γ denotes the number of generators of $\mathcal{G}$, *i.e.* $\mathcal{G} \simeq (\mathbb{Z}/2\mathbb{Z})^\gamma$;
- r_0 denotes the degree of the invariant code with non repeated entries, which is alternant according to Theorem 3.

Remark 1. The indexes 1, 3 and 5 in the parameters names correspond to security levels according to NIST's call. Level 1, corresponds to 128 bits security with a classical computer, Level 3 to 192 bits security and Level 5 to 256 bits security.

In addition to the set of parameters of Table 1, we introduce self chosen smaller parameters listed in Table 2. They **do not** correspond to claimed secure instantiations of the scheme but permitted to test some of our assumptions by computer aided calculations.

3   Schur Products

From now on and unless otherwise specified, the extension degree m will be equal to 2. This is the context of any proposed parameters in DAGS.

Table 2. Small scale parameters, **not** proposed in DAGS.

Name	q	m	n	n_0	k	k_0	γ	r_0
DAGS_0	2^4	2	240	15	80	5	4	5

3.1   Product of Vectors

The component wise product of two vectors in $\mathbb{F}_q^n$ is denoted by

$$\boldsymbol{a} \star \boldsymbol{b} \stackrel{\text{def}}{=} (a_1 b_1, \ldots, a_n b_n).$$

Next, for any positive integer t we define $\boldsymbol{a}^{\star t}$ as

$$\boldsymbol{a}^{\star t} \stackrel{\text{def}}{=} \underbrace{\boldsymbol{a} \star \cdots \star \boldsymbol{a}}_{t \text{ times}}.$$

More generally, given a polynomial $P \in \mathbb{F}_q[z]$ we define $P(\boldsymbol{a})$ as the vector $(P(a_1), \ldots, P(a_n))$. In particular, given $\boldsymbol{a} \in \mathbb{F}_{q^2}^n$, we denote by $\text{Tr}(\boldsymbol{a})$ and $\text{N}(\boldsymbol{a})$ the vectors obtained by applying respectively the trace and the norm map component by component:

$$\text{Tr}(\boldsymbol{a}) \stackrel{\text{def}}{=} (a_1 + a_1^q, \ldots, a_n + a_n^q)$$
$$\text{N}(\boldsymbol{a}) \stackrel{\text{def}}{=} (a_1^{q+1}, \ldots, a_n^{q+1}).$$

Finally, the all one vector $(1, \ldots, 1)$, which is the unit vector of the algebra $\mathbb{F}_q^n$ with operations $+$ and $\star$ is denoted by $\boldsymbol{1}$.

3.2   Schur Product of Codes

The *Schur product* of two codes $\mathscr{A}$ and $\mathscr{B} \subseteq \mathbb{F}_q^n$ is defined as

$$\mathscr{A} \star \mathscr{B} \stackrel{\text{def}}{=} \langle \boldsymbol{a} \star \boldsymbol{b} \mid \boldsymbol{a} \in \mathscr{A}, \ \boldsymbol{b} \in \mathscr{B} \rangle_{\mathbb{F}_q}.$$

In particular, $\mathscr{A}^{\star 2}$ denotes the *square code* of a code $\mathscr{A}$: $\mathscr{A}^{\star 2} \stackrel{\text{def}}{=} \mathscr{A} \star \mathscr{A}$.

3.3   Schur Products of GRS and Alternant Codes

The behaviour of GRS and of some alternant codes with respect to the Schur product is very different from that of random codes. This provides a manner to distinguish GRS codes from random ones and leads to a cryptanalysis of GRS based encryption schemes [9,13,31]. Some alternant codes, namely Wild Goppa codes with extension degree 2 have been also subject to a cryptanalysis based on Schur products computations [11,12].

Here we recall an elementary but crucial result.

Theorem 4. *Let $x \in \mathbb{F}_{q^m}^n$ be a support and $y, y' \in \mathbb{F}_{q^m}^n$ be multipliers. Let k, k' be two positive integers, then*

$$\mathbf{GRS}_k(x, y) \star \mathbf{GRS}_{k'}(x, y') = \mathbf{GRS}_{k+k'-1}(x, y \star y').$$

Proof. See for instance [9, Proposition 6]. □

4 Conductors

In this section, we introduce a fundamental object in the attack to follow. This object was already used in [10,12] without being named. We chose here to call it *conductor*. The rationale behind this terminology is explained in Remark 2.

Definition 10. *Let $\mathscr{C}$ and $\mathscr{D}$ be two codes of length n over $\mathbb{F}_q$. The conductor of $\mathscr{D}$ into $\mathscr{C}$ is defined as the largest code $\mathscr{X} \subseteq \mathbb{F}_q^n$ such that $\mathscr{D} \star \mathscr{X} \subseteq \mathscr{C}$. That is:*

$$\mathbf{Cond}(\mathscr{D}, \mathscr{C}) \stackrel{def}{=} \{u \in \mathbb{F}_q^n \mid u \star \mathscr{D} \subseteq \mathscr{C}\}.$$

Proposition 4. *Let $\mathscr{D}, \mathscr{C} \subseteq \mathbb{F}_q^n$ be two codes, then*

$$\mathbf{Cond}(\mathscr{D}, \mathscr{C}) = \left(\mathscr{D} \star \mathscr{C}^{\perp}\right)^{\perp}.$$

Proof. See [10,12]. □

Remark 2. The terminology *conductor* has been borrowed from number theory in which the conductor of two subrings $\mathcal{O}, \mathcal{O}'$ of the ring of integers $\mathcal{O}_K$ of a number field K is the largest ideal $\mathfrak{P}$ of $\mathcal{O}_K$ such that $\mathfrak{P} \cdot \mathcal{O} \subseteq \mathcal{O}'$.

4.1 Conductors of GRS Codes

Proposition 5. *Let $x, y \in \mathbb{F}_{q^m}^n$ be a support and a multiplier. Let $k \leqslant k'$ be two integers less than n. Then,*

$$\mathbf{Cond}(\mathbf{GRS}_k(x, y), \mathbf{GRS}_{k'}(x, y)) = \mathbf{RS}_{k'-k+1}(x).$$

Proof. Let $\mathscr{E}$ denote the conductor. From Proposition 4 and Lemma 1,

$$\mathscr{E}^{\perp} = \mathbf{GRS}_k(x, y) \star \mathbf{GRS}_{n-k'}(x, y^{\perp}) = \mathbf{GRS}_{n-k'+k-1}(x, y \star y^{\perp}).$$

Note that

$$y \star y^{\perp} = \left(\frac{1}{\pi'_x(x_1)}, \ldots, \frac{1}{\pi'_x(x_n)}\right).$$

Then, using Lemma 1 again, we get

$$\mathscr{E} = \mathbf{GRS}_{k'-k+1}(x, (y \star y^{\perp})^{\perp}) = \mathbf{RS}_{k'-k+1}(x).$$

□

Let us emphasize a very interesting aspect of Proposition 4. We considered the conductor of a GRS code into another one having the same support and multiplier. The point is that the conductor **does not depend on y**. Hence the computation of a conductor permits to get rid of the multiplier and to obtain a much easier code to study: a Reed-Solomon code.

4.2 An Illustrative Example: Recovering the Structure of GRS Codes Using Conductors

Before presenting the attack on QD-alternant codes, we propose first to describe a manner to recover the structure of a GRS code. This may help the reader to understand the spirit the attack to follow.

Suppose we know a generator matrix of a code $\mathscr{C}_k = \mathbf{GRS}_k(\boldsymbol{x}, \boldsymbol{y})$ where $(\boldsymbol{x}, \boldsymbol{y})$ are unknown. In addition, suppose that we know a generator matrix of the subcode $\mathscr{C}_{k-1} = \mathbf{GRS}_{k-1}(\boldsymbol{x}, \boldsymbol{y})$ which has codimension 1 in $\mathscr{C}_k$. First compute the conductor

$$\mathscr{X} = \mathbf{Cond}(\mathscr{C}_{k-1}, \mathscr{C}_k).$$

From Proposition 5, the conductor $\mathscr{X}$ equals $\mathbf{RS}_2(\boldsymbol{x})$. This code has dimension 2 and is spanned by $\mathbf{1}$ and $\boldsymbol{x}$. We claim that, from the knowledge of $\mathscr{X}$, a pair $(\boldsymbol{x}', \boldsymbol{y}')$ such that $\mathscr{C}_k = \mathbf{GRS}_k(\boldsymbol{x}', \boldsymbol{y}')$ can be found easily by using techniques which are very similar from those presented further in Sect. 6.6.

Of course, there is no reason that we could know both $\mathbf{GRS}_k(\boldsymbol{x}, \boldsymbol{y})$ and $\mathbf{GRS}_{k-1}(\boldsymbol{x}, \boldsymbol{y})$. However, we will see further that the quasi-dyadic structure permits to find interesting subcodes whose conductor may reveal the secret structure of the code.

4.3 Conductors of Alternant Codes

When dealing with alternant codes, having an exact description of the conductors like in Proposition 5 becomes difficult. We can at least prove the following theorem.

Proposition 6. *Let $\boldsymbol{x}, \boldsymbol{y} \in \mathbb{F}_{q^2}^n$ be a support and a multiplier. Let $r' \geqslant r$ be two positive integers. Then,*

$$\mathbf{RS}_{r'-r+1}(\boldsymbol{x}) \cap \mathbb{F}_q^n \subseteq \mathbf{Cond}(\mathscr{A}_{r'}(\boldsymbol{x}, \boldsymbol{y}), \mathscr{A}_r(\boldsymbol{x}, \boldsymbol{y})). \tag{4}$$

Proof. Consider the Schur product

$$\begin{aligned}
\left(\mathbf{RS}_{r'-r+1}(\boldsymbol{x}) \cap \mathbb{F}_q^n\right) &\star \mathscr{A}_{r'}(\boldsymbol{x}, \boldsymbol{y}) \\
&= \left(\mathbf{RS}_{r'-r+1}(\boldsymbol{x}) \cap \mathbb{F}_q^n\right) \star \left(\mathbf{GRS}_{n-r'}(\boldsymbol{x}, \boldsymbol{y}^\perp) \cap \mathbb{F}_q^n\right) \\
&\subseteq \left(\mathbf{RS}_{r'-r+1}(\boldsymbol{x}) \star \mathbf{GRS}_{n-r'}(\boldsymbol{x}, \boldsymbol{y}^\perp)\right) \cap \mathbb{F}_q^n.
\end{aligned}$$

Next, using Theorem 4,

$$\begin{aligned}
\left(\mathbf{RS}_{r'-r+1}(\boldsymbol{x}) \cap \mathbb{F}_q^n\right) \star \mathscr{A}_{r'}(\boldsymbol{x}, \boldsymbol{y}) &\subseteq \mathbf{GRS}_{n-r}(\boldsymbol{x}, \boldsymbol{y}^\perp) \cap \mathbb{F}_q^n \\
&\subseteq \mathscr{A}_r(\boldsymbol{x}, \boldsymbol{y}).
\end{aligned}$$

The last inclusion is a consequence of Lemma 1 and Definition 4.   □

4.4 Why the Straightforward Generalisation Of the Illustrative Example Fails for Alternant Codes

Compared to Proposition 5, Proposition 6 provides only an inclusion. However, it turns out that we experimentally observed that the equality frequently holds.

On the other hand, even if inclusion (4) was an equality, the attack described in Sect. 3.2 could not be straightforwardly generalised to alternant codes. Indeed, suppose we know two alternant codes with consecutive degrees $\mathscr{A}_{r+1}(x, y)$ and $\mathscr{A}_r(x, y)$. Then, Proposition 6 would yield

$$\mathbf{RS}_2(x) \cap \mathbb{F}_q^n \subseteq \mathbf{Cond}(\mathscr{A}_{r+1}(x, y), \mathscr{A}_r(x, y)). \tag{5}$$

Suppose that the above inclusion is actually an equality; as we just said this is in general what happens. The point is that as soon as x has one entry in $\mathbb{F}_{q^2} \setminus \mathbb{F}_q$, then $\mathbf{RS}_2(x) \cap \mathbb{F}_q^n$ is reduced to the code spanned by $\mathbf{1}$ and hence cannot provide any relevant information.

The previous discussion shows that, if we want to generalise the toy attack described in Sect. 4.2 to alternant codes, we cannot use a pair of alternant codes with consecutive degrees. In light of Proposition 6, the gap between the degrees r and r' of the two alternant codes should be large enough to provide a non trivial conductor. A sufficient condition for this is that $\mathbf{RS}_{r'-r+1}(x) \cap \mathbb{F}_q^n$ is non trivial. This motivates the introduction of a code we called the *norm trace code*.

4.5 The Norm-Trace Code

Notation 6. In what follows, we fix $\alpha \in \mathbb{F}_{q^2}$ such that $\mathrm{Tr}(\alpha) = 1$. In particular, $(1, \alpha)$ forms an $\mathbb{F}_q$-basis of $\mathbb{F}_{q^2}$.

Definition 11 (Norm trace code). *Let $x \in \mathbb{F}_{q^2}^n$ be a support. The* norm-trace code $\mathscr{N\!T}(x) \subseteq \mathbb{F}_q^n$ *is defined as*

$$\mathscr{N\!T}(x) \stackrel{def}{=} \langle \mathbf{1}, \mathit{Tr}(x), \mathit{Tr}(\alpha x), N(x) \rangle_{\mathbb{F}_q}.$$

This *norm trace code* turns out to be the code we will extract from the public key by conductor computations. To relate it with the previous discussions, we have the following statement whose proof is straightforward.

Proposition 7. *Let $x \in \mathbb{F}_{q^2}^n$ be a support. Then, for any $k > q + 1$, we have*

$$\mathscr{N\!T}(x) \subseteq \mathbf{RS}_k(x) \cap \mathbb{F}_q^n. \tag{6}$$

Remark 3. It addition to this statement, we observed experimentally that for $2q + 1 > k > q + 1$ inclusion (6) is in general an equality.

4.6   Summary and a Heuristic

First, let us summarise the previous discussions.

– If we know a pair of alternant codes $\mathscr{A}_r(\boldsymbol{x}, \boldsymbol{y})$ and $\mathscr{A}_{r'}(\boldsymbol{x}, \boldsymbol{y})$ such that $q < r' - r$, then $\mathbf{Cond}(\mathscr{A}_{r'}(\boldsymbol{x}, \boldsymbol{y}), \mathscr{A}_r(\boldsymbol{x}, \boldsymbol{y}))$ is non trivial since, according to Proposition 6 and to (6), it contains the norm-trace code.
– Experimentally, we observed that if $q < r' - r < 2q$, then, almost every time, we have

$$\mathbf{Cond}(\mathscr{A}_{r'}(\boldsymbol{x}, \boldsymbol{y}), \mathscr{A}_r(\boldsymbol{x}, \boldsymbol{y})) = \mathscr{N}\mathscr{T}(\boldsymbol{x}).$$

– One problem remains: given an alternant code $\mathscr{A}_r(\boldsymbol{x}, \boldsymbol{y})$, how to get a subcode $\mathscr{A}_{r'}(\boldsymbol{x}, \boldsymbol{y})$ in order to apply the previous results? This will be explained in Sects. 5 and 6 in which we show that for quasi-dyadic alternant codes it is possible to get a subcode $\mathscr{D} \subseteq \mathscr{A}_r(\boldsymbol{x}, \boldsymbol{y})$ such that $\mathscr{D} \subseteq \mathscr{A}_{r'}(\boldsymbol{x}, \boldsymbol{y})$ for some r' satisfying $r' - r > q + 1$.
Moreover, it turns out that $\mathscr{A}_{r'}(\boldsymbol{x}, \boldsymbol{y})$ can be replaced by a subcode without changing the result of the previous discussions. This is what is argued in the following heuristic.

Heuristic 1. *In the context of Proposition 6, suppose that $q < r - r' < 2q$. Let $\mathscr{D}$ be a subcode of $\mathscr{A}_{r'}(\boldsymbol{x}, \boldsymbol{y})$ such that*

(i) $\dim \mathscr{D} \cdot \dim \mathscr{A}_r(\boldsymbol{x}, \boldsymbol{y})^{\perp} \geqslant n$;
(ii) $\mathscr{D} \not\subset \mathscr{A}_{r'+1}(\boldsymbol{x}, \boldsymbol{y})$;
(iii) a generator matrix of $\mathscr{D}$ has no zero column.

Then, with a high probability,

$$\mathbf{Cond}(\mathscr{D}, \mathscr{A}_r(\boldsymbol{x}, \boldsymbol{y})) = \mathscr{N}\mathscr{T}(\boldsymbol{x}).$$

Let us give some evidences for this heuristic. From Proposition 4,

$$\mathbf{Cond}(\mathscr{D}, \mathscr{A}_r(\boldsymbol{x}, \boldsymbol{y})) = \left(\mathscr{D} \star \mathscr{A}_r(\boldsymbol{x}, \boldsymbol{y})^{\perp}\right)^{\perp}.$$

From (2), we have $\mathscr{A}_r(\boldsymbol{x}, \boldsymbol{y})^{\perp} = \mathrm{Tr}_{\mathbb{F}_{q^2}/\mathbb{F}_q}(\mathbf{GRS}_r(\boldsymbol{x}, \boldsymbol{y}))$. Since $\mathscr{D}$ is a code over $\mathbb{F}_q$ and by the $\mathbb{F}_q$-linearity of the trace map, we get

$$\mathscr{D} \star \mathscr{A}_r(\boldsymbol{x}, \boldsymbol{y})^{\perp} = \mathrm{Tr}_{\mathbb{F}_{q^2}/\mathbb{F}_q}\left(\mathscr{D} \star \mathbf{GRS}_r(\boldsymbol{x}, \boldsymbol{y})\right).$$

Since $\mathscr{D} \subseteq \mathscr{A}_{r'}(\boldsymbol{x}, \boldsymbol{y})$ then, from (1), it is a subset of a GRS code. Namely,

$$\mathscr{D} \subseteq \mathbf{GRS}_{n-r'}(\boldsymbol{x}, \boldsymbol{y}^{\perp}), \quad \text{where} \quad \boldsymbol{y}^{\perp} = \left(\frac{1}{\pi'_{\boldsymbol{x}}(x_1)y_1}, \ldots, \frac{1}{\pi'_{\boldsymbol{x}}(x_n)y_n}\right).$$

Therefore, thanks to Theorem 4, we get

$$\mathscr{D} \star \mathscr{A}_r(\boldsymbol{x}, \boldsymbol{y})^{\perp} \subseteq \mathrm{Tr}_{\mathbb{F}_{q^2}/\mathbb{F}_q}\left(\mathbf{GRS}_{n-r'+r-1}(\boldsymbol{x}, \boldsymbol{y} \star \boldsymbol{y}^{\perp})\right). \tag{7}$$

Note that $\mathscr{D} \star \mathscr{A}_r(\boldsymbol{x}, \boldsymbol{y})^{\perp}$ is spanned by $\dim \mathscr{D} \cdot \dim \mathscr{A}_r(\boldsymbol{x}, \boldsymbol{y})^{\perp}$ generators which are obtained by computing the Schur products of elements of a basis of $\mathscr{D}$ by elements of a basis of $\mathscr{A}_r(\boldsymbol{x}, \boldsymbol{y})^{\perp}$. By (i), the number of such generators exceeds n. For this reason, it is reasonable to hope that this Schur product fills in the target code and that,

$$\mathscr{D} \star \mathscr{A}_r(\boldsymbol{x}, \boldsymbol{y})^{\perp} = \mathrm{Tr}_{\mathbb{F}_{q^2}/\mathbb{F}_q} \left(\mathbf{GRS}_{n-r'+r-1}(\boldsymbol{x}, \boldsymbol{y} \star \boldsymbol{y}^{\perp}) \right).$$

Next, we have

$$\boldsymbol{y} \star \boldsymbol{y}^{\perp} = \left(\frac{1}{\pi'_{\boldsymbol{x}}(x_1)}, \dots, \frac{1}{\pi'_{\boldsymbol{x}}(x_n)} \right).$$

Therefore, using Lemma 1, we conclude that

$$\left(\mathscr{D} \star \mathscr{A}_r(\boldsymbol{x}, \boldsymbol{y})^{\perp} \right)^{\perp} = \mathbf{RS}_{r'-r+1}(\boldsymbol{x}) \cap \mathbb{F}_q^n.$$

Using Remark 3, we get the result.

Remark 4. Assumption (ii) permits to avoid the situation where the conductor could be the subfield subcode of a larger Reed-Solomon code. Assumption (iii) permits to avoid the presence of words of weight 1 in the conductor that would not be elements of a Reed-Solomon code.

Further Discussion on the Heuristic. In all our computer experiments, we never observed any phenomenon contradicting this heuristic.

5   Fundamental Degree Properties of the Invariant Subcode of a QD Alternant Code

A crucial statement for the attack is:

Theorem 5. *Let* $\boldsymbol{x}, \boldsymbol{y} \in \mathbb{F}_{q^2}^n$ *be a support and a multiplier. Let* s *be an integer of the form* $s = 2^\gamma s_0$. *Suppose that* $\mathscr{A}_{s_0}(\psi_{\mathcal{G}}(\boldsymbol{x}), \overline{\boldsymbol{y}})$ *is fully non degenerate (see Definition 5 and Sect. 2.5 for notation* $\psi_{\mathcal{G}}$ *and* $\overline{\boldsymbol{y}}$). *Then,*

(a) $\mathscr{A}_s(\boldsymbol{x}, \boldsymbol{y})^{\mathcal{G}} \subseteq \mathscr{A}_{s+|\mathcal{G}|-1}(\boldsymbol{x}, \boldsymbol{y})$;
(b) $\mathscr{A}_s(\boldsymbol{x}, \boldsymbol{y})^{\mathcal{G}} \not\subseteq \mathscr{A}_{s+|\mathcal{G}|}(\boldsymbol{x}, \boldsymbol{y})$.

Proof. From (1), we have

$$\mathscr{A}_s(\boldsymbol{x}, \boldsymbol{y}) = \left\{ \left(\frac{1}{y_i \pi'_{\boldsymbol{x}}(x_i)} f(x_i) \right)_{i=1,\dots,n} \;\middle|\; f \in \mathbb{F}_{q^2}[z]_{<n-s} \right\} \cap \mathbb{F}_q^n.$$

This code is obtained by evaluation of polynomials of degree up to

$$n - s - 1 = (2^\gamma(n_0 - s_0) - 1).$$

From Theorem 2, the invariant codewords of $\mathscr{A}_s(\boldsymbol{x}, \boldsymbol{y})$ come from evaluations of polynomials of the form $h \circ \psi_{\mathcal{G}}$. Such polynomials have a degree that is a multiple of $\deg \psi_{\mathcal{G}} = 2^\gamma$ and hence their degree cannot exceed $2^\gamma(n_0 - s_0 - 1)$. Thus, they should lie in $\mathbb{F}_{q^2}[z]_{\leqslant n - s - |\mathcal{G}|} = \mathbb{F}_{q^2}[z]_{< n - s - |\mathcal{G}| + 1}$. This leads to

$$\mathscr{A}_s(\boldsymbol{x}, \boldsymbol{y})^{\mathcal{G}} \subseteq \left\{ \left(\frac{1}{y_i \pi'_{\boldsymbol{x}}(x_i)} f(x_i) \right)_{i=1,\dots,n} \ \middle| \ f \in \mathbb{F}_{q^2}[z]_{< n - s - |\mathcal{G}| + 1} \right\} \cap \mathbb{F}_q^n$$

$$\subseteq \mathscr{A}_{s + |\mathcal{G}| - 1}(\boldsymbol{x}, \boldsymbol{y}).$$

This proves (a).

To prove (b), note that the assumption on $\mathscr{A}_{s_0}(\overline{\psi_{\mathcal{G}}(\boldsymbol{x})}, \overline{\boldsymbol{y}})$ asserts the existence of $f \in \mathbb{F}_{q^2}[z]_{< n_0 - s_0}$ such that $\deg f = n_0 - s_0 - 1$ and $f(\overline{\psi_{\mathcal{G}}(\boldsymbol{x})}) \in \mathbb{F}_q^{n_0}$. Thus, $f(\psi_{\mathcal{G}}(\boldsymbol{x})) \in \mathbb{F}_q^n$ and $\deg(f \circ \psi_{\mathcal{G}}) = n - s - |\mathcal{G}|$. Therefore $f(\psi(\boldsymbol{x})) \in \mathscr{A}_s(\boldsymbol{x}, \boldsymbol{y})^{\mathcal{G}}$ and $\mathscr{A}_s(\boldsymbol{x}, \boldsymbol{y})^{\mathcal{G}}$ contains an element of $\mathscr{A}_{s + |\mathcal{G}| - 1}(\boldsymbol{x}, \boldsymbol{y})$ that is not in $\mathscr{A}_{s + |\mathcal{G}|}(\boldsymbol{x}, \boldsymbol{y})$. □

6   Presentation of the Attack

6.1   Context

Recall that the extension degree is always $m = 2$. The public code is the QD alternant code

$$\mathscr{C}_{\text{pub}} \overset{\text{def}}{=} \mathscr{A}_r(\boldsymbol{x}, \boldsymbol{y}),$$

with a permutation group $\mathcal{G}$ of cardinality $|\mathcal{G}| = 2^\gamma$. As in Sect. 2.6, the code has a length $n = n_0 2^\gamma$, dimension k and is defined over a field $\mathbb{F}_q$ and $q = 2^\ell$ for some positive integer ℓ. The degree r of the alternant code is also a multiple of $|\mathcal{G}| = 2^\gamma$ and hence is of the form $r = r_0 2^\gamma$. We suppose from now on that the classical lower bound on the dimension k is reached, i.e. $k = n - 2r$. This always holds in the parameters proposed in [3]. We finally set $k_0 = k/2^\gamma$. In summary, we have the following notation

$$n = n_0 2^\gamma, \quad k = k_0 2^\gamma, \quad r = r_0 2^\gamma. \tag{8}$$

6.2   The Subcode $\mathscr{D}$

We introduce a subcode $\mathscr{D}$ of $\mathscr{C}_{\text{pub}}$ and prove that its knowledge permits to compute the norm trace code. This code $\mathscr{D}$ is unknown by the attacker and we will see in Sect. 7 that the time consuming part of the attack consists in guessing it.

Definition 12. *Suppose that $|\mathcal{G}| \leqslant q$. We define the code $\mathscr{D}$ as*

$$\mathscr{D} \overset{\text{def}}{=} \mathscr{A}_{r+q}(\boldsymbol{x}, \boldsymbol{y})^{\mathcal{G}}.$$

Remark 5. For parameters suggested in DAGS, we always have $|\mathcal{G}| \leqslant q$, with strict inequality for DAGS_1 and DAGS_3 and equality for DAGS_5.

Remark 6. The case $q < |\mathcal{G}|$ which never holds in DAGS suggested parameters would be particularly easy to treat. In such a situation, replacing possibly $\mathcal{G}$ by a subgroup, one can suppose that $|\mathcal{G}| = 2q$. Next, according to Theorem 5, and Heuristic 1, we would have

$$\mathbf{Cond}((\mathscr{C}_{\mathrm{pub}})^{\mathcal{G}}, \mathscr{C}_{\mathrm{pub}}) = \mathscr{N}\mathscr{T}(\boldsymbol{x}),$$

which would provide a very simple manner to compute $\mathscr{N}\mathscr{T}(\boldsymbol{x})$.

The following results are the key of the attack. Theorem 6 explains why this subcode $\mathscr{D}$ is of deep interest and how it can be used to recover the norm-trace code, from which the secret key can be recovered (see Sect. 6.6). Theorem 7 explains why this subcode $\mathscr{D}$ can be computed in a reasonable time thanks to the QD structure. Indeed, it shows that even if $\mathscr{D}$ has a large codimension as a subcode of $\mathscr{C}_{\mathrm{pub}}$ its codimension in $(\mathscr{C}_{\mathrm{pub}})^{\mathcal{G}}$ is much smaller. This is why the QD structure plays a crucial role in this attack (Table 3).

Theorem 6. *Under Heuristic 1 and assuming that* $\overline{\mathscr{A}_{r+q}(\boldsymbol{x}, \boldsymbol{y})}^{\mathcal{G}}$ *is fully non degenerate (see Definition 5), we have*

$$\mathbf{Cond}(\mathscr{D}, \mathscr{C}_{pub}) = \mathscr{N}\mathscr{T}(\boldsymbol{x}).$$

Proof. It is a direct consequence of Theorem 5 and Heuristic 1.   □

Theorem 7. *The code $\mathscr{D}$ has codimension* $\leqslant \frac{2q}{|\mathcal{G}|} = 2^{\ell-\gamma+1}$ *in* $(\mathscr{C}_{pub})^{\mathcal{G}}$.

Proof. Using Theorem 3, we know that $\mathscr{D}$ has the same dimension as $\mathscr{A}_{r_0+\frac{q}{|\mathcal{G}|}}(\psi_{\mathcal{G}}(\boldsymbol{x}), \overline{\boldsymbol{y}})$. This code has dimension $\geqslant n_0 - 2(r_0 + \frac{q}{|\mathcal{G}|})$. Since $\dim(\mathscr{C}_{\mathrm{pub}})^{\mathcal{G}} = k_0 = n_0 - 2r_0$, we get the result.   □

Remark 7. Actually the codimension equals $2^{\ell-\gamma+1}$ almost all the time.

Table 3. Numerical values for the code $\mathscr{D}$

Proposal	$\mathscr{D}$	Codimension in $(\mathscr{C}_{\mathrm{pub}})^{\mathcal{G}}$
DAGS_1	$\mathscr{A}_{240}(\boldsymbol{x}, \boldsymbol{y})^{\mathcal{G}}$	4
DAGS_3	$\mathscr{A}_{416}(\boldsymbol{x}, \boldsymbol{y})^{\mathcal{G}}$	4
DAGS_5	$\mathscr{A}_{768}(\boldsymbol{x}, \boldsymbol{y})^{\mathcal{G}}$	2

6.3   Description of the Attack

The attack can be summarised as follows:

(1) Compute $(\mathscr{C}_{\mathrm{pub}})^{\mathcal{G}}$;
(2) Guess the subcode $\mathscr{D}$ of $(\mathscr{C}_{\mathrm{pub}})^{\mathcal{G}}$ of codimension $\frac{2q}{|\mathcal{G}|}$ such that

$$\mathbf{Cond}(\mathscr{D}, \mathscr{C}_{\mathrm{pub}}) = \mathscr{N}\mathscr{T}(\boldsymbol{x});$$

(3) Determine $\boldsymbol{x}$ from $\mathscr{N}\mathscr{T}(\boldsymbol{x})$ and then $\boldsymbol{y}$ from $\boldsymbol{x}$.

The difficult part is clearly the second one: how to guess $\mathscr{D}$? We present two manners to realise this guess.

– The first one consists in performing exhaustive search on subcodes of codimension $\frac{2q}{|\mathcal{G}|}$ of $(\mathscr{C}_{\mathrm{pub}})^{\mathcal{G}}$.
– The second one consists in finding both $\mathscr{D}$ and $\mathscr{N}\mathscr{T}(\boldsymbol{x})$ by solving a system of equations of degree 2 using Gröbner bases.

The first approach has a significant cost but which remains far below the expected security level of DAGS proposed parameters. For the second approach, we did not succeed to get a relevant estimate of the work factor but its practical implementation permits to break DAGS_1 in about 20 min and DAGS_5 in less than one minute (see Sect. 8 for further details on the implementation). We did not succeed to break DAGS_3 parameters using the second approach. On the other hand the first approach would have a work factor of $\approx 2^{80}$ for keys with an expected security of 192 bits.

The remainder of this section is devoted to detail the different steps of the attack.

6.4   First Approach, Brute Force Search of $\mathscr{D}$

A first way of getting $\mathscr{D}$ and then of obtaining $\mathscr{N}\mathscr{T}(\boldsymbol{x})$ consists in enumerating all the subspaces $\mathscr{X} \subseteq (\mathscr{C}_{\mathrm{pub}})^{\mathcal{G}}$ of codimension $\frac{2q}{|\mathcal{G}|}$ until we find one such that $\mathbf{Cond}(\mathscr{X}, \mathscr{C}_{\mathrm{pub}})$ has dimension 4. Indeed, for an arbitrary $\mathscr{X}$ the conductor will have dimension 1 and be generated by $\mathbf{1}$, while for $\mathscr{X} = \mathscr{D}$ the conductor will be $\mathscr{N}\mathscr{T}(\boldsymbol{x})$ which has dimension 4.

The number of subspaces to enumerate is in $O(q^{(2q/|\mathcal{G}|)(k_0 - 2q/|\mathcal{G}|)})$ which is in general much too large to make the attack practical. It is however possible to reduce the cost of brute force attack as follows.

Using Random Subcodes of Dimension 2. For any parameter set proposed in DAGS, the public code has a rate k/n less than $1/2$. Hence, its dual has rate larger than $1/2$. Therefore, according to Heuristic 1, given a random subcode $\mathscr{D}_0$ of $\mathscr{D}$ of dimension 2, then $\mathbf{Cond}(\mathscr{D}_0, \mathscr{C}_{\mathrm{pub}}) = \mathscr{N}\mathscr{T}(\boldsymbol{x})$ with a high probability.

Thus, one can proceed as follows

- Pick two independent vectors $c, c' \in (\mathscr{C}_{\text{pub}})^{\mathcal{G}}$ at random and compute $\mathbf{Cond}(\langle c, c' \rangle, \mathscr{C}_{\text{pub}})$;
- If the conductor has dimension 4, you probably found $\mathcal{NT}(x)$, then pursue the attack as explained in Sect. 6.6.
- Else, try again.

The probability that $c, c' \in \mathscr{D}$ equals $q^{-\frac{4q}{|\mathcal{G}|}}$. Therefore, one may have found $\mathcal{NT}(x)$ after $O(q^{\frac{4q}{|\mathcal{G}|}})$ computations of conductors.

Example 1. The average number of computations of conductors will be

- $O(q^8) = O(2^{40})$ for DAGS_1;
- $O(q^8) = O(2^{48})$ for DAGS_3;
- $O(q^4) = O(2^{24})$ for DAGS_5.

Using Shortened Codes. Another manner consists in replacing the public code by one of its shortenings. For that, we shorten $\mathscr{C}_{\text{pub}} = \mathscr{A}_r(x, y)$ at a set of $a = a_0 2^\gamma$ positions which is a union of blocks, so that the shortened code remains QD. We choose the integer a such that the invariant subcode of the shortened code has dimension $2 + \frac{2q}{|\mathcal{G}|}$ and hence the shortening of $\mathscr{D}$ has dimension 2. Let $\mathcal{I}$ be such a subset of positions. To determine $\mathcal{S}_{\mathcal{I}}(\mathscr{D})$, we can enumerate any subspace $\mathcal{X}$ of dimension 2 of $\mathcal{S}_{\mathcal{I}}(\mathscr{C}_{\text{pub}})$ and compute $\mathbf{Cond}(\mathcal{X}, \mathcal{S}_{\mathcal{I}}(\mathscr{C}_{\text{pub}}))$. In general, we get the trivial code spanned by the all-one codeword $\mathbf{1}$. If the conductor has dimension 4 it is highly likely that we found $\mathcal{S}_{\mathcal{I}}(\mathscr{D})$ and that the computed conductor equals $\mathcal{NT}(x_{\mathcal{I}})$.

The number of such spaces we enumerate is in $O(q^{\frac{4q}{|\mathcal{G}|}})$, which is very similar to the cost of the previous method.

6.5   Second Approach, Solving Polynomial System of Degree 2

An alternative approach to recover $\mathscr{D}$ and $\mathcal{NT}(x)$ consists in solving a polynomial system. We proceed as follows. Since $\text{Tr}(x) \in \mathbf{Cond}(\mathscr{D}, \mathscr{C}_{\text{pub}})$ and, from Proposition 4, $\mathbf{Cond}(\mathscr{D}, \mathscr{C}_{\text{pub}}) = (\mathscr{D} \star \mathscr{C}_{\text{pub}}^\perp)^\perp$, then

$$G_{\mathscr{D} \star \mathscr{C}_{\text{pub}}^\perp} \cdot \text{Tr}(x)^\top = 0,$$

where $G_{\mathscr{D} \star \mathscr{C}_{\text{pub}}^\perp}$ denotes a generator matrix of $\mathscr{D} \star \mathscr{C}_{\text{pub}}^\perp$. The above identity holds true when replacing $\text{Tr}(x)$ by $\text{Tr}(\beta x)$ for any $\beta \in \mathbb{F}_{q^2}$. Hence,

$$G_{\mathscr{D} \star \mathscr{C}_{\text{pub}}^\perp} \cdot x^\top = 0. \tag{9}$$

The above identity provides the system we wish to solve. We have two type of unknowns: the code $\mathscr{D}$ and the vector x. Set $c \stackrel{\text{def}}{=} \frac{2q}{|\mathcal{G}|}$ the codimension of $\mathscr{D}$

in $(\mathscr{C}_{\mathrm{pub}})^{\mathcal{G}}$. For $\mathscr{D}$, let us introduce $(k_0 - c)k_0$ formal variables $U_{11}, \ldots, U_{1,c}$, $\ldots, U_{k_0-c,1}, \ldots, U_{k_0-c,c}$ and set

$$
\boldsymbol{U} \stackrel{\text{def}}{=} \begin{pmatrix} U_{11} & \cdots & U_{1,c} \\ \vdots & & \vdots \\ U_{k_0-c,1} & \cdots & U_{k_0-c,c} \end{pmatrix} \qquad \text{and} \qquad \boldsymbol{G}(U_{ij}) \stackrel{\text{def}}{=} \left(\boldsymbol{I}_{k_0-c} \mid \boldsymbol{U} \right) \cdot \boldsymbol{G}^{\mathrm{inv}},
$$

where $\boldsymbol{I}_{k_0-c}$ denotes the $(k_0 - c) \times (k_0 - c)$ identity matrix and $\boldsymbol{G}^{\mathrm{inv}}$ denotes a $k_0 \times n_0$ generator matrix of $(\mathscr{C}_{\mathrm{pub}})^{\mathcal{G}}$. It is probable that $\mathscr{D}$ has a generator matrix of the form $\boldsymbol{G}(u_{ij})$ for some special values $u_{11}, \ldots, u_{k_0-c,c} \in \mathbb{F}_q$. The case where $\mathscr{D}$ has no generator matrix of this form is rare and can be addressed by choosing another generator matrix for $(\mathscr{C}_{\mathrm{pub}})^{\mathcal{G}}$.

Now, let $\boldsymbol{H}$ be a parity-check matrix of $\mathscr{C}_{\mathrm{pub}}$. A generator matrix of $\mathscr{D} \star \mathscr{C}_{\mathrm{pub}}^{\perp}$ can be obtained by constructing a matrix whose rows list all the possible Schur products of one row of a generator matrix of $\mathscr{D}$ by one row of a parity-check matrix of $\mathscr{C}_{\mathrm{pub}}$. Therefore, let $\boldsymbol{R}(U_{ij})$ be a matrix with entries in $\mathbb{F}_q[U_{1,1}, \ldots, U_{k_0-c,c}]$ whose rows list all the possible Schur products of one row of $\boldsymbol{G}(U_{i,j})$ and one row of $\boldsymbol{H}$. Hence, there is a specialisation $u_{11}, \ldots, u_{k_0-c,c} \in \mathbb{F}_q$ of the variables U_{ij} such that $\boldsymbol{R}(u_{ij})$ is a generator matrix of $\mathscr{D} \star \mathscr{C}_{\mathrm{pub}}^{\perp}$.

The second set of variables $X_1, \ldots, X_n$ corresponds to the entries of $\boldsymbol{x}$. Using (9), the polynomial system we have to solve is nothing but

$$
\boldsymbol{R}(U_{ij}) \cdot \begin{pmatrix} X_1 \\ \vdots \\ X_n \end{pmatrix} = 0. \tag{10}
$$

Reducing the Number of Variables. Actually, it is possible to reduce the number of variables using three different tricks.

1. Since the code is QD, the vector $\boldsymbol{x}$ is a union of orbits under the action of the additive group $\mathcal{G}$. Therefore, one can introduce formal variables $A_1, \ldots, A_\gamma$ corresponding to the generators of $\mathcal{G}$. Then, one can replace $(X_1, \ldots, X_n)$ by

$$
(T_1, \ T_1 + A_1, \ \ldots, \ T_1 + A_1 + \cdots + A_\gamma, \ T_2, T_2 + A_1, \ \ldots). \tag{11}
$$

   for some variables $T_1, \ldots, T_{n_0}$.
2. Without loss of generality and because of the 2-transitive action of the affine group on $\mathbb{F}_{q^2}$, one can suppose that the first entries of $\boldsymbol{x}$ are 0 and 1 respectively (see for instance [12, Appendix A]). Therefore, in (11), one can replace T_1 by 0 and A_1 by 1.
3. Similarly to the approach of Sect. 6.4, one can shorten the codes so that $\mathscr{D}$ has only dimension 2, which reduces the number of variables U_{ij} to $2c$ and also reduces the length of the support we seek and hence reduces the number of the variables T_i.

On the Structure of the Polynomial System. The polynomial equations have all the following features:

- Any equation is the sum of an affine and a bilinear form;
- Any degree 2 monomial is either of the form $U_{ij}A_k$ or of the form $U_{ij}T_k$.

Table 4 lists for the different proposals the number of variables of type U, A and T of the system when we use the previously described shortening trick.

Table 4. Number of variables of type U, A and T of the system

Proposal	Number of U_{ij}'s	Number of A_i's	Number of T_i's
DAGS_1	8	3	31
DAGS_3	8	4	27
DAGS_5	4	5	25

6.6   Finishing the Attack

When the previous step of the attack is over, then, if we used the first approach based on a brute force search of $\mathscr{D}$, we know at least $\mathscr{NT}(\boldsymbol{x})$ or $\mathscr{NT}(\boldsymbol{x}_{\mathcal{I}})$ for some set $\mathcal{I}$ of positions. If we used the second approach, then $\boldsymbol{x}$ is already computed, or at least $\boldsymbol{x}_{\mathcal{I}}$ for some set of indexes $\mathcal{I}$. Thus, there remains to be able to

(1) recover $\boldsymbol{x}$ from $\mathscr{NT}(\boldsymbol{x})$ or $\boldsymbol{x}_{\mathcal{I}}$ from $\mathscr{NT}(\boldsymbol{x}_{\mathcal{I}})$;
(2) recover $\boldsymbol{y}$ from $\boldsymbol{x}$ or $\boldsymbol{y}_{\mathcal{I}}$ from $\boldsymbol{x}_{\mathcal{I}}$;
(3) recover $\boldsymbol{x}, \boldsymbol{y}$ from $\boldsymbol{x}_{\mathcal{I}}, \boldsymbol{y}_{\mathcal{I}}$.

Recovering $\boldsymbol{x}$ from $\mathscr{NT}(\boldsymbol{x})$. The code $\mathscr{NT}(\boldsymbol{x})$ has dimension 4 over $\mathbb{F}_q$ and is spanned by $\mathbf{1}, \mathrm{Tr}(\boldsymbol{x}), \mathrm{Tr}(\alpha\boldsymbol{x}), \mathrm{N}(\boldsymbol{x})$. It is not difficult to prove that

$$\mathscr{NT}(\boldsymbol{x}) \otimes \mathbb{F}_{q^2} = \langle \mathbf{1}, \boldsymbol{x}, \boldsymbol{x}^{\star q}, \boldsymbol{x}^{\star(q+1)} \rangle,$$

where $\mathscr{NT}(\boldsymbol{x}) \otimes \mathbb{F}_{q^2}$ denotes the $\mathbb{F}_{q^2}$-linear code contained in $\mathbb{F}_{q^2}^n$ and spanned over $\mathbb{F}_{q^2}$ by the elements of $\mathscr{NT}(\boldsymbol{x})$.

Because of the 2-transitivity of the affine group on $\mathbb{F}_{q^2}$, without loss of generality, one can suppose that the first entry of $\boldsymbol{x}$ is 0 and the second one is 1 (see for instance [12, Appendix A]). Therefore, after shortening $\mathscr{NT}(\boldsymbol{x}) \otimes \mathbb{F}_{q^2}$ we get a code that we call $\mathscr{S}$, which is of the form

$$\mathscr{S} \overset{\text{def}}{=} S_{\{1\}}\left(\mathscr{NT}(\boldsymbol{x}) \otimes \mathbb{F}_{q^2}\right) = \langle \boldsymbol{x}, \boldsymbol{x}^{\star q}, \boldsymbol{x}^{\star(q+1)} \rangle_{\mathbb{F}_{q^2}}.$$

Next, a simple calculation shows that

$$\mathscr{S} \cap \mathscr{S}^{\star 2} = \langle \boldsymbol{x}^{\star(q+1)} \rangle.$$

Since, the second entry of $\boldsymbol{x}$ has been set to 1, we can deduce the value of $\boldsymbol{x}^{\star(q+1)}$.

Remark 8. Actually, both $\mathscr{S}$ and $\mathscr{NT}(\boldsymbol{x})$ have a basis defined over $\mathbb{F}_q$, therefore, to get $\langle \boldsymbol{x}^{\star(q+1)} \rangle_{\mathbb{F}_q}$ it is sufficient to perform any computation on codes defined over $\mathbb{F}_q$.

Now, finding $\boldsymbol{x}$ is easy: enumerate the affine subspace of $\mathscr{NT}(\boldsymbol{x}) \otimes \mathbb{F}_{q^2}$ of vectors whose first entry is 0 and second entry is 1 (or equivalently, the affine subspace of vectors of $\mathscr{S}$ whose first entry equals 1). For any such vector $\boldsymbol{c}$, compute $\boldsymbol{c}^{\star(q+1)}$. If $\boldsymbol{c}^{\star(q+1)} = \boldsymbol{x}^{\star(q+1)}$, then $\boldsymbol{c}$ equals either $\boldsymbol{x}$ or $\boldsymbol{x}^{\star q}$. Since $\mathscr{A}_r(\boldsymbol{x}, \boldsymbol{y}) = \mathscr{A}_r(\boldsymbol{x}^{\star q}, \boldsymbol{y}^{\star q})$ (see for instance [12, Lemma 39]), taking $\boldsymbol{x}$ or $\boldsymbol{x}^{\star q}$ has no importance. Thus, without loss of generality, one can suppose $\boldsymbol{x}$ has been found.

Recovering $\boldsymbol{y}$ from $\boldsymbol{x}$. This is very classical calculation. The public code $\mathscr{C}_{\text{pub}}$ is alternant, and hence is well-known to have a parity-check matrix defined over $\mathbb{F}_{q^2}$ of the form

$$\boldsymbol{H}_{\text{pub}} = \begin{pmatrix} y_1 & \cdots & y_n \\ x_1 y_1 & \cdots & x_n y_n \\ \vdots & & \vdots \\ x_1^{r-1} y_1 & \cdots & x_n^{r-1} y_n \end{pmatrix}. \tag{12}$$

Denote by $\boldsymbol{G}_{\text{pub}}$ a generator matrix of $\mathscr{C}_{\text{pub}}$. Then, since the x_i's are known, then the $y_i's$ can be computed by solving the linear system

$$\boldsymbol{H}_{\text{pub}} \cdot \boldsymbol{G}_{\text{pub}}^{\top} = 0.$$

Recovering $\boldsymbol{x}, \boldsymbol{y}$ from $\boldsymbol{x}_{\mathcal{I}}, \boldsymbol{y}_{\mathcal{I}}$. After a suitable reordering of the indexes, one can suppose that $\mathcal{I} = \{s, s+1, \ldots, n\}$. Hence, the entries $x_1, \ldots, x_{s-1}$ of $\boldsymbol{x}$ and $y_1, \ldots, y_{s-1}$ are known. Set $\mathcal{I}' \overset{\text{def}}{=} \mathcal{I} \setminus \{s\}$. Thus, let $\boldsymbol{G}(\mathcal{I}')$ be a generator matrix of $\mathscr{A}_r(\boldsymbol{x}_{\mathcal{I}'}, \boldsymbol{y}_{\mathcal{I}'})$, which is nothing by $\mathcal{S}_{\mathcal{I}'}(\mathscr{C}_{\text{pub}})$. Using (12), we have

$$\begin{pmatrix} y_1 & \cdots & y_s \\ x_1 y_1 & \cdots & x_s y_s \\ \vdots & & \vdots \\ x_1^{r-1} y_1 & \cdots & x_s^{r-1} y_s \end{pmatrix} \cdot \boldsymbol{G}(\mathcal{I}') = 0.$$

In the above identity, all the $x_i's$ and $y_i's$ are known but x_s, y_s. The entry y_s can be found by solving the linear system

$$(y_1 \cdots y_s) \cdot \boldsymbol{G}(\mathcal{I}') = 0.$$

Then, x_s can be deduced by solving the linear system

$$(x_1 y_1 \cdots x_s y_s) \cdot \boldsymbol{G}(\mathcal{I}') = 0.$$

By this manner, we can iteratively recover the entries $x_{s+1}, \ldots, x_n$ and $y_{s+1}, \ldots, y_n$. The only constraint is that $\mathcal{I}$ should be small enough so that $\mathcal{S}_{\mathcal{I}}(\mathscr{C}_{\text{pub}})$ is nonzero. But this always holds true for the choices of $\mathcal{I}$ we made in the previous sections.

6.7 Comparison with a Previous Attack

First, let us recall the attack on Wild Goppa codes over quadratic extensions [12]. This attack concerns some subclass of alternant codes called *wild Goppa codes*. For such codes a distinguisher exists which permits to compute a filtration of the public code. Hence, after some computations, we obtain the subcode $\mathscr{A}_{r+q+1}(\boldsymbol{x}, \boldsymbol{y})$ of the public code $\mathscr{A}_r(\boldsymbol{x}, \boldsymbol{y})$. Then, according to Heuristic 1, the computation of a conductor permits to get the code $\mathscr{N}\mathscr{T}(\boldsymbol{x})$. As soon as $\mathscr{N}\mathscr{T}(\boldsymbol{x})$ is known, the recovery of the secret is easy. Note that, the use of the techniques of Sect. 6.6 can significantly simplify the end of the attack of [12] which was rather technical.

We emphasise that, out of the calculation of $\mathscr{N}\mathscr{T}(\boldsymbol{x})$ by computing a conductor which appears in our attack so that in [12], the two attacks remain very different. Indeed, the way one gets a subcode whose conductor into the public code provides $\mathscr{N}\mathscr{T}(\boldsymbol{x})$ is based in [12] on a distinguisher which does not work for general alternant codes which are not Goppa codes. In addition, in the present attack, the use of the permutation group is crucial, while it was useless in [12].

7 Complexity of the First Version of the Attack

As explained earlier, we have not been able to provide a complexity analysis of the approach based on polynomial system solving. In particular because the Macaulay matrix in degree 2 of the system turned out to have a surprisingly low rank, showing that this polynomial system was far from being generic. Consequently, we limit our analysis to the first approach based on performing a brute force search on the subcode $\mathscr{D}$.

Since we look for approximate work factors, we will discuss an upper bound on the complexity and not only a big O.

7.1 Complexity of Calculation of Schur Products

A Schur product $\mathscr{A} \star \mathscr{B}$ of two codes $\mathscr{A}, \mathscr{B}$ of length n and respective dimensions k_a, k_b is computed as follows.

1. Take bases $\boldsymbol{a}_1, \ldots, \boldsymbol{a}_{k_a}$ and $\boldsymbol{b}_1, \ldots, \boldsymbol{b}_{k_b}$ of $\mathscr{A}$ and $\mathscr{B}$ respectively and construct a matrix $\boldsymbol{M}$ whose rows are all the possible products $\boldsymbol{a}_i \star \boldsymbol{b}_j$, for $1 \leqslant i \leqslant k_a$ and $1 \leqslant j \leqslant k_b$. This matrix has $k_a k_b$ rows and n columns.
2. Perform Gaussian elimination to get a reduced echelon form of $\boldsymbol{M}$.

The cost of the computation of a reduced echelon form of a $s \times n$ matrix is $ns \min(n, s)$ operations in the base field. The cost of the computation of the matrix $\boldsymbol{M}$ is the cost of $k_a k_b$ Schur products of vectors, i.e. $nk_a k_b$ operations in the base field. This leads to an overall calculation of the Schur product equal to

$$nk_a k_b + nk_a k_b \min(n, k_a k_b)$$

operations in the base field. When $k_a k_b \geqslant n$, the cost of the Schur product can be reduced using a probabilistic shortcut described in [10]. It consists in computing an $n \times n$ submatrix of $\boldsymbol{M}$ by choosing some random subset of products $\boldsymbol{a}_i \star \boldsymbol{b}_j$. This permits to reduce the cost of computing a generator matrix in row echelon form of $\mathscr{A} \star \mathscr{B}$ to $2n^3$ operations in the base field.

7.2   Cost of a Single Iteration of the Brute Force Search

Computing the conductor $\mathbf{Cond}(\mathscr{X}, \mathscr{C}_{\mathrm{pub}})$ consists in computing the code $(\mathscr{X} \star \mathscr{C}_{\mathrm{pub}}^{\perp})^{\perp}$. Since our attack consists in computing such conductors for various $\mathscr{X}$'s, one can compute a generator matrix of $\mathscr{C}_{\mathrm{pub}}^{\perp}$ once for good. Hence, one can suppose a generator matrix for $\mathscr{C}_{\mathrm{pub}}^{\perp}$ is known. Then, according to Sect. 7.1, the calculation of a generator matrix of $\mathscr{X} \star \mathscr{C}_{\mathrm{pub}}^{\perp}$ costs at most $2n^3$ operations in $\mathbb{F}_q$.

7.3   Complexity of finding $\mathscr{D}$ and $\mathscr{N}\mathscr{T}(x)$

According to Sect. 6.4, the average number of iterations of the brute force search is $q^{2\mathrm{Codim}\mathscr{D}}$, that is $q^{\frac{4q}{|\mathscr{G}|}}$. Thus, we get an overall cost of the first step bounded above by

$$2n^3 q^{\frac{4q}{|\mathscr{G}|}} \text{ operations in } \mathbb{F}_q.$$

Since, $n = \Theta(q^2)$, we get a complexity in $O(n^{3+\frac{2q}{|\mathscr{G}|}})$ operations in $\mathbb{F}_q$ for the computation of $\mathscr{N}\mathscr{T}(\boldsymbol{x})$.

7.4   Complexity of deducing x, y from $\mathscr{N}\mathscr{T}(x)$

A simple analysis shows that the final part of the attack is negligible compared to the previous step. Indeed,

- the computation of $\mathscr{N}\mathscr{T}(\boldsymbol{x})^{\star 2}$ costs $O(n^2)$ operations in $\mathbb{F}_q$ (because of Remark 8, one can perform these computations over $\mathbb{F}_q$) since the code has dimension 4;
- the computation of $\mathscr{N}\mathscr{T}(\boldsymbol{x})^{\star 2} \cap \mathscr{N}\mathscr{T}(\boldsymbol{x})$ boils down to linear algebra and costs $O(n^3)$ operations in $\mathbb{F}_q$;
- The enumeration of the subset of $\mathscr{N}\mathscr{T}(\boldsymbol{x}) \otimes \mathbb{F}_{q^2}$ of elements whose first entry is 0 an second one is 1 and computation of their norm costs $O(q^4 n) = O(n^3)$ operations in $\mathbb{F}_{q^2}$. Indeed the affine subspace of $\mathscr{N}\mathscr{T}(\boldsymbol{x}) \otimes \mathbb{F}_{q^2}$ which is enumerated has dimension 2 over $\mathbb{F}_{q^2}$ and hence has q^4 elements, while the computation of the component wise norm of a vector costs $O(n)$ operations assuming that the Frobenius $z \mapsto z^q$ can be computed in constant time in $\mathbb{F}_{q^2}$.
- The recovery of $\boldsymbol{y}$ from $\boldsymbol{x}$ boils down to linear algebra and hence can also be done in $O(n^3)$ operations in $\mathbb{F}_{q^2}$. If we have to recover $\boldsymbol{x}, \boldsymbol{y}$ from $\boldsymbol{x}_{\mathcal{I}}, \boldsymbol{y}_{\mathcal{I}}$, it can be done iteratively by solving a system of a constant number of equations, hence the cost of one iteration is in $O(n^2)$ operations in $\mathbb{F}_{q^2}$.

Thus, the overall cost remains in $O(n^3)$ operations in $\mathbb{F}_{q^2}$.

7.5   Overall Complexity

As a conclusion, the attack has an approximate work factor of

$$2n^3 q^{\frac{4q}{|\mathcal{G}|}} \text{ operations in } \mathbb{F}_q. \tag{13}$$

7.6   Approximate Work Factors of the First Variant Of the Attack on DAGS Parameters

We assume that operations in $\mathbb{F}_q$ can be done in constant time. Indeed, the base fields of the public keys of DAGS proposal are $\mathbb{F}_{32}$ and $\mathbb{F}_{64}$. For such a field, it is reasonable to store a multiplication and inversion table.

Therefore, we list in Table 5 some approximate work factors for DAGS according to (13). The second column recalls the security levels claimed in [3] for the best possible attack. The last column gives the approximate work factors for the first variant of our attack.

Table 5. Work factors of the first variant of the attack

Name	Claimed security level	Work factor of our attack
DAGS_1	128 bits	$\approx 2^{70}$
DAGS_3	192 bits	$\approx 2^{80}$
DAGS_5	256 bits	$\approx 2^{58}$

8   Implementation

Tests have been done using Magma [8] on an Intel® Xeon 2.27 GHz.

Since the first variant of the attack had too significant costs to be tested on our machines, we tested it on the toy parameters DAGS_0. We performed 20 tests, which succeeded in an average time of 2 h.

On the other hand, we tested the second variant based on solving a polynomial system on DAGS_1, _3 and _5. We have not been able to break DAGS_3 keys using this variant of the attack, on the other hand about 100 tests have been performed for DAGS_1 and DAGS_5. The average running times are listed in Table 6.

Table 6. Average times for the second variant of the attack.

Name	Claimed security level	Average time
DAGS_1	128 bits	19 mn
DAGS_5	256 bits	< 1 mn

Acknowledgements. The authors are supported by French *Agence nationale de la* recherche grants ANR-15-CE39-0013-01 *Manta* and ANR-17-CE39-0007 *CBCrypt*. Computer aided calculations have been performed using software MAGMA [8]. The authors express their deep gratitude to Jean-Pierre Tillich and Julien Lavauzelle for very helpful comments.

References

1. Baldi, M., Bianchi, M., Chiaraluce, F.: Security and complexity of the McEliece cryptosystem based on QC-LDPC codes. IET Inf. Secur. **7**(3), 212–220 (2013)
2. Baldi, M., Bianchi, M., Chiaraluce, F., Rosenthal, J., Schipani, D.: Enhanced public key security for the McEliece cryptosystem. J. Cryptol. **29**(1), 1–27 (2016)
3. Banegas, G., et al.: DAGS : key encapsulation for dyadic GS codes, November 2017. First round submission to the NIST post-quantum cryptography call. https://csrc.nist.gov/CSRC/media/Projects/Post-Quantum-Cryptography/documents/round-1/submissions/DAGS.zip
4. Barelli, E.: On the security of some compact keys for McEliece scheme. In: WCC Workshop on Coding and Cryptography, September 2017. http://wcc2017.suai.ru/Proceedings_WCC2017.zip
5. Berger, T.P., Cayrel, P.-L., Gaborit, P., Otmani, A.: Reducing key length of the McEliece cryptosystem. In: Preneel, B. (ed.) AFRICACRYPT 2009. LNCS, vol. 5580, pp. 77–97. Springer, Heidelberg (2009). https://doi.org/10.1007/978-3-642-02384-2_6
6. Berger, T.P., Loidreau, P.: How to mask the structure of codes for a cryptographic use. Des. Codes Cryptogr. **35**(1), 63–79 (2005)
7. Berlekamp, E., McEliece, R., van Tilborg, H.: On the inherent intractability of certain coding problems. IEEE Trans. Inf. Theory **24**(3), 384–386 (1978)
8. Bosma, W., Cannon, J., Playoust, C.: The Magma algebra system I: the user language. J. Symbolic Comput. **24**(3/4), 235–265 (1997)
9. Couvreur, A., Gaborit, P., Gauthier-Umaña, V., Otmani, A., Tillich, J.P.: Distinguisher-based attacks on public-key cryptosystems using Reed-Solomon codes. Des. Codes Cryptogr. **73**(2), 641–666 (2014). https://doi.org/10.1007/s10623-014-9967-z
10. Couvreur, A., Márquez-Corbella, I., Pellikaan, R.: Cryptanalysis of McEliece cryptosystem based on algebraic geometry codes and their subcodes. IEEE Trans. Inf. Theory **63**(8), 5404–5418 (2017)
11. Couvreur, A., Otmani, A., Tillich, J.P.: Polynomial time attack on wild McEliece over quadratic extensions. In: Nguyen, P.Q., Oswald, E. (eds.) EUROCRYPT 2014. LNCS, vol. 8441, pp. 17–39. Springer, Heidelberg (2014). https://doi.org/10.1007/978-3-642-55220-5_2
12. Couvreur, A., Otmani, A., Tillich, J.P.: Polynomial time attack on wild McEliece over quadratic extensions. IEEE Trans. Inf. Theory **63**(1), 404–427 (2017). https://doi.org/10.1109/TIT.2016.2574841
13. Couvreur, A., Otmani, A., Tillich, J.-P., Gauthier–Umaña, V.: A polynomial-time attack on the BBCRS scheme. In: Katz, J. (ed.) PKC 2015. LNCS, vol. 9020, pp. 175–193. Springer, Heidelberg (2015). https://doi.org/10.1007/978-3-662-46447-2_8
14. Delsarte, P.: On subfield subcodes of modified Reed-Solomon codes. IEEE Trans. Inf. Theory **21**(5), 575–576 (1975)

15. Faugère, J.C., Otmani, A., Perret, L., de Portzamparc, F., Tillich, J.P.: Folding alternant and Goppa Codes with non-trivial automorphism groups. IEEE Trans. Inform. Theory **62**(1), 184–198 (2016). https://doi.org/10.1109/TIT.2015.2493539
16. Faugère, J.-C., Otmani, A., Perret, L., Tillich, J.-P.: Algebraic cryptanalysis of McEliece variants with compact keys. In: Gilbert, H. (ed.) EUROCRYPT 2010. LNCS, vol. 6110, pp. 279–298. Springer, Heidelberg (2010). https://doi.org/10.1007/978-3-642-13190-5_14
17. Faugère, J.-C., Perret, L., de Portzamparc, F.: Algebraic attack against variants of McEliece with goppa polynomial of a special form. In: Sarkar, P., Iwata, T. (eds.) ASIACRYPT 2014. LNCS, vol. 8873, pp. 21–41. Springer, Heidelberg (2014). https://doi.org/10.1007/978-3-662-45611-8_2
18. Gaborit, P.: Shorter keys for code based cryptography. In: Proceedings of the 2005 International Workshop on Coding and Cryptography (WCC 2005), Bergen, Norway, pp. 81–91, March 2005
19. Goss, D.: Basic Structures of Function Field arithmetic, Ergebnisse der Mathematik und ihrer Grenzgebiete (3) [Results in Mathematics and Related Areas (3)], vol. 35. Springer, Berlin (1996)
20. MacWilliams, F.J., Sloane, N.J.A.: The Theory of Error-Correcting Codes, 5th edn. North-Holland, Amsterdam (1986)
21. McEliece, R.J.: A Public-Key System Based on Algebraic Coding Theory, pp. 114–116. Jet Propulsion Lab (1978), dSN Progress Report 44
22. Misoczki, R., Barreto, P.: Compact McEliece keys from Goppa codes. In: Selected Areas in Cryptography, Calgary, Canada (2009)
23. Misoczki, R., Tillich, J.P., Sendrier, N., Barreto, P.S.L.M.: MDPC-McEliece: new McEliece variants from moderate density parity-check codes. In: Proceedings of the IEEE International Symposium on Information Theory - ISIT, pp. 2069–2073 (2013)
24. Niederreiter, H.: Knapsack-type cryptosystems and algebraic coding theory. Probl. Control. Inf. Theory **15**(2), 159–166 (1986)
25. Otmani, A., Tillich, J.P., Dallot, L.: Cryptanalysis of McEliece cryptosystem based on quasi-cyclic LDPC codes. In: Proceedings of First International Conference on Symbolic Computation and Cryptography, pp. 69–81. LMIB Beihang University, Beijing, April 2008
26. Persichetti, E.: Compact McEliece keys based on quasi-dyadic Srivastava codes. J. Math. Cryptol. **6**(2), 149–169 (2012)
27. de Portzamparc, F.U.: Algebraic and physical security in code-based cryptography. (Sécurités algébrique et physique en cryptographie fondée sur les codes correcteurs d'erreurs). Ph.D. thesis, Pierre and Marie Curie University, Paris, France (2015)
28. Sidelnikov, V.M., Shestakov, S.: On the insecurity of cryptosystems based on generalized Reed-Solomon codes. Discrete Math. Appl. **1**(4), 439–444 (1992)
29. Wang, Y.: Quantum resistant random linear code based public key encryption scheme RLCE. In: Proceedings of the IEEE International Symposium on Information Theory - ISIT 2016, pp. 2519–2523. IEEE, Barcelona (2016). https://doi.org/10.1109/ISIT.2016.7541753
30. Wieschebrink, C.: Two NP-complete problems in coding theory with an application in code based cryptography. In: Proceedings of the IEEE International Symposium on Information Theory - ISIT, pp. 1733–1737 (2006)
31. Wieschebrink, C.: Cryptanalysis of the Niederreiter public key scheme based on GRS subcodes. In: Sendrier, N. (ed.) PQCrypto 2010. LNCS, vol. 6061, pp. 61–72. Springer, Heidelberg (2010). https://doi.org/10.1007/978-3-642-12929-2_5

Encrypted Storage

Pattern Matching on Encrypted Streams

Nicolas Desmoulins[1], Pierre-Alain Fouque[2], Cristina Onete[3],
and Olivier Sanders[4(✉)]

[1] Orange Labs, Applied Crypto Group, Caen, France
`nicolas.desmoulins@orange.com`
[2] Université de Rennes 1 & Institut Universitaire de France, Rennes, France
[3] Université de Limoges, CNRS UMR 7252, Limoges, France
[4] Orange Labs, Applied Crypto Group, Cesson-Sévigné, France
`olivier.sanders@orange.com`

Abstract. Pattern matching is essential in applications such as deep-packet inspection (DPI), searching on genomic data, or analyzing medical data. A simple task to do on plaintext data, pattern matching is much harder to do when the privacy of the data must be preserved. Existent solutions involve searchable encryption mechanisms with at least one of these three drawbacks: requiring an exhaustive (and static) list of keywords to be prepared before the data is encrypted (like in symmetric searchable encryption); requiring *tokenization, i.e.,* breaking up the data to search into substrings and encrypting them separately (*e.g.,* like BlindBox); relying on symmetric-key cryptography, thus implying a token-regeneration step for each encrypted-data source (*e.g.,* user). Such approaches are ill-suited for pattern-matching with evolving patterns (*e.g.,* updating virus signatures), variable searchword lengths, or when a single entity must filter ciphertexts from multiple parties.

In this work, we introduce Searchable Encryption with Shiftable Trapdoors (SEST): a new primitive that allows for pattern matching with universal tokens (usable by all entities), in which keywords of arbitrary lengths can be matched to arbitrary ciphertexts. Our solution uses public-key encryption and bilinear pairings.

In addition, very minor modifications to our solution enable it to take into account regular expressions, such as fully- or partly-unknown characters in a keyword (wildcards and interval/subset searches). Our trapdoor size is at most linear in the keyword length (and independent of the plaintext size), and we prove that the leakage to the searcher is only the trivial one: since the searcher learns whether the pattern occurs and where, it can distinguish based on different search results of a single trapdoor on two different plaintexts.

To better show the usability of our scheme, we implemented it to run DPI on all the SNORT rules. We show that even for very large plaintexts, our encryption algorithm scales well. The pattern-matching algorithm is slower, but extremely parallelizable, and it can thus be run even on very large data. Although our proofs use a (marginally) interactive assumption, we argue that this is a relatively small price to pay for the flexibility and privacy that we are able to attain.

© International Association for Cryptologic Research 2018
T. Peyrin and S. Galbraith (Eds.): ASIACRYPT 2018, LNCS 11272, pp. 121–148, 2018.
https://doi.org/10.1007/978-3-030-03326-2_5

1 Introduction

Learning whether a given pattern occurs in a larger input string (and where exactly that happens) has many applications, such as when searching on genomic data, in deep-packet inspection (DPI), or when delegating searches in databases. In such cases, the entity performing the search, usually called the *gateway*, is only semi-trusted by the owner of the input data. Indeed, in all the three scenarios above, it is of paramount importance to preserve the *privacy* of the input data[1].

Consider the case of a middlebox, such as a virus scan or a firewall. A user who may trust the middlebox to scan its data for viruses might not, in fact, be comfortable revealing the full contents of its data to that middlebox. Similarly, a person might trust a laboratory to check whether their genome contains a particular substring (indicating, *e.g.*, a genetic predisposition to a disease); however, the laboratory should not, in this way, come into possession of that person's full genome. Such concerns have been exacerbated lately by threats of mass-surveillance, following the revelations of Edward Snowden. As a consequence, data *encryption* is slowly becoming an *a priori* pre-requisite for pattern matching.

In cryptography, pattern matching on encrypted data is closely related to Searchable Encryption, either Symmetric [16–18,32] or Public-Key [9]. Many Searchable Encryption solutions, however, only allow to search for pre-chosen keywords, which are hard-coded in the encrypted input. Searching for a new keyword – not indicated *a priori* – in that same (already encrypted) data would yield a false negative, even if that keyword is, in fact contained in the input data. Correctly matching the new pattern to the data requires that the latter be re-encrypted. Therefore this solution is ill-suited to more dynamic environments, like DPI. We provide a full comparison with related literature, including searchable encryption, in Sect. 1.2.

Pattern matching with non-static patterns can be achieved through symmetric-key techniques and so-called *tokenization* [31]. In this approach, a sliding-window technique is used to encode keywords of a given, fixed length, which can then be matched by the searcher. This allows searches to be performed for arbitrarily-chosen keywords; however, a disadvantage is that each instantiation requires a new generation of tokens. Moreover, this only works for a fixed keyword length and different ciphertexts are required to handle different pattern sizes. This is less than ideal for many use-cases such as DPI, since for instance SNORT rules [1] include patterns of many different lengths. In this paper, our goal is to improve on this solution, specifically by allowing to search on encrypted data, with patterns that are non-static (flexible), of variable length, and universal (no need to re-tokenize). In particular, we achieve secure pattern-matching on encrypted data with *universal tokens*.

---

[1] By contrast, in many cases, the patterns themselves may be publicly known.

1.1 Our Contributions

We opt for a solution in a public-key setting (which immediately achieves universality for our patterns). The gateway will be able to search for *keywords* on encrypted data using *trapdoors* that are unforgeable. More specifically, our construction can support pattern matching for keywords that can be adaptively chosen and which can have variable lengths. Moreover, the size of the trapdoors corresponding to those keywords does not depend on the length of the input data (our trapdoors are short, even when we are searching in very large input data). We support regular expressions, such as the presence of wildcards or matching encrypted input to general data-subsets. Thus, our solution is well suited to deep packet inspection or delegated searches on medical data.

Intuitively, in our construction we *project* each coordinate of the plaintext S (and then of the keyword W) on a geometric basis consisting of some values z^i, for $i = 0, \dots, |S| - 1$. We prevent malleability of trapdoors by embedding the exact order of the bits of W into a polynomial, which cannot be forged without the secret key. A fundamental part of the searching algorithm that we propose is the way in which the middlebox will be able to *shift* from one part of the ciphertext to another, when searching for a match with W. Thus, our scheme can be viewed as an anonymous predicate encryption scheme where one could derive the secret keys for $(*, w_1, \dots, w_\ell, *, \dots, *), \dots, (*, \dots, *, w_1, \dots, w_\ell)$ from the secret key for $(w_1, \dots, w_\ell, *, \dots, *)$.

Such changes require the definition of a new primitive that we call Searchable Encryption with Shiftable Trapdoors (SEST). We provide a formal security model for the latter, which ensures that even a malicious gateway knowing trapdoors $\mathsf{td}_{W_1}, \dots, \mathsf{td}_{W_q}$ does not learn any information from an encrypted string S beyond the presence of the keyword W_k in S, for $k \in [1, q]$.

Our construction is – to our knowledge – the first SEST scheme, and thus can be taken as a proof-of-concept construction. We guarantee the desired properties by only using asymmetric prime order bilinear groups (*i.e.* a set of 3 groups $\mathbb{G}_1$, $\mathbb{G}_2$ and $\mathbb{G}_T$ along with an efficient bilinear map $e : \mathbb{G}_1 \times \mathbb{G}_2 \to \mathbb{G}_T$) for which very efficient implementations have been proposed (*e.g.* [7]). Encryption of plaintexts S only requires operations in the group $\mathbb{G}_1$, while detection of the keyword W is done by performing pairings. The former operation requires only the public key while the latter additionally needs the corresponding trapdoor; only the trapdoor-issuing algorithm requires the corresponding secret key.

We are able to allow for pattern-matching when some of the contents of the keywords are either fully-unknown, *i.e.*, wildcards, or partially-unknown, *i.e.*, in an interval. Searches for such regular expressions remain fully-compatible with our original solution. In the first case, the only difference is that when issuing the trapdoor, instead of fully randomizing it we choose special randomness – equal to 0 – for the "coefficients" of the polynomial that we project the wildcards or unknown subsets to. For the scenario of partially-known trapdoors, we require a more complex key-generation process since we use different values on which to (uniformly) project the unclear values to. These will be used in the trapdoor generation step, ensuring that if a partially-known input is used, that coefficient of the trapdoor will still "vanish".

In particular, our pattern-matching algorithm is very similar to that of Rabin-Karp and consequently, we can use it to solve similar problems. In addition to the previous use-cases, our technique can also be used to perform 2D pattern matching in images, or searching subtrees in rooted, labelled trees. However, note that due to the privacy-preserving goal of our work, we cannot benefit from many of the tricks used by Rabin-Karp, thus yielding a scheme with limited efficiency.

We also analyze how well our scheme performs when applied to DPI. We implemented our scheme to search for all the SNORT rules in input data of varying sizes. Even for large data, the encryption algorithm is very efficient. Moreover, while the testing (pattern matching) step scales less well with increasing input-data size, that particular step is highly parallelizable, and thus the running time can be much reduced.

Impact and Limitations. Our scheme allows for a flexible searchable encryption mechanism, in which encrypters do not have to embed a list of possible keywords into their ciphertexts. Moreover, we also provide a great deal of flexibility with respect to searching for keywords of arbitrary lengths. In this sense, our technique allows for searchable encryption with *universal tokens*, which can be used in deep-packet inspection, applications on genomic and medical data, or matching subtrees in labelled trees.

One limitation of our scheme is the size of our public keys. We require a public key of size linear in the size of the plaintext to be encrypted (which is potentially very large). This is mostly due to the need to shift the ciphertext each time in order to detect the presence of the keyword. We also require a large ciphertext, consisting of a number of elements that is again linear in the size of the plaintext; however, the same inefficiency is inherent also to solutions such as BlindBox [31], in which we must encrypt many "windows" of the data, of same size. Finally, the search of a keyword of size ℓ in a plaintext of size n requires at least $2(n - \ell + 1)$ pairing computations.

Furthermore, we are only able to prove the security of our construction under an interactive assumption, unless we severely restrict the size n of the message space. Indeed, we need an assumption which offers enough flexibility to provide shiftable trapdoors for all possible keywords except the one that allow trivial distinction of the encrypted string. We modify the GDH assumption [8] in a minimal way, to allow the adversary to request the values on which the reduction will break this assumption. We could remove the need for this flexibility, by, for instance reducing the value of n so that the simulator could guess the strings targeted by the adversary but this strongly limits the applications of our construction.

We argue that despite this interactive assumption, the intrinsic value of our construction lies in its flexibility, namely in the fact that we are able to search for arbitrary keywords. This significantly improves existing solutions of, *e.g.*, detecting viruses on encrypted traffic over HTTPS [24,25,31].

Moreover, we emphasize that we achieve this high level of flexibility without using complex (and costly) cryptographic tools such as fully homomorphic encryption. We simply need pairings which have become quite standard in cryptography and which can be implemented very efficiently [7]. We therefore argue that our scheme, when compared to solutions providing the same features (see Sect. 1.3 for more details), offers a practical improvement over the state of the art.

1.2 Related Work

How Searchable Encryption Works. In searchable encryption (SE) [9,16–18,32], any party that is given a trapdoor td_W associated with a keyword W is able to search for that keyword within a given ciphertext. The ideal privacy guarantee required is that searching reveals nothing else on the underlying plaintext (other than the presence or absence of the keyword). Routing encrypted emails, querying encrypted database or running an antivirus on encrypted traffic are typical applications which require such a functionality.

In general, SE searches are usually performed by the middlebox on keywords that have been pre-chosen by the party encrypting the ciphertexts (*i.e.*, the encrypter). In particular, an encrypted string containing W can be detected by the middlebox knowing td_W only if the sender has selected W as a keyword and has encrypted it using the SE scheme. Such approaches are still suitable for some types of database searches (in which documents are already indexed by keywords), or in the case of emailing applications – for which natural keywords can be the sender's identity, the subject line, or flags such as "urgent". Unfortunately, in cases such as messaging applications, or just for common Internet browsing, the keywords are much harder to find, and can include expressions that are not sequences of words *per se*, but rather something of the kind "http://www.example.com/index.php?username=1".

Our solution allows for better flexibility in terms of searching for arbitrarily-chosen keywords, even after the plaintext has been encrypted and sent. In fact, it is not even necessary that the encrypter be the same person as the party which issues the trapdoors. This makes our solution much better suited to DPI scenarios, whereas SE is typically better suited to database searches.

Tokenization. The solution proposed in [31] to search keywords of length ℓ is to split the string $S = s_0 \dots s_{n-1}$ into $[s_0 \dots s_{\ell-1}], [s_1 \dots s_\ell], \dots, [s_{n-\ell} \dots s_{n-1}]$ and then to encrypt each of these substrings using a searchable encryption scheme (the substrings are thus the keywords associated with S). However, this solution has a drawback: it works well if all the searchable keywords $W_1, \dots, W_q$ have the same length but this is usually not the case. In the worst case, if all searchable keyword W_k are of different length ℓ_k, the sender will have, for each $k \in [1, q]$, to split S in substrings of size ℓ_k and encrypt them, which quickly becomes cumbersome. One solution could be to split the searchable keywords W_k into smaller keywords of the same length $\ell_{min} = min_k(\ell_k)$. For example, if $\ell_{min} = 3$ the searchable keyword "execute" could be split into "exe", "cut" and "ute" for which specific trapdoors would be issued. Unfortunately, this severely harms privacy since these smaller keywords will match many more strings S. Moreover, repeating this procedure for every keyword W_k will allow the gateway to receive trapdoors for a large fraction of the set of strings of length ℓ_{min} and so to recover large parts of S with significant probability.

We note that Canard *et al.* [14] recently proposed a public key variant of the Blindbox [31] approach which therefore suffers from the same limitations. Moreover, their performance corresponds to the "delimiter-based" version of their protocol that consists in splitting a string $s = s_0 \ldots s_{n-1}$ into t substrings $[s_0 \ldots s_{n_1-1}]$, $[s_{n_1} \ldots s_{n_2-1}]$, ..., $[s_{n_{t-1}} \ldots s_{n-1}]$ which are then independently encrypted using searchable encryption. While this dramatically reduces complexity, we stress that this only allows to detect patterns that perfectly match one of the substrings. In particular, a pattern cannot be detected if it straddles two substrings.

By contrast, our scheme addresses the main drawback of this tokenization technique: we allow for universal trapdoors of arbitrary length to be matched against the encrypted data, without false negatives or positives. This comes at a cost in performance; however, we show in our implementation that our scheme remains practical.

Generic Evaluation of Functions on Ciphertexts. Evaluation of functions over encrypted data is a major topic in cryptography, which has known very important results over the past decade. Generic solutions (*e.g.*, fully homomorphic encryption [22], functional encryption [3,4], etc.), supporting a wide class of functions, have been proposed; however, their very high complexity makes such solutions impractical. In practice, it is then better to use a scheme specifically designed for the function(s) that one wants to evaluate.

Several recent publications study secure substring search and text processing [5,21,23,26,28,29,33], specifically in two-party settings. Some of these papers provide applications to genomic data, specifically matching substrings of DNA to encrypted genomes. This was done by using secure multi-party computation or fully-homomorphic encryption. However, the former solution requires interaction between the searcher and the encrypter, whereas the use of FHE induces a relatively high complexity. Of particular interest here is the approach by Lauter et al. [28], which presents an application to genomic data. The authors here go much further than just matching patterns with some regular expressions, however, they require fully-homomorphic encryption (FHE) for their applications. We leave it as future work to investigate in how far we can modify our technique with universal tokens in order to provide some support to the algorithms presented by Lauter et al. for genomic matching.

At first sight, anonymous predicate encryption (*e.g.* [27]) or hidden vector encryption [11] provide an elegant solution to the problem of searching on encrypted streams. Indeed, the sender could use one of these schemes to produce a ciphertext for some attributes $s_0, \ldots, s_{n-1}$ which together make up a word S, while the middlebox, knowing the suitable secret keys, could detect whether S contains a substring W. The encryption process would then not depend on the searchable keywords and the anonymity property of these schemes would ensure that the ciphertext does not leak more information on S.

However, another issue arises with this solution. Indeed, $W = w_1 \ldots w_\ell$ can be contained at any position in S. Therefore, the gateway should receive the secret keys for $(w_1, \ldots, w_\ell, *, \ldots, *)$, $(*, w_1, \ldots, w_\ell, *, \ldots, *)$, $\ldots$, $(*, \ldots, *, w_1, \ldots, w_\ell)$, where "$*$" plays the role of a wildcard, to take into account all the possible offsets. So, for each searchable keyword of size ℓ, the gateway would have to store $n - \ell + 1$ keys, which is obviously a problem for large strings S.

DPI with Multi-context Key-Distribution. Naylor et al. [30] recently presented a multi-context key-exchange over the TLS protocol, which aims to allow middleboxes (read, write, or no) access to specific ciphertext fragments that they are entitled to see. This type of solution has some important merits, such as the fact that it is relatively easy to put into practice and allows the middlebox to perform its task with a very low overhead (the cost of a simple decryption). In addition, the parties sending and receiving messages need not deviate from the protocols they employ (such as TLS/SSL).

However, such solutions also have important disadvantages. The first of these is that the privacy they offer is not ideal. Instead of simply learning whether a specific content is contained within a given message or not, the middlebox learns entire chunks of messages. Moreover, the access-control scheme associated to the key-exchange scheme is relatively inflexible. The middlebox is given read or write access to a number of message fragments, and this is not easily modifiable (except by running the key-distribution algorithm once more). Finally, despite the efficiency of the search step (once the key-repartition is done), the finer-grained the access control is – thus offering more privacy – the more keys will have to be generated and stored by the various participating entities.

1.3   Benefits of SEST

Pattern matching on encrypted data is a very frequently-encountered problem, which can be addressed by many different primitives. In this context, the benefits of our new primitive (SEST) might not seem obvious. To better understand the intrinsic differences between all these approaches, we provide in Fig. 1 a comparison of their asymptotic complexities. We choose to only consider the most relevant alternatives, namely Searchable Encryption (both Symmetric and Public-Key) and Predicate Encryption/Hidden Vector Encryption. Other solutions do exist, as explained above; however, they induce high complexity, interactivity or weaker privacy.

As we explained, searching substrings at any position using SSE or ASE requires a tokenization process which must be repeated for each possible length of keyword, hence the $O(n \cdot L)$ size of the ciphertext. ASE performance is an adaptation of the tokenization idea of BlindBox to the Public Key Encryption with Keyword Search of Boneh *et al.* [9].

Conversely, PE and HVE offer a $O(n)$ complexity for the ciphertext but at the cost of generating and storing $n \cdot q$ trapdoors (to handle any possible offset).

We therefore argue that SEST is an interesting middle way which almost provides the best of the previous two types. Its only drawback compared to SSE and to ASE is the size of the public parameters but we believe this is a reasonable price to pay to achieve all the other features.

1.4   Pattern Matching and Privacy

At first sight, the ability to search patterns within a ciphertext may seem harmful to users' privacy, compared to standard end-to-end encryption. However, we stress that it is a lesser evil in many use-cases.

For example, in current solutions for DPI [25], the middlebox acts as a man in the middle to decrypt all traffic, which means that end-to-end encryption is gone anyway. Using SEST, the users can at least control which information can be leaked from their traffic since they are the only ones who can issue trapdoors. In particular, they can check that the keywords submitted by the middlebox are legitimate. For example, as we describe in Sect. 6.2, they could agree to issue trapdoors only for patterns associated to malwares, using public rules such as the ones provided by SNORT [1].

More generally, the incompatibility of standard encryption with any data processing often jeopardizes users' privacy since it gives no other choice than complete decryption of the traffic. We therefore argue that SEST is far from being a threat to privacy and can actually be used to improve it.

Outline. Our paper has the following structure. We begin in Sect. 2 by formally defining our new primitive, Searchable Encryption with Shiftable Trapdoors (SEST). Then, in Sect. 3, we describe an instantiation of this primitive, which relies on public-key encryption and bilinear pairings. In Sect. 4, we describe under which assumptions our scheme achieves provable security, and provide a security proof. We then describe how our construction can be used to handle regular expressions (wildcards and value intervals) in Sect. 5. Handling regular expressions is important in real-world applications, including DPI. In Sect. 6 we discuss the efficiency of our protocol and provide implementation results for pattern matching of all the SNORT rules on encrypted data of various sizes. Finally, we discuss our results and make some concluding remarks in Sect. 7.

Primitives	Issue	Public Parameters	Ciphertext	Trapdoors
SSE	$O(s \cdot q)$	$O(1)$	$O(n \cdot L)$	$O(s \cdot q)$
ASE	$O(q)$	$O(1)$	$O(n \cdot L)$	$O(q)$
PE/HVE	$O(n \cdot q)$	$O(n)$	$O(n)$	$O(n \cdot q)$
SEST (this work)	$O(q)$	$O(n)$	$O(n)$	$O(q)$

Fig. 1. Complexity comparison between related work and our primitive. The Issue process refers to the generation of trapdoors. The complexity indicated in the last three columns is the size complexity. The integers n, q, L, s denote respectively the length of the message to encrypt, the number of issued trapdoors, the number of different lengths among the q trapdoors and the number of users communicating with the receiver.

2   Searchable Encryption with Shiftable Trapdoors

We begin by presenting the syntax of our SEST primitive. Note that in addition to indicating whether the keyword was found in the (encrypted) plaintext, this scheme also outputs the position(s) at which the keyword is found. This is one advantage of shiftable trapdoors[2], namely yielding the exact position, within the target plaintext, of the search word. Such a knowledge is indeed necessary for some use-cases (see Sect. 6.2).

To keep our model as general as possible we consider strings $S = s_0 \ldots s_{m-1}$ whose characters s_i belong to a finite set $\mathcal{S}$. Since $\mathcal{S}$ is finite, we may assume that each of its elements s can be simply indexed by a unique integer $f(s)$ between 0 and $|\mathcal{S}| - 1$. For sake of simplicity, we will omit in the following the function f and will then directly use s as an index (for example $T[f(s)]$ will be denoted by $T[s]$).

2.1   Syntax

A searchable encryption scheme with shiftable trapdoors is defined by 5 algorithms that we call Setup, Keygen, Issue, Encrypt and Test. The first three of these are run by an entity called the receiver, while Encrypt is run by a sender and Test by a gateway.

- Setup($1^k, n$): This probabilistic algorithm takes as input a security parameter k and an integer n defining the maximum size of the strings that one can encrypt. It returns the public parameters pp that will be taken in input by all the other algorithms. In the following, pp will be considered as an implicit input to all algorithms and so will be omitted.
- Keygen($\mathcal{S}$): This probabilistic algorithm run by the receiver takes as input a finite set $\mathcal{S}$ and returns a key pair (sk, pk). The former value is secret and only known to the receiver, while the latter is public.
- Issue(W, sk): This probabilistic algorithm takes as input a string W of any size $0 < \ell \leq n$, along with the receiver's secret key, and returns a trapdoor td_W.
- Encrypt(S, pk): This probabilistic algorithm takes as input the receiver's public key along with a string $S = s_0 \ldots s_{m-1}$ of size $0 < m \leq n$ such that $s_i \in \mathcal{S}$ for all $i \in [0, m-1]$ and returns a ciphertext C.
- Test(C, td_W): This deterministic algorithm takes as input a ciphertext C encrypting a string $S = s_0 \ldots s_{m-1}$ of size m along with a trapdoor td_W for a string $W = w_0 \ldots w_{\ell-1}$ of size ℓ. If $m > n$ or $\ell > m$, then the algorithm returns $\bot$. Else, the algorithm returns a set (potentially empty) $\mathcal{J} \subset \{0, m-\ell\}$ of indexes j s.t. $s_j \ldots s_{j+\ell-1} = w_0 \ldots w_{\ell-1}$.

---

[2] Solutions using tokenization, such as Blindbox, also output the position. Here we compare with standard searchable encryption that usually does not reveal this information.

Remark 1. Notice that searchable encryption, *e.g.*, [2,11], usually does not consider a decryption algorithm which takes as input sk and a ciphertext C encrypting S and which returns S. Indeed, this functionality can easily be added by also encrypting S under a conventional encryption scheme. Nevertheless, one can note that decryption can be performed by issuing a trapdoor for all characters $s \in \mathcal{S}$ and running the Test algorithm on C for each of them.

2.2 Security Model

Correctness. As in [2], we divide correctness into two parts. The first one stipulates that the Test algorithm run on (C, td_W) will always return j if S contains the substring W at index j (no false negatives). More formally, this means that, for any string S of size $m \leq n$ and any W of length $\ell \leq m$: whenever $s_j \ldots s_{j+\ell-1} = w_0 \ldots w_{\ell-1}$,

$$\Pr[j \in \mathtt{Test}(\mathtt{Encrypt}(S, \mathsf{pk}), \mathtt{Issue}(W, \mathsf{sk}))] = 1,$$

where the probability is taken over the choice of the pair $(\mathsf{sk}, \mathsf{pk})$.

The second part of the correctness property requires that false positives (*i.e.*, when the Test algorithm returns j despite the fact $s_j \ldots s_{j+\ell-1} \neq w_0 \ldots w_{\ell-1}$) only occur with negligible probability. More formally, this means that, for any string S of size $m \leq n$ and any string W of length $\ell \leq m$:

$$\Pr\left[\begin{array}{c} j \in \mathtt{Test}(\mathtt{Encrypt}(S, \mathsf{pk}), \mathtt{Issue}(W, \mathsf{sk})) \\ \&\quad s_j \ldots s_{j+\ell-1} \neq w_0 \ldots w_{\ell-1} \end{array} \right] \leq \mu(k)$$

where μ is a negligible function.

Indistinguishability (SEST-IND-CPA). For the security requirement of Searchable Encryption with Shiftable Trapdoors (SEST), we adapt the standard notion of IND-CPA to this case (hence the name SEST-IND-CPA). Informally, this notion requires that no adversary $\mathcal{A}$, even with access to an oracle $\mathcal{O}\mathtt{Issue}$ which returns a trapdoor td_W for any queried string W, can decide whether a ciphertext C encrypts S_0 or S_1 as long as the trapdoors issued by the oracle do not allow trivial distinction of these two strings. This is formally defined by the experiment $\mathtt{Exp}_{\mathcal{A}}^{ind-cpa-\beta}(1^k, n)$, where $\beta \in \{0, 1\}$ as described in Fig. 2. The set $\mathcal{W}$ is the set of all the strings W submitted to $\mathcal{O}\mathtt{Issue}$.

We define the advantage of such an adversary as $\mathtt{Adv}_{\mathcal{A}}^{ind-cpa}(1^k, n) = |\Pr[\mathtt{Exp}_{\mathcal{A}}^{ind-cpa-1}(1^k, n)] - \Pr[\mathtt{Exp}_{\mathcal{A}}^{ind-cpa-0}(1^k, n)]|$. A searchable encryption scheme with shiftable trapdoors is SEST-IND-CPA secure if this advantage is negligible for any polynomial-time adversary.

We note that this security notion is very similar to the *attribute hiding* property of predicate encryption [27]. However, we cannot directly use this latter property because of the differences between predicate encryption and our primitive (*e.g.*, the lack of decryption algorithm), hence the need for a new security game.

$\mathrm{Exp}_{\mathcal{A}}^{ind-cpa-\beta}(1^k, n)$

1. $pp \leftarrow \mathtt{Setup}(1^k, n)$
2. $\mathsf{pk} \leftarrow \mathtt{Keygen}(\mathcal{S})$
3. $(S_0, S_1) \leftarrow \mathcal{A}^{\mathcal{O}\mathtt{Issue}}(\mathsf{pk})$, with $S_i = s_0^{(i)} \dots s_{m-1}^{(i)}$ for some $m \leq n$
4. $C \leftarrow \mathtt{Encrypt}(S_\beta, \mathsf{pk})$
5. $\beta' \leftarrow \mathcal{A}^{\mathcal{O}\mathtt{Issue}}(C, \mathsf{pk})$
6. If $\exists W = w_0 \dots w_{\ell_W-1} \in \mathcal{W}$ and j such that:

$$s_j^{(i)} \dots s_{j+\ell_W-1}^{(i)} = w_0 \dots w_{\ell_W-1} \neq s_j^{(1-i)} \dots s_{j+\ell_W-1}^{(1-i)}$$

   then return 0
7. Return $(\beta = \beta')$

Fig. 2. SEST-IND-CPA security game

The restriction in step 6 simply ensures that if S_i contains $W \in \mathcal{W}$ at offset j, then this is also the case for S_{1-i}. Otherwise, running the Test algorithm on (C, td_W) would enable $\mathcal{A}$ to trivially win this experiment.

Although this kind of restriction is very common in predicate/functionnal encryption schemes (e.g. [27]), we stress that, in practice, one must take care that it does not lead to situations where security becomes meaningless. For example, if the adversary gets a trapdoor for every character $s \in \mathcal{S}$, then it will always fail the experiment (it will not be able to output two strings S_0 and S_1 complying with the requirement of step 6) while being able to decrypt any ciphertext (see Remark 1).

This example highlights the implicit restrictions placed on the set of trapdoors. This is obviously a limitation of the security model (that also applies to all predicate or searchable encryption schemes) but we believe that these restrictions are very hard to formalize and should rather be considered on a case-by-case basis. For example, in the context of DPI, the receiver could assess once and for all the set of rules to check that the leakage remains reasonable.

Selective-Indistinguishability (SEST-sIND-CPA). We also need a weaker security notion in which the adversary commits to S_0 and S_1 at the beginning of the experiment, before seeing pp and pk. Such a restriction is quite standard and is usually referred to as *selective* security [15].

Remark 2. We recall that in a public-key setting, it is always possible to recover W from td_W: one simply has to encrypt the $2^{|W|}$ strings of size $|W|$ and then run $\mathtt{Test}(., \mathsf{td}_W)$ on each resulting ciphertext. The correctness property ensures (with overwhelming probability) that one will always get an empty set, except for the encryption of W.

Therefore, unless we place restrictions on the set of keywords that one can query (in particular on its min-entropy, as in [10]), we cannot achieve relevant privacy notions for the trapdoor td_W itself. However, this is not a problem for, say, deep-packet inspection, in which many of the keywords can even be public [1].

Finally, we note that one can achieve interesting privacy notions for the trapdoors in the private-key setting (*e.g.* [13]).

3   Our Construction

We are able to construct our SEST scheme by "projecting" both the keyword and the plaintext onto a multiplicative basis of the type z^i for some secret integer z. We encrypt the plaintext character-by-character, using secret encodings α_s for each $s \in \mathcal{S}$. The latter are also used to generate the trapdoors associated with the keyword. By using a *bilinear mapping* we are able to shift into the ciphertext and compare a given fragment of suitable length to the trapdoor.

Note that in order to achieve the security notion of SEST-(s)IND-CPA, we need to at least guarantee that, given some trapdoors td_{W_i} for words W_i, the adversary is not able to forge a trapdoor for some fresh word W^*. By projecting keywords on a polynomial in a secret value z, we ensure that trapdoors on keywords W are essentially un-malleable.

We describe our construction in detail in what follows, prefacing our scheme by a brief introduction to bilinear groups and pairings.

3.1   Bilinear Groups

Bilinear groups are a set of three cyclic groups, $\mathbb{G}_1$, $\mathbb{G}_2$, and $\mathbb{G}_T$, of prime order p, along with a bilinear map $e : \mathbb{G}_1 \times \mathbb{G}_2 \to \mathbb{G}_T$ with the following properties:

1. for all $g \in \mathbb{G}_1, \widetilde{g} \in \mathbb{G}_2$ and $a, b \in \mathbb{Z}_p$, $e(g^a, \widetilde{g}^b) = e(g, \widetilde{g})^{a \cdot b}$;
2. for any $g \neq 1_{\mathbb{G}_1}$ and $\widetilde{g} \neq 1_{\mathbb{G}_2}$, $e(g, \widetilde{g}) \neq 1_{\mathbb{G}_T}$;
3. the map e is efficiently computable.

Galbraith, Paterson, and Smart [20] defined three types of pairings: in type 1, $\mathbb{G}_1 = \mathbb{G}_2$; in type 2, $\mathbb{G}_1 \neq \mathbb{G}_2$ but there exists an efficient homomorphism $\phi : \mathbb{G}_2 \to \mathbb{G}_1$, while no efficient one exists in the other direction; in type 3, $\mathbb{G}_1 \neq \mathbb{G}_2$ and no efficiently computable homomorphism exists between $\mathbb{G}_1$ and $\mathbb{G}_2$, in either direction.

The security of our construction holds as long as no efficient homomorphism exists from $\mathbb{G}_1$ to $\mathbb{G}_2$. Our system must therefore be instantiated with pairings of type 2 or 3. However, in the following, we will only consider the latter type since it allows simpler security proofs thanks to the separation between the two groups $\mathbb{G}_1$ and $\mathbb{G}_2$. We stress that this is not a significant restriction since type 3 pairings offer the best performances among the three types.

3.2   Intuition

Intuitively, our scheme associates each element s of $\mathcal{S}$ with a secret encoding α_s. A trapdoor for a string $w_0 \ldots w_{\ell-1}$ is associated with a polynomial $V = \sum_{i=0}^{\ell-1} v_i \cdot \alpha_{w_i} \cdot z^i$ where v_i are random secret scalars whose purpose is to prevent forgeries of new trapdoors. The trapdoor then consists in the elements $\widetilde{g}^V$ and $\widetilde{g}^{v_i}$

for $i = 0, \ldots, \ell - 1$. In the meantime, a ciphertext encrypting a string $s_0 \cdots s_{n-1}$ is the sequence of "monomials" $C'_j = g^{a \cdot \alpha_{s_j} \cdot z^j}$ where a is a random factor (the Keygen algorithm will ensure that this can be done by only using elements from the public key). By using the bilinear map e, one can derive from the ciphertext and the trapdoor elements of the form $e(g, \widetilde{g})^U$ where U is a polynomial whose coefficients depends on the encodings α_{s_i} and on the scalars v_i.

In this encoding, if $s_0 \cdots s_{n-1}$ contains the pattern $w_0 \cdots w_{\ell-1}$ at offset j (i.e. if $s_{j+i} = w_i$ for $i = 0, \ldots, \ell - 1$) one can generate $e(g, \widetilde{g})^U = \prod_{i=0}^{\ell-1} e(C'_{j+i}, \widetilde{g}^{v_i})$ where $U = a \cdot z^j \cdot V$. Therefore, by extending the ciphertext with the elements $C_j = g^{a \cdot z^j}$, one can simply test the presence of W. By contrast, a difference $s_{j+i} \neq w_i$ or the combination of non-successive ciphertext elements will lead to a random-looking polynomial which would be useless to the adversary.

However, using this solution to search for a pattern of length ℓ within a string of length m requires $(\ell + 1)(m - \ell + 1)$ pairings, which quickly becomes prohibitive. While it seems natural that the complexity depends on the size m (since we have to search at every position), one could hope to reduce the factor $(\ell + 1)$.

A first attempt could be to set $v_i = v$ for all $i \in [0, \ell - 1]$ for some secret scalar v. Indeed, thanks to the bilinearity of e, the ℓ pairings $\prod_{i=0}^{\ell-1} e(C'_{j+i}, \widetilde{g}^{v_i})$ could be replaced by only one: $e(\prod_{i=0}^{\ell-1} C'_{j+i}, \widetilde{g}^v)$. Unfortunately, such a solution is insecure as proven by the following example.

Let C be a ciphertext encrypting a string $S = s_0 \cdots s_{m-1}$ and let us assume that W is a keyword such that $w_i = s$ for all $i \in [0, \ell - 1]$ (i.e. W is a sequence of identical values, equal to s). Then, for any $0 < j \leq \ell - 1$

$$e(C_0 \cdot C_j^{-1}, \widetilde{g}^{V_W}) = e(g, \widetilde{g})^{a(1-z^j)V_W} = e(g, \widetilde{g})^{aV'},$$

with

$$V' = \sum_{k=0}^{j-1} v \cdot \alpha_s \cdot z^k - \sum_{k=\ell}^{\ell+j-1} v \cdot \alpha_s \cdot z^k.$$

Therefore, $e(g, \widetilde{g})^{aV'}$ can be used to check whether

$$s_0 \ldots s_{j-1} = \overbrace{s \ldots s}^{j \text{ times}} \wedge s_\ell \ldots s_{\ell+j-1} = \overbrace{1 \ldots 1}^{j \text{ times}}.$$

Using td_W, a gateway is then able to get more information on S than the presence of W as a substring, which breaks the security of the construction.

However, this attack does not mean that we necessarily have to select different scalars v_i but simply that the generation process needs to be more subtle. We indeed prove that one can "recycle" the random elements v_i within the same trapdoor without jeopardizing security. More specifically, the issuing process that we describe in the next section is based on the observation that the secret encodings α_s already add some variability to the coefficients of the polynomial V. This therefore means that this variability need not exclusively rely on the random scalars v_i. In particular when $w_i \neq w_j$, the coefficients $v_i \cdot \alpha_{w_i}$ and $v_j \cdot \alpha_{w_j}$ will be different even if $v_i = v_j$. In such a case, there is no need to chose distinct scalars, which allows us to batch the corresponding pairings for the test. Compared to the solution with random scalars v_i, this divides the whole number of pairings by up to $|\mathcal{S}|$ (*e.g.*, 256 if we consider bytestrings).

3.3   The Protocol

- Setup($1^k, n$): Let $(\mathbb{G}_1, \mathbb{G}_2, \mathbb{G}_T, e)$ be the description of type 3 bilinear groups of prime order p, this algorithm selects $g \xleftarrow{\$} \mathbb{G}_1$ and $\widetilde{g} \xleftarrow{\$} \mathbb{G}_2$ and returns $pp \leftarrow (\mathbb{G}_1, \mathbb{G}_2, \mathbb{G}_T, e, g, \widetilde{g}, n)$.
- Keygen($\mathcal{S}$): On input a finite set $\mathcal{S}$, this algorithm selects $|\mathcal{S}| + 1$ random scalars $z, \{\alpha_s\}_{s \in \mathcal{S}}$ and computes $g_i \leftarrow g^{z^i}$ along with $\{g_i^{\alpha_s}\}_{s \in \mathcal{S}}$ for $i = 0, \ldots, n - 1$. The public key pk is set as $\{(g_i, \{g_i^{\alpha_s}\}_{s \in \mathcal{S}})\}_{i=0}^{n-1}$ whereas sk is set as $(z, \{\alpha_s\}_{s \in \mathcal{S}})$.
- Encrypt($S, $ pk): To encrypt a string $S = s_0 \ldots s_{m-1}$, where $m \leq n$ the user selects a random scalar a and returns $C = \{(C_i, C_i')\}_{i=0}^{m-1}$, where $C_i \leftarrow g_i^a$ and $C_i' \leftarrow g_i^{a \cdot \alpha_{s_i}}$ for $i = 0 \ldots m - 1$.
- Issue($W, $ sk): To issue a trapdoor td_W for a string $W = w_0 \ldots w_{\ell-1}$ of length $\ell \leq n$, one uses the following algorithm.

$\mathsf{Ind}[s] = 0$ for all $s \in \mathcal{S}$;
$L[i] = 0$ for all $i \in [0, \ell - 1]$;
$V = 0, c = 0$;
for $i = 0, \ldots, \ell - 1$ do
    if $L[\mathsf{Ind}[w_i]] = 0$ then
        $L[c] \xleftarrow{\$} \mathbb{Z}_p, \mathcal{I}_c \leftarrow \{i\}$;
        $c = c + 1$;
    else
        $\mathcal{I}_{\mathsf{Ind}[w_i]} = \mathcal{I}_{\mathsf{Ind}[w_i]} \cup \{i\}$;
    end
    $V = V + z^i \cdot \alpha_{w_i} \cdot L[\mathsf{Ind}[w_i]]$;
    $\mathsf{Ind}[w_i] = \mathsf{Ind}[w_i] + 1$;
end
$\mathsf{td}_W \leftarrow (c, \{\mathcal{I}_j\}_{j=0}^{c-1}, \{\widetilde{g}^{L[j]}\}_{j=0}^{c-1}, \widetilde{g}^V)$;

Algorithm 1: Issue

Our Issue algorithm formalizes the following principle: the random scalars (stored in L) can be re-used as long as the coefficients of the polynomial V are all distinct. In particular, if we write V as $\sum_{i=0}^{\ell-1} v_i \cdot \alpha_{w_i} \cdot z^i$, then $v_i \neq v_j$ if $w_i = w_j$.

- Test(C, td_W): To test whether the string S encrypted by C contains the substring W, the algorithm parses td_W as $(c, \{\mathcal{I}_j\}_{j=0}^{c-1}, \{\widetilde{g}^{L[j]}\}_{j=0}^{c-1}, \widetilde{g}^V)$ and C

as $\{(C_i, C_i')\}_{i=0}^{m-1}$ and checks, for $j = 0, \ldots, m - \ell$, if the following equation holds:

$$\prod_{t=0}^{c-1} e(\prod_{i \in \mathcal{I}_t} C_{j+i}', \widetilde{g}^{L[t]}) = e(C_j, \widetilde{g}^V).$$

It then returns the (potentially empty) set $\mathcal{J}$ of indexes j for which there is a match.

Correctness. First note that, if S contains the substring W at index j (*i.e.*, $s_{j+i} = w_i \ \forall i = 0, \ldots, \ell - 1$), then:

$$\prod_{t=0}^{c-1} e(\prod_{i \in \mathcal{I}_t} C_{j+i}', \widetilde{g}^{L[t]}) = \prod_{t=0}^{c-1} e(\prod_{i \in \mathcal{I}_t} g^{a \cdot \alpha_{s_{j+i}} \cdot z^{j+i}}, \widetilde{g}^{L[t]})$$

$$= \prod_{t=0}^{c-1} e(g^a, \widetilde{g}^{L[t] \cdot \sum_{i \in \mathcal{I}_t} \alpha_{w_i} \cdot z^{j+i}})$$

$$= \prod_{t=0}^{c-1} e(g^a, \widetilde{g}^{\sum_{i \in \mathcal{I}_t} L[t] \cdot \alpha_{w_i} \cdot z^{j+i}})$$

$$= e(g, \widetilde{g})^{a \cdot z^j \cdot V} = e(C_j, \widetilde{g}^V)$$

The set $\mathcal{J}$ returned by Test contains j.

Now, let us assume that $\mathcal{J}$ contains j but that $s_j \ldots s_{j+\ell-1} \neq w_0 \ldots w_{\ell-1}$, *i.e.*, the algorithm returns a false positive. Let $\mathcal{I}_{\neq}$ be the (non-empty) set of indexes i such that $s_{j+i} \neq w_i$. For all $i \in [0, \ell - 1]$, we define $v_i = L[t_i]$ where t_i is such that $i \in \mathcal{I}_{t_i}$. Since j has been returned by Test, we have,

$$\prod_{t=0}^{c-1} e(\prod_{i \in \mathcal{I}_t} C_{j+i}', \widetilde{g}^{L[t]}) = e(C_j, \widetilde{g}^V)$$

$$\Leftrightarrow \qquad \prod_{i=0}^{\ell-1} e(C_{j+i}', \widetilde{g}^{v_i}) = e(C_j, \widetilde{g}^V)$$

$$\Leftrightarrow \qquad \prod_{i \in \mathcal{I}_{\neq}} e(C_{j+i}', \widetilde{g}^{v_i}) = e(C_j, \widetilde{g}^{\sum_{i \in \mathcal{I}_{\neq}} v_i \cdot \alpha_{w_i} \cdot z^i})$$

$$\Leftrightarrow \qquad \prod_{i \in \mathcal{I}_{\neq}} e(g, \widetilde{g})^{a \cdot v_i \cdot \alpha_{s_{j+i}} z^{i+j}} = e(g, \widetilde{g})^{a \cdot z^j \sum_{i \in \mathcal{I}_{\neq}} v_i \cdot \alpha_{w_i} \cdot z^i}$$

$$\Leftrightarrow \qquad \sum_{i \in \mathcal{I}_{\neq}} v_i \cdot \alpha_{s_{j+i}} z^i = \sum_{i \in \mathcal{I}_{\neq}} v_i \cdot \alpha_{w_i} \cdot z^i$$

$$\Leftrightarrow \qquad \sum_{i \in \mathcal{I}_{\neq}} v_i (\alpha_{s_{j+i}} - \alpha_{w_i}) \cdot z^i = 0.$$

Since $\alpha_{s_{j+i}} \neq \alpha_{w_i}$ for all $i \in \mathcal{I}_{\neq}$, this amounts to evaluating the probability that a random scalar z is a root of a non-zero polynomial of degree at most $\ell - 1$. The probability that Test returns a false positive j is thus at most $\frac{\ell-1}{p}$, which is negligible.

Remark 3. Our construction achieves the goals that we define at the beginning of Sect. 1.1. Indeed, the Encrypt procedure does not depend on the keywords W, and the latter may have distinct lengths. In particular, the size of C only depends on the length of the message it encrypts. Moreover, the trapdoors td_W allow to search the word W in $S = s_0 \dots s_{m-1}$ at any possible offset, while being of size independent of m.

All these features are provided using only asymmetric prime order bilinear groups, which can be very efficiently implemented on a computer (*e.g.*, [7]). We refer to Sect. 6 for a more thorough analysis of the efficiency of our protocol.

Remark 4. As explained in Sect. 2.1, public-key searchable encryption schemes often assume that the sender will also encrypt the string S by using a conventional encryption scheme Π. Such a solution enables fast decryption but should be used cautiously in some contexts, such as DPI, where the sender is likely to be malicious. Indeed, nothing prevents the latter from encrypting an harmless string S using the searchable encryption scheme while encrypting a different S' using Π. The message (S) checked by the gateway would then be different from the one forwarded to the receiver (S'), which would make the inspection pointless.

It is therefore necessary to check that both ciphertexts decrypt to the same string S, which can easily be done by the receiver. Indeed, after decrypting the conventional ciphertext, the latter (who knows sk) can verify whether $\{(C_i, C_i')\}_{i=0}^{m-1}$ encrypts $S = s_0 \dots s_{m-1}$ by testing if $C_i' = C_i^{\alpha_{s_i}}$ for $i \in [0, m-1]$. One can also perform such tests only for a limited number $N \leq m$ of indexes i, but the probability of detecting cheating sender will become $\frac{N}{m}$.

4   Security Analysis

4.1   Complexity Assumptions

Let us consider an adversary $\mathcal{A}$ which, knowing q trapdoors td_{W_k}, would like to decide if a ciphertext C encrypts S_0 or S_1. The natural restrictions imposed by the security model imply that there is at least one index i^* such that $s_{i^*}^{(0)} \neq s_{i^*}^{(1)}$ and that, for all $k \in [1, q]$ and all $j \in [0, \ell_k - 1]$ (where ℓ_k is the length of W_k), $s_{i^*-\ell_k+1+j}^{(0)} \dots s_{i^*+j}^{(0)}$ and $s_{i^*-\ell_k+1+j}^{(1)} \dots s_{i^*+j}^{(1)}$ both differ from $w_{k,0}, \dots, w_{k,\ell_k-1}$. In other words, any substring of S_0 (or respectively S_1) of length ℓ_k containing $s_{i^*}^{(0)}$ (resp. $s_{i^*}^{(1)}$) must be different from W_k, for all $k \in [1, q]$.

If we focus on the index i^*, $\mathcal{A}$ must then distinguish whether the discrete logarithm of C_{i^*}' in base g_{i^*} is $a \cdot \alpha_{s_{i^*}^{(0)}}$ or $a \cdot \alpha_{s_{i^*}^{(1)}}$. To this end, the attacker has access to many elements of $\mathbb{G}_1$ (the public parameters and the other elements of the ciphertext) and of $\mathbb{G}_2$ (the trapdoors td_{W_k}). All of them are of the form $g^{P_u(a,\alpha_s,z)}$ or $\widetilde{g}^{Q_v(\alpha_s,z,v_{i,k})}$ for a polynomial number of multivariate polynomials P_u and Q_v. The assumption underlying the security of our scheme is thus related to the General Diffie-Hellman GDH problem [8], whose asymmetric version [12] is recalled below.

Definition 1 (GDH assumption). *Let r, s, t and c be four positive integers and $\mathsf{R} \in \mathbb{F}_p[X_1,\ldots,X_c]^r$, $\mathsf{S} \in \mathbb{F}_p[X_1,\ldots,X_c]^s$, and $\mathsf{T} \in \mathbb{F}_p[X_1,\ldots,X_c]^t$ be three tuples of multivariate polynomials over $\mathbb{F}_p$. Let $R^{(i)}$, $S^{(i)}$ and $T^{(i)}$ denote the i-th polynomial contained in R, S, and T. For any polynomial $f \in \mathbb{F}_p[X_1,\ldots,X_c]$, we say that f is dependent on $<\mathsf{R},\mathsf{S},\mathsf{T}>$ if there are $\{a_j\}_{i=1}^s \in \mathbb{F}_p^s \setminus \{(0,\ldots,0)\}$, $\{b_{i,j}\}_{i,j=1}^{i=r,j=s} \in \mathbb{F}_p^{r\cdot s}$ and $\{c_k\}_{k=1}^t \in \mathbb{F}_p^t$ such that*

$$f(\sum_j a_j S^{(j)}) = \sum_{i,j} b_{i,j} R^{(i)} S^{(j)} + \sum_k c_k T^{(k)}.$$

Let $(x_1,\ldots,x_c)$ be a secret vector. The GDH assumption states that, given the values $\{g^{R^{(i)}(x_1,\ldots,x_c)}\}_{i=1}^r$, $\{\widetilde{g}^{S^{(i)}(x_1,\ldots,x_c)}\}_{i=1}^s$ and $\{e(g,\widetilde{g})^{T^{(i)}(x_1,\ldots,x_c)}\}_{i=1}^t$, it is hard to decide whether $U = g^{f(x_1,\ldots,x_c)}$ or U is random if f is independent of $<\mathsf{R},\mathsf{S},\mathsf{T}>$.

Unfortunately, we cannot directly make use of this assumption unless we severely restrict the size n of the strings that one can encrypt. In our proof, presented in Sect. 4.2, one of the main important steps is showing that, even given a number of keyword trapdoors (and in particular, the polynomials V associated with those keywords), the adversary is unable to detect the presence of a fresh keyword; consequently, we can bound the leakage on the input plaintexts by only considering the adversary's queries to the issuing oracle. This can be mapped to an instance of GDH, but we will need the adversary to choose which of those polynomials are input to the GDH instance.

If we did bound the size n of the plaintext, by making a guess on the string $S_\beta = s_1^{(\beta)} \ldots s_m^{(\beta)}$, one could define a GDH instance providing all the elements of the public parameters, the trapdoors for every word W that does not match any of the substrings of S_β containing $s_{i^*}^{(\beta)}$, the elements $\{g_i^a\}_{i=0}^{n-1}$ and $\{g_i^{a\cdot\alpha_{s_i}}\}_{i\in[0,n-1]\setminus\{i^*\}}$ along with the challenge element $U \in \mathbb{G}_1$ associated with the polynomial $f = a \cdot z^{i^*} \cdot \alpha_{s_{i^*}}$.

With such a GDH instance, the security proof becomes straightforward and only requires a proof that f does not depend on the polynomials underlying the provided elements. However, the reduction does not abort only if the initial guess is valid, which occurs with probability $\frac{1}{2^n}$.

So either we require n to be small (say $n \leq 30$, for example) or we choose to rely on an interactive variant of the GDH assumption, in which the elements $g^{R^{(i)}(x_1,\ldots,x_c)}$, $\widetilde{g}^{S^{(i)}(x_1,\ldots,x_c)}$ and $e(g,\widetilde{g})^{T^{(i)}(x_1,\ldots,x_c)}$ can be queried to specific oracles, to offer enough flexibility to the simulator.

The latter solution is less than ideal because it essentially makes the GDH instance interactive and consequently our construction will end up offering less security than a static assumption. Nevertheless, we argue that this solution remains of interest for two reasons. The first is that it allows to construct a quite efficient scheme with remarkable features: the size of the ciphertext is independent of the ones of the searchable strings, and the size of the trapdoors is independent of the size of the messages. Achieving this while being able to handle any trapdoor query is not obvious and may justify the use of an interactive assumption.

A second reason is that, intrinsically, the hardness of the GDH problem (proven in the generic group model [8]) relies on the same argument as its interactive variant : as long as the "challenge" polynomial f does not depend on $<\mathsf{R},\mathsf{S},\mathsf{T}>$, $g^{f(x_1,\dots,x_c)}$ is indistinguishable from a random element of $\mathbb{G}_1$. The fact that the sets R, S, and T are defined in the assumption or by the queries to oracles does not fundamentally impact the proof. We therefore define the interactive-GDH (i-GDH) assumption and show that our scheme can be proven secure under it.

Definition 2 (i-GDH assumption). *Let* r, s, t, c, *and* k *be five positive integers and* $\mathsf{R} \in \mathbb{F}_p[X_1,\dots,X_c]^r$, $\mathsf{S} \in \mathbb{F}_p[X_1,\dots,X_c]^s$ *and* $\mathsf{T} \in \mathbb{F}_p[X_1,\dots,X_c]^t$ *be three tuples of multivariate polynomials over* $\mathbb{F}_p$*. Let* $\mathcal{O}^{\mathsf{R}}$ *(resp.* $\mathcal{O}^{\mathsf{S}}$ *and* $\mathcal{O}^{\mathsf{T}}$*) be oracles that, on input* $\{\{a_{i_1,\dots,i_c}^{(k)}\}_{i_j=0}^{d_k}\}_k$*, add the polynomials* $\{\sum_{i_1,\dots,i_c} a_{i_1,\dots,i_c}^{(k)} \prod_j X_j^{i_j}\}_k$ *to* R *(resp.* S *and* T*).*

Let $(x_1,\dots,x_c)$ *be a secret vector and* q_{R} *(resp* q_{S}*) (resp.* q_{T}*) be the number of queries to* $\mathcal{O}^{\mathsf{R}}$ *(resp.* $\mathcal{O}^{\mathsf{S}}$*) (resp.* $\mathcal{O}^{\mathsf{T}}$*). The i-GDH assumption states that, given the values* $\{g^{R^{(i)}(x_1,\dots,x_c)}\}_{i=1}^{r+k\cdot q_{\mathsf{R}}}$*,* $\{\widetilde{g}^{S^{(i)}(x_1,\dots,x_c)}\}_{i=1}^{s+k\cdot q_{\mathsf{S}}}$ *and* $\{e(g,\widetilde{g})^{T^{(i)}(x_1,\dots,x_c)}\}_{i=1}^{t+k\cdot q_{\mathsf{T}}}$*, it is hard to decide whether* $U = g^{f(x_1,\dots,x_c)}$ *or* U *is random if* f *is independent of* $<\mathsf{R},\mathsf{S},\mathsf{T}>$*.*

4.2   Security Results

Theorem 3. *The scheme described in Sect. 3 is* SEST-sIND-CPA *secure under the* i-GDH *assumption for* R*,* S*, and* T *initially set as* $\mathsf{R} = \{(z^i, x_j \cdot z^i, a \cdot z^i)\}_{i=0,j=0}^{i=2n-1,j=|\mathcal{S}|-1}$*,* $\mathsf{S} = \mathsf{T} = \emptyset$ *and* $f = a \cdot x_0 \cdot z^n$*.*

Proof. Let $G_0^{(\beta)}$ denote the $\mathrm{Exp}_{\mathcal{A}}^{sind-cpa-\beta}$ game, as described in Sect. 2.2 – recall that this is the *selective* version of the IND-CPA security notion. Moreover, let $S_0 = s_0^{(0)}\dots s_{m-1}^{(0)}$ and $S_1 = s_0^{(1)}\dots s_{m-1}^{(1)}$ be the two substrings returned by $\mathcal{A}$ at the beginning of the game. Our proof uses a sequence of games $G_j^{(\beta)}$, for $j = 1,\dots,n$, to argue that the advantage of $\mathcal{A}$ is negligible. This is a standard hybrid argument, in which at each game hop we randomize another element of the challenge ciphertext.

Let $\mathcal{I}_{\neq}$ be the set of indexes i such that $s_i^{(0)} \neq s_i^{(1)}$ and $\mathcal{I}_{\neq}^{(j)}$ be the subset containing the first j indexes of $\mathcal{I}_{\neq}$ (if $j > |\mathcal{I}_{\neq}|$, then $\mathcal{I}_{\neq}^{(j)} = \mathcal{I}_{\neq}$). For $j = 1,\dots,n$, game $G_j^{(\beta)}$ modifies $G_0^{(\beta)}$ by switching the elements C_i' of the challenge ciphertext to random elements of $\mathbb{G}_1$, for $i \in \mathcal{I}_{\neq}^{(j)}$. Ultimately, in the last game, $G_n^{(\beta)}$, the challenge ciphertext contains no meaningful information about $s_i^{(\beta)}$ $\forall i \in \mathcal{I}_{\neq}$, so the adversary cannot distinguish whether it plays $G_n^{(0)}$ or $G_n^{(1)}$.

In particular, we can write:

$$
\begin{aligned}
&\mathsf{Adv}_{\mathcal{A}}^{sind-cpa}(1^k, n) \\
&= |\Pr[\mathsf{Exp}_{\mathcal{A}}^{sind-cpa-1}(1^k, n)] - \Pr[\mathsf{Exp}_{\mathcal{A}}^{sind-cpa-0}(1^k, n)]| \\
&= |G_0^{(1)}(1^k, n) - G_0^{(0)}(1^k, n)| \\
&\leq \sum_{j=0}^{n-1} |G_j^{(1)}(1^k, n) - G_{j+1}^{(1)}(1^k, n)| \\
&\quad + |G_n^{(1)}(1^k, n) - G_n^{(0)}(1^k, n)| \\
&\quad + \sum_{j=0}^{n-1} |G_{j+1}^{(0)}(1^k, n) - G_j^{(0)}(1^k, n)| \\
&\leq \sum_{j=0}^{n-1} |G_j^{(1)}(1^k, n) - G_{j+1}^{(1)}(1^k, n)| \\
&\quad + \sum_{j=0}^{n-1} |G_{j+1}^{(0)}(1^k, n) - G_j^{(0)}(1^k, n)|.
\end{aligned}
$$

In order to bound this result, we must prove that $\mathcal{A}$ cannot distinguish $G_j^{(\beta)}$ from $G_{j+1}^{(\beta)}$, which is formally stated by the lemma below.

Assuming that this lemma were proved, each term above is negligible under the i-GDH assumption, which concludes the proof.

Lemma 4. *For all $j = 0, \ldots, n-1$ and $\beta \in \{0, 1\}$, the difference $|\Pr[G_j^{\beta}(1^k, n) = 1] - \Pr[G_{j+1}^{\beta}(1^k, n) = 1]|$ is negligible under the i-GDH assumption for R, S, and T initially set as follows: $\mathrm{R} = \{(z^i, x_j \cdot z^i, a \cdot z^i)\}_{i=0, j=0}^{i=2n-1, j=|S|-1}$, $\mathrm{S} = \mathrm{T} = \emptyset$ and $f = a \cdot x_0 \cdot z^n$.*

The proof is provided in the full version [19].

5 Handling Regular Expressions

Our solution, introduced in Sect. 3, allows for pattern matching of keywords of arbitrary lengths, for ciphertexts emitted from arbitrary sources (we call this having universal tokens). In this section, we extend our notion of keyword-search to a more generic case, in which some of the keyword characters are fully-unknown (wildcards) and some are only partially-unknown (in an interval of size greater than 1).

Consider the general case in which one wants to search for substrings of the form $W = w_0 \ldots w_{t-1} w_t^{(\mathcal{S}_t)} w_{t+1} \ldots w_{\ell-1}$ where $w_t^{(\mathcal{S}_t)}$ denotes any element from the set $\mathcal{S}_t \subset \mathcal{S}$. For example, $\mathcal{S}_t$ can be the set [0-9] of all integers between 0 and 9.

A trivial solution could be to issue a trapdoor for every possible value of w_t but this would imply, for the gateway, to store the $|\mathcal{S}_t|$ resulting trapdoors and to test each of them separately. This not only raises a question of efficiency, but it also gives the gateway much more information on the input string. Intuitively, at the end of the search, the gateway will not only be able to tell that a given character is within a certain subset, but also which particular element of the subset it corresponds to.

In the following, we show how to modify our construction to allow for two notable regular expressions: wildcards and interval searches, without leaking any additional information, and with a minimal efficiency loss.

5.1   Handling Wildcards

The first case we consider assumes $W = w_0 \ldots w_{i_1}^{(\mathcal{S}_{i_1})} \ldots w_{i_r}^{(\mathcal{S}_{i_r})} \ldots w_{\ell-1}$ with $\mathcal{S}_{i_1} = \ldots = \mathcal{S}_{i_r} = \mathcal{S}$, which means that $w_{i_1}^{(\mathcal{S}_{i_1})}, \ldots, w_{i_r}^{(\mathcal{S}_{i_r})}$ can take any value from the set $\mathcal{S}$ and can consequently be seen as "wildcards".

Informally, this implies that the $(j+i_1)$-th,...,$(j+i_r)$-th ciphertext elements must not be taken into account when testing if $C_j \ldots C_{j+\ell-1}$ encrypts W. This leads to the following variant of our main protocol where only the Issue and the Test algorithms differ (slightly) from the original ones.

- Issue(W, sk): Let $\mathcal{D} = \{i_1, \ldots, i_r\}$. The issuance process of a trapdoor td_W for $W = w_0 \ldots w_{i_1}^{(\mathcal{S}_{i_1})} \ldots w_{i_r}^{(\mathcal{S}_{i_r})} \ldots w_{\ell-1}$ is described by Algorithm 2.
  The only difference with the original Issue algorithm is the additional condition $i \notin \mathcal{D}$ which ensures that V will have no monomial of degree i for $i \in \mathcal{D}$.

$\mathbf{Ind}[s] = 0$ for all $s \in \mathcal{S}$;
$L[i] = 0$ for all $i \in [0, \ell - 1]$;
$V = 0, c = 0$;
for $i = 0, \ldots, \ell - 1$ **do**
   if $i \notin \mathcal{D}$ **then**
      if $L[\mathbf{Ind}[w_i]] = 0$ **then**
         $L[c] \xleftarrow{\$} \mathbb{Z}_p, \mathcal{I}_c \leftarrow \{i\}$;
         $c = c + 1$;
      else
         $\mathcal{I}_{\mathbf{Ind}[w_i]} = \mathcal{I}_{\mathbf{Ind}[w_i]} \cup \{i\}$;
      end
      $V = V + z^i \cdot \alpha_{w_i} \cdot L[\mathbf{Ind}[w_i]]$;
      $\mathbf{Ind}[w_i] = \mathbf{Ind}[w_i] + 1$;
   end
end
$\mathsf{td}_W \leftarrow (c, \mathcal{D}, \{\mathcal{I}_j\}_{j=0}^{c-1}, \{\widetilde{g}^{L[j]}\}_{j=0}^{c-1}, \widetilde{g}^V)$;

Algorithm 2: Issue supporting wildcards

- Test(C, td_W): this algorithm remains unchanged except that the trapdoor now contains the set $\mathcal{D}$. The process still consists of checking if the equality

$$(1) \quad \prod_{t=0}^{c-1} e(\prod_{i \in \mathcal{I}_t} C'_{j+i}, \widetilde{g}^{L[t]}) = e(C_j, \widetilde{g}^V).$$

holds for $j = 0, \ldots, m - \ell$.

One can note that this variant does not increase the complexity of our scheme. Actually, this is the opposite: all the indexes in $\mathcal{D}$ are discarded in the product of (1). Regarding security, one can note that the proof of Sect. 4 still applies here, since the latter does not require the coefficients v_i to be different from 0.

5.2 Handling General Subsets

Now let us consider the general case where the substring W one wants to search contains $w_i^{(\mathcal{S}_i)}$ for a subset $\mathcal{S}_i \subsetneq \mathcal{S}$. For example, $\mathcal{S}_i$ can be the set $[0,9]$ of all the integers $x \in [0,9]$ or the set $\{a, \dots, z\}$ of the letters of the Latin alphabet. Our construction can actually be modified to handle this kind of searches provided that: (1) the searchable sets $\mathcal{S}_i$ are known in advance, and can be used during the Keygen process; and (2) all these subsets are disjoint. We argue that both conditions are reasonable since this is often the case for regular expressions.

5.3 The Protocol

- Setup$(1^k, n)$: Let $(\mathbb{G}_1, \mathbb{G}_2, \mathbb{G}_T, e)$ be the description of type 3 bilinear groups of prime order p, this algorithm selects $g \xleftarrow{\$} \mathbb{G}_1$ and $\tilde{g} \xleftarrow{\$} \mathbb{G}_2$ and returns $pp \leftarrow (\mathbb{G}_1, \mathbb{G}_2, \mathbb{G}_T, e, g, \tilde{g}, n)$.
- Keygen$(\mathcal{S}, \mathcal{S}^{(1)}, \dots, \mathcal{S}^{(k)})$: This algorithm now takes as input k disjoint subsets of $\mathcal{S}$. We can assume, without loss of generality, that $\mathcal{S} = \mathcal{S}^{(1)} \cup \dots \cup \mathcal{S}^{(k)}$ since we can simply add the complement of all previous sets if this is not the case. The function $f : \mathcal{S} \to \{1, \dots, k\}$ which maps any element $s \in \mathcal{S}$ to the index of the set $\mathcal{S}^{(j)}$ which contains it is thus perfectly defined. The algorithm then selects $|\mathcal{S}| + k + 1$ random scalars $\{\alpha_s\}_{s \in \mathcal{S}}, \beta_1, \dots, \beta_k, z \xleftarrow{\$} \mathbb{Z}_p$ and computes $g_i \leftarrow g^{z^i}$ for $i = 0, \dots, n-1$ along with $(g_i^{\alpha_s}, g_i^{\beta_d})$ for $d = 1, \dots, k$ and all $s \in \mathcal{S}^{(d)}$. The public key is then set to $\{g_i\}_{i=0}^{n-1} \cup_{d=1}^{k} \{(g_i^{\alpha_s}, g_i^{\beta_d})\}_{i \in [0, n-1], s \in \mathcal{S}^{(d)}}$ and sk as $\{\alpha_s\}_{s \in \mathcal{S}}, \beta_1, \dots, \beta_k, z$.
- Encrypt(S, pk): To encrypt a string $S = s_0 \dots s_{m-1}$, where $m \leq n$ the user selects a random scalar a and returns $C = \{(C_i, C_i^{(1)}, C_i^{(2)})\}_{i=0}^{m-1}$, where $C_i \leftarrow g_i^a$, $C_i^{(1)} \leftarrow (g_i^{\alpha_{s_i}})^a$ and $C_i^{(2)} \leftarrow (g_i^{\beta_{f(s_i)}})^a$, for $i = 1 \dots m$.
- To issue a trapdoor td_W for a string $W = w_1 \dots w_{i_1}^{(\mathcal{S}_{i_1})} \dots w_{i_r}^{(\mathcal{S}_{i_r})} \dots w_\ell$ of length $\ell \leq n$, the algorithm first checks that all the involved subsets have been taken as input by the Keygen algorithm, i.e. $\mathcal{S}_{i_j} \in \{\mathcal{S}^{(1)}, \dots, \mathcal{S}^{(k)}\}$ for $j = 1, \dots, r$, and returns $\bot$ otherwise. The function h which maps every index i_j to the integer $d \in \{1, \dots, k\}$ such that $\mathcal{S}_{i_j} = \mathcal{S}^{(d)}$ is thus correctly defined. Let $\mathcal{D} = \{i_1, \dots, i_r\}$, we modify the original Issue procedure as described in Algorithm 3.
- Test(C, td_W): To test whether the string S encrypted by C contains the substring W, the algorithm parses td_W as $(c, \mathcal{D}, \{\mathcal{I}_j\}_{j=0}^{c-1}, \{\tilde{g}^{L[j]}\}_{j=0}^{c-1}, \tilde{g}^V)$ and C as $\{(C_i, C_i^{(1)}, C_i^{(2)})\}_{i=0}^{m-1}$ and checks, for $j = 0, \dots, m - \ell$, if the following equation holds:

$\texttt{Ind}[s] = 0$ for all $s \in \mathcal{S}$;
$\texttt{Ind}'[k] = 0$ for all $k \in [0, d-1]$;
$L[i] = 0$ for all $i \in [0, \ell - 1]$;
$V = 0$, $c = 0$;
for $i = 0, \ldots, \ell - 1$ **do**

    if $i \notin \mathcal{D}$ **then**

        if $L[\texttt{Ind}[w_i]] = 0$ **then**

            $L[c] \xleftarrow{\$} \mathbb{Z}_p$, $\mathcal{I}_c \leftarrow \{i\}$;

            $c = c + 1$;

        else

            $\mathcal{I}_{\texttt{Ind}[w_i]} = \mathcal{I}_{\texttt{Ind}[w_i]} \cup \{i\}$;

        end

        $V = V + z^i \cdot \alpha_{w_i} \cdot L[\texttt{Ind}[w_i]]$;

        $\texttt{Ind}[w_i] = \texttt{Ind}[w_i] + 1$;

    else

        if $L[\texttt{Ind}'[h(i) - 1]] = 0$ **then**

            $L[c] \xleftarrow{\$} \mathbb{Z}_p$, $\mathcal{I}_c \leftarrow \{i\}$;

            $c = c + 1$;

        else

            $\mathcal{I}_{\texttt{Ind}'[h(i)-1]} = \mathcal{I}_{\texttt{Ind}'[h(i)-1]} \cup \{i\}$;

        end

        $V = V + z^i \cdot \beta_{h(i)} \cdot L[\texttt{Ind}'[h(i) - 1]]$;

        $\texttt{Ind}'[h(i) - 1] = \texttt{Ind}'[h(i) - 1] + 1$;

    end

end
$\texttt{td}_W \leftarrow (c, \mathcal{D}, \{\mathcal{I}_j\}_{j=0}^{c-1}, \{\widetilde{g}^{L[j]}\}_{j=0}^{c-1}, \widetilde{g}^V)$;

Algorithm 3: Issue supporting general subsets

$$\prod_{t=0}^{c-1} e((\prod_{i \in \mathcal{I}_t \wedge i \notin \mathcal{D}} C_{j+i}^{(1)})(\prod_{i \in \mathcal{I}_t \wedge i \in \mathcal{D}} C_{j+i}^{(2)}), \widetilde{g}^{L[t]}) = e(C_j, \widetilde{g}^V).$$

It then returns the set (potentially empty) $\mathcal{J}$ of indexes j for which there is a match.

The values β_j defined in this protocol can be seen as an encoding of the subset $\mathcal{S}^{(j)}$, in the same way as the scalars α_s encode the characters $s \in \mathcal{S}$. Actually, it is as if we worked with a larger set $\mathcal{S}'$ containing $\mathcal{S}$ but also the "characters" $\mathcal{S}^{(j)}$. The fact that one encrypts using both encodings makes the ciphertext compatible with any kind of trapdoors: if the i-th element of W is of the form w_j, we use $C_j^{(1)}$, whereas we use $C_j^{(2)}$ for an element of the form $w_j^{(\mathcal{S}_j)}$. Correctness and security follow directly from the original construction.

Regarding efficiency, encrypting for both encodings adds an element of $\mathbb{G}_1$ by character to the ciphertext. Nevertheless, as we explain in the next section, working with a larger set $\mathcal{S}'$ allows to reduce the number of random scalars that we need to generate the trapdoors, which leads to a faster Test procedure.

6   The Complexity of Our Scheme

We describe in this section the timings one can get for different parameters. But first we discuss the different strategies for choosing the set $\mathcal{S}$.

6.1   Generic Complexity

When considering data streams, the most relevant sets are the one of bits (*i.e.* $\mathcal{S} = \{0, 1\}$) or the one of bytes (*i.e.* $\mathcal{S} = \{0, \ldots, 255\}$). Larger sets (for example the one containing all sequences of r bytes for some $r > 1$) would improve the efficiency of the Test procedure but would harm our ability to detect all patterns. We focus on four specific points: the sizes of (1) the public key, of (2) the ciphertext and of (3) the trapdoor along with (4) the number of pairings required to detect the presence of a pattern of size ℓ.

1. **The size of pk.** Let n be the maximum number of bytes one can encrypt with the protocol of Sect. 3.3. If $\mathcal{S} = \{0, 1\}$, then the public key contains $(1+2)8n$ elements of $\mathbb{G}_1$ which amounts to $768n$ bytes using Barreto-Naehrig (BN) [6] curves. If we now consider bytestrings (*i.e.* $\mathcal{S} = \{0, \ldots, 255\}$), then pk contains $(1 + 256)n$ elements of $\mathbb{G}_1$ which amounts to $8224n$ bytes using the same curves.
2. **The length of the ciphertext.** Each character is encrypted by 2 elements of $\mathbb{G}_1$ that represent 64 bytes. Therefore, encrypting m bytes requires $512m$ bytes if $\mathcal{S} = \{0, 1\}$ and $64m$ bytes if $\mathcal{S} = \{0, \ldots, 255\}$.
3. **The size of td_W.** Our algorithm makes this evaluation much more difficult to perform. Indeed, the fact that we can reuse the same random scalar for two different characters $w_i \neq w_j$ implies that the size of td_W strongly depends on the keyword W itself. For example, a "constant" keyword $W = s \ldots s$ of size ℓ would entail a trapdoor containing $\ell+1$ elements of $\mathbb{G}_2$. Conversely, a keyword $W = w_0 \ldots w_{\ell-1}$ with $w_i \neq w_j$ for $i \neq j$ would only require to store 2 elements of $\mathbb{G}_2$. Nevertheless, we notice that larger sets decrease the probability of having equal characters. More specifically, assuming uniform distribution of the characters within a keyword, a trapdoor contains, on average, $(1 + \lceil \ell/2 \rceil)$ elements of $\mathbb{G}_2$ if $\mathcal{S} = \{0, 1\}$ and only $(1 + \lceil \ell/256 \rceil)$ if $\mathcal{S} = \{0, \ldots, 255\}$. We can then hope to gain a factor 128 in the latter case.
4. **The number of pairings.** The number of pairings one must compute to test the presence of a keyword W of length ℓ within an encrypted string is related to the size of the corresponding trapdoor td_W. More specifically, if td_W contains N elements of $\mathbb{G}_2$, then one must perform $N(m-\ell+1)$ pairings, where m is the length of the encrypted string. Therefore, a shorter trapdoor implies a more efficient Test procedure, which means that it is better to work with $\mathcal{S} = \{0, \ldots, 255\}$ than with $\mathcal{S} = \{0, 1\}$.

Public key aside, we note that working on bytes instead of bits allows to significantly decrease complexity. Our timings then correspond to the case where $\mathcal{S} = \{0, \ldots, 255\}$.

6.2 Implementation of SEST for DPI

As we explain, evaluating the size of the trapdoors, and therefore the number of pairings requires to make assumptions about the distribution of the keywords. Previous estimations assumed a uniform distribution of the latter, which is unlikely in practice. We therefore evaluate our protocol on the SNORT public rules set [1] to provide a more concrete estimation[3].

The SNORT rules set contains thousands of rules which mostly consist in searching some specific patterns in a stream. We parsed all these rules and got 6048 different patterns. Figure 3 describes the sizes of the corresponding trapdoors.

Trapdoors of size	2	3	4	5	6	7	8	9	10	11	12	13	14	15	18	23	27
Number	2067	1879	705	745	361	140	69	32	20	19	3	2	1	2	1	1	1

Fig. 3. Number of trapdoors of size N, where N is the number of elements of $\mathbb{G}_2$. In other words, among the 6048 trapdoors generated for the SNORT rules set, 2076 contain 2 elements of $\mathbb{G}_2$, 1879 contain 3 elements of $\mathbb{G}_2$, and so on.

This table highlights the advantage of our issuing protocol: even for large patterns we manage to keep most of the time short trapdoors thanks to the re-use (when possible) of the random scalars. The whole trapdoors set thus only amounts to 1.35 MB.

Since the number of pairings is related to the size of the trapdoors, one could try to deduce from this table the total number of pairings required to test all SNORT patterns. However, we stress that this would only be a quite inaccurate upper bound. First, because many of these patterns are part of the same rule which enables to avoid unnecessary tests: if there is no match for a pattern defined by a rule, then it is pointless to test the other ones within the same rule. Second, because many rules include parameters called "depth", "offset", "distance" or "within" which allow to reduce the search to a smaller part of the stream.

The number of pairings for the whole SNORT rules set is thus significantly smaller than the one we could expect from the complexity evaluation we provide in Sect. 6.1. Moreover, we recall that the optimal Ate pairing [34] that we use to instantiate the map e can be split into two parts that are usually called the

---

[3] We stress that the only goal of this section is to provide timings on a concrete and non-artificial set of patterns. We chose the DPI use-case for which searching on encrypted streams is particularly relevant. But we obviously do not claim that our solution is practical enough to handle all Internet traffic worldwide.

String length (B)	1500	3000	5000	10000	30000
Encrypt (s)	0.08	0.15	0.27	0.5	1.5
Test (s)	0.6	1.2	1.6	3.3	11.1

Fig. 4. Timings for encrypting a string of m bytes and searching a pattern of 100 bytes within it.

Miller loop and the *final exponentiation*. The latter, which roughly represents half of the computational cost of a pairing, can be performed once for all the pairings involved in the same equality test, which allows to further reduce the complexity of the Test procedure.

We ran an experiment on a stream of 1500 bytes using a computer running Linux 4.13 and equipped with an Intel E5-1620 3.70 GHz processor. Testing all Snort rules took 28 min. This is obviously too much for online analysis but we stress that alternatives (*e.g.* FHE) offering the same features would be even more complex. Moreover, this corresponds to testing thousands of patterns on a single computer: by using parallelization and more powerful hardware, one could hope to dramatically reduce these timings.

Finally, we provide in Fig. 4 the timings of the Encrypt and the Test algorithms for larger strings (up to 30 KB). It shows that encryption remains quite efficient even for large strings. The Test algorithm is obviously slower since it implies pairings computations but it takes (approximatively) only one second for strings of few kilobytes.

7   Conclusion

In this work, we introduced the concept of searchable encryption with shiftable trapdoors (SEST). This type of construction provides a practical solution to the generic problem of pattern matching with universal tokens. Notably, we are the first to provide a searchable encryption alternative that allows for arbitrarily-chosen keywords of arbitrary length, which can be applied to any ciphertext encrypted with the generated public key in this system. In particular, since we do not rely on symmetric keys, multiple entities can use the same public key to encrypt. Moreover, our construction is also highly usable for encrypted *streams* of data (we need no backtracking), and it returns the exact position at which the pattern occurs. Our instantiation of the SEST primitive uses bilinear pairings, and we allow for some regular expressions such as wildcards, or partial keywords in which we know some entries to be within a given interval.

Beyond applications in deep-packet inspection, the fact that our algorithm essentially follows the approach of Rabin-Karp allows us to also use that same algorithm for application scenarios such as searching on structured data, matching subtrees to labelled trees, delegated searches on medical data (compiled from multiple institutions), or 2D searches.

We propose a main construction, which we adapt to accounting for wildcards and for interval searches. The former adaptation is relatively simple, since the issued trapdoor just contains zero coefficients for the wildcards. For the interval searches we need to modify our key generation algorithm, providing special elements that we map interval characters to; however, this only works for intervals which are known in advance.

Our scheme provides trapdoors for the keywords which are at most linear in the size of the keywords *only*, and the size of the ciphertexts is linear in the size of the plaintext size. Although our public keys are large (linear in the size of the maximal plaintext size), we do achieve a complete decorrelation between the plaintext encryption and the trapdoor generation for the keywords. Our scheme provides in practice an almost linear – in the size of the plaintext – complexity (in terms of the number of pairings). Our implementation results for the publicly-given SNORT rules show that while the encryption algorithm scales well with the plaintext size, the testing algorithm – which is slower – will benefit from the fact that it is fully parallelizable.

We prove the security of our scheme under an interactive version of the GDH assumption. Our modification of this assumption is relatively minor, allowing the adversary to choose on which input to play the GDH instance. We also argue that our construction offers an interesting tradeoff between the secure, but quite cumbersome, systems based on existing cryptographic primitives and the fast, but unsecure, current solutions where the gateway decrypts the traffic. Moreover, we hope that the practical applications of this primitive will incite new work on this subject, in particular to construct new schemes which would rely on standard assumptions.

Acknowledgments. Nicolas Desmoulins and Olivier Sanders were supported in part by the French ANR Project ANR-16-CE39-0014 PERSOCLOUD. Pierre-Alain Fouque and Cristina Onete are grateful for the support of the ANR through project 16 CE39 0012 (SafeTLS).

References

1. https://www.snort.org/
2. Abdalla, M., et al.: Searchable encryption revisited: consistency properties, relation to anonymous IBE, and extensions. In: Shoup, V. (ed.) CRYPTO 2005. LNCS, vol. 3621, pp. 205–222. Springer, Heidelberg (2005). https://doi.org/10.1007/11535218_13
3. Abdalla, M., Bourse, F., De Caro, A., Pointcheval, D.: Simple functional encryption schemes for inner products. In: Katz, J. (ed.) PKC 2015. LNCS, vol. 9020, pp. 733–751. Springer, Heidelberg (2015). https://doi.org/10.1007/978-3-662-46447-2_33
4. Agrawal, S., Gorbunov, S., Vaikuntanathan, V., Wee, H.: Functional encryption: new perspectives and lower bounds. In: Canetti, R., Garay, J.A. (eds.) CRYPTO 2013. LNCS, vol. 8043, pp. 500–518. Springer, Heidelberg (2013). https://doi.org/10.1007/978-3-642-40084-1_28
5. Baron, J., El Defrawy, K., Minkovich, K., Ostrovsky, R., Tressler, E.: 5PM: secure pattern matching. In: Visconti, I., De Prisco, R. (eds.) SCN 2012. LNCS, vol. 7485, pp. 222–240. Springer, Heidelberg (2012). https://doi.org/10.1007/978-3-642-32928-9_13

6. Barreto, P.S.L.M., Naehrig, M.: Pairing-friendly elliptic curves of prime order. In: Preneel, B., Tavares, S. (eds.) SAC 2005. LNCS, vol. 3897, pp. 319–331. Springer, Heidelberg (2006). https://doi.org/10.1007/11693383_22
7. Beuchat, J.-L., González-Díaz, J.E., Mitsunari, S., Okamoto, E., Rodríguez-Henríquez, F., Teruya, T.: High-speed software implementation of the optimal ate pairing over Barreto–Naehrig curves. In: Joye, M., Miyaji, A., Otsuka, A. (eds.) Pairing 2010. LNCS, vol. 6487, pp. 21–39. Springer, Heidelberg (2010). https://doi.org/10.1007/978-3-642-17455-1_2
8. Boneh, D., Boyen, X., Goh, E.-J.: Hierarchical identity based encryption with constant size ciphertext. In: Cramer, R. (ed.) EUROCRYPT 2005. LNCS, vol. 3494, pp. 440–456. Springer, Heidelberg (2005). https://doi.org/10.1007/11426639_26
9. Boneh, D., Di Crescenzo, G., Ostrovsky, R., Persiano, G.: Public key encryption with keyword search. In: Cachin, C., Camenisch, J.L. (eds.) EUROCRYPT 2004. LNCS, vol. 3027, pp. 506–522. Springer, Heidelberg (2004). https://doi.org/10.1007/978-3-540-24676-3_30
10. Boneh, D., Raghunathan, A., Segev, G.: Function-private identity-based encryption: hiding the function in functional encryption. In: Canetti, R., Garay, J.A. (eds.) CRYPTO 2013. LNCS, vol. 8043, pp. 461–478. Springer, Heidelberg (2013). https://doi.org/10.1007/978-3-642-40084-1_26
11. Boneh, D., Waters, B.: Conjunctive, subset, and range queries on encrypted data. In: Vadhan, S.P. (ed.) TCC 2007. LNCS, vol. 4392, pp. 535–554. Springer, Heidelberg (2007). https://doi.org/10.1007/978-3-540-70936-7_29
12. Boyen, X.: The uber-assumption family. In: Galbraith, S.D., Paterson, K.G. (eds.) Pairing 2008. LNCS, vol. 5209, pp. 39–56. Springer, Heidelberg (2008). https://doi.org/10.1007/978-3-540-85538-5_3
13. Brakerski, Z., Segev, G.: Function-private functional encryption in the private-key setting. In: Dodis, Y., Nielsen, J.B. (eds.) TCC 2015. LNCS, vol. 9015, pp. 306–324. Springer, Heidelberg (2015). https://doi.org/10.1007/978-3-662-46497-7_12
14. Canard, S., Diop, A., Kheir, N., Paindavoine, M., Sabt, M.: BlindIDS: market-compliant and privacy-friendly intrusion detection system over encrypted traffic. In: Karri, R., Sinanoglu, O., Sadeghi, A.-R., Yi, X. (eds.) Proceedings of the 2017 ACM on Asia Conference on Computer and Communications Security, AsiaCCS 2017, Abu Dhabi, United Arab Emirates, 2–6 April 2017, pp. 561–574. ACM (2017)
15. Canetti, R., Halevi, S., Katz, J.: A forward-secure public-key encryption scheme. In: Biham, E. (ed.) EUROCRYPT 2003. LNCS, vol. 2656, pp. 255–271. Springer, Heidelberg (2003). https://doi.org/10.1007/3-540-39200-9_16
16. Chase, M., Kamara, S.: Structured encryption and controlled disclosure. In: Abe, M. (ed.) ASIACRYPT 2010. LNCS, vol. 6477, pp. 577–594. Springer, Heidelberg (2010). https://doi.org/10.1007/978-3-642-17373-8_33
17. Chase, M., Shen, E.: Substring-searchable symmetric encryption. PoPETs **2015**(2), 263–281 (2015)
18. Curtmola, R., Garay, J.A., Kamara, S., Ostrovsky, R.: Searchable symmetric encryption: improved definitions and efficient constructions. In: Juels, A., Wright, R.N., De Capitani di Vimercati, S. (eds.) ACM CCS 06, pp. 79–88. ACM Press, October/November 2006
19. Desmoulins, N., Fouque, P.-A., Onete, C., Sanders, O.: Pattern matching on encrypted streams (full version). IACR Cryptology ePrint Archive 2017:148 (2017)
20. Galbraith, S.D., Paterson, K.G., Smart, N.P.: Pairings for cryptographers. Discrete Appl. Math. **156**(16), 3113–3121 (2008)
21. Gennaro, R., Hazay, C., Sorensen, J.S.: Automata evaluation and text search protocols with simulation-based security. J. Cryptol. **29**(2), 243–282 (2016)

22. Gentry, C.: Fully homomorphic encryption using ideal lattices. In: Mitzenmacher, M. (ed.) 41st ACM STOC, pp. 169–178. ACM Press, May/June 2009

23. Hazay, C., Lindell, Y.: Efficient protocols for set intersection and pattern matching with security against malicious and covert adversaries. J. Cryptol. **23**(3), 422–456 (2010)

24. Huang, L.-S., Rice, A., Ellingsen, E., Jackson, C.: Analyzing forged SSL certificates in the wild. In: 2014 IEEE Symposium on Security and Privacy, pp. 83–97. IEEE Computer Society Press, May 2014

25. Jarmoc, J.: SSL/TLS interception proxies and transitive trust. Presentation at Black Hat Europe (2012)

26. Katz, J., Malka, L.: Secure text processing with applications to private DNA matching. In: Al-Shaer, E., Keromytis, A.D., Shmatikov, V. (eds.) ACM CCS 10, pp. 485–492. ACM Press, October 2010

27. Katz, J., Sahai, A., Waters, B.: Predicate encryption supporting disjunctions, polynomial equations, and inner products. J. Cryptol. **26**(2), 191–224 (2013)

28. Lauter, K., López-Alt, A., Naehrig, M.: Private computation on encrypted genomic data. In: Aranha, D.F., Menezes, A. (eds.) LATINCRYPT 2014. LNCS, vol. 8895, pp. 3–27. Springer, Cham (2015). https://doi.org/10.1007/978-3-319-16295-9_1

29. Mohassel, P., Niksefat, S., Sadeghian, S., Sadeghiyan, B.: An efficient protocol for oblivious DFA evaluation and applications. In: Dunkelman, O. (ed.) CT-RSA 2012. LNCS, vol. 7178, pp. 398–415. Springer, Heidelberg (2012). https://doi.org/10.1007/978-3-642-27954-6_25

30. Naylor, D., et al.: Multi-context TLS (mcTLS): enabling secure in-network functionality in TLS. In: Proceedings of SIGCOMM 2015, pp. 199–212. ACM (2015)

31. Sherry, J., Lan, C., Popa, R.A., Ratnasamy, S.: BlindBox: deep packet inspection over encrypted traffic. In: Uhlig, S., Maennel, O., Karp, B., Padhye, J. (eds.) SIGCOMM 2015, pp. 213–226. ACM, August 2015

32. Song, D.X., Wagner, D., Perrig, A.: Practical techniques for searches on encrypted data. In: 2000 IEEE Symposium on Security and Privacy, pp. 44–55. IEEE Computer Society Press, May 2000

33. Troncoso-Pastoriza, J.R., Katzenbeisser, S., Celik, M.: Privacy preserving error resilient DNA searching through oblivious automata. In: Ning, P., De Capitani di Vimercati, S., Syverson, P.F. (eds.) ACM CCS 07, pp. 519–528. ACM Press, October 2007

34. Vercauteren, F.: Optimal pairings. IEEE Trans. Inf. Theory **56**(1), 455–461 (2010)

SQL on Structurally-Encrypted Databases

Seny Kamara$^{(\boxtimes)}$ and Tarik Moataz

Brown University, Providence, USA
{seny,tarik_moataz}@brown.edu

Abstract. We show how to encrypt a relational database in such a way that it can efficiently support a large class of SQL queries. Our construction is based solely on structured encryption (STE) and does not make use of any property-preserving encryption (PPE) schemes such as deterministic and order-preserving encryption. As such, our approach leaks considerably less than PPE-based solutions which have recently been shown to reveal a lot of information in certain settings (Naveed et al., *CCS '15*). Our construction is efficient and—under some conditions on the database and queries—can have asymptotically-optimal query complexity. We also show how to extend our solution to be dynamic while maintaining the scheme's optimal query complexity.

1 Introduction

The problem of encrypted search has received attention from industry, academia and government due to its potential applications to cloud computing and database security. Most of the progress in this area, however, has been in the setting of keyword search on encrypted documents. While this has many applications in practice (e.g., email, NoSQL databases, desktop search engines, cloud document storage), much of the data produced and consumed in practice is stored and processed in *relational databases*. A relational database is, roughly speaking, a set of tables with rows representing entities/items and columns representing their attributes. The relational database model was proposed by Codd [18] and most relational DBs are queried using the structured query language (SQL) which is a special-purpose declarative language introduced by Chamberlain and Boyce [14].

The problem of encrypted relational DBs is one of the "holy-grails" of database security. As far as we know, it was first explicitly considered by Hacigümüş et al. [25] who described a quantization-based approach which leaks the range within which an item falls. In [37], Popa, Redfield, Zeldovich and Balakrishnan describe a system called CryptDB that can support a non-trivial subset of SQL without quantization. CryptDB achieves this in part by making use of property-preserving encryption (PPE) schemes like deterministic and order-preserving (OPE) encryption, which reveal equality and order, respectively. The high-level approach is to replace the plaintext operations needed to execute a SQL query (e.g., equality tests and comparisons) by the same operations on PPE-encrypted ciphertexts. This approach was later adopted by other

T. Peyrin and S. Galbraith (Eds.): ASIACRYPT 2018, LNCS 11272, pp. 149–180, 2018.
https://doi.org/10.1007/978-3-030-03326-2_6

systems including Cipherbase [3] and SEEED [23]. While this leads to systems that are efficient and legacy-friendly, it was shown by Naveed et al. [34] that PPE-based EDB systems can leak a lot of information when used in certain settings like electronic medical records (EMRs). In light of this result, the major open problem in encrypted search and, more generally, in database security is whether it is possible to efficiently execute SQL queries on encrypted DBs with less leakage than the PPE-based solutions.

Our Contributions. In this work, we address this problem and propose the first solution for SQL on encrypted DBs that does not make use of either PPE or general-purpose primitives like fully-homomorphic encryption (FHE) or oblivious RAM (ORAM).[1] As such, our scheme leaks less than any of the previously-known practical approaches and is more practical than any solution based on FHE or ORAM. Our approach is efficient and handles a sub-class of SQL queries and an even larger class if we allow for a small amount of post-processing at the client.

More precisely, our construction handles the class of *conjunctive queries*[2] [15] which corresponds to SQL queries of the form

$$\text{Select } attributes \text{ From } tables \text{ Where } \left(\text{att}_1 = X_1 \wedge \cdots \wedge \text{att}_\ell = X_\ell\right),$$

where att_1 through att_ℓ are attributes in the DB schema and X_1 through X_n are either attributes or constants. For ease of exposition, we mainly focus on conjunctive queries with Where predicates that are *uncorrelated* which, very roughly speaking, means that the attributes are not the same across terms (we refer the reader to Sect. 5 for a precise definition). The case of correlated predicates is quite involved so it is deferred to the full version of this work. While the class of conjunctive queries is smaller than the class supported by the PPE-based solutions, it is one of the most well-studied and useful classes of queries. Furthermore, as mentioned above, if one allows for a small amount of post-processing at the client, we show how to extend the expressiveness of our solution to a wider sub-class.

With respect to efficiency, we show that the query complexity of our scheme is asymptotically optimal in time and space when $(s_1 + \cdots + s_t)/h = O(1)$, where t denotes the number of tables in the query, s_i denotes the number of

---

[1] In the full version of this work, we present a dynamic variant of our construction that makes use of ORAM to achieve forward-security, but it is only used to store and manage one of several data structures needed by the scheme. In other words, ORAM is not used to store and manage the entire database.

[2] We stress that conjunctive queries in the context of relational databases (and as used throughout this work) is conceptually unrelated to conjunctive *keyword* queries as studied in the searchable encryption literature (e.g., in [12,28]). In particular, our scheme does not make use of any searchable encryption schemes for conjunctive keyword queries and our problem cannot be solved by applying these schemes directly on tables. However it is worth mentioning that some of the techniques in the expressive SSE literature could possibly be leveraged to achieve a better leakage profile.

columns in the ith table and h denotes the number of attributes in the Select term of the query. Towards analyzing the asymptotic complexity of our solution, we precisely characterize the result size of an SPC query as a function of the query and of the underlying relational database. This analysis, deferred to the full version of this work, could be of independent interest.

We also show how to extend our construction to be dynamic and to support two traditional SQL update operations: row addition and row deletions. Surprisingly, our dynamic construction has the same asymptotic efficiency as our static construction. Finally, we show how to extend our dynamic construction to be forward-secure at the cost of a poly-logarithmic overhead for updates but maintaining the same query complexity.

1.1 Possible Approaches

PPE-Based. The PPE-based approach to EDBs essentially replaces the plaintext execution of a SQL query with an encrypted execution of the query by executing the server's low-level operations (i.e., comparisons and equality tests) directly on the encrypted cells. This can be done thanks to the properties of PPE which guarantee that operations on plaintexts can be done on ciphertexts as well. This "plug-and-play" approach makes the design of EDBs relatively straightforward since the only requirement is to replace plaintext cells with PPE-encrypted cells. This approach however has been shown to leak a lot of information in certain scenarios [34].

SSE-Based. Searchable symmetric encryption (SSE) allows one to perform search queries on an encrypted document collection. While SSE constructions do not yield an encrypted relational database, they could be used to handle a very small subset of SQL. By applying SSE to a column one could handle queries of the form

$$\text{Select } attribute \text{ From } table \text{ Where att} = X,$$

where att is the attribute that has been indexed with SSE and X is a constant. If the SSE scheme supports ranges this would extend to queries of the form

$$\text{Select } attribute \text{ From } table \text{ Where att} \ominus X,$$

where $\ominus \in \{=, <, >\}$ and if it supports conjunctions it would extend to

$$\text{Select } attribute \text{ From } table \text{ Where } \big(\text{att} = X_1 \wedge \cdots \wedge \text{att} = X_\ell\big).$$

Note that the supported queries in both cases are limited to a *single* column and a *single* table, and *don't support joins or projections*. This is, unfortunately, far from what is expected from a relational database. In addition, extending existing expressive SSE schemes (e.g., OXT [12], BlindSeer [36] or IEX [28]) to handle SQL operations would be highly non-trivial—unless one used the naive approach of executing many simple queries and having the server build the response (e.g., like the naive approach to conjunctions or disjunctions) which would leak a lot more. In general, expressiveness in SSE does not imply the same level of expressiveness in the relational setting, i.e., we cannot use an expressive SSE scheme in a "plug-and-play" fashion (similar to PPE) to handle the same level of expressiveness in relational databases.

Generic Approaches. Fully-homomorphic encryption (FHE) or oblivious RAM (ORAM) could be used in a black-box fashion to handle *full* SQL. However, these approaches would be inefficient due the inherent cost of the primitives.

1.2   Our Techniques

Conceptual Approach. Our first step towards a solution is in isolating some of the conceptual difficulties of the problem. Relational DBs are relatively simple from a data structure perspective since they just consist of a set of two-dimensional arrays. The high-level challenge stems from SQL and, in particular, from its complexity (it can express first-order logic) and the fact that it is *declarative*. To overcome this we restrict ourselves to a simpler but widely applicable and well-studied subset of SQL queries (see above) and we take a more procedural view. More precisely, we work with the *relational algebra* formulation of SQL which is more amenable to cryptographic techniques. The relational algebra was introduced by Codd [18] as a way to formalize queries on relational databases. Roughly speaking, it consists of all the queries that can be expressed from a set of basic operations. It was later shown by Chandra and Merlin [15] that three of these operations (selection, projection and cross product) capture a large class of useful queries called *conjunctive queries* that have particularly nice theoretical properties. Since their introduction, conjunctive queries have been studied extensively in the database literature.

The subset of the relational algebra expressed by the selection, projection and cross product operators is also called the *SPC algebra*. By working in the SPC algebra, we not only get a procedural representation of SQL queries, but we also reduce the problem to handling just three basic operations. Conceptually, this is reminiscent of the benefits one gets by working with circuits in secure multi-party computation and FHE. Another important advantage of working in the SPC algebra is that it admits a *normal form*; that is, every SPC query can be written in a standard form. By working with this normal form, we get another benefit of general-purpose solutions which are that we can design and analyze a *single* construction that handles *all* SPC queries. Note, however, that like circuit representations the SPC normal form is not always guaranteed to be the most efficient.

The SPC Algebra. As mentioned, the SPC algebra consists of all queries that can be expressed by a combination of the select, project and cross product operators which, at a high-level, work as follows. The select operator σ_Ψ takes as input a table T and outputs the rows of T that satisfy the predicate Ψ. The project operator $\pi_{\mathsf{att}_1,\dots,\mathsf{att}_h}$ takes as input a table T and outputs the columns of T indexed by $\mathsf{att}_1,\dots,\mathsf{att}_h$. Finally, the cross product operator $\mathsf{T}_1 \times \mathsf{T}_2$ takes two tables as input and outputs a third table consisting of rows in the cross product of T_1 and T_2 when viewed as sets of rows. An SPC query in normal form over a database $\mathsf{DB} = (\mathsf{T}_1,\dots,\mathsf{T}_n)$ has the form,

$$\pi_{\mathsf{att}_1,\cdots,\mathsf{att}_h}\left([a_1] \times \cdots \times [a_f] \times \sigma_\Psi(\mathsf{T}_{i_1} \times \cdots \times \mathsf{T}_{i_t})\right),$$

where $[a_j]$ is a 1×1 table that holds a constant a_j for all $j \in [f]$, Ψ is of the form $\mathsf{att}_1 = X_1 \wedge \cdots \wedge \mathsf{att}_\ell = X_\ell$ where $\mathsf{att}_1,\dots,\mathsf{att}_\ell$ are attributes in the schema of DB and $X_1,\dots,X_\ell$ are either attributes or constants. So, concretely, our problem reduces to the problem of encrypting a relational database $\mathsf{DB} = (\mathsf{T}_1,\dots,\mathsf{T}_n)$ in such a way that it can support SPC queries in normal form.

Structured Encryption and Constructive Queries. The main difficulty in the case of relational DBs and, in particular, in handling SPC queries is that queries are *constructive* in the sense that they produce new data structures from the original base structure. Intuitively, handling constructive queries (without interaction) is particularly challenging because the intermediate and final structures that have to be created by the server to answer the query are *dependent* on the query and, therefore, cannot be constructed by the client in the setup/pre-processing phase. An important observation about relational DBs that underlies our approach, however, is that while SPC queries are constructive, they are not arbitrarily so. In other words, the tables needed to answer an SPC query are not completely arbitrary but are structured in a way that can be predicted at setup. What is query-dependent is the *content* of these tables but, crucially, all of that content is already stored in the original database. So the challenge then is to provide the server with the means to construct the appropriate intermediate and final tables and to design encrypted structures that will allow it to efficiently find the (encrypted) content it needs to create those tables.

Handling SPC Normal Form Queries. By taking a closer look at the SPC normal form, one can see that the first intermediate table needed to answer a query is the cross product $\mathsf{T}' = \mathsf{T}_{i_1} \times \cdots \times \mathsf{T}_{i_t}$. Ignoring the cross products with $[a_1],\dots,[a_f]$ for ease of exposition, the remaining intermediate tables as well as the final table are "sub-tables" of T' that result from selecting a subset of rows (according to Ψ) and keeping a subset of columns (according to $\mathsf{att}_1,\dots,\mathsf{att}_h$). Handling such a query naively requires one to first compute the cross product of the tables which can be prohibitively large. As we show in Sect. 5, however, SPC normal form queries can be rewritten in a different and optimized form we introduce called the heuristic normal form (HNF). We then show how to encrypt the database in such a way that we can handle queries in their HNF form. At a high level, we achieve this by creating a set of encrypted structures that store different representations of the database. For example, one of the encrypted structures stores a row-wise representation of the database whereas another stores a column-wise representation. By using these various representations and by combining them in an appropriate manner, we can generate tokens for the server to recover the encrypted database rows needed for it to process the query in its HNF form.

The SPX Framework. We describe and analyze our scheme using algorithms that make black-box use of several lower-level STE schemes (e.g., multi-map and dictionary encryption schemes). As such, our construction is more of a framework that can be used to design encrypted relational databases with various efficiency/leakage trade-offs. In fact, in Sect. 7.1, we describe an instantiations of our framework with a zero-leakage variant of the TWORAM-based construction of Garg et al. [20] which results in a very low-leakage construction at the cost of an additional poly-logarithmic overhead.

Dynamism. We show how to extend our static construction to be dynamic. This is challenging as we want to maintain the scheme's query complexity while not introducing additional leakage. From a functionality perspective, we restrict our attention to row additions and deletions and leave as important open problem the handling of more complex update operations. While real-world databases also handle edits, we note that these two update operations are already interesting in practice and non-trivial to achieve. As discussed above, we store different encrypted representations of the database. One of these representations, however, stores parts of the database that are highly inter-correlated. The difficulty this poses is that we cannot simply add or remove items from this structure as any change affects all the other items stored in the structure. We introduce a two-party protocol to solve this challenge without the client having to trivially download the entire structure and without leaking too much information to the server. We then show how to extend this solution to be forward-secure at the cost of a poly-logarithmic blowup (for updates). This is achieved by storing and managing one of the structures in an oblivious RAM.

A Note on Our Techniques. We stress that our approach to handle the SPC algebra is very different from how these queries are handled on plaintext databases. In other words, our approach does not simply replicate standard data structures and algorithms from the database literature. In fact, our approach to handling SPC queries could be of independent interest for plaintext relational databases.

2   Related Work

Searchable and Structured Encryption. Encrypted search was first considered explicitly by Song et al. in [38] which introduced the notion of searchable symmetric encryption (SSE). Goh provided the first security definition for SSE and a solution based on Bloom filters with linear search complexity. Curtmola et al. introduced and formulated the notion of adaptive semantic security for SSE [19] together with optimal-time and optimal-space constructions. Chase and Kamara introduced the notion of structured encryption which generalizes SSE to arbitrary data structures [16]. Cash et al. [11] show how to construct optimal-time SSE schemes with low I/O complexity and Cash and Tessaro [13] gave lower bounds on the locality of adaptively-secure SSE schemes. Asharov et al. build SSE schemes with optimal locality, optimal space overhead and nearly-optimal read efficiency [4]. Garg et al. [20] presented a new SSE construction with reduced leakage leveraging oblivious RAM and garbled RAM techniques. Bost [9] proposed an efficient forward-secure SSE construction based on trapdoor permutations. SSE has also been considered in the multi-user setting [19,27]. Pappas et al. [36] proposed a multi-user SSE construction based on garbled circuits and Bloom filters that can support Boolean formulas, ranges and stemming. Other approaches for encrypted search include oblivious RAMs (ORAM) [22], secure multi-party computation [6], functional encryption [8] and fully-homomorphic encryption [21] as well as solutions based on deterministic encryption [5] and order-preserving encryption (OPE) [7].

Encrypted Relational Databases. As far as we know the first encrypted relational DB solution was proposed by Hacigümüş et al. [25] and was based on quantization. Roughly speaking, the attribute space of each column is partitioned into bins and each element in the column is replaced with its bin number. Popa et al. proposed CryptDB [37]. CryptDB was the first non-quantization-based solution and can handle a large subset of SQL. Instead of quantization, CryptDB relies on PPE like deterministic encryption [5] and OPE [2,7]. The CryptDB design influenced the Cipherbase system from Arasu *et al.* [3] and the SEEED system from Grofig *et al.* [23]. In [34], Naveed et al. study the security of these PPE-based solutions in the context of medical data. Recently, Grubbs et al. [24] point out pitfalls in integrating encrypted database solutions in real-world database management systems (DBMS).

Attacks on SSE. While we do not consider the problem of designing an SSE scheme in this work, we can use SSE schemes as building blocks to instantiate SPX. Several works have proposed attacks that try to exploit the leakage of SSE. This includes the query-recovery attacks of Islam et al. [26], of Cash et al. [10] and of Zhang et al. [40]. Recently, Abdelraheem et al. [33], presented attacks on encrypted relational databases. We briefly mention here that although the attacks in [33] are ostensibly on relational EDBs, they are not related to or applicable to our construction. For more details on these attacks and their relation to our work we refer the reader to Sect. 7.3.

3 Preliminaries

Notation. The set of all binary strings of length n is denoted as $\{0,1\}^n$, and the set of all finite binary strings as $\{0,1\}^*$. $[n]$ is the set of integers $\{1,\ldots,n\}$. We write $x \leftarrow \chi$ to represent an element x being sampled from a distribution χ, and $x \xleftarrow{\$} X$ to represent an element x being sampled uniformly at random from a set X. The output x of an algorithm $\mathcal{A}$ is denoted by $x \leftarrow \mathcal{A}$. Given a sequence $\mathbf{v}$ of n elements, we refer to its ith element as v_i or $\mathbf{v}[i]$. If S is a set then $\#S$ refers to its cardinality. If s is a string then $|s|$ refers to its bit length.

Basic Structures. We make use of several basic data types including dictionaries and multi-maps which we recall here. A dictionary DX of capacity n is a collection of n label/value pairs $\{(\ell_i, v_i)\}_{i \leq n}$ and supports get and put operations. We write $v_i := \mathsf{DX}[\ell_i]$ to denote getting the value associated with label ℓ_i and $\mathsf{DX}[\ell_i] := v_i$ to denote the operation of associating the value v_i in DX with label ℓ_i. A multi-map MM with capacity n is a collection of n label/tuple pairs $\{(\ell_i, \mathbf{t}_i)\}_{i \leq n}$ that supports get and put operations. Similarly to dictionaries, we write $\mathbf{t}_i := \mathsf{MM}[\ell_i]$ to denote getting the tuple associated with label ℓ_i and $\mathsf{MM}[\ell_i] := \mathbf{t}_i$ to denote operation of associating the tuple $\mathbf{t}_i$ to label ℓ_i. Note that tuples may have different lengths. Multi-maps are the abstract data type instantiated by an inverted index. In the encrypted search literature multi-maps are sometimes referred to as indexes, databases or tuple-sets (T-sets). We refer to the set of all possible queries a data structure supports as its *query space* and to the set of its possible responses as its *response space*. For some data structure DS we sometimes write $\mathsf{DS} : \mathbf{Q} \rightarrow \mathbf{R}$ to mean that DS has query and response spaces $\mathbf{Q}$ and $\mathbf{R}$, respectively.

Relational Databases. A relational database $\mathsf{DB} = (\mathsf{T}_1, \ldots, \mathsf{T}_n)$ is a set of *tables* where each table T_i is a two-dimensional array with rows corresponding to an entity (e.g., a customer or an employee) and columns corresponding to attributes (e.g., age, height, salary). For any given attribute, we refer to the set of all possible values that it can take as its *domain* (e.g., integers, booleans, strings). We define the *schema* of a table T to be its set of attributes and denote it $\mathbb{S}(\mathsf{T})$. The schema of a database $\mathsf{DB} = (\mathsf{T}_1, \ldots, \mathsf{T}_n)$ is then the set $\mathbb{S}(\mathsf{DB}) = \bigcup_i \mathbb{S}(\mathsf{T}_i)$. We assume the attributes in $\mathbb{S}(\mathsf{DB})$ are unique and represented as positive integers. We denote a table T's number of rows as $\|\mathsf{T}\|_r$ and its number of columns as $\|\mathsf{T}\|_c$.

We sometimes view tables as a tuple of rows and write $\mathbf{r} \in \mathsf{T}$ and sometimes as a tuple of columns and write $\mathbf{c} \in \mathsf{T}^\mathsf{T}$. Similarly, we write $\mathbf{r} \in \mathsf{DB}$ and $\mathbf{c} \in \mathsf{DB}^\mathsf{T}$ for $\mathbf{r} \in \bigcup_i \mathsf{T}_i$ and $\mathbf{c} \in \bigcup_i \mathsf{T}_i^\mathsf{T}$, respectively. For a row $\mathbf{r} \in \mathsf{T}_i$, its table identifier $\mathsf{tbl}(\mathbf{r})$ is i and its row rank $\mathsf{rrk}(\mathbf{r})$ is its position in T_i when viewed as a tuple of rows. Similarly, for a column $\mathbf{c} \in \mathsf{T}_i^\mathsf{T}$, its table identifier $\mathsf{tbl}(\mathbf{c})$ is i and its column rank $\mathsf{crk}(\mathbf{c})$ is its position in T_i when viewed as a tuple of columns. For any row $\mathbf{r} \in \mathsf{DB}$ and column $\mathbf{c} \in \mathsf{DB}^\mathsf{T}$, we refer to the pairs $\chi(\mathbf{r}) \stackrel{def}{=} (\mathsf{tbl}(\mathbf{r}), \mathsf{rrk}(\mathbf{r}))$

and $\chi(\mathbf{c}) \overset{def}{=} (\mathsf{tbl}(\mathbf{c}), \mathsf{crk}(\mathbf{c}))$, respectively, as their *coordinates* in DB. Similarly, we denote by $\chi(\mathsf{att})$ the coordinate of column $\mathbf{c}$ with attribute $\mathsf{att} \in \mathbb{S}(\mathsf{DB})$ such that $\chi(\mathsf{att}) = \chi(\mathbf{c})$. We write $\mathbf{r}[i]$ and $\mathbf{c}[i]$ to refer to the ith element of a row $\mathbf{r}$ and column $\mathbf{c}$. The coordinate of the jth cell in row $\mathbf{r} \in \mathsf{T}_i$ is the triple $(i, \mathsf{rrk}(\mathbf{r}), j)$. Given a column $\mathbf{c} \in \mathsf{DB}^\mathsf{T}$, we denote its corresponding attribute by $\mathsf{att}(\mathbf{c})$. For any pair of attributes $\mathsf{att}_1, \mathsf{att}_2 \in \mathbb{S}(\mathsf{DB})$ with the same domain such that $\mathsf{dom}(\mathsf{att}_1) = \mathsf{dom}(\mathsf{att}_2)$, $\mathsf{DB}_{\mathsf{att}_1 = \mathsf{att}_2}$ denotes the set of row pairs $\{(\mathbf{r}_1, \mathbf{r}_2) \in \mathsf{DB}^2 : \mathbf{r}_1[\mathsf{att}_1] = \mathbf{r}_2[\mathsf{att}_2]\}$. For any attribute $\mathsf{att} \in \mathbb{S}(\mathsf{DB})$ and constant $a \in \mathsf{dom}(\mathsf{att})$, $\mathsf{DB}_{\mathsf{att} = a}$ is the set of rows $\{\mathbf{r} \in \mathsf{DB} : \mathbf{r}[\mathsf{att}] = a\}$.

SQL. In practice, relational databases are queried using the special-purpose language SQL, introduced by Chamberlain and Boyce [14]. SQL is a declarative language and can be used to modify and query a relational DB. In this work, we only focus on its query operations. Informally, SQL queries typically have the form

Select attributes From tables Where condition,

where *attributes* is a set of attributes/columns, *tables* is a set of tables and *condition* is a predicate over the rows of *tables* and can itself contain a nested SQL query. More complex queries can be obtained using Group-by, Order-by and aggregate operators (i.e., max, min, average etc.) but the simple form above already captures a large subset of SQL. The most common class of queries on relational DBs are *conjunctive queries* [15] which have the above form with the restriction that *condition* is a conjunction of equalities over attributes and constants. In particular, this means there are no nested queries in *condition*. More precisely, conjunctive queries have the form

Select attributes From tables Where $\left(\mathsf{att}_1 = X_1 \wedge \cdots \wedge \mathsf{att}_\ell = X_\ell\right),$

where att_i is an attribute in $\mathbb{S}(\mathsf{DB})$ and X_i can be either an attribute or a constant.

The SPC Algebra. It was shown by Chandra and Merlin [15] that conjunctive queries could be expressed as a subset of Codd's relational algebra which is an imperative query language based on a set of basic operators. In particular, they showed that three operators *select*, *project* and *cross product* were enough. The *select* operator σ_Ψ is parameterized with a predicate Ψ and takes as input a table T and outputs a new table T' that includes the rows of T that satisfy the predicate Ψ. The *projection* operator $\pi_{\mathsf{att}_1, \ldots, \mathsf{att}_h}$ is parameterized by a set of attributes $\mathsf{att}_1, \ldots, \mathsf{att}_h$ and takes as input a table T and outputs a table T' that consists of the columns of T indexed by att_1 through att_n. The *cross product* operator $\times$ takes as input two tables T_1 and T_2 and outputs a new table $\mathsf{T}' = \mathsf{T}_1 \times \mathsf{T}_2$ such that each row of T' is an element of the cross product between the set of rows of T_1 and the set of rows of T_2. The query language that results from any combination of select, project and cross product is referred to as the *SPC algebra*. We formalize this in Definition 1 below.

Definition 1 (SPC algebra). *Let* $\mathsf{DB} = (\mathsf{T}_1, \ldots, \mathsf{T}_n)$ *be a relational database. The SPC algebra consists of any query that results from the combination of the following operators:*

- $\mathsf{T}' \leftarrow \sigma_\Psi(\mathsf{T})$: *the* select *operator is parameterized with a predicate* Ψ *of form* $\mathsf{att}_1 = X_1 \wedge \cdots \wedge \mathsf{att}_\ell = X_\ell$, *where* $\mathsf{att}_i \in \mathbb{S}(\mathsf{DB})$ *and* X_i *is either a constant equal to* a *in the domain of* att_i *(type-1) or an attribute* $\mathsf{x}_j \in \mathbb{S}(\mathsf{DB})$ *(type-2). It takes as input a table* $\mathsf{T} \in \mathsf{DB}$ *and outputs a table* $\mathsf{T}' = \{\mathbf{r} \in \mathsf{T} : \Psi(\mathbf{r}) = 1\}$, *where terms of the form* $\mathsf{att}_i = \mathsf{x}_j$ *are satisfied if* $\mathbf{r}[\mathsf{att}_i] = \mathbf{r}[\mathsf{x}_j]$ *and terms of the form* $\mathsf{att}_i = a$ *are satisfied if* $\mathbf{r}[\mathsf{att}_i] = a$.
- $\mathsf{T}' \leftarrow \pi_{\mathsf{att}_1, \ldots, \mathsf{att}_h}(\mathsf{T})$: *the* project *operator is parameterized by a set of attributes* $\mathsf{att}_1, \ldots, \mathsf{att}_h \in \mathbb{S}(\mathsf{DB})$. *It takes as input a table* $\mathsf{T} \in \mathsf{DB}$ *and outputs a table* $\mathsf{T}' = \{\langle \mathbf{r}[\mathsf{att}_1], \ldots, \mathbf{r}[\mathsf{att}_h] \rangle : \mathbf{r} \in \mathsf{T}\}$.
- $\mathsf{R} \leftarrow \mathsf{T}_1 \times \mathsf{T}_2$: *the* cross product *operator takes as input two tables* T_1 *and* T_2 *and outputs a result table* $\mathsf{R} = \{\langle \mathbf{r}, \mathbf{v} \rangle : \mathbf{r} \in \mathsf{T}_1 \text{ and } \mathbf{v} \in \mathsf{T}_2\}$, *where* $\langle \mathbf{r}, \mathbf{v} \rangle$ *is the concatenation of rows* $\mathbf{r}$ *and* $\mathbf{v}$.

Intuitively, the connection between conjunctive SQL queries and the SPC algebra can be seen as follows: Select corresponds to the projection operator, From to the cross product and Where to the (SPC) select operator.

SPC Normal Form. Any query in the SPC algebra can be reduced to a *normal form* using a certain set of well-known identities. The normal form of an SPC query over a relational database $\mathsf{DB} = (\mathsf{T}_1, \ldots, \mathsf{T}_n)$ has the form:

$$\pi_{\mathsf{att}_1, \cdots, \mathsf{att}_h}\left([a_1] \times \cdots \times [a_f] \times \sigma_\Psi(\mathsf{T}_{i_1} \times \cdots \times \mathsf{T}_{i_t})\right),$$

where $a_1, \ldots, a_f \in \bigcup_{\mathsf{att} \in \mathbb{S}(\mathsf{DB})} \mathsf{dom}(\mathsf{att})$ and $[a_j]$ is the 1×1 table that holds a_j. The 1×1 tables are needed for the normal form to have enough expressive power to capture the SPC algebra (for more details see [1]). Here, the attributes $\mathsf{att}_1, \ldots, \mathsf{att}_h$ in the projection are either in $\mathbb{S}(\mathsf{DB})$ or refer to the columns generated by $[a_1]$ through $[a_f]$. In the latter case, we say that they are *virtual attributes* and are in $\mathbb{S}(\mathsf{VDB})$, where VDB is the *virtual database* defined as $\mathsf{VDB} = ([a_1], \ldots, [a_f])$.

One of the advantages of working in the relational algebra is that it allows for powerful optimization techniques. Given a query, we can use several identities to rewrite the query so that it can be executed more efficiently. The topic of query optimization is a large and important area of research in both database theory and engineering and real-world database management systems crucially rely on sophisticated query optimization algorithms. The main disadvantage of working with SPC queries in normal form is that their execution is extremely expensive, i.e., exponential in t. Furthermore, it is a-priori unclear how one could use standard query optimization techniques over encrypted data. We will see in Sect. 5, however, that these challenges can be overcome.

We note that while executing normal form SPC queries is prohibitively expensive, converting conjunctive SQL queries to normal form SPC queries is a well-studied problem with highly-optimized solutions. In particular, the queries that result from such a translation are "compact" in the sense that the number of projects, selects and cross products in the resulting SPC query is the same as the number of attributes, tables and conditions, respectively, in the original SQL query (for an overview of SQL-to-SPC translation we refer the reader to [39]).

Basic Cryptographic Primitives. We make use of encryption schemes that are random-ciphertext-secure against chosen-plaintext attacks (RCPA). RCPA-secure encryption can be instantiated practically using either the standard PRF-based private-key encryption scheme or, e.g., AES in counter mode.

4 Definitions

In this Section, we define the syntax and security of STE schemes. A STE scheme encrypts data structures in such a way that they can be privately queried. There are several natural forms of structured encryption. The original definition of [16] considered schemes that encrypt both a structure and a set of associated data items (e.g., documents, emails, user profiles etc.). In [17], the authors also describe *structure-only* schemes which only encrypt structures. Another distinction can be made between *interactive* and *non-interactive* schemes. Interactive schemes produce encrypted structures that are queried through an interactive two-party protocol, whereas non-interactive schemes produce structures that can be queried by sending a single message, i.e, the token. One can also distinguish between *response-hiding* and *response-revealing* schemes: the latter reveal the query response to the server whereas the former do not.

Our main construction, SPX, is response-hiding but makes use of response-revealing schemes as building blocks. Furthermore, SPX's building blocks can be instantiated using either non-interactive or interactive schemes. We define response-hiding and response-revealing schemes below, but only for the non-interactive setting. The definitions, however, can be naturally extended to the interactive case. At a high-level, non-interactive STE works as follows. During a setup phase, the client constructs an encrypted structure EDS under a key K from a plaintext structure DS. The client then sends EDS to the server. During the query phase, the client constructs and sends a token tk generated from its query q and secret key K. The server then uses the token tk to query EDS and recover either a response r or an encryption ct of r depending on whether the scheme is response-revealing or response-hiding.

Definition 2 (Response-revealing structured encryption [16]). *A response-revealing structured encryption scheme $\Sigma = $ (Setup, Token, Query) consists of three polynomial-time algorithms that work as follows:*

- *$(K, \text{EDS}) \leftarrow \text{Setup}(1^k, \text{DS})$: is a probabilistic algorithm that takes as input a security parameter 1^k and a structure DS and outputs a secret key K and an encrypted structure EDS.*
- *tk $\leftarrow \text{Token}(K, q)$: is a (possibly) probabilistic algorithm that takes as input a secret key K and a query q and returns a token tk.*

- $\{\bot, r\} \leftarrow$ Query(EDS, tk): *is a deterministic algorithm that takes as input an encrypted structure* EDS *and a token* tk *and outputs either* $\bot$ *or a response.*

We say that a response-revealing structured encryption scheme Σ *is correct if for all* $k \in \mathbb{N}$, *for all* poly(k)*-size structures* DS : $\mathbf{Q} \rightarrow \mathbf{R}$, *for all* (K, EDS) *output by* Setup$(1^k, \mathsf{DS})$ *and all sequences of* $m = $ poly(k) *queries* $q_1, \ldots, q_m$, *for all tokens* tk$_i$ *output by* Token(K, q_i), Query(EDS, tk$_i$) *returns* DS(q_i) *with all but negligible probability.*

Definition 3 (Response-hiding structured encryption [16]). *A response-hiding structured encryption scheme* $\Sigma = $ (Setup, Token, Query, Dec) *consists of four polynomial-time algorithms such that* Setup *and* Token *are as in Definition 2 and* Query *and* Dec *are defined as follows:*

- $\{\bot, ct\} \leftarrow$ Query(EDS, tk): *is a deterministic algorithm that takes as input an encrypted structured* EDS *and a token* tk *and outputs either* $\bot$ *or a ciphertext* ct.
- $r \leftarrow$ Dec(K, ct): *is a deterministic algorithm that takes as input a secret key* K *and a ciphertext* ct *and outputs a response* r.

We say that a response-hiding structured encryption scheme Σ *is correct if for all* $k \in \mathbb{N}$, *for all* poly(k)*-size structures* DS : $\mathbf{Q} \rightarrow \mathbf{R}$, *for all* (K, EDS) *output by* Setup$(1^k, \mathsf{DS})$ *and all sequences of* $m = $ poly(k) *queries* $q_1, \ldots, q_m$, *for all tokens* tk$_i$ *output by* Token(K, q_i), Dec$_K$(Query(EDS, tk$_i$)) *returns* DS(q_i) *with all but negligible probability.*

Security. The standard notion of security for structured encryption guarantees that an encrypted structure reveals no information about its underlying structure beyond the setup leakage $\mathcal{L}_S$ and that the query algorithm reveals no information about the structure and the queries beyond the query leakage $\mathcal{L}_Q$. If this holds for non-adaptively chosen operations then this is referred to as non-adaptive semantic security. If, on the other hand, the operations are chosen adaptively, this leads to the stronger notion of adaptive semantic security. This notion of security was introduced by Curtmola et al. in the context of SSE [19] and later generalized to structured encryption in [16].

Definition 4 (Adaptive semantic security [16,19]). *Let* $\Sigma = $ (Setup, Token, Query) *be a response-revealing structured encryption scheme and consider the following probabilistic experiments where* $\mathcal{A}$ *is a stateful adversary,* $\mathcal{S}$ *is a stateful simulator,* $\mathcal{L}_S$ *and* $\mathcal{L}_Q$ *are leakage profiles and* $z \in \{0, 1\}^*$:

Real$_{\Sigma, \mathcal{A}}(k)$: *given* z *the adversary* $\mathcal{A}$ *outputs a structure* DS. *It receives* EDS *from the challenger, where* $(K, \mathsf{EDS}) \leftarrow$ Setup$(1^k, \mathsf{DS})$. *The adversary then adaptively chooses a polynomial number of queries* $q_1, \ldots, q_m$. *For all* $i \in [m]$, *the adversary receives* tk $\leftarrow$ Token(K, q_i). *Finally,* $\mathcal{A}$ *outputs a bit* b *that is output by the experiment.*

Ideal$_{\Sigma, \mathcal{A}, \mathcal{S}}(k)$: *given* z *the adversary* $\mathcal{A}$ *generates a structure* DS *which it sends to the challenger. Given* z *and leakage* $\mathcal{L}_S(\mathsf{DS})$ *from the challenger, the simulator*

$\mathcal{S}$ returns an encrypted data structure EDS to $\mathcal{A}$. The adversary then adaptively chooses a polynomial number of operations $q_1, \ldots, q_m$. For all $i \in [m]$, the simulator receives a tuple $\big(\mathsf{DS}(q_i), \mathcal{L}_Q(\mathsf{DS}, q_i)\big)$ and returns a token tk_i to $\mathcal{A}$. Finally, $\mathcal{A}$ outputs a bit b that is output by the experiment.

We say that Σ is adaptively $(\mathcal{L}_S, \mathcal{L}_Q)$-semantically secure if there exists a PPT *simulator $\mathcal{S}$ such that for all* PPT *adversaries $\mathcal{A}$, for all $z \in \{0,1\}^*$, the following expression is negligible in k:*

$$\big| \Pr\left[\, \mathbf{Real}_{\Sigma,\mathcal{A}}(k) = 1 \,\right] - \Pr\left[\, \mathbf{Ideal}_{\Sigma,\mathcal{A},\mathcal{S}}(k) = 1 \,\right] \big|$$

The security definition for *response-hiding* schemes can be derived from Definition 4 by giving the simulator $\big(\bot, \mathcal{L}_Q(\mathsf{DS}, q_i)\big)$ instead of $\big(\mathsf{DS}(q_i), \mathcal{L}_Q(\mathsf{DS}, q_i)\big)$.

5   SPX: A Relational Database Encryption Scheme

In this Section we describe our main construction SPX. We start by giving a high-level overview of two of the main techniques we rely on. The first is how we index the DB to in order to handle HNF queries efficiently. The second is how we use the "chaining" technique from [16] to build complex encrypted structures from simpler ones.

Database Indexing. The first step of our construction is to build different representations of the database, each designed to handle a particular operation of the SPC algebra. These representations are designed—when combined in an appropriate manner—to support the *efficient* processing of SPC queries. We use four representations. The first is a *row-wise* representation of the database instantiated as a multi-map MM_R that maps the coordinate of every row in the DB (recall that a coordinate is a row rank/table identifier pair) to the contents of the row. The second representation is a *column-wise* representation of the DB. Similarly, we create a multi-map MM_C that maps the coordinate of every column to the contents of that. The third representation, contrary to MM_R and MM_C, does not store any content of the table but the equality relation among values in the database. For this, we create a multi-map MM_V that maps each value in every column to all the rows that contain the same value. Finally, the fourth representation is a set of multi-maps, one for every column $\mathbf{c}$ in the DB. Each multi-map, $\mathsf{MM}_{\mathbf{c}}$, maps a pair of column coordinates to all the rows that have the same value in both those columns. Now, using multi-map and dictionary encryption schemes, we encrypt all these representations. This results in the encrypted multi-maps $\mathsf{EMM}_R, \mathsf{EMM}_C, \mathsf{EMM}_V$ and an encrypted dictionary EDX (which stores all the all EMM_c's).

Chaining and Constructive Queries. The different representations we just described are designed so that, given an SPC query, the server can generate the intermediate (encrypted) tables needed to produce the final (encrypted) result/table. To do this, the server will need to make further intermediate queries on these (intermediate) encrypted tables. This type of query evaluation is *constructive* in the sense that the intermediate and final encrypted tables are not the result of pre-processing at setup time but are constructed at query time by the server as a function of the query and the underlying DB. To handle this, we use the chaining technique of [16]. At a high level, the idea is to store query tokens for one encrypted structure as the responses of another encrypted structure. By carefully chaining the various encrypted multi-maps (EMMs) described above, we can handle constructive queries by first querying some subset of the EMMs to recover either tokens for EMMs further down the chain or encrypted content which we will use to populate intermediate tables. This process proceeds further down the chain until the final result/table is constructed.

Security and Efficiency. The database representations we choose along with the careful chaining of their encryptions provide us a way to control both the efficiency and the security of scheme. While intermediate results/tables will vary depending on the query, the chaining sequence remains the same for any SPC query written in our heuristic normal form. The chaining sequence is important because it determines the leakage profile of the construction. We analyze the security of our scheme in black-box manner; that is, we provide a black-box leakage profile that is a function of the leakage profile of the underlying encrypted multi-map and encrypted dictionaries used. This allows us to isolate the leakage that is coming from the underlying building blocks and the leakage that is coming directly from our construction. This further enables us to reason about and decide which concrete instantiations to use as building blocks so that we can choose the kind of leakage/performance tradeoff that is most appropriate.

From an efficiency standpoint, we show that when SPX is instantiated with optimal-time encrypted multi-map and dictionary schemes, it can achieve optimal query complexity and linear storage complexity (in the size of the DB) under natural assumptions about the database.

5.1   (Plaintext) Database Indexing

As detailed above, SPX relies on several ideas and techniques. Some of these are cryptographic and some are not. To better explain these techniques we will progressively build our solution; starting with a naive plaintext algorithm for evaluating SPC queries and ending with a detailed description of SPX.

The Naive SPC Algorithm. The naive way to evaluate an SPC normal form query

$$\pi_{\mathsf{att}_1,\cdots,\mathsf{att}_h}\left([a_1] \times \cdots [a_f] \times \sigma_\Psi(\mathsf{T}_{i_1} \times \cdots \times \mathsf{T}_{i_t})\right)$$

on a database $\mathsf{DB} = (\mathsf{T}_1, \ldots, \mathsf{T}_n)$ is to first compute $\mathsf{R}_1 := \mathsf{T}_{i_1} \times \cdots \times \mathsf{T}_{i_t}$, then $\mathsf{R}_2 := \sigma_\Psi(\mathsf{R}_1)$, then $\mathsf{R}_3 := [a_1] \times \cdots \times [a_f] \times \mathsf{R}_2$ and finally $\mathsf{R} := \pi_{\mathsf{att}_1,\ldots,\mathsf{att}_h}(\mathsf{R}_3)$.

This algorithm is dominated by the cross product computation which is $O(m^t \cdot \sum_{i=1}^t s_i)$, where $m = \max_{i=1}^t \|T_i\|_r$ and $s_i = \|T_i\|_c$. The exponential blowup in t is the main reason normal form SPC queries are never used in practice. In addition, since m is usually very large the naive algorithm is prohibitive even for small t.

The benefit of working with the SPC normal form is generality; that is, we can handle an entire class of queries by finding a solution for a single well-specified query form. The disadvantage, however, is that normal form queries take exponential time to evaluate even on a plaintext database.

Heuristic Normal Form (HNF). We show that certain optimizations can be applied to the SPC normal form so that its evaluation time only induces a multiplicative factor of $\sum_{i=1}^t s_i/h$ over the optimal evaluation time on a plaintext database. We refer to this new normal form as the *heuristic normal form*. In some cases, this multiplicative factor is a constant as it does not depend on the size of the result and, in such cases, the HNF evaluation is optimal. The idea is inspired by a query optimization heuristic from database theory which takes advantage of a distributive property between the select and cross product operators. For example, if the predicate $\Psi = (\mathsf{att}_1 = a_1 \wedge \cdots \wedge \mathsf{att}_\ell = a_\ell)$ is only composed of type-1 terms and if, for all $i \in [\ell]$, $\mathsf{att}_i \in T_i$, and the number of terms in Ψ equals the number of tables in the cross product, $\ell = t$, then we have the identity

$$\sigma_\Psi(T_1 \times \cdots \times T_t) = \sigma_{\mathsf{att}_1=a_1}(T_1) \times \cdots \times \sigma_{\mathsf{att}_t=a_t}(T_t).$$

In the database literature this is known as "pushing selects through products" and, depending on the selectivity of the terms, it can greatly reduce the cost of the evaluation. We extend this approach to arbitrary conjunctive predicates which can have both type-1 and type-2 terms. Optimizing these queries is quite involved because the terms can have complex dependencies. In the following, we say that a query is *correlated* if its predicate Ψ satisfies any of the following properties: (1) two or more type-2 terms share a common attribute; (2) a type-1 and type-2 term share a common attribute; (3) the attributes of two or more type-2 terms are from the same table; and (4) the attributes from a type-1 and type-2 term are from the same table. We say that a query is *uncorrelated* if it is not correlated. For ease of exposition, we only describe here how to handle uncorrelated queries and treat the case of correlated queries in the full version of this work.

HNF for Uncorrelated Queries. If Ψ is uncorrelated, we process each term of Ψ and apply the following rules. Let φ be an empty query. If there are $p \geq 1$ type-1 terms $\mathsf{att}_1 = a_1, \ldots, \mathsf{att}_p = a_p$ from some table T, then we set

$$\varphi := \varphi \times \left(\sigma_{\mathsf{att}_1=a_1}(T) \cap \cdots \cap \sigma_{\mathsf{att}_p=a_p}(T) \right),$$

and remove these terms from Ψ. If the term has form $\mathsf{att}_1 = \mathsf{att}_2$ (i.e., is type-2), where att_1 and att_2 are from tables T_1 and T_2, respectively, then we set

$$\varphi := \varphi \times \sigma_{\mathsf{att}_1 = \mathsf{att}_2}(\mathsf{T}_1 \times \mathsf{T}_2).$$

Note that if att_1 and att_2 are from the same table T, then $\mathsf{T}_1 = \mathsf{T}_2 = \mathsf{T}$ above.

At the end of this rewriting process, we say that the query

$$\pi_{\mathsf{att}_1, \cdots, \mathsf{att}_h}\left([a_1] \times \cdots [a_f] \times \varphi \right)$$

is in the heuristic SPC normal form or simply the heuristic normal form.

Indexing. In database systems, select and project operations can be executed in one of two ways: with or without an index. In an unindexed execution, the database management system evaluates the operation using sequential scan. For example, to evaluate the operation $\sigma_{\mathsf{att}=a}(\mathsf{T})$, it scans the rows of T and returns the ones that satisfy $\mathsf{att} = a$. In an indexed execution, on the other hand, the database management system uses a pre-computed data structure (e.g., an index) to find the relevant rows in sub-linear time. Here, we give an overview of how one can index the database to support efficient heuristic normal form queries. Note that our indexing strategy is really designed so that we can support heuristic normal form queries on encrypted data (which we discuss below) so it is not necessarily the most natural way to index a plaintext database.

Given a database $\mathsf{DB} = (\mathsf{T}_1, \ldots, \mathsf{T}_n)$, we first create a multi-map MM_R that stores, for all $\mathbf{r} \in \mathsf{DB}$, the pair

$$\left(\chi(\mathbf{r}), \mathbf{r} \right).$$

In other words, the multi-map MM_R maps row coordinates to rows. We then create a second multi-map MM_C that maps column coordinates to columns. Following this, we build a third multi-map, MM_V, that maps every value/column pair $(v, \chi(\mathbf{c}))$ in the database to the coordinates of the rows that hold v in column $\mathbf{c}$. That is, for all columns $\mathbf{c} \in \mathsf{DB}^\mathsf{T}$ and all values $v \in \mathbf{c}$, MM_V stores the pair

$$\left(\Big\langle v, \chi(\mathbf{c}) \Big\rangle, \Big(\chi(\mathbf{r}) \Big)_{\mathbf{r} \in \mathsf{DB}_{\mathsf{att}(\mathbf{c})=v}} \right).$$

Finally, we build a set of multi-maps for every column $\mathbf{c} \in \mathsf{DB}^\mathsf{T}$. More precisely, for all columns $\mathbf{c} \in \mathsf{DB}^\mathsf{T}$ we create the multi-map $\mathsf{MM}_{\mathbf{c}}$ which maps the coordinates of $\mathbf{c}$ and any other column $\mathbf{c}'$ that has the same domain as $\mathbf{c}$, to the coordinates of rows $\mathbf{r}$ and $\mathbf{r}'$ such that $\mathbf{r}[\mathbf{c}] = \mathbf{r}'[\mathbf{c}']$. More precisely, for all $\mathbf{c}' \in \mathsf{DB}^\mathsf{T}$ such that $\mathsf{dom}(\mathbf{c}') = \mathsf{dom}(\mathbf{c})$, $\mathsf{MM}_{\mathbf{c}}$ stores pairs

$$\left(\Big\langle \chi(\mathbf{c}), \chi(\mathbf{c}') \Big\rangle, \Big(\chi(\mathbf{r}), \chi(\mathbf{r}') \Big)_{(\mathbf{r},\mathbf{r}') \in \mathsf{DB}_{\mathsf{att}(\mathbf{c})=\mathsf{att}(\mathbf{c}')}} \right).$$

To speed up access to the multi-map $\mathsf{MM_c}$, we store it in a dictionary DX. That is, for all $\mathbf{c} \in \mathsf{DB^T}$, we set

$$\mathsf{DX}[\chi(\mathbf{c})] := \mathsf{MM_c}.$$

Note that, in practice, we could store a pointer to $\mathsf{MM_c}$ in the dictionary instead.

Indexed Execution of HNF Queries. We now show how to perform an *indexed* execution of heuristic normal form queries using these structures.[3] For clarity, we use a small database composed of two tables and a simple SQL query. We hope that this example clarifies some of the ideas behind our construction.

Recall that HNF queries have form

$$\pi_{\mathsf{att}_1, \cdots, \mathsf{att}_h} \Big([a_1] \times \cdots \times [a_f] \times \varphi \Big),$$

where $\varphi = \varphi_1 \times \cdots \times \varphi_d$ with each φ_i having form either $\sigma_{\mathsf{att}_1 = a_1}(\mathsf{T}) \cap \cdots \cap \sigma_{\mathsf{att}_p = a_p}(\mathsf{T})$ or $\sigma_{\mathsf{att}_1 = \mathsf{att}_2}(\mathsf{T}_1 \times \mathsf{T}_2)$. We process each φ_i and create a set R_i of rows as follows:

– **(Case 1)** If φ_i has form $\sigma_{\mathsf{att}_1 = a_1}(\mathsf{T}) \cap \cdots \cap \sigma_{\mathsf{att}_p = a_p}(\mathsf{T})$ we recover for each term $\sigma_{\mathsf{att}_j = a_j}(\mathsf{T})$ a set R'_j by computing

$$\Big(\chi(\mathbf{r}) \Big)_{\mathbf{r} \in \mathsf{DB}_{\mathsf{att}_j = a_j}} := \mathsf{MM}_V \Big[\Big\langle a_j, \chi(\mathsf{att}_j) \Big\rangle \Big]$$

and querying MM_R on each of the returned row coordinates. We then set

$$R_i = R'_1 \cap \cdots \cap R'_p.$$

– **(Case 2)** If φ_i has form $\sigma_{\mathsf{att}_1 = \mathsf{att}_2}(\mathsf{T}_1 \times \mathsf{T}_2)$, we first compute $\mathsf{MM}_{\mathsf{att}_1} := \mathsf{DX}[\chi(\mathsf{att}_1)]$ and

$$\Big(\chi(\mathbf{r}_1), \chi(\mathbf{r}_2) \Big)_{(\mathbf{r}_1, \mathbf{r}_2) \in \mathsf{DB}_{\mathsf{att}_1 = \mathsf{att}_2}} := \mathsf{MM}_{\mathsf{att}_1} \Big[\Big\langle \chi(\mathsf{att}_1), \chi(\mathsf{att}_2) \Big\rangle \Big].$$

Then we query MM_R on all of the returned row coordinates to produce a set

$$R_i := \Big\{ \mathbf{r}_1 \times \mathbf{r}_2 \Big\}_{(\mathbf{r}_1, \mathbf{r}_2) \in \mathsf{DB}_{\mathsf{att}_1 = \mathsf{att}_2}}.$$

After processing $\varphi_1, \ldots, \varphi_d$, we compute a temporary table

$$\mathsf{S} := [a_1] \times \cdots \times [a_f] \times R_1 \times \cdots \times R_d.$$

---

[3] In the full version of this work, we provide a concrete example that walks through our indexed HNF algorithm.

We then consider the set of attributes in the project operation that are in tables that appear in the select operation. Specifically, this is the set:

$$I = \left\{ \mathsf{att} \in S : \mathsf{att} \in \bigcup_{j=1}^{t} \mathbb{S}(\mathsf{T}_{i_j}) \right\},$$

where $S \overset{def}{=} \{\mathsf{att}_1, \dots, \mathsf{att}_h\}$. Suppose I has $z \geq 1$ elements which we denote $(\mathsf{att}_1^i, \dots, \mathsf{att}_z^i)$. We compute

$$\mathsf{W} := \pi_{\mathsf{att}_1^i, \dots, \mathsf{att}_z^i}(S).$$

We then consider the attributes in the project operation that are not in the tables that appear in the select operation; that is, the set $O = S \setminus I$. Suppose O has $h - z$ elements which we denote $(\mathsf{att}_1^o, \dots, \mathsf{att}_{h-z}^o)$. For all $1 \leq j \leq h - z$, we compute

$$\mathbf{c}_j := \mathsf{MM}_c\big[\chi(\mathsf{att}_j^o)\big].$$

Finally, we generate the result table

$$\mathsf{R} := \mathbf{c}_1 \times \cdots \times \mathbf{c}_{h-z} \times \mathsf{W},$$

where the $\mathbf{c}_j$'s are viewed as single-column tables.

5.2 Detailed Construction

We now describe our SPX construction at a high-level. Due to space limitations, we defer the pseudo-code to the full version of this work. The scheme makes black-box use of a response-revealing multi-map encryption scheme $\Sigma_{\mathsf{MM}} = (\mathsf{Setup}, \mathsf{Token}, \mathsf{Get})$, of a response-revealing dictionary encryption scheme $\Sigma_{\mathsf{DX}} = (\mathsf{Setup}, \mathsf{Token}, \mathsf{Get})$, of a symmetric-key encryption scheme $\mathsf{SKE} = (\mathsf{Gen}, \mathsf{Enc}, \mathsf{Dec})$. Note that encrypted multi-maps and dictionaries can be instantiated using a variety of schemes [11,12,16,19,30,35].

Overview. At a high-level, the Setup algorithm takes as input a database $\mathsf{DB} = (\mathsf{T}_1, \dots, \mathsf{T}_n)$, creates the multi-maps MM_R, MM_C, MM_V, $\{\mathsf{MM}_\mathbf{c}\}_{\mathbf{c} \in \mathsf{DB}^\intercal}$ and the dictionary DX, as described above, and then encrypts each structure with the appropriate structured encryption scheme. The Token algorithm works by parsing the heuristic normal form query and generating appropriate tokens for each structure so as to enable the server to perform an indexed execution of the query (over encrypted data) as described in the previous paragraph.

Setup. The Setup algorithm takes as input a relational database $\mathsf{DB} = (\mathsf{T}_1, \dots, \mathsf{T}_n)$ and indexes it as above. This results in three multi-maps MM_R, MM_V and MM_C and a dictionary DX that stores pointers to an additional set of multi-maps

$\{MM_c\}_{c \in DB^T}$. The algorithm then encrypts every row $\mathbf{r}$ in MM_R using SKE. In other words, MM_R now holds value/tuple pairs of the form

$$\left(\chi(\mathbf{r}), \left(\mathsf{Enc}_{K_1}(r_1), \ldots, \mathsf{Enc}_{K_1}(r_{\#\mathbf{r}}) \right) \right),$$

where $K_1 \xleftarrow{\$} \{0,1\}^k$. It then encrypts MM_R with Σ_{MM} which results in a key K_R and an encrypted multi-map EMM_R. It then encrypts every column $\mathbf{c}$ in MM_C using SKE in the same manner as above and encrypts MM_C with Σ_{MM}. This results in K_C and an encrypted multi-map EMM_C.

Now for all $\mathbf{r} \in DB$, it replaces all occurrences of $\chi(\mathbf{r})$ in MM_V and $\{MM_c\}_{c \in DB^T}$ with

$$\mathsf{rtk}_{\mathbf{r}} := \Sigma_{MM}.\mathsf{Token}(K_R, \chi(\mathbf{r})).$$

It then encrypts MM_V and $\{MM_c\}_{c \in DB}$ with Σ_{MM} which results in keys K_V and $\{K_c\}_{c \in DB^T}$ and encrypted multi-maps EMM_V and $\{EMM_c\}_{c \in DB^T}$. It then stores pairs $\left(\chi(\mathbf{c}), EMM_c \right)_{c \in DB^T}$ in a dictionary DX and encrypts DX with Σ_{DX} which results in a key K_D and an encrypted dictionary EDX.

Finally, the Setup algorithms then outputs the key

$$K = (K_1, K_R, K_V, K_C, K_D, \{K_c\}_{c \in DB^T}),$$

and the encrypted database

$$EDB = (EMM_R, EMM_C, EMM_V, EDX).$$

Token. The Token algorithm takes as input a secret key K and a query q in SPC normal form. It first transforms it in heuristic normal form:

$$\pi_{\mathsf{att}_1, \cdots, \mathsf{att}_h} \left([a_1] \times \cdots [a_f] \times \varphi_1 \times \cdots \times \varphi_d \right).$$

For all $i \in [h]$, if the project attribute att_i does not appear in $\varphi_1 \times \cdots \times \varphi_d$, the algorithm computes

$$\mathsf{ptk}_i := \Sigma_{MM}.\mathsf{Token}\left(K_C, \chi(\mathsf{att}_i) \right),$$

and sets $\mathsf{ytk}_i = (\mathsf{ptk}_i, \mathsf{out})$; otherwise it sets

$$\mathsf{ptk}_i := \mathsf{pos}_i,$$

where $\mathsf{pos}_i \in \left[\sum_{j=1}^{t} \| T_{i_j} \|_c \right]$ denotes the position of the attribute in the tables referenced in $\varphi_1 \times \cdots \times \varphi_d$. It then sets $\mathsf{ytk}_i = (\mathsf{ptk}_i, \mathsf{in})$.

For every constant a_1 through a_f it computes $e_1 \leftarrow \mathsf{Enc}_{K_1}(a_1)$ through $e_f \leftarrow \mathsf{Enc}_{K_1}(a_f)$. It then processes φ_1 through φ_d and for each φ_i it does the following:

- **(Case 1)** if φ_i has form $\sigma_{att_1 = a_1}(\mathsf{T}) \cap \cdots \cap \sigma_{att_p = a_p}(\mathsf{T})$, it sets

$$\mathsf{stk}_i := (\mathsf{itk}_1, \ldots, \mathsf{itk}_p),$$

where, for all $j \in [p]$,

$$\mathsf{itk}_j := \Sigma_{\mathsf{MM}}.\mathsf{Token}\big(K_V, \langle a_j, \chi(att_j) \rangle\big).$$

- **(Case 2)** if φ_i has form $\sigma_{att_1 = att_2}(\mathsf{T}_1 \times \mathsf{T}_2)$ it sets $\mathsf{stk}_i := (\mathsf{dtk}_i, \mathsf{jtk}_i)$, where

$$\mathsf{dtk}_i := \Sigma_{\mathsf{DX}}.\mathsf{Token}\big(K_D, \chi(att_1)\big)$$

and

$$\mathsf{jtk}_i := \Sigma_{\mathsf{MM}}.\mathsf{Token}\left(K_{\mathbf{c}}, \Big\langle \chi(att_1), \chi(att_2) \Big\rangle\right).$$

Finally, it outputs the token

$$\mathsf{tk} = \left(\big(\mathsf{ytk}_i\big)_{i \in [h]}, \big(e_i\big)_{i \in [f]}, \big(\mathsf{stk}_i\big)_{i \in [d]} \right).$$

Query. The Query algorithm works like the plaintext indexed HNF query evaluation algorithm we described above. Given a token

$$\mathsf{tk} = \left(\big(\mathsf{ytk}_i\big)_{i \in [z]}, \big(e_i\big)_{i \in [f]}, \big(\mathsf{stk}_i\big)_{i \in [d]} \right)$$

as input, it process the sub-tokens $(\mathsf{stk}_1, \ldots, \mathsf{stk}_d)$. For each stk_i it recovers a set of encrypted rows R_i as follows:

- **(Case 1)** if stk_i has form $(\mathsf{itk}_1, \ldots, \mathsf{itk}_p)$, then it recovers, for all $j \in [p]$, a set R'_j by first computing

$$(\mathsf{rtk}_1, \ldots, \mathsf{rtk}_s) := \Sigma_{\mathsf{MM}}.\mathsf{Get}(\mathsf{EMM}_V, \mathsf{itk}_j).$$

It then computes

$$\mathbf{ct}_1 := \Sigma_{\mathsf{MM}}.\mathsf{Get}(\mathsf{EMM}_R, \mathsf{rtk}_1), \ldots, \mathbf{ct}_s := \Sigma_{\mathsf{MM}}.\mathsf{Get}(\mathsf{EMM}_R, \mathsf{rtk}_s),$$

and sets $R'_j := \{\mathbf{ct}_1, \ldots, \mathbf{ct}_s\}$. Finally, it sets $R_i = R'_1 \cap \cdots \cap R'_p$.
- **(Case 2)** if stk_i has form $(\mathsf{dtk}_i, \mathsf{jtk}_i)$ it first computes

$$\mathsf{EMM}_{\mathbf{c}} := \Sigma_{\mathsf{DX}}.\mathsf{Get}(\mathsf{EDX}, \mathsf{dtk}_i)$$

and

$$\left((\mathsf{rtk}_1, \mathsf{rtk}'_1), \ldots, (\mathsf{rtk}_s, \mathsf{rtk}'_s) \right) := \Sigma_{\mathsf{MM}}.\mathsf{Get}(\mathsf{EMM}_{\mathbf{c}}, \mathsf{jtk}_i).$$

It then computes

$$\mathbf{ct}_1 := \Sigma_{\mathsf{MM}}.\mathsf{Get}(\mathsf{EMM}_R, \mathsf{rtk}_1), \ldots, \mathbf{ct}_s := \Sigma_{\mathsf{MM}}.\mathsf{Get}(\mathsf{EMM}_R, \mathsf{rtk}_s),$$

and

$$\mathbf{ct}_1' := \Sigma_{\mathsf{MM}}.\mathsf{Get}(\mathsf{EMM}_R, \mathsf{rtk}_1'), \ldots, \mathbf{ct}_s' := \Sigma_{\mathsf{MM}}.\mathsf{Get}(\mathsf{EMM}_R, \mathsf{rtk}_s').$$

Finally, it sets $R_i = \left\{ \mathbf{ct}_j \times \mathbf{ct}_j' \right\}_{j \in [s]}$.

After processing stk_1 through stk_d, it creates the temporary encrypted table

$$\mathsf{S} = \mathsf{e}_{a_1} \times \cdots \times \mathsf{e}_{a_f} \times R_1 \times \cdots \times R_d.$$

Let $(\mathsf{ytk}_1^i, \ldots, \mathsf{ytk}_z^i)$ be the ytk sub-tokens with form $(\mathsf{ptk}_i, \mathsf{in})$. It then computes

$$\mathsf{W} := \pi_{\mathsf{ptk}_1, \cdots, \mathsf{ptk}_z}(\mathsf{S}).$$

Let $(\mathsf{ytk}_1^o, \ldots, \mathsf{ytk}_{h-z}^o)$ be the ytk sub-tokens with form $(\mathsf{ptk}_i, \mathsf{out})$. For all $i \in [h - z]$, it computes

$$\mathbf{ct}_i := \Sigma_{\mathsf{MM}}.\mathsf{Get}(\mathsf{EMM}_C, \mathsf{ptk}_i).$$

Finally, it generates the response table

$$\mathsf{R} := \mathbf{ct}_1 \times \cdots \times \mathbf{ct}_{h-z} \times \mathsf{W},$$

where the encrypted column $\mathbf{ct}_i$ is viewed as a single-column table.

Decryption. The Dec algorithm takes as input a secret key K and the response table R returned by the server and simply decrypts each cell of R.

5.3   Efficiency

We now turn to analyzing the search and storage efficiency of our construction.

Search Complexity. Consider an SPC query written in its heuristic normal form

$$\pi_{\mathsf{att}_1, \cdots, \mathsf{att}_h}\left([a_1] \times \cdots [a_f] \times \varphi_1 \times \cdots \times \varphi_d \right).$$

We show in the full version of this work that the size of the result table over a plaintext database (in cells) is linear in

$$\#\mathsf{R} = h \cdot \left(m^{h-z} \cdot \prod_{i=1}^{d} \#R_i \right), \tag{1}$$

where $z = \#\left\{ \mathsf{att} \in S : \mathsf{att} \in \bigcup_{j=1}^{t} \mathbb{S}(\mathsf{T}_{i_j}) \right\}$ and $S \overset{def}{=} \{\mathsf{att}_1, \ldots, \mathsf{att}_h\}$, and R_i is the set of rows returned by the evaluation of the term φ_i.

Theorem 1. *If Σ_{DX} and Σ_{MM} are optimal dictionary and multi-map encryption schemes, then the time and space complexity of the* Query *algorithm presented in Sect. 5.2 is*

$$O\left(\frac{\#R}{h} \cdot \sum_{i=1}^{t} s_i\right),$$

where h is the number of selected attributes, s_i the number of attributes of the ith table for all $i \in [t]$, and $\#R$ is the size of the result table over plaintext database as shown in Eq. 1.

We defer the proof of Theorem 1 to the full version of this work.

Corollary 1. *If $h^{-1} \cdot \sum_{i=1}^{t} s_i$ is a constant in $\#R$, then both time and space complexity are in $O(\#R)$, which is optimal.*

The corollary follows simply from Theorem 1. Optimality here refers to query complexity that is linear in the size of the response table, which is the minimum time needed to return it. This is similar to the SSE setting where optimal solutions are linear in the number of documents that hold the keyword.

Storage Complexity. For a database $DB = (T_1, \ldots, T_n)$, SPX produces four encrypted multi-maps EMM_R, EMM_C, EMM_V and EDX. For ease of exposition, we again assume each table has m rows. Finally, note that standard multi-map encryption schemes [11,12,19,30] produce encrypted structures with storage overhead that is linear in sum of the tuple sizes. Using such a scheme as the underlying multi-map encryption scheme, we have that EMM_R and EMM_C will be $O(\sum_{r \in DB} \#r)$ and $O(\sum_{c \in DB^T} \#c)$, respectively, since the former maps the coordinates of each row in DB to their (encrypted) row and the latter maps the coordinates of very column to their (encrypted) columns. Since EMM_V maps each cell in DB to tokens for the rows that contain the same value, it requires $O(\sum_{c \in DB^T} \sum_{v \in c} \#DB_{att(c)=v})$ storage. EDX maps the coordinates of each column $c \in DB^T$ to an encrypted multi-map EMM_c which in turn maps each pair of form (c, c') such that $dom(att(c)) = dom(att(c'))$ to a tuple of tokens for rows in $DB_{att(c)=att(c')}$. As such, EDX will have size

$$O\left(\sum_{c \in DB^T} \sum_{c':dom(att(c'))=dom(att(c))} \#DB_{att(c)=att(c')}\right).$$

Note that the expression will vary greatly depending on the number of columns in DB with the same domain. In the worst case, all columns will have a common domain and the expression will be a sum of $O\left(\left(\sum_i \|T_i\|_c\right)^2\right)$ terms of the form $\#DB_{att(c)=att(c')}$. In the best case, none of the columns will share a domain and EDX will be empty. In practice, however, we expect there to be some relatively small number of columns with common domains. In the full version of the paper, we provide a concrete example of the storage overhead of an encrypted database.

6   Black-Box Security and Leakage of SPX

We show that our construction is adaptively-secure with respect to a well-specified leakage profile. Part of the subtlety in our security analysis is that some of the leakage is "black-box" in the sense that it comes from the underlying building blocks and part of it is "non-black-box" in the sense that it comes directly from the SPX construction.

6.1   Setup Leakage

The setup leakage of SPX captures what an adversary can learn before performing any query operation. The setup leakage of SPX is

$$\mathcal{L}_S^{\mathsf{spx}}(\mathsf{DB}) = \left(\mathcal{L}_S^{\mathsf{dx}}(\mathsf{DX}), \mathcal{L}_S^{\mathsf{mm}}(\mathsf{MM}_R), \mathcal{L}_S^{\mathsf{mm}}(\mathsf{MM}_C), \mathcal{L}_S^{\mathsf{mm}}(\mathsf{MM}_V) \right),$$

where $\mathcal{L}_S^{\mathsf{dx}}$ and $\mathcal{L}_S^{\mathsf{mm}}$ are the setup leakages of Σ_{DX} and Σ_{MM}, respectively. If the latter are instantiated with standard encrypted multi-map constructions, the setup leakage of SPX will consist of the number of rows and columns in DB and the size of the dictionary. Note that standard encrypted dictionary constructions leak only the maximum size of the values they store so the size of the $\mathsf{EMM_c}$'s will be hidden (up to the maximum size).

6.2   Query Leakage

The query leakage is more complex and is defined as follows,

$$\mathcal{L}_Q^{\mathsf{spx}}(\mathsf{DB}, q) = \left(\mathrm{XPP}(\mathsf{DB}, q), \mathrm{PrP}(\mathsf{DB}, q), \mathrm{SelP}(\mathsf{DB}, q) \right),$$

where each individual pattern is described next.

Cross Product. The first leakage pattern is the *cross product* pattern which is defined as

$$\mathrm{XPP}(\mathsf{DB}, q) = \left\{ (|a_i|)_{i \in [f]} \right\},$$

and includes the size of the virtual attributes.

Projection. The second leakage pattern is the *projection pattern* which is defined as

$$\mathrm{PrP}(\mathsf{DB}, q) = \left(\mathcal{P}(\mathsf{att}_1), \ldots, \mathcal{P}(\mathsf{att}_h) \right),$$

where

$$\mathcal{P}(\mathsf{att}_i) = \begin{cases} \left(\mathsf{out}, \mathcal{L}_Q^{\mathsf{mm}}\left(\mathsf{MM}_C, \chi(\mathsf{att}_i) \right), (|c_j|)_{j \in [\#\mathbf{c}_i]}, \mathrm{AccP}(\mathbf{c}_i) \right) & \text{if } \mathsf{att}_i \in S \setminus I; \\ \left(\mathsf{in}, \mathsf{att}_i \right) & \text{otherwise,} \end{cases}$$

where $I = \left\{ \text{att} \in S : \text{att} \in \bigcup_{j=1}^{t} \mathbb{S}(\mathsf{T}_{i_j}) \right\}$ and $S \stackrel{def}{=} \{\text{att}_1, \ldots, \text{att}_h\}$, $\mathbf{c}_i \in \mathsf{DB}^\mathsf{T}$
denotes the column with attribute att_i and $\mathrm{AccP}(\mathbf{c}_i)$ indicates the access pattern,
i.e., if and when the column $\mathbf{c}_i$ has been accessed before. PrP captures the leakage
produced when the server queries MM_C and for every attribute att_i reveals
whether the attribute was in or out of the set composed of the attributes in
the predicate Ψ. If it is out, it also reveals the size of the items in the projected
column and if and when this column has been accessed before. Notice that it also
reveals the Σ_{MM} query leakage on the coordinates of the projected attribute. If
the attribute is in, it just reveals the attribute.[4]

Selection. The third leakage pattern is the *selection pattern* which is defined as

$$\mathrm{SelP}(\mathsf{DB}, q) = \left(\mathcal{Z}(\varphi_1), \ldots, \mathcal{Z}(\varphi_d) \right).$$

If φ_i has form $\sigma_{\text{att}_{i,1}=a_{i,1}}(\mathsf{T}) \cap \cdots \cap \sigma_{\text{att}_{i,p_i}=a_{i,p_i}}(\mathsf{T})$, then $\mathcal{Z}(\varphi_i)$ is defined as

$$\mathcal{Z}(\varphi_i) = \left(\text{case-1}, p_i, \left(\mathcal{L}_\mathsf{Q}^{\mathsf{mm}}\left(\mathsf{MM}_V, \left\langle X_{i,j}, \chi(\text{att}_{i,j}) \right\rangle \right), \right.\right.$$
$$\left.\left. \left\{ \mathcal{L}_\mathsf{Q}^{\mathsf{mm}}\left(\mathsf{MM}_R, \chi(\mathbf{r}) \right), \mathrm{AccP}(\mathbf{r}) \right\}_{\mathbf{r} \in \mathsf{DB}_{\text{att}_{i,j}=X_{i,j}}} \right)_{j \in [p_i]} \right),$$

where $\mathrm{AccP}(\mathbf{r})$ indicates whether the row $\mathbf{r}$ has been accessed before, and *case-1*
refers to the first form of φ_i as introduced in Sect. 5.1. $\mathcal{Z}(\varphi_i)$ captures the leakage
produced when the server queries MM_V and uses the resulting row tokens to then
query MM_R. It reveals whether the selection term is of case-1, the Σ_{MM} query
leakage on the constant a_j, and the coordinates of the attribute $\text{att}_{i,j}$, for all
$j \in [p_i]$ where p_i represents the number of attributes $\text{att}_{i,j}$ that are in the same
table T. In addition, it also leaks the Σ_{MM} query leakage on the coordinates of
the rows in $\mathsf{DB}_{\text{att}_{i,j}=a_{i,j}}$ as well as if and when they have been accessed before,
for all $j \in [p_i]$.

If, on the other hand, φ_i has form $\sigma_{\text{att}_{i,1}=\text{att}_{i,2}}(\mathsf{T}_{i,1} \times \mathsf{T}_{i,2})$, then $\mathcal{Z}(\varphi_i)$ is
defined as

$$\mathcal{Z}(\varphi_i) = \left(\text{case-2}, \mathcal{L}_\mathsf{Q}^{\mathsf{dx}}\left(\mathsf{DX}, \chi(\text{att}_{i,1}) \right), \mathcal{L}_\mathsf{S}^{\mathsf{mm}}(\mathsf{MM}_{\text{att}_{i,1}}), \mathrm{AccP}(\mathsf{EMM}_{\text{att}_{i,1}}), \right.$$
$$\mathcal{L}_\mathsf{Q}^{\mathsf{mm}}\left(\mathsf{MM}_{\text{att}_{i,1}}, \left\langle \chi(\text{att}_{i,1}), \chi(\text{att}_{i,2}) \right\rangle \right), \left\{ \mathcal{L}_\mathsf{Q}^{\mathsf{mm}}\left(\mathsf{MM}_R, \chi(\mathbf{r}_1) \right), \right.$$
$$\left.\left. \mathrm{AccP}(\mathbf{r}_1), \mathcal{L}_\mathsf{Q}^{\mathsf{mm}}\left(\mathsf{MM}_R, \chi(\mathbf{r}_2) \right), \mathrm{AccP}(\mathbf{r}_2) \right\}_{(\mathbf{r}_1, \mathbf{r}_2) \in \mathsf{DB}_{\text{att}_{i,1}=\text{att}_{i,2}}} \right),$$

where $\mathrm{AccP}(\mathbf{r}_1)$, $\mathrm{AccP}(\mathbf{r}_2)$ and $\mathrm{AccP}(\mathsf{EMM}_{\text{att}_i})$ indicate if and when $\mathbf{r}_1$, $\mathbf{r}_2$ and
$\mathsf{EMM}_{\text{att}_{i,1}}$ have been accessed before, and *case-2* refers to the second form of φ_i as

---

[4] To be more precise, it reveals *only* the position of the attribute in the heuristic
normal form. The position, however, is independent of the attribute itself.

introduced in Sect. 5.1. In this case, $\mathcal{Z}(\varphi_i)$ captures the leakage produced when the server queries EDX to retrieve some $\mathsf{EMM}_{\mathsf{att}_{i,1}}$ which it in turn queries to retrieve row tokens with which to query EMM_R. It reveals whether the selection term is of case-2, the Σ_{DX} query leakage on the coordinates of $\mathsf{att}_{i,1}$, the Σ_{MM} *setup* leakage on $\mathsf{MM}_{\mathsf{att}_{i,1}}$ and if and when $\mathsf{EMM}_{\mathsf{att}_{i,1}}$ has been accessed in the past. In addition, it reveals the query leakage of Σ_{MM} on the coordinates of $\mathsf{att}_{i,1}$ and $\mathsf{att}_{i,2}$ and, for every pair of rows $(\mathbf{r}_1, \mathbf{r}_2)$ in $\mathsf{DB}_{\mathsf{att}_{i,1}=\mathsf{att}_{i,2}}$, their Σ_{MM} query leakage if and when they were accessed in the past.

6.3   Black-Box Security of SPX

We show that SPX is adaptively semantically-secure with respect to the leakage profile described in the previous sub-section.

Theorem 2. *If* SKE *is RCPA secure,* Σ_{DX} *is adaptively* $\left(\mathcal{L}_\mathsf{S}^{\mathsf{dx}}, \mathcal{L}_\mathsf{Q}^{\mathsf{dx}}\right)$*-semantically secure and* Σ_{MM} *is adaptively* $\left(\mathcal{L}_\mathsf{S}^{\mathsf{mm}}, \mathcal{L}_\mathsf{Q}^{\mathsf{mm}}\right)$*-secure, then* SPX *is* $\left(\mathcal{L}_\mathsf{S}^{\mathsf{spx}}, \mathcal{L}_\mathsf{Q}^{\mathsf{spx}}\right)$*-semantically secure.*

The proof of Theorem 2 is in the full version of the paper.

7   Concrete Security and Leakage of SPX

7.1   With Zero-Leakage Building Blocks

Here, we are interested in the leakage profile of SPX when the underlying building blocks are ZL. By a ZL encrypted structure, we mean that its query operations only reveals information that can be derived from the security parameter or other public parameters. We write this as $\mathcal{L}_\mathsf{Q}(\mathsf{DS}, q) = \perp$, for any query q in its corresponding query space. When instantiated with ZL building blocks, the query leakage of SPX decreases considerably but its setup leakage remains the same. Specifically, the projection pattern becomes $\mathrm{PrP}(\mathsf{DB}, q) = \left(\mathcal{P}(\mathsf{att}_1), \ldots, \mathcal{P}(\mathsf{att}_h) \right)$, where

$$\mathcal{P}(\mathsf{att}_i) = \begin{cases} \left(\mathsf{out}, \left(|c_j| \right)_{j \in [\#\mathbf{c}_i]}, \mathrm{AccP}(\mathbf{c}_i) \right) & \text{if } \mathsf{att}_i \in S \setminus I; \\ \left(\mathsf{in}, \mathsf{att}_i \right) & \text{otherwise.} \end{cases}$$

The selection pattern SelP becomes $\mathrm{SelP}(\mathsf{DB}, q) = \left(\mathcal{Z}(\varphi_1), \ldots, \mathcal{Z}(\varphi_d) \right)$, where if φ_i has form $\sigma_{\mathsf{att}_{i,1}=a_{i,1}}(\mathsf{T}) \cap \cdots \cap \sigma_{\mathsf{att}_{i,p_i}=a_{i,p_i}}(\mathsf{T})$, then $\mathcal{Z}(\varphi_i)$ is defined as

$$\mathcal{Z}(\varphi_i) = \left(\mathsf{case\text{-}1}, p_i, \left\{ \mathrm{AccP}(\mathbf{r}) \right\}_{\mathbf{r} \in \mathsf{DB}_{\mathsf{att}_{i,j}=X_{i,j}}, j \in [p_i]} \right),$$

Otherwise if, φ_i has form $\sigma_{att_{i,1}=att_{i,2}}(T_{i,1} \times T_{i,2})$, then $\mathcal{Z}(\varphi_i)$ is defined as

$$\mathcal{Z}(\varphi_i) = \Bigg(\text{case-2}, \mathcal{L}_S^{mm}(MM_{att_{i,1}}), \text{AccP}(EMM_{att_{i,1}}),$$

$$\Big\{ \text{AccP}(r_1), \text{AccP}(r_2) \Big\}_{(r_1,r_2) \in DB_{att_{i,1}=att_{i,2}}} \Bigg).$$

We are aware of two ZL encrypted multi-map constructions. The first can be derived from an SSE construction of Garg, Mohassel and Papamanthou [20] that itself is based on the TWORAM construction. We note that the SSE scheme proposed in that work is not ZL (since it reveals the response length) but it can be made so with a careful parametrization of its block size. The second construction is FZL by Kamara, Moataz and Ohromenko [29]. Of course, ZL schemes come with an additional efficiency overhead. For example, if the TWORAM-based construction is used in SPX its time and space complexity would incur an additive overhead of

$$\widetilde{O}\Bigg((2\ell + h) \cdot m \cdot \log{(n \cdot m)} + d \cdot m^2 \cdot \log{\Bigg(\sum_{i \in [n]} \|T_i\|_c \cdot m \Bigg)} \Bigg),$$

where n is the number of tables in DB. Note that SPX becomes interactive if it is instantiated with any of the currently-known ZL constructions.

7.2   With Standard Building Bocks

In this section, we describe the leakage profile of SPX when instantiated with encrypted dictionary or multi-map schemes with the "standard" leakage profile [11,12,16,19,30,35]. A standard response-revealing encrypted multi-map or dictionary encryption reveals the search pattern SP and access pattern AP, whereas a standard response-hiding encrypted multi-map or dictionary reveals the search pattern SP and the response length RL. The search pattern reveals if and when a query is repeated, the access pattern reveals the responses, and the response length reveals the length of the response. The query leakage of SPX when instantiated with standard STE schemes is the one detailed in Sect. 6.2 except that we replace $\mathcal{L}_Q^{mm}$ with the patterns detailed above depending on whether the underlying scheme is response-revealing or response-hiding. In the following, we provide a high level description of both the projection and selection patterns of SPX.

Projection. The projection pattern discloses the frequency of accesses made to a particular attribute. An adversary can learn the size of the accessed columns, and therefore the number of entries that a specific table has. The impact of such leaked information depends on the auxiliary information the attacker possesses. In some settings, just knowing the size of the table can be sufficient for an adversary to know the targeted information, but this is a general problem that can be addressed by padding, for instance.

Selection. Of all the leakage patterns of SPX, the selection pattern is the one that leaks the most. If φ_i is of case-1, then an adversary can know the number of rows that contain the same value at a particular column(s), and this applies to all the p_i attributes in φ_i. The adversary can also learn the frequency with which a particular row has been accessed, and also the size of that row. If many queries have been performed on the same table and the same column, then the adversary can build a frequency histogram of that specific column's contents. Otherwise if φ_i is of case-2, then the server learns how many rows are equal to each other in both columns.

7.3 SPX and SSE Attacks

As mentioned, *one* of the possible instantiation SPX makes use of standard SSE to implement the underlying encrypted multi-maps. There are several known attacks that try to exploit the leakage of various SSE schemes such as the inference attacks of Islam et al. [26] and of Cash et al. [10] and the file injection attacks of Cash et al. [10] and Zhang et al. [40]. It is not exactly clear what the impact of these attacks would be to our setting since our construction handles more complex objects and has a different leakage profile than standard SSE schemes. What is clear, however, is that our scheme leaks *more* than standard SSE schemes so presumably the techniques from these works could be extended to apply to our construction.

We note, however, that the attacks in [10,26] rely on strong assumptions including knowledge of a large fraction of the client's data and knowledge of some client queries[5]. Specifically, for IKK, the adversary needs to know about 90% of the client's data in order to recover about 10% of its queries. Similarly, the Count attack from [10] requires the adversary to know 80% of the client's data and 5% of its queries in order to recover 40% of the client's queries (note that the success rate of the counting attack is not linear so knowing even 75% of the client's data is not enough for the adversary to learn even 1% of the client's queries). With 90% of the data and 2% of the queries, the Count attack does not work at all. Another limitation of these attacks is related to how the adversary can recover client data in practice. Recall that in an outsourced storage setting the client is assumed to erase its data after storing it in encrypted form on the server (that is the purpose of outsourcing). It is therefore not clear how the adversary can recover, say 80%, of client data unless the client encrypts publicly-known data—in which case it should use a different primitive like private information retrieval. In a model where the adversary does not know any of the client's data a-priori—which is the standard model for SSE and structured encryption—neither the IKK attack nor the Count attack can recover *any* queries at all.

Unlike the previously mentioned attacks, the file injection attacks of [40] are effective in practice but are only applicable against dynamic SSE schemes and in scenarios where the adversary can inject data into the encrypted structure. This

---

[5] While the Count attack is not described as a known-query attack in [10], it has come to our attention that this was an error and will be fixed by the authors.

is the case, for example, if one were to use a dynamic SSE scheme to encrypt an email archive since the server/adversary could send the client malicious emails. In our setting, we assume the data is generated by the client and is not publicly modifiable *after the setup*. However, if our dynamic scheme SPX$^+$ were used in a setting where row injections are possible then, presumably, attacks like those of [40] could be designed and some queries could be disclosed. As suggested in [40], one countermeasure in this case is to use forward-secure constructions. In the full version of this work, we discuss how to make SPX$^+$ forward-secure.

Recently, Abdelraheem et al. [33] presented an attack on relational databases encrypted with SSE. We stress, however, that the attack of [33] only applies to a very specific and naive SSE-based relational EDB construction described in that work and first used for experiments in [12] (e.g., the construction does not handle any non-trivial SQL query). While it is not clear at all how this attack would apply to our construction, we point out that the attack relies on strong assumptions. In particular, it works only for databases with attributes whose domain sizes are unique. In addition, it relies on the adversary knowing the attributes in the database and their domain sizes. Furthermore, the adversary also needs to know, for each attacked column, which domain element appears the most frequently, the second most frequently etc. Finally, the attack needs to solve an NP-complete problem that can be solved in pseudo-polynomial time only for databases with a small number of rows and small attribute domains (experimental results were conducted for databases with 32, 561 rows and domain sizes that range from 2 to 41 and execution times were not reported).

7.4   Comparison to PPE-Based Solutions

As mentioned in Sect. 1, PPE-based solutions can handle a large class of SQL queries which includes conjunctive queries. To support conjunctive queries, however, these solutions have to rely on deterministic encryption. For example, to handle a case-1 query on a table T, they will reveal a deterministic encryptions of all the accessed attributes **c** in T (i.e., every element of every column is encrypted under the same key). To handle a case-2 query between two columns c_1 and c_2, they will reveal deterministic encryptions of both columns (under the same key). In turn, this will provide the *frequency* information on the entire columns to the server. Depending on the setting, frequency patterns can be particularly dangerous, as shown in [34].

SPX leaks considerably less. First, it does not leak any frequency information on entire columns or rows. For case-1 queries, it only leaks information about the attributes in the query and the rows that match the term. For case-2 queries, it only leaks information about the pair of attributes $(\mathsf{att}_{i,1}, \mathsf{att}_{i,2})$ in the select and the rows that match the term. Note that this leakage is only a function of the attributes in the query and of the rows that match it, whereas the leakage in PPE-based solutions is a function of entire columns. Moreover, in the case of SPX, if the underlying multi-map and dictionary schemes are instantiated with standard constructions, the information leaked about the attributes and matching rows is "repetition" type of information, i.e., if and when they have appeared in the past. Analogously, the project operations in SPX only leak information about the attributes in the project and the columns that match it and the information being leaked "repetition" type of information.

Formally, the setup leakage of PPE-based solutions like CryptDB is

$$\mathcal{L}_S^{\mathsf{ppe}}(\mathsf{DB}) = \Big(\|\mathsf{T}_i\|_c, \|\mathsf{T}_i\|_r \Big)_{i\in[n]},$$

where n is the number of tables in DB. Given a SQL query q, the query leakage is

$$\mathcal{L}_Q^{\mathsf{ppe}}(\mathsf{DB}, q) = \Big(\mathrm{XPP}(\mathsf{DB}, q), \mathrm{PrP}(\mathsf{DB}, q), \mathrm{SelP}(\mathsf{DB}, q), \mathrm{FrP}(\mathsf{DB}, q) \Big),$$

where XPP, PrP and SelP are the cross product, projection and selection patterns (defined as in the leakage profile of SPX), and $\mathrm{FrP}(\mathsf{DB}, q)$ is the frequency pattern which leaks frequency information on all queried columns. It is easy to see that even when SPX is instantiated with non-ZL building blocks, its query leakage is a subset of the query leakage of the PPE-based solutions. Note that, not only is FrP relatively easy to exploit [34], it is also *persistent* in the sense that it is available not only to an adversary that has the query tokens and witnesses or executes the query operation but also to a "snapshot" adversary which only has access to the encrypted DB. This is not the case for SPX.

A Remark on Leakage. Ideally, one would hope to better understand how significant the leakage of practical encrypted search solutions are but we currently lack any theoretical framework to conduct such an analysis. In other words, the best we can currently do is to give a precise leakage profile and prove that our constructions do not leak anything beyond that profile. For the same reason, the best we can currently do to compare two leakage profiles is to show that one is a subset of the other (and in some cases, this is not even possible).

8   Extensions

In the full version of the paper, we show how to extend SPX to handle additional post-processing operations including Group-by, Order-by and various aggregate functions such as Sum, Average, Median, Count, Mode, Max and Min.

In addition, due to its modularity, SPX can be extended to be dynamic without re-designing it entirely. We refer to the dynamic version of SPX as SPX$^+$ and describe it in the full version of this work. Note that SPX$^+$ maintains the same query complexity and query leakage as SPX. We also discuss how to use ORAM to make SPX$^+$ forward-secure at the cost of a poly-logarithmic overhead for updates and without affecting the query complexity.

9   Future Directions and Open Problems

In this work, we proposed the first encrypted relational database scheme purely based on STE techniques. As such, our construction offers more security than the PPE-based solutions and are more efficient than solutions based on general-purpose techniques like ORAM simulation or FHE. Our work leaves open several interesting questions. The first is whether our techniques can be extended to handle the *full* relational algebra which, effectively, is the entire SQL. To achieve this, our solution would have to be extended to handle negations and disjunctions (set unions) in the Where clause of the SQL query. We believe this to be challenging. A second problem is to handle SQL queries with ranges in the Where clause. A first step towards achieving this would be to improve the state of the art in encrypted range queries. In particular, finding schemes with improved leakage profiles is important since recent work [31,32] has described powerful attacks against the state of the art encrypted search solutions (under some assumptions on the data and queries).

References

1. Abiteboul, S., Hull, R., Vianu, V.: Foundations of Databases: The Logical Level. Addison-Wesley Longman Publishing Co., Inc, Boston (1995)
2. Agrawal, R., Kiernan, J., Srikant, R., Xu, Y.: Order preserving encryption for numeric data. In: ACM SIGMOD International Conference on Management of Data, pp. 563–574 (2004)
3. Arasu, A., Blanas, S., Eguro, K., Kaushik, R., Kossmann, D., Ramamurthy, R., Venkatesan, R.: Orthogonal security with cipherbase. In: CIDR (2013)
4. Asharov, G., Naor, M., Segev, G., Shahaf, I.: Searchable symmetric encryption: optimal locality in linear space via two-dimensional balanced allocations. In: ACM on Symposium on Theory of Computing (STOC 2016) (2016)
5. Bellare, M., Boldyreva, A., O'Neill, A.: Deterministic and efficiently searchable encryption. In: Menezes, A. (ed.) CRYPTO 2007. LNCS, vol. 4622, pp. 535–552. Springer, Heidelberg (2007). https://doi.org/10.1007/978-3-540-74143-5_30
6. Ben-David, A., Nisan, N., Pinkas, B.: Fairplaymp: a system for secure multi-party computation. In: ACM Conference on Computer and Communications Security (CCS 2008), pp. 257–266. ACM (2008)
7. Boldyreva, A., Chenette, N., Lee, Y., O'Neill, A.: Order-preserving symmetric encryption. In: Joux, A. (ed.) EUROCRYPT 2009. LNCS, vol. 5479, pp. 224–241. Springer, Heidelberg (2009). https://doi.org/10.1007/978-3-642-01001-9_13
8. Boneh, D., Di Crescenzo, G., Ostrovsky, R., Persiano, G.: Public key encryption with keyword search. In: Cachin, C., Camenisch, J.L. (eds.) EUROCRYPT 2004. LNCS, vol. 3027, pp. 506–522. Springer, Heidelberg (2004). https://doi.org/10.1007/978-3-540-24676-3_30
9. Bost, R.: Sophos - forward secure searchable encryption. In: ACM Conference on Computer and Communications Security (CCS 2016) (2016)
10. Cash, D., Grubbs, P., Perry, J., Ristenpart, T.: Leakage-abuse attacks against searchable encryption. In: ACM Conference on Communications and Computer Security (CCS 2015), pp. 668–679. ACM (2015)

11. Cash, D., et al.: Dynamic searchable encryption in very-large databases: data structures and implementation. In: Network and Distributed System Security Symposium (NDSS 2014) (2014)
12. Cash, D., Jarecki, S., Jutla, C., Krawczyk, H., Roşu, M.-C., Steiner, M.: Highly-scalable searchable symmetric encryption with support for boolean queries. In: Canetti, R., Garay, J.A. (eds.) CRYPTO 2013. LNCS, vol. 8042, pp. 353–373. Springer, Heidelberg (2013). https://doi.org/10.1007/978-3-642-40041-4_20
13. Cash, D., Tessaro, S.: The locality of searchable symmetric encryption. In: Nguyen, P.Q., Oswald, E. (eds.) EUROCRYPT 2014. LNCS, vol. 8441, pp. 351–368. Springer, Heidelberg (2014). https://doi.org/10.1007/978-3-642-55220-5_20
14. Chamberlin, D.D., Boyce, R.F.: SEQUEL: a structured English query language. In: SIGMOD 1974 (1974)
15. Chandra, A., Merlin, P.: Optimal implementation of conjunctive queries in relational data bases. In: STOC 1977 (1977)
16. Chase, M., Kamara, S.: Structured encryption and controlled disclosure. In: Abe, M. (ed.) ASIACRYPT 2010. LNCS, vol. 6477, pp. 577–594. Springer, Heidelberg (2010). https://doi.org/10.1007/978-3-642-17373-8_33
17. Chase, M., Kamara, S.: Structured encryption and controlled disclosure. Technical report 2011/010.pdf, IACR Cryptology ePrint Archive (2010)
18. Codd, E.: A relational model of data for large shared data banks. Commun. ACM 13(6), 377–387 (1970)
19. Curtmola, R., Garay, J., Kamara, S., Ostrovsky, R.: Searchable symmetric encryption: improved definitions and efficient constructions. In: ACM Conference on Computer and Communications Security (CCS 2006), pp. 79–88. ACM (2006)
20. Garg, S., Mohassel, P., Papamanthou, C.: TWORAM: efficient oblivious RAM in two rounds with applications to searchable encryption. In: Robshaw, M., Katz, J. (eds.) CRYPTO 2016. LNCS, vol. 9816, pp. 563–592. Springer, Heidelberg (2016). https://doi.org/10.1007/978-3-662-53015-3_20
21. Gentry, C.: A fully homomorphic encryption scheme. Ph.D. thesis, Stanford University (2009)
22. Goldreich, O., Ostrovsky, R.: Software protection and simulation on oblivious RAMs. J. ACM 43(3), 431–473 (1996)
23. Grofig, P., et al.: Experiences and observations on the industrial implementation of a system to search over outsourced encrypted data. In: Sicherheit, pp. 115–125 (2014)
24. Grubbs, P., Ristenpart, T., Shmatikov, V.: Why your encrypted database is not secure. In: HotOS (2017)
25. Hacigümüş, H., Iyer, B., Li, C., Mehrotra, S.: Executing SQL over encrypted data in the database-service-provider model. In: SIGMOD 2002 (2002)
26. Islam, M.S., Kuzu, M., Kantarcioglu, M.: Access pattern disclosure on searchable encryption: ramification, attack and mitigation. In: Network and Distributed System Security Symposium (NDSS 2012) (2012)
27. Jarecki, S., Jutla, C., Krawczyk, H., Rosu, M., Steiner, M.: Outsourced symmetric private information retrieval. In: ACM Conference on Computer and Communications Security (CCS 2013), pp. 875–888 (2013)
28. Kamara, S., Moataz, T.: Boolean searchable symmetric encryption with worst-case sub-linear complexity. In: Coron, J.-S., Nielsen, J.B. (eds.) EUROCRYPT 2017. LNCS, vol. 10212, pp. 94–124. Springer, Cham (2017). https://doi.org/10.1007/978-3-319-56617-7_4

29. Kamara, S., Moataz, T., Ohrimenko, O.: Structured encryption and leakage suppression. In: Shacham, H., Boldyreva, A. (eds.) CRYPTO 2018. LNCS, vol. 10991, pp. 339–370. Springer, Cham (2018). https://doi.org/10.1007/978-3-319-96884-1_12

30. Kamara, S., Papamanthou, C., Roeder, T.: Dynamic searchable symmetric encryption. In: ACM Conference on Computer and Communications Security (CCS 2012). ACM Press (2012)

31. Kellaris, G., Kollios, G., Nissim, K., Neill, A.O.: Generic attacks on secure outsourced databases. In: ACM Conference on Computer and Communications Security (CCS 2016) (2016)

32. Lacharité, M., Minaud, B., Paterson, K.G.: Improved reconstruction attacks on encrypted data using range query leakage. In: 2018 IEEE Symposium on Security and Privacy, SP, pp. 297–314 (2018)

33. Abdelraheem, M.A., Andersson, T., Gehrmann, C.: Inference and record-injection attacks on searchable encrypted relational databases. Technical report 2017/024 (2017). http://eprint.iacr.org/2017/024

34. Naveed, M., Kamara, S., Wright, C.V.: Inference attacks on property-preserving encrypted databases. In: ACM Conference on Computer and Communications Security (CCS), CCS 2015, pp. 644–655. ACM (2015)

35. Naveed, M., Prabhakaran, M., Gunter, C.: Dynamic searchable encryption via blind storage. In: IEEE Symposium on Security and Privacy (S&P 2014) (2014)

36. Pappas, V., et al.: Blind seer: a scalable private DBMS. In: 2014 IEEE Symposium on Security and Privacy (SP), pp. 359–374. IEEE (2014)

37. Popa, R.A., Redfield, C., Zeldovich, N., Balakrishnan, H.: CryptDB: protecting confidentiality with encrypted query processing. In: ACM Symposium on Operating Systems Principles (SOSP), pp. 85–100 (2011)

38. Song, D., Wagner, D., Perrig, A.: Practical techniques for searching on encrypted data. In: IEEE Symposium on Research in Security and Privacy (2000)

39. Van den Bussche, J., Vansummeren, S.: Translating SQL into the relational algebra (2009). http://cs.ulb.ac.be/public/_media/teaching/infoh417/sql2alg_eng.pdf

40. Zhang, Y., Katz, J., Papamanthou, C.: All your queries are belong to us: the power of file-injection attacks on searchable encryption. In: USENIX Security Symposium (2016)

Parameter-Hiding Order Revealing Encryption

David Cash[1], Feng-Hao Liu[2], Adam O'Neill[3], Mark Zhandry[4],
and Cong Zhang[5(✉)]

[1] Department of Computer Science, University of Chicago, Chicago, USA
davidcash@cs.uchicago.edu
[2] Department of Computer and Electrical Engineering and Computer Science,
Florida Atlantic University, Boca Raton, USA
[3] Department of Computer Science, Georgetown University, Washington, D.C., USA
[4] Department of Computer Science, Princeton University, Princeton, USA
[5] Department of Computer Science, Rutgers University, New Brunswick, USA
cz200@cs.rutgers.edu

Abstract. Order-revealing encryption (ORE) is a primitive for outsourcing encrypted databases which allows for efficiently performing range queries over encrypted data. Unfortunately, a series of works, starting with Naveed *et al.* (CCS 2015), have shown that when the adversary has a good estimate of the distribution of the data, ORE provides little protection. In this work, we consider the case that the database entries are drawn identically and independently from a distribution of known shape, but for which the mean and variance are not (and thus the attacks of Naveed *et al.* do not apply). We define a new notion of security for ORE, called *parameter-hiding ORE*, which maintains the secrecy of these parameters. We give a construction of ORE satisfying our new definition from bilinear maps.

Keywords: Encryption · Order-revealing encryption

1 Introduction

An emerging area of cryptography concerns the design and analysis of "leaky" protocols (see *e.g.* [11,33,36] and additional references below), which are protocols that deliberately give up some level of security in order to achieve better efficiency. One important tool in this area is *order-revealing encryption* [7,8][1]. Order-revealing encryption (ORE) is a special type of symmetric encryption which leaks the order of the underlying plaintexts through a *public* procedure Comp. In practice, ORE allows for a client to store a database on an untrusted server in encrypted form, while still permitting the server to efficiently perform various operations such as range queries on the encrypted data without the secret decryption key. ORE has been implemented and used in real-world encrypted database systems, including CryptDB [36].

---

[1] In [7], it was called efficiently-orderable encryption.

© International Association for Cryptologic Research 2018
T. Peyrin and S. Galbraith (Eds.): ASIACRYPT 2018, LNCS 11272, pp. 181–210, 2018.
https://doi.org/10.1007/978-3-030-03326-2_7

Various notions of ORE have been proposed. The strongest, called "ideal" ORE, insists that everything about the plaintexts is hidden, except for their order. For example, it should be impossible to distinguish between encryptions of 1, 2, 3 and 1, 4, 9. Such ideal ORE can be constructed from multilinear maps [8], showing that in principle ideal ORE is achievable. However, current multilinear maps are quite inefficient, and moreover have been subject to numerous attacks (e.g. [16,17,32]).

In order to develop efficient schemes, one can relax the security requirements to allow for more leakage. Order-preserving encryption (OPE) [1,6]—which actually predates ORE—is one example, where Comp is simply integer comparison. Very efficient constructions of OPE are known [6]. However, OPE necessarily leaks much more information about the plaintexts [6] than ideal ORE; intuitively, the difference between ciphertexts can be used to approximate the difference between the plaintexts. More recently, there have been efforts to achieve better security without sacrificing too much efficiency: Chenette, Lewi, Weis and Wu (CLWW) [15] recently gave an ORE construction which leaks only the position of the most significant differing bits of the plaintexts.

Unfortunately, even hypothetical ideal ORE has recently been shown insecure for various use cases [3,10,19,20,22,24–26,30,34]. This is even if the scheme itself reveals nothing but the order of the plaintexts. The problem is that just the order of plaintexts alone can already reveal a significant amount of information about the data. For example, if the data is chosen uniformly from the entire domain, then even *ideal* ORE will leak the most significant bits. As the most significant bits are often the most important ones, this is troubling.

The problem is that the definitions of ORE, while precise and provable, do not immediately provide any "semantically meaningful" guarantees for the privacy of the underlying data. Indeed, the above attacks show that when the adversary has a strong estimate of the prior distribution the data is drawn from, essentially no security is possible. However, we contend that there are scenarios (see below) where the adversary lacks this knowledge. A core problem in such scenarios is that the privacy of one message is inherently dependent on what other ciphertexts the adversary sees. Analyzing these correlations under arbitrary sources of data, even for ideal ORE, can be quite difficult. Only very mild results are known, for example the fact that either CLWW leakage or ideal leakage provably hides the *least* significant bits of uniformly chosen data. Unfortunately, these bits are probably of less importance (e.g. for salaries).

Therefore, a central goal of this paper is to devise a semantically meaningful notion of privacy for the underlying data in the case that the adversary does not have a strong estimate of the prior distribution, and develop a construction attaining this notion not based on multilinear maps.

We stress that we are not trying to devise a scheme that is secure in the use cases of the attacks above, as many of the attacks above would apply to *any* ORE scheme; we are instead aiming to identify settings where the attacks do not apply, and then provide a scheme satisfying a given notion of security in this setting.

1.1   This Work: Parameter-Hiding ORE

In this work, we give one possible answer to the question above. Rather than focusing on the individual data records, we instead ask about the privacy of the distribution they came from. We show how to protect some information about the underlying data distribution.

Motivating Example. To motivate our notion, consider the following setting. A large university wants to outsource its database of student GPAs. For simplicity, we will assume each student's academic ability is independent of other students, and that this is reflected in the GPA. Thus, we will assume that each GPA is sampled independently and identically according to some underlying distribution. The university clearly wants to keep each individual's GPA hidden. It also may want aggregate statistics such as mean and variance to be hidden, perhaps to avoid getting a reputation for handing out very high or very low grades.

Distribution-Hiding ORE. This example motivates a notion of distribution-hiding ORE, where all data is sampled independently and identically from some underlying distribution D, and we wish to hide as much as possible about D. We would ideally like to handle arbitrary distributions D, but in many cases will accept handling certain special classes of distributions. Notice that if the distribution itself is completely hidden, then so too is every individual record, since any information about a record is also information about D.

We begin with the following trivial observation: if D has high min-entropy (namely, super-logarithmic), then the ideal ORE leakage is just a random ordering with no equalities, since there are no collisions with overwhelming probability. In particular, this leakage is independent of the distribution D; as such, ideal ORE leakage hides everything about the underlying distribution, except for the super-logarithmic lower bound on min-entropy. Thus, we can use the multilinear map-based scheme of [8] to achieve distribution-hiding ORE for any distribution with high min-entropy.

We note the min-entropy requirement is critical, since for smaller min-entropies, the leakage allows for determining the frequency of the most common elements, hence learning non-trivial information about D.[2]

Unfortunately, the only way we know to build distribution-hiding ORE is using ideal leakage as above; as such, we do not know of a construction not based on multilinear maps. Instead, in hopes of building such a scheme, we will allow some information about the distribution to leak.

---

[2] This min-entropy requirement may be somewhat problematic in some settings. GPAs for example, probably have fewer than 10 bits of entropy. However, adding small random noise to the data before encrypting (much smaller than the precision of the data) will force the data to have high min-entropy without changing the order of data, with the exception that identical data will appear different when comparing. In many cases (such as answering range queries) it is totally acceptable to fail to identify identical data.

Parameter-Hiding ORE. We recall that in many settings, data follows a known type of distribution. For example, the central limit theorem implies that many quantities such as various physical, biological, and financial quantities are (approximately) normally distributed. It is also common practice to assign grades on an approximately normal distribution, so GPAs might reasonably be conjectured to be normal. For a different example, insurance claims are often modeled according to the Gamma distribution.

Therefore, since the general shape of the distribution is typically known, a reasonable relaxation of distribution-hiding ORE is what we will call *parameter-hiding ORE*. Here, we will assume the distribution has a *known, public* "shape" (*e.g.* normal, uniform, Laplace *etc.*) but it may be shifted or scaled. We will allow the overall shape to be revealed; our goal instead is to completely hide the shifting and scaling information. More precisely, we consider a distribution D over $[0, 1]$ which will describe the general shape of the family of distributions in question. For example, if the shape in consideration is the set of uniform distributions over an interval, we may take D to be uniform distribution over $[0, 1]$; if the shape is the normal distribution, we will take D be the normal distribution with mean $1/2$, and standard deviation small enough so that the vast majority of the mass is in $[0, 1]$. Let $D_{\alpha,\beta}$ be the distribution defined as: first sample $x \leftarrow D$, and then output $\lfloor \alpha x + \beta \rfloor$. We will call α the scaling term and β the shift. The adversary receives a polynomial number of encryptions of plaintext sampled iid from $D_{\alpha,\beta}$ for some α, β. We will call a scheme *parameter hiding* if the scale and shift are hidden from any computationally bounded adversary. Our main theorem is that it is possible to construct such parameter-hiding ORE from bilinear maps:

Theorem 1 (Informal). *Assuming bilinear maps, it is possible to construct parameter-hiding ORE for any "smooth" distribution D, provided the scaling term is "large enough."*

We note the restrictions to large scalings are inherent: any small scaling will lead to a distribution with low min-entropy. As discussed above, even with ideal ORE, it is possible to estimate the min-entropy of low min-entropy distributions, and hence it would be possible to recover the scaling term if the scaling term is small. Some restrictions on the shape of D are also necessary, as certain shapes can yield low min-entropy even for large scalings. "Smoothness" (which we will define as having a bounded derivative) guarantees high min-entropy at large scales, and is also important technically for our analysis.

1.2 Technical Overview

As a starting point, we will consider the leakage profile of Chenette, Lewi, Weis and Wu [15] (henceforth referred to as CLWW), which reveals the position of the most significant differing bit between any two plaintexts. This is quite a lot of information: for example, it can be used to get rough bounds on the difference between two plaintexts. Thus, CLWW cannot be parameter hiding, since the scaling term is not hidden. However, CLWW will be a useful starting point, as it will allow us to construct *shift-hiding* ORE, where we only care about hiding the shift term. To help illustrate our approach, we will therefore first describe an equivalent formulation of CLWW leakage, which we will then explain how to extend to get full parameter-hiding ORE.

An Alternative View of CLWW Leakage. Consider the plaintext space $\{0, 1, 2, \ldots, 2^{\ell} - 1\}$. We will think of the plaintexts as leaves in a full binary tree of depth ℓ. In this tree, the position of the most significant differing bit between two plaintexts corresponds to the depth of their nearest ancestor. The leakage of CLWW can therefore can be seen as revealing the tree consisting of all given plaintexts, their ancestors in the tree up to the lowest common ancestor, and the order of the leaves, with all other information removed. See Fig. 1 for an illustration.

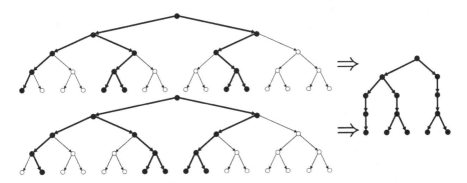

Fig. 1. CLWW Leakage. The two sets of plaintext $\{0, 4, 5, 10, 11\}$ and $\{1, 6, 7, 8, 9\}$ correspond to equivalent subtrees. If the message space extends beyond 15, the CLWW leakage remains the same as depicted, since the leakage only reveals the tree up to the most recent ancestor.

Now, suppose all plaintext elements are in the range $[0, 2^i)$ for some i. This means they all belong in the same subtree at height i; in particular, the CLWW leakage will only have depth at most i. Now, suppose we add a multiple of 2^i to every plaintext. This will simply shift all the plaintexts to being in a different subtree, but otherwise keep the same structure. Therefore, the CLWW leakage will remain the same.

Therefore, while CLWW is not shift hiding, it is *shift periodic*. In particular, if imagine a distribution D whose support is on $[0, 2^i)$, and consider shifting D by β. Consider an adversary A, which is given the CLWW leakage from q plaintexts sampled from the shifted D, and outputs a bit. If we plot the probability $p(\beta)$ that A outputs 1 as a function of β, we will see that the function is periodic with period 2^i.

Shift-Hiding ORE/OPE. With this periodicity, it is simple to construct a scheme that is shift hiding. To get a shift-hiding scheme for message space $[0, 2^\ell)$, we instantiate CLWW with message space $[0, 2^{\ell+1})$. We also include as part of the secret key a random shift γ chosen uniformly in $[0, 2^\ell)$. We then encrypt a message m as $\mathsf{Enc}(m + \gamma)$. Adding a random shift can be seen as convolving the signal $p(\beta)$ with the rectangular function

$$q(\beta) = \begin{cases} 2^{-\ell} & \text{if } \beta \in [0, 2^\ell) \\ 0 & \text{otherwise} \end{cases}$$

Since the rectangular function's support matches the period of p, the result is that the convolved signal $\hat{p}$ is *constant*. In other words, the adversary always has the same output distribution, regardless of the shift β. Thus, we achieve shift hiding.

When the comparison algorithm of an ORE scheme is simple integer comparison, we say the scheme is an *order-preserving encryption* (OPE) scheme. OPE is preferable because it can be used with fewer modifications to a database server. We recall that CLWW can be made into an OPE scheme — where ciphertexts are integers and comparision is integer comparison — while maintaining the CLWW leakage profile. Our conversion to shift-hiding preserves the OPE property, so we similarly achieve a shift-hiding OPE scheme.

Scale-Hiding ORE/OPE. We note that we can also turn any shift-hiding ORE into a scale-hiding ORE. Simply take the logarithm of the input before encrypting; now multiplying by a constant corresponds to shifting by a constant. Of course, taking the logarithm will result in non-integers; this can easily be fixed by rounding to the appropriate level of precision (enough precision to guarantee no collisions over the domain) and scaling up to make the plaintexts integral. Similarly, we can also obtain scale-hiding OPE if we start with an OPE scheme.

Impossibility of Parameter-Hiding OPE. One may hope to achieve both shift-hiding and scale-hiding by some combination of the two above schemes. For example, since order *preserving* encryption schemes can be composed, one can imagine composing a shift-hiding scheme with a scale-hiding scheme. Interestingly, this does not give a parameter-hiding scheme. The reason is that shifts/scalings of the plaintext do not correspond to shifts/scalings of the ciphertexts. Therefore, while the outer OPE may provide, say, shift-hiding for its inputs, this will not translate to shift-hiding of the inner OPE's inputs.

Nonetheless, one may hope that tweaks to the above may give a scheme that is simultaneously scale and shift hiding. Perhaps surprisingly, we show that this is actually impossible. Namely, we show that *OPE cannot possibly be parameter-hiding*. Due to space limit, we put the rigorous proof in our full version [12].

This impossibility shows that strategies leveraging CLWW leakage are unlikely to yield parameter-hiding ORE schemes. Interestingly, all ORE schemes we are aware of that can be constructed from symmetric crypto can also be made into OPE schemes. Thus, this suggests we need stronger tools than those used by previous efficient schemes.

Parameter Hiding via Smoothed CLWW Leakage. Motivated by the above, we must seek a different leakage profile if we are to have any hope of achieving parameter-hiding ORE. We therefore first describe a "dream" leakage that will allow us to perform similar tricks as in the shift hiding case in order to achieve both scale and shift hiding simultaneously. Our dream leakage will be a "smoothed" CLWW leakage, where all nodes of degree exactly 2 are replaced with an edge between the two neighbors. In other words, the dream leakage is the smallest graph that is "homeomorphic" to the CLWW leakage. See Fig. 2 for an illustration.

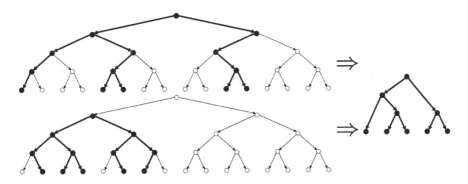

Fig. 2. Smoothed CLWW Leakage. The two sets of plaintext $\{0, 4, 5, 10, 11\}$ and $\{1, 2, 3, 5, 6\}$ correspond to equivalent smoothed subtrees. Notice that the CLWW leakage for these two trees is different.

Our key observation is that this smoothed CLWW leakage now exhibits additional periodicity. Namely, if we multiply every plaintext by 2, every edge in the bottom layer of the CLWW leakage will get subdivided into a path of length 2, but smoothing out the leakage will result in the same exact graph. This means that smoothed CLWW leakage is periodic in the *log* domain.

In particular, consider a distribution D with support on $[0, 2^i)$, and suppose it is multiplied by α. Consider an adversary A, which is given the smoothed CLWW leakage from q plaintexts sampled from a scaled D, and outputs a bit. If we plot the probability $p(\log_2 \alpha)$ that A outputs 1 as a function of α, we will see that the function is periodic with period 1.

Therefore, we can perform a similar trick as above. Namely, we convolve p with the uniform distribution over the period of p in the log domain. We accomplish this by including a random scalar α as part of the secret key, and multiplying by α before encrypting. However, this time several things are different:

- Since we are working in the log domain, the logarithm of the random scalar α has to be uniform. In other words, α is log-uniform
- Since we are working over integers instead of real numbers, many issues arise.

- First, α needs to be an integer to guarantee that the scaled plaintexts are still integers. This means we cannot choose α at log-uniformly over a single log period, since then α only has support on $\{1, 2\}$. Instead, we need to choose α log-uniformly over a sufficiently large multiple of the period that α approximates the continuous log-uniform distribution sufficiently well.

- Second, unlike the shift case, sampling at random from D and then scaling is not the same as sampling from a scaled version of D, since the rounding step does not commute with scaling. For example, for concreteness consider the normal distribution. If we sample from a normal distribution (and round) and then scale, the resulting plaintexts will all be multiples of α. However, if we sample directly from a scaled normal distribution (and then round), the support of the distribution will include integers which are not multiples of α.

  To remedy this issue, we observe that if the plaintexts are sampled from a wide enough distribution, their differing bits will not be amongst the lowest significant bits. Hence, the leakage will actually be independent of the lower order bits. For example, this means that while the rounding does not commute with the scaling, the leakage actually does not depend on the order in which the two operations are carried out.

- The above arguments can be made to work for, say, the normal distribution. However, we would like to have a proof that works for any distribution. Unfortunately, for distributions that oscillate rapidly, we may run into trouble with the above arguments, since rounding such distributions can cause odd behaviors at all scales. This problem is actually unavoidable, as quickly oscillating distributions may have actually have low min-entropy even at large scales. Therefore, we must restrict to "smooth" functions that have a bounded derivative.

  Using a careful analysis, we are able to show for smooth distributions that we achieve the desired scale hiding.

- Finally, we want to have a scheme that is both scale and shift hiding. This is slightly non-trivial, since once we introduce, say, a random shift, we have modified the leakage of the scheme, and cannot directly appeal to the arguments above to obtain scale hiding as well. Instead, we distill a set of specific requirements on the leakage that will work for both shift hiding and scale hiding. We show that our shift hiding scheme above satisfies the requirements needed in order for us to introduce a random scale and additionally prove scale hiding.

Achieving Smoothed CLWW Leakage. Next we turn to actually constructing ORE with smoothed CLWW leakage. Of course, ideal ORE has better than (smoothed) CLWW leakage, so we can construct such ORE based on multilinear maps. However, we want a construction that uses standard tools.

We therefore provide a new construction of ORE using pairings that achieves smoothed CLWW leakage. We believe this construction is of interest on its own, as it is achieves the to-date smallest leakage of any non-multilinear-map-based scheme.

CLWW ORE and How to Reduce its Leakage. Our construction builds on the ideas of CLWW, so we first briefly recall the ORE scheme of CLWW. In their (basic) scheme, the encryption key is just a PRF key K. To encrypt a plaintext $x \in \{0,1\}^n$, for each prefix $p_i = x[1, \ldots, i]$, the scheme computes

$$y_i = \mathsf{PRF}_K(p_i) + x_{i+1}$$

where x_{i+1} is the $(i + 1)$-st bit of x, and the output of $\mathsf{PRF} \in \{0,1\}^\lambda$ is treated as an integer (we will take λ to be the security parameter). The ORE ciphertext is then $(y_1 \ldots, y_n)$. To compare two ciphertexts $(y_1 \ldots, y_n)$ and $(y'_1 \ldots, y'_n)$, one finds the smallest index i such that $y_i \neq y'_i$, and outputs 1 if $y'_i - y_i = 1$. This naturally reveals the index of the bit where the plaintexts differ.

Our approach to reducing the leakage is to attempt to hide the index i where the plaintexts differ. As a naive attempt at this, first consider what happens if we modify the scheme to simply randomly permute the outputs $(y_1 \ldots, y_n)$ (with a fresh permutation chosen for each encryption). We can still compare ciphertexts by appropriately modifying the comparison algorithm: now given $c = (y_1 \ldots, y_n)$ and $c' = (y'_1 \ldots, y'_n)$ (permuted as above), it will look for indices i, j such that either $y'_i - y_j = 1$, in which case it outputs 1, or $y_j - y'_i = 1$, in which case it outputs 0. (If we choose the output length of the PRF to be long enough then this check will be correct with overwhelming probability).

This modification, however, does not actually reduce leakage: an adversary can still determine the most significant differing bit by counting how many elements c and c' have in common.

We can however recover this approach by preventing an adversary from detecting how many elements c and c' have in common. To do so, we introduce and employ the new notion of *property-preserving hashing* (PPH). Intuitively, a PPH is a randomized hashing scheme that is designed to publicly reveal a particular predicate P on pairs of inputs.

PPH can be seen as the hashing (meaning, no decryption) analogue of the notion of property-preserving encryption, a generalization of order-revealing encryption to arbitrary properties due to Pandey and Rouselakis [35]. (This can also be seen as a symmetric-key version of the notion of "relational hash" due to Mandal and Roy [31].)

Specifically, we construct and employ a PPH for the property

$$P_1(x, x') = \begin{cases} 1 & \text{if } x = x' + 1 \\ 0 & \text{otherwise} \end{cases}$$

(Here x, x' are not plaintexts of the ORE scheme, think of them as other inputs determined below.) Security requires that this is *all* that is leaked; in particular, input equality is *not* leaked by the hash values (which requires a randomized hashing algorithm).

Now, the idea is to modify the scheme to include a key K_H for such a PPH $\mathcal{H}$, and the encryption algorithm to not only randomly permute the y_i's but hash them as well, i.e., output $(h_1, \ldots, h_n)$ where $h_i = \mathcal{H}_{K_H}(y_i)$ for the permuted y_i's.[3] The comparison algorithm can again be modified appropriately, namely to not to check if $y_i' - y_j = 1$ but rather if their h_i' and h_j' hash values satisfy P_1 via the PPH (and similarly for the check $y_j - y_i' = 1$).

For any two messages, the resulting ORE scheme is actually ideal: it only reveals the order of the underlying plaintexts, but nothing else. However, for three messages m, m', m'' we see that some additional information is leaked. Namely, if we find that $y_i' - y_j = 1$ $y_k'' - y_j = 1$, then we know that $y_j' = y_k''$. We choose the range of the PRF large enough so that this can only happen if y_j' and y_k' are both $\mathsf{PRF}_K(p_\ell) + x_{\ell+1}$ for the same prefix p_ℓ and same bit $x_{\ell+1}$, and y_j' corresponds to the most significant bit where m' differs from m, y_k'' corresponds to the most significant bit where m'' differs from m, and moreover these positions are the same. Therefore, the adversary learns whether these most-significant differing bits are the same. It is straightforward to show that this leakage is exactly equivalent to the smoothed CLWW leakage we need. Proving this ORE scheme secure wrt. this leakage based on an achievable notion of security for the PPH turns out to be technically challenging. Nevertheless, we manage to prove it "non-adaptively secure," meaning the adversary is required to non-adaptively choose the dataset, which is realistic for a passive adversary in the outsourced database setting.

Property-Preserving Hash From Bilinear Maps. Next we turn to constructing a property-preserving hash (PPH) for the property $P_1(x, x') = x = x' + 1$. For this, we adapt techniques from perfectly one-way hash functions [9,31] to the symmetric-key setting and use asymmetric bilinear groups. Roughly, in our construction the key for the hash function is a key K for a pseudorandom function PRF and, letting $e \colon G_1 \times G_2 \to G_T$ be an asymmetric bilinear map on prime order cyclic groups G_1, G_2 with generators g_1, g_2, the hash of x is

$$\mathcal{H}_K(x) = (g_1^{r_1}, g_1^{r_1 \mathsf{PRF}_K(x)}, g_2^{r_2}, g_2^{r_2 \mathsf{PRF}_K(x+1)})$$

for fresh random $r_1, r_2 \in \mathbb{Z}_p$. (Thus, the PRF is also pushed to our PPH construction and can be dropped from the higher-level ORE scheme when our hash function is plugged-in). The bilinear map allows testing whether $P_1(x, x')$ from $\mathcal{H}_K(x), \mathcal{H}_K(x')$, and intuitively our use of asymmetric bilinear groups prevents testing other relations such as equality (formally we use the XSDH assumption). We prove the construction secure under an indistinguishability-based notion in which the adversary has to distinguish between the hash of a random challenge x^* and a random hash value, and can query for hash values of inputs x of its

---

[3] A minor issue here is that we now lose decryptability for the resulting ORE scheme; however, this can easily be added back in a generic way by also encrypting the plaintext separately under a semantically secure scheme.

choice as long as $P_1(x, x^*)$ and $P_1(x^*, x)$ are both 0. Despite being restricted,[4], this notion suffices in our ORE scheme above.

When our PPH is plugged into our ORE scheme, ciphertexts consist of $4n$ group elements, and order comparison requires $n(n-1)$ pairing computations on average. We also note that CLWW gave an improved version of their scheme where ciphertexts are size $O(n)$ rather than $O(n\lambda)$ for security parameter λ, however, we have reason to believe this may be difficult for schemes with our improved leakage profile, see below.

Piecing everything together, we obtain a parameter-hiding ORE from bilinear maps. We note that, as parameter-hiding OPE is impossible, we achieve the first construction of ORE without multilinear maps secure with a security notion that is impossible for OPE.

Generalizing Our ORE Scheme. In our full version [12], we also show several extensions to our smoothed CLWW ORE scheme. In one direction, we achieve an improved level of leakage by considering blocks of bits at a time(encrypting message block by block, rather than bit by bit). We show that if the block size is only 2, then we improve security and efficiency simultaneously, while for larger block sizes the leakage continues to reduce but the efficiency compared to the basic scheme (in terms of both ciphertext size and pairings required for comparison) decreases.

On the other direction, we also show how to improve efficiency while sacrificing some security. We give a more efficient version of the scheme than above (only need $O(n)$ pairings for each comparison), that is still sufficient for achieving parameter-hiding ORE using our conversion.

In addition, we also show how our ORE scheme easily gives a *left/right ORE* as defined by [29] that also improves on their leakage. In left/right ORE, ciphertexts can be generated in either the left mode or right mode, and the comparison algorithm only compares a left and a right ciphertext. Security requires that no information is leaked amongst left and right ciphertexts in isolation.

1.3   Discussion and Perspective

The original OPE scheme of [6] leaks "whatever a random order-preserving function leaks." Unfortunately, this notion does not say anything about what such leakage actually looks like. The situation has been improved in recent works on OPE such as CLWW which define a precise "leakage profile" for their scheme. However, such leakage profiles are still of limited use, since they do not obviously say anything about the actual privacy of the underlying data.

We instead study ORE with a well-defined privacy notion for the underlying plaintexts. A key part of our results is showing how to translate sufficiently strong leakage profiles into such privacy notions. Nonetheless, we do not claim

---

[4] More generally, following [35] one could allow the adversary to choose two challenge inputs and make queries that do not allow it to trivially distinguish them, but we are unable to prove our construction secure under this stronger notion.

that our new ORE scheme is safe to use in general higher-level protocols. We only claim security as long all that is sensitive is the scale and shift of the underlying plaintext distributions. If, for example, if the shape of the distribution is highly sensitive, or if there are correlations to other data available to the attacker, our notion is insufficient.

However, our construction provably has better leakage than existing efficient schemes, and it at least shows some meaningful security for specific situations. Moreover we suspect that the scheme can be shown to be useful in many other settings by extending our techniques.

1.4   Related Work

Work done on "leaky cryptography" includes work on multiparty computation [33], searchable symmetric and structured encryption [11,13,14,18,21,28, 37], and property-preserving encryption [5,6,35]. In the database community, the problem of querying an encrypted database was introduced by Hacigümüş, Iyer, Li and Mehrotra [23], leading to a variety of proposals there but mostly lacking formal security analysis. Proposals of specific outsourced database systems based on property-preserving encryption like ORE include CryptDB [36], Cipherbase [2], and TrustedDB [4].

Besides, in [29], the authors give an efficient ORE construction based on PRFs, while their leakage profile cannot achieve shift hiding and scale hiding simultaneously, which means their scheme cannot meet our privacy notion. Moreover, in [27], the authors give an alternative ORE construction, based on function revealing encryption for simple functions, namely orthogonality testing and intersection cardinality, while their leakage needs further analysis.

2   Background

NOTATION. All algorithms are assumed to be polynomial-time in the security parameter (though we will sometimes refer to efficient algorithms explicitly). We will denote the security parameter by λ. For a random variable Y, we write $y \xleftarrow{\$} Y$ to denote that y is sampled according to Y's distribution, moreover, let D be Y's distribution, we abuse notation $y \xleftarrow{\$} D$ to mean that y is sampled according to D. For an algorithm A, by $y \xleftarrow{\$} A(x)$ we mean that A is executed on input x and the output is assigned to y, furthermore, if A is randomized, then we write $y \xleftarrow{\$} \mathcal{A}(x)$ to denote running $\mathcal{A}$ on input x with a fresh random tape and letting y be the random variable induced by its output. We denote by $\Pr[A(x) = y : x \xleftarrow{\$} X]$ the probability that A outputs y on input x when x is sampled according to X. We say that an adversary $\mathcal{A}$ has advantage ϵ in distinguishing X from Y if $\Pr[A(x) = 1 : x \xleftarrow{\$} X]$ and $\Pr[A(y) = 1 : y \xleftarrow{\$} Y]$ differ by at most ϵ.

When more convenient, we use the following probability-theoretic notation instead. We write $P_X(x)$ to denote the probability that X places on x, i.e.

$P_X(x) = \Pr[X = x]$, and we say $P_X(x)$ is the probability density function (PDF) of X's distribution. The *statistical distance* between X and Y is given by $\Delta = \frac{1}{2}\sum_x |P_X(x) - P_Y(x)|$. If $\Delta(X,Y)$ is at most ϵ then we say X, Y are ϵ-close. It is well-known that if X, Y are ϵ-close then any (even computationally unbounded) adversary A has advantage at most ϵ in distinguishing X from Y.

The *min-entropy* of a random variable X is $H_\infty(X) = -\log(\max_x P_X(x))$. A value $\nu \in \mathbb{R}$ depending on λ is called *negligible* if its absolute value goes to 0 faster than any polynomial in λ, i.e. $\forall c > 0 \; \exists \lambda^* \in \mathbb{N} \; \forall \lambda \geq \lambda^* : |\nu| \leq \frac{1}{\lambda^c}$. We let $[M] = \{1, \ldots, M\}$, $[M]' = \{0, \ldots, M-1\}$ and $[M, N] = \{M, \ldots, N\}$. We write $\boldsymbol{m}$ as a vector of plaintexts and $|\boldsymbol{m}|$ as the vector's length, namely $\boldsymbol{m} = (m_1, \ldots, m_s)$ and $|\boldsymbol{m}| = s$. For a vector $\boldsymbol{m}$, by $a\boldsymbol{m}$ we mean $(am_1, \ldots, am_s)$ and we write $\boldsymbol{m}+b$ to denote $(m_1+b, \ldots, m_s+b)$. Let x be a real number, we write $\lfloor x \rfloor$ as the largest integer s.t. $\lfloor x \rfloor \leq x$, and $\lceil x \rceil$ as the smallest integer s.t. $\lceil x \rceil \geq x$. By $\lfloor x \rceil$, we mean rounding x to the nearest integer, namely $-1/2 \leq \lfloor x \rceil - x < 1/2$. If P is a predicate, we write $\mathbf{1}(P)$ for the function that takes the inputs to P and returns 1 if P holds and 0 otherwise.

PRFs. We use the standard notion of a PRF. A function $F : \{0,1\}^\lambda \times D \to \{0,1\}^\lambda$ is said to be a *PRF with domain D* if for all efficient $\mathcal{A}$ we have that

$$| \Pr[\mathcal{A}^{F(K,\cdot)}(1^\lambda) = 1] - \Pr[\mathcal{A}^{g(\cdot)}(1^\lambda) = 1] |$$

is a negligible function of λ, where K is uniform over $\{0,1\}^\lambda$ and g is uniform over all functions from D to $\{0,1\}^\lambda$.

ORE. The following definition of syntax for order-revealing encryption makes explicit that comparison may use helper information (e.g. a description of a particular group) by incorporating a *comparison key*, denote ck.

Definition 2 (ORE). *A ORE scheme is a tuple of algorithms $\Pi = (\mathcal{K}, \mathcal{E}, \mathcal{C})$ with the following syntax.*

- *The key generation algorithm $\mathcal{K}$ is randomized, takes inputs $(1^\lambda, M)$, and always emits two outputs $(\mathsf{sk}, \mathsf{ck})$. We refer to the first output sk as the* secret key *and the second output ck as the* comparison key.
- *The encryption algorithm $\mathcal{E}$ is randomized, takes inputs (sk, m) where $m \in [M]$, and always emits a single output c, that we refer to as a* ciphertext.
- *The comparison algorithm $\mathcal{C}$ is deterministic, takes inputs (ck, c_1, c_2), and always emits a bit.*

If the comparison algorithm $\mathcal{C}$ is simple integer comparison (i.e., if $\mathcal{C}(\mathsf{ck}, c_1, c_2)$ is a canonical algorithm that treats its the ciphertexts and binary representations of integers and tests which is greater) then the scheme is said to be an order-preserving encryption (OPE) *scheme.*

CORRECTNESS OF ORE SCHEMES. Intuitively, an ORE scheme is correct if the comparison algorithm can output the order of the underlying plaintext, by taking ck and two ciphertexts as inputs.

Our constructions will only be *computationally* correct, i.e. correct with overwhelming probability when the input messages are provided by an efficient process, under hardness assumptions. Formally, we define correctness using the game $\mathrm{COR}_{\Pi}^{\mathrm{ore}}(\mathcal{A})$, which is defined as follows: The game starts by running $(\mathsf{sk}, \mathsf{ck}) \xleftarrow{\$} \mathcal{K}(1^\lambda, M)$, and it gives ck to $\mathcal{A}$. The adversary $\mathcal{A}$ then outputs two messages $x, y \in [M]$. The game computes $c_1 \xleftarrow{\$} \mathcal{E}(\mathsf{sk}, x)$ and $c_2 \xleftarrow{\$} \mathcal{E}(\mathsf{sk}, y)$, outputs 1 if $x < y$ but $\mathcal{C}(\mathsf{ck}, c_1, c_2) = 0$.

We say that an ORE scheme Π is *computationally correct* if for all efficient adversaries $\mathcal{A}$, all $M = \mathrm{poly}(\lambda)$, we have that $\Pr[\mathrm{COR}_{P_i}^{\mathrm{ore}}(\mathcal{A}) = 1]$ is a negligible function in the security parameter.

SECURITY OF ORE SCHEMES. The following simulation-based security definition is due to Chenette et al. [15]. Here a *leakage profile* is any randomized algorithm. The definition refers to games given in Fig. 3, which we review now. In the real game, key generation is run and the adversary is given the comparison key and oracle access to the encryption algorithm with the corresponding secret key. The adversary eventually outputs a bit that the game uses as its own output. In the ideal simulation game, the adversary is interacting with the same oracle, but the comparison key is generated by a stateful simulator, and the oracle responses are generated by the simulator which receives leakage from the stateful leakage algorithm $\mathcal{L}$.

Game $\mathrm{REAL}_{\Pi}^{\mathrm{ore}}(\mathcal{A})$:	Game $\mathrm{SIM}_{\Pi,\mathcal{L}}^{\mathrm{ore}}(\mathcal{A}, \mathcal{S})$:
$(\mathsf{sk}, \mathsf{ck}) \xleftarrow{\$} \mathcal{K}(1^\lambda, M); b \xleftarrow{\$} \mathcal{A}^{\mathrm{ENC}}(\mathsf{ck})$	$\mathsf{st}_\ell \leftarrow \bot; (\mathsf{ck}, \mathsf{st}_s) \xleftarrow{\$} S(1^\lambda); b \xleftarrow{\$} \mathcal{A}^{\mathrm{ENC}}(\mathsf{ck})$
Return b	Return b
$\mathrm{ENC}(m)$:	$\mathrm{ENC}(m)$:
Return $\mathcal{E}(\mathsf{sk}, m)$	$(L, \mathsf{st}_\ell) \xleftarrow{\$} \mathcal{L}(\mathsf{st}_\ell, m); (c, \mathsf{st}_s) \xleftarrow{\$} \mathcal{S}(L, \mathsf{st}_s)$
	Return c

Fig. 3. Games $\mathrm{REAL}^{\mathrm{ore}}\Pi(\mathcal{A})$ (left) and $\mathrm{SIM}_{\Pi,\mathcal{L}}^{\mathrm{ore}}(\mathcal{A}, \mathcal{S})$ (right), where $\Pi = (\mathcal{E}, \mathcal{C})$ is an ORE scheme, $\mathcal{L}$ is a leakage profile, $\mathcal{A}$ is an adversary, and $\mathcal{S}$ is a simulator.

Definition 3 ($\mathcal{L}$-simulation-security for ORE). *For an ORE scheme Π, an adversary $\mathcal{A}$, a simulator $\mathcal{S}$, and leakage profile $\mathcal{L}$, we define the games* $\mathrm{REAL}_{\Pi}^{\mathrm{ore}}(\mathcal{A})$ *and* $\mathrm{SIM}_{\Pi,\mathcal{L}}^{\mathrm{ore}}(\mathcal{A})$ *in Fig. 3. The advantage of $\mathcal{A}$ with respect to $\mathcal{S}$ is defined as*

$$\mathsf{Adv}_{\Pi,\mathcal{L},\mathcal{A},\mathcal{S}}^{\mathrm{ore}}(\lambda) = \left| \Pr[\mathrm{REAL}_{\Pi}^{\mathrm{ore}}(\mathcal{A}) = 1] - \Pr[\mathrm{SIM}_{\Pi,\mathcal{L}}^{\mathrm{ore}}(\mathcal{A}, \mathcal{S}) = 1] \right|.$$

We say that Π is $\mathcal{L}$-simulation-secure if for every efficient adversary $\mathcal{A}$ there exists an efficient simulator $\mathcal{S}$ such that $\mathsf{Adv}_{\Pi,\mathcal{L},\mathcal{A},\mathcal{S}}^{\mathrm{ore}}(\lambda)$ *is a negligible function.*

We also define non-adaptive *variants of the games where $\mathcal{A}$ gets a single query to an oracle that accepts a vector of messages of unbounded size. In the real* game $\text{REAL}_{\Pi}^{\text{ore-na}}(\mathcal{A})$, *the oracle returns the encryptions applied independently to each message. In the ideal game* $\text{SIM}_{\Pi}^{\text{ore-na}}(\mathcal{A})$, *the leakage function gets the entire vector of messages as input and produces an output L that is then given to $\mathcal{S}$ which produces a vector of ciphertexts, which are returned by the oracle.*

We define the non-adaptive advantage *of $\mathcal{A}$ with respect to $\mathcal{S}$ analogously, and denote it* $\text{Adv}_{\Pi,\mathcal{L},\mathcal{A},\mathcal{S}}^{\text{ore-na}}(\lambda)$. *Non-adaptive $\mathcal{L}$-simulation security is defined analogously.*

Ideal ORE. Ideal ORE is the case where the leakage profile $\mathcal{L}$ is simply the list of results of comparisons between the plaintexts. We note that such a $\mathcal{L}$ is *always* revealed by the comparison algorithm, so ideal ORE is the best one can hope for. Ideal ORE can be constructed from multilinear maps [8].

CLWW Leakage. As an example of a non-ideal leakage profile, consider the leakage $\mathcal{L}_{\text{clww}}$ of Chenette, Lewi, Weis and Wu [15]. For $m_0, m_1 \in \{0,1\}^n$, we define the most significant differing bit of m_1 and m_2, denoted $\text{msdb}(m_0, m_1)$, as the index of first bit where m_0, m_1 differ, or $n+1$ if $m_1 = m_2$.

The CLWW leakage profile $\mathcal{L}_{\text{clww}}$ takes in input a vector of plaintext $\boldsymbol{m} = (m_1, \ldots, m_q)$ and produce the following:

$$\mathcal{L}_{\text{clww}}(m_1, \ldots, m_q) := (\forall 1 \le i, j \le n, \mathbf{1}(m_i < m_j), \text{msdb}(m_i, m_j))$$

3   New Security Notions for ORE

In this section, we propose four meaningful notions of privacy: *distribution-hiding, parameter-hiding, scale-hiding* and *shift-hiding*; in those notions, we are considering the privacy of the underlying *distribution* of data records, rather than the individual data records, and show how to protect information about the underlying data distribution.

DISTRIBUTION-HIDING FOR ORE. We assume that all database entries are independently and identically distributed according to some distribution D^5, and the notion of distribution-hiding refers to game defined in Fig. 4. In the interactive game, after receiving the public parameter and comparison key, adversary $\mathcal{A}$ picks two distributions D_0, D_1 and sends to challenger $\mathcal{C}$, $\mathcal{C}$ then flips a coin b, samples a sequence of entries from D_b, and sends back the encrypted entries. Eventually $\mathcal{A}$ outputs a bit, and we say adversary wins if it guesses b correctly. We note that if either of D_b has low min-entropy, it is possible for an adversary to estimate the min-entropy by looking for collisions in its ciphertexts. Therefore, we must restrict D_b to have high min-entropy.

Definition 4 (Distribution-Hiding for ORE). *For an ORE scheme Π, an adversary $\mathcal{A}$, function $q = q(\lambda)$ we define the games* $\text{DH}_{\Pi,q}(\mathcal{A}, \lambda)$ *in Fig. 4. The*

---

[5] By D, here we mean a sampling algorithm, such that the outputs of this algorithm obey the distribution D, for ease we denote $\max D$ as the maximum item in D's support.

Game $\mathsf{DH}_{\Pi,q}(\mathcal{A}, \lambda)$:

$(\mathsf{sk}, \mathsf{ck}) \xleftarrow{\$} \mathcal{K}(1^\lambda, M); \ D_0, D_1 \leftarrow \mathcal{A}(1^\lambda, \mathsf{ck}) \ \text{s.t.} \ H_\infty(D_b) \geq \omega(\log \lambda)$

$b \xleftarrow{\$} \{0, 1\}, \boldsymbol{m} \xleftarrow{\$} D_b \ \text{s.t.} \ |\boldsymbol{m}| = q; \max D_b \leq M; \boldsymbol{c} = \mathcal{E}(\mathsf{sk}, \boldsymbol{m})$

$b' = \mathcal{A}(\mathsf{ck}, \boldsymbol{c}); \ \text{Return} \ (b \overset{?}{=} b')$

Fig. 4. Games $\mathsf{DH}_{\Pi,q}(\mathcal{A}, \lambda)$, where $\Pi = (\mathcal{K}, \mathcal{E}, \mathcal{C})$ is an ORE scheme, $q = \mathsf{poly}(\lambda)$, and $\mathcal{A}$ is an adversary.

advantage of $\mathcal{A}$ is defined as $\mathbf{Adv}_{\Pi,q}^{\mathsf{DH}}(\mathcal{A}, \lambda) = |\Pr[\mathsf{DH}_{\Pi,q}(\mathcal{A}, \lambda) - \frac{1}{2}]|$. We say that Π is distribution-hiding if for every efficient adversary $\mathcal{A}$, and any polynomial $q = \mathsf{poly}(\lambda)$, $\mathbf{Adv}_{\Pi,q}^{\mathsf{DH}}(\mathcal{A}, \lambda)$ is a negligible function.

We immediately observe that ideal ORE achieves distribution hiding, while for other known leakier ORE schemes, it's seems unfeasible to achieve this privacy guarantee. However, in many settings, the general shape of the distribution is often known (that is, if the distribution is normal, uniform, Laplace, etc.), and it is reasonable to allow the overall shape to be reveal but hide its mean and/or variance completely, subject to certain restrictions. Before formalize these notion, we firstly introduce some notations.

For a continuous random variable X, where D is X's distribution, we abuse notation $p_D(x) = p_X(x)$. Now we introduce three alternative distributions: $D_{\mathsf{scale}}^\delta, D_{\mathsf{shift}}^\ell, D_{\mathsf{aff}}^{\delta,\ell}$ with parameter δ, ℓ, where the corresponding probability density function is defined as:

$$p_{D_{\mathsf{scale}}} = \frac{p_D(\frac{x}{\delta})}{\delta}; \ \ p_{D_{\mathsf{shift}}}(x) = p_D(x - \ell); \ \ p_{D_{\mathsf{aff}}} = \frac{p_D(\frac{x-\ell}{\delta})}{\delta}$$

In other words, $D_{\mathsf{scale}}^\delta$ scales the shape of D by a factor of δ; D_{shift} shifts D by ℓ and D_{aff} does both.

ROUNDED DISTRIBUTION. As our plaintexts are integers, we need map real number to its rounded integer, namely $x \to \lceil x \rceil$. More precisely, let D be a distribution over real numbers between α and β; we induce a rounded distribution $R_D^{\alpha,\beta}$ on $[\lceil \alpha \rceil, \lfloor \beta \rfloor]$ which samples from D and then rounds. Its probability density function is:

$$p_{R_D^{\alpha,\beta}}(k) = \begin{cases} \frac{\int_\alpha^{\lceil\alpha\rceil+1/2} p_D(x)dx}{\int_\alpha^\beta p_D(x)dx} & k = \alpha \\ \frac{\int_{k-1/2}^{k+1/2} p_D(x)dx}{\int_\alpha^\beta p_D(x)dx} & k \in [\lceil \alpha+1 \rceil, \lfloor \beta-1 \rfloor] \\ \frac{\int_{\lfloor\beta\rfloor-1/2}^{\beta} p_D(x)dx}{\int_\alpha^\beta p_D(x)dx} & k = \beta \\ 0 & Otherwise \end{cases}$$

In the case of $D_{\mathsf{scale}}^\delta$, D_{shift}^ℓ, or $D_{\mathsf{aff}}^{\delta,\ell}$, we will use the notation $\lfloor D_{\mathsf{scale}}^\delta \rceil$, $\lfloor D_{\mathsf{shift}}^\ell \rceil$, and $\lfloor D_{\mathsf{aff}}^{\delta,\ell} \rceil$ to denote the respective rounded distributions.

Now, we present the notion "(γ, D)-parameter-hiding" ORE, referring to the game defined in Fig. 5. Here, D is a distribution over $[0, 1]$, which represents the description of the known shape of the distribution of plaintexts. γ is a lower-bound on the scaling that is allowed. Then key generation is run and adversary is given the public parameter, (γ, D), and the comparison key. Then, the adversary $\mathcal{A}$ sends two pairs of parameters $(\delta_0, \ell_0), (\delta_1, \ell_1)$ to challenger $\mathcal{C}$. Next, $\mathcal{C}$ flips a coin b, checks whether the parameter is proper($\mathbf{1}(\delta_0 \geq \gamma \cap \delta_1 \geq \gamma)$), then samples a sequence of data entries from the rounded distribution $\lfloor D_{\mathsf{aff}}^{\delta_b, \ell_b} \rceil$ and sends back encrypted data. Eventually $\mathcal{A}$ outputs a bit, and we say adversary wins if it guesses b correctly.

Game (γ, D)-para-hid$_{\Pi,q}(\mathcal{A}, \lambda)$:

$(\mathsf{sk}, \mathsf{ck}) \xleftarrow{\$} \mathcal{K}(1^\lambda, M); \delta_0, \ell_0, \delta_1, \ell_1 \leftarrow \mathcal{A}(\mathsf{ck}, D)$

If $\delta_0 < \gamma$ or $\delta_1 < \gamma$, output a random bit and abort,

else, $b \xleftarrow{\$} \{0, 1\}, \boldsymbol{m} \xleftarrow{\$} \lfloor D_{\mathsf{aff}}^{\delta_b, \ell_b} \rceil, s.t. |\boldsymbol{m}| = q; \max \lfloor D_{\mathsf{aff}}^{\delta_b, \ell_b} \rceil \leq M; \boldsymbol{c} = \mathcal{E}(\mathsf{sk}, \boldsymbol{m})$

$b' = \mathcal{A}(\mathsf{ck}, \boldsymbol{c})$ Return $(b \stackrel{?}{=} b')$

Fig. 5. Games para-hid$_{\Pi,q}(\mathcal{A}, \lambda)$, where $\Pi = (\mathcal{E}, \mathcal{C})$ is an ORE scheme, D is a distribution on $[0, 1]$, $\mathcal{A}$ is an adversary

Definition 5 ($((\gamma, D)$-parameter hiding for ORE). *For an ORE scheme Π, an adversary $\mathcal{A}$, a distribution D, and function $q = q(\lambda)$, we define the games (γ, D)-para-hid$_{\Pi,q}(\mathcal{A}, \lambda)$ in Fig. 5. The advantage of $\mathcal{A}$ is defined as*

$$\mathbf{Adv}_{\Pi,q,\gamma,D}^{\mathsf{para\text{-}hid}}(\mathcal{A}, \lambda) = |\Pr[(\gamma, D)\text{-para-hid}_{\Pi,q}(\mathcal{A}, \lambda) - \frac{1}{2}]|$$

We say that Π is (γ, D)-parameter hiding if for every efficient adversary $\mathcal{A}$ and polynomial q $\mathbf{Adv}_{\Pi,q,\gamma,D}^{\mathsf{para\text{-}hid}}(\mathcal{A}, \lambda)$ is a negligible function.

Similarly, we define (γ, D)-scale hiding and (γ, D)-shift hiding with little change as above. More precisely, in the game of (γ, D)-scale hiding, we add the restriction $\ell_0 = \ell_1 = 0$ and in the game of (γ, D)-shift hiding, we add the restriction $\delta_0 = \delta_1$. Due to the space limit, we skip the formal definitions here.

We note that these three notions are distribution dependent, and we would like they work for any distribution. Unfortunately, quickly oscillating distributions do not fit into our case, as they may have actually low min-entropy for their discretized distributions on integers, even at large scales. Hence, we place additional restrictions. We place the following restriction, which is sufficient, but potentially stronger than necessary:

(η, μ)-SMOOTH DISTRIBUTION. We let D be a distribution where its support mainly on $[0, 1]$ ($\Pr[x \notin [0, 1] : x \leftarrow D] \leq \mathsf{negl}(\lambda)$), we denote $p_D(x)$ as its derivative, and we say that D is (η, μ)-smooth if (1) $\forall x \in [0, 1], p_D(x) \leq \eta$; (2) $|p'_D(x)| \leq \eta$ for all $x \in [0, 1]$ except for μ points.

Definition 6 ((γ, η, μ)-parameter hiding for ORE). *For an ORE scheme Π, we say Π is (γ, η, μ)-parameter hiding if for every efficient adversary $\mathcal{A}$, polynomial q, and any (η, μ)-smooth distribution D, $\mathbf{Adv}_{\Pi,q,\gamma,D}^{\mathsf{para\text{-}hid}}(\mathcal{A}, \lambda)$ is a negligible function.*

4   Parameter Hiding ORE

In this section, we will assume we are given an ORE $\Pi = (\mathcal{K}, \mathcal{E}, \mathcal{C})$ with a "smoothed" version of CLWW leakage, defined below. Later, in Sect. 5, we will show how to instantiate such a scheme from bilinear maps.

We show how to convert a scheme with smoothed CLWW leakage into a parameter-hiding ORE scheme by simply composing with a linear function: namely, for any plaintext m, the ciphertext has form $\mathcal{E}(\alpha m + \beta)$, where α, β are the same across all messages and are sampled as part of the secret key. Intuitively, α helps to hide the scale parameter and β hides the shift. We need to be careful about the distributions of α and β; α needs to be drawn from a "discrete log uniform" distribution of appropriate domain, and β needs to be chosen from a uniform distribution of appropriate domain.

The discrete log uniform distribution D on $[A, B]$ ($\mathsf{logU}(A, B)$) has probability density function:

$$
p_D(k) = \begin{cases} \frac{1/k}{\sum_{i=A}^{B} 1/i} & i \in [A, B] \\ 0 & Otherwise \end{cases}
$$

We say a leakage function $\mathcal{L}$ is smoothed CLWW if:

1. For any two plaintext sequences $\boldsymbol{m_0}, \boldsymbol{m_1}$, if $\mathcal{L}_{\mathsf{clww}}(\boldsymbol{m_0}) = \mathcal{L}_{\mathsf{clww}}(\boldsymbol{m_1})$, then $\mathcal{L}(\boldsymbol{m_0}) = \mathcal{L}(\boldsymbol{m_1})$ (in other words, it leaks no more information that CLWW);
2. For any plaintext sequence $\boldsymbol{m}$, $\mathcal{L}(\boldsymbol{m}) = \mathcal{L}(2\boldsymbol{m})$

4.1   Parameter-Hiding ORE

In this part, we give the formal description of parameter-hiding ORE. To simplify our exposition, we first specify some parameters. We will assume we are given:

$$
q = \mathsf{poly}(\lambda), M = 2^{\mathsf{poly}(\lambda)}, \gamma = 2^{\omega(\log \lambda)}, \eta, \mu \leq O(1)
$$

We will assume γ and M are exactly powers of 2 without loss of generality by rounding up. We define:

$$
\tau = \gamma, \xi = \gamma^2, U = 4\xi M, T = \gamma^2 \times U, K = 2 \times T
$$

Let $\Pi = (\mathcal{K}, \mathcal{E}, \mathcal{C})$ be an ORE scheme on message space $[K]$ with smoothed CLWW leakage $\mathcal{L}$. We define our new ORE $\Pi_{\mathsf{aff}} = (\mathcal{K}_{\mathsf{aff}}, \mathcal{E}_{\mathsf{aff}}, \mathcal{C}_{\mathsf{aff}})$ on message space $[M]$ as follows:

- $\mathcal{K}_{\mathsf{aff}}(1^\lambda, M, \Pi)$: On input the security parameter λ, message space $[M]$ and Π, the algorithm picks a super-polynomial $\gamma = 2^{\omega(\log \lambda)}$ as a global parameter, and computes parameters above. Then it runs $(\mathsf{ck}, \mathsf{sk}) \leftarrow \mathcal{K}(1^\lambda, K)$, draws $\alpha \stackrel{\$}{\leftarrow} \mathsf{logU}(\xi, 2\xi - 1)$ and β from discrete uniform on $[T]'$ and outputs $\mathsf{sk}_{\mathsf{aff}} = (\mathsf{sk}, \alpha, \beta), \mathsf{ck}_{\mathsf{aff}} = \mathsf{ck}$;
- $\mathcal{E}_{\mathsf{aff}}(\mathsf{sk}_{\mathsf{aff}}, m)$. On input the secret key $\mathsf{sk}_{\mathsf{aff}}$ and a message $m \in [M]$, it outputs

$$\mathsf{CT}_{\mathsf{aff}} = \mathcal{E}(\alpha m + \beta)$$

By our choice of message space $[K]$ for Π, the input to $\mathcal{E}$ is guaranteed to be in the message space.

- $\mathcal{C}_{\mathsf{aff}}(\mathsf{ck}_{\mathsf{aff}}, \mathsf{CT}^0_{\mathsf{aff}}, \mathsf{CT}^1_{\mathsf{aff}})$: On inputs the comparison key $\mathsf{ck}_{\mathsf{aff}}$, two ciphertexts $\mathsf{CT}^0_{\mathsf{aff}}, \mathsf{CT}^1_{\mathsf{aff}}$, it outputs $\mathcal{C}(\mathsf{ck}_{\mathsf{aff}}, \mathsf{CT}^0_{\mathsf{aff}}, \mathsf{CT}^1_{\mathsf{aff}})$

Here we also give the description of composted schemes that only achieve "scale-hiding" or "shift-hiding". Formally, we define $\Pi_{\mathsf{scale}} = (\mathcal{K}_{\mathsf{scale}}, \mathcal{E}_{\mathsf{scale}}, \mathcal{C}_{\mathsf{scale}})$ and $\Pi_{\mathsf{shift}} = (\mathcal{K}_{\mathsf{shift}}, \mathcal{E}_{\mathsf{shift}}, \mathcal{C}_{\mathsf{shift}})$, respectively:

- $\mathcal{K}_{\mathsf{scale}}(1^\lambda, M, \Pi)$: On input the security parameter λ, the message space $[M]$ and Π, the algorithm picks a super-polynomial $\gamma = 2^{\omega(\log \lambda)}$ as a global parameter, and computes parameters above. Then it runs $(\mathsf{ck}, \mathsf{sk}) \leftarrow \mathcal{K}(1^\lambda, K)$, draws $\alpha \stackrel{\$}{\leftarrow} \mathsf{logU}(\xi, 2\xi - 1)$ and outputs $\mathsf{sk}_{\mathsf{scale}} = (\mathsf{sk}, \alpha), \mathsf{ck}_{\mathsf{scale}} = \mathsf{ck}$;
- $\mathcal{E}_{\mathsf{scale}}(\mathsf{sk}_{\mathsf{scale}}, m)$. On input the secret key $\mathsf{sk}_{\mathsf{scale}}$ and a message $m \in [M]$, it outputs

$$\mathsf{CT}_{\mathsf{scale}} = \mathcal{E}(\alpha m)$$

- $\mathcal{C}_{\mathsf{scale}}(\mathsf{ck}_{\mathsf{scale}}, \mathsf{CT}^0_{\mathsf{scale}}, \mathsf{CT}^1_{\mathsf{scale}})$: On inputs the comparison key $\mathsf{ck}_{\mathsf{scale}}$, two ciphertexts $\mathsf{CT}^0_{\mathsf{scale}}, \mathsf{CT}^1_{\mathsf{scale}}$, it outputs $\mathcal{C}(\mathsf{ck}_{\mathsf{scale}}, \mathsf{CT}^0_{\mathsf{scale}}, \mathsf{CT}^1_{\mathsf{scale}})$.
- $\mathcal{K}_{\mathsf{shift}}(1^\lambda, M, \Pi)$: On input the security parameter λ, the message space $[M]$ and Π, the algorithm picks a super-polynomial $\gamma = 2^{\omega(\log \lambda)}$ as a global parameter, and computes parameters above. Then it runs $(\mathsf{ck}, \mathsf{sk}) \leftarrow \mathcal{K}(1^\lambda)$, draws β from discrete uniform on $[T]'$ and outputs $\mathsf{sk}_{\mathsf{shift}} = (\mathsf{sk}, \alpha), \mathsf{ck}_{\mathsf{shift}} = \mathsf{ck}$;
- $\mathcal{E}_{\mathsf{shift}}(\mathsf{sk}_{\mathsf{shift}}, m)$. On input the secret key $\mathsf{sk}_{\mathsf{shift}}$ and a message $m \in [M]$, it outputs

$$\mathsf{CT}_{\mathsf{shift}} = \mathcal{E}(m + b)$$

- $\mathcal{C}_{\mathsf{shift}}(\mathsf{ck}_{\mathsf{shift}}, \mathsf{CT}^0_{\mathsf{shift}}, \mathsf{CT}^1_{\mathsf{shift}})$: On inputs the comparison key $\mathsf{ck}_{\mathsf{shift}}$, two ciphertexts $\mathsf{CT}^0_{\mathsf{shift}}, \mathsf{CT}^1_{\mathsf{shift}}$, it outputs $\mathcal{C}(\mathsf{ck}_{\mathsf{shift}}, \mathsf{CT}^0_{\mathsf{shift}}, \mathsf{CT}^1_{\mathsf{shift}})$.

The correctness of $\Pi_{\mathsf{aff}}, \Pi_{\mathsf{scale}}$ and Π_{shift} is directly held by correctness of Π, and what is more interesting is the privacy that those scheme can guarantee.

4.2   Main Theorem

In the part, we prove Π_{aff} is parameter hiding, formally:

Theorem 7 (Main Theorem). *Assuming Π has $\mathcal{L}$-simulation-security where $\mathcal{L}$ is smoothed CLWW, then for any $\gamma = 2^{\omega(\log \lambda)}$, Π_{aff} is (γ, η, μ)-parameter hiding.*

Proof. According to the security notions, it is straightforward that if an ORE scheme is (γ, η, μ)-parameter hiding, then it is also (γ, η, μ)-scale hiding and (γ, η, μ)-shift hiding. Next we claim the converse proposition holds.

CLAIM. If an ORE scheme Π achieves (γ, η, μ)-scale hiding and (γ, η, μ)-shift hiding simultaneously, then Π is (γ, η, μ)-parameter hiding.

We sketch the proof by hybrid argument. For any $\gamma = 2^{\omega(\log \lambda)}$ and (η, μ)-smooth distribution D, firstly, by shift-hiding, there is no efficient adversary that distinguish (δ_0, ℓ_0) from $(\delta_0, 0)$ with non-negligible probability. Then due to scale-hiding, no efficient adversary can differ $(\delta_0, 0)$ from $(\delta_1, 0)$ with non-negligible probability. Thirdly, same as the first argument, any efficient adversary can distinguish $(\delta_1, 0)$ from (δ_1, ℓ_1) with only negligible advantage. Combining together, Π achieves (γ, η, μ)-parameter hiding.

Thus, it suffices to show Π_{aff} is both (γ, η, μ)-scale hiding and (γ, η, μ)-shift hiding, due to space limit, we put the rigorous proof in our full version [12].

5   ORE with Smoothed CLWW Leakage

We start by defining the security we target via a smoothed CLWW leakage function. Then we recall a primitive for our construction called a *property-preserving hash (PPH) function*, and state and analyze our ORE construction using a PPH. In a later section we instantiate the PPH to complete the construction. Next, we give variant constructions with trade-offs between efficiency and leakage.

Now We define the non-adaptive version of the leakage profile for our construction. The leakage profile takes in input a vector of messages $\boldsymbol{m} = (m_1, \ldots, m_q)$ and produces the following:

$$\mathcal{L}_f(m_1, \ldots, m_q) := (\forall 1 \leq i, j, k \leq q, \mathbf{1}(m_i < m_j), \mathbf{1}(\mathsf{msdb}(m_i, m_j) = \mathsf{msdb}(m_i, m_k)))$$

By definition, it's easy to note that $\mathcal{L}_f$ leaks strictly less than CLWW. Except for the order of underlying plaintexts, it only leaks whether the position of $\mathsf{msdb}(m_i, m_j)$ and $\mathsf{msdb}(m_i, m_j)$ are the same, therefore the leakage profile preserve consistent if we left-shift all the plaintexts by one bit, which referring to $\mathcal{L}_f(\boldsymbol{m}) = \mathcal{L}_f(2\boldsymbol{m})$. Thus, $\mathcal{L}_f$ is smoothed CLWW.

5.1   Property Preserving Hash

Our construction will depend on a tool – *property preserving hash (PPH)*, which is essentially a property-preserving encryption scheme [35] without the decryption algorithm. In this section we recall the syntax and security of a PPH.

Definition 8. *A property-preserving hash (PPH) scheme is a tuple of algorithms $\Gamma = (\mathcal{K}_h, \mathcal{H}, \mathcal{T})$ with the following syntax:*

- *The key generation algorithm $\mathcal{K}_h$ is randomized, takes as input 1^λ and emits two outputs $(\mathsf{hk}, \mathsf{tk})$ that we refer to as the* hash key hk *and* test key tk. *These implicitly define a domain D and range R for the hash.*
- *The evaluation algorithm $\mathcal{H}$ is randomized, takes as input the hash key hk, an input $x \in D$, and emits a single output $h \in R$ that we refer to as the* hash *of x.*
- *The test algorithm $\mathcal{T}$ is deterministic, takes as input the test key tk and two hashes h_1, h_2, and emits a bit.*

CORRECTNESS OF PPH SCHEMES. Let P be a predicate on pairs of inputs. We define correctness of a PPH Γ with respect to P via the game $\mathrm{COR}^{\mathsf{pph}}_{\Gamma,P}(\mathcal{A})$, which is as follows: It starts by running $(\mathsf{hk}, \mathsf{tk}) \xleftarrow{\$} \mathcal{K}_h(1^\lambda)$ and gives tk to $\mathcal{A}$. Then $\mathcal{A}$ outputs x, y. The game computes $h \xleftarrow{\$} \mathcal{H}(\mathsf{hk}, x), h' \xleftarrow{\$} \mathcal{H}(\mathsf{hk}, y)$ and outputs 1 if $\mathcal{T}(\mathsf{tk}, h, h') \neq P(x, y)$. We say that Γ is *computationally correct with respect to P* if for all efficient $\mathcal{A}$, $\Pr[\mathrm{COR}^{\mathsf{pph}}_{\Gamma,P}(\mathcal{A}) = 1]$ is a negligible function of λ.

SECURITY OF PPH SCHEMES. We recall a simplified version of the security definition for PPH that is a weaker version of PPE security defined by Pandey and Rouselakis [35]. The definition is a sort of semantic security for random messages under chosen-plaintext attacks, except that the adversary is restricted from making certain queries.

Game $\mathrm{IND}^{\mathsf{pph}}_{\Gamma,P}(\mathcal{A})$:

$(\mathsf{hk}, \mathsf{tk}) \xleftarrow{\$} \mathcal{K}_h(1^\lambda)$; $x^* \xleftarrow{\$} \mathcal{A}(\mathsf{tk})$
$h_0 \xleftarrow{\$} \mathcal{H}(\mathsf{hk}, x^*)$; $h_1 \xleftarrow{\$} R$; $b \xleftarrow{\$} \{0, 1\}$; $b' \xleftarrow{\$} \mathcal{A}^{\mathrm{HASH}}(\mathsf{tk}, x^*, h_b)$
Return $(b \overset{?}{=} b')$
$\mathrm{HASH}(x)$:

If $P(x^*, x) = 1$ or $P(x, x^*) = 1$, then $h \leftarrow \bot$, Else $h \xleftarrow{\$} \mathcal{H}(\mathsf{hk}, x)$
Return h

Fig. 6. Game $\mathrm{IND}^{\mathsf{pph}}_{\Gamma,P}(\mathcal{A})$.

Definition 9. *Let P be some predicate and $\Gamma = (\mathcal{K}_h, \mathcal{H}, \mathcal{T})$ be a PPH scheme with respect to P. For an adversary $\mathcal{A}$ we define the game $\mathrm{IND}^{\mathsf{pph}}_{\Gamma,P}(\mathcal{A})$ in Fig. 6. The* restricted-chosen-input *advantage of $\mathcal{A}$ is defined to be $\mathsf{Adv}^{\mathsf{pph}}_{\Gamma,P,\mathcal{A}}(\lambda) = 2\Pr[\mathrm{IND}^{\mathsf{pph}}_{\Gamma,P}(\mathcal{A}) = 1] - 1$. We say that Γ is* restricted-chosen-input *secure if for all efficient adversaries $\mathcal{A}$, $\mathsf{Adv}^{\mathsf{pph}}_{\Gamma,P,\mathcal{A}}(\lambda)$ is negligible.*

5.2   ORE from PPH

CONSTRUCTION. Let $F : K \times ([n] \times \{0, 1\}^n) \to \{0, 1\}^\lambda$ be a secure PRF. Let $P(x, y) = \mathbf{1}(x = y + 1)$ be the predicate that outputs 1 if and only if $x = y + 1$, and let $\Gamma = (\mathcal{K}_h, \mathcal{H}, \mathcal{T})$ be a PPH scheme with respect to P. In our construction, we interpret the output of F as a λ-bit integer, which is also the input domain of the PPH Γ. We define our ORE scheme $\Pi = (\mathcal{K}, \mathcal{E}, \mathcal{C})$ as follows:

- $\mathcal{K}(1^\lambda, M)$: On input the security parameter and message space $[M]$, the algorithm chooses a key k uniformly at random for F, and runs the key generation algorithm of the property preserving hash function $\Gamma.\mathcal{K}_h$ to obtain the hash and test keys (hk, tk). It sets $\mathsf{ck} \leftarrow \mathsf{tk}$, $\mathsf{sk} \leftarrow (k, \mathsf{hk})$ and outputs (ck, sk).
- $\mathcal{E}(\mathsf{sk}, m)$: On input the secret key sk and a message m, the algorithm writes the binary representation as m as $(b_1, \ldots, b_n)$, and then for $i = 1, \ldots, n$, it computes:

$$u_i = F(k, (i, b_1 b_2 \cdots b_{i-1} \| 0^{n-i+1})) + b_i \mod 2^\lambda, \quad t_i = \Gamma.\mathcal{H}(\mathsf{hk}, u_i).$$

We note that u_i is computed by treating the PRF output as a member of $\{0, \ldots, 2^\lambda - 1\}$. Then it chooses a random permutation $\pi : [n] \to [n]$, and sets $v_i = t_{\pi(i)}$. The algorithm outputs $\mathsf{CT} = (v_1, \ldots, v_n)$.
- $\mathcal{C}(\mathsf{ck}, \mathsf{CT}_1, \mathsf{CT}_2)$: on input the public parameter, two ciphertexts $\mathsf{CT}_1, \mathsf{CT}_2$ where $\mathsf{CT}_1 = (v_1, \ldots, v_n), \mathsf{CT}_2 = (v'_1, \ldots, v'_n)$, the algorithm runs $\Gamma.\mathcal{T}(\mathsf{tk}, v_i, v'_j)$ and $\Gamma.\mathcal{T}(\mathsf{tk}, v'_i, v_j)$ for every $i, j \in [n]$. If there exists a pair (i^*, j^*) such that $\Gamma.\mathcal{T}(\mathsf{tk}, v_{i^*}, v'_{j^*}) = 1$, then the algorithm outputs 1, meaning $m_1 > m_2$; else if there exists a pair (i^*, j^*) such that $\Gamma.\mathcal{T}(\mathsf{tk}, v'_{i^*}, v_{j^*}) = 1$, then the algorithm outputs 0, meaning $m_1 < m_2$; otherwise it outputs $\perp$, meaning $m_1 = m_2$.

CORRECTNESS. For two messages m_1, m_2, let $(b_1, \ldots b_n)$ and $(b'_1, \ldots, b'_n)$ be their binary representations. Assuming $m_1 > m_2$, there must exists a unique index $i^* \in [n]$ such that $u_i = u'_i + 1$. Therefore correctness of Π is followed by correctness of PPH. We can use the same argument for the case $m_1 = m_2$ and $m_1 < m_2$. What is more interesting is its simulation based security, as it is the foundation for parameter hiding ORE, formally:

Theorem 10. *Assuming F is a secure PRF and Γ is restricted-chosen-input secure, Π is $\mathcal{L}_f$-non-adaptively-simulation secure.*

Proof. We use a hybrid argument, and define a sequence of hybrid games as follows:

- H_{-1}: Real game $\mathrm{REAL}_\Pi^{\mathsf{ore}}(\mathcal{A})$;
- H_0: Same as H_{-1}, except replacing PRF $F_k(\cdot)$ by a truely random function F^* in the encryption oracle;
- $H_{i \cdot q + j}$ Depend on a predicate $\mathsf{Switch}_{(i,j)}$ which is define below. If $\mathsf{Switch}_{(i,j)} = 0$, then $H_{i \cdot q + j} = H_{i \cdot q + j - 1}$, else in procedure of $\mathcal{E}(m_j)$, u_i^j is replaced by a random string.

From the high level, we establish the proof by showing show that any adjacent hybrids are indistinguishable, and then we construct an efficient simulator S such that the output of H_{qn} and $SIM^{ore}_{\Pi,\mathcal{L}_f}(\mathcal{A},\mathcal{S})$ are statistically identical. For the predicate, we say $Switch_{i,j} = 1$ if $\forall k \in [q], msdb(m_j, m_k) \neq i$, and 0 otherwise. We note that when $Switch_{i,j} = 0$, there exists u_i^k such that $u_i^j = u_i^k \pm 1$, the relation which can be detected by the test algorithm of PPH(for the i-th bit of m_j, we call such a bit a leaky bit), which means we cannot replace it with random string, otherwise adversary can trivially distinguish it. In the following we firstly prove any adjacent objects are computational indistinguishable.

Lemma 11. *Assuming Γ is restricted-chosen-input secure, for any $k \in [qn]$ $H_{k-1} \overset{comp}{\approx} H_k$.*

Proof. Due to the security of PRF, it's trivial that $H_{-1} \overset{comp}{\approx} H_0$, and for any $k > 0$ (for ease, $k = i^* \cdot q + j^*$ where $i^* \in [n-1], j^* \in [q]$), it suffices to show $H_{k-1} \overset{comp}{\approx} H_k$ under the condition $Switch_{i^*,j^*} = 1(Switch_{i^*,j^*} = 0$ implies $H_{k-1} = H_k$). We prove that if there exists adversary $\mathcal{A}$ that distinguish H_k from H_{k-1} with noticeable advantage ϵ, then we can construct a simulator $\mathcal{B}$ wins the restricted-chosen-input game with ϵ-negl. Here is the description of $\mathcal{B}$. Firstly it runs IND^{pph}_{Γ}, and sends tk as the comparison key ck to $\mathcal{A}$. After receiving a sequence of plaintext $m_1, \ldots, m_q$, it picks a random function F^*(using the lazy sampling technique for instance), sets $X^* = F^*(i^*, b_1^{j^*} b_2^{j^*} \cdots b_{i^*-1}^{j^*} || 0^{n-i^*+1}) + b_{i^*}^{j^*}$ where b_i^j is the i-th bit of m_j. Then it sends X^* to its challenger in restricted-chosen-input game and gets back T as the challenge term. To simulate the encryption oracle, $\mathcal{B}$ works as follows:

1. $(i',j') > (i^*,j^*)$(here using a natural order for tuples, $(i,j) > (i',j')$ iff $iq+j > i'q + j'$), $\mathcal{B}$ computes:
$$u_{i'}^{j'} = F^*(i^*, b_1^{j'} b_2^{j'} \cdots b_{i'-1}^{j'} || 0^{n-i'+1}) + b_{i'}^{j'}; t_{i'}^{j'} = \Gamma.\mathcal{H}(hk, u_{i'}^{j'})$$

2. $(i',j') < (i^*,j^*) \cap Switch_{i',j'} = 0$, then same as above, else $u_{i'}^{j'} \overset{\$}{\leftarrow} \{0,1\}^\lambda, t_{i'}^{j'} = \Gamma.\mathcal{H}(hk, u_{i'}^{j'})$.

3. sets $t_{i^*}^{j^*} = T$, and $\forall j \in [q]$, picks a random permutation π_j and outputs the ciphertexts $CT_j = (t_{\pi_j(1)}^j, \ldots, t_{\pi_j(n)}^j)$.

Finally, $\mathcal{B}$ outputs whatever $\mathcal{A}$ outputs[6].

Since F^* is a random function, $Pr[u_{i'}^{j'} = X^* \pm 1]$ is negligible for all $(i',j') \neq (i^*,j^*)$, which means $\mathcal{B}$ fails to simulate the encryption oracle with only negligible probability. Besides, when $T = \Gamma.\mathcal{H}(hk, X^*)$, $\mathcal{B}$ properly simulates H_{k-1}, and if T is random, then $\mathcal{B}$ simulates H_k(due to the PRF security, the distribution of $\Gamma.\mathcal{H}(hk, r) : r \overset{\$}{\leftarrow} \{0,1\}^\lambda$ is computationally close to a random variable that uniformly sampled from the range of Γ). Hence, if $\mathbf{Adv}(\mathcal{A})$ is noticeable, then $\mathcal{B}$'s advantage is also noticeable. □

In the following, we describe an efficient simulator S such that the output of H_{qn} and $SIM^{ore}_{\Pi,\mathcal{L}_f}(\mathcal{A},\mathcal{S})$ are statistically identical. Roughly speaking, we note

---

[6] We note that $\mathcal{B}$ does not have hk, what it does is to call the hash oracle.

that $\mathsf{Switch}_{i,j} = 1$ means that i-th bit of m_j is not a leaky bit, indicating that its value would not affect the leakage profile whp. Hence, it suffices to only simulate the leaky bit of each individual message, which can be extracted by $\mathcal{L}_f$, and sets the rest just as random string. Due to the final random permutations, H_{qn} and $\mathrm{SIM}^{\mathrm{ore}}_{\Pi,\mathcal{L}_f}(\mathcal{A},\mathcal{S})$ are statistically identical. Formally:

Description of the simulator. For fixed a message set $\mathcal{M} = \{m_1,\ldots,m_q\}$ (without loss of generality, we assume $m_1 > \ldots > m_q$), the simulator $\mathcal{S}$ is given the leakage information $\mathcal{L}_f(m_1,\ldots,m_q)$. $\mathcal{S}$ firstly keeps a $q \times n$ matrix $\mathcal{B}$ and runs a recursive algorithm $\mathsf{FillMatrix}(1,1,q)$ to fill in the entries, as follows:

- If $j = k$, then $\forall i' \in [i,n]$, $\mathcal{B}[j][i'] = r$ where $r \xleftarrow{\$} \{0,1\}^\lambda$;
- Else, it proceeds as follows:
  - searches the smallest $j^* \in [j,k]$ s.t. $P(m_j,m_{j^*}) = P(m_j,m_k)$;
  - sets $\mathcal{B}[j'][i] = r', \forall j' \in [j,j^*-1]$; $\mathcal{B}[j'][i] = r'-1, \forall j' \in [j^*,k]$, where $r' \xleftarrow{\$} \{0,1\}^\lambda$;
  - runs $\mathsf{FillMatrix}(i+1,j,j'-1)$ and $\mathsf{FillMatrix}(i+1,j',k)$ recursively.

More concretely, our recursive algorithm is to fill in the entries by

$$\mathsf{FillMatrix}(i,j,k), \ \forall i \in [n], j \leq k \in [q]$$

Then $\mathcal{S}$ runs $\Gamma.\mathcal{K}_h(1^\lambda)$ and gets the keys tk,hk, and sets $t_{i,j} = \Gamma.\mathcal{H}(\mathsf{hk},\mathcal{B}[j][i])$, $\forall i \in [n], j \in [q]$. Finally, $\mathcal{S}$ samples random permutations π_j, outputs CT_j as $\mathsf{CT}_j = (t^j_{\pi_j(1)},\ldots,t^j_{\pi_j(n)})$ We note that the FillMatrix algorithm terminates after at most qn steps as each cell will not be written twice, hence $\mathcal{S}$ is an efficient simulator.

Finally we claim that $\mathcal{S}$ properly simulates the relevant games. We first observe that the simulator identifies how many leaked bits (prefixes) there are for the messages $m_1,\ldots,m_q$. Recall that if messages $m_1,\ldots,m_q$ share the same prefix up to the $\ell-1$-th bit, and if there exists (the first) i^* such that $\mathsf{msdb}(m_1,m_{i^*}) = \mathsf{msdb}(m_1,m_q)$, then we can conclude that $\{m_1,\ldots,m_{i^*-1}\}$ has 1 on their ℓ-th bit, and $\{m_{i^*},\ldots,m_q\}$ has 0 on their ℓ-th bit. This way the ℓ-th bit of these messages are leaked. The simulator recursively identifies other leaked bits for these two sets. At the end, for each message, how many prefixes whose next bits are leaked will be identified. As this information will also be identified in the hybrid H_{qn}. So a random permutation (for H_{qn} and the simulation) will hide these leaked prefixes, except the total number. Thus, our simulation is identical to H_{qn}, and we establish the entire proof. $\qquad\square$

5.3   More Efficient Comparisons

The construction above needs to run $O(n^2)$ times PPH test algorithm for one single comparison, which is very expensive for real application. In this part, we present a variant ORE achieving better efficiency but with a weaker leakage profile, which only requires $O(n)$ pairings in each individual comparison. And what's more interesting is that this weaker leakage profile is also smoothed

CLWW, that means we can still construct a parameter hiding ORE based on it, along with better efficiency. From the high level, we fix a permutation for all encryptions(this permutation is part of the secret key now), rather than sampling fresh permutation for each ciphertext. Therefore, in the comparison, we only need run the PPH test for pairs that share the same index, which means only $O(n)$ pairings for one comparison. Formally:

CONSTRUCTION. Let F be a secure PRF with the same syntax as above, let $P(x,y) = \mathbf{1}(x = y + 1)$ be the relation predicate that outputs 1 if and only if $x = y+1$, and let $\Gamma = (\mathcal{K}_h, \mathcal{H}, \mathcal{T})$ be a PPH scheme with respect to P, as before. We define our ORE scheme $\Pi = (\mathcal{K}, \mathcal{E}, \mathcal{C})$ as follows:

- $\mathcal{K}(1^\lambda, M)$: On input the security parameter and message space $[M]$, the algorithm chooses a key k uniformly at random for F, runs $\Gamma.\mathcal{K}_h$ to obtain the hash and test keys $(\mathsf{hk}, \mathsf{tk})$, and samples a random permutation $\pi : [n] \to [n]$. It sets $\mathsf{ck} \leftarrow \mathsf{tk}$, $\mathsf{sk} \leftarrow (k, \mathsf{hk}, \pi)$ and outputs $(\mathsf{ck}, \mathsf{sk})$.
- $\mathcal{E}(\mathsf{sk}, m)$: On input the secret key SK and a message m, the algorithm computes the binary representation of $m = (b_1, \ldots, b_n)$, and then calculates:

$$u_i = F(k, (i, b_1 b_2 \cdots b_{i-1} || 0^{n-i+1})) + b_i, \quad t_i = \Gamma.\mathcal{H}(\mathsf{hk}, u_i).$$

  Then it sets $v_i = t_{\pi(i)}$ and outputs $\mathsf{CT} = (v_1, \ldots, v_n)$.
- $\mathcal{C}(\mathsf{ck}, \mathsf{CT}_1, \mathsf{CT}_2)$: on input the public parameter, two ciphertexts $\mathsf{CT}_1, \mathsf{CT}_2$ where $\mathsf{CT}_1 = (v_1, \ldots, v_n), \mathsf{CT}_2 = (v'_1, \ldots, v'_n)$, the algorithm runs $\Gamma.\mathcal{T}(\mathsf{tk}, v_i, v'_i)$ for every $i \in [n]$. If there exists i^* such that $\Gamma.\mathcal{T}(\mathsf{tk}, v_{i^*}, v'_{i^*}) = 1$, then the algorithm outputs 1, meaning $m_1 > m_2$; else if there exists a pair i^* such that $\Gamma.\mathcal{T}(\mathsf{tk}, v'_{i^*}, v_{i^*}) = 1$, then the algorithm outputs 0, meaning $m_1 < m_2$; otherwise it outputs it outputs $\perp$, meaning $m_1 = m_2$.

Now, we give the description of the leakage profile, which takes $\boldsymbol{m} = \{m_1, \ldots, m_q\}$ as input and produces:

$$\mathcal{L}'_f(m_1, \ldots, m_q) := (\forall 1 \leq i, j, k, l \leq q, \mathbf{1}(m_i < m_j), \mathbf{1}(\mathsf{msdb}(m_i, m_j) = \mathsf{msdb}(m_k, m_l)))$$

Compared to $\mathcal{L}_f$, $\mathcal{L}'_f$ gives extra information that $\mathbf{1}(\mathsf{msdb}(m_i, m_j) = \mathsf{msdb}(m_k, m_l))$ even when $i \neq k$. However, $\mathcal{L}'_f$ is still strictly stronger than CLWW, and for any $\boldsymbol{m}$, it's obvious that $\mathcal{L}'_f(\boldsymbol{m}) = \mathcal{L}'_f(2\boldsymbol{m})$, which gives evidence that $\mathcal{L}'_f$ is also smoothed CLWW. And for its simulation based security, applying exactly the same argument as the proof of Theorem 10, we can establish the following theorem.

Theorem 12. *The ORE scheme Π is $\mathcal{L}'_f$-non-adaptive-simulation secure, assuming F is a secure PRF and Γ is restricted-chosen-input secure.*

Therefore, to achieve the privacy of parameter hiding, we can use this efficient scheme as an alternative, such that we only need $O(n)$ pairings for each comparison.

6   PPH from Bilinear Maps

We construct a PPH scheme for the predicate P required in our ORE construction. That is, $P(x, y) = 1$ if and only if $x = y + 1$.

We let $F : \{0, 1\}^\lambda \times \{0, 1\}^\lambda \to \mathbb{Z}_p$ be a PRF, where p is a prime to be determined at key generation.

CONSTRUCTION. We now define our PPH $\Gamma = (\mathcal{K}_h, \mathcal{H}, \mathcal{T})$.

- $\mathcal{K}_h(1^\lambda)$ This algorithm takes the security parameter as input. It samples descriptions of prime-order p groups $\mathbb{G}, \hat{\mathbb{G}}, \mathbb{G}_T$, generators $g \in \mathbb{G}, \hat{g} \in \hat{\mathbb{G}}$, a bilinear map $e : \mathbb{G} \times \hat{\mathbb{G}} \to \mathbb{G}_T$. It then chooses $k \xleftarrow{\$} \{0, 1\}^\lambda$. It sets the hash key $\mathsf{hk} \leftarrow (k, g, \hat{g})$, the test key $\mathsf{tk} \leftarrow (\mathbb{G}, \hat{\mathbb{G}}, \mathbb{G}_T, e)$, a description of the bilinear map and groups, and outputs $(\mathsf{hk}, \mathsf{tk})$.
- $\mathcal{H}(\mathsf{hk}, x)$ This algorithm takes as input the hash key hk, an input x, picks two random non-zero $r_1, r_2 \in \mathbb{Z}_p$ and outputs

$$\mathcal{H}(\mathsf{hk}, x) = (g^{r_1}, g^{r_1 \cdot F(k,x)}, \hat{g}^{r_2}, \hat{g}^{r_2 \cdot F(k,x+1)}).$$

- $\mathcal{T}(\mathsf{tk}, h_1, h_2)$ To test two hash values (A_1, A_2, B_1, B_2) and (C_1, C_2, D_1, D_2), $\mathcal{T}$ outputs 1 if

$$e(A_1, D_2) = e(A_2, D_1),$$

and otherwise it outputs 0.

Hence the domain D is $\{0, 1\}^\lambda$ and the range R is $(\mathbb{G}^2, \hat{\mathbb{G}}^2)$

CORRECTNESS. Correctness reduces to testing if $F(k, y + 1) = F(k, x)$. If $x = y + 1$ then this always holds. If not, then it is easily shown that finding x, y with this property (and without knowing the key) with non-negligible probability leads to an adversary that contradicts the assumption that F is a PRF.

SECURITY. We prove that PPH is restricted-chosen-input secure, assuming that F is a PRF and that the following assumption holds.

Definition 13. *Let $\mathbb{G}, \hat{\mathbb{G}}, \mathbb{G}_T$ be prime-order p groups, g be generator of $\mathbb{G}$ and $\hat{g}$ be a generator of $\hat{\mathbb{G}}$, tand $e : \mathbb{G} \times \hat{\mathbb{G}} \to \mathbb{G}_T$ be a bilinear pairing. We say the symmetric external Diffie-Hellman assumption holds with respect to these groups and pairing if for all efficient $\mathcal{A}$,*

$$|\Pr[\mathcal{A}(g, g^a, g^b, g^{ab}) = 1] \Pr[\mathcal{A}(g, g^a, g^b, T) = 1]|$$

and

$$|\Pr[\mathcal{A}(\hat{g}, \hat{g}^a, \hat{g}^b, \hat{g}^{ab}) = 1] \Pr[\mathcal{A}(\hat{g}, \hat{g}^a, \hat{g}^b, T) = 1]|$$

are negligible functions of λ, where a, b, c are uniform over $\mathbb{Z}_p$ and T is uniform over G_T.

We can now state and prove our security theorem.

Theorem 14. *Our PPH Γ is restricted-chosen-input secure, assuming F is a PRF and the SXDH assumption hold with respect to the appropriate groups and pairing.*

Proof. We use a hybrid argument. Let $(A_1, A_2, B_1, B_2) \in \mathbb{G}^2 \times \hat{\mathbb{G}}^2$ denote the challenge hash value given to the adversary during the real game $\mathsf{H}_0 = \mathsf{IND}_{\Gamma,P}^{\mathsf{pph}}(\mathcal{A})$. Additionally, let R be a random element of $\mathbb{G}$, $\hat{R}$ be a random element of $\hat{\mathbb{G}}$, both independent of the rest of the random variables under consideration. Then we define the following hybrid experiments:

- H_1: At the start of the game, a uniformly random function $F^* \xleftarrow{R} \mathsf{Funs}[\{0,1\}^\lambda, \{0,1\}^\lambda]$ is sampled instead of the PRF key K, the rest remain unchanged.
- H_2: The challenge hash value is (A_1, R, B_1, B_2), where $R \xleftarrow{\$} \hat{\mathbb{G}}$.
- H_3: The challenge hash value is $(A_1, R, B_1, \hat{R})$, where $R \xleftarrow{\$} \hat{\mathbb{G}}$.

In H_3, the adversary is given a random element from the range $\mathcal{R}$. Therefore,

$$\mathsf{Adv}_{\Gamma,P,\mathcal{A}}^{\mathsf{pph}}(\lambda) = |Pr[\mathsf{H}_0 = 1] - Pr[\mathsf{H}_3 = 1]|$$

To prove H_0 is indistinguishable from H_3, we show that each step of the hybrid is indistinguishable from the next. First, it is apparent that H_0 and H_1 are computational indistinguishable by the PRF security, then:

Lemma 15. $\mathsf{H}_1 \approx \mathsf{H}_2$ *under the SXDH assumption.*

Let $\mathcal{A}$ be an adversary playing the PPH security game, and let

$$\epsilon = |Pr[\mathsf{H}_1 = 1] - Pr[\mathsf{H}_2 = 1]|.$$

Then we can build adversary $\mathcal{B}$ that solves SXDH with advantage ϵ. $\mathcal{B}$ is given as input $(g, \hat{g}, B, C)$ and the challenge term T. $\mathcal{B}$ works as follows:

- $\mathcal{B}$ sets $\mathsf{tk} = (\mathbb{G}, \hat{\mathbb{G}}, \mathbb{G}_T, e)$ and sends it to $\mathcal{A}$. After receiving $x^* \xleftarrow{\$} \mathcal{A}(\mathsf{tk})$ it simulates a random function F^* via lazy sampling, and it will implicitly set $F^*(x^*) = b$, the discrete logarithm of B. It prepares the challenge as by selecting $r^* \xleftarrow{\$} \mathbb{Z}_p$ and computing

$$A_1 = g^c, A_2 = T, B_1 = \hat{g}^{r^*}, B_2 = \hat{g}^{r^* F^*(x^*+1)}$$

  and runs $\mathcal{A}$ on input $\mathsf{tk}, x^*, (A_1, A_2, B_1, B_2)$.
- To answer hash query for $x \neq x^*$ from $\mathcal{A}$, $\mathcal{B}$ calculates $F^*(x)$ and $F^*(x+1)$ (note that $x, x+1 \neq x^*$). Then $\mathcal{B}$ picks r_1, r_2 randomly and computes:

$$\mathcal{H}(x) = g^{r_1}, g^{r_1 \cdot F^*(x)}, \hat{g}^{r_2}, \hat{g}^{r_2 \cdot F^*(x+1)};$$

If $\mathcal{A}$ queries $x = x^*$, $\mathcal{B}$ calculates $F^*(x^*+1)$, picks $r_1', r_2' \xleftarrow{\$} \mathbb{Z}_p$, and computes

$$\mathcal{H}(x^*) = g^{r_1'}, B^{r_1'}, \hat{g}^{r_2'}, \hat{g}^{r_2' \cdot F^*(x^*+1)};$$

– Finally $\mathcal{B}$ outputs whatever $\mathcal{A}$ outputs.

We note that in $\mathcal{A}$'s view, without querying $\mathcal{A}(x^* - 1)$, $\mathcal{B}$ simulates the game properly. If $T = g^{bc}$, then $\mathcal{B}$ simulates H_1, and if T s random then it simulates H_2. Hence if $\mathcal{A}$ has an advantage ϵ in distinguishing H_1 and H_2, then $\mathcal{B}$ has the same advantage to break SXDH assumption.

We also have the following lemma:

Lemma 16. $\mathsf{H}_2 \approx \mathsf{H}_3$ *under the SXDH assumption.*

The proof is exactly the same as the prior hybrid step, except in the group $\hat{\mathbb{G}}$ part of the hash instead of $\mathbb{G}$. We omit the details.

Collecting the steps completes the proof of Theorem 14.

Acknowledgments. David Cash is supported by NSF CNS-1453132. Feng-Hao Liu is supported by NSF CNS-1657040. Adam O'Neill is supported in part by NSF CNS-1650419. Mark Zhandry is supported by NSF. David Cash and Cong Zhang are partially supported by DARPA and SSC Pacific under contract N66001-15-C-4070. Any opinions, findings, and conclusions or recommendations expressed in this material are those of the author(s) and do not necessarily reflect the views of NSF, DARPA or SSC Pacific.

References

1. Agrawal, R., Kiernan, J., Srikant, R., Xu, Y.: Order preserving encryption for numeric data. In: SIGMOD (2004)
2. Arasu, A., Blanas, S., Eguro, K., Kaushik, R., Kossmann, D., Ramamurthy, R., Venkatesan, R.: Orthogonal security with cipherbase. In: CIDR (2013)
3. Arasu, A., Eguro, K., Kaushik, R., Ramamurthy, R.: Querying encrypted data (tutorial). In: ICDE (2013)
4. Bajaj, S., Sion, R.: TrustedDB: a trusted hardware-based database with privacy and data confidentiality. TKDE **26**(3), 752–765 (2014)
5. Bellare, M., Boldyreva, A., O'Neill, A.: Deterministic and efficiently searchable encryption. In: Menezes, A. (ed.) CRYPTO 2007. LNCS, vol. 4622, pp. 535–552. Springer, Heidelberg (2007). https://doi.org/10.1007/978-3-540-74143-5_30
6. Boldyreva, A., Chenette, N., Lee, Y., O'Neill, A.: Order-preserving symmetric encryption. In: Joux, A. (ed.) EUROCRYPT 2009. LNCS, vol. 5479, pp. 224–241. Springer, Heidelberg (2009). https://doi.org/10.1007/978-3-642-01001-9_13
7. Boldyreva, A., Chenette, N., O'Neill, A.: Order-preserving encryption revisited: improved security analysis and alternative solutions. In: Rogaway, P. (ed.) CRYPTO 2011. LNCS, vol. 6841, pp. 578–595. Springer, Heidelberg (2011). https://doi.org/10.1007/978-3-642-22792-9_33
8. Boneh, D., Lewi, K., Raykova, M., Sahai, A., Zhandry, M., Zimmerman, J.: Semantically secure order-revealing encryption: multi-input functional encryption without obfuscation. In: Oswald, E., Fischlin, M. (eds.) EUROCRYPT 2015. LNCS, vol. 9057, pp. 563–594. Springer, Heidelberg (2015). https://doi.org/10.1007/978-3-662-46803-6_19
9. Canetti, R.: Towards realizing random oracles: hash functions that hide all partial information. In: Kaliski, B.S. (ed.) CRYPTO 1997. LNCS, vol. 1294, pp. 455–469. Springer, Heidelberg (1997). https://doi.org/10.1007/BFb0052255

10. Cash, D., Grubbs, P., Perry, J., Ristenpart, T.: Leakage-abuse attacks against searchable encryption. In: CCS (2015)
11. Cash, D., Jarecki, S., Jutla, C., Krawczyk, H., Roşu, M.-C., Steiner, M.: Highly-scalable searchable symmetric encryption with support for boolean queries. In: Canetti, R., Garay, J.A. (eds.) CRYPTO 2013. LNCS, vol. 8042, pp. 353–373. Springer, Heidelberg (2013). https://doi.org/10.1007/978-3-642-40041-4_20
12. Cash, D., Liu, F.-H., O'Neill, A., Zhandry, M., Zhang, C.: Parameter-hiding order revealing encryption. Cryptology ePrint Archive, Report 2018/698 (2018). https://eprint.iacr.org/2018/698
13. Chang, Y.-C., Mitzenmacher, M.: Privacy preserving keyword searches on remote encrypted data. In: Ioannidis, J., Keromytis, A., Yung, M. (eds.) ACNS 2005. LNCS, vol. 3531, pp. 442–455. Springer, Heidelberg (2005). https://doi.org/10.1007/11496137_30
14. Chase, M., Kamara, S.: Structured encryption and controlled disclosure. In: Abe, M. (ed.) ASIACRYPT 2010. LNCS, vol. 6477, pp. 577–594. Springer, Heidelberg (2010). https://doi.org/10.1007/978-3-642-17373-8_33
15. Chenette, N., Lewi, K., Weis, S.A., Wu, D.J.: Practical order-revealing encryption with limited leakage. In: Peyrin, T. (ed.) FSE 2016. LNCS, vol. 9783, pp. 474–493. Springer, Heidelberg (2016). https://doi.org/10.1007/978-3-662-52993-5_24
16. Cheon, J.H., Han, K., Lee, C., Ryu, H., Stehlé, D.: Cryptanalysis of the multilinear map over the integers. In: Oswald, E., Fischlin, M. (eds.) EUROCRYPT 2015. LNCS, vol. 9056, pp. 3–12. Springer, Heidelberg (2015). https://doi.org/10.1007/978-3-662-46800-5_1
17. Coron, J.-S., Lee, M.S., Lepoint, T., Tibouchi, M.: Cryptanalysis of GGH15 multilinear maps. In: Robshaw, M., Katz, J. (eds.) CRYPTO 2016. LNCS, vol. 9815, pp. 607–628. Springer, Heidelberg (2016). https://doi.org/10.1007/978-3-662-53008-5_21
18. Curtmola, R., Garay, J., Kamara, S., Ostrovsky, R.: Searchable symmetric encryption: improved definitions and efficient constructions. In: CCS (2006)
19. Dautrich Jr., J.L., Ravishankar, C.V.: Compromising privacy in precise query protocols. In: EDBT (2013)
20. Durak, F.B., DuBuisson, T.M., Cash, D.: What else is revealed by order-revealing encryption? In: ACM CCS (2016)
21. Goh, E.-J., et al.: Secure indexes. IACR Cryptology ePrint Archive 2003:216 (2003)
22. Grubbs, P., Sekniqi, K., Bindschaedler, V., Naveed, M., Ristenpart, T.: Leakage-abuse attacks against order-revealing encryption. Cryptology ePrint Archive, Report 2016/895 (2016). http://eprint.iacr.org/2016/895
23. Hacigümüş, H., Iyer, B., Li, C., Mehrotra, S.: Executing SQL over encrypted data in the database-service-provider model. In: Proceedings of the 2002 ACM SIGMOD International Conference on Management of Data, SIGMOD 2002, pp. 216–227. ACM, New York (2002)
24. Hore, B., Mehrotra, S., Canim, M., Kantarcioglu, M.: Secure multidimensional range queries over outsourced data. VLDBJ 21(3), 333–358 (2012)
25. Islam, M.S., Kuzu, M., Kantarcioglu, M.: Access pattern disclosure on searchable encryption: ramification, attack and mitigation. In: NDSS (2012)
26. Islam, M.S., Kuzu, M., Kantarcioglu, M.: Inference attack against encrypted range queries on outsourced databases. In: CODASPY (2014)
27. Joye, M., Passelègue, A.: Function-revealing encryption (2016)
28. Kamara, S., Moataz, T.: SQL on structurally-encrypted databases. Cryptology ePrint Archive, Report 2016/453 (2016). http://eprint.iacr.org/

29. Lewi, K., Wu, D.J.: Order-revealing encryption: new constructions, applications, and lower bounds. In: ACM CCS (2016)
30. Liu, C., Zhu, L., Wang, M., Tan, Y.-A.: Search pattern leakage in searchable encryption: attacks and new construction. Inf. Sci. **265**, 176–188 (2014)
31. Mandal, A., Roy, A.: Relational hash: probabilistic hash for verifying relations, secure against forgery and more. In: Gennaro, R., Robshaw, M. (eds.) CRYPTO 2015. LNCS, vol. 9215, pp. 518–537. Springer, Heidelberg (2015). https://doi.org/10.1007/978-3-662-47989-6_25
32. Miles, E., Sahai, A., Zhandry, M.: Annihilation attacks for multilinear maps: cryptanalysis of indistinguishability obfuscation over GGH13. In: Robshaw, M., Katz, J. (eds.) CRYPTO 2016. LNCS, vol. 9815, pp. 629–658. Springer, Heidelberg (2016). https://doi.org/10.1007/978-3-662-53008-5_22
33. Mohassel, P., Franklin, M.: Efficiency tradeoffs for malicious two-party computation. In: Yung, M., Dodis, Y., Kiayias, A., Malkin, T. (eds.) PKC 2006. LNCS, vol. 3958, pp. 458–473. Springer, Heidelberg (2006). https://doi.org/10.1007/11745853_30
34. Naveed, M., Kamara, S., Wright, C.V.: Inference attacks on property-preserving encrypted databases. In: CCS (2015)
35. Pandey, O., Rouselakis, Y.: Property preserving symmetric encryption. In: Pointcheval, D., Johansson, T. (eds.) EUROCRYPT 2012. LNCS, vol. 7237, pp. 375–391. Springer, Heidelberg (2012). https://doi.org/10.1007/978-3-642-29011-4_23
36. Popa, R.A., Redfield, C.M.S., Zeldovich, N., Balakrishnan, H.: CryptDB: protecting confidentiality with encrypted query processing. In: SOSP (2011)
37. Song, D.X., Wagner, D., Perrig, A.: Practical techniques for searches on encrypted data. In: SP (2000)

Symmetric-Key Constructions

Revisiting Key-Alternating Feistel Ciphers for Shorter Keys and Multi-user Security

Chun Guo[1] and Lei Wang[2,3]([✉])

[1] ICTEAM/ELEN/Crypto Group, Université Catholique de Louvain,
Louvain-la-Neuve, Belgium
chun.guo.sc@gmail.com
[2] Shanghai Jiao Tong University, Shanghai, China
wanglei_hb@sjtu.edu.cn
[3] Westone Cryptologic Research Center, Beijing, China

Abstract. Key-Alternating Feistel (KAF) ciphers, a.k.a. Feistel-2 models, refer to Feistel networks with round functions of the form $F_i(k_i \oplus x_i)$, where k_i is the (secret) round-key and F_i is a *public* random function. This model roughly captures the structures of many famous Feistel ciphers, and the most prominent instance is DES.

Existing provable security results on KAF assumed independent round-keys and round functions (ASIACRYPT 2004 & FSE 2014). In this paper, we investigate how to achieve security under simpler and more realistic assumptions: with round-keys derived from a short main-key, and hopefully with identical round functions.

For birthday-type security, we consider 4-round KAF, investigate the minimal conditions on the way to derive the four round-keys, and prove that when such adequately derived keys and the same round function are used, the 4-round KAF is secure up to $2^{n/2}$ queries.

For beyond-birthday security, we focus on 6-round KAF. We prove that when the adjacent round-keys are independent, and independent round-functions are used, the 6 round KAF is secure up to $2^{2n/3}$ queries. To our knowledge, this is the first beyond-birthday security result for KAF without assuming completely independent round-keys.

Our results hold in the multi-user setting as well, constituting the first non-trivial multi-user provable security results on Feistel ciphers. We finally demonstrate applications of our results on designing key-schedules and instantiating keyed sponge constructions.

Keywords: Blockcipher · Provable security · Multi-user security
Key-alternating cipher · Feistel cipher · Key-schedule design
Keyed sponge

The full version is available [28].

© International Association for Cryptologic Research 2018
T. Peyrin and S. Galbraith (Eds.): ASIACRYPT 2018, LNCS 11272, pp. 213–243, 2018.
https://doi.org/10.1007/978-3-030-03326-2_8

1   Introduction

Overview. We extend provable security of models of practical Feistel ciphers along multi-axes. First, we (significantly) reduce the key-sizes needed for super pseudorandom security. Second, we provide the first non-trivial multi-user provable results. We also exhibit applications of our results: on designing key-schedules for practical Feistel ciphers, and on instantiating keyed sponges.

Background. Practical iterative blockcipher (BC) designs roughly fall into two classes (with some rare exceptions such as IDEA), namely *Feistel ciphers and their generalizations*, and *substitution-permutation networks* (SPNs). In a Feistel cipher, in the i-th round, the intermediate state $x = x_L \| x_R$ is updated according to $x_L \| x_R \mapsto x_R \| x_L \oplus G_i(k_i, x_R)$, where G_i is called the i-th round function. On the other hand, their counterpart SPNs could be further abstracted as the *iterated Even-Mansour* (IEM) *ciphers*, or *key-alternating ciphers*, which consist of alternatively applying round-key additions and keyless round permutations, i.e. $\mathsf{IEM}_{k_0,k_1,\dots,k_t}^{P_1,\dots,P_t}(M) = k_t \oplus P_t(\dots(k_1 \oplus P_1(k_0 \oplus M)))$.

The traditional security notion for BCs is *pseudorandomness*: for any adversary with reasonable resources (e.g. polynomial complexity), the BC with *a random and secret key* should be indistinguishable from a truly random permutation. Proving such security for concrete BCs such as AES seems out of the reach of current techniques. Yet, by idealizing the underlying round functions, security could be proved. Following this line, both idealized Feistel [36,38] and IEM [11,22] have been proposed and analyzed.

To obtain a $2n$-bit BC, the IEM model requires $2n$-bit permutations. Whereas following the Feistel approach, several n-to-n-bit functions suffice. Moreover, these functions need *not* to be *invertible* (this might be the reason why Feistel ciphers were extremely popular before 1990s). In all, Feistel ciphers could be built upon primitives with smaller domain and less structural properties, which is particularly appealing from a theoretical point of view. From the security point of view, without any additional hardness assumption other than the idealness of round functions, provable security is limited by the domain-size of the round functions [49]. Therefore, IEM benefits from the use of larger primitives: with t independent $2n$-bit random permutations and $2tn$ key bits, t-round IEM is provably secure up to $2^{\frac{2tn}{t+1}}$ adversarial queries [15] which approaches 2^{2n} for large t. In contrast, Feistel models can only be secure against at most 2^n queries [49], which is far less than its domain-size 2^{2n}. This upper bound is very unsatisfying. Despite this limitation as well as the gap between the idealized model and the rather weak round functions in practice, this provable approach supplies insights into the BC structures, excludes generic attacks, and may help refine designs. Due to these, this approach is valuable and has received a lot of attention.

The Luby-Rackoff (LR) Scheme, in reference to the seminal work of Luby and Rackoff [38], might be the most popular model for Feistel ciphers so far. In this model, the round functions $G_i(k_i, x_R)$ are *pseudorandom functions* (PRFs). Via a standard hybrid argument, this is transposed to the Feistel networks formed by uniformly random and *Secret* round functions $SG_i(x_R)$. Following [38], a long series of work established either better security (maybe using a larger number of rounds)—with [3,31,40,44,49] to name a few,—or reduced complexity for security [45–47,52].

Key-Alternating Feistel Ciphers. Works along the line of Luby and Rackoff are very generic and could cover all possible forms of round functions. On the opposite side, the LR model falls short of showing how to concretely design *keyed* primitives (BCs) from (conceptually) simpler *keyless* primitives—it just "defers" the task to designing *keyed* round functions $G_i(k_i, x_R)$, which is, however, not known to be simpler than designing the BCs themselves.

In reality, general purpose Feistel ciphers usually employ length-preserving keyless round functions, and xor each round-key before applying the corresponding round function. Examples include DES, GOST, Camellia variant without FL/FL^{-1} functions [9], MIBS [34], and two recent designs LBlock [57] and Twine [55] (they are multi-line generalizations of Feistel). This idea corresponds to Feistel networks with round functions instantiated in the probably simplest form of $G_i(k_i, x_i) = F_i(k_i \oplus x_i)$, where F_i is *keyless and public*; and at the i-th round, the intermediate state is updated according to

$$x_L \| x_R \to x_R \| x_L \oplus F_i(k_i \oplus x_R).$$

This model was named *Key-Alternating Feistel* (KAF) by Lampe and Seurin [36], and is also known as *Feistel-2* schemes according to IACR Tikz library. It has been extensively studied by the cryptanalytic community [9,29,33], and frequently became the instructive example for new attacks [2,10].

The gap between LR and KAF ciphers is non-negligible. For example, with less than 2^{2n} complexity, the best known generic key recovery attacks break 4-round LR [33] which is in sharp contrast with 6-round KAF [29]. Moreover, 6- or even 5-round LR model is already sufficient for optimal information theoretic security against 2^n queries [44, Chap. 17]. However, for KAF we exhibit a generic *distinguishing attack* against t rounds using $O(\frac{(t-2)n}{t-1})$ queries, which means $O(n)$ number of rounds are necessary for optimal security. These indicate the LR model misses some important structural properties in practical Feistel ciphers, and KAF is likely to be a better model for the reality.

By the above, theoretical analysis of the KAF model is of significance. In this respect, one would assume the (keyless) round functions F_i as *public* random functions that can be queried by the adversary in a black-box way, and try to establish indistinguishability for the worlds $(\text{KAF}_k, F_1, \ldots, F_t)$ and $(P, F_1, \ldots, F_t)$ in the random oracle model, i.e. the cipher KAF with a secret random key k is indistinguishable from a random permutation P even if given the access of the t random round functions $F_1, \ldots, F_t$. This is very similar to the setting introduced for IEM [11]. In this vein, we are only aware of two works. First, an early work of Gentry and Ramzan (GR) [24] proved a birthday-type security for a 4-round keyless Feistel scheme with pre- and post-whitening keys, which can be translated into a 4-round KAF variant. Then, a recent work of Lampe and Seurin (LS) [36] proved beyond-birthday security up to $2^{\frac{tn}{t+1}}$

adversarial queries for $6t$-round KAF, assuming the round functions and round-keys are *both completely independent* [36].[1]

Our Problem. The secret-key analyzes of KAF of GR [24] and LS [36] mentioned before leave two remarkable gaps. The first gap lies between the models and ciphers in practice. In detail, both LS and GR assumed completely Independent Round-Keys (INDRK). In contrast, BCs in practice utilize identical round functions as well as round-keys derived from a short main-key (thus highly correlated rather than completely independent). Security arguments with correlated round-keys are desired to bridge this gap.

On the theoretical side, arguments with correlated round-keys reduce the amount of key required by secure cryptosystems, and sometimes lead to minimal designs [14,21]. Therefore, such arguments are of great importance from both practical and theoretical points of view, and while the INDRK assumption is common in seminal theoretical results, e.g. LR [38], IEM [11], and models for SPNs [41], subsequent works usually tried to remove it. For example, Patarin et al. analyzed the possibility of designing secure LR variants using a single random function (which is equivalent to pseudorandom function with a single round-key) [45–48,52]; Chen et al. analyzed 2-round IEM with **correlated** round-keys and even *identical* permutations [14]; and Dodis et al. proved results for SPN models with correlated round-keys [20].

Regarding the round complexity for beyond-birthday security, there is one more gap. While optimal security up to 2^n queries *cannot* be achieved by a small constant number of rounds of KAF (as discussed before), the optimal security of 6-round LR motivates ones to expect that the **6**-round KAF is at least beyond-birthday secure. However, LS only proved (beyond-birthday) security against $2n/3$ queries for **12**-round KAF, which is twice as the expected rounds.

Contribution I: Security with Correlated Round-Keys. We narrow the above gaps, and make the first step towards minimizing sufficient conditions for the provable security of KAF models. The results consist of two parts depending on the security goal.

BIRTHDAY-TYPE SECURITY: MINIMAL SOLUTION WITH 4 ROUNDS. In this regime, we consider the KAF ciphers with all the **round functions identical**, as depicted in Fig. 1 (left), and denote it KAFSF to make a clear distinction. For such variants, if the round-keys are also identical, then for $S\|T = \mathsf{KAFSF}(L\|R)$ it always holds $\mathsf{KAFSF}^{-1}(T\|S) = R\|L$, which means it can be distinguished by 2 queries (more severely, this allows ruining the secrecy of the plaintext in the CPA setting). Consequently, there have to be some non-trivial correlations between the round-keys. To unveil this, we investigate the minimal conditions on the round-keys that suffice for security. We prove that for the four n-bit round keys (k_1, k_2, k_3, k_4), as long as k_1, k_4, and $k_1 \oplus k_4$ are all uniform (a quite mild requirement), the 4-round KAFSF is secure up to $2^{n/2}$ queries. The bound is tight, since any 4-round Feistel can be distinguished by $2^{n/2}$ queries [45].

---

[1] A more recent work of Gilboa et al. [25] analyzed a variant of 2-round IEM, which corresponds to a KAF variant *with whitening keys*. We'll elaborate later.

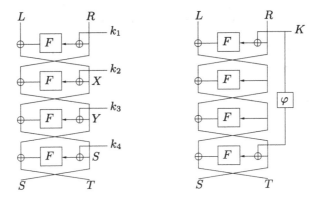

Fig. 1. (Left) The general 4-round KAFSF cipher in question. F is a *public* random function. (Right) the "minimal" KAFSF scheme with birthday-type provable security. φ is a fixed orthomorphism of $\mathbb{F}_2^n$.

This general result on the round-keys allows us to derive them from a short main-key in various ways. For the best efficiency, one could drop k_2 and k_3, and set $k_1 \leftarrow K$ and $k_4 \leftarrow \varphi(K)$, where φ is an orthomorphism of $\mathbb{F}_2^n$, cf. Fig. 1 (right).[2] This yields a super pseudorandom KAF cipher from a single random function and an n-bit main-key. This construction is theoretically "minimal" in the sense that removing *any* of the components ruins security: removing φ brings the severe weakness $\mathsf{KAFSF}(L\|R) = S\|T \Leftrightarrow \mathsf{KAFSF}^{-1}(T\|S) = R\|L$ back, while removing any call to F brings us back to a 3-round Feistel network, which is not super pseudorandom. While it appears crazy to completely drop k_2 and k_3, this actually matches an early theoretical result of Ramzan and Reyzin [50], which will be discussed later. However, we stress our "minimal" scheme is of mainly theoretical interest. Most importantly, we are **not** advocating following **it** to design general purpose Feistel ciphers.

Birthday-type security is now usually deemed as quite weak. For example, general purpose Feistel BCs usually take $2n = 128$, for which a birthday-bound merely ensures 32-bit security. Though, we believe it's of significance to deepen the understanding of birthday-type security, shape existing results, and derive theoretically minimal constructions.

BEYOND-BIRTHDAY SECURITY: IMPROVED RESULTS WITH 6 ROUNDS. For KAF built upon **independent** round functions, see Fig. 2 (left), we prove security up to $2^{2n/3}$ adversarial queries as long as the six round-keys $(k_1, k_2, k_3, k_4, k_5, k_6)$ are uniform and *adjacent round-keys are independent*. It seems such a sequence of round-keys can be easily derived from a $2n$-bit main-key $K\|K'$ via the "word-aligned", feedback-shift-register-based key-schedules that are widely adopted.

---

[2] A permutation φ of $\mathbb{F}_2^n$ is an orthomorphism if $K \mapsto K \oplus \varphi(K)$ is also a permutation. The Feistel-like linear transformation $\varphi(K_L\|K_R) = K_L \oplus K_R\|K_L$ is a very efficient instance. Orthomorphisms have found many cryptographic applications, particularly in minimizing LR [52] and IEM models [14].

As far as we know, this is the first beyond-birthday result on KAF without INDRK assumption.

More generally, when k_1, k_3, and k_5 are uniform in 2^n values, while k_2, k_4, and k_6 are uniform in only 2^{n-r} values, security is up to $2^{(2n-r)/3}$ queries. While such round-keys appear quite artificial, it's valuable for two reasons: first, it appears the first step towards modeling key-schedules of the form $\{0,1\}^{cn} \rightarrow \{0,1\}^{tn}$ for non-integers c; second, it cinches interesting implications on "partial-key" Even-Mansour and keyed sponges, which will be discussed latter.

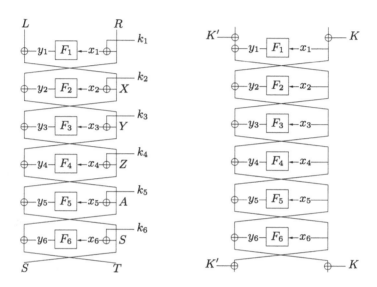

Fig. 2. (Left) The 6-round KAF ciphers with notations used in this paper. $F_1, \ldots, F_6$ are six independent public random functions. (Right) The single-key Even-Mansour cipher based on a 6-round keyless Feistel permutation LR_6.

Application: A Concret Proposal for KAF Key-Schedules. Although our results turn heuristic once instantiated [13], we believe they shed some light on how to design key-schedules for practical Feistel ciphers, which appear quite non-trivial. In particular, key-schedules of KAF ciphers need not to be overly strong nor "one-way", and actually key-schedules with some simple combinatorial properties could be a good starting point (a similar conclusion has been made for the IEM ciphers [14]).

To further illustrate, based on our results and some additional intuitions, we propose to consider key-schedules that produce *pair-wise independent round-keys*[3] in KAF ciphers. We further demonstrate examples of such key-schedules.

---

[3] This should be distinguished from complete independence. For example, given the main-key $K\|K'$, the round-keys $K, K', K \oplus K'$ are pair-wise independent, but they aren't completely independent. In fact, appealing to pair-wise independence instead of complete independence is an approach to derandomization [37].

However, we stress that these proposals only serve as *starting points for further research*, and should *not* be used without deeper investigations.

Multi-User (MU) Setting. The discussed super pseudorandomness model is now termed as *single-user* (SU) setting. It has been noticed that in practice, cryptosystems are typically deployed en masse and attackers are often satisfied with compromising some users among many, which can be substantially easier [8]. In fact, massively parallel attacks on many keys at once have been considered as the most promising way to break AES-128 [6]. These motivated the *multi-user* (MU) security notion [5] and a lot of follow up works—please see [12] and the references therein. For BCs, this could even affect higher-level systems: frequently rekeying is sometimes used in BC-based modes in order to achieve better security bounds [26] or leakage resilience [54], and the security of such modes inherently relies on the MU security of the underlying BCs.

According to Mouha and Luykx [42], the MU security of BCs was formalized as $m > 1$ instances of BCs with m independent user-keys being indistinguishable from m *independent random permutations*. This could be related to the SU security: with m independent keys, a generic reduction shows the MU security is $\log m$ bits less than the SU security (Jager et al. showed that this is unavoidable for generic reductions [35]). This is quantitatively weaker. Yet, interestingly, dedicated analyzes could usually establish MU bounds that are quantitatively the *same* as SU bounds [32,42,56].

Contribution II: MU Security of KAF. As mentioned, the MU security may be quantitatively weaker than the MU security. Yet, our positive results are proved via establishing the so-called *point-wise proximity* of Hoang and Tessaro [32], and our bounds satisfy their "super-additiveness" requirement. Therefore, by their general transition, these establish MU security against $2^{n/2}$ queries at 4 rounds and against $2^{(2n-r)/3}$ queries at 6 rounds. To our knowledge, these constitute the first non-trivial MU provable results on Feistel ciphers.

We remark that it's not as trivial as it appears to ensure "super-additiveness" during the analysis. For example, this requires to get rid of terms of the form $f(q_f)$ or $f(q_f) \cdot \sqrt{q_e}$. In particular, our proof follows a "two-step" approach used by Cogliati et al. for analyzing tweakable Even-Mansour [16,17], yet neither of the bounds given in these works fulfills this requirement. To resolve this, we eschew many concrete approaches used in [16,17] (in particular, the use of Markov inequality), and extensively use the expectation method from [32] instead, to derive more "smooth" bounds.

As a final remark, Hoang and Tessaro proved that the SU and MU security bounds of IEM with INDRK are quantitatively the same [32]. While our results appear to indicate the same conclusion, we don't expect this to be true for KAF in general. A deeper investigation is left for future.

Implications. As multi-user secure BCs, our provable KAF constructions could be plugged into many BC-based (secret-key) modes to reduce the size of (ideal) primitives in use, or to drop the requirement on the invertibility of the underlying ideal primitives. The latter is particularly attractive in the multi-party computation setting, in which invertibility could be quite expensive [51]. In addition, depending on the concrete parameters, in some cases, e.g. truncated CBC [23], this even does not result in a security loss.

Less obviously, our general results on 6-round KAF imply that it's secure to alternatively use an n-bit key K and another $(n - r)$-bit key K' at each round. With such an alternating key-schedule, the 6-round KAF collapses to a 1-round IEM with key $0^r \| K' \| K$ and the permutation instantiated by a 6-round keyless Feistel permutation LR_6, as in Fig. 2 (right). Therefore, this shows *instantiating the permutation π in the 1-round "Partial-Key" Even-Mansour*

$$\mathsf{PKEM}^\pi_{0^r\|K'\|K}(M) = (0^r \| K' \| K) \oplus \pi((0^r \| K' \| K) \oplus M) \qquad (1)$$

by a 6-round keyless Feistel permutation LR_6 preserves security, and for $r > n/2$ the security is beyond-birthday with respect to the domain-size of the underlying ideal primitives. This extends the birthday-type result of GR [24] (two more Feistel rounds for beyond-birthday security).

This results in even more interesting implications. Sponge functions are versatile cryptographic primitives [7]. Keyed sponges can be used for encryption and message authentication. Many variants of lightweight keyed sponges can be rewritten as a construction built upon the aforementioned $\mathsf{PKEM}^\pi_{0^r\|K'\|K}$ cipher, and the sponge is secure as long as $\mathsf{PKEM}^\pi_{0^r\|K'\|K}$ is secure (maybe in the MU setting) [1,23,43]. Thus by the above implication, such keyed sponges could rely on $\mathsf{PKEM}^{\mathsf{LR}_6}_{0^r\|K'\|K}$ instead of $\mathsf{PKEM}^\pi_{0^r\|K'\|K}$. With the keys canceled, we obtain a sponge built upon LR_6. Therefore, our results indicate: *the random permutation underlying many keyed sponge variants could be securely instantiated with a 6-round keyless Feistel permutation LR_6.* For concrete security results please see Sect. 7.

We stress that these results *cannot* be derived from existing provable results on IEM/keyed sponges and keyless Feistel via general transitions. The most relevant results are the correlation intractability [39] and CP-indifferentiability [53] positive results on LR_6. But they are quantitatively weak: $q^4/2^n$ for correlation intractability of LR_6 [39], and $q^6/2^n$ for CP-indifferentiability of LR_5 [53].

Table 1. Comparison to existing provable results on KAF. We stress that our results include more general ones that allow deriving the round-keys in flexible ways. And rows 4 and 5 are the *theoretically best possible* ones derived from the general ones.

Key size	Rounds	Num. of rand. func	SU bound	MU bound	Reference
$4n$	4	2	$n/2$	Missed	GR [24]
$12n$	12	12	$2n/3$	Missed	LS [36]
$6tn$	$6t$	$6t$	$tn/(t+1)$	Missed	LS [36]
n	4	1	$n/2$	$n/2$	Sect. 4
$2n$	6	6	$2n/3$	$2n/3$	Sect. 5

Discussion, and Comparison to Related Works. It would be tempting to ask how we are able to halve the round complexity for $2n/3$ security (compared with LS [36]). Briefly, LS divided a KAF cipher into two halves, proved NCPA (non-adaptive chosen-plaintext attack) security for each half, and then applied a composition to obtain CCA security. And (informally) their *coupling* argument could only reduce certain collision probability every 3 rounds. Consequently, they only obtained $2n/3$ NCPA security at 6 rounds and $2n/3$ CCA security at 12 rounds. In comparison, we follow a "two-step" approach [16,17] for analyzing the *transcripts* of queries and answers of the distinguisher, transform the transcripts into input-output pairs of the inner four rounds, and then employ a more fine-grained and dedicated analysis. This allows us to remove much redundancy from the structures and successfully halve the rounds. Due to the randomness of the 1st and 6th round functions, every resulted input-output pair of the inner four rounds would only be involved in a single collision (one could see Fig. 4 for illustration), and this significantly simplifies the analysis. Still, the analysis for 4 rounds remains complicated, and the complexity is further increased by the aim of "super-additiveness" (as mentioned). We remark that such an analysis for 4-round KAF seems missing in the literature—Patarin's mirror theory-based analysis for 4-round LR [44, Chap. 17] does not seem to be transposable to KAF.

On the other hand, our 6-round construction(s) could probably be further simplified while retaining $2n/3$-bit security. However, we figured out some difficulties, see the full version. Since verifiability of the proof is equally important, we favored the current construction and its relatively simpler proof. Despite this, our 6-round construction with $2n$-bit main-keys has significantly improved upon existing results. In Table 1, we make comparison with the results of LS [36] and GR [24]. We remark that GR's main motivation was to deepen the understanding of the Even-Mansour cipher [22], rather than to study KAF ciphers.

Also, we list the relevant results on the popular LR and IEM models in Table 2 for comparison. We remark that LR results are in the *standard model*, and are better than the *ideal model* results on IEM and KAF in some theoretical sense. Yet, as emphasized before, KAF is closer to reality.

The results in Table 2 in particular include the aforementioned work of Gilboa et al., which proved $n/2$ security for a 2-round IEM variant with identical round-permutations and identical round-keys [25]. Moreover, the round-permutation is instantiated with a 2-round LR construction built upon *a public random permutation*. This construction is somewhat related to KAF: but it can only be transformed into a KAF variant with whitening keys rather than the "bare" KAF model studied in this paper (thus we denote KAFSP*). Consequently, our result on 4-round KAFSF—as well as the usefulness of orthomorphisms in this setting—could not be derived from [25].

In addition, Ramzan and Reyzin proved birthday-type security for a variant of 4-round LR, in which the middle two round functions are *public* rather than secret [50]. As mentioned before, an interesting fact is that our 4-round minimal construction also captures the idea of leaving the middle two round functions "unprotected" (as the middle two round-keys are absent). In this sense, our

Table 2. Comparison to LR and IEM *super pseudorandom* provable results. For the LR results, κ is the key-size of the underlying PRFs. For the first row: the proof used the mirror theory [44, Chap. 14], and was only sketched in [44, Chap. 17.5]. For row 2: it's the best result to our knowledge. For row 4 & 5, the MU bounds of EMIP and EMSP models were not given, yet are trivial: (a) with $2n$ key bits, it $\leq n$-bit [8], while (b) it $\geq n$-bit, which is the MU security of the 1-round single-key IEM [32].

Model	Block size	Prim. size	Key size	Rounds	Number of prim	SU bound	MU bound	Reference
LR	$2n$	n	5κ	5	5	$\approx n$	Missed	[44]
LR	$2n$	n	κ	4	1	$n/2$	Missed	Nandi [45]
IEM	$2n$	$2n$	$2tn$	t	t	$2tn/(t+1)$	$2tn/(t+1)$	CS and HT [15,32]
EMIP	$2n$	$2n$	$2n$	2	2	$4n/3$	n	Chen et al. [14]
EMSP	$2n$	$2n$	$2n$	1	2	$4n/3$	n	Chen et al. [14]
KAFSP*	$2n$	n	$2n$	4	1	$n/2$	Missed	Gilboa et al. [25]
KAF	$2n$	n	$6tn$	$6t$	$6t$	$tn/(t+1)$	Missed	LS [36]
KAFSF	$2n$	n	n	4	1	$n/2$	$n/2$	Sect. 4
KAF	$2n$	n	$2n$	6	6	$2n/3$	$2n/3$	Sect. 5

minimal construction also deepen the understanding of the secrecy of round functions in Feistel ciphers.

Last, a series of papers analyzed idealized BCs in the indifferentiability framework, which is a different security model. Please see [19] and the references therein. Among them is a positive result [27] on a variant of KAF abstracted from NSA's cipher SIMON [4]. These works shed lights on designing key-schedules from a different point of view, and are thus complementary to ours.

Organization. Section 2 supplies notations and definitions. Section 3 describes the generic distinguishing attack against any number of rounds. Then, Sects. 4 and 5 respectively present our results on 4-round KAFSF and 6-round KAF and their security proofs. After these, based on our results, Sect. 6 presents our key-schedule proposal, while Sect. 7 makes discussion on the implications.

2   Preliminaries

Notation and General Definitions. In all the following, we fix an integer $n \geq 1$ and denote $N = 2^n$. Further denote $\mathcal{F}(n)$ the set of all functions of domain $\{0,1\}^n$ and range $\{0,1\}^n$, and $\mathcal{P}(2n)$ the set of all permutations on $\{0,1\}^{2n}$. For a random variable $\epsilon(s)$ that relies on another random variable s, we denote by $\mathbb{E}_{s\in\mathcal{S}}[\epsilon(s)]$ the expectation of $\epsilon(s)$ taken over all $s \in \mathcal{S}$, and $\mathbb{E}_s[\epsilon(s)]$ for short when the set $\mathcal{S}$ is clear from the context. For $X, Y \in \{0,1\}^n$, $X\|Y$ or simply XY denotes their concatenation.

Assume that the i-th round function of KAF is $F_i : \{0,1\}^n \rightarrow \{0,1\}^n$, and the corresponding n-bit round-key is k_i, then the i-th round transformation of KAF is the permutation on $\{0,1\}^{2n}$ defined as

$$\Psi_{k_i}^{F_i}(W_{i-1}\|W_i) = W_i\|W_{i+1} = W_i\|W_{i-1} \oplus F_i(K_i \oplus W_i),$$

where W_{i-1} and W_i are the left and right n-bit halves of the inputs of the i-th round respectively. And the t-round KAF is specified by t public round functions $F = (F_1, \ldots, F_t)$ and a round-key vector $k = (k_1, \ldots, k_t)$:

$$\mathsf{KAF}_k^F(W_0\|W_1) = \Psi_{k_t}^{F_t} \circ \ldots \circ \Psi_{k_1}^{F_1}(W_0\|W_1).$$

These functions may be completely independent, or correlated, or even identical. To highlight, we denote by KAFSF the variant with identical round function, i.e.

$$\mathsf{KAFSF}_k^F(M) = \Psi_{k_t}^{F} \circ \ldots \circ \Psi_{k_1}^{F}(M).$$

Note that the key spaces of these schemes are not fixed, and depend on the concrete contexts.

As noted in [18], a KAF cipher with an even number of rounds can be seen as a special case of an *IEM cipher*. In detail, two rounds of a KAF cipher can be rewritten as:

$$\Psi_{k_{i+1}}^{F_{i+1}} \circ \Psi_{k_i}^{F_i}(W_{i-1}\|W_i) = (k_{i+1}\|k_i) \oplus \Psi_0^{F_{i+1}} \circ \Psi_0^{F_i}((k_{i+1}\|k_i) \oplus (W_{i-1}\|W_i)),$$

where $\Psi_0^{F_{i+1}} \circ \Psi_0^{F_i}$ is a two-round keyless Feistel permutation. As a consequence, *in general*, KAF ciphers should *avoid* using identical round-key, as otherwise the round-keys would cancel each other and the cipher would collapse to a single round IEM cipher using a keyless Feistel as the permutation and $k\|k$ as the pre- and post-whitening key.[4]

For convenience—in particular, to simplify subscripts,—we follow a classical notation system (which has been used for Luby-Rackoff schemes [49]):

- for 4-round KAF(SF), we take L, R, X, Y, S, T as $W_0, W_1, W_2, W_3, W_4, W_5$ correspondingly, as depicted in Fig. 1 (left);
- for 6-round KAF(SF), we take L, R, X, Y, Z, A, S, T as $W_0, W_1, \ldots, W_6, W_7$ correspondingly, as in Fig. 2 (left).

Multi-User (MU) Security of Blockciphers. We concentrate on the MU security with m users. The SU security definition corresponds to the special case of $m = 1$. Concretely, consider a t-round KAF built from t n-to-n-bit function oracles $\mathbf{F} = (\mathbf{F}_1, \ldots, \mathbf{F}_t)$. Only the round-key vectors k with certain context-dependent properties (will be identified) can ensure security. We denote by $\mathcal{K}$ the set of all k with such desired properties. To study the indistinguishability, we consider a distinguisher D interacting with $\mathbf{F}$. In the MU setting, D has access to additional m $2n$-bit permutation oracles, which are either m instances $\mathsf{KAF}_{k^{(1)}}^{\mathbf{F}}, \ldots, \mathsf{KAF}_{k^{(m)}}^{\mathbf{F}}$ with m independent keys uniformly picked from $\mathcal{K}$, or m independent random permutations $\mathbf{P}^{(1)}, \ldots, \mathbf{P}^{(m)}$. The goal of D is to tell apart the two worlds $(\mathsf{KAF}_{k^{(1)}}^{\mathbf{F}}, \ldots, \mathsf{KAF}_{k^{(m)}}^{\mathbf{F}}, \mathbf{F})$ (termed the *real world*) and $(\mathbf{P}^{(1)}, \ldots, \mathbf{P}^{(m)}, \mathbf{F})$ (the *ideal world*) by adaptively making forward and backward

---

[4] In page 8, we indeed take the implication on PKEM as an interesting one. But that implication concentrates on *specific theoretical models*, and does not intend to say anything about *general purpose* Feistel ciphers.

queries to each of the permutations and the functions. Formally, D's distinguishing advantage is defined as

$$\mathbf{Adv}_{\mathsf{KAF}}^{\mathrm{MU}}(D) = \Pr[(\mathbf{P}^{(1)}, \ldots, \mathbf{P}^{(m)}) \xleftarrow{\$} (\mathcal{P}(2n))^m, \mathbf{F} \xleftarrow{\$} (\mathcal{F}(n))^t : D^{\mathbf{P}_1, \ldots, \mathbf{P}_m, \mathbf{F}} = 1]$$
$$- \Pr[(k^{(1)}, \ldots, k^{(m)}) \xleftarrow{\$} (\mathcal{K})^m, \mathbf{F} \xleftarrow{\$} (\mathcal{F}(n))^t : D^{\mathsf{KAF}_{k^{(1)}}^{\mathbf{F}}, \ldots, \mathsf{KAF}_{k^{(m)}}^{\mathbf{F}}, \mathbf{F}} = 1].$$

Furthermore, we consider computationally unbounded distinguishers, and we assume without loss of generality that the distinguisher is deterministic and never makes redundant queries. For non-negative integers q_f and q_e, we define the insecurity of the idealized KAF cipher as:

$$\mathbf{Adv}_{\mathsf{KAF}}^{\mathrm{MU}}(q_f, q_e) = \max_D \mathbf{Adv}_{\mathsf{KAF}}^{\mathrm{MU}}(D),$$

where the maximum is taken over all distinguishers D making exactly q_f queries to each function oracle and in total q_e queries to the permutation oracles (termed as (q_f, q_e)-distinguishers).

If a collision occurs among the m user keys, e.g. $k^{(i)} = k^{(j)}$, then D can easily distinguish: in the real world, $\mathsf{KAF}_{k^{(i)}}^{\mathbf{F}}$ and $\mathsf{KAF}_{k^{(j)}}^{\mathbf{F}}$ are the same, while in the ideal world the corresponding oracles $\mathbf{P}^{(i)}$ and $\mathbf{P}^{(j)}$ are independent. For (q_f, q_e)-distinguishers, the number of involved users m cannot exceed q_e. Thus such a collision happens with probability at most $\frac{q_e^2}{2|\mathcal{K}|}$. For simplicity, throughout the remaining, we only consider the MU setting in which all the involved user keys are *distinct*; and the bounds in the "normal" MU setting can be derived as our bounds plus the term $\frac{q_e^2}{2|\mathcal{K}|}$ (this approach resembles [32]).

As mentioned, setting $m \leftarrow 1$, we obtain $\mathbf{Adv}_{\mathsf{KAF}}^{\mathrm{SU}}$, which measures the advantage of D on distinguishing one KAF instance from a random permutation.

H-Coefficients. We utilize the H-coefficient technique [15,47], and follow the paradigm of Hoang and Tessaro (HT) [32]. For this, we summarize the interaction of D with its oracles in the *queries transcripts*. Suppose D making q_i queries to the i-th permutation oracle ($\mathbf{P}^{(i)}$ or $\mathsf{KAF}_{k^{(i)}}^{\mathbf{F}}$), which are recorded as a set

$$\mathcal{Q}_{E_i} = \{(L_1 R_1, S_1 T_1), \ldots, (L_{q_i} R_{q_i}, S_{q_i} T_{q_i})\},$$

where for $j = 1, \ldots, q_i$ the tuples $(L_j R_j, S_j T_j) \in \{0,1\}^{2n} \times \{0,1\}^{2n}$ indicate the queries and answers. On the other hand, for $i = 1, \ldots, t$, the queries made to F_i are recorded as

$$\mathcal{Q}_{F_i} = \{(x_{i,1}, y_{i,1}), \ldots, (x_{i,q_f}, y_{i,q_f})\},$$

in which for each $j \in [1, \ldots, q_f]$, it indicates F_i was queried on $x_{i,j}$ and answered with $y_{i,j}$. Let $\mathcal{Q}_E = (\mathcal{Q}_{E_1}, \ldots, \mathcal{Q}_{E_m})$ and $\mathcal{Q}_F = (\mathcal{Q}_{F_1}, \ldots, \mathcal{Q}_{F_t})$. Then the pair $\tau = (\mathcal{Q}_E, \mathcal{Q}_F)$ will be called the *transcript* of the distinguisher in the MU setting: it contains all the information obtained by D during the interaction. In the SU setting, we have to focus on only one permutation oracle; therefore, we drop the index i and simply write $\mathcal{Q}_E = \{(L_1 R_1, S_1 T_1), \ldots, (L_{q_i} R_{q_i}, S_{q_i} T_{q_i})\}$ for the permutation query transcript and write $\tau = (\mathcal{Q}_E, \mathcal{Q}_F)$. Note that queries are recorded in a directionless (for permutation queries) and unordered fashion, but since D is assumed deterministic, there is a one-to-one mapping between this representation and the raw transcript of the interaction of D with its oracles (a formal proof could be found in [15]). Also, the output of D is a deterministic function of τ.

Given a set $\mathcal{Q}_{F_i}$ of function queries and a function $\mathbf{F}_i$, we say that $\mathbf{F}_i$ *extends* $\mathcal{Q}_{F_i}$, denoted $\mathbf{F}_i \vdash \mathcal{Q}_{F_i}$, if $\mathbf{F}_i(x) = y$ for all $(x,y) \in \mathcal{Q}_{F_i}$. Similarly, given a transcript of permutation queries $\mathcal{Q}_{E_i}$ and a permutation $\mathbf{P}^{(i)}$, we say $\mathbf{P}^{(i)}$ *extends* $\mathcal{Q}_{E_i}$, denoted $\mathbf{P}^{(i)} \vdash \mathcal{Q}_{E_i}$, if $\mathbf{P}^{(i)}(LR) = ST$ for all $(LR, ST) \in \mathcal{Q}_{E_i}$. The latter definition also extends to the t-round KAF cipher built upon $\mathbf{F}$ and a key $k^{(i)}$; in that case, we write $\mathsf{KAF}^{\mathbf{F}}_{k^{(i)}} \vdash \mathcal{Q}_{E_i}$. Finally, for $\mathcal{Q}_F = (\mathcal{Q}_{F_1}, \dots, \mathcal{Q}_{F_t})$ and $\mathbf{F} = (\mathbf{F}_1, \dots, \mathbf{F}_t)$, if $\mathbf{F}_1 \vdash \mathcal{Q}_{F_1} \wedge \dots \wedge \mathbf{F}_t \vdash \mathcal{Q}_{F_t}$, then $\mathbf{F} \vdash \mathcal{Q}_F$.

For all possible transcript τ that describes a possible interaction with either a tuple of oracles $(\mathbf{P}^{(1)}, \dots, \mathbf{P}^{(m)}, \mathbf{F})$ or $(\mathsf{KAF}^{\mathbf{F}}_{k^{(1)}}, \dots, \mathsf{KAF}^{\mathbf{F}}_{k^{(m)}}, \mathbf{F})$, we denote $\mathrm{Pr}_{re}(\tau)$, resp. $\mathrm{Pr}_{id}(\tau)$, the probability that D's interaction with the real world, resp. the ideal world, produces τ. Formally,

$$\mathrm{Pr}_{re}(\tau) = \mathrm{Pr}[(k^{(1)}, \dots, k^{(m)}) \xleftarrow{\$} (\mathcal{K})^m, \mathbf{F} \xleftarrow{\$} (\mathcal{F}(n))^t :$$
$$\mathsf{KAF}^{\mathbf{F}}_{k^{(1)}} \vdash \mathcal{Q}_{E_1} \wedge \dots \wedge \mathsf{KAF}^{\mathbf{F}}_{k^{(m)}} \vdash \mathcal{Q}_{E_m} \wedge \mathbf{F} \vdash \mathcal{Q}_F],$$

$$\mathrm{Pr}_{id}(\tau) = \mathrm{Pr}[(\mathbf{P}^{(1)}, \dots, \mathbf{P}^{(m)}) \xleftarrow{\$} (\mathcal{P}(2n))^m, \mathbf{F} \xleftarrow{\$} (\mathcal{F}(n))^t :$$
$$\mathbf{P}^{(1)} \vdash \mathcal{Q}_{E_1} \wedge \dots \wedge \mathbf{P}^{(m)} \vdash \mathcal{Q}_{E_m} \wedge \mathbf{F} \vdash \mathcal{Q}_F].$$

With these definitions, the core lemma of the H-coefficients technique states that the distinguishing advantage could be inferred from the ratio of $\mathrm{Pr}_{re}(\tau)$ and $\mathrm{Pr}_{id}(\tau)$ (which is a function of q_f and q_e).

Lemma 1 (From [32]). *Assume that in the atk setting (atk $\in \{SU, MU\}$), there is a function $\varepsilon(q_f, q_e) > 0$ such that for every possible transcript τ with q_e and q_f queries of the two types it holds*

$$\mathrm{Pr}_{id}(\tau) - \mathrm{Pr}_{re}(\tau) \le \mathrm{Pr}_{id}(\tau) \cdot \varepsilon(q_f, q_e), \tag{2}$$

then it holds

$$\mathbf{Adv}^{atk}_{KAF}(q_f, q_e) \le \varepsilon(q_f, q_e).$$

Following [32], the lower bound (2) is named "ε-point-wise proximity" of τ. We partition the key set $\mathcal{K}$ into two disjoint subsets $\mathcal{K}_{good}$ and $\mathcal{K}_{bad}$ such that $\mathcal{K} = \mathcal{K}_{good} \cup \mathcal{K}_{bad}$. Let $\mathrm{Pr}_{re}(\tau, k)$ be the probability that D interacts with the real world, where $k \in \mathcal{K}$ is sampled as the key, and receives a transcript τ. Moreover, we assume there is a fake key variable k in the ideal world that is uniformly selected from the key space $\mathcal{K}$, i.e., $k \xleftarrow{\$} \mathcal{K}$, and define $\mathrm{Pr}_{id}(\tau, k)$ similarly. It is trivial that $\mathrm{Pr}_{id}(\tau, k) = \mathrm{Pr}_{id}(\tau) \times \mathrm{Pr}[k \xleftarrow{\$} \mathcal{K}]$. With these, HT provided a general lemma for establishing point-wise proximity.

Lemma 2 (Lemma 1 of [32]). *Fix a transcript τ with $\mathrm{Pr}_{id}(\tau) > 0$. Assume that: (i) $\mathrm{Pr}[k \in \mathcal{K}_{bad}] \le \delta$, and (ii) there is a function $g : \mathcal{K} \to [0, \infty)$ such that for all $k \in \mathcal{K}_{good}$, it holds $\frac{\mathrm{Pr}_{re}(\tau, k)}{\mathrm{Pr}_{id}(\tau, k)} \ge 1 - g(k)$. Then we have*

$$\mathrm{Pr}_{id}(\tau) - \mathrm{Pr}_{re}(\tau) \le \mathrm{Pr}_{id}(\tau) \cdot (\delta + \mathbb{E}_{k \in \mathcal{K}}[g(k)]). \tag{3}$$

HT also proved that once such point-wise proximity results have been established for the SU setting, similar results could be established for the MU setting via a general transformation. For this we restate Lemma 3 of [32] in our KAF setting.

Lemma 3. *Let t be the number of calls to $\mathbf{F}$ that a single call to KAF/KAF^{-1} makes. Let $\varepsilon : \mathbb{N} \times \mathbb{N} \to \mathbb{R}^{\ge 0}$ be a function such that*

- *$\varepsilon(q_f, q_e) + \varepsilon(q_f, q'_e) \le \varepsilon(q_f, q_e + q'_e)$ for every $q_f, q_e, q'_e \in \mathbb{N}$, and*
- *$\varepsilon(\cdot, q)$ and $\varepsilon(q, \cdot)$ are non-decreasing functions on $\mathbb{N}$ for every $q \in \mathbb{N}$.*

Assume that in the SU setting, for every transcript τ with q_f and q_e queries of the two types, one has

$$\mathrm{Pr}_{id}(\tau) - \mathrm{Pr}_{re}(\tau) \le \mathrm{Pr}_{id}(\tau) \cdot \varepsilon(q_f, q_e),$$

then in the MU setting, for every transcript τ with q_f and q_e queries, one has

$$\mathrm{Pr}_{id}(\tau) - \mathrm{Pr}_{re}(\tau) \le \mathrm{Pr}_{id}(\tau) \cdot 2\varepsilon(q_f + t \cdot q_e, q_e).$$

3   Security Upper Bound: A Distinguishing Attack

Combining the idea of *enumerating all the possible round-keys* from [11] and the *(round) function reduction* technique of [33], the t-round KAF can be *distinguished* by $O(N^{\frac{t-2}{t-1}})$ queries:

(1) Chooses λ plaintexts $L_1 R_1, \ldots, L_\lambda R_\lambda$, with $L_1, \ldots, L_\lambda$ pair-wise distinct, and $R_1 = \ldots = R_\lambda = R$, and makes λ encryption queries $\mathrm{ENC}_k(L_1, R_1) \to (S_1, T_1)$, ..., $\mathrm{ENC}_k(L_\lambda, R_\lambda) \to (S_\lambda, T_\lambda)$;

(2) For ℓ from 2 to $t - 1$, asks λ arbitrary distinct queries $x_\ell^{(1)}, x_\ell^{(2)}, \ldots, x_\ell^{(\lambda)}$ to F_ℓ:
   - $F_\ell(x_\ell^{(1)}) \to y_\ell^{(1)}$,
   - $\ldots$
   - $F_\ell(x_\ell^{(\lambda)}) \to y_\ell^{(\lambda)}$;

(3) Denote $CON = F_1(k_1 \oplus R)$. For all $k = (k_1, \ldots, k_t) \in \mathcal{K}$ and all 2^n possible values of CON, if there exists $t - 1$ query-answer pairs $(L_i R, S_i T_i)$, (x_2, y_2), (x_3, y_3), ..., (x_{t-1}, y_{t-1}) such that an almost completed computation chain is formed:
   - $k_2 \oplus CON = L_i \oplus x_2$, and
   - $k_3 = R \oplus y_2 \oplus x_3$, and
   - $\ldots$
   - $k_{\ell+1} = (k_{\ell-1} \oplus x_{\ell-1}) \oplus y_\ell \oplus x_{\ell+1}$, and

– ...
– $k_{t-1} = (k_{t-3} \oplus x_{t-3}) \oplus y_{t-2} \oplus x_{t-1}$,

and further $S = (k_{t-2} \oplus x_{t-2}) \oplus y_{t-1}$, then outputs 1 to indicates it's the real world (otherwise 0).

When $\lambda = N^{\frac{t-2}{t-1}}$ and thus $\frac{\lambda^{t-1}}{N^{t-2}} = 1$, the probability of forming a chain is approximately 1. By this, a 6-round KAF ensure at most $4n/5$-bit security. This should be contrasted with the results on the classical LR model (as discussed in the Introduction).

We also note that the t-round IEM ciphers built upon n-bit random permutations and *independent* round-keys tightly ensure $\frac{tn}{t+1}$-bit security [32], which is better than the upper bound $\frac{(t-2)n}{t-1}$-bit here. This matches the folklore that compared to IEM ciphers, Feistel ciphers have more structural properties that are helpful for attacks (as a consequence, to ensure the same amount of security, KAF needs more rounds). Tight security bounds for t-round KAF remains an open problem.

4   Four Rounds for Birthday-Type Security

We first present a general positive result for 4-round KAFSF in Subsect. 4.1. Then in Subsect. 4.2, we discuss how to schedule the desired round-keys from a short main-key, and present our "minimal" provably secure construction.

4.1   A General Positive Result

The first step is to specify conditions on the round-key vector that will allow us to upper bound the probability to obtain a round-bad key vector in the ideal world (the definition of bad key vectors will appear later).

Definition 1 (Suitable Round-Key Vector for 4 Rounds). *A round-key vector $k = (k_1, k_2, k_3, k_4)$ is suitable if it satisfies the following conditions:*

(i) k_1 and k_4 are uniform in $\{0,1\}^n$ (but they need not to be independent);
(ii) $k_1 \oplus k_4$ is also uniformly distributed in $\{0,1\}^n$.

If condition (i) is seriously compromised, the cipher would essentially lost 1 or 2 rounds. E.g., when k_1 is only uniform in n possibilities, an adversary could derive the second-round intermediate value $X = L \oplus F(k_1 \oplus R)$ with n guesses. The less obvious condition (ii) is intended to prevent palindrome-like relations in the derived round-keys, which have been found harmful [45]. To further help understanding, in the full version we present attacks against some round-keys that do not fulfill condition (ii).

Instantiated with such a suitable round-key vector, KAFSF ensures birthday security.

Theorem 1. *For the 4-round idealized KAFSF cipher with a suitable round-key vector as specified in Definition 1, it holds*

$$\mathbf{Adv}_{KAFSF}^{SU}(q_f, q_e) \leq \frac{9q_e^2 + 4q_e q_f}{N}, \text{ and } \mathbf{Adv}_{KAFSF}^{MU}(q_f, q_e) \leq \frac{50q_e^2 + 8q_e q_f}{N}.$$

Proof. We devote to prove that in the SU setting, for any transcript τ, it holds

$$\mathrm{Pr}_{id}(\tau) - \mathrm{Pr}_{re}(\tau) \leq \mathrm{Pr}_{id}(\tau) \cdot \frac{9q_e^2 + 4q_e q_f}{N}. \tag{4}$$

This along with Lemmas 1 and 3 would yield the two main claims. Due to page limits, the proof of Eq. (4) is deferred to the full version [28].   □

4.2   How to Schedule the Key: The Minimal Construction

By Definition 1, it can be seen that if pair-wise independence is ensured between round-keys, then the key vector is suitable. We refer to Sect. 6 for how to derive such round-keys. Here it would be tempting to ask how to schedule a single n-bit key K into a suitable key vector. Below we identify a condition on a key-schedule $\gamma = (\gamma_1, \gamma_2, \gamma_3, \gamma_4)$ (setting $k_i = \gamma_i(K)$ for $i = 1, 2, 3, 4$) that suffices for this purpose. We call such key-schedules *good*:

Definition 2 (Good Key-Schedule for 4-Round KAFSF). *We say that a key-schedule $\gamma = (\gamma_1, \gamma_2, \gamma_3, \gamma_4)$, where $\gamma_i : \{0,1\}^n \to \{0,1\}^n$, is good if γ_1, γ_4, and $\gamma_1 \oplus \gamma_4$ are all bijective maps of $\mathbb{F}_2^n$.*

As mentioned in the Introduction, one could take for γ_1 the identity, and $\gamma_4 = \varphi$, where φ is an orthomorphism of $\mathbb{F}_2^n$, as in Fig. 1 (right).

5   Six Rounds for Beyond-Birthday Security

Similarly to Sect. 4, we also specify conditions on the round-key vectors first.

Definition 3 (Suitable Round-Key Vector for 6 Rounds). *A round-key vector $k = (k_1, k_2, k_3, k_4, k_5, k_6)$ is suitable if it satisfies the following conditions:*

(i) k_1, k_3, and k_5 are uniformly distributed in $\{0,1\}^n$;
(ii) k_2, k_4, and k_6 are uniformly distributed in 2^{n-r} possibilities;
(iii) for $(i, j) \in \{(1,2), (2,3), (4,5), (5,6), (1,6)\}$, k_i and k_j are independent.

Unlike Sect. 4, in the subsequent analysis we find the uniformness of every round-key crucial. This is why we require all of them to be uniform (this is also understandable, since beyond-birthday security requires various types of collisions can be bounded by small enough probability, and thus requiring a larger amount of randomness). The (mild) independence is also crucially used in the analysis. To further understand the necessity, please see [28, Appendix A].

Instantiated with such a suitable round-key vector, KAF ensures beyond-birthday security.

Theorem 2. *For the 6-round idealized cipher* KAF *with a suitable round-key vector as specified in Definition 3, it holds*

$$\mathbf{Adv}_{KAF}^{SU}(q_f, q_e) \leq \frac{7q_e^3 + 13q_e q_f^2 + 22q_e^2 q_f}{N^2} + \frac{2^r(8q_e q_f^2 + 2q_e^2 q_f)}{N^2}, \text{ and}$$

$$\mathbf{Adv}_{KAF}^{MU}(q_f, q_e) \leq \frac{1214q_e^3 + 26q_e q_f^2 + 356q_e^2 q_f}{N^2} + \frac{2^r(600q_e^3 + 16q_e q_f^2 + 196q_e^2 q_f)}{N^2}.$$

Note that when $r < n/2$, the security is beyond-birthday—and when $r = 0$, the bound is of "typical" beyond-birthday form $O(\frac{q^3}{N^2})$.

We devote to prove the following point-wise proximity result for the SU setting: for any transcript τ, it holds

$$\mathrm{Pr}_{id}(\tau) - \mathrm{Pr}_{re}(\tau) \leq \mathrm{Pr}_{id}(\tau) \cdot \frac{7q_e^3 + 13q_e q_f^2 + 22q_e^2 q_f + 2^r(8q_e q_f^2 + 2q_e^2 q_f)}{N^2}. \quad (5)$$

Gathering this and Lemmas 1 and 3 yields the claims.

Fix a transcript $\tau = (\mathcal{Q}_E, \mathcal{Q}_F)$ with $\mathcal{Q}_F = (\mathcal{Q}_{F_1}, \mathcal{Q}_{F_2}, \mathcal{Q}_{F_3}, \mathcal{Q}_{F_4}, \mathcal{Q}_{F_5}, \mathcal{Q}_{F_6})$, $|\mathcal{Q}_E| = q_e$, and $|\mathcal{Q}_{F_i}| = q_f$ for $i = 1, \ldots, 6$, we first define bad key-vectors, then lower bound the probability $\mathrm{Pr}_{re}(\tau, k)$. These two steps correspond to the following two subsections respectively.

5.1 Bad Round-Key Vectors and Probability

Similarly to Subsect. 4.1, for any $x_i \in \{0,1\}^n$, if there exists a corresponding record (x_i, y_i) in $\mathcal{Q}_{F_i}$, then we write $x_i \in Dom\mathcal{F}_i$ (and $x_i \notin Dom\mathcal{F}_i$ otherwise), and write $ImgF_i(x_i)$ for the corresponding y_i. Now, the definition is as follows.

Definition 4 (Bad Round-Key Vector for 6 Rounds). *With respect to* $\tau = (\mathcal{Q}_E, \mathcal{Q}_F)$, *a suitable key vector k fulfilling one of the conditions is bad:*

- *(B-1) there exists $(LR, ST) \in \mathcal{Q}_E$, $(x_1, y_1) \in \mathcal{Q}_{F_1}$, and $(x_6, y_6) \in \mathcal{Q}_{F_6}$ such that $k_1 = R \oplus x_1$ and $k_6 = S \oplus x_6$;*
- *(B-2) there exists $(LR, ST) \in \mathcal{Q}_E$, $(x_1, y_1) \in \mathcal{Q}_{F_1}$, and $(x_2, y_2) \in \mathcal{Q}_{F_2}$ such that $k_1 = R \oplus x_1$ and $k_2 = L \oplus y_1 \oplus x_2$;*
- *(B-3) there exists $(LR, ST) \in \mathcal{Q}_E$, $(x_5, y_5) \in \mathcal{Q}_{F_5}$, and $(x_6, y_6) \in \mathcal{Q}_{F_6}$ such that $k_6 = S \oplus x_6$ and $k_5 = T \oplus y_6 \oplus x_5$.*

Otherwise we say k is good. Denote by $\mathcal{K}_{bad}$ the set of bad key vectors.

We now prove

$$\mathrm{Pr}[k \xleftarrow{\$} \mathcal{K} : k \in \mathcal{K}_{bad}] \leq \frac{3 \cdot 2^r \cdot q_e q_f^2}{N^2}. \quad (6)$$

Consider (B-1) first. Since we have at most $q_e q_f^2$ choices for $(LR, ST) \in \mathcal{Q}_E$ and $(x_1, y_1) \in \mathcal{Q}_{F_1}$ and $(x_6, y_6) \in \mathcal{Q}_{F_6}$ and since k_1, resp. k_6, is uniform in 2^n, resp. 2^{n-r} possibilities, and further since k_1 and k_6 are independent (cf. Definition 3), it holds $\mathrm{Pr}[(\text{B-1})] \leq \frac{q_e q_f^2}{2^{2n-r}} \leq \frac{2^r q_e q_f^2}{N^2}$.

Similarly, since k_1 and k_2 are random and independent, and we have at most $q_e q_f^2$ choices for $(LR, ST) \in \mathcal{Q}_E$ and $(x_1, y_1) \in \mathcal{Q}_{F_1}$ and $(x_2, y_2) \in \mathcal{Q}_{F_2}$, we have $\mathrm{Pr}[(\text{B-2})] \leq \frac{2^r q_e q_f^2}{N^2}$; by symmetry, $\mathrm{Pr}[(\text{B-3})] \leq \frac{2^r q_e q_f^2}{N^2}$. The sum yields (6).

5.2   Analysis for Good Keys

Fix a good round-key vector k, we are to derive a lower bound for the probability $\Pr[\mathbf{F} \xleftarrow{\$} (\mathcal{F}(n))^6 : \mathsf{KAF}_k^{\mathbf{F}} \vdash \mathcal{Q}_E \mid \mathbf{F} \vdash \mathcal{Q}_F]$. It consists of two steps. In the first step, we will lower bound the probability that a pair of functions $(\mathbf{F}_1, \mathbf{F}_6)$ satisfies certain "bad" conditions that will be defined. With the values given by a "good" pair of functions $(\mathbf{F}_1, \mathbf{F}_6)$, a transcript of the distinguisher on 6 rounds can be transformed into a special transcript on 4 rounds; in this sense, we "peel off" the outer two rounds. Then in the second step, assuming $(\mathbf{F}_1, \mathbf{F}_6)$ is good, we analyze the induced 4-round transcript to yield the final bounds. In the following, each step would take a subsubsection. As mentioned in the Introduction, this two-step approach is motivated by Cogliati et al. [16,17].

Peeling Off the Outer Two Rounds. Pick a pair of functions $(\mathbf{F}_1, \mathbf{F}_6)$ such that $\mathbf{F}_1 \vdash \mathcal{Q}_{F_1}$ and $\mathbf{F}_6 \vdash \mathcal{Q}_{F_6}$, and for each $(LR, ST) \in \mathcal{Q}_E$ we set $X \leftarrow L \oplus \mathbf{F}_1(k_1 \oplus R)$ and $A \leftarrow T \oplus \mathbf{F}_6(k_6 \oplus S)$. In this way we obtain q_e tuples of the form (RX, AS); for convenience we denote the set of such induced tuples by $\mathcal{Q}_E^*(\mathbf{F}_1, \mathbf{F}_6)$. We further denote by $\mathcal{EQ}(X)$ the set that contains all such induced tuples with their second coordinate equaling X—formally,

- $\mathcal{EQ}(X) = \{(RX, AS) : (RX, AS) \in \mathcal{Q}_E^*(\mathbf{F}_1, \mathbf{F}_6)\}$.
- Similarly, $\mathcal{EQ}(A) = \{(RX, AS) : (RX, AS) \in \mathcal{Q}_E^*(\mathbf{F}_1, \mathbf{F}_6)\}$.

And we define several key-dependent quantities characterizing τ:

$$\alpha_1(k) \xlongequal{\text{def}} |\{((LR, ST), (x_1, y_1)) \in \mathcal{Q}_E \times \mathcal{Q}_{F_1} : k_1 = R \oplus x_1\}|,$$

$$\alpha_2(k) \xlongequal{\text{def}} |\{((LR, ST), (x_6, y_6)) \in \mathcal{Q}_E \times \mathcal{Q}_{F_6} : k_6 = S \oplus x_6\}|,$$

$$\alpha_{2,3}(k) \xlongequal{\text{def}} |\{((LR, ST), (x_2, y_2), (x_3, y_3)) \in \mathcal{Q}_E \times \mathcal{Q}_{F_2} \times \mathcal{Q}_{F_3} : k_3 = R \oplus y_2 \oplus x_3\}|,$$

$$\alpha_{4,5}(k) \xlongequal{\text{def}} |\{((LR, ST), (x_4, y_4), (x_5, y_5)) \in \mathcal{Q}_E \times \mathcal{Q}_{F_4} \times \mathcal{Q}_{F_5} : k_4 = S \oplus y_5 \oplus x_4\}|.$$

Then we define a predicate $\mathsf{Bad}(\mathbf{F}_1, \mathbf{F}_6)$ on the pair $(\mathbf{F}_1, \mathbf{F}_6)$, which holds if the corresponding induced set $\mathcal{Q}_E^*(\mathbf{F}_1, \mathbf{F}_6)$ fulfills at least one of the following five "collision" conditions (see Fig. 3 for illustration):

- (C-1) there exists three records $(RX, AS) \in \mathcal{Q}_E^*(\mathbf{F}_1, \mathbf{F}_6)$, $(x_2, y_2) \in \mathcal{Q}_{F_2}$, and $(x_5, y_5) \in \mathcal{Q}_{F_5}$ such that $k_2 = X \oplus x_2$ and $k_5 = A \oplus x_5$;
- (C-2) there exists three records $(RX, AS) \in \mathcal{Q}_E^*(\mathbf{F}_1, \mathbf{F}_6)$, $(x_2, y_2) \in \mathcal{Q}_{F_2}$, and $(x_3, y_3) \in \mathcal{Q}_{F_3}$ such that $k_2 = X \oplus x_2$ and $k_3 = R \oplus y_2 \oplus x_3$;
- (C-3) there exists three records $(RX, AS) \in \mathcal{Q}_E^*(\mathbf{F}_1, \mathbf{F}_6)$, $(x_4, y_4) \in \mathcal{Q}_{F_4}$, and $(x_5, y_5) \in \mathcal{Q}_{F_5}$ such that $k_5 = A \oplus x_5$ and $k_4 = S \oplus y_5 \oplus x_4$;
- (C-4) there exists two distinct (RX, AS), $(R'X', A'S')$ in $\mathcal{Q}_E^*(\mathbf{F}_1, \mathbf{F}_6)$, and a pair (x_2, y_2) in $\mathcal{Q}_{F_2}$ such that $X = X'$ and $k_2 = X \oplus x_2$; or, symmetrically, two distinct (RX, AS), $(R'X', A'S')$ in $\mathcal{Q}_E^*(\mathbf{F}_1, \mathbf{F}_6)$ and a pair (x_5, y_5) in $\mathcal{Q}_{F_5}$ such that $A = A'$ and $k_5 = A \oplus x_5$;

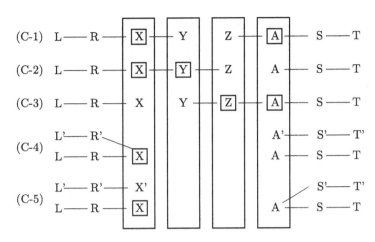

Fig. 3. The five "collision" conditions characterizing a pair of functions $(\mathbf{F}_1, \mathbf{F}_6)$ such that $\mathsf{Bad}(\mathbf{F}_1, \mathbf{F}_6)$ holds. The values X, Y, Z, A in squares satisfy $k_2 \oplus X \in Dom\mathcal{F}_2$, $k_3 \oplus Y \in Dom\mathcal{F}_3$, $k_4 \oplus Z \in Dom\mathcal{F}_4$, and $k_5 \oplus A \in Dom\mathcal{F}_5$ respectively.

– (C-5) there exists two distinct (RX, AS), $(R'X', A'S')$ in $\mathcal{Q}_E^*(\mathbf{F}_1, \mathbf{F}_6)$ and a pair (x_2, y_2) in $\mathcal{Q}_{F_2}$ such that $A = A'$ and $k_2 = X \oplus x_2$; or, symmetrically, two distinct (RX, AS), $(R'X', A'S')$ in $\mathcal{Q}_E^*(\mathbf{F}_1, \mathbf{F}_6)$ and a pair (x_5, y_5) in $\mathcal{Q}_{F_5}$ such that $X = X'$ and $k_5 = A \oplus x_5$.

For convenience, if $\mathsf{Bad}(\mathbf{F}_1, \mathbf{F}_6)$ does not hold, then we say $(\mathbf{F}_1, \mathbf{F}_6)$ is *good*; in this case, the induced tuples (RX, AS) are easier to analyze. For $\Pr[\mathsf{Bad}(\mathbf{F}_1, \mathbf{F}_6)]$ we have the following bound.

Lemma 4. *It holds*

$$\Pr_{\mathbf{F}_1, \mathbf{F}_6}[\mathit{Bad}(\mathbf{F}_1, \mathbf{F}_6) \mid \mathbf{F}_1 \vdash \mathcal{Q}_{F_1} \wedge \mathbf{F}_6 \vdash \mathcal{Q}_{F_6}]$$
$$\leq \frac{q_e q_f^2}{N^2} + \frac{4q_e^2 q_f}{N^2} + \frac{\alpha_{2,3}(k) + \alpha_{4,5}(k)}{N} + \frac{q_f(\alpha_1(k) + \alpha_2(k))}{N}.$$

Proof. Due to page limits please see the full version [28] for the proofs for:

$$\Pr[(\text{C-1})] \leq \frac{q_e q_f^2}{N^2}, \quad \Pr[(\text{C-2})] \leq \frac{\alpha_{2,3}(k)}{N}, \quad \Pr[(\text{C-3})] \leq \frac{\alpha_{4,5}(k)}{N},$$
$$\Pr[(\text{C-4})] \leq \frac{2q_e^2 q_f}{N^2}, \text{ and } \Pr[(\text{C-5})] \leq \frac{2q_e^2 q_f}{N^2} + \frac{q_f(\alpha_1(k) + \alpha_2(k))}{N}.$$

Summing over them gives the result. All the arguments rely on the uniformness of entries of $\mathbf{F}$, which are uniform in 2^n values rather than 2^{n-r}. This clarifies why the bounds have nothing to do with the term 2^r. $\square$

Analyzing the Inner Four Rounds. Let $\mathbf{F}^* = (\mathbf{F}_2, \mathbf{F}_3, \mathbf{F}_4, \mathbf{F}_5)$. We denote

$$\mathsf{p}(\tau, \mathbf{F}_1, \mathbf{F}_6) = \Pr[\mathbf{F}^* \xleftarrow{\$} (\mathcal{F}(n))^4 : \mathsf{KAF}_k^{\mathbf{F}^*} \vdash \mathcal{Q}_E^*(\mathbf{F}_1, \mathbf{F}_6) \mid \mathbf{F}_i \vdash \mathcal{Q}_{F_i}, i = 1, 2, 3, 4, 5, 6].$$

This captures the probability that the inner four rounds of KAF "extend" the tuples in $\mathcal{Q}_E^*(\mathbf{F}_1, \mathbf{F}_6)$. The probability $\Pr_{re}(\tau, k)$ can be related to it.

Lemma 5. *Assume that there exists a function* $\epsilon : (\mathcal{F}(n))^2 \times \mathcal{K} \to [0, \infty)$ *such that for any good* $(\mathbf{F}_1, \mathbf{F}_6)$*, it holds*

$$p(\tau, \mathbf{F}_1, \mathbf{F}_6) \Big/ \prod_{i=0}^{q_e-1} \left(\frac{1}{N^2 - i} \right) \geq 1 - \epsilon(\mathbf{F}_1, \mathbf{F}_6, k). \tag{7}$$

Then we have

$$\frac{\Pr_{re}(\tau, k)}{\Pr_{id}(\tau, k)} \geq 1 - \Pr[Bad(\mathbf{F}_1, \mathbf{F}_6) \mid \mathbf{F}_1 \vdash \mathcal{Q}_{F_1}, \mathbf{F}_6 \vdash \mathcal{Q}_{F_6}]$$
$$- \mathbb{E}_{\mathbf{F}_1, \mathbf{F}_6}[\epsilon(\mathbf{F}_1, \mathbf{F}_6, k) \mid \mathbf{F}_1 \vdash \mathcal{Q}_{F_1}, \mathbf{F}_6 \vdash \mathcal{Q}_{F_6}].$$

Proof. Define $p(\mathbf{F}_1, \mathbf{F}_6) \stackrel{\text{def}}{=\!=} \Pr[(\mathbf{F}_1^*, \mathbf{F}_6^*) \xleftarrow{\$} (\mathcal{F}(n))^2 : (\mathbf{F}_1^*, \mathbf{F}_6^*) = (\mathbf{F}_1, \mathbf{F}_6)]$ for convenience. Then, clearly, once $\mathbf{F}_1$ and $\mathbf{F}_6$ are fixed such that $\mathbf{F}_1 \vdash \mathcal{Q}_{F_1}$ and $\mathbf{F}_6 \vdash \mathcal{Q}_{F_6}$, the event $\mathsf{KAF}_k^{\mathbf{F}} \vdash \mathcal{Q}_E$ is equivalent to $\mathsf{KAF}_k^{\mathbf{F}^*} \vdash \mathcal{Q}_E^*(\mathbf{F}_1, \mathbf{F}_6)$. Hence

$$\Pr_{re}(\tau, k) \geq \sum_{\mathbf{F}_1 \vdash \mathcal{Q}_{F_1}, \mathbf{F}_6 \vdash \mathcal{Q}_{F_6} : (\mathbf{F}_1, \mathbf{F}_6) \text{ good}} p(\mathbf{F}_1, \mathbf{F}_6) \cdot \frac{p(\tau, \mathbf{F}_1, \mathbf{F}_6)}{|\mathcal{K}| \cdot N^{4q_f}}.$$

Therefore,

$$\frac{\Pr_{re}(\tau, k)}{\Pr_{id}(\tau, k)} \geq \frac{\sum_{\mathbf{F}_1 \vdash \mathcal{Q}_{F_1}, \mathbf{F}_6 \vdash \mathcal{Q}_{F_6} : (\mathbf{F}_1, \mathbf{F}_6) \text{ good}} p(\mathbf{F}_1, \mathbf{F}_6) \cdot p(\tau, \mathbf{F}_1, \mathbf{F}_6)}{\Pr[\mathbf{F}_1 \vdash \mathcal{Q}_{F_1}, \mathbf{F}_6 \vdash \mathcal{Q}_{F_6}] \cdot \prod_{i=0}^{q_e-1} \frac{1}{N^2 - i}}$$

$$\geq \frac{\sum_{\mathbf{F}_1 \vdash \mathcal{Q}_{F_1}, \mathbf{F}_6 \vdash \mathcal{Q}_{F_6} : (\mathbf{F}_1, \mathbf{F}_6) \text{ good}} p(\mathbf{F}_1, \mathbf{F}_6)(1 - \epsilon(\mathbf{F}_1, \mathbf{F}_6, k))}{\Pr[\mathbf{F}_1 \vdash \mathcal{Q}_{F_1}, \mathbf{F}_6 \vdash \mathcal{Q}_{F_6}]} \quad \text{(by (7))}$$

$$\geq 1 - \Pr[Bad(\mathbf{F}_1, \mathbf{F}_6) \mid \mathbf{F}_1 \vdash \mathcal{Q}_{F_1}, \mathbf{F}_6 \vdash \mathcal{Q}_{F_6}]$$

$$- \underbrace{\sum_{\mathbf{F}_1 \vdash \mathcal{Q}_{F_1}, \mathbf{F}_6 \vdash \mathcal{Q}_{F_6}} p(\mathbf{F}_1, \mathbf{F}_6) \epsilon(\mathbf{F}_1, \mathbf{F}_6, k)}_{=\mathbb{E}_{\mathbf{F}_1, \mathbf{F}_6}[\epsilon(\mathbf{F}_1, \mathbf{F}_6, k) \mid \mathbf{F}_1 \vdash \mathcal{Q}_{F_1}, \mathbf{F}_6 \vdash \mathcal{Q}_{F_6}]}.$$

as claimed. □

We now prove the assumption of Lemma 5.

Lemma 6. *For any fixed good tuple* $(\mathbf{F}_1, \mathbf{F}_6)$*, there exists a function* $\epsilon(\mathbf{F}_1, \mathbf{F}_6, k)$ *of the function pair and the round-key vector* k *such that the inequality (7) mentioned in Lemma 5 holds. Moreover,*

$$\mathbb{E}_{\mathbf{F}_1, \mathbf{F}_6, k}[\epsilon(\mathbf{F}_1, \mathbf{F}_6, k)] \leq \frac{7q_e^3 + 10q_e q_f^2 + 18q_e^2 q_f + 3 \cdot 2^r \cdot q_e q_f^2 + 2 \cdot 2^r \cdot q_e^2 q_f}{N^2}. \tag{8}$$

Proof. The general expression of $\epsilon(\mathbf{F}_1, \mathbf{F}_6, k)$ is a function of several variables defined before, which suffers from a bad readability. Therefore, we directly establish (and present) the bound on its expectation. However, due to space constraints, the full proof has to be deferred to [28].

Below we present a sketch and the core results. According to the type of the involved collisions, we divide the tuples in $\mathcal{Q}_E^*(\mathbf{F}_1, \mathbf{F}_6)$ into four groups (see Fig. 4 for an illustration):

- $\mathcal{G}_1 = \{(RX, AS) \in \mathcal{Q}_E^*(\mathbf{F}_1, \mathbf{F}_6) : |\mathcal{EQ}(X)| = |\mathcal{EQ}(A)| = 1,$ and further $k_2 \oplus X \notin Dom\mathcal{F}_2 \wedge k_5 \oplus A \notin Dom\mathcal{F}_5\}$,
- $\mathcal{G}_2 = \{(RX, AS) \in \mathcal{Q}_E^*(\mathbf{F}_1, \mathbf{F}_6) : k_2 \oplus X \in Dom\mathcal{F}_2\}$,
- $\mathcal{G}_3 = \{(RX, AS) \in \mathcal{Q}_E^*(\mathbf{F}_1, \mathbf{F}_6) : k_5 \oplus A \in Dom\mathcal{F}_5\}$,
- $\mathcal{G}_4 = \{(RX, AS) \in \mathcal{Q}_E^*(\mathbf{F}_1, \mathbf{F}_6) : |\mathcal{EQ}(X)| \geq 2,$ or $|\mathcal{EQ}(A)| \geq 2\}$.

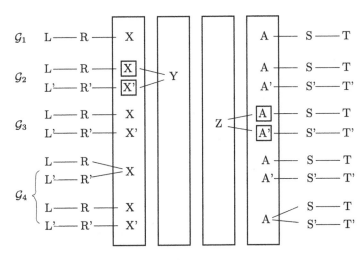

Fig. 4. Partition of the tuples in $\mathcal{Q}_E^*(\mathbf{F}_1, \mathbf{F}_6)$. The value X, resp. A, in square satisfies $k_2 \oplus X \in Dom\mathcal{F}_2$, resp. $k_5 \oplus A \in Dom\mathcal{F}_5$.

Let $\beta_1 = |\mathcal{G}_2|$, $\beta_2 = |\mathcal{G}_3|$, and $\beta_3 = |\mathcal{G}_4|$. Note that by definition, these sets form a partition of $\mathcal{Q}_E^*(\mathbf{F}_1, \mathbf{F}_6)$:

- $\mathcal{G}_1 \cap \mathcal{G}_2 = \mathcal{G}_1 \cap \mathcal{G}_3 = \mathcal{G}_1 \cap \mathcal{G}_4 = \emptyset$ by definition;
- $\mathcal{G}_2 \cap \mathcal{G}_3 = \emptyset$ since otherwise $\mathcal{Q}_E^*(\mathbf{F}_1, \mathbf{F}_6)$ would satisfy (C-1);
- $\mathcal{G}_2 \cap \mathcal{G}_4 = \emptyset$, since for any $(RX, AS) \in \mathcal{G}_2$, $|\mathcal{EQ}(X)| \geq 2$ would imply $\mathcal{Q}_E^*(\mathbf{F}_1, \mathbf{F}_6)$ fulfilling (C-4), while $|\mathcal{EQ}(A)| \geq 2$ would imply (C-5);
- $\mathcal{G}_3 \cap \mathcal{G}_4 = \emptyset$, since for any $(RX, AS) \in \mathcal{G}_3$, $|\mathcal{EQ}(X)| \geq 2$ implies (C-5), while $|\mathcal{EQ}(A)| \geq 2$ implies (C-4).

We denote respectively $\mathsf{E}_{\mathcal{G}_1}$, $\mathsf{E}_{\mathcal{G}_2}$, $\mathsf{E}_{\mathcal{G}_3}$, and $\mathsf{E}_{\mathcal{G}_4}$ the event that $\mathsf{KAF}_k^{\mathbf{F}^*} \vdash \mathcal{G}_1, \mathcal{G}_2,$ $\mathcal{G}_3$, and $\mathcal{G}_4$. It can be seen

$$\mathsf{p}(\tau, \mathbf{F}_1, \mathbf{F}_6) = \Pr[\mathsf{E}_{\mathcal{G}_1} \wedge \mathsf{E}_{\mathcal{G}_2} \wedge \mathsf{E}_{\mathcal{G}_3} \wedge \mathsf{E}_{\mathcal{G}_4} \mid \mathbf{F} \vdash \mathcal{Q}_F].$$

We next analyze the four groups in turn. The first one, i.e. $\Pr[\mathsf{E}_{\mathcal{G}_1} \mid \mathbf{F} \vdash \mathcal{Q}_F]$, involves the most complicated analysis. Briefly, for each tuple (RX, AS) in $\mathcal{G}_1$, it consists of three cases:

(i) In the first case, neither of the two corresponding intermediate values Y and Z derived from $\mathbf{F}_2$ and $\mathbf{F}_5$ collides with values that have been in the history. The probability that $\mathsf{KAF}_k^{\mathbf{F}}$ extends (RX, AS) in this case is roughly at least

$$\left(1 - \frac{q_f + q_e + \beta_1}{N}\right)\left(1 - \frac{q_f + q_e + \beta_2}{N}\right)\frac{1}{N^2}.$$

(ii) In the second case, the corresponding intermediate value Y collides with some "existing" values, yet the further derived Z is "free". The probability that $\mathsf{KAF}_k^{\mathbf{F}}$ extends (RX, AS) in this case is roughly at least

$$\left(\frac{q_f + q_e}{N} - O\left(\frac{2^r \cdot q_f^2}{N^2} + \frac{(q_f + q_e)^2}{N^2}\right)\right)\frac{1}{N^2}.$$

(iii) The third case is symmetrical to the second one: Z collides with "existing" values, yet Y is "free". The probability is roughly at least

$$\left(\frac{q_f + q_e}{N} - O\left(\frac{(q_f + q_e)^2}{N^2}\right)\right)\frac{1}{N^2}.$$

Summing over the above, we obtain

$$\Pr[\mathsf{E}_{\mathcal{G}_1} \mid \mathbf{F} \vdash \mathcal{Q}_F] \geq \prod_{\ell=1}^{|\mathcal{G}_1|}\left(1 - \frac{\beta_1}{N} - \frac{\beta_2}{N} - O\left(\frac{2^r \cdot q_f^2}{N^2} + \frac{(q_f + q_e)^2}{N^2}\right)\right)\frac{1}{N^2}.$$

Yet, the above results are oversimplified due to the page limits. We in fact used many additional notations, cf. [28]. The concrete bound is

$$\mathbb{E}_k\left[\Pr[\mathsf{E}_{\mathcal{G}_1} \mid \mathbf{F} \vdash \mathcal{Q}_F]\right]$$
$$\geq \left(1 - \frac{2^r \cdot q_e q_f^2}{N^2} - \frac{2q_e(2q_f + q_e)(q_f + q_e)}{N^2} - \frac{(q_f + 2q_e)(\beta_1 + \beta_2)}{N}\right)\frac{1}{N^{2|\mathcal{G}_1|}}. \quad (9)$$

To analyze $\mathsf{E}_{\mathcal{G}_2}$, $\mathsf{E}_{\mathcal{G}_3}$, and $\mathsf{E}_{\mathcal{G}_4}$, we again apply the bad predicate approach. These groups involve collisions, and have relatively small sizes: $|\mathcal{G}_2|, |\mathcal{G}_3|, |\mathcal{G}_4| = O(2^r \cdot q^2/N)$ (will be proved later). Therefore, any collisions between tuples in these groups and values related to $\mathcal{Q}_F$ or $\mathcal{G}_1$ can be included in the bad predicates: for each tuple in these three groups the probability would be $O(q/N)$ with $q = \max\{q_e, q_f\}$, yet it remains $O(q/N) \cdot O(2^r \cdot q^2/N) = O(2^r \cdot q^3/N^2)$ in total. See [28] for the formal analyzes. In all, the results are

$$\Pr[\mathsf{E}_{\mathcal{G}_2} \wedge \mathsf{E}_{\mathcal{G}_3} \mid \mathsf{E}_{\mathcal{G}_1} \wedge \mathbf{F} \vdash \mathcal{Q}_F] \geq \left(1 - \frac{(\beta_1 + \beta_2)(q_f + q_e)}{N}\right)\frac{1}{N^{2(|\mathcal{G}_2| + |\mathcal{G}_3|)}}, \quad (10)$$

$$\Pr[\mathsf{E}_{\mathcal{G}_4} \mid \mathsf{E}_{\mathcal{G}_1} \wedge \mathsf{E}_{\mathcal{G}_2} \wedge \mathsf{E}_{\mathcal{G}_3} \wedge \mathbf{F} \vdash \mathcal{Q}_F] \geq \left(1 - \frac{2\beta_3(q_f + q_e)}{N}\right)\frac{1}{N^{2|\mathcal{G}_4|}}. \quad (11)$$

Summing Up would yield a lower bound of the form

$$\mathsf{p}(\tau, \mathbf{F}_1, \mathbf{F}_6) = \Pr[\mathsf{E}_{\mathcal{G}_1} \wedge \mathsf{E}_{\mathcal{G}_2} \wedge \mathsf{E}_{\mathcal{G}_3} \wedge \mathsf{E}_{\mathcal{G}_4} \mid \mathbf{F} \vdash \mathcal{Q}_F]$$

$$\geq (1 - \epsilon_1)(1 - \epsilon_2)(1 - \epsilon_3) \frac{1}{N^{2(|\mathcal{G}_1| + |\mathcal{G}_2| + |\mathcal{G}_3| + |\mathcal{G}_4|)}}$$

$$\geq (1 - (\epsilon_1 + \epsilon_2 + \epsilon_3)) \frac{1}{N^{2q_e}} \text{ (since } |\mathcal{G}_1| + |\mathcal{G}_2| + |\mathcal{G}_3| + |\mathcal{G}_4| = q_e),$$

where ϵ_1, ϵ_2, ϵ_3 are in (9), (10), and (11) respectively. We note

$$\frac{1}{N^{2q_e}} \bigg/ \left(\prod_{i=0}^{q_e - 1} \frac{1}{N^2 - i} \right) \geq \left(1 - \frac{q_e}{N^2} \right)^{q_e} \geq 1 - \frac{q_e^2}{N^2} \geq 1 - \frac{q_e^3}{N^2},$$

Thus using $(1 - A)(1 - B) \geq 1 - (A + B)$ we obtain

$$\frac{\mathsf{p}(\tau, \mathbf{F}_1, \mathbf{F}_6)}{\prod_{i=0}^{q_e - 1} \frac{1}{N^2 - i}} \geq 1 - \epsilon(\mathbf{F}_1, \mathbf{F}_2, k),$$

for which

$$\mathbb{E}_k \left[\epsilon(\mathbf{F}_1, \mathbf{F}_6, k) \right] \leq \frac{(2q_f + 3q_e)(\beta_1 + \beta_2) + 2\beta_3(q_f + q_e)}{N}$$

$$+ \frac{2^r \cdot q_e q_f^2}{N^2} + \frac{2q_e(2q_f + q_e)(q_f + q_e) + q_e^3}{N^2}.$$

We now derive $\mathbb{E}_{\mathbf{F}_1, \mathbf{F}_6}[\mathbb{E}_k[\epsilon(\mathbf{F}_1, \mathbf{F}_2, k)] \mid \mathbf{F}_1 \vdash \mathcal{Q}_{F_1}, \mathbf{F}_6 \vdash \mathcal{Q}_{F_6}]$. To this end, note that by definition, β_1, β_2, and β_3 are quantities that depend on $(\mathbf{F}_1, \mathbf{F}_6)$:

$$\beta_1 = |\{(RX, AS) \in \mathcal{Q}_E^*(\mathbf{F}_1, \mathbf{F}_6) : k_2 \oplus X = k_2 \oplus L \oplus \mathbf{F}_1(k_1 \oplus R) \in Dom\mathcal{F}_2\}|,$$

$$\beta_2 = |\{(RX, AS) \in \mathcal{Q}_E^*(\mathbf{F}_1, \mathbf{F}_6) : k_5 \oplus A = k_5 \oplus T \oplus \mathbf{F}_6(k_6 \oplus S) \in Dom\mathcal{F}_5\}|,$$

$$\beta_3 = |\{(RX, AS) \in \mathcal{Q}_E^*(\mathbf{F}_1, \mathbf{F}_6) : \exists(R'X', A'S') \text{ such that } X = X', \text{ or:}$$
$$\exists(R'X', A'S') \in \mathcal{Q}_E^*(\mathbf{F}_1, \mathbf{F}_6) \text{ such that } A = A'\}|.$$

We consider β_1 first. For each $(RX, AS) \in \mathcal{Q}_E^*(\mathbf{F}_1, \mathbf{F}_6)$, if $k_1 \oplus R \in Dom\mathcal{F}_1$, then $k_2 \oplus X \notin Dom\mathcal{F}_2$ by $\neg$(B-2). Thus conditioned on $\mathbf{F}_1 \vdash \mathcal{Q}_{F_1}$, $\mathbf{F}_1(k_1 \oplus R)$ remains uniform, and $\Pr[k_2 \oplus L \oplus \mathbf{F}_1(k_1 \oplus R) \in Dom\mathcal{F}_2] \leq \frac{q_f}{N}$. Therefore,

$$\mathbb{E}_k[\beta_1] \leq \frac{q_e q_f}{N}.$$

Similarly by symmetry, using the randomness supplied by $\mathbf{F}_6$, $\mathbb{E}_k[\beta_2] \leq \frac{q_e q_f}{N}$.

Then we consider β_3. We fix a record (LR, ST) such that $k_1 \oplus R \notin Dom\mathcal{F}_1$, and consider another $(L'R', S'T')$. If $R = R'$ then it has to be $L \neq L'$ and thus $X \neq X'$. Otherwise, as $k_1 \oplus R \notin Dom\mathcal{F}_1$, $\mathbf{F}_1(k_1 \oplus R)$ remains random conditioned on $\mathbf{F}_1 \vdash \mathcal{Q}_{F_1}$, and $\Pr[X = X'] = \Pr[\mathbf{F}_1(k_1 \oplus R) = L \oplus L' \oplus \mathbf{F}_1(k_1 \oplus R')] = \frac{1}{N}$. The number of distinct pairs of such tuples is at most q_e^2. Thus we know the expectation of the number of pairs $((RX, AS), (R'X', A'S'))$ such that $X = X'$ is at most $\frac{q_e^2}{N}$. Thus

$$\mathbb{E}_k[|\{(RX, AS) : k_1 \oplus R \notin Dom\mathcal{F}_1, \text{ and } \exists(R'X', A'S') \text{ s.t. } X = X'\}|] \leq \frac{q_e^2}{N}.$$

As the number of (LR, ST) such that $k_1 \oplus R \in Dom\mathcal{F}_1$ is $\alpha_1(k)$, we obtain

$$\mathbb{E}_k[|\{(RX, AS) : \exists(R'X', A'S') \text{ s.t. } X = X'\}|] \leq \frac{q_e^2}{N} + \alpha_1(k).$$

Symmetrically, $\mathbb{E}_k[|\{(RX, AS) : \exists(R'X', A'S') \text{ s.t. } A = A'\}|] \leq \frac{q_e^2}{N} + \alpha_2(k)$. Thus $\mathbb{E}_k[\beta_3] \leq \frac{2q_e^2}{N} + \alpha_1(k) + \alpha_2(k)$.

Finally, since k_1, resp. k_6, are uniform in 2^n, resp. 2^{n-r} possibilities,

$$\mathbb{E}_k[\alpha_1(k)] = \sum_{(LR,ST)\in\mathcal{Q}_E} \sum_{(x_1,y_1)\in\mathcal{Q}_{F_1}} \Pr[k_1 = R \oplus x_1] \leq \frac{q_e q_f}{N}$$

and $\mathbb{E}_k[\alpha_2(k)] \leq \frac{2^r \cdot q_e q_f}{N}$. Gathering all the above yields

$$\mathbb{E}_{\mathbf{F}_1,\mathbf{F}_6,k}\big[\epsilon(\mathbf{F}_1, \mathbf{F}_6, k)\big] \leq \frac{4q_e q_f^2 + 6q_e^2 q_f}{N^2} + \frac{2(q_e + q_f)(2q_e^2 + q_e q_f + 2^r q_e q_f)}{N^2}$$
$$+ \frac{2^r \cdot q_e q_f^2}{N^2} + \frac{2q_e(2q_f + q_e)(q_f + q_e) + q_e^3}{N^2}$$
$$= \frac{7q_e^3 + 10q_e q_f^2 + 18q_e^2 q_f + 3 \cdot 2^r \cdot q_e q_f^2 + 2 \cdot 2^r \cdot q_e^2 q_f}{N^2},$$

as claimed in (8).   □

5.3   Concluding the Point-Wise Proximity Proof

Gathering Lemma 2, Lemma 5, and (6), we obtain

$$\frac{\Pr_{re}(\tau)}{\Pr_{id}(\tau)} \geq 1 - \left(\frac{3 \cdot 2^r q_e q_f^2}{N^2} + \mathbb{E}_k\big[\Pr[\mathsf{Bad}(\mathbf{F}_1, \mathbf{F}_6) \mid \mathbf{F}_1 \vdash \mathcal{Q}_{F_1}, \mathbf{F}_6 \vdash \mathcal{Q}_{F_6}]\big]\right.$$
$$\left. + \mathbb{E}_k\big[\mathbb{E}_{\mathbf{F}_1,\mathbf{F}_6}[\epsilon(\mathbf{F}_1, \mathbf{F}_6, k) \mid \mathbf{F}_1 \vdash \mathcal{Q}_{F_1}, \mathbf{F}_6 \vdash \mathcal{Q}_{F_6}]\big]\right),$$

where $\epsilon(\mathbf{F}_1, \mathbf{F}_6, k)$ is the function specified in (7). Note that its expectation has been bounded in Lemma 6.

For $\mathbb{E}_k[\Pr[\mathsf{Bad}(\mathbf{F}_1, \mathbf{F}_6) \mid \mathbf{F}_1 \vdash \mathcal{Q}_{F_1}, \mathbf{F}_6 \vdash \mathcal{Q}_{F_6}]]$, since k_3 and k_4 are both uniformly distributed (in 2^n and 2^{n-r} values, respectively), we have

$$\mathbb{E}_k[\alpha_{2,3}(k)] \leq \frac{q_e q_f^2}{N}, \text{ and } \mathbb{E}_k[\alpha_{4,5}(k)] \leq \frac{2^r q_e q_f^2}{N}.$$

At the end of the previous subsection we have shown $\mathbb{E}_k[\alpha_1(k)] \leq q_e q_f/N$ and $\mathbb{E}_k[\alpha_2(k)] \leq 2^r q_e q_f/N$. Injecting them into the bound of Lemma 4 yields

$$\mathbb{E}_k[\Pr[\mathsf{Bad}(\mathbf{F}_1, \mathbf{F}_6) \mid \mathbf{F}_1 \vdash \mathcal{Q}_{F_1}, \mathbf{F}_6 \vdash \mathcal{Q}_{F_6}]] \leq \frac{3q_e q_f^2}{N^2} + \frac{2 \cdot 2^r q_e q_f^2}{N^2} + \frac{4q_e^2 q_f}{N^2}.$$

Gathering all the above eventually establishes (5).

5.4 $(2n - r)/3$-bit Security from $2n - r$ Bits Main-Key, and PKEM

According to Definition 3, a suitable round-key vector could be derived from two independent main keys K and K', where $|K| = n$ and $|K'| = n - r$. A specific case is to alternatively apply the two keys. In this case, the construction collapses to a "partial-key" Even-Mansour variant

$$\mathsf{PKEM}^{\mathsf{LR}_6}_{0^r\|K'\|K}(M) = (0^r\|K'\|K) \oplus \mathsf{LR}_6((0^r\|K'\|K) \oplus M) \tag{12}$$

for LR_6 the 6-round keyless Feistel permutation built from 6 independent random functions; see Fig. 2 (right). On the other hand, with an orthomorphisms φ one could set the key vector to $(K, K', \varphi(K), \varphi(K'), K, K')$, with which the KAF would be a "normal" Feistel cipher rather than "collapsing" to PKEM.

6   Application: A Proposal for **KAF** Key-Schedules

To further demonstrate the usefulness of our theoretical results, we propose some concrete key-schedules for KAF ciphers. In detail, we propose to consider key-schedules with produced round-keys $(k_1, \ldots, k_t)$ satisfying the following three conditions:

(i) *Uniformness*: every k_i is uniform in $\{0, 1\}^n$;
(ii) *Pair-Wise Independence (PWI)*: any two round-keys k_i and k_j are independent;
(iii) *Distinctness*: it's hard to find weak keys K that gives rise to identical round-keys $k_1 = \ldots = k_t$.

The considerations behind PWI are two-fold. First, such round-keys satisfy both Definitions 1 and 3, and are thus supported by our theoretical results. Second, it's intuitively good: independence between round-keys plays a crucial role in our analysis, and would probably help simplify the proof for tighter bounds for 5 and 6 rounds.

The property *distinctness* is rather informal. It's intended to prevent the KAF cipher from collapsing to 1-round IEM. Note that PWI is able to prevent such collapsing with "significant probability"; however, this is not enough, since the number of (weak) main-keys that would cause such collapsing may not be small enough from the viewpoint of practitioners; see [28] for an example.

As discussed in the Introduction, common "word-aligned" key-schedules usually ensure *independence between adjacent round-keys*. This deviates from PWI, and the latter is not clear to be achieved by ad hoc designs. Fortunately, the three properties can be achieved from a $2n$-bit main-key $K = K_1\|K_2$ by efficient linear functions [37]. Below we exhibit an example. Let $\mathbb{F}_2^n$ be the set $\{0, 1\}^n$ seen as the field with 2^n elements defined by some irreducible polynomial of degree n over $\mathbb{F}_2$, the field with two elements, and denote $a \otimes b$ the field multiplication of two elements $a, b \in \mathbb{F}_2^n$. In addition, for $1 \leq t \ll 2^n$, let the constants a_t and

a_{t+1} be the t and $(t+1)^{\text{th}}$ values in the prime sequence $1, 2, 3, 5, 7, 11, 13, \ldots$ respectively. Then, for $t \ll 2^n$ rounds (which is usually the case), one can set

$$
\begin{aligned}
k_1 &= K_1 + 2 \otimes K_2, & k_2 &= 2 \otimes K_1 + 3 \otimes K_2, \\
k_3 &= 3 \otimes K_1 + 5 \otimes K_2, & k_4 &= 5 \otimes K_1 + 7 \otimes K_2, \\
\ldots, & & k_t &= a_t \otimes K_1 + a_{t+1} \otimes K_2,
\end{aligned}
$$

The proof for PWI is quite simple, and is given in the full version [28].

PWI cannot be achieved from $\kappa < 2n$ main-key bits. However, nowadays it's rather uncommon for a BC to have key-size smaller than its block-size. On the other hand, instances of Feistel ciphers with $2n$-bit blocks *and* $2n$-bit keys do exist: e.g. SIMON96/96 and SIMON128/128 [4].

More generally, with a cn-bit main-key for c integer we conjecture c-wise independent round-keys are desirable. This is however not revealed by our results. We leave this as an interesting future direction.

7   Other Implications

As multi-user secure BCs, our provable KAF constructions could be plugged into many BC-based modes to reduce the size of (ideal) primitives in use. In some cases, this even does not result in a security loss.

For example, Gaži et al. proved that when the adversary makes q queries of length $\ell < 2^{n/4}$, the PRF security bound of the truncated CBC mode built upon a $2n$-bit random permutation is roughly $\frac{q(q+\ell)}{2^{2n-d}} + \frac{\ell q^2}{2^{2n}}$, where d is the length of the output [23]. By this, instantiated with our 6-round KAF (with $r = 0$), the resulted bound is

$$
\frac{(\ell q)^3}{2^{2n}} + \frac{(\ell q)^2 q_f}{2^{2n}} + \frac{(\ell q) q_f^2}{2^{2n}} + \frac{q(q+\ell)}{2^{2n-d}} + \frac{\ell q^2}{2^{2n}},
$$

where q_f is the number of adversarial function queries. It can be seen that this is the same as the original when $d \geq 7n/6$ (i.e. the output is sufficiently long) and $q_f \ll 2^{2n/3}$.

7.1   Lightweight Keyed Sponges

A more interesting implication is on keyed sponges. Many lightweight keyed sponges with permutation π have their security rely on the (MU) security of the Even-Mansour variant $\mathsf{PKEM}^{\pi}_{0^r \| K' \| K}$ defined in (1) [1, 23, 43]. As our results imply the MU security of $\mathsf{PKEM}^{\mathsf{LR}_6}_{0^r \| K' \| K}$ (Subsect. 5.4, (12)), these keyed sponges could be based on $\mathsf{PKEM}^{\mathsf{LR}_6}_{0^r \| K' \| K}$ instead. And after the keys are canceled, we obtain keyed sponge variants using LR_6 as the permutation. This means the permutation underlying many keyed sponges can be securely instantiated with LR_6. This results in an improved implementation efficiency (maybe at the expense of a decreased security). And when $r < n/2$, security of resulted construction is beyond-birthday with respect to n, the size of the underlying ideal functions. This is usually fulfilled in lightweight sponges, since relatively large $c = 2n - r$ is desired: e.g. all the members in the Photon family [30].

Concretely, consider the "inner-keyed" sponge with a $2n$-bit permutation π first. By [1], for any distinguisher making q_c queries to the sponge and q_π queries to π, the corresponding distinguishing advantage (from a random oracle) is $\frac{q_c^2}{2^{2n-r}} + \mathbf{Adv}_{\mathsf{PKEM}^\pi_{0^r \| K \| K'}}^{\mathsf{SU}}(q_\pi, \sigma)$, where σ is the total number of blocks in the q_c construction queries. Therefore, by our results, the security bound of the inner-keyed sponge with LR_6 is

$$\frac{q_c^2}{2^{2n-r}} + \frac{\sigma^3}{2^{2n}} + \frac{\sigma^2 q_f}{2^{2n}} + \frac{\sigma q_f^2}{2^{2n}},$$

where q_f is the number of adversarial random function queries. It's not hard to see similar implications can be derived on "outer-keyed" sponge; however, we are unable to derive concrete bounds.

Another example is Chaskey [43], which is a sponge-like MAC of Mouha et al. With a $2n$-bit permutation π, the designers proved that the MAC security bound of Chaskey$^\pi$ is (roughly) $\frac{\sigma^2}{2^{2n}} + \frac{1}{d} + \mathbf{Adv}_{\mathsf{PKEM}^\pi_{K \| K'}}^{\mathsf{MU}}(q_\pi, \sigma)$, where d is the tag size, σ is total number of blocks in the adversarial MAC queries, and q_π is the number of adversarial queries to π. Therefore, the security bound of the variant Chaskey$^{\mathsf{LR}_6}$ is $\frac{\sigma^2}{2^{2n}} + \frac{1}{d} + \frac{\sigma^3}{2^{2n}} + \frac{\sigma^2 q_f}{2^{2n}} + \frac{\sigma q_f^2}{2^{2n}}$, where q_f is the number of adversarial random function queries.

Acknowledgements. We thank the reviewers for invaluable comments, and for pointing [25] to us. Chun Guo is funded in part by the ERC project 724725 (acronym SWORD), and would like to thank François-Xavier Standaert for the invaluable support. Lei Wang is supported by National Natural Science Foundation of China (61602302, 61472250, 61672347), Natural Science Foundation of Shanghai (16ZR1416400), Shanghai Excellent Academic Leader Funds (16XD1401300), 13th five-year National Development Fund of Cryptography (MMJJ20170114).

Finally we thank Yaobin Shen for identifying a flaw (in Lemma 5) in an earlier version of the proof, and Christian Rechberger and Damian Vizár for the discussion on multi-party computation.

References

1. Andreeva, E., Daemen, J., Mennink, B., Van Assche, G.: Security of keyed sponge constructions using a modular proof approach. In: Leander, G. (ed.) FSE 2015. LNCS, vol. 9054, pp. 364–384. Springer, Heidelberg (2015). https://doi.org/10.1007/978-3-662-48116-5_18

2. Bar-On, A., Biham, E., Dunkelman, O., Keller, N.: Efficient slide attacks. J. Cryptol. **31**(3), 641–670 (2017)

3. Barbosa, M., Farshim, P.: The related-key analysis of Feistel constructions. In: Cid, C., Rechberger, C. (eds.) FSE 2014. LNCS, vol. 8540, pp. 265–284. Springer, Heidelberg (2015). https://doi.org/10.1007/978-3-662-46706-0_14

4. Beaulieu, R., Shors, D., Smith, J., Treatman-Clark, S., Weeks, B., Wingers, L.: The SIMON and SPECK families of lightweight block ciphers. Cryptology ePrint Archive, Report 2013/404 (2013). https://eprint.iacr.org/2013/404.pdf
5. Bellare, M., Boldyreva, A., Micali, S.: Public-key encryption in a multi-user setting: security proofs and improvements. In: Preneel, B. (ed.) EUROCRYPT 2000. LNCS, vol. 1807, pp. 259–274. Springer, Heidelberg (2000). https://doi.org/10.1007/3-540-45539-6_18
6. Bellare, M., Tackmann, B.: The multi-user security of authenticated encryption: AES-GCM in TLS 1.3. In: Robshaw, M., Katz, J. (eds.) CRYPTO 2016, part I. LNCS, vol. 9814, pp. 247–276. Springer, Heidelberg (2016). https://doi.org/10.1007/978-3-662-53018-4_10
7. Bertoni, G., Daemen, J., Peeters, M., Van Assche, G.: Sponge functions. In: Ecrypt Hash Workshop 2007 (2007)
8. Biham, E.: How to decrypt or even substitute DES-encrypted messages in 2^{28} steps. Inf. Process. Lett. **84**(3), 117–124 (2002)
9. Biryukov, A., Nikolić, I.: Complementing Feistel ciphers. In: Moriai, S. (ed.) FSE 2013. LNCS, vol. 8424, pp. 3–18. Springer, Heidelberg (2014). https://doi.org/10.1007/978-3-662-43933-3_1
10. Biryukov, A., Wagner, D.: Advanced slide attacks. In: Preneel, B. (ed.) EUROCRYPT 2000. LNCS, vol. 1807, pp. 589–606. Springer, Heidelberg (2000). https://doi.org/10.1007/3-540-45539-6_41
11. Bogdanov, A., Knudsen, L.R., Leander, G., Standaert, F.-X., Steinberger, J., Tischhauser, E.: Key-alternating ciphers in a provable setting: encryption using a small number of public permutations. In: Pointcheval, D., Johansson, T. (eds.) EUROCRYPT 2012. LNCS, vol. 7237, pp. 45–62. Springer, Heidelberg (2012). https://doi.org/10.1007/978-3-642-29011-4_5
12. Bose, P., Hoang, V.T., Tessaro, S.: Revisiting AES-GCM-SIV: multi-user security, faster key derivation, and better bounds. In: Nielsen, J.B., Rijmen, V. (eds.) EUROCRYPT 2018, part I. LNCS, vol. 10820, pp. 468–499. Springer, Cham (2018). https://doi.org/10.1007/978-3-319-78381-9_18
13. Canetti, R., Goldreich, O., Halevi, S.: The random Oracle methodology. Revisit. J. ACM **51**(4), 557–594 (2004)
14. Chen, S., Lampe, R., Lee, J., Seurin, Y., Steinberger, J.: Minimizing the Two-Round Even-Mansour cipher. J. Cryptol. **31**(4), 1064–119 (2018)
15. Chen, S., Steinberger, J.: Tight security bounds for key-alternating ciphers. In: Nguyen, P.Q., Oswald, E. (eds.) EUROCRYPT 2014. LNCS, vol. 8441, pp. 327–350. Springer, Heidelberg (2014). https://doi.org/10.1007/978-3-642-55220-5_19
16. Cogliati, B., Lampe, R., Seurin, Y.: Tweaking Even-Mansour ciphers. In: Gennaro, R., Robshaw, M. (eds.) CRYPTO 2015, part I. LNCS, vol. 9215, pp. 189–208. Springer, Heidelberg (2015). https://doi.org/10.1007/978-3-662-47989-6_9
17. Cogliati, B., Seurin, Y.: Beyond-birthday-bound security for tweakable Even-Mansour ciphers with linear tweak and key mixing. In: Iwata, T., Cheon, J.H. (eds.) ASIACRYPT 2015, part II. LNCS, vol. 9453, pp. 134–158. Springer, Heidelberg (2015). https://doi.org/10.1007/978-3-662-48800-3_6
18. Daemen, J., Rijmen, V.: Probability distributions of correlation and differentials in block ciphers. J. Math. Cryptol. **1**(3), 221–242 (2007)
19. Dai, Y., Seurin, Y., Steinberger, J., Thiruvengadam, A.: Indifferentiability of iterated even-mansour ciphers with non-idealized key-schedules: five rounds are necessary and sufficient. In: Katz, J., Shacham, H. (eds.) CRYPTO 2017, part III. LNCS, vol. 10403, pp. 524–555. Springer, Cham (2017). https://doi.org/10.1007/978-3-319-63697-9_18

20. Dodis, Y., Katz, J., Steinberger, J., Thiruvengadam, A., Zhang, Z.: Provable security of substitution-permutation networks. Cryptology ePrint Archive, Report 2017/016 (2017). http://eprint.iacr.org/2017/016.pdf
21. Dunkelman, O., Keller, N., Shamir, A.: Slidex attacks on the Even-Mansour encryption scheme. J. Cryptol. **28**(1), 1–28 (2015)
22. Even, S., Mansour, Y.: A construction of a cipher from a single pseudorandom permutation. J. Cryptol. **10**(3), 151–161 (1997)
23. Gaži, P., Pietrzak, K., Tessaro, S.: The exact PRF security of truncation: tight bounds for keyed sponges and truncated CBC. In: Gennaro, R., Robshaw, M. (eds.) CRYPTO 2015, part I. LNCS, vol. 9215, pp. 368–387. Springer, Heidelberg (2015). https://doi.org/10.1007/978-3-662-47989-6_18
24. Gentry, C., Ramzan, Z.: Eliminating random permutation oracles in the Even-Mansour cipher. In: Lee, P.J. (ed.) ASIACRYPT 2004. LNCS, vol. 3329, pp. 32–47. Springer, Heidelberg (2004). https://doi.org/10.1007/978-3-540-30539-2_3
25. Gilboa, S., Gueron, S., Nandi, M.: Balanced permutations Even-Mansour ciphers. Cryptography **1**(1), 2 (2017)
26. Gueron, S., Lindell, Y.: Better bounds for block cipher modes of operation via nonce-based key derivation. CCS **2017**, 1019–1036 (2017)
27. Guo, C., Lin, D.: On the indifferentiability of key-alternating Feistel ciphers with no key derivation. In: Dodis, Y., Nielsen, J.B. (eds.) TCC 2015, part I. LNCS, vol. 9014, pp. 110–133. Springer, Heidelberg (2015). https://doi.org/10.1007/978-3-662-46494-6_6
28. Guo, C., Wang, L.: Revisiting key-alternating Feistel ciphers for shorter keys and multi-user security. Cryptology ePrint Archive, Report 2018/816 (2018). http://eprint.iacr.org/2018/816.pdf. The full version of this paper
29. Guo, J., Jean, J., Nikolić, I., Sasaki, Y.: Meet-in-the-middle attacks on generic Feistel constructions. In: Sarkar, P., Iwata, T. (eds.) ASIACRYPT 2014, part I. LNCS, vol. 8873, pp. 458–477. Springer, Heidelberg (2014). https://doi.org/10.1007/978-3-662-45611-8_24
30. Guo, J., Peyrin, T., Poschmann, A.: The PHOTON family of lightweight hash functions. In: Rogaway, P. (ed.) CRYPTO 2011. LNCS, vol. 6841, pp. 222–239. Springer, Heidelberg (2011). https://doi.org/10.1007/978-3-642-22792-9_13
31. Hoang, V.T., Rogaway, P.: On generalized Feistel networks. In: Rabin, T. (ed.) CRYPTO 2010. LNCS, vol. 6223, pp. 613–630. Springer, Heidelberg (2010). https://doi.org/10.1007/978-3-642-14623-7_33
32. Hoang, V.T., Tessaro, S.: Key-alternating ciphers and key-length extension: exact bounds and multi-user security. In: Robshaw, M., Katz, J. (eds.) CRYPTO 2016, part I. LNCS, vol. 9814, pp. 3–32. Springer, Heidelberg (2016). https://doi.org/10.1007/978-3-662-53018-4_1
33. Isobe, T., Shibutani, K.: Generic key recovery attack on Feistel scheme. In: Sako, K., Sarkar, P. (eds.) ASIACRYPT 2013, part I. LNCS, vol. 8269, pp. 464–485. Springer, Heidelberg (2013). https://doi.org/10.1007/978-3-642-42033-7_24
34. Izadi, M., Sadeghiyan, B., Sadeghian, S.S., Khanooki, H.A.: MIBS: a new lightweight block cipher. In: Garay, J.A., Miyaji, A., Otsuka, A. (eds.) CANS 2009. LNCS, vol. 5888, pp. 334–348. Springer, Heidelberg (2009). https://doi.org/10.1007/978-3-642-10433-6_22
35. Jager, T., Stam, M., Stanley-Oakes, R., Warinschi, B.: Multi-key authenticated encryption with corruptions: reductions are lossy. In: Kalai, Y., Reyzin, L. (eds.) TCC 2017. LNCS, vol. 10677, pp. 409–441. Springer, Cham (2017). https://doi.org/10.1007/978-3-319-70500-2_14

36. Lampe, R., Seurin, Y.: Security analysis of key-alternating Feistel ciphers. In: Cid, C., Rechberger, C. (eds.) FSE 2014. LNCS, vol. 8540, pp. 243–264. Springer, Heidelberg (2015). https://doi.org/10.1007/978-3-662-46706-0_13

37. Luby, M., Wigderson, A.: Pairwise independence and derandomization. Found. Trends Theor. Comput. Sci. **1**(4), 237–301 (2005)

38. Luby, M.G., Rackoff, C.: Pseudo-random permutation generators and cryptographic composition. In: Proceedings of the Eighteenth Annual ACM Symposium on Theory of Computing, STOC 1986, pp. 356–363. ACM, New York (1986)

39. Mandal, A., Patarin, J., Seurin, Y.: On the public indifferentiability and correlation intractability of the 6-round Feistel construction. In: Cramer, R. (ed.) TCC 2012. LNCS, vol. 7194, pp. 285–302. Springer, Heidelberg (2012). https://doi.org/10.1007/978-3-642-28914-9_16

40. Maurer, U., Pietrzak, K.: The security of many-round Luby-Rackoff pseudorandom permutations. In: Biham, E. (ed.) EUROCRYPT 2003. LNCS, vol. 2656, pp. 544–561. Springer, Heidelberg (2003). https://doi.org/10.1007/3-540-39200-9_34

41. Miles, E., Viola, E.: Substitution-permutation networks, pseudorandom functions, and natural proofs. In: Safavi-Naini, R., Canetti, R. (eds.) CRYPTO 2012. LNCS, vol. 7417, pp. 68–85. Springer, Heidelberg (2012). https://doi.org/10.1007/978-3-642-32009-5_5

42. Mouha, N., Luykx, A.: Multi-key security: the even-mansour construction revisited. In: Gennaro, R., Robshaw, M. (eds.) CRYPTO 2015, part I. LNCS, vol. 9215, pp. 209–223. Springer, Heidelberg (2015). https://doi.org/10.1007/978-3-662-47989-6_10

43. Mouha, N., Mennink, B., Van Herrewege, A., Watanabe, D., Preneel, B., Verbauwhede, I.: Chaskey: an efficient MAC algorithm for 32-bit microcontrollers. In: Joux, A., Youssef, A. (eds.) SAC 2014. LNCS, vol. 8781, pp. 306–323. Springer, Cham (2014). https://doi.org/10.1007/978-3-319-13051-4_19

44. Nachef, V., Patarin, J., Volte, E.: Feistel Ciphers. Security Proofs and Cryptanalysis. Springer, Cham (2017). https://doi.org/10.1007/978-3-319-49530-9

45. Nandi, M.: The characterization of Luby-Rackoff and its optimum single-key variants. In: Gong, G., Gupta, K.C. (eds.) INDOCRYPT 2010. LNCS, vol. 6498, pp. 82–97. Springer, Heidelberg (2010). https://doi.org/10.1007/978-3-642-17401-8_7

46. Nandi, M.: On the optimality of non-linear computations of length-preserving encryption schemes. In: Iwata, T., Cheon, J.H. (eds.) ASIACRYPT 2015, part II. LNCS, vol. 9453, pp. 113–133. Springer, Heidelberg (2015). https://doi.org/10.1007/978-3-662-48800-3_5

47. Patarin, J.: How to construct pseudorandom and super pseudorandom permutations from one single pseudorandom function. In: Rueppel, R.A. (ed.) EUROCRYPT 1992. LNCS, vol. 658, pp. 256–266. Springer, Heidelberg (1993). https://doi.org/10.1007/3-540-47555-9_22

48. Patarin, J.: Improved security bounds for pseudorandom permutations. In: CCS 1997, pp. 142–150. ACM (1997)

49. Patarin, J.: Security of random Feistel schemes with 5 or more rounds. In: Franklin, M. (ed.) CRYPTO 2004. LNCS, vol. 3152, pp. 106–122. Springer, Heidelberg (2004). https://doi.org/10.1007/978-3-540-28628-8_7

50. Ramzan, Z., Reyzin, L.: On the round security of symmetric-key cryptographic primitives. In: Bellare, M. (ed.) CRYPTO 2000. LNCS, vol. 1880, pp. 376–393. Springer, Heidelberg (2000). https://doi.org/10.1007/3-540-44598-6_24

51. Rotaru, D., Smart, N.P., Stam, M.: Modes of operation suitable for computing on encrypted data. IACR Trans. Symmetric Cryptol. **2017**(3), 294–324 (2017)

52. Sadeghiyan, B., Pieprzyk, J.: A construction for super pseudorandom permutations from a single pseudorandom function. In: Rueppel, R.A. (ed.) EUROCRYPT 1992. LNCS, vol. 658, pp. 267–284. Springer, Heidelberg (1993). https://doi.org/10.1007/3-540-47555-9_23

53. Soni, P., Tessaro, S.: Public-seed pseudorandom permutations. In: Coron, J.-S., Nielsen, J.B. (eds.) EUROCRYPT 2017, part II. LNCS, vol. 10211, pp. 412–441. Springer, Cham (2017). https://doi.org/10.1007/978-3-319-56614-6_14

54. Standaert, F.-X., Pereira, O., Yu, Y.: Leakage-resilient symmetric cryptography under empirically verifiable assumptions. In: Canetti, R., Garay, J.A. (eds.) CRYPTO 2013. LNCS, vol. 8042, pp. 335–352. Springer, Heidelberg (2013). https://doi.org/10.1007/978-3-642-40041-4_19

55. Suzaki, T., Minematsu, K., Morioka, S., Kobayashi, E.: *TWINE*: a lightweight block cipher for multiple platforms. In: Knudsen, L.R., Wu, H. (eds.) SAC 2012. LNCS, vol. 7707, pp. 339–354. Springer, Heidelberg (2013)

56. Tessaro, S.: Optimally secure block ciphers from ideal primitives. In: Iwata, T., Cheon, J.H. (eds.) ASIACRYPT 2015, part II. LNCS, vol. 9453, pp. 437–462. Springer, Heidelberg (2015). https://doi.org/10.1007/978-3-662-48800-3_18

57. Wu, W., Zhang, L.: LBlock: a lightweight block cipher. In: Lopez, J., Tsudik, G. (eds.) ACNS 2011. LNCS, vol. 6715, pp. 327–344. Springer, Heidelberg (2011). https://doi.org/10.1007/978-3-642-21554-4_19

Short Variable Length Domain Extenders with Beyond Birthday Bound Security

Yu Long Chen[1(✉)], Bart Mennink[2], and Mridul Nandi[3]

[1] imec -COSIC, KU Leuven, Leuven, Belgium
yulong.chen@kuleuven.be
[2] Digital Security Group, Radboud University, Nijmegen, The Netherlands
b.mennink@cs.ru.nl
[3] Indian Statistical Institute, Kolkata, India
mridul.nandi@gmail.com

Abstract. Length doublers are cryptographic functions that transform an n-bit cryptographic primitive into an efficient and secure cipher that length-preservingly encrypts strings of length in $[n, 2n-1]$. All currently known constructions are only proven secure up to the birthday bound, and for all but one construction this bound is known to be tight. We consider the remaining candidate, LDT by Chen et al. (ToSC 2017(3)), and prove that it achieves beyond the birthday bound security for the domain $[n, 3n/2)$. We generalize the construction to multiple rounds and demonstrate that by adding one more encryption layer to LDT, beyond the birthday bound security can be achieved for all strings of length in $[n, 2n-1]$: security up to around $2^{2n/3}$ for the encryption of strings close to n and security up to around 2^n for strings of length close to $2n$. The security analysis of both schemes is performed in a modular manner through the introduction and analysis of a new concept called "harmonic permutation primitives."

Keywords: Length doublers · LDT · Beyond birthday bound
Harmonic primitives · Chi-squared

1 Introduction

Block ciphers are keyed deterministic functions that encrypt bit strings of a fixed size n bits to ciphertext blocks of the same size. They play a predominant role in cryptography, and yet, most cryptographic applications deal with arbitrary-length messages. To achieve this, the applications evaluate a block cipher in a certain mode of operation.

A simple example of this is counter mode encryption. Given block cipher E_K on n bits, counter mode encrypts a message M of arbitrary length as follows. First, the message is partitioned into blocks $M_1, \ldots, M_\ell$, where the first $\ell - 1$ are of size n bits, and the last one may be smaller. Second, the message is encrypted as

$$C_i = E_k(\text{ctr} + i) \oplus M_i \text{ for } i = 1, \ldots, \ell,$$

© International Association for Cryptologic Research 2018
T. Peyrin and S. Galbraith (Eds.): ASIACRYPT 2018, LNCS 11272, pp. 244–274, 2018.
https://doi.org/10.1007/978-3-030-03326-2_9

where the ℓ-th ciphertext block is truncated to have the same size as M_ℓ, and where ctr is a carefully specified counter.

Counter mode is unique in the sense that it allows for easy length-preservation due to its "streaming" property. Whereas this property is fine in some use cases, in many others it is lacking. For example, stream cipher encryption is inapplicable to disk sector encryption for security reasons. Alternative encryption modes like CBC [47], OCB [26,38,39], XTS [15], and TC3 [41], however, feed the message to the block cipher and there is no easy way of keeping length preservation. One often pads input to size a multiple of n-blocks and takes ciphertext expansion for granted [1,2,26,28]. Ciphertext expansion is, in many cases, not desirable: it creates overhead, making it unsuitable for disk encryption and low-bandwidth network protocols.

A generic method for length-preserving variable-length encryption is ciphertext stealing [13,40]. Informally, it encrypts the first $\ell - 1$ blocks as is, but to encrypt the non-integral ℓ-th block, it is first expanded to n bits by scraping sufficiently many ciphertext bits from the $(\ell - 1)$-th block and gluing these to M_ℓ. The approach is appealing, but it only works on modes of use for which ciphertext blocks can be decrypted independently of each other: otherwise one cannot recover the ciphertext bits scraped off of $C_{\ell-1}$.

Besides these two generic solutions, many dedicated designs that support variable-length encryption have appeared, e.g., EME [20], TET [21], HEH [43], HCTR [46], HCH [10], and XCB [27], but a golden method for generically transforming an existing block cipher mode of operation for integral data to one for arbitrary-length data was long due.

1.1 Length Doublers

In 2007, Ristenpart and Rogaway [37] introduced *length doublers* as an elegant way of achieving variable-length encryption. A length doubler is a length-preserving encryption mode on the set of bit strings of size between n and $2n-1$ bits, where n is the state size of the underlying primitive.

By allowing flexibility of the size of the second block, length doublers suit well as modular building blocks for variable-length encryption and authenticated encryption. For example, whereas the possibility to apply ciphertext stealing depends on the mode in consideration, length doubling can be used generically for black-box authenticated encryption schemes as demonstrated by Chen et al. [11]. We discuss further applications of length doublers in Sect. 1.4.

Alongside the formalization, Ristenpart and Rogaway introduced the XLS length doubler, based on three block cipher calls and two evaluations of a so-called ϵ-*good mixing function*. It found application in first-round CAESAR submission AES-COPA [2,3]. Only 7 years after its introduction, Nandi found an attack on XLS [32], an attack that also rendered the solution in the COPA mode insecure [34]. Nandi further proved that a secure length doubler must make at least four block cipher calls [33]. Other length doublers introduced after XLS are DE by Nandi [31] and HEM by Zhang [48], both of which make four block cipher calls and match the lower bound of [33].

Chen et al. considered the design of length doublers from tweakable block ciphers and introduced LDT [11]. It makes two calls to a tweakable block cipher and uses a *pure mixing function*, noting that an ϵ-good mixing function is pure but not necessarily vice versa. The transition to using tweakable block ciphers is a natural one: 18 initial submissions to the CAESAR competition were based on tweakable block ciphers, various novel cryptographic authentication and/or encryption modes use a tweakable block cipher as black box [23,35,41,45], and dedicated tweakable block ciphers like TWEAKEY [24] and SKINNY [5] are gaining traction. The recently announced ARMv8.3 [36] uses an implementation of the lightweight tweakable blockcipher QARMA [4]. The approach allows for more modular (and thus simpler) security proofs.

1.2 Towards Beyond Birthday Bound Security

All of the length doublers mentioned so far, barring XLS, are proven secure up to $2^{n/2}$. For DE and HEM this bound is tight as there is an attack matching this complexity. For LDT, Chen et al. [11] derived an attack in approximately $2^{n-s/2}$ queries, as long as all queries are of size at least $n+s$. The bound suggests tightness for $s = n - 1$, but it leaves the possibility of proving beyond birthday bound security for $s \ll n - 1$ open.

Although all length doublers known to date have only birthday bound proven security, beyond birthday bound secure length doublers are relevant for various scenarios. First, consider the case of a cryptographic mode that uses a length doubler in a black-box manner and achieves beyond birthday bound security. If it is instantiated with any off-the-shelf solution (DE, HEM, LDT) the provable security guarantee degrades to birthday bound security. Second, considering the case of format-preserving encryption and electronic product code tag encryption (see Sect. 1.4), using a birthday bound secure length doubler with a lightweight 64-bit block cipher yields 32-bit security at best. A beyond birthday bound secure length doubler would guarantee security up to well beyond 32 bits.

1.3 Our Contribution

We challenge the problem of proving beyond birthday bound security of length doublers. The starting point of our work is Chen et al.'s LDT: it is simple, modular, and so far the only existing candidate that may offer beyond birthday bound security.

As first contribution, we prove in Sect. 5 that the original LDT achieves beyond the birthday security for queries of size in $[n, 3n/2)$: if only evaluations of size around n are permitted, $2n/3$-bit security is achieved, but if evaluations of size around $3n/2$ are permitted, the proven security bound degrades to $n/2$. The bound is not tight, but we recall that Chen et al. [11] already demonstrated a birthday bound attack if $s = n - 1$, testifying of the fact that the security *decreases* with s. As second and main contribution, we generalize the mode to r-round LDT, recalling that the original construction consists of 2 rounds, and prove in Sect. 6 that 3-round LDT achieves beyond the birthday bound security for the entire domain $[n, 2n-1]$. As proven so far, the security of 3-round LDT *increases* with s: for evaluations of size around n we achieve $2n/3$-bit security, and for evaluations of size around $2n$ we get optimal n-bit security. Figure 1 plots the simplified security results of 2-LDT and 3-LDT for bit strings of length in $\{n, 5n/4, 3n/2, 7n/4, 2n-1\}$ (these data are taken from the discussion in Sects. 5 and 6). In aforementioned example of an 80-bit cipher using a 64-bit primitive, 3-LDT achieves $2^{3n/4} = 2^{48}$ security.

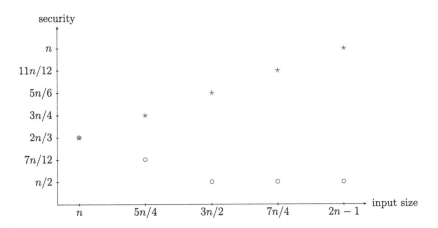

Fig. 1. Security bound of 2-LDT and 3-LDT for various choices of input size, where $\circ$ stands for 2-LDT and $\star$ stands for 3-LDT.

Central to our proofs is the introduction and usage of a new concept: "harmonic permutation primitives." These can be seen as lazily-sampled permutations where one part of the state is always sampled uniformly at random and the other part in such a way that permutation consistency is maintained. We describe two harmonic primitives: a harmonic tweakable permutation in Sect. 4.1 and a harmonic variable-length pseudorandom permutation in Sect. 4.2.

These harmonic permutation primitives allow for compact, neat, and modular security proofs of both 2-round and 3-round LDT. Both proofs use the two harmonic permutation primitives of Sect. 4 in a different setting, but using the chi-squared method by Dai et al. [14] and properties of the hypergeometric distribution, security of both LDT modes is reduced to the security of the harmonic permutation primitives. What then remains is an analysis of these primitives in Sects. 7 and 8.

Inspired by the proof approach in this work, one may likewise use the two harmonic permutation primitives to prove security of r-round LDT for $r \geq 4$. However, it would only render marginal improvement of the bound, with a large efficiency penalty. It nevertheless appears that the idea of harmonic permutation primitives and our proof technique may be broadly applicable beyond LDT, for example in the direction of sponge functions [7].

1.4   Application

An example use case of length doublers is format-preserving encryption, a field that got significant attention recently in light of the standardization [16] of FF1 [6] and FF3 [8]. Format-preserving encryption considers the problem of encrypting data from a small domain that does not fit the parameters of standardized block ciphers. For example, there is no practical way to length-preservingly encrypt 80-bit strings using AES-128 (other than streaming-based). Whereas the standardized FF1 and FF3 are made to facilitate arbitrary types of domains, for certain cases this can equally well be resolved using a length doubler. Above example of 80-bit strings can be resolved with a birthday bound secure length doubler on top of a lightweight 64-bit tweakable block cipher, but that would only give 32-bit security. As shown in Fig. 1, for this scenario 2-LDT would achieve around 37-bit security and 3-LDT even 48-bit security.

A more concrete example is that of electronic product code tag encryption, which is considered as a replacement for bar codes using low-cost passive RFID-tags. The standard EPC Class 1 Gen 2 RFID tag [18] proposes to use a unique 96-bit identifier for any physical item [19]. As for above generic case, a birthday bound secure length doubler on top of a 64-bit block cipher would give 32-bit security at best. Our bound of 2-LDT does not improve for this regime (see Fig. 1), but 3-LDT does achieve beyond birthday bound security: instantiated with a 64-bit tweakable block cipher, it reaches around 53-bit security.

It is straightforward to transform r-LDT into a *tweakable* length doubler, where the tweak is fed as additional tweak input to the underlying tweakable block ciphers (this requires extending the tweak space of the underlying primitive). This observation has two implications. First, one can obtain multi-user security of r-LDT by considering user IDs as tweak inputs and feeding those to the underlying tweakable block cipher. Second, r-LDT is an interesting and non-obvious generalization of the tweakable block cipher based domain extender of Coron et al. [12]. Stated simply, Coron et al. considered the problem of transforming a tweakable block cipher with $2n$-bit tweaks and n-bit blocks into a domain extender with n-bit tweaks and $2n$-bit blocks. They presented a 2-round scheme (achieving birthday bound security) and a 3-round scheme (achieving optimal n-bit security). Our tweakable length doublers, instead, transform that tweakable block cipher into a length doubler with n-bit tweaks and $[n, 2n - 1]$-bit blocks, therewith enabling support for variable length input. For the specific case of $s \approx n$, our schemes achieve the same level of security as those of [12].

Finally, we remark that if one considers 2-LDT for fixed s, and sandwiches it by two universal hash functions in a specific way, the resulting construction is identical to the Small-Block Cipher (SBC) construction proposed by Minematsu and Iwata [30] (an extension of ENR [29]). As SBC is designed to achieve beyond birthday bound security quite efficiently, it makes sense to compare it with 3-LDT. It turns out that 3-LDT compares favorably in various aspects. First, Minematsu and Iwata showed that SBC achieves $(n + s)/2$-bit security, whereas 3-LDT achieves $(2n + s)/3$-bit security for any fixed s (see also the last column of Table 1 in Sect. 6). Second, SBC uses two tweakable block ciphers and two universal hash functions, whereas 3-LDT uses three tweakable block ciphers. The latter could be beneficial for implementation on constrained devices. Finally, SBC is ultimately still a fixed input length cipher, whereas 3-LDT allows for inputs of size $[n, 2n - 1]$.

2 Preliminaries

For $n \in \mathbb{N}$, we denote the set of all bit strings of length n as $\{0,1\}^n$, and the set of all bit strings of arbitrary length as $\{0,1\}^*$. For $m \in \mathbb{N}$ and $m \leq n$ we define $\{0,1\}^{[m,n]} = \bigcup_{m \leq i \leq n} \{0,1\}^i$. Given two bit strings $X, Y \in \{0,1\}^*$, we use both $X\|Y$ and XY interchangeably to denote their concatenation. The length of X is denoted $|X|$, and if X and Y satisfy $|X| = |Y|$, we denote their bitwise addition as $X \oplus Y$. For $X \in \{0,1\}^n$, we denote $\mathsf{left}_m(X)$ the m leftmost bits of X and $\mathsf{right}_m(X)$ the m rightmost bits of X, in such a way that $X = \mathsf{left}_{n-m}(X)\|\mathsf{right}_m(X)$.

For $n \in \mathbb{N}$ and $X \in \{0,1\}^{[0,n-1]}$, we define a padding function $\mathsf{pad}(X) = X\|10^{n-|X|-1}$. We denote its inverse unpad that on input of a string of length n removes the rightmost string 10^* and returns the resulting string. Note that unpad is an injective mapping.

The expression $S \leftarrow T$ denotes the assignment of the value T to variable S, $\mathcal{L} \xleftarrow{\cup} S$ the addition of S to list $\mathcal{L}$, and $S \xleftarrow{\$} \mathcal{S}$ for finite set $\mathcal{S}$ the uniformly random sampling of S from $\mathcal{S}$. For an algorithm $\mathcal{D}$ and a function/oracle $\mathcal{O}$, $\mathcal{D}^{\mathcal{O}}$ represents the evaluation of $\mathcal{D}$ with oracle interaction to $\mathcal{O}$, and $\Delta_{\mathcal{D}}\left(\mathcal{O} ; \mathcal{P}\right)$ represents the advantage of $\mathcal{D}$ in distinguishing $\mathcal{O}$ from an oracle $\mathcal{P}$.

2.1 (Tweakable) Block Ciphers

For arbitrary finite key space $\mathcal{K}$ and $n \in \mathbb{N}$, a block cipher is a function $E : \mathcal{K} \times \{0,1\}^n \to \{0,1\}^n$ such that for every fixed key $K \in \mathcal{K}$, $E_K(\cdot) = E(K, \cdot)$ is a permutation on $\{0,1\}^n$. We denote its inverse for fixed key K by $E_K^{-1}(\cdot) = E^{-1}(K, \cdot)$. Denote by $\mathrm{Perm}(n)$ the set of all permutations on $\{0,1\}^n$. Tweakable block ciphers generalize over ordinary block ciphers by input of a t-bit tweak, for $t \in \mathbb{N}$. More detailed, a tweakable block cipher is a function $\tilde{E} : \mathcal{K} \times \{0,1\}^t \times \{0,1\}^n \to \{0,1\}^n$ such that for every fixed key $K \in \mathcal{K}$ and tweak $T \in \{0,1\}^t$, $\tilde{E}_K(T, \cdot) = \tilde{E}(K, T, \cdot)$ is a permutation on $\{0,1\}^n$. Its inverse for fixed key K and tweak T is denoted by $\tilde{E}_K^{-1}(T, \cdot) = \tilde{E}^{-1}(K, T, \cdot)$. Denote by $\widetilde{\mathrm{Perm}}(t, n)$ the set of all families of permutations $\tilde{\pi} : \{0,1\}^t \times \{0,1\}^n \to \{0,1\}^n$ indexed by tweak $T \in \{0,1\}^t$.

The security of a tweakable block cipher $\tilde{E}$ is measured by considering a distinguisher $\mathcal{D}$ that has two-sided query access to either $\tilde{E}_K$ for a randomly drawn key $K \xleftarrow{\$} \mathcal{K}$, or a random tweakable permutation $\tilde{\pi} \xleftarrow{\$} \widetilde{\mathrm{Perm}}(t, n)$, and its goal is try to distinguish the real construction from the ideal one:

$$\mathbf{Adv}_{\tilde{E}}^{\widetilde{\mathrm{sprp}}}(\mathcal{D}) = \left| \Pr\left[K \xleftarrow{\$} \mathcal{K} : \mathcal{D}^{\tilde{E}_K^{\pm}} = 1 \right] - \Pr\left[\tilde{\pi} \xleftarrow{\$} \widetilde{\mathrm{Perm}}(t, n) : \mathcal{D}^{\tilde{\pi}^{\pm}} = 1 \right] \right|.$$

For the left probability, the key space $\mathcal{K}$ is a fair representation of the randomness of $\tilde{E}_{\mathcal{K}}^{\pm}$. Often, it is the set of k-bit strings, where k is the key size. In proofs, specifically in hybrid arguments within proofs, one regularly considers tweakable block ciphers with idealized primitives. For example, one may consider the construction of a tweakable block cipher $\tilde{E}$ from a secret permutation (that could, in turn, be instantiated using a block cipher with secret key). In this case, the key space of $\tilde{E}$ is $\mathcal{K} = \mathrm{Perm}(n)$. More involved examples appear if the construction internally consists of lazy sampling, as will for instance be the case with our harmonic tweakable SPRP in Sect. 4.1.

2.2 Chi-Squared Method

Our proof will rely on the chi-squared method by Dai et al. [14].

Consider two stateless systems $\mathcal{O}_0, \mathcal{O}_1$ and any computationally unbounded deterministic distinguisher $\mathcal{D}$ that has query access to either of these systems. The distinguisher's goal is to distinguish both systems. If we denote the maximum amount of queries by q, we can define a transcript $\boldsymbol{\tau} = (\tau^{(1)}, \ldots, \tau^{(q)})$ and let $\boldsymbol{\tau}^{(i)} = (\tau^{(1)}, \ldots, \tau^{(i)})$ for every $i \leq q$. Distinguisher $\mathcal{D}$ can make its queries adaptively, but as it makes them in a deterministic manner, the $(i+1)$-th query input is determined by the first i query-responses $\boldsymbol{\tau}^{(i)}$.

For system $\mathcal{O} \in \{\mathcal{O}_0, \mathcal{O}_1\}$ and fixed tuple $\boldsymbol{\tau}^{(i)}$, we denote by $p_{\mathcal{O}, \mathcal{D}}(\boldsymbol{\tau}^{(i)})$ the probability that distinguisher $\mathcal{D}$ interacting with $\mathcal{O}$ obtains transcript $\boldsymbol{\tau}^{(i)}$ for its first i queries. If $p_{\mathcal{O}, \mathcal{D}}(\boldsymbol{\tau}^{(i)}) > 0$, then we denote by $p_{\mathcal{O}, \mathcal{D}}(Y^{(i+1)} \mid \boldsymbol{\tau}^{(i)})$ the conditional probability that $\mathcal{D}$ receives response $Y^{(i+1)}$ upon its $(i+1)$-th query, given transcript $\boldsymbol{\tau}^{(i)}$ of the first i queries (that deterministically fixes the input to the $(i+1)$-th query). Define for any $i \in \{1, \ldots, q\}$ and any query-response tuple $\boldsymbol{\tau}^{(i)}$:

$$\chi^2(\boldsymbol{\tau}^{(i-1)}) = \sum_{Y^{(i)}} \frac{\left(p_{\mathcal{O}_1, \mathcal{D}}(Y^{(i)} \mid \boldsymbol{\tau}^{(i-1)}) - p_{\mathcal{O}_0, \mathcal{D}}(Y^{(i)} \mid \boldsymbol{\tau}^{(i-1)})\right)^2}{p_{\mathcal{O}_0, \mathcal{D}}(Y^{(i)} \mid \boldsymbol{\tau}^{(i-1)})}, \qquad (1)$$

where the sum is taken over all $Y^{(i)}$ in the support of the distribution $p_{\mathcal{O}_0, \mathcal{D}}(\cdot \mid \boldsymbol{\tau}^{(i-1)})$. The chi-squared method states the following:

Lemma 1 (Chi-squared method [14]). *Consider a fixed deterministic distinguisher $\mathcal{D}$ and two systems $\mathcal{O}_0, \mathcal{O}_1$. Suppose that for any $i \in \{1, \ldots, q\}$ and any query-response tuple $\boldsymbol{\tau}^{(i)}$, $p_{\mathcal{O}_0, \mathcal{D}}(\boldsymbol{\tau}^{(i)}) > 0$ whenever $p_{\mathcal{O}_1, \mathcal{D}}(\boldsymbol{\tau}^{(i)}) > 0$. Then:*

$$\Delta_{\mathcal{D}}\left(\mathcal{O}_0 ; \mathcal{O}_1\right) = \|p_{\mathcal{O}_0, \mathcal{D}}(\cdot) - p_{\mathcal{O}_1, \mathcal{D}}(\cdot)\| \leq \left(\frac{1}{2} \sum_{i=1}^{q} \mathrm{Exp}[\chi^2(\boldsymbol{\tau}^{(i-1)})]\right)^{1/2}, \qquad (2)$$

where the expectation is taken over $\boldsymbol{\tau}^{(i-1)}$ of the $i-1$ first answers sampled according to interaction with $\mathcal{O}_1$.

2.3   Hypergeometric Distribution

The hypergeometric distribution $\mathrm{HG}(N, K, n)$ considers the case of n draws without replacement from a set of size N elements, denote by K the total number of successes out of N and h the number of successes present in a sample of size n. It is well-known that for $h \sim \mathrm{HG}(N, K, n)$,

$$\mathrm{Exp}[h] = n \cdot \frac{K}{N},$$

$$\mathrm{Var}[h] = n \cdot \frac{K}{N} \cdot \frac{(N - K)}{N} \cdot \frac{N - n}{N - 1}.$$

3   Length Doublers and LDT

Following Chen et al. [11], we recall the formalization of length doublers in Sect. 3.1, and present generalized LDT in Sect. 3.2.

3.1   Length Doublers

For arbitrary finite key space $\mathcal{K}$ and $n \in \mathbb{N}$, a length doubler is a function $\mathcal{E} : \mathcal{K} \times \{0, 1\}^{[n, 2n-1]} \to \{0, 1\}^{[n, 2n-1]}$ such that for every fixed key $K \in \mathcal{K}$, $\mathcal{E}_K(\cdot) = \mathcal{E}(K, \cdot)$ is a length preserving invertible function on $\{0, 1\}^{[n, 2n-1]}$. We denote its inverse for fixed key K by $\mathcal{E}_K^{-1}(\cdot) = \mathcal{E}^{-1}(K, \cdot)$. Note that $\mathcal{E}$ should behave like a random permutation for every length input in $[n, 2n - 1]$. Denote by $\mathrm{VPerm}([n, 2n - 1])$ the set of all length-preserving and invertible functions on $\{0, 1\}^{[n, 2n-1]}$. The security of $\mathcal{E}$ is measured by considering a distinguisher $\mathcal{D}$ that has two-sided query access to either $\mathcal{E}_K$ for a randomly drawn key $K \xleftarrow{\$} \mathcal{K}$, or a random length-preserving permutation $\rho \xleftarrow{\$} \mathrm{VPerm}([n, 2n-1])$, and its goal is to try to distinguish the real construction from the ideal one:

$$\mathbf{Adv}_{\mathcal{E}}^{\mathrm{vsprp}}(\mathcal{D}) = \left| \Pr\left[K \xleftarrow{\$} \mathcal{K} : \mathcal{D}^{\mathcal{E}_K^{\pm}} = 1 \right] - \right.$$
$$\left. \Pr\left[\rho \xleftarrow{\$} \mathrm{VPerm}([n, 2n - 1]) : \mathcal{D}^{\rho^{\pm}} = 1 \right] \right|.$$

As in Sect. 2.1, the key space $\mathcal{K}$ corresponds to the source of randomness of the construction $\mathcal{E}_K^{\pm}$. It may take various shapes, but it will always be clear from the context.

3.2   Generalized LDT

Chen et al. [11] introduced length doubler LDT that internally makes two calls to an underlying tweakable block cipher, separated by an evaluation of a "pure mixing function" (a weaker variant of a multipermutation [44]) on part of the state. In this work, we will consider a generalization of LDT to multiple rounds, but we simplify it by discarding the pure mixing function and replacing it by the simplest possible option: $\text{mix}(A, B) = (B, A)$, i.e., a function that swaps the two halves of its input. This simplification is without loss of generality: all results in this work generalize to arbitrary pure mixing functions with some notational overhead. For completeness, we describe pure mixing functions as defined by Chen et al. [11] in Appendix A.

Algorithm 1. Round function $F[\tilde{E}_K]$	**Algorithm 2.** Round function $F^{-1}[\tilde{E}_K]$
Input: $K \in \mathcal{K}$, $M \in \{0,1\}^{[n,2n-1]}$	**Input:** $K \in \mathcal{K}$, $C \in \{0,1\}^{[n,2n-1]}$
Output: $C \in \{0,1\}^{|M|}$	**Output:** $M \in \{0,1\}^{|C|}$
1: $s \leftarrow |M| - n$	1: $s \leftarrow |C| - n$
2: $M_1 \leftarrow \text{left}_n(M)$, $M_2 \leftarrow \text{right}_s(M)$	2: $C_1 \leftarrow \text{left}_n(C)$, $C_2 \leftarrow \text{right}_s(C)$
3: $Y \leftarrow \tilde{E}_K(\text{pad}(M_2), M_1)$	3: $Y \leftarrow \text{left}_{n-s}(C_1)\|C_2$
4: $C \leftarrow \text{left}_{n-s}(Y)\|M_2\|\text{right}_s(Y)$	4: $M \leftarrow \tilde{E}_K^{-1}(\text{pad}(\text{right}_s(C_1)), Y)\|\text{right}_s(C_1)$
5: **return** C	5: **return** M

Consider finite key space $\mathcal{K}$ and let $n \in \mathbb{N}$. Let $\tilde{E} : \mathcal{K} \times \{0,1\}^n \times \{0,1\}^n \to \{0,1\}^n$ be a tweakable block cipher. Consider the round function F (and its inverse) that uses $\tilde{E}_K$ for secret key $K \in \mathcal{K}$, and length-preservingly transforms a plaintext $M \in \{0,1\}^{[n,2n-1]}$ (resp. a ciphertext $C \in \{0,1\}^{[n,2n-1]}$) into a ciphertext C (resp. a plaintext M) as in Algorithm 1 (resp. Algorithm 2). For $r \geq 2$, the r-round length doubler r-LDT is defined as

$$r\text{-LDT}_K(M) = F_{K_r} \circ \cdots \circ F_{K_1}(M), \tag{3}$$

where $\boldsymbol{K} = (K_1, \ldots, K_r) \in \mathcal{K}^r$ and $M \in \{0,1\}^{[n,2n-1]}$. In this evaluation, the mixing of the last round function evaluation is irrelevant for the scheme's security and therefore ignored. For $r = 2$ and $r = 3$, the doubler r-LDT is depicted in Fig. 2.

Chen et al. proved that two rounds of LDT (with arbitrary pure mixing) is secure against any adversary making around $2^{n/2}$ queries.

Proposition 1 (Chen et al. [11]). *Let $\tilde{E} : \mathcal{K} \times \{0,1\}^n \times \{0,1\}^n \to \{0,1\}^n$ be a tweakable block cipher. Consider two-round 2-LDT. For any distinguisher $\mathcal{D}$ making at most q queries, there exist distinguishers $\mathcal{D}_1'$ and $\mathcal{D}_2'$ with the same query complexity such that*

$$\mathbf{Adv}_{2\text{-LDT}}^{\text{vsprp}}(\mathcal{D}) \leq \mathbf{Adv}_{\tilde{E}}^{\widetilde{\text{sprp}}}(\mathcal{D}_1') + \mathbf{Adv}_{\tilde{E}}^{\widetilde{\text{sprp}}}(\mathcal{D}_2') + \frac{q(q-1)}{2^n}. \tag{4}$$

Chen et al. also presented a distinguisher against 2-LDT that succeeds in approximately $2^{n-s/2}$ queries, where the distinguisher makes queries of size $n + s$ bits. The analysis of this attack supports on earlier proofs and attacks by Hall et al. [22] and Gilboa and Gueron [17] on the truncated permutation construction. The attack only works if the distinguisher takes large enough $s \gg 0$ [11]. In addition, it shows that the birthday bound security analysis is tight for $s \approx n-1$, and that we may only be able to prove beyond birthday bound security for $s \ll n - 1$. Based on these observations, in future analyses we will explicitly limit s to a certain range by using lower and upper bounds $s_{\min}$ and $s_{\max}$.

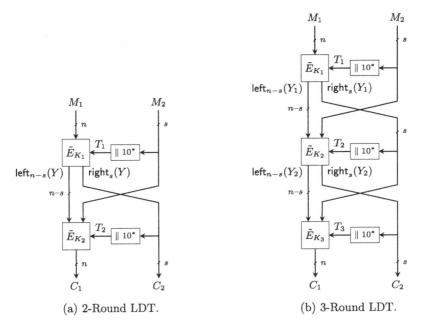

Fig. 2. Depiction of 2-round and 3-round LDT. Here, $s = |M| - n$.

4 Harmonic Permutation Primitives

In this section we introduce two harmonic permutation primitives: a tweakable SPRP in Sect. 4.1 and a variable SPRP in Sect. 4.2.

4.1 Harmonic Tweakable SPRP $G_{a,b}$

We introduce a tweakable pseudorandom permutation $G_{a,b}$ parameterized by $a, b \in \{0, 1\}$. The primitive will be used as intermediate in the analysis of 2-LDT (for $(a, b) = (1, 0)$ and $(a, b) = (0, 1)$) and in the analysis of 3-LDT (for $(a, b) = (1, 1)$).

$G_{a,b}$ is a tweakable permutation with n-bit tweaks and data blocks (so $G_{a,b} \in \widetilde{\mathrm{Perm}}(n, n)$). It maintains an initially empty list $\mathcal{L}$ to store all query-response tuples (T, X, Y). For $T \in \{0, 1\}^n$, write $\mathrm{dom}(\mathcal{L}_T) = \{X \mid (T, X, \cdot) \in \mathcal{L}\}$ and $\mathrm{rng}(\mathcal{L}_T) = \{Y \mid (T, \cdot, Y) \in \mathcal{L}\}$. The tweakable pseudorandom permutation $G_{a,b}$ on input of a new query is described in Algorithm 3 (forward) and Algorithm 4 (inverse).

Algorithm 3. Harmonic $G_{a,b}$	**Algorithm 4.** Harmonic $G_{a,b}^{-1}$
Input: $T \in \{0,1\}^n \backslash \{0^n\}, X \in \{0,1\}^n$	**Input:** $T \in \{0,1\}^n \backslash \{0^n\}, Y \in \{0,1\}^n$
Output: $Y \in \{0,1\}^n$	**Output:** $X \in \{0,1\}^n$
1: $s \leftarrow \|\mathsf{unpad}(T)\|$	1: $s \leftarrow \|\mathsf{unpad}(T)\|$
2: **if** $a = 0$ **then**	2: **if** $b = 0$ **then**
3: $Y \xleftarrow{\$} \{0,1\}^n \backslash \mathsf{rng}(\mathcal{L}_T)$	3: $X \xleftarrow{\$} \{0,1\}^n \backslash \mathsf{dom}(\mathcal{L}_T)$
4: **if** $a = 1$ **then**	4: **if** $b = 1$ **then**
5: $Z \xleftarrow{\$} \{0,1\}^s$	5: $Z \xleftarrow{\$} \{0,1\}^s$
6: $Y \xleftarrow{\$} \{\{0,1\}^{n-s}\|Z\} \backslash \mathsf{rng}(\mathcal{L}_T)$	6: $X \xleftarrow{\$} \{\{0,1\}^{n-s}\|Z\} \backslash \mathsf{dom}(\mathcal{L}_T)$
7: $\mathcal{L} \xleftarrow{\cup} (T, X, Y)$	7: $\mathcal{L} \xleftarrow{\cup} (T, X, Y)$
8: **return** Y	8: **return** X

In our work, $G_{a,b}$ will never be called for tweak $T = 0^n$, hence the assignment $s \leftarrow \|\mathsf{unpad}(T)\|$ is sound. If $a = b = 0$, $G_{0,0}$ describes a randomly drawn tweakable permutation from $\widetilde{\mathrm{Perm}}(n,n)$ (lazily sampled). We will use $G_{a,b}$ for the case where a or b is 1.

Lemma 2. *Let $a, b \in \{0,1\}$, and consider $G_{a,b}$. Let $s_{min}, s_{max} \in [0, n-1]$ such that $s_{min} \leq s_{max}$. Let $1 \leq \theta \leq 2^{n-s_{max}-2}$ be an integral threshold. For any distinguisher $\mathcal{D}$ making at most $q \leq 2^{n-1}$ queries, all with tweaks satisfying $\|\mathsf{unpad}(T)\| \in [s_{min}, s_{max}]$, and restricted to making at most θ inverse queries per tweak (if $a = 1$) and at most θ forward queries per tweak (if $b = 1$), we have*

$$\mathbf{Adv}_{G_{a,b}}^{\widetilde{\mathrm{sprp}}}(\mathcal{D}) \leq \begin{cases} 0 & \text{if } (a,b) = (0,0), \\ \left(\dfrac{2q^3}{2^{2n-s_{max}}}\right)^{1/2} + \binom{q}{\theta}\dfrac{1}{2^{(\theta-1)s_{min}}}, & \text{if } (a,b) \in \{(1,0),(0,1)\}, \\ \left(\dfrac{4\left(\theta + \theta^2\right)q}{2^{2n-s_{max}}}\right)^{1/2}, & \text{if } (a,b) = (1,1). \end{cases}$$

Note that no limitation is put on the number of times a single tweak is queried in forward direction in case $a = 0$ or in inverse direction in case $b = 0$. The proof will be given in Sect. 7.

4.2 Harmonic VSPRP Permutation H

We introduce a variable pseudorandom permutation H, that operates similarly as $G_{1,1}$, but on domain $\{0,1\}^{[n,2n-1]}$ and without tweak input. H likewise maintains an initially empty list $\mathcal{L}$ to store all query-response tuples (X, Y). For $s \in [0, n-1]$, write $\mathsf{dom}(\mathcal{L}_s) = \{X \in \{0,1\}^{n+s} \mid (X, \cdot) \in \mathcal{L}\}$ and $\mathsf{rng}(\mathcal{L}_s) = \{Y \in \{0,1\}^{n+s} \mid (\cdot, Y) \in \mathcal{L}\}$. The variable pseudorandom permutation H on input of a new query is described in Algorithm 5 (forward) and Algorithm 6 (inverse).

Algorithm 5. Harmonic H	**Algorithm 6.** Harmonic H^{-1}
Input: $X \in \{0,1\}^{[n,2n-1]}$	**Input:** $Y \in \{0,1\}^{[n,2n-1]}$
Output: $Y \in \{0,1\}^{\lvert X \rvert}$	**Output:** $X \in \{0,1\}^{\lvert Y \rvert}$
1: $s \leftarrow \lvert X \rvert - n$	1: $s \leftarrow \lvert Y \rvert - n$
2: $Z \xleftarrow{\$} \{0,1\}^s$	2: $Z \xleftarrow{\$} \{0,1\}^s$
3: $Y \xleftarrow{\$} \{\{0,1\}^n \Vert Z\} \backslash \mathrm{rng}(\mathcal{L}_s)$	3: $X \xleftarrow{\$} \{\{0,1\}^n \Vert Z\} \backslash \mathrm{dom}(\mathcal{L}_s)$
4: $\mathcal{L} \xleftarrow{\cup} (X,Y)$	4: $\mathcal{L} \xleftarrow{\cup} (X,Y)$
5: return Y	5: return X

Lemma 3. *Consider H. Let $s_{min} \in [0, n-1]$. For any distinguisher $\mathcal{D}$ making at most $q \leq 2^{n-1}$ queries, all of length in $[n + s_{min}, 2n - 1]$ bits, we have*

$$\mathbf{Adv}_H^{\mathrm{vsprp}}(\mathcal{D}) \leq \left(\frac{2q^3}{2^{2n+s_{min}}} \right)^{1/2} .$$

The proof will be given in Sect. 8.

5   2-Round LDT

As main result on 2-LDT, we derive the following reduction to harmonic primitives $G_{a,b}$ and H.

Theorem 1. *Let $\tilde{E} : \mathcal{K} \times \{0,1\}^n \times \{0,1\}^n \to \{0,1\}^n$ be a tweakable block cipher. Consider two-round 2-LDT. Let $s_{min}, s_{max} \in [0, n-1]$ such that $s_{min} \leq s_{max}$. Let $1 \leq \theta \leq 2^{n - s_{max} - 2}$ be an integral threshold. For any distinguisher $\mathcal{D}$ making at most q queries, all of length in $[n + s_{min}, n + s_{max}]$ bits, there exist distinguishers $\mathcal{D}'_1, \ldots, \mathcal{D}'_5$ with the same query complexity such that*

$$\mathbf{Adv}_{2\text{-}\mathrm{LDT}}^{\mathrm{vsprp}}(\mathcal{D}) \leq \mathbf{Adv}_{\tilde{E}}^{\widetilde{\mathrm{sprp}}}(\mathcal{D}'_1) + \mathbf{Adv}_{\tilde{E}}^{\widetilde{\mathrm{sprp}}}(\mathcal{D}'_2) + \mathbf{Adv}_H^{\mathrm{vsprp}}(\mathcal{D}'_3) \tag{5a}$$

$$+ \mathbf{Adv}_{G_{1,0}}^{\widetilde{\mathrm{sprp}}}(\mathcal{D}'_4) + \mathbf{Adv}_{G_{0,1}}^{\widetilde{\mathrm{sprp}}}(\mathcal{D}'_5) + \binom{q}{\theta} \frac{1}{2^{(\theta-1)s_{min}}} , \tag{5b}$$

where $\mathcal{D}'_4$ may make at most θ inverse queries per tweak and $\mathcal{D}'_5$ at most θ forward queries per tweak.

We will prove Theorem 1 in Sect. 5.1. Plugging the bounds of Lemmas 2 and 3 into the equation yields the following corollary.

Corollary 1. *Let $\tilde{E} : \mathcal{K} \times \{0,1\}^n \times \{0,1\}^n \to \{0,1\}^n$ be a tweakable block cipher. Consider two-round 2-LDT. Let $s_{min}, s_{max} \in [0, n-1]$ such that $s_{min} \leq s_{max}$. Let $1 \leq \theta \leq 2^{n - s_{max} - 2}$ be an integral threshold. For any distinguisher $\mathcal{D}$ making at most q queries, all of length in $[n + s_{min}, n + s_{max}]$ bits, there exist distinguishers $\mathcal{D}'_1, \mathcal{D}'_2$ with the same query complexity such that*

$$\mathbf{Adv}_{2\text{-}\mathrm{LDT}}^{\mathrm{vsprp}}(\mathcal{D}) \leq \mathbf{Adv}_{\tilde{E}}^{\widetilde{\mathrm{sprp}}}(\mathcal{D}'_1) + \mathbf{Adv}_{\tilde{E}}^{\widetilde{\mathrm{sprp}}}(\mathcal{D}'_2)$$

$$+ \left(\frac{2q^3}{2^{2n+s_{min}}} \right)^{1/2} + 2 \left(\frac{2q^3}{2^{2n-s_{max}}} \right)^{1/2} + 3 \binom{q}{\theta} \frac{1}{2^{(\theta-1)s_{min}}} .$$

The first two advantages represent the security of the underlying tweakable block cipher $\tilde{E}$. By Stirling's approximation, if $s_{\min} \leq \theta$, the last term satisfies

$$3 \binom{q}{\theta} \frac{1}{2^{(\theta-1)s_{\min}}} \leq 3 \cdot 2^{s_{\min}} \cdot \left(\frac{qe}{\theta 2^{s_{\min}}} \right)^{\theta} \leq 3 \left(\frac{2qe}{\theta 2^{s_{\min}}} \right)^{\theta} .$$

As the term decreases with θ but θ is limited by side condition $\theta \leq 2^{n-s_{\max}-2}$, it makes sense to choose $\theta = 2^{n-s_{\max}-2}$, and this term equals

$$3 \left(\frac{8qe}{2^{n+s_{\min}-s_{\max}}} \right)^{\theta} .$$

We obtain security up to approximately $\min \left\{ \frac{2n+s_{\min}}{3}, \frac{2n-s_{\max}}{3}, n + s_{\min} - s_{\max} \right\}$ bits, provided that $s_{\min} \leq 2^{n-s_{\max}-2}$. For $s_{\max} \geq n/2$, the middle term dominates and we achieve $n/2$-bit security at most. In this case, the bound of Chen et al. [11] is better. For $s_{\max} < n/2$, our bound guarantees up to at most $2n/3$ bits of security, depending of the choice of $s_{\max}$, where $s_{\min}$ is adapted to $s_{\min} \leq 2^{n-s_{\max}-2}$.

5.1   Proof of Theorem 1

Consider any distinguisher $\mathcal{D}$ making at most q queries, all of length in $[n + s_{\min}, n + s_{\max}]$ bits. It has access to either 2-LDT$_K$ for $\boldsymbol{K} = (K_1, K_2) \xleftarrow{\$} \mathcal{K}^2$ or a random length-preserving invertible permutation $\rho \xleftarrow{\$} \mathrm{VPerm}([n \ldots 2n - 1])$. For ease of discussion, write

$$\text{2-LDT}_K = \mathcal{E}[\tilde{E}_{K_1}, \tilde{E}_{K_2}] .$$

Let $\tilde{\pi}_1, \tilde{\pi}_2 \xleftarrow{\$} \widetilde{\mathrm{Perm}}(n, n)$. We have

$$\mathbf{Adv}_{\text{2-LDT}}^{\text{vsprp}}(\mathcal{D}) = \Delta_{\mathcal{D}} \left(\mathcal{E}[\tilde{E}_{K_1}, \tilde{E}_{K_2}]^{\pm} \ ; \ \rho^{\pm} \right)$$

$$\leq \Delta_{\mathcal{D}_1'} \left(\tilde{E}_{K_1}^{\pm} \ ; \ \tilde{\pi}_1^{\pm} \right) + \Delta_{\mathcal{D}_2'} \left(\tilde{E}_{K_2}^{\pm} \ ; \ \tilde{\pi}_2^{\pm} \right) + \Delta_{\mathcal{D}} \left(\mathcal{E}[\tilde{\pi}_1, \tilde{\pi}_2]^{\pm} \ ; \ \rho^{\pm} \right)$$

$$= \mathbf{Adv}_{\tilde{E}}^{\widetilde{\mathrm{sprp}}}(\mathcal{D}_1') + \mathbf{Adv}_{\tilde{E}}^{\widetilde{\mathrm{sprp}}}(\mathcal{D}_2') + \Delta_{\mathcal{D}} \left(\mathcal{E}[\tilde{\pi}_1, \tilde{\pi}_2]^{\pm} \ ; \ \rho^{\pm} \right), \qquad (6)$$

for some distinguishers $\mathcal{D}_1'$ and $\mathcal{D}_2'$ with the same query complexity as $\mathcal{D}$.

We will focus on the remaining distance in (6). Without loss of generality, we will consider computationally unbounded and deterministic distinguishers. Consider three harmonic primitives, $G_{1,0}$ and $G_{0,1}$ of Sect. 4.1 and H of Sect. 4.2. We obtain via the triangle inequality:

$$\Delta_{\mathcal{D}} \left(\mathcal{E}[\tilde{\pi}_1, \tilde{\pi}_2]^{\pm} \ ; \ \rho^{\pm} \right) \leq \Delta_{\mathcal{D}} \left(\mathcal{E}[\tilde{\pi}_1, \tilde{\pi}_2]^{\pm} \ ; \ \mathcal{E}[G_{1,0}, G_{0,1}]^{\pm} \right)$$

$$+ \Delta_{\mathcal{D}} \left(\mathcal{E}[G_{1,0}, G_{0,1}]^{\pm} \ ; \ H^{\pm} \right) + \Delta_{\mathcal{D}} \left(H^{\pm} \ ; \ \rho^{\pm} \right)$$

$$= \Delta_{\mathcal{D}} \left(\mathcal{E}[\tilde{\pi}_1, \tilde{\pi}_2]^{\pm} \ ; \ \mathcal{E}[G_{1,0}, G_{0,1}]^{\pm} \right)$$

$$+ \Delta_{\mathcal{D}} \left(\mathcal{E}[G_{1,0}, G_{0,1}]^{\pm} \ ; \ H^{\pm} \right) + \mathbf{Adv}_H^{\text{vsprp}}(\mathcal{D}_3'), \qquad (7)$$

for some distinguisher $\mathcal{D}_3'$ with the same query complexity as $\mathcal{D}$ (in fact, $\mathcal{D}_3' = \mathcal{D}$).

Below two claims bound the remaining distances in (7) and complete the proof.

Claim. We have $\Delta_{\mathcal{D}}\left(\mathcal{E}[G_{1,0}, G_{0,1}]^{\pm} \; ; \; H^{\pm}\right) = 0$.

Proof (of claim). For any query to H of length $n + s$ bits (either forward or inverse), the last s bits of the response are drawn uniformly at random from $\{0,1\}^s$ and the first n bits are drawn uniformly at random in such a way that the permutativity of H is retained (see Algorithms 5 and 6). Consider any query to $\mathcal{E}[G_{1,0}, G_{0,1}]$, without loss of generality a forward query of length $n + s$ bits. The s rightmost bits of the output equal the s rightmost bits of $G_{1,0}$, and are generated uniformly at random (see Algorithm 3). Denote this s-bit block by C_2. The remaining n bits of the response, say C_1, come from the evaluation of $G_{0,1}$ for tweak C_2, on input of a data block that never appeared for this tweak before. As can be deduced from Algorithm 3, $G_{0,1}$ behaves like a tweakable permutation: for every tweak input, it behaves like a permutation. Therefore, C_1 is generated uniformly at random in such a way that $C_1 \| C_2$ has never appeared before. Concluding, $\mathcal{E}[G_{1,0}, G_{0,1}]^{\pm}$ and $H^{\pm}$ follow identical distributions.   □

Claim. We have

$$\Delta_{\mathcal{D}}\left(\mathcal{E}[\tilde{\pi}_1, \tilde{\pi}_2]^{\pm} \; ; \; \mathcal{E}[G_{1,0}, G_{0,1}]^{\pm}\right) \leq \mathbf{Adv}_{G_{1,0}}^{\widetilde{\mathrm{sprp}}}(\mathcal{D}'_4) + \mathbf{Adv}_{G_{0,1}}^{\widetilde{\mathrm{sprp}}}(\mathcal{D}'_5) + \binom{q}{\theta}\frac{1}{2^{(\theta-1)s_{\min}}},$$

for some distinguishers $\mathcal{D}'_4$ and $\mathcal{D}'_5$ with the same query complexity as $\mathcal{D}$, where $\mathcal{D}'_4$ may make at most θ inverse queries per tweak and $\mathcal{D}'_5$ at most θ forward queries per tweak.

Proof (of claim). Consider a computationally unbounded and deterministic distinguisher $\mathcal{D}$ making at most q queries. It has access to either $\mathcal{E}[\tilde{\pi}_1, \tilde{\pi}_2]^{\pm}$ or $\mathcal{E}[G_{1,0}, G_{0,1}]^{\pm}$. Summarize the queries in a transcript $\tau = (\tau^{(1)}, \ldots, \tau^{(q)})$, where the i-th tuple $\tau^{(i)} = (\ell^{(i)}, X^{(i)}, Y^{(i)})$ is comprised of a bit $\ell^{(i)} \in \{-1, 1\}$ denoting the direction of the query, $X^{(i)}$ is the query input and $Y^{(i)}$ the query output, in such a way $Y^{(i)} = \mathcal{O}^{\ell^{(i)}}(X^{(i)})$. Write $s^{(i)} = |X^{(i)}| - n$. We assume that the distinguisher $\mathcal{D}$ does not repeat any query, which means that $\tau^{(i)}$ does not contain duplicate elements.

For the threshold θ of the theorem statement, define the following bad event:

$$\mathsf{BAD} : \max_{\ell \in \{-1,1\}} \max_{s \in [s_{\min}, s_{\max}]} \max_{Z \in \{0,1\}^s} \left|\{i \mid \ell^{(i)} = \ell \wedge s^{(i)} = s \wedge \mathsf{right}_s(Y^{(i)}) = Z\}\right| > \theta .$$

Clearly, writing $\mathcal{O}_{\tilde{\pi}} = \mathcal{E}[\tilde{\pi}_1, \tilde{\pi}_2]^{\pm}$ and $\mathcal{O}_G = \mathcal{E}[G_{1,0}, G_{0,1}]^{\pm}$ for brevity,

$$
\begin{aligned}
\Delta_{\mathcal{D}}\left(\mathcal{O}_{\tilde{\pi}} \; ; \; \mathcal{O}_G\right) &= \left|\Pr\left[\mathcal{D}^{\mathcal{O}_{\tilde{\pi}}} = 1\right] - \Pr\left[\mathcal{D}^{\mathcal{O}_G} = 1\right]\right| \\
&\leq \left|\Pr\left[\mathcal{D}^{\mathcal{O}_{\tilde{\pi}}} = 1 \wedge \neg\mathsf{BAD}\right] - \Pr\left[\mathcal{D}^{\mathcal{O}_G} = 1 \wedge \neg\mathsf{BAD}\right]\right| \\
&\quad + \left|\Pr\left[\mathcal{D}^{\mathcal{O}_{\tilde{\pi}}} = 1 \wedge \mathsf{BAD}\right] - \Pr\left[\mathcal{D}^{\mathcal{O}_G} = 1 \wedge \mathsf{BAD}\right]\right| \\
&\leq \left|\Pr\left[\mathcal{D}^{\mathcal{O}_{\tilde{\pi}}} = 1 \wedge \neg\mathsf{BAD}\right] - \Pr\left[\mathcal{D}^{\mathcal{O}_G} = 1 \wedge \neg\mathsf{BAD}\right]\right| \\
&\quad + \max\left\{\Pr\left[\mathcal{O}_{\tilde{\pi}} \text{ sets } \mathsf{BAD}\right], \Pr\left[\mathcal{O}_G \text{ sets } \mathsf{BAD}\right]\right\}. \quad (8)
\end{aligned}
$$

Denoting the distance in (8) by $\Delta_{\mathcal{D}}^{\neg\mathsf{BAD}}\left(\mathcal{O}_{\tilde{\pi}} \; ; \; \mathcal{O}_G\right)$ for brevity, a straightforward triangle argument shows that

$$
\Delta_{\mathcal{D}}^{\neg\mathsf{BAD}}\left(\mathcal{O}_{\tilde{\pi}} \; ; \; \mathcal{O}_G\right) \leq \mathbf{Adv}_{G_{1,0}}^{\widetilde{\mathrm{sprp}}}(\mathcal{D}_4') + \mathbf{Adv}_{G_{0,1}}^{\widetilde{\mathrm{sprp}}}(\mathcal{D}_5'), \quad (9)
$$

for some distinguishers $\mathcal{D}_4'$ and $\mathcal{D}_5'$ with the same query complexity as $\mathcal{D}$, where $\mathcal{D}_4'$ may make at most θ inverse queries per tweak and $\mathcal{D}_5'$ at most θ forward queries per tweak. These two restrictions follow from the way $\mathcal{E}$ evaluates its primitives ($\tilde{\pi}_1, \tilde{\pi}_2$ in the left oracle and $G_{1,0}, G_{0,1}$ in the right oracle) and from the conditioning of the bad event.

Consider the max-term in (8). Consider any $\ell \in \{-1, 1\}$ and $s \in [s_{\min}, s_{\max}]$, and denote the number of queries with $\ell^{(i)} = \ell$ and $s^{(i)} = s$ by $q_{\ell,s}$. For $\mathcal{O}_G$, in forward queries the $\mathsf{right}_s(Y^{(i)})$-values come from the evaluation of $G_{1,0}$ and are always uniformly randomly drawn (see Algorithm 3), whereas in inverse queries they come from evaluations of $G_{0,1}^{-1}$ and are also uniformly randomly drawn (see Algorithm 4). Therefore,

$$
\Pr\left[\mathcal{O}_G \text{ sets } \mathsf{BAD} \text{ for } (\ell, s)\right] \leq \binom{q_{\ell,s}}{\theta} \frac{1}{2^{(\theta-1)s}}.
$$

On the other hand, for $\mathcal{O}_{\tilde{\pi}}$, the $\mathsf{right}_s(Y^{(i)})$-values come from a truncated permutation evaluation, and we find

$$
\Pr\left[\mathcal{O}_{\tilde{\pi}} \text{ sets } \mathsf{BAD} \text{ for } (\ell, s)\right] = \binom{q_{\ell,s}}{\theta} \cdot 2^s \cdot \prod_{i=0}^{\theta-1} \frac{2^{n-s} - i}{2^n - i} \leq \binom{q_{\ell,s}}{\theta} \frac{1}{2^{(\theta-1)s}}.
$$

We thus obtain

$$
\max\left\{\Pr\left[\mathcal{O}_{\tilde{\pi}} \text{ sets } \mathsf{BAD}\right], \Pr\left[\mathcal{O}_G \text{ sets } \mathsf{BAD}\right]\right\} \leq \binom{q}{\theta} \frac{1}{2^{(\theta-1)s_{\min}}}, \quad (10)
$$

using that $\binom{q_a}{\theta} + \binom{q_b}{\theta} \leq \binom{q_a + q_b}{\theta}$ and the distinguisher maximizes its probability for $s = s_{\min}$. The proof is concluded by combining (8), (9), and (10). $\qquad\square$

6   3-Round LDT

We derive the following reduction from the security of 3-LDT to harmonic primitives $G_{a,b}$ and H.

Theorem 2. *Let $\tilde{E} : \mathcal{K} \times \{0,1\}^n \times \{0,1\}^n \to \{0,1\}^n$ be a tweakable block cipher. Consider three-round 3-LDT. Let $s_{min}, s_{max} \in [0, n-1]$ such that $s_{min} \leq s_{max}$. Let $1 \leq \theta \leq 2^{n-s_{max}-2}$ be an integral threshold. For any distinguisher $\mathcal{D}$ making at most q queries, all of length in $[n+s_{min}, n+s_{max}]$ bits, there exist distinguishers $\mathcal{D}'_1, \ldots, \mathcal{D}'_5$ with the same query complexity such that*

$$\mathbf{Adv}^{\mathrm{vsprp}}_{\text{3-LDT}}(\mathcal{D}) \leq \mathbf{Adv}^{\widetilde{\mathrm{sprp}}}_{\tilde{E}}(\mathcal{D}'_1) + \mathbf{Adv}^{\widetilde{\mathrm{sprp}}}_{\tilde{E}}(\mathcal{D}'_2) + \mathbf{Adv}^{\widetilde{\mathrm{sprp}}}_{\tilde{E}}(\mathcal{D}'_3) \tag{11a}$$

$$+ \mathbf{Adv}^{\mathrm{vsprp}}_{H}(\mathcal{D}'_4) + \mathbf{Adv}^{\widetilde{\mathrm{sprp}}}_{G_{1,1}}(\mathcal{D}'_5) + \binom{q}{\theta} \frac{1}{2^{(\theta-1)s_{min}}}, \tag{11b}$$

where $\mathcal{D}'_5$ may make at most θ forward and θ inverse queries per tweak.

We will prove Theorem 2 in Sect. 6.1.

The improvement of the bound of 3-LDT over that of 2-LDT of Theorem 1 is readily visible: $\mathbf{Adv}^{\widetilde{\mathrm{sprp}}}_{G_{1,0}} + \mathbf{Adv}^{\widetilde{\mathrm{sprp}}}_{G_{0,1}}$ has been replaced with $\mathbf{Adv}^{\widetilde{\mathrm{sprp}}}_{G_{1,1}}$, which by Lemma 2 achieves a better bound. Plugging the bounds of Lemmas 2 and 3 into the equation yields the following corollary.

Corollary 2. *Let $\tilde{E} : \mathcal{K} \times \{0,1\}^n \times \{0,1\}^n \to \{0,1\}^n$ be a tweakable block cipher. Consider three-round 3-LDT. Let $s_{min}, s_{max} \in [0, n-1]$ such that $s_{min} \leq s_{max}$. Let $1 \leq \theta \leq 2^{n-s_{max}-2}$ be an integral threshold. For any distinguisher $\mathcal{D}$ making at most q queries, all of length in $[n+s_{min}, n+s_{max}]$ bits, there exist distinguishers $\mathcal{D}'_1, \mathcal{D}'_2, \mathcal{D}'_3$ with the same query complexity such that*

$$\mathbf{Adv}^{\mathrm{vsprp}}_{\text{3-LDT}}(\mathcal{D}) \leq \mathbf{Adv}^{\widetilde{\mathrm{sprp}}}_{\tilde{E}}(\mathcal{D}'_1) + \mathbf{Adv}^{\widetilde{\mathrm{sprp}}}_{\tilde{E}}(\mathcal{D}'_2) + \mathbf{Adv}^{\widetilde{\mathrm{sprp}}}_{\tilde{E}}(\mathcal{D}'_3)$$

$$+ \left(\frac{2q^3}{2^{2n+s_{min}}} \right)^{1/2} + \left(\frac{4\left(\theta + \theta^2\right)q}{2^{2n-s_{max}}} \right)^{1/2} + \binom{q}{\theta} \frac{1}{2^{(\theta-1)s_{min}}} .$$

The first three advantages represent the security of the underlying tweakable block cipher $\tilde{E}$. Two of the terms in the remaining portion of the bound depend on θ: the first one increases with θ whereas the latter decreases with θ. Recalling from Sect. 5 that, for $s_{min} \leq \theta$,

$$\binom{q}{\theta} \frac{1}{2^{(\theta-1)s_{min}}} \leq \left(\frac{2qe}{\theta 2^{s_{min}}} \right)^{\theta},$$

equating the two θ-dependent fractions in the corollary gives $\theta \approx 2^{(2n-s_{max}-s_{min})/3}$. This threshold value still has to obey to the condition $s_{min} \leq \theta \leq 2^{n-s_{max}-2}$, or stated differently,

$$s_{max} \leq \min\left\{ (n - 6 + s_{min})/2, \, 2n - s_{min} - 3\log_2(s_{min}) \right\}. \tag{12}$$

Table 1. Interpretation of the bound of Corollary 2 for various choices of $s_{\min}$, where *const* is a constant to make the bound meaningful. Small constants are omitted in the security upper bound.

$s_{\min}$	security up to		
	arbitrary $s_{\max}$	$s_{\max} \approx \frac{n+s_{\min}}{2}$ of (12)	$s_{\max} \approx s_{\min}$
const	$\min\left\{\dfrac{8n}{12}, \dfrac{4n}{6} - \dfrac{s_{\max}}{3}\right\}$	$\dfrac{n}{2}$	$\dfrac{2n}{3}$
$\dfrac{n}{4}$	$\min\left\{\dfrac{9n}{12}, \dfrac{5n}{6} - \dfrac{s_{\max}}{3}\right\}$	$\dfrac{5n}{8}$	$\dfrac{3n}{4}$
$\dfrac{n}{2}$	$\min\left\{\dfrac{10n}{12}, \dfrac{6n}{6} - \dfrac{s_{\max}}{3}\right\}$	$\dfrac{3n}{4}$	$\dfrac{5n}{6}$
$\dfrac{3n}{4}$	$\min\left\{\dfrac{11n}{12}, \dfrac{7n}{6} - \dfrac{s_{\max}}{3}\right\}$	$\dfrac{7n}{8}$	$\dfrac{11n}{12}$
$n - 2\log_2(n)$	$\min\left\{\dfrac{12n}{12}, \dfrac{8n}{6} - \dfrac{s_{\max}}{3}\right\}$	n	n

The minimum is achieved for its left element as long as $s_{\min} \leq n - 2\log_2(n)$. In Table 1, we list the simplified security bound of Corollary 2 (omitting constants) for $s_{\min} \in \{const, n/4, n/2, 3n/4, n-2\log_2(n)\}$ and three possible choices of $s_{\max}$: arbitrary, $s_{\max} \approx (n + s_{\min})/2$ of (12), and $s_{\max} \approx s_{\min}$. For $s_{\min}$ approaching n, n-bit security is achieved.

Note that these two choices of $s_{\max}$ set its two extremes: for given $s_{\min}$, we require that $s_{\min} \leq s_{\max} \leq (n + s_{\min})/2$. The security bounds for the two extremes are plotted in Fig. 3: the level of security given by Corollary 2 is in the shaded area of Fig. 3 and depends on $s_{\min}$ and $s_{\max}$. For example, fixing $s_{\min} = n/2$, the security bound of Corollary 2 lies between $3n/4$ (for $s_{\max} \approx (n+s_{\min})/2$) and $5n/6$ (for $s_{\max} \approx s_{\min}$), using that $s_{\min} \leq s_{\max} \leq (n+s_{\min})/2$ by condition.

6.1 Proof of Theorem 2

The first steps of the proof resemble those of Sect. 5.1. Consider any distinguisher $\mathcal{D}$ making at most q queries. It has access to either 3-LDT$_K$ for $\boldsymbol{K} = (K_1, K_2, K_3) \xleftarrow{\$} \mathcal{K}^3$ or a random length-preserving invertible permutation $\rho \xleftarrow{\$} \text{VPerm}([n \ldots 2n - 1])$. For ease of discussion, write

$$3\text{-LDT}_K = \mathcal{E}[\tilde{E}_{K_1}, \tilde{E}_{K_2}, \tilde{E}_{K_3}].$$

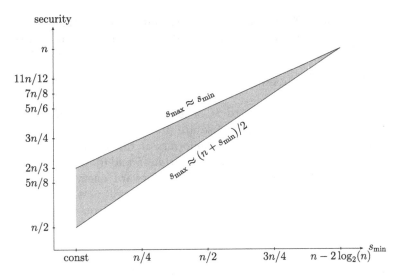

Fig. 3. Simplified security bound of 3-LDT for various choices of $s_{\min}$. Lower line is for $s_{\max} \approx (n + s_{\min})/2$, upper line for $s_{\max} \approx s_{\min}$. Security of 3-LDT is indicated by the shaded area and depends on $s_{\min}$ and $s_{\max}$, where $s_{\min} \leq s_{\max} \leq (n + s_{\min})/2$.

Let $\tilde{\pi}_1, \tilde{\pi}_2, \tilde{\pi}_3 \xleftarrow{\$} \widetilde{\text{Perm}}(n, n)$. We have

$$
\begin{aligned}
\mathbf{Adv}^{\text{vsprp}}_{\text{3-LDT}}(\mathcal{D}) &= \Delta_{\mathcal{D}}\left(\mathcal{E}[\tilde{E}_{K_1}, \tilde{E}_{K_2}, \tilde{E}_{K_3}]^{\pm} \; ; \; \rho^{\pm}\right) \\
&\leq \Delta_{\mathcal{D}'_1}\left(\tilde{E}^{\pm}_{K_1} \; ; \; \tilde{\pi}^{\pm}_1\right) + \Delta_{\mathcal{D}'_2}\left(\tilde{E}^{\pm}_{K_2} \; ; \; \tilde{\pi}^{\pm}_2\right) + \Delta_{\mathcal{D}'_3}\left(\tilde{E}^{\pm}_{K_3} \; ; \; \tilde{\pi}^{\pm}_3\right) \\
&\quad + \Delta_{\mathcal{D}}\left(\mathcal{E}[\tilde{\pi}_1, \tilde{\pi}_2, \tilde{\pi}_3]^{\pm} \; ; \; \rho^{\pm}\right) \\
&= \mathbf{Adv}^{\widetilde{\text{sprp}}}_{\tilde{E}}(\mathcal{D}'_1) + \mathbf{Adv}^{\widetilde{\text{sprp}}}_{\tilde{E}}(\mathcal{D}'_2) + \mathbf{Adv}^{\widetilde{\text{sprp}}}_{\tilde{E}}(\mathcal{D}'_3) \\
&\quad + \Delta_{\mathcal{D}}\left(\mathcal{E}[\tilde{\pi}_1, \tilde{\pi}_2, \tilde{\pi}_3]^{\pm} \; ; \; \rho^{\pm}\right),
\end{aligned}
\tag{13}
$$

for some distinguishers $\mathcal{D}'_1$, $\mathcal{D}'_2$, and $\mathcal{D}'_2$ with the same query complexity as $\mathcal{D}$.

We will focus on the remaining distance in (13). Without loss of generality, we will consider computationally unbounded and deterministic distinguishers. Consider two harmonic primitives, $G_{1,1}$ of Sect. 4.1 and H of Sect. 4.2. We obtain via the triangle inequality:

$$
\begin{aligned}
\Delta_{\mathcal{D}}\left(\mathcal{E}[\tilde{\pi}_1, \tilde{\pi}_2, \tilde{\pi}_3]^{\pm} \; ; \; \rho^{\pm}\right) &\leq \Delta_{\mathcal{D}}\left(\mathcal{E}[\tilde{\pi}_1, \tilde{\pi}_2, \tilde{\pi}_3]^{\pm} \; ; \; \mathcal{E}[\tilde{\pi}_1, G_{1,1}, \tilde{\pi}_3]^{\pm}\right) \\
&\quad + \Delta_{\mathcal{D}}\left(\mathcal{E}[\tilde{\pi}_1, G_{1,1}, \tilde{\pi}_3]^{\pm} \; ; \; H^{\pm}\right) + \Delta_{\mathcal{D}}\left(H^{\pm} \; ; \; \rho^{\pm}\right) \\
&= \Delta_{\mathcal{D}}\left(\mathcal{E}[\tilde{\pi}_1, \tilde{\pi}_2, \tilde{\pi}_3]^{\pm} \; ; \; \mathcal{E}[\tilde{\pi}_1, G_{1,1}, \tilde{\pi}_3]^{\pm}\right) \\
&\quad + \Delta_{\mathcal{D}}\left(\mathcal{E}[\tilde{\pi}_1, G_{1,1}, \tilde{\pi}_3]^{\pm} \; ; \; H^{\pm}\right) + \mathbf{Adv}^{\text{vsprp}}_{H}(\mathcal{D}'_4),
\end{aligned}
\tag{14}
$$

for some distinguisher $\mathcal{D}_4'$ with the same query complexity as $\mathcal{D}$ (in fact, $\mathcal{D}_4' = \mathcal{D}$).

Below two claims bound the remaining distances in (14) and complete the proof.

Claim. We have $\Delta_{\mathcal{D}}\left(\mathcal{E}[\tilde{\pi}_1, G_{1,1}, \tilde{\pi}_3]^{\pm} \; ; \; H^{\pm}\right) = 0.$

Proof (of claim). For any query to H of length $n + s$ bits (either forward or inverse), the last s bits of the response are drawn uniformly at random from $\{0,1\}^s$ and the first n bits are drawn uniformly at random in such a way that the permutativity of H is retained (see Algorithms 5 and 6). Consider any query to $\mathcal{E}[\tilde{\pi}_1, G_{1,1}, \tilde{\pi}_3]$, without loss of generality a forward query of length $n + s$ bits. The s rightmost bits of the output equal the s rightmost bits of $G_{1,1}$, and are generated uniformly at random (see Algorithm 3; here, we make explicit use of the fact that $G_{1,1}$ never receives the same input twice). Denote this s-bit block by C_2. The remaining n bits of the response, say C_1, come from the evaluation of $\tilde{\pi}_3$ for tweak C_2 on input of a data block that never appeared for this tweak before. For every tweak input, the tweakable permutation $\tilde{\pi}_3$ behaves like a permutation. Therefore, C_1 is generated uniformly at random in such a way that $C_1 \| C_2$ has never appeared before. Concluding, $\mathcal{E}[\tilde{\pi}_1, G_{1,1}, \tilde{\pi}_3]^{\pm}$ and $H^{\pm}$ follow identical distributions. $\square$

Claim. We have

$$\Delta_{\mathcal{D}}\left(\mathcal{E}[\tilde{\pi}_1, \tilde{\pi}_2, \tilde{\pi}_3]^{\pm} \; ; \; \mathcal{E}[\tilde{\pi}_1, G_{1,1}, \tilde{\pi}_3]^{\pm}\right) \leq \mathbf{Adv}_{G_{1,1}}^{\widetilde{\mathrm{sprp}}}(\mathcal{D}_5') + \binom{q}{\theta}\frac{1}{2^{(\theta-1)s_{\min}}},$$

for some distinguisher $\mathcal{D}_5'$ with the same query complexity as $\mathcal{D}$, but that may make at most θ forward and θ inverse queries per tweak.

Proof (of claim). The first part of the proof resembles that of the corresponding claim in Sect. 5.1.

Consider a computationally unbounded and deterministic distinguisher $\mathcal{D}$ making at most q queries. It has access to either $\mathcal{E}[\tilde{\pi}_1, \tilde{\pi}_2, \tilde{\pi}_3]^{\pm}$ or $\mathcal{E}[\tilde{\pi}_1, G_{1,1}, \tilde{\pi}_3]^{\pm}$. Summarize the queries in a transcript $\boldsymbol{\tau} = (\tau^{(1)}, \ldots, \tau^{(q)})$, where the i-th tuple $\tau^{(i)} = (\ell^{(i)}, X^{(i)}, Y^{(i)})$ is comprised of a bit $\ell^{(i)} \in \{-1, 1\}$ denoting the direction of the query, $X^{(i)}$ is the query input and $Y^{(i)}$ the query output, in such a way $Y^{(i)} = \mathcal{O}^{\ell^{(i)}}(X^{(i)})$. Write $s^{(i)} = |X^{(i)}| - n$. We further denote by $Z^{(i)}$ the last s bits of the output of $\tilde{\pi}_1$ (which is also the last s bits of the input of $\tilde{\pi}_3$) in forward queries, and the last s bits of the output of $\tilde{\pi}_3^{-1}$ (which is also the last s bits of the input of $\tilde{\pi}_1^{-1}$) in inverse queries. We assume that the distinguisher $\mathcal{D}$ does not repeat any query, which means that $\tau^{(i)}$ does not contain duplicate elements.

For the threshold θ of the theorem statement, define the following bad event:

BAD : $\displaystyle\max_{\ell \in \{-1,1\}} \max_{s \in [s_{\min}, s_{\max}]} \max_{Z \in \{0,1\}^s} \left| \{i \mid \ell^{(i)} = \ell \wedge s^{(i)} = s \wedge Z^{(i)} = Z\} \right| > \theta.$

As before, writing $\mathcal{O}_{\tilde{\pi}} = \mathcal{E}[\tilde{\pi}_1, \tilde{\pi}_2, \tilde{\pi}_3]^{\pm}$ and $\mathcal{O}_G = \mathcal{E}[\tilde{\pi}_1, G_{1,1}, \tilde{\pi}_3]^{\pm}$,

$$\Delta_{\mathcal{D}}\left(\mathcal{O}_{\tilde{\pi}} \; ; \; \mathcal{O}_G\right) \leq \left|\Pr\left[\mathcal{D}^{\mathcal{O}_{\tilde{\pi}}} = 1 \wedge \neg \mathsf{BAD}\right] - \Pr\left[\mathcal{D}^{\mathcal{O}_G} = 1 \wedge \neg \mathsf{BAD}\right]\right|$$
$$+ \max\left\{\Pr\left[\mathcal{O}_{\tilde{\pi}} \text{ sets } \mathsf{BAD}\right], \Pr\left[\mathcal{O}_G \text{ sets } \mathsf{BAD}\right]\right\}. \quad (15)$$

Denoting the distance in (15) by $\Delta_{\mathcal{D}}^{\neg \mathsf{BAD}}\left(\mathcal{O}_{\tilde{\pi}} \; ; \; \mathcal{O}_G\right)$ for brevity, a straightforward triangle argument shows that

$$\Delta_{\mathcal{D}}^{\neg \mathsf{BAD}}\left(\mathcal{O}_{\tilde{\pi}} \; ; \; \mathcal{O}_G\right) \leq \mathbf{Adv}_{G_{1,1}}^{\widetilde{\mathrm{sprp}}}(\mathcal{D}_5'), \quad (16)$$

for some distinguisher $\mathcal{D}_5'$ with the same query complexity as $\mathcal{D}$, but that may make at most θ forward and θ inverse queries per tweak. These two restrictions follow from the way $\mathcal{E}$ evaluates its primitives ($\tilde{\pi}_2$ in the left oracle and $G_{1,1}$ in the right oracle) and from the conditioning of the bad event.

Consider the max-term in (15). Consider any $\ell \in \{-1, 1\}$ and $s \in [s_{\min}, s_{\max}]$, and denote the number of queries with $\ell^{(i)} = \ell$ and $s^{(i)} = s$ by $q_{\ell,s}$. For both $\mathcal{O}_{\tilde{\pi}}$ and $\mathcal{O}_G$, the $Z^{(i)}$-values come from a truncated permutation evaluation, and we find for $\mathcal{O} \in \{\mathcal{O}_{\tilde{\pi}}, \mathcal{O}_G\}$:

$$\Pr\left[\mathcal{O} \text{ sets } \mathsf{BAD} \text{ for } (\ell, s)\right] = \binom{q_{\ell,s}}{\theta} \cdot 2^s \cdot \prod_{i=0}^{\theta-1} \frac{2^{n-s} - i}{2^n - i} \leq \binom{q_{\ell,s}}{\theta} \frac{1}{2^{(\theta-1)s}}.$$

We thus obtain

$$\max\left\{\Pr\left[\mathcal{O}_{\tilde{\pi}} \text{ sets } \mathsf{BAD}\right], \Pr\left[\mathcal{O}_G \text{ sets } \mathsf{BAD}\right]\right\} \leq \binom{q}{\theta} \frac{1}{2^{(\theta-1)s_{\min}}}, \quad (17)$$

as before. The proof is concluded by combining (15), (16), and (17). $\qquad \square$

7   Proof of Lemma 2 on $G_{a,b}$

For $a = b = 0$, the lemma is trivial. Let $a, b \in \{0, 1\}$ such that $a + b \geq 1$, and consider any distinguisher $\mathcal{D}$ making at most q queries, all with tweaks satisfying $|\mathrm{unpad}(T)| \in [s_{\min}, s_{\max}]$, and it makes at most θ inverse queries per tweak (if $a = 1$) and at most θ forward queries per tweak (if $b = 1$). The distinguisher has access to either random system $G_{a,b}$ or $\tilde{\pi} \xleftarrow{\$} \widetilde{\mathrm{Perm}}(n, n)$, and without loss of generality, $\mathcal{D}$ is computationally unbounded and deterministic.

We will use the chi-squared method of Sect. 2.2, with $\mathcal{O}_2 = G_{a,b}$ being the real system and $\mathcal{O}_0 = \tilde{\pi}$ the ideal system. Define an intermediate world $\mathcal{O}_1$ that implements $\mathcal{O}_2$, unless some event "BAD" (defined below) happens, from which point it implements $\mathcal{O}_0$. Summarize the communication of $\mathcal{D}$ with its oracle in a transcript $\boldsymbol{\tau} = (\tau^{(1)}, \ldots, \tau^{(q)})$, where $\tau^{(i)} = (\ell^{(i)}, T^{(i)}, X^{(i)}, Y^{(i)})$ consists of a bit $\ell^{(i)} \in \{-1, 1\}$ indicating the direction of the query (1 means forward, and

-1 means inverse), a tweak value $T^{(i)}$, an input value $X^{(i)}$, and a response $Y^{(i)}$, in such a way that $O^{\ell^{(i)}}(T^{(i)}, X^{(i)}) = Y^{(i)}$ for $O \in \{O_0, O_2\}$.

By a triangle inequality,

$$\mathbf{Adv}_{G_{a,b}}^{\widetilde{\mathrm{sprp}}}(\mathcal{D}) = \|p_{O_0, \mathcal{D}}(\cdot) - p_{O_2, \mathcal{D}}(\cdot)\|$$

$$\leq \|p_{O_0, \mathcal{D}}(\cdot) - p_{O_1, \mathcal{D}}(\cdot)\| + \|p_{O_1, \mathcal{D}}(\cdot) - p_{O_2, \mathcal{D}}(\cdot)\|. \qquad (18)$$

Let $\mathcal{T}$ denote the set of all possible transcripts, and $\mathcal{T}_{\mathrm{bad}}$ the set of all transcripts that satisfy BAD. We have that $p_{O_1, \mathcal{D}}(\tau) = p_{O_2, \mathcal{D}}(\tau)$ for any $\tau \in \mathcal{T} \backslash \mathcal{T}_{\mathrm{bad}}$, and hence,

$$\|p_{O_1, \mathcal{D}}(\cdot) - p_{O_2, \mathcal{D}}(\cdot)\| = \sum_{\tau \in \mathcal{T}} \max\{0, p_{O_1, \mathcal{D}}(\tau) - p_{O_2, \mathcal{D}}(\tau)\}$$

$$= \sum_{\tau \in \mathcal{T}_{\mathrm{bad}}} \max\{0, p_{O_1, \mathcal{D}}(\tau) - p_{O_2, \mathcal{D}}(\tau)\}$$

$$\leq \sum_{\tau \in \mathcal{T}_{\mathrm{bad}}} p_{O_1, \mathcal{D}}(\tau) = \Pr[O_1 \text{ sets BAD}].$$

We obtain from (18):

$$\mathbf{Adv}_{G_{a,b}}^{\widetilde{\mathrm{sprp}}}(\mathcal{D}) \leq \|p_{O_0, \mathcal{D}}(\cdot) - p_{O_1, \mathcal{D}}(\cdot)\| + \Pr[O_1 \text{ sets BAD}]. \qquad (19)$$

We will formalize and analyze BAD in Sect. 7.1 and analyze the remaining distance using the chi-squared technique in Sect. 7.2. These will immediately conclude the proof by (19).

7.1 Bad Transcripts

For the threshold θ of the theorem statement, define the following bad events:

BAD$_1$: $\displaystyle \max_{s \in [s_{\min}, s_{\max}]} \max_{Z, Z' \in \{0,1\}^s} \left| \{i \mid a = 1 \wedge \ell^{(i)} = 1 \wedge \mathsf{unpad}(T^{(i)}) = Z \wedge \mathsf{right}_s(Y^{(i)}) = Z'\} \right| > \theta$,

BAD$_2$: $\displaystyle \max_{s \in [s_{\min}, s_{\max}]} \max_{Z, Z' \in \{0,1\}^s} \left| \{i \mid a = 1 \wedge \ell^{(i)} = -1 \wedge \mathsf{unpad}(T^{(i)}) = Z \wedge \mathsf{right}_s(X^{(i)}) = Z'\} \right| > \theta$,

BAD$_3$: $\displaystyle \max_{s \in [s_{\min}, s_{\max}]} \max_{Z, Z' \in \{0,1\}^s} \left| \{i \mid b = 1 \wedge \ell^{(i)} = 1 \wedge \mathsf{unpad}(T^{(i)}) = Z \wedge \mathsf{right}_s(X^{(i)}) = Z'\} \right| > \theta$,

BAD$_4$: $\displaystyle \max_{s \in [s_{\min}, s_{\max}]} \max_{Z, Z' \in \{0,1\}^s} \left| \{i \mid b = 1 \wedge \ell^{(i)} = -1 \wedge \mathsf{unpad}(T^{(i)}) = Z \wedge \mathsf{right}_s(Y^{(i)}) = Z'\} \right| > \theta$.

Define BAD $=$ BAD$_1 \vee$ BAD$_2 \vee$ BAD$_3 \vee$ BAD$_4$.

The bad events look complicated, but in fact they are not. If $(a, b) = (0, 0)$, none of the four bad events are satisfied, and BAD does not hold by construction. On the other hand, if $(a, b) = (1, 1)$, the distinguisher makes at most θ forward queries per tweak and at most θ inverse queries per tweak, and also in this case BAD does not hold by construction. The cases $(a, b) = (1, 0), (0, 1)$ are symmetric, and we treat the former only. If $(a, b) = (1, 0)$, BAD$_3$, BAD$_4$ do not hold as $b = 0$, and BAD$_2$ does not hold as the distinguisher makes at most θ inverse queries. We are left with BAD$_1$. Consider any $s \in [s_{\min}, s_{\max}]$ and any

$Z \in \{0,1\}^s$, and denote the number of queries with $\ell^{(i)} = 1$ and $\mathsf{unpad}(T^{(i)}) = Z$ by $q_{s,Z}$. The $\mathsf{right}_s(Y^{(i)})$-values come from the evaluation of $G_{1,0}$ and are always uniformly randomly drawn (see Algorithm 3). Therefore,

$$\Pr\left[\mathcal{O}_1 \text{ sets BAD for } (s,Z)\right] \leq \binom{q_{s,Z}}{\theta} \frac{1}{2^{(\theta-1)s}} .$$

We thus obtain

$$\Pr\left[\mathcal{O}_1 \text{ sets BAD}\right] \leq \binom{q}{\theta} \frac{1}{2^{(\theta-1)s_{\min}}} , \qquad (20)$$

using that $\binom{q_a}{\theta} + \binom{q_b}{\theta} \leq \binom{q_a+q_b}{\theta}$ and the distinguisher maximizes its probability for $s = s_{\min}$. Recalling that the case of $(a,b) = (0,1)$ is symmetric and that BAD is not set for $(a,b) = (0,0),(1,1)$, we obtain

$$\Pr\left[\mathcal{O}_1 \text{ sets BAD}\right] \leq |a - b| \cdot \binom{q}{\theta} \frac{1}{2^{(\theta-1)s_{\min}}} .$$

7.2   Distance Between $\mathcal{O}_0$ and $\mathcal{O}_1$

Our aim is to bound the term of (1). Consider a given transcript $\tau^{(i-1)}$, which in turn determines the values $\ell^{(i)}$, $T^{(i)}$, and $X^{(i)}$. Let $s = |\mathsf{unpad}(T^{(i)})|$, and consider any value $Y^{(i)}$. As both oracles behave independently for different tweaks, it suffices to focus on earlier queries of the same tweak. We additionally refine into the number of queries with the same or opposite query direction. Let

$$i_{\mathrm{pos}} = \left| \left\{ j \in \{1,\dots,i-1\} \mid T^{(j)} = T^{(i)} \wedge \ell^{(j)} = \ell^{(i)} \right\} \right| ,$$

$$i_{\mathrm{neg}} = \left| \left\{ j \in \{1,\dots,i-1\} \mid T^{(j)} = T^{(i)} \wedge \ell^{(j)} = -\ell^{(i)} \right\} \right| ,$$

and write $i' = i_{\mathrm{pos}} + i_{\mathrm{neg}}$ for brevity. Let

$$h_{\mathrm{pos}}(Y^{(i)}) = \left| \left\{ j \in \{1,\dots,i-1\} \mid T^{(j)} = T^{(i)} \wedge \ell^{(j)} = \ell^{(i)} \wedge \mathsf{right}_s(Y^{(j)}) = \mathsf{right}_s(Y^{(i)}) \right\} \right| ,$$

$$h_{\mathrm{neg}}(Y^{(i)}) = \left| \left\{ j \in \{1,\dots,i-1\} \mid T^{(j)} = T^{(i)} \wedge \ell^{(j)} = -\ell^{(i)} \wedge \mathsf{right}_s(X^{(j)}) = \mathsf{right}_s(Y^{(i)}) \right\} \right| ,$$

where $h_{\mathrm{pos}}(Y^{(i)}) \leq i_{\mathrm{pos}}$ and $h_{\mathrm{neg}}(Y^{(i)}) \leq i_{\mathrm{neg}}$, and write $h(Y^{(i)}) = h_{\mathrm{pos}}(Y^{(i)}) + h_{\mathrm{neg}}(Y^{(i)})$. We can distinct the following cases.

(1) $\ell^{(i)} = 1$ (forward query) and $Y^{(i)} \in \mathsf{rng}(\mathcal{L}_T)$. This case is excluded as $Y^{(i)}$ is not in the support of both probabilities;
(2) $\ell^{(i)} = 1$ (forward query) and $Y^{(i)} \notin \mathsf{rng}(\mathcal{L}_T)$.
    (a) $a = 0$. We have $p_{\mathcal{O}_0,\mathcal{D}}(Y^{(i)}|\tau^{(i-1)}) = p_{\mathcal{O}_1,\mathcal{D}}(Y^{(i)}|\tau^{(i-1)}) = \frac{1}{2^n - i'}$, as the response is drawn uniformly at random from a set of size 2^n minus the amount of earlier queries for the same tweak;

(b) $a = 1$. We have $p_{\mathcal{O}_0, \mathcal{D}}(Y^{(i)} \mid \tau^{(i-1)}) = \frac{1}{2^n - i'}$ as before, and $p_{\mathcal{O}_1, \mathcal{D}}(Y^{(i)} \mid \tau^{(i-1)}) = \frac{1}{2^s(2^{n-s} - h(Y^{(i)}))}$ as $\mathsf{right}_s(Y^{(i)})$ is generated uniformly at random, and $\mathsf{left}_{n-s}(Y^{(i)})$ from a set of size 2^{n-s} minus $h(Y^{(i)})$. For later usage, note that this case fixes $(\ell^{(i)}, T^{(i)}, Y^{(i)})$, and we have $h_{\mathrm{pos}}(Y^{(i)}) \le \theta$ by $\neg\mathsf{BAD}_1$ and $h_{\mathrm{neg}}(Y^{(i)}) \le \theta$ by $\neg\mathsf{BAD}_2$. Therefore, in this case, we have $h(Y^{(i)}) \le 2\theta$.

(3) $\ell^{(i)} = -1$ (inverse query) and $Y^{(i)} \in \mathrm{dom}(\mathcal{L}_T)$. The case is symmetric to (1).

(4) $\ell^{(i)} = -1$ (inverse query) and $Y^{(i)} \notin \mathrm{dom}(\mathcal{L}_T)$.

(a) $b = 0$. The case is symmetric to (2a).

(b) $b = 1$. The case is symmetric to (2b), where now we rely on the fact that by $\neg(\mathsf{BAD}_3 \vee \mathsf{BAD}_4)$, $h(Y^{(i)}) \le 2\theta$.

Cases (2b) and (4b) dominate the chi-squared technique, and we obtain for $\chi^2(\tau^{(i-1)})$ of (1):

$$\chi^2(\tau^{(i-1)}) = \sum_{Y^{(i)}} \frac{\left(\frac{1}{2^n - i'} - \frac{1}{2^s(2^{n-s} - h(Y^{(i)}))} \right)^2}{\frac{1}{2^n - i'}}$$

$$= \sum_{Y^{(i)}} (2^n - i') \cdot \left(\frac{1}{2^n - i'} - \frac{1}{2^s(2^{n-s} - h(Y^{(i)}))} \right)^2$$

$$= \sum_{Y^{(i)}} \frac{1}{(2^n - i')(2^{n-s} - h(Y^{(i)}))^2} \cdot \left(h(Y^{(i)}) - \frac{i'}{2^s} \right)^2$$

$$\le \frac{1}{(2^n - i')(2^{n-s} - 2\theta)^2} \cdot \sum_{Y^{(i)}} \left(h(Y^{(i)}) - \frac{i'}{2^s} \right)^2$$

$$\le \frac{8}{2^{3n-2s}} \cdot \sum_{Y^{(i)}} \left(h(Y^{(i)}) - \frac{i'}{2^s} \right)^2 ,$$

using that $h(Y^{(i)}) \le 2\theta$ by $\neg\mathsf{BAD}$ (see above), and $i' \le 2^{n-1}$ and $\theta \le 2^{n-s_{\max}-2}$. We find for its expectation:

$$\mathrm{Exp}[\chi^2(\tau^{(i-1)})] \le \frac{8}{2^{3n-2s}} \cdot \sum_{Y^{(i)}} \mathrm{Exp}\left[\left(h(Y^{(i)}) - \frac{i'}{2^s} \right)^2 \right] . \tag{21}$$

Recalling that $i' = i_{\text{pos}} + i_{\text{neg}}$ and $h(Y^{(i)}) = h_{\text{pos}}(Y^{(i)}) + h_{\text{neg}}(Y^{(i)})$, the remaining expectation satisfies:

$$
\begin{aligned}
\text{Exp}\left[\left(h(Y^{(i)}) - \frac{i'}{2^s}\right)^2\right] &= \text{Exp}\left[\left(h_{\text{pos}}(Y^{(i)}) + h_{\text{neg}}(Y^{(i)}) - \frac{i_{\text{pos}} + i_{\text{neg}}}{2^s}\right)^2\right] \\
&= \text{Exp}\left[\left(h_{\text{pos}}(Y^{(i)}) - \frac{i_{\text{pos}}}{2^s}\right)^2\right] + \text{Exp}\left[\left(h_{\text{neg}}(Y^{(i)}) - \frac{i_{\text{neg}}}{2^s}\right)^2\right] \\
&\quad + 2 \cdot \text{Exp}\left[\left(h_{\text{pos}}(Y^{(i)}) - \frac{i_{\text{pos}}}{2^s}\right)\left(h_{\text{neg}}(Y^{(i)}) - \frac{i_{\text{neg}}}{2^s}\right)\right] \\
&= \text{Exp}\left[\left(h_{\text{pos}}(Y^{(i)}) - \frac{i_{\text{pos}}}{2^s}\right)^2\right] + \left(h_{\text{neg}}(Y^{(i)}) - \frac{i_{\text{neg}}}{2^s}\right)^2 \\
&\quad + 2 \cdot \left(\text{Exp}\left[h_{\text{pos}}(Y^{(i)})\right] - \frac{i_{\text{pos}}}{2^s}\right)\left(h_{\text{neg}}(Y^{(i)}) - \frac{i_{\text{neg}}}{2^s}\right). \quad (22)
\end{aligned}
$$

As $h_{\text{pos}}(Y^{(i)}) \sim \text{HG}(2^n, 2^{n-s}, i_{\text{pos}})$, by Sect. 2.3 it satisfies

$$
\text{Exp}[h_{\text{pos}}(Y^{(i)})] = \frac{i_{\text{pos}}}{2^s},
$$

$$
\text{Var}[h_{\text{pos}}(Y^{(i)})] = \frac{i_{\text{pos}}}{2^s} \cdot \left(1 - \frac{1}{2^s}\right) \cdot \frac{2^n - i_{\text{pos}}}{2^n - 1},
$$

and we obtain that

$$
\begin{aligned}
\text{Exp}\left[\left(h(Y^{(i)}) - \frac{i'}{2^s}\right)^2\right] &= \frac{i_{\text{pos}}}{2^s} \cdot \left(1 - \frac{1}{2^s}\right) \cdot \frac{2^n - i_{\text{pos}}}{2^n - 1} + \left(h_{\text{neg}}(Y^{(i)}) - \frac{i_{\text{neg}}}{2^s}\right)^2 \\
&\leq \frac{i_{\text{pos}}}{2^s} + \left(h_{\text{neg}}(Y^{(i)}) - \frac{i_{\text{neg}}}{2^s}\right)^2. \quad (23)
\end{aligned}
$$

We furthermore claim the following.

Claim. We have $\sum_{Y^{(i)}} \left(h_{\text{neg}}(Y^{(i)}) - \frac{i_{\text{neg}}}{2^s}\right)^2 \leq i_{\text{neg}}^2 2^{n-s}$.

Proof (of claim). We have

$$
\sum_{Y^{(i)}} \left(h_{\text{neg}}(Y^{(i)}) - \frac{i_{\text{neg}}}{2^s}\right)^2 = \sum_{Z^{(i)}} \sum_{Y^{(i)} = *\|Z^{(i)}} \left(h_{\text{neg}}(Y^{(i)}) - \frac{i_{\text{neg}}}{2^s}\right)^2.
$$

As $h_{\text{neg}}(Y^{(i)}) = h_{\text{neg}}(Y^{(i)\prime})$ for $\text{right}_s(Y^{(i)}) = \text{right}_s(Y^{(i)\prime})$, we subsequently have

$$\sum_{Y^{(i)}} \left(h_{\text{neg}}(Y^{(i)}) - \frac{i_{\text{neg}}}{2^s} \right)^2 = \sum_{Z^{(i)}} 2^{n-s} \left(h_{\text{neg}}(0^{n-s} \| Z^{(i)}) - \frac{i_{\text{neg}}}{2^s} \right)^2$$

$$= 2^{n-s} \sum_{Z^{(i)}} \left(\left(h_{\text{neg}}(0^{n-s} \| Z^{(i)}) \right)^2 \right.$$

$$\left. - 2h_{\text{neg}}(0^{n-s} \| Z^{(i)}) \frac{i_{\text{neg}}}{2^s} + \left(\frac{i_{\text{neg}}}{2^s} \right)^2 \right)$$

$$\leq 2^{n-s} \left(i_{\text{neg}}^2 - \frac{2i_{\text{neg}}^2}{2^s} + \frac{2^s i_{\text{neg}}^2}{2^{2s}} \right)$$

$$= 2^{n-s} \left(i_{\text{neg}}^2 - \frac{i_{\text{neg}}^2}{2^s} \right) \leq i_{\text{neg}}^2 2^{n-s}.$$

□

Equations (21) and (23), alongside above claim, constitute to

$$\text{Exp}[\chi^2(\tau^{(i-1)})] \leq \frac{8}{2^{3n-2s}} \cdot \left(i_{\text{pos}} 2^{n-s} + i_{\text{neg}}^2 2^{n-s} \right)$$

$$= \frac{8 \left(i_{\text{pos}} + i_{\text{neg}}^2 \right)}{2^{2n-s}}. \tag{24}$$

If $(a, b) \in \{(1,0), (0,1)\}$, we have $i_{\text{pos}}, i_{\text{neg}} \leq (i-1)$ and

$$(24) \leq \frac{8 \left((i-1) + (i-1)^2 \right)}{2^{2n-s}}.$$

This bound is independent of the direction of the i-th query ($\ell^{(i)} \in \{-1, 1\}$), but the parameter s depends on the query, as $s = |\text{unpad}(T^{(i)})|$. The adversary maximizes its chances by sticking to the maximal s. This, finally, gives by Lemma 1:

$$\|p_{\mathcal{O}_0, \mathcal{D}}(\cdot) - p_{\mathcal{O}_1, \mathcal{D}}(\cdot)\| \leq \left(\frac{1}{2} \sum_{i=1}^{q} \frac{8 \left((i-1) + (i-1)^2 \right)}{2^{2n - s_{\max}}} \right)^{1/2}$$

$$= \left(\frac{4}{3} \frac{q^3 - q}{2^{2n - s_{\max}}} \right)^{1/2} \leq \left(\frac{2q^3}{2^{2n - s_{\max}}} \right)^{1/2}.$$

On the other hand, if $(a, b) = (1, 1)$, we have $i_{\text{pos}}, i_{\text{neg}} \leq \theta$ and

$$(24) \leq \frac{8 \left(\theta + \theta^2 \right)}{2^{2n-s}}.$$

Again sticking to the maximal s, this gives by Lemma 1:

$$\|p_{\mathcal{O}_0, \mathcal{D}}(\cdot) - p_{\mathcal{O}_1, \mathcal{D}}(\cdot)\| \leq \left(\frac{1}{2} \sum_{i=1}^{q} \frac{8 \left(\theta + \theta^2 \right)}{2^{2n - s_{\max}}} \right)^{1/2} = \left(\frac{4 \left(\theta + \theta^2 \right) q}{2^{2n - s_{\max}}} \right)^{1/2}.$$

8   Proof of Lemma 3 on H

Consider any distinguisher $\mathcal{D}$ making at most $q \leq 2^{n-1}$ queries, all of length in $[n + s_{\min}, 2n - 1]$ bits. The distinguisher has access to either random system H or $\rho \xleftarrow{\$} \mathrm{VPerm}([n, 2n - 1])$, and without loss of generality, $\mathcal{D}$ is computationally unbounded and deterministic.

We will use the chi-squared method of Sect. 2.2, with $\mathcal{O}_0 = H$ being the real system and $\mathcal{O}_1 = \rho$ the ideal system. Summarize the communication of $\mathcal{D}$ with its oracle in a transcript $\boldsymbol{\tau} = (\tau^{(1)}, \ldots, \tau^{(q)})$, where $\tau^{(i)} = (\ell^{(i)}, X^{(i)}, Y^{(i)})$ consists of a bit $\ell^{(i)} \in \{-1, 1\}$ indicating the direction of the query (1 means forward, and -1 means inverse), an input value $(X^{(i)})$, and a response $Y^{(i)}$, in such a way that $O^{\ell^{(i)}}(X^{(i)}) = Y^{(i)}$ for $\mathcal{O} \in \{\mathcal{O}_0, \mathcal{O}_1\}$.

Unlike the proof of Sect. 7, we will not rely on additional bad events, and there is no need to perform a hybrid argument and to upper bound the probability of bad events. We immediately move to bounding the term of (1), and the proof is very similar to that in Sect. 7.2. Consider a given transcript $\boldsymbol{\tau}^{(i-1)}$, which in turn determines the values $\ell^{(i)}$ and $X^{(i)}$. Let $s = |X^{(i)}| - n$, and consider any value $Y^{(i)}$. As both oracles behave independently for different input lengths, it suffices to focus on earlier queries of the same size. We additionally refine into the number of queries with the same or opposite query direction. Let

$$i_{\mathrm{pos}} = \left| \left\{ j \in \{1, \ldots, i - 1\} \mid |X^{(j)}| = |X^{(i)}| \wedge \ell^{(j)} = \ell^{(i)} \right\} \right|,$$

$$i_{\mathrm{neg}} = \left| \left\{ j \in \{1, \ldots, i - 1\} \mid |X^{(j)}| = |X^{(i)}| \wedge \ell^{(j)} = -\ell^{(i)} \right\} \right|,$$

and write $i' = i_{\mathrm{pos}} + i_{\mathrm{neg}}$. Let

$$h_{\mathrm{pos}}(Y^{(i)}) = \left| \left\{ j \in \{1, \ldots, i - 1\} \mid |X^{(j)}| = |X^{(i)}| \wedge \ell^{(j)} = \ell^{(i)} \wedge \mathsf{right}_s(Y^{(j)}) = \mathsf{right}_s(Y^{(i)}) \right\} \right|,$$

$$h_{\mathrm{neg}}(Y^{(i)}) = \left| \left\{ j \in \{1, \ldots, i - 1\} \mid |X^{(j)}| = |X^{(i)}| \wedge \ell^{(j)} = -\ell^{(i)} \wedge \mathsf{right}_s(X^{(j)}) = \mathsf{right}_s(Y^{(i)}) \right\} \right|,$$

where $h_{\mathrm{pos}}(Y^{(i)}) \leq i_{\mathrm{pos}}$ and $h_{\mathrm{neg}}(Y^{(i)}) \leq i_{\mathrm{neg}}$, and write $h(Y^{(i)}) = h_{\mathrm{pos}}(Y^{(i)}) + h_{\mathrm{neg}}(Y^{(i)})$. We can distinct the following cases.

(1) $\ell^{(i)} = 1$ (forward query) and $Y^{(i)} \in \mathrm{rng}(\mathcal{L}_s)$. This case is excluded as $Y^{(i)}$ is not in the support of both probabilities;
(2) $\ell^{(i)} = 1$ (forward query) and $Y^{(i)} \notin \mathrm{rng}(\mathcal{L}_s)$. We have $p_{\mathcal{O}_0, \mathcal{D}}(Y^{(i)} \mid \boldsymbol{\tau}^{(i-1)}) = \frac{1}{2^{n+s} - i'}$ as the response is drawn uniformly at random from a set of size 2^{n+s} minus the amount of earlier queries for the same tweak, and $p_{\mathcal{O}_1, \mathcal{D}}(Y^{(i)} \mid \boldsymbol{\tau}^{(i-1)}) = \frac{1}{2^s (2^n - h(Y^{(i)}))}$ as $\mathsf{right}_s(Y^{(i)})$ is generated uniformly at random, and $\mathsf{left}_n(Y^{(i)})$ from a set of size 2^n minus $h(Y^{(i)})$.
(3) $\ell^{(i)} = -1$ (inverse query) and $Y^{(i)} \in \mathrm{dom}(\mathcal{L}_s)$. The case is symmetric to (1).
(4) $\ell^{(i)} = -1$ (inverse query) and $Y^{(i)} \notin \mathrm{dom}(\mathcal{L}_s)$. The case is symmetric to (2).

Cases (2) and (4) dominate the chi-squared technique, and we obtain for $\chi^2(\tau^{(i-1)})$ of (1):

$$\chi^2(\tau^{(i-1)}) = \sum_{Y^{(i)}} \frac{\left(\frac{1}{2^{n+s}-i'} - \frac{1}{2^s(2^n-h(Y^{(i)}))}\right)^2}{\frac{1}{2^{n+s}-i'}}$$

$$= \sum_{Y^{(i)}} (2^{n+s} - i') \cdot \left(\frac{1}{2^{n+s}-i'} - \frac{1}{2^s(2^n-h(Y^{(i)}))}\right)^2$$

$$= \sum_{Y^{(i)}} \frac{1}{(2^{n+s}-i')(2^n-h(Y^{(i)}))^2} \cdot \left(h(Y^{(i)}) - \frac{i'}{2^s}\right)^2$$

$$\leq \frac{1}{(2^{n+s}-i')(2^n-i')^2} \cdot \sum_{Y^{(i)}} \left(h(Y^{(i)}) - \frac{i'}{2^s}\right)^2$$

$$\leq \frac{8}{2^{3n+s}} \cdot \sum_{Y^{(i)}} \left(h(Y^{(i)}) - \frac{i'}{2^s}\right)^2,$$

using that $h(Y^{(i)}) \leq i'$, and $i' \leq 2^{n-1}$. We find for its expectation:

$$\mathrm{Exp}[\chi^2(\tau^{(i-1)})] \leq \frac{8}{2^{3n+s}} \cdot \sum_{Y^{(i)}} \mathrm{Exp}\left[\left(h(Y^{(i)}) - \frac{i'}{2^s}\right)^2\right]. \tag{25}$$

Recalling that $i' = i_{\mathrm{pos}} + i_{\mathrm{neg}}$ and $h(Y^{(i)}) = h_{\mathrm{pos}}(Y^{(i)}) + h_{\mathrm{neg}}(Y^{(i)})$, the remaining expectation satisfies (identically to (22)):

$$\mathrm{Exp}\left[\left(h(Y^{(i)}) - \frac{i'}{2^s}\right)^2\right] = \mathrm{Exp}\left[\left(h_{\mathrm{pos}}(Y^{(i)}) - \frac{i_{\mathrm{pos}}}{2^s}\right)^2\right] + \left(h_{\mathrm{neg}}(Y^{(i)}) - \frac{i_{\mathrm{neg}}}{2^s}\right)^2$$

$$+ 2 \cdot \left(\mathrm{Exp}\left[h_{\mathrm{pos}}(Y^{(i)})\right] - \frac{i_{\mathrm{pos}}}{2^s}\right)\left(h_{\mathrm{neg}}(Y^{(i)}) - \frac{i_{\mathrm{neg}}}{2^s}\right).$$

As $h_{\mathrm{pos}}(Y^{(i)}) \sim \mathrm{HG}(2^{n+s}, 2^n, i_{\mathrm{pos}})$, by Sect. 2.3 it satisfies

$$\mathrm{Exp}[h_{\mathrm{pos}}(Y^{(i)})] = \frac{i_{\mathrm{pos}}}{2^s},$$

$$\mathrm{Var}[h_{\mathrm{pos}}(Y^{(i)})] = \frac{i_{\mathrm{pos}}}{2^s} \cdot \left(1 - \frac{1}{2^s}\right) \cdot \frac{2^{n+s} - i_{\mathrm{pos}}}{2^{n+s} - 1},$$

and we obtain that

$$\mathrm{Exp}\left[\left(h(Y^{(i)}) - \frac{i'}{2^s}\right)^2\right] = \frac{i_{\mathrm{pos}}}{2^s} \cdot \left(1 - \frac{1}{2^s}\right) \cdot \frac{2^{n+s} - i_{\mathrm{pos}}}{2^{n+s} - 1} + \left(h_{\mathrm{neg}}(Y^{(i)}) - \frac{i_{\mathrm{neg}}}{2^s}\right)^2$$

$$\leq \frac{i_{\mathrm{pos}}}{2^s} + \left(h_{\mathrm{neg}}(Y^{(i)}) - \frac{i_{\mathrm{neg}}}{2^s}\right)^2. \tag{26}$$

We furthermore claim the following.

Claim. We have $\sum_{Y^{(i)}} \left(h_{\text{neg}}(Y^{(i)}) - \frac{i_{\text{neg}}}{2^s} \right)^2 \leq i_{\text{neg}}^2 2^n$.

Proof (of claim). The proof is identical to that of the claim in Sect. 7.2, except that now $(n+s)$-bit values $Y^{(i)}$ are involved.   □

Equations (25) and (26), alongside above claim, constitute to

$$\text{Exp}[\chi^2(\tau^{(i-1)})] \leq \frac{8}{2^{3n+s}} \cdot \left(i_{\text{pos}} 2^n + i_{\text{neg}}^2 2^n \right)$$

$$= \frac{8 \left(i_{\text{pos}} + i_{\text{neg}}^2 \right)}{2^{2n+s}}$$

$$\leq \frac{8 \left((i-1) + (i-1)^2 \right)}{2^{2n+s}} .$$

This bound is independent of the direction of the i-th query ($\ell^{(i)} \in \{-1,1\}$), but the parameter s depends on the query, as $s = |X^{(i)}| - n$. The adversary maximizes its chances by sticking to the minimal s. This, finally, gives by Lemma 1:

$$\mathbf{Adv}_H^{\text{vsprp}}(\mathcal{D}) = \|p_{\mathcal{O}_0,\mathcal{D}}(\cdot) - p_{\mathcal{O}_1,\mathcal{D}}(\cdot)\| \leq \left(\frac{1}{2} \sum_{i=1}^{q} \frac{8 \left((i-1) + (i-1)^2 \right)}{2^{2n+s_{\min}}} \right)^{1/2}$$

$$= \left(\frac{4}{3} \frac{q^3 - q}{2^{2n+s_{\min}}} \right)^{1/2} \leq \left(\frac{2q^3}{2^{2n+s_{\min}}} \right)^{1/2} .$$

Acknowledgments. This work was supported in part by the Research Council KU Leuven: GOA TENSE (C16/15/058). Yu Long Chen is supported by a Ph.D. Fellowship from the Research Foundation - Flanders (FWO). Bart Mennink is supported by a postdoctoral fellowship from the Netherlands Organisation for Scientific Research (NWO) under Veni grant 016.Veni.173.017. Mridul Nandi is supported by the Wisekey Project in the R.C.Bose Centre of Cryptology and Security. The authors would like to thank the anonymous reviewers for their comments and suggestions.

A   Example Mixing Functions

Chen et al. [11] defined pure mixing functions as follows.

Definition 1. *Let $m, n \in \mathbb{N}$ such that $m \leq n$, and let $\text{mix} : \cup_{s=m}^{n}(\{0,1\}^s)^2 \to \cup_{s=m}^{n}(\{0,1\}^s)^2$ be a length-preserving permutation. Define mix_L as the left half of its evaluation and mix_R as its right half. The mixing function is called* pure *if for all $s \in [m,n]$:*

- *$\text{mix}_L(A, \cdot)$ is a permutation for all $A \in \{0,1\}^s$, and*
- *$\text{mix}_R(\cdot, B)$ is a permutation for all $B \in \{0,1\}^s$.*

Chen et al. already pointed out that the simplest possible pure mixing function, $\text{mix}(A, B) = (B, A)$, is sufficient for LDT.

272 Y. L. Chen et al.

References

1. Andreeva, E., et al.: COLM v1 (2016), submission to CAESAR competition
2. Andreeva, E., Bogdanov, A., Luykx, A., Mennink, B., Tischhauser, E., Yasuda, K.: Parallelizable and Authenticated Online Ciphers. In: Sako and Sarkar [42], pp. 424–443
3. Andreeva, E., Bogdanov, A., Luykx, A., Mennink, B., Tischhauser, E., Yasuda, K.: AES-COPA v. 1 (2015), submission to CAESAR competition
4. Avanzi, R.: The QARMA block cipher family. Almost MDS matrices over rings with zero divisors, nearly symmetric even-mansour constructions with non-involutory central rounds, and search heuristics for low-latency s-boxes. IACR Trans. Symmetric Cryptol. **2017**(1), 4–44 (2017). https://doi.org/10.13154/tosc.v2017.i1.4-44
5. Beierle, C., Jean, J., Kölbl, S., Leander, G., Moradi, A., Peyrin, T., Sasaki, Y., Sasdrich, P., Sim, S.M.: The SKINNY family of block ciphers and its low-latency variant MANTIS. In: Robshaw, M., Katz, J. (eds.) CRYPTO 2016. LNCS, vol. 9815, pp. 123–153. Springer, Heidelberg (2016). https://doi.org/10.1007/978-3-662-53008-5_5
6. Bellare, M., Rogaway, P., Spies, T.: The FFX Mode of Operation for Format-Preserving Encryption (2010), submission to NIST
7. Bertoni, G., Daemen, J., Peeters, M., Van Assche, G.: Sponge functions. In: ECRYPT Hash Workshop 2007, May 2007
8. Brier, E., Peyrin, T., Stern, J.: BPS: A Format-Preserving Encryption Proposal (2010), submission to NIST
9. Canteaut, A., Viswanathan, K. (eds.): INDOCRYPT 2004. LNCS, vol. 3348. Springer, Heidelberg (2005). https://doi.org/10.1007/b104579
10. Chakraborty, D., Sarkar, P.: HCH: a new tweakable enciphering scheme using the hash-encrypt-hash approach. In: Barua, R., Lange, T. (eds.) INDOCRYPT 2006. LNCS, vol. 4329, pp. 287–302. Springer, Heidelberg (2006). https://doi.org/10.1007/11941378_21
11. Chen, Y., Luykx, A., Mennink, B., Preneel, B.: Efficient length doubling from tweakable block ciphers. IACR Trans. Symmetric Cryptol. **2017**(3), 253–270 (2017)
12. Coron, J.-S., Dodis, Y., Mandal, A., Seurin, Y.: A domain extender for the ideal cipher. In: Micciancio, D. (ed.) TCC 2010. LNCS, vol. 5978, pp. 273–289. Springer, Heidelberg (2010). https://doi.org/10.1007/978-3-642-11799-2_17
13. Daemen, J.: Hash Function and Cipher Design: Strategies Based on Linear and Differential Cryptanalysis. Ph.D. thesis, Katholieke Universiteit Leuven, Leuven, Belgium (1995)
14. Dai, W., Hoang, V.T., Tessaro, S.: Information-Theoretic Indistinguishability via the Chi-Squared Method. In: Katz and Shacham [25], pp. 497–523
15. Dworkin, M.: NIST SP 800–38E: Recommendation for Block Cipher Modes of Operation: The XTS-AES Mode for Confidentiality on Storage Devices (2010)
16. Dworkin, M.: NIST SP 800–38G: Recommendation for Block Cipher Modes of Operation: Methods for Format-Preserving Encryption (2016)
17. Gilboa, S., Gueron, S.: Distinguishing a truncated random permutation from a random function. Cryptology ePrint Archive, Report 2015/773 (2015)
18. GS1: EPC[TM] Radio-Frequency Identity Protocols Generation-2 UHF RFID, Version 2.0.1 (2015). https://www.gs1.org/sites/default/files/docs/epc/Gen2_Protocol_Standard.pdf
19. GS1: EPC Tag Data Standard, Version 1.11 (2017). https://www.gs1.org/sites/default/files/docs/epc/GS1_EPC_TDS_i1_11.pdf

20. Halevi, S.: EME*: extending EME to handle arbitrary-length messages with associated data. In: Canteaut and Viswanathan [9], pp. 315–327
21. Halevi, S.: Invertible universal hashing and the TET encryption mode. In: Menezes, A. (ed.) CRYPTO 2007. LNCS, vol. 4622, pp. 412–429. Springer, Heidelberg (2007). https://doi.org/10.1007/978-3-540-74143-5_23
22. Hall, C., Wagner, D., Kelsey, J., Schneier, B.: Building PRFs from PRPs. In: Krawczyk, H. (ed.) CRYPTO 1998. LNCS, vol. 1462, pp. 370–389. Springer, Heidelberg (1998). https://doi.org/10.1007/BFb0055742
23. Iwata, T., Minematsu, K., Peyrin, T., Seurin, Y.: ZMAC: A Fast Tweakable Block Cipher Mode for Highly Secure Message Authentication. In: Katz and Shacham [25], pp. 34–65
24. Jean, J., Nikolić, I., Peyrin, T.: Tweaks and keys for block ciphers: the TWEAKEY framework. In: Sarkar, P., Iwata, T. (eds.) ASIACRYPT 2014. LNCS, vol. 8874, pp. 274–288. Springer, Heidelberg (2014). https://doi.org/10.1007/978-3-662-45608-8_15
25. Katz, J., Shacham, H. (eds.): CRYPTO 2017. LNCS, vol. 10403. Springer, Cham (2017). https://doi.org/10.1007/978-3-319-63697-9
26. Krovetz, T., Rogaway, P.: The software performance of authenticated-encryption modes. In: Joux, A. (ed.) FSE 2011. LNCS, vol. 6733, pp. 306–327. Springer, Heidelberg (2011). https://doi.org/10.1007/978-3-642-21702-9_18
27. McGrew, D.A., Fluhrer, S.R.: The security of the extended codebook (XCB) mode of operation. In: Adams, C., Miri, A., Wiener, M. (eds.) SAC 2007. LNCS, vol. 4876, pp. 311–327. Springer, Heidelberg (2007). https://doi.org/10.1007/978-3-540-77360-3_20
28. McGrew, D.A., Viega, J.: The security and performance of the galois/counter mode (GCM) of operation. In: Canteaut and Viswanathan [9], pp. 343–355
29. Minematsu, K.: Beyond-birthday-bound security based on tweakable block cipher. In: Dunkelman, O. (ed.) FSE 2009. LNCS, vol. 5665, pp. 308–326. Springer, Heidelberg (2009). https://doi.org/10.1007/978-3-642-03317-9_19
30. Minematsu, K., Iwata, T.: Building blockcipher from tweakable blockcipher: extending fse 2009 proposal. In: Chen, L. (ed.) IMACC 2011. LNCS, vol. 7089, pp. 391–412. Springer, Heidelberg (2011). https://doi.org/10.1007/978-3-642-25516-8_24
31. Nandi, M.: A generic method to extend message space of a strong pseudorandom permutation. Computación y Sistemas 12(3), 285–296 (2009)
32. Nandi, M.: XLS is not a strong pseudorandom permutation. In: Sarkar, P., Iwata, T. (eds.) ASIACRYPT 2014. LNCS, vol. 8873, pp. 478–490. Springer, Heidelberg (2014). https://doi.org/10.1007/978-3-662-45611-8_25
33. Nandi, M.: On the optimality of non-linear computations of length-preserving encryption schemes. In: Iwata, T., Cheon, J.H. (eds.) ASIACRYPT 2015. LNCS, vol. 9453, pp. 113–133. Springer, Heidelberg (2015). https://doi.org/10.1007/978-3-662-48800-3_5
34. Nandi, M.: Revisiting security claims of XLS and COPA. Cryptology ePrint Archive, Report 2015/444 (2015)
35. Peyrin, T., Seurin, Y.: Counter-in-Tweak: authenticated encryption modes for tweakable block ciphers. In: Robshaw, M., Katz, J. (eds.) CRYPTO 2016. LNCS, vol. 9814, pp. 33–63. Springer, Heidelberg (2016). https://doi.org/10.1007/978-3-662-53018-4_2
36. Qualcomm: Pointer Authentication on ARMv8.3 – Design and Analysis of the New Software Security Instructions (2017). https://www.qualcomm.com/media/documents/files/whitepaper-pointer-authentication-on-armv8-3.pdf

37. Ristenpart, T., Rogaway, P.: How to enrich the message space of a cipher. In: Biryukov, A. (ed.) FSE 2007. LNCS, vol. 4593, pp. 101–118. Springer, Heidelberg (2007). https://doi.org/10.1007/978-3-540-74619-5_7

38. Rogaway, P.: Efficient instantiations of tweakable blockciphers and refinements to modes OCB and PMAC. In: Lee, P.J. (ed.) ASIACRYPT 2004. LNCS, vol. 3329, pp. 16–31. Springer, Heidelberg (2004). https://doi.org/10.1007/978-3-540-30539-2_2

39. Rogaway, P., Bellare, M., Black, J., Krovetz, T.: OCB: a block-cipher mode of operation for efficient authenticated encryption. In: Reiter, M.K., Samarati, P. (eds.) ACM CCS 2001, pp. 196–205. ACM (2001)

40. Rogaway, P., Wooding, M., Zhang, H.: The security of ciphertext stealing. In: Canteaut, A. (ed.) FSE 2012. LNCS, vol. 7549, pp. 180–195. Springer, Heidelberg (2012). https://doi.org/10.1007/978-3-642-34047-5_11

41. Rogaway, P., Zhang, H.: Online ciphers from tweakable blockciphers. In: Kiayias, A. (ed.) CT-RSA 2011. LNCS, vol. 6558, pp. 237–249. Springer, Heidelberg (2011). https://doi.org/10.1007/978-3-642-19074-2_16

42. Sako, K., Sarkar, P. (eds.): ASIACRYPT 2013. LNCS, vol. 8269. Springer, Heidelberg (2013). https://doi.org/10.1007/978-3-642-42033-7

43. Sarkar, P.: Improving upon the TET mode of operation. In: Nam, K.-H., Rhee, G. (eds.) ICISC 2007. LNCS, vol. 4817, pp. 180–192. Springer, Heidelberg (2007). https://doi.org/10.1007/978-3-540-76788-6_15

44. Schnorr, C.P., Vaudenay, S.: Parallel FFT-hashing. In: Anderson, R. (ed.) FSE 1993. LNCS, vol. 809, pp. 149–156. Springer, Heidelberg (1994). https://doi.org/10.1007/3-540-58108-1_18

45. Shrimpton, T., Terashima, R.S.: A modular framework for building variable-input-length tweakable ciphers. In: Sako and Sarkar [42], pp. 405–423

46. Wang, P., Feng, D., Wu, W.: HCTR: a variable-input-length enciphering mode. In: Feng, D., Lin, D., Yung, M. (eds.) CISC 2005. LNCS, vol. 3822, pp. 175–188. Springer, Heidelberg (2005). https://doi.org/10.1007/11599548_15

47. Ehrsam, W.F., Meyer, C.H.W., Smith, J.L., Tuchman, W.L.: Message verification and transmission error detection by block chaining. US Patent 40,740,66 (1976)

48. Zhang, H.: Length-Doubling ciphers and tweakable ciphers. In: Bao, F., Samarati, P., Zhou, J. (eds.) ACNS 2012. LNCS, vol. 7341, pp. 100–116. Springer, Heidelberg (2012). https://doi.org/10.1007/978-3-642-31284-7_7

Building Quantum-One-Way Functions from Block Ciphers: Davies-Meyer and Merkle-Damgård Constructions

Akinori Hosoyamada$^{(\boxtimes)}$ and Kan Yasuda

NTT Secure Platform Laboratories, 3-9-11, Midori-cho Musashino-shi,
Tokyo 180-8585, Japan
{hosoyamada.akinori,yasuda.kan}@lab.ntt.co.jp

Abstract. We present hash functions that are almost optimally one-way in the quantum setting. Our hash functions are based on the Merkle-Damgård construction iterating a Davies-Meyer compression function, which is built from a block cipher. The quantum setting that we use is a natural extention of the classical ideal cipher model. Recent work has revealed that symmetric-key schemes using a block cipher or a public permutation, such as CBC-MAC or the Even-Mansour cipher, can get completely broken with quantum superposition attacks, in polynomial time of the block size. Since many of the popular schemes are built from a block cipher or a permutation, the recent findings motivate us to study such schemes that are provably secure in the quantum setting. Unfortunately, no such schemes are known, unless one relies on certain algebraic assumptions. In this paper we present hash constructions that are provably one-way in the quantum setting without algebraic assumptions, solely based on the assumption that the underlying block cipher is ideal. To do this, we reduce one-wayness to a problem of finding a fixed point and then bound its success probability with a distinguishing advantage. We develop a generic tool that helps us prove indistinguishability of two quantum oracle distributions.

Keywords: Symmetric key cryptography · Provable security
Merkle-Damgård · Davies-Meyer · One-wayness · Non-invertibility
Preimage-resistance · Derangement · Fixed point
Indistinguishability · Quantum ideal cipher model

1 Introduction

The epoch-making work by Shor [25] revealed that widely used cryptographic schemes such as RSA, DSA and ECDSA would become insecure when a practical quantum computer becomes available. Since then, researchers have become increasingly interested in so-called *post-quantum* cryptography. Today there exist several schemes that claim to provide post-quantum security. Some of them are based on computational problems that are seemingly hard to solve even with

© International Association for Cryptologic Research 2018
T. Peyrin and S. Galbraith (Eds.): ASIACRYPT 2018, LNCS 11272, pp. 275–304, 2018.
https://doi.org/10.1007/978-3-030-03326-2_10

quantum computers, like the lattice-based cryptography based on the shortest vector problem or its variants. Others are based on the assumption that there exist post-quantum-secure symmetric-key primitives, e.g. digital signatures based on one-way hash functions.

Two Levels of Post-Quantum Security. There are two notions of security against adversaries with quantum computers: *standard* security and *quantum* security [33]. In this paper we focus on the quantum security, because it is stronger. In the standard-security setting we assume that adversaries have quantum computers but can make only classical queries to the oracles. On the other hand, in the quantum-security setting, adversaries are allowed to make quantum superposition queries. In other words, that a scheme provides quantum security means that it will remain secure even in the far future when all computations and communications are done in quantum superposition states.

Post-Quantum Insecurity of Symmetric-Key Constructions. On the negative side, it has turned out that a number of symmetric-key constructions as well as many public-key schemes can be broken in polynomial time (of the block size) if adversaries are allowed to make quantum superposition queries. For example, such adversaries can distinguish 3-round Feistel ciphers from random [18], recover keys of Even-Mansour ciphers [19], forge various message authentication codes like CBC-MAC [16], by making only polynomially many queries. These attacks tell us that in general there is no guarantee that the classical security of a symmetric-key scheme implies its quantum security.

Quantum-Secure Schemes Based on One-Way Functions. On the positive side, previous work [7,26,33] has shown that, if we assume the existence of one-way functions that are hard to invert even with quantum computers, then we can come up with a wide range of quantum-secure schemes. These include pseudo-random functions, message authentication codes, universal one-way hash functions, one-time signatures, and EU-CMA signature schemes. Thus, the existence of quantum-secure one-way functions is fundamental, just as in the classical setting, and the cryptographic hash functions in use like SHA-3 [22] and SHA-2 [21] are considered to be possible candidates also for the instantiation of these quantum-secure one-way functions.

Cryptographic Hash Functions Revisited. Recall that cryptographic hash functions are normally constructed only with public, "keyless" primitives, either from a public permutation or a block cipher having no secret keys (i.e. key inputs are public). For example, SHA-3 is constructed from a public permutation, and SHA-2 is essentially based on a public block cipher. The generic security (indifferentiability) of the sponge construction used in SHA-3 is proven in the random permutation model, and the security (one-wayness and collision resistance) of Davies-Meyer construction adopted by the SHA-2 compression function is proven in the ideal cipher model.

However, as mentioned above, we should carefully note that the classical provable security of these hash functions may not carry over to the quantum setting. For example, recently Carstens et al. [9] gave an evidence that SHA-3 is not indifferentiable in the quantum setting, based on a conjecture. Therefore, here we would like to pose a fundamental question: do we have a provably quantum-secure construction of one-way hash functions?

1.1   Our Contributions

Our answer is positive; in this paper we show that the Merkle-Damgård iteration with the Davies-Meyer compression function is a quantum-secure one-way hash function. This has been a popular design used in MD5, SHA-1 and SHA-2. Indeed, our construction is essentially identical to the modes of operation used in these traditional hash functions, except for minor differences in padding rules, initialization vectors, and input-size restrictions on the underlying block cipher.

Our contributions come in three steps. First, we fix a security model in which we prove our main result. Second, we develop a generic tool for bounding quantum oracle indistinguishability. Finally, we use the tool to prove our main result.

1. **Introducing the Quantum Ideal Cipher Model.** As the first step we introduce the *quantum ideal cipher* model, which, as the name suggests, naturally extends the ideal cipher model in the classical setting. Similarly to the classical case, we treat the underlying block cipher as an ideal cipher E, i.e., E_k is a random permutation for each key k. We then allow quantum adversaries to make both forward and backward queries to the cipher. In our model, a table of all values for the ideal cipher E is determined at the beginning of each game, and the oracle that computes $E_{(\cdot)}(\cdot)$ and $E_{(\cdot)}^{-1}(\cdot)$ are given to the adversary. Following the style of previous work in the classical setting, we consider (quantum) information-theoretic adversaries that have no limitation on computational resources, such as time or the number of available qubits. We only bound the number q of queries that the adversary makes to its oracles.

2. **A Generic Tool for Quantum Indistinguishability.** The second step is to develop a proof tool to upper-bound quantum oracle distinguishing advantages. The tool can be applied to any pair (D_1, D_2) of distributions on an arbitrary (finite) set of functions (Proposition 3.1.) The tool enables us to obtain an upper bound by mere combinatorial enumeration and associated probability computations. There is a simplified version of the tool corresponding to the special case when D_1 and D_2 are distributions on a set of boolean functions (having some fixed domain size) with D_2 being a degenerate distribution at the zero function (Proposition 3.2.) In fact this simplified version suffices to prove our main result. Our tool is developed by generalizing and integrating several existing techniques [2,5,15,27] corresponding to some limited cases of the simplified version. However, previous work treats only

the case that D_1 is some specific distributions, and no previous work seems suitable to our situation. We developed our tool so that it looks familiar to researchers on symmetric-key provable security (like coefficient-H technique).

3. **One-Wayness of Merkle-Damgård with Davies-Meyer.** The final but main contribution of this paper is to give almost optimal security bound for quantum one-wayness of the Merkle-Damgård construction with a Davies-Meyer compression function. That is, any quantum query adversary needs to make about $2^{n/2}$ queries to invert the function with n-bit output. This bound is almost optimal since the Grover search can find a preimage of random functions with $O(2^{n/2})$ quantum queries, and it is proven that the Grover search is optimal strategy to find a preimage of random functions [15]. In our proof, the input length of functions can be exponentially long but must be fixed. We stress that this is the first proof for quantum security on symmetric key schemes based on public block ciphers.

Technical Details. In this paper we give exact security bounds without any asymptotic notation, because security parameters of symmetric-key schemes are usually fixed to some constant.

This paper considers two security notions: non-invertibility and one-wayness. When we say $h : \{0,1\}^s \rightarrow \{0,1\}^n$ has one-wayness, we mean that any adversary cannot find a preimage of $y = h(x)$, where x is randomly chosen from $\{0,1\}^s$.[1] On the other hand, when we say h has non-invertibility, we mean that any adversary cannot find a preimage of y, where y is randomly chosen from $\{0,1\}^n$. These are similar but independent notions.

We firstly show non-invertibility of permutation with feedforward in the quantum ideal permutation model, secondly show both non-invertibility and one-wayness of Davies-Meyer constructions, and finally show both non-invertibility and one-wayness of Merkle-Damgård constructions. It might be unexpected that permutation with feedforward is non-invertible in the quantum setting although it uses only public permutation and XOR operation, which seems similar to the Even-Mansour ciphers that are broken by quantum superposition attacks.

Due to a technical reason, we need some restriction on usage of keys in Davies-Meyer construction. Similarly, we need a padding function for Merkle-Damgård construction. However, these do not mean restriction on available block ciphers. As a subsidiary result, we also show that any quantum query adversary needs to make about $2^{n/2}$ queries to find a fixed point of a public random permutation (which allow adversaries to make both forward and backward quantum queries). This is the first result on quantum query lower bound for a property related to public random permutations.

Our proof strategy is to reduce the problem of breaking security notions to the problem of distinguishing oracle distributions on boolean functions. A similar strategy can be found in [15]. Then indistinguishability between quantum oracle distributions is shown using our new proof tool described above. To reduce problems on public random permutations to problems on boolean functions,

---

[1] This security notion is also called *preimage resistance* (see [24] for example).

we try to approximate the uniform distribution on random permutations by combining distributions on boolean functions with the uniform distribution on derangements (permutations without fixed points).

1.2 Related Work

There already exist powerful tools that aim to give quantum security bounds for cryptographic schemes. These tools include "one-way to hiding" lemma and quantum random oracle programming by Unruh [28,29], the rank method and oracle indistinguishability frameworks by Zhandry [7,33,34]. These tools do not seem to consider the situation where adversaries can make both forward and backward queries to public permutations or block ciphers. There exists previous work [1] that proves quantum security of Even-Mansour ciphers in a model where adversaries make both forward and backward queries to the underlying permutation, but it should be noted that the proof [1] requires a quantum computational hardness assumption (the hidden shift problem).

A quantum version of the random oracle model is proposed by Boneh et al., [6], and many schemes are proven to be secure in this model ([28,34], for example). Regarding symmetric key schemes, several papers on quantum security already exist. They include work on quantum security of Carter-Wegman MACs [7], quantum PRP-PRF switching lemma [35], quantum security of the CBC, OFB, CTR, and XTS modes of operation [3], quantum generic security of random hash functions [15], and quantum security of NMAC [27]. With a computational assumption that *hidden shift problem* is hard to solve even with quantum computers, it is shown that Even-Mansour ciphers and CBC-MAC, which are broken in polynomial time with quantum queries, can be modified to have quantum security [1]. For standard security, i.e., with the assumption that adversaries have quantum computers but can make only classical queries, XOR of PRPs are proven to be secure [20]. Unruh introduced a security notion named *collapsing*, which is a generalized notion of collision-resistant in the quantum setting [31]. Unruh showed that Merkle-Damgård constructions are collapsing if underlying constructions are collapsing [30]. Czajkowski et al. showed that sponge constructions are also collapsing [10] (Note that they assume building permutations are one-way permutations or functions, and do not treat the usual sponge functions that are constructed from public permutations). Recently Zhandry [32] showed indifferentiability of the Merkle-Damgård construction in the quantum random oracle model (compression functions are assumed to be random functions).

2 Preliminaries

In this section we describe notation and definitions. For readers who are not familiar with quantum terminology, a brief explanation on quantum computation is given in this paper's full version [14].

Notation. Let $[i, \ldots, j]$ denote the set of integers $\{i, i+1, \ldots, j\}$ for $i < j$, and $[N]$ denote the set $[1, \ldots, N]$. For sets X and Y, let $\mathsf{Func}(X, Y)$ be the set of functions from X to Y. For a set X, let $\mathsf{Perm}(X)$ be the set of permutations on X. Let $\mathsf{Ciph}(m, n)$ denote the set

$$\{E \in \mathsf{Func}(\{0,1\}^m \times \{0,1\}^n, \{0,1\}^n) \mid E(k, \cdot) \in \mathsf{Perm}(\{0,1\}^n) \text{ for each } k\},$$

where "$\cdot$" means arbitrary inputs.

We call an element of $\mathsf{Ciph}(m, n)$ an *n-bit block cipher* with an *m-bit key*. For each $E \in \mathsf{Ciph}(m, n)$ and $k \in \{0,1\}^m$, let E_k denote the permutation $E(k, \cdot)$. For a distribution D, let $\mathrm{Pr}_{x \sim D}[\text{event}]$ denote the probability that event occurs when x is sampled according to the distribution D. For two distributions D_1 and D_2, let $\Delta(D_1, D_2)$ denote the total variation distance D_1 and D_2. Let $\mathsf{td}(\rho_1, \rho_2)$ denote the trace distance between density matrices ρ_1 and ρ_2. For a random variable V that takes values in a set X, define a distribution $D_V : X \to [0, 1]$ by $D_V(x) = \Pr[V = x]$ for each $x \in X$. We call D_V the distribution of V. If we write $x \xleftarrow{D} X$, then it means to sample x according to the distribution D on X.

Derangements. A permutation $P_0 \in \mathsf{Perm}(X)$ is called a *derangement* if P_0 has no fixed point, i.e. if there is no element $x \in X$ such that $P_0(x) = x$. The set of derangements on a set X is denoted as $\mathsf{Der}(X)$. The number of derangements on a set of size N is written as $!N$. The following formula is well-known [13]:

Lemma 2.1. *We have* $!N = N! \cdot \sum_{i=0}^{N} \frac{(-1)^i}{i!} = \left\lfloor \frac{N!}{e} + \frac{1}{2} \right\rfloor$, *where* $\lfloor \cdot \rfloor$ *is the floor function.*

A proof of this lemma is given in this paper's full version [14].

Davies-Meyer and Merkle-Damgård Constructions. For an n-bit block cipher E with an m-bit key, we define a function $\mathsf{DM}^E \in \mathsf{Func}(\{0,1\}^m \times \{0,1\}^n, \{0,1\}^n)$ by $\mathsf{DM}^E(z, x) = E_z(x) \oplus x$. We call DM^E the *Davies-Meyer construction* made from $E \in \mathsf{Ciph}(m, n)$. For a permutation $P \in \mathsf{Perm}(\{0,1\}^n)$, we define a function $\mathsf{FF}^P \in \mathsf{Func}(\{0,1\}^n)$ by $\mathsf{FF}^P(x) := P(x) \oplus x$. We call the function FF^P as *permutation P with feedforward*. The function FF can be regarded as a "fixed-key" version of DM.

For a function $h : \{0,1\}^m \times \{0,1\}^n \to \{0,1\}^n$ and an integer $\ell > 0$, the *Merkle-Damgård construction* $\mathsf{MD}_\ell^h : \{0,1\}^n \times \{0,1\}^{m\ell} \to \{0,1\}^n$ is defined by

$$\mathsf{MD}_\ell^h(x, z_1, \ldots, z_\ell) := h(z_\ell, h(z_{\ell-1}, \cdots, h(z_2, h(z_1, x)) \cdots)), \tag{1}$$

where $z_i \in \{0,1\}^m$ for each i. We consider the special case when h is the Davies-Meyer compression function, i.e., $h(z, x) = \mathsf{DM}^E(z, x)$ for an n-bit block cipher $E \in \mathsf{Ciph}(m, n)$. Figure 1 illustrates $\mathsf{MD}_\ell^{\mathsf{DM}^E}$, the combination of a Davies-Meyer compression function with the Merkle-Damgård iteration.

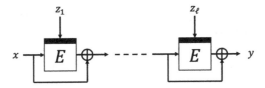

Fig. 1. The Merkle-Damgård construction with a Davies-Meyer compression function

Quantum Oracles and Quantum Adversaries. For a function $f \in$ $\mathsf{Func}(\{0,1\}^a, \{0,1\}^b)$, quantum oracle of f is defined as the unitary operator O_f such that $O_f |x\rangle |y\rangle = |x\rangle |y \oplus f(x)\rangle$ for arbitrary $x \in \{0,1\}^a, y \in \{0,1\}^b$. By an abuse of notation, let O_f also denote the $(a + b + c)$-qubit unitary operator $O_f \otimes I_c$ that maps $|x\rangle |y\rangle |z\rangle$ to $|x\rangle |y \oplus f(x)\rangle |z\rangle$ for any c.

This paper discusses on information theoretic quantum query adversary. That is, we fix a constant q and assume that a quantum adversary $\mathcal{A}$ can make at most q quantum queries, but we assume no other limitation for $\mathcal{A}$ about quantum computational resources such as time or the number of available qubits. Following the previous works that treat quantum oracle query adversary ([4,6,7,27,33,34], for example), we model $\mathcal{A}$ as a sequence of unitary operators $U_q O_f U_{q-1} \cdots O_f U_0$. We write $\mathcal{A}^O(x) = y$ for the event that a quantum adversary $\mathcal{A}$ takes x as input, makes quantum queries to O, and finally outputs y.

If quantum oracle O is dependent on some distribution, then the state of a quantum query algorithm $\mathcal{A}$ is described as a density operator. Suppose $O = O_f$ for a function f, which is sampled according to a distribution D_1 on $\mathsf{Func}(\{0,1\}^a, \{0,1\}^b)$. Then, the state of $\mathcal{A}$ with input x after the i-th query becomes $|\phi_f^i\rangle := U_i O_f U_{i-1} O_f \cdots O_f U_0 |0, x, 0\rangle$ with probability $p_1^f := \mathrm{Pr}_{F \sim D_1}[F = f]$. This mixed state is described as

$$\rho_1^i = \sum_f p_1^f |\phi_f^i\rangle \langle \phi_f^i| . \tag{2}$$

Quantum Oracle Distinguishing Advantage. Following previous works (see [33], for example), we define quantum oracle distinguishing advantage as follows. Let D_1, D_2 be two distributions on a set of functions. Assume that a quantum algorithm $\mathcal{A}$ is allowed to access the quantum oracle of a function that is chosen according to either D_1 or D_2. Suppose $\mathcal{A}$ can make at most q queries, and finally outputs the result 1 or 0. Then, we define the distinguishing advantage of $\mathcal{A}$ by

$$\mathsf{Adv}_{D_1,D_2}^{\mathrm{dist}}(\mathcal{A}) := \left| \Pr_{f \sim D_1} [\mathcal{A}^{O_f}() = 1] - \Pr_{g \sim D_2} [\mathcal{A}^{O_g}() = 1] \right| .$$

In addition, we define

$$\mathsf{Adv}_{D_1,D_2}^{\mathrm{dist}}(q) := \max_{\mathcal{A}} \left\{ \mathsf{Adv}_{D_1,D_2}^{\mathrm{dist}}(\mathcal{A}) \right\} ,$$

where the maximum is taken over all quantum-query algorithms, each making at most q quantum queries.

Distinguishing advantages can be bounded by the trace distance and total variational distance. Let ρ_1^i be the density operator defined by (2), and ρ_2^i be the density operator that is similarly defined according to the distribution D_2. Then we can show the following lemma:

Lemma 2.2. *For any quantum algorithm $\mathcal{A}$ that makes at most q queries,*

$$\mathsf{Adv}_{D_1,D_2}^{\mathsf{dist}}(\mathcal{A}) \leq \mathsf{td}(\rho_1^q, \rho_2^q) \tag{3}$$

and

$$\mathsf{td}(\rho_1^q, \rho_2^q) \leq \Delta(D_1, D_2) \tag{4}$$

hold.

The inequality (4) trivially follows from definitions and the proof of inequality (3) is also straightforward, but a proof of the lemma is given in this paper's full version [14] for readers who are not used to quantum computation.

2.1 Modeling Public Random Permutations and Block Ciphers in the Quantum Setting

To model public ideal permutations and block ciphers, here we introduce quantum ideal permutation model and quantum ideal cipher model, which are quantum versions of the classical ideal permutation model and ideal cipher model, respectively. There already exist works on quantum provable security [1] in the models that are essentially same to our quantum random permutation model. However, this is the first paper on provable security that treats ideal cipher model in the quantum setting. We begin with formalizing quantum oracles of public permutations and block ciphers, and then introduce quantum ideal permutation model and quantum ideal cipher model.

Quantum Oracles of Public Permutations and Ciphers. Here we describe how to formalize quantum oracles of public permutations and block ciphers. For an n-bit public permutation P, we define a function $P^{\pm} : \{0,1\} \times \{0,1\}^n \to \{0,1\}^n$ by

$$P^{\pm}(b,x) = \begin{cases} P(x) & if\ b = 0, \\ P^{-1}(x) & if\ b = 1. \end{cases}$$

For a distribution D on $\mathsf{Perm}(\{0,1\}^n)$, let $D^{\pm}$ be the associated distribution on $\mathsf{Func}(\{0,1\} \times \{0,1\}^n, \{0,1\}^n)$ defined by $D^{\pm}(f) = \Pr_{P \sim D}[P^{\pm} = f]$. For any public permutation P, we assume that the quantum oracle $O_{P^{\pm}}$ is available. This models the situation that both of forward and backward quantum queries to the public permutation P are allowed.

Similarly, if E is an n-bit block cipher with m-bit key, then we define a function $E^{\pm} : \{0,1\} \times \{0,1\}^m \times \{0,1\}^n \to \{0,1\}^n$ by

$$E^{\pm}(b,k,x) = \begin{cases} E_k(x) & if\ b=0, \\ E_k^{-1}(x) & if\ b=1. \end{cases}$$

For a distribution D on $\mathsf{Ciph}(m,n)$, let $D^{\pm}$ be the associated distribution on $\mathsf{Func}(\{0,1\}\times\{0,1\}^m\times\{0,1\}^n, \{0,1\}^n)$ defined by $D^{\pm}(f) = \Pr_{E\sim D}[E^{\pm} = f]$. For any public block cipher E, we assume that the quantum oracle $O_{E^{\pm}}$ is available. This models the situation that both of forward and backward quantum queries to a block cipher E are allowed.

Quantum Ideal Permutation Model. Assume that P is a public permutation which is chosen from $\mathsf{Perm}(\{0,1\}^n)$ uniformly at random, and an adversary $\mathcal{A}$ is allowed to make at most q quantum queries to $P^{\pm}$, for some fixed number q. We call this model as *quantum ideal permutation model*. We say that a scheme constructed from a public permutation is secure (with regard to some quantum security notion) up to q quantum queries if no such quantum information theoretic adversary can break the security notion. We say that P is an ideal permutation if we assume the situation that quantum adversaries can access quantum oracle of P, and P is chosen from $\mathsf{Perm}(\{0,1\}^n)$ uniformly at random.

Quantum Ideal Cipher Model. Assume that E is a public block cipher which is chosen from $\mathsf{Ciph}(m,n)$ uniformly at random, and an adversary $\mathcal{A}$ is allowed to make at most q quantum queries to $E^{\pm}$, for some fixed number q. We call this model as *quantum ideal cipher model*. Security in this model is defined similarly as in the quantum ideal permutation model. Similarly, we say that E is an ideal cipher if we assume the situation that quantum adversaries can access quantum oracle of E, and E is chosen from $\mathsf{Ciph}(m,n)$ uniformly at random.

2.2   Two Security Notions: Non-invertibility and One-Wayness

This paper considers two security notions: non-invertibility and one-wayness. These are similar but independent notions (we give a separation proof in this paper's full version [14] for completeness). Let $h^F : \{0,1\}^s \to \{0,1\}^n$ be a function that is constructed from a function (or permutation) F, and O be a quantum oracle that is defined depending on F. We assume F is chosen from a set of functions $\mathcal{S}_F$ uniformly at random. The set $\mathcal{S}_F$ and how the oracle O is related to F depend on security models.

If we consider the quantum ideal permutation model, then $\mathcal{S}_F = \mathsf{Perm}(\{0,1\}^n)$, and O is defined as the oracle of $P^{\pm}$. We will consider the case that h^F is a permutation with feedforward. Similarly, if we consider the quantum ideal cipher model, then $\mathcal{S}_F = \mathsf{Ciph}(m,n)$, and O is defined as the oracle of $E^{\pm}$. We will consider the case that h^F is the Davies-Meyer constructions or Merkle-Damgård constructions.

Non-invertibility. For any quantum oracle query adversary $\mathcal{A}$, define the advantage of $\mathcal{A}$ to invert the function h^F by

$$\mathsf{Adv}_{h^F}^{inv}(\mathcal{A}) := \Pr_{F,y}[\mathcal{A}^O(y) = x \wedge h^F(x) = y], \tag{5}$$

where $F \in \mathcal{S}_F$ and $y \in \{0,1\}^n$ are chosen uniformly at random. In addition, we define

$$\mathsf{Adv}_{h^F}^{inv}(q) := \max_{\mathcal{A}}\{\mathsf{Adv}_{h^F}^{inv}(\mathcal{A})\}, \tag{6}$$

where the maximum is taken over all quantum-query algorithms, each making at most q quantum queries.

One-wayness. Similarly, define the advantage of $\mathcal{A}$ to break the one-wayness of the function h^F by

$$\mathsf{Adv}_{h^F}^{ow}(\mathcal{A}) := \Pr_{F,x'}[\mathcal{A}^O(h^F(x')) = x \wedge h^F(x) = h^F(x')], \tag{7}$$

where $F \in \mathcal{S}_F$ and $x' \in \{0,1\}^s$ are chosen uniformly at random. In addition, we define

$$\mathsf{Adv}_{h^F}^{ow}(q) := \max_{\mathcal{A}}\{\mathsf{Adv}_{h^F}^{ow}(\mathcal{A})\}, \tag{8}$$

where the maximum is taken over all quantum-query algorithms, each making at most q quantum queries.

Trivial Upper Bounds. We note here that there are trivial upper bounds of quantum query complexity for non-invertibility and one-wayness, if h^F is sufficiently random. The bound is given by simple application of the Grover search or its generalizations [8,12]. Given y, let consider to find x such that $h^F(x) = y$. Then, if $2^s/|(h^F)^{-1}(y)| \approx 2^n$, (which is the case when h^F is a truly random function and message space $\{0,1\}^s$ is much larger than range $\{0,1\}^n$) then we can find x such that $h^F(x) = y$ with about $\sqrt{2^n}$ quantum queries to h^F. We say h^F is almost optimally non-invertible or one-way if $\mathsf{Adv}_{h^F}^{inv}(q) = \tilde{O}(q/\sqrt{2^n})$ or $\mathsf{Adv}_{h^F}^{ow}(q) = \tilde{O}(q/\sqrt{2^n})$, respectively, since these imply that there is no way which is significantly better than the generic attack (the Grover search) to break one-wayness of h^F.

3   A Tool for Quantum Oracle Indistinguishability

Here we give a tool to upper bound quantum oracle distinguishing advantages $\mathsf{Adv}_{D_1,D_2}^{dist}$ with only classical probability calculation and purely combinatorial enumeration (Proposition 3.1). Our tool can be applied to *any* distributions D_1, D_2 on *any* (finite) set of functions $\mathsf{Func}(\{0,1\}^n, \{0,1\}^c)$. In later sections, to show non-invertibility and one-wayness of functions, we treat only the cases that $c = 1$ and D_2 is the degenerate distribution with support on the zero function. Our tool can be somewhat simplified in those cases, and thus we give a simplified version of our tool (Proposition 3.2) for later use. We believe that the generalized version (Proposition 3.1) itself is also useful to give some quantum security bound for other schemes or other security notions. To show that the generalized version is also useful, an application is given in this paper's full version [14].

There already exist techniques to bound quantum oracle distinguishing advantages in the situations which are similar to our simplified version ($c = 1$ and D_2 is the degenerate distribution with support on the zero function), but existing works treat only the case that D_1 is some specific distributions. (See proof of Lemma 37 in [2], proof of Lemma C.1 in [27], for example. Theorem 1 in [15] gives similar result as Lemma 37 in [2], but uses different analyzing technique by Zhandry [33].) On the other hand, our simplified tool (Proposition 3.2) enables us to treat *any* distribution D_1 on a (finite) set of boolean functions.

This section is organized as follows. First, we explain our motivations to develop quantum proof tools. Second, we describe our main tool. Third, we briefly explain how to apply them to give quantum security bounds in later sections.

3.1   Motivations: The Coefficient H Technique

In the classical setting, there exist several proof tools to prove oracle indistinguishability of symmetric key schemes. The *coefficient-H technique* developed by Patarin [23] is one of the most powerful tools. Below we explain essence of the technique.

Suppose we want to upper bound $\mathsf{Adv}_{D_1,D_2}^{dist}(\mathcal{A})$ for a (classical) information theoretic adversary $\mathcal{A}$, and distributions D_1, D_2. The technique allows $\mathcal{A}$ to obtain *transcripts* including all input-output pairs defined by queries. Let T_1, T_2 be the transcripts that correspond to the oracle distributions D_1 and D_2, respectively. Then, $\mathsf{T}_1, \mathsf{T}_2$ define distributions on a set of transcript $\mathcal{T}$. The coefficient-H technique divides $\mathcal{T}$ into a *good* set good and *bad* set bad. Roughly speaking, the technique gives a bound $\mathsf{Adv}_{D_1,D_2}^{dist}(\mathcal{A}) \leq \epsilon + \Pr[\mathsf{T}_2 \in \mathsf{bad}]$. The parameter ϵ is a small number that satisfies $\Pr[\mathsf{T}_1 = \tau]/\Pr[\mathsf{T}_2 = \tau] \geq 1 - \epsilon$ for any good transcript $\tau \in \mathsf{good}$. How good bound we can achieve depends on how well we define the set of transcripts $\mathcal{T}$, good sets good, and bad sets bad.

3.2   Our Main Tool

Following the classical coefficient-H technique, we aim to develop a quantum proof tool so that: 1. It uses some good and bad sets, and 2. It gives an upper bound as a sum of an amount related to good events (like ϵ in the coefficient-H technique), and a bad probability. In addition, we make our tool so that we can obtain an upper bound with only classical probability calculation and purely combinatorial enumeration. We first describe a generalized version that D_1 and D_2 can be any distributions, and then explain how it is simplified in the case $c = 1$ and D_2 is the degenerate distribution.

Generalized Version. Let D_1, D_2 be *any* distributions on *any* (finite) set of functions $\mathsf{Func}(\{0,1\}^n, \{0,1\}^c)$. In addition, let $\bar{D}$ be an *arbitrary* distribution on the product space $\mathsf{Func}(\{0,1\}^n, \{0,1\}^c) \times \mathsf{Func}(\{0,1\}^n, \{0,1\}^c)$ that satisfies

$$D_1(f) = \sum_g \bar{D}(f,g) \text{ for any } f \wedge D_2(g) = \sum_f \bar{D}(f,g) \text{ for any } g. \quad (9)$$

(In applications, even though D_1 and D_2 are given as indipendent distributions, we try to find a convenient distribution $\bar{D}$, just like we do so in the (classical) game-playing proof technique. See this paper's full version for a concrete example.)

For each $f, g \in \mathsf{Func}(\{0,1\}^n, \{0,1\}^c)$, let $p_1^f, p_2^g, p^{f,g}$ denote $\Pr_{F \sim D_1}[F = f]$, $\Pr_{G \sim D_1}[G = g]$, and $\Pr_{(F,G) \sim \bar{D}}[(F,G) = (f,g)]$, respectively. In addition, define a boolean function $\delta(f,g) : \{0,1\}^n \to \{0,1\}$ by $\delta(f,g)(x) = 1$ if and only if $f(x) \neq g(x)$ for each pair (f,g). Let $\mathbf{0} \in \mathsf{Func}(\{0,1\}^n, \{0,1\})$ be the zero function that maps x to 0 for any x. For each $g \in \mathsf{Func}(\{0,1\}^n, \{0,1\}^c)$, let $\delta D|_g$ be the conditional distribution on $\mathsf{Func}(\{0,1\}^n, \{0,1\})$ defined by $(\delta D|_g)(\gamma) = \Pr_{(F,G) \sim \bar{D}}[\delta(F,G) = \gamma | G = g]$ for any $\gamma \in \mathsf{Func}(\{0,1\}^n, \{0,1\})$.

For each $g \in \mathsf{Func}(\{0,1\}^n, \{0,1\}^c)$, take a "bad" set $\mathsf{bad}^g \subset \mathsf{Func}(\{0,1\}^n, \{0,1\}) \setminus \{\mathbf{0}\}$ arbitrarily (actually we select bad^g such that $\Pr_{\Gamma \sim \delta D|_g}[\Gamma \in \mathsf{bad}^g]$ is small), and define "good" set by $\mathsf{good}^g := \mathsf{Func}(\{0,1\}^n, \{0,1\}) \setminus (\{\mathbf{0}\} \cup \mathsf{bad}^g)$. Furthermore, decompose the good set good^g into smaller subsets $\{\mathsf{good}_\alpha^g\}_{\alpha \in A_g}$ (i.e. $\mathsf{good}^g = \bigcup_\alpha \mathsf{good}_\alpha^g$ and $\mathsf{good}_\alpha^g \cap \mathsf{good}_\beta^g = \emptyset$ for $\alpha \neq \beta$) such that the conditional probability $\Pr_{\Gamma \sim \delta D|_g}[\Gamma = \gamma | \Gamma \in \mathsf{good}_\alpha^g]$ is independent of γ (in other words, for each $\alpha \in A_g$, $\Pr_{\Gamma \sim \delta D|_g}[\Gamma = \gamma] = \Pr_{\Gamma \sim \delta D|_g}[\Gamma = \gamma']$ holds for $\gamma, \gamma' \in \mathsf{good}_\alpha^g$). In addition, define $\mathsf{bad}_{all} \subset (\mathsf{Func}(\{0,1\}^n, \{0,1\}^c))^2$ by $\mathsf{bad}_{all} := \{(f,g) | \delta(f,g) \in \mathsf{bad}^g\}$. For each g, $\alpha \in A_g$ and $\gamma \in \mathsf{Func}(\{0,1\}^n, \{0,1\})$, let $p_{\delta D|_g}^{\mathsf{good}_\alpha^g} := \Pr_{\Gamma \sim \delta D|_g}[\Gamma \in \mathsf{good}_\alpha^g]$ and $p_{\delta D|_g}^{\gamma | \mathsf{good}_\alpha^g} := \Pr_{\Gamma \sim \delta D|_g}[\Gamma = \gamma | \Gamma \in \mathsf{good}_\alpha^g]$ (by assumption, $p_{\delta D|_g}^{\gamma | \mathsf{good}_\alpha^g}$ is independent of γ). Then the following proposition holds.

Proposition 3.1 (Generalized version). *Let D_1, D_2 be any distributions on $\mathsf{Func}(\{0,1\}^n, \{0,1\}^c)$, and $\bar{D}$ be any distribution that satisfies (9). Let $\mathsf{bad}_{all}, \mathsf{bad}^g, \mathsf{good}^g$, and $\{\mathsf{good}_\alpha^g\}_{\alpha \in A_g}$ be the sets as stated above. Then, for any quantum algorithm $\mathcal{A}$ that makes at most q quantum queries, $\mathsf{Adv}_{D_1, D_2}^{\mathsf{dist}}(\mathcal{A})$ is upper bounded by*

$$2q \cdot \mathbf{E}_{G \sim D_2} \left[\sum_{\alpha \in A_G} p_{\delta D|_G}^{\mathsf{good}_\alpha^G} \sqrt{p_{\delta D|_G}^{\gamma | \mathsf{good}_\alpha^G}} \cdot \max_x \left| \{\gamma \in \mathsf{good}_\alpha^G \mid \gamma(x) = 1\} \right| \right]$$

$$+ 2q \cdot \Pr_{(F,G) \sim \bar{D}}[(F,G) \in \mathsf{bad}_{all}]. \quad (10)$$

A proof of this proposition is given in this paper's full version [14].

In later sections, we apply our tool only to the cases that $c = 1$ and D_2 is the degenerate distribution with support on the zero function $\mathbf{0}$. Description of our tool can be somewhat simplified in such cases, and below we give the simplified version for later use. To show that the generalized version itself is also useful, an application of Proposition 3.1 is given in this paper's full version [14].

Simplified Version. Now we describe a simplified version of our tool. Let D_1, D_2 be distributions on a set of boolean functions $\mathsf{Func}(\{0,1\}^n, \{0,1\})$, and D_2 be the degenerate distribution with support on the zero function $\mathbf{0}$. D_1 can be any distribution.

Take a "bad" set $\mathsf{bad} \subset \mathsf{Func}(\{0,1\}^n, \{0,1\}) \setminus \{\mathbf{0}\}$ arbitrarily (actually we select bad such that $\Pr_{F \sim D_1}[F \in \mathsf{bad}]$ will be small), and define "good" set by $\mathsf{good} := \mathsf{Func}(\{0,1\}^n, \{0,1\}) \setminus (\{\mathbf{0}\} \cup \mathsf{bad})$. Furthermore, decompose the good set good into smaller subsets $\{\mathsf{good}_\alpha\}_\alpha$ (i.e. $\mathsf{good} = \bigcup_\alpha \mathsf{good}_\alpha$ and $\mathsf{good}_\alpha \cap \mathsf{good}_\beta = \emptyset$ for $\alpha \neq \beta$) such that the conditional probability $\Pr_{F \sim D_1}[F = f | F \in \mathsf{good}_\alpha]$ is independent of f (in other words, for each α, $\Pr_{F \sim D_1}[F = f] = \Pr_{F \sim D_1}[F = f']$ holds for $f, f' \in \mathsf{good}_\alpha$). Let $p_1^{\mathsf{good}_\alpha} := \Pr_{F \sim D_1}[F \in \mathsf{good}_\alpha]$ and $p_1^{f|\mathsf{good}_\alpha} := \Pr_{F \sim D_1}[F = f | F \in \mathsf{good}_\alpha]$ (by assumption, $p_1^{f|\mathsf{good}_\alpha}$ is independent of f). Then, the following proposition holds, which enables us to bound advantages of quantum adversaries with only classical probability calculations and purely combinatorial enumeration, without any quantum arguments.

Proposition 3.2 (Simplified version). *Let D_1 be any distribution on the set of boolean functions $\mathsf{Func}(\{0,1\}^n, \{0,1\})$, and D_2 be the degenerate distribution with support on the zero function. Let $\mathsf{bad}, \mathsf{good}$, and $\{\mathsf{good}_\alpha\}_\alpha$ be the subsets of $\mathsf{Func}(\{0,1\}^n, \{0,1\})$ as stated above. Then, for any quantum algorithm $\mathcal{A}$ that makes at most q quantum queries, $\mathsf{Adv}^{\mathsf{dist}}_{D_1, D_2}(\mathcal{A})$ is upper bounded by*

$$2q \sum_\alpha p_1^{\mathsf{good}_\alpha} \sqrt{p_1^{f|\mathsf{good}_\alpha} \cdot \max_x |\{f \in \mathsf{good}_\alpha \mid f(x) = 1\}|} + 2q \Pr_{F \sim D_1}[F \in \mathsf{bad}].$$

(11)

This proposition follows as an immediate corollary of the generalized version Proposition 3.1 as below.

Proof (of Proposition 3.2). Now, D_1 and D_2 are distributions on a set of boolean functions $\mathsf{Func}(\{0,1\}^n, \{0,1\})$, and D_2 is the degenerate distribution with support on the zero function $\mathbf{0}$. Let $\mathsf{bad}, \mathsf{good}$, and $\{\mathsf{good}_\alpha\}_\alpha$ be the sets in Proposition 3.2.

We translate notations in Proposition 3.2 to those in Proposition 3.1. Let $\bar{D}$ be the product distribution $D_1 \times D_2$. Let $\mathsf{bad}^g := \emptyset$, $\mathsf{good}^g_\alpha := \mathsf{Func}(\{0,1\}^n, \{0,1\}) \setminus \{\mathbf{0}\}$ for $g \neq \mathbf{0}$, and $\mathsf{bad}^{\mathbf{0}} := \mathsf{bad}$, $\mathsf{good}^{\mathbf{0}}_\alpha := \mathsf{good}_\alpha$.

Then, $\delta(f, \mathbf{0}) = f$ holds for any boolean function f, $\Pr_{G \sim D_2}[G = g] = 1$ holds if and only if $g = \mathbf{0}$, and $\delta D|_{\mathbf{0}} = D_1$ holds. In addition, we have $p_{\delta D|_{\mathbf{0}}}^{\mathsf{good}^{\mathbf{0}}_\alpha} = p_1^{\mathsf{good}_\alpha}$, and $p_{\delta D|_{\mathbf{0}}}^{f|\mathsf{good}^{\mathbf{0}}_\alpha} = p_1^{f|\mathsf{good}_\alpha}$ for any boolean function f. Moreover, $\mathsf{bad}_{all} = \{(f, \mathbf{0}) | f \in \mathsf{bad}^{\mathbf{0}}\}$ holds, which implies that $\Pr_{(F,G) \sim \bar{D}}[(F,G) \in \mathsf{bad}_{all}] = \Pr_{F \sim D_1}[F \in \mathsf{bad}]$. Therefore Proposition 3.2 follows from Proposition 3.1. $\qquad \square$

Remark 3.1. We do not claim that our tool is all-around. Actually the condition that the probability $p_{\delta D|_g}^{\gamma|\text{good}_\alpha^g}$ is independent of γ (in the generalized version) and $p_1^{f|\text{good}_\alpha}$ is independent of f (in the simplified version) implicitly means that D_1 must have some "uniform" structure to obtain a good bound with our tool. See proofs of Lemmas 4.3 and 5.1 for concrete examples.

3.3 How to Give Quantum Security Bound with Our Tool

Next, we describe how we apply Proposition 3.2 in later sections to give quantum security bounds, in a high-level fashion. Roughly speaking, we try to reduce a target problem to a problem of bounding distinguishing advantage between two distributions on a set of boolean functions, and then apply Proposition 3.2. This strategy itself is not new, but we believe our tool enables us to take the strategy for wider applications.

Let $\mathcal{A}$ be a quantum query algorithm, and suppose that a problem to give a security proof is reduced to a problem to upper bound some distinguishing advantage $\mathsf{Adv}_{G_{\text{real}}, G_{\text{ideal}}}^{\text{dist}}(\mathcal{A})$. We introduce intermediate distributions (i.e. intermediate games) $G_1 = G_{\text{ideal}}, G_2, \ldots, G_t = G_{\text{real}}$ such that $\mathsf{Adv}_{G_i, G_{i+1}}^{\text{dist}}(\mathcal{A})$ can be bounded using other techniques for $1 \leq i \leq t - 2$. In addition, we assume $\mathsf{Adv}_{G_{t-1}, G_t}^{\text{dist}}(\mathcal{A})$ can be bounded by $\mathsf{Adv}_{D_1, D_2}^{\text{dist}}(\mathcal{B})$ for some distributions D_1, D_2 on $\mathsf{Func}(\{0, 1\}^n, \{0, 1\})$, and another quantum query algorithm $\mathcal{B}$. Then we have

$$\mathsf{Adv}_{G_{\text{real}}, G_{\text{ideal}}}^{\text{dist}}(\mathcal{A}) \leq \mathsf{Adv}_{G_{t-1}, G_t}^{\text{dist}}(\mathcal{A}) + \sum_{i=1}^{t-2} \mathsf{Adv}_{G_i, G_{i+1}}^{\text{dist}}(\mathcal{A})$$

$$\leq \mathsf{Adv}_{D_1, D_2}^{\text{dist}}(\mathcal{B}) + \sum_{i=1}^{t-2} \mathsf{Adv}_{G_i, G_{i+1}}^{\text{dist}}(\mathcal{A}) \qquad (12)$$

Hence, if $\mathsf{Adv}_{G_i, G_{i+1}}^{\text{dist}}(\mathcal{A})$ can be upper bounded by other approaches for $1 \leq i \leq t - 2$, then the remaining term can be bounded without any quantum argument, by using our tool. In later sections, we will upper bound $\mathsf{Adv}_{G_i, G_{i+1}}^{\text{dist}}(\mathcal{A})$ by total variation distance $\Delta(G_i, G_{i+1})$. (Remember that $\mathsf{Adv}_{D, D'}^{\text{dist}}(\mathcal{A}) \leq \Delta(D, D')$ holds for any distributions D and D' from Lemma 2.2.) Thus we upper bound the advantage $\mathsf{Adv}_{G_{\text{real}}, G_{\text{ideal}}}^{\text{dist}}(\mathcal{A})$ by purely combinatorial enumerating arguments.

4   Non-invertibility of Permutation with Feedforward in the Quantum Ideal Permutation Model

Now we apply the technique of Sect. 3 to show that permutation with feedforward is optimally non-invertible in the ideal permutation model. As one step in our proof, we also prove the difficulty to find a fixed point of random permutations (Proposition 4.1). We stress that this is the first results on quantum query lower bound for some property of random permutation P or some scheme constructed from P, in the model that both of forward and backward queries to permutation P are allowed. The goal of this section is to prove the following theorem.

Theorem 4.1. *Let $n \geq 32$. For any quantum algorithm $\mathcal{A}$ that makes at most q forward or backward queries to a public permutation P,*

$$\mathsf{Adv}_{\mathsf{FF}^P}^{inv}(\mathcal{A}) \leq \frac{4(e+1)(q+1)}{2^{n/2}} + \epsilon(n) \tag{13}$$

holds, where $\epsilon(n) = \frac{8n^3}{2^n - 2n + 1} + \frac{48n^3}{2^n} + \frac{3(e+1)}{n!}$. In particular, $\mathcal{A}$ cannot invert FF^P with constant probability for $q \ll 2^{n/2}$.

Remark 4.1. We need the condition $n \geq 32$ for technical reasons. This assumption is reasonable since block lengths of block ciphers usually satisfy it.

To show the above theorem, we begin with reducing the problem of finding a preimage of permutation with feedforward in the ideal permutation model to the problem of finding a fixed point of an ideal permutation. Let us define the advantage of a quantum algorithm $\mathcal{A}$ to find a fixed point of an ideal permutation by

$$\mathsf{Adv}_P^{fixpt}(\mathcal{A}) := \Pr_P[\mathcal{A}^{O_{P\pm}}() = x \wedge P(x) = x],$$

here P is chosen uniformly at random, and

$$\mathsf{Adv}_P^{fixpt}(q) := \max_{\mathcal{A}} \left\{ \mathsf{Adv}_P^{fixpt}(\mathcal{A}) \right\},$$

where the maximum is taken over all quantum-query algorithms, each making at most q quantum queries.

Lemma 4.1. *For a quantum algorithm $\mathcal{A}$ that makes at most q quantum queries to $O_{P\pm}$, there exists a quantum algorithm $\mathcal{B}$ that makes at most q quantum queries to $O_{P\pm}$ such that $\mathsf{Adv}_{\mathsf{FF}^P}^{inv}(\mathcal{A}) = \mathsf{Adv}_P^{fixpt}(\mathcal{B})$.*

Proof. Given such algorithm $\mathcal{A}$, we construct $\mathcal{B}$ with the desired properties. Firstly, before making queries, $\mathcal{B}$ chooses $y \in \{0,1\}^n$ uniformly at random. $\mathcal{B}$ is given the oracle $O_{P\pm}$ of the permutation P. Define another permutation P' by $P'(x) = P(x) \oplus y$. Then, the pair (P', y) follows the uniform distribution. If x satisfies $\mathsf{FF}_{P'}(x) = y$, then $P(x) = x$ holds. In addition, $\mathcal{B}$ can simulate the quantum oracle $O_{P'\pm}$ using $O_{P\pm}$ with no simulation overhead.

Then $\mathcal{B}$ runs $\mathcal{A}$, giving y as the target image. If $\mathcal{A}$ makes queries, then $\mathcal{B}$ answers using the oracle $O_{P'\pm}$. Finally $\mathcal{B}$ outputs the final output of $\mathcal{A}$. This algorithm $\mathcal{B}$ obviously satisfies the desired property. □

From the above lemma, it suffices to upper bound Adv_P^{fixpt} to prove Theorem 4.1. Below we show the following proposition.

Proposition 4.1. *Let $n \geq 32$. For any quantum algorithm $\mathcal{A}$ that makes at most q forward or backward queries to a public permutation P,*

$$\mathsf{Adv}_P^{fixpt}(\mathcal{A}) \leq \frac{4(e+1)(q+1)}{2^{n/2}} + \epsilon(n) \tag{14}$$

holds, where $\epsilon(n) = \frac{8n^3}{2^n - 2n + 1} + \frac{48n^3}{2^n} + \frac{3(e+1)}{n!}$. In particular, $\mathcal{A}$ cannot find a fixed point of P with constant probability for $q \ll 2^{n/2}$.

Next, we reduce the problem of finding a fixed point of permutations to the problem of distinguishing two oracle distributions: random permutations and random derangements (permutations without fixed point). Let U be the uniform distribution on $\mathsf{Perm}(\{0,1\}^n)$, and U_0 be the uniform distribution on $\mathsf{Der}(\{0,1\}^n) \subseteq \mathsf{Perm}(\{0,1\}^n)$. Then

$$\mathsf{Adv}_P^{fixpt}(q) \leq \mathsf{Adv}_{U^\pm, U_0^\pm}^{dist}(q+1) \tag{15}$$

holds, since we can distinguish a permutation from derangements if we find its fixed point.

To upper bound $\mathsf{Adv}_{U^\pm, U_0^\pm}^{dist}(q+1)$, we apply the technique introduced in Sect. 3. That is, we reduce the problem of distinguishing $U^\pm$ and $U_0^\pm$ to the problem of distinguishing two distributions Λ and Λ_0 on $\mathsf{Func}(\{0,1\}^n, \{0,1\})$, introducing intermediate distributions (or games). Λ is the distribution which is defined according to the distribution of fixed points of random permutations, and Λ_0 is the degenerate distribution with support on the zero-function. To this end, in addition to Λ, Λ_0, below we define functions Φ : $\mathsf{Der}(\{0,1\}^n) \times \mathsf{Func}(\{0,1\}^n, \{0,1\}) \rightarrow \mathsf{Perm}(\{0,1\}^n)$, Φ' : $\mathsf{Der}(\{0,1\}^n) \times$ $\mathsf{Func}(\{0,1\}^n, \{0,1\}) \rightarrow \mathsf{Func}(\{0,1\}^n, \{0,1\}^n)$, and distributions D_{num} on $[0,\ldots,2^n]$, U_1' on $\mathsf{Perm}(\{0,1\}^n)$, and U_2' on $\mathsf{Func}(\{0,1\} \times \{0,1\}^n, \{0,1\}^n)$. In the notation of Sect. 3, $G_1 = G_{\mathsf{ideal}} = U^\pm$, $G_2 = U_1'^\pm$, $G_3 = U_2'$, and $G_4 = G_{\mathsf{real}} = U_0^\pm$, and $D_1 = \Lambda, D_2 = \Lambda_0$.

Here we briefly explain motivations to introduce U_1', U_2' and Φ, Φ'. Our goal is to reduce the problem of distinguishing $U^\pm$ from $U_0^\pm$ to the problem of distinguishing Λ from Λ_0. That is, we want a technique to simulate the oracle that follows the distribution $U^\pm$ or $U_0^\pm$ on $\mathsf{Func}(\{0,1\} \times \{0,1\}^n, \{0,1\}^n)$, given the oracle that follows the distribution Λ or Λ_0 on $\mathsf{Func}(\{0,1\}^n, \{0,1\})$, respectively, without any knowledge that which of Λ and Λ_0 is given. However, it is difficult to directly construct such a technique. Thus, we define an intermediate distribution U_1' that is close to U, and so that we can construct such a technique between $U_1'^\pm$ and $U_0^\pm$. The technique is as follows. Firstly, we define a map $\Phi: \mathsf{Der}(\{0,1\}^n) \times \mathsf{Func}(\{0,1\}^n, \{0,1\}) \rightarrow \mathsf{Perm}(\{0,1\}^n)$ such that $\Phi(P_0, f)$ follows U_1' if (P_0, f) follows (U_0, Λ), and $\Phi(P_0, f)$ follows U_0 if (P_0, f) follows (U_0, Λ_0), respectively (actually Φ is firstly defined and then U_1' is defined using Φ). Secondly, given an oracle f that follows Λ or Λ_0, we choose $P_0 \in \mathsf{Der}(\{0,1\}^n)$ uniformly at random, and simulate the oracle of $(\Phi(P_0, f))^\pm$. Then, we can simulate the distributions $U_1'^\pm$ or $U_0^\pm$ according to which of Λ or Λ_0 is given. However, there is a problem: simulation cost of $U_1'^\pm$ might become very high. Thus we introduce another distribution U_2' and map Φ', to overcome the problem of simulation overhead. Details on simulation overhead will be explained later.

Now we give formal description of intermediate distributions and maps Φ, Φ'. In what follows, we identify a function $F \in \mathsf{Func}(\{0,1\}^n, \{0,1\}^n)$ with the associated graph G_F of which vertexes are n-bit strings. In the graph G_F, there is an edge from a vertex x to another vertex y if and only if $F(x) = y$. If F is a permutation P, then each connected component of G_P is a cycle, and isolated points correspond to fixed points of P.

Distribution D_{num}. Distribution D_{num} on $[0, \ldots, 2^n]$ is the distribution of the number of fixed points of random permutations. D_{num} is formally defined by $D_{num}(\lambda) := \Pr_{P \sim U}[\lambda = |\{x|P(x) = x\}|]$. In other words, D_{num} is the distribution of the random variable that takes values in $[0, \ldots, 2^n]$ which is defined according to the following sampling.

1. $P \xleftarrow{\$} \mathsf{Perm}(\{0,1\}^n)$
2. $\lambda \leftarrow |\{x|P(x) = x\}|$
3. Return λ.

Distribution Λ. Distribution Λ on $\mathsf{Func}(\{0,1\}^n, \{0,1\})$ is defined according to the distribution of fixed points of random permutations. For $P \in \mathsf{Perm}(\{0,1\}^n)$, define $f_P \in \mathsf{Func}(\{0,1\}^n, \{0,1\})$ by $f_P(x) = 1$ if and only if $P(x) = x$. Then, Λ is formally defined by $\Lambda(f) := \Pr_{P \sim U}[f = f_P]$. In other words, Λ is the distribution of the random variable that takes values in $\mathsf{Func}(\{0,1\}^n, \{0,1\})$, which is defined according to the following sampling:

1. $P \xleftarrow{\$} \mathsf{Perm}(\{0,1\}^n)$
2. $f \leftarrow f_P$
3. Return f.

Distribution Λ_0. Distribution Λ_0 on $\mathsf{Func}(\{0,1\}^n, \{0,1\})$ is the degenerate distribution with support on the zero-function $\mathbf{0}$, which maps x to 0 for any x. Formally, Λ_0 is defined by $\Lambda_0(g) := 1$ if and only if $g = \mathbf{0}$.

Function Φ. Taking $P_0 \in \mathsf{Der}(\{0,1\}^n)$ and $f \in \mathsf{Func}(\{0,1\}^n, \{0,1\})$ as inputs, we want to construct another permutation $P = \Phi(P_0, f)$ which has, informally speaking, the following properties:

1. $P(x) = x$ if and only if $f(x) = 1$ holds with high probability when P_0 and f are chosen uniformly at random.
2. If $f(x) = 0$, then $P(x) = P_0(x)$ for almost all x.

This function Φ is used later to approximate U by using U_0 and Λ.
   Formally, function $\Phi : \mathsf{Der}(\{0,1\}^n) \times \mathsf{Func}(\{0,1\}^n, \{0,1\}) \to \mathsf{Perm}(\{0,1\}^n)$ is defined by the following process.

1. Take $P_0 \in \mathsf{Perm}(\{0,1\}^n), f \in \mathsf{Func}(\{0,1\}^n)$ as inputs.
2. For each $x \in \{0,1\}^n$, define $P(x)$ by:
3.   If $f(x) = 1$
4. $P(x) \leftarrow x$
5.   Else
6.   Calculate $\min\{i \mid f(P_0^i(x)) = 0\}$, $\mathsf{cnt} \leftarrow \min\{i \mid f(P_0^i(x)) = 0\}$
7. $P(x) \leftarrow P_0^{\mathsf{cnt}}(x)$
8.   End If
9. $\Phi(P_0, f) \leftarrow P$

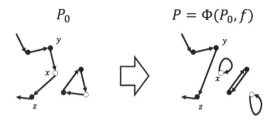

P_0 $P = \Phi(P_0, f)$

Fig. 2. How $P = \Phi(P_0, f)$ is generated. White circle are the preimages of 1 by f.

Figure 2 illustrates how $P = \Phi(P_0, f)$ is generated from P_0 and f. Each element x such that $f(x) = 1$ is converted to isolated points, and the edges $y \to x, x \to z$ are converted to new edges $y \to z, x \to x$. By definition, images of Φ are certainly in $\mathsf{Perm}(\{0,1\}^n)$. Note that $\Phi(P_0, f)^{-1} = \Phi(P_0^{-1}, f)$ holds.

Function Φ'. Φ' is a function which is defined to approximate U using U_0 and Λ similarly as Φ, but the approximation of Φ' is more rough than that of Φ. While outputs of Φ are always permutations, outputs of Φ' might not be permutations, although $\Phi(P_0, f) = \Phi'(P_0, f)$ holds with high probability when P_0 and f are sampled following U_0 and Λ. See this paper's full version [14] for more details.

Formally, function $\Phi' : \mathsf{Der}(\{0,1\}^n) \times \mathsf{Func}(\{0,1\}^n, \{0,1\}) \to \mathsf{Func}(\{0,1\}^n, \{0,1\}^n)$ is defined by the following process.

1. Take $P_0 \in \mathsf{Perm}(\{0,1\}^n), f \in \mathsf{Func}(\{0,1\}^n)$ as inputs.
2. For each $x \in \{0,1\}^n$, define $P(x)$ by:
3.   If $f(x) = 1$
4. $P(x) \gets x$
5.   Else If $f(P_0(x)) = 1$
6. $P(x) \gets P_0^2(x)$
7.   Else
8. $P(x) \gets P_0(x)$
9.   End If
10. $\Phi'(P_0, f) \gets P$

We defined not only Φ but also Φ' to achieve low simulation overhead: Suppose we are given the oracle of $f \in \mathsf{Func}(\{0,1\}^n, \{0,1\})$. Then, for any $P_0 \in \mathsf{Der}(\{0,1\}^n)$ which we choose ourselves, we can operate one evaluation of the function $\Phi'(P_0, f)$ with only two queries to f. On the other hand, we might need a lot of queries to f to evaluate $\Phi(P_0, f)$ in Step 6 of the definition of Φ (we need about 2^n queries in the worst case). This is the reason why we introduced Φ'.

For fixed P_0 and f, we define $P_2'^{\pm} : \{0,1\} \times \{0,1\}^n \to \{0,1\}^n$ by

$$P_2'^{\pm}(b, x) := \begin{cases} \Phi'(P_0, f)(x) & \text{if } b = 0, \\ \Phi'(P_0^{-1}, f)(x) & \text{if } b = 1. \end{cases}$$

$P_2'^{\pm}$ can be regarded as an approximation of the function $\Phi^{\pm}(P_0, f) \in$ $\mathsf{Func}(\{0,1\} \times \{0,1\}^n, \{0,1\}^n)$, which is defined by $\Phi^{\pm}(P_0, f)(0, x) = \Phi(P_0, f)(x)$ and $\Phi^{\pm}(P_0, f)(1, x) = \Phi(P_0^{-1}, f)(x)$.

Distribution U_1'. Distribution U_1' on $\mathsf{Perm}(\{0,1\}^n)$ is an approximation of the uniform distribution U that combines U_0 with Λ. Formally, U_1' is defined by $U_1'(P) = \mathrm{Pr}_{P_0 \sim U_0, f \sim \Lambda}[P = \Phi(P_0, f)]$. In other words, U_1' is the distribution of the random variable that takes values in $\mathsf{Perm}(\{0,1\}^n)$ which is defined according to the following sampling:

1. $P_0 \xleftarrow{U_0} \mathsf{Perm}(\{0,1\}^n)$, $f \xleftarrow{\Lambda} \mathsf{Func}(\{0,1\}^n, \{0,1\})$
2. $P \leftarrow \Phi(P_0, f)$

Note that if P is sampled following U_1', we assume that a quantum adversary $\mathcal{A}$ is given a quantum oracle of $P^{\pm} : \{0,1\} \times \{0,1\}^n \to \{0,1\}^n$ (see Sect. 2.1).

Distribution U_2'. Distribution U_2' on $\mathsf{Func}(\{0,1\} \times \{0,1\}^n, \{0,1\}^n)$ is another approximation of U, which is more "rough" than U_1'. Below, for $F \in \mathsf{Func}(\{0,1\} \times \{0,1\}^n, \{0,1\}^n)$, the n-bit functions $F(0, \cdot), F(1, \cdot)$ are denoted by F^+ and F^-. Then, formally, U_2' is defined by $U_2'(F) = \mathrm{Pr}_{P_0 \sim U_0, f \sim \Lambda}[F^+ = \Phi'(P_0, f) \wedge F^- = \Phi'(P_0^{-1}, f)]$. In other words, U_2' is the distribution of the random variable that takes values in $\mathsf{Func}(\{0,1\} \times \{0,1\}^n, \{0,1\}^n)$ which is defined according to the following sampling:

1. $P_0 \xleftarrow{U_0} \mathsf{Perm}(\{0,1\}^n)$, $f \xleftarrow{\Lambda} \mathsf{Func}(\{0,1\}^n, \{0,1\})$
2. $F^+ \leftarrow \Phi'(P_0, f), F^- \leftarrow \Phi'(P_0^{-1}, f)$

Now the preparation to use the technique in Sect. 3 is completed. We reduce the problem of distinguishing U from U_0 to the problem of distinguishing Λ and Λ_0. Now we have the following inequalities.

$$\mathsf{Adv}_{U^{\pm}, U_0^{\pm}}^{dist}(\mathcal{A}) \leq \mathsf{Adv}_{U^{\pm}, U_1'^{\pm}}^{dist}(\mathcal{A}) + \mathsf{Adv}_{U_1'^{\pm}, U_2'}^{dist}(\mathcal{A}) + \mathsf{Adv}_{U_2', U_0^{\pm}}^{dist}(\mathcal{A})$$

$$\leq \Delta(U^{\pm}, U_1'^{\pm}) + \Delta(U_1'^{\pm}, U_2') + \mathsf{Adv}_{U_2', U_0^{\pm}}^{dist}(\mathcal{A}). \qquad (16)$$

Next, we show the following lemma.

Lemma 4.2. *For a quantum algorithm $\mathcal{A}$ to distinguish U_2' from $U_0^{\pm}$ that makes at most q quantum queries, we can construct a quantum algorithm $\mathcal{B}$ to distinguish Λ from Λ_0 that makes at most $2q$ queries and satisfies*

$$\mathsf{Adv}_{U_2', U_0^{\pm}}^{dist}(\mathcal{A}) = \mathsf{Adv}_{\Lambda, \Lambda_0}^{dist}(\mathcal{B}).$$

Proof. We give a quantum algorithm $\mathcal{B}$ that satisfies the desired properties. $\mathcal{B}$ is given a quantum oracle O_f, where f is sampled according to Λ or Λ_0. Before making queries, $\mathcal{B}$ chooses a derangement P_0 uniformly at random. Then, $\mathcal{B}$ runs $\mathcal{A}$. $\mathcal{B}$ answers to queries of $\mathcal{A}$ by calculating $\Phi'(P_0, f)$ and $\Phi'(P_0^{-1}, f)$. By definition of Φ', $\mathcal{B}$ can calculate one evaluation of $\Phi'(P_0, f)$ (and $\Phi'(P_0^{-1}, f)$) with two queries to O_f. Finally, $\mathcal{B}$ outputs what $\mathcal{A}$ outputs.

Since $\mathcal{A}$ makes at most q queries, $\mathcal{B}$ makes at most $2q$ queries. $\mathcal{B}$ perfectly simulates the distributions U_2' and $U_0^{\pm}$ according to which of Λ and Λ_0 is given. Thus $\mathsf{Adv}_{U_2',U_0^{\pm}}^{dist}(\mathcal{A}) = \mathsf{Adv}_{\Lambda,\Lambda_0}^{dist}(\mathcal{B})$ holds. □

From the above lemma and the inequalities (16), we have

$$\mathsf{Adv}_{U^{\pm},U_0^{\pm}}^{dist}(q) \le \Delta(U^{\pm}, U_1'^{\pm}) + \Delta(U_1'^{\pm}, U_2') + \mathsf{Adv}_{\Lambda,\Lambda_0}^{dist}(2q). \qquad (17)$$

The three terms in the right hand side are upper bounded as in the following lemmas.

Lemma 4.3. $\mathsf{Adv}_{\Lambda,\Lambda_0}^{dist}(q) \le \frac{2(e+1)q}{2^{n/2}}$

Lemma 4.4. $\Delta(U^{\pm}, U_1'^{\pm}) \le \frac{8n^3}{2^n - 2n + 1} + \frac{16n^3}{2^n} + \frac{e+1}{n!}$ for $n \ge 32$.

Lemma 4.5. $\Delta(U_1'^{\pm}, U_2') \le \frac{32n^3}{2^n} + \frac{2(e+1)}{n!}$ for $n \ge 32$.

Thus we have

$$\mathsf{Adv}_{U^{\pm},U_0^{\pm}}^{dist}(q) \le \frac{4(e+1)q}{2^{n/2}} + \frac{8n^3}{2^n - 2n + 1} + \frac{48n^3}{2^n} + \frac{3(e+1)}{n!}.$$

Combining this inequality and inequality (15), we obtain the desired bound (14) in Theorem 4.1.

To complete the proof, we give a proof of Lemma 4.3. Proofs of Lemma 4.4 and 4.5 are given in this paper's full version [14].

Proof of Lemma 4.3. To prove the Lemma 4.3, we use Proposition 3.2. Let us define a set of functions $\mathsf{good}, \mathsf{bad} \subset \mathsf{Func}(\{0,1\}^n, \{0,1\})$ by $\mathsf{good} := \mathsf{Func}(\{0,1\}^n, \{0,1\})\backslash\{\mathbf{0}\}$, and $\mathsf{bad} := \emptyset$. In addition, for each integer $\lambda > 0$, define $\mathsf{good}_\lambda \subset \mathsf{good}$ by $f \in \mathsf{good}_\lambda$ if and only if $|f^{-1}(1)| = \lambda$. Then, $\bigcup_\lambda \mathsf{good}_\lambda = \mathsf{good}$ and $\mathsf{good}_{\lambda_1} \cap \mathsf{good}_{\lambda_2} = \emptyset$ for $\lambda_1 \neq \lambda_2$. Moreover, the conditional probability $\Pr_{F \sim \Lambda}[F = f | F \in \mathsf{good}_\lambda]$ is independent on f due to the symmetry of the distribution Λ. Therefore we can apply Proposition 3.2.

Let $p_1^{\mathsf{good}_\lambda} := \Pr_{F \sim \Lambda}[F \in \mathsf{good}_\lambda]$ and $p_1^{f|\mathsf{good}_\lambda} := \Pr_{F \sim \Lambda}[F = f \mid F \in \mathsf{good}_\lambda]$. For each fixed x, the number of boolean function f such that $f(x) = 1 \wedge |f^{-1}(1)| = \lambda$ is exactly $\binom{2^n - 1}{\lambda - 1}$. Hence we have

$$\max_x |\{f \in \mathsf{good}_\lambda \mid f(x) = 1\}| = \binom{2^n - 1}{\lambda - 1}. \qquad (18)$$

In addition,

$$p_1^{f|\mathsf{good}_\lambda} = \frac{1}{\binom{2^n}{\lambda}}. \qquad (19)$$

hold.

Next, we upper bound $p_1^{\text{good}_\lambda} = \Pr_{f \sim \Lambda}[f \in \text{good}_\lambda] = \Pr_{a \sim D_{num}}[a = \lambda]$. For any fixed λ, we have

$$
\begin{aligned}
\Pr_{a \sim D_{num}}[a = \lambda] &= \frac{\binom{2^n}{\lambda} \cdot !(2^n - \lambda)}{2^n!} = \frac{!(2^n - \lambda)}{(2^n - \lambda)!} \cdot \frac{1}{\lambda!} \le \frac{(2^n - \lambda)!/e + 1}{(2^n - \lambda)!} \cdot \frac{1}{\lambda!} \\
&= \left(1 + \frac{e}{(2^n - \lambda)!}\right) \cdot \frac{1}{e} \cdot \frac{1}{\lambda!} \le \frac{1 + e}{e} \cdot \frac{1}{\lambda!}
\end{aligned}
\tag{20}
$$

(Remember that $!N$ denotes the number of derangements on a set of size N and $!N = \lfloor \frac{N!}{e} + \frac{1}{2} \rfloor$ holds. See Sect. 2.) Thus we have

$$
p_1^{\text{good}_\lambda} = \Pr_{f \sim \Lambda}[f \in \text{good}_\lambda] \le \frac{1 + e}{e} \cdot \frac{1}{\lambda!}.
\tag{21}
$$

From Proposition 3.2, equality (18), (19), and inequality (21), since $\Pr_{f \sim \Lambda}[f \in \text{bad}] = 0$ we have

$$
\begin{aligned}
\text{Adv}_{\Lambda, \Lambda_0}^{\text{dist}}(q) &\le 2q \cdot \sum_{0 < \lambda} p_1^{\text{good}_\lambda} \sqrt{p_1^{f | \text{good}_\lambda} \cdot \max_x \{|\{f \mid f(x) = 1 \land f \in \text{good}_\lambda\}|\}} \\
&\le 2q \cdot \sum_{0 < \lambda} \frac{1 + e}{e} \cdot \frac{1}{\lambda!} \sqrt{\frac{\binom{2^n - 1}{\lambda - 1}}{\binom{2^n}{\lambda}}} \le \frac{2q(1 + e)}{e} \cdot \sum_{0 < \lambda} \frac{1}{\lambda!} \sqrt{\frac{\lambda}{2^n}} \\
&= \frac{2q(1 + e)}{e} \cdot \sum_{0 < \lambda} \frac{1}{\sqrt{\lambda}(\lambda - 1)!} \sqrt{\frac{1}{2^n}} \\
&\le \frac{2q(1 + e)}{e} \cdot \sum_{0 \le \lambda} \frac{1}{\lambda!} \sqrt{\frac{1}{2^n}} = \frac{2(e + 1)q}{\sqrt{2^n}},
\end{aligned}
\tag{22}
$$

which is the desired bound. Hence Lemma 4.3 follows. $\square$

Remark 4.2. In this section we showed the non-invertibility of FF^P but did not show the one-wayness, because it seems difficult to reduce the one-wayness to the non-invertibility for the case of a permutation with feedforward. For Davies-Meyer construction, on the other hand, we can reduce its one-wayness to the non-invertibility by upper-bounding the total variation distance between the distribution of the game to break the one-wayness and that of the game to break the non-invertibility. Unfortunately, for permutations with feedforward, this strategy cannot be applied since the total variation distance between the two corresponding distributions would become very large.

5   Security of Davies-Meyer Constructions in the Quantum Ideal Cipher Model

This section gives proofs for security of Davies-Meyer constructions in the quantum ideal cipher model. We begin with showing non-invertibility, and then prove one-wayness. Our result in this section is the first proof for quantum security of functions based on public block ciphers.

5.1 Non-invertibility of Davies-Meyer

Non-invertibility in the ideal cipher model is shown in the similar way as in the proof for non-invertibility of permutation with feedforward in Sect. 4. We show the following theorem.

Theorem 5.1 (Non-invertibility of Davies-Meyer). *Let $n \geq 32$. For any quantum algorithm $\mathcal{A}$ that makes at most q queries to a block cipher E,*

$$\mathsf{Adv}_{\mathsf{DM}^E}^{inv}(\mathcal{A}) \leq 4(q+1)\left(\frac{n^{1/2}}{2^{n/2}} + \frac{2^m(e+1)}{n!}\right) + 2^m \epsilon(n) \tag{23}$$

holds, where $\epsilon(n) = \frac{8n^3}{2^n - 2n + 1} + \frac{48n^3}{2^n} + \frac{3(e+1)}{n!}$. In particular, $\mathcal{A}$ cannot invert DM^E with constant probability if $\frac{2^m}{2^n} \ll 1$ and $q \ll 2^{n/2}/n^{1/2}$.

Remark 5.1. In the above theorem, security bound is valid only for the case that key length m is less than block length n. (We do not know if there exist any attacks that exploit long key lengths. The condition that key length should be shorter than the block length comes from limitation of our proof technique.) However, even if $m \geq n$, then we can achieve the same bound if we restrict key space. That is, if we are given n-bit block ciphers with m-bit key and $m \geq n$, we use only the keys of which all bits are 0 except for the first $n/2$-bits, for example. Then we can construct non-invertible functions with $3n/2$-bit input and n-bit output.

We cannot get rid of this restriction on usage of key space since there are terms of order $O(n^3 \cdot 2^{m-n})$ in our bound (23), which come from Lemmas 4.4 and 4.5. The bound of Lemma 4.4 cannot be essentially improved, since $\Delta(U, U_1') \geq \frac{1}{4e \cdot 2^n}$ holds (see this paper's full version [14] for more details). Thus, if we want to get rid of the restriction, then we have to use other proof strategies.

Let U_E be the uniform distribution on $\mathsf{Ciph}(m, n)$, and $U_{E,0}$ be the distribution on $\mathsf{Ciph}(m, n)$ defined by $U_{E_0}(E) = \prod_k U_0(E_k)$ (i.e., when E is sampled according to $U_{E,0}$, then E_k is sampled according to U_0 for each key k.) We say that a pair (z, x) is a fixed point of a block cipher E if $E_z(x) = x$. Let us define the advantage of a quantum algorithm $\mathcal{A}$ to find a fixed point of an ideal block cipher E by

$$\mathsf{Adv}_E^{fixpt}(\mathcal{A}) := \Pr_{E \sim U_E}[\mathcal{A}^{O_{E^{\pm}}}() = (z, x) \wedge E_z(x) = x],$$

and

$$\mathsf{Adv}_E^{fixpt}(q) := \max_{\mathcal{A}}\left\{\mathsf{Adv}_E^{fixpt}(\mathcal{A})\right\},$$

where the maximum is taken over all quantum-query algorithms, each making at most q quantum queries.

Then, similarly as in the proof for permutation with feedforward, we have

$$\mathsf{Adv}_{\mathsf{DM}^E}^{inv}(q) \leq \mathsf{Adv}_E^{fixpt}(q) \leq \mathsf{Adv}_{U_E^{\pm}, U_{E,0}^{\pm}}^{dist}(q+1). \tag{24}$$

To upper bound $\mathsf{Adv}^{dist}_{U^\pm_E, U^\pm_{E,0}}$, we introduce distributions $D_{E,num}, \Lambda_E, \Lambda_{E,0}, U'_{E,1}$, $U'_{E,2}$, which are essentially product distributions of $D_{num}, \Lambda, \Lambda_0, U'_1, U'_2$, respectively.

Distribution $D_{E,num}$. Distribution $D_{E,num}$ on $([0,\ldots,2^n])^{\times 2^m}$ is the product distribution $D_{num} \times \cdots \times D_{num}$, i.e. $D_{E,num}$ is defined by $D_{E,num}(\lambda_0,\ldots,\lambda_{2^m-1}) := D_{num}(\lambda_0) \times \cdots \times D_{num}(\lambda_{2^m-1})$. $D_{E,num}$ can be regarded as the distribution of the number of fixed points of ideal ciphers.

Distribution Λ_E. Distribution Λ_E on the set $\mathsf{Func}(\{0,1\}^m \times \{0,1\}^n, \{0,1\})$ $= (\mathsf{Func}(\{0,1\}^n, \{0,1\}))^{2^m}$ is defined as the product distribution $\Lambda \times \cdots \times \Lambda$, i.e. Λ_E is defined by $\Lambda_E(F) := \Lambda_E(F(0,\cdot)) \times \Lambda_E(F(1,\cdot)) \times \cdots \times \Lambda_E(F(2^m - 1,\cdot))$. Λ_E can be regarded as the distribution of fixed points of ideal ciphers.

Distribution $\Lambda_{E,0}$. Distribution $\Lambda_{E,0}$ on $\mathsf{Func}(\{0,1\}^m \times \{0,1\}^n, \{0,1\})$ is the degenerate distribution with support on the zero-function $\mathbf{0}$.

Distribution $U'_{E,1}$. Distribution $U'_{E,1}$ on $\mathsf{Ciph}(m,n)$ is defined by $U'_{E,1}(E) := \prod_{k\in\{0,1\}^m} U'_1(E_k)$. That is, when E is sampled according to $U'_{E,1}$, then E_k is chosen according to U'_1 independently for each key k. Similarly as U'_1 is an approximation of U, $U'_{E,1}$ can be regarded as an approximation of U_E.

Distribution $U'_{E,2}$. Distribution $U'_{E,2}$ on $\mathsf{Func}(\{0,1\}\times\{0,1\}^m\times\{0,1\}^n, \{0,1\}^n)$ is defined by $U'_{E,2}(F) = \prod_{k\in\{0,1\}^m} U'_2(F(\cdot,k,\cdot))$. That is, $U'_{E,2}$ is the distribution of the random variable that is defined by the following sampling.

1. For each $z \in \{0,1\}^m$, do:
2. $\quad G_z \xleftarrow{U'_2} \mathsf{Func}(\{0,1\} \times \{0,1\}^n, \{0,1\}^n)$
3. $F(b,z,x) \leftarrow G_z(b,x)$ for each $b \in \{0,1\}, z \in \{0,1\}^m, x \in \{0,1\}^n$.
4. Return F

Similarly as U'_2 is a rough approximation of $U^\pm$, $U'_{E,2}$ can be regarded as a rough approximation of $U^\pm_E$.

Now we apply the technique introduced in Sect. 3. Similarly as inequality (17), we can show that

$$\mathsf{Adv}^{dist}_{U^\pm_E, U^\pm_{E,0}}(q) \le \Delta(U^\pm_E, U'^\pm_{E,1}) + \Delta(U'^\pm_{E,1}, U'_{E,2}) + \mathsf{Adv}^{dist}_{\Lambda_E, \Lambda_{E,0}}(2q),$$

holds. In addition, since $U, U'_{E,1}, U'_{E,2}$ are essentially the product distributions of U, U'_1, U'_2, from Lemmas 4.4 and 4.5 we have

$$\mathsf{Adv}^{dist}_{U^\pm_E, U^\pm_{E,0}}(q) \le 2^m \Delta(U^\pm, U'^\pm_1) + 2^m \Delta(U'^\pm_1, U'_2) + \mathsf{Adv}^{dist}_{\Lambda_E, \Lambda_{E,0}}(2q)$$

$$\le 2^m \left(\frac{8n^3}{2^n - 2n + 1} + \frac{48n^3}{2^n} + \frac{3(e+1)}{n!} \right) + \mathsf{Adv}^{dist}_{\Lambda_E, \Lambda_{E,0}}(2q). \tag{25}$$

Thus, to prove Theorem 5.1, it suffices to show the following lemma.

Lemma 5.1

$$\mathsf{Adv}^{dist}_{\Lambda_E, \Lambda_{E,0}}(q) \leq 2q \left(\frac{n^{1/2}}{2^{n/2}} + \frac{2^m(e+1)}{n!} \right)$$

Proof. To prove the Lemma 5.1, again we use our tool in Sect. 3. Let us define a set of functions $\mathsf{good} \subset \mathsf{Func}(\{0,1\}^m \times \{0,1\}^n, \{0,1\})$ by $f \in \mathsf{good}$ if and only if $f \neq \mathbf{0}$ and $\lambda_z = |f_z^{-1}(1)| < n$ for all $z \in \{0,1\}^m$, where $f_z(\cdot) = f(z, \cdot)$. Let $\mathsf{bad} := \mathsf{Func}(\{0,1\}^m \times \{0,1\}^n, \{0,1\}) \backslash (\mathsf{good} \cup \{\mathbf{0}\})$. In addition, for each sequence of integers $\lambda_S = (\lambda_0, \lambda_1, \ldots, \lambda_{2^m-1})$, define $\mathsf{good}_{\lambda_S} \subset \mathsf{good}$ by $f \in \mathsf{good}_{\lambda_S}$ if and only if $f_z^{-1}(1) = \lambda_z$ for all $0 \leq z \leq 2^m - 1$. For simplicity, we write $\lambda_S < n$ if and only if $\lambda_z < n$ for all $0 \leq z \leq 2^m - 1$. Similarly, we write $0 < \lambda_S$ if and only if $\lambda_z > 0$ for all $0 \leq z \leq 2^m - 1$. Then, $\bigcup_{0 < \lambda_S < n} \mathsf{good}_{\lambda_S} = \mathsf{good}$ and $\mathsf{good}_{\lambda_S} \cap \mathsf{good}_{\lambda_{S'}} = \emptyset$ for $\lambda_S \neq \lambda_{S'}$. The conditional probability $\mathrm{Pr}_{F \sim \Lambda_E}[F = f | f \in \mathsf{good}_{\lambda_S}]$ is independent on f due to the symmetry of the distribution Λ_E. Therefore we can apply Proposition 3.2 with $D_1 = \Lambda_E$ and $D_2 = \Lambda_{E,0}$.

Define

$$p_1^{\mathsf{good}_{\lambda_S}} := \Pr_{f \sim \Lambda_E} \left[f \in \mathsf{good}_{\lambda_S} \right] \tag{26}$$

and

$$p_1^{f|\mathsf{good}_{\lambda_S}} := \Pr_{F \sim \Lambda_E} \left[F = f \mid F \in \mathsf{good}_{\lambda_S} \right]. \tag{27}$$

Now we upper bound $\mathrm{Pr}_{f \sim \Lambda_E}[f \in \mathsf{bad}]$. Note that $\mathrm{Pr}_{f \sim \Lambda_E}[f \in \mathsf{bad}] \leq 2^m \mathrm{Pr}_{f \sim \Lambda}[|f^{-1}(1)| \geq n]$ holds since Λ_E is product distribution of Λ. In addition, from inequality (21) we have

$$\Pr_{f \sim \Lambda}[|f^{-1}(1)| \geq \lambda_0] \leq \frac{e+1}{e} \sum_{\lambda \geq \lambda_0} \frac{1}{\lambda!} \leq \frac{e+1}{e} \frac{e}{\lambda_0!} = \frac{e+1}{\lambda_0!}, \tag{28}$$

where we used the fact $\sum_{\lambda \geq \lambda_0} \frac{1}{\lambda!} \leq \frac{e}{\lambda_0!}$. Thus we have

$$\Pr_{f \sim \Lambda_E}[f \in \mathsf{bad}] \leq \frac{2^m(1+e)}{n!}. \tag{29}$$

Next, we upper bound $p_1^{f|\mathsf{good}_{\lambda_S}} \cdot \max_{(z,x)} |\{f \in \mathsf{good}_{\lambda_S} \mid f(z,x) = f_z(x) = 1\}|$. For each fixed $w \in \{0,1\}^m, x \in \{0,1\}^n$ and $\lambda_S = (\lambda_0, \ldots, \lambda_{2^m-1})$, the number of boolean function $f \in \mathsf{good}_{\lambda_S}$ such that $f_w(x) = 1$ is equal to

$$\binom{2^n - 1}{\lambda_w - 1} \cdot \prod_{z \neq w \in \{0,1\}^m} \binom{2^n}{\lambda_z} = \frac{\lambda_w}{2^n} \cdot \prod_{z \in \{0,1\}^m} \binom{2^n}{\lambda_z}. \tag{30}$$

Thus for each sequence $\lambda_S < n$ we have

$$\max_{(z,x)} |\{f \in \mathsf{good}_{\lambda_S} \mid f(z,x) = f_z(x) = 1\}| = \max_{(z,x)} \left\{ \frac{\lambda_z}{2^n} \cdot \prod_{z \in \{0,1\}^m} \binom{2^n}{\lambda_z} \right\}$$

$$\leq \frac{n}{2^n} \cdot \prod_{z \in \{0,1\}^m} \binom{2^n}{\lambda_z} \tag{31}$$

Hence, for each sequence $\lambda_S < n$ we have

$$p_{\Delta}^{f|\mathsf{good}_{\lambda_S}} \cdot \max_{(z,x)} \left| \{ f \in \mathsf{good}_{\lambda_S} \mid f(z,x) = f_z(x) = 1 \} \right|$$

$$\leq \frac{1}{\prod_{z \in \{0,1\}^m} \binom{2^n}{\lambda_z}} \cdot \frac{n}{2^n} \cdot \prod_{z \in \{0,1\}^m} \binom{2^n}{\lambda_z} = \frac{n}{2^n}. \tag{32}$$

From Proposition 3.2, and inequalities (29) and (32), $\mathsf{Adv}_{\Lambda,\Lambda_0}^{\mathsf{dist}}(q)$ is upper bounded by

$$2q \cdot \sum_{\lambda_S < n} p_1^{\mathsf{good}_{\lambda_S}} \sqrt{p_1^{f|\mathsf{good}_{\lambda_S}} \cdot \max_{(z,x)} \left| \{ f \in \mathsf{good}_{\lambda_S} \mid f_z(x) = 1 \} \right|}$$

$$+ \, 2q \cdot \Pr_{f \sim \Lambda_E} [f \in \mathsf{bad}]$$

$$\leq 2q \cdot \sum_{\lambda_S < n} p_1^{\mathsf{good}_{\lambda_S}} \sqrt{\frac{n}{2^n}} + 2q \cdot \frac{2^m(e+1)}{n!} \leq 2q \left(\sqrt{\frac{n}{2^n}} + \frac{2^m(e+1)}{n!} \right), \tag{33}$$

which completes the proof. $\square$

5.2 One-Wayness of Davies-Meyer

Next, we show that Davies-Meyer constructions are also quantum one-way in the quantum ideal cipher model.

Theorem 5.2 (One-wayness of Davies-Meyer). *Let* $n \geq 32$ *and* $m \leq n^2$. *For any quantum algorithm* $\mathcal{A}$ *that makes at most* q *queries to a block cipher* E,

$$\mathsf{Adv}_{\mathsf{DM}^E}^{ow}(\mathcal{A}) \leq 4(q+1) \left(\frac{n^{1/2}}{2^{n/2}} + \frac{2^m(e+1)}{n!} \right) + 2^m \epsilon(n) + \frac{2n+1}{2^{m/3+1}} + \frac{n^2}{2^{m-2}} \tag{34}$$

holds, where $\epsilon(n) = \frac{8n^3}{2^n - 2n + 1} + \frac{48n^3}{2^n} + \frac{3(e+1)}{n!}$. *In particular,* $\mathcal{A}$ *cannot find a preimage of* DM^E *with constant probability if* $\frac{2^m}{2^n} \ll 1$ *and* $q \ll 2^{n/2}/n^{1/2}$.

Remark 5.2. Here we need an additional condition $m \leq n^2$ for technical reasons. This assumption is reasonable since usual block ciphers satisfy it.

Proof. Let U_n be the uniform distribution on $\{0,1\}^n$ and V be the distribution on $\mathsf{Ciph}(m,n) \times \{0,1\}^n$ which is defined by $V(E,y) = \Pr_{e \sim U_E, (z,x) \sim U_{m+n}}[e = E \wedge \mathsf{DM}^E(z,x) = y]$. That is, V is the distribution of the random variable which is defined by the following sampling:

1. $E \xleftarrow{U_E} \mathsf{Ciph}(m,n)$, $z \xleftarrow{\$} \{0,1\}^m, x \xleftarrow{\$} \{0,1\}^n$
2. $y \leftarrow \mathsf{DM}^E(z,x)$
3. Return (E,y)

Then $\mathsf{Adv}_{\mathsf{DM}^E}^{ow}(\mathcal{A}) = \Pr_{(E,y)\sim V}[\mathcal{A}^{O_{E^\pm}}(y) = (z', x') \wedge \mathsf{DM}^E(z', x') = y]$ is upper bounded by

$$\Pr_{E\sim U_E, y\sim U_n}[\mathcal{A}^{O_{E^\pm}}(y) = (z', x') \wedge \mathsf{DM}^E(z', x') = y]$$

$$+ \left| \Pr_{(E,y)\sim V}[\mathcal{A}^{O_{E^\pm}}(y) = (z', x') \wedge \mathsf{DM}^E(z', x') = y] \right.$$

$$\left. - \Pr_{E\sim U_E, y\sim U_n}[\mathcal{A}^{O_{E^\pm}}(y) = (z', x') \wedge \mathsf{DM}^E(z', x') = y] \right|$$

$$\leq \mathsf{Adv}_{\mathsf{DM}^E}^{inv}(\mathcal{A}) + \Delta(V, (U_E, U_n)). \tag{35}$$

Hence Theorem 5.2 follows from Theorem 5.1 and the following lemma.

Lemma 5.2. $\Delta(V, (U_E, U_n)) \leq \frac{2n+1}{2^{m/3+1}} + \frac{n^2}{2^{m-2}}$ for $n \geq 32$ and $m \leq n^2$.

A proof of this lemma is given in this paper's full version [14]. □

6 Security of Merkle-Damgård with Davies-Meyer Constructions

This section shows that the combination of Davies-Meyer constructions with the Merkle-Damgård constructions are optimally non-invertible and one-way in the quantum ideal cipher model.

Merkle-Damgård construction is the most basic construction to convert compression functions, which have fixed input length, to a function with (variable) long input lengths. In particular, lots of popular hash functions like SHA-2 [21] are based on the Merkle-Damgård constructions, and use Davies-Meyer constructions as compression functions. Merkle-Damgård construction with MD-compliant padding is proven to be collision resistant hash function when underlying compression function is collision-resistant [11]. However, there is no guarantee that Merkle-Damgård constructions (with MD-compliant padding) become one-way (preimage resistant) or second preimage resistant hash functions even if underlying compression functions are one-way (preimage resistant) or second preimage resistant. Actually there is an attack that finds a second preimage with complexity less than 2^n [17].

Since usual Merkle-Damgård constructions do not guarantee one-wayness even in classical settings, in this paper we fix input length. Input length can be very long (actually we will construct functions of which input bit length are exponential of n), but must be fixed.

This section assumes that we are given an ideal block cipher $E \in \mathsf{Ciph}(m, n)$ with $m \leq n^2$. For a positive number r (r means "rate") with $1 < r < n$ and $\ell \geq 1$, define a padding function $\mathsf{pad}_{r,\ell} : \{0,1\}^n \times \{0,1\}^{\frac{n}{r} \cdot \ell} \to \{0,1\}^n \times \{0,1\}^{m\ell}$ by

$$\mathsf{pad}_{r,\ell} : x\|z_1\| \cdots \|z_\ell \mapsto x\|z_1\|0\| \cdots \|z_i\|(i-1)\| \cdots z_\ell\|(\ell-1),$$

where $z_i \in \{0,1\}^{\frac{n}{r}}$ and we assume that each integer i is expressed as an $(m-n/r)$-bit string. Let us define a function $H_{r,\ell}^E : \{0,1\}^{n+\frac{n}{r} \cdot \ell} \to \{0,1\}^n$ by

$$H_{r,\ell}^E(M) := \mathsf{MD}_\ell^{\mathsf{DM}^E}(\mathsf{pad}_{r,\ell}(M)).$$

The following theorem claims that $H_{r,\ell}^E$ has both non-invertibility and one-wayness.

Theorem 6.1 (Security of Merkle-Damgård with Davies-Meyer). *Let $n \geq 32$ and $m \leq n^2$. Assume $E \in \mathsf{Ciph}(m, n)$ is an ideal cipher. For any quantum adversary $\mathcal{A}$ that makes at most q queries to E,*

$$\mathsf{Adv}_{H_{r,\ell}^E}^{inv}(\mathcal{A}) \leq 4(q+1) \left(\frac{n^{1/2}}{2^{n/2}} + \frac{2^{n/r}(e+1)}{n!} \right) + \epsilon(r, n) \tag{36}$$

and

$$\mathsf{Adv}_{H_{r,\ell}^E}^{ow}(\mathcal{A}) \leq 4(q+1) \left(\frac{n^{1/2}}{2^{n/2}} + \frac{2^{n/r}(e+1)}{n!} \right) + \epsilon(r, n) + \delta(r, \ell, n) \tag{37}$$

holds, where $\epsilon(r, n) = 2^{n/r} \left(\frac{8n^3}{2^n - 2n + 1} + \frac{48n^3}{2^n} + \frac{3(e+1)}{n!} \right)$ and $\delta(r, \ell, n) = \ell \cdot \left(\frac{2n+1}{2^{n/3r+1}} + \frac{n^2}{2^{n/r-2}} \right)$. In particular, if $\ell \ll 2^{\frac{n}{3r}}$, then $\mathcal{A}$ cannot find a preimage of $H_{r,\ell}^E$ with constant probability for $q \ll 2^{n/2}/n^{1/2}$.

Remark 6.1. We need padding function $\mathsf{pad}_{r,\ell}$ to restrict key space for each message block (see Remark 5.1). Our padding function pads different numbers for different message blocks so that the i-th compression function and the j-th compression function become essentially independent for $i \neq j$.

Proof. Firstly we show non-invertibility, i.e. inequality (36). Non-invertibility of $H_{r,\ell}^E$ is reduced to non-invertibility of the Davies-Meyer construction of the last block. By using an adversary $\mathcal{A}$ to invert $H_{r,\ell}^E$, we construct an adversary $\mathcal{B}$ to invert a Davies-Meyer construction $\mathsf{DM}^{E'}$, where $E' \in \mathsf{Ciph}(n/r, n)$.

At the beginning of a game, $\mathcal{B}$ receives randomly chosen $y \in \{0, 1\}^n$ as an input. In addition, $\mathcal{B}$ has oracle access to an ideal cipher $E' \in \mathsf{Ciph}(n/r, n)$. $\mathcal{B}$ simulates an oracle of ideal cipher $E \in \mathsf{Ciph}(m, n)$ as follows. $\mathcal{B}$ chooses $\tilde{E} \in \mathsf{Ciph}(m, n)$ uniformly at random, and define $E \in \mathsf{Ciph}(m, n)$ by

$$E(k, x) = \begin{cases} E'(z, x) & \text{if } k = z\|\ell \text{ for some } z \in \mathsf{Ciph}(n/r, n), \\ \tilde{E}(k, x) & \text{otherwise.} \end{cases} \tag{38}$$

The distribution of E equals to the uniform distribution. $\mathcal{B}$ runs $\mathcal{A}$, giving y as the target image. $\mathcal{B}$ answers queries of $\mathcal{A}$ by using E. After $\mathcal{A}$ outputs a message $M = x\|z_1\| \cdots \|z_\ell \in \{0, 1\}^{n + \frac{n}{r} \cdot \ell}$, $\mathcal{B}$ calculates $x_{\ell-1} := H_{r,\ell-1}^E(x\|z_1\| \cdots \|z_{\ell-1})$ and outputs $(z_\ell, x_{\ell-1})$. Note that calculation of $x_{\ell-1}$ does not need any query to E'. Since $\mathsf{DM}^{E'}(z_\ell\|\ell, H_{r,\ell-1}^E(x\|z_1\| \cdots \|z_{\ell-1})) = H_{r,\ell}^E(M) = y$ holds, we have $\mathsf{Adv}_{H_{r,\ell}^E}^{inv}(\mathcal{A}) = \mathsf{Adv}_{\mathsf{DM}^{E'}}^{inv}(\mathcal{B})$, and we obtain the desired bound (36) from Theorem 5.1.

Next we show one-wayness, i.e. inequality (37). Similarly as in Sect. 5, we reduce one-wayness to non-invertibility. Again, let U_n be the uniform distribution on $\{0, 1\}^n$. Let V_1 be the distribution of the random variable which takes values in $\mathsf{Ciph}(m, n) \times \{0, 1\}^n$ and is defined by the following sampling:

A. Hosoyamada and K. Yasuda

1. $E \xleftarrow{U_E} \mathsf{Ciph}(m,n)$, $M \xleftarrow{\$} \{0,1\}^{n+\frac{n}{r}\cdot\ell}$
2. $y \leftarrow H_{r,\ell}^E(M)$
3. return (E,y)

Then we have

$$\mathsf{Adv}_{H_{r,\ell}^E}^{ow}(\mathcal{A}) \leq \mathsf{Adv}_{H_{r,\ell}^E}^{inv}(\mathcal{A}) + \Delta(V_1, (U_E, U_n)). \tag{39}$$

Below we upper bound $\Delta(V_1, (U_E, U_n))$ by using intermediate distributions $V_2, \ldots, V_\ell$. For $2 \leq i \leq \ell$, let V_i be the distribution of the random variable which takes values in $\{0,1\}^n$ and is defined by the following sampling:

1. $x\|z_i\|\cdots\|z_\ell \xleftarrow{\$} \{0,1\}^{n+\frac{n}{r}(\ell-i+1)}$
2. $h_{i-1} \leftarrow x$
3. For $j = i, \ldots, \ell$, do:
4. $\qquad h_j \leftarrow \mathsf{DM}^E((z_i\|i), h_{j-1})$
5. $y \leftarrow h_\ell$

Note that the above definition is valid even for $i = 1$, and the resulting distribution is equal to V_1. By definition of our padding function pad, function distributions of the compression functions which process the i-th block and j-th block are essentially independent for $i \neq j$. Thus, by Lemma 5.2 we have

$$\Delta(V_i, V_{i+1}), \Delta(V_\ell, (U_E, U_n)) \leq \frac{2n+1}{2^{n/3r+1}} + \frac{n^2}{2^{n/r-2}} \tag{40}$$

for $1 \leq i \leq \ell - 1$. Hence $\Delta(V_1, (U_E, U_n))$ is upper bounded by

$$\sum_{i=1}^{\ell-1} \Delta(V_i, V_{i+1}) + \Delta(V_\ell, (U_E, U_n)) \leq \ell \cdot \left(\frac{2n+1}{2^{n/3r+1}} + \frac{n}{2^{n/r-2}}\right). \tag{41}$$

Thus inequality (37) follows from inequality (39) and (41). □

References

1. Alagic, G., Russell, A.: Quantum-secure symmetric-key cryptography based on hidden shifts. In: Coron, J.-S., Nielsen, J.B. (eds.) EUROCRYPT 2017. LNCS, vol. 10212, pp. 65–93. Springer, Cham (2017). https://doi.org/10.1007/978-3-319-56617-7_3
2. Ambainis, A., Rosmanis, A., Unruh, D.: Quantum attacks on classical proof systems: the hardness of quantum rewinding. In: 55th IEEE Annual Symposium on Foundations of Computer Science, FOCS 2014, Philadelphia, PA, USA, 18–21 October 2014, pp. 474–483 (2014)
3. Anand, M.V., Targhi, E.E., Tabia, G.N., Unruh, D.: Post-quantum security of the CBC, CFB, OFB, CTR, and XTS modes of operation. In: Takagi, T. (ed.) PQCrypto 2016. LNCS, vol. 9606, pp. 44–63. Springer, Cham (2016). https://doi.org/10.1007/978-3-319-29360-8_4

4. Beals, R., Buhrman, H., Cleve, R., Mosca, M., de Wolf, R.: Quantum lower bounds by polynomials. In: 39th Annual Symposium on Foundations of Computer Science, FOCS 1998, 8–11 November 1998, Palo Alto, California, USA, pp. 352–361 (1998)
5. Bennett, C.H., Bernstein, E., Brassard, G., Vazirani, U.V.: Strengths and weaknesses of quantum computing. SIAM J. Comput. **26**(5), 1510–1523 (1997)
6. Boneh, D., Dagdelen, Ö., Fischlin, M., Lehmann, A., Schaffner, C., Zhandry, M.: Random oracles in a quantum world. In: Lee, D.H., Wang, X. (eds.) ASIACRYPT 2011. LNCS, vol. 7073, pp. 41–69. Springer, Heidelberg (2011). https://doi.org/10.1007/978-3-642-25385-0_3
7. Boneh, D., Zhandry, M.: Quantum-secure message authentication codes. In: Johansson, T., Nguyen, P.Q. (eds.) EUROCRYPT 2013. LNCS, vol. 7881, pp. 592–608. Springer, Heidelberg (2013). https://doi.org/10.1007/978-3-642-38348-9_35
8. Boyer, M., Brassard, G., Høyer, P., Tapp, A.: Tight bounds on quantum searching. Fortsch. Phys. **46**(4–5), 493–505 (1998)
9. Carstens, T.V., Ebrahimi, E., Tabia, G.N., Unruh, D.: On quantum indifferentiability. IACR Cryptology ePrint Archive, Report 2018/257 (2018)
10. Czajkowski, J., Groot Bruinderink, L., Hülsing, A., Schaffner, C., Unruh, D.: Post-quantum security of the sponge construction. In: Lange, T., Steinwandt, R. (eds.) PQCrypto 2018. LNCS, vol. 10786, pp. 185–204. Springer, Cham (2018). https://doi.org/10.1007/978-3-319-79063-3_9
11. Goldwasser, S., Bellare, M.: Lecture notes on cryptography. Summer course "Cryptography and computer security" at MIT (1996–2008)
12. Grover, L.K.: A fast quantum mechanical algorithm for database search. In: Proceedings of the Twenty-Eighth Annual ACM Symposium on the Theory of Computing, Philadelphia, Pennsylvania, USA, 22–24 May 1996, pp. 212–219 (1996)
13. Hassani, M.: Derangements and applications. J. Integer Sequences **6**(2) (2003)
14. Hosoyamada, A., Yasuda, K.: Building quantum-one-way functions from block ciphers: Davies-Meyer and Merkle-Damgård constructions. IACR Cryptology ePrint Archive, Report 2018/841 (2018)
15. Hülsing, A., Rijneveld, J., Song, F.: Mitigating multi-target attacks in hash-based signatures. In: Cheng, C.-M., Chung, K.-M., Persiano, G., Yang, B.-Y. (eds.) PKC 2016. LNCS, vol. 9614, pp. 387–416. Springer, Heidelberg (2016). https://doi.org/10.1007/978-3-662-49384-7_15
16. Kaplan, M., Leurent, G., Leverrier, A., Naya-Plasencia, M.: Breaking symmetric cryptosystems using quantum period finding. In: Robshaw, M., Katz, J. (eds.) CRYPTO 2016. LNCS, vol. 9815, pp. 207–237. Springer, Heidelberg (2016). https://doi.org/10.1007/978-3-662-53008-5_8
17. Kelsey, J., Schneier, B.: Second preimages on n-bit hash functions for much less than 2^n work. In: Cramer, R. (ed.) EUROCRYPT 2005. LNCS, vol. 3494, pp. 474–490. Springer, Heidelberg (2005). https://doi.org/10.1007/11426639_28
18. Kuwakado, H., Morii, M.: Quantum distinguisher between the 3-round Feistel cipher and the random permutation. In: IEEE International Symposium on Information Theory, ISIT 2010, 13–18 June 2010, Austin, Texas, USA, Proceedings, pp. 2682–2685 (2010)
19. Kuwakado, H., Morii, M.: Security on the quantum-type Even-Mansour cipher. In: Proceedings of the International Symposium on Information Theory and its Applications, ISITA 2012, Honolulu, HI, USA, 28–31 October 2012, pp. 312–316 (2012)

20. Mennink, B., Szepieniec, A.: XOR of PRPs in a quantum world. In: Lange, T., Takagi, T. (eds.) PQCrypto 2017. LNCS, vol. 10346, pp. 367–383. Springer, Cham (2017). https://doi.org/10.1007/978-3-319-59879-6_21
21. NIST: Fips pub 180–2. National Institute of Standards and Technology (2002)
22. NIST: Fips pub 202. National Institute of Standards and Technology (2014)
23. Patarin, J.: The "coefficients H" technique. In: Avanzi, R.M., Keliher, L., Sica, F. (eds.) SAC 2008. LNCS, vol. 5381, pp. 328–345. Springer, Heidelberg (2009). https://doi.org/10.1007/978-3-642-04159-4_21
24. Rogaway, P., Shrimpton, T.: Cryptographic hash-function basics: definitions, implications, and separations for preimage resistance, second-preimage resistance, and collision resistance. In: Roy, B., Meier, W. (eds.) FSE 2004. LNCS, vol. 3017, pp. 371–388. Springer, Heidelberg (2004). https://doi.org/10.1007/978-3-540-25937-4_24
25. Shor, P.W.: Polynomial-time algorithms for prime factorization and discrete logarithms on a quantum computer. SIAM J. Comput. **26**(5), 1484–1509 (1997)
26. Song, F.: A note on quantum security for post-quantum cryptography. In: Mosca, M. (ed.) PQCrypto 2014. LNCS, vol. 8772, pp. 246–265. Springer, Cham (2014). https://doi.org/10.1007/978-3-319-11659-4_15
27. Song, F., Yun, A.: Quantum security of NMAC and related constructions. In: Katz, J., Shacham, H. (eds.) CRYPTO 2017. LNCS, vol. 10402, pp. 283–309. Springer, Cham (2017). https://doi.org/10.1007/978-3-319-63715-0_10
28. Unruh, D.: Quantum position verification in the random oracle model. In: Garay, J.A., Gennaro, R. (eds.) CRYPTO 2014. LNCS, vol. 8617, pp. 1–18. Springer, Heidelberg (2014). https://doi.org/10.1007/978-3-662-44381-1_1
29. Unruh, D.: Revocable quantum timed-release encryption. In: Nguyen, P.Q., Oswald, E. (eds.) EUROCRYPT 2014. LNCS, vol. 8441, pp. 129–146. Springer, Heidelberg (2014). https://doi.org/10.1007/978-3-642-55220-5_8
30. Unruh, D.: Collapse-binding quantum commitments without random oracles. In: Cheon, J.H., Takagi, T. (eds.) ASIACRYPT 2016. LNCS, vol. 10032, pp. 166–195. Springer, Heidelberg (2016). https://doi.org/10.1007/978-3-662-53890-6_6
31. Unruh, D.: Computationally binding quantum commitments. In: Fischlin, M., Coron, J.-S. (eds.) EUROCRYPT 2016. LNCS, vol. 9666, pp. 497–527. Springer, Heidelberg (2016). https://doi.org/10.1007/978-3-662-49896-5_18
32. Zhandry, M.: How to record quantum queries, and applications to quantum indifferentiability. IACR Cryptology ePrint Archive, Report 2018/276 (2018)
33. Zhandry, M.: How to construct quantum random functions. In: 53rd Annual IEEE Symposium on Foundations of Computer Science, FOCS 2012, New Brunswick, NJ, USA, 20–23 October 2012, pp. 679–687 (2012)
34. Zhandry, M.: Secure identity-based encryption in the quantum random oracle model. In: Safavi-Naini, R., Canetti, R. (eds.) CRYPTO 2012. LNCS, vol. 7417, pp. 758–775. Springer, Heidelberg (2012). https://doi.org/10.1007/978-3-642-32009-5_44
35. Zhandry, M.: A note on the quantum collision and set equality problems. Quantum Info. Comput. **15**(7–8), 557–567 (2015)

Tweakable Block Ciphers Secure Beyond the Birthday Bound in the Ideal Cipher Model

ByeongHak Lee$^{(\boxtimes)}$ and Jooyoung Lee$^{(\boxtimes)}$

KAIST, Daejeon, Korea
{lbh0307,hicalf}@kaist.ac.kr

Abstract. We propose a new construction of tweakable block ciphers from standard block ciphers. Our construction, dubbed XHX2, is the cascade of two independent XHX block ciphers, so it makes two calls to the underlying block cipher using tweak-dependent keys. We prove the security of XHX2 up to $\min\{2^{2(n+m)/3}, 2^{n+m/2}\}$ queries (ignoring logarithmic factors) in the ideal cipher model, when the block cipher operates on n-bit blocks using m-bit keys. The XHX2 tweakable block cipher is the first construction that achieves beyond-birthday-bound security with respect to the input size of the underlying block cipher in the ideal cipher model.

Keywords: Tweakable block cipher
Beyond-birthday-bound security · Ideal cipher model

1 Introduction

Tweakable block ciphers, first introduced in [9], are a generalization of standard block ciphers that accept extra inputs called *tweaks*. The tweak, providing inherent variability to the block cipher, makes it easy to design various higher level cryptographic schemes such as message authentication codes and modes of operation.

Tweakable block ciphers can either be designed from scratch [4,5,17], or be built upon off-the-shelf cryptographic primitives such as block ciphers and (public) permutations [3,8,11,14]. In this work, we will specifically focus on block cipher-based constructions; one of the advantages of such constructions is that the trust in extensively-studied block ciphers can be transferred to the tweakable block ciphers via security reductions. In this line of research, it has been suggested that changing tweaks should be cheaper than changing keys. Following this principle, early proposals including LRW1 and LRW2 [8,9], and their cascades used their underlying block ciphers with fixed keys, namely *tweak*

Jooyoung Lee was supported by a National Research Foundation of Korea (NRF) grant funded by the Korean government (Ministry of Science and ICT), No. NRF-2017R1E1A1A03070248.

T. Peyrin and S. Galbraith (Eds.): ASIACRYPT 2018, LNCS 11272, pp. 305–335, 2018.
https://doi.org/10.1007/978-3-030-03326-2_11

independent keys. So changing tweaks does not require rekeying the underlying block cipher. The security of tweakable block ciphers without tweak-rekeying has typically been analyzed in the standard model, where the block cipher with a secret random key is replaced by a secret random permutation.

Recently, a unified vision for the tweak and key inputs has been proposed within the TWEAKEY framework [6]. From this point of view, tweakable block ciphers using *tweak dependent keys* have been studied [10,18]. By using tweak dependent keys, one might expect a higher level of security (than using fixed keys), whereas the security of such constructions is typically analyzed in the ideal cipher model.

OUR RESULTS. Suppose that a κ-bit key tweakable block cipher TBC has been built on an m-bit key n-bit block cipher E (modeled as an ideal cipher). Typically, each evaluation of TBC would need a fixed number of calls to the underlying block cipher E, and hence $O(2^\kappa)$ block cipher queries will be sufficient to mount an exhaustive key search on TBC. However, if $n + m < \kappa$, then one would be able to find its secret key (in an information theoretic sense) by making all possible 2^{n+m} block cipher queries. Therefore, TBC will not be provably secure beyond $2^{\min\{\kappa, n+m\}}$ queries in the ideal cipher model. In this line of research, recent work has been aimed at achieving security beyond $2^{n/2}$ (precisely, 2^n) assuming $\kappa = m = n$ [10,18]. This level of security is optimal, but still it is only the birthday bound with respect to the input size of the ideal cipher, namely $n + m$. If a tweakable block cipher accepts sufficiently large keys (for example, if $\kappa > n = m$), then one might expect security beyond 2^n. The problem that we tackle in this paper is to construct a tweakable block cipher secure beyond the birthday bound with respect to the input size of the underlying block cipher in the ideal cipher model (as the counterpart of LRW2[2] in the standard model), assuming $\kappa > n + m$.[1]

We begin with XHX proposed by Jha et al. [7]. Let $E : \{0,1\}^m \times \{0,1\}^n \to \{0,1\}^n$ be an m-bit key n-bit block cipher, let $\mathcal{T}$ be a tweak space, and let $\mathcal{G}$ and $\mathcal{H}$ be families of functions $g : \mathcal{T} \to \{0,1\}^n$ and $h : \mathcal{T} \to \{0,1\}^m$, respectively. Then the XHX tweakable block cipher accepts a key $(g, h) \in \mathcal{G} \times \mathcal{H}$ and a tweak $t \in \mathcal{T}$, and encrypts a plaintext $x \in \{0,1\}^n$ by computing

$$E_{h(t)}(x \oplus g(t)) \oplus g(t).$$

If $\mathcal{G}$ is δ-almost uniform and δ-almost XOR-universal, and if $\mathcal{H}$ is δ'-almost uniform and δ'-almost universal with $\delta \approx 1/2^n$ and $\delta' \approx 1/2^m$, then XHX is proved to be secure up to $2^{(n+m)/2}$ queries in the ideal cipher model.

Our main contribution is to prove the security of the cascade of two independent XHX constructions (see Fig. 1), dubbed XHX2, up to

$$\min\{2^{\frac{2(n+m)}{3}}, 2^{n+\frac{m}{2}-\log_2 n}\}$$

---

[1] This assumption is similar to the study of key length extension, where the key size of the entire scheme is sometimes larger than the input size of the underlying block cipher.

queries. To the best of our knowledge, this is the first construction of a tweakable block cipher that achieves beyond-birthday-bound security with respect to the input size of the underlying block cipher.

For simplicity, we will prove the security of XHX2 under the assumption that the first and the second block cipher calls are made to independent block ciphers. However, in the ideal cipher model, a single key bit will be sufficient to separate a single block cipher into two independent ones with negligible security loss.

We believe that our results are not only of theoretical interest, but also practically relevant in certain environments, in particular where stronger security is required with block ciphers operating on (relatively) small blocks (e.g., CAST-128 [1], KATAN, KTANTAN [2], Simeck [19]). For example, CAST-128 (used in GPG and PGP) operates on 64-bit blocks using 128-bit keys. Based on this block cipher, the resulting XHX2 provides 128-bit security (ignoring log factors and constants), while this level of security would not be achieved with any other existing construction. On the other hand, the key schedule of the underlying block cipher should not be too simple (being secure against related-key and known-/chosen-key distinguishing attacks) since every block cipher key is supposed to define an independent permutation in our security model.

COMPARISON. A comparison of XHX2 with the existing tweakable block ciphers is given in Table 1. In this table, security is evaluated by the threshold number of queries in $\log_2$. In Min, $|t|$ denotes the fixed tweak length. All the constructions with tweak-rekeying are analyzed in the ideal cipher model, while the constructions without tweak-rekeying are in the standard model. Efficiency is evaluated by the number of block cipher calls, the number of multiplications or universal hashes, and the use of tweak dependent keys (represented by TDK).

Table 1. Comparison of XHX2 with existing tweakable block ciphers.

Construction	Key size	Security ($\log_2$)	Efficiency E	$\otimes/\mathcal{H}$	TDK	References
LRW1	n	$n/2$	2	0		[9]
LRW2, XEX	$2n$	$n/2$	1	1	$\boldsymbol{\times}$	[9, 16]
LRW2[2]	$4n$	$2n/3$	2	2		[3]
LRW2[s]	$2sn$	$sn/(s+2)$	s	s		[3]
Min	n	$\max\{n/2, n-|t|\}$	2	0		[12]
$\widetilde{F}[1]$	n	$2n/3$	1	1		[10]
$\widetilde{F}[2]$	n	n	2	0	$\checkmark$	[10, 18]
$\widetilde{E1},\ldots,\widetilde{E32}$	$n(2n)$	n	2(1)	0		[18]
XHX	$n+m$	$(n+m)/2$	1	2		[7]
XHX2	$2n+2m$	$\min\{2(n+m)/3, n+m/2\}$	2	4		This work

DISCUSSION. It is notable that our result for XHX2 implies beyond-birthday-bound security for the cascade of two independent XTX [13] constructions (for the first time).

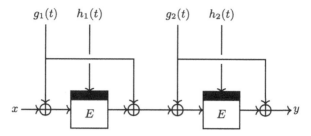

Fig. 1. Tweakable block cipher XHX2.

In typical TBC-based modes of operation (such as TBC, TAE [9] and SCT [15]), nonces and counters are placed into the tweak; when the tweak size is limited to the key size of the underlying block cipher, the hash computation can be defined as a single multiplication, namely $t \cdot k$ for a hash key k and a tweak t. In this case, different tweaks map to different block cipher keys, removing the possibility of (C-14), and hence the term $2^{n+m/2}$ from the security bound.

OVERVIEW OF THE PROOF. Our security proof is based on the standard H-coefficient technique. We begin by defining a set of bad transcripts. The badness will be determined solely by the choice of hash keys g_1, g_2, h_1 and h_2. Once the hash keys are fixed, we can associate each construction query (t, x, y) with a 5-tuple $(h_1(t), h_2(t), x \oplus g_1(t), y \oplus g_2(t), g_1(t) \oplus g_2(t))$, which will be called a "reduced query". As long as the hash keys are not bad, the reduced queries will be all distinct. Let $k = h_1(t)$, $l = h_2(t)$, $u = x \oplus g_1(t)$, $v = y \oplus g_2(t)$ and $\Delta = g_1(t) \oplus g_2(t)$. The relation between a reduced query (k, l, u, v, Δ) and its original query (t, x, y) can be pictorially represented as follows.

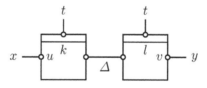

The core of the proof is to show that the probabilities to obtain any good transcript are close in the real and in the ideal world, or particularly, to tightly lower bound the probability of obtaining a good transcript in the real world. In the real world, randomness comes only from the underlying ideal ciphers E_1 and E_2. For example, suppose that $E_1(k, u)$ has been determined by a block cipher query (i.e., query history $\mathcal{Q}_E$). Then the probability that E_1 and E_2 complete the reduced query (k, l, u, v, Δ) becomes the probability that E_2 maps $E_1(k, u) \oplus \Delta$ to v with key l, where we can assume that $E_2(l, E_1(k, u) \oplus \Delta)$ and $E_2^{-1}(l, v)$ have not been fixed excluding bad keys (of (C-9) and (C-10)). Fixing $E_2(l, E_1(k, u) \oplus \Delta) = v$ might affect the freedom of other construction queries, making the analysis complicated. The notion of a reduced query helps systematically dealing with this problem; we will carefully classify the reduced queries into five classes, and compute the (conditional) probability of completing each class of queries one by one. This classification will be defined in detail at Sect. 3.3.

2 Preliminaries

BASIC NOTATION. In all the following, we fix positive integers m and n, and denote $N = 2^n$. Given a non-empty set $\mathcal{X}$, $x \leftarrow_\$ \mathcal{X}$ denotes that x is chosen uniformly at random from $\mathcal{X}$. For a set $\mathcal{X}$ and an integer $b \geq 1$, we write $x_1, \ldots, x_b \in^{\neq} \mathcal{X}$ to mean that $x_1, \ldots, x_b$ are pairwise distinct elements of $\mathcal{X}$. The set of all sequences that consist of b pairwise distinct elements of $\mathcal{X}$ is denoted $\mathcal{X}^{*b}$. For integers $1 \leq b \leq a$, we will write $(a)_b = a(a-1)\cdots(a-b+1)$ and $(a)_0 = 1$ by convention. If $|\mathcal{X}| = a$, then $(a)_b$ becomes the size of $|\mathcal{X}^{*b}|$. When two sets $\mathcal{X}$ and $\mathcal{Y}$ are disjoint, we denote $\mathcal{X} \sqcup \mathcal{Y}$ their (disjoint) union.

USEFUL LEMMA. The following lemma, viewed as a generalization of Lemma 5 in [3], will be used in the security proof of XHX2.

Lemma 1. *Let N, a, b, c, d be positive integers such that $a + b \leq N/2$, $a + c \leq N/2$, $d \leq b$ and $d \leq c$. Then*

$$\frac{(N-d)_a(N-b-c+d)_a}{(N-b)_a(N-c)_a} \geq 1 - \frac{4a(b-d)(c-d)}{N^2}.$$

Due to the space limit, the proof of this lemma will be given in the full version.

UNIFORM, UNIVERSAL AND XOR-UNIVERSAL HASH FUNCTIONS. We will need the following definitions of almost uniform, almost universal (AU) and almost XOR-universal (AXU) hash functions.

Definition 1. *Let $\delta > 0$, and let $\mathcal{H}$ be a family of functions $h : \mathcal{T} \rightarrow \mathcal{Y}$ for non-empty sets $\mathcal{T}$ and $\mathcal{Y}$.*

1. *$\mathcal{H}$ is said to be δ-almost uniform if for any $x \in \mathcal{T}$ and any $y \in \mathcal{Y}$,*

$$\Pr[h \leftarrow_\$ \mathcal{H} : h(x) = y] \leq \delta.$$

2. *$\mathcal{H}$ is said to be δ-almost universal (δ-AU) if for any distinct x and $x' \in \mathcal{T}$,*

$$\Pr[h \leftarrow_\$ \mathcal{H} : h(x) = h(x')] \leq \delta.$$

3. *When $\mathcal{Y} = \{0,1\}^n$, $\mathcal{H}$ is said to be δ-almost XOR-universal (δ-AXU) if for any distinct $x, x' \in \mathcal{T}$ and any $y \in \mathcal{Y}$,*

$$\Pr[h \leftarrow_\$ \mathcal{H} : h(x) \oplus h(x') = y] \leq \delta.$$

Remark 1. Hash functions in $\mathcal{H}$ are typically indexed by keys in a certain key space, written as $\mathcal{H} : \mathcal{K} \times \mathcal{T} \rightarrow \mathcal{Y}$ for a key space $\mathcal{K}$. For example, let $\mathcal{K} = \mathcal{Y} = \{0,1\}^n$ and let $\mathcal{T} = \{0,1\}^{dn} \setminus \{(0, \ldots, 0)\}$ for a positive integer d. Identifying

$\{0,1\}^n$ with a finite field $\mathbf{GF}(2^n)$ with 2^n elements and representing an element $t \in \mathcal{T}$ as a concatenation of n-bit elements $t_d, \ldots, t_1$, define

$$\mathcal{H} : \mathcal{K} \times \mathcal{T} \longrightarrow \{0,1\}^n$$
$$(k, t_d \| \ldots \| t_1) \longmapsto t_d \cdot k^d + \cdots + t_1 \cdot k.$$

Then it is not hard to show that $\mathcal{H}$ is $\frac{d}{2^n}$-almost uniform and $\frac{d}{2^n}$-almost XOR-universal. As seen in this example, for any n, one can define a δ-almost uniform and δ-almost XOR-universal family of functions with n-bit key, n-bit output, and $\delta \approx 1/2^n$ (ignoring d).

THE IDEAL CIPHER MODEL. A block cipher with key space $\mathcal{K}$ and message space $\mathcal{X}$ is a mapping $E : \mathcal{K} \times \mathcal{X} \to \mathcal{X}$ such that, for any key $k \in \mathcal{K}$, $x \mapsto E(k, x)$ is a permutation of $\mathcal{X}$. Throughout this paper, we will fix $\mathcal{K} = \{0,1\}^m$ and $\mathcal{X} = \{0,1\}^n$, and write $\mathsf{BC}(m,n)$ to mean the set of all such block ciphers.

In the ideal cipher model, a block cipher E is chosen from $\mathsf{BC}(m,n)$ uniformly at random. It allows for two types of oracle queries $E(k,x)$ and $E^{-1}(k,y)$ for $x, y \in \{0,1\}^n$ and $k \in \{0,1\}^m$. The response to an inverse query $E^{-1}(k,y)$ is $x \in \{0,1\}^n$ such that $E(k,x) = y$.

TWEAKABLE BLOCK CIPHERS. A tweakable permutation with tweak space $\mathcal{T}$ and message space $\mathcal{X}$ is a mapping $\widetilde{P} : \mathcal{T} \times \mathcal{X} \to \mathcal{X}$ such that, for any tweak $t \in \mathcal{T}$, $x \mapsto \widetilde{P}(t,x)$ is a permutation of $\mathcal{X}$. Throughout the paper, we will fix $\mathcal{X} = \{0,1\}^n$, and write $\mathsf{Perm}(\mathcal{T}, n)$ to mean the set of all tweakable permutations with tweak space $\mathcal{T}$ and message space $\{0,1\}^n$.

A tweakable block cipher TBC with key space $\mathcal{K}$, tweak space $\mathcal{T}$ and message space $\mathcal{X}$ is a mapping $\mathsf{TBC} : \mathcal{K} \times \mathcal{T} \times \mathcal{X} \to \mathcal{X}$ such that for any key $\mathbf{k} \in \mathcal{K}$, $(t,x) \mapsto \mathsf{TBC}(\mathbf{k}, t, x)$ is a tweakable permutation with tweak space $\mathcal{T}$ and message space $\mathcal{X}$.

INDISTINGUISHABILITY. For $s \geq 1$, we will consider a tweakable block cipher TBC based on a set of block ciphers

$$\mathcal{E} = (E_1, \ldots, E_s) \in \mathsf{BC}(m,n)^s.$$

So each key $\mathbf{k} \in \mathcal{K}$ and a set of block ciphers $\mathcal{E} = (E_1, \ldots, E_s) \in \mathsf{BC}(m,n)^s$ define a tweakable permutation, denoted $\mathsf{TBC}_{\mathbf{k}}[\mathcal{E}]$, with tweak space $\mathcal{T}$ and message space $\mathcal{X}$. Specifically, we have $s = 1$ for XHX and $s = 2$ for XHX2, and $\mathcal{X} = \{0,1\}^n$ for both constructions.

In the *real* world, a secret key $\mathbf{k} \in \mathcal{K}$ is chosen uniformly at random. A set of s block ciphers $E_1, \ldots, E_s$ are also chosen independently at random from $\mathsf{BC}(m,n)$. A distinguisher $\mathcal{D}$ is given oracle access to $\mathsf{TBC}_{\mathbf{k}}[\mathcal{E}]$ as well as $\mathcal{E} = (E_1, \ldots, E_s)$. In the *ideal* world, $\mathcal{D}$ is given a random tweakable permutation $\widetilde{P} \in \mathsf{Perm}(\mathcal{T}, n)$ instead of $\mathsf{TBC}_{\mathbf{k}}[\mathcal{E}]$. However, oracle access to $\mathcal{E} = (E_1, \ldots, E_s)$ is still allowed in this world.

The adversarial goal is to tell apart the two worlds $(\mathsf{TBC_k}[\mathcal{E}], \mathcal{E})$ and $(\widetilde{P}, \mathcal{E})$ by adaptively making forward and backward queries to the construction and each of the block ciphers. Formally, $\mathcal{D}$'s distinguishing advantage is defined by

$$\mathbf{Adv}_{\mathsf{TBC}}(\mathcal{D}) = \Pr\left[\widetilde{P} \leftarrow_\$ \mathsf{Perm}(\mathcal{T}, n), \mathcal{E} \leftarrow_\$ \mathsf{BC}(m, n)^s : 1 \leftarrow \mathcal{D}^{\mathcal{E}, \widetilde{P}}\right]$$

$$- \Pr\left[\mathbf{k} \leftarrow_\$ \mathcal{K}, \mathcal{E} \leftarrow_\$ \mathsf{BC}(m, n)^s : 1 \leftarrow \mathcal{D}^{\mathcal{E}, \mathsf{TBC_k}[\mathcal{E}]}\right].$$

For $p, q > 0$, we define

$$\mathbf{Adv}_{\mathsf{TBC}}(p, q) = \max_{\mathcal{D}} \mathbf{Adv}_{\mathsf{TBC}}(\mathcal{D})$$

where the maximum is taken over all adversaries $\mathcal{D}$ making at most p queries to each of the block ciphers and at most q queries to the outer tweakable permutation.

H-COEFFICIENT TECHNIQUE. Suppose that a distinguisher $\mathcal{D}$ makes p queries to each of the block ciphers, and q queries to the construction oracle. The queries made to the construction oracle are recorded in a query history

$$\mathcal{Q}_C = (t_i, x_i, y_i)_{1 \le i \le q}.$$

So according to the instantiation, it would imply either $\mathsf{TBC_k}[\mathcal{E}](t_i, x_i) = y_i$ or $\widetilde{P}(t_i, x_i) = y_i$. For $j = 1, \ldots, s$, the queries made to E_j are recorded in a query history

$$\mathcal{Q}_{E_j} = (j, k_{j,i}, u_{j,i}, v_{j,i})_{1 \le i \le p},$$

where $(j, u_{j,i}, v_{j,i})$ represents the evaluation $E_j(k_{j,i}, u_{j,i}) = v_{j,i}$ obtained by the i-th query to E_j. We will often omit the index j when it is clear from context. Let

$$\mathcal{Q}_E = \mathcal{Q}_{E_1} \cup \cdots \cup \mathcal{Q}_{E_s}.$$

Then the pair of query histories $\tau = (\mathcal{Q}_C, \mathcal{Q}_E)$ will be called the *transcript* of the attack: it contains all the information that $\mathcal{D}$ has obtained at the end of the attack. In this work, we will only consider information theoretic distinguishers. Therefore we can assume that a distinguisher is deterministic without making any redundant query, and hence the output of $\mathcal{D}$ can be regarded as a function of τ, denoted $\mathcal{D}(\tau)$ or $\mathcal{D}(\mathcal{Q}_C, \mathcal{Q}_E)$.

Fix a transcript $\tau = (\mathcal{Q}_C, \mathcal{Q}_E)$, a key $\mathbf{k} \in \mathcal{K}$, a tweakable permutation $\widetilde{P} \in \mathsf{Perm}(\mathcal{T}, n)$, a tuple of block ciphers $\mathcal{E} = (E_1, \ldots, E_s) \in \mathsf{BC}(m, n)^s$ and $j \in \{1, \ldots, s\}$: if $\mathsf{TBC_k}[\mathcal{E}](t_i, x_i) = y_i$ (resp. $\widetilde{P}(t_i, x_i) = y_i$) for every $i = 1, \ldots, q$, then we will write $\mathsf{TBC_k}[\mathcal{E}] \vdash \mathcal{Q}_C$ (resp. $\widetilde{P} \vdash \mathcal{Q}_C$). Similarly, if $E_j(k_{j,i}, u_{j,i}) = v_{j,i}$ for every $i = 1, \ldots, p$, then we will write $E_j \vdash \mathcal{Q}_{E_j}$. We will write $\mathcal{E} \vdash \mathcal{Q}_E$ if $E_j \vdash \mathcal{Q}_{E_j}$ for every $j = 1, \ldots, s$.

If there exist $\widetilde{P} \in \mathsf{Perm}(\mathcal{T}, n)$ and $\mathcal{E} \in \mathsf{BC}(m, n)^s$ that outputs τ at the end of the interaction with $\mathcal{D}$, then we will call the transcript τ *attainable*. So for any attainable transcript $\tau = (\mathcal{Q}_C, \mathcal{Q}_E)$, there exist $\widetilde{P} \in \mathsf{Perm}(\mathcal{T}, n)$ and

$\mathcal{E} \in \mathsf{BC}(m,n)^s$ such that $\widetilde{P} \vdash \mathcal{Q}_C$ and $\mathcal{E} \vdash \mathcal{Q}_E$. For an attainable transcript $\tau = (\mathcal{Q}_C, \mathcal{Q}_E)$ and a key $\mathbf{k} \in \mathcal{K}$, let

$$\mathsf{p}_{\mathsf{id}}(\mathcal{Q}_C | \mathcal{Q}_E) = \Pr\left[\widetilde{P} \leftarrow_\$ \mathsf{Perm}(\mathcal{T}, n), \mathcal{E} \leftarrow_\$ \mathsf{BC}(m,n)^s : \widetilde{P} \vdash \mathcal{Q}_C \middle| \mathcal{E} \vdash \mathcal{Q}_E\right],$$

$$\mathsf{p}_{\mathsf{re}}(\mathcal{Q}_C | \mathcal{Q}_E) = \Pr\left[\mathbf{k} \leftarrow_\$ \mathcal{K}, \mathcal{E} \leftarrow_\$ \mathsf{BC}(m,n)^s : \mathsf{TBC}_\mathbf{k}[\mathcal{E}] \vdash \mathcal{Q}_C \middle| \mathcal{E} \vdash \mathcal{Q}_E\right],$$

$$\mathsf{p}_{\mathsf{re}}^\mathbf{k}(\mathcal{Q}_C | \mathcal{Q}_E) = \Pr\left[\mathcal{E} \leftarrow_\$ \mathsf{BC}(m,n)^s : \mathsf{TBC}_\mathbf{k}[\mathcal{E}] \vdash \mathcal{Q}_C \middle| \mathcal{E} \vdash \mathcal{Q}_E\right].$$

With respect to an attainable transcript $\tau = (\mathcal{Q}_C, \mathcal{Q}_E)$, we will define a set of "bad" keys, denoted $\mathcal{K}_{\mathsf{bad}}$, such that the probability of a uniform random key being bad is small, while the ratio $\mathsf{p}_{\mathsf{re}}^\mathbf{k}(\mathcal{Q}_C | \mathcal{Q}_E)/\mathsf{p}_{\mathsf{id}}(\mathcal{Q}_C | \mathcal{Q}_E)$ is close to 1 for any "good" key $\mathbf{k} \in \mathcal{K} \setminus \mathcal{K}_{\mathsf{bad}}$. With these definitions, the following lemma, the core of the H-coefficients technique, will be also used in our security proof.

Lemma 2. *Let $\varepsilon_1, \varepsilon_2 > 0$. Suppose that for any attainable transcript $\tau = (\mathcal{Q}_C, \mathcal{Q}_E)$, there exists $\mathcal{K}_{\mathsf{bad}} \subset \mathcal{K}$ such that $|\mathcal{K}_{\mathsf{bad}}|/|\mathcal{K}| \leq \varepsilon_1$ and for any $\mathbf{k} \in \mathcal{K} \setminus \mathcal{K}_{\mathsf{bad}}$*

$$\mathsf{p}_{\mathsf{re}}^\mathbf{k}(\mathcal{Q}_C | \mathcal{Q}_E) \geq (1 - \varepsilon_2)\mathsf{p}_{\mathsf{id}}(\mathcal{Q}_C | \mathcal{Q}_E).$$

Then one has

$$\mathbf{Adv}_{\mathsf{TBC}}(\mathcal{D}) \leq \varepsilon_1 + \varepsilon_2.$$

3   Security Proof for **XHX2**

Let $E_1, E_2 : \{0,1\}^m \times \{0,1\}^n \to \{0,1\}^n$ be m-bit key n-bit block ciphers, let $\mathcal{T}$ be a tweak space, and let $\mathcal{G}$ and $\mathcal{H}$ be families of hash functions $g : \mathcal{T} \to \{0,1\}^n$ and $h : \mathcal{T} \to \{0,1\}^m$, respectively. The XHX2 tweakable block cipher accepts a key $\mathbf{k} = (g_1, h_1, g_2, h_2) \in \mathcal{K} =^{\mathrm{def}} \mathcal{G} \times \mathcal{H} \times \mathcal{G} \times \mathcal{H}$ and a tweak $t \in \mathcal{T}$, and encrypts a plaintext $x \in \{0,1\}^n$ by computing

$$E_2\left(h_2(t), E_1(h_1(t), x \oplus g_1(t)) \oplus g_1(t) \oplus g_2(t)\right) \oplus g_2(t).$$

Theorem 1. *Let $\delta, \delta' > 0$, let $\mathcal{G}$ be a δ-almost uniform and universal family of hash functions from $\mathcal{T}$ to $\{0,1\}^n$ and let $\mathcal{H}$ be a δ'-almost uniform and XOR-universal family of hash functions from $\mathcal{T}$ to $\{0,1\}^m$. Then for any integers p and q, one has*

$$\mathbf{Adv}_{\mathsf{XHX2}}(p,q) \leq 64p^{\frac{2}{3}}q^{\frac{2}{3}}\delta\delta' + \frac{256(8q^3 + 2pq^2)^{\frac{1}{2}}\delta^{\frac{1}{2}}\delta'}{N^{\frac{1}{2}}} + \frac{160(16q^3 + 8pq^2 + p^2q)^{\frac{1}{2}}\delta'}{N}$$

$$+ 256(16q^3 + 8pq^2 + 2q^2 + 3p^2q)\delta^2(\delta')^2 + \frac{131072n^2q^2\delta'}{N^2}.$$

3.1 Giving Free Queries to the Distinguisher

For the security proof of XHX2, we will make an additional assumption on the attack model; a distinguisher $\mathcal{D}$ will be given free queries at the end of the attack by the following rule.

1. If $\mathcal{D}$ has made $N/4$ or more block cipher queries to E_1 (resp. E_2) for a fixed key $k \in \{0,1\}^m$, then $\mathcal{D}$ will be given $E_1(k,u)$ (resp. $E_2(k,u)$) for all unqueried u (if any).
2. If $\mathcal{D}$ has made $N/16$ or more queries to the construction oracle C for a fixed tweak $t \in \mathcal{T}$, then $\mathcal{D}$ will be given $C(t,x)$ for all unqueried x (if any).

This modification would not degrade the adversarial distinguishing advantage since $\mathcal{D}$ is free to ignore the additional information. Suppose that $\mathcal{D}$ makes at most p queries to each of the block ciphers and at most q queries to the outer tweakable permutation. Then the number of free queries given to $\mathcal{D}$ is upper bounded by $3p$ for each block cipher, and by $15q$ for the tweakable permutation. So this assumption can be viewed as transforming $\mathcal{D}$ into a new distinguisher $\mathcal{D}'$ that

(i) makes at most $4p$ queries to each of the block ciphers and at most $16q$ queries to the outer tweakable permutation;
(ii) makes either all N queries or less than $N/4$ queries for each key and each of the block ciphers;
(iii) makes either all N queries or less than $N/16$ construction queries for each tweak.

Let

$$\mathbf{Adv}^*_{\mathsf{TBC}}(p,q) = \max_{\mathcal{D}'} \mathbf{Adv}_{\mathsf{TBC}}(\mathcal{D}')$$

where the maximum is taken over all adversaries $\mathcal{D}'$ that make at most p queries to each of the block ciphers and at most q queries to the outer tweakable permutation *satisfying conditions (ii) and (iii)*. Then we have

$$\mathbf{Adv}_{\mathsf{XHX2}}(p,q) \leq \mathbf{Adv}^*_{\mathsf{XHX2}}(4p, 16q). \tag{1}$$

Henceforth, we will assume that a modified adversary $\mathcal{D}'$ makes p primitive queries to each of the block ciphers and q construction queries.

For an attainable transcript $\tau = (\mathcal{Q}_C, \mathcal{Q}_E)$, we will use the following notations: for $r, s \in \{0,1\}^m$, and $w \in \mathcal{T}$,

$$\mathcal{Q}_{E_1}(r) = \{(k,u,v) \in \mathcal{Q}_{E_1} : k = r\},$$
$$\mathcal{Q}_{E_2}(s) = \{(l,u,v) \in \mathcal{Q}_{E_2} : l = s\},$$
$$\mathcal{Q}_C(w) = \{(t,x,y) \in \mathcal{Q}_C : t = w\}.$$

Note that either $|\mathcal{Q}_{E_i}(r)| < N/4$ or $|\mathcal{Q}_{E_i}(r)| = N$ for any $r \in \{0,1\}^m$ and $i = 1,2$. Similarly, we have either $|\mathcal{Q}_C(w)| < N/16$ or $|\mathcal{Q}_C(w)| = N$ for any $w \in \mathcal{T}$. In particular, we will write

$$\mathcal{T}^* = \{t \in \mathcal{T} : |\mathcal{Q}_C(t)| = N\}, \qquad \mathcal{Q}^*_C = \bigsqcup_{t \in \mathcal{T}^*} \mathcal{Q}_C(t).$$

3.2   Bad Keys

Fix an attainable transcript $\tau = (\mathcal{Q}_C, \mathcal{Q}_E)$, and positive integers M_1, M_2, M_3 (that will be optimized later). Let

$$\mathcal{A}_1 = \{((t,x,y),(k,u,v)) \in \mathcal{Q}_C \times \mathcal{Q}_{E_1} : (h_1(t), x \oplus g_1(t)) = (k,u)\},$$

$$\mathcal{A}_2 = \{((t,x,y),(k,u,v)) \in \mathcal{Q}_C \times \mathcal{Q}_{E_2} : (h_2(t), y \oplus g_2(t)) = (k,v)\},$$

$$\mathcal{B}_1 = \{((t,x,y),(t',x',y')) \in \mathcal{Q}_C^{*2} : \exists (t'',x'',y'') \neq (t,x,y),(t',x',y') \text{ such that}$$
$$x \oplus g_1(t) = x'' \oplus g_1(t''), \ h_1(t) = h_1(t''), \ h_2(t) = h_2(t')\},$$

$$\mathcal{B}_2 = \{((t,x,y),(t',x',y')) \in \mathcal{Q}_C^{*2} : \exists (t'',x'',y'') \neq (t,x,y),(t',x',y') \text{ such that}$$
$$y \oplus g_2(t) = y'' \oplus g_2(t''), \ h_2(t) = h_2(t''), \ h_1(t) = h_1(t')\},$$

$$\mathcal{B}_3 = \{((t,x,y),(k,u,v)) \in \mathcal{Q}_C \times \mathcal{Q}_{E_1} : \exists (t',x',y') \neq (t,x,y) \text{ such that}$$
$$y \oplus g_2(t) = y' \oplus g_2(t'), \ h_2(t) = h_2(t'), \ h_1(t) = k\},$$

$$\mathcal{B}_4 = \{((t,x,y),(k,u,v)) \in \mathcal{Q}_C \times \mathcal{Q}_{E_2} : \exists (t',x',y') \neq (t,x,y) \text{ such that}$$
$$x \oplus g_1(t) = x' \oplus g_1(t'), \ h_1(t) = h_1(t'), \ h_2(t) = k\},$$

$$\mathcal{C}_1 = \{((t,x,y),(t',x',y'),(t'',x'',y'')) \in \mathcal{Q}_C^3 :$$
$$t \neq t', \ t \neq t'', \ h_1(t) = h_1(t'), \ h_2(t) = h_2(t'')\},$$

$$\mathcal{C}_2 = \{((t,x,y),(t',x',y'),(k,u,v)) \in \mathcal{Q}_C^2 \times \mathcal{Q}_{E_1} :$$
$$t \neq t', \ h_2(t) = h_2(t'), \ h_1(t) = k\},$$

$$\mathcal{C}_3 = \{((t,x,y),(t',x',y'),(k,u,v)) \in \mathcal{Q}_C^2 \times \mathcal{Q}_{E_2} :$$
$$t \neq t', \ h_1(t) = h_1(t'), \ h_2(t) = k\},$$

$$\mathcal{C}_4 = \{((t,x,y),(k,u,v),(k',u',v')) \in \mathcal{Q}_C \times \mathcal{Q}_{E_1} \times \mathcal{Q}_{E_2} : h_1(t) = k, h_2(t) = k'\}.$$

A key $\mathbf{k} = (g_1, h_1, g_2, h_2) \in \mathcal{K}$ is defined to be *bad* if one of the following conditions is fulfilled:

(C-1) $|\mathcal{A}_i| \geq M_1$ for some $i = 1, 2$;

(C-2) there exist $(t,x,y),(t',x',y') \in^{\neq} \mathcal{Q}_C$ and $(k,u,v),(k',u',v') \in \mathcal{Q}_{E_1}$ such that

$$(h_1(t), x \oplus g_1(t)) = (k,u),$$
$$(h_1(t'), x' \oplus g_1(t')) = (k',u'),$$
$$(h_2(t), v \oplus g_1(t) \oplus g_2(t)) = (h_2(t'), v' \oplus g_1(t') \oplus g_2(t'));$$

(C-3) there exist $(t,x,y),(t',x',y') \in^{\neq} \mathcal{Q}_C$ and $(k,u,v),(k',u',v') \in \mathcal{Q}_{E_2}$ such that

$$(h_2(t), y \oplus g_2(t)) = (k,v),$$
$$(h_2(t'), y' \oplus g_2(t')) = (k',v'),$$
$$(h_1(t), u \oplus g_1(t) \oplus g_2(t)) = (h_1(t'), u' \oplus g_1(t') \oplus g_2(t'));$$

(C-4) $|\mathcal{B}_i| \geq M_2$ for some $i = 1, 2, 3, 4$;

(C-5) $|\mathcal{C}_i| \geq M_3$ for some $i = 1, 2, 3, 4$;

(C-6) there exist $(t, x, y), (t', x', y'), (t'', x'', y'') \in \mathcal{Q}_C$ such that $(t, x, y) \neq (t', x', y')$, $(t, x, y) \neq (t'', x'', y'')$ and

$$(h_1(t), x \oplus g_1(t)) = (h_1(t'), x' \oplus g_1(t')),$$
$$(h_2(t), y \oplus g_2(t)) = (h_2(t''), y'' \oplus g_2(t''));$$

(C-7) there exist $(t, x, y), (t', x', y') \in^{\neq} \mathcal{Q}_C$ such that

$$(h_1(t), x \oplus g_1(t)) = (h_1(t'), x' \oplus g_1(t')),$$
$$(h_2(t), g_1(t) \oplus g_2(t)) = (h_2(t'), g_1(t') \oplus g_2(t'));$$

(C-8) there exist $(t, x, y), (t', x', y') \in^{\neq} \mathcal{Q}_C$ such that

$$(h_1(t), g_1(t) \oplus g_2(t)) = (h_1(t'), g_1(t') \oplus g_2(t')),$$
$$(h_2(t), y \oplus g_2(t)) = (h_2(t'), y' \oplus g_2(t'));$$

(C-9) there exist $(t, x, y) \in \mathcal{Q}_C$, $(k, u, v) \in \mathcal{Q}_{E_1}$ and $(k', u', v') \in \mathcal{Q}_{E_2}$ such that

$$(h_1(t), x \oplus g_1(t)) = (k, u),$$
$$(h_2(t), y \oplus g_2(t)) = (k', v');$$

(C-10) there exist $(t, x, y) \in \mathcal{Q}_C$, $(k, u, v) \in \mathcal{Q}_{E_1}$ and $(k', u', v') \in \mathcal{Q}_{E_2}$ such that

$$(h_1(t), x \oplus g_1(t)) = (k, u),$$
$$(h_2(t), v \oplus g_1(t) \oplus g_2(t)) = (k', u');$$

(C-11) there exist $(t, x, y) \in \mathcal{Q}_C$, $(k, u, v) \in \mathcal{Q}_{E_1}$ and $(k', u', v') \in \mathcal{Q}_{E_2}$ such that

$$(h_1(t), u' \oplus g_1(t) \oplus g_2(t)) = (k, v),$$
$$(h_2(t), y \oplus g_2(t)) = (k', v');$$

(C-12) there exist $(t, x, y), (t', x', y') \in^{\neq} \mathcal{Q}_C$ and $(k, u, v) \in \mathcal{Q}_{E_1}$ such that

$$(h_1(t), x \oplus g_1(t)) = (k, u),$$
$$(h_2(t), y \oplus g_2(t)) = (h_2(t'), y' \oplus g_2(t'));$$

(C-13) there exist $(t, x, y), (t', x', y') \in^{\neq} \mathcal{Q}_C$ and $(k, u, v) \in \mathcal{Q}_{E_2}$ such that

$$(h_1(t), x \oplus g_1(t)) = (h_1(t'), x' \oplus g_1(t')),$$
$$(h_2(t), y \oplus g_2(t)) = (k, v);$$

(C-14) there exist $k \in \{0, 1\}^m$ and $h \in \{h_1, h_2\}$ such that

$$\frac{N}{4} \leq |\{(t, x, y) \in \mathcal{Q}_C \setminus \mathcal{Q}_C^* : h(t) = k\}|.$$

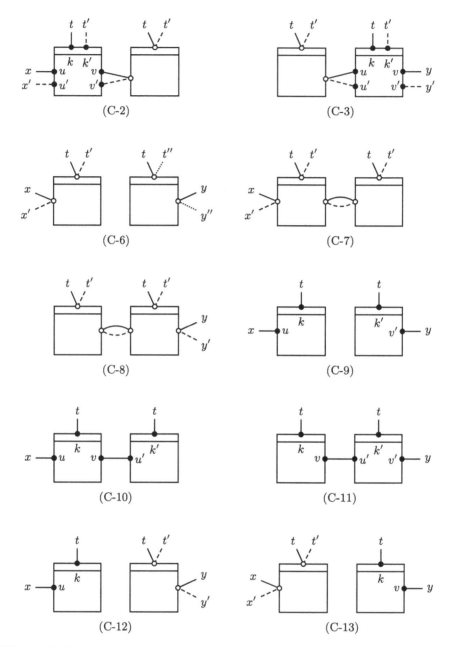

Fig. 2. Reduced queries that make bad conditions (C-2), (C-3) and (C-6) to (C-13). Black dots (resp. white dots) represent values fixed by $\mathcal{Q}_{E_1}$ and $\mathcal{Q}_{E_2}$ (resp. free values).

Figure 2 pictorially represents bad conditions (C-2), (C-3) and (C-6) to (C-13) in terms of reduced queries (as defined in Sect. 3.3). The probability of having bad keys in the ideal world is upper bounded as follows.

Lemma 3. *For an attainable transcript* $\tau = (\mathcal{Q}_C, \mathcal{Q}_E)$, *let* $\mathcal{K}_{bad}$ *be the set of bad keys defined as above. Then we have*

$$\frac{|\mathcal{K}_{bad}|}{|\mathcal{K}|} \le \frac{2pq\delta\delta'}{M_1} + 2M_1^2\delta\delta' + \frac{(2q^3 + 2pq^2)\delta(\delta')^2}{M_2} + \frac{(q^3 + 2pq^2 + p^2q)(\delta')^2}{M_3}$$

$$+ (q^3 + 2pq^2 + 2q^2 + 3p^2q)\delta^2(\delta')^2 + \frac{512n^2q^2\delta'}{N^2}.$$

For $i = 1, \dots, 14$, let E_i denote the event that a uniform random key $\mathbf{k} \in \mathcal{K}$ satisfies condition (C-i). Then we have

$$\frac{|\mathcal{K}_{bad}|}{|\mathcal{K}|} \le \Pr[\mathsf{E}_1 \vee \mathsf{E}_2 \vee \mathsf{E}_3] + \sum_{i=4}^{14} \Pr[\mathsf{E}_i]. \tag{2}$$

Here we only upper bound $\Pr[\mathsf{E}_{14}]$; the analysis of the other events are rather straightforward. Due to the space limit, the complete proof will be given in the full version.

UPPER BOUNDING. $\Pr[\mathsf{E}_{14}]$. Let

$$\mathcal{T}^i = \{w \in \mathcal{T} : 2^{i-1} \le |\mathcal{Q}_C(w)| < 2^i\},$$
$$\mathcal{Q}_C^i = \{(t, x, y) \in \mathcal{Q}_C(w) : w \in \mathcal{T}^i\},$$

for $i = 1, \dots, n-4$. Then we have

$$\mathcal{T} \setminus \mathcal{T}^* = \bigsqcup_{i=1}^{n-4} \mathcal{T}^i, \qquad \mathcal{Q}_C \setminus \mathcal{Q}_C^* = \bigsqcup_{i=1}^{n-4} \mathcal{Q}_C^i.$$

For each $h \in \{h_1, h_2\}$ and $i \in \{1, \dots, n-4\}$, we define two random variables

$$X_i = |\{(t, t') \in (\mathcal{T}^i)^{*2} : h(t) = h(t')\}|,$$
$$Y_i = \max_{\substack{\exists t_1, \dots, t_\ell \in \neq \mathcal{T}^i \text{ s.t.} \\ h(t_1) = \dots = h(t_\ell)}} \ell.$$

Since $|\mathcal{T}^i| \le \frac{q}{2^{i-1}}$ and by the δ'-almost uniformity of $\mathcal{H}$, we have

$$\mathbf{E}[X_i] \le |\mathcal{T}^i|(|\mathcal{T}^i| - 1)\delta' \le \left(\frac{q}{2^{i-1}}\right)^2 \delta'$$

for $i = 1, \dots, n-4$. Since $Y_i(Y_i - 1) \le X_i$ and by Markov's inequality, we have

$$\Pr\left[Y_i \ge \frac{q\sqrt{C\delta'}}{2^{i-1}} + 1\right] \le \Pr\left[Y_i(Y_i - 1) \ge \left(\frac{q\sqrt{C\delta'}}{2^{i-1}}\right)^2\right]$$

$$\le \Pr\left[X_i \ge C\left(\frac{q}{2^{i-1}}\right)^2 \delta'\right] \le \frac{1}{C}$$

for any $C > 0$. Therefore, for each $k \in \{0,1\}^m$ and $h \in \{h_1, h_2\}$, we have

$$|\{(t,x,y) \in \mathcal{Q}_C \setminus \mathcal{Q}_C^* : h(t) = k\}| < \sum_{i=1}^{n-4} Y_i 2^i < \sum_{i=1}^{n-4} \left(\frac{q\sqrt{C\delta'}}{2^{i-1}} + 1 \right) 2^i$$

$$< 2nq\sqrt{C\delta'} + \frac{N}{8}$$

except with probability at most n/C. By letting $C = \left(\frac{N}{16nq} \right)^2 \frac{1}{\delta'}$ (satisfying $2nq\sqrt{C\delta'} = N/8$), we have

$$\Pr\left[\mathsf{E}_{14}\right] \leq \frac{512n^2 q^2 \delta'}{N^2}. \tag{3}$$

3.3   Lower Bounding $\mathsf{p}_{\mathsf{re}}^{\mathsf{k}}(\mathcal{Q}_C | \mathcal{Q}_E)/\mathsf{p}_{\mathsf{id}}(\mathcal{Q}_C | \mathcal{Q}_E)$ For a Good Key

This section will be devoted to the proof of the following lemma.

Lemma 4. *For an attainable transcript* $\tau = (\mathcal{Q}_C, \mathcal{Q}_E)$ *and a good key* $\mathbf{k} = (g_1, h_1, g_2, h_2) \in \mathcal{K}$, *one has*

$$\frac{\mathsf{p}_{\mathsf{re}}^{\mathsf{k}}(\mathcal{Q}_C | \mathcal{Q}_E)}{\mathsf{p}_{\mathsf{id}}(\mathcal{Q}_C | \mathcal{Q}_E)} \geq 1 - \left(\frac{16M_2}{N} + \frac{16M_3}{N^2} \right).$$

3.3.1   Useful Definitions and Properties

Let

$$\overline{\mathcal{Q}_C} = \{(h_1(t), h_2(t), x \oplus g_1(t), y \oplus g_2(t), g_1(t) \oplus g_2(t)) : (t,x,y) \in \mathcal{Q}_C\}.$$

The elements of $\overline{\mathcal{Q}_C}$ will be called *reduced queries* (or simply queries). The reduced queries of $\overline{\mathcal{Q}_C}$ are all distinct, namely, if $(t,x,y) \neq (t', x', y')$, then

$$(h_1(t), h_2(t), x \oplus g_1(t), y \oplus g_2(t), g_1(t) \oplus g_2(t))$$
$$\neq (h_1(t'), h_2(t'), x \oplus g_1(t'), y \oplus g_2(t'), g_1(t') \oplus g_2(t'))$$

since $\mathbf{k}$ does not satisfy condition (C-6). Let

$$\mathcal{Q}^{(1)} = \{(k, l, u, v, \Delta) \in \overline{\mathcal{Q}_C} : (k, u, *) \in \mathcal{Q}_{E_1} \text{ for some } * \in \{0,1\}^n\},$$

$$\mathcal{Q}^{(2)} = \{(k, l, u, v, \Delta) \in \overline{\mathcal{Q}_C} : (l, *, v) \in \mathcal{Q}_{E_2} \text{ for some } * \in \{0,1\}^n\},$$

$$\mathcal{Q}^{(3)} = \{(k, l, u, v, \Delta) \in \overline{\mathcal{Q}_C} : \exists (k', l', u', v', \Delta') \in \overline{\mathcal{Q}_C} \text{ such that}$$
$$(k', l', u', v', \Delta') \neq (k, l, u, v, \Delta), \ (k', u') = (k, u)\} \setminus \mathcal{Q}^{(1)},$$

$$\mathcal{Q}^{(4)} = \{(k, l, u, v, \Delta) \in \overline{\mathcal{Q}_C} : \exists (k', l', u', v', \Delta') \in \overline{\mathcal{Q}_C} \text{ such that}$$
$$(k', l', u', v', \Delta') \neq (k, l, u, v, \Delta), \ (l', v') = (l, v)\} \setminus \mathcal{Q}^{(2)},$$

$$\mathcal{Q}^{(5)} = \overline{\mathcal{Q}_C} \setminus \left(\bigcup_{i=1}^{4} \mathcal{Q}^{(i)} \right).$$

Each class of queries are pictorially represented in Fig. 3.

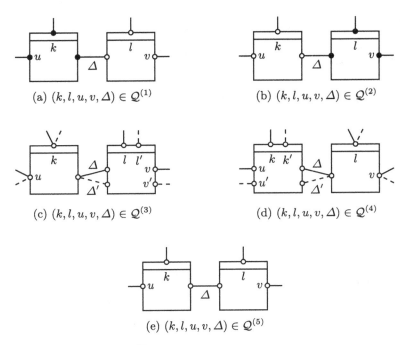

Fig. 3. Reduced queries in $\mathcal{Q}^{(i)}$, $i = 1, 2, 3, 4, 5$. Black dots represent values fixed by $\mathcal{Q}_{E_1}$ and $\mathcal{Q}_{E_2}$, while white dots are "free". Two distinct dots on each side do not necessarily correspond to distinct values.

Property 1. Sets $\mathcal{Q}^{(i)}$, $i = 1, 2, 3, 4, 5$, partition $\overline{\mathcal{Q}_C}$, namely,

$$\overline{\mathcal{Q}_C} = \bigsqcup_{i=1}^{5} \mathcal{Q}^{(i)}.$$

Proof. The union of $\mathcal{Q}^{(i)}$, $i = 1, 2, 3, 4, 5$, is $\overline{\mathcal{Q}_C}$ by the definition of $\mathcal{Q}^{(5)}$. Furthermore, they are pairwise disjoint; in particular,

1. $\mathcal{Q}^{(1)} \cap \mathcal{Q}^{(2)} = \emptyset$ by excluding bad keys satisfying (C-9);
2. $\mathcal{Q}^{(1)} \cap \mathcal{Q}^{(4)} = \emptyset$ by excluding bad keys satisfying (C-12);
3. $\mathcal{Q}^{(2)} \cap \mathcal{Q}^{(3)} = \emptyset$ by excluding bad keys satisfying (C-13);
4. $\mathcal{Q}^{(3)} \cap \mathcal{Q}^{(4)} = \emptyset$ by excluding bad keys satisfying (C-6).

□

We will further classify the queries and count each class using the following notations.

1. For $r, s \in \{0, 1\}^m$, $d \in \{0, 1\}^n$ and $i \in \{1, 2, 3, 4, 5\}$, let

$$\mathcal{Q}^{(i)}_{r,s,d} = \{(k, l, u, v, \Delta) \in \mathcal{Q}^{(i)} : (k, l, \Delta) = (r, s, d)\},$$

and let

$$\mathcal{Q}_{r,s}^{(i)} = \bigsqcup_{d \in \{0,1\}^n} \mathcal{Q}_{r,s,d}^{(i)}, \quad \mathcal{Q}_{r,*}^{(i)} = \bigsqcup_{l \in \{0,1\}^m} \mathcal{Q}_{r,l}^{(i)}, \quad \mathcal{Q}_{*,s}^{(i)} = \bigsqcup_{k \in \{0,1\}^m} \mathcal{Q}_{k,s}^{(i)}.$$

2. For $w \in \mathcal{T}$, $r, s \in \{0,1\}^m$, $d \in \{0,1\}^n$ and $i \in \{1,2,3,4,5\}$, let

$$q_w = |\mathcal{Q}_C(w)|, \qquad p_{r,*} = |\mathcal{Q}_{E_1}(r)|, \qquad p_{*,s} = |\mathcal{Q}_{E_2}(s)|,$$
$$q_{r,s,d}^{(i)} = |\mathcal{Q}_{r,s,d}^{(i)}|, \qquad q_{r,s}^{(i)} = |\mathcal{Q}_{r,s}^{(i)}|,$$
$$q_{r,*}^{(i)} = |\mathcal{Q}_{r,*}^{(i)}|, \qquad q_{*,s}^{(i)} = |\mathcal{Q}_{*,s}^{(i)}|.$$

Given the partition of the queries, we can also define the following sets.

1. For $r, s \in \{0,1\}^m$, let

$$U_1(r) = \{u \in \{0,1\}^n : \exists v \in \{0,1\}^n \text{ such that } (u,v) \in \mathcal{Q}_{E_1}(r)\},$$
$$V_1(r) = \{v \in \{0,1\}^n : \exists u \in \{0,1\}^n \text{ such that } (u,v) \in \mathcal{Q}_{E_1}(r)\},$$
$$U_2(s) = \{u \in \{0,1\}^n : \exists v \in \{0,1\}^n \text{ such that } (u,v) \in \mathcal{Q}_{E_2}(s)\},$$
$$V_2(s) = \{v \in \{0,1\}^n : \exists u \in \{0,1\}^n \text{ such that } (u,v) \in \mathcal{Q}_{E_2}(s)\}.$$

2. For $r, s \in \{0,1\}^m$ and $i \in \{1,2,3,4,5\}$, let

$$U_1^{(i)}(r) = \{u \in \{0,1\}^n : \exists s, v, \Delta \text{ such that } (r,s,u,v,\Delta) \in \mathcal{Q}^{(i)}\},$$
$$V_2^{(i)}(s) = \{v \in \{0,1\}^n : \exists r, u, \Delta \text{ such that } (r,s,u,v,\Delta) \in \mathcal{Q}^{(i)}\}.$$

Sets $U_1^{(i)}(r)$ and $V_2^{(i)}(s)$, $i = 1,2,3,4,5$, are pictorially represented in Fig. 4. We have the following properties on these sets.

Property 2. For $r, s \in \{0,1\}^m$, one has

1. $U_1^{(1)}(r) \subset U_1(r)$;
2. $U_1(r)$ and $U_1^{(i)}(r)$, $i = 2,3,4,5$, are pairwise disjoint;
3. $V_2^{(1)}(s) \subset V_2(s)$;
4. $V_2(s)$ and $V_2^{(i)}(s)$, $i = 1,3,4,5$, are pairwise disjoint.

Proof. By definition, $U_1^{(1)}(r) \subset U_1(r)$. $U_1(r)$ and $U_1^{(2)}(r)$ are disjoint by excluding bad keys of (C-9); $U_1(r)$ and $U_1^{(3)}(r)$ are disjoint since $\mathcal{Q}^{(1)}$ and $\mathcal{Q}^{(3)}$ are disjoint; $U_1(r)$ and $U_1^{(4)}(r)$ are disjoint by excluding bad keys of (C-12); $U_1^{(2)}(r)$ and $U_1^{(3)}(r)$ are disjoint by excluding bad keys of (C-13); $U_1^{(2)}(r)$ and $U_1^{(4)}(r)$ are disjoint by excluding bad keys of (C-13) and since $\mathcal{Q}^{(2)}$ and $\mathcal{Q}^{(4)}$ are disjoint; $U_1^{(3)}(r)$ and $U_1^{(4)}(r)$ are disjoint by excluding bad keys of (C-6). Since $\mathcal{Q}^{(1)} \cup \mathcal{Q}^{(2)} \cup \mathcal{Q}^{(3)} \cup \mathcal{Q}^{(4)}$ and $\mathcal{Q}^{(5)}$ are disjoint, $U_1^{(1)}(r) \cup U_1^{(2)}(r) \cup U_1^{(3)}(r) \cup U_1^{(4)}(r)$ and $U_1^{(5)}(r)$ are also disjoint. The remaining properties are proved similarly. □

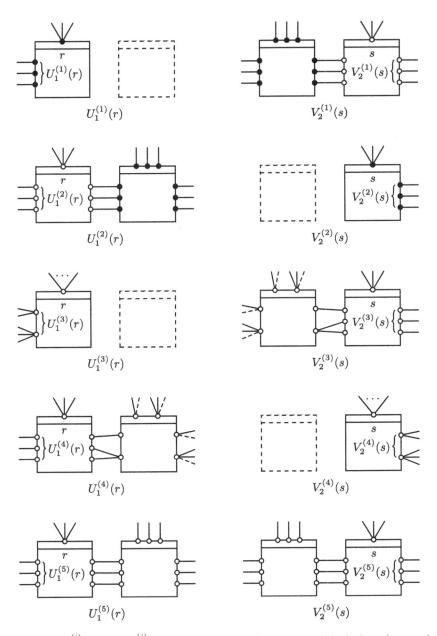

Fig. 4. Sets $U_1^{(i)}(r)$ and $V_2^{(i)}(s)$, $i = 1, 2, 3, 4, 5$. As in Fig. 3, black dots (resp. white dots) represent values fixed by $\mathcal{Q}_{E_1}$ and $\mathcal{Q}_{E_2}$ (resp. free values). Distinct dots on each side do not necessarily correspond to distinct values.

Property 3. For $r, s \in \{0,1\}^m$, one has

1. $|U_1(r)| = |V_1(r)| = p_{r,*}$;
2. $|U_2(s)| = |V_2(s)| = p_{*,s}$;
3. $|U_1^{(i)}(r)| = q_{r,*}^{(i)}$ for $i = 2, 4, 5$;
4. $|V_2^{(i)}(s)| = q_{*,s}^{(i)}$ for $i = 1, 3, 5$.

Proof. It is straightforward to prove the first two properties. Every $(k, l, u, v, \Delta) \in \mathcal{Q}_{r,*}^{(2)}$ (resp. $\mathcal{Q}_{r,*}^{(4)}$) contains a distinct u since otherwise we would find queries satisfying (C-13) (resp. (C-6)), which implies $|U_1^{(2)}(r)| = q_{r,*}^{(2)}$ (resp. $|U_1^{(4)}(r)| = q_{r,*}^{(4)}$). We also have $|U_1^{(5)}(r)| = q_{r,*}^{(5)}$ since $\mathcal{Q}^{(5)}$ and $\mathcal{Q}^{(3)}$ are disjoint. The last property is proved similarly. □

We define $a_{r,*}^{(3)} = |U_1^{(3)}(r)|$ and $a_{*,s}^{(4)} = |V_2^{(4)}(s)|$.

Property 4. For $r, s \in \{0,1\}^m$ and $d \in \{0,1\}^n$, one has

1. $p_{r,*} \geq q_{r,s,d}^{(1)}$;
2. $p_{*,s} \geq q_{r,s,d}^{(2)}$;
3. $a_{r,*}^{(3)} \geq q_{r,s,d}^{(3)}$;
4. $a_{*,s}^{(4)} \geq q_{r,s,d}^{(4)}$.

Proof. Every $(k, l, u, v, \Delta) \in \mathcal{Q}_{r,s,d}^{(1)}$ contains a distinct u since otherwise we would find queries satisfying (C-7). Therefore we have $p_{r,*} = |U_1(r)| \geq q_{r,s,d}^{(1)}$. The other properties are proved similarly. □

For a subset $\mathcal{Q} \subset \overline{\mathcal{Q}_C}$, we will write $(E_1, E_2) \vdash \mathcal{Q}$ if

$$E_2(l, E_1(k, u) \oplus \Delta) = v$$

for every $(k, l, u, v, \Delta) \in \mathcal{Q}$. With this notation, let

$$\mathsf{p}_1 = \Pr\left[(E_1, E_2) \vdash \mathcal{Q}^{(1)} \cup \mathcal{Q}^{(2)} \,\middle|\, E_1 \vdash \mathcal{Q}_{E_1} \wedge E_2 \vdash \mathcal{Q}_{E_2}\right],$$

$$\mathsf{p}_2 = \Pr\left[(E_1, E_2) \vdash \mathcal{Q}^{(3)} \cup \mathcal{Q}^{(4)} \,\middle|\, E_1 \vdash \mathcal{Q}_{E_1} \wedge E_2 \vdash \mathcal{Q}_{E_2} \wedge (E_1, E_2) \vdash \mathcal{Q}^{(1)} \cup \mathcal{Q}^{(2)}\right],$$

$$\mathsf{p}_3 = \Pr\left[(E_1, E_2) \vdash \mathcal{Q}^{(5)} \,\middle|\, E_1 \vdash \mathcal{Q}_{E_1} \wedge E_2 \vdash \mathcal{Q}_{E_2} \wedge (E_1, E_2) \vdash \bigcup_{i=1}^{4} \mathcal{Q}^{(i)}\right].$$

Then we have

$$\mathsf{p}_{\mathsf{re}}^{\mathsf{k}}(\mathcal{Q}_C | \mathcal{Q}_E) = \Pr\left[(E_1, E_2) \vdash \overline{\mathcal{Q}_C} \,\middle|\, E_1 \vdash \mathcal{Q}_{E_1} \wedge E_2 \vdash \mathcal{Q}_{E_2}\right] = \mathsf{p}_1 \cdot \mathsf{p}_2 \cdot \mathsf{p}_3. \quad (4)$$

3.3.2   Computing p_1

Suppose that $(k, l, u, v, \Delta) \in \mathcal{Q}^{(1)}$. It means that $E_1(k, u)$ has been already determined by $\mathcal{Q}_{E_1}$. In order for (E_1, E_2) to complete this query, E_2 should map $E_1(k, u) \oplus \Delta$ to v with key l. In this situation, the following properties are noteworthy.

1. Not either $E_2^{-1}(l, v)$ or $E_2(l, E_1(k, u) \oplus \Delta)$ has been determined by $\mathcal{Q}_{E_2}$ since $\mathbf{k}$ does not satisfy either (C-9) or (C-10).
2. There is no collision on the input to E_2 by the queries of $\mathcal{Q}^{(1)}$; precisely, for any (k, l, u, v, Δ), $(k', l', u', v', \Delta') \in^{\neq} \mathcal{Q}^{(1)}$ such that $l = l'$, we have $E_1(k, u) \oplus \Delta \neq E_1(k', u') \oplus \Delta'$ since $\mathbf{k}$ does not satisfy (C-2).
3. There is no collision on the output from E_2 by any other query of $\overline{\mathcal{Q}_C}$; precisely, for any distinct queries $(k, l, u, v, \Delta) \in \mathcal{Q}^{(1)}$ and $(k', l', u', v', \Delta') \in \overline{\mathcal{Q}_C}$ such that $l = l'$, we have $v \neq v'$ since $\mathbf{k}$ does not satisfy (C-12).

For a fixed $s \in \{0, 1\}^m$, $\mathcal{Q}_{E_2}$ determines $p_{*,s}$ evaluations of $E_2(s, \cdot)$. On the other hand, the number of queries $(k, l, u, v, \Delta) \in \mathcal{Q}^{(1)}$ such that $l = s$ is $q_{*,s}^{(1)}$ (by definition). Such queries determine all different inputs and outputs of $E_2(s, \cdot)$, so $E_2(s, \cdot)$ would complete the queries with probability $1/(N - p_{*,s})_{q_{*,s}^{(1)}}$. Therefore we have

$$\Pr\left[(E_1, E_2) \vdash \mathcal{Q}^{(1)} \,\middle|\, E_1 \vdash \mathcal{Q}_{E_1} \wedge E_2 \vdash \mathcal{Q}_{E_2}\right] = \prod_{s \in \{0,1\}^m} \frac{1}{(N - p_{*,s})_{q_{*,s}^{(1)}}}.$$

Applying a similar argument to $\mathcal{Q}^{(2)}$ (excluding bad key satisfying (C-3), (C-9), (C-11) or (C-13)), we have

$$\mathsf{p}_1 = \prod_{r \in \{0,1\}^m} \frac{1}{(N - p_{r,*})_{q_{r,*}^{(2)}}} \cdot \prod_{s \in \{0,1\}^m} \frac{1}{(N - p_{*,s})_{q_{*,s}^{(1)}}}. \tag{5}$$

3.3.3 Computing p_2

Subject to

$$E_1 \vdash \mathcal{Q}_{E_1} \wedge E_2 \vdash \mathcal{Q}_{E_2} \wedge (E_1, E_2) \vdash \mathcal{Q}^{(1)} \cup \mathcal{Q}^{(2)},$$

we will lower bound the probability of completing the reduced queries of $\mathcal{Q}^{(3)} \cup \mathcal{Q}^{(4)}$ when extending the evaluations of E_1 and E_2. For $r, s \in \{0, 1\}^m$, we can fix

$$V_1^{(2)}(r) \stackrel{\text{def}}{=} \{E_1(r, u) : u \in U_1^{(2)}(r)\},$$

$$U_2^{(1)}(s) \stackrel{\text{def}}{=} \{E_2^{-1}(s, v) : v \in V_2^{(1)}(s)\}.$$

Property 5. For any $r \in \{0, 1\}^m$ such that $U_1^{(3)}(r) \neq \emptyset$, $|V_1(r) \cup V_1^{(2)}(r)| < N/2$.

Proof. We distinguish two cases.

Case (1) There exists no tweak $w \in \mathcal{T}^*$ such that $h_1(w) = r$. In this case,
(i) $|V_1(r)| < N/4$ since we have modified the adversary so that the number of block cipher queries is either N or less than $N/4$ (for any fixed key), and $U_1^{(3)}(r)$ being nonempty implies that the number of block cipher queries cannot be N, and

(ii) $|V_1^{(2)}(r)| < N/4$ since we are excluding bad keys of (C-14) (with no tweak w in $\mathcal{T}^*$ such that $h_1(w) = r$).

Therefore we have

$$|V_1(r) \cup V_1^{(2)}(r)| \leq |V_1(r)| + |V_1^{(2)}(r)| < \frac{N}{4} + \frac{N}{4} = \frac{N}{2}.$$

Case (2) There exists $w \in \mathcal{T}^*$ such that $h_1(w) = r$; we again distinguish three cases. Let $s = h_2(w)$.

(i) $|\mathcal{Q}_{E_1}(r)| = N$; we have $U_1(r) = \{0,1\}^n$, and hence $U_1^{(3)}(r) = \emptyset$.

(ii) $|\mathcal{Q}_{E_2}(s)| = N$; since $w \in \mathcal{T}^*$, all possible N construction queries are made with tweak w, and they are all contained in $\mathcal{Q}^{(2)}$ since $|\mathcal{Q}_{E_2}(s)| = N$ for $s = h_2(w)$. This means that $U_1^{(2)}(r) = \{0,1\}^n$. Since $U_1^{(2)}(r)$ and $U_1^{(3)}(r)$ are disjoint by Property 2, we have $U_1^{(3)}(r) = \emptyset$.

(iii) $|\mathcal{Q}_{E_1}(r)|, |\mathcal{Q}_{E_2}(s)| < N/4$; there is no query $(k, l, u, v, \Delta) \in \mathcal{Q}^{(2)}$ such that $k = r$ and $l \neq s$ since otherwise we will see queries satisfying (C-13). Therefore $|V_1^{(2)}(r)|$ counts the number of queries $(k, l, u, v, \Delta) \in \mathcal{Q}^{(2)}$ such that $k = r$ and $l = s$. Such queries correspond to queries in $\mathcal{Q}_{E_2}(s)$, where $|\mathcal{Q}_{E_2}(s)| < N/4$. Since $|V_1(r)| \leq |\mathcal{Q}_{E_1}(r)| < N/4$, we have $|V_1(r) \cup V_1^{(2)}(r)| < N/2$.   □

Similarly, we can prove the following property.

Property 6. For any $s \in \{0,1\}^m$ such that $V_2^{(4)}(s) \neq \emptyset$, $|U_2(s) \cup U_2^{(1)}(s)| < N/2$.

In order to estimate the probability that E_1 and E_2 complete $\mathcal{Q}^{(3)} \cup \mathcal{Q}^{(4)}$, we will choose an (ordered) set of $a_{r,*}^{(3)}(= |U_1^{(3)}(r)|)$ elements, denoted $V_1^{(3)}(r)$, from $\{0,1\}^n \setminus (V_1(r) \cup V_1^{(2)}(r))$ for each $r \in \{0,1\}^m$. Once $V_1^{(3)}(r)$ is chosen, we will compute the probability that the queries of $\mathcal{Q}^{(3)}$ are completed satisfying $E_1(r, U_1^{(3)}(r)) = V_1^{(3)}(r)$.[2] Similarly, for each $s \in \{0,1\}^m$, we will choose a set of $a_{*,s}^{(4)}$ elements, denoted $U_2^{(4)}(s)$, from $\{0,1\}^n \setminus (U_2(s) \cup U_2^{(1)}(s))$, and compute the probability that the queries of $\mathcal{Q}^{(4)}$ are completed via the elements of $U_2^{(4)}(s)$ (as $E_2^{-1}(l, v)$).

Without any restriction, the number of ways of choosing $V_1^{(3)}(r)$ and $U_2^{(4)}(s)$ (over all the keys $r, s \in \{0,1\}^m$) would be

$$\prod_{r \in \{0,1\}^m} (N - p_{r,*} - q_{r,*}^{(2)})_{a_{r,*}^{(3)}} \cdot \prod_{s \in \{0,1\}^m} (N - p_{*,s} - q_{*,s}^{(1)})_{a_{*,s}^{(4)}}.$$

However, in order to make the analysis simpler, we will avoid certain bad conditions when choosing $V_1^{(3)}(r)$ and $U_2^{(4)}(s)$; suppose that y has been chosen as $E_1(r, u)$ from $\{0,1\}^n \setminus (V_1(r) \cup V_1^{(2)}(r))$ for a query $(r, s, u, v, \Delta) \in \mathcal{Q}^{(3)}$. In order

---

[2] $U_1^{(3)}(r)$ and $V_1^{(3)}(r)$ are viewed as ordered sets, and $E_1(r, U_1^{(3)}(r)) = V_1^{(3)}(r)$ means that each element of $U_1^{(3)}(r)$ is mapped to the corresponding element of $V_1^{(3)}(r)$ (with respect to the ordering) under $E_1(r, \cdot)$.

for E_2 complete this query, one should have $E_2(s, y \oplus \Delta) = v$. Here we would like the element $y \oplus \Delta$ to be "free", namely to lie outside $U_2(s) \cup U_2^{(1)}(s) \cup U_2^{(4)}(s)$. We would also like the elements $y \oplus \Delta$ to be all distinct for each key of E_2. Similarly, for each element x that has been chosen as $E_2^{-1}(s, v)$ for a query $(r, s, u, v, \Delta) \in \mathcal{Q}^{(4)}$, we would like $x \oplus \Delta$ to be outside $V_1(r) \cup V_1^{(2)}(r) \cup V_1^{(3)}(r)$. For each key of E_1, there should be no collision between $x \oplus \Delta$. More precisely, the undesirable "colliding" events can be classified as follows.[3]

$\mathsf{Col}_1 \Leftrightarrow$ there exist $(k, l, u, v, \Delta) \in \mathcal{Q}^{(3)}$ and $(l', u', v') \in \mathcal{Q}_{E_2}$ such that
$l = l'$ and $E_1(k, u) \oplus \Delta = u'$.

$\mathsf{Col}_2 \Leftrightarrow$ there exist $(k, l, u, v, \Delta) \in \mathcal{Q}^{(3)}$ and $(k', l', u', v', \Delta') \in \mathcal{Q}^{(1)}$ such that
$l = l'$ and $E_1(k, u) \oplus \Delta = E_2^{-1}(l', v')$.

$\mathsf{Col}_3 \Leftrightarrow$ there exist $(k, l, u, v, \Delta), (k', l', u', v', \Delta') \in^{\neq} \mathcal{Q}^{(3)}$ such that
$l = l'$ and $E_1(k, u) \oplus \Delta = E_1(k', u') \oplus \Delta'$.

$\mathsf{Col}_4 \Leftrightarrow$ there exist $(k, l, u, v, \Delta) \in \mathcal{Q}^{(3)}$ and $(k', l', u', v', \Delta') \in \mathcal{Q}^{(4)}$ such that
$l = l'$ and $E_1(k, u) \oplus \Delta = E_2^{-1}(l', v')$.

$\mathsf{Col}_5 \Leftrightarrow$ there exist $(k, l, u, v, \Delta) \in \mathcal{Q}^{(4)}$ and $(k', u', v') \in \mathcal{Q}_{E_1}$ such that
$k = k'$ and $E_2^{-1}(l, v) \oplus \Delta = v'$.

$\mathsf{Col}_6 \Leftrightarrow$ there exist $(k, l, u, v, \Delta) \in \mathcal{Q}^{(4)}$ and $(k', l', u', v', \Delta') \in \mathcal{Q}^{(2)}$ such that
$k = k'$ and $E_2^{-1}(l, v) \oplus \Delta = E_1(k', u')$.

$\mathsf{Col}_7 \Leftrightarrow$ there exist $(k, l, u, v, \Delta) \in \mathcal{Q}^{(4)}$ and $(k', l', u', v', \Delta') \in \mathcal{Q}^{(3)}$ such that
$k = k'$ and $E_2^{-1}(l, v) \oplus \Delta = E_1(k', u')$.

$\mathsf{Col}_8 \Leftrightarrow$ there exist $(k, l, u, v, \Delta), (k', l', u', v', \Delta') \in^{\neq} \mathcal{Q}^{(4)}$ such that
$k = k'$ and $E_2^{-1}(l, v) \oplus \Delta = E_2^{-1}(l', v') \oplus \Delta'$.

Property 7. The probabilities of Col_i, $i = 1, \ldots, 8$, (over random choices of $V_1^{(3)}(r)$ and $U_2^{(4)}(s)$) are all upper bounded by $2M_2/N$.

Proof. To estimate the probability of Col_3, consider pairs of distinct queries (k, l, u, v, Δ), $(k', l', u', v', \Delta') \in \mathcal{Q}^{(3)}$ such that $l = l'$. The set of such pairs can be partitioned into the following two types;

1. there exists a query $(k'', l'', u'', v'', \Delta'')$ such that $(k'', u'') = (k, u)$ and
$$(k'', l'', u'', v'', \Delta'') \notin \{(k, l, u, v, \Delta), (k', l', u', v', \Delta')\};$$

2. there exists no query $(k'', l'', u'', v'', \Delta'')$ such that $(k'', u'') = (k, u)$ and
$$(k'', l'', u'', v'', \Delta'') \notin \{(k, l, u, v, \Delta), (k', l', u', v', \Delta')\}.$$

---

[3] For $(k, l, u, v, \Delta) \in \mathcal{Q}^{(3)} \cup \mathcal{Q}^{(4)}$, we will write $E_1(k, u)$ and $E_2^{-1}(l, v)$ to denote the elements determined by the choice of $V_1^{(3)}(k)$ and $U_2^{(4)}(l)$, respectively.

Since $(k, l, u, v, \Delta) \in \mathcal{Q}^{(3)}$, one always has a query $(k^*, l^*, u^*, v^*, \Delta^*)$ such that $(k^*, u^*) = (k, u)$ and $(k^*, l^*, u^*, v^*, \Delta^*) \neq (k, l, u, v, \Delta)$, so if a pair of queries falls into the second type, then it means that $(k^*, l^*, u^*, v^*, \Delta^*) = (k', l', u', v', \Delta')$, and hence $(k, l, u) = (k', l', u')$. Then by excluding bad keys of (C-7), we have $\Delta \neq \Delta'$. So for any pair of queries of the second type, it cannot be the case that $E_1(k, u) \oplus \Delta = E_1(k', u') \oplus \Delta'$. On the other hand, the number of the pairs of the first type is upper bounded by $|\mathcal{B}_1|$, which is smaller than M_2 by excluding bad keys of (C-4). For each pair, the probability that $E_1(k, u) \oplus \Delta = E_1(k', u') \oplus \Delta'$ is upper bounded by $2/N$ (since $|\{0, 1\}^n \setminus (V_1(r) \cup V_1^{(2)}(r))| > N/2$ by Property 5). Therefore, we have

$$\Pr[\mathsf{Col}_3] \leq \frac{2M_2}{N}.$$

The other bounds are proved similarly.   □

The number of ways of choosing $V_1^{(3)}(r)$ and $U_2^{(4)}(s)$ over all $r, s \in \{0, 1\}^m$, without fulfilling any of the bad conditions Col_i, $i = 1, \ldots, 8$, is lower bounded by

$$\prod_{r \in \{0,1\}^m} (N - p_{r,*} - q_{r,*}^{(2)})_{a_{r,*}^{(3)}} \cdot \prod_{s \in \{0,1\}^m} (N - p_{*,s} - q_{*,s}^{(1)})_{a_{*,s}^{(4)}} \cdot \left(1 - \sum_{i=1}^{8} \Pr[\mathsf{Col}_i]\right). \quad (6)$$

For each of "good" choices for $V_1^{(3)}(r)$ and $U_2^{(4)}(s)$, (E_1, E_2) complete the queries of $\mathcal{Q}^{(3)}$ and $\mathcal{Q}^{(4)}$ (via $V_1^{(3)}(r)$ and $U_2^{(4)}(s)$, respectively) with probability

$$\frac{1}{\prod_{r \in \{0,1\}^m} (N - p_{r,*} - q_{r,*}^{(2)})_{a_{r,*}^{(3)} + q_{r,*}^{(4)}} \cdot \prod_{s \in \{0,1\}^m} (N - p_{*,s} - q_{*,s}^{(1)})_{a_{*,s}^{(4)} + q_{*,s}^{(3)}}}. \quad (7)$$

By (6), (7) and Property 7, we have

$$p_2 \geq \frac{\prod\limits_{r \in \{0,1\}^m} (N - p_{r,*} - q_{r,*}^{(2)})_{a_{r,*}^{(3)}} \cdot \prod\limits_{s \in \{0,1\}^m} (N - p_{*,s} - q_{*,s}^{(1)})_{a_{*,s}^{(4)}} \cdot \left(1 - \sum\limits_{i=1}^{8} \Pr[\mathsf{Col}_i]\right)}{\prod\limits_{r \in \{0,1\}^m} (N - p_{r,*} - q_{r,*}^{(2)})_{a_{r,*}^{(3)} + q_{r,*}^{(4)}} \cdot \prod\limits_{s \in \{0,1\}^m} (N - p_{*,s} - q_{*,s}^{(1)})_{a_{*,s}^{(4)} + q_{*,s}^{(3)}}}$$

$$\geq \frac{1}{\prod\limits_{r \in \{0,1\}^m} (N - p_{r,*} - q_{r,*}^{(2)} - a_{r,*}^{(3)})_{q_{r,*}^{(4)}} \cdot \prod\limits_{s \in \{0,1\}^m} (N - p_{*,s} - q_{*,s}^{(1)} - a_{*,s}^{(4)})_{q_{*,s}^{(3)}}}$$

$$\times \left(1 - \frac{16M_2}{N}\right). \quad (8)$$

3.3.4 Computing p_3

Subject to

$$E_1 \vdash \mathcal{Q}_{E_1} \wedge E_2 \vdash \mathcal{Q}_{E_2} \wedge (E_1, E_2) \vdash \bigcup_{i=1}^{4} \mathcal{Q}^{(i)}, \tag{9}$$

we can fix

$$b_r \overset{\text{def}}{=} p_{r,*} + q_{r,*}^{(2)} + a_{r,*}^{(3)} + q_{r,*}^{(4)} \tag{10}$$

evaluations of $E_1(r, \cdot)$ and

$$c_s \overset{\text{def}}{=} p_{*,s} + q_{*,s}^{(1)} + q_{*,s}^{(3)} + a_{*,s}^{(4)} \tag{11}$$

evaluations of $E_2(s, \cdot)$ for each $(r, s) \in \{0, 1\}^m \times \{0, 1\}^m$. Let

$$\mathcal{Q}_1^{(5)} = \{(r, s, u, v, \Delta) \in \mathcal{Q}^{(5)} : r = h_1(t) \text{ and } s = h_2(t) \text{ for some } t \in \mathcal{T}^*\},$$
$$\mathcal{Q}_2^{(5)} = \{(r, s, u, v, \Delta) \in \mathcal{Q}^{(5)} : r \neq h_1(t) \text{ and } s \neq h_2(t) \text{ for every } t \in \mathcal{T}^*\}.$$

Let

$$\mathcal{R} = \{r \in \{0, 1\}^m : r = h_1(t) \text{ for some } t \in \mathcal{T}^*\},$$
$$\mathcal{S} = \{s \in \{0, 1\}^m : s = h_2(t) \text{ for some } t \in \mathcal{T}^*\},$$

and let $\mathcal{R}' = \{0, 1\}^m \setminus \mathcal{R}$ and $\mathcal{S}' = \{0, 1\}^m \setminus \mathcal{S}$.

Property 8. With the above definitions, the following hold:

1. $\mathcal{Q}^{(5)}$ is partitioned into $\mathcal{Q}_1^{(5)}$ and $\mathcal{Q}_2^{(5)}$, namely, $\mathcal{Q}^{(5)} = \mathcal{Q}_1^{(5)} \sqcup \mathcal{Q}_2^{(5)}$;

2. $\mathcal{Q}_1^{(5)} = \displaystyle\bigsqcup_{(r,s) \in \mathcal{R} \times \mathcal{S}} \mathcal{Q}_{r,s}^{(5)}$;

3. $\mathcal{Q}_2^{(5)} = \displaystyle\bigsqcup_{(r,s) \in \mathcal{R}' \times \mathcal{S}'} \mathcal{Q}_{r,s}^{(5)}$;

4. $\mathcal{Q}_{r,s}^{(5)} = \emptyset$ for $(r, s) \notin (\mathcal{R} \times \mathcal{S}) \cup (\mathcal{R}' \times \mathcal{S}')$.

Proof. By definition, we have

$$\mathcal{Q}_1^{(5)} \subset \bigsqcup_{(r,s) \in \mathcal{R} \times \mathcal{S}} \mathcal{Q}_{r,s}^{(5)}, \qquad\qquad \mathcal{Q}_2^{(5)} \subset \bigsqcup_{(r,s) \in \mathcal{R}' \times \mathcal{S}'} \mathcal{Q}_{r,s}^{(5)},$$

$$\mathcal{Q}_1^{(5)} \cup \mathcal{Q}_2^{(5)} \subset \mathcal{Q}^{(5)} = \bigsqcup_{(r,s) \in (\mathcal{R} \cup \mathcal{R}') \times (\mathcal{S} \cup \mathcal{S}')} \mathcal{Q}_{r,s}^{(5)}. \tag{12}$$

Therefore it is obvious that $\mathcal{Q}_1^{(5)}$ and $\mathcal{Q}_2^{(5)}$ are disjoint. If $(r, s, u, v, \Delta) \in \mathcal{Q}^{(5)} \setminus \mathcal{Q}_2^{(5)}$, then it should be the case that either $r = h_1(t)$ or $s = h_2(t)$ for some $t \in \mathcal{T}^*$; if $r = h_1(t)$ for some $t \in \mathcal{T}^*$, then we would have a query $(r', s', u', v', \Delta') \in \overline{\mathcal{Q}_C}$ such that $u' = u$, $r' = h_1(t) = r$ and $s' = h_2(t)$. Since $\mathcal{Q}^{(5)}$ is disjoint from $\mathcal{Q}^{(3)}$, it must be the case that $(r', s', u', v', \Delta') = (r, s, u, v, \Delta)$. Since $r = r' = h_1(t)$ and $s = s' = h_2(t)$, we have $(r, s, u, v, \Delta) \in \mathcal{Q}_1^{(5)}$. With a similar argument for the case that $s = h_2(t)$ for some $t \in \mathcal{T}^*$, we have $\mathcal{Q}^{(5)} = \mathcal{Q}_1^{(5)} \sqcup \mathcal{Q}_2^{(5)}$. The remaining properties are immediate from the first one (combined with the observation (12)). $\qquad\square$

Let

$$\mathsf{p}'_3 = \Pr\left[(E_1(r,\cdot), E_2(s,\cdot)) \vdash \mathcal{Q}^{(5)}_{r,s} \text{ for every } (r,s) \in \mathcal{R} \times \mathcal{S}\right],$$

$$\mathsf{p}''_3 = \Pr\left[(E_1(r,\cdot), E_2(s,\cdot)) \vdash \mathcal{Q}^{(5)}_{r,s} \text{ for every } (r,s) \in \mathcal{R}' \times \mathcal{S}'\right], \qquad (13)$$

where both probabilities are conditioned on (9). Then by Property 8, we have

$$\mathsf{p}_3 = \mathsf{p}'_3 \cdot \mathsf{p}''_3. \qquad (14)$$

COMPUTING. p'_3. We begin with the following property.

Property 9. For $(r, s) \in \mathcal{R} \times \mathcal{S}$, one has

1. $q^{(1)}_{r,*} = q^{(1)}_{*,s} = q^{(1)}_{r,s} = p_{r,*}$;
2. $q^{(2)}_{r,*} = q^{(2)}_{*,s} = q^{(2)}_{r,s} = p_{*,s}$;
3. $q^{(3)}_{*,s} = a^{(3)}_{r,*} = q^{(3)}_{r,s}$;
4. $q^{(4)}_{r,*} = a^{(4)}_{*,s} = q^{(4)}_{r,s}$;
5. $q^{(1)}_{r,s} + q^{(2)}_{r,s} + q^{(3)}_{r,s} + q^{(4)}_{r,s} + q^{(5)}_{r,s} = N$;
6. $b_r = c_s = N - q^{(5)}_{r,s}$.

Proof. Define a function

$$\phi : \mathcal{Q}^{(1)}_{r,s} \longrightarrow U_1(r)$$
$$(k, l, u, v, \Delta) \longmapsto u.$$

Since $r = h_1(t)$ for some $t \in \mathcal{T}^*$, ϕ is surjective. Suppose that $(k, l, u, v, \Delta) \neq (k', l', u', v', \Delta') \in \mathcal{Q}^{(1)}_{r,s}$ with $(k, l) = (k', l') = (r, s)$ and $u = u'$. If their original queries contain an identical tweak in $\mathcal{T}$, then we have $\Delta = \Delta'$, which is a contradiction since we are excluding bad keys of (C-7). If their original queries contain different tweaks in $\mathcal{T}$, then we would be able to find queries satisfying (C-6). So ϕ is injective. This implies that $q^{(1)}_{r,s} = p_{r,*}$. Since $U^{(1)}_1(r) = U_1(r)$, we also have $q^{(1)}_{r,*} = p_{r,*}$. Furthermore, for any $r' \in \{0,1\}^m$ such that $r' \neq r$, we have $q^{(1)}_{r',s} = 0$ since otherwise we could find queries satisfying (C-12). So we have $q^{(1)}_{*,s} = q^{(1)}_{r,s}$. The second property is proved similarly.

Define a function

$$\psi : \mathcal{Q}^{(3)}_{r,s} \longrightarrow U^{(3)}_1(r)$$
$$(k, l, u, v, \Delta) \longmapsto u.$$

Since $s = h_2(t)$ for some $t \in \mathcal{T}^*$, ψ is surjective. Suppose that $(k, l, u, v, \Delta) \neq (k', l', u', v', \Delta') \in \mathcal{Q}^{(3)}_{r,s}$ with $(k, l) = (k', l') = (r, s)$ and $u = u'$. If their original queries contain an identical tweak in $\mathcal{T}$, then we have $\Delta = \Delta'$, which is a contradiction since we are excluding bad keys of (C-7). If their original queries contain different tweaks in $\mathcal{T}$, then we would be able to find queries satisfying

(C-6). So ϕ is injective. This implies that $q_{*,s}^{(3)} = a_{r,*}^{(3)}$. Furthermore, for any $r' \in \{0,1\}^m$ such that $r' \neq r$, we have $q_{r',s}^{(3)} = 0$ since otherwise we could find queries satisfying (C-12). So we have $q_{*,s}^{(3)} = q_{r,s}^{(3)}$. The remaining properties are proved similarly. □

Fix $(r,s) \in \mathcal{R} \times \mathcal{S}$. If $q_{r,s}^{(5)} = 0$, then we have $N - b_r = 0$. If $q_{r,s}^{(5)} > 0$, then there would exist $w \in \mathcal{T}^*$ such that $r = h_1(w)$ and $s = h_2(w)$, and $E_1(r, \cdot)$ and $E_2(s, \cdot)$ might complete the queries in $\mathcal{Q}_{r,s}^{(5)}$ that contain w (in their original forms). In this case, it cannot be the case that either $r \neq h_1(w')$ or $s \neq h_2(w')$ for any $w' \in \mathcal{T}^*$ such that $w' \neq w$ since the existence of such a tweak would imply $\mathcal{Q}_{r,s}^{(5)} = \emptyset$. Note that

$$V_2(s) \cup \bigcup_{i=1,3,4} V_2^{(i)}(s) = \left\{ E_2(s, E_1(r,u) \oplus \Delta) : u \in U_1(r) \cup \bigcup_{i=2,3,4} U_1^{(i)}(r) \right\},$$

where $\Delta = g_1(w) \oplus g_2(w)$, and $q_{r,s}^{(5)} = N - b_r = N - c_s$. So the probability that $E_1(r, \cdot)$ and $E_2(s, \cdot)$ complete all the queries of $\mathcal{Q}_{r,s}^{(5)}$ is $1/(N - b_r)!$, and hence

$$\mathsf{p}_3' = \prod_{(r,s)\in\mathcal{R}\times\mathcal{S}} \frac{1}{(N - b_r)!}. \tag{15}$$

COMPUTING. p_3''. We first fix a lexicographical order on $\mathcal{R}' \times \mathcal{S}' \times \{0,1\}^n$; $(r,s,d) < (r',s',d')$ if and only if $r < r'$ or $(r = r'$ and $s < s')$ or $(r = r'$, $s = s'$ and $d < d')$.

Next, we fix $(r,s,d) \in \mathcal{R}' \times \mathcal{S}' \times \{0,1\}^n$, and suppose that E_1 and E_2 have completed all the queries of $\mathcal{Q}_{r',s',d'}^{(5)}$ for $(r',s',d') < (r,s,d)$. Subject to this event, let

$$B_{r,s,d} = V_1(r) \cup \left\{ E_1(k,u) : (k,l,u,v,\Delta) \in \bigcup_{i=2,3,4} \mathcal{Q}_{r,*}^{(i)} \cup \bigcup_{\substack{(r',s',d')<(r,s,d) \\ r'=r}} \mathcal{Q}_{r',s',d'}^{(5)} \right\},$$

$$C_{r,s,d} = \{x \oplus d : x \in U_2(s)\}$$

$$\cup \left\{ E_2^{-1}(l,v) \oplus d : (k,l,u,v,\Delta) \in \bigcup_{i=1,3,4} \mathcal{Q}_{*,s}^{(i)} \cup \bigcup_{\substack{(r',s',d')<(r,s,d) \\ s'=s}} \mathcal{Q}_{r',s',d'}^{(5)} \right\},$$

be the set of all elements y for which $E_1^{-1}(r,y)$ have been determined, and the set of all elements y for which $E_2(s, y \oplus d)$ have been determined, respectively. We will choose an (ordered) set of $q_{r,s,d}^{(5)}$ elements, denoted Y, from $\{0,1\}^n \setminus (B_{r,s,d} \cup C_{r,s,d})$ and consider the probability that each $(r,s,u,v,d) \in \mathcal{Q}_{r,s,d}^{(5)}$ is completed with $E_1(r,u) = y$ and $E_2(s, y \oplus d) = v$ for a distinct $y \in Y$.

Let $b_{r,s,d} = |B_{r,s,d}|$ and $c_{r,s,d} = |C_{r,s,d}|$. Then we have

$$b_{r,s,d} = b_r + \sum_{i<s} q_{r,i}^{(5)} + \sum_{j<d} q_{r,s,j}^{(5)},$$

$$c_{r,s,d} = c_s + \sum_{i<r} q_{i,s}^{(5)} + \sum_{j<d} q_{r,s,j}^{(5)}.$$

Define a function

$$\phi : \bigsqcup_{i=1}^{4} \mathcal{Q}_{r,s,d}^{(i)} \longrightarrow B_{r,s,d} \cap C_{r,s,d}$$

$$(k, l, u, v, \Delta) \longmapsto E_1(k, u),$$

where $E_1(k, u)$ has already been determined. Suppose that (k, l, u, v, Δ) and $(k', l', u', v', \Delta')$ are mapped to the same $E_1(k, u) = E_1(k', u')$. Since both queries are contained in $\bigsqcup_{i=1}^{4} \mathcal{Q}_{r,s,d}^{(i)}$, we have $(k, l, \Delta) = (k', l', \Delta') = (r, s, d)$. It implies that $u = u'$ and $v = E_2(l, E_1(k, u) \oplus \Delta) = E_2(l', E_1(k', u') \oplus \Delta') = v'$, and hence $(k, l, u, v, \Delta) = (k', l', u', v', \Delta')$. So we see that ϕ is injective. Therefore we have

$$|B_{r,s,d} \cup C_{r,s,d}| = |B_{r,s,d}| + |C_{r,s,d}| - |B_{r,s,d} \cap C_{r,s,d}|$$
$$\leq b_{r,s,d} + c_{r,s,d} - e_{r,s,d},$$

where

$$e_{r,s,d} \stackrel{\text{def}}{=} \left| \bigsqcup_{i=1}^{4} \mathcal{Q}_{r,s,d}^{(i)} \right| = q_{r,s,d}^{(1)} + q_{r,s,d}^{(2)} + q_{r,s,d}^{(3)} + q_{r,s,d}^{(4)}.$$

Overall, the number of ways of choosing Y so that $E_1^{-1}(r, y)$ and $E_2(s, y \oplus d)$ have not been determined for any $y \in Y$ is at least

$$(N - b_{r,s,d} - c_{r,s,d} + e_{r,s,d})_{q_{r,s,d}^{(5)}}.$$

Property 10. For $(r, s, d) \in \mathcal{R}' \times \mathcal{S}' \times \{0, 1\}^n$ such that $\mathcal{Q}_{r,s,d}^{(5)} \neq \emptyset$, one has

1. $q_{r,s,d}^{(5)} + b_{r,s,d} < N/2$;
2. $q_{r,s,d}^{(5)} + c_{r,s,d} < N/2$.

Proof. Note that

$$q_{r,s,d}^{(5)} + b_{r,s,d} = q_{r,s,d}^{(5)} + p_{r,*} + q_{r,*}^{(2)} + a_{r,*}^{(3)} + q_{r,*}^{(4)} + \sum_{i<s} q_{r,i}^{(5)} + \sum_{j<d} q_{r,s,j}^{(5)},$$

where $p_{r,*} < N/4$ (since $\mathcal{Q}_{r,s,d}^{(5)} \neq \emptyset$), and the sum of the remaining summands is upper bounded by the number of queries (k, l, u, v, Δ) such that $k = r$, which is smaller than $N/4$ since there is no tweak $t \in \mathcal{T}^*$ such that $r = h_1(t)$ and by excluding bad keys of (C-14). Therefore we have $q_{r,s,d}^{(5)} + b_{r,s,d} < N/2$. The second property is proved similarly. $\qquad\square$

Thanks to Property 10, we can apply Lemma 1 to lower bound the probability that E_1 and E_2 complete the queries of $\mathcal{Q}_{r,s,d}^{(5)}$ by

$$\frac{(N - b_{r,s,d} - c_{r,s,d} + e_{r,s,d})_{q_{r,s,d}^{(5)}}}{(N - b_{r,s,d})_{q_{r,s,d}^{(5)}} (N - c_{r,s,d})_{q_{r,s,d}^{(5)}}}$$

$$\geq \frac{1}{(N - e_{r,s,d})_{q_{r,s,d}^{(5)}}} \left(1 - \frac{4 q_{r,s,d}^{(5)} (b_{r,s,d} - e_{r,s,d})(c_{r,s,d} - e_{r,s,d})}{N^2}\right).$$

Therefore we have

$$\mathsf{p}_3'' \geq \prod_{\substack{(r,s) \in \mathcal{R}' \times \mathcal{S}' \\ d \in \{0,1\}^n}} \frac{1}{(N - e_{r,s,d})_{q_{r,s,d}^{(5)}}} \left(1 - \frac{4 q_{r,s,d}^{(5)} (b_{r,s,d} - e_{r,s,d})(c_{r,s,d} - e_{r,s,d})}{N^2}\right)$$

$$\geq \prod_{\substack{(r,s) \in \mathcal{R}' \times \mathcal{S}' \\ d \in \{0,1\}^n}} \frac{1}{(N - e_{r,s,d})_{q_{r,s,d}^{(5)}}}$$

$$\times \left(1 - \frac{\sum\limits_{\substack{(r,s) \in \mathcal{R}' \times \mathcal{S}' \\ d \in \{0,1\}^n}} 4 q_{r,s,d}^{(5)} (b_{r,s,d} - e_{r,s,d})(c_{r,s,d} - e_{r,s,d})}{N^2}\right) \tag{16}$$

By replacing $(b_{r,s,d} - e_{r,s,d})$ and $(c_{r,s,d} - e_{r,s,d})$ by $(p_{r,*} + (b_{r,s,d} - p_{r,*} - e_{r,s,d}))$ and $(p_{*,s} + (c_{r,s,d} - p_{*,s} - e_{r,s,d}))$, respectively, we have

$$\sum_{\substack{(r,s) \in \mathcal{R}' \times \mathcal{S}' \\ d \in \{0,1\}^n}} q_{r,s,d}^{(5)} (b_{r,s,d} - e_{r,s,d})(c_{r,s,d} - e_{r,s,d})$$

$$= \sum_{\substack{(r,s) \in \mathcal{R}' \times \mathcal{S}' \\ d \in \{0,1\}^n}} q_{r,s,d}^{(5)} p_{r,*} p_{*,s} + \sum_{\substack{(r,s) \in \mathcal{R}' \times \mathcal{S}' \\ d \in \{0,1\}^n}} q_{r,s,d}^{(5)} (b_{r,s,d} - p_{r,*} - e_{r,s,d}) p_{*,s}$$

$$+ \sum_{\substack{(r,s) \in \mathcal{R}' \times \mathcal{S}' \\ d \in \{0,1\}^n}} q_{r,s,d}^{(5)} (c_{r,s,d} - p_{*,s} - e_{r,s,d}) p_{r,*}$$

$$+ \sum_{\substack{(r,s) \in \mathcal{R}' \times \mathcal{S}' \\ d \in \{0,1\}^n}} q_{r,s,d}^{(5)} (b_{r,s,d} - p_{r,*} - e_{r,s,d})(c_{r,s,d} - p_{*,s} - e_{r,s,d}). \tag{17}$$

Each term of (17) is upper bounded as follows.

Property 11. One has the following upper bounds:

1. $\displaystyle \sum_{\substack{(r,s) \in \mathcal{R}' \times \mathcal{S}' \\ d \in \{0,1\}^n}} q_{r,s,d}^{(5)} p_{r,*} p_{*,s} \leq M_3;$

2.
$$\sum_{\substack{(r,s)\in\mathcal{R}'\times\mathcal{S}'\\ d\in\{0,1\}^n}} q^{(5)}_{r,s,d}(b_{r,s,d}-p_{r,*}-e_{r,s,d})p_{*,s} \le M_3;$$

3.
$$\sum_{\substack{(r,s)\in\mathcal{R}'\times\mathcal{S}'\\ d\in\{0,1\}^n}} q^{(5)}_{r,s,d}(c_{r,s,d}-p_{*,s}-e_{r,s,d})p_{r,*} \le M_3;$$

4.
$$\sum_{\substack{(r,s)\in\mathcal{R}'\times\mathcal{S}'\\ d\in\{0,1\}^n}} q^{(5)}_{r,s,d}(b_{r,s,d}-p_{r,*}-e_{r,s,d})(c_{r,s,d}-p_{*,s}-e_{r,s,d}) \le M_3.$$

Proof. We will prove the third upper bound; the other bounds are proved similarly.

Consider

$$\bigsqcup_{\substack{(r,s)\in\mathcal{R}'\times\mathcal{S}'\\ d\in\{0,1\}^n}} \left(\mathcal{Q}^{(5)}_{r,s,d}\times\left(\bigsqcup_{i=1,3,4}\mathcal{Q}^{(i)}_{*,s}\cup\bigsqcup_{i<r}\mathcal{Q}^{(5)}_{i,s}\cup\bigsqcup_{j<d}\mathcal{Q}^{(5)}_{r,s,j}\setminus\bigsqcup_{i=1,3,4}\mathcal{Q}^{(i)}_{r,s,d}\right)\times\mathcal{Q}_{E_1}(r)\right).$$

A triple of queries from this set corresponds to a triple

$$((t,x,y),(t',x',y'),(k,u,v))\in\mathcal{Q}^2_C\times\mathcal{Q}_{E_1}$$

(in their original forms) such that $t\ne t'$, $h_2(t)=h_2(t')$ and $h_1(t)=k$. (Note that if two queries (r,s,u,v,d) and (r',s',u',v',d') share a common tweak, then we would have $(r,s,d)=(r',s',d')$.) Since such a triple is contained in $\mathcal{C}_2$ and $|\mathcal{C}_2|\le M_3$ by excluding bad keys of (C-5), the size of this set is also upper bounded by M_3.

For $(r,s)\in\mathcal{R}'\times\mathcal{S}'$ and $d\in\{0,1\}^n$, we have

$$\left|\bigsqcup_{i=1,3,4}\mathcal{Q}^{(i)}_{*,s}\cup\bigsqcup_{i<r}\mathcal{Q}^{(5)}_{i,s}\cup\bigsqcup_{j<d}\mathcal{Q}^{(5)}_{r,s,j}\setminus\bigsqcup_{i=1,3,4}\mathcal{Q}^{(i)}_{r,s,d}\right|$$
$$=(q^{(1)}_{*,s}-q^{(1)}_{r,s,d})+(q^{(3)}_{*,s}-q^{(3)}_{r,s,d})+(a^{(4)}_{*,s}-q^{(4)}_{r,s,d})+\sum_{i<r}q^{(5)}_{i,s}+\sum_{j<d}q^{(5)}_{r,s,j}$$
$$\ge c_{r,s,d}-p_{*,s}-e_{r,s,d}.$$

Therefore we have

$$\sum_{\substack{(r,s)\in\mathcal{R}'\times\mathcal{S}'\\ d\in\{0,1\}^n}} q^{(5)}_{r,s,d}(c_{r,s,d}-p_{*,s}-e_{r,s,d})p_{r,*} \le |\mathcal{C}_2| \le M_3.$$

$\square$

By (17) and Property 11, we have

$$\sum_{\substack{(r,s)\in\mathcal{R}'\times\mathcal{S}'\\ d\in\{0,1\}^n}} q^{(5)}_{r,s,d}(b_{r,s,d}-e_{r,s,d})(c_{r,s,d}-e_{r,s,d}) \le 4M_3,$$

and by plugging it into (16), we obtain

$$\mathsf{p}_3'' \geq \left(1 - \frac{16M_3}{N^2}\right) \cdot \prod_{\substack{(r,s)\in\mathcal{R}'\times\mathcal{S}' \\ d\in\{0,1\}^n}} \frac{1}{(N - e_{r,s,d})_{q_{r,s,d}^{(5)}}}. \tag{18}$$

3.3.5 Lower Bounding the Ratio

For each $(r,s,d) \in \{0,1\}^m \times \{0,1\}^m \times \{0,1\}^n$, let

$$\mathcal{T}(r,s,d) = \{w \in \mathcal{T} : (h_1(w), h_2(w), g_1(w) \oplus g_2(w)) = (r,s,d)\}.$$

Then we have a partition of $\mathcal{T}$, namely,

$$\mathcal{T} = \bigsqcup_{\substack{r,s\in\{0,1\}^m \\ d\in\{0,1\}^n}} \mathcal{T}(r,s,d).$$

Since $\sum_{w\in\mathcal{T}(r,s,d)} q_w = q_{r,s,d}^{(1)} + q_{r,s,d}^{(2)} + q_{r,s,d}^{(3)} + q_{r,s,d}^{(4)} + q_{r,s,d}^{(5)}$, we have

$$\mathsf{p}_{\mathsf{id}}(\mathcal{Q}_C|\mathcal{Q}_E) = \prod_{w\in\mathcal{T}} \frac{1}{(N)_{q_w}} \leq \prod_{\substack{r,s\in\{0,1\}^m \\ d\in\{0,1\}^n}} \frac{1}{(N)_{\sum\limits_{w\in\mathcal{T}(r,s,d)} q_w}}$$

$$= \prod_{\substack{r,s\in\{0,1\}^m \\ d\in\{0,1\}^n}} \frac{1}{(N)_{q_{r,s,d}^{(1)}+q_{r,s,d}^{(2)}+q_{r,s,d}^{(3)}+q_{r,s,d}^{(4)}+q_{r,s,d}^{(5)}}}. \tag{19}$$

By (4), (5), (8), (13), (14), (15), (18), (19), we can prove

$$\frac{\mathsf{p}_{\mathsf{re}}^{\mathsf{k}}(\mathcal{Q}_C|\mathcal{Q}_E)}{\mathsf{p}_{\mathsf{id}}(\mathcal{Q}_C|\mathcal{Q}_E)} \geq 1 - \left(\frac{16M_2}{N} + \frac{16M_3}{N^2}\right), \tag{20}$$

which completes the proof of Lemma 4. The detailed computation will be given in the full version of this paper.

3.4 Putting the Pieces Together

Theorem 1 follows from (1), Lemma 2, Lemma 3 and Lemma 4 with

$$M_1 = p^{\frac{1}{3}}q^{\frac{1}{3}},$$

$$M_2 = \frac{1}{4}(2q^3 + 2pq^2)^{\frac{1}{2}}N^{\frac{1}{2}}\delta^{\frac{1}{2}}\delta',$$

$$M_3 = \frac{1}{2}(q^3 + 2pq^2 + p^2q)^{\frac{1}{2}}N\delta'.$$

References

1. Adams, C.M.: Constructing symmetric ciphers using the CAST design procedure. Des. Codes Cryptogr. **12**(3), 283–316 (1997)
2. De Cannière, C., Dunkelman, O., Knežević, M.: KATAN and KTANTAN — a family of small and efficient hardware-oriented block ciphers. In: Clavier, C., Gaj, K. (eds.) CHES 2009. LNCS, vol. 5747, pp. 272–288. Springer, Heidelberg (2009). https://doi.org/10.1007/978-3-642-04138-9_20
3. Cogliati, B., Lampe, R., Seurin, Y.: Tweaking even-mansour ciphers. In: Gennaro, R., Robshaw, M. (eds.) CRYPTO 2015, Part I. LNCS, vol. 9215, pp. 189–208. Springer, Heidelberg (2015). https://doi.org/10.1007/978-3-662-47989-6_9
4. Crowley, P.: Mercy: a fast large block cipher for disk sector encryption. In: Goos, G., Hartmanis, J., van Leeuwen, J., Schneier, B. (eds.) FSE 2000. LNCS, vol. 1978, pp. 49–63. Springer, Heidelberg (2001). https://doi.org/10.1007/3-540-44706-7_4
5. Ferguson, N., et al.: The skein hash function family. In: Submission to NIST (round 3), **7**(7.5), 3 (2010)
6. Jean, J., Nikolić, I., Peyrin, T.: Tweaks and keys for block ciphers: the TWEAKEY framework. In: Sarkar, P., Iwata, T. (eds.) ASIACRYPT 2014, Part II. LNCS, vol. 8874, pp. 274–288. Springer, Heidelberg (2014). https://doi.org/10.1007/978-3-662-45608-8_15
7. Jha, A., Mishra, S., List, E., Minematsu, K., Nandi, M.: XHX - a framework for optimally secure tweakable block ciphers from classical block ciphers and universal hashing. In: Latincrypt (2017, to appear). https://eprint.iacr.org/2017/1075.pdf
8. Landecker, W., Shrimpton, T., Terashima, R.S.: Tweakable blockciphers with beyond birthday-bound security. In: Safavi-Naini, R., Canetti, R. (eds.) CRYPTO 2012. LNCS, vol. 7417, pp. 14–30. Springer, Heidelberg (2012). https://doi.org/10.1007/978-3-642-32009-5_2
9. Liskov, M., Rivest, R.L., Wagner, D.: Tweakable block ciphers. In: Yung, M. (ed.) CRYPTO 2002. LNCS, vol. 2442, pp. 31–46. Springer, Heidelberg (2002). https://doi.org/10.1007/3-540-45708-9_3
10. Mennink, B.: Optimally secure tweakable blockciphers. In: Leander, G. (ed.) FSE 2015. LNCS, vol. 9054, pp. 428–448. Springer, Heidelberg (2015). https://doi.org/10.1007/978-3-662-48116-5_21
11. Mennink, B.: XPX: generalized tweakable even-mansour with improved security guarantees. In: Robshaw, M., Katz, J. (eds.) CRYPTO 2016, Part I. LNCS, vol. 9814, pp. 64–94. Springer, Heidelberg (2016). https://doi.org/10.1007/978-3-662-53018-4_3
12. Minematsu, K.: Beyond-birthday-bound security based on tweakable block cipher. In: Dunkelman, O. (ed.) FSE 2009. LNCS, vol. 5665, pp. 308–326. Springer, Heidelberg (2009). https://doi.org/10.1007/978-3-642-03317-9_19
13. Minematsu, K., Iwata, T.: Tweak-length extension for tweakable blockciphers. In: Groth, J. (ed.) IMACC 2015. LNCS, vol. 9496, pp. 77–93. Springer, Cham (2015). https://doi.org/10.1007/978-3-319-27239-9_5
14. Naito, Y.: Tweakable blockciphers for efficient authenticated encryptions with beyond the birthday-bound security. IACR Trans. Symmetric Cryptol. **2017**(2), 1–26 (2017)
15. Peyrin, T., Seurin, Y.: Counter-in-Tweak: authenticated encryption modes for tweakable block ciphers. In: Robshaw, M., Katz, J. (eds.) CRYPTO 2016, Part I. LNCS, vol. 9814, pp. 33–63. Springer, Heidelberg (2016). https://doi.org/10.1007/978-3-662-53018-4_2

16. Rogaway, P.: Efficient instantiations of tweakable blockciphers and refinements to modes OCB and PMAC. In: Lee, P.J. (ed.) ASIACRYPT 2004. LNCS, vol. 3329, pp. 16–31. Springer, Heidelberg (2004). https://doi.org/10.1007/978-3-540-30539-2_2

17. Schroeppel, R., Orman, H.: The hasty pudding cipher. In: AES Candidate Submitted to NIST, p. M1 (1998)

18. Wang, L., Guo, J., Zhang, G., Zhao, J., Gu, D.: How to build fully secure tweakable blockciphers from classical blockciphers. In: Cheon, J.H., Takagi, T. (eds.) ASIACRYPT 2016, Part I. LNCS, vol. 10031, pp. 455–483. Springer, Heidelberg (2016). https://doi.org/10.1007/978-3-662-53887-6_17

19. Yang, G., Zhu, B., Suder, V., Aagaard, M.D., Gong, G.: The Simeck family of lightweight block ciphers. In: Güneysu, T., Handschuh, H. (eds.) CHES 2015. LNCS, vol. 9293, pp. 307–329. Springer, Heidelberg (2015). https://doi.org/10.1007/978-3-662-48324-4_16

ZCZ – Achieving n-bit SPRP Security with a Minimal Number of Tweakable-Block-Cipher Calls

Ritam Bhaumik[1](✉), Eik List[2](✉), and Mridul Nandi[1](✉)

[1] Indian Statistical Institute, Kolkata, India
bhaumik.ritam@gmail.com, mridul.nandi@gmail.com
[2] Bauhaus-Universität Weimar, Weimar, Germany
eik.list@uni-weimar.de

Abstract. Strong Pseudo-random Permutations (SPRPs) are important for various applications. In general, it is desirable to base an SPRP on a single-keyed primitive for minimizing the implementation costs. For constructions built on classical block ciphers, Nandi showed at ASIACRYPT'15 that at least two calls to the primitive per processed message block are required for SPRP security, assuming that all further operations are linear. The ongoing trend of using tweakable block ciphers as primitive has already led to MACs or encryption modes with high security and efficiency properties. Thus, three interesting research questions are hovering in the domain of SPRPs: (1) if and to which extent the bound of two calls per block can be reduced with a tweakable block cipher, (2) how concrete constructions could be realized, and (3) whether full n-bit security is achievable from primitives with n-bit state size.

The present work addresses all three questions. Inspired by Iwata et al.'s ZHash proposal at CRYPTO'17, we propose the ZCZ (ZHash-Counter-ZHash) construction, a single-key variable-input-length SPRP based on a single tweakable block cipher whose tweak length is at least its state size. ZCZ possesses close to optimal properties with regards to both performance and security: not only does it require only asymptotically $3\ell/2$ calls to the primitive for ℓ-block messages; we show that this figure is close to the minimum by an PRP distinguishing attack on any construction with tweak size of $\tau = n$ bits and fewer than $(3\ell - 1)/2$ calls to the same primitive. Moreover, it provides optimal n-bit security for a primitive with n-bit state and tweak size.

Keywords: Symmetric-key cryptography · Provable security
Variable-input-length sprp · Tweakable block cipher · Encryption

Full version: https://eprint.iacr.org/2018/819.pdf.
The research by Mridul Nandi has been supported by the Wisekey project at the R. C. Bose Centre for Cryptology and Security, Indian Statistical Institute, Kolkata.

T. Peyrin and S. Galbraith (Eds.): ASIACRYPT 2018, LNCS 11272, pp. 336–366, 2018.
https://doi.org/10.1007/978-3-030-03326-2_12

1   Introduction

SPRPs. Strong Pseudo-Random Permutations (or wide-block ciphers), are important symmetric-key schemes for protecting the privacy of variable-length messages. Their tweakable variants (STPRPs) are useful to build strong authenticated encryption [12,31] or onion AE [30]. During the previous two decades, the symmetric-key community proposed a considerable corpus of SPRPs. From a high-level point of view, existing constructions could be categorized into (1) Generalized Feistel networks, (2) Encrypt-Mix-Encrypt, (3) Hash-ECB-Hash, (4) Hash-Counter-Hash, and (5) miscellaneous designs.

OPTIMIZATION GOALS. The primary goals for optimizations in cryptographic schemes are, in general, low implementation costs, high provable security guarantees, and high performance. For the first criterion, it is desirable to construct higher-level schemes from a single well-analyzed primitive without large internal state and with a single key.

High security is essential in many domains that have to process large amounts of data without the ability of frequent re-keying. In most constructions, however, it comes at the cost of decreased performance. Unsurprisingly, the challenges of combining high security guarantees with high performance have been identified among the hot topics of symmetric-key cryptography at the ESC 2017 workshop [5]. Often, high security is associated with security *beyond the birthday bound*. In the areas of authentication (e.g., [19,32,33]), encryption, as well as authenticated encryption (e.g., [13,14,28]), beyond-birthday security has undergone a long line of research. In the area of SPRPs, however, the security of the vast majority of existing constructions is still limited by the birthday bound of $n/2$ bits, where n is the state size of the underlying primitive. So, the privacy guarantees are lost if $q \simeq 2^{n/2}$ message blocks have been encrypted under the same key. Assuming the AES as primitive, this would imply that significantly fewer than 2^{64} blocks could safely be encrypted under a single key.

SECURITY OF SPRPs: STATE OF THE ART. Among the earlier proposals, the LARGEBLOCK1 and LARGEBLOCK2 constructions by Minematsu and Iwata [23] as well as TCT$_2$ by Shrimpton and Terashima [31] are exceptional for their security guarantees. The LARGEBLOCK designs can achieve optimal n-bit security, whereas TCT$_2$ is limited by $2n/3$ bits. Both share similarities to the Ψ_2 and Ψ_3 constructions from Coron et al. [9], which use two and three calls to a tweakable block cipher. Both LARGEBLOCK2 and TCT$_2$ possess a sandwich structure, where an encryption layer is wrapped by two layers of hashing. In the former, the encryption layer is an application of Ψ_2 in ECB-mode; the hashing layers employs two calls to a polynomial hash of $2(\ell - 1)$ multiplications each. TCT$_2$ can be seen as an unbalanced version of Ψ_3, where also $2(\ell-1)$ of ℓ input blocks are hashed in each hashing layer. Both constructions are remarkable for their time. To be comparably efficient, however, they required two primitives, a block cipher and a universal hash function.

A different direction is followed by HHFHFH [2] and its instantiations (e.g., [3]), which is a four-round unbalanced Feistel network, built on a large-state primitive. Instead of providing beyond-birthday security, it possesses large security margins due to a larger birthday bound of their internal primitives. However, the large state size limits its efficiency.

The only approach we are aware of that almost combines both security and performance desiderata is SIMPIRA (v2) [10], a family of Feistel-like constructions built upon the AES round function. Its authors claim 128-bit security and high performance on current processors with support for AES native instructions. However, SIMPIRA's security claim stems purely from heuristics, which will demand intensive further cryptanalysis to increase trust into it.

TWEAKABLE BLOCK CIPHERS. One established approach for achieving higher security without considerably sacrificing performance is to use a tweakable block cipher (TBC) [18] as underlying primitive. At the core, tweakable block ciphers employ an additional public input called tweak, which allows to efficiently separate the domains of different calls to the primitive. This fact can reduce the impact of internal collisions on the security of the scheme built around them. For message authentication codes (MACs), a series of recent works pushed the security bounds further [8,15,24], but a similar trend is also observable in the domain of encryption modes and authenticated encryption schemes [14,17,21,28,29]. This approach has also been used earlier for SPRPs [9,20,22,23,31] – those proposals, however, originate from at least half a decade ago where TBCs used to be constructed in cumbersome fashion from classical block ciphers. Nowadays, we have the option of using efficient dedicated TBCs, such as DEOXYS-BC, JOLTIK-BC [16], or SKINNY [1].

The application of TBCs can also boost the efficiency of constructions, as has been demonstrated recently for MACs. At CRYPTO'17, Iwata et al. [15] introduced ZMAC, a TBC-based parallelizable, single-key single-primitive MAC whose internal hash function ZHASH processed the message in both the tweak and plaintext simultaneously. The additional message bits per primitive call render ZMAC more efficient than previous MACs and suggest the adoption of the approach to other domains.

OPEN RESEARCH QUESTIONS. When abstracting away the details of the primitive, the number of calls to it per input block becomes the main efficiency metric. From Encrypt-Mix-Encrypt-based constructions, it is well-known that the bound is at most two calls per block (plus some minor overhead), assuming all further operations are linear. Thus, it is an interesting question if SPRPs can be built from fewer calls to a single-keyed primitive. Moreover, a strongly related question is that for the minimal number of calls necessary for SPRP security.

From a theoretical perspective, Nandi [26] showed that constructions built from a classical single-keyed block cipher require 2ℓ calls for ℓ-block messages for SPRP security. Though, it seems as though this bound is reducible if one used a TBC instead as the underlying primitive. For Hash-Counter-Hash-based constructions, the most efficient (T)BC-based hash function we are aware of is ZHASH. For a TBC with n-bit state and τ-bit tweak length, it would yield a construction of about $\ell + 2 \lceil \sigma/(n + \tau) \rceil$ calls for messages of σ bits. For dedi-

Table 1. Asymptotic #primitive calls for SPRP paradigms. We assume that hash functions and encryption layers use a single-keyed (tweakable) block cipher with n-bit state and τ-bit tweak size to encrypt an ℓ-block message of σ bits in total. We assume the hashing layers use ZHASH (as the most efficient blockcipher-based hash function we are aware of).

Paradigm	#Block-cipher calls			
	Top	Middle	Bottom	Total (asympt.)
LARGEBLOCK2	$2\lceil(\ell-1)/2\rceil$	ℓ	$2\lceil(\ell-1)/2\rceil$	$4\lceil(\ell-1)/2\rceil+\ell$
TCT$_2$	$2\lceil(\ell-1)/2\rceil$	$2(\ell-1)$	$2\lceil(\ell-1)/2\rceil$	$4\lceil(\ell-1)/2\rceil+2\ell$
Encrypt-Mix-Encrypt	ℓ	$\lceil\ell/n\rceil$	ℓ	$2\ell+\lceil\ell/n\rceil$
Hash-ECB-Hash	ℓ	ℓ	ℓ	3ℓ
Hash-Counter-Hash	$\lceil\sigma/(n+\tau)\rceil$	ℓ	$\lceil\sigma/(n+\tau)\rceil$	$\ell+2\lceil\sigma/(n+\tau)\rceil$
ZCZ	$\ell/2$	$\ell/2+\lceil\ell/2n\rceil$	$\ell/2$	$3\ell/2+\lceil\ell/2n\rceil$

cated TBCs, such as DEOXYS-BC-128-384 or SKINNY-128-384, this figure still implies that approximately $5\ell/3$ calls are necessary. Regarding the other design principles, it is unclear if similar results are applicable to constructions based on the Encrypt-Mix-Encrypt or Hash-ECB-Hash paradigms. We estimate that Hash-ECB-Hash constructions would need about ℓ primitive calls in each hashing layer, plus ℓ calls in the encryption layer. An instantiation of LARGEBLOCK2 with ZHASH instead of multiplications would yield $2\lceil(\ell-1)/2\rceil$ calls in each hashing layer, plus ℓ calls in the middle, or 3ℓ calls in sum. TCT$_2$ could use a ZHASH layer each for both top and bottom hashing layer. While further modifications could make it more efficient, its proposal employed $2\ell-2$ calls in the middle. We compare the approaches in Table 1. Altogether, three interesting research questions remain: (1) to which extent can the number of primitive calls be reduced when employing a tweakable block cipher, (2) how can a specific construction be realized, and (3) can it be built with high provable security guarantees.

CONTRIBUTION. This work tries to answer all three questions above: for the theoretical interest, (1) we show that 1.5ℓ primitive calls per message block is close to minimal by a generic distinguisher on any construction that employs fewer than $(3\ell-1)/2$ calls to a single-keyed primitive per message block, where all further operations are linear. For the practitioner's interest, (2) we propose ZCZ (ZHash-Counter-ZHash), an almost fully parallelizable variable-input-length SPRP based on a single-keyed TBC with n-bit state and n-bit tweak size. ZCZ matches approximately the optimal number of 1.5ℓ calls to the primitive for an ℓ-block message, plus a small overhead. Finally, we show (3) that ZCZ achieves optimal n-bit security, i.e., the SPRP advantage of any adversary that asks at most q queries of σ blocks in total is in $O(\sigma^2/2^{2n})$.

We note that instantiations of Hash-Counter-Hash with ZHASH and a TBC with large tweaks of $\tau = 3n$, the number of primitive calls could become equal to that of ZCZ. However, such primitives would introduce a significant slowdown, be it due to the requirements of more rounds in a TWEAKEY-like cipher, or due to the need of calling an additional universal hash function for compressing the tweak. Concerning practical tweak sizes $\tau < 3n$, the number of calls is significantly lower for our construction.

YET ANOTHER ENCRYPTION SCHEME? It may appear that ZCZ is yet another encryption scheme after all, and with hundreds of encryption schemes already being present in the literature, it is difficult get excited about another one, notwithstanding small improvements in performance and security. We beg to differ on this point primarily for two reasons: (1) very few existing encryption schemes built upon a primitive with an n-bit output provide n-bit security — most in fact are only secure up to the birthday bound. As such, the improvement by ZCZ in terms of security is not a small step, but rather a leap. Since there is a considerable interest in the (still) small group of constructions that achieve this security, we believe that our encryption scheme is an exciting addition to this group. (2) Even more significant is the way that ZCZ exploits the randomness generated by a tweakable blockcipher. While most previous approaches were based on generic replacements of two or more blockcipher calls by a single call to a tweakable block cipher, the approach used by ZCZ is not a corollary of any previous work. Given its efficiency, we believe it can lead to exciting new directions in research on tweakable-blockcipher modes.

OUTLINE. The remainder is structured as follows: first, Sect. 2 briefly summarizes the necessary preliminaries. Given a primitive with an effective tweak size[1] $\tau = n$, Sect. 3 illustrates that every PRP with fewer than $3\ell - 1$ primitive calls for 2ℓ-block messages is insecure, which was the core motivation for our search for constructions with about 1.5ℓ calls. Subsequently, Sect. 4 defines our basic construction, which is first described for messages whose length is a positive multiple of $2n$ bits. Thereupon, Sect. 5 extends our definition to messages of more general lengths. Section 6 provides the details of our security analysis.

We provide further insights on the starting point of our research in the full version of this work [4]. Therein, we also discuss attacks on insecure preliminary variants that motivated our studies towards the final design of ZCZ.

2   Preliminaries

GENERAL NOTATION. We use lowercase letters x for indices and integers, uppercase letters X, Y for binary strings and functions, and calligraphic uppercase letters $\mathcal{X}, \mathcal{Y}$ for sets. We denote the concatenation of binary strings X and Y by $X \parallel Y$; we mostly treat bit strings as representations of elements in the finite field $\mathbb{F}_{2^n}$, which is the Galois Field $\mathbb{GF}(2^n)$ with a fixed irreducible polynomial $p(\mathbf{x})$. There, we interpret a bit string $(x_{n-1} \ldots x_1 x_0)$ as polynomial $\sum_{i=0}^{n-1} a_i \cdot \mathbf{x}^i$ in $\mathbb{F}_{2^n}$. Bit x_i represents the coefficient $a_i \in \{0, 1\}$, for $0 \le i \le n - 1$, and the most significant bit is the leftmost, and the least significant bit is the rightmost bit. We

---

[1] By effective tweak size, we mean the usable tweak domain without bits that are used for other purposes such as domain separation.

denote the result of the addition of two elements as $X + Y$, which is equivalent to the XOR of X and Y. For tuples of bit strings $(X_1, \ldots, X_x)$, $(Y_1, \ldots, Y_x)$ of equal domain, we denote by $(X_1, \ldots, X_x) + (Y_1, \ldots, Y_x)$ the element-wise XOR, i.e., $(X_1 + Y_1, \ldots, X_x + Y_x)$. Unless stated otherwise, we consider all additions of n-bit values to be in $\mathbb{F}_2^n$. Moreover, we will use $\oplus$ for the XOR of bit strings in illustrations. However, all additions and subtractions in sub- and superscripts that denote indices represent integer additions. We indicate the length of a bit string X in bits by $|X|$, and write X_i for the i-th block. Moreover, we denote by $X \twoheadleftarrow \mathcal{X}$ that X is chosen independently uniformly at random from the set $\mathcal{X}$. We define three sets of particular interest: $\mathsf{Func}(\mathcal{X}, \mathcal{Y})$ be the set of all functions $F : \mathcal{X} \to \mathcal{Y}$, $\mathsf{Perm}(\mathcal{X})$ the set of all permutations over $\mathcal{X}$, and $\widetilde{\mathsf{Perm}}(\mathcal{T}, \mathcal{X})$ for the set of tweaked permutations over $\mathcal{X}$ with associated tweak space $\mathcal{T}$.

$(X_1, \ldots, X_x) \overset{n}{\twoheadleftarrow} X$ denotes that X is split into the minimal number of n-bit blocks possible i.e., $X_1 \| \ldots \| X_x = X$, and $|X_i| = n$ for $1 \le i \le x - 1$, and $|X_x| \le n$. So, when $|X| > 0$, then $|X_x| > 0$. If $|X| = 0$, $Y \overset{x}{\twoheadleftarrow} X$ sets Y to the empty string. $\langle X \rangle_n$ denotes an encoding of an integer $X \in \mathbb{Z}_n$ as an n-bit string. For two sets $\mathcal{X}$ and $\mathcal{Y}$, a uniform random function $\rho : \mathcal{X} \to \mathcal{Y}$ maps inputs $X \in \mathcal{X}$ independently and uniformly at random to outputs $Y \in \mathcal{Y}$. For an event E, we denote by $\Pr[E]$ the probability of E; ε is the empty string. For a given set $\mathcal{X}$ and integer x, we define $\mathcal{X}^{\le x} = \bigcup_{i=1}^{x} \mathcal{X}^i$ and $\mathcal{X}^+ = \bigcup_{j=1}^{\infty} \mathcal{X}^j$. For two integers n, k with $n \ge k \ge 1$, we denote the falling factorial as $(n)_k = \prod_{i=0}^{k-1} (n - i)$.

ADVERSARIES. An adversary $\mathbf{A}$ is an efficient Turing machine that interacts with a given set of oracles that appear as black boxes to $\mathbf{A}$. We denote by $\mathbf{A}^{\mathcal{O}}$ the output of $\mathbf{A}$ after interacting with some oracle $\mathcal{O}$. We write $\Delta_{\mathbf{A}}(\mathcal{O}^1; \mathcal{O}^2) := |\Pr[\mathbf{A}^{\mathcal{O}^1} \Rightarrow 1] - \Pr[\mathbf{A}^{\mathcal{O}^2} \Rightarrow 1]|$ for the advantage of $\mathbf{A}$ to distinguish between oracles $\mathcal{O}^1$ and $\mathcal{O}^2$. All probabilities are defined over the random coins of the oracles and those of $\mathbf{A}$, if any. W.l.o.g., we assume that $\mathbf{A}$ never asks queries to which it already knows the answer.

A block cipher E with associated key space $\mathcal{K}$ and message space $\mathcal{M}$ is a mapping $E : \mathcal{K} \times \mathcal{M} \to \mathcal{M}$ such that for every key $K \in \mathcal{K}$, it holds that $E(K, \cdot)$ is a permutation over $\mathcal{M}$. A tweakable block cipher $\widetilde{E}$ with additional tweak space $\mathcal{T}$ is a mapping $\widetilde{E} : \mathcal{K} \times \mathcal{T} \times \mathcal{M} \to \mathcal{M}$ such that for every key $K \in \mathcal{K}$ and tweak $T \in \mathcal{T}$, it holds that $\widetilde{E}(K, T, \cdot)$ is a permutation over $\mathcal{M}$. We also write $\widetilde{E}_K^T(\cdot)$ as short form. In this work, we assume that SPRPs allow variable-length inputs, i.e., there is no single fixed length, but the length of the ciphertext always equals that of the plaintext and vice versa; moreover, over all inputs of equal length, the construction is a permutation. The advantage is defined as follows.

Definition 1 (SPRP Advantage). Let $\mathcal{K}$ be a non-empty set and $\mathcal{M} \subset \{0, 1\}^*$. Let $\Pi : \mathcal{K} \times \mathcal{M} \to \mathcal{M}$ be a length-preserving permutation. Let $\pi \twoheadleftarrow \mathsf{Perm}(\mathcal{M})$ be sampled from the set of all length-preserving permutations of $\mathcal{M}$, and $K \twoheadleftarrow \mathcal{K}$. Then, the SPRP advantage of $\mathbf{A}$ with respect to Π is defined as
$$\mathbf{Adv}_{\Pi}^{\mathrm{SPRP}}(\mathbf{A}) \overset{\mathrm{def}}{=} \Delta_{\mathbf{A}}(\Pi_K, \Pi_K^{-1}; \pi, \pi^{-1}).$$

Definition 2 (STPRP Advantage). Let $\mathcal{K}$ and $\mathcal{T}$ be non-empty sets and let $\widetilde{E} : \mathcal{K} \times \mathcal{T} \times \{0,1\}^n \to \{0,1\}^n$ denote a tweakable block cipher. Let $\widetilde{\pi} \leftarrow \widetilde{\mathsf{Perm}}(\mathcal{T}, \{0,1\}^n)$ and $K \leftarrow \mathcal{K}$. Then, the STPRP advantage of $\mathbf{A}$ w.r.t. $\widetilde{E}$ is defined as $\mathbf{Adv}_{\widetilde{E}}^{\mathrm{STPRP}}(\mathbf{A}) \overset{\text{def}}{=} \Delta_{\mathbf{A}}(\widetilde{E}_K, \widetilde{E}_K^{-1}; \widetilde{\pi}, \widetilde{\pi}^{-1})$.

Definition 3 (Almost-XOR-Universal Hash Function). Let $\mathcal{K}$, $\mathcal{X}$, and $\mathcal{Y} \subseteq \{0,1\}^*$ be non-empty sets. Let $H : \mathcal{K} \times \mathcal{X} \to \mathcal{Y}$ be a function keyed by $K \in \mathcal{K}$. We call H ϵ-almost-XOR-universal (ϵ-AXU) if, for all distinct $X, X' \in \mathcal{X}$ and any $\Delta \in \mathcal{Y}$, it holds that $\mathrm{Pr}_{K \leftarrow \mathcal{K}}[H_K(X) - H_K(X') = \Delta] \leq \epsilon$, where subtraction is in $\mathbb{F}_{2^n}$.

THE H-COEFFICIENT TECHNIQUE. The H-coefficient technique is a proof method by Patarin [27]. It assumes that the results of the interaction of an adversary $\mathbf{A}$ with its oracles are collected in a transcript τ of the attack: $\tau = \langle (M_1, C_1, d_1), \ldots, (M_q, C_q, d_q) \rangle$. (M_i, C_i) denotes the in- and output of the i-th query of $\mathbf{A}$; a Boolean variable d_i denotes the query direction: $d_i = 1$ indicates that C_i was result of an encryption query, and $d_i = 0$ that M_i was the result of a decryption query. The task of $\mathbf{A}$ is to distinguish the real world $\mathcal{O}_{\mathrm{real}}$ from the ideal world $\mathcal{O}_{\mathrm{ideal}}$. A transcript τ is called *attainable* if the probability to obtain τ in the ideal world is non-zero. We denote by Θ_{real} and Θ_{ideal} the distribution of transcripts in the real and the ideal world, respectively. Then, the fundamental Lemma of the H-coefficients technique, whose proof is given in [6,27], states:

Lemma 1 (Fundamental Lemma of the H-coefficient Technique [27]). Assume that the set of attainable transcripts is partitioned into two disjoint sets GOODT and BADT. Further assume that there exist $\epsilon_1, \epsilon_2 \geq 0$ such that for any transcript $\tau \in$ GOODT, it holds that

$$\frac{\mathrm{Pr}[\Theta_{\mathrm{real}} = \tau]}{\mathrm{Pr}[\Theta_{\mathrm{ideal}} = \tau]} \geq 1 - \epsilon_1, \quad \text{and} \quad \mathrm{Pr}[\Theta_{\mathrm{ideal}} \in \mathrm{BADT}] \leq \epsilon_2.$$

Then, for all adversaries $\mathbf{A}$, it holds that $\Delta_{\mathbf{A}}(\mathcal{O}_{\mathrm{real}}; \mathcal{O}_{\mathrm{ideal}}) \leq \epsilon_1 + \epsilon_2$.

3   On the Minimal Number of Required Primitive Calls

This section shows that any PRP with fewer than $3\ell - 1$ calls for messages of 2ℓ blocks to a primitive with n-bit tweak size and n-bit state size is insecure. We follow the approach by [26], who proved that an SPRP based on a single-keyed classical block cipher needs at least 2ℓ calls to the primitive for ℓ-block messages.

3.1   Generic Construction

Define positive integers n, τ, and ℓ, and let $\mathcal{M} \subseteq \{0,1\}^*$ denote a space for which $(\{0,1\}^n)^{2\ell} \subseteq \mathcal{M}$. Let $r \leq 3\ell - 2$ and let $\widetilde{\pi}_i : \{0,1\}^\tau \times \{0,1\}^n \to \{0,1\}^n$, for all $1 \leq i \leq r$, denote tweakable permutations with tweak space $\{0,1\}^\tau$ and state

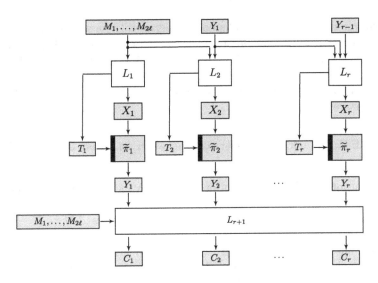

Fig. 1. Generic model of a PRP that consists of at most $r \leq 3\ell - 2$ calls to tweakable block ciphers $\widetilde{\pi}_i$ for messages of 2ℓ blocks.

size n. Let $\Pi[\widetilde{\pi}_1, \ldots, \widetilde{\pi}_r] : \mathcal{M} \to \mathcal{M}$ be a length-preserving cipher that employs as its only non-linear functions in total r calls to the permutations $\widetilde{\pi}_1, \ldots, \widetilde{\pi}_r$. For simplicity, we also write Π as short form, hereafter. All further components of Π are linear over $\mathbb{F}_{2^n}$. For any such construction, we can formulate this as follows. Let X_i denote the input to π_i, T_i the tweak to π_i, and let $Y_i \leftarrow \pi_i(X_i)$ denote its output. The linear operations in Π must be describable as non-zero linear functions $L_i : \mathcal{M} \times (\{0,1\}^n)^{i-1} \to \{0,1\}^n \times \{0,1\}^r$, for $1 \leq i \leq r$, and an additional non-zero linear function $L_{r+1} : \mathcal{M} \times (\{0,1\}^n)^r \to \mathcal{M}$ that, for all given inputs $(M, Y_1, \ldots, Y_r) \in \mathcal{M} \times (\{0,1\}^n)^r$, outputs C s.t. it holds that $|C| = |M|$. Then, we can describe the encryption with $\Pi(M)$ as

$$(X_i, T_i) \leftarrow L_i(M, Y_1, \ldots, Y_{i-1}), \qquad \text{for all } 1 \leq i \leq r,$$
$$Y_i \leftarrow \widetilde{\pi}^{T_i}(X_i), \qquad \text{for all } 1 \leq i \leq r, \text{ and}$$
$$C \leftarrow L_{r+1}(M, Y_1, \ldots, Y_r).$$

Π must be correct for all inputs, i.e., for all $M, C \in \mathcal{M}$, it must hold that $\Pi^{-1}(\Pi(M)) = M$ and $\Pi(\Pi^{-1}(C)) = C$. Figure 1 gives an illustration.

Remark 1. It may not be instantaneously clear why the generic construction above covers all considered schemes. Note that it computes the values X_i and T_i by a non-zero linear function of $M, Y_1, Y_2, \ldots, Y_{i-1}$. So, the previous values Y_i can also be used to generate X_i. Indeed, it is generic enough to include all such constructions where the only non-linear components are the permutation calls.

For simplicity, we consider independent permutations with tweak domain $\mathbb{F}_2^\tau$ in this section. For efficiency, our proposal later in this work will employ only a single tweakable primitive with a composite tweak domain $\mathcal{T}_D = \mathcal{D} \times \mathbb{F}_2^\tau$, where $\mathcal{D}$ is a non-empty set of domains. So, this approach achieves the same goal of having independent permutations. We consider that τ is the effectively usable size of the tweaks without domains.

3.2 A PRP Attack on Constructions with at Most $3\ell - 2$ Calls

CASE $\tau = n$. Let $\mathbf{A}$ be an adversary with the goal to distinguish the outputs of a variable-input-length PRP Π under a secret key as above from an ideal PRP. First, $\mathbf{A}$ chooses two messages M and M' of 2ℓ blocks each, i.e., $M = (M_1, \ldots, M_{2\ell})$ and $M' = (M_1', \ldots, M_{2\ell}')$. We define the differences $\Delta M = M - M'$, and analogously the differences ΔX_i, ΔY_i, and ΔC in the obvious manner. Choose M and M' such that it holds that $\Delta X_i = 0$ and $\Delta T_i = 0$, for $1 \leq i \leq \ell - 1$. Note that such a choice of M and M' must be possible since these variables correspond to $2\ell - 2$ equations ($\ell - 1$ equations for adjusting the values ΔX_i and $\ell - 1$ equations for adjusting the values ΔT_i) and there exist 2ℓ blocks ΔM_i. For instance, the adversary can efficiently derive an element N from the null space of $L_1, \ldots, L_{2(\ell-1)}$. It chooses M arbitrarily and derives $M' = M + N$.

From $\Delta X_i = 0^n$ and $\Delta T_i = 0^\tau$ for $1 \leq i \leq \ell - 1$, it follows that $\Delta Y_i = \widetilde{\pi}^{T_i}(X_i) \oplus \widetilde{\pi}^{T_i}(X_i') = 0^n$, for all $1 \leq i \leq \ell - 1$. The non-linear layer of calls to the tweakable block cipher maps $(\Delta X_1, \ldots, \Delta X_r)$ to $(\Delta Y_1, \ldots, \Delta Y_r)$. We obtain

$$L_{r+1}(\Delta M, \underbrace{\Delta Y_1, \ldots, \Delta Y_{\ell-1}}_{= (0, \ldots, 0)}, \Delta Y_\ell, \ldots, \Delta Y_r) = \Delta C.$$

Since $\mathbf{A}$ fixed ΔM and chose M and M' so that $\Delta X_1 = \ldots = \Delta X_{\ell-1} = 0^n$ and $\Delta T_1 = \ldots = \Delta T_{\ell-1} = 0^\tau$, we obtain $\Delta Y_1, \ldots, \Delta Y_{\ell-1} = 0^n$. So, there are at most $2\ell - 1$ free variables $\Delta Y_\ell, \ldots \Delta Y_r$, and 2ℓ equations for $\Delta C_1, \ldots, \Delta C_{2\ell}$, which implies that 2ℓ blocks of ΔC are a linear combination of $2\ell - 1$ values $\Delta Y_\ell, \ldots, \Delta Y_r$. So, in the real construction, L_{r+1} defines a map from $2\ell - 1$ to 2ℓ n-bit variables, and $\mathbf{A}$ can efficiently derive a solution $\Delta Y_\ell, \ldots, \Delta Y_r$ from the null space of the equation system. This becomes a distinguishing event happening with probability one in the real construction and with probability $1/2^n$ in the ideal world for this example. The distinguishing advantage is hence $1 - 1/2^n$. $\mathbf{A}$ can query it with two messages as above and output real if such a non-zero linear function L exists and random otherwise, as summarized in Algorithm 1.

FOR GENERAL VALUES OF τ. A similar attack is applicable for general values of τ. Though, we have to consider linearity over $\mathbb{F}_2$ then. Define

$$s = \left\lfloor \frac{2\ell n}{n + \tau} \right\rfloor - 1.$$

The adversary chooses $M \in (\mathbb{F}_2^n)^{2\ell}$ arbitrarily, and $M' \in (\mathbb{F}_2^n)^{2\ell}$ with $M \neq M'$ s. t. $\Delta X_1 = \ldots \Delta X_s = 0^n$ and $\Delta T_1 = \ldots = \Delta T_s = 0^\tau$. Note that we consider

---

Algorithm 1. PRP attack on generic constructions Π with at most $3\ell - 2$ primitive calls, here for $\tau = n$.

1: **function $\mathbf{A}^{\Pi}$**
2:     Choose M_i for $1 \leq i \leq 2\ell$ arbitrarily
3:     Choose M_i' for $\ell \leq i \leq 2\ell$ s. t. it holds that
4:     $L_i(\Delta M_i) = (\Delta X_i, \Delta T_i) = (0^n, 0^\tau)$, for $1 \leq i \leq 2(\ell - 1)$
5:     Ask for the encryption of $C = \Pi(M)$ and $C' = \Pi(M')$
6:     Derive $\Delta C = C' - C$
7:     **if** there exists $(\Delta Y_\ell, \ldots, \Delta Y_r)$, s. t. $L_{r+1}(\Delta M, \Delta Y) = \Delta C$ **then**
8:         **return** "Real"
9:     **return** "Random"

---

the inputs $X_i \in \mathbb{F}_2^n$ and the tweaks $T_i \in \mathbb{F}_2^\tau$ as blocks. Again, such a choice of M' exists for the same reason as above and can be found efficiently from the null space of the linear functions $L_1, L_2, \ldots$ that are involved in the computation of $\Delta X_1, \ldots, \Delta X_s$ and $\Delta T_1, \ldots, \Delta T_s$. Again, we obtain $\Delta Y_i = 0^n$, for $1 \leq i \leq s$ for the real construction. We obtain the equation

$$L_{r+1}(\Delta M, \underbrace{\Delta Y_1, \ldots, \Delta Y_s}_{= (0, \ldots, 0)}, \Delta Y_{s+1}, \ldots, \Delta Y_r) = \Delta C.$$

The blocks $\Delta Y_{s+1}, \ldots, \Delta Y_r$ contain $(r - s)n$ bits, that are mapped through L_{r+1} to $\Delta C_{2\ell n}$ bits. For all schemes Π that use r calls to the primitive with

$$(r - s) \cdot n < 2\ell n, \qquad \text{which leads to} \qquad r < 2\ell \left(1 + \frac{n}{n + \tau}\right) - 1,$$

we obtain a compressing mapping. Then, there exist are more equations than variables, and the distinguisher as before applies. However, the advantage may be smaller and depends on the values of r, n, and τ.

4   Definition of the Basic ZCZ Construction

This section defines the basic ZCZ scheme. First, we consider messages that consist of at most $2n$ blocks, and will extend it thereupon to all messages whose length is a multiple of $2n$ bits. The subsequent section will then further define it for messages whose lengths are not necessarily multiples of $2n$ bits.

PARAMETERS. Let $n, \tau, k, d \geq 1$ be integers with $d \ll n$ and $n = \tau$; we define $N \stackrel{\text{def}}{=} 2^n$ as an alias. Let $\mathcal{B} = \{0,1\}^{2n}$ define a *di-block* (or dual block, double block), i.e., $2n$ bits. We define non-empty sets of tweaks $\mathcal{T} = \{0,1\}^\tau$, keys $\mathcal{K} = \{0,1\}^k$, domains $\mathcal{D} = \{\mathsf{t}, \mathsf{s}, \mathsf{c}, \mathsf{b}, \mathsf{t\$}, \mathsf{s\$}, \mathsf{c\$}, \mathsf{b\$}, \mathsf{xl}, \mathsf{xr}, \mathsf{yl}, \mathsf{yr}, \mathsf{p}, \mathsf{kd}\} \subseteq \{0,1\}^d$, and a set of indices $\mathcal{I} \subseteq \{1, \ldots, 2^n - 1\}$. The purpose of domains and indices is to define an extended tweak set $\mathcal{T}_{D,I} = \mathcal{D} \times \mathcal{I} \times \mathcal{T}$ for a tweakable block cipher $\widetilde{E} : \mathcal{K} \times \mathcal{T}_{D,I} \times \{0,1\}^n \to \{0,1\}^n$.

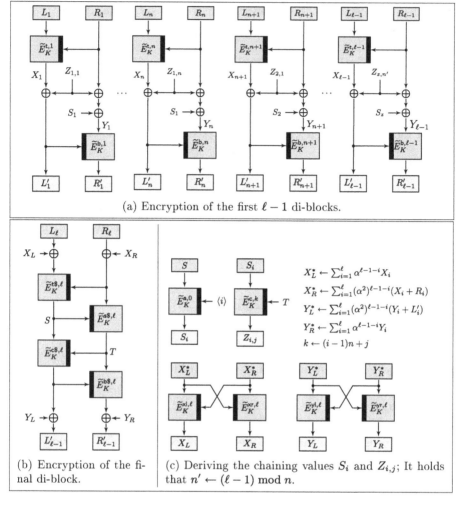

(a) Encryption of the first $\ell - 1$ di-blocks.

(b) Encryption of the final di-block.

(c) Deriving the chaining values S_i and $Z_{i,j}$; It holds that $n' \leftarrow (\ell - 1) \bmod n$.

Fig. 2. Encryption of a message with ℓ complete di-blocks with $\mathrm{ZCZ}[\widetilde{E}_K]$.

OVERVIEW. The basic $\mathrm{ZCZ}[\widetilde{E}_K]$ construction takes as input a secret key $K \in \mathcal{K}$ and a plaintext $M \in \mathcal{B}^{\leq n}$ that is split into $\ell \in [1..n]$ di-blocks. The design can be split into a top, middle, and a bottom layer. In the top layer, the first $\ell - 1$ complete di-blocks (L_i, R_i) are processed similarly as in the $\mathbb{ZHASH}$ construction by Iwata et al. [15]. The TBC outputs X_i are accumulated by an MDS code to two values X_L^* and X_R^* using the Horner rule, which are finally encrypted in a butterfly-like structure [24] to $X_L \leftarrow \widetilde{E}_K^{\mathrm{xl},\ell,X_R^*}(X_L^*)$ and $X_R \leftarrow \widetilde{E}_K^{\mathrm{xr},\ell,X_L^*}(X_R^*)$. X_L and X_R are used to mask the branches of the final di-block, L_ℓ and R_ℓ. The final di-block is processed by a four-round Feistel-like network of four TBC calls in the spirit of the constructions by Coron et al. [9].

This four-round network generates two intermediate values S and T after the first and second call to $\widetilde{E}$. The middle layer derives from S and T a value $S_1 \leftarrow \widetilde{E}_K^{\mathsf{s},0,1}(S)$ and a series of $\ell - 1$ chaining values $Z_{1,j} \leftarrow \widetilde{E}^{\mathsf{c},j,T}(S_1)$. For the j-th di-block, the chaining value $Z_{1,j}$ is added to both branches of the j-th block. Moreover, S_1 is also added to the right branch of each di-block: $L'_j \leftarrow X_j + Z_{i,j}$ and $Y_j \leftarrow R_j + Z_{1,j} + S_1$. So, this middle layer ensures that each di-block depends on all others. Finally, the middle layer generates from the blocks Y_j and L'_j two values Y_L and Y_R symmetrically as X_L and X_R, from the values Y_j.

The bottom layer is then a symmetric version of the top layer. The $\ell - 1$ di-blocks are processed by another ZHASH layer to compute the ciphertext blocks: $L'_j \leftarrow X_j$ and $R'_j \leftarrow \widetilde{E}_K^{\mathsf{b},i,L'_j}(Y_j)$. The final complete di-block is processed by two further Feistel rounds before Y_L added to the left branch, and Y_R is added to the right branch of the ℓ-th di-block. The resulting values L'_i, R'_i, for $1 \leq i \leq \ell$, are concatenated and returned as the ciphertext. The details of the encryption with $\text{ZCZ}[\widetilde{E}_K]$ is given in Algorithm 2, and is illustrated in parts in Fig. 2, already for more than n complete di-blocks.

RATIONALE. The structure is inspired by ZHASH [15] and AEZ [12]. The use of α and α^2 prevents that a collision in X_L would automatically lead to a collision also in X_R and vice versa; considering also the tweak values R_i for X_R renders birthday collisions in X_i from separate tweaks ineffective. Encrypting X_L^*, X_R^*, Y_L^*, and Y_R^* avoids that differences in the masks cancel differences in the final di-block. Finally, adding S_i and $Z_{i,j}$ prevents adversaries from observing differences $\Delta Z_{1,j}$. Using the masks X_L, X_R, Y_L, and Y_R in the final block makes its outputs depend on all blocks; Using S and T for the counter mode in the middle layer creates a dependency of each di-block on all others. We elaborate on attacks on preliminary versions of ZCZ in the full version of this work. We employ pairwise distinct domains for all calls to $\widetilde{E}$ to prevent dependencies between the calls.

EXTENSION TO LONGER MESSAGES. Messages with more than n di-blocks are partitioned into *chunks*. The i-th (complete) chunk denotes the series of the n consecutive di-blocks $(L_{(i-1)n+1}, R_{(i-1)n+1}, \ldots L_{i \cdot n}, R_{i \cdot n})$, and employs the chaining values S_i and $Z_{i,j}$. We derive all chaining values under distinct domains as before. Furthermore, we derive $\ell - 1$ chaining values $Z_{i,j}$ by a TBC call each from S. For the i-th chunk, S_i is computed as $S_i \leftarrow \widetilde{E}_K^{\mathsf{s},0,i}(S)$. Then, for $j \in [1..n]$, $Z_{i,j}$ for the j-th block of the i-th chunk is generated as $Z_{i,j} \leftarrow \widetilde{E}_K^{\mathsf{c},0,n(i-1)+j}(S_i)$. $Y_{n(i-1)+j}$ is then computed as $Y_{n(i-1)+j} \leftarrow R_{n(i-1)+j} + S_i + Z_{n(i-1)+j}$. The rest of the computations remain unchanged. Letting j take any value in $[1..\ell]$, we can rewrite this as

$$Y_j \leftarrow R_j + S_{\lceil j/n \rceil} + Z_j. \tag{2'}$$

The encryption of $\text{ZCZ}[\widetilde{E}_K]$ is defined in Algorithm 2, and illustrated in parts in Fig. 2, already for more than n complete di-blocks. The figure employs bold bars in the blocks of $\widetilde{E}$ to indicate the parts of the tweaks that stem from T. The decryption is defined in the obvious way.

Algorithm 2. Definition of the encryption algorithm of $\mathrm{ZCZ}[\widetilde{E}]$ given a tweakable block cipher $\widetilde{E}$. The code in the boxes is only part of $\mathrm{ZCZ}^*[\widetilde{E}]$ in Algorithm 3.

```
10: function ZCZ[Ẽ_K](M)                          50: procedure LastTopEnc[Ẽ_K](X_L, X_R)
11:     r ← |M| mod 2n                            51:     S ← Ẽ_K^{t$,ℓ,R_ℓ+X_R}(L_ℓ + X_L)
12:     ℓ ← (|M| − r)/2n                          52:     T ← Ẽ_K^{s$,ℓ,S}(R_ℓ + X_R)
13:     z ← ⌈(ℓ−1)/n⌉
14:     L'_* ← ε; R'_* ← ε                        60: procedure BotEnc[Ẽ_K]
15:     Parse(M, ℓ)                               61:     Y_L^* ← 0^n
16:     TopEnc[Ẽ_K]()                             62:     Y_R^* ← 0^n
17:     if r > 0 then                             63:     for i ← 1 . . . z − 1 do
18:         ┌PartialTopEnc[Ẽ_K]()┐                64:         for j ← 1 . . . n do
19:     LastTopEnc[Ẽ_K](X_L, X_R)                 65:             k ← (i − 1)n + j
20:     MidLayer[Ẽ_K](S, T)                       66:             L'_k ← X_k + Z_{i,j}
21:     BotEnc[Ẽ_K]()                             67:             Y_k ← R_k + Z_{i,j} + S_i
22:     LastBotEnc[Ẽ_K](Y_L, Y_R)                 68:             R'_k ← Ẽ_K^{b,k,L'_k}(Y_k)
23:     if r > 0 then                             69:             Y_L^* ← Y_L^* + (α^2)^{ℓ−1−k}(Y_k+L'_k)
24:         ┌PartialBotEnc[Ẽ_K]()┐                70:             Y_R^* ← Y_R^* + (α)^{ℓ−1−k}Y_k
25:     C                              ←          71:         for j ← 1 . . . ℓ − 1 − (z − 1)n do
            (L'_1‖R'_1‖ · · · ‖L'_ℓ‖R'_ℓ‖L'_*‖R'_*)   72:             k ← (z − 1)n + j
26:     return C                                  73:             L'_k ← X_k + Z_{z,j}
                                                  74:             Y_k ← R_k + Z_{z,j} + S_z
30: procedure TopEnc[Ẽ_K]                         75:             R'_k ← Ẽ_K^{b,k,L'_k}(Y_k)
31:     X_L^* ← X_R^* ← 0^n                       76:             Y_L^* ← Y_L^* + (α^2)^{ℓ−1−k}(Y_k + L'_k)
32:     for i ← 1 . . . ℓ − 1 do                  77:             Y_R^* ← Y_R^* + α^{ℓ−1−k}Y_k
33:         X_i ← Ẽ_K^{t,i,R_i}(L_i)              78:     Y_L ← Ẽ_K^{yl,ℓ,Y_R^*}(Y_L^*)
34:         X_L^* ← X_L^* + α^{ℓ−1−i}X_i          79:     Y_R ← Ẽ_K^{yr,ℓ,Y_L^*}(Y_R^*)
35:         X_R^* ← X_R^* + (α^2)^{ℓ−1−i}(X_i +
                R_i)                              80: procedure LastBotEnc[Ẽ_K](Y_L, Y_R)
36:     X_L ← Ẽ_K^{xl,ℓ,X_R^*}(X_L^*)            81:     L'_ℓ ← Ẽ_K^{c$,ℓ,T}(S) + Y_L
37:     X_R ← Ẽ_K^{xr,ℓ,X_L^*}(X_R^*)            82:     R'_ℓ ← Ẽ_K^{b$,ℓ,T}(L'_ℓ + Y_L) + Y_R

40: procedure MidLayer[Ẽ_K](S, T)                90: procedure Parse(M, ℓ)
41:     S_0 ← S                                   91:     i ← ℓ · 2n
42:     for i ← 1 . . . z do                      92:     (L_1,R_1,· · · ,L_ℓ,R_ℓ) ←ⁿ M[0..i − 1]
43:         S_i ← Ẽ_K^{s,0,i}(S_{i−1})            93:     if r > 0 then
44:     for i ← 1 . . . z do                      94:         (L_*, R_*) ←ⁿ M[i..|M|]
45:         for j ← 1 . . . n do
46:             Z_{i,j} ← Ẽ_K^{c,(i−1)n+j,T}(S_i)
```

5 ZCZ* for Messages with Partial Final Di-block

We extend the definition of ZCZ to messages whose length is not a multiple of $2n$ bits. We denote the last $r \leftarrow |M| \bmod 2n$ bits as *partial di-block*. Our approach for ZCZ* is inspired by the DE domain extender from [25]. Therefore, we briefly recap it.

THE DOMAIN EXTENDER DE$[\Pi, F, H] : \{0,1\}^{\geq n} \to \{0,1\}^{\geq n}$ [25] takes a blockwise-operating length-preserving permutation $\Pi : (\{0,1\}^n)^+ \to (\{0,1\}^n)^+$, a

Algorithm 3. Functions of the encryption algorithm of $\mathrm{ZCZ}^*[\widetilde{E}]$ for messages whose length is not necessarily a multiple of $2n$ bit (but at least $2n$ bit). Recall that $r = |M| \bmod 2n$.

10: **procedure** PARTIALTOPENC[$\widetilde{E}_K$]	40: **procedure** PARTIALBOTENC[$\widetilde{E}_K$]
11: $M_\ell \leftarrow L_\ell \,\|\, R_\ell$	41: $(P, Q) \leftarrow \mathcal{H}[\widetilde{E}_K, 2](L_\ell + L_\ell', R_\ell + R_\ell')$
12: $M_* \leftarrow \mathsf{pad}_{2n}(L_* \,\|\, R_*)$	42: $W \leftarrow \mathsf{msb}_r(P \,\|\, Q) \,\|\, 0^{2n-r}$
13: $(\overline{L}_*, \overline{R}_*) \xleftarrow{n} M_*$	43: $(P_*, Q_*) \xleftarrow{n} W$
14: $(U_\ell, V_\ell) \leftarrow \mathcal{H}[\widetilde{E}_K, 0](\overline{L}_*, \overline{R}_*)$	44: $L_*' \leftarrow L_* + P_*$
15: $L_\ell \leftarrow L_\ell + U_\ell$	45: $R_*' \leftarrow R_* + Q_*$
16: $R_\ell \leftarrow R_\ell + V_\ell$	46: $(\overline{L}_*', \overline{R}_*') \xleftarrow{n} \mathsf{pad}_{2n}(L_*' \,\|\, R_*')$
	47: $(U_\ell', V_\ell') \leftarrow \mathcal{H}[\widetilde{E}_K, 4](\overline{L}_*', \overline{R}_*')$
20: **function** $\mathsf{msb}_x(X)$	48: $L_\ell' \leftarrow L_\ell' + U_\ell'$
21: **return** $X[0..x-1]$	49: $R_\ell' \leftarrow R_\ell' + V_\ell'$
	50: **function** $\mathcal{H}[\widetilde{E}_K, i](U, V)$
30: **function** $\mathsf{pad}_x(X)$	51: $U' \leftarrow \widetilde{E}_K^{\mathsf{p},i,V}(U)$
31: **return** $X \,\|\, 1 \,\|\, 0^{x-|X|-1}$	52: $V' \leftarrow \widetilde{E}_K^{\mathsf{p},i+1,V}(U)$
	53: **return** (U', V')

PRF $F : \{0,1\}^n \to \{0,1\}^n$, and an XOR-universal hash function $H : \{0,1\}^n \times \{0,1\}^{2n} \to \{0,1\}^n$. It produces a length-preserving permutation over bit strings of any length $\geq n$ bits. A message $M \in \{0,1\}^{\geq 2n}$ is split into blocks $(M_1, \ldots, M_\ell)$; $\mathrm{DE}[\Pi, F, H]$ computes the corresponding ciphertext $C = (C_1, \ldots, C_\ell)$ as: (1) $M_{\ell-1}^* \leftarrow H(M_{\ell-1}, M_\ell)$, (2) $(C_1, \ldots, C_{\ell-2}, C_{\ell-1}^*) \leftarrow \Pi(M_1, \ldots, M_{\ell-2}, M_{\ell-1}^*)$, (3) $C_\ell \leftarrow F(M_{\ell-1}^* + C_{\ell-1}^*) +_{|M_\ell|} M_\ell$, and (4) $C_{\ell-1} \leftarrow H(C_{\ell-1}^*, C_\ell)$. Where

$$x +_n y \stackrel{\mathrm{def}}{=} \mathsf{msb}_n(x) + y$$

for any $x, y \in \{0,1\}^*$ and integer n. To obtain that DE is a permutation, the hash function H must satisfy $H(H(M_{\ell-1}, M_\ell), M_\ell) = M_{\ell-1}$ for any allowed input $M_{\ell-1}$, M_ℓ (see [25, Remark 2]).

OVERVIEW OF ZCZ^*. Our extension ZCZ^* requires that the message length is still at least $2n$ bits. Let $M_* = (L_*, R_*)$ be the partial message di-block that follows after ℓ complete di-blocks. Further assume that the partial di-block consists of $\geq n$ bits that are split into $|L_*| = n$ and $|R_*| < n$. The right part is padded to n bits by a single 1 and as many zero bits as necessary to extend it to n bits: $\overline{R}_* \leftarrow \mathsf{pad}_n(R_*)$. The values are given as inputs to a hash function $\mathcal{H}[\widetilde{E}_K, i]$, with $i = 0$, that is illustrated on the right side of Fig. 3. $\{H\}$ uses one of the two n-bit values as state and the other one as tweak input for two calls to $\widetilde{E}_K$ under distinct tweaks: $U' \leftarrow \widetilde{E}_K^{\mathsf{p},i,V}(U)$ and $V' \leftarrow \widetilde{E}_K^{\mathsf{p},i+1,V}(U)$. The $2n$-bit output (U', V') is added to the final complete di-block. The resulting final di-block (L_ℓ, R_ℓ) is then processed by $\mathrm{ZCZ}[\widetilde{E}_K]$. The sum of $(L_\ell, R_\ell) + (L_\ell', R_\ell')$ is then given again into $\mathcal{H}[\widetilde{E}_K, i]$, with $i = 2$ to produce a $2n$-bit value (P_ℓ', Q_ℓ'). The most significant r bits of it are added to the final partial di-block to obtain the partial ciphertext di-block M_*'. M_*' is again padded to $2n$ bits and given

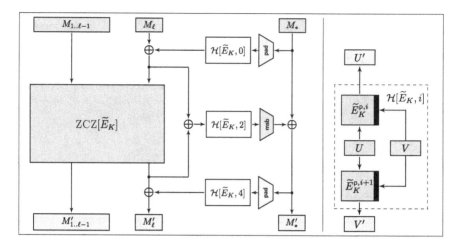

Fig. 3. Encryption of a partial message $M_1, \ldots, M_\ell, M^*$ whose length is not a multiple of $2n$ bit with $ZCZ^*[\widetilde{E}_K]$. All preceeding di-blocks $M_1, \ldots, M_\ell$ are processed with $ZCZ[\widetilde{E}_K]$ as before.

as input to a third call to $\mathcal{H}[\widetilde{E}_K, i]$, with $i = 4$. The hash output is added to the final ciphertext di-block to produce M_ℓ'. If the partial di-block consists of less than n bits, it is also padded to $2n$ bits and processed analogously. So, the hash function H from the original definition of $DE[\Pi, F, H]$ is given by $H(M_\ell, M_*) \stackrel{\text{def}}{=} M_\ell + \mathcal{H}[\widetilde{E}_K, i](\text{pad}_{2n}(M_*))$. One can see that the requirement from above holds for arbitrary M_ℓ and M_*: $H\left(H\left(M_\ell, M_*\right), M_*\right) = M_\ell$.

Remark 2. Note that ZCZ^* still requires messages to consist of at least $2n$ bits. A further minor improvement in future work could be the integration of smaller messages. For instance, the use of the very recent length-doubling construction LDT [7] could reduce the minimal message length to $n + 1$ bits. Though, this step would require an appropriate integration and ZCZ^* is already a variable-input-length SPRP for lengths $\geq 2n$ bit.

6   Security Analysis of ZCZ and ZCZ*

This section studies the SPRP security of ZCZ and ZCZ*. Figure 4 provides a high-level overview on ZCZ. A given message M is split an input message into (M_L, M_R), where M_R consists of one $2n$-bit di-block, and M_L of the remaining di-blocks; the major part M_L is then processed by a variant of ZHASH, that is denoted ZHASH* here. It differs from ZHASH in two aspects: ZHASH* omits the XOR of the TBC output to the tweak input blocks. More prominently, ZHASH* does not compress the input to two hash values, but is a permutation over $(n + \tau)^*$. So, the top layer returns the TBC outputs and the tweaks. $\widetilde{V}_1$ and $\widetilde{V}_2$ represent tweakable permutations. Internally, they can use the same primitive

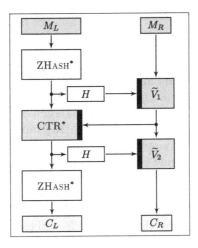

Fig. 4. High-level view on our proposal of ZCZ.

as also for ZHASH*, and the tweakable variant of Counter mode, CTR*. H symbolizes an error-correcting code that sums up the inputs to $2n$ bits.

This high-level view allows to give a rationale for a dedicated analysis. A straight-forward use of a rate-1 counter mode would allow to apply a standard generic proof as for HCTR. Though, such an approach would yield 2ℓ calls to the primitive alone in the counter mode. In combination with ZHASH*, this approach would need 4ℓ calls to the primitive for messages of 2ℓ blocks. ZCZ considers a special variant of counter mode that uses only ℓ blocks of entropy to mask 2ℓ blocks, similar as has been used in AEZ from version 2 [12]. However, this counter mode disallows to simply adopt the analysis from HCTR-like constructions when the goal is showing n-bit security. So, a dedicated analysis is needed, which is a major contribution of the present work. In the following, we study the security of the basic construction before we consider the extensions for inputs whose length is not necessarily a multiple of $2n$ bits, but at least $2n$ bits. We show the security of the extension ZCZ* at the end of this section.

6.1 Security of the Basic Construction

Theorem 1. Let $\widetilde{\pi} \twoheadleftarrow \widetilde{\mathsf{Perm}}(\mathcal{T}_{D,I}, \{0,1\}^n)$. Let $\mathbf{A}$ be an SPRP adversary on ZCZ$[\widetilde{\pi}]$, s.t. $\mathbf{A}$ asks at most q queries of domain $\mathcal{B}^{\leq n}$, that sum up to at most σ di-blocks in total. Then

$$\mathbf{Adv}_{\mathrm{ZCZ}[\widetilde{\pi}]}^{\mathrm{SPRP}}(\mathbf{A}) \leq \frac{3\sigma^2 + 9q^2}{2N^2}.$$

Proof. The queries 1 through q by $\mathbf{A}$ are collected in a transcript τ where we define two disjoint sets of indices E and D s.t. $[1..q] = E \sqcup D$, and it holds that E consists of exactly those indices i s.t. the i-th query of $\mathbf{A}$ is an encryption query; similarly, D consists of exactly those indices i s.t. the i-th query of $\mathbf{A}$ is an decryption query. We define ℓ^i to be the number of di-blocks in the i-query, where $\ell^i \leq n$.

In both worlds, the adversary's queries are answered immediately with the corresponding outputs; certain internal parts of the transcript will be revealed to the adversary after it made all its queries, but before it outputs its decision bit that represents its guess of which world it interacted with. The internal parts consist of $S^i, T^i, S^i_1, X^i_L, X^i_R, Y^i_L, Y^i_R$ for $i \in [1..q]$ and $Z^i_{1,j}$ for $i \in [1..q], j \in [1..\ell^i - 1]$; for ease of notation, we write Z^i_j to refer to $Z^i_{1,j}$.

We will subsequently define certain transcripts to be *good*. More specifically, we describe a mechanism for the ideal oracle to sample the internal values to be given to the adversary at the end of the query phase, and define the event bad as the union of five events badA, badB, badC, badD and badE. We call a transcript good if it can be obtained by the ideal oracle without encountering the event bad. Now we state two lemmas.

Lemma 2. $\Pr\left[bad\right] \leq \dfrac{3\sigma^2 + 8q^2}{N^2}.$

Lemma 3. For any good transcript τ,

$$\frac{\Pr\left[\Theta_{\mathrm{real}} = \tau\right]}{\Pr\left[\Theta_{\mathrm{ideal}} = \tau\right]} \geq 1 - \frac{q^2}{N^2}.$$

Then, the proof follows from Lemmas 1, 2, and 3.   □

For proving Lemmas 2 and 3, we first define the sampling mechanism of the ideal oracle and the bad events.

EQUATIONS. First, we write the internal variables X^i_j, Y^i_j for $i \in [1..q], j \in [1..\ell^i]$ and $U^i_L, U^i_R, V^i_L, V^i_R$ for $i \in [1..q]$ in terms of $S^i, T^i, S^i_1, X^i_L, X^i_R, Y^i_L, Y^i_R, Z^i_j$:

$$X^i_j = L'^i_j + Z^i_j, \tag{1}$$
$$Y^i_j = R^i_j + Z^i_j + S^i_1,. \tag{2}$$

Moreover, we define four auxiliary variables to easier referral:

$$U^i_L = L^i_\ell + X^i_L, \tag{3}$$
$$U^i_R = R^i_\ell + X^i_R, \tag{4}$$
$$V^i_L = L'^i_\ell + Y^i_L, \tag{5}$$
$$V^i_R = R'^i_\ell + Y^i_R. \tag{6}$$

IDENTIFYING A BASIS. A basis is the set of variables (internal to the constructions) which can be sampled uniformly and independently in the ideal oracles after fixing the inputs and outputs that are known to adversary. By looking at the construction and eliminating the relationships between the internal variables, plaintexts, and ciphertexts, some internal variables can be chosen almost freely, and still the real construction will behave indistinguishable from the ideal world for the adversary even after observing the plain- and ciphertexts. We call those variables a basis. For $i \in [1..q], j \in [1..\ell^i]$, we define (i, j) to be *fresh* if either of the following is true:

- $i \in E$, and for any $i' \in [1..i-1]$: $(L_j^{i'}, R_j^{i'}) \neq (L_j^i, R_j^i)$;
- $i \in D$, and for any $i' \in [1..i-1]$: $(L_j'^{i'}, R_j'^{i'}) \neq (L_j'^i, R_j'^i)$.

For $i \in [2..q], i' \in [1..i-1]$, we say i is *akin* to i' if either of the following holds:

- $\ell^i = \ell^{i'}$, $i \in E$, and for any $j \in [1..\ell^i - 1]$: $(L_j^{i'}, R_j^{i'}) = (L_j^i, R_j^i)$;
- $\ell^i = \ell^{i'}$, $i \in D$, and for any $j \in [1..\ell^i - 1]$: $(L_j'^{i'}, R_j'^{i'}) = (L_j'^i, R_j'^i)$;

We say i is *new* if it is not akin to any $i' \in [1..i-1]$. Now we define the basis as follows: for $i \in [1..q]$,

- For $j \in [1..\ell^i - 1]$, Z_j^i is in the basis if (i, j) is fresh;
- X_L^i and X_R^i are in the basis if $i \in D$, or if $i \in E$ and i is new;
- Y_L^i and Y_R^i are in the basis if $i \in E$, or if $i \in D$ and i is new;
- S^i, T^i, and S_1^i are in the basis.

Let σ_F represent the total number of fresh pairs in the set $\{(i, j) \mid i \in [q], j \in [\ell^i - 1]\}$. Moreover, let q_ν be the total number of new queries in $[1..q]$. Then, the size of the basis is $\sigma_F + 2q_\nu + 5q$.

EXTENSION FROM BASIS. Now we show how all the internal variables X_j^i, Y_j^i for $i \in [1..q], j \in [1..\ell^i]$ and $U_L^i, U_R^i, V_L^i, V_R^i$ for $i \in [1..q]$ can be written in terms of basis variables. Since we have already seen how to write them in terms of $S^i, T^i, S_1^i, X_L^i, X_R^i, Y_L^i, Y_R^i$ for $i \in [1..q]$ and Z_j^i for $i \in [1..q], j \in [1..\ell^i - 1]$, and S^i, T^i, S_1^i for $i \in [1..q]$ are already in the basis, it suffices to show that Z_j^i for $i \in [1..q], j \in [1..\ell^i - 1]$ and $X_L^i, X_R^i, Y_L^i, Y_R^i$ for $i \in [1..q]$ can be written in terms of basis variables. An expression of an internal variable in terms of basis variables and the oracle inputs and outputs will be called the *extension expression* of the basis variable. Thus, whenever we sample all the basis elements, we can extend this through these equations to assign values to all the internal variables.

For $i \in E, j \in [1..\ell^i]$, let i' be such that (i', j) is fresh, and $(L_j^{i'}, R_j^{i'}) = (L_j^i, R_j^i)$. Then, i' is called the *j-predecessor* of i, denoted $i : j$. Similarly, for $i \in D, j \in [1..\ell^i]$, if for some i' we have (i', j) fresh and $(L_j'^{i'}, R_j'^{i'}) = (L_j'^i, R_j'^i)$, we set $i : j = i'$. (Thus, when (i, j) is fresh, $i : j$ is i itself.) For $i \in E, j \in [1..\ell^i]$ we have from (1) that $X_j^i = X_j^{i:j} = L_j'^{i:j} + Z_j^{i:j}$, so

$$Z_j^i = L_j'^{i:j} + L_j'^i + Z_j^{i:j}; \tag{7}$$

and for $i \in D, j \in [1..\ell^i]$ we have from (2)

$$Y_j^i = Y_j^{i:j} = R_j^{i:j} + Z_j^{i:j} + S_j^{i:j},$$

so

$$Z_j^i = R_j^{i:j} + R_j^i + Z_j^{i:j} + S_1^{i:j} + S_1^i. \tag{8}$$

Now if i and $i : j$ are both in E or both in D, $Z_j^{i:j}$ is a basis element. (In particular, when $i : j = i$, Z_j^i is a basis element.) Otherwise, we can go back one step further to $(i : j) : j$, the j-predecessor of $i : j$, denoted $i : j^2$. We call (1) and (2) the *extension equations*. They will serve useful in the later proofs. Note that it does not hold in general that $(i : j) : j = i : j$. This holds only if $i : j$ and i are both in E or both in D, or when $i : j$ points to a fresh input block.

For $i \in [2..q]$, the smallest query index in $[1..i-1]$ which i is akin to is called the *origin* of i, denoted $\bar{i}$. We also define the origin of 1 to be 1 itself. Thus, for $i \in E$,

$$X_L^i = X_L^{\bar{i}}, \tag{9}$$
$$X_R^i = X_R^{\bar{i}}; \tag{10}$$

and for $i \in D$,

$$Y_L^i = Y_L^{\bar{i}}, \tag{11}$$
$$Y_R^i = Y_R^{\bar{i}}. \tag{12}$$

Since for $i \in E$, $X_L^{\bar{i}}$ and $X_R^{\bar{i}}$ are in the basis, and for $i \in D$, $Y_L^{\bar{i}}$ and $Y_R^{\bar{i}}$ are in the basis, this completes the extensions.

ORACLES AND BAD EVENTS. The real oracle employs $\mathsf{ZCZ}[\tilde{\pi}]$ to answer the queries of $\mathbf{A}$. In the ideal world, the encryption oracle samples and returns $L_j'^i, R_j'^i$ for $i \in E, j \in [1..\ell^i]$ uniformly at random; the decryption oracle samples and returns L_j^i, R_j^i for $i \in D$, $j \in [1..\ell^i]$ uniformly at random. Once the interaction phase is over, the ideal world oracle samples and returns each basis element uniformly at random from $\{0,1\}^n$, with two exceptions:

– For $i \in E$, S^i is drawn uniformly from the set
  $\{0,1\}^n \setminus \left\{ S^{i'} \mid i \text{ is akin to } i', R^i = R^{i'} \right\}$;
– For $i \in D$, T^i is drawn uniformly from the set
  $\{0,1\}^n \setminus \left\{ T^{i'} \mid i \text{ is akin to } i', L'^i = L'^{i'} \right\}$.

The real world releases the values of the basis variables to the adversary. (Thus, from the extension equations, $\mathbf{A}$ can calculate the values of the inputs, tweaks, and outputs of all internal TBC calls.) $\mathbf{A}$ shall distinguish the real world $\mathcal{O}_{\text{real}}$

from the ideal world $\mathcal{O}_{\text{ideal}}$, given a transcript τ of its interaction with the available oracles. We say that the event bad occurs when one of the following occurs:

- badA occurs when one of the following holds:
  - For some $i \in E, j \in [1..\ell^i]$, there exists $i' \in [1..i-1]$ with $\ell^{i'} \geq j$ such that $(L_j'^{i'}, R_j'^{i'}) = (L_j'^i, R_j'^i)$;
  - For some $i \in D, j \in [1..\ell^i]$, there exists $i' \in [1..i-1]$ with $\ell^{i'} \geq j$ such that $(L_j^{i'}, R_j^{i'}) = (L_j^i, R_j^i)$;
- badB occurs when for some $i \in [2..q]$ there exists $i' \in [1..i-1]$ with $\ell^i = \ell^{i'}$ such that one of the following holds:
  - $(U_L^i, U_R^i) = (U_L^{i'}, U_R^{i'})$;
  - $(S^i, U_R^i) = (S^{i'}, U_R^{i'})$;
  - $(S^i, T^i) = (S^{i'}, T^{i'})$;
  - $(V_L^i, T^i) = (V_L^{i'}, T^{i'})$;
  - $(V_L^i, V_R^i) = (V_L^{i'}, V_R^{i'})$;
- badC occurs when one of the following holds:
  - For some $i \in [1..q]$, there exists $i' \in [1..i-1]$ such that $(S_1^i, T^i) = (S_1^{i'}, T^{i'})$;
  - For some $i \in [1..q], j \in [1..\ell^i-1]$, there exists $i' \in [1..i-1]$ with $\ell^{i'} \geq j+1$ such that $(Z_j^i, T^i) = (Z_j^{i'}, T^{i'})$;
- badD occurs when one of the following holds:
  - For some $i \in E, j \in [1..\ell^i - 1]$, there exists $i' \in [1..i-1]$ with $\ell^{i'} \geq j+1$ such that $(L_j'^i, Y_j^i) = (L_j'^{i'}, Y_j^{i'})$;
  - For some $i \in D, j \in [1..\ell^i - 1]$, there exists $i' \in [1..i-1]$ with $\ell^{i'} \geq j+1$ such that $(R_j^i, X_j^i) = (R_j^{i'}, X_j^{i'})$;
- badE occurs when for some $i \in [2..q]$, there exists $i' \in [1..i-1]$ such that i is not akin to i' and yet one of the following holds:
  - $(X_L^{*i}, X_R^{*i}) = (X_L^{*i'}, X_R^{*i'})$;
  - $(Y_L^{*i}, Y_R^{*i}) = (Y_L^{*i'}, Y_R^{*i'})$;

Thus, bad $\stackrel{\text{def}}{=}$ badA $\vee$ badB $\vee$ badC $\vee$ badD $\vee$ badE. Clearly,

$$\Pr[\text{bad}] \leq \Pr[\text{badA}] + \Pr[\text{badB}] + \Pr[\text{badC}] + \Pr[\text{badD}] + \Pr[\text{badE}]. \qquad (13)$$

Now, we are in a position to prove Lemmas 2 and 3.

Proof of Lemma 2. Below, we show that each of the collision-pairs that would result in one of the bad events has a joint probability of $\leq 1/N^2$. Clearly, we need the assumption that all basis elements are uniformly sampled from $\{0,1\}^n$ for this purpose. Moreover, the values S^i and T^i are sampled without replacement under certain circumstances, their bound is at most $1/N(N-1)$, which can be upper bounded by $1/N(N-1) < 2/N^2$. Thus, for bounding the bad events, we simply need to bound the number of candidate collision-pairs.

For badA, there can be:

- at most $\sigma_E^2/2$ collision events of the form $(L_j'^{i'}, R_j'^{i}) = (L_j'^{i}, R_j'^{i})$;
- at most $\sigma_D^2/2$ collision events of the form $(L_j^{i'}, R_j^{i'}) = (L_j^{i}, R_j^{i})$;

where σ_E is the total number of encryption query blocks and σ_D is the total number of decryption query blocks, so that $\sigma_E^2 + \sigma_D^2 \leq \sigma^2$. Thus

$$\Pr[\mathsf{badA}] \leq \frac{\sigma^2}{N^2}. \tag{14}$$

For badB, there can be:

- at most $q^2/2$ collision events of the form $(U_L^i, U_R^i) = (U_L^{i'}, U_R^{i'})$;
- at most $q^2/2$ collision events of the form $(S^i, U_R^i) = (S^{i'}, U_R^{i'})$;
- at most $q^2/2$ collision events of the form $(S^i, T^i) = (S^{i'}, T^{i'})$;
- at most $q^2/2$ collision events of the form $(V_L^i, T^i) = (V_L^{i'}, T^{i'})$;
- at most $q^2/2$ collision events of the form $(V_L^i, V_R^i) = (V_L^{i'}, V_R^{i'})$;

Thus

$$\Pr[\mathsf{badB}] \leq \frac{5q^2}{N^2}. \tag{15}$$

For badC, there can be:

- at most $q^2/2$ collision events of the form $(S_1^i, T^i) = (S_1^{i'}, T^{i'})$.
- at most $\sigma^2/2$ collision events of the form $(Z_j^i, T^i) = (Z_j^{i'}, T^{i'})$;

Thus

$$\Pr[\mathsf{badC}] \leq \frac{q^2 + \sigma^2}{N^2}. \tag{16}$$

For badD, there can be:

- at most $\sigma_E^2/2$ collision events of the form $(L_j'^{i}, Y_j^i) = (L_j'^{i'}, Y_j^{i'})$;
- at most $\sigma_D^2/2$ collision events of the form $(R_j^i, X_j^i) = (R_j^{i'}, X_j^{i'})$.

Thus

$$\Pr[\mathsf{badD}] \leq \frac{\sigma^2}{N^2}. \tag{17}$$

For badE, there can be:

- at most $q^2/2$ collision events of the form $(X_L^{*i}, X_R^{*i}) = (X_L^{*i'}, X_R^{*i'})$;
- at most $q^2/2$ collision events of the form $(Y_L^{*i}, Y_R^{*i}) = (Y_L^{*i'}, Y_R^{*i'})$.

Thus

$$\Pr[\mathsf{badE}] \leq \frac{2q^2}{N^2}. \tag{18}$$

The lemma follows from (13)–(18).

Now, all that is left to do is to establish our claim that each of the collision-pairs that would result in one of the bad events has a joint probability $\leq 1/N^2$.

This is to be done by examining each bad event separately. badA, badB and badC are fairly straightforward, and we leave out the proofs. badD is more interesting; we provide below a complete analysis of it. The trickiest case is badE; here, due to space constraints, we only examine two of its main subcases in detail. The complete case-by-case analysis, along with a short analysis of badA, badB and badC, can be found in the Appendix of the full version [4].

FULL ANALYSIS OF badD. We consider the two cases separately:

- $(L_j^{\prime i}, Y_j^i) = (L_j^{\prime i'}, Y_j^{i'})$, $i \in E$, $i' < i$: We will show that $Y_j^i = Y_j^{i'}$ always leads to an equation containing at least one basis variable that cannot get canceled out. The required bound follows since the basis variable and $L_j^{\prime i}$ are independently sampled. From (2) we have

$$R_j^i + Z_j^i + S_1^i = R_j^{i'} + Z_j^{i'} + S_1^{i'}. \tag{19}$$

Note that S_1^i cannot occur in the expansion of $Z_j^{i:j}$, since $i \in E$. Now we have two options of i':

• $i' \in E$: From (7) and (19) we have

$$R_j^i + L_j^{\prime i:j} + L_j^{\prime i} + Z_j^{i:j} + S_1^i = R_j^{i'} + L_j^{\prime i':j} + L_j^{\prime i'} + Z_j^{i':j} + S_1^{i'}.$$

Here the basis element S_1^i cannot be canceled out, since $i' < i$.

• $i' \in D$: From (7), (8) and (19), we have

$$R_j^i + L_j^{\prime i:j} + L_j^{\prime i} + Z_j^{i:j} + S_1^i = R_j^{i'} + R_j^{i':j} + R_j^{i'} + Z_j^{i':j} + S_1^{i':j}.$$

Again, the basis element S_1^i cannot be canceled out since $i' : j \le i' < i$.

- $(R_j^i, X_j^i) = (R_j^{i'}, X_j^{i'})$, $i \in D$, $i' < i$: As above, we show that $X_j^i = X_j^{i'}$ always leads to an equation containing at least one basis variable that cannot get canceled out, and the required bound follows since the basis variable and R_j^i are independently sampled. From (1), we have

$$L_j^{\prime i} + Z_j^i = L_j^{\prime i'} + Z_j^{i'}. \tag{20}$$

Now, we have two options of i':

• $i' \in E$: From (8), (7) and (20), we have

$$L_j^{\prime i} + R_j^{i:j} + R_j^i + Z_j^{i:j} + S_1^{i:j} + S_1^i = L_j^{\prime i':j} + Z_j^{i':j}.$$

When $i : j < i$, the basis element S_1^i cannot be canceled out, and when $i = i : j$, we have $i' : j \le i' < i = i : j$, so the basis element $Z_j^{i:j} = Z_j^i$ cannot be canceled out.

• $i' \in D$: From (8) and (19), we have

$$L_j^{\prime i} + R_j^{i:j} + R_j^i + Z_j^{i:j} + S_1^{i:j} + S_1^i = L_j^{\prime i'} + R_j^{i':j} + R_j^{i'} + Z_j^{i':j} + S_1^{i':j} + S_1^{i'},$$

Here again, either S_1^i or the basis element Z_j^i cannot be canceled out, and the argument is identical to the above.

PARTIAL ANALYSIS OF badE. This is trickier than the other bad events, and requires some careful case analysis. We examine the two most difficult sub-cases here. Let $i' < i$ and $\ell \stackrel{\text{def}}{=} \ell^{i'} = \ell^i$, and let $\alpha_j(\cdot)$ and $\alpha_j^2(\cdot)$ be linear functions defined as

$$\alpha_j(x) \stackrel{\text{def}}{=} \alpha^{\ell-1-j} \cdot x \quad \text{and} \quad \alpha_j^2(x) \stackrel{\text{def}}{=} (\alpha^2)^{\ell-1-j} \cdot x.$$

Both the sub-cases we examine here fall under the case of $(X_L^{*i}, X_R^{*i}) = (X_L^{*i'}, X_R^{*i'})$. We can write this collision as

$$\sum_{j=0}^{\ell-1} \alpha_j(X_j^i + X_j^{i'}) = 0 \quad \text{and} \quad \sum_{j=0}^{\ell-1} \alpha_j^2(X_j^i + X_j^{i'}) = \sum_{j=0}^{\ell-1} \alpha_j^2(R_j^i + R_j^{i'}).$$

Using (1) we can rewrite these as

$$\sum_{j=0}^{\ell-1} \alpha_j(Z_j^i + Z_j^{i'}) = \sum_{j=0}^{\ell-1} \alpha_j(L_j'^i + L_j'^{i'}), \tag{21}$$

$$\sum_{j=0}^{\ell-1} \alpha_j^2(Z_j^i + Z_j^{i'}) = \sum_{j=0}^{\ell-1} \alpha_j^2(L_j'^i + L_j'^{i'} + R_j^i + R_j^{i'}). \tag{22}$$

We first observe that since i is not akin to i', $X_j^i + X_j^{i'}$ cannot trivially disappear for all $j \in [1, .., \ell - 1]$. Also, since $\alpha_j(X_j^i + X_j^{i'})$ sum to 0, there must be at least two indices in $[1, .., \ell - 1]$ where $X_j^i + X_j^{i'}$ does not trivially disappear; let j_0 and j_1 be the two largest such indices, with $j_0 > j_1$. Now, we first consider the sub-case $i \in E, i' \in E$. From (7), (21) and (22) we have

$$\sum_{j=0}^{\ell-1} \alpha_j(Z_j^{i:j} + Z_j^{i':j}) = \sum_{j=0}^{\ell-1} \alpha_j(L_j'^{i:j} + L_j'^{i':j}), \tag{23}$$

$$\sum_{j=0}^{\ell-1} \alpha_j^2(Z_j^{i:j} + Z_j^{i':j}) = \sum_{j=0}^{\ell-1} \alpha_j^2(L_j'^{i:j} + L_j'^{i':j} + R_j^{i:j} + R_j^{i':j}). \tag{24}$$

By choice of j_0, $i : j_0 \neq i' : j_0$. Suppose $i : j_0 > i' : j_0$. If $i : j_0 \in D$, using (8), we replace $Z_{j_0}^{i:j_0}$ by $R_{j_0}^{i:j_0^2} + R_{j_0}^{i:j_0} + Z_{j_0}^{i:j_0^2} + S_1^{i:j_0^2} + S_1^{i:j_0}$. The basis element $S_1^{i:j_0}$ does not get canceled out; moreover, $R_{j_0}^{i:j_0}$ remains only in the top equation, while it gets canceled out in the bottom equation. Since $i : j = i' : j$ for all $j > j_0$, none of the adversary-queried blocks remaining in either equation came after $R_{j_0}^{i:j_0}$, so it is independent of the rest of the equation; along with the basis element $S_1^{i:j_0}$ (which appears in both equations), this makes the two collisions independent, thus occurring jointly with a probability $1/N^2$.

If $i : j_0 \in E$, $Z_{j_0}^{i:j_0}$ is in the basis, and does not cancel out. On the right hand side of both equations, $L_{j_0}'^{i:j_0}$ remains uncanceled as well, while all later adversary queries get canceled. Thus, the two equations can become dependent with probability at most $1/N$; then, the common collision can occur with probability at most $1/N$. Thus, in either case, the joint collision can occur with a probability of more than $1/N^2$. The analysis is similar when $i : j_0 < i : j_0$; then we focus on the latter instead.

The other sub-case we consider is $i \in E, i' \in D$. From (7), (8), (21) and (22) we have

$$\sum_{j=0}^{\ell-1} \alpha_j(Z_j^{i:j} + Z_j^{i':j} + S_1^{i'} + S_1^{i':j}) = \sum_{j=0}^{\ell-1} \alpha_j(L_j^{'i:j} + L_j^{'i':j} + R_j^{i'} + R_j^{i':j}), \quad (25)$$

$$\sum_{j=0}^{\ell-1} \alpha_j^2(Z_j^{i:j} + Z_j^{i':j} + S_1^{i'} + S_1^{i':j}) = \sum_{j=0}^{\ell-1} \alpha_j^2(L_j^{'i:j} + L_j^{'i':j} + R_j^{i:j} + R_j^{i':j}). \quad (26)$$

By choice of j_0 and j_1, $i : j_0 \neq i'$ and $i : j_1 \neq i'$. Suppose $i : j_0 < i'$. Then $S_1^{i'}$ and $R_{j_0}^{i'}$ remain uncanceled in (25), and no adversary query block queried after $R_{j_0}^{i'}$ remains uncanceled; in (26), $S_1^{i'}$ remains uncanceled again, but there is no $R_{j_0}^{i'}$ and no adversary query block queried after it. Thus these two can occur jointly with a probability at most $1/N^2$.

A symmetric argument can be used when $i : j_0 > i'$ and $i : j_0 \in D$: we replace $Z_{j_0}^{i:j_0}$ by $R_{j_0}^{i:j_0} + R_{j_0}^{i:j_0} + Z_{j_0}^{i:j_0^2} + S_1^{i:j_0^2} + S_1^{i:j_0}$ using (8), and observe that $S_1^{i:j_0}$ remains uncanceled in either equation, while $R_{j_0}^{i:j_0}$ remains uncanceled in (25), but gets canceled out in (26), and no adversary query block queried after it remains in either equation.

When $i : j_0 > i'$ and $i : j_0 \in E$, but $i : j_1$ satisfied one of the above two conditions, we can argue as above using $i : j_1$ instead. If we also have $i : j_1 > i'$ and $i : j_1 \in E$, we observe that $Z_{j_0}^{i:j_0}$ and $Z_{j_1}^{i:j_1}$ are basis elements that do not get canceled out in either equation. Their combined contribution to the left-hand side of (25) is $\alpha^{\ell-1-j_0} \cdot Z_{j_0}^{i:j_0} + \alpha^{\ell-1-j_1} \cdot Z_{j_1}^{i:j_1}$ and to the left-hand side of (26) is $(\alpha^2)^{\ell-1-j_0} \cdot Z_{j_0}^{i:j_0} + (\alpha^2)^{\ell-1-j_1} \cdot Z_{j_1}^{i:j_1}$. These two collisions are independent since $\alpha^{\ell-1-j_0} \cdot (\alpha^2)^{\ell-1-j_1} \neq \alpha^{\ell-1-j_1} \cdot (\alpha^2)^{\ell-1-j_0}$, and thus can occur with a probability at most $1/N^2$. The rest of the subcases can be analysed similarly. This completes the proof of Lemma 2.   □

Proof of Lemma 3. Let τ be a good transcript, i.e., none of the events badA, badB, badC, badD, or badE occurred. Then, in the ideal world, there are 2σ samplings for generating the query responses and $\sigma_F + 2q_\nu + 5q$ for generating the basis elements. In the ideal world, the basis elements are sampled uniformly at random and independently from each other. Hence, the probability for those is given by $1/N^{\sigma_F + 2q_\nu + 5q}$. The situation differs for the outputs of the scheme. The ideal world is an ideal SPRP; hence, the outputs are sampled without replacement. Since all queries are from the domain $\mathcal{B}^{\leq n}$, we can group encryption and decryption queries into disjoint sets $\mathcal{L}^1, \ldots, \mathcal{L}^n$ s.t. their union contains all queries, and Set $\mathcal{L}^i$ contains exactly the queries of length i di-blocks. We define by LOAD $(\mathcal{L}^i)$ the number of queries in Set $\mathcal{L}^i$, for all $1 \leq i \leq n$.

The probability for ciphertext outputs from encryption queries and plaintext outputs from decryption queries is

$$\prod_{i=1}^{n} \frac{1}{(N^{2i})_{\text{LOAD}(\mathcal{L}^i)}}.$$

Since each query has at least $2n$ bits, we can lower bound the probability by

$$\prod_{i=1}^{n} \frac{1}{(N^{2i})_{\text{LOAD}(\mathcal{L}^i)}} \leq \frac{1}{(N^2)_{2q}} \cdot \frac{1}{N^{2\sigma-2q}}.$$

We obtain that

$$\Pr\left[\Theta_{\text{ideal}} = \tau\right] \leq \frac{1}{N^{\sigma_F + 2q_\nu + 3q + 2\sigma}} \cdot \frac{1}{(N^2)_q}. \tag{27}$$

In the real world, the construction employs a permutation $\widetilde{\pi}^{\mathsf{T}}(\cdot)$ for each tweak $\mathsf{T} \in \mathcal{T}_{\mathcal{D} \times \mathcal{I}}$ that was used in the transcript, . We write the set of all occurred tweaks of all di-blocks of all queries in the transcript and write it as $\{\mathsf{T}^1, \ldots, \mathsf{T}^\theta\}$. We further define by $\text{LOAD}(\mathsf{T})$ the load of a tweak T, i.e., the number of distinct inputs used for it over all queries and di-blocks of the transcript. It holds that $\sum_{i=1}^{\theta} \text{LOAD}(\mathsf{T}^i) = \sigma_F + 2\sigma + 2q_\nu + 5q$. We adopt the notion of transcript-compatible permutations from [6]. We call $\widetilde{\pi}$ *compatible* with τ if for all queries, $\widetilde{\pi}$ produced all intermediate variables as well as all outputs in τ. Let $\text{Comp}(\tau)$ denote the set of tweakable permutations $\widetilde{\pi}$ that are compatible with τ. Thus

$$\Pr\left[\Theta_{\text{real}} = \tau\right] = \Pr\left[\widetilde{\pi} \leftarrow \widetilde{\text{Perm}}\left(\mathcal{T}_{D,I}, \{0,1\}^n\right) : \widetilde{\pi} \in \text{Comp}(\tau)\right].$$

For a fixed tweak T, the fraction of compatible permutations is

$$\prod_{i=0}^{\text{LOAD}(\mathsf{T})-1} \frac{1}{N-i} = \frac{1}{(N)_{\text{LOAD}(\mathsf{T})}}.$$

Over all tweaks T^i, for $1 \leq i \leq \theta$, the fraction of compatible permutations is given by

$$\prod_{i=1}^{\theta} \frac{1}{(N)_{\text{LOAD}(\mathsf{T}^i)}}$$

It is hard to work with this probability directly. Instead, since we are interested in a bound for the real-world probability of transcripts, we can lower bound the probability of all $\sigma_F + 2q_\nu + 5q$ basis variables by the naive probability that they are all computed from fresh tweaks: $1/N^{\sigma_F + 2q_\nu + 5q}$. For the ciphertext and plaintext outputs, we can employ similar sets $\mathcal{L}^i$, for $1 \leq i \leq n$, as we had for the ideal world, where Set $\mathcal{L}^i$ again consists of all queries of length i di-blocks. The probability of outputs in the real world can then be lower bounded by

$$\prod_{i=1}^{n} \frac{1}{(N^{2i})_{\text{LOAD}(\mathcal{L}^i)}}.$$

Now, we can upper bound the ratio of the probability of our transcripts by

$$\frac{\Pr\left[\Theta_{\text{real}} = \tau\right]}{\Pr\left[\Theta_{\text{ideal}} = \tau\right]} \geq \frac{\frac{1}{N^{\sigma_F + 2q\nu + 5q}} \cdot \prod_{i=1}^{n} \frac{1}{(N^{2i})_{\text{LOAD}(\mathcal{L}^i)}}}{\frac{1}{N^{\sigma_F + 2q\nu + 5q}} \cdot \frac{1}{N^{2\sigma - 2q}} \cdot \frac{1}{(N^2)_q}}$$

$$\geq \frac{\prod_{i=1}^{n} \frac{1}{(N^{2i})_{\text{LOAD}(\mathcal{L}^i)}}}{\frac{1}{(N^2)_q} \cdot \frac{1}{N^{2\sigma - 2q}}} \geq \frac{(N^2)_q \cdot N^{2\sigma - 2q}}{N^{2\sigma}} = \frac{(N^2)_q}{(N^2)^q}$$

$$= \frac{(N^2)(N^2 - 1) \cdots \cdots (N^2 - q + 1)}{(N^2)^q} \geq \left(\frac{N^2 - q + 1}{N^2}\right)^q$$

$$\geq \left(\frac{N^2 - q}{N^2}\right)^q = \left(1 - \frac{q}{N^2}\right)^q \geq 1 - \frac{q^2}{N^2},$$

where the last inequality is Bernoulli's. So, we obtain our claim in Lemma 3. □

6.2 Proof Sketch for Messages with Arbitrary Number of Complete Di-blocks

Theorem 2. Let $\widetilde{\pi} \leftarrow \widetilde{\mathsf{Perm}}(\mathcal{T}_{D,I}, \{0,1\}^n)$. Let **A** be an SPRP adversary on $\mathsf{ZCZ}[\widetilde{\pi}]$ that asks at most q queries queries of domain $\mathcal{B}^+$, whose lengths sum up to at most σ di- blocks in total, and **A** runs in time at most TIME. Then

$$\mathbf{Adv}_{\mathsf{ZCZ}[\widetilde{\pi}]}^{\mathrm{SPRP}}(\mathbf{A}) \leq \frac{4\sigma^2 + 8q^2}{N^2}.$$

Proof Sketch. The proof follows a similar strategy as that of Theorem 1. So, we only consider the equations in the analysis of bad events that differ. We add each S_k^i, $i \in [1..q]$, $k \in \left[1.. \lceil \ell^i/n \rceil\right]$ to the basis. The ideal oracle samples the additional basis elements along with the original basis elements in the second step, and the definitions of the bad cases do not change. From the Eqs. (1)–(6) that we began with, only (2) is now replaced by

$$Y_j^i = R_j^i + Z_j^i + S_{\lceil j/n \rceil}^i. \tag{2'}$$

In the extension equations, this changes only (8), which is replaced by

$$Z_j^i = R_j^{i:j} + R_j^i + Z_j^{i:j} + S_{\lceil j/n \rceil}^{i:j} + S_{\lceil j/n \rceil}^i. \tag{8'}$$

The definitions of the bad cases remain the same except badC, which now occurs when:

- For some $i \in [1..q], k \in \left[1.. \lceil \ell^i/n \rceil\right]$, there exists $i' \in [1..i-1]$ with $\ell^{i'} \geq n(k-1)$ s.t. $(S_k^i, T^i) = (S_k^{i'}, T^{i'})$;
- For some $i \in [1..q], j \in [1..\ell^i - 1]$, there exists $i' \in [1..i-1]$ with $\ell^{i'} \geq j+1$ s.t. $(Z_{k,c}^i, T^i) = (Z_{k,c}^{i'}, T^{i'})$, where $k = \lceil j/n \rceil, c = j - n(k-1)$.

Of these, the counting does not change for the latter; for the former, there are now at most $c_{\max}q^2/2$ possible collision pairs now, where $c_{\max}$ is the maximum number of chunks in one query; we generously bound this by $\sigma^2/2$. This adds $(\sigma^2 - q^2)/2N$ to our earlier bound, to obtain the new bound for the extended version. To ensure that the counting argument for badE still goes through, we only note that for $k \in [1..\lceil \ell/n \rceil]$, S_k^i can only occur in any of the collision equations from badE with coefficients $\beta^{\ell-1-j}$ for $j \in [n(k-1)+1..nk]$, where β is either α or α^2, and for any choice of k, a non-empty subset of these coefficients cannot add to 0.

6.3   Proof Sketch for the Security of ZCZ*

Theorem 3. Let $\widetilde{\pi} \twoheadleftarrow \widetilde{\mathsf{Perm}}(\mathcal{T}_{D,I}, \{0,1\}^n)$. Let $\mathbf{A}$ be an SPRP adversary on ZCZ*$[\widetilde{\pi}]$ that asks at most q queries of domain $\{0,1\}^{\geq 2n}$, whose lengths sum up to at most σ di-blocks in total, q' of which contains an incomplete di-block at the end. Then

$$\mathbf{Adv}_{\mathrm{ZCZ}^*[\widetilde{\pi}]}^{\mathrm{SPRP}}(\mathbf{A}) \leq \frac{4\sigma^2 + 8q^2 + 9q'^2}{N^2}.$$

Proof Sketch. The ideal oracle's sampling mechanism for the tweakable blockcipher outputs for the partial di-block messages is slightly trickier. Let $\mathcal{I}$ denote the indices of the queries with incomplete di-blocks. Instead of simulating an ideal permutation, the ideal oracle simulates what [11] calls an $\pm$**rnd** oracle, which always returns random bits, as long as no pointless queries are asked. (It is easy to argue for our construction why not permitting pointless queries does not diminish the adversary's power, so we can confine our attention to the no-pointless-query scenario.)

We use the notation $(U,V), (U_m, V_m), (U', V')$ for outputs of the blockcipher calls in the top, middle, and bottom layers respectively. M_j denotes (L_j, R_j), and $*$ denotes the index of the incomplete di-block.

- For the smallest $i \in \mathcal{I}$, $U_*^i, V_*^i, U_*'^i, V_*^i$ are sampled uniformly from $\{0,1\}^n$;
- For each i in $\mathcal{I}$ such that for no i' in $\mathcal{I}$ with $i' < i$ we have $(L_*^i, R_*^i) \neq (L_*^{i'}, R_*^{i'})$:
  - U_*^i is sampled uniformly from $\{0,1\}^n \setminus \left\{ U_*^{i'} \mid i' \in \mathcal{I}, i' < i \right\}$;
  - V_*^i is sampled uniformly from $\{0,1\}^n \setminus \left\{ V_*^{i'} \mid i' \in \mathcal{I}, i' < i \right\}$;
- For each i in $\mathcal{I}$ such that for no i' in $\mathcal{I}$ with $i' < i$ we have $(L_*'^i, R_*'^i) \neq (L_*'^{i'}, R_*'^{i'})$:
  - $U_*'^i$ is sampled uniformly from $\{0,1\}^n \setminus \left\{ U_*'^{i'} \mid i' \in \mathcal{I}, i' < i \right\}$;
  - $V_*'^i$ is sampled uniformly from $\{0,1\}^n \setminus \left\{ V_*'^{i'} \mid i' \in \mathcal{I}, i' < i \right\}$;
- For each $i \in \mathcal{I}$ the $(2n-s)$-bit suffix R^i of (U_{m*}^i, V_{m*}^i) is sampled uniformly from $\{0,1\}^{2n-s}$, and (U_{m*}^i, V_{m*}^i) is set to $(M_*^i + M_*'^i) \| R^i$.

The new bad cases are:

- For some distinct i, i' in $\mathcal{I}$ with $\ell^i = \ell^{i'} = \ell$ we have

$$(M^i_{1..\ell-1}, M^i_\ell + (U^i_*, V^i_*)) = (M^{i'}_{1..\ell-1}, M^{i'}_\ell + (U^{i'}_*, V^{i'}_*));$$

- For some distinct i, i' in $\mathcal{I}$ with $\ell^i = \ell^{i'} = \ell$ we have

$$(M'^i_{1..\ell-1}, M'^i_\ell + (U'^i_*, V'^i_*)) = (M'^{i'}_{1..\ell-1}, M'^{i'}_\ell + (U'^{i'}_*, V'^{i'}_*));$$

- For some distinct i, i' in $\mathcal{I}$ with $\ell^i = \ell^{i'} = \ell$ we have

$$(L^i_\ell + L'^i_\ell + U^i_* + U'^i_*, R^i_\ell + R'^i_\ell + V^i_* + V'^i_*)$$
$$= (L^{i'}_\ell + L'^{i'}_\ell + U^{i'}_* + U'^{i'}_*, R^{i'}_\ell + R'^{i'}_\ell + V^{i'}_* + V'^{i'}_*);$$

- For some distinct i, i' in $\mathcal{I}$ with $\ell^i = \ell^{i'} = \ell$ we have

$$(R^i_\ell + R'^i_\ell + V^i_* + V'^i_*, U^i_{m*}) = (R^{i'}_\ell + R'^{i'}_\ell + V^{i'}_* + V'^{i'}_*, U^{i'}_{m*});$$

- For some distinct i, i' in $\mathcal{I}$ with $\ell^i = \ell^{i'} = \ell$ we have

$$(R^i_\ell + R'^i_\ell + V^i_* + V'^i_*, V^i_{m*}) = (R^{i'}_\ell + R'^{i'}_\ell + V^{i'}_* + V'^{i'}_*, V^{i'}_{m*}).$$

The probabilities of these bad cases can be bounded by $q'^2/2N'^2$, $q'^2/2N'^2$, $q'^2/2N'^2$, $q'^2/2NN'$, $q'^2/2NN'$ in that order, where $N' = N - q'$. With the reasonable assumption that $q' \leq N/2$, we can replace N' with $N/2$ in these bounds and have them sum to $8q'^2/N^2$, which is our bound for the combined probability of the new bad cases. The theorem follows from Theorem 2 and Lemma 6 of [11].

Our results in Theorems 1 and 3 had considered the instantiation with an ideal random tweaked permutation $\widetilde{\pi} \twoheadleftarrow \mathsf{Perm}(\mathcal{T}_{I,D}, \{0,1\}^n)$. Corollaries 1 and 2 yield the resulting security bounds when ZCZ and ZCZ* are instantiated with a given tweakable block cipher $\widetilde{E}_K : \mathcal{K} \times \mathcal{T}_{I,D} \times \{0,1\}^n \to \{0,1\}^n$ be a tweakable block cipher with $K \twoheadleftarrow \mathcal{K}$.

Corollary 1. Let $\mathbf{A}$ be an SPRP adversary on $\mathsf{ZCZ}[\widetilde{E}_K]$, s.t. $\mathbf{A}$ asks at most q queries of domain $\mathcal{B}^{\leq n}$, that sum up to at most σ di-blocks in total, and $\mathbf{A}$ runs in time at most TIME. Then

$$\mathbf{Adv}^{\mathrm{SPRP}}_{\mathsf{ZCZ}[\widetilde{E}_K]}(\mathbf{A}) \leq \frac{3\sigma^2 + 10q^2}{2N^2} + \mathbf{Adv}^{\mathrm{STPRP}}_{\widetilde{E}_K, \widetilde{E}_K^{-1}}(\mathbf{A}'),$$

where $\mathbf{A}'$ is an STPRP adversary against $\widetilde{E}_K$ that asks at most $a' = 3\sigma + \lceil \sigma/n \rceil + 6q$ queries and runs in time at most TIME $+ O(a')$.

364 R. Bhaumik et al.

Corollary 2. Let $\mathbf{A}$ be an SPRP adversary on $\mathrm{ZCZ}^*[\widetilde{E}_K]$ that asks at most q queries of domain $\{0,1\}^{\geq 2n}$, whose lengths sum up to at most σ di-blocks in total, q' of which contains an incomplete di-block at the end, and $\mathbf{A}$ runs in time at most TIME. Then

$$\mathbf{Adv}^{\mathrm{SPRP}}_{\mathrm{ZCZ}^*[\widetilde{E}_K]}(\mathbf{A}) \leq \frac{4\sigma^2 + 8q^2 + 9q'^2}{N^2} + \mathbf{Adv}^{\mathrm{STPRP}}_{\widetilde{E}_K, \widetilde{E}_K^{-1}}(\mathbf{A}'),$$

where $\mathbf{A}'$ is an STPRP adversary against $\widetilde{E}_K$ that asks at most $a' = 3\sigma + \lceil \sigma/n \rceil + 6q + 6q'$ queries and runs in time at most TIME $+ O(a')$.

Acknowledgments. The authors thank all anonymous reviewers for their fruitful comments that greatly helped to improve this work.

References

1. Beierle, C., et al.: The SKINNY family of block ciphers and its low-latency variant MANTIS. In: Robshaw, M., Katz, J. (eds.) CRYPTO 2016. LNCS, vol. 9815, pp. 123–153. Springer, Heidelberg (2016). https://doi.org/10.1007/978-3-662-53008-5_5
2. Bernstein, D.J.: Some challenges in heavyweight cipher design. Technical report, January 2016. https://cr.yp.to/talks/2016.01.15/slides-djb-20160115-a4.pdf
3. Bertoni, G., Daemen, J., Hoffert, S., Peeters, M., Assche, G.V., Keer, R.V.: Farfalle: parallel permutation-based cryptography. IACR Trans. Symmetric Cryptol. **2017**(4), 1–38 (2017)
4. Bhaumik, R., List, E., Nandi, M.: ZCZ - achieving n-bit SPRP security with a minimal number of tweakable-block-cipher calls. Cryptology ePrint Archive, Report 2018/819 (2018). http://eprint.iacr.org/2018/819
5. Biryukov, A., Daemen, J., Lucks, S., Vaudenay, S.: Topics and research directions for symmetric cryptography. In: Early Symmetric Crypto Workshop, vol. 2017 (2017). https://www.cryptolux.org/mediawiki-esc2017/images/9/9a/ASJS-Topics_SymCrypto-ESC17.pdf
6. Chen, S., Steinberger, J.: Tight security bounds for key-alternating ciphers. In: Nguyen, P.Q., Oswald, E. (eds.) EUROCRYPT 2014. LNCS, vol. 8441, pp. 327–350. Springer, Heidelberg (2014). https://doi.org/10.1007/978-3-642-55220-5_19
7. Chen, Y.L., Luykx, A., Mennink, B., Preneel, B.: Efficient length doubling from tweakable block ciphers. IACR Trans. Symmetric Cryptol. **2017**(3), 253–270 (2017)
8. Cogliati, B., Lee, J., Seurin, Y.: New constructions of MACs from (tweakable) block ciphers. IACR Trans. Symmetric Cryptol. **2017**, 27–58 (2017)
9. Coron, J.-S., Dodis, Y., Mandal, A., Seurin, Y.: A domain extender for the ideal cipher. In: Micciancio, D. (ed.) TCC 2010. LNCS, vol. 5978, pp. 273–289. Springer, Heidelberg (2010). https://doi.org/10.1007/978-3-642-11799-2_17
10. Gueron, S., Mouha, N.: Simpira v2: a family of efficient permutations using the AES round function. In: Cheon, J.H., Takagi, T. (eds.) ASIACRYPT 2016, part I. LNCS, vol. 10031, pp. 95–125. Springer, Heidelberg (2016). https://doi.org/10.1007/978-3-662-53887-6_4
11. Halevi, S., Rogaway, P.: A tweakable enciphering mode. In: Boneh, D. (ed.) CRYPTO 2003. LNCS, vol. 2729, pp. 482–499. Springer, Heidelberg (2003). https://doi.org/10.1007/978-3-540-45146-4_28

12. Hoang, V.T., Krovetz, T., Rogaway, P.: Robust authenticated-encryption AEZ and the problem that it solves. In: Oswald, E., Fischlin, M. (eds.) EUROCRYPT 2015. LNCS, vol. 9056, pp. 15–44. Springer, Heidelberg (2015). https://doi.org/10.1007/978-3-662-46800-5_2

13. Iwata, T.: New blockcipher modes of operation with beyond the birthday bound security. In: Robshaw, M. (ed.) FSE 2006. LNCS, vol. 4047, pp. 310–327. Springer, Heidelberg (2006). https://doi.org/10.1007/11799313_20

14. Iwata, T., Minematsu, K.: Stronger security variants of GCM-SIV. IACR Trans. Symmetric Cryptol. **2016**(1), 134–157 (2016)

15. Iwata, T., Minematsu, K., Peyrin, T., Seurin, Y.: ZMAC: a fast tweakable block cipher mode for highly secure message authentication. In: Katz, J., Shacham, H. (eds.) CRYPTO 2017, part III. LNCS, vol. 10403, pp. 34–65. Springer, Cham (2017). https://doi.org/10.1007/978-3-319-63697-9_2

16. Jean, J., Nikolić, I., Peyrin, T.: Tweaks and keys for block ciphers: the TWEAKEY framework. In: Sarkar, P., Iwata, T. (eds.) ASIACRYPT 2014. LNCS, vol. 8874, pp. 274–288. Springer, Heidelberg (2014). https://doi.org/10.1007/978-3-662-45608-8_15

17. Jean, J., Nikolić, I., Peyrin, T.: Deoxys v1.41. In: Third-Round Submission to the CAESAR Competition (2016). https://competitions.cr.yp.to/round3/deoxysv141.pdf

18. Liskov, M., Rivest, R.L., Wagner, D.: Tweakable block ciphers. In: Yung, M. (ed.) CRYPTO 2002. LNCS, vol. 2442, pp. 31–46. Springer, Heidelberg (2002). https://doi.org/10.1007/3-540-45708-9_3

19. Luykx, A., Preneel, B., Tischhauser, E., Yasuda, K.: A MAC mode for lightweight block ciphers. In: Peyrin, T. (ed.) FSE 2016. LNCS, vol. 9783, pp. 43–59. Springer, Heidelberg (2016). https://doi.org/10.1007/978-3-662-52993-5_3

20. Minematsu, K.: Beyond-birthday-bound security based on tweakable block cipher. In: Dunkelman, O. (ed.) FSE 2009. LNCS, vol. 5665, pp. 308–326. Springer, Heidelberg (2009). https://doi.org/10.1007/978-3-642-03317-9_19

21. Minematsu, K.: Parallelizable rate-1 authenticated encryption from pseudorandom functions. In: Nguyen, P.Q., Oswald, E. (eds.) EUROCRYPT 2014. LNCS, vol. 8441, pp. 275–292. Springer, Heidelberg (2014). https://doi.org/10.1007/978-3-642-55220-5_16

22. Minematsu, K.: Building blockcipher from small-block tweakable blockcipher. Des., Code Cryptogr. **74**(3), 645–663 (2015)

23. Minematsu, K., Iwata, T.: Building blockcipher from tweakable blockcipher: extending FSE 2009 proposal. In: Chen, L. (ed.) IMACC 2011. LNCS, vol. 7089, pp. 391–412. Springer, Heidelberg (2011). https://doi.org/10.1007/978-3-642-25516-8_24

24. Naito, Y.: Full PRF-secure message authentication code based on tweakable block cipher. In: Au, M.-H., Miyaji, A. (eds.) ProvSec 2015. LNCS, vol. 9451, pp. 167–182. Springer, Cham (2015). https://doi.org/10.1007/978-3-319-26059-4_9

25. Nandi, M.: A generic method to extend message space of a strong pseudorandom permutation. Computación y Sistemas **12**(3) (2009). http://cys.cic.ipn.mx/ojs/index.php/CyS/article/view/1204

26. Nandi, M.: On the optimality of non-linear computations of length-preserving encryption schemes. In: Iwata, T., Cheon, J.H. (eds.) ASIACRYPT 2015. LNCS, vol. 9453, pp. 113–133. Springer, Heidelberg (2015). https://doi.org/10.1007/978-3-662-48800-3_5

27. Patarin, J.: The "Coefficients H" technique. In: Avanzi, R.M., Keliher, L., Sica, F. (eds.) SAC 2008. LNCS, vol. 5381, pp. 328–345. Springer, Heidelberg (2009). https://doi.org/10.1007/978-3-642-04159-4_21

28. Peyrin, T., Seurin, Y.: Counter-in-tweak: authenticated encryption modes for tweakable block ciphers. In: Robshaw, M., Katz, J. (eds.) CRYPTO 2016. LNCS, vol. 9814, pp. 33–63. Springer, Heidelberg (2016). https://doi.org/10.1007/978-3-662-53018-4_2

29. Rogaway, P.: Efficient instantiations of tweakable blockciphers and refinements to modes OCB and PMAC. In: Lee, P.J. (ed.) ASIACRYPT 2004. LNCS, vol. 3329, pp. 16–31. Springer, Heidelberg (2004). https://doi.org/10.1007/978-3-540-30539-2_2

30. Rogaway, P., Zhang, Y.: Onion-AE: foundations of nested encryption. PoPETs **2018**(2), 85–104 (2018)

31. Shrimpton, T., Terashima, R.S.: A modular framework for building variable-input-length tweakable ciphers. In: Sako, K., Sarkar, P. (eds.) ASIACRYPT 2013. LNCS, vol. 8269, pp. 405–423. Springer, Heidelberg (2013). https://doi.org/10.1007/978-3-642-42033-7_21

32. Yasuda, K.: A new variant of PMAC: beyond the birthday bound. In: Rogaway, P. (ed.) CRYPTO 2011. LNCS, vol. 6841, pp. 596–609. Springer, Heidelberg (2011). https://doi.org/10.1007/978-3-642-22792-9_34

33. Zhang, L., Wu, W., Sui, H., Wang, P.: 3kf9: enhancing 3GPP-MAC beyond the birthday bound. In: Wang, X., Sako, K. (eds.) ASIACRYPT 2012. LNCS, vol. 7658, pp. 296–312. Springer, Heidelberg (2012). https://doi.org/10.1007/978-3-642-34961-4_19

Lattice-Based Cryptography

Measuring, Simulating and Exploiting the Head Concavity Phenomenon in BKZ

Shi Bai[1(✉)], Damien Stehlé[2(✉)], and Weiqiang Wen[2(✉)]

[1] Department of Mathematical Sciences,
Florida Atlantic University, Boca Raton, USA
shih.bai@gmail.com
[2] ENS de Lyon and Laboratoire LIP
(U. Lyon, CNRS, ENS de Lyon, INRIA, UCBL), Lyon, France
{damien.stehle,weiqiang.wen}@ens-lyon.fr

Abstract. The Blockwise-Korkine-Zolotarev (BKZ) lattice reduction algorithm is central in cryptanalysis, in particular for lattice-based cryptography. A precise understanding of its practical behavior in terms of run-time and output quality is necessary for parameter selection in cryptographic design. As the provable worst-case bounds poorly reflect the practical behavior, cryptanalysts rely instead on the heuristic BKZ simulator of Chen and Nguyen (Asiacrypt'11). It fits better with practical experiments, but not entirely. In particular, it over-estimates the norm of the first few vectors in the output basis. Put differently, BKZ performs better than its Chen–Nguyen simulation.

In this work, we first report experiments providing more insight on this shorter-than-expected phenomenon. We then propose a refined BKZ simulator by taking the distribution of short vectors in random lattices into consideration. We report experiments suggesting that this refined simulator more accurately predicts the concrete behavior of BKZ. Furthermore, we design a new BKZ variant that exploits the shorter-than-expected phenomenon. For the same cost assigned to the underlying SVP-solver, the new BKZ variant produces bases of better quality. We further illustrate its potential impact by testing it on the SVP-120 instance of the Darmstadt lattice challenge.

1 Introduction

A (full-rank) lattice $\mathcal{L}$ of dimension n can be generated by a basis $\mathbf{B}$ made of linearly independent vectors $\mathbf{b}_1, \cdots, \mathbf{b}_n \in \mathbb{R}^n$ via integer combinations: $\mathcal{L}(\mathbf{B}) = \sum_{i \leq n} \mathbb{Z}\mathbf{b}_i$. Lattice reduction aims to compute a basis made of relatively short vectors from an arbitrary input basis. Quantitatively, one measure of quality is the so-called Hermite factor $\mathrm{HF}(\mathbf{B}) = \|\mathbf{b}_1\|/|\det \mathbf{B}|^{1/n} = \|\mathbf{b}_1\|/(\det \mathcal{L})^{1/n}$. Understanding the practical behavior and limits of reduction algorithms is important for setting parameters in lattice-based cryptography. Indeed, the best known attacks against lattice-based schemes typically consist in finding short vectors/bases of lattices provided by publicly available data [APS15].

© International Association for Cryptologic Research 2018
T. Peyrin and S. Galbraith (Eds.): ASIACRYPT 2018, LNCS 11272, pp. 369–404, 2018.
https://doi.org/10.1007/978-3-030-03326-2_13

In [SE94], Schnorr and Euchner proposed a practical lattice reduction algorithm, named the Block Korkine-Zolotarev (BKZ) algorithm. It is parameterized by a block-size $\beta \geq 2$: the larger the block-size β, the more expensive in terms of running-time, but the smaller the output Hermite factor. This is because it internally relies on an algorithm that solves the Shortest Vector Problem (SVP) in dimension β, i.e., which can find a shortest non-zero vector in any β-dimensional lattice. Since then, several optimizations of BKZ have been investigated, such as early termination [HPS11] and progressive reduction [CN11, AWHT16]. In [HPS11] (see also [Neu17]), it was shown that in the worst case, BKZ_β (with early termination) achieves a Hermite factor of $\beta^{O(n/\beta)}$ within a polynomial number of calls to the SVP solver, for $\beta = o(n)$ and n growing to infinity. It was shown in [HS08] that there exist bases with such Hermite factors (up to a constant factor in the exponent) which are left unchanged when given as inputs to BKZ_β. Unfortunately, these worst-case bounds are quantitatively very far from experimental data.

The BKZ algorithm proceeds by improving the Gram–Schmidt orthogonalization $\mathbf{B}^* = (\mathbf{b}_1^*, \cdots, \mathbf{b}_n^*)$ of the current basis $\mathbf{B} = (\mathbf{b}_1, \cdots, \mathbf{b}_n)$. More precisely, it aims at updating $\mathbf{B}$ such that the norms $\|\mathbf{b}_1^*\|, \cdots, \|\mathbf{b}_n^*\|$ of the Gram–Schmidt vectors do not decrease too fast. In [Sch03], Schnorr presented a heuristic on the shape of the Gram–Schmidt norms of the output basis, named the Geometric Series Assumption (GSA). It states that there exists a constant $r > 1$ such that the output basis satisfies $\|\mathbf{b}_i^*\|/\|\mathbf{b}_{i+1}^*\| \approx r$ for all $i < n$. Among others, this implies that $\text{HF}(\mathbf{B}) \approx r^{(n-1)/2}$. It was argued in [CN11] (see also [Che09, Chp. 4]) that for β small compared to n, one should have $r \approx (\frac{\beta}{2\pi e}(\pi\beta)^{\frac{1}{\beta}})^{\frac{1}{\beta-1}}$. The latter value is derived by relying on the Gaussian heuristic[1] to estimate the smallest non-zero norm in a β-dimensional lattice $\mathcal{L}$ by $\text{GH}(\mathcal{L}) := ((\det L)/v_\beta)^{1/\beta}$, where v_β denotes the volume of the β-dimensional unit ball. It was experimentally observed that the GSA is a good first approximation to the practical behavior of BKZ. Nevertheless, it does not provide an exact fit: for $\beta \gtrsim 30$, the typical BKZ output basis has its first few Gram–Schmidt norms and its last $\approx \beta$ Gram–Schmidt norms violate this assumption. These first and last Gram–Schmidt norms are respectively called the *head* and the *tail*, the rest being the *body*. In [CN11], Chen and Nguyen refined the sandpile model from [HPS11] and provided a BKZ simulator based on the Gaussian heuristic (with a modification for the tail, see Subsect. 2.3). Their BKZ simulator captures the body and tail behaviors of the Gram–Schmidt norms very precisely [CN11, YD17]. However, as investigated in [CN11, AWHT16, YD17], the Chen–Nguyen simulator fails to capture the head phenomenon: the head almost follows the GSA in the simulations, whereas, in the experiments, the logarithmic Gram–Schmidt norms form a concave curve (instead of a line). Put plainly, BKZ finds shorter vectors than predicted by the Chen–Nguyen simulator. Refer to Figs. 1 and 2 for an example: we run BKZ with block-size 45 on 100-dimensional lattices (generated by the

---

[1] The Gaussian heuristic states that a measurable $\mathcal{S} \subseteq \mathbb{R}^n$ should contain $\approx \text{vol}(\mathcal{S})/\det(\mathcal{L})$ points of $\mathcal{L}$.

Darmstadt lattice challenge generator)[2] and record the Gram–Schmidt norms of the reduced bases after 2000 tours (each data is averaged over 100 trials). This inaccuracy may lead to overestimated security evaluations in cryptographic design. Understanding the head concavity phenomenon was put forward as an important open problem in [YD17], for assessing the bit-security of concrete lattice-based cryptosystems.

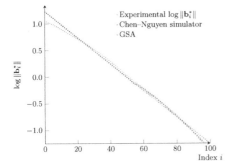

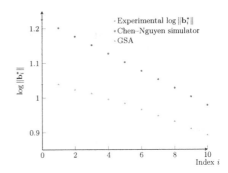

Fig. 1. Gram–Schmidt log-norms for BKZ$_{45}$ at tour $2,000$.

Fig. 2. Same as left hand side, but zoomed in.

Contributions. Our first main contribution is the design of a more accurate BKZ simulator, relying on a probabilistic version of the Gaussian heuristic. More precisely, we take into account the fact that the norm of a shortest non-zero vector of a random lattice is not a fixed quantity driven by the Gaussian heuristic, but a random variable. Concretely, we use a distribution derived from the result on the distribution of short vectors in random lattices by Södergren [Söd11]. We compare our probabilistic simulator and experimental BKZ, and observe that our simulator provides accurate predictions of the head region, while maintaining a good approximation on both body and tail regions. If we focus on the head region, the new simulator is always more precise than the Chen–Nguyen simulator, and similarly accurate for body and tail. Therefore, the Hermite factors estimated by the new simulator are more accurate and fit the experimental results more precisely. This is established through extensive experiments designed to measure the head concavity phenomenon. Such understanding also allows to efficiently assess how it scales for larger block-sizes: when β increases, the head phenomenon decreases, i.e., the GSA is followed more closely.

Our second main contribution is an algorithmic exploitation of the fact that BKZ performs better than the GSA for its first output vectors. We propose a new variant of BKZ, pressed-BKZ, that aims to exploit the head phenomenon everywhere in the graph of Gram–Schmidt norms. To do so, we proceed iteratively: we run BKZ between indices 1 and n, then we freeze the first basis vector

---

[2] https://www.latticechallenge.org/svp-challenge/.

and run BKZ between indices 2 and n (i.e., on the appropriately projected basis), then we freeze the first two basis vectors and run BKZ between 3 and n, etc. The bonus of being at the start of the basis is exploited at every position. The output basis tightly follows the GSA in the head and body regions. The gain is that the logarithmic Gram–Schmidt slope is better than that from the original BKZ. Overall, for the same block-size as in BKZ, pressed-BKZ produces lattice bases of improved quality. We adapt our BKZ simulator to pressed-BKZ, and again, the simulation seems quite accurate, giving further confidence that our simulation correctly captures the head phenomenon.

Another way to exploit the head phenomenon was suggested in [AWHT16]. As the first BKZ blocks are more reduced, solving the corresponding SVP instances is easier. In [AWHT16], Aono *et al.* propose using a larger block-size in the head region than in the rest of the basis. The purpose is to make the head region even better, without increasing the overall cost significantly. We combine this "adaptive block-size" strategy with pressed-BKZ. This allows to accelerate the convergence of pressed-BKZ towards its typical output quality.

Finally, we demonstrate the usefulness of the BKZ variant by testing it on an SVP-120 instance obtained with the Darmstadt lattice challenge generator. We also compare the quality of pressed-BKZ_{60} reduced bases with standard BKZ_β-reduced bases for various block-sizes β.

Impact. For concrete lattice-based cryptosystems with parameters set using the Chen–Nguyen simulator (or the corresponding GSA ratio), the head phenomenon is a potential security risk: as BKZ performs better than what has been taken into account while setting parameters, the parameters were potentially set too low for the targeted bit-security levels. Our simulator, which accurately predicts the head phenomenon, suggests that the head phenomenon vanishes when the block-size becomes large. We conjecture this is because the distribution of the first minimum in random lattices has a standard deviation that decreases to 0 relatively quickly when the lattice dimension increases (this lattice dimension corresponds to the BKZ block-size β). Quantitatively, the phenomenon has almost fully disappeared for $\beta \approx 200$. It is also less important when n is much larger than β. Concrete figures are provided at the end of Subsect. 4.4.

The lattice-based submissions to the NIST post-quantum standardization process[3] use conservative security estimates. In particular, they rely on lower bounds for the cost of solving SVP in dimension β, which are significantly below what can currently be achieved in practice (we refer to [ACD+18] for concrete figures). Note that this seems unrelated to the head phenomenon: the BKZ block-sizes needed to break the scheme are often in the hundreds, a range of block-sizes for which the head phenomenon has already vanished. The NIST candidates most impacted are those that were more aggressive in setting their parameters, though the impact remains limited even for them.

Oppositely, for block-sizes that can be handled in practice (e.g., $\beta \lesssim 100$), the head concavity phenomenon is non-negligible, and can be exploited. Our work can then help make concrete cryptanalysis more accurate. By allowing one

---

[3] https://csrc.nist.gov/Projects/Post-Quantum-Cryptography.

to solve SVP in larger dimensions β using pressed-BKZ$_{\beta'}$ with $\beta' < \beta$ as a pre-processing, our work should allow one to perform BKZ in larger block-sizes β. It is well-known that for small block-sizes (say $\beta \lesssim 35$), the BKZ output quality is inaccurately predicted by the Gaussian Heuristic (see [CN11], for example). This phenomenon vanishes when the block-size becomes higher. But then BKZ$_\beta$ benefits from the head concavity phenomenon. As a result, extrapolating concrete experiments in such block-sizes to draw conclusions in much larger block-sizes seems to amount to wild guessing. On the other hand, we have a better simulation of the head phenomenon for BKZ with practical block-sizes. By exploiting the head phenomenon, we can hope to reach higher block-sizes, for which such small block-size effects do not occur anymore. In this smoother regime, extrapolating experiments should become sounder.

Related Works. The first simulator for predicting the Gram–Schmidt norms of a BKZ-reduced basis was proposed by Chen and Nguyen in [CN11]. It relies on the assumption that each SVP-solver in the projected local block finds a lattice vector whose norm exactly matches its Gaussian heuristic estimate for that local block, except for a few blocks at the end of the basis. It is a good first approximation, but remains inaccurate in two ways. First, it does not capture the head concavity phenomenon (which is reported nevertheless in the experiments of [CN11]). Second, it does not take into account that in practice it is preferable to use heuristic SVP-solvers which may miss the optimal solutions. The main such heuristic SVP-solver is pruned enumeration, introduced in [SE94] and refined and improved in [GNR10]. It consists of pruning the enumeration tree by keeping only the nodes that are most likely to lead to interesting leaves. As a result, only a subset of lattice points are enumerated within the required radius, and the optimal solution may be missed. Extreme pruning [GNR10] goes even further: it decreases the probability of finding a shortest non-zero vector to lower the time/probability ratio, and runs the process several times to boost the success probability. Each time, the lattice basis is re-randomized and reduced with a lower block-size to prepare for the enumeration. An alternative approach for solving SVP is lattice sieving. The fast sieving variants, such as [NV08, MV10, Duc18, BDGL16], are also not guaranteed to return a shortest non-zero lattice vector.

In [AWHT16], Aono *et al.* described the so-called progressive-BKZ. The main new ingredient is that the latter tries to avoid the re-randomization/preprocessing overheads by using a single enumeration in any SVP call. For this, the authors increase the search radius in the enumeration, aiming to find a short vector but not necessarily a shortest one by pruning the enumeration tree. This search radius is adaptively derived from the current basis quality. Since the authors are not in the regime of finding a shortest non-zero vector, to estimate the success probability, the authors model lattice points of norm below the search radius as random points in the ball of that radius (see [AWHT16, Lemma 1]). This pruned enumeration with increased search radius heuristically produces a non-zero vector in lattice Λ of norm $\frac{\beta}{\beta+1} \cdot \alpha \cdot \mathrm{GH}(\Lambda)$ for some $\alpha \geq 1$, using their random point model. For $\alpha = 1$, we obtain an expectation for the first minimum that is lower than the Gaussian heuristic. Aono *et al.* also adapted the Chen–Nguyen simulator by modifying the expected norm found by the SVP-solver using the random points model rather than the Gaussian heuristic value. Note that the updated simulator takes some probabilistic phenomenon into account but remains deterministic. In particular, it does not capture the head concavity phenomenon. Finally, as mentioned earlier, Aono *et al.* also experimentally observed the head concavity phenomenon, and proposed to exploit it by using BKZ with larger block-size on the first few blocks.

Yu and Ducas [YD17] ran extensive experiments to assess the practical behavior of BKZ. They have two main experimental observations. First, the distribution of differences $v_i := \log \|\mathbf{b}_i^*\| - \log \|\mathbf{b}_{i+1}^*\|$ between two consecutive Gram–Schmidt log-norms, varies as a function of the index i when i belongs to the head and tail regions (and it does not in the body region). Second, the covariance between v_i and v_{i+2} is 0 for all i, but v_i and v_{i+1} are negatively correlated: in the head and tail regions, their covariance depends on both i and the block-size β, but in the body region only the block-size β contributes to their covariance. These observations quantify the head concavity phenomenon more precisely.

Software. The BKZ experiments were run using the `fplll` [dt16] (version 5.2.0) and `fpylll` [dt17] (version 0.4.0dev) open-source libraries. The efficiency of these libraries for large block sizes $\beta \geq 50$ was essential for obtaining useful statistics. Our simulator, coded in Python, and the BKZ variants, coded in C++, are freely available.

As mentioned earlier, we report experiments on pressed-BKZ with an adaptive block-size strategy, for the SVP-120 challenge. We expect our BKZ improvements to be useful in larger dimensions as well (e.g., SVP-150), if given sufficient computational resources. We want to stress that our primary goal is to model, predict and exploit the head phenomenon, the SVP-120 experiment being an illustration of its relevance.

Auxiliary material. We provide a significant amount of material to make our results reproducible and to report experimental observations in more details. Concretely, we provide codes (as mentioned above), experimental raw data, graphs that could not fit within the page limit and video files. Data and links are provided on the authors' webpages.

2   Preliminaries

In this section, we recall some basic facts on lattices and lattice reduction. We refer the reader to the survey [NV09] for more background. We first introduce the notations used throughout the paper.

Notations. We let lower-case bold letters denote (column) vectors and upper-case bold letters denote matrices. For a vector $\mathbf{x}$, we use $\|\mathbf{x}\|$ to denote its ℓ_2-norm. Similarly, a matrix $\mathbf{B} = (\mathbf{b}_1, \cdots, \mathbf{b}_n)$ is also parsed column-wise. For $n \geq 1$ and $r > 0$, we let $V_n(r)$ denote the volume of an n-dimensional ball with radius r and v_n the volume of an n-dimensional unit ball. Correspondingly, we let c_n

denote the radius of an n-dimensional ball of unit volume. Logarithms are in base 2. For $\lambda > 0$, we let $\text{Expo}(\lambda)$ denote the exponential distribution with density function proportional to $x \mapsto \lambda e^{-\lambda x}$, up to a normalization factor. We let log denotes the natural logarithm with base e.

2.1 Euclidean Lattices

Let $\mathbf{B} \in \mathbb{R}^{n \times n}$ be full rank. The lattice $\mathcal{L}$ generated by $\mathbf{B}$ is $\mathcal{L}(\mathbf{B}) = \{\mathbf{B}\mathbf{x} \mid \mathbf{x} \in \mathbb{Z}^n\}$, and the matrix $\mathbf{B}$ is called a basis of $\mathcal{L}$. We let $\mathbf{B}^* = (\mathbf{b}_1^*, \cdots, \mathbf{b}_n^*)$ denote the Gram–Schmidt orthogonalization of $\mathbf{B}$. The determinant of a lattice $\mathcal{L}$ with basis $\mathbf{B}$ is defined as $\det(\mathcal{L}) = \prod_{i \leq n} \|\mathbf{b}_i^*\|$. The norm of a shortest non-zero vector in $\mathcal{L}$ is denoted by $\lambda_1(\mathcal{L})$ and called the minimum of $\mathcal{L}$. Minkowski's theorem asserts that $\lambda_1(\mathcal{L}) \leq 2 \cdot v_n^{-1/n} \cdot \det(\mathcal{L})^{1/n}$. For $i \leq n$, we let π_i denote the orthogonal projection onto the linear subspace $(\mathbf{b}_1, \cdots, \mathbf{b}_{i-1})^{\perp}$. For $i < j \leq n$, we let $\mathbf{B}_{[i,j]}$ denote the local block $(\pi_i(\mathbf{b}_i), \cdots, \pi_i(\mathbf{b}_j))$, and $\mathcal{L}_{[i,j]}$ denote the lattice generated by $\mathbf{B}_{[i,j]}$.

Lattice Reduction. A lattice basis $\mathbf{B}$ is called size-reduced, if it satisfies $|\mu_{i,j}| \leq 1/2$ for $j < i \leq n$ where $\mu_{i,j} = \langle \mathbf{b}_i, \mathbf{b}_j^* \rangle / \langle \mathbf{b}_j^*, \mathbf{b}_j^* \rangle$. A basis $\mathbf{B}$ is HKZ-reduced if it is size-reduced and further satisfies:

$$\|\mathbf{b}_i^*\| = \lambda_1(\mathcal{L}_{[i,n]}), \ \forall i \leq n.$$

A basis $\mathbf{B}$ is BKZ-β reduced for block size $\beta \geq 2$ if it is size-reduced and satisfies:

$$\|\mathbf{b}_i^*\| = \lambda_1(\mathcal{L}_{[i,\min(i+\beta-1,n)]}), \ \forall i \leq n.$$

Heuristics. Lattice reduction algorithms and their analyses often rely on heuristic assumptions. Let $\mathcal{L}$ be an n-dimensional lattice and $\mathcal{S}$ a measurable set in the real span of $\mathcal{L}$. The *Gaussian Heuristic* states that the number of lattice points in $\mathcal{S}$, denoted $|\mathcal{L} \cap \mathcal{S}|$, is about $\text{vol}(\mathcal{S})/\det(\mathcal{L})$. In particular, taking $\mathcal{S}$ as a centered n-ball of radius R, the number of lattice points contained in the n-ball is about $V_n(R)/\det(\mathcal{L})$. Furthermore, by setting $V_n(R) \approx \det(\mathcal{L})$, we see that $\lambda_1(\mathcal{L})$ is about $\text{GH}(\mathcal{L}) := v_n^{-1/n} \cdot \det(\mathcal{L})^{1/n}$. Note that this is a factor of 2 smaller than the rigorous upper bound provided by Minkowski's theorem. In [Sch03], Schnorr introduced the *Geometric Series Assumption* (GSA), which states that the Gram-Schmidt norms $\{\|\mathbf{b}_i^*\|\}_{i \leq n}$ of a BKZ-reduced basis behave as a geometric series, i.e., there exists $r > 1$ such that $\|\mathbf{b}_i^*\|/\|\mathbf{b}_{i+1}^*\| \approx r$ for all $i < n$.

Random Lattices. We use $\Gamma_n = \{\mathcal{L} \in \mathbb{R}^n \mid \text{vol}(\mathcal{L}) = 1\}$ to denote the set of all full-rank lattices of rank n with unit volume. The distribution of short(est) vectors in random lattices uniformly chosen in Γ_n was studied, among others, in [Rog56, Sch59, Söd11]. In [Che09], Chen proposed the following statement as a direct corollary of [Söd11, Theorem 1].

Theorem 1. *[Che09, Corollary 3.1.4] Sample $\mathcal{L}$ uniformly in Γ_n. The distribution of $v_n \cdot \lambda_1(\mathcal{L})^n$ converges in distribution to $\text{Expo}(1/2)$ as $n \to \infty$.*

If we set $\lambda_1(\mathcal{L})$ as a random variable $Y = X^{1/n} \cdot \mathrm{GH}(\mathcal{L})$, with X sampled from $\mathrm{Expo}(1/2)$, then the expected value of λ_1 is

$$\mathbb{E}(\lambda_1(\mathcal{L})) = 2^{1/n} \cdot \Gamma\left(1 + 1/n\right) \cdot \mathrm{GH}(\mathcal{L}).$$

In lattices of unit volume, the $\mathrm{GH}(\mathcal{L})$ term can be replaced by $v_n^{-1/n}$. In the rest of this paper, we refer to this quantity as the minimum expectation. For large n, this is $\approx (1 + 0.116/n + o(1/n)) \cdot \mathrm{GH}(\mathcal{L})$. It can be also seen that the variance is

$$\mathbb{V}(\lambda_1(\mathcal{L})) = 2^{2/n} \cdot \left(\Gamma\left(1 + 2/n\right) - (\Gamma\left(1 + 1/n\right))^2\right) \cdot \left(\mathrm{GH}(\mathcal{L})\right)^2,$$

which is $\approx \frac{\pi^2}{6n^2}(1 + o(1)) \cdot (\mathrm{GH}(\mathcal{L}))^2$ for large n.

2.2   The BKZ Algorithm

The Schnorr-Euchner BKZ algorithm [SE94] takes as inputs a block-size β and a basis $\mathbf{B} = (\mathbf{b}_1, \cdots, \mathbf{b}_n)$ of a lattice Λ, and outputs a basis which is "close" to being BKZ_β-reduced (up to numerical inaccuracies, as the underlying Gram–Schmidt orthogonalization is computed in floating-point arithmetic, and up to the progress parameter $\delta < 1$). BKZ can be seen as a practical variant of Schnorr's algorithm from [Sch87]. BKZ starts by LLL-reducing the input basis, then calls an SVP-solver on consecutive local blocks $\mathbf{B}_{[k,\min(k+\beta-1,n)]}$ for $k = 1, \cdots, n - 1$. This is called a *BKZ tour*. After each execution of the SVP-solver, if we have $\lambda_1(\Lambda_{[k,\min(k+\beta-1,n)]}) < \delta \cdot \|\mathbf{b}_k^*\|$, then BKZ updates the block $\mathbf{B}_{[k,\min(k+\beta-1,n)]}$ by inserting the vector found by the SVP-solver between indices $k-1$ and k, and LLL-reducing the updated block (in this case, the input is a generating set instead of a basis). Otherwise, we LLL-reduce the local block directly, without any insertion. The procedure terminates when no change occurs at all during a tour. We refer to Algorithm 1 for a complete description of the BKZ algorithm.

Algorithm 1. The Schnorr and Euchner BKZ algorithm

Input: A basis $\mathbf{B} = \{\mathbf{b}_1, \cdots, \mathbf{b}_n\}$, a block size $\beta \geq 2$ and a constant $\delta < 1$.
Output: A BKZ_β-reduced basis of $\Lambda(\mathbf{B})$.

1: **repeat**
2:     **for** $k = 1$ to $n - 1$ **do**
3:         Find any $\mathbf{b}$ such that $\|\pi_k(\mathbf{b})\| = \lambda_1(\Lambda_{[k,\min(k+\beta-1,n)]})$
4:         **if** $\delta \cdot \|\mathbf{b}_k^*\| > \|\mathbf{b}\|$ **then**
5:             LLL-reduce$(\mathbf{b}_1, \cdots, \mathbf{b}_{k-1}, \mathbf{b}, \mathbf{b}_k, \cdots, \mathbf{b}_{\min(k+\beta,n)})$.
6:         **else**
7:             LLL-reduce$(\mathbf{b}_1, \cdots, \mathbf{b}_{\min(k+\beta,n)})$.
8:         **end if**
9:     **end for**
10: **until** no change occurs.

For practical reasons, there are diverse BKZ variants.

- Early-abort. The BKZ reduction aborts when a selected number of tours are completed or when a desired output quality has been reached [HPS11].
- SVP-solver. BKZ could be run with any SVP solver; in practice for typical block sizes, the fastest one is lattice enumeration [Kan83, FP83]; the latter can be significantly accelerated with tree pruning [SE94] and even further with extreme pruning [GNR10]. In the case of enumeration with pruning, the SVP solver is not guaranteed to return a shortest non-zero vector in its input lattice. Furthermore, one can set the enumeration radius to either $\|\mathbf{b}_i^*\|$ or Gaussian heuristic (whichever is smaller). In the experiments of Sects. 3 and 4, we use the enumeration radius $0.99 \cdot \|\mathbf{b}_i^*\|$, which is the default choice in the implementation of BKZ in fplll [dt16]. In the experiments of Sect. 5.4, we set the enumeration radius to be 1.05 times the Gaussian heuristic of the local block. In all these cases, the SVP solver is not guaranteed to return a shortest non-zero vector.
- Pre-processing and post-processing. Pre-processing is performed *before* the call to the SVP solver. In the pre-processing step, some strategies (e.g., BKZ with a smaller block size) are chosen to further improve the basis. Post-processing is executed *after* the call to the SVP-solver, e.g., running LLL on indices 1 to $\min(k + \beta - 1, n)$, in order to propagate the progress made at index k.

2.3   The Chen–Nguyen Simulator

In [CN11], Chen and Nguyen proposed a simulator to capture the practical behavior of BKZ with relatively large block size (e.g., $\beta \geq 45$). The goal was to estimate the practical behavior of BKZ for hard-to-solve instances. Overall, the simulation proceeds closely to BKZ. It considers successive tours. For each tour, it computes new Gram-Schmidt log-norms $\hat{\ell}_1, \ldots, \hat{\ell}_n$ from current Gram-Schmidt log-norms $\ell_1, \ldots, \ell_n$. At the beginning of each BKZ tour, a boolean flag τ is initialized to be true. To update each local block, the simulator first (deterministically) compute the Gaussian heuristic value $\mathrm{GH}(\mathbf{B}_{[k, \min(k+\beta-1, n)]})$ as an estimation of first miminum, by looking at the Gram–Schmidt norms of the current local block (except for small blocks in the end). This corresponds to Line 8 of Algorithm 2, we recall that the v_d denotes the volume of d-dimensional unit ball. The computed Gaussian heuristic value is then used to update the current local block, if it is smaller than the current $\|\mathbf{b}_k^*\|$ (as written in Line 10--11). Else, the local block is kept unchanged. To update, the first Gram–Schmidt norm is replaced by the selected value, and the boolean flag τ is flipped once such an update occurs (as written in Line 12). Once the boolean flag τ is changed, all the remaining Gram–Schmidt norms, of indices $k' \in [k + 1, n - 45]$ are updated one by one to $\mathrm{GH}(\mathbf{B}_{[k', \min(k'+\beta-1, n)]})$, independently of whether the current $\|\mathbf{b}_k^*\|$ is already small enough or not (as written in Line 15). At the end of each tour, there is an additional update of the tail block of length 45 (as written in Line 19--21). The Gram–Schmidt norms in this tail block are simulated with the experimental Gram–Schmidt norms of HKZ-reduced bases of 45-dimensional unit-volume lattices. The experimental Gram–Schmidt norms are prepared in

Line 1--2 of Algorithm 2. This length of 45 was chosen because the minimum of blocks of dimension ≥ 45 within BKZ follows the Gaussian heuristic quite well (as observed by the extensive experiments of [CN11]). This special treatment on the tail block also make the simulator more precise for capturing the practical behavior of BKZ compared to GSA assumption.

Algorithm 2. The Chen–Nguyen BKZ simulator

Input: The Gram–Schmidt log-norms $\{\ell_i = \log \|\mathbf{b}_i^*\|\}_{i \leq n}$ and an integer $N \geq 1$.
Output: A prediction of the Gram–Schmidt log-norms $\{\widehat{\ell_i} = \log \|\mathbf{b}_i^*\|\}_{i \leq n}$ after N
    tours of BKZ.

 1: **for** $i = 1$ **to** 45 **do** $r_i \leftarrow \mathbb{E}[\log \|\mathbf{b}_k^*\| : \mathbf{B}$ HKZ-reduced basis of $\Lambda \leftarrow \Gamma_{45}]$
 2: **end for**
 3: **for** $j = 1$ **to** N **do**
 4:    $\tau \leftarrow$ **true**
 5:    **for** $k = 1$ **to** $n - 45$ **do**
 6:        $d \leftarrow \min(\beta, n - k + 1); e \leftarrow k + d - 1$
 7:        $\log \mathrm{vol}(\Lambda_{[k,e]}) \leftarrow \sum_{i=1}^{e} \ell_i - \sum_{i=1}^{k-1} \widehat{\ell_i}$
 8:        $g \leftarrow \left(\log \mathrm{vol}(\Lambda_{[k,e]}) - \log v_d\right)/d$
 9:        **if** τ = **true then**
10:           **if** $g < \ell_k$ **then**
11:             $\widehat{\ell_k} \leftarrow g$
12:             $\tau \leftarrow$ **false**
13:           **end if**
14:        **else**
15:           $\widehat{\ell_k} \leftarrow g$
16:        **end if**
17:    **end for**
18:    $\log \mathrm{vol}(\Lambda_{[k,e]}) \leftarrow \sum_{i=1}^{n} \ell_i - \sum_{i=1}^{n-45} \widehat{\ell_i}$
19:    **for** $k' = n - 44$ **to** n **do**
20:        $\widehat{\ell_{k'}} \leftarrow \frac{\log \mathrm{vol}(\Lambda_{[k,e]})}{45} + r_{k'+45-n}$
21:    **end for**
22:    $\{\ell_1, \cdots, \ell_n\} \leftarrow \{\widehat{\ell_1}, \cdots, \widehat{\ell_n}\}$
23: **end for**

---

3   Measuring the Head Concavity

In this section, we describe in detail the concavity phenomenon in the leading Gram–Schmidt log-norms. In particular, we report experiments on the quality of bases output by BKZ_β and on the evolution of Gram–Schmidt norms during the execution of the algorithm.

In our experiments, we consider the knapsack-type lattice bases generated by the Darmstadt lattice challenge generator. In dimension n, the generator selects a prime p of bitsize $10 \cdot n$ and sets the first basis vector as $(p, 0, \cdots, 0)$. For $i > 1$, the i-th basis vector starts with a uniformly chosen integer modulo p, and all other entries are 0 except the i-th entry which is 1. When using the generator file, the `seed` is from the set $\{0, \cdots, k-1\}$, where k is total number of samples in the experiment, which enables reproducibility. We always run LLL reduction before a BKZ reduction. We use the default LLL in `fplll` of parameter $\delta = 0.99$.

3.1 BKZ Output Quality

In our first set of experiments, we measure the output quality of the BKZ algorithm. We consider the final reduced basis, for increasing block sizes β. We let BKZ run until it fully stops and use a full enumeration as SVP-solver (without pruning), to avoid side-effects. We then measure the Gram–Schmidt log-norms $\{\log \|\mathbf{b}_i^*\|\}_{i \leq n}$ of the reduced basis $\mathbf{B}$. In particular, when BKZ completes, the vector $\mathbf{b}_i^*$ is a shortest non-zero vector of the lattice $\Lambda_{[i,i+\min(i+\beta-1,n)]}$ (up to the 0.99 factor), for every i (see Subsect. 2.2).

As we use BKZ until exhaustion with full enumeration, the experiments are quite lengthy. We restricted them to dimension $n = 100$, with selected block sizes β ranging from 4 to 40. For each choice of β, we conduct the experiment 100 times using input lattices generated with different seeds. For each experiment, we normalize the $\log \|\mathbf{b}_i^*\|$'s of the reduced basis by substracting one hundredth of the logarithmic determinants of its input lattice, such that the summation of the new logarithmic Gram–Schmidt norms is normalized to be 0. This step helps eliminate the small differences of determinants of all generated lattices. We then average $\log \|\mathbf{b}_i^*\|$ for each i over the 100 samples.

We plotted the results for the various block sizes in Figs. 3, 4, 5, 6, 7 and 8. The x-axis corresponds to the basis vector at index i and the y-axis is the Gram–Schmidt log-norm. Each figure contains several plots: the red dots are the (averaged) experimental $\log \|\mathbf{b}_i^*\|$'s; the brown dots are obtained by applying the first Minkowski's theorem to each one of the experimentally obtained local blocks $\mathbf{B}_{[i,i+\min(i+\beta-1,n)]}$ of the output basis; the purple dots are the values obtained by replacing Minkowski's theorem by the Gaussian heuristic value $\mathrm{GH}(\Lambda_{[i,i+\min(i+\beta-1,n)]})$, and the blue dots are the expected $\lambda_1(\Lambda_{[i,i+\min(i+\beta-1,n)]})$ (see Subsect. 2.1).

The experiments highlight that the Gaussian heuristic and expected value of first minimum are not very accurate for predicting the output of the BKZ algorithm (and neither is Minkowski's theorem, but that is less surprising). For small block sizes, the experimental Gram–Schmidt log-norms are above the Gaussian heuristic values. Notice this even appears to happen for the tail blocks for large β. When the block size increases, the Gaussian heuristic and first minimum expectation get closer to each other (except in the tail region), but still do not accurately predict the genuine BKZ output. In particular, the experimental Gram–Schmidt log-norms are concave in the head region (the other curves are also somewhat concave, but less so, as they are smoothed versions of the experimental curve). This is essentially the same as the phenomenon we already observed in Sect. 1, which we refer to as head concavity. It starts being quite noticeable with $\beta \approx 30$.

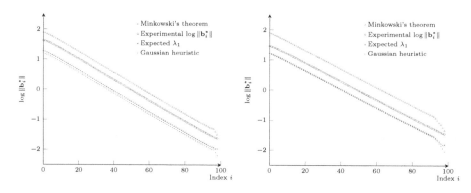

Fig. 3. Output of BKZ_4.   **Fig. 4.** Output of BKZ_8.

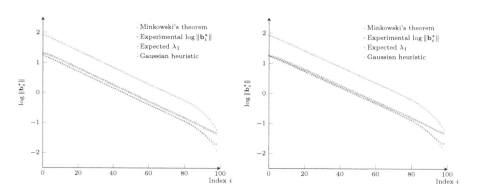

Fig. 5. Output of BKZ_{16}.   **Fig. 6.** Output of BKZ_{20}.

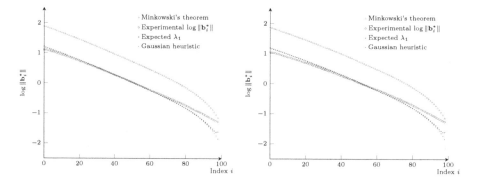

Fig. 7. Output of BKZ_{30}.   **Fig. 8.** Output of BKZ_{40}.

3.2   Enumeration Costs in Local Blocks

The enumeration cost for SVP in each local block is also an interesting quantity for evaluating the extent of the head concavity of a BKZ-reduced basis. As explained in [HS07], under the Gaussian heuristic, the full enumeration cost (in terms of number of nodes enumerated, denoted by "# nodes") of a d-dimensional lattice using enumeration radius $\|\mathbf{b}_1^*\|$ can be estimated by

$$\sum_{k=1}^{d} \frac{1}{2} \cdot \frac{V_k(\|\mathbf{b}_1^*\|)}{\prod_{i=d-k+1}^{d} \|\mathbf{b}_i^*\|}. \tag{1}$$

We take the (averaged) BKZ_{40} preprocessed basis from the previous subsection and compute the local SVP costs of BKZ_{50} and BKZ_{60} on the BKZ_{40}-preprocessed basis. We also compute the local SVP costs of BKZ_{40} which can be considered as the cost for checking that the basis is indeed BKZ_{40}-reduced. In Fig. 9, we plot the logarithm of the quantity above for each local block of SVP_{40}, SVP_{50} and SVP_{60}. It can be seen that the local SVP costs in the first few blocks are cheaper. The enumeration costs keep increasing until the last $\beta - 1$ blocks. These last blocks are of smaller dimensions, explaining why their enumeration costs become lower. As cheaper enumeration reflects stronger reducedness, Fig. 9 hints at a concavity of the $\log \|\mathbf{b}_i^*\|$'s in the head.

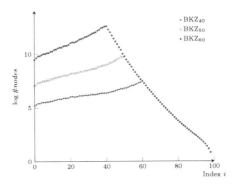

Fig. 9. Estimated enumeration costs (of each local block) for BKZ_{40}, BKZ_{50} and BKZ_{60} on a BKZ_{40} reduced basis.

3.3   Evolution of the Gram–Schmidt Norms During the Execution

The previous experiments suggest that the Gaussian heuristic may be inaccurate for a BKZ-reduced basis in the head region. Below, we further investigate the *evolution* of the accuracy of the Gaussian heuristic for each local block $\Lambda_{[i,\min(i+\beta,n)]}$ during the running of the BKZ algorithm. We focus on the evolution of the BKZ_{40} experiments from Subsect. 3.1. After each BKZ tour, we record $\{\mathbf{b}_i^*\}_{i\in[n]}$ for each experiment. Again we use a full enumeration as SVP-solver (without pruning), to avoid side-effects and wait until BKZ completes.

In Fig. 10, we plot the Gram–Schmidt log-norms after each tour (for the first 1000 tours, plus those of the initial LLL-reduced input). For each BKZ_{40} experiment, we normalize the log-norms after each tour as in Subsect. 3.1. Furthermore, we take the average of the log-norms for the 100 experiments (one individual graph would be less smooth). Finally, we plot the log-norms for the first 1000 tours (one BKZ instance completes before 1000 tours; and after this one completes, for a given tour number, we take the average over the BKZ experiments that are running for more than 1000 tours). The dots corresponding to the earlier tours are colored in blue, and those corresponding to the later tours are colored in red (the color changes gradually).

The plot shows the evolution of the log-norms across tours. However, it does not clearly highlight the evolution of the relation between the $\|\mathbf{b}_i^*\|$'s and the Gaussian heuristic values. Hence we further compute the quantities

$$\frac{\|\mathbf{b}_i^*\|}{GH(\Lambda_{[i,\min(i+\beta,n)]})} \quad \text{for } i \leq n.$$

Note that this should be expected to be close to 1 for a random lattice, under the Gaussian heuristic. For each tour, for all indices i, we record all the (averaged) quantities at i's across the 100 experiments. We plot a line for each tour and hence Fig. 11 contains 1001 lines. In Fig. 11, the x-axis corresponds to the index i; the y-axis corresponds to the quantities above. Note that for each i, there are 1001 dots vertically, corresponding to the number of BKZ tours plus the initial LLL-reduced input.

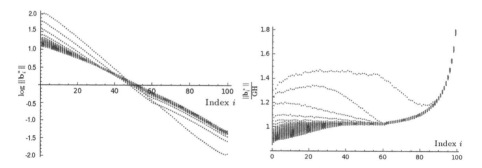

Fig. 10. Evolution of the Gram–Schmidt log-norms during BKZ_{40}'s execution.

Fig. 11. Evolution of the $\|\mathbf{b}_i^*\|$/GH's during BKZ_{40}'s execution.

As observed in prior works, BKZ distorts the distribution of the projected lattices: the first projected sublattices are denser (the minimum is smaller) and the last projected sublattices are sparser. This can be seen from Fig. 11 since the red points are significantly lower than 1 in the first indices. Further, this distortion occurs often quickly during the execution of BKZ, sometimes within a few tours.

3.4   Evolution of Root Hermite Factor of the Basis

We now consider the asymptote of the root Hermite factor of the basis being BKZ-reduced, as the number of BKZ tours increases. A similar experiment was done in [HPS11]. We compare the experimental behavior to the Chen–Nguyen simulator. Note that the root Hermite factor only measures the head concavity phenomenon for the first basis vector. We fix the block size at $\beta = 45$ and run BKZ_{β} on 100 random instances. After each tour, we record the average root Hermite factor. In Fig. 23 (we also duplicate it here for convenience, as Fig. 12), we plot the averaged root Hermite factors over all experiments. The root Hermite factor δ is computed as:

$$\delta = (\|\mathbf{b}_1^*\| / (\det \Lambda)^{1/n})^{1/n}.$$

It can be seen that the evolution of the root Hermite factor does not match with its prediction by the Chen–Nguyen simulator. Indeed, the root Hermite factor obtained with the Chen–Nguyen simulator does not further improve after the first few tours; while it keeps improving in the actual experiments. It should also be noted that in the first few tours, the root Hermite factors in the actual experiments are worse than those of the Chen–Nguyen simulation. In the experiments, we do not use pruned enumeration nor early-abort. One potential reason is that the local SVP solver used only attempts to find a vector slightly smaller than $\|\mathbf{b}_i^*\|$ (instead of the Gaussian heuristic value). As the number of tours increases, the root Hermite factors in experiments become smaller than those obtained by the Chen–Nguyen simulator.

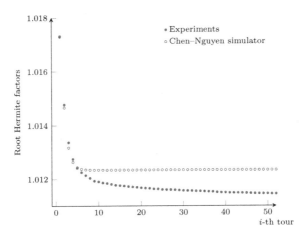

Fig. 12. Evolution of Root Hermite factors during the execution of BKZ_{45}.

3.5   BKZ with Pruning

All of the previous experiments used BKZ without pruning to avoid side-effects on the quality. The purpose of this subsection is to show that using extreme pruning within the enumeration indeed affects the behavior of BKZ to some extent (this was also observed in [YD17]). Nevertheless, the head concavity phenomenon remains visible even in pruned-enumeration BKZ. Again we run the BKZ experiments until they fully complete (i.e., no early-abort).

We consider two experiments. First, we run BKZ_{40} with pruned enumeration and compare it with standard BKZ_{40}. We used the default pruning strategy of fpll1. We note that there is no known canonically best way to prune, and the experimental results may vary a little across different pruning strategies. We see by comparing Fig. 13 (with pruned enumeration) with Fig. 8 (without) that the extent of the head concavity phenomenon is less than without pruned enumeration. In the second experiment, we run BKZ with pruned enumeration with larger block size, which is also more relevant to cryptanalysis. In particular, we run BKZ_{60} with pruned enumeration and then plot the evolution of the corresponding $\|\mathbf{b}_i^*\|/GH$'s (for the first 500 tours) in Fig. 14. This is to be compared with Fig. 11. We can conclude that the head concavity phenomenon still exists for practical versions of BKZ with larger block sizes.

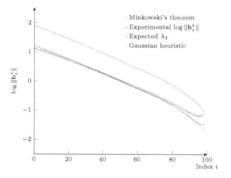

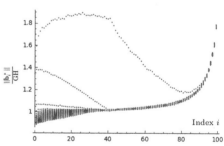

Fig. 13. Output Gram–Schmidt log-norms for BKZ_{40} with pruning.

Fig. 14. Evolution of the $\|\mathbf{b}_i^*\|/GH$'s during the execution of BKZ_{60} with pruning.

4 A Refined BKZ Simulator

In this section, we describe a refined BKZ simulator, and report on experiments indicating that the simulation is quite accurate, in particular in capturing the head concavity phenomenon.

4.1 The Refined Simulator

Our probabilistic BKZ simulator aims to provide a more accurate simulation of the experimental behavior of the BKZ algorithm. Our simulator has similar structure as the Chen–Nguyen simulator (refer to Subsect. 2.2), in particular, we also consider the Gram–Schmidt log-norms. There are several differences with the Chen–Nguyen simulator.

The main difference is the emulation of the probabilistic nature of the minimum in random lattices. Theorem 1 provides the distribution of the minimum of a uniform unit-volume lattice. The new BKZ simulator, given as Algorithm 3, is probabilistic. It takes this distribution into consideration when updating each local block. In more detail, suppose that we are updating the local block $\Lambda_{[k,e]} = \Lambda(\mathbf{B}_{[k,e]})$ for some $k \leq n - 45$ and $e = \min(k + \beta - 1, n)$ with dimension $d = \min(\beta, n - k + 1)$. Let us assume this is a random lattice. By Theorem 1, we have that $\lambda_1(\Lambda_{[k,e]})$ is distributed as

$$\lambda_1(\Lambda_{[k,e]}) = \left(\frac{X \cdot \mathrm{vol}(\Lambda_{[k,e]})}{v_d} \right)^{1/d},$$

where X is sampled with distribution $\mathrm{Expo}[1/2]$. Recall that v_d is the volume of n-dimensional unit ball. Now we can take the logarithm to obtain

$$\log \lambda_1(\Lambda_{[k,e]}) = \frac{\log X + \log \mathrm{vol}(\Lambda_{[k,e]}) - \log v_d}{d}.$$

This explains Line 14 in Algorithm 3. In Line 15, the simulator checks whether a value sampled as above, e.g., $\log \|\mathbf{b}_k^*\|$, is smaller than the current $\log \|\mathbf{b}_k^*\|$. If it is indeed smaller, then the value of $\log \|\mathbf{b}_k^*\|$ is updated. Else the former one is kept. This is corresponding to the main step in the BKZ algorithm (Line 4--7): once the found vector (in the SVP call) is shorter than current $\mathbf{b}_i^*$ in current local block, then the found vector will be used to replace $\mathbf{b}_i$, thus $\mathbf{b}_i^*$ is updated. Otherwise the found vector will be discarded, and the simulation assumes that $\mathbf{b}_i^*$ is not changed during the LLL-reduction.

A further difference with the Chen–Nguyen simulator is the way we handle the remaining Gram–Schmidt log-norms in the current local block in case $\log \|\mathbf{b}_k^*\|$ has been updated. In the Chen–Nguyen simulator, after updating the first Gram–Schmidt log-norms $\log \|\mathbf{b}_k^*\|$ in the current local block, all the remaining log-norms $\log \|\mathbf{b}_i^*\|$ for $i > k$ will be updated by using the Gaussian heuristic directly without further checking whether the estimated value gives an improvement or not (refer to Algorithm 2). In our simulator, we consider a refined update of the remaining $\log \|\mathbf{b}_i^*\|$'s of the block. Concretely, we update all the remaining indices in the current local block by increasing them by a common amount chosen so that the volume of current block is preserved (it compensates for the decrease of $\log \|\mathbf{b}_k^*\|$). There is one further subtlety in the actual update applied by the simulator. For the second Gram–Schmidt log-norm of the block, it sets $\widehat{\ell}_{k+1} \leftarrow \ell_k + \log(\sqrt{1 - 1/d})$ rather than increasing it by the same amount as for the $d - 2$ remaining log-norms. The quantity $\sqrt{1 - 1/d}$ is used to simulate the change in norm for the old vector $\mathbf{b}_k^*$ after being projected with respect to a new vector (the shortest vector of the local block inserted). We assume that the coefficients of the shortest vector in terms of the normalized Gram–Schmidt basis $(\mathbf{b}_1^*/ \|\mathbf{b}_1^*\|, \mathbf{b}_2^*/ \|\mathbf{b}_2^*\|, \cdots, \mathbf{b}_n^*/ \|\mathbf{b}_n^*\|)$ looks like a uniformly distributed vector of the same norm. This twist also occurs in experiments: the updated second Gram–Schmidt norm is almost always a bit smaller than the old first Gram–Schmidt norm of the block. Such a strategy also makes the simulator more flexible. In the new simulator, it is not necessary to update all the remaining blocks with the value estimated by the Gaussian heuristic once we have an update: the simulator makes an update only when needed, i.e., when an improving Gram–Schmidt norm is sampled.

We also use two sets of boolean values $\{t_0^{(i)}\}_{i \leq n}$ and $\{t_1^{(i)}\}_{i \leq n}$, to record if there is a change of $\log \|\mathbf{b}_i^*\|$ in the last and the current tours, respectively. If we know there was no change at all in current local block during the last tour, we simply skip the current block and go to the next one. Correspondingly, in BKZ, it means that the found shortest vector in current block in this tour will be the same as the one in current block in last tour. As it was not used to make an update during the last tour, so will it not be used in this tour.

Algorithm 3. The probabilistic BKZ simulator

Input: The Gram–Schmidt log-norms $\{\ell_i = \log \|\mathbf{b}_i^*\|\}_{i \leq n}$ and an integer $N \geq 1$.
Output: A prediction of the Gram–Schmidt log-norms after N tours of BKZ.

1: **for** $i = 1$ **to** 45 **do** $r_i \leftarrow \mathbb{E}[\log \|\mathbf{b}_k^*\| : \mathbf{B}$ HKZ-reduced basis of $\Lambda \leftarrow \Gamma_{45}]$
2: **end for**
3: $t_0^{(i)} \leftarrow$ **true**, $\forall i \leq n$
4: **for** $j = 1$ **to** N **do**
5:      $t_1^{(i)} \leftarrow$ **false**, $\forall i \leq n$
6:      **for** $k = 1$ **to** $n - 45$ **do**
7:          $d \leftarrow \min(\beta, n - k + 1);\ e \leftarrow k + d$
8:          $\tau \leftarrow$ **false**
9:          **for** $k' = k$ **to** e **do** $\tau \leftarrow \tau \| t_0^{(k')}$
10:          **end for**
11:          $\log \text{vol}(\Lambda_{[k,e]}) \leftarrow \sum_{i=1}^{e-1} \ell_i - \sum_{i=1}^{k-1} \widehat{\ell}_i$
12:          **if** $\tau =$ **true then**
13:             $X \hookleftarrow \text{Expo}[1/2]$
14:             $g \leftarrow (\log X + \log \text{vol}(\Lambda_{[k,e]}) - \log v_d)/d$
15:             **if** $g < \ell_k$ **then**
16:                 $\widehat{\ell}_k = g$
17:                 $\widehat{\ell}_{k+1} \leftarrow \ell_k + \log(\sqrt{1 - 1/d})$
18:                 $\gamma \leftarrow (\ell_k + \ell_{k+1}) - (\widehat{\ell}_k + \widehat{\ell}_{k+1})$
19:                 **for** $k' = k + 2$ **to** e **do**
20:                     $\widehat{\ell}_{k'} \leftarrow \ell_{k'} + \gamma/(d - 2)$
21:                     $t_1^{(k')} \leftarrow$ **true**
22:                 **end for**
23:                 $\tau \leftarrow$ **false**
24:             **end if**
25:          **end if**
26:          $\{\ell_k, \cdots, \ell_{e-1}\} \leftarrow \{\widehat{\ell}_k, \cdots, \widehat{\ell}_{e-1}\}$
27:      **end for**
28:      $\log \text{vol}(\Lambda_{[k,e]}) \leftarrow \sum_{i=1}^{n} \ell_i - \sum_{i=1}^{n-45} \widehat{\ell}_i$
29:      **for** $k' = n - 44$ **to** n **do**
30:          $\widehat{\ell}_{k'} \leftarrow \dfrac{\log \text{vol}(\Lambda_{[k,e]})}{45} + r_{k'+45-n}$
31:          $t_1^{(k')} \leftarrow$ **true**
32:      **end for**
33:      $\{\ell_1, \cdots, \ell_n\} \leftarrow \{\widehat{\ell}_1, \cdots, \widehat{\ell}_n\}$
34:      $\{t_0^{(1)}, \cdots, t_0^{(n)}\} \leftarrow \{t_1^{(1)}, \cdots, t_1^{(n)}\}$
35: **end for**

As the Chen–Nguyen simulator is deterministic, it terminates relatively fast, within a few hundreds of tours typically. Oppositely, our probabilistic simulator may perform far more tours and continue making further (though smaller and smaller) Gram–Schmidt progress. Another difference between the behaviors of the simulators comes from the fact that the expectation of a given sample (g in Line 14 of Algorithm 3) for updating each local block in our simulator is slightly larger than the one used in the Chen–Nguyen simulator that uses the Gaussian heuristic (but they are closer to each other as the block size increases). As a result, the sampled value for the first minimum of a local block can be slightly larger than in the Chen–Nguyen simulator. However (and more importantly), the chosen value can also be smaller than the Gaussian heuristic, and in fact smaller than the current value even if that one is already quite small. This is exactly what makes the Gram–Schmidt log-norms progress further in the simulations and makes the simulations closer to the practical behavior of BKZ.

4.2   Heuristic Justification

We now give a heuristic explanation as to why the probabilistic simulator (and BKZ) keeps making progress even after some significant amount of time. Every time it considers a block, it keeps trying to find a shorter vector than the current first vector of the block, thanks to fresh random sampling. Let $X \hookleftarrow \mathrm{Expo}(1/2)$ and $Y = X^{1/n}$. Assume for simplicity that there is only one block (i.e., $n = \beta$) and that the lattice Λ has been scaled so that the volume of the lattice is 1, which implies that $\lambda_1(\Lambda)$ has the same distribution as Y. The CDF of Y is

$$F(y) = 1 - e^{-y^n/2}.$$

Let $Y_{\min,K}$ be the minimum among K independent Y_i's. Its CDF and PDF are

$$F_{\min,K}(y) = 1 - e^{-Ky^n/2} \quad \text{and} \quad f_{\min,K}(y) = Kny^{n-1}e^{-Ky^n/2}/2,$$

respectively. We can hence compute the expected value

$$\mathbb{E}(Y_{K,min}) = (2/K)^{1/n} \cdot \Gamma(1 + 1/n) = \mathbb{E}(\lambda_1(\Lambda))/K^{1/n}.$$

One sees that the expectancy keeps decreasing, although much more slowly as K increases. Notice that K here can be regarded as proportional to the number of tours in our probabilistic simulator. We conjecture that BKZ is enjoying a similar phenomenon.

This simple model does not work for explaining BKZ with a single block (because for a single block, once the SVP instance has been solved, it cannot be improved further). In the more interesting case where $\beta < n$, the fact there are many intertwined blocks helps as an improvement for one block 'refreshes' the neighbouring blocks, which then have a chance to be improved. In this case, however, this simple model does not capture the impact of one block on the neighbouring blocks, nor the fact that the SVP instances across blocks are not statistically independent (in particular, the blocks overlap).

4.3   Quality of the New Simulator

In this subsection, we describe experiments aiming to assess the accuracy of our probabilistic BKZ simulator. We measure the quality of our simulator by comparing with the practical BKZ and the Chen–Nguyen simulator using two quantities: the Gram–Schmidt log-norms after certain tours and the root Hermite factors. We then describe some limitations of our simulator.

(a) **Graph of Gram–Schmidt Log-norms.** In practice, the full sequence of Gram–Schmidt log-norms is important for evaluating the quality of a basis. For example, if we extrapolate the log-norms by a straight line, the slope of the line can be used to indicate whether the basis is of good quality or not. For this reason, we are interested in how accurately the simulator predicts the evolution of the full sequence of Gram–Schmidt log-norms during the BKZ execution. We consider the following two experiments: (1) The input lattices are SVP-100 instances and we use BKZ_{45} without pruned enumeration up to $2,000$ tours. For this experiment, the setup is the same as the one used in Subsect. 3.4. We plot the averaged Gram–Schmidt log-norms at tours 50 and $2,000$. (2) The input lattices are SVP-150 instances and we use BKZ_{60} with pruned enumeration up to $20,000$ tours. Note some experiments (and simulation) completes before $20,000$ tours. In such cases, we take the Gram–Schmidt log-norms of the basis obtained at completion. We plot the averaged Gram–Schmidt log-norms at tours 50 and $20,000$ (or the last Gram–Schmidt log-norms if it completes before $20,000$ tours). We record the full log-norm sequences at the end of selected tours. As shown in Figs. 15, 16, 17, 18, 19, 20, 21 and 22, after a few tours, both the new BKZ simulator and the Chen–Nguyen simulator approach the experimental behavior of BKZ. As the number of BKZ tours increases, both the experimental BKZ and the probabilistic BKZ simulator evolve, and the corresponding log-norms eventually become concave in the head region. However, the Chen–Nguyen simulator stops making progress after a few tours. By comparison, the new simulator fits the experimental results quite accurately in both situations.

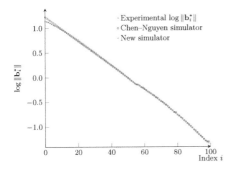 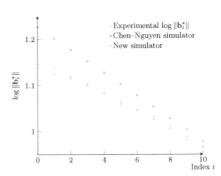

Fig. 15. Gram–Schmidt log-norms for BKZ_{45} at tour 50.

Fig. 16. Same as left hand side, but zoomed in.

(b) **Root Hermite Factor.** In Subsect. 3.4, we have seen that the asymptotes (for a large number of tours) of the root Hermite factors obtained with the genuine BKZ algorithm and the Chen–Nguyen simulator diverge. Here in Figs. 23 and 24, we investigate the behavior of the root Hermite factor obtained with the new probabilistic simulator, when the number of tours increases. One can observe that, after a few tours, the probabilistic simulator predicts the experimental data

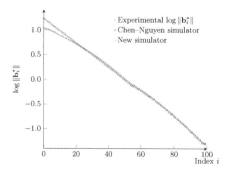

Fig. 17. Gram–Schmidt log-norms for BKZ$_{45}$ at tour 2,000.

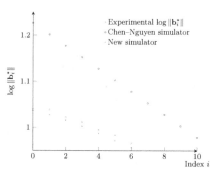

Fig. 18. Same as left hand side, but zoomed in.

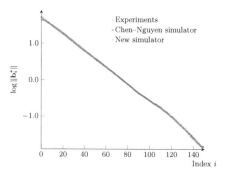

Fig. 19. Gram–Schmidt log-norms for BKZ$_{60}$ at tour 50.

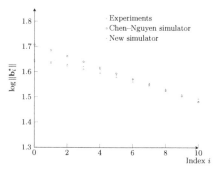

Fig. 20. Same as left hand side, but zoomed in.

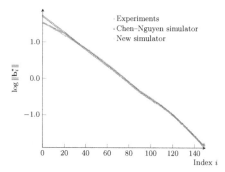

Fig. 21. Gram–Schmidt log-norms for BKZ$_{60}$ at tour 20,000.

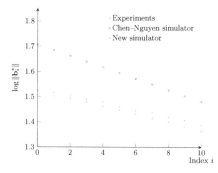

Fig. 22. Same as left hand side, but zoomed in.

more closely. One can also observe that, in the very first several tours, neither the Chen–Nguyen simulator nor the probabilistic simulator is very accurate. In the case of pruned enumeration, the experimental root Hermite factors seem to drop faster than in the simulators; while with non-pruned enumeration, the root Hermite factors in experiments evolve more slowly. This may be due to the algorithmic and implementation complications brought by the pre-processing, the SVP solver, pruning and post-processing.

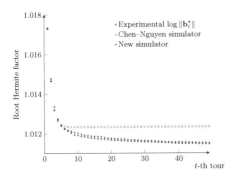 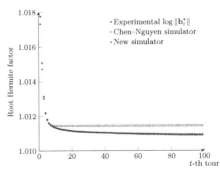

Fig. 23. Evolution of the root Hermite factor during the execution of BKZ_{45} (no pruned enumeration) on SVP-100.

Fig. 24. Evolution of the root Hermite factor during the execution of BKZ_{60} (with pruned enumeration) on SVP-150.

(c) Limitations of the New Simulator. The probabilistic simulator does not fully match with the experimental behavior of BKZ in the first few tours. In particular, the progress of the real Gram–Schmidt log-norms with BKZ with non-pruned enumeration is slower than the simulator's (refer to Fig. 23). One potential reason is the local SVP solver only attempts to find a vector slightly smaller than $\|\mathbf{b}_i^*\|$ (instead of the Gaussian heuristic value). On the other hand, it may be observed that the progress of the real Gram–Schmidt log-norms is a bit faster than the simulated log-norms in the very first BKZ tours, for BKZ with pruned enumeration (refer to Fig. 24) in these experiments. One potential reason could be that the pruned enumeration uses extensive pre-processing in a local block (which is not captured by the simulator), and this helps to lower the root Hermite factor in the beginning of the execution. However, as soon as the number of tours increases, the probabilistic phenomenon seems to weigh more and the new simulator becomes accurate.

Next, we verify if the preprocessing indeed helps make the experimental root Hermite factor decrease faster than the corresponding quality in the simulator. To verify the impact of preprocessing in pruned enumeration, we run BKZ_{60} (with pruned enumeration) without pre-processing on SVP_{150} instances. We plot the root Hermite factor of the basis after each tours (up to 100 tours). Each data is taken averaged over 100 results. As shown in Fig. 25, the BKZ variant without pre-processing makes progress no faster than the simulator. This suggests that pre-processing indeed accelerates the progress made by BKZ. On the other hand, we can also observe that without preprocessing, the root Hermite factor decrease slower than the corresponding quality in the simulator. One possible reason for this could be that the vector found by extreme pruning in each local block may be longer than the minimum of the local lattice.

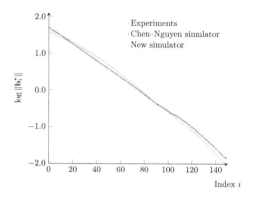

Fig. 25. Comparison of Gram–Schmidt log-norms obtained by the simulators and BKZ_{60} (no pre-processing) on SVP-150, after 4,000 tours.

In conclusion, it seems quite difficult to use the simulator to estimate the precise evolution of Gram–Schmidt log-norms for the first few tours due to the following two reasons: (1) we are not clear about how much improvement is provided by the pre-processing; (2) we do not have a precise understanding on the distribution of norms of vectors output by the enumeration (ideally with pruning). On other hand, after the first few tours, the simulator seems to be more accurate when estimating the Hermite factors, which is important for cryptographic applications.

4.4   Predicting the Root Hermite Factor for Large Block Sizes

As our proposed simulator predicts real BKZ quite well for the range of block sizes for which such experiments can be run, we expect that our simulator keeps this accuracy for larger block sizes. This is in particular relevant in cryptanalysis and for security analyses of concrete lattice-based cryptosystems. Indeed, many of the existing security analyses rely on the root Hermite factor predicted by the Chen–Nguyen simulator (see [ACD+18] and the references therein), which, as we have seen, is an over-estimate. We thus run the simulators for large block sizes and large dimensions, to assess how the discrepancy scales.

In this experiment, we consider two cases:

(1) the dimension n is much larger than the block-size β.
(2) the dimension n is a small constant times larger than the block-size β.

The Case (1) is a scenario often considered to assess the quality of BKZ-type algorithms (see, e.g., [CN11]). On the other hand, in practice, we are also interested in Case (2) where the dimension/block-size ratio is small. This is a typical situation for the lattice-based NIST candidates (see [ACD+18]). Concretely, in the first case, we run our simulator of BKZ with block-size $\beta \in [50, 250]$ on 1000-dimensional lattices and our simulator on BKZ with block-size $\beta \in [260, 300]$ in 2000-dimensional lattices, both with 20,000 tours. In the second case, we run the same experiment as above except with a fixed ratio of 3 between dimension and block-size. Each data point is averaged over 10 samples. We plot the root Hermite factor corresponding to the Gram–Schmidt log-norms output by our simulator.

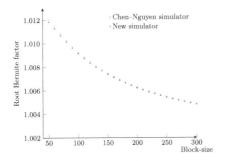
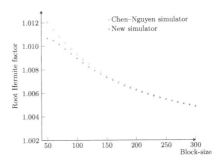

Fig. 26. Root Hermite factor for selected $\beta \in \{50, 60, \cdots, 300\}$. Here the dimension is 1000 for $\beta \in [50, 250]$ and 2000 for $\beta \in [260, 300]$.

Fig. 27. Root Hermite factor for selected $\beta \in \{50, 60, \cdots, 300\}$. Here the dimension is $3 \cdot \beta$.

As can be seen in Figs. 26 and 27, for large block sizes, the discrepancy vanishes: both simulators converge to the same root Hermite factors. This may be explained by considering the distribution of the minimum of a uniform unit-volume lattice, used in the probabilistic simulator. The expectation is $2^{1/\beta} \cdot \Gamma(1 + 1/\beta)$, which converges to 1, the Gaussian heuristic value (when β grows to infinity). Further, as we have seen in Subsect. 2.1, the variance of the selected value is $2^{2/\beta} \cdot \left(\Gamma(1 + 2/\beta) - (\Gamma(1 + 1/\beta))^2\right) \cdot v_\beta^{-2/\beta}$, which decreases to 0 as $O(1/\beta^2)$, making the distribution "more concentrated" and lowering the chance of being "lucky" in finding unexpectedly short vectors in local lattices.

5   Pressing the Concavity

In this section, we propose a new BKZ variant. For practical purposes, we further twist this new algorithm with several different strategies. We also quantify the quality of the obtained lattice bases.

5.1 Pressed-BKZ

Below, we first describe the new BKZ variant, pressed-BKZ, and then explain why it provides an improvement. Pressed-BKZ is described as Algorithm 4.

Algorithm 4. The pressed-BKZ algorithm

Input: A basis $\mathbf{B} = \{\mathbf{b}_1, \cdots, \mathbf{b}_n\}$, a block-size $\beta \geq 2$ and a constant $\delta < 1$.
Output: A basis of $\Lambda(\mathbf{B})$.
1: **for** $s = 1$ **to** $n - \beta + 1$ **do**   // progressive starting point
2:     Re-randomize the projected lattice $\Lambda_{[s,n]}$.
3:     **repeat**
4:         **for** $k = s$ **to** $n - 1$ **do**
5:             Find $\mathbf{b}$ such that $\|\pi_k(\mathbf{b})\| = \lambda_1(\Lambda_{[k,\min(k+\beta-1,n)]})$
6:             **if** $\delta \cdot \|\mathbf{b}_k^*\| > \|\mathbf{b}\|$ **then**
7:                 LLL-reduce($\mathbf{b}_1, \cdots, \mathbf{b}_{k-1}, \mathbf{b}, \mathbf{b}_k, \cdots, \mathbf{b}_{\min(k+\beta,n)}$).
8:             **else**
9:                 LLL-reduce($\mathbf{b}_1, \cdots, \mathbf{b}_{\min(k+\beta,n)}$).
10:             **end if**
11:         **end for**
12:     **until** no change occurs (or other condition).
13: **end for**

The pressed-BKZ algorithm runs standard BKZ on block $\Lambda_{[s,n]}$ with an incrementally increased starting index $s \in [1, n - \beta + 1]$. In particular, in the case of $s = 1$, pressed-BKZ executes standard BKZ. Note that in Line 12, "no change occurs" means that no local block was updated during the last tour (from $k = s$ to $k = n - 1$). The difference between pressed-BKZ and standard BKZ starts with $s > 1$. At that stage, it does not run BKZ on the full lattice basis anymore. Instead, it freezes the first $s - 1$ lattice vectors $\{\mathbf{b}_i\}_{i \in [1, s-1]}$ and re-randomizes the projected lattice $\Lambda_{[s,n]}$, then runs stardard BKZ on the projected lattice. Note that the re-randomization is necessary, otherwise after the BKZ reduction on $\Lambda_{[1,n]}$, no improvement will happen in BKZ reduction on $\Lambda_{[2,n]}$ in the second iteration and either in the following iterations. In particular, in the second iteration, the re-randomization helps randomize the basis vectors of the projected lattice $\Lambda_{[2,n]}$, thus gives a chance of generating a denser leading block of $\Lambda_{[2,n]}$ via BKZ reduction. The re-randomization on the projected lattice is done via tranforming the basis of the projected lattice with a unimodular matrix. Here, we use the unimodular matrix generated in the fplll library.

The design rationale is as follows. Suppose BKZ creates a head concavity for the Gram–Schmidt log-norms. Then the first iteration with $s = 1$ will help to lower $\log \|\mathbf{b}_1^*\|$. The iteration with $s = 2$ will preserve $\log \|\mathbf{b}_1^*\|$ and help to lower $\log \|\mathbf{b}_2^*\|$, etc. This explains the name of the algorithm.

5.2 On the Behavior of Pressed-BKZ

The goal of pressed-BKZ is to further improve the quality of bases obtained by the original BKZ algorithm without a block-size increase. In order to illustrate the idea, we run standard BKZ_{60} on 120-dimensional random lattices (generated in the same way as mentioned at the start of Sect. 4) with 500 tours (i.e., with early-abort) first, and then run pressed-BKZ with the same number of tours in each iteration with start index $s = 2$. Each data point is averaged over 100 samples. As shown in Fig. 28, pressed-BKZ successfully presses the "head concavity" that was produced by the standard BKZ algorithm.

From the experiment above, we can already see that pressed-BKZ produces a basis with better quality, as its corresponding Gram–Schmidt log-norms achieve a smaller slope. Next, we try to assess by how much pressed-BKZ improves standard BKZ in this respect. We first adapt the simulator for BKZ from Sect. 4 in the direct way to simulate pressed-BKZ. Before we go further, we check the accuracy of our simulator when simulating the behavior of pressed-BKZ by running the same experiment above, but with the simulator. As shown in Fig. 29, our simulator produces a result that is close to the one experimentally obtain with pressed-BKZ.

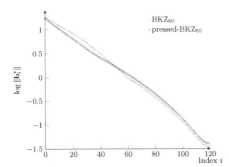

Fig. 28. Full sequences of Gram–Schmidt log-norms of bases returned by BKZ_{60} and pressed-BKZ_{60}.

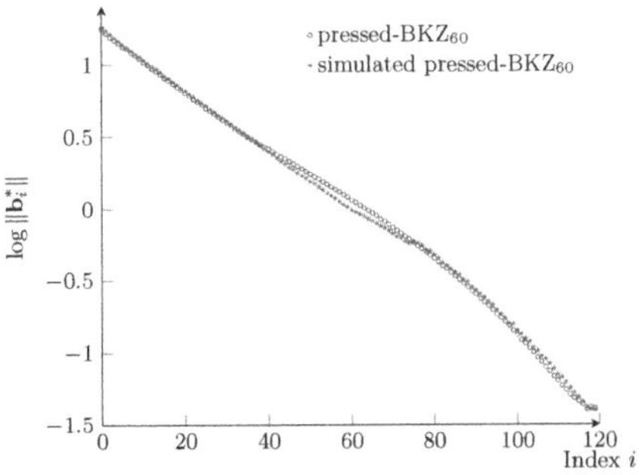

Fig. 29. Full sequences of Gram–Schmidt log-norms of bases returned by BKZ_{60}, pressed-BKZ_{60} and simulated pressed-BKZ_{60}.

Now we have an accurate simulator for pressed-BKZ, we can proceed to check the behavior of pressed-BKZ further. For this, we run our simulator of pressed-BKZ for block-sizes between 50 and 300, with many tours. We again consider two cases: (1) the dimension n is much larger than the block-size β; (2) the dimension n is a small constant times larger than the block-size β. In the first case, we simulate pressed-BKZ with block-size $\beta \in [50, 250]$ on 1,000-dimensional lattices with 5,000 tours for each iteration, and pressed-BKZ with block-size $\beta \in [260, 300]$ on 2,000-dimensional lattices with 10,000 tours. Each data is averaged over 10 samples. In the second case, we run the same experiment as above except with the dimension/block-size ratio set to 3. Further, we recall the Chen–Nguyen simulator for a comparison. Note that we can also adapt the Chen–Nguyen simulator for pressed-BKZ, which however, gives a same result as the simulation for standard BKZ. Here, we use the extrapolated slope to evaluate the quality of a reduced basis. To compute the slope, we fit the Gram–Schmidt log-norms with a line using the least square method of fplll and fpylll. Note that the default implementation in fplll and fpylll computes the slope using the Gram–Schmidt log-norms multiplied by 2. Here we compute the slope using the Gram–Schmidt log-norms only. As we can see in Fig. 30, there is a difference between our simulator for pressed-BKZ and the Chen–Nguyen simulator (for standard BKZ), which means our simulator for pressed-BKZ may be used to make a severer cryptanalysis on lattice-based cryptography compared to the Chen–Nguyen simulator.

As can be seen in Fig. 31, when the dimension is relatively close to the block-size, our simulator for pressed-BKZ outputs the Gram–Schmidt norms with slope more significantlly better than the one output by the Chen–Nguyen simulator. In particular, for small block-size $\beta = 50$, our simulator for pressed-BKZ can produce Gram–Schmidt norms with slope almost equal to the one produced by the Chen–Nguyen simulator for standard BKZ with block-size 85. Thus we earn almost 35 dimensions while only relying on an SVP solver in dimension 50. The difference becomes very small when the block-size considered is larger than 200.

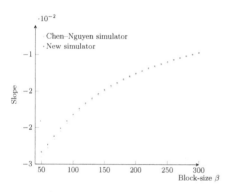

Fig. 30. Comparison of the slopes of Gram–Schmidt log-norms between our simulator for pressed-BKZ and the Chen–Nguyen simulator for standard BKZ for selected $\beta \in \{50, 60, \cdots, 300\}$. Here the dimension is 1000 for $\beta \in [50, 250]$ and 2000 for $\beta \in [260, 300]$.

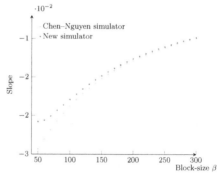

Fig. 31. Comparison of the slopes of Gram–Schmidt log-norms between our simulator for pressed-BKZ and the Chen–Nguyen simulator for standard BKZ for selected $\beta \in \{50, 60, \cdots, 300\}$. Here the dimension is $3 \cdot \beta$.

5.3   Variable Block-Size Strategy

Pressed-BKZ helps improve the quality of the basis such that its Gram–Schmidt log-norms approximate a line. However, the concavity phenomenon may still exist within each iteration during pressed-BKZ. Concretely, in the BKZ_β reduction for each projected sub-lattice $\Lambda_{[s,n]}$ for $s \in [1, \cdots, n - \beta + 1]$, one can still observe the head concavity phenomenon after a few tours of the BKZ algorithm. As a result, the costs of solving SVP instances in the leading blocks become less than those for the middle blocks (we refer to Subsect. 3.2 for the correspondence between quality of basis and enumeration cost for SVP).

We adapt the variable block-size strategy from [AWHT16]. The principle of the variable block-size strategy is to adaptively use larger block-sizes for the leading blocks, so that their enumeration costs match the enumeration costs for the middle blocks. We use the following simple variant: for the case of BKZ_β on the projected $(n - s + 1)$-dimensional sub-lattice, we always take the specific block $\Lambda_{[k,e]}$ in the middle with $k = \lfloor n/2 \rfloor - \lfloor \beta/2 \rfloor + \lfloor s/2 \rfloor + 1$ and $e = \lfloor n/2 \rfloor + \lfloor \beta/2 \rfloor + \lfloor s/2 \rfloor$ as the standard SVP cost for comparison. When the estimated SVP cost for any leading block is smaller than the cost of this middle block, we progressively increase the block-size of the current leading block until its SVP cost matches the standard SVP cost. Correspondingly, we only use the variable block-size strategy for those leading blocks, with starting index not exceeding k (the starting index of the selected middle block).

Note that if such variable block-size strategy improves standard BKZ, then it is likely to improve pressed-BKZ: if the variable block-size strategy can decrease the first Gram–Schmidt norm of the projected lattice $\Lambda_{[k,n]}$ (for k from 1 to $n - \beta + 1$) a little more (compared to standard BKZ without such a strategy), then the improvement from each iteration will eventually contribute to the final pressed-BKZ reduced basis. Thus we will only consider such variable block-size strategy with standard BKZ. As our simulator seems to be precise on the quality of BKZ, we first compare BKZ with and without such a variable block-size strategy using our simulator.

We run the simulation (100 instances) for BKZ_{60} (with and without the variable block-size strategy) and plot the average root Hermite factor after each tour. As shown in Figs. 32 and 33, BKZ with variable block-size makes the root Hermite factor decrease slightly faster. It seems that the difference becomes smaller when the number of tours increases. However, we also notice that after sufficiently many tours, such a difference reoccurs as shown in Fig. 33. One can observe that the largest gap in Fig. 33 is less than 0.0001. Thus we may conclude that the variable block-size strategy helps improve the root Hermite factor faster. However, it does not seem to give a significant improvement on the root Hermite factor itself.

Next, we run experiment to verify if the variable block-size strategy indeed helps decreasing the root Hermite factor faster (and check if this matches the simulated results). We run standard BKZ_{60} with and without variable block-size on an SVP-120 instance from the Darmstadt lattice challenge. We plot the average root Hermite factor (over 100 samples) after each tour. As can be seen in Figs. 34 and 35, the convergence of root Hermite factor of basis output by the standard BKZ_{60} with variable block-size is slightly better than the one output by BKZ_{60} without such strategy.

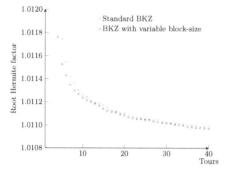

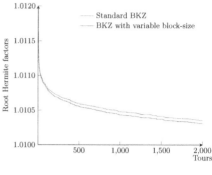

Fig. 32. Comparison of root Hermite factors of simulated BKZ with and without variable block-size. The simulation is performed with our new simulator up to 40 tours.

Fig. 33. Comparison of root Hermite factors of simulated BKZ with and without variable block-size. The simulation is performed with our new simulator up to 2,000 tours.

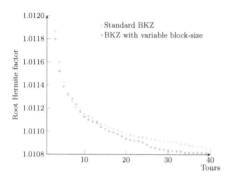

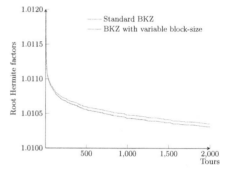

Fig. 34. Comparison of root Hermite factors of standard BKZ_{60} with and without variable block-size within 40 tours.

Fig. 35. Comparison of root Hermite factors of standard BKZ_{60} with and without variable block-size within 2,000 tours.

5.4   Solving SVP-120 with Pressed-BKZ

In this subsection, we use pressed-BKZ for the preprocessing phase to solve an SVP-120 challenge, to demonstrate its practical relevance. We are interested in the quality of pressed-BKZ-reduced bases as reflected by the total enumeration cost, i.e., the sum the preprocessing and enumeration costs, divided by the success probability. In the experiment, we consider an SVP challenge of dimension 120 (generated using the Darmstadt lattice challenge generator) and preprocess it using pressed-BKZ_{60} with the adaptive block-size strategy described in the previous subsection. The preprocessing took a total 5×10^5 s on an Intel Xeon processor of 2.67GHz (the enumeration speed is 2×10^7 nodes per second and hence the runtime corresponds to an enumeration tree of 1×10^{13} nodes).

Comparison with Standard BKZ. We first investigate the quality of the pressed-BKZ$_{60}$-reduced basis in terms of BKZ-reducedness. The aim is to find the block-sizes β (and the number of tours) for which the output of standard BKZ$_\beta$ would be of similar quality. This suggests that the bases produced by pressed-BKZ$_{60}$ and standard BKZ$_\beta$ have similar full enumeration cost.

We have to determine some criterion for the quality of bases. Essentially, one wants to compare the *pruned* enumeration cost of the pressed-BKZ$_{60}$-reduced basis with the pruned enumeration cost of the standard BKZ$_\beta$-reduced basis. As a first approximation, we compute the *full* enumeration cost of BKZ$_\beta$-reduced basis (right after each BKZ tour) and stop as soon as it is close to the *full* enumeration cost for the pressed-BKZ-reduced basis. This also gives us roughly the number of tours needed for BKZ with the corresponding block-size to achieve a similar quality as our basis reduced by pressed-BKZ$_{60}$. A better approach, which we did not implement, would be to invoke the pruning optimizer right after each local SVP to estimate the enumeration cost and stop as soon as it is close to the pruned enumeration cost for the pressed-BKZ reduced basis.

Instead of doing the actual BKZ$_\beta$ experiment for all candidate blocksizes, we first use simulation to find the most competitive blocksizes. As investigated in Sect. 4, the probabilistic simulator seems quite precise after the first few tours: if the number of tours involved in the simulation is tiny, we conduct true BKZ experiments for confirmation. After we have determined the most appropriate blocksizes β, we conduct true BKZ experiments for these blocksizes to double-check their quality and run-time (as opposed to simulation).

To start with, we have to determine some suitable searching range for the block-size β. As we already saw, in the case where the dimension is not much larger than the block-size, the quality of a basis reduced by pressed-BKZ$_{60}$ can be quite superior to that obtained by using BKZ$_\beta$ for $\beta > 60$. Thus we try several larger blocksizes starting for $\beta = 70, 75, 80, 85, 90$. For each blocksize β, the Gram–Schmidt norms of standard BKZ$_\beta$ are simulated by the probabilistic simulator. We start with the LLL-reduced basis of the SVP-120 input and average over the 100 simulations for each β. We set a maximum of $50,000$ tours in the simulator but break as soon as (if possible) the full enumeration cost is smaller than the full enumeration cost of our reduced pressed-BKZ$_{60}$.

For blocksizes 70 and 75, the full enumeration cost cannot beat the full enumeration cost of pressed-BKZ$_{60}$ reduced basis within the limit of $50,000$ tours and therefore terminates. For other blocksizes, after the simulator terminates, we compute the (average) minimum number of tours needed. They are listed in the legend of Fig. 36. In Fig. 36, we also plot the Gram–Schmidt log-norms of the pressed-BKZ$_{60}$-reduced basis along with the average simulated Gram–Schmidt log-norms of the output bases of standard BKZ$_\beta$ (for the relevant numbers of tours). One can observe that, at the point of termination, the simulated Gram–Schmidt log-norms have comparable shape as the pressed-BKZ$_{60}$ reduced basis. We confirm this by examining their full enumeration cost in Table 1. The full

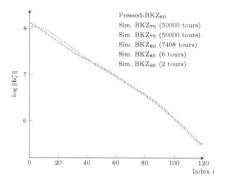 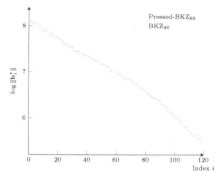

Fig. 36. Gram–Schmidt log-norms of simulated pressed-BKZ$_{60}$ and simulated BKZ$_{\beta}$.

Fig. 37. Gram–Schmidt log-norms of experimental pressed-BKZ$_{60}$ and BKZ$_{90}$ (28 tours).

enumeration cost is tabulated for each (averaged) simulated basis. As a conclusion, it can be seen that the most competitive blocksizes are 85 and 90: the number of tours involved for blocksizes 70, 75, 80 are too large.

So far, we have only judged the quality of the preprocessed basis using simulation. It should be noted that the probabilistic simulator may not to be accurate when the number of tours involved are tiny (see Subsect. 4.3). This is the case for blocksizes 85 and 90. Therefore, instead of simulation, we conduct actual BKZ$_{85}$ and BKZ$_{90}$ experiments with the LLL-reduced basis as input: we used a parallel implementation of the BKZ algorithm implemented in `fpylll` and ran BKZ$_{90}$ on the LLL-reduced basis with 280 cores. The local SVP solver attempts to find a vector smaller than 1.05 times the Gaussian heuristic of the local block. Also, if too many trials have been attempted without a success, then it moves to the next block. Therefore, the number of tours in experiments could be larger than in simulations (but each local SVP takes less time).

In the experiments, we aborted the BKZ$_{90}$ execution right after the full enumeration cost of the current basis is similar to (if possible) that of the pressed-BKZ$_{60}$-reduced basis. Then we used the previous BKZ tour (where the full enumeration cost was slightly larger than that of the pressed-BKZ$_{60}$-reduced basis). BKZ$_{90}$ took 28 tours to reach a similar full enumeration cost and the overall runtime was 5×10^6 s (the number of cores is taken into account). In Fig. 37, we plot the Gram–Schmidt log-norms of this BKZ$_{90}$-reduced basis and compare it with pressed-BKZ$_{60}$. This confirms that their qualities are analogous. For BKZ$_{85}$, we aborted the computation after 100 tours as the overall run-time was already 8×10^6 s. Note that both are already much larger than the cost we spent on the pressed-BKZ$_{60}$ preprocessing, of 5×10^5 s. The full enumeration costs of BKZ$_{90}$ and BKZ$_{85}$-reduced bases is computed in Table 1. Note that the experiments for BKZ$_{90}$ (and BKZ$_{85}$) took much more tours to achieve the same quality (if possible) compared to simulation. This might be due to the facts that our implementation is greedy as mentioned above and does not always solve the local SVP problem.

Table 1. Estimated enumeration cost to solve the SVP-120 instance. The row "Full of Sim." records the full enumeration cost (number of nodes) based on the simulated preprocessed basis. The row "Full of Exp." records the full enumeration cost on BKZ_{85} and BKZ_{90}-reduced bases (from experiments) after 100 tours and 28 tours respectively. The row "Prune of Exp." records the cost for pruned enumeration for Pressed-BKZ_{60} and BKZ_{90} reduced basis (from experiments): it includes the costs of all trial enumerations and the cost of preprocessing before each trial enumeration (but excludes the initial preprocessing cost).

	Pressed-BKZ_{60}	BKZ_{70}	BKZ_{75}	BKZ_{80}	BKZ_{85}	BKZ_{90}
Full of Sim.	n/a	6.83×10^{27}	3.21×10^{27}	1.17×10^{27}	1.15×10^{27}	0.83×10^{27}
Full of Exp.	1.21×10^{27}	n/a	n/a	n/a	2.64×10^{27}	1.35×10^{27}
Prune of Exp.	5.9×10^{13}	n/a	n/a	n/a	n/a	6.3×10^{13}

So far, we have only used the full enumeration cost to measure the quality. We confirm this using a pruner to estimate the enumeration cost (for Pressed-BKZ_{60} and BKZ_{90}-reduced bases). A pruner optimizes the pruning coefficients to minimize the overall run-time of preprocessing plus enumeration divided by the success probability. The general strategy in extreme pruning [CN11] is to preprocess the basis using BKZ and then run the enumeration with a certain success probability p. If the enumeration fails, it rerandomizes the basis and then conducts the preprocessing and enumeration again. The expected number of repetitions to succeed in the enumeration is $\approx 1/p$. It remains to determine the preprocessing time before each enumeration. It should be noted if the first enumeration fails, one usually runs a mild re-randomization before the next preprocessing, thus the next preprocessing will be faster than the first preprocessing, since it still benefits from the BKZ reduction in last preprocessing.

We determine the preprocessing time with the following experiment. For the BKZ_{90}-reduced basis, after re-randomization, the full enumeration cost increases from 1.35×10^{27} to 1.56×10^{27}. We re-preprocess the randomized basis using BKZ_{80} until the full enumeration cost decreases to around 1.35×10^{27}. Here we just used BKZ_{80} for simplicity (there could be other strategies). The re-preprocessing took 1.7×10^{5} s (i.e., 3.4×10^{12} nodes). We use this preprocessing cost (the preprocessing before each trial enumeration except the initial preprocessing) as input to the pruner (for both Pressed-BKZ_{60} and BKZ_{90}-reduced bases). The total pruned enumeration cost estimate in fpylll, tabulated in Table 1, confirms that Pressed-BKZ_{60} and BKZ_{90}-reduced bases indeed have similar quality as they all admit similar total pruned enumeration costs. In general, the pruner seems to be quite precise in practice (hence so are the estimates in Table 1). Thus it suffices to compare the initial preprocessing cost between Pressed-BKZ_{60} and BKZ_{90}: pressed-BKZ_{60} (5×10^{5} s) took less time compared to BKZ_{90} (28 tours in 5×10^{6} s).

In this subsection, we have only considered a straightforward strategy, BKZ plus enumeration, for solving the SVP-120 instance. In the following we will further compare with progressive-BKZ [AWHT16].

Comparison with Progressive-BKZ. The main idea of progressive-BKZ is to preprocess the basis using BKZ with progressively increased blocksizes and use local enumeration with high success probability to avoid the overheads brought in by the preprocessing. Furthermore, a progressive blocksize strategy (optimized based on their adaptation of the Chen–Nguyen simulator for their progressive-BKZ algorithm) was used for preprocessing before a final enumeration. In particular, [AWHT16, Table 4] gives the cost of solving SVP challenges using their blocksize strategy: this table is to be understood as the cost of an idealized algorithm and is hence optimistic compared to current algorithms. We re-investigate the estimates in that table by combining their progressive-BKZ method with our pressed-BKZ algorithm.

Given the pressed-BKZ$_{60}$ reduced basis, we use the progressive-BKZ method in the `bkz2_sweet_spot`[4] branch in `fplll`. Note that it implements a variant of progressive-BKZ: the progressive strategy differs from that of [AWHT16] but it suffices for our comparison. It should be noted that our pressed-BKZ$_{60}$ reduced basis is already quite reduced so we start progressive-BKZ with blocksize ≈ 75 to avoid a superfluous re-computation. We used 80 cores for the computation on the pressed-BKZ$_{60}$ reduced basis. We spent 5.78 core days (5×10^5 s) on the initial pressed-BKZ$_{60}$ and 1.21 core days for the progressive-BKZ to complete the SVP instance. In total, we completed the computation in a total of 6.99 core days (with enumeration speed of $\approx 2 \times 10^7$ nodes per second), faster than the 14.94 lower bound (with enumeration speed of 6×10^7 nodes per second) in [AWHT16, Table 4].

For further comparison, we also ran the same experiment using an LLL-reduced basis instead of pressed-BKZ$_{60}$ reduced basis in the beginning. The overall run-time was 8.75 core days. This implies that `bkz2_sweet_spot` is faster than the estimates in [AWHT16]. Compared to this LLL-based experiment, the pressed-BKZ$_{60}$-reduced basis helps to reduce the overall run-time by about 20%.

It should be noted that we only provide one such strategy that lowers the estimates in [AWHT16, Table 4] and demonstrate the usefulness of the pressed-BKZ algorithm. It is quite possible that this is far from an optimal strategy, which could combine variants of progressive preprocessing, extreme pruning and adaptive choices based on simulation. For instance, it may be better to also use pressed-BKZ inside progressive-BKZ (recursively for any preprocessing) to better maintain the shape of the pressed-BKZ preprocessed basis. Also, we only conducted two SVP-120 experiments, which is not statistically significant. We leave the question of how to optimize the strategy based on the existing approaches open for future work.

---

[4] https://github.com/fplll/fpylll/tree/bkz2_sweet_spot.

Acknowledgments. We thank the reviewers for detailed comments and suggestions. We acknowledge the Research Computing at Florida Atlantic University and the PSMN (Pôle Scientifique de Modélisation Numérique) of ENS Lyon for providing computing facilities. This work has been supported in part by ERC Starting Grant ERC-2013-StG-335086-LATTAC, by the European Union PROMETHEUS project (Horizon 2020 Research and Innovation Program, grant 780701) and by BPI-France in the context of the national project RISQ (P141580).

References

[ACD+18] Albrecht, M.R., et al.: Estimate all the {LWE, NTRU} schemes! In SCN, pp. 351–357 (2018)

[APS15] Albrecht, M.R., Player, R., Scott, S.: On the concrete hardness of learning with errors. J. Math. Cryptol. **9**(3), 169–203 (2015)

[AWHT16] Aono, Y., Wang, Y., Hayashi, T., Takagi, T.: Improved progressive BKZ algorithms and their precise cost estimation by sharp simulator. In: Fischlin, M., Coron, J.-S. (eds.) EUROCRYPT 2016. LNCS, vol. 9665, pp. 789–819. Springer, Heidelberg (2016). https://doi.org/10.1007/978-3-662-49890-3_30

[BDGL16] Becker, A., Ducas, L., Gama, N., Laarhoven, T.: New directions in nearest neighbor searching with applications to lattice sieving. In: SODA, pp. 10–24 (2016)

[Che09] Chen Y.: Réduction de réseau et sécurité concrète du chiffrement complètement homomorphe. Ph.D. thesis, Université Paris Diderot (2009)

[CN11] Chen, Y., Nguyen, P.Q.: BKZ 2.0: better lattice security estimates. In: Lee, D.H., Wang, X. (eds.) ASIACRYPT 2011. LNCS, vol. 7073, pp. 1–20. Springer, Heidelberg (2011). https://doi.org/10.1007/978-3-642-25385-0_1

[dt16] The FPLLL development team. fplll, a lattice reduction library (2016). https://github.com/fplll/fplll

[dt17] The FPYLLL development team. fpylll, a Python interface to fplll (2017). https://github.com/fplll/fpylll

[Duc18] Ducas, L.: Shortest vector from lattice sieving: a few dimensions for free. In: Nielsen, J.B., Rijmen, V. (eds.) EUROCRYPT 2018. LNCS, vol. 10820, pp. 125–145. Springer, Cham (2018). https://doi.org/10.1007/978-3-319-78381-9_5

[FP83] Fincke, U., Pohst, M.: A procedure for determining algebraic integers of given norm. In: van Hulzen, J.A. (ed.) EUROCAL 1983. LNCS, vol. 162, pp. 194–202. Springer, Heidelberg (1983). https://doi.org/10.1007/3-540-12868-9_103

[GNR10] Gama, N., Nguyen, P.Q., Regev, O.: Lattice enumeration using extreme pruning. In: Gilbert, H. (ed.) EUROCRYPT 2010. LNCS, vol. 6110, pp. 257–278. Springer, Heidelberg (2010). https://doi.org/10.1007/978-3-642-13190-5_13

[HPS11] Hanrot, G., Pujol, X., Stehlé, D.: Analyzing blockwise lattice algorithms using dynamical systems. In: Rogaway, P. (ed.) CRYPTO 2011. LNCS, vol. 6841, pp. 447–464. Springer, Heidelberg (2011). https://doi.org/10.1007/978-3-642-22792-9_25

[HS07] Hanrot, G., Stehlé, D.: Improved analysis of Kannan's shortest lattice vector algorithm. In: Menezes, A. (ed.) CRYPTO 2007. LNCS, vol. 4622, pp. 170–186. Springer, Heidelberg (2007). https://doi.org/10.1007/978-3-540-74143-5_10

[HS08] Hanrot, G., Stehlé, D.: Worst-case Hermite-Korkine-Zolotarev reduced lattice bases. CoRR, abs/0801.3331 (2008)

[Kan83] Kannan, R.: Improved algorithms for integer programming and related lattice problems. In: STOC, pp. 99–108. ACM (1983)

[MV10] Micciancio, D., Voulgaris, P.: Faster exponential time algorithms for the shortest vector problem. In: SODA. ACM (2010)

[Neu17] Neumaier, A.: Bounding basis reduction properties. Des. Codes Cryptogr. **84**(1–2), 237–259 (2017)

[NV08] Nguyen, P.Q., Vidick, T.: Sieve algorithms for the shortest vector problem are practical. J. Math. Cryptol. **2**(2), 181–207 (2008)

[NV09] Nguyen, P.Q., Vallée, B.: The LLL Algorithm: Survey and Applications. Information Security and Cryptography. Springer, Heidelberg (2009)

[Rog56] Rogers, C.A.: The number of lattice points in a set. Proc. London Math. Soc. **3**(6), 305–320 (1956)

[Sch59] Schmidt, W.: Masstheorie in der Geometrie der Zahlen. Acta Math. **102**(3–4), 159–224 (1959)

[Sch87] Schnorr, C.-P.: A hierarchy of polynomial lattice basis reduction algorithms. Theor. Comput. Science **53**, 201–224 (1987)

[Sch03] Schnorr, C.P.: Lattice reduction by random sampling and birthday methods. In: Alt, H., Habib, M. (eds.) STACS 2003. LNCS, vol. 2607, pp. 145–156. Springer, Heidelberg (2003). https://doi.org/10.1007/3-540-36494-3_14

[SE94] Schnorr, C.-P., Euchner, M.: Lattice basis reduction: improved practical algorithms and solving subset sum problems. Math. Program. **66**, 181–199 (1994)

[Söd11] Södergren, A.: On the Poisson distribution of lengths of lattice vectors in a random lattice. Math. Z. **269**(3), 945–954 (2011)

[YD17] Yu, Y., Ducas, L.: Second order statistical behavior of LLL and BKZ. In: Adams, C., Camenisch, J. (eds.) SAC 2017. LNCS, vol. 10719, pp. 3–22. Springer, Cham (2018). https://doi.org/10.1007/978-3-319-72565-9_1

Quantum Lattice Enumeration and Tweaking Discrete Pruning

Yoshinori Aono[1], Phong Q. Nguyen[2,3(✉)], and Yixin Shen[3,4]

[1] National Institute of Information and Communications Technology, Tokyo, Japan
[2] Inria, Paris, France
Phong.Nguyen@inria.fr
[3] CNRS, JFLI, University of Tokyo, Tokyo, Japan
[4] IRIF, Univ Paris Diderot, CNRS, Paris, France

Abstract. Enumeration is a fundamental lattice algorithm. We show how to speed up enumeration on a quantum computer, which affects the security estimates of several lattice-based submissions to NIST: if T is the number of operations of enumeration, our quantum enumeration runs in roughly $\sqrt{T}$ operations. This applies to the two most efficient forms of enumeration known in the extreme pruning setting: cylinder pruning but also discrete pruning introduced at Eurocrypt '17. Our results are based on recent quantum tree algorithms by Montanaro and Ambainis-Kokainis. The discrete pruning case requires a crucial tweak: we modify the preprocessing so that the running time can be rigorously proved to be essentially optimal, which was the main open problem in discrete pruning. We also introduce another tweak to solve the more general problem of finding close lattice vectors.

1 Introduction

The main two hard lattice problems are finding short lattice vectors (SVP) and close lattice vectors (CVP), either exactly or approximately. Both have been widely used in cryptographic design for the past twenty years: Ajtai's SIS [2] and Regev's LWE [38] are randomized variants of respectively SVP and CVP.

With the NIST standardization of post-quantum cryptography and the development of fully-homomorphic encryption, there is a need for convincing security estimates for lattice-based cryptosystems. Yet, in the past ten years, there has been regular progress in the design of lattice algorithms, both in theory (*e.g.* [1,20,31]) and practice (*e.g.* [10,17,19,21,25,32,35]), which makes security estimates tricky. Lattice-based NIST submissions use varying cost models, which gives rise to a wide range of security estimates [5]. The biggest source of divergence is the cost assessment of a subroutine to find nearly shortest lattice vectors in certain dimensions (typically the blocksize of reduction algorithms), which is chosen among two families: sieving [3,15,25,32,35] and enumeration.

Enumeration is the simplest algorithm to solve SVP/CVP: it outputs $L \cap B$, given a lattice L and an n-dimensional ball $B \subseteq \mathbb{R}^n$. Dating back to the early

© International Association for Cryptologic Research 2018
T. Peyrin and S. Galbraith (Eds.): ASIACRYPT 2018, LNCS 11272, pp. 405–434, 2018.
https://doi.org/10.1007/978-3-030-03326-2_14

1980s [24,37], it has been significantly improved in practice in the past twenty years, thanks to pruning methods introduced by Schnorr *et al.* [40–42], and later revisited and generalized as cylinder pruning [21] and discrete pruning [10]: these methods offer a trade-off by enumerating over a subset $S \subseteq B$, at the expense of missing solutions. One may only be interested in finding one point in $L \cap S$ (provided it exists), or the 'best' point in $L \cap S$, *i.e.* a point minimizing the distance to a target. Enumeration and cylinder pruning compute $L \cap S$ by a depth-first search of a tree with super-exponentially many nodes. Discrete pruning is different, but the computation of S uses special enumerations.

The choice between sieving and enumeration for security estimates is not straightforward. On the one hand, sieving methods run in time $2^{O(n)}$ much lower than enumeration's $2^{O(n \log n)}$, but require exponential space. On the other hand, until very recently [6], the largest lattice numerical challenges had all been solved by pruned enumeration, either directly or as a subroutine: cylinder pruning [21] for NTRU challenges [43] (solved by Ducas-Nguyen) and Darmstadt's lattice challenges [28] (solved by Aono-Nguyen), and discrete pruning [10,19] for Darmstadt's SVP challenges [39] (solved by Kashiwabara-Teruya). Among all lattice-based submissions [5,36] to NIST, the majority chose sieving over enumeration based on the analysis of NewHope [8, Sect. 6], which states that sieving is more efficient than enumeration in dimension ≥ 250 for both classical and quantum computers. But this analysis is debatable: [8] estimates the cost of sieving by a lower bound (ignoring sub-exponential terms) and that of enumeration by an upper bound (either [17, Table 4] or [16, Table 5.2]), thereby ignoring the lower bound of [17] (see [11] for improved bounds).

The picture looks even more blurry when considering the impact of quantum computers. The quantum speed-up is rather limited for sieving: the best quantum sieve algorithm runs in heuristic time $2^{0.265n+o(n)}$, only slighty less than the best classical (heuristic) time $2^{0.292n+o(n)}$ [15,25]. And the quantum speed-up for enumeration is unclear, as confirmed by recent discussions on the NIST mailing-list [4]. In 2015, Laarhoven *et al.* [26, Sect. 9.1] noticed that quantum search algorithms do not apply to enumeration: indeed, Grover's algorithm assumes that the possible solutions in the search space can be indexed and that one can find the i-th possible solution efficiently, whereas lattice enumeration explores a search tree of an unknown structure which can only be explored locally. Three recent papers [7,8,18] mention in a short paragraph that Montanaro's quantum backtracking algorithm [33] can speed up enumeration, by decreasing the number T of operations to $\sqrt{T}$. However, no formal statement nor details are given in [7,8,18]. Furthermore, none of the lattice-based submissions to NIST cite Montanaro's algorithm [33]: the only submission that mentions enumeration in a quantum setting is NTRU-HSS-KEM [23], where it is speculated that enumeration might have a $\sqrt{T}$ quantum variant.

Our Results. We show that lattice enumeration and its cylinder and discrete pruning variants can all be quadratically sped up on a quantum computer, unlike sieving. This is done by a careful interpretation and analysis of enumeration as tree algorithms. Interestingly, we show that this speedup also applies to extreme pruning [21] where one repeats enumeration over many reduced bases: a naive approach would only decrease the classical cost mt (where m is the number of bases and t is the number of operations of a single enumeration) to $m\sqrt{t}$ quantum operations, but we bring it down to $\sqrt{mt}$.

First, we clarify the application of Montanaro's algorithm [33] to enumeration with cylinder pruning: the analysis of [33] assumes that the degree of the tree is bounded by a constant, which is tailored for constraint satisfaction problems, but is not the setting of lattice enumeration. To tackle enumeration, we add basic tools such as binary tree conversion and dichotomy: we obtain that if a lattice enumeration (with or without cylinder pruning) searches over a tree with T nodes, the best solution can be found by a quantum algorithm using roughly $\sqrt{T}$ poly-time operations, where there is a polynomial overhead, which can be decreased if one is only interested in finding one solution. This formalizes earlier brief remarks of [7,8,18], and applies to both SVP and CVP.

Our main result is that the quantum quadratic speed-up also applies to the recent discrete pruning enumeration introduced by Aono and Nguyen [10] as a generalization of Schnorr's sampling algorithm [40]. To do so, we tweak discrete pruning and use an additional quantum algorithm, namely that of Ambainis and Kokainis [9] from STOC '17 to estimate the size of trees. Roughly speaking, given a parameter T, discrete pruning selects T branches (optimizing a certain metric) in a larger tree, and derives T candidate short lattice vectors from them. Our quantum variant directly finds the best candidate in roughly $\sqrt{T}$ operations.

As mentioned previously, we show that the quadratic speed-up of both enumerations also applies to the extreme pruning setting (required to exploit the full power of pruning): if one runs cylinder pruning over m trees, a quantum enumeration can run in $\sqrt{T}$ poly-time operations where T is the sum of the m numbers of nodes, rather than $\sqrt{mT}$ naively; and there is a similar phenomenon for discrete pruning.

As a side result, we present two tweaks to discrete pruning [10], to make it more powerful and more efficient. The first tweak enables to solve CVP in such a way that most of the technical tools introduced in [10] can be reused. This works for the approximation form of CVP, but also its exact version formalized by the *Bounded Distance Decoding* problem (BDD), which appears in many cryptographic applications such as LWE. In BDD, the input is a lattice basis and a lattice point shifted by some small noise whose distribution is crucial. We show how to handle the most important noise distributions, such as LWE's Gaussian distribution and finite distributions used in GGH [22] and lattice attacks on DSA [34]. Enumeration, which was historically only described for SVP, can trivially be adapted to CVP, and so does [21]'s cylinder pruning [29]. However, discrete pruning [10] appears to be less simple.

The second tweak deals with the selection of optimal discrete pruning parameters, and is crucial for our quantum variant. Intuitively, given an integer $T > 0$, the problem is to find the T "best" integral vectors $t \in \mathbb{N}^n$ which minimize some objective function $f(t)$. Aono and Nguyen [10] introduced a fast practical algorithm to do so for a very special useful choice of f, but the algorithm was heuristic: no good bound on the running time was known. We show that their algorithm can actually behave badly in the worst case, *i.e.* it may take exponential time. But we also show that by a careful modification, the algorithm becomes provably efficient and even optimal for that f, and heuristically for more general choices of f: the running time becomes essentially T operations.

Our theoretical analysis has been validated by experiments, which show that in practical BDD situations, discrete pruning is as efficient as cylinder pruning. Since discrete pruning has interesting features (such as an easier parallelization and an easier generation of parameters), it might become the method of choice for large-scale blockwise lattice reduction.

Impact. Figure 1 illustrates the impact of our quantum enumeration on security estimates: the red and yellow curves show $\sqrt{\#bases * N}$ where N is an upper bound cost, i.e., number of nodes of enumeration with extreme pruning with probability $1/\#bases$. The upper bounds for HKZ/Rankin bases are computed by the method of [11]. Here, we omitted the polynomial overhead factor because small factors in quantum sieve have also never been investigated. Note that the estimate $2^{(0.187\beta \log \beta - 1.019\beta + 16.1)/2}$ (called Q-Enum in [5]) of a hypothetical quantum enumeration in NTRU-HSS-KEM [23], which is the square-root of a numerical interpolation of the upper bound of [16,17], is higher than our HKZ estimate: however, both are less than 2^{128} until blocksize roughly 400.

Quantum enumeration with extreme pruning would be faster than quantum sieve up to higher dimensions than previously thought, around 300 if we assume that 10^{10} quasi-HKZ-bases can be obtained for a cost similar as enumeration, or beyond 400 if 10^{10} Rankin-bases (see [17]) can be used instead. Such ranges would affect the security estimates of between 11 and 17 NIST submissions (see Fig. 2), depending on which basis model is considered: these submissions state that the best attack runs BKZ with a blocksize seemingly lower than our threshold between quantum enumeration and quantum sieving, except in the case of S/L NTRU Prime, for which the blocksize 528 corresponds to less than 2^{200} in Fig. 1, whereas the target NIST category is 5.

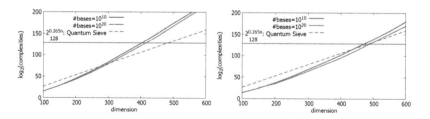

Fig. 1. Q-sieve vs Q-enum: (Left) Using HKZ bases (Right) Using Rankin bases

Furthermore, we note that our quantum speedup might actually be more than quadratic. Indeed, the number T of enumeration nodes is actually a random variable: the average quantum running time is $\mathbb{E}(\sqrt{T})$, which is $\leq \sqrt{\mathbb{E}(T)}$ and potentially much less (*e.g.* a log-normal distribution). It would be useful to identify the distribution of T: it cannot be log-normal for LLL bases (unlike what

Name	NIST category	Blocksize
EMBLEM	1	260/337
uRound2	1	286/302/304
Ding Key Exchange	1	330-366
R EMBLEM	1	345/383
CRYSTALSDilithium	1	347
uRound2	2	355/358/386/397
CRYSTALSKyber	1	386
NewHope	1	386
uRound2	3	394/401/427/425
NTRUEncrypt	1	319
S/L NTRU Prime	5	528

Fig. 2. Lattice-based NIST submissions affected by quantum enumeration

seems to be suggested in [44]), because it would violate the provable running time $2^{O(n^2)}$ of enumeration with LLL bases.

On the other hand, we stress that this is just a first assessment of quantum enumeration. If one is interested in more precise estimates, such as the number of quantum gates, one would need to assess the quantum cost of the algorithm of Montanaro [33] and that of Ambainis and Kokainis [9].

Related Work. Babai's nearest plane algorithm [14] can be viewed as the first form of BDD discrete pruning, using only a single cell. Lindner-Peikert's algorithm [27] generalizes it using exponentially many cells, and is the BDD analogue of Schnorr's random sampling [40] (see [29]). But for both [27,40], the selection of cells is far from being optimal. In 2003, Ludwig [30] applied Grover search to speed up [40] quantumly.

Roadmap. Section 2 provides background. Section 3 gives a general description of enumeration to find close lattice vectors. In Sect. 4, we speed up cylinder pruning enumeration on a quantum computer, using [33]. In Sect. 5, we adapt lattice enumeration with discrete pruning to CVP. In Sect. 6, we show how to efficiently select the best parameters for discrete pruning, by modifying the orthogonal enumeration of [10]. In Sect. 7, we speed up discrete pruning enumeration on a quantum computer, using [9,33]. Supplementary material is given in the full version [12], including proofs and experimental results.

2 Preliminaries

We follow the notations of [10].

General. $\mathbb{N}$ is the set of integers ≥ 0. For any finite set U, its number of elements is $\#U$. For any measurable subset $S \subseteq \mathbb{R}^n$, its volume is $\mathrm{vol}(S)$. We use row representations of matrices. The Euclidean norm of a vector $v \in \mathbb{R}^n$ is $\|v\|$. We denote by $\mathrm{Ball}_n(c, R)$ the n-dim Euclidean ball of radius R and center c, whose volume is $\mathrm{vol}(\mathrm{Ball}_n(R)) = R^n \frac{\pi^{n/2}}{\Gamma(n/2+1)}$. If c is omitted, we mean $c = 0$.

Lattices. A *lattice* L is a discrete subgroup of $\mathbb{R}^m$, or equivalently the set $L(b_1, \ldots, b_n) = \{\sum_{i=1}^n x_i b_i : x_i \in \mathbb{Z}\}$ of all integer combinations of n linearly independent vectors $b_1, \ldots, b_n \in \mathbb{R}^m$. Such b_i's form a *basis* of L. All the bases have the same number n of elements, called the dimension or rank of L, and the same n-dimensional volume of the parallelepiped $\{\sum_{i=1}^{n} a_i \boldsymbol{b}_i \ : \ a_i \in [0,1)\}$ they generate. We call this volume the co-volume of L, denoted by $\mathrm{covol}(L)$. The lattice L is said to be *full-rank* if $n = m$. The *shortest vector problem* (SVP) asks to find a non-zero lattice vector of minimal Euclidean norm. The *closest vector problem* (CVP) asks to find a lattice vector closest to a target vector.

Orthogonalization. For a basis $B = (\boldsymbol{b}_1, \ldots, \boldsymbol{b}_n)$ of a lattice L and $i \in \{1, \ldots, n\}$, we denote by π_i the orthogonal projection on $\mathrm{span}(\boldsymbol{b}_1, \ldots, \boldsymbol{b}_{i-1})^{\perp}$. The *Gram-Schmidt orthogonalization* of the basis B is defined as the sequence of orthogonal vectors $B^{\star} = (\boldsymbol{b}_1^{\star}, \ldots, \boldsymbol{b}_n^{\star})$, where $\boldsymbol{b}_i^{\star} := \pi_i(\boldsymbol{b}_i)$. We can write each $\boldsymbol{b}_i$ as $\boldsymbol{b}_i^{\star} + \sum_{j=1}^{i-1} \mu_{i,j} \boldsymbol{b}_j^{\star}$ for some unique $\mu_{i,1}, \ldots, \mu_{i,i-1} \in \mathbb{R}$. Thus, we may represent the $\mu_{i,j}$'s by a lower-triangular matrix μ with unit diagonal. $\pi_i(L)$ is a lattice of rank $n + 1 - i$ generated by $\pi_i(\boldsymbol{b}_i), \ldots, \pi_i(\boldsymbol{b}_n)$, with $\mathrm{covol}(\pi_i(L)) = \prod_{j=i}^{n} \|\boldsymbol{b}_j^{\star}\|$.

Gaussian Heuristic. The classical Gaussian Heuristic provides an estimate on the number of lattice points inside a "nice enough" set:

Heuristic 1. *Given a full-rank lattice $L \subseteq \mathbb{R}^n$ and a measurable set $S \subseteq \mathbb{R}^n$, the number of points in $S \cap L$ is approximately $\mathrm{vol}(S)/\mathrm{covol}(L)$.*

Both rigorous results and counter-examples are known (see [10]). One should therefore experimentally verify its use, especially for pruned enumeration which relies on strong versions of the heuristic, where the set S is not fixed, depending on a basis of L.

Statistics. We denote by $\mathbb{E}()$ the expectation and $\mathbb{V}()$ the variance of a random variable. For discrete pruning, it is convenient to extend $\mathbb{E}()$ to any measurable set C of $\mathbb{R}^n$ by using the squared norm, that is $\mathbb{E}\{C\} := \mathbb{E}_{\boldsymbol{x} \in C}(\|\boldsymbol{x}\|^2)$.

Gaussian Distribution. The CDF of the Gaussian distribution of expectation 0 and variance σ^2 is $\frac{1}{2}(1 + \mathrm{erf}(\frac{x}{\sigma\sqrt{2}}))$ where the error function is $\mathrm{erf}(z) := \frac{2}{\sqrt{\pi}} \int_0^z e^{-t^2} dt$. The multivariate Gaussian distribution over $\mathbb{R}^m$ of parameter σ selects each coordinate with Gaussian distribution.

Quantum Tree Algorithms. Like in [9], a tree $\mathcal{T}$ is locally accessed given:

1. the root r of $\mathcal{T}$.
2. a black box which, given a node v, returns the number of children $d(v)$ for this node. If $d(v) = 0$, v is called a leaf.
3. a black box which, given a node v and $i \in [d(v)]$, returns the i-th child of v.

We denote by $V(\mathcal{T})$ its set of nodes, $L(\mathcal{T})$ its set of leaves, $d(\mathcal{T}) = \max_{v \in V(\mathcal{T})} d(v)$ its degree and $n(\mathcal{T})$ an upper-bound of its depth. When there is no ambiguity, we use d and n directly without the argument $\mathcal{T}$. We also denote by $\#\mathcal{T}$ the number of nodes of the tree $\mathcal{T}$.

Backtracking is a classical algorithm for solving problems such as constraint satisfaction problems, by performing a tree search in depth-first order. Each node represents a partial candidate and its children say how to extend a candidate. There is a black-box function $\mathcal{P} : V(\mathcal{T}) \to \{true, false, indeterminate\}$ such that $\mathcal{P}(v) \in \{true, false\}$ iff v is a leaf: a node $v \in V(\mathcal{T})$ is called marked if $\mathcal{P}(v) = true$. Backtracking determines whether $\mathcal{T}$ contains a marked node, or outputs one or all marked nodes. Classically, this can be done in $\#V(\mathcal{T})$ queries. Montanaro [33] studied the quantum case:

Theorem 2 ([33]). *There is a quantum algorithm* **ExistSolution**$(\mathcal{T}, T, \mathcal{P}, n, \varepsilon)$ *which given $\varepsilon > 0$, a tree $\mathcal{T}$ such that $d(\mathcal{T}) = O(1)$, a black box function $\mathcal{P}$, and upper bounds T and n on the size and the depth of $\mathcal{T}$, determines if $\mathcal{T}$ contains a marked node by making $O(\sqrt{Tn}\log(1/\varepsilon))$ queries to $\mathcal{T}$ and to the black box function $\mathcal{P}$, with a probability of correct answer $\geq 1 - \varepsilon$. It uses $O(1)$ auxiliary operations per query and uses* poly(n) *qubits.*

Theorem 3 ([33]). *There is a quantum algorithm* **FindSolution**$(\mathcal{T}, \mathcal{P}, n, \varepsilon)$ *which, given $\varepsilon > 0$, a tree $\mathcal{T}$ such that $d(\mathcal{T}) = O(1)$, a black box function $\mathcal{P}$, and an upper bound n on the depth of $\mathcal{T}$, outputs x such that $\mathcal{P}(x)$ is true, or "not found" if no such x exists by making $O(\sqrt{\#V(\mathcal{T})}n^{3/2}\log(n)\log(1/\varepsilon))$ queries to $\mathcal{T}$ and to the black box function $\mathcal{P}$, with correctness probability at least $1 - \varepsilon$. It uses $O(1)$ auxiliary operations per query and uses* poly(n) *qubits.*

Notice that Theorem 3 does not require an upper-bound on $\#V(\mathcal{T})$ as input.

Ambainis and Kokainis [9] gave a quantum algorithm to estimate the size of trees, with input a tree $\mathcal{T}$ and a candidate upper bound T_0 on $\#V(\mathcal{T})$. The algorithm must output an estimate for $\#V(\mathcal{T})$, *i.e.* either a number of $\hat{T} \in [T_0]$ or a claim "$\mathcal{T}$ contains more than T_0 vertices". The estimate is δ-correct if:

1. the estimate is $\hat{T} \in [T_0]$ which satisfies $|T - \hat{T}| \leq \delta T$ where T is the actual number of vertices;
2. the estimate is "$\mathcal{T}$ contains more than T_0 vertices" and the actual number of vertices T satisfies $(1 + \delta)T > T_0$.

An algorithm solves the tree size estimation problem up to precision $1 \pm \delta$ with correctness probability at least $1 - \varepsilon$ if for any $\mathcal{T}$ and any T_0, the probability that it outputs a δ-correct estimate is at least $1 - \varepsilon$.

Theorem 4 ([9]). *There is a quantum algorithm* **TreeSizeEstimation**$(\mathcal{T}, T_0, \delta, \varepsilon)$ *which, given $\varepsilon > 0$, a tree $\mathcal{T}$, and upper bounds d and n on the degree and the depth of $\mathcal{T}$, solves tree size estimation up to precision $1 \pm \delta$, with correctness probability at least $1 - \varepsilon$. It makes $O\left(\frac{\sqrt{nT_0}}{\delta^{1.5}}d\log^2(\frac{1}{\varepsilon})\right)$ queries to $\mathcal{T}$ and $O(\log(T_0))$ non-query transformations per query. The algorithm uses* poly$(n, \log(d), \log(T_0), \log(\delta), \log(\log(1/\varepsilon)))$ *qubits.*

3 Enumeration with Pruning

We give an overview of lattice enumeration and pruning, for the case of finding close lattice vectors, rather than finding short lattice vectors: this revisits the analysis model of both [21] and [10].

3.1 Finding Close Vectors by Enumeration

Let L be a full-rank lattice in $\mathbb{R}^n$. Given a target $u \in \mathbb{Q}^n$, a basis $B = (b_1, \ldots, b_n)$ of L and a radius $R > 0$, enumeration [24,37] outputs $L \cap S$ where $S = \mathrm{Ball}_n(u, R)$: by comparing all the distances to u, one extracts a lattice vector closest to u. It performs a recursive search using projections, to reduce the dimension of the lattice: if $\|v\| \leq R$, then $\|\pi_k(v)\| \leq R$ for all $1 \leq k \leq n$. One can easily enumerate $\pi_n(L) \cap S$. And if one enumerates $\pi_{k+1}(L) \cap S$ for some $k \geq 1$, one derives $\pi_k(L) \cap S$ by enumerating the intersection of a one-dimensional lattice with a suitable ball, for each point in $\pi_{k+1}(L) \cap S$. Concretely, it can be viewed as a depth-first search of the enumeration tree $\mathcal{T}$: the nodes at depth $n + 1 - k$ are the points of $\pi_k(L) \cap S$. The running-time of enumeration depends on R and B, but is typically super-exponential in n, even if $L \cap S$ is small.

3.2 Finding Close Vectors by Enumeration with Pruning

We adapt the general form of enumeration with pruning introduced by [10]: pruned enumeration uses a pruning set $P \subseteq \mathbb{R}^n$, and outputs $L \cap (u + P)$. The advantage is that for suitable choices of P, enumerating $L \cap (u + P)$ is much cheaper than $L \cap S$, and if we further intersect $L \cap (u + P)$ with S, we may have found non-trivial points of $L \cap S$. Note that we use $u + P$ rather than P, because it is natural to make P independent of u, and it is what happens when one uses the pruning of [21] to search for close vectors. Following [21], we view the pruning set P as a random variable: it depends on the choice of basis B.

We distinguish two cases, which were considered separately in [10,21]:

Approximation setting: This was studied in [10], but not in [21]. Here, we are interested in finding any point in $L \cap S \cap (u + P)$ by enumerating $L \cap (u + P)$ then intersect it with the ball S, so we define the success probability as:

$$\Pr_{\mathrm{succ}} = \Pr_{P,u}(L \cap S \cap (u + P) \neq \emptyset), \qquad (1)$$

which is the probability that it outputs at least one point in $L \cap S$. By (slightly) adapting the reasoning of [10] based on the Gaussian heuristic, we estimate that (1) is heuristically

$$\Pr_{\mathrm{succ}} \approx \min(1, \mathrm{vol}(S \cap (u + P))/\mathrm{covol}(L)), \qquad (2)$$

and that the number of elements of $L \cap S \cap (u + P)$ is roughly $\mathrm{vol}(S \cap (u + P))/\mathrm{covol}(L)$. This corresponds to approximating the closest vector problem in a lattice, whose hardness is used in most lattice-based signature schemes.

Unique setting: Here, we know that the target u is unusually close to the lattice, that is $L \cap S$ is a singleton, and we want to find the closest lattice point to u: this is the so-called *Bounded Distance Decoding* problem (BDD), whose hardness is used in most lattice-based encryption schemes. Thus, u is of the form $u = v + e$ where $v \in L$ and $e \in \mathbb{R}^n$ is very short, and we want to recover v. This was implicitly studied in [21], but not in [10]: [21] studied the exact SVP case, where one wants to recover a shortest lattice vector (in our setting, if the target $u \in L$, the BDD solution would be u, but one could alternatively ask for the closest distinct lattice point, which can be reduced to finding a shortest lattice vector). We are only interested in finding the closest lattice point $v \in L$, so we define the success probability as:

$$\Pr_{\text{succ}} = \Pr_{P,u}(v \in L \cap (u + P)), \tag{3}$$

because we are considering the probability that the solution v belongs to the enumerated set $L \cap (u + P)$. Usually, the target u is derived from the noise e, which has a known distribution, then we can rewrite (3) as:

$$\Pr_{\text{succ}} = \Pr_{P,e}(0 \in e + P) = \Pr_{P,e}(-e \in P). \tag{4}$$

In the context of SVP, we would instead define $\Pr_{\text{succ}} = \Pr_P(v \in P)$ where v is a shortest lattice vector. In general, it is always possible to make u depend solely on e: one can take a canonical basis of L, like the HNF, and use it to reduce u modulo L, which only depends on e. Whether $\Pr_{P,e}(-e \in P)$ can be evaluated depends on the choice of P and the distribution of the noise e. For instance, if the distribution of $-e$ is uniform over some measurable set E, then:

$$\Pr_{P,e}(-e \in P) = \frac{\text{vol}(E \cap P)}{\text{vol}(E)}.$$

We discuss other settings in Sect. 5.6. This can be adapted to a discrete distribution. If the distribution of $-e$ is uniform over a finite set $E \cap \mathbb{Z}^n$, then:

$$\Pr_{P,e}(-e \in P) = \frac{\#(E \cap P \cap \mathbb{Z}^n)}{\#(E \cap \mathbb{Z}^n)},$$

where $\#(E \cap P \cap \mathbb{Z}^n)$ is heuristically $\approx \text{vol}(E \cap P)$ by the Gaussian heuristic, and $\#(E \cap \mathbb{Z}^n)$ is usually given by the specific choice of E.

When it fails, we can simply repeat the process with many different P's until we solve the problem, in the approximation-setting or the unique-setting.

We have discussed ways to estimate the success probability of pruned enumeration. To estimate the running time of the full algorithm, we need more information, which depends on the choice of pruning:

- An estimate of the cost of enumerating $L \cap S \cap (u + P)$.
- An estimate of the cost of computing the (random) reduced basis B.

3.3 Cylinder Pruning

The first pruning set P ever used is the following generalization [21] of pruned enumeration of [41,42]. There, P is defined by a function $f : \{1, \dots, n\} \to [0, 1]$, a radius $R > 0$ and a lattice basis $B = (b_1, \dots, b_n)$ as follows:

$$P_f(B, R) = \{x \in \mathbb{R}^n \text{ s.t. } \|\pi_{n+1-i}(x)\| \le f(i)R \text{ for all } 1 \le i \le n\}, \tag{5}$$

where the π_i's are the Gram-Schmidt projections defined by B. We call *cylinder pruning* this form of enumeration, because $P_f(B, R)$ is an intersection of cylinders: each inequality $\|\pi_{n+1-i}(\boldsymbol{x})\| \leq f(i)R$ defines a cylinder. Cylinder pruning was introduced in the SVP setting, but its adaptation to CVP is straightforward [29].

Gama *et al.* [21] showed how to efficiently compute tight lower and upper bounds for $\mathrm{vol}(P_f(B, R))$, thanks to the Dirichlet distribution and special integrals. Then we can do the same for $\mathrm{vol}(P_f(B, R) \cap S)$ if S is any zero-centered ball. Using the shape of $P_f(B, R)$, [21] also estimated of the cost of enumerating $L \cap S \cap P_f(B, R)$, using the Gaussian heuristic on projected lattices $\pi_i(L)$: these estimates are usually accurate in practice, and they can also be used in the CVP case [29]. To optimize the whole selection of parameters, one finally needs to take into account the cost of computing the (random) reduced basis B: for instance, this is done in [13,17].

4   Quantum Speed-Up of Cylinder Pruning

4.1   Tools

The analysis of quantum tree algorithms requires the tree to have constant degree $d = O(1)$. Without this assumption, there is an extra $\mathtt{poly}(d)$ term in the complexity bound like in Theorem 4. Instead, it is more efficient to first convert the tree into a binary tree, so that the overhead is limited to $\mathtt{poly}(\log d)$. We will use the following conversion (illustrated by Fig. 3):

Theorem 5. *One can transform any tree $\mathcal{T}$ of depth n and degree d into a binary one $\mathcal{T}_2$ so that: $\mathcal{T}_2$ can be explored locally; $\mathcal{T}$ and $\mathcal{T}_2$ have roughly the same number of nodes, namely $\#\mathcal{T} \leq \#\mathcal{T}_2 \leq 2\#\mathcal{T}$; the leaves of $\mathcal{T}$ and $\mathcal{T}_2$ are identical; the depth of $\mathcal{T}_2$ is $\leq n \log d$. Moreover, a black-box function $\mathcal{P}$ over $\mathcal{T}$ can be adapted a black box $\mathcal{P}_2$ for $\mathcal{T}_2$, so that the marked nodes of $\mathcal{T}$ and $\mathcal{T}_2$ are the same. One query to $\mathcal{P}_2$ requires at most one query to $\mathcal{P}$ with additional $O(\log d)$ auxiliary operations.*

In the context of enumeration with pruning, instead of enumerating the whole set $L \cap S$, we may only be interested in the 'best' vector in $L \cap S$, *i.e.* minimizing some distance. In terms of tree, this means that given a tree $\mathcal{T}$ with marked leafs defined by a predicate $\mathcal{P}$, we want to find a marked leaf minimizing an integral function g which is defined on the marked leaves of $\mathcal{T}$. We know that $L(\mathcal{T}) = L(\mathcal{T}_2)$. g is thus also defined on the marked leaves of $\mathcal{T}_2$. We denote by g_V the predicate which returns true on a node $\mathcal{N}$ if and only if it is a marked leaf and $g(\mathcal{N}) \leq V$. We first find a parameter R such that there is at least one marked leaf $\mathcal{N}$ such that $g(\mathcal{N}) \leq R$. Then we decrease R by dichotomy using Theorem 3 with different marking functions. We thus obtain **FindMin1**$(\mathcal{T}, \mathcal{P}, g, R, d, \varepsilon)$ (Algorithm 1), which is a general algorithm to find a leaf minimizing the function g with error probability ε, using the binary tree $\mathcal{T}_2$.[1]

---

[1] The access to $\mathcal{T}_2$ is guaranteed by Theorem 5 via the access to $\mathcal{T}$.

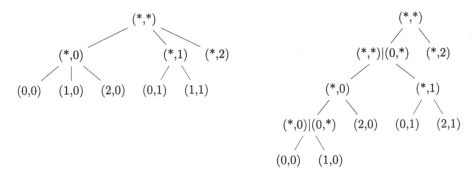

Fig. 3. An example of the transformation in Theorem 5

Algorithm 1. Finding a minimum: **FindMin1**$(T, P, g, R, d, \varepsilon)$

Input: A tree T with marked leaves defined by the predicate P. An integral function g defined on the marked leaves of T. A parameter R, such that $g(N) \leq R$ has at least one solution over all of the marked leaves. An upper-bound d of the number of children of a node in T.

Output: A marked leaf N such that g takes its minimum on N among all the marked leaves explored by the backtracking algorithm.

1: $T_2 \leftarrow$ the corresponding binary tree of T. (see Footnote 1)
2: $N \leftarrow R$, $N' \leftarrow 0$, $Round \leftarrow \lceil \log_2 R \rceil$, $\mathbf{v} \leftarrow (0, \cdots, 0)$
3: **while** $N' < N - 1$ **do**
4:    Call **FindSolution**$(T_2, g_{\lfloor (N+N')/2 \rfloor}, n \log d, \varepsilon / Round)$
5:    **if** **FindSolution**$(T_2, g_{\lfloor (N+N')/2 \rfloor}, n \log d, \varepsilon / Round)$ returns $\mathbf{x}$ **then**
6:       $\mathbf{v} \leftarrow \mathbf{x}$, $N \leftarrow \lfloor (N + N')/2 \rfloor$
7:    **else**
8:       $N' \leftarrow \lfloor (N + N')/2 \rfloor$
9:    **end if**
10: **end while**
11: **return** $\mathbf{v}$

Theorem 6. *Let* $\varepsilon > 0$. *Let* T *be a tree with its marked leaves defined by a predicate* P. *Let* d *be an upper-bound on the degree of* T. *Let* g *be an integral function defined on the marked leaves such that* $g(N) \leq R$ *has at least one solution over all of the marked leaves. Then Algorithm 1 outputs* $N \in T$ *such that* g *takes its minimum on* N *among all of the marked leaves of* T, *with probability at least* $1 - \varepsilon$. *It requires* $O(\sqrt{T}(n \log d)^{3/2} \log(n \log d) \log(\lceil \log_2 R \rceil / \varepsilon) \lceil \log_2 R \rceil)$ *queries on* T *and on* P, *where* $T = \#T$. *Each query on* T *requires* $O(\log d)$ *auxiliary operations. The algorithm needs* poly$(n \log d, \log R)$ *qubits.*

Proof. Correctness is trivial. Regarding the query complexity, there are in total $Round = \lceil \log_2 R \rceil$ calls to **FindSolution**. According to Theorem 3, each call requires $O(\sqrt{T}(n \log d)^{3/2} \log(n \log d) \log(Round/\varepsilon))$ queries on the local structure of T_2 and on g. Thus according to Theorem 5, in total, we need

$O(\sqrt{T}(n \log d)^{3/2} \log(n \log d) \log(\lceil \log_2 R \rceil / \varepsilon) \lceil \log_2 R \rceil)$ queries on the local structure of $\mathcal{T}$ and on g. Each query on $\mathcal{T}$ requires $O(\log d)$ auxiliary operations. For each call, we need $\mathtt{poly}(n \log d)$ qubits. In total, we need $\mathtt{poly}(n \log d, \log R)$ qubits.   □

If we know an upper-bound of T of the number of nodes in the tree $\mathcal{T}$, we can speed up the algorithm by replacing **FindSolution** by **ExistSolution** in lines 4, 5: the new algorithm **FindMin2**$(\mathcal{T}, \mathcal{P}, g, R, d, T, \varepsilon)$ is given and analyzed in the full version [12].

4.2 Application to Cylinder Pruning

Lemma 1. *Let* $(b_1, \cdots, b_n)$ *be an LLL-reduced basis. Let* $\mathcal{T}$ *be the backtracking tree corresponding to the cylinder pruning algorithm for SVP with radius* $R \leq \|b_1\|$ *and bounding function* f. *Then the degree of the tree satisfies:* $d(\mathcal{T}) \leq 2^n$.

Proof. In $\mathcal{T}$, the number of children of a node $\mathcal{N}$ of depth k can be upper-bounded by $d_k = 2f(k)\frac{\|b_1\|}{\|b_{n-k+1}^\star\|} + 1 \leq 2^{(n-k)/2+1} + 1$. The result follows from the fact that an LLL-reduced basis satisfies: $\frac{\|b_1\|^2}{\|b_i^\star\|^2} \leq 2^{i-1}$ for all $1 \leq i \leq n$.   □

Theorem 7. *There is a quantum algorithm which, given* $\varepsilon > 0$, *an LLL-reduced basis* $B = (b_1, \cdots, b_n)$ *of a lattice* L *in* $\mathbb{Z}^n$, *a radius* $R \leq \|b_1\|$ *and a bounding function* $f : \{1, \cdots, n\} \to [0, 1]$, *outputs with correctness probability* $\geq 1 - \varepsilon$:

1. *a non-zero vector* v *in* $L \cap P_f(B, R)$, *in time* $O(\sqrt{T}n^3\mathtt{poly}(\log(n), \log(1/\varepsilon))))$, *if* $L \cap P_f(B, R) \not\subseteq \{0\}$.
2. *all vectors in* $L \cap P_f(B, R)$, *in time* $O(\#(L \cap P_f(B, R))\sqrt{T}n^3 \log(n)$ $\mathtt{poly}(\log(\#(L \cap P_f(B, R))), \log(1/\varepsilon)))$.
3. *a shortest non-zero vector* v *in* $L \cap P_f(B, R)$, *in time* $O(\sqrt{T}n^3\beta$ $\mathtt{poly}(\log(n), \log(1/\varepsilon), \log(\beta)))$, *if* $L \cap P_f(B, R) \not\subseteq \{0\}$. *Here* β *is the bitsize of the vectors of* B.

Here T *is the total number of nodes in the enumeration tree* $\mathcal{T}$ *searched by the cylinder pruning algorithm over* $P_f(B, R)$.

Proof. Let $\mathcal{T}$ be the enumeration tree searched by the cylinder pruning algorithm in which a node of depth i, where $1 \leq i \leq n$, is encoded as $(*, \cdots, *, x_{n-i+1}, \cdots, \cdots, x_n)$ and where the root is encoded as $(*, \cdots, *)$. Let $\mathcal{T}_2$ be the corresponding binary tree. Let $\mathcal{P}$ be a predicate which returns true only on the nodes encoded as $(x_1, \cdots, x_n)$ in $\mathcal{T}_2$ (*i.e.* the leaves of $\mathcal{T}_2$, where all the variables are assigned), such that $\|\sum_{i=1}^n x_i b_i\|^2 \leq R^2$ and $(x_1, \cdots, x_n) \neq (0, \cdots, 0)$.

For 1, if $L \cap P_f(B, R) \neq \emptyset$, we apply **FindSolution**$(\mathcal{T}_2, \mathcal{P}, n \log d, \varepsilon)$. For 2, we find all marked nodes by simply repeating the algorithm **FindSolution**, modifying the oracle operator to strike out previously seen marked elements, which requires space complexity $O(\#(L \cap P_f(B, R)))$.

For 3, if $L \cap P_f(B, R) \neq \emptyset$, we apply Theorem 6 to $\mathbf{FindMin1}(\mathcal{T}, \mathcal{P}, \| \cdot \|^2, R^2, 2^n + 1, \varepsilon)$. In $\mathcal{T}_2$, the height of the tree can be upper-bounded by $n \log d = O(n^2)$. We also have $Round = O(\beta)$. The time complexity is $O(\sqrt{T} n^3 \beta \mathtt{poly}(\log(n), \log(1/\varepsilon), \log(\beta)))$.   □

As corollary, we obtain the following quantum speed-up of Kannan's algorithm for the shortest vector problem:

Theorem 8. *There is a quantum algorithm which, given $\varepsilon > 0$, and a basis B of a full-rank lattice L in $\mathbb{Z}^n$, with entries of bitlength$\leq \beta$, outputs a shortest non-zero vector of L, with error probability at most ε, in time $(n^{\frac{n}{4e}} + o(n)) \cdot \mathtt{poly}(\log(n), \log(1/\varepsilon), \beta)$ using $\mathtt{poly}(\mathrm{n}, \beta)$ qubits.*

We can also apply the quantum tree algorithms to extreme pruning. If we run cylinder pruning over m trees, we can combine these trees into a global one and apply the quantum tree algorithms on it.

Theorem 9 (Quantum speed-up for SVP extreme pruning). *There is a quantum algorithm which, given $\varepsilon > 0$, m LLL-reduced bases $B_1, \cdots B_m$ of a lattice L in $\mathbb{Z}^n$, a radius $R \leq \min_i \|\boldsymbol{b}_{1,i}\|$ where $\boldsymbol{b}_{1,i}$ is the first vector of B_i and a bounding function $f : \{1, \cdots, n\} \rightarrow [0, 1]$, outputs with correctness probability $\geq 1 - \varepsilon$ a shortest non-zero vector $\boldsymbol{v}$ in $L \cap (\cup P_f(B_i, R))$, in time $O(\sqrt{T} n^3 \beta \mathtt{poly}(\log(n), \log(1/\varepsilon), \log(\beta), \log(m)))$, if $L \cap (\cup P_f(B_i, R) \not\subseteq \{0\}$. Here β is a bound on the bitsize of vectors of B_i's, T is the sum of number of nodes in the enumeration trees $\mathcal{T}_i$ searched by cylinder pruning over $P_f(B_i, R)$ for all $1 \leq i \leq m$.*

In the case of CVP with target vector $\boldsymbol{u}$, we use the cylinder pruning algorithm with radius $R \leq \sqrt{\sum_{i=1}^{n} \|\boldsymbol{b}_i^\star\|^2}/2$ and bounding function f. The degree of the tree is now upper-bounded by $d = \max \sqrt{\sum_{i=1}^{n} \|\boldsymbol{b}_i^\star\|^2}/\|\boldsymbol{b}_j^\star\| + 1$. We have $\log d = O(\beta + n)$ where β is the bitsize of the vectors of the basis B. We can obtain a similar theorem as Theorem 7 with different overheads. For exemple for the first case, the time complexity becomes $O(\sqrt{T} n^{3/2} (n + \beta)^{3/2} \mathtt{poly}(\log(n), \log(1/\varepsilon), \log(\beta)))$.

For the extreme pruning for CVP the time complexity is $O(\sqrt{T} n^{3/2} (n + \beta)^{3/2} \beta \mathtt{poly}(\log(n), \log(1/\varepsilon), \log(\beta), \log(m)))$.

5   BDD Enumeration with Discrete Pruning

We adapt Aono-Nguyen's discrete pruning [10] to the BDD case.

5.1   Discrete Pruning for the Enumeration of Short Vectors

Discrete pruning is based on lattice partitions defined as follows. Let L be a full-rank lattice in $\mathbb{Q}^n$. An L-partition is a partition $\mathcal{C}$ of $\mathbb{R}^n$ such that:

- The partition is countable: $\mathbb{R}^n = \cup_{t \in T} \mathcal{C}(t)$ where T is a countable set, and $\mathcal{C}(t) \cap \mathcal{C}(t') = \emptyset$ whenever $t \neq t'$.

- Each cell $\mathcal{C}(t)$ contains a single lattice point, which can be found efficiently: given any $t \in T$, one can "open" the cell $\mathcal{C}(t)$, i.e. compute $\mathcal{C}(t) \cap L$ in polynomial time. In other words, the partition defines a function $g : T \to L$ where $\mathcal{C}(t) \cap L = \{g(t)\}$, and one can compute g in polynomial time.

Discrete pruning is obtained by selecting the pruning set P as the union of finitely many cells $\mathcal{C}(t)$, namely $P = \cup_{t \in U} \mathcal{C}(t)$ for some finite $U \subseteq T$. Then $L \cap P = \cup_{t \in U} (L \cap \mathcal{C}(t))$ can be enumerated by opening each cell $\mathcal{C}(t)$ for $t \in U$.

[10] presented two useful L-partitions: Babai's partition where $T = \mathbb{Z}^n$ and each cell $\mathcal{C}(t)$ is a box of volume $\mathrm{covol}(L)$; and the natural partition where $T = \mathbb{N}^n$ and each cell $\mathcal{C}(t)$ is a union of non-overlapping boxes, with total volume $\mathrm{covol}(L)$. The natural partition is preferable, and [10] explained how to select good cells for the natural partition. In theory, one would like to select the cells $\mathcal{C}(t)$ which maximize $\mathrm{vol}(\mathcal{C}(t) \cap S)$: [10] shows how to compute $\mathrm{vol}(\mathcal{C}(t) \cap S)$, but an exhaustive search to derive the best $\mathrm{vol}(\mathcal{C}(t) \cap S)$ exactly would be too expensive. Instead, [10] shows how to approximate efficiently the optimal selection, by selecting the cells $\mathcal{C}(t)$ minimizing $\mathbb{E}(\mathcal{C}(t))$: given m, it is possible to compute in practice the m cells which minimize $\mathbb{E}(\mathcal{C}(t))$.

5.2   Universal Lattice Partitions

Unfortunately, in the worst case, L-partitions are not sufficient for our framework: if $P = \cup_{t \in U} \mathcal{C}(t)$, then $L \cap (P + u) = \cup_{t \in U} (L \cap (\mathcal{C}(t) + u))$ but the number of elements in $L \cap (\mathcal{C}(t) + u)$ is unclear, and it is also unclear how to compute in $L \cap (\mathcal{C}(t) + u)$ efficiently. To fix this, we could compute instead $L \cap P \cap S = \cup_{t \in U} (L \cap \mathcal{C}(t)) \cap S$, but that creates two issues:

- In the unique setting, it is unclear how we would evaluate success probabilities. Given a tag t and a target $u = v + e$ where e is the noise and $v \in L$, we would need to estimate the probability that $v \in \mathcal{C}(t)$, i.e. $u - e \in \mathcal{C}(t)$.
- We would need to select the tag set U depending on the target u, without knowing how to evaluate success probabilities.

BDD asks to find the lattice point $v \in L$ closest to some target vector $u \in \mathbb{Q}^n$, unusually close to L. To adapt discrete pruning to BDD, the most natural solution would be to subtract u to the lattice L as follows.

Definition 1. *Let L be a full-rank lattice in $\mathbb{Q}^n$. An L-partition $\mathcal{C}$ is* universal *if for all $u \in \mathbb{Q}^n$, the shifted partition $\mathcal{C} + u$ is an L-partition, i.e.:*

- *The partition is countable: $\mathbb{R}^n = \cup_{t \in T} \mathcal{C}(t)$ where T is a countable set, and $\mathcal{C}(t) \cap \mathcal{C}(t') = \emptyset$ whenever $t \neq t'$.*
- *For any $u \in \mathbb{Q}^n$, each cell $\mathcal{C}(t)$ contains a single point in $L - u = \{v - u, v \in L\}$, which can be found efficiently: given any $t \in T$ and $u \in \mathbb{Q}^n$, one can "open" the cell $u + \mathcal{C}(t)$, i.e. compute $(u + \mathcal{C}(t)) \cap L$ in polynomial time.*

Unfortunately, an L-partition is not necessarily universal, even in dimension one. Indeed, consider the L-partition $\mathcal{C}$ with $T = \mathbb{Z}$ defined as follows: $\mathcal{C}(0) =$

$[-1/2, 1/2]$; For any $k > 0$, $\mathcal{C}(k) = (k - 1/2, k + 1/2]$; For any $k < 0$, $\mathcal{C}(k) = [k - 1/2, k+1/2)$. It can be checked that $\mathcal{C}$ is not universal: the shifted cell $\mathcal{C}(0) + 1/2$ contains two lattice points, namely 0 and 1. Fortunately, we show in the full version that the two L-partitions (related to Gram-Schmidt orthogonalization) introduced in [10] for discrete pruning are actually universal:

Lemma 2. *Let B be a basis of a full-rank lattice L in $\mathbb{Z}^n$. Let $T = \mathbb{Z}^n$ and for any $t \in T$, $\mathcal{C}_{\mathbb{Z}}(t) = tB^\star + \mathcal{D}$ where $\mathcal{D} = \{\sum_{i=1}^n x_i b_i^\star \text{ s.t. } -1/2 \le x_i < 1/2\}$. Then Babai's L-partition $(\mathcal{C}_{\mathbb{Z}}(), T)$ is universal.*

Lemma 3. *Let B be a basis of a full-rank lattice L in $\mathbb{Z}^n$. Let $T = \mathbb{N}^n$ and for any $t = (t_1, \ldots, t_n) \in T$, $\mathcal{C}_{\mathbb{N}}(t) = \{\sum_{i=1}^n x_i b_i^\star \text{ s.t. } -(t_i + 1)/2 < x_i \le -t_i/2 \text{ or } t_i/2 < x_i \le (t_i + 1)/2\}$. Then the natural partition $(\mathcal{C}_{\mathbb{N}}(), T)$ is universal.*

5.3   BDD Discrete Pruning from Universal Lattice Partitions

Any universal L-partition $(\mathcal{C}, T)$ and any vector $u \in \mathbb{Q}^n$ define a partition $\mathbb{R}^n = \cup_{t \in T}(u + \mathcal{C}(t))$. Following the SVP case, discrete pruning opens finitely many cells $u + \mathcal{C}(t)$, as done by Algorithm 2: discrete pruning is parametrized by a finite set $U \subseteq T$ of tags, specifying which cells $u + \mathcal{C}(t)$ to open. It is therefore a pruned CVP enumeration with pruning set $P = \cup_{t \in U}\mathcal{C}(t)$.

Algorithm 2. Close-Vector Discrete Pruning from Universal Lattice Partitions

---

Input: A target vector $u \in \mathbb{Q}^n$, a universal lattice partition $(\mathcal{C}(), T)$, a finite subset $U \subseteq T$ and if we are in the approximation setting, a radius R.
Output: $L \cap (u + (S \cap P))$ where $S = \text{Ball}_n(R)$ and $P = \cup_{t \in U}\mathcal{C}(t)$.
1: $\mathcal{R} = \emptyset$
2: **for** $t \in U$ **do**
3:    Compute $L \cap (u + \mathcal{C}(t))$ by opening $u + \mathcal{C}(t)$: in the approx setting, check if the output vector is within distance $\le R$ to u, then add the vector to the set $\mathcal{R}$. In the unique setting, check if the output vector is the solution.
4: **end for**
5: Return $\mathcal{R}$.

The algorithm performs exactly k cell openings, where $k = \#U$ is the number of cells, and each cell opening runs in polynomial time. So the running time is $\#U$ poly-time operations: one can decide how much time should be spent.

Since the running time is easy to evaluate like in the SVP case, there are only two issues: how to estimate the success probability and how to select U, in order to maximize the success probability.

5.4   Success Probability

Following Sect. 3.2, we distinguish two cases:

Approximation setting: Based on (2), the success probability can be derived from:

$$\text{vol}(S \cap (\boldsymbol{u} + P)) = \sum_{t \in U} \text{vol}(\text{Ball}_n(R) \cap \mathcal{C}(\boldsymbol{t})). \tag{6}$$

This is exactly the same situation as in the SVP case already tackled by [10]. They showed how to compute $\text{vol}(\text{Ball}_n(R) \cap \mathcal{C}(\boldsymbol{t}))$ for Babai's partition and the natural partition by focusing on the intersection of a ball with a box $H = \{(x_1, \ldots, x_n) \in \mathbb{R}^n \text{ s.t. } \alpha_i \leq x_i \leq \beta_i\}$:

- In the case of Babai's partition, each cell $\mathcal{C}_{\mathbb{Z}}(\boldsymbol{t})$ is a box.
- In the case of the natural partition, each cell $\mathcal{C}_{\mathbb{N}}(\boldsymbol{t})$ is the union of 2^j symmetric (non-overlapping) boxes, where j is the number of non-zero coefficients of $\boldsymbol{t}$. It follows that $\text{vol}(\mathcal{C}_{\mathbb{N}}(\boldsymbol{t}) \cap \text{Ball}_n(\mathbb{R})) = 2^j \text{vol}(H \cap S)$, where H is any of these 2^j boxes.

And they also showed to approximate a sum $\sum_{t \in U} \text{vol}(\text{Ball}_n(R) \cap \mathcal{C}(\boldsymbol{t}))$ in practice, without having to compute separately each volume.

Unique setting: Based on (4), if the noise vector is $\boldsymbol{e}$, then the success probability is

$$\Pr_{\text{succ}} = \Pr_{P,e}(-\boldsymbol{e} \in P) = \sum_{t \in U} \Pr_{P,e}(-\boldsymbol{e} \in \mathcal{C}(\boldsymbol{t})) \tag{7}$$

It therefore suffices to compute the cell probability $\Pr_{P,e}(\boldsymbol{e} \in \mathcal{C}(\boldsymbol{t}))$, instead of an intersection volume. Similarly to the approximation setting, we might be able to approximate the sum $\sum_{t \in U} \Pr_{P,e}(\boldsymbol{e} \in \mathcal{C}(\boldsymbol{t}))$ without having to compute individually each probability. In Sect. 5.6, we focus on the natural partition: we discuss ways to compute the cell probability $\Pr_{P,e}(\boldsymbol{e} \in \mathcal{C}(\boldsymbol{t}))$ depending on the distribution of the noise $\boldsymbol{e}$.

In both cases, we see that the success probability is of the form:

$$\Pr_{\text{succ}} = \sum_{t \in U} f(\boldsymbol{t}), \tag{8}$$

for some function $f() : T \to [0, 1]$ such that $\sum_{t \in T} f(\boldsymbol{t}) = 1$, where (8) is rigorous for the unique setting, and heuristic for the approximation setting due to the Gaussian heuristic. If ever the computation of $f()$ is too slow to compute individually each term of $\sum_{t \in U} f(\boldsymbol{t})$, we can use the statistical inference techniques of [10] to approximate (8) from the computation of a small number of $f(\boldsymbol{t})$. Note that if we know that the probability is reasonably large, say > 0.01, we can alternatively use Monte-Carlo sampling to approximate it.

5.5 Selecting Parameters

We would like to select the finite set U of tags to maximize $\mathrm{Pr}_{\mathrm{succ}}$ given by (8). Let us assume that we have a function $g : T \to \mathbb{R}^+$ such that $\sum_{t \in T} g(t)$ converges. If (8) provably holds, then $\sum_{t \in T} f(t) = 1$, so the sum indeed converges. Since T is infinite, this implies that for any $B > 0$, the set $\{t \in T \text{ s.t. } f(t) > B\}$ is finite, which proves the following elementary result:

Lemma 4. *Let T be an infinite countable set. Let $f : T \to \mathbb{R}^+$ be a function such that $\sum_{t \in T} f(t)$ converges. Then for any integer $m > 0$, there is a finite subset $U \subseteq T$ of cardinal m such that $f(t) \leq \min_{u \in U} f(u)$ for all $t \in T \setminus U$. Such a subset U maximizes $\sum_{u \in U} f(u)$ among all m-size subsets of T.*

Any such subset U would maximize $\mathrm{Pr}_{\mathrm{succ}}$ among all m-size subsets of T, so we would ideally want to select such a U for any given m. And m quantifies the effort we want to spend on discrete pruning, since the bit-complexity of discrete pruning is exactly m poly-time operations.

Now that we know that optimal subsets U exist, we discuss how to find such subsets U efficiently. In the approximation setting of [10], the actual function $f()$ is related to volumes: we want to select the k cells which maximize $\mathrm{vol}(\mathrm{Ball}_n(R)\cap \mathcal{C}(t))$ among all the cells. This is too expensive to do exactly, but [10] provides a fast heuristic method for the natural partition, by selecting the cells $\mathcal{C}(t)$ minimizing $\mathbb{E}\{\mathcal{C}_{\mathbb{N}}(t)\}$: given as input m, it is possible to compute efficiently in practice the tags of the m cells which minimize

$$\mathbb{E}\{\mathcal{C}_{\mathbb{N}}(t)\} = \sum_{i=1}^{n} \left(\frac{t_i^2}{4} + \frac{t_i}{4} + \frac{1}{12} \right) \| b_i^{\star} \|^2 .$$

In other words, this is the same as replacing the function $f()$ related to volumes by the function

$$h(t) = e^{-\sum_{i=1}^{n} \left(\frac{t_i^2}{4} + \frac{t_i}{4} + \frac{1}{12} \right) \| b_i^{\star} \|^2} ,$$

and it can be verified that $\sum_{t \in \mathbb{N}^n} h(t)$ converges. In practice (see [10]), the m cells maximizing $h(t)$ (*i.e.* minimizing $\mathbb{E}\{\mathcal{C}_{\mathbb{N}}(t)\}$) are almost the same as the cells maximizing $\mathrm{vol}(\mathrm{Ball}_n(R) \cap \mathcal{C}(t))$.

However, the method of [10] was only heuristic. In Sect. 6, we modify that method to make it fully provable: for any integer $m > 0$, we can provably find the best m cells in essentially m polynomial-time operations and polynomial space (the m solutions are output as a stream).

5.6 Noise Distributions in the Unique Setting

We discuss how to evaluate the success probability of BDD discrete pruning in the unique setting for the natural partition. This can easily be adapted to Babai's partition, because it also relies on boxes. Following (7), it suffices to evaluate:

$$p(t) = \Pr_{P,e}(e \in -\mathcal{C}(t)), \tag{9}$$

where P is the (random) pruning set, e is the BDD noise and $\mathcal{C}(t)$ is the cell of the tag t. We now analyze the most frequent distributions for e.

LWE and Gaussian Noise. The most important BDD case is LWE [38]. However, there are many variants of LWE using different distributions of the noise e. We will use the continuous Gaussian distribution over $\mathbb{R}^n$, like in [38]. Many schemes actually use a discrete distribution, such as some discrete Gaussian distribution over $\mathbb{Z}^n$ (or something easier to implement): because this is harder to analyze, cryptanalysis papers such as [27, 29] prefer to ignore this difference, and perform experiments to check if it matches with the theoretical analysis. The main benefit of the Gaussian distribution over $\mathbb{R}^n$ is that for any basis, each coordinate is a one-dimensional Gaussian.

Lemma 5. *Let* $t = (t_1, \ldots, t_n) \in \mathbb{N}^n$ *be a tag of the natural partition* $\mathcal{C}_{\mathbb{N}}()$ *with basis* $B = (b_1, \ldots, b_n)$. *If the noise* e *follows the multivariate Gaussian distribution over* $\mathbb{R}^n$ *with parameter* σ, *then:*

$$p(t) = \prod_{i=1}^{n} \left(\mathrm{erf}\left(\frac{1}{\sqrt{2}\sigma} \cdot \frac{t_i + 1}{2} \cdot \|b_i^\star\| \right) - \mathrm{erf}\left(\frac{1}{\sqrt{2}\sigma} \cdot \frac{t_i}{2} \cdot \|b_i^\star\| \right) \right) \qquad (10)$$

Spherical Noise. If the noise e is uniformly distributed over a centered ball, we can reuse the analysis of [10]:

Lemma 6. *Let* $(\mathcal{C}, T)$ *be a universal L-partition. Let* $t \in T$ *be a tag. If the noise* e *is uniformly distributed over the n-dimensional centered ball of radius* R, *then:*

$$p(t) = \frac{\mathrm{vol}(\mathcal{C}(t) \cap \mathrm{Ball}_n(R))}{\mathrm{vol}(\mathrm{Ball}_n(R))} \qquad (11)$$

For both Babai's partition $\mathcal{C}_{\mathbb{Z}}$ and the natural partition $\mathcal{C}_{\mathbb{N}}$, $\mathcal{C}(t)$ is the union of disjoint symmetric boxes, so the evaluation of (11) is reduced to the computation of the volume of a ball-box intersection, which was done in [10].

Product of Finite Distributions. We now consider a general distribution $\mathcal{D}$ for the noise e where each coordinate e_i is independently sampled from the uniform distribution over some finite set. This includes the box distribution, which is the uniform distribution over a set of the form $\prod_{i=1}^{n} \{a_i, \ldots, b_i\}$. The continuous Gaussian distribution and the uniform distribution over a ball are both invariant by rotation. But if the noise distribution $\mathcal{D}$ is not invariant by rotation, the tag probability $p(t)$ may take different values for the same $(\|b_1^\star\|, \ldots, \|b_n^\star\|)$, which is problematic for analysing the success probability. To tackle this issue, we reuse the following heuristic assumption introduced in [21]:

Heuristic 10 *([21, Heuristic 3]) The distribution of the normalized Gram-Schmidt orthogonalization* $(b_1^\star / \|b_1^\star\|, \ldots, b_n^\star / \|b_n^\star\|)$ *of a random reduced basis* $(b_1, \ldots, b_n)$ *looks like that of a uniformly distributed orthogonal matrix.*

We obtain:

Lemma 7. *Let* $\mathcal{C}_{\mathbb{N}}$ *be the natural partition. Let* $\boldsymbol{t} \in \mathbb{N}^n$ *be a tag. If the distribution of the noise* $\boldsymbol{e}$ *has finite support, then under Heuristic 10:*

$$p(\boldsymbol{t}) = \sum_{r \in E} \Pr_{\boldsymbol{e}}(\|\boldsymbol{e}\| = r) \times \Pr_{\boldsymbol{x} \leftarrow S_n} (\boldsymbol{x} \in \mathcal{C}(\boldsymbol{t})/r) \tag{12}$$

where $E \subseteq \mathbb{R}_{\geq 0}$ *denotes the finite set formed by all possible values of* $\|\boldsymbol{e}\|$ *and* S_n *denotes the* n*-dimensional unit sphere.*

6   Linear Optimization for Discrete Pruning

We saw in Sect. 5.6 how to compute or approximate the probability $p(\boldsymbol{t})$ that the cell of the tag $\boldsymbol{t}$ contains the BDD solution. From Lemma 4, we know that for any integer $m > 0$, there are m tags which maximize $p(\boldsymbol{t})$ in the sense that any other tag must have a lower $p(\boldsymbol{t})$. To select optimal parameters for BDD discrete pruning, we want to find these m tags as fast as possible, possibly in m operations and polynomial-space (by outputting the result as a stream).

6.1   Reduction to Linear Optimization

We distinguish two cases:

- Selection based on expectation. Experiments performed in [10] show that in practice, the m tags $\boldsymbol{t}$ which maximize $\mathrm{vol}(\mathcal{C}_{\mathbb{N}}(\boldsymbol{t}) \cap \mathrm{Ball}_n(R))$ are essentially the ones which minimize the expectation $\mathbb{E}\{\mathcal{C}_{\mathbb{N}}(\boldsymbol{t})\}$ where $\mathbb{E}\{C\} := \mathbb{E}_{\boldsymbol{x} \in C}(\|\boldsymbol{x}\|^2)$ over the uniform distribution. Cor. 3 in [10] shows that this expectation is:

$$\mathbb{E}\{\mathcal{C}_{\mathbb{N}}(\boldsymbol{t})\} = \sum_{i=1}^{n} \left(\frac{t_i^2}{4} + \frac{t_i}{4} + \frac{1}{12} \right) \|\boldsymbol{b}_i^{\star}\|^2.$$

  So we can assume that for a noise uniformly distributed over a ball (see Lemma 6), the m tags $\boldsymbol{t}$ maximizing $p(\boldsymbol{t})$ are the tags minimizing $\mathbb{E}\{\mathcal{C}_{\mathbb{N}}(\boldsymbol{t})\}$.
- Gaussian noise. If the noise distribution is the continuous multivariate Gaussian distribution, Lemma 5 shows that $p(\boldsymbol{t})$ is given by (10). This implies that the m tags $\boldsymbol{t}$ which maximize $p(\boldsymbol{t})$ are the ones which minimize $-\log p(\boldsymbol{t})$

In both cases, we want to find the m tags $\boldsymbol{t} \in \mathbb{N}^n$ which minimize an objective function g of the form $g(\boldsymbol{t}) = \sum_{i=1}^{n} f(i, t_i)$, where $f(i, t_i) \geq 0$. The fact that the objective function can be decomposed as a sum of individual positive functions in each coordinate allows us to view this problem as a *linear optimization*. We will see that in the case that g has integral outputs, it is possible to provably find the best m tags which minimize such a function g in essentially m operations. If g is not integral, it is nevertheless possible to enumerate all solutions such that $g(\boldsymbol{t}) \leq R$ where R is an input, in time linear in the number of solutions. A special case is the problem of enumerating smooth numbers below a given number.

In practice, it is more efficient to rely on the expectation, because it is faster to evaluate. Figure 4 shows how similar are the best tags with respect to one indicator compared to another: to compare two sets A and B formed by the best M tags, the graph displays $\#(A \cap B)/M$. For instance, the top curve confirms the experimental result of [10] that the m tags t which maximize $\mathrm{vol}(\mathcal{C}_{\mathbb{N}}(t) \cap \mathrm{Ball}_n(R))$ are almost the same as the ones which minimize the expectation $\mathbb{E}\{\mathcal{C}_{\mathbb{N}}(t)\}$. The top second curve shows that the best tags that maximize the LWE probability are very close to those minimizing the expectation. The bottom two curves compare with the finite noise distribution arising in GGH challenges [22] (see the full version for details). In all cases, at most 10% of the best tags are different, and more importantly, we report that the global success probabilities are always very close, with a relative error typically $\leq 1\%$.

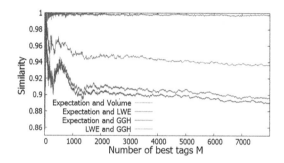

Fig. 4. Similarity between optimal sets of tags, depending on the objective function.

We conclude that in practice, the expectation is a very good indicator to select the best tags for the distributions studied in Sect. 5.6.

6.2   Limits of Orthogonal Enumeration

Aono and Nguyen [10, Sect. 6] presented a heuristic method to solve this linear optimization problem in the special case: $g(t) = \mathbb{E}\{\mathcal{C}_{\mathbb{N}}(t)\} = \sum_{i=1}^{n} \left(\frac{t_i^2}{4} + \frac{t_i}{4} + \frac{1}{12} \right) \|b_i^\star\|^2$, by noticing that $\mathbb{E}\{\mathcal{C}_{\mathbb{N}}(t)\}$ was the squared distance between a target point and a special lattice with a known orthogonal basis. This allowed to find all $t \in \mathbb{N}^n$ such that $\mathbb{E}\{\mathcal{C}_{\mathbb{N}}(t)\} \leq R$ for any R, using a variant [10, Alg. 6] of enumeration. And by using a binary search based on an early-abort variant, it was also possible to find an R yielding slightly more than m solutions.

[10, Sect. 6] reported that this algorithm worked very well in practice: if ℓ is the number of $t \in \mathbb{N}^n$ such that $\mathbb{E}\{\mathcal{C}_{\mathbb{N}}(t)\} \leq R$, the number of nodes L of the enumeration algorithm [10, Alg. 6] seemed to be bounded by $O(\ell n)$, perhaps even $\ell \times n$. This was in contrast with the usual situation where the number of nodes of the enumeration tree is exponentially larger than the number of solutions. However, no rigorous result could be proved in [10], leaving it as an open problem to show the efficiency of [10, Alg. 6].

Surprisingly, we solve this open problem of [10] in the negative. More precisely, we show that there are cases where the number of nodes L of enumeration [10, Alg. 6] is exponentially larger than the number of solutions ℓ. To see this, consider the orthogonal lattice $\mathbb{Z}^n$ with the canonical basis. Then: $\mathbb{E}\{\mathcal{C}_{\mathbb{N}}(t)\} = \sum_{i=1}^{n} \left(\frac{t_i^2}{4} + \frac{t_i}{4} + \frac{1}{12} \right)$. But we have:

Lemma 8. *Let $R = \frac{n}{12} + \frac{1}{2}$ and $n' = \lfloor n/10 \rfloor$. Then the number ℓ of $t \in \mathbb{N}^n$ such that $\sum_{i=1}^{n} \left(\frac{t_i^2}{4} + \frac{t_i}{4} + \frac{1}{12} \right) \leq R$ is exactly $n + 1$. But the number ℓ' of $(x_{n-n'+1}, \ldots, x_n) \in \mathbb{N}^{n'}$ such that $\sum_{i=n-n'+1}^{n} \left(\frac{x_i^2}{4} + \frac{x_i}{4} + \frac{1}{12} \right) \leq R$ is $\geq 2^{n'}$.*

Proof. For the choice $R = \frac{n}{12} + \frac{1}{2}$, we have $\sum_{i=1}^{n} \left(\frac{t_i^2}{4} + \frac{t_i}{4} + \frac{1}{12} \right) \leq R$ if and only if all the t_i's are equal to zero, except at most one, which must be equal to one. Furthermore, for any $(x_{n-n'+1}, \ldots, x_n) \in \{0,1\}^{n'}$, we have:

$$\sum_{i=n-n'+1}^{n} \left(\frac{x_i^2}{4} + \frac{x_i}{4} + \frac{1}{12} \right) \leq n' \left(\frac{1}{2} + \frac{1}{12} \right) \leq \frac{n}{10} \frac{7}{12} = \frac{7n}{120} < R.$$

$\square$

It follows in this case that the number of nodes L of the enumeration algorithm [10, Alg. 6] for that R is at least exponential in n, though the number of solutions is linear in n.

6.3   Solving Linear Optimization

We show that a slight modification of orthogonal enumeration can solve the more general problem of linear optimization essentially optimally. This is based on two key ideas. The first idea is that when solving linear optimization, we may assume without loss of generality that each function $f(i,)$ is sorted by increasing value, with a starting value equal to zero, which changes the tree: $f(i,0) = 0$ and $f(i,j) \leq f(i,j')$ whenever $j \leq j'$. Indeed, it suffices to sort the values of $f(i,)$ if necessary and subtract the minimal value: however, note that for both the expectation $\mathbb{E}\{\mathcal{C}_{\mathbb{N}}(t)\} = \sum_{i=1}^{n} \left(\frac{t_i^2}{4} + \frac{t_i}{4} + \frac{1}{12} \right) \|b_i^\star\|^2$ and for $-\sum_{i=1}^{n} \log \left(\mathrm{erf}\left(\frac{1}{\sqrt{2}\sigma} \cdot \frac{t_i+1}{2} \cdot \|b_i^\star\| \right) - \mathrm{erf}\left(\frac{1}{\sqrt{2}\sigma} \cdot \frac{t_i}{2} \cdot \|b_i^\star\| \right) \right)$, the values of $f(i,)$ are already sorted. For instance, $\frac{t_i^2}{4} + \frac{t_i}{4} + \frac{1}{12}$ is an increasing function of t_i.

The second idea is that we may assume to simplify that f has integral values, which allows us to bound the running time of dichotomy. This is not directly true for the expectation $\mathbb{E}\{\mathcal{C}_{\mathbb{N}}(t)\} = \sum_{i=1}^{n} \left(\frac{t_i^2}{4} + \frac{t_i}{4} + \frac{1}{12} \right) \|b_i^\star\|^2$. However, because we deal with integer lattices, the basis B is integral, the $\|b_i^\star\|^2$'s are rational numbers with denominator $\mathrm{covol}(L(b_1, \ldots, b_{i-1}))^2$, so we can transform the expectation into an integer, by multiplying with a suitable polynomial-size integer.

First, we present a slight modification Algorithm 3 of [10, Alg. 6], whose running time is provably essentially proportional to the number of solutions:

Theorem 11. *Assume that $f : \{1,\ldots,n\} \times \mathbb{N} \to \mathbb{R}$ satisfies $f(i,0) = 0$ and $f(i,j) \geq f(i,j')$ for all i and $j > j'$. Given as input a number $R > 0$, Algorithm 3 outputs all $(v_1,\ldots,v_n) \in \mathbb{N}^n$ such that $\sum_{i=1}^n f(i,v_i) \leq R$ using $O(nN+1)$ arithmetic operations and $\leq (2n-1)N+1$ calls to the function $f()$, where the number N is the number of $(v_1,\ldots,v_n) \in \mathbb{N}^n$ such that $\sum_{i=1}^n f(i,v_i) \leq R$.*

Proof. To analyze the complexity of Algorithm 3, let n_k denote the number of times we enter Lines 3–18, depending on the value of k, which is ≥ 1 and $\leq n$ at each Line 3. Then n_k can be decomposed as $n_k = a_k + b_k$, where a_k (resp. b_k) denotes the number of times we enter Lines 5–10 (resp. Lines 12–17). Notice that $a_{n+1} = 0$ and a_1 is exactly the number N of $(v_1,\ldots,v_n) \in \mathbb{N}^n$ such that $\sum_{i=1}^n f(i,v_i) \leq R$. And if $1 < i \leq n$, then a_i is the number of times that the variable k is decremented from i to $i-1$. Similarly, $b_n = 1$, and if $1 \leq i \leq n$, then b_i is the number of times that the variable k is incremented from i to $i+1$. By Line 1 (resp. 14), the initial (resp. final) value of k is n (resp. $n+1$). Therefore, for any $1 \leq i \leq n-1$, the number of times k is incremented from i to $i+1$ must be equal to the number of times k is decremented from $i+1$ to i, in other words: $b_i = a_{i+1}$. Thus, the total number of loop iterations is:

$$\sum_{i=1}^n n_i = \sum_{i=1}^n (a_i + b_i) = N + 1 + 2\sum_{i=2}^n a_i.$$

Note that because $f(i,0) = 0$, any partial assignment $\sum_{i=i_0}^n f(i,v_i) \leq R$ can be extended to a larger partial assignment $\sum_{i=1}^n f(i,v_i) \leq R$, which implies that $a_1 \geq a_2 \geq \ldots a_n$. It follows that the total number of loop iterations is:

$$\sum_{i=1}^{n+1} n_i \leq N + 1 + 2(n-1)N = (2n-1)N + 1.$$

For each loop iteration (Lines 3–18), the number of arithmetic operations performed is $O(1)$ and the number of calls to $f()$ is exactly one. It follows that the total number of arithmetic operations is $O(nN+1)$ and the number of calls to $f()$ is $\leq (2n-1)N+1$. □

We showed that the number of nodes in the search tree is linear in the number of solutions. Next, we present Algorithm 4, which is a counting version of Algorithm 3:

Theorem 12. *Assume that $f : \{1,\ldots,n\} \times \mathbb{N} \to \mathbb{R}$ satisfies $f(i,0) = 0$ and $f(i,j) \geq f(i,j')$ for all i and $j > j'$. Given as input two numbers $R > 0$ and $M > 0$, Algorithm 4 decides if is $N \geq M$ or $N < M$, where N is the number of $(v_1,\ldots,v_n) \in \mathbb{N}^n$ such that $\sum_{i=1}^n f(i,v_i) \leq R$. Furthermore, if $N \geq M$, the number of arithmetic operations is $O(N)$, and otherwise, the number of arithmetic operations is $O(nN+1)$, and the algorithms outputs N.*

Proof. Similarly to the proof of Theorem 11, let n_k denote the number of times we enter Lines 3–17, depending on the value of k, which is ≥ 1 and $\leq n$ at each

Line 3. Then n_k can be decomposed as $n_k = a_k + b_k$, where a_k (resp. b_k) denotes the number of times we enter Lines 5–9 (resp. Lines 11–16).

Let M be the number of $(v_1, \ldots, v_n) \in \mathbb{N}^n$ such that $\sum_{i=1}^n f(i, v_i) \le R$. If $M \le N$, then Algorithm 4 will perform the same operations as Algorithm 3 (except Line. 6), so the cost is $O(nM + 1) \le O(nN + 1)$ arithmetic operations. Otherwise, $M > N$, which means that the while loop will stop after exactly N iterations, and the total number of operations is therefore $O(N)$. $\square$

Our main result states that if the function f is integral, given any M, Algorithm 5 finds the best N assignments in time M where $M \le N \le (n+1)M$:

Theorem 13. *Assume that* $f : \{1, \ldots, n\} \times \mathbb{N} \to \mathbb{N}$ *satisfies* $f(i, 0) = 0$ *and* $f(i, j) < f(i, j')$ *for all* i *and* $j > j'$. *Assume that* $f(i, j) \le j^{O(1)} 2^{n^{O(1)}}$. *Given as input a number* $M > 1$, *Algorithm 5 outputs the* N *assignments* $(v_1, \ldots, v_n) \in \mathbb{N}^n$ *which minimize* $\sum_{i=1}^n f(i, v_i)$ *in time* $O(n(n+1)M) + n^{O(1)} + O(\log_2 M)$, *where the number* N *satisfies*: $M \le N \le (n+1)M$.

Proof. We have the following invariant at the beginning of each loop iteration: the number of $(v_1, \ldots, v_n) \in \mathbb{N}^n$ such that $\sum_{i=1}^n f(i, v_i) \le R_0$ is $< M$, and the number of $(v_1, \ldots, v_n) \in \mathbb{N}^n$ such that $\sum_{i=1}^n f(i, v_i) \le R_1$ is $\ge M$. Initially, this holds because the number of $(v_1, \ldots, v_n) \in \mathbb{N}^n$ such that $\sum_{i=1}^n f(i, v_i) \le 0$ is 1 and the number of $(v_1, \ldots, v_n) \in \mathbb{N}^n$ such that $\sum_{i=1}^n f(i, v_i) \le \sum_{i=1}^n f(i, \lceil M^{1/n} \rceil)$ is $\ge (M^{1/n})^n = M$. Furthermore, the loop preserves the invariant by definition of the loop. Since the length $R_1 - R_0$ decreases by a factor two, it follows that the number of loop iterations is $\le \log_2(\sum_{i=1}^n f(i, \lceil M^{1/n} \rceil))$.

After the loop, we must have $R_0 = R_1 - 1$. Let N_1 (resp. N_0) be the number of $(v_1, \ldots, v_n) \in \mathbb{N}^n$ such that $\sum_{i=1}^n f(i, v_i) \le R_1$ (resp. R_0) after the loop. By the invariant, we know that $N_0 < M \le N_1$. We claim that $(N_1 - N_0) \le nM$, which implies that $N_1 \le (n+1)M$. Notice that $N_1 - N_0$ is the number of $(v_1, \ldots, v_n) \in \mathbb{N}^n$ such that $\sum_{i=1}^n f(i, v_i) = R_1$. For any such assignment, one of the v_i's must be ≥ 1: if we decrement that v_i, we get a cost $< R_1$, so it must be $\le R_0$ because $R_0 = R_1 - 1$, which means that this assignment is counted by N_0. Since we have at most n possibilities for i, it follows that $N_1 - N_0 \le nM$. $\square$

Furthermore, Algorithm 5 uses negligible space, except that the output is linear in M: the best tags are actually output as a stream. If we sort the N tags, which requires space, we could output exactly the best M tags.

7   Quantum Speed-Up of Discrete Pruning

We present a quadratic quantum speed-up for discrete pruning, namely:

Theorem 14. *There is a quantum algorithm which, given* $\varepsilon > 0$, *a number* $M > 0$, *and an LLL-reduced basis* B *of a full-rank lattice* L *in* $\mathbb{Z}^n$, *outputs the shortest non-zero vector in* $L \cap P$ *in time* $O(n^2 \sqrt{M}) \mathtt{poly}(\log(n), \log(M), \log(1/\epsilon), \beta)$ *with error probability* ε. *Here*, β *denotes the bitsize of the vectors of* B, $P = \cup_{t \in U} \mathcal{C}_{\mathbb{N}}(t)$

Algorithm 3. Enumeration of low-cost assignments

Input: A function $f : \{1, \ldots, n\} \times \mathbb{N} \to \mathbb{R}_{\geq 0}$ such that $f(i, 0) = 0$ and $f(i, j) \geq f(i, j')$
   for all i and $j > j'$; a bound $R > 0$.
Output: All $(v_1, \ldots, v_n) \in \mathbb{N}^n$ such that $\sum_{i=1}^{n} f(i, v_i) \leq R$.
1: $v_1 = v_2 = \cdots = v_n = 0$ and $\rho_{n+1} = 0$ and $k = n$
2: **while** true **do**
3:    $\rho_k = \rho_{k+1} + f(k, v_k)$ // cost of the tag $(0, \ldots, 0, v_k, \ldots, v_n)$
4:    **if** $\rho_k \leq R$ **then**
5:       **if** $k = 1$ **then**
6:          **return** $(v_1, \ldots, v_n)$; (solution found)
7:          $v_k \leftarrow v_k + 1$
8:       **else**
9:          $k \leftarrow k - 1$ and $v_k \leftarrow 0$ // going down the tree
10:      **end if**
11:   **else**
12:      $k \leftarrow k + 1$ // going up the tree
13:      **if** $k = n + 1$ **then**
14:         **exit** (no more solutions)
15:      **else**
16:         $v_k \leftarrow v_k + 1$
17:      **end if**
18:   **end if**
19: **end while**

Algorithm 4. Counting low-cost assignments

Input: A function $f : \{1, \ldots, n\} \times \mathbb{N} \to \mathbb{R}_{\geq 0}$ such that $f(i, 0) = 0$ and $f(i, j) \geq f(i, j')$
   for all i and $j > j'$; a bound $R > 0$ and a number $M \geq 0$.
Output: Decide if the number of $(v_1, \ldots, v_n) \in \mathbb{N}^n$ such that $\sum_{i=1}^{n} f(i, v_i) \leq R$ is
   $\geq M$ or $< M$.
1: $v_1 = v_2 = \cdots = v_n = 0$ and $\rho_{n+1} = 0$ and $k = n$ and $m = 0$
2: **while** $m < M$ **do**
3:    $\rho_k = \rho_{k+1} + f(k, v_k)$ // cost of the tag $(0, \ldots, 0, v_k, \ldots, v_n)$
4:    **if** $\rho_k \leq R$ **then**
5:       **if** $k = 1$ **then**
6:          $m \leftarrow m + 1$ and $v_k \leftarrow v_k + 1$ (one more solution)
7:       **else**
8:          $k \leftarrow k - 1$ and $v_k \leftarrow 0$ // going down the tree
9:       **end if**
10:   **else**
11:      $k \leftarrow k + 1$ // going up the tree
12:      **if** $k = n + 1$ **then**
13:         **return** $m < M$ // no more solutions
14:      **else**
15:         $v_k \leftarrow v_k + 1$
16:      **end if**
17:   **end if**
18: **end while**
19: **return** $m \geq M$

Algorithm 5. Enumeration of lowest-cost assignments

Input: A function $f : \{1, \ldots, n\} \times \mathbb{N} \to \mathbb{R}_{\geq 0}$ such that $f(i, 0) = 0$ and $f(i, j) \geq f(i, j')$
for all i and $j > j'$; a number $M > 0$.
Output: Output the N assignments $(v_1, \ldots, v_n) \in \mathbb{N}^n$ that minimize $\sum_{i=1}^{n} f(i, v_i)$,
where $M \leq N \leq nM$.
1: $R_0 \leftarrow 0$ and $R_1 \leftarrow \sum_{i=1}^{n} f(i, \lceil M^{1/n} \rceil)$;
2: **while** $R_0 < R_1 - 1$ **do**
3:    Call Alg. 4 with $R = \lfloor (R_0 + R_1)/2 \rceil$ and M
4:    **if** number of solutions $\geq M$ **then**
5:       $R_1 \leftarrow R$
6:    **else**
7:       $R_0 \leftarrow R$
8:    **end if**
9: **end while**
10: Call Alg. 3 with R_1.

---

where $\mathcal{C}_{\mathbb{N}}()$ is the natural partition with respect to B, U is formed by the N tags t minimizing $\mathbb{E}\{\mathcal{C}_{\mathbb{N}}(t)\}$, for some $M \leq N \leq 32n^2M$ with probability at least $1 - \varepsilon/2$. If the algorithm is further given a target $\boldsymbol{u} \in \mathbb{Z}^n$, it also outputs the shortest vector in $(L - \boldsymbol{u}) \cap P$.

By comparison, opening all the cells returned by Algorithm 5 of Sect. 6 does the same in $O(M)$ poly-time operations, except that the upper bound on N is slightly lower. The proof of Theorem 14 has two parts: first, we show how to determine the best N cells without computing them, for some N close to M, with high probability; then we find the best candidate inside these N cells. Both rely on a tree interpretation. Algorithm 3 can be seen as a backtracking algorithm on a tree $\mathcal{T}(R)$, where each node can be encoded as $(*, \cdots, *, v_k, \cdots, v_n)$. The root is encoded as $(*, \cdots, *)$. Given a node $(*, \cdots, *, v_k, \cdots, v_n)$, if $k = 1$, then it is a leaf. If $\sum_{i=k}^{n} f(i, v_i) > R$, then it is also a leaf. If $\sum_{i=k}^{n} f(i, v_i) \leq R$, then its children are $(*, \cdots, *, v_{k-1}, v_k, \cdots, v_n)$, where v_{k-1} can take all integer values between 0 and $\rho_{v_k, \cdots, v_n}$. Here $\rho_{v_k, \cdots, v_n}$ is the smallest integer such that $f(i - 1, \rho_{v_k, \cdots, v_n}) + \sum_{i=k}^{n} f(i, v_i) > R$. In case of discrete pruning, f is quadratic. We can compute $\rho_{v_k, \cdots, v_n}$ and build the black-box on $\mathcal{T}(R)$.

7.1   Determining the Best Cells Implicitly

Given a number $M > 0$, Algorithm 5 finds (in time essentially M) the best N vectors $\boldsymbol{t} \in \mathbb{N}^n$ (for some N close to M) minimizing $\mathbb{E}\{\mathcal{C}_{\mathbb{N}}(t)\} = \sum_{i=1}^{n} \left(\frac{t_i^2}{4} + \frac{t_i}{4} + \frac{1}{12} \right) \|\boldsymbol{b}_i^\star\|^2$ by minimizing instead the function:

$$g(v_1, \cdots, v_n) = \sum_{i=1}^{n} f(i, v_i) = \sum_{i=1}^{n} v_i(v_i + 1) \|\boldsymbol{b}_i^\star\|^2 = \sum_{i=1}^{n} \alpha_i v_i(v_i + 1).$$

This is done by finding a suitable radius R by dichotomy, based on logarithmically many calls to Algorithm 4 until the number of solutions is close to M, and eventually enumerating the marked leaves of a search tree by Algorithm 3. Both Algorithm 3 and Algorithm 4 can be viewed as algorithms exploring a tree $\mathcal{T}(R)$ depending on a radius $R > 0$: Algorithm 4 decides if the number $\#S(\mathcal{T}(R))$ of marked leaves (*i.e.* the number of outputs returned by Algorithm 3) is $\geq$ or $<$ than an input number; Algorithm 3 returns all the marked leaves.

This tree interpretation gives rise to Algorithm 6, which is our quantum analogue of Algorithm 5 with the following differences: we are only interested in finding a suitable radius R such that $N = \#S(\mathcal{T}(R))$ is close to M up to a factor of $32n^2$, with correctness probability at least $1 - \varepsilon/2$, because enumerating all the marked leaves would prevent any quadratic speed up. We replace Algorithm 4 by the quantum tree size estimation algorithm of [9]: this gives a quadratic speed up, but approximation errors slightly worsens the upper bound on N. The input $(\alpha_1, \cdots, \alpha_n)$ of Algorithm 6 corresponds to $(\|\boldsymbol{b}_1^\star\|^2, \cdots, \|\boldsymbol{b}_n^\star\|^2)$, where $(\boldsymbol{b}_1, \cdots, \boldsymbol{b}_n)$ is an integer basis. We know that $(\|\boldsymbol{b}_1^\star\|^2, \cdots, \|\boldsymbol{b}_n^\star\|^2) \in \mathbb{Q}^n$, but by suitable multiplication preserving polynomial sizes, we may assume that $(\|\boldsymbol{b}_1^\star\|^2, \cdots, \|\boldsymbol{b}_n^\star\|^2) \in \mathbb{N}^n$. The order between the $\|\boldsymbol{b}_i^\star\|^2$'s doesn't matter in our analysis. We can assume that $\|\boldsymbol{b}_1^\star\|^2 \leq \cdots \leq \|\boldsymbol{b}_n^\star\|^2$. We show that Algorithm 6 finds a radius R corresponding to the best M cells in approximately $\sqrt{M}$ quantum operations:

Algorithm 6. Computing implicitly the best cells quantumly

Input: $\varepsilon, M > 0$ and $(\alpha_1, \cdots, \alpha_n) \in \mathbb{N}^n$ with $\alpha_1 \leq \cdots \leq \alpha_n$ such that the input
$\quad f : \{1, \cdots, n\} \times \mathbb{N} \to \mathbb{N}$ of Alg. 3 satisfies $f(i, x) = \alpha_i x(x + 1)$
Output: R such that $M \leq \#S(\mathcal{T}(R)) \leq 32n^2 M$ with probability $\geq 1 - \varepsilon$
1: $r \leftarrow \lceil \log_2(\sum_{i=1}^n f(i, \lceil (4nM)^{1/n} \rceil)) \rceil$ and $R \leftarrow \sum_{i=1}^n f(i, \lceil (4nM)^{1/n} \rceil)$ and $R_0 \leftarrow 0$
$\quad$ and $R_1 \leftarrow R$
2: **while** $R_1 - R_0 > 1$ **do**
3: $\quad$ Call **TreeSizeEstimation**$(\mathcal{T}_2(R), 16n^2 M, 1/2, \varepsilon r/2, 2)$
4: $\quad$ **if** the answer is "$\mathcal{T}_2(R)$ contains more than $16n^2 M$ vertices" **then**
5: $\quad\quad$ $R_1 \leftarrow R$ and $R \leftarrow \lfloor (R_0 + R_1)/2 \rfloor$
6: $\quad$ **else if** the answer is "$\mathcal{T}_2(R)$ contains $\hat{T}$ vertices" with $\hat{T} < 3(2n - 1)M$ **then**
7: $\quad\quad$ $R_0 \leftarrow R$ and $R \leftarrow \lfloor (R_0 + R_1)/2 \rceil$
8: $\quad$ **else**
9: $\quad\quad$ Return R
10: $\quad$ **end if**
11: **end while**
12: Return R_0

Theorem 15. *The output R of Algorithm 6 satisfies $M \leq \#S(\mathcal{T}(R)) \leq 32n^2 M$ with probability $\geq 1 - \varepsilon/2$. Algorithm 6 runs in quantum time $O(n^2 \sqrt{M} \texttt{poly}(\log(n), \log(M), \log(1/\varepsilon), \beta))$ where β is the bitsize of the basis vectors $(\mathbf{b}_1, \cdots, \mathbf{b}_n)$. The algorithm needs $O(\texttt{poly}(n, \log(M), \log(1/\epsilon)))$ qubits.*

7.2   Finding the Best Lattice Vector

We now know R such that the number N of $(v_1, \cdots, v_n) \in \mathbb{N}^n$ which satisfies $\sum_{i=1}^{n} f(i, v_i) \leq R$ is in $[M, 32n^2 M]$ with probability at least $1 - \varepsilon/2$. All these solutions are leaves of the tree $\mathcal{T}(R)$ and they form the set U of the best N tags minimizing t minimizing $\mathbb{E}\{\mathcal{C}_{\mathbb{N}}(t)\}$. Let $P = \cup_{t \in U} \mathcal{C}_{\mathbb{N}}(t)$ where $\mathcal{C}_{\mathbb{N}}()$ is the natural partition with respect to the input basis B. We would like to find a shortest non-zero vector in $L \cap P$ for the SVP setting, or the shortest vector in $(L - u) \cap P$ in the CVP setting, when we are further given target $u \in \mathbb{Z}^n$. To do this, we notice that it suffices to apply **FindMin2** (in App), provided that the basis $(\mathbf{b}_1, \cdots, \mathbf{b}_n)$ is LLL-reduced. More precisely, we call **FindMin2**$(\mathcal{T}(R), \mathcal{P}, h, \|\mathbf{b}_1\|^2, d, 32n^2 M, \varepsilon/2)$. Here $\mathcal{P}$ is the predicate which returns true on a node iff it is a leaf encoded as $(x_1, \cdots, x_n)$ such that $g(x_1, \cdots, x_n) = \sum_{i=1}^{n} f(i, x_i) \leq R$. $h_V(x_1, \cdots, x_n)$ is the predicate which indicates if the square of the norm of the lattice vector in the cell of tag $(x_1, \cdots, x_n)$ is $\leq V$. The time complexity is $O(n^2 \sqrt{M}\mathtt{poly}(\log(n), \log(M), \log(1/\varepsilon), \beta))$.

Since the subroutine of determining the best cells and the one of finding a shortest non-zero vector, both have an error probability $\varepsilon/2$, by union bound, the total error probability is ε. We thus have proved Theorem 14.

7.3   The Case of Extreme Pruning

In this section, we explain how to tackle the extreme pruning case, where one wants to run discrete pruning over many reduced bases. Due to space limitations, we only give a proof sketch, but the main ideas are the same.

Given m LLL-reduced bases $(\mathbf{B}_1, \cdots, \mathbf{B}_m)$ of the same integer lattice L of rank n, we define for each basis $\mathbf{B}_i$ a function $g_i : \mathbb{N}^n \to \mathbb{Q}$ such that $g_i(x_1, \cdots, x_n) = \sum_{j=1}^{n} \|\mathbf{b}_{i,j}^\star\|^2 x_i(x_i + 1)$, where $(\mathbf{b}_{i,1}^\star, \cdots, \mathbf{b}_{i,n}^\star)$ is the Gram-Schmidt orthogonalization of the basis $\mathbf{B}_i$. Here, we want to first find the $\mathtt{poly}(n) * M$ best cells with respect to all of the functions g_i altogether, and then find the shortest vector in these cells. Both steps have complexity $O(\sqrt{M}\mathtt{poly}(n, \log M, \log 1/\varepsilon, \beta))$, where ε is the total error probability and where β is the bitsize of the vectors of the input bases.

Theorem 16. *There is a quantum algorithm which, given $\varepsilon > 0$, a number $M > 0$, and m LLL-reduced bases $(\mathbf{B}_1, \cdots, \mathbf{B}_m)$ of an n-rank integer lattice L, outputs the shortest non-zero vector in $L \cap P$ in time $O(\sqrt{M}\mathtt{poly}(n, \log M, \log 1/\varepsilon, \beta))$ with error probability ε. Here, β denotes the maximum bitsize of the vectors of all given bases, $P = \cup_{(i,t) \in U} \mathcal{C}_{\mathbb{N}}(i, t)$ where $\mathcal{C}_{\mathbb{N}}(i, \cdot)$ is the natural partition with respect to B_i, U is formed by the N tuples $(i, t) \in \{1, \cdots, m\} \times \mathbb{N}^n$ minimizing $g_i(t)$ among all tuples, for some $N = \mathtt{poly}(n) * M$ with probability at least $1 - \varepsilon/2$. If the algorithm is further given a target $u \in \mathbb{Z}^n$, it also outputs the shortest vector in $(L - u) \cap P$.*

The main idea of the proof is the following. For each basis $\mathbf{B}_i$, there is a back-tracking tree with respect to the function g_i as we explained in the previous section. We put all these trees together and obtain one single tree. We first apply the **TreeSizeEstimation** algorithm several times to find a good common radius R for all functions g_i by dichotomy, such that the total number of good cells in all trees is $\texttt{poly}(n) * M$. After that, we apply **FindMin2** to find the shortest vector among all these cells. Remark that in the previous section, we required the function g to have integral values, and this was achieved by multiplying all $\|\boldsymbol{b}_i^\star\|^2$ by a common denominator. Instead, we here want to keep the output rational, which is proved sufficient by the following lemma:

Lemma 9. *Given a basis* $(\mathbf{b}_1, \cdots, \mathbf{b}_n)$ *of an integer lattice* L, $g : \mathbb{N}^n \to \mathbb{Q}$ *such that* $g(x_1, \cdots, x_n) = \sum_{i=1}^n \|\boldsymbol{b}_i^\star\|^2 x_i(x_i+1)$, *we denote* $\mathcal{T}(R)$ *the backtracking tree for finding all solutions of* $g(x_1, \cdots, x_n) \leq R$, $\mathcal{T}_2(R)$ *the corresponding binary tree. For all* $R \in \mathbb{R}^+$, $\#S(\mathcal{T}_2(R+\delta)) \leq 2n\#S(\mathcal{T}_2(R))$, *where* $\delta = \frac{1}{\prod_{i=1}^n \Delta_i}$ *and* $\Delta_i = \mathrm{covol}(\mathbf{b}_1, \cdots, \mathbf{b}_i)^2 = \prod_{j=1}^i \|\boldsymbol{b}_i^\star\|^2$.

The proof of this lemma is the same as the proof of a similar lemma in the full version by noticing that $\prod_{i=1}^n \Delta_i$ is a common denominator of all $\|\boldsymbol{b}_i^\star\|^2$.

For each basis $\mathbf{B}_i$, we define δ_i as in Lemma 9. In the dichotomy step, we stop when the difference of the two terms is smaller than $\min_{j \in \{1, \cdots, m\}} \delta_j$. The other steps are the same as in the previous section.

Acknowledgements. This work was supported by JSPS KAKENHI Grant Numbers 16H02780 and 16H02830, and partially supported by a mobility scholarship of the third author at the University of Tokyo in the frame of the Erasmus Mundus Action 2 Project TEAM Technologies for Information and Communication Technologies, funded by the European Commission. This publication reflects the view only of the authors, and the Commission cannot be held responsible for any use which may be made of the information contained therein. We thank Frédéric Magniez for helpful discussions.

References

1. Aggarwal, D., Dadush, D., Regev, O., Stephens-Davidowitz, N.: Solving the shortest vector problem in 2^n time using discrete gaussian sampling: extended abstract. In: Proceedings of 47th ACM STOC, pp. 733–742 (2015)
2. Ajtai, M.: Generating hard instances of lattice problems. In: Proceedings of 28th ACM STOC, pp. 99–108 (1996)
3. Ajtai, M., Kumar, R., Sivakumar, D.: A sieve algorithm for the shortest lattice vector problem. In: Proceedings of 33rd STOC, pp. 601–610. ACM (2001)
4. Albrecht, M., Schanck, J., Bernstein, D.: Messages on the NIST pqc mailing-list, May 2018
5. Albrecht, M.R., et al.: Estimate all the LWE, NTRU schemes! posted on the pqc-forum, 1 February 2018. https://estimate-all-the-lwe-ntru-schemes.github.io/paper.pdf
6. Albrecht, M.R., Ducas, L., Herold, G., Kirshanova, E., Postlethwaite, E., Stevens, M.: New records for lattice SVP challenges (2018)
7. Alkim, E., et al.: Revisiting TESLA in the quantum random oracle model. In: Lange, T., Takagi, T. (eds.) PQCrypto 2017. LNCS, vol. 10346, pp. 143–162. Springer, Cham (2017). https://doi.org/10.1007/978-3-319-59879-6_9

8. Alkim, E., Ducas, L., öppelmann, T.P., Schwabe, P.: Post-quantum key exchange - a new hope. In: Proceedings of 25th USENIX, pp. 327–343. USENIX (2016)
9. Ambainis, A., Kokainis, M.: Quantum algorithm for tree size estimation, with applications to backtracking and 2-player games. In: Proceedings of STOC 2017. ACM (2017)
10. Aono, Y., Nguyen, P.Q.: Random sampling revisited: lattice enumeration with discrete pruning. In: Coron, J.-S., Nielsen, J.B. (eds.) EUROCRYPT 2017. LNCS, vol. 10211, pp. 65–102. Springer, Cham (2017). https://doi.org/10.1007/978-3-319-56614-6_3
11. Aono, Y., Nguyen, P.Q., Seito, T., Shikata, J.: Lower bounds on lattice enumeration with extreme pruning. In: Shacham, H., Boldyreva, A. (eds.) CRYPTO 2018. LNCS, vol. 10992, pp. 608–637. Springer, Cham (2018). https://doi.org/10.1007/978-3-319-96881-0_21
12. Aono, Y., Nguyen, P.Q., Shen, Y.: Quantum lattice enumeration and tweaking discrete pruning. Cryptology ePrint Archive, Report 2018/546 (2018)
13. Aono, Y., Wang, Y., Hayashi, T., Takagi, T.: Improved progressive BKZ algorithms and their precise cost estimation by sharp simulator. In: Fischlin, M., Coron, J.-S. (eds.) EUROCRYPT 2016. LNCS, vol. 9665, pp. 789–819. Springer, Heidelberg (2016). https://doi.org/10.1007/978-3-662-49890-3_30
14. Babai, L.: On Lovász' lattice reduction and the nearest lattice point problem. In: Mehlhorn, K. (ed.) STACS 1985. LNCS, vol. 182, pp. 13–20. Springer, Heidelberg (1985). https://doi.org/10.1007/BFb0023990
15. Becker, A., Ducas, L., Gama, N., Laarhoven, T.: New directions in nearest neighbor searching with applications to lattice sieving. In: Proceedings of 27th ACM-SIAM Symposium on Discrete Algorithms (SODA), pp. 10–24 (2016)
16. Chen, Y.: Réduction de réseau et sécurité concrète du chiffrement complètement homomorphe. Ph.D. thesis, Univ. Paris 7 (2013)
17. Chen, Y., Nguyen, P.Q.: BKZ 2.0: better lattice security estimates. In: Lee, D.H., Wang, X. (eds.) ASIACRYPT 2011. LNCS, vol. 7073, pp. 1–20. Springer, Heidelberg (2011). https://doi.org/10.1007/978-3-642-25385-0_1
18. del Pino, R., Lyubashevsky, V., Pointcheval, D.: The whole is less than the sum of its parts: constructing more efficient lattice-based AKEs. In: Zikas, V., De Prisco, R. (eds.) SCN 2016. LNCS, vol. 9841, pp. 273–291. Springer, Cham (2016). https://doi.org/10.1007/978-3-319-44618-9_15
19. Fukase, M., Kashiwabara, K.: An accelerated algorithm for solving SVP based on statistical analysis. JIP **23**(1), 67–80 (2015)
20. Gama, N., Nguyen, P.Q.: Predicting lattice reduction. In: Smart, N. (ed.) EUROCRYPT 2008. LNCS, vol. 4965, pp. 31–51. Springer, Heidelberg (2008). https://doi.org/10.1007/978-3-540-78967-3_3
21. Gama, N., Nguyen, P.Q., Regev, O.: Lattice enumeration using extreme pruning. In: Gilbert, H. (ed.) EUROCRYPT 2010. LNCS, vol. 6110, pp. 257–278. Springer, Heidelberg (2010). https://doi.org/10.1007/978-3-642-13190-5_13
22. Goldreich, O., Goldwasser, S., Halevi, S.: Public-key cryptosystems from lattice reduction problems. In: Kaliski, B.S. (ed.) CRYPTO 1997. LNCS, vol. 1294, pp. 112–131. Springer, Heidelberg (1997). https://doi.org/10.1007/BFb0052231
23. Hülsing, A., Rijneveld, J., Schanck, J.M., Schwabe, P.: NTRU-HRSS-KEM: algorithm specifications and supporting documentation. NIST submission
24. Kannan, R.: Improved algorithms for integer programming and related lattice problems. In: Proceedings of 15th ACM STOC, pp. 193–206 (1983)

25. Laarhoven, T.: Sieving for shortest vectors in lattices using angular locality-sensitive hashing. In: Gennaro, R., Robshaw, M. (eds.) CRYPTO 2015. LNCS, vol. 9215, pp. 3–22. Springer, Heidelberg (2015). https://doi.org/10.1007/978-3-662-47989-6_1
26. Laarhoven, T., Mosca, M., van de Pol, J.: Finding shortest lattice vectors faster using quantum search. Des. Codes Crypt. **77**(2–3), 375–400 (2015)
27. Lindner, R., Peikert, C.: Better key sizes (and attacks) for LWE-based encryption. In: Kiayias, A. (ed.) CT-RSA 2011. LNCS, vol. 6558, pp. 319–339. Springer, Heidelberg (2011). https://doi.org/10.1007/978-3-642-19074-2_21
28. Lindner, R., Rückert, M.: TU Darmstadt lattice challenge. http://www.latticechallenge.org/
29. Liu, M., Nguyen, P.Q.: Solving BDD by enumeration: an update. In: Dawson, E. (ed.) CT-RSA 2013. LNCS, vol. 7779, pp. 293–309. Springer, Heidelberg (2013). https://doi.org/10.1007/978-3-642-36095-4_19
30. Ludwig, C.: A faster lattice reduction method using quantum search. In: Ibaraki, T., Katoh, N., Ono, H. (eds.) ISAAC 2003. LNCS, vol. 2906, pp. 199–208. Springer, Heidelberg (2003). https://doi.org/10.1007/978-3-540-24587-2_22
31. Micciancio, D., Voulgaris, P.: A deterministic single exponential time algorithm for most lattice problems based on Voronoi cell computations. In: Proceedings of 42nd ACM Symposium on Theory of Computing (STOC) (2010)
32. Micciancio, D., Voulgaris, P.: Faster exponential time algorithms for the shortest vector problem. In: Proceedings of ACM-SIAM SODA, pp. 1468–1480 (2010)
33. Montanaro, A.: Quantum walk speedup of backtracking algorithms. ArXiv (2015)
34. Nguyen, P.Q., Shparlinski, I.: The insecurity of the digital signature algorithm with partially known nonces. J. Crypt. **15**(3), 151–176 (2002)
35. Nguyen, P.Q., Vidick, T.: Sieve algorithms for the shortest vector problem are practical. J. Math. Crypt. **2**(2), 181–207 (2008)
36. NIST: Round 1 submissions for post-quantum cryptography standardization. https://csrc.nist.gov/projects/post-quantum-cryptography/round-1-submissions
37. Pohst, M.: On the computation of lattice vectors of minimal length, successive minima and reduced bases with applications. SIGSAM Bull. **15**(1), 37–44 (1981)
38. Regev, O.: On lattices, learning with errors, random linear codes, and cryptography. In: Proceedings of 37th ACM STOC, pp. 84–93 (2005)
39. Schneider, M., Gama, N.: SVP challenge. http://www.latticechallenge.org/svp-challenge/
40. Schnorr, C.P.: Lattice reduction by random sampling and birthday methods. In: Alt, H., Habib, M. (eds.) STACS 2003. LNCS, vol. 2607, pp. 145–156. Springer, Heidelberg (2003). https://doi.org/10.1007/3-540-36494-3_14
41. Schnorr, C.-P., Euchner, M.: Lattice basis reduction: improved practical algorithms and solving subset sum problems. Math. Programm. **66**, 181–199 (1994)
42. Schnorr, C.P., Hörner, H.H.: Attacking the chor-rivest cryptosystem by improved lattice reduction. In: Guillou, L.C., Quisquater, J.-J. (eds.) EUROCRYPT 1995. LNCS, vol. 921, pp. 1–12. Springer, Heidelberg (1995). https://doi.org/10.1007/3-540-49264-X_1
43. Security Innovation. NTRU challenge. https://www.securityinnovation.com/products/ntru-crypto/ntru-challenge
44. Yu, Y., Ducas, L.: Second order statistical behavior of LLL and BKZ. In: Proceedings of SAC 2017, pp. 3–22 (2017)

On the Hardness of the Computational Ring-LWR Problem and Its Applications

Long Chen[1,2], Zhenfeng Zhang[1,3(✉)], and Zhenfei Zhang[4]

[1] TCA Laboratory, State Key Laboratory of Computer Science,
Institute of Software, Chinese Academy of Sciences, Beijing, China
{chenlong,zfzhang}@tca.iscas.ac.cn
[2] New Jersey Institute of Technology, Newark, USA
[3] University of Chinese Academy of Sciences, Beijing, China
[4] OnBoard Security Inc., Wilmington, USA
zzhang@onboardsecurity.com

Abstract. In this paper, we propose a new assumption, the *Computational Learning With Rounding over rings*, which is inspired by the computational Diffie-Hellman problem. Assuming the hardness of R-LWE, we prove this problem is hard when the secret is small, uniform and invertible. From a theoretical point of view, we give examples of a key exchange scheme and a public key encryption scheme, and prove the worst-case hardness for both schemes with the help of a random oracle. Our result improves both speed, as a result of not requiring Gaussian secret or noise, and size, as a result of rounding. In practice, our result suggests that decisional R-LWR based schemes, such as SABER, ROUND2 and LIZARD, which are among the most efficient solutions to the NIST post-quantum cryptography competition, stem from a provable secure design. There are no hardness results on the decisional R-LWR with polynomial modulus prior to this work, to the best of our knowledge.

1 Introduction

Organizations and research groups are looking for candidate algorithms to replace RSA and ECC based schemes [48,49] due to the threat of quantum computers [58]. Among all candidates, lattice based solutions seem to offer the most promising solutions. One of the fundamental features enabled by the Learning With Errors (LWE) [39,57]/the Small Integer Solution (SIS) [1,45] family of problems, is that the *average-case* security of the cryptosystem stems from the *worst-case* hardness of well studied lattice problems [2,16,39,45,51,55,57].

The celebrated work of worst-case/average-case reductions was firstly presented in [51,57] for LWE and in [39] for R-LWE. In both cases, the errors follow a rounded Gaussian distribution. Albeit great improvements in a sequence of work [3,13,28–30,35,47,52,56], Gaussian sampling is still the most intricate part to implementing (R-)LWE based schemes.

© International Association for Cryptologic Research 2018
T. Peyrin and S. Galbraith (Eds.): ASIACRYPT 2018, LNCS 11272, pp. 435–464, 2018.
https://doi.org/10.1007/978-3-030-03326-2_15

436 L. Chen et al.

An average-case/worse-case reduction without Gaussian sampling is a long standing problem. It has been studied by a series of works from different angles [9,12,26,43,44]. Generally, there are two ways to solve this problem. One may either reduce LWE to LWE with uniform/binary errors [9,26,43,44], or reduce LWE to the Learning With Rounding (LWR) problem [4,5,10,12]. Here the (R-)LWR problem, introduced in [10], is a variant of (R-)LWE where random errors are replaced by a deterministic rounding function. Interestingly, there exists a reduction from LWE with uniform errors to LWR [12] that indicates a connection between the aforementioned two solutions.

In addition to avoiding Gaussian sampling, it is also common to resort to a ring setting [39,41,55]. However, the above methods are no longer applicable, since the reductions from generic LWE to "binary LWE" in [9,26,43,44] all rely on a search-to-decision reduction from [43]. How to carry over this reduction to the ring setting is still an open problem. Moreover, there is no reduction from R-LWE to the decisional version of R-LWR when the modulus is polynomial, to our best knowledge.[1]

Another obstacle of deploying (R-)LWE based cryptosystems is that the sizes of public keys and the ciphertexts are significantly larger than those of RSA and ECC [13]. One direction to lower the size of public keys/ciphertexts, is to choose a smaller modulus q. However, a smaller q leads to a higher (and sometime non-negligible) decryption error rate. In some cases, this may result in an invalidation of a security proof. For example, in [3], the failure probability is around 2^{-61} for a security level of 128. The security proof in [3,13,14] only provides an indistinguishability between a session key derived by Bob and a uniformly random string. Now that Alice and Bob may derive different session keys with a non-negligible probability, it is also essential to prove the pseudorandomness of Alice's key. This is not captured by the existing proofs. In addition, many schemes rely on the Fujisaki-Okamoto transformation [33] to achieve CCA-2 security. This also requires a negligible failure probability [36]. In history we have seen non-negligible failure lead to attacks, such as [37].

A trivial solution to decryption errors is to perform key validation. This, however, needs additional round trips for the protocol. An alternative solution is to further tuning the parameters. For example, to use a narrower secret/error. However, the worst-case hardness theorems for R-LWE [39,55] require the widths of the error distributions to exceed certain $\Omega(\sqrt{n})$ bounds, where n is the degree of the secret polynomial. On the other hand, if the errors are smaller than $\sqrt{n}$, LWE can be solved in polynomial time using the Arora-Ge's algorithm [7] with $m = O(n^2)$ samples. There is a natural extension of this attack to R-LWE by viewing each R-LWE instance as n LWE samples. In general, as pointed out in [54], error distributions that are too far from the provably hard ones shall not be used, to avoid weak instances of the R-LWE problem [17,18,31,32].

---

[1] [10] proved hardness of decisional Ring-LWR for super-polynomial q is as secure as decisional Ring-LWE for super-polynomial q. However, the hardness of decisional Ring-LWE for super-polynomial q is not well understood yet.

Due to its great simplicity and efficiency, R-LWR based constructions, namely, SABER [24], ROUND2 [8], LIZARD [21], ROUND5 [11] and OKCN [38], are among the most promising candidates to the NIST post-quantum cryptography competition [48]. See [42] for a comparison of performance versus security among all lattice based candidates. Specifically, SABER [24] provides a decisional module-LWR based KEM, to which R-LWR can be viewed as a special case. The KEM and PKE algorithms in ROUND2 [8] may be based on *either* decisional LWR or decisional R-LWR, while the algorithms in the ring version of LIZARD [21] is based on *both* of decisional R-LWE and decisional R-LWR. Thus, the hardness of R-LWR is a long await result in the community, to show that those three schemes indeed stem from a provable secure design.

1.1   Our Contributions

In the literature, there exists a reduction from search R-LWE to search R-LWR [12], using the tool of Rényi Divergence (RD). However, it is hard to instantiate a scheme directly from this result since cryptosystems are usually based on decisional problems. On the other hand, it seems very difficult to provide a reduction from decisional R-LWE to decisional R-LWR when the modulus is polynomial, due to the limitation of RD in dealing with decisional problems [9].

To bridge this gap, we propose a new assumption, the Computational Learning With Rounding over rings (R-CLWR) in this paper, in analogy to the Computational Diffie-Hellman (CDH) assumption. Next, we provide a reduction from decisional R-LWE to R-CLWR when the secret of the R-LWE instances is uniform from the set of all invertible elements whose coefficients lie in a small interval $[-\beta, \beta]^n$ for some integer $\beta < q$. Combining the existing average-case/worst-case reduction for R-LWE [39,55], we prove that the R-CLWR problem is hard, assuming the hardness of some worst-case lattice problems.

Applications. We give two applications of R-CLWR, a public key encryption (PKE) scheme in Sect. 5 and a Diffie-Hellman type key exchange scheme in Sect. 6. *Asymptotically speaking*, our scheme improves a classical R-LWE based solutions in two ways:

1. we allow for smaller size of public keys/ciphertexts as a result of rounding;
2. we remove the cumbersome Gaussian samplings.

We remark that it is hard to find overlaps between the concrete world and the asymptotic world. In *practice*, most of the NIST submissions and other schemes [3,13,14] only consider the best known cryptanalytic attacks [20,42] and ignore the average-case/worst-case proof. For the same reason, none of the Ring-LWE/LWR based NIST candidates sample errors from rounded Gaussian. Our result is asymptotic. Thus, we do not provide a direct comparison between our scheme and the NIST submissions in this paper. Instead, we give asymptotic parameters for both R-LWE scheme and our R-CLWR based scheme for a fair comparison. In addition, we also assume that the decryption failure probability needs to be exponentially small within this asymptotic world.

	R-LWE	R-CLWR
Samples - KEYGEN	2	1
Samples - ENCRYPT	3	1
Sampler	Gaussian	Uniform & Invertible
Modulus	$\Omega(n^{5.5}\log^{0.5} n)$	$\Omega(n^{3.75}\log^{0.25} n)$

- A R-LWE based scheme needs to proceed two Gaussian samplings during key generation and three Gaussian samplings during encryption. The modulus of the public key and the ciphertext is $q = \Omega(n^{5.5}\log^{0.5} n)$.
- A R-CLWR based scheme needs to proceed one sampling during the key generation and one sampling during the encryption. The sampling procedure is to simply draw an element from a small interval and output when it is invertible, The modulus of the public key and the ciphertext is $p = \Omega(n^{3.75}\log^{0.25} n)$.

To show the power of our result, we give security proofs for a variant of SABER and ROUND2, as well as LIZARD, based on the R-CLWR assumption. Nonetheless, since the worst-case connection does not imply definite security for any concrete choice of parameters, our proofs will be based on asymptotic simplifications of their original algorithms.

Technique Overview. The notion of R-CLWR is inspired by the following observation. Decisional Diffie-Hellman (DDH) based schemes, such as ELGAMAL [34], are provable secure under the CDH assumption and the random oracle model (ROM). There, instead of distinguishing the ciphertexts of different plaintexts, the adversary needs to find a pre-image of the hash function using the public key and ciphertexts. Therefore, with the help of ROM, one converts the underlying decisional problem into a computational problem. At a high level, we apply same methodology to lattice based cryptography and reduce the security of the cryptosystem (a decisional problem) to a computational problem. In doing so, we are able to utilize the tool of RD. A similar idea is also used in the secure analysis of Newhope [3].

To present the R-CLWR problem, first, let us present a set of *interactive experiments* between a challenger $\mathcal{C}$ and an adversary $\mathcal{A}$. There exist a source $\mathcal{S}$ where the $\mathcal{C}$ gets all its input from. For simplicity, assuming all sources $\mathcal{S}$ can be partitioned in two parts: a variable part *var* that is different for distinct sources, and a constant part *con* that remains the same for all sources. We view the challenger as a function that takes inputs $X \leftarrow var$ and $aux \leftarrow con$, and outputs two quantities, Input and Target (from $\mathcal{A}$'s point of view).

Next, we are ready to describe a computational assumption based on the above experiments. Suppose there are two experiments, namely, Exp_1 and Exp_2. In Exp_1, X_1 contains a set of R-LWR samples that are sampled from var_1. In Exp_2, X_2 contains a set of uniform samples from var_2. Assuming all the rest variables in those experiments remain identical (i.e., $\mathcal{A}$ and $\mathcal{C}$), if the success probability in Exp_2 is negligible for any adversary, then, that in Exp_1 will also be negligible. Intuitively, this definition captures that, assuming all rest variables remain the same, $\mathcal{A}$ cannot learn more information from R-LWR samples than from uniform samples.

In what it follows, we provide definitions for the R-CLWR assumption (Definition 7) and the R-CRLWE assumption (Definition 8), along with the following reductions:

$$\text{R-LWE (decisional)} \Longrightarrow \text{R-CRLWE} \Longrightarrow \text{R-CLWR}.$$

As stated earlier, the first "$\Longrightarrow$" allows us to convert a decisional problem into a computational problem, so that RD becomes applicable to the second "$\Longrightarrow$". Then, the key becomes to show that RD between an R-LWR sample $(a, \lfloor as \rfloor_p)$ and a *rounded* R-LWE sample $(a, \lfloor as + e \rfloor_p)$ is small. A natural way to obtain this result is to extend the estimation of [12] to meet the requirement of the average-case/worst-case reduction for R-LWE [39,55]. We highlight the challenge for this task at a high level. For R-LWE, [12] requires the error distribution to be bounded, the coefficients to be independent, and the secret to be invertible over the ring. By contrast, in the first "$\Longrightarrow$" the worst case hardness results [39,55] require the error to follow rounded Gaussian over the H space (see Sect. 2) where the secret is not necessarily invertible unless the ring R_q is also a finite field. This rules out common rings such as $x^n + 1$ with n a power of 2. We solve this issue with rejection sampling arguments. We will provide more details in Sect. 4.

It is also worth pointing out that conversions between R-LWE instances and R-LWR instances are not straightforward. For simplicity, let $(a, as+e) \in R_q^2$ be an R-LWE instance, and $(a', \lfloor a's' \rfloor_p) \in R_q \times R_p$ be an R-LWR instance. Notice that a and $as+e$ are both in R_q, while $\lfloor a's' \rfloor_p$ is in R_p. In a security proof, we need to replace $as + e$ with a random element u, and pass u to the next R-LWE instance as a public input. In comparison, for R-LWR, $\lfloor as \rfloor_p$ is in R_p instead of R_q; and it will not be a valid public input to the next R-LWR instance, unless we change the modulus for the hardness assumption from q to p. This is indeed an issue for ROUND2 [8], whose proof only works when q dividable by p. We solve this problem by introducing a new probabilistic function $\text{INV}(\cdot)$ in this paper that "lifts" an R_p element back to R_q. Particularly, we have $\lfloor \text{INV}(\lfloor a \rfloor_p) \rfloor_p = \lfloor a \rfloor_p$ and $\text{INV}(\lfloor a \rfloor_p)$ is uniform in R_q when a is uniform in R_q. Note that q is not required to be dividable by p. This allows for NTT friendly prime q-s for efficient implementations. We will provide details in Sect. 5.

2   Preliminaries

For a set S and a probability distribution χ over S, denote by $x \leftarrow_\$ \chi$ sampling $x \in S$ according to χ. When χ is a uniform distribution over S, denote by $x \leftarrow_\$ \mathcal{U}(S)$ to sample x uniformly at random from S. For simplicity, we sometimes write it as $x \leftarrow_\$ S$. Additionally, we use $\mathcal{U}(\lfloor \mathbb{Z}_q \rfloor_p)$ to denote the distribution of $\lfloor x \rfloor_p$ where $x \leftarrow_\$ \mathcal{U}(\mathbb{Z}_q)$.

2.1   The Rounding Function

For any integer modulus $q \geq 2$, $\mathbb{Z}_q$ denotes the quotient ring of integers modulo q. We define a (floor) rounding function $\lfloor \cdot \rceil_p : \mathbb{Z}_q \to \mathbb{Z}_p$ as $\lfloor x \rceil_p = \lfloor (p/q) \cdot \bar{x} \rfloor \bmod p$, where $q \geq p \geq 2$ will be apparent from the context, $\bar{x}$ is an integer congruent to $x \bmod q$. We extend $\lfloor \cdot \rceil_p$ componentwise to vectors and matrices over $\mathbb{Z}_q$, and coefficient-wise (with respect to the "power basis") to the quotient ring R_q. Note that in [4,10,12], LWR is defined with the function $\lfloor \cdot \rceil_p$, while it can be extended directly to $\lfloor \cdot \rfloor_p$ with a similar definition while preserving the proof. We opt to use $\lfloor \cdot \rfloor_p$ for the following reason: in the implementation when q and p are both powers of some common base b (e.g., 2), $\lfloor \cdot \rfloor_p$ is equivalent to dropping the least-significant digit(s) in base b. Moreover, $\lfloor x \rfloor_p$ is uniformly random in $\mathbb{Z}_p$ if x is uniformly random in $\mathbb{Z}_q$ when p divides q.

2.2   Rényi Divergence

In [9], Bai et al. show that Rényi divergence (RD) is a powerful tool to improve or generalize security reductions in lattice-based cryptography. The formal definition is shown below.

Definition 1 (Rényi divergence). *Let $\mathcal{P}$, $\mathcal{Q}$ be two distributions s.t. $Supp(\mathcal{P}) \subseteq Supp(\mathcal{Q})$. For $a \in (1, +\infty)$, the Rényi divergence of order a is defined by*

$$\mathsf{RD}_a(\mathcal{P}\|\mathcal{Q}) = \left(\sum_{x \in Supp(\mathcal{P})} \left(\mathcal{P}(x)^a / \mathcal{Q}(x)^{a-1} \right) \right)^{\frac{1}{a-1}}.$$

Specifically, the Rényi divergence of order $+\infty$ is given by

$$\mathsf{RD}_\infty(\mathcal{P}\|\mathcal{Q}) = \max_{x \in Supp(\mathcal{P})} \left(\mathcal{P}(x)/\mathcal{Q}(x) \right).$$

The Rényi divergence has following useful properties.

Lemma 1 ([9]). *For two distributions $\mathcal{P}$, $\mathcal{Q}$ and two families of distributions $(\mathcal{P}_i)_i$, $(\mathcal{Q}_i)_i$, the Rényi divergence verifies the following properties:*

- *__Data processing inequality.__ For any function f, $RD_a(\mathcal{P}_f\|\mathcal{Q}_f) \leq RD_a(\mathcal{P}\|\mathcal{Q})$.*
- *__Multiplicativity.__ $RD_a(\prod_i \mathcal{P}_i \| \prod_i \mathcal{Q}_i) = \prod_i RD_a(\mathcal{P}_i\|\mathcal{Q}_i)$.*
- *__Probability preservation.__ For any event $E \subseteq Supp(\mathcal{Q})$ and $a \in (1, +\infty)$,*

$$\mathcal{Q}(E) \geq \mathcal{P}(E)^{a/(a-1)}/RD_a(\mathcal{P}\|\mathcal{Q}),$$

$$\mathcal{Q}(E) \geq \mathcal{P}(E)/RD_\infty(\mathcal{P}\|\mathcal{Q}).$$

2.3   Lattice and Algebra

Now we are ready to present a few well-known results related to lattice based cryptography. For more details, see [39,40,46,54,55].

Lattice. A (full-rank) lattice is a set of the form $L = \sum_{i \leq n} \mathbb{Z} \mathbf{b}_i$, where $\mathbf{b}_i$'s are linearly independent vectors in $\mathbb{R}^n$. The integer n is called the *lattice dimension*, and the $\mathbf{b}_i$'s are called a *basis* of L. The *first minimum* $\lambda_1(L)$ (resp. $\lambda_1^\infty(L)$) is the Euclidean (resp. infinity) norm of any shortest non-zero vector of L. If $\mathfrak{B} = (\mathbf{b}_i)_i$ is a basis matrix of L, the fundamental parallelepiped of $\mathfrak{B}$ is the set $P(\mathfrak{B}) = \left\{ \sum_{i \leq n} c_i \mathbf{b}_i : c_i \in [0,1) \right\}$. The volume $|\det(\mathfrak{B})|$ of $P(\mathfrak{B})$ is an invariant of the lattice L, denoted by $\det(L)$. Minkowski's theorem states that $\lambda_1(L) \leq \sqrt{n}(\det L)^{1/n}$. The k-th successive minima $\lambda_k(L)$ for any $k \leq n$ is defined as the smallest r such that L contains at least k linearly independent non-zero vectors of norm $\leq r$. The dual lattice of L is defined as $L^* = \{\mathbf{c} \in \mathbb{R}^n : \forall i, \langle \mathbf{c}, \mathbf{b}_i \rangle \in \mathbb{Z}\}$.

H **Space.** We follow the framework of [39] by working over the *H Space* to deal with ideal lattices. Recall that $H \subseteq \mathbb{R}^{s_1} \times \mathbb{C}^{s_2}$ is defined as

$$H := (x_1, \ldots, x_n) \in \mathbb{R}^{s_1} \times \mathbb{C}^{2s_2} : x_{s_1 + s_2 + j} = \overline{x_{s_1 + j}}, \; \forall j \in 1, \ldots, s_2$$

for some nonnegative integers s_1, s_2 with $n = s_1 + 2s_2$. As shown in [39], H is isomorphic to $\mathbb{R}^n$.

Let $f(x) \in \mathbb{Q}[x]$ be a (monic) polynomial of degree n that is irreducible over $\mathbb{R}$, and ζ be a root of $f(x)$ such that $f(\zeta) = 0$. A *number field* is then a field extension $K = \mathbb{Q}(\zeta)$ obtained by adjoining an element ζ to the rationals. There exists an isomorphism between $K \cong \mathbb{Q}[X]/(f(X))$, given by $\zeta \mapsto X$. Hence, elements in K can be represented with polynomials, using *the power basis* $\{1, \zeta, \ldots, \zeta^{n-1}\}$.

The Ring of Integers of a cyclotomic number field, denoted by R, is the set of all algebraic integers in the number field K. Hence, $R \subset K$ forms a ring under the same operations in K. In addition $\mathbb{Z}[\zeta] \cong \mathbb{Z}[X]/f(X)$ under the above isomorphism. In other words, the power basis $\{1, \zeta, \ldots, \zeta^{n-1}\}$ for R has a $\mathbb{Z}$-basis. Looking ahead, we will use $R_q = R/qR$ to denote the localisation of R, for some modulus q. When dealing with R_q, we assume that the coefficients are in $[-q/2, q/2)$ (except for R_2 where the coefficients are in $\{0,1\}$).

Canonical Embedding. For a given f, there are n none-necessarily distinct roots or power basis. This allows us to define n embeddings $\sigma_i : K \to \mathbb{C}$ by sending ζ to one of the roots of f. The *canonical embedding* $\sigma : K \to \mathbb{C}^n$ is the concatenation of all the embeddings for n, i.e. $\sigma(a) = (\sigma_i(a))_{i \in n}, a \in K$. Let $\mathbf{R}$ be an $n \times n$ Vandermonde matrix

$$\mathbf{R} = \begin{pmatrix} 1, & \sigma_1(\zeta), & \ldots, & \sigma_1^{n-1}(\zeta) \\ & \vdots & & \vdots \\ 1, & \sigma_n(\zeta), & \ldots, & \sigma_n^{n-1}(\zeta) \end{pmatrix}.$$

Then $\sigma(a) = \mathbf{R}\mathbf{a}$, where $\mathbf{a}$ is the vector of the coefficients of the polynomial a.

The *trace* and *norm* are the sum and product, respectively, of the canonical embeddings: $Tr(x) = \sum_{i \in [n]} \sigma_i(x)$ and $\mathcal{N}(x) = \prod_{i \in [n]} \sigma_i(x)$. The norm of an ideal I is its index as an additive subgroup of R, i.e., $\mathcal{N}(I) = |R/I|$.

In addition, with a proper indexation, the image H of σ is the $\mathbb{Q}$ vector space generated by the columns of $\sqrt{2} \cdot \mathbf{T}$ where:

$$\mathbf{T} = \frac{1}{\sqrt{2}} \begin{pmatrix} \mathbf{I}_{\phi(m)/2} & i\mathbf{I}_{\phi(m)/2} \\ \mathbf{I}_{\phi(m)/2} & -i\mathbf{I}_{\phi(m)/2} \end{pmatrix}$$

with $i = \sqrt{-1}$ and $\mathbf{I}$ is the identity matrix. In other words, for any element $x \in \mathbb{Q}(\zeta)$, there exists a vector $\mathbf{v} \in \mathbb{Q}^n$ such that $\sigma(x) = \mathbf{Rx} = \sqrt{2}\mathbf{Tv}$, and vice versa. For the rest of the paper, we will refer to the column vectors of $\mathbf{T}$ as *the canonical basis* for the embedding space H.

Defining

$$\mathbf{B} := 1/\sqrt{2} \cdot \mathbf{T}^{-1}\mathbf{R} \tag{1}$$

the transformation matrix from the canonical basis to the power basis, then, for any $a \in \mathbb{Q}(\zeta)$, there exists a corresponding vector $\mathbf{v} = \mathbf{Ba}$ where $\mathbf{a}$ is the vector form of a. It is straightforward to see that $\mathbf{B}$ is invertible since both $\mathbf{R}$ and $\mathbf{T}$ are nonsingular. Hence we also have $\mathbf{v} = \mathbf{B}^{-1}\mathbf{x}$. This allows us to bound the norm of $\mathbf{v}$ in functions of $\mathbf{x}$. According to the results in the functional analysis[2], there are positive constants c_1 and c_2 such that

$$c_1\|\mathbf{x}\| \leq \|\mathbf{B}^{-1}\mathbf{x}\| \leq c_2\|\mathbf{x}\| \tag{2}$$

for any $\mathbf{x}$. The absolute values of c_1 and c_2 depends solely on $\mathbf{B}$ which is only determined by the ring R, and $c_1^n \leq \det(\mathbf{B}^{-1}) \leq c_2^n$.

For cyclotomic rings $\mathbb{Z}[x]/(x^n + 1)$ where n is a power of 2, we have $c_1 = c_2$ since $\mathbf{B}$ is an orthogonal matrix [27]. Estimating the asymptotic bounds for other rings is still an open problem, although it was shown in [23], that even if c_1 and c_2 were not bounded by some constant, they seems to grow very slowly in n. Hence in this paper, we assume that

$$c_2 \leq (1 + 1/n)^{\tau_1} c_1 \tag{3}$$

for some constant τ_1, c_1 and c_2.

The Ideal Lattice. We follow [39] by viewing an ideal I in R as a lattices with a $\mathbb{Z}$-basis $U = \{u_1, ..., u_n\}$, under the canonical embedding σ. Correspondingly, denote the volume $vol(I) := vol(\sigma(I))$ of an ideal, the minimum distance $\lambda_1(I) := \lambda_1(\sigma(I))$, etc.

The (absolute) discriminant $\Delta_K = vol(R)^2$ of a number field K is the squared volume of its ring of integers $R = O_K$, viewed as a lattice; equivalently,

$$\Delta_K = |\det(Tr(u_i \cdot u_j))| = |\det(\mathbf{U}^* \cdot \mathbf{U})|$$

---

[2] The following statement can be found in most functional analysis textbooks. Here we refer to [50] Corollary 2.3.1.: Let X, Y be two Banach space, if $T : X \rightarrow Y$ is a one-to-one onto bounded linear operator, there are two positive numbers $a, b > 0$, such that $a\|x\| \leq \|Tx\| \leq b\|x\|$, $\forall x \in X$.

where $\mathbf{U} = \sigma(U)$ for an arbitrary $\mathbb{Z}$-basis $U = (u_1, \ldots, u_n)$ of R. A useful dimension-normalized quantity is the *root discriminant* $\delta_K := \sqrt{\Delta_K}^{1/n} = vol(R)^{1/n}$ (sometimes also denoted δ_R). It is a measurement of the "sparsity" of the algebraic integers in K. It follows directly from the definition that $vol(I) = \mathcal{N}(I) \cdot \sqrt{\Delta_K}$ for any fractional ideal I in K. The following standard fact is an immediate consequence of Minkowski's first theorem (for the upper bound) and the arithmetic mean-geometric mean inequality (for the lower bound).

Lemma 2 ([54]). *For any fractional ideal I in a number field K of degree n,*

$$\sqrt{n} \cdot \mathcal{N}(I)^{1/n} \leq \lambda_1(I) \leq \sqrt{n} \cdot \mathcal{N}(I)^{1/n} \cdot \delta_K.$$

Dual Lattice. For any lattice L in K (i.e., for the $\mathbb{Z}$-span of any $\mathbb{Q}$-basis of K), its dual is defined as $L^\vee = \{x \in K : Tr(xL) \in \mathbb{Z}\}$. Recall that the ring of integers of $\mathbb{Q}(\zeta)$ is $\mathbb{Z}[\zeta] := \mathbb{Z}[X]/(f)$. Let $I^\vee \subset K$ be the dual fractional ideal of I. Under the canonical embedding, $I^\vee$ embeds as the complex conjugate of the (usual defined) dual lattice of I, i.e., $\sigma(I^\vee) = \overline{\sigma(I)^*}$. Specifically, the dual (or codifferent ideal) of $\mathbb{Z}[\zeta]$, denoted by $\mathbb{Z}[\zeta]^\vee$, is the fractional ideal $\frac{1}{f'(\zeta)}\mathbb{Z}[\zeta]$, where f' is the derivative of f [22]. That is, given a vector $\mathbf{a}$ corresponding to $a \in R^\vee$, we can injectively map a to $b = f'(\zeta)a \in R$ though a linear transformation $\mathbf{Da} = \mathbf{b}$. Similar to matrix $\mathbf{B}$, here, the matrix $\mathbf{D}$ is determined by the ring R, and there exist constants c_3 and c_4 such that

$$c_3 \|\mathbf{x}\| \leq \|\mathbf{D}^{-1}\mathbf{x}\| \leq c_4 \|\mathbf{x}\| \tag{4}$$

for any $\mathbf{x}$. Again, it is an open problem to give asymptotical bounds for c_3 and c_4, except for the case of cyclotomic ring $\mathbb{Z}[x]/(x^n + 1)$ with n is a power of 2, where $c_3 = c_4 = 1/n$. Therefore, for the rest of rings, we assume that

$$c_4 \leq (1 + 1/n)^{\tau_2} c_3 \tag{5}$$

for some constant τ_2, c_3 and c_4.

For a function $\mathcal{F}$ that maps lattices to non-negative reals, the *bounded distance decoding problem* (BDD) over H is defined as given a lattice $L \subset H$, a distance bound $d \leq \mathcal{F}(L)$, and a coset $\mathbf{e} + L$ where $\|\mathbf{e}\| \leq d$, find $\mathbf{e}$.

2.4   Gaussian Distribution

For $\alpha > 0$, the *continuous* Gaussian distribution D_α^H of parameter (or width) α over H is defined to by a probability density function $f(\mathbf{x}) = \frac{1}{\alpha^n}\rho_\alpha(\mathbf{x}) = \frac{1}{\alpha^n}\exp\left(-\pi\frac{\langle\mathbf{x},\mathbf{x}\rangle}{\alpha^2}\right)$. This naturally induce a distribution over the field tensor product $K_\mathbb{R} = K \otimes_\mathbb{Q} \mathbb{R}$ with respect to the canonical basis. When converting to the power basis, the random vector $\mathbf{y} = \mathbf{Bx}$ follows a probability density function $f'(\mathbf{y}) = \frac{1}{\alpha^n\sqrt{\Sigma}}\exp\left(-\pi\frac{\mathbf{y}^T\Sigma^{-1}\mathbf{y}}{\alpha^2}\right)$, where $\Sigma = \mathbf{BB}^T$ for $\mathbf{B}$ defined in (1). The *rounded Gaussian*, denoted by $\bar{D}_\alpha^H$, is the distribution $\lfloor x \rceil \bmod q \in R_q$ where $x \leftarrow D_\alpha^H$ and the rounding is performed over the power basis.

Next we recall an important definition, the *smoothing parameter* [46], and its various related lattice quantities.

Definition 2. *For a lattice L and positive real $\varepsilon > 0$, the smoothing parameter $\eta_\varepsilon(L)$ is defined to be the smallest r such that $\rho_{1/r}(L^*/\{0\}) \leq \varepsilon$.*

Lemma 3 ([46]). *For any n-dimensional lattice L, we have $\eta_{2^{-2n}}(L) \leq \sqrt{n}/\lambda_1(L^*)$, and $\eta_\varepsilon(L) \leq \sqrt{\ln(n/\varepsilon)}\lambda_n(L)$ for all $0 < \varepsilon < 1$.*

Lemma 4 ([46]). *For any lattice L, $\varepsilon > 0$, $r \geq \eta_\varepsilon(L)$, and $\mathbf{c} \in H$, the statistical distance between $(D_r + \mathbf{c}) \bmod L$ and uniform distribution modulo L is at most ε.*

The next lemma describes the tail cutting property of a Gaussian distribution.

Lemma 5 (Tail Cutting). *A one-dimensional Gaussian D_α over $\mathbb{R}$ satisfies the tail bound $\Pr_{x \leftarrow D_\alpha}[|x| \geq B] \leq 2\exp(-\pi(B/\alpha)^2)$ for any $B \geq 0$. Particularly, if $B > \sqrt{n}\alpha$ for some integer n, $\Pr_{x \leftarrow D_\alpha}[|x| \geq B]$ is exponentially small in n.*

2.5 The Learning with Errors Problem over the Ring

The first hardness result for decisional R-LWE problem is for cyclotomic fields [39,40], assuming that the BDD problem is hard. In [55], the result is extended to any ring, with the help of a *discrete Gaussian sampling* problem.

Let K be some number field of dimension n. Let $R = \mathcal{O}_K$ be its ring of integers which embeds as a lattice. $R^\vee \subset K$ is the dual fractional ideal of R. For simplicity and convenience for our applications, we present the problem in its discretized, "normal" form [6], where the secret are drawn from the same distribution with the error. See [40,41,54] for more general forms.

Definition 3 (R-LWE **Distribution**). *For an $s \in R_q^\vee$ and a distribution χ over the field tensor product $K_\mathbb{R} = K \otimes_\mathbb{Q} \mathbb{R}$, a sample from the R-LWE distribution $\mathcal{O}_{s,\chi}$ over $R_q \times K_\mathbb{R}/qR^\vee$ is generated by choosing $a \leftarrow R_q$ uniformly at random, choosing $e \leftarrow \chi$, and outputting $(a, b = a \cdot s + e)$.*

Definition 4 (R-LWE **Average-Case Decisional Problem**). *The decision version of the R-LWE problem, denoted by $R\text{-DLWE}_{q,\chi',\chi}$, is to distinguish with non-negligible advantage between independent samples from $\mathcal{O}_{s,\chi}$ for some s chosen from χ', and the same number of uniformly random and independent samples from $R_q \times K_\mathbb{R}/qR^\vee$.*

The claim that $R\text{-DLWE}_{q,\chi',\chi}$ is hard for any probabilistic polynomial time distinguisher $\mathcal{A}$ is equivalent to the following statement: Let $\Pr(\mathcal{A}^{\mathcal{O}_{\chi,s}} = 1) = p_0(s)$ and $\Pr(\mathcal{A}^{\mathcal{U}(R_q \times R_q)} = 1) = p_1$. Denote by S_ε the set where for any elements $s \in S$, $|p_0(s) - p_1| > \varepsilon$ except for some negligible ε. Then there is a negligible δ such that $\Pr(s \in S | s \leftarrow \chi') < \delta$.

Theorem 1 ([40,41]). *Let K be the m-th cyclotomic number field with dimension $n = \psi(m)$ and $R = \mathcal{O}_K$ be its ring of integers. Let $\xi = \xi(n) > 0$, and let $q = q(n) \geq 2$, $q = 1 \bmod m$ be a poly(n)-bounded prime such that*

$\xi q \geq \omega(\sqrt{\log n})$. Then there is a polynomial-time quantum reduction from $\tilde{O}(\sqrt{n}/\xi)$-approximate SIVP (or SVP) on ideal lattices in K to the problem of solving R-DLWE$_{q,D_\alpha}$, given $l - 1$ samples, where $\alpha = q\xi \cdot (nl/log(nl))^{1/4}$.

The theorem above captures reductions from ideal lattice GapSVP (GapSIVP) to R-LWE. To guarantee an average-case/worst-case reduction as in [40], the error distribution χ needs to be a continuous Gaussian distribution D_α^H over H. In practice, it is more convenient to work with a discretized "non-dual" form of R-LWE [27], where the secret and the error are both in R_q instead of $R_q^\vee$. Accordingly, samples will be of the form $(a_i, b_i = s \cdot a_i + e_i \bmod qR) \in R_q \times R_q$. To achieve so, we multiply the error distribution by $t = f'(\zeta)$, then discretize it by rounding each coefficient in the power basis to the nearest integer. Consequently, the error distribution becomes $t \cdot D_\alpha^H$ over R. In the paper we adapt the "normal" form R-LWE [6], i.e., the secret is also drawn from the distribution $\overline{t \cdot D_\alpha^H}$.

3   Warm up

Our computational assumption is defined by the success probability among multiple experiments, where each experiment is a sequence of interactions between a challenger $\mathcal{C}$ and an adversary $\mathcal{A}$ as defined in Definition 5. In addition, we use a third party, the Source, denoted by $\mathcal{S}$, who is responsible for generating the samples for $\mathcal{C}$, as illustrated in Fig. 1.

Definition 5 (Exp($\mathcal{C}, \mathcal{A}$)). *The experiment is defined as a sequence of interactions as follows:*

1. $\mathcal{S}$ *samples from var and con to obtain a sample* (X, aux), *and sends it to* $\mathcal{C}$;
2. $\mathcal{C}$ *computes* (Input, Target) $\leftarrow \mathcal{C}(X, aux)$, *and sends* Input *to the* $\mathcal{A}$;
3. $\mathcal{A}$ *replies with a guess* Output.

The adversary wins the experiment if Target = Output.

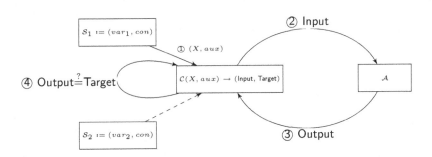

Fig. 1. Data flow for our experiments

We claim that the success probability of $\mathcal{A}$ will depend on three factors: (a), the distribution of the source var; (b) the distribution of the Target; and (c) the connection between Input and Target, i.e., the combination of $\mathcal{C}$ and $\mathcal{A}$. Our goal is to ensure that, for variance Exp_i, the success probability of $\mathcal{A}_i$ will only depend on the distribution of the source $\mathcal{S}_i$. To achieve so, we use a same challenger $\mathcal{C}$ and adversary $\mathcal{A}$ pair throughout the experiments.

As a result, those experiments will reveal the impact of different $\mathcal{S}$-s on $\mathcal{A}$'s success probability. If $\mathcal{A}$ successfully guesses an Output for an X_i, we can deduce that $\mathcal{C}$ leaks enough information about $\mathcal{S}$ for the adversary to compute Target. Thus, for two sources $\mathcal{S}_1$ and $\mathcal{S}_2$, our definition captures that, no matter what information is leaked through $\mathcal{C}$, if an adversary cannot compute Target from X_1 for source $\mathcal{S}_1$, then it cannot compute Target from X_2 for source $\mathcal{S}_2$. That is, the adversary cannot learn more information from $\mathcal{S}_1$ than from $\mathcal{S}_2$ for a fixed $\mathcal{C}$.

Then, for any PPT challenger $\mathcal{C}$, if the success probability of any adversary $\mathcal{A}$ in Exp_1 of Table 1 is negligible, so does $\mathcal{A}$ in Exp_2.

Table 1. Exp_1 v.s. Exp_2

$\mathsf{Exp}_1(\mathcal{C}, \mathcal{A})$	$\mathsf{Exp}_2(\mathcal{C}, \mathcal{A})$
$X_1 \leftarrow var_1$	$X_2 \leftarrow var_2$
$aux \leftarrow con$	$aux \leftarrow con$
$\mathsf{Input}_1, \mathsf{Target}_1 \leftarrow \mathcal{C}(X_1, aux)$	$\mathsf{Input}_2, \mathsf{Target}_2 \leftarrow \mathcal{C}(X_2, aux)$
$\mathsf{Output}_1 \leftarrow \mathcal{A}(\mathsf{Input}_1)$	$\mathsf{Output}_2 \leftarrow \mathcal{A}(\mathsf{Input}_2)$
Success if $\mathsf{Output}_1 = \mathsf{Target}_1$	Success if $\mathsf{Output}_2 = \mathsf{Target}_2$

To show that the above model is useful in a security proof, let us present a proof of an (informal) Diffie-Hellman version of the assumption within the above model. Looking ahead, we will use a similar approach to proof R-CLWR.

Definition 6 (The Diffie-Hellman analogue to our assumption). *Let $\mathbb{G}$ be a group. Let $\mathcal{Z}_s$ be the distribution of $(a, b) = (g, g^s)$ where $g \leftarrow_\$ \mathbb{G}$ is a randomly chosen group element and s is an randomly chosen and fixed index. Accordingly, let $\mathcal{U}$ be the distribution of $(a, b) = (g, u)$ where $g, u \leftarrow_\$ \mathbb{G}$. Let var_1 denote the distribution $\mathcal{Z}_s^l$ and var_2 denote the distribution $\mathcal{U}^l$. Let con be an arbitrary distribution over $\{0, 1\}^*$ which is independent of var_1 and var_2. For a fixed PPT challenger $\mathcal{C}$, $\mathring{P}_\mathcal{C}(\mathcal{A})$ is the probability for a PPT adversary $\mathcal{A}$ to win the $\mathsf{Exp}_1(\mathcal{C}, \mathcal{A})$ with $\mathcal{S}_1$ in Table 1, while $\mathring{Q}_\mathcal{C}(\mathcal{A})$ is that for $\mathcal{A}$ to the $\mathsf{Exp}_2(\mathcal{C}, \mathcal{A})$ with $\mathcal{S}_2$. Then, if $\mathring{Q}_\mathcal{C}$ is negligible for any PPT adversary $\mathcal{A}$, so is $\mathring{P}_\mathcal{C}$.*

We claim that this assumption implies the CDH assumption. Recall that CDH says that given g^x and g^y for a randomly chosen element g, no PPT adversary is able to compute g^{xy}. Slightly different with the traditional CDH assumption, here we require g is randomly chosen from a cyclic group instead of a fixed element. So $g, g^x, g^y g^{xy}$ all can be as distributions. We sketch a reduction through the following games.

Game 1. The Input for $\mathcal{A}$ is (g^x, g^y), and the Target is g^{xy}.

Game 2. The Input for $\mathcal{A}$ is (u, g^y) for some random u, and the Target is u^y.

Game 3. The Input for $\mathcal{A}$ is (u, v) for some random u and v, and the Target is w for some random w.

Observe that, in Game 3, u, v and w are independent, therefore the success probability of the adversary will be $1/|\mathbb{G}|$, which is negligible.

In the rest of the reduction, we will firstly proof the success probability of the adversary in Game 2 is also negligible. To meet the notation, we set var_1 to be the distribution of $((a_1, b_1), (a_2, b_2))$ for $(a_1, b_1) = (g, g^y)$ and $(a_2, b_2) = (u, u^y)$, and var_2 to be that for $(a_1, b_1) = (g, v)$ and $(a_2, b_2) = (u, w)$. Set con to be dummy. $\mathcal{C}$ is then defined as given $X = ((a_1, b_1), (a_2, b_2))$, compute Input $= (a_2, b_1)$ and Target $= b_2$. As per Definition 6, if the success probability of Exp_2 in Table 2 is negligible, so is that of Exp_1. Therefore, the success probability of the adversary in Game 2 is negligible.

Table 2. Reduction between Game 2 and 3

	$\mathsf{Exp}_1(\mathcal{C}, \mathcal{A})$	$\mathsf{Exp}_2(\mathcal{C}, \mathcal{A})$
	$((g, g^y), (u, u^y)) \leftarrow var_1$	$((g, v), (u, w)) \leftarrow var_2$
Source	$\perp \leftarrow con$	$\perp \leftarrow con$
Challenger	$X_1 \leftarrow ((g, g^y), (u, u^y)), \perp)$	$X_2 \leftarrow (((g, v), (u, w)), \perp)$
	$\mathsf{Input}_1 \leftarrow (u, g^y)$	$\mathsf{Input}_2 \leftarrow (u, v)$
	$\mathsf{Target}_1 \leftarrow u^y$	$\mathsf{Target}_2 \leftarrow w$
Attacker	$\mathsf{Output}_1 \leftarrow \mathcal{A}((u, g^y))$	$\mathsf{Output}_2 \leftarrow \mathcal{A}(u, v)$
	Success if $\mathsf{Output}_1 = u^y$	Success if $\mathsf{Output}_2 = w$

Then we will proof the success probability of the adversary in Game 1 is also negligible. Let con be the distribution of choosing an arbitrary index y; var_1 be the distribution of (a_1, b_1) for $(a_1, b_1) = (g, g^x)$; and var_2 be that for $(a_1, b_1) = (g, v)$. Accordingly, $\mathcal{C}$ is defined as given $X = ((a_1, b_1), y)$ and computes Input $= (b_1, a_1^y)$ and Target $= b_1^y$. As per Definition 6, if the success probability of Exp_2 in Table 3 is negligible, so is that of Exp_1. Therefore, the success probability of the adversary in Game 1 is negligible.

Table 3. Reduction between Game 1 and 2

	$\mathsf{Exp}_1(\mathcal{C}, \mathcal{A})$	$\mathsf{Exp}_2(\mathcal{C}, \mathcal{A})$
	$(g, g^x) \leftarrow var_1$	$(g, u) \leftarrow var_2$
Source	$y \leftarrow con$	$y \leftarrow con$
Challenger	$X_1 \leftarrow ((g, g^x), y)$	$X_2 \leftarrow ((g, u), y)$
	$\mathsf{Input}_1 \leftarrow (g^x, g^y)$	$\mathsf{Input}_2 \leftarrow (u, g^y)$
	$\mathsf{Target}_1 \leftarrow g^{xy}$	$\mathsf{Target}_2 \leftarrow u^y$
Attacker	$\mathsf{Output}_1 \leftarrow \mathcal{A}(g^x, g^y)$	$\mathsf{Output}_2 \leftarrow \mathcal{A}(u, g^y)$
	Success if $\mathsf{Output}_1 = g^{xy}$	Success if $\mathsf{Output}_2 = u^y$

In the next section, we will give more details on how to instantiate the framework as per Definition 6 where the underlying discrete log problem is replaced by a lattice problem.

4 The Computational Ring-LWR Assumption

For simplicity, we make use of the following additional notations. We refer to a uniformly distribution over $[-\beta, \beta]$ as U_β. Accordingly, denote by U_β^n the distribution over R_q where each coefficient is no greater than β. For a distribution χ over K, we say $\bar{\chi}$ is the discretization distribution over R, which is obtained by rounding each coefficient in the power basis to the nearest integer. For a distribution χ' over R, denote by $(\chi')^\times$ the distribution of the output of the following process: sample an element $a \leftarrow \chi'$, output a if a is invertible; repeat until an output is obtained.

Now we are ready to give a formal definition of the R-CLWR assumption. This definition, as hinted in previous section, allows us to prove that an adversary cannot learn more information from R-CLWR sample inputs than from uniform inputs. Our definition follows the framework of the Table 1. The only variation here is on the definitions of var_1 and var_2.

Definition 7 (Computational Ring-LWR Assumption). *Let q, p and l be positive integers. Fix an s that is chosen from a distribution χ over R. Denote by $\mathcal{X}_s$ the distribution of $(a, \lfloor as \rfloor_p)$ where $a \leftarrow_\$ R_q$; and denote by $\mathcal{U}$ the distribution of $(a, \lfloor b \rfloor_p)$ where $a, b \leftarrow_\$ R_q$. Let $\mathcal{S}_i = (var_i, con)$, where var_1 denotes the distribution $\mathcal{X}_s^l$; var_2 denote the distribution $\mathcal{U}^l$; and con is an arbitrary distribution over $\{0,1\}^*$ which is independent from var_1 and var_2. For a fixed PPT challenger $\mathcal{C}$, let $P_{\mathcal{C},\mathcal{A}}(\chi)$ be the probability for a PPT adversary $\mathcal{A}$ to win $\mathsf{Exp}_1(\mathcal{C}, \mathcal{A})$ with $\mathcal{S}_1$, while $Q_{\mathcal{C},\mathcal{A}}$ be that for $\mathcal{A}$ to win $\mathsf{Exp}_2(\mathcal{C}, \mathcal{A})$ with $\mathcal{S}_2$.*

The computational ring-LWR assumption with regard to a secret distribution χ, denoted by R-CLWR$_{p,q,l,\chi}$, or R-CLWR$_\chi$ for short, is that for any challenger $\mathcal{C}$, if $Q_{\mathcal{C},\mathcal{A}}$ is negligible for any PPT adversary $\mathcal{A}$, so is $P_{\mathcal{C},\mathcal{A}}$.

Correspondingly, we also define the *computational rounded learning with errors over the ring* (R-CRLWE) assumption. Notice its difference from a computational LWE over the ring assumption, which, by the analogy to R-CLWR, replaces R-LWR samples ($\lfloor as \rfloor_p$) with R-LWE samples ($as + e$). By contrast, in R-CRLWE, one replaces R-LWR samples with *rounded* R-LWE samples ($\lfloor as + e \rfloor_p$).

Definition 8 (Computational Ring-RLWE Assumption). *Let q, p, l, s, χ and $\mathcal{U}$ be the same as Definition 7. Denote by $\mathcal{Y}_{s,\chi'}$ the distribution of $(a, \lfloor as + e \rfloor_p)$ where $a \leftarrow_\$ R_q$ and $e \leftarrow \chi'$ over R. Let $\mathcal{S}_i = (var_i, con)$, where var_1 denotes the distribution $\mathcal{Y}_{s,\chi'}^l$; var_2 denotes the distribution $\mathcal{U}^l$; con denotes an arbitrary distribution over $\{0,1\}^*$ which is independent of S_1 and S_2. For a fixed PPT challenger $\mathcal{C}$, let $P'_{\mathcal{C},\mathcal{A}}(\chi, \chi')$ be the probability for a PPT adversary $\mathcal{A}$ to $\mathsf{Exp}_1(\mathcal{C}, \mathcal{A})$ with $\mathcal{S}_1$, while $Q_{\mathcal{C},\mathcal{A}}$ to be that for $\mathcal{A}$ to win $\mathsf{Exp}_2(\mathcal{C}, \mathcal{A})$ with $\mathcal{S}_2$.*

The computational ring-RLWE assumption with a secret distribution χ and an error distribution χ', denoted by R-CRLWE$_{p,q,l,\chi,\chi'}$ or R-CRLWE$_{\chi,\chi'}$ for short, *is that for any challenger* $\mathcal{C}$*, if* $Q_{\mathcal{C},\mathcal{A}}$ *is negligible for any PPT adversary* $\mathcal{A}$*, so is* $P'_{\mathcal{C},\mathcal{A}}(\chi,\chi')$*.*

This definition suggests that the adversary cannot learn more information from R-CRLWE inputs than from uniform inputs. Next, we show that the R-CLWR assumption holds for uniform secrets, assuming the hardness of the decisional R-LWE assumption. Formally, we will have the following theorem.

Theorem 2 (Main Theorem). *Following the notions in Definitions 7 and 8. For any ring* R *satisfying (3) and (5), the largest degree of the irreducible factors modulo integer* q *of the polynomial* f *is less than* k_q*. If* l *is a constant,* $\alpha \geq c_2 c_4 \sqrt{n \ln(2n)} q^{k_q/n} \cdot \delta_K$*,* $\beta = \Omega(nl\alpha)$ *and* $q/p = \Omega(nl\alpha/c_2 c_4)$*, there is a reduction from the decisional ring-LWE assumption* $R\text{-LWE}_{q,\overline{t \cdot D_\alpha^H},t \cdot D_\alpha^H}$ *to the computational ring-LWR assumption* $R\text{-CLWR}_{p,q,l,(U_\beta^n)^\times}$ *(Fig. 2).*

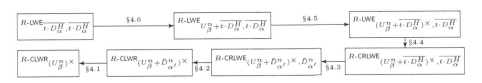

Fig. 2. Reduction flow from R-LWE to R-CLWR

Combing with the worst-case/average-case reduction in Theorem 1, the hardness of our R-CLWR problem will be based on the worse-case hardness of lattice problems. It is worth pointing out that, the majority of practical cryptosystems uses a cyclotomic ring $R = \mathbb{Z}[x]/(x^n + 1)$ where n is a power of 2. For this ring, we have the following result.

Corollary 1. *Following the same notations. For* $R = \mathbb{Z}[x]/(x^n + 1)$ *where* n *is a power of 2, if* l *is a constant,* $\alpha \geq 2\sqrt{n \ln(2n)} \cdot q^{2/n}$*,* $\beta = \Omega(nl\alpha)$ *and* $q/p = \Omega(n^2 l\alpha)$*, there is a reduction from the decisional ring-LWE assumption* $R\text{-LWE}_{q,t \cdot D_\alpha^H,t \cdot D_\alpha^H}$ *to the computational ring-LWR assumption* $R\text{-CLWR}_{p,q,l,(U_\beta^n)^\times}$*.*

4.1 From $R\text{-CLWR}_{(U_\beta^n + \bar{D}_{\alpha'}^n)^\times}$ to $R\text{-CLWR}_{(U_\beta^n)^\times}$

We begin with proving the following lemma which shows the RD between the two distributions on $\mathbb{Z}$, namely U_β and $U_\beta + \bar{D}_\alpha$, is bounded by $1 + 1/n$.

Lemma 6. *Following the same notion. In addition, let* U_β *be a uniform distribution from* $[-\beta, \beta]$ *over* $\mathbb{Z}$ *where* $\beta > \alpha$*. Let the distribution* $\psi = \bar{D}_\alpha + U_\beta$*. Then* $\text{RD}_2(U_\beta \| \psi) \leq 1 + \frac{\alpha}{c\beta}$ *where* $c = \frac{(1-\exp(-\pi))^2}{2} \approx 0.4577$*. Specifically, when* $\beta > n\alpha/c$*,* $\text{RD}_2(U_\beta \| \psi) < 1 + 1/n$*.*

Proof. Please see the full version [19].

With Lemma 6, we are ready to proof the first reduction.

Lemma 7. *Following the same notation, if* $\beta = \Omega(nl\alpha)$, $P_{\mathcal{C},\mathcal{A}}(U_\beta^n) \leq 2P_{\mathcal{C}}(U_\beta^n + \bar{D}_\alpha^n)$. *Hence there is a reduction from* $R\text{-}CLWR_{(U_\beta^n + \bar{D}_\alpha^n)^\times}$ *to* $R\text{-}CLWR_{(U_\beta^n)^\times}$.

Proof. Note that $P_{\mathcal{C},\mathcal{A}}((U_\beta^n)^\times) \leq P_{\mathcal{C},\mathcal{A}}((U_\beta^n + \bar{D}_\alpha^n)^\times) \cdot RD_2\left(U_\beta\|U_\beta + \bar{D}_\alpha\right)^{nl}$. Lemma 6 says $RD_2\left(U_\beta\|U_\beta + \bar{D}_\alpha\right)^{nl} \leq 2$ when $\beta = \Omega(nl\alpha)$. On the other hand, assuming the hardness of $R\text{-}CLWR_{(U_\beta^n + \bar{D}_\alpha^n)^\times}$, we have that for any challenger $\mathcal{C}$, $P_{\mathcal{C},\mathcal{A}}((U_\beta^n + \bar{D}_\alpha^n)^\times)$ is negligible when $Q_{\mathcal{C},\mathcal{A}}$ is negligible. By the above result, $P_{\mathcal{C},\mathcal{A}}((U_\beta^n)^\times)$ is also negligible. So the assumption $R\text{-}CLWR_{(U_\beta^n)^\times}$ holds. $\square$

4.2 From $R\text{-}CRLWE_{(U_\beta^n + \bar{D}_\alpha^n)^\times, \bar{D}_\alpha^n}$ to $R\text{-}CLWR_{(U_\beta^n + \bar{D}_\alpha^n)^\times}$

The following lemma is adapted from [12] with a slight modification on the noise distribution. We provide a proof for completeness.

Lemma 8 ([12]). *Assume* $B < q/2p$. *For every unit* $s \in R_q$ *and noise distribution* χ *that is balanced over* R_q *and each coefficient is bounded by* B *with probability larger than* δ, *we have* $RD_2(\mathcal{X}_s\|\mathcal{Y}_s) \leq (1 + 2pB/q)^n/\delta^n$ *where* $\mathcal{X}_s$ *is the random variable* $(a, \lfloor a \cdot s \rceil_p)$ *and* $\mathcal{Y}_s$ *is the random variable* $(a, \lfloor a \cdot s + e \rceil_p)$ *with* $a \leftarrow R_q$ *and* $e \leftarrow \chi$.

Proof. By the definition,

$$RD_2(\mathcal{X}_s\|\mathcal{Y}_s) = E_{a \leftarrow R_q} \frac{Pr(\mathcal{X}_s = (a, \lfloor a \cdot s \rceil_p))}{Pr(\mathcal{Y}_s = (a, \lfloor a \cdot s + e \rceil_p))}$$

$$= E_{a \leftarrow R_q} \frac{1}{Pr_{e \leftarrow \chi}\left(\lfloor a \cdot s + e \rceil_p = \lfloor a \cdot s \rceil_p\right)}.$$

We define the set $border_{p,q}(B) = \left\{x \in \mathbb{Z}_q : \left|x - \frac{q}{p}\lfloor x \rceil_p\right| < B\right\}$. For a ring element $a \in R_q$, we use a_i to denote the ith coefficient in the power basis. For fixed s and for any $t \in [n]$, we define the set

$$BAD_{s,t} = \left\{a \in R_q : |\{i \in [n], (a \cdot s)_i \in border_{p,q}(B)\}| = t\right\}.$$

These are candidate a-s for which $a \cdot s$ has exactly t coefficients which are dangerously close to the rounding boundary. Fix an arbitrary t and $a \in BAD_{s,t}$. For any $i \in [n]$ such that $(a \cdot s)_i \notin border_{p,q}(B)$, $Pr_{e_i}[\lfloor (as)_i + e_i \rceil_p = \lfloor (as)_i \rceil_p] \geq \delta$. For any $i \in [n]$ such that $(a \cdot s)_i \in border_{p,q}(B)$, we still have $\lfloor (a \cdot s)_i + e_i \rceil_p = \lfloor (a \cdot s)_i \rceil_p$ as long as $e_i \in [-B, \ldots, 0]$. By the assumption on the noise distribution, we have $Pr_{e_i}[\lfloor (a \cdot s)_i + e_i \rceil_p = \lfloor (a \cdot s)_i \rceil_p] \geq 1/2$. Because e is independent over all coefficients and a has exactly t coefficients in $border_{p,q}(B)$, $Pr_{e \leftarrow \chi}\left(\lfloor a \cdot s + e \rceil_p = \lfloor a \cdot s \rceil_p\right) \geq \frac{1}{2^t}\delta^{n-t} \geq \frac{1}{2^t}\delta^n$.

Since s is a unit in R_q, $a \cdot s$ will be uniform over R_q and

$$Pr\left[a \in BAD_{s,t}\right] \leq \binom{n}{t}\left(1 - \frac{|border_{p,q}(B)|}{q}\right)^{n-t}\left(\frac{|border_{p,q}(B)|}{q}\right)^t.$$

Conditioning on the event $a \in BAD_{s,t}$, we conclude

$$\mathsf{RD}_2(X_s \| Y_s) \le \delta^{-n} \sum_{t=0}^{n} 2^t \cdot \Pr[a \in BAD_{s,t}] = \delta^{-n} \left(1 + \frac{|border_{p,q}(B)|}{q}\right)^n.$$

$\square$

Lemma 9. *Adopt the same notions and symbols in Definitions 7 and 8. If $p > \frac{q\sqrt{\pi}}{2nl\alpha\sqrt{\ln(2nl)}}$, we have $P_{\mathcal{C},\mathcal{A}}(U_\beta^n + \bar{D}_\alpha^n)^\times \le e^2 P'_{\mathcal{C},\mathcal{A}}(U_\beta^n + \bar{D}_\alpha^n)^\times$. Hence there is a reduction from $R\text{-}CRLWE_{(U_\beta^n + \bar{D}_{\alpha'}^n)^\times, \bar{D}_{\alpha'}^n}$ to $R\text{-}CLWR_{(U_\beta^n + \bar{D}_{\alpha'}^n)^\times}$.*

Proof. We have $P_{\mathcal{C},\mathcal{A}}(U_\beta^n + \bar{D}_\alpha^n) \le P'_{\mathcal{C},\mathcal{A}}(U_\beta^n + \bar{D}_\alpha^n) \cdot \mathsf{RD}_2(X_s \| Y_s)^l$. Note that a one-dimensional Gaussian D_α over $\mathbb{R}$ satisfies the tail bound $\Pr_{x \leftarrow D_\alpha}[|x| \ge B] \le 2\exp(-\pi(B/\alpha)^2)$ for any $B \ge 0$. We set $B = \sqrt{\frac{\ln(2nl)}{\pi}}\alpha$, so $2\exp(-\pi(B/\alpha)^2) \le 1/nl$ and $\delta \ge 1 - \frac{1}{nl}$. Also we set $p > q/2nlB$, then we have

$$\mathsf{RD}_2(X_s \| Y_s)^l \le (1 + 2pB/q)^{nl}/\delta^{nl} \le \frac{(1+1/nl)^{nl}}{(1-1/nl)^{nl}} \le e^2 \tag{6}$$

Assuming $R\text{-}CRLWE_{(U_\beta^n + \bar{D}_{\alpha'}^n)^\times, \bar{D}_{\alpha'}^n}$ assumption holds, then for any $\mathcal{C}$ and $\mathcal{A}$, $P'_{\mathcal{C},\mathcal{A}}\left((U_\beta^n + \bar{D}_{\alpha'}^n)^\times, \bar{D}_{\alpha'}^n\right)$ is negligible so long as $Q_{\mathcal{C},\mathcal{A}}$ is negligible. By the result of (6), $P_{\mathcal{C},\mathcal{A}}(U_\beta^n + \bar{D}_{\alpha'}^n)^\times$ is also negligible. This proves the $R\text{-}CLWR_{(U_\beta^n + \bar{D}_{\alpha'}^n)^\times}$ assumption. $\square$

4.3 From $R\text{-}CRLWE_{(U_\beta^n + \overline{t \cdot D_\alpha^H})^\times, \overline{t \cdot D_\alpha^H}}$ to $R\text{-}CRLWE_{(U_\beta^n + \bar{D}_{\alpha'}^n)^\times, \bar{D}_{\alpha'}^n}$

Lemma 10. *Following the same notations. Additionally, let $\overline{t \cdot D_\alpha^H}$ be the discretization of $t \cdot D_\alpha^H$, where D_α^H is the continuous Gaussian with width α over the H space. $\bar{D}_{\alpha'}^n$ is the discretization of the continuous Gaussian with width α according to the power basis. $\mathcal{Y}'_{\overline{t \cdot D_\alpha^H}, \overline{t \cdot D_\alpha^H}}$ is the random variable $(a, \lfloor a \cdot s + e \rceil_p)$ with $a \leftarrow_\$ R_q$ and $s, e \leftarrow \overline{t \cdot D_\alpha^H}$, and $\mathcal{Y}'_{\bar{D}_{\alpha'}^n, \bar{D}_{\alpha'}^n}$ is the random variable $(a, \lfloor a \cdot s + e \rceil_p)$ with $a \leftarrow_\$ R_q$ and $s, e \leftarrow \bar{D}_{\alpha'}^n$. For any ring R satisfying (3) and (5), when $\alpha/c_1 c_3 \le \alpha' \le \left(1 + \frac{1}{n}\right)^{\tau_1 + \tau_2} \alpha/c_2 c_4$, we have $\mathsf{RD}_\infty\left(\mathcal{Y}'_{\overline{t \cdot D_\alpha^H}, \overline{t \cdot D_\alpha^H}} \| \mathcal{Y}'_{\bar{D}_{\alpha'}^n, \bar{D}_{\alpha'}^n}\right) \le e^{\tau_1 + \tau_2}$.*

Proof. According to the data processing inequality of Rényi divergence, it is sufficient to show $\mathsf{RD}_\infty\left(D_\alpha^n \| t \cdot D_\alpha^H\right) \le e^{\tau_1 + \tau_2}$. So we need to prove for all $\mathbf{x} \in \mathbb{R}^n$, $\rho(\mathbf{x})/\rho'(\mathbf{x}) \le e^{\tau_1 + \tau_2}$. Recall that $t \cdot D_\alpha^H$ has the probability density function over the power basis $\rho(\mathbf{x}) = (\alpha^n \det(\mathbf{D}) \det(\mathbf{B}))^{-1} \exp\left(-\pi \mathbf{x}^T \left(\mathbf{D}^{-1}\right)^T \mathbf{\Sigma}^{-1} \mathbf{D}^{-1} \mathbf{x}/\alpha^2\right)$, and D_α^n has the probability density function over the power basis $\rho'(\mathbf{x}) = \alpha'^{-n} \exp\left(-\pi \mathbf{x}^T \mathbf{x}/\alpha'^2\right)$. Hence,

$$\frac{\rho(\mathbf{x})}{\rho'(\mathbf{x})} = \frac{\alpha'^n}{\alpha^n \det(\mathbf{D}) \det(\mathbf{B})} \exp\left(\pi\left(\frac{\mathbf{x}^T \mathbf{x}}{\alpha'^2} - \frac{\mathbf{x}^T \left(\mathbf{D}^{-1}\right)^T \mathbf{\Sigma}^{-1} \mathbf{D}^{-1} \mathbf{x}}{\alpha^2}\right)\right).$$

According to (2) and (4), $\Sigma = \mathbf{B}^T\mathbf{B}$, $\|\mathbf{D}^{-1}\mathbf{x}\| \geq c_1\|\mathbf{x}\|$ for any $\mathbf{x} \in \mathbb{R}^n$ and $\|\mathbf{B}^{-1}\mathbf{y}\| \geq c_3\|\mathbf{y}\|$ for any $\mathbf{y} \in \mathbb{R}^n$. If $\alpha' \geq \alpha/c_1 c_3$, we have $\dfrac{\mathbf{x}^T(\mathbf{D}^{-1})^T\Sigma^{-1}\mathbf{D}^{-1}\mathbf{x}}{\alpha^2} \geq \dfrac{c_1^2 c_3^2 \mathbf{x}^T\mathbf{x}}{\alpha^2} \geq \dfrac{\mathbf{x}^T\mathbf{x}}{\alpha'^2}$. Therefore,

$$\frac{\rho(\mathbf{x})}{\rho'(\mathbf{x})} \leq \frac{\alpha'^n}{\alpha^n \det(\mathbf{D})\det(\mathbf{B})} \leq e^{\tau_1 + \tau_2}$$

when $\alpha' \leq \left(1 + \frac{1}{n}\right)^{\tau_1 + \tau_2} \alpha c_2 c_4 \leq \left(1 + \frac{1}{n}\right)^{\tau_1 + \tau_2} \alpha|\det(\mathbf{D})|^{1/n}|\det(\mathbf{B})|^{1/n}$. According to (3) and (5), we have $c_2 \leq \left(1 + \frac{1}{n}\right)^{\tau_1} c_1$ and $c_3 \leq \left(1 + \frac{1}{n}\right)^{\tau_2} c_4$. Therefore there must exist at least an α' that satisfies $\alpha/c_1 c_3 \leq \alpha' \leq \left(1 + \frac{1}{n}\right)^{\tau_1 + \tau_2} \alpha/c_2 c_4$.
□

Lemma 11. *Adopt the same notions and symbols as above. For any ring R satisfying (3) and (5), when $\alpha/c_1 c_3 \leq \alpha' \leq (1 + 1/n)^{\tau_1 + \tau_2} \alpha/c_2 c_4$, we have*
$$P'_{\mathcal{C},\mathcal{A}}\left(\left(U_\beta^n + \overline{t \cdot D_\alpha^H}\right)^\times, \overline{t \cdot D_\alpha^H}\right) \leq e^{l(\tau_1 + \tau_2)} P'_{\mathcal{C},\mathcal{A}}\left(\left(U_\beta^n + \bar{D}_\alpha^n\right)^\times, \bar{D}_\alpha^n\right).$$ *Hence there is a reduction from $R\text{-CRLWE}_{(U_\beta^n + \overline{t \cdot D_\alpha^H})^\times, \overline{t \cdot D_\alpha^H}}$ to $R\text{-CRLWE}_{(U_\beta^n + \bar{D}_{\alpha'}^n)^\times, \bar{D}_{\alpha'}^n}$.*

4.4   From $R\text{-LWE}_{(U_\beta^n + \overline{t \cdot D_\alpha^H})^\times, \overline{t \cdot D_\alpha^H}}$ to $R\text{-CRLWE}_{(U_\beta^n + \overline{t \cdot D_\alpha^H})^\times, \overline{t \cdot D_\alpha^H}}$

Lemma 12. *Adopt the same notions and symbols in Definitions 7 and 8. Assume the advantage of any probabilistic polynomial time algorithm to solve the decisional $R\text{-LWE}$ problem $R\text{-LWE}_{(U_\beta^n + \overline{t \cdot D_\alpha^H})^\times, \overline{t \cdot D_\alpha^H}}$ is less than ε, then we have $\left| P'_{\mathcal{C},\mathcal{A}}\left(\left(U_\beta^n + \overline{t \cdot D_\alpha^H}\right)^\times, \overline{t \cdot D_\alpha^H}\right) - Q_{\mathcal{C},\mathcal{A}} \right| < \varepsilon$ for any PPT adversary $\mathcal{A}$.*

Proof. We construct an adversary $\mathcal{B}$ who breaks the decisional R-LWE problem as follows. At the high level, $\mathcal{B}$ will play the role as the challenger $\mathcal{C}$ in the experiment. Given samples $(x_1, y_1), \ldots, (x_l, y_l)$, the algorithm $\mathcal{B}$ sets $a_i = x_i$ and $b_i = \lfloor y_i \rfloor_p$ for $i \leq l$, and $X = (a_1, b_1), \ldots, (a_l, b_l)$. Since $\mathcal{B}$ can obtain all the view of any challenger $\mathcal{C}$, $\mathcal{B}$ can simulate all the behaviors of $\mathcal{C}$ and compute the corresponding Input and Target. $\mathcal{B}$ also check whether the Output of $\mathcal{A}$ equals the Target. If the check is passed, $\mathcal{B}$ outputs 1; otherwise it outputs 0.

When $(x_1, y_1), \ldots, (x_l, y_l)$ are R-LWE samples,

$$\Pr(\mathcal{B}((x_1, y_1), \ldots, (x_l, y_l)) = 1) = P'_{\mathcal{C},\mathcal{A}}\left(\left(U_\beta^n + \overline{t \cdot D_\alpha^H}\right)^\times, \overline{t \cdot D_\alpha^H}\right);$$

by contrast, when $(x_1, y_1), \ldots, (x_l, y_l)$ are uniform samples,

$$\Pr(\mathcal{B}((x_1, y_1), \ldots, (x_l, y_l)) = 1) = Q_{\mathcal{C},\mathcal{A}}$$

for adversary $\mathcal{A}$. Thus, assuming the hardness of decisional ring-LWE, we have $\left| P'_{\mathcal{C},\mathcal{A}}\left(\left(U_\beta^n + \overline{t \cdot D_\alpha^H}\right)^\times, \overline{t \cdot D_\alpha^H}\right) - Q_{\mathcal{C},\mathcal{A}} \right| < \varepsilon$ for negligible ε.

□

4.5   From $R\text{-LWE}_{U_\beta^n + \overline{t \cdot D_\alpha^H}, t \cdot D_\alpha^H}$ to $R\text{-LWE}_{(U_\beta^n + \overline{t \cdot D_\alpha^H})^\times, \overline{t \cdot D_\alpha^H}}$

Lemma 13. *Let $D_{\hat\alpha}^n$ be a continuous Gaussian with width $\hat\alpha$ and D_α^H be a continuous Gaussian over H with width α. Let $t = f'(\zeta)$. If the assumption (3) and (5) holds, when $\frac{\alpha}{(1+1/n)^{\tau_1 + \tau_2} c_1 c_3} \le \hat\alpha \le \frac{\alpha}{c_2 c_4}$, we have $RD_\infty(D_{\hat\alpha}^n | t \cdot D_\alpha^H) \le e^{\tau_1 + \tau_2}$.*

The proof is similar to Lemma 10. We omit the details and recommend readers to refer the full version [19].

Lemma 14. *Let $D_{\hat\alpha}^n$ be a continuous Gaussian distribution over $K_{\mathbb{R}}$ where $K \cong \mathbb{Q}[X]/(f(X))$. The largest degree of the irreducible factors modulo integer q of the polynomial f is less than k_q. Let $\hat\alpha \ge \sqrt{n \ln(n/\varepsilon)} q^{k_q/n} \cdot \delta_K$ and β is any positive integer. If $a \leftarrow U_\beta^n + \overline{D_{\hat\alpha}^n}$, the probability of that a is invertible is larger than $1 - q^{-k_q} - \varepsilon$.*

Proof. Our goal is to bound the probability that a is in $\mathcal{I} := \langle q, \phi \rangle$ by $q^{-n/k_q} + \varepsilon$, for any $k \le k_q$, when $a \leftarrow U_\beta^n + \overline{D_{\hat\alpha}^n}$. Specifically, denote $a := a_1 + a_2$ where $a_1 \leftarrow U_\beta^n$ and $a_2 \leftarrow \overline{D_{\hat\alpha}^n}$. We have $\mathcal{N}(\mathcal{I}) \ge q^{k_q}$. By Minkowski's theorem, this implies $\lambda_1(\mathcal{I}) \le \sqrt{n} q^{k_q/n}$. Since $\mathcal{I}$ is an ideal of R, we have $\lambda_n(\mathcal{I}) = \lambda_1(\mathcal{I})$. Then, in Lemma 2, we have $\lambda_n(\mathcal{I}) \le \sqrt{n} q^{k_q/n} \cdot \delta_K$, and in Lemma 3, we have $\eta_\varepsilon(\mathcal{I}) \le \sqrt{\ln(n/\varepsilon)} \lambda_n(\mathcal{I}) \le \sqrt{n \ln(n/\varepsilon)} q^{k_q/n} \cdot \delta_K$. In addition, Lemma 4 shows that the statistical distance between $b \bmod \mathcal{I}$ and a uniform distribution modulo $\mathcal{I}$ is less than ε for $b \leftarrow D_{\hat\alpha}^n$. Since $a_1 = \lfloor b \rceil \in R$ and $\mathcal{I} \subseteq R$, a_1 will be uniform in $R \bmod \mathcal{I}$ with a statistical distance ε. This implies that $a = a_1 + a_2$ is uniform in $R \bmod \mathcal{I}$ with statistical distance ε. So we have $a = 0 \bmod \mathcal{I}$ with probability less than $q^{-k_q} + \varepsilon$. When we set $\varepsilon = 1/2$, we get the desired result. $\square$

Lemma 15. *Following the above notations. For any ring R satisfying (3) and (5), when $\alpha \ge c_2 c_4 \sqrt{n \ln(2n)} q^{2/n} \cdot \delta_K$, there is a reduction from $R\text{-LWE}_{U_\beta^n + \overline{t \cdot D_\alpha^H}, t \cdot D_\alpha^H}$ to $R\text{-LWE}_{(U_\beta^n + \overline{t \cdot D_\alpha^H})^\times, \overline{t \cdot D_\alpha^H}}$.*

Proof. Let $\Pr(\mathcal{A}^{\mathcal{O}_{x,s}} = 1) = p_0(s)$, $\Pr(\mathcal{A}^{\mathcal{U}(R_q \times R_q)} = 1) = p_1$ and the set S_ε denote the all s that $|p_0(s) - p_1| > \varepsilon$ for any non-negligible ε, then we have

$$\Pr\left(s \in S_\varepsilon | s \leftarrow U_\beta^n + \overline{t \cdot D_\alpha^H} \right)$$

$$= \Pr\left(s \in S_\varepsilon | s \leftarrow \left(U_\beta^n + \overline{t \cdot D_\alpha^H} \right)^\times \right) \Pr\left(s \in R_q^\times | s \leftarrow U_\beta^n + \overline{t \cdot D_\alpha^H} \right)$$

$$+ \Pr\left(s \in S_\varepsilon | s \leftarrow U_\beta^n + \bar{D}_\alpha^H \text{and output when } s \text{ not invertible} \right)$$

$$\Pr\left(s \text{ is not invertible} | s \leftarrow U_\beta^n + \bar{D}_\alpha^H \right)$$

$$\ge \Pr\left(s \in S_\varepsilon | s \leftarrow \left(U_\beta^n + \overline{t \cdot D_\alpha^H} \right)^\times \right) \Pr\left(s \in R_q^\times | s \leftarrow U_\beta^n + \overline{t \cdot D_\alpha^H} \right).$$

Next, Lemma 13 says for $\frac{\alpha}{(1+1/n)^{\tau_1+\tau_2} c_1 c_3} \leq \hat{\alpha} \leq \frac{\alpha}{c_2 c_4}$,

$$\Pr\left(s \in R_q^\times | s \leftarrow U_\beta^n + \overline{t \cdot D_\alpha^H}\right) \geq \frac{\Pr\left(s \in R_q^\times | s \leftarrow U_\beta^n + \overline{D_{\hat{\alpha}}^n}\right)}{RD_\infty(D_{\hat{\alpha}}^n \parallel t \cdot D_\alpha^H)}$$

$$\geq \frac{\Pr\left(s \in R_q^\times | s \leftarrow U_\beta^n + \overline{D_{\hat{\alpha}}^n}\right)}{\exp(\tau_1 + \tau_2)}$$

In addition, in Lemma 14 we have proved $\Pr\left(s \in R_q^\times | s \leftarrow U_\beta^n + \overline{D_{\hat{\alpha}}^n}\right)$ is non-negligible for $\hat{\alpha} \geq \sqrt{n \ln(n/\varepsilon)} q^{k_q/n} \cdot \delta_K$. So $\Pr\left(s \in R_q^\times | s \leftarrow U_\beta^n + \overline{t \cdot D_\alpha^H}\right)$ is also non-negligible. This implies $\Pr\left(s \in S | s \leftarrow U_\beta^n + \overline{t \cdot D_\alpha^H}\right)$ is non-negligible as long as $\Pr\left(s \in S | s \leftarrow \left(U_\beta^n + \overline{t \cdot D_\alpha^H}\right)^\times\right)$ is also non-negligible, i.e. an adversary can solve $R\text{-LWE}_{U_\beta^n + \overline{t \cdot D_\alpha^H}, \overline{t \cdot D_\alpha^H}}$ so long as it can solve $R\text{-LWE}_{\left(U_\beta^n + \overline{t \cdot D_\alpha^H}\right)^\times, \overline{t \cdot D_\alpha^H}}$. $\square$

4.6   From $R\text{-LWE}_{\overline{t \cdot D_\alpha^H}, \overline{t \cdot D_\alpha^H}}$ to $R\text{-LWE}_{U_\beta^n + \overline{t \cdot D_\alpha^H}, \overline{t \cdot D_\alpha^H}}$

Lemma 16. *Let $\psi = \overline{t \cdot D_\alpha^H} + U_\beta^n$ be a distribution. If there is a PPT algorithm $\mathcal{A}'$ that distinguishes $\mathcal{O}_{s,\chi}$ from $\mathcal{U}$ within m queries for $s \leftarrow \psi$, then there is a PPT algorithm $\mathcal{A}$ which distinguishes $\mathcal{O}_{s,\chi}$ from $\mathcal{U}$ within m queries for $s \leftarrow \overline{t \cdot D_\alpha^H}$.*

Proof. Given m elements $(a_i, b_i) \in R_q \times R_q$, drawn from either $\left(\mathcal{O}_{s,\bar{D}_\alpha}\right)^m$ for $s \leftarrow \overline{t \cdot D_\alpha^H}$, or $\left(\mathcal{U}(R_q \times R_q)\right)^m$, the reduction algorithm chooses $s' \leftarrow U_\beta^n$ and outputs m elements $(a_i, b_i + a_i s') \in R_q \times R_q$. Obviously, when (a_i, b_i) are drawn from $\mathcal{O}_{s,\bar{D}_\alpha}$, $(a_i, b_i + a_i s')$ are drawn from $\mathcal{O}_{s+s',\bar{D}_\alpha}$ and the distribution of $s + s'$ will be $\psi = \overline{t \cdot D_\alpha^H} + U_\beta^n$. When (a_i, b_i) are all drawn from $\mathcal{U}(R_q \times R_q)$, $(a_i, b_i + a_i s')$ are also drawn from $\mathcal{U}(R_q \times R_q)$. $\square$

5   Application I: A Public Key Encryption

In this section, we will provide an IND-CPA secure PKE scheme based on the R-CLWR assumption. Our scheme improves R-LWE based schemes in both time and space efficiency. At a high level, our scheme uses the standard KEM-DEM approach, where the KEM, similar to that of [53], stems from an IND-CPA secure scheme.

5.1   Reconciliation Mechanism

Reconciliation was firstly proposed by [25], and has a few variants, for example, [3,53]. In this paper, for the ease of presentation, we will follow the work of [53].

Let us define the reconciliation rounding function as $[\cdot]_{2,q} : x \rightarrow \left\lfloor \frac{2}{q} \cdot x \right\rceil$ mod 2, and the reconciliation cross-rounding function as $\langle \cdot \rangle_{2,q} : x \rightarrow \left\lfloor \frac{4}{q} \cdot x \right\rfloor$ mod 2. Then the algorithm REC will be defined as follows. On input $y \in \mathbb{Z}_q$ and $z \in \{0,1\}$, REC(y, z) outputs $[x]_{2,q}$, where x is the closest element to y such that $\langle x \rangle_{2,q} = z$. First, when q is even, we have following results.

Lemma 17. *If $x \in \mathbb{Z}_q$ is uniformly random, $[x]_{2,q}$ is uniformly random given $\langle x \rangle_{2,q}$.*

Lemma 18. *If $|x - y| < q/8$, then we have REC$(y, \langle x \rangle_{2,q}) = [x]_{2,q}$.*

On the other hand, when the modulus q is odd, we make use of a randomized doubling function: let DBL $: \mathbb{Z}_q \rightarrow \mathbb{Z}_{2q}, x \mapsto$ DBL$(x) = 2x - e$, where e is sampled from $\{-1, 0, 1\}$ with probabilities $p_{-1} = p_1 = 1/4$ and $p_0 = 1/2$. We have two similar lemmas.

Lemma 19. *For odd q, if $x \in \mathbb{Z}_q$ is uniformly random and $\bar{x} \leftarrow_\$ $ DBL(x), then $[\bar{x}]_{2,2q}$ is uniformly random given $\langle \bar{x} \rangle_{2,2q}$.*

Lemma 20. *For odd q, let $|x - y| < q/8$ for $x, y \in \mathbb{Z}_q$. Let $\bar{x} = $ DBL(x). Then REC $\left(y, \langle \bar{x} \rangle_{2,2q} \right) = [\bar{x}]_{2,2q}$.*

Moreover, the above reconciliation mechanism can be extended coefficient-wise to R_q with respect to the power basis.

5.2   PKE Schemes

Before describing our R-CLWR based PKE, let us recall a variant of the R-LWE based scheme in [53]. This scheme slightly differentiate from [53] in that the element a in a public key is derived from a PRNG which can be modeled as a random oracle. This modification is adopted by many (R-)LWE based schemes such as [3,13,15]. For simplicity, we choose the ring $R = \mathbb{Z}[x]/(x^n + 1)$ where n is a power of 2. Here q is odd, since Theorem 1 requires a prime q.

Ring-LWE Based PKE. Let $\mathcal{H} : \{0,1\}^n \rightarrow \{0,1\}^k$ be a hash function for integer k. $\mathcal{G} : \{0,1\}^{k'} \rightarrow R_q$ be a pusedorandom generator. The R-LWE based scheme consists of the following three algorithms.

- RLWE.KeyGen(1^λ): Given the security parameter λ, choose $seed \leftarrow \{0,1\}^{k'}$, $a = \mathcal{G}(seed) \in R_q$ and $s, e_1 \leftarrow \overline{t \cdot D_\alpha^H}$. Output $(seed, b = sa + e_1) \in \{0,1\}^{k'} \times R_q$ as the public key and s as the secret key.
- RLWE.Encryption$(pk = (seed, b), m \in \{0,1\}^k)$: Given the message m, choose $r, e_2, e_3 \leftarrow \overline{t \cdot D_\alpha^H}$. Compute $\hat{v} = br + e_2$ and $v = \langle$DBL$(\hat{v})\rangle_{2,2q}$. Also compute $a = \mathcal{G}(seed)$, $u = ra + e_3$ and $w = \mathcal{H}([$DBL$(\hat{v})]_{2,2q}) \oplus m$. The ciphertext is $ct = (u, v, w) \in R_q \times \{0,1\}^n \times \{0,1\}^k$.
- RLWE.Decryption$(ct = (u, v, w), sk = s)$: Compute $v' = su$ and output $m' = w \oplus \mathcal{H}(REC(v', v))$.

Correctness. In fact, $\hat{v} = br + e_2 = (as + e_1)r + e_2 = asr + (e_1r + e_2)$ and $v' = su = (ar + e_3)s = asr + se_3$. Suppose each coefficient of e_1, e_2, e_3, r, s is bounded by B with overwhelming probability, we have $|e_2r + e_1| \leq nB^2 + B$ and $|se_3| \leq nB^2$. To ensure correctness, we need to make sure $|\hat{v} - v'| < q/8$, hence we require

$$2nB^2 + B < q/8. \tag{7}$$

Ring-CLWR Based PKE. Next, we describe the R-CLWR version of the above scheme. Firstly, as mentioned in the Sect. 1.1, we make use of a probabilistic function $\text{INV}(\cdot) : \mathbb{Z}_p \to \mathbb{Z}_q$ that takes $x \in \mathbb{Z}_p$ as input and uniform randomly chooses an element from the set $\{u \in \mathbb{Z}_q | \lfloor u \rfloor_p = x\}$ as the output. Apparently, we have $\lfloor \text{INV}(\lfloor x \rfloor_p) \rfloor_p = \lfloor x \rfloor_p$ and $\text{INV}(\lfloor x \rfloor_p)$ is uniform in $\mathbb{Z}_q$ when x is uniform in $\mathbb{Z}_q$. We extend $\text{INV}(\cdot)$ coefficient-wisely to R_q with respect to the power basis. Also note that both $\text{INV}(\cdot)$ and its extension to R_q are polynomial time algorithms. so long as p, q and n are of polynomial size.

- RCLWR.KeyGen(1^λ): Given the security parameter λ, choose a *seed* $\leftarrow \{0,1\}^{k'}$ and $a = \mathcal{G}(seed) \in R_q$. Then, sample s from $(U_\beta^n)^\times$ by repeating $s \leftarrow U_\beta^n$ until s is invertible. Output $(seed, b = \lfloor sa \rfloor_p)$ as the public key and s as the secret key.
- RCLWR.Encryption($pk = (seed, b)$, $m \in \{0,1\}^k$): Given a message m, sample r from $(U_\beta^n)^\times$ by repeating $r \leftarrow U_\beta^n$ until r is invertible. Compute $\bar{v} = \lfloor \text{INV}(b)r \rfloor_p$, $\hat{v} = \text{INV}(\bar{v})$ and $v = \langle \text{DBL}(\hat{v}) \rangle_{2,2q}$. Also compute $a = \mathcal{G}(seed)$, $u = \lfloor ra \rfloor_p$ and $w = \mathcal{H}([\text{DBL}(\hat{v})]_{2,2q}) \oplus m$. The ciphertext is $ct = (u, v, w) \in R_p \times \{0,1\}^n \times \{0,1\}^k$.
- RCLWR.Decryption($ct = (u, v, w)$, $sk = s$): Compute $v' = s\text{INV}(u)$ and output $m' = w \oplus \mathcal{H}(\text{REC}(v', v))$.

Correctness. To show the correctness of the scheme, we need to make sure $|\hat{v} - v'| < q/4$. Specifically, we have

$$\hat{v} = \text{INV}(\bar{v}) = \text{INV}(b)r + e_1 = (as + e_2)r + e_1 = asr + (e_2r + e_1)$$

and

$$v' = s\text{INV}(u) = (ar + e_3)s = asr + se_3.$$

When the secret is drawn from a uniform distribution U_β^n, we have $|e_1| \leq q/p$, $|e_2| \leq q/p$ $|e_3| \leq q/p$, $|r| \leq \beta$, $|s| \leq \beta$. We have $|e_2r + e_1| \leq n\beta q/p + q/p$ and $|se_3| \leq n\beta q/p$, hence we require

$$2n\beta q/p + q/p < q/8. \tag{8}$$

5.3 Security Proof

In this subsection, we prove the IND-CPA security of the above PKE based on R-CLWR assumption as per Definition 7.

First, we will reduce the IND-CPA security to searching the pre-image of a hash function $\mathcal{H}$ through the following Game.

1. The challenger $\mathcal{C}$ gives the adversary $\mathcal{A}$ the public key pk.
2. $\mathcal{A}$ chooses two messages m_0 and m_1 and gives them to the challenger.
3. $\mathcal{C}$ chooses a random bit b and gives $\mathcal{A}$ a ciphertext ct_b that encrypts m_b.
4. The adversary $\mathcal{A}$ outputs a bit b' as a guess of b.

Since $\mathcal{H}$ is modeled as a random oracle, the adversary $\mathcal{A}$ will successfully guess the bit b with probability $1/2$, unless he has previously queried the value $[\mathrm{DBL}(\hat{v})]_{2,2q}$ corresponding to the challenge ciphertext to the random oracle. Therefore, we can construct an adversary $\mathcal{A}'$ from $\mathcal{A}$, which, upon inputting the public key pk and $(u, v) \in R_p \times \{0, 1\}^n$, outputs the value $[\mathrm{DBL}(\hat{v})]_{2,2q}$. In a bit more details, when $\mathcal{A}'$ receives pk and $(u, v) \in R_p \times \{0, 1\}^n$, it returns pk to $\mathcal{A}$. When $\mathcal{A}$ generates the message pair (m_0, m_1), $\mathcal{A}'$ chooses $r \leftarrow \{0, 1\}^n$, $b \leftarrow \{0, 1\}$ and sends $\mathcal{A}$ the ciphertexts $(u, v, m_b \oplus r)$. In the meantime, $\mathcal{A}'$ answers the $\mathcal{H}$ queries of $\mathcal{A}$ by keeping a random oracle table. Since we have assumed that $\mathcal{A}$ successfully guesses the bit b with a non-negligible advantage, the value of $[\mathrm{DBL}(\hat{v})]_{2,2q}$ must be queried by $\mathcal{A}$ with a non-negligible probability. Consequently, $\mathcal{A}'$ can successfully output the value $[\mathrm{DBL}(\hat{v})]_{2,2q}$ with a non-negligible probability.

Next, we will show that the success probability of $\mathcal{A}'$ is negligible under the R-CLWR assumption. Specifically, we can construct following games.

Game 1. Choose $a \leftarrow R_q$ and $s, r \leftarrow (U_\beta^n)^\times$. $b = \lfloor sa \rfloor_p$, $\bar{v} = \lfloor \mathrm{INV}(b)r \rfloor_p$, $\hat{v} = \mathrm{INV}(\bar{v})$, $v = \langle \mathrm{DBL}(\hat{v}) \rangle_{2,2q}$ and $u = \lfloor ra \rfloor_p$. $\mathcal{A}'$ is given (u, v) and its target is to compute $[\mathrm{DBL}(\hat{v})]_{2,2q}$.

Game 2. Choose $a \leftarrow R_q$ and $s, r \leftarrow (U_\beta^n)^\times$. $b \leftarrow \mathcal{U}(\lfloor R_q \rfloor_p)$, $\bar{v} = \lfloor \mathrm{INV}(b)r \rfloor_p$, $\hat{v} = \mathrm{INV}(\bar{v})$, $v = \langle \mathrm{DBL}(\hat{v}) \rangle_{2,2q}$ and $u = \lfloor ra \rfloor_p$. $\mathcal{A}'$ is given (u, v) and its target is to compute $[\mathrm{DBL}(\hat{v})]_{2,2q}$.

Game 3. Choose $a \leftarrow R_q$ and $s, r \leftarrow (U_\beta^n)^\times$. $c \leftarrow R_q$, $\bar{v} = \lfloor cr \rfloor_p$, $\hat{v} = \mathrm{INV}(\bar{v})$, $v = \langle \mathrm{DBL}(\hat{v}) \rangle_{2,2q}$ and $u = \lfloor ra \rfloor_p$. $\mathcal{A}'$ is given (u, v) and its target is to compute $[\mathrm{DBL}(\hat{v})]_{2,2q}$.

Game 4. Choose $a \leftarrow R_q$ and $s, r \leftarrow (U_\beta^n)^\times$. $c \leftarrow R_q$, $\bar{v} \leftarrow \mathcal{U}(\lfloor R_q \rfloor_p)$, $\hat{v} = \mathrm{INV}(\bar{v})$, $v = \langle \mathrm{DBL}(\hat{v}) \rangle_{2,2q}$ and $u \leftarrow \mathcal{U}(\lfloor R_q \rfloor_p)$. $\mathcal{A}'$ is given (u, v) and its target is to compute $[\mathrm{DBL}(\hat{v})]_{2,2q}$.

Firstly, we define var_1, var_2, con and $\mathcal{C}$ as follows. We set con as the distribution of choosing r from $(U_\beta^n)^\times$. Let var_1 be the distribution of (a, b) where $b = \lfloor sa \rfloor_p$ and var_2 be the distribution of (a, b) where $b \leftarrow \mathcal{U}(\lfloor R_q \rfloor_p)$. The challenger $\mathcal{C}$ computes $\mathsf{Input} = (\lfloor ra \rfloor_p, \langle \mathrm{DBL}(\mathrm{INV}(\lfloor \mathrm{INV}(b)r \rfloor_p)) \rangle_{2,2q}) = (u, v)$ and $\mathsf{Target} = [\mathrm{DBL}(\mathrm{INV}(\lfloor \mathrm{INV}(b)r \rfloor_p))]_{2,2q}$. According to the R-CLWR assumption, if the success probability for any $\mathcal{A}$ is negligible when $b \leftarrow \mathcal{U}(\lfloor R_q \rfloor_p)$, that is also negligible when (a, b) is an R-LWR instance. Therefore, the success probability of Game 1 is negligible if that of Game 2 is negligible.

Secondly, the success probability of Game 2 and that of Game 3 are same, since $\mathrm{INV}(b)$ is uniform in R_q for $b \leftarrow \mathcal{U}(\lfloor R_q \rfloor_p)$, and the views and the goals of the adversary in both games remain the same.

Thirdly, we define var_1, var_2, con and $\mathcal{C}$ as follows. We set con to be dummy. Let var_1 be the distribution of $((c, \bar{v}), (a, u))$ where $\bar{v} = \lfloor cr \rfloor_p$ and $u = \lfloor ra \rfloor_p$, while S_2 to be the distribution of $((c, \bar{v}), (a, u))$ where $\bar{v}, u \leftarrow \mathcal{U}(\lfloor R_q \rfloor_p)$. The challenger $\mathcal{C}$ computes the Input $= (u, \langle \mathrm{DBL}(\mathrm{INV}(\bar{v})) \rangle_{2,2q}) = (u, v)$ and Target $=$ $[\mathrm{DBL}(\mathrm{INV}(\bar{v}))]_{2,2q}$.

According to the R-CLWR assumption, if the success probability for any $\mathcal{A}$ is negligible when $\bar{v}, u \leftarrow \mathcal{U}(\lfloor R_q \rfloor_p)$, then that is also negligible when $((c, \bar{v}), (a, u))$ is an R-LWR instance. Therefore, the success probability of Game 3 is negligible if that of Game 4 is negligible.

Finally, u and $\bar{v}$ are independent in Game 4. Since $\bar{v} \leftarrow \mathcal{U}(\lfloor R_q \rfloor_p)$, $\mathrm{INV}(\bar{v})$ is uniform in R_q. According to Lemma 19, $[\mathrm{DBL}(\mathrm{INV}(\bar{v}))]_{2,2q}$ is uniformly random given $\langle \mathrm{DBL}(\mathrm{INV}(\bar{v})) \rangle_{2,2q}$, so the success probability of Game 4 is negligible.

Combining all above analyses, we conclude that the success probability of $\mathcal{A}'$ in Game 1 is negligible under the R-CLWR assumption. In other words, the R-CLWR based PKE scheme is IND-CPA secure.

5.4   Parameters and Comparisons

Time Complexity. As discussed in the introduction, the sampling subroutine is usually the most intricate part during the implementations. In an R-LWE based scheme, one needs to produce two samplings during the key generation and three samplings during the encryption. In comparison, in an R-CLWR based scheme, one only needs to proceed a single sampling for each key generation and encryption. Moreover, an R-LWE based scheme needs to sample from rounded Gaussian, while we can simply sample uniformly from a small interval and reject when it is non-invertible for an R-CLWR based scheme.

In terms of efficiency, we believe that our sampling subroutine will be much more efficient for the following reasons. First, it allows us to save a huge amount of entropy in practice. Secondly, and more importantly, a single sampling routing becomes more efficient in our case as we only require uniform sampling.

Nonetheless one may be concerned that the overall improvement may not be as much due to the required rejection sampling. Here, we give two arguments. Firstly, the total number of samples required to generate a valid one will be small according to Hoeffding's inequality. This is shown in Lemma 21. In the meantime, the invertibitiy check for a ring element can be carried out efficiently through the extended GCD algorithm.

Lemma 21. *Let $D_{\hat{\alpha}}^n$ be a continuous Gaussian distribution over $K_{\mathbb{R}}$ where $K \cong \mathbb{Q}[X]/(f(X))$. The largest degree of the irreducible factors modulo integer q of the polynomial f is less than k_q. Let $\hat{\alpha} \geq \sqrt{n \ln(n/\varepsilon)} q^{k_q/n} \cdot \delta_K$ and $\beta > 3n\hat{\alpha}$. If $b \leftarrow U_\beta^n$, the probability of that b is invertible is larger than $1 - 2q^{-k_q} - 2\varepsilon$.*

Proof. According to Lemma 14, when $a \leftarrow U_\beta^n + \overline{D_{\hat{\alpha}}^n}$, the probability of that a is non-invertible is smaller than $q^{-k_q} + \varepsilon$. According to Lemma 6, $\mathrm{RD}_2(U_\beta^n \parallel U_\beta^n + \overline{D_{\hat{\alpha}}^n}) = \mathrm{RD}_2(U_\beta \parallel U_\beta + \overline{D_{\hat{\alpha}}})^n \leq 2$. So

$$\Pr(b \text{ is non-inv}) \leq \Pr(a \text{ is non-inv}) \cdot \mathrm{RD}_2\left(U_\beta^n \parallel U_\beta^n + \overline{D_{\hat{\alpha}}^n}\right) \leq 2q^{-k_q} + 2\varepsilon.$$

$\square$

Space Complexity. Next, we will choose the parameters for these two schemes to deliver a fair comparison. As motivated in the introduction, we aim to keep decryption failure probability less than $O(1/e^n)$.

For the R-LWE based scheme, as per average-case/worst-case reduction in Theorem 3, $\alpha = \Omega(n^{1/4}\log^{1/4} n)$. Since $R = \mathbb{Z}[x]/(x^n + 1)$, we have $c_1 = c_2 = 1/\sqrt{n}$, $c_3 = c_4 = 1/n$. Since $t = n \cdot \zeta^{n-1}$, each coefficient of the error from $\overline{t \cdot D_\alpha^H}$ is one-dimensional rounded Gaussian with width $\alpha' = n^{1.5}\alpha$, which is smaller than $B = \Omega(n^{0.5}\alpha') = \Omega(n^{0.5}\alpha/c_2c_4) = \Omega(n^{2.25}\log^{1/4} n)$ with probability $1 - O(e^{-n})$. To make sure that (7) holds with probability $1 - O(e^{-n})$, we must choose $q = \Omega(n^{5.5}\log^{0.5} n)$. If we set $q = n^{5.5}\log^{0.5} n$, the public key has size of $k' + n\log(q) = k' + 2.75 \cdot n\log n$ and the ciphertext has size of $k + n + n\log(q) = k + n + 2.75 \cdot n\log n$.

For the R-CLWR based scheme with uniform secret, according to the reductions, $\beta = \Omega(n\alpha') = \Omega(n^{2.75}\log^{1/4} n)$ and $q/p = \Omega(n^{2.75}\log^{0.75} n)$. To make sure that (8) holds with overwhelming probability, we can choose $q = n^{6.5}\log n$ and $p = n^{3.75}\log^{1/4} n$. That results in the public key of size $k' + n\log(p) = k' + 0.9375 \cdot n\log n$ and the ciphertext of size $k + n + n\log(p) = k + n + 0.9375 \cdot n\log n$.

6 Application II: Diffie-Hellman Type Key Exchange

For completeness, we also describe a key exchange protocol based on R-CLWR with binary secret. The protocol is described in Table 4. Alice and Bob previously share the public ring element $a \in R_q$. For every new exchange instance, Alice and Bob generate their secret ring elements s, s' respectively, which are uniformly over $(U_\beta^n)^\times$. κ and κ' are the session key which are finally acquired by Alice and Bob respectively.

Table 4. A key exchange protocol based on R-CLWR.

Alice	Bob
$s \leftarrow_\$ (U_\beta^n)^\times$	
$b = \lfloor as \rceil_p \in R_p$	
$\xrightarrow{\quad b \quad}$	
	$s' \leftarrow_\$ (U_\beta^n)^\times$
	$w' = \lfloor \text{INV}(b)s' \rangle\rfloor_p$
	$b' = \lfloor as' \rceil_p \in R_p^k$
	$c = \langle \text{DBL}(\text{INV}(w'))\rangle_{2,q}$
	$km' = [\text{DBL}(\text{INV}(w'))]_{2,2q}$
	$\kappa' = \mathcal{H}(km')$
$\xleftarrow{\quad b',c \quad}$	
$d = \left\lceil \frac{q}{p}b' \right\rfloor s$	
$km = \text{REC}(\text{DBL}(d), c)$	
$\kappa = \mathcal{H}(km)$	

The security proof is similar to the PKE scheme in Sect. 5, since the pusedo-randomness of κ' can be reduced from the computational problem that $\mathcal{A}'$ inputs (b, b', c) and outputs km'. So the proof is similar to the PKE scheme.

7 Application III: New Proofs for Variant Schemes

In this section, we will prove the IND-CPA security of a variant of SABER and ROUND2, under the R-CLWR assumption, for proper parameters and distributions. Below we give an asymptotic simplification of their algorithms. There are two differences between the scheme to be presented and SABER/ROUND2. First, our scheme does not encrypt the message m directly, instead, we encrypt a bit string g and mask m by a one-time pad. Second, during the encryption, we lifted b to R_q before multiplying it by r and rounding. These two modifications make the scheme suitable for our computational assumption.

Theorem 3. *The simplified Round2 and Saber scheme is IND-CPA secure under the R-CLWR assumption R-CLWR$_{p,q,1,\chi}$ and R-CLWR$_{p,q,2,\chi'}$ under the random oracle model.*

The proof is similar to Subsect. 5.3, and please refer to the full version [19].

Similarly, we can prove the IND-CPA security of the PKE scheme of the ring version of Lizard under R-LWE and R-CLWR, for proper parameters and distributions. We also need an asymptotic simplification of the algorithm that is similar to the scheme in previous subsection.

Theorem 4. *The simplified Lizard scheme is IND-CPA secure under the ring-CLWR assumption R-LWE$_{q,\chi}$ and R-CLWR$_{p,q,2,\chi'}$ in the random oracle model.*

The proof can be found in the full version [19].

8 Conclusion

The learning with rounding over the ring problem is the most practical variants within the (R-)LWX family of problems. However, it is yet still unclear on how to build a proof for polynomial modulus and uniform secret. In this paper, we take an alternative approach by proposing the computational learning with rounding problem over the ring and show that variance practical schemes, including those that are among most practical solutions in NIST PQC competitions, can be derived from this provable secure framework.

Acknowledgements. The authors would like to thank Jiang Zhang, Jeffrey Hoffstein and Yunlei Zhao for thoughtful discussions. Also we would like to thank the anonymous reviewers for their valuable comments. This work is supported by the National Key Research and Development Program of China (No. 2017YFB0802000), the National Natural Science Foundation of China (No. U1536205).

References

1. Ajtai, M.: Generating hard instances of lattice problems (extended abstract). In: Proceedings of the Twenty-Eighth Annual ACM Symposium on the Theory of Computing, Philadelphia, Pennsylvania, USA, 22–24 May 1996, pp. 99–108 (1996)
2. Ajtai, M., Dwork, C.: A public-key cryptosystem with worst-case/average-case equivalence. In: Proceedings of the Twenty-Ninth Annual ACM Symposium on the Theory of Computing, El Paso, Texas, USA, 4–6 May 1997, pp. 284–293 (1997)
3. Alkim, E., Ducas, L., Pöppelmann, T., Schwabe, P.: Post-quantum key exchange - a new hope. In: 25th USENIX Security Symposium, USENIX Security 2016, Austin, TX, USA, 10–12 August 2016, pp. 327–343 (2016)
4. Alperin-Sheriff, J., Apon, D.: Dimension-preserving reductions from LWE to LWR. IACR Cryptology ePrint Archive 2016:589 (2016)
5. Alwen, J., Krenn, S., Pietrzak, K., Wichs, D.: Learning with rounding, revisited. In: Canetti, R., Garay, J.A. (eds.) CRYPTO 2013, Part I. LNCS, vol. 8042, pp. 57–74. Springer, Heidelberg (2013). https://doi.org/10.1007/978-3-642-40041-4_4
6. Applebaum, B., Cash, D., Peikert, C., Sahai, A.: Fast cryptographic primitives and circular-secure encryption based on hard learning problems. In: Halevi, S. (ed.) CRYPTO 2009. LNCS, vol. 5677, pp. 595–618. Springer, Heidelberg (2009). https://doi.org/10.1007/978-3-642-03356-8_35
7. Arora, S., Ge, R.: New algorithms for learning in presence of errors. In: Aceto, L., Henzinger, M., Sgall, J. (eds.) ICALP 2011. LNCS, vol. 6755, pp. 403–415. Springer, Heidelberg (2011). https://doi.org/10.1007/978-3-642-22006-7_34
8. Baan, H.: Round2: KEM and PKE based on GLWR. Cryptology ePrint Archive, Report 2017/1183 (2017). https://eprint.iacr.org/2017/1183
9. Bai, S., Langlois, A., Lepoint, T., Stehlé, D., Steinfeld, R.: Improved security proofs in lattice-based cryptography: using the Rényi divergence rather than the statistical distance. In: Iwata, T., Cheon, J.H. (eds.) ASIACRYPT 2015, Part I. LNCS, vol. 9452, pp. 3–24. Springer, Heidelberg (2015). https://doi.org/10.1007/978-3-662-48797-6_1
10. Banerjee, A., Peikert, C., Rosen, A.: Pseudorandom functions and lattices. In: Pointcheval, D., Johansson, T. (eds.) EUROCRYPT 2012. LNCS, vol. 7237, pp. 719–737. Springer, Heidelberg (2012). https://doi.org/10.1007/978-3-642-29011-4_42
11. Bhattacharya, S.: Round5: compact and fast post-quantum public-key encryption. Submitted for publication, August 2018
12. Bogdanov, A., Guo, S., Masny, D., Richelson, S., Rosen, A.: On the hardness of learning with rounding over small modulus. In: Kushilevitz, E., Malkin, T. (eds.) TCC 2016, Part I. LNCS, vol. 9562, pp. 209–224. Springer, Heidelberg (2016). https://doi.org/10.1007/978-3-662-49096-9_9
13. Bos, J.W., et al.: Take off the ring! practical, quantum-secure key exchange from LWE. In: Proceedings of the 2016 ACM SIGSAC Conference on Computer and Communications Security, Vienna, Austria, 24–28 October 2016, pp. 1006–1018 (2016)
14. Bos, J. W., Costello, C., Naehrig, M., Stebila, D.: Post-quantum key exchange for the TLS protocol from the ring learning with errors problem. In: 2015 IEEE Symposium on Security and Privacy, SP 2015, San Jose, CA, USA, 17–21 May 2015, pp. 553–570 (2015)
15. Bos, J.W., et al.: CRYSTALS - Kyber: a CCA-secure module-lattice-based KEM. IACR Cryptology ePrint Archive 2017:634 (2017)

16. Brakerski, Z., Langlois, A., Peikert, C., Regev, O., Stehlé, D.: Classical hardness of learning with errors. In Symposium on Theory of Computing Conference, STOC 2013, Palo Alto, CA, USA, 1–4 June 2013, pp. 575–584 (2013)

17. Chen, H., Lauter, K.E., Stange, K.E.: Attacks on search RLWE. IACR Cryptology ePrint Archive 2015:971 (2015)

18. Chen, H., Lauter, K.E., Stange, K.E.: Vulnerable galois RLWE families and improved attacks. IACR Cryptology ePrint Archive 2016:193 (2016)

19. Chen, L., Zhang, Z., Zhang, Z.: On the hardness of the computational Ring-LWR problem and its applications. Cryptology ePrint Archive, Report 2018/536 (2018). https://eprint.iacr.org/2018/536

20. Chen, Y., Nguyen, P.Q.: BKZ 2.0: better lattice security estimates. In: Lee, D.H., Wang, X. (eds.) ASIACRYPT 2011. LNCS, vol. 7073, pp. 1–20. Springer, Heidelberg (2011). https://doi.org/10.1007/978-3-642-25385-0_1

21. Cheon, J. H., Kim, D., Lee, J., Song, Y.: Lizard: Cut off the tail! Practical post-quantum public-key encryption from LWE and LWR. IACR Cryptology ePrint Archive, 2016:1126 (2016)

22. Conrad, K.: The different ideal. Expository papers/Lecture notes (2009). http://www.math.uconn.edu/kconrad/blurbs/gradnumthy/different.pdf

23. Damgård, I., Pastro, V., Smart, N., Zakarias, S.: Multiparty computation from somewhat homomorphic encryption. In: Safavi-Naini, R., Canetti, R. (eds.) CRYPTO 2012. LNCS, vol. 7417, pp. 643–662. Springer, Heidelberg (2012). https://doi.org/10.1007/978-3-642-32009-5_38

24. D'Anvers, J.-P., Karmakar, A., Sinha Roy, S., Vercauteren, F.: Saber: module-LWR based key exchange, CPA-secure encryption and CCA-secure KEM. In: Joux, A., Nitaj, A., Rachidi, T. (eds.) AFRICACRYPT 2018. LNCS, vol. 10831, pp. 282–305. Springer, Cham (2018). https://doi.org/10.1007/978-3-319-89339-6_16

25. Ding, J.: A simple provably secure key exchange scheme based on the learning with errors problem. IACR Cryptology ePrint Archive 2012:688 (2012)

26. Döttling, N., Müller-Quade, J.: Lossy codes and a new variant of the learning-with-errors problem. In: Johansson, T., Nguyen, P.Q. (eds.) EUROCRYPT 2013. LNCS, vol. 7881, pp. 18–34. Springer, Heidelberg (2013). https://doi.org/10.1007/978-3-642-38348-9_2

27. Ducas, L., Durmus, A.: Ring-LWE in polynomial rings. In: Fischlin, M., Buchmann, J., Manulis, M. (eds.) PKC 2012. LNCS, vol. 7293, pp. 34–51. Springer, Heidelberg (2012). https://doi.org/10.1007/978-3-642-30057-8_3

28. Ducas, L., Durmus, A., Lepoint, T., Lyubashevsky, V.: Lattice signatures and bimodal Gaussians. In: Canetti, R., Garay, J.A. (eds.) CRYPTO 2013. LNCS, vol. 8042, pp. 40–56. Springer, Heidelberg (2013). https://doi.org/10.1007/978-3-642-40041-4_3

29. Ducas, L., Nguyen, P.Q.: Faster Gaussian lattice sampling using lazy floating-point arithmetic. In: Wang, X., Sako, K. (eds.) ASIACRYPT 2012. LNCS, vol. 7658, pp. 415–432. Springer, Heidelberg (2012). https://doi.org/10.1007/978-3-642-34961-4_26

30. Dwarakanath, N.C., Galbraith, S.D.: Sampling from discrete Gaussians for lattice-based cryptography on a constrained device. Appl. Algebra Eng. Commun. Comput. **25**(3), 159–180 (2014)

31. Eisenträger, K., Hallgren, S., Lauter, K.: Weak instances of PLWE. In: Joux, A., Youssef, A. (eds.) SAC 2014. LNCS, vol. 8781, pp. 183–194. Springer, Cham (2014). https://doi.org/10.1007/978-3-319-13051-4_11

32. Elias, Y., Lauter, K.E., Ozman, E., Stange, K.E.: Provably weak instances of ring-LWE. In: Gennaro, R., Robshaw, M. (eds.) CRYPTO 2015. LNCS, vol. 9215, pp. 63–92. Springer, Heidelberg (2015). https://doi.org/10.1007/978-3-662-47989-6_4
33. Fujisaki, E., Okamoto, T.: Secure integration of asymmetric and symmetric encryption schemes. In: Wiener, M. (ed.) CRYPTO 1999. LNCS, vol. 1666, pp. 537–554. Springer, Heidelberg (1999). https://doi.org/10.1007/3-540-48405-1_34
34. ElGamal, T.: A public key cryptosystem and a signature scheme based on discrete logarithms. In: Blakley, G.R., Chaum, D. (eds.) CRYPTO 1984. LNCS, vol. 196, pp. 10–18. Springer, Heidelberg (1985). https://doi.org/10.1007/3-540-39568-7_2
35. Micciancio, D., Peikert, C.: Trapdoors for lattices: simpler, tighter, faster, smaller. In: Pointcheval, D., Johansson, T. (eds.) EUROCRYPT 2012. LNCS, vol. 7237, pp. 700–718. Springer, Heidelberg (2012). https://doi.org/10.1007/978-3-642-29011-4_41
36. Hofheinz, D., Hövelmanns, K., Kiltz, E.: A modular analysis of the Fujisaki-Okamoto transformation. In: Kalai, Y., Reyzin, L. (eds.) TCC 2017, Part I. LNCS, vol. 10677, pp. 341–371. Springer, Cham (2017). https://doi.org/10.1007/978-3-319-70500-2_12
37. Howgrave-Graham, N., et al.: The impact of decryption failures on the security of NTRU encryption. In: Boneh, D. (ed.) CRYPTO 2003. LNCS, vol. 2729, pp. 226–246. Springer, Heidelberg (2003). https://doi.org/10.1007/978-3-540-45146-4_14
38. Jin, Z., Zhao, Y.: Optimal key consensus in presence of noise. arXiv preprint arXiv:1611.06150 (2016)
39. Lyubashevsky, V., Peikert, C., Regev, O.: On ideal lattices and learning with errors over rings. In: Gilbert, H. (ed.) EUROCRYPT 2010. LNCS, vol. 6110, pp. 1–23. Springer, Heidelberg (2010). https://doi.org/10.1007/978-3-642-13190-5_1
40. Lyubashevsky, V., Peikert, C., Regev, O.: On ideal lattices and learning with errors over rings. J. ACM (JACM) **60**(6), 43 (2013)
41. Lyubashevsky, V., Peikert, C., Regev, O.: A toolkit for ring-LWE cryptography. In: Johansson, T., Nguyen, P.Q. (eds.) EUROCRYPT 2013. LNCS, vol. 7881, pp. 35–54. Springer, Heidelberg (2013). https://doi.org/10.1007/978-3-642-38348-9_3
42. Deo, A., et al.: Estimate all the LWE, NTRU schemes! https://estimate-all-the-lwe-ntru-schemes.github.io/docs/. Accessed 4 May 2018
43. Micciancio, D., Mol, P.: Pseudorandom knapsacks and the sample complexity of LWE search-to-decision reductions. In: Rogaway, P. (ed.) CRYPTO 2011. LNCS, vol. 6841, pp. 465–484. Springer, Heidelberg (2011). https://doi.org/10.1007/978-3-642-22792-9_26
44. Micciancio, D., Peikert, C.: Hardness of SIS and LWE with small parameters. In: Canetti, R., Garay, J.A. (eds.) CRYPTO 2013. LNCS, vol. 8042, pp. 21–39. Springer, Heidelberg (2013). https://doi.org/10.1007/978-3-642-40041-4_2
45. Micciancio, D., Regev, O.: Worst-case to average-case reductions based on Gaussian measures. In: 45th Symposium on Foundations of Computer Science (FOCS 2004), 17–19 October 2004, Rome, Italy, Proceedings, pp. 372–381 (2004)
46. Micciancio, D., Regev, O.: Worst-case to average-case reductions based on gaussian measures. SIAM J. Comput. **37**(1), 267–302 (2007)
47. Micciancio, D., Walter, M.: Gaussian sampling over the integers: Efficient, generic, constant-time. IACR Cryptology ePrint Archive 2017:259 (2017)
48. NIST. Post-Quantum Cryptography - Round 1 Submissions. https://csrc.nist.gov/Projects/Post-Quantum-Cryptography/Round-1-Submissions
49. NSA. Information Assurance. https://www.nsa.gov/what-we-do/information-assurance/

50. Peide, L.: Functional Analysis Foundation. Wuhan University Press (2001)
51. Peikert, C.: Public-key cryptosystems from the worst-case shortest vector problem. In: Proceedings of the Forty-First Annual ACM Symposium on Theory of Computing, pp. 333–342. ACM (2009)
52. Peikert, C.: An efficient and parallel Gaussian sampler for lattices. In: Rabin, T. (ed.) CRYPTO 2010. LNCS, vol. 6223, pp. 80–97. Springer, Heidelberg (2010). https://doi.org/10.1007/978-3-642-14623-7_5
53. Peikert, C.: Lattice cryptography for the internet. In: Mosca, M. (ed.) PQCrypto 2014. LNCS, vol. 8772, pp. 197–219. Springer, Cham (2014). https://doi.org/10.1007/978-3-319-11659-4_12
54. Peikert, C.: How (Not) to instantiate Ring-LWE. In: Zikas, V., De Prisco, R. (eds.) SCN 2016. LNCS, vol. 9841, pp. 411–430. Springer, Cham (2016). https://doi.org/10.1007/978-3-319-44618-9_22
55. Peikert, C., Regev, O., Stephens-Davidowitz, N.: Pseudorandomness of ring-LWE for any ring and modulus. In: Proceedings of the 49th Annual ACM SIGACT Symposium on Theory of Computing, STOC 2017, Montreal, QC, Canada, 19–23 June 2017, pp. 461–473 (2017)
56. Pöppelmann, T., Ducas, L., Güneysu, T.: Enhanced lattice-based signatures on reconfigurable hardware. In: CHES, pp. 353–370 (2014)
57. Regev, O.: On lattices, learning with errors, random linear codes, and cryptography. In: Proceedings of the 37th Annual ACM Symposium on Theory of Computing, Baltimore, MD, USA, 22–24 May 2005, pp. 84–93 (2005)
58. Shor, P.W.: Polynomial-time algorithms for prime factorization and discrete logarithms on a quantum computer. SIAM Rev. **41**(2), 1484–1509 (1996)

On the Statistical Leak of the GGH13 Multilinear Map and Some Variants

Léo Ducas[1] and Alice Pellet-Mary[2(✉)]

[1] Cryptology Group, CWI, Amsterdam, The Netherlands
leo.ducas@cwi.nl
[2] Univ Lyon, CNRS, ENS de Lyon, Inria, UCBL, LIP, Lyon, France
alice.pellet__mary@ens-lyon.fr

Abstract. At EUROCRYPT 2013, Garg, Gentry and Halevi proposed a candidate construction (later referred as GGH13) of cryptographic multilinear map (MMap). Despite weaknesses uncovered by Hu and Jia (EUROCRYPT 2016), this candidate is still used for designing obfuscators.

The naive version of the GGH13 scheme was deemed susceptible to averaging attacks, i.e., it could suffer from a statistical leak (yet no precise attack was described). A variant was therefore devised, but it remains heuristic. Recently, to obtain MMaps with low noise and modulus, two variants of this countermeasure were developed by Döttling et al. (EPRINT:2016/599).

In this work, we propose a systematic study of this statistical leakage for all these GGH13 variants. In particular, we confirm the weakness of the naive version of GGH13. We also show that, among the two variants proposed by Döttling et al., the so-called conservative method is not so effective: it leaks the same value as the unprotected method. Luckily, the leakage is more noisy than in the unprotected method, making the straightforward attack unsuccessful. Additionally, we note that all the other methods also leak values correlated with secrets.

As a conclusion, we propose yet another countermeasure, for which this leakage is made unrelated to all secrets. On our way, we also make explicit and tighten the hidden exponents in the size of the parameters, as an effort to assess and improve the efficiency of MMaps.

Keywords: Cryptanalysis · Multilinear maps · Statistical leakages
Ideal lattices

1 Introduction

Since their introduction in cryptographic constructions by Joux in 2000 [25], cryptographic bilinear maps, as provided by pairings on elliptic curves, have enabled the construction of more and more advanced cryptographic protocols, starting with the Identity-Based Encryption scheme of Boneh and Franklin [8]. More abstractly, a group equipped with an efficient bilinear map, and on which

© International Association for Cryptologic Research 2018
T. Peyrin and S. Galbraith (Eds.): ASIACRYPT 2018, LNCS 11272, pp. 465–493, 2018.
https://doi.org/10.1007/978-3-030-03326-2_16

some discrete-logarithm like problems are hard (such as the bilinear Diffie-Hellmann problem), provides foundation for a whole branch of cryptography. A natural open question is whether it can be generalized to degrees higher than 2 while ensuring hardness of generalizations of the Diffie-Hellmann problem. Such hypothetical objects are referred to as *Cryptographic Multilinear Maps* (or, for short, MMaps).

In 2013, Garg, Gentry and Halevi [17] proposed a candidate construction for MMaps related to ideal-lattices, yet without a clearly identified underlying hard lattice problem. It differs from the pairing case in the sense that elements in the low-level groups have no canonical representation, and that the representation is noisy. Yet, these differences are not too problematic on the functionality front.

On the security front, it rapidly turned out that this construction was insecure, at least in its original set-up. In particular, the natural one-round k-partite protocol based on this MMap was broken by the zeroizing attack of Hu and Jia [24]: this construction fails to securely mimic the tripartite protocol of [25]. More generally, the mere knowledge of a non-trivial representative of 0 tends to make constructions based on this MMap insecure. Orthogonally, it has been discovered that solving over-stretched versions of the NTRU problem (whose intractability is necessary for the security of the GGH MMap) was significantly easier than previously thought, due to the presence of an unusually dense sublattice [1,12,26], yet this can be compensated at the cost of increasing parameters. Also, due to recent algorithms for the Principal Ideal Problem [6,7] and Short generator recovery [10,14], the GGH MMap can be broken[1] in quantum polynomial time, and classical subexponential time $\exp(\tilde{O}(\sqrt{n}))$, where n is the dimension of the used ring.

Nevertheless, this candidate MMap was still considered in a weaker form,[2] to attempt realizing indistinguishability obfuscation (or, for short, iO). Several iO candidates were broken by attacks that managed to build low-level encodings of zero even if no such encodings were directly given (this is referred to as zeroizing attacks, see e.g. [11,13]). To try to capture and prevent such attacks, a Weak MMap model was devised in [18,34].

Some iO constructions come with a security proof based on assumptions in the standard model [2,29,30], but cannot be securely instantiated with the GGH13 MMap as they require low-level encodings of 0. Others are proved secure in a non-standard model (the Generic MMap model [4,9] or the Weak MMap Model [15,18]). These models remain not fully satisfactory, as they imply Virtual-Black-Box Obfuscation [9,18], a provably impossible primitive [5]. The latest candidate of Lin and Tessaro [31] did escape these pitfalls by relying on pairings, but it required special Pseudo-Random Generators that were rapidly proved not to exist [3,32].

---

[1] The secret value h can be recovered exactly, allowing in particular to construct zero-tester at larger levels.

[2] Without providing any low-level encoding of 0, and keeping the order of the multilinear group secret.

Statistical leaks in lattice-based cryptography. Early signature schemes based on lattices [21–23] suffered from statistical leaks, which led to devastating attacks [20, 35]. Those leaks can be fixed in a provably secure way using a *Gaussian Sampling* algorithm from Klein [27], as proven in [19]: the samples available to the adversary are made statistically independent from the secret key.

Similar leaks are a worry in the original construction of [17], and therefore, a candidate countermeasure was developed, making use of Klein's sampling procedure. Nevertheless, no formal statement was made on what this countermeasure prevents: the countermeasure is heuristic. This particular countermeasure turned out to be a difficulty when considering variants of the original scheme, as done in [15]. This candidate obfuscator aims at reaching polynomially small errors and modulus (in order to improve both efficiency and security of the GGH map, especially in the light of the dense sublattice attacks [1, 12, 26]) and hence cannot use the original sampling methods from [17]. Two modified versions of [17] are then proposed in [15], a so-called conservative one, leading to quite efficient parameters, and a so-called aggressive one.

Ideally, one wishes to make provable statements about those four variants, as done in other contexts [19]. Unfortunately, in the context of MMaps, it is not even clear what the statement should exactly be. The next best guarantee is a precise understanding of what can be done from a cryptanalytic point of view, as initiated in [17].

The analysis of the leak of [17] focuses on the covariance of products of encodings of zero. One can (informally) argue that this analysis captures all the information of the leakage. Indeed, up to discretization, such a product is the product of several centered Gaussian distributions (non necessary spherical), and such a distribution is fully identified by its covariance. The countermeasure proposed in Sect. 6.4 of [17] attempts to make this covariance proportional to the identity matrix (and therefore unrelated to all secrets) by sampling each element of the product according to a spherical distribution, that is a distribution whose covariance is proportional to the identity matrix. As we shall see, this attempt is unsuccessful, as one of the factors of the product (namely, the one related to the zero-testing parameter) is fixed. Obtaining several independent multiples of it, with covariance proportional to the identity matrix, then reveals an approximation of this factor.

Contributions. Our main contribution is to give a systematic study of the statistical leakage in the GGH13 scheme and its variants, in a simple framework we define. We first suggest a common formalism that encompasses all the variants at hand, by parametrising the sampling procedure for encodings by an arbitrary covariance matrix. Following the nomenclature of [15, 17], except for the second one that had no clear name, we consider:

1. The simplistic method: the GGH MMap without countermeasure [17, Sect. 4.1]. This method was only given for simplicity of exposition and was already highly suspected to be insecure;

2. The exponential method:[3] the GGH MMap with countermeasure [17, Sect. 6.4];
3. The conservative method, proposed in [15]—which we partly revisit to tackle some of its limitations;
4. The aggressive method, proposed in [15]—we note that this method is specific to the iO construction of [15], and is not applicable to all constructions over the GGH MMap.

In order to formalize our study of the leakage, we propose a simple setting of the GGH multilinear map. Indeed, due to the attacks in presence of encodings of zero, the exact set-up for the analysis of the leakage in [17] is not relevant anymore. We adjust their setting to not provide low-level encodings of zero directly. Still, some relations between encodings are needed for the MMaps to be non-trivial; to ensure that those relations do not allow zeroizing attacks, we provide a security proof in the weak multilinear map model of [15,18,34]. For ease of exposure, we restrict ourselves to degree $\kappa = 2$, yet our analysis easily extends to higher degrees.

Using this framework, we are able to analyse a particular averaging attack against the GGH multilinear map. On the one hand, our analysis shows that Method 3 leads to the same leakage as Method 1. We also prove that with Method 1, a polynomial-time attack can be mounted using the leakage. Interestingly, it does not require the Gentry-Szydlo algorithm [20], unlike the approach discussed in [17, Sects. 6.3.2 and 7.6]. Nevertheless, we did not manage to extend the attack to Method 3: while the same quantity is statistically leaked, the number of samples remains too low for the attack to go through completely. On the other hand, we show that the statistical leakage of Method 4 is similar to the one of Method 2: perhaps surprisingly the aggressive method seems more secure than the conservative one.

Finally, having built a better understanding of which information is leaked, we devise a countermeasure that we deem more adequate than all the above:

5. The compensation method.

This method is arguably simpler, and provides better parameters. More importantly, applying the same leakage attack than above, one only obtains a distribution whose covariance is independent of all secrets. We wish to clarify that this is in no way a formal statement of security. The statistical attacks considered in this work are set up in a minimalistic setting, and extensions could exist beyond this minimalistic setting. For example, one could explore what can be done by varying the zero-tested polynomial, or by keeping certain encodings fixed between several successful zero-tests.

As a secondary contribution, we also make explicit and tighten many hidden constants present in the previous constructions, in an effort to evaluate and improve the efficiency of GGH13-like MMaps.

---

[3] The naming reflects the fact that this method leads to a modulus q which is exponential in the number ℓ of so-called *atoms*.

Impact. This result may be useful in pursuit of an underlying hard problem on which one could based the GGH multilinear map. Indeed, we show here that it is possible to recover some information about secret elements, for all the previously proposed sampling methods. Hence, an underlying hard problem (or the security reduction) should capture this leak. This enables us to get a bit more insight into what could be (or could not be) an underlying hard problem for the GGH map. In that regard, finding such a hard underlying problem could be easier with our new method, since one specific leak has been sealed. Again, we *do not* claim that no other leaks exist.

Further, our analysis shows that the weak multilinear map model does not capture averaging attacks. This is not surprising, as the weak multilinear map model only allows to evaluate polynomials in the post-zero-test values, while we need to average on them for this attack. But proving that averaging cannot be achieved by evaluating polynomials is not so immediate. Interestingly, our results prove it. Indeed, using averaging techniques, we were able to mount a polynomial time attack against our setting when using the simplistic sampling method (Method 1), but we also proved that in the weak multilinear map model, no polynomial time attacks could be mounted. This proves that the weak multilinear map model does not capture averaging attacks.[4]

Finally, our new method severely decreases the length of encodings in the GGH13 multilinear map, which substentially contribute to their practical feasibility.

Outline of the article. In Sect. 2, we recall some mathematical background about cyclotomic number fields and statistics. We also describe the GGH multilinear map and detail the size of its parameters. In Sect. 3, we describe different sampling methods for the GGH multilinear map, which come from [15,17], using a common formalism so as to factor the later analysis. We describe our simple setting and analyse the leakage in Sect. 4. The security proof of this simple setting in the weak multilinear map model can be found in the full version of this article [16]. Finally, we discuss the design of sampling methods in Sect. 5, and propose a design we deem more rational.

2 Preliminaries

2.1 Mathematical Background

Rings. We denote by R the ring of integers $\mathbb{Z}[X]/(X^n + 1)$ for some n which is a power of 2 and $K = \mathbb{Q}[X]/(X^n + 1)$ its fraction field. We denote by $\sigma_j :$ $K \to \mathbb{C}$, with $1 \leq j \leq n$, the complex embeddings of K in $\mathbb{C}$. We also denote $K_\mathbb{R} = \mathbb{R}[X]/(X^n + 1)$ the topological closure of K. For $x \in K_\mathbb{R}$, we denote $x_i \in \mathbb{R}$ its i-th coefficient, so that $x = \sum_{i=0}^{n-1} x_i X^i$. For $g \in K$ (or even $K_\mathbb{R}$) we denote gR the ideal generated by g: $gR = \{gx | x \in R\}$. The complex conjugation over R

---

[4] The precise component of the attack which is not captured by the weak multilinear map model is the rounding operation performed at the end.

and K is denoted $\bar{\cdot}$. It is the automorphism of R sending X to X^{-1}. We denote S the subring of $K_{\mathbb{R}}$ of symmetric elements, that is $S = \{x \in K_{\mathbb{R}} | x = \bar{x}\}$. We set S^+ the subset of symmetric positive elements of S, defined by $S^+ = \{x\bar{x} | x \in K_{\mathbb{R}}\}$. Alternatively, S is the completion of the real subfield of K, and S^+ is (the completion of) the set of elements of K whose embeddings are all non-negative real numbers. Note that S^+ is closed under addition, multiplication, division, but not under subtraction. The elements of S^+ also admit one and exactly one square root (resp. k-th root) in S^+, which we denote $\sqrt{\cdot}$ (resp. $\sqrt[k]{\cdot}$) . Finally, we call $x\bar{x} \in S^+$ the autocorrelation[5] of $x \in K_{\mathbb{R}}$, and denote it $A(x)$. For $\Sigma \in S^+$ it holds that $A(\sqrt{\Sigma}) = \Sigma$. We also define equivalence over S^+ up to scaling by reals, and write $x \sim y$ for invertible elements $x, y \in S^+$ if $x = \alpha y$ for some positive real $\alpha > 0$. Let q be a prime congruent to 1 modulo $2n$. We denote by R_q the quotient ring $R/(qR)$. For $x \in R$, we denote by $[x]_q$ (or $[x]$ when there is no ambiguity) the coset of the element x in R_q. We will often lift back elements from R_q to R, in which case we may implicitly mean that we choose the representative with coefficients in the range $[-q/2, q/2]$. To avoid confusion, we will always write x^{-1} for the inversion in R_q, and keep the fraction symbols $1/x$ and $\frac{1}{x}$ for inversion in K and $K_{\mathbb{R}}$.

Geometry. Because we work in the ring $\mathbb{Z}[X]/(X^n + 1)$, the canonical geometry of the coefficients embeddings is equivalent, up to scaling, to the geometry of the Minkowski embeddings. We stick with the former, following the literature on multilinear maps. More precisely, the inner product of two elements $x, y \in K$ is defined by $\langle x, y \rangle = \sum x_i y_i$. The Euclidean norm (or ℓ_2-norm) is defined by $\|x\| = \sqrt{\langle x, x \rangle}$. The ℓ_∞-norm is noted $\|x\|_\infty = \max |x_i|$.

We recall the following inequalities:

$$\|xy\| \leq \sqrt{n} \cdot \|x\| \cdot \|y\| \tag{1}$$

$$\|x\|_\infty \leq \|x\| \leq \sqrt{n} \cdot \|x\|_\infty \tag{2}$$

$$\|x\|^2 \leq \|x\bar{x}\|_\infty \tag{3}$$

$$\|\bar{x}\| = \|x\| \text{ and } \|\bar{x}\|_\infty = \|x\|_\infty. \tag{4}$$

Statistics. We denote by $\Pr[E]$ the probability of an event E. For a random variable x over $K_{\mathbb{R}}$, we denote by $\mathbb{E}[x]$ the expectation of x, and by $\mathbb{V}[x] = \mathbb{E}[x\bar{x}] - \mathbb{E}[x]\mathbb{E}[\bar{x}]$ its variance. It should be noted that $\mathbb{V}[x] \in S^+$ for any random variable x over $K_{\mathbb{R}}$. A random variable x is said centered if $\mathbb{E}[x] = 0$, and isotropic if $\mathbb{V}[x] \sim 1$. We recall Hoeffding's inequality.

Theorem 1 (Hoeffding's inequality). *Let* $Y_1, \cdots, Y_m$ *be independent random variables in* $\mathbb{R}$ *with the same mean* $\mu \in \mathbb{R}$ *and such that* $|Y_i| \leq B$ *for all i's.*

---

[5] In an algebraic context, this would be more naturally described as the norm of x relative to the maximal real subfield of K, yet for our purposes it is more adequate to use the vocabulary of statistics.

Then for all $t > 0$,

$$Pr\left[\left\|\frac{1}{m}\sum_{i=1}^{m}Y_i - \mu\right\| \geq t\right] < 2e^{-\frac{mt^2}{2B^2}}.$$

Hoeffding's inequality, as given above, applies to random variables in $\mathbb{R}$. In this article, we will be interested in random variables in R. We will then see our elements in R as vectors in $\mathbb{R}^n$ and apply Hoeffding's inequality coefficient-wise.

Corollary 1 (Hoeffding's inequality in R). *Let $Y_1, \cdots, Y_m$ be independent random variables in R with the same mean $\mu \in K_\mathbb{R}$ and such that $\|Y_i\|_\infty \leq B$ for all i's. Let $\varepsilon > 0$, then*

$$Pr\left[\left\|\frac{1}{m}\sum_{i=1}^{m}Y_i - \mu\right\|_\infty \geq B\sqrt{\frac{2(\ln n - \ln \varepsilon)}{m}}\right] < 2\varepsilon.$$

Proof. For $1 \leq i \leq m$ and $0 \leq j \leq n-1$, define $Y_{i,j}$ to be the j-th coefficient of the variable $Y_i \in R$ and μ_j to be the j-th coefficient of μ. For a fixed j, the variables $Y_{i,j}$ (where only i varies) are independent random variables in $\mathbb{R}$ of mean μ_j. Moreover, as $\|Y_i\|_\infty \leq B$ for all i's, the coefficients $Y_{i,j}$ are also bounded by B. We can then apply Hoeffding's inequality (Theorem 1) to them. We obtain

$$Pr\left[\left\|\frac{1}{m}\sum_{i=1}^{m}Y_i - \mu\right\|_\infty \geq B\sqrt{\frac{2(\ln n - \ln \varepsilon)}{m}}\right]$$

$$= Pr\left[\exists j : \left|\frac{1}{m}\sum_{i=1}^{m}Y_{i,j} - \mu_j\right| \geq B\sqrt{\frac{2(\ln n - \ln \varepsilon)}{m}}\right]$$

$$\leq \sum_{j=0}^{n-1} Pr\left[\left|\frac{1}{m}\sum_{i=1}^{m}Y_{i,j} - \mu_j\right| \geq B\sqrt{\frac{2(\ln n - \ln \varepsilon)}{m}}\right]$$

$$< \sum_{j=0}^{n-1} 2e^{-\frac{2mB^2(\ln n - \ln \varepsilon)}{2B^2 m}} = \sum_{j=0}^{n-1} 2\frac{\varepsilon}{n} = 2\varepsilon.$$

We used the union bound and Hoeffding's inequality with $t = B\sqrt{\frac{2(\ln n - \ln \varepsilon)}{m}}$. $\square$

Discrete Gaussians. For $\Sigma \in S^+$ and $x_0 \in K_\mathbb{R}$, we define the *Gaussian weight function* on $K_\mathbb{R}$ as

$$\rho_{\sqrt{\Sigma}, x_0} : x \mapsto \exp\left(-\frac{1}{2}\left\|\frac{x - x_0}{\sqrt{\Sigma}}\right\|^2\right).$$

For any shifted ideal $I + c$, $I \subset K$, $c \in K_\mathbb{R}$, we define the *discrete Gaussian distribution* over $I + c$ of parameter $\sqrt{\Sigma}$, centered in x_0 by:

$$\forall x \in I + c, \ D_{I+c,\sqrt{\Sigma},x_0}(x) = \frac{\rho_{\sqrt{\Sigma},x_0}(x)}{\rho_{\sqrt{\Sigma},x_0}(I + c)}.$$

For concision, we write $D_{I+c,\sqrt{\Sigma}}$ instead of $D_{I+c,\sqrt{\Sigma},0}$ and $\rho_{\sqrt{\Sigma}}$ instead of $\rho_{\sqrt{\Sigma},0}$.

Theorem 2 (Reformulation of [19, Theorem 4.1.]). *There exists a PPT algorithm that given $g \in R$, $c \in K_\mathbb{R}$ and a parameter Σ such that $\|g/\sqrt{\Sigma}\| \leq o(1/\sqrt{\log n})$, outputs x from a distribution negligibly close to $D_{gR+c,\sqrt{\Sigma}}$.*

This reformulation simply relies on the identity $D_{gR+c,\sqrt{\Sigma}} = \frac{\sqrt{\Sigma}}{\sigma} \cdot D_{(gR+c)/\sqrt{\Sigma},\sigma}$. We also recall that, above the smoothing parameter [33], a discrete Gaussian resembles the continuous Gaussian, in particular it is almost centered at 0, and of variance almost Σ.

Lemma 1. *For any $g \in K$, $\Sigma \in S^+$, $c \in K_\mathbb{R}$ such that $\|g/\sqrt{\Sigma}\| \leq o(1/\sqrt{\log n})$, if $x \leftarrow D_{gR+c,\sqrt{\Sigma}}$, then $\|\mathbb{E}[x]\| \leq \varepsilon \cdot \|\sqrt{\Sigma}\|$ and $\|\mathbb{V}[x] - \Sigma\| \leq \varepsilon \cdot \|\Sigma\|$ for some negligible function $\varepsilon(n)$.*

The proof of this result, using [33, Lemma 4.2], can be found in the full version [16].

2.2   The GGH13 Multilinear Map

We describe in this section the GGH13 multilinear map [17], in its asymmetric setting. The GGH13 multilinear map encodes elements of a ring of integers R, modulo a secret small element $g \in R$. More concretely, an authority generates the following parameters:

- an integer n which is a power of 2 (serving as the security parameter).
- a (small) element g in R. We denote by $I = gR$ the ideal generated by g in R.
- a (large) positive integer q such that $q \equiv 1 \mod 2n$. Originally, q was chosen exponentially large in n [17], but variants were proposed for polynomially sized q [15,28].
- ℓ invertible elements $[z_i] \in R_q^\times$, for $1 \leq i \leq \ell$, chosen uniformly at random in $R_q^\times$.
- a zero-testing parameter $[p_{zt}] = [hz^*g^{-1}]$ where $[z^*] = [\prod_{1 \leq i \leq \ell} z_i]$ and h is a random element in R, generated according to a Gaussian distribution of standard deviation approximately $\sqrt{q}$.

We detail in Sect. 2.2 the size of the parameters described above (we will choose them to ensure the correctness of the scheme). The elements n, q and p_{zt} are public while the parameters h, g and the z_i's are kept secret.

Encoding of an element. The GGH13 multilinear map allows to encode cosets of the form $a + I$ for some element a in R. Let $\boldsymbol{v} \in \{0,1\}^\ell$ be a vector of size ℓ. An encoding of the coset $a + I$ at level $\boldsymbol{v}$ is an element of R_q of the form

$$u = \left[(a + rg) \cdot z_{\boldsymbol{v}}^{-1} \right]$$

where $[z_{\boldsymbol{v}}] = [\prod_{i, \boldsymbol{v}[i]=1} z_i]$ and $a + rg$ is a small element in the coset $a + I$. We call $\boldsymbol{v}$ the level of the encoding.[6] We abuse notation by saying that u is an encoding of a (instead of an encoding of the coset $a + I$).

An encoding generated by the authority is called a fresh encoding, by opposition to encodings that are obtained by adding or multiplying other encodings. The precise distribution of $a + rg$ for a fresh encoding will be a discrete Gaussian distribution over the coset $a + I$, but not necessarily a spherical one: $a + rg \leftarrow D_{a+I, \sqrt{\Sigma_{\boldsymbol{v}}}}$. The shape $\Sigma_{\boldsymbol{v}}$ of this Gaussian is essentially what distinguishes the variants that we will discuss in Sect. 3.

Adding and multiplying encodings. If u_1 and u_2 are two encodings of elements a_1 and a_2 at the same level $\boldsymbol{v}$ then $u_1 + u_2$ is an encoding of $a_1 + a_2$ at level $\boldsymbol{v}$.

If u_1 and u_2 are two encodings of elements a_1 and a_2 at levels $\boldsymbol{v}$ and $\boldsymbol{w}$ with $\boldsymbol{v}[i] \cdot \boldsymbol{w}[i] = 0$ for all $1 \leq i \leq \ell$, then $u_1 \cdot u_2$ is an encoding of $a_1 \cdot a_2$ at level $\boldsymbol{v} + \boldsymbol{w}$ (where the addition is the usual addition on vectors of size ℓ).

Zero-testing. We denote by $\boldsymbol{v}^* = (1, \dots, 1)$ the maximum level of an encoding. The zero testing parameter allows us to test if an encoding u at level $\boldsymbol{v}^*$ is an encoding of zero, by computing

$$[w] = [u \cdot p_{zt}].$$

If w is small compared to q (the literature usually requires its coefficients to be less than $q^{3/4}$), then u is an encoding of zero. Otherwise, it is not.

Size of the parameters and correctness. We define Q such that $q = n^Q$ and L such that $\ell = n^L$ (the elements Q and L are not necessarily integers). The bounds below on the size of g and h come from [17]. The secret generator g is sampled so that:

$$\|g\| = O(n), \quad \|1/g\| = O(n^2). \tag{5}$$

Remark. There seems to be some inconsistencies in [17] about the size of g, which is on page 10 sampled with width $\sigma = \tilde{O}(\sqrt{n})$, while on page 13 the width σ is set to $\sqrt{n\lambda}$ to ensure the smoothing condition $\sigma \geq \eta_{2^{-\lambda}}(\mathbb{Z}^n)$ (where $\lambda = O(n)$ denote the security parameter). Yet, according to [33, Lemma 3.3], it holds that $\eta_{2^{-\lambda}}(\mathbb{Z}^n) \leq O(\sqrt{\lambda} + \log n)$, so $\sigma = O(\sqrt{n})$ is sufficient, and we do have $\|g\| \leq O(n)$ with overwhelming probability by [33, Lemma 4.4].

---

[6] Remark that we could define encodings of level $\boldsymbol{v}$ even if $\boldsymbol{v}$ is not binary (but still has non negative integer coefficients). This is not necessary for a honest use of the GGH13 map, but we will use it in Sect. 4 for our attack.

474 L. Ducas and A. Pellet-Mary

The numerator $c = a + rg$ of a fresh encoding of $a + I$ at level $\boldsymbol{v}$ is sampled such that

$$\|c\| = \Theta(n^{\gamma + \eta \cdot \|\boldsymbol{v}\|_1 + \nu L}), \tag{6}$$

where γ, η and ν are positive reals, and depend on the sampling method, such as the ones proposed in [15] (depending on the method, η and ν may be zero). We describe later the different sampling methods and the values of γ, η and ν associated to each method. When we do not need to focus on the dependence on $\|\boldsymbol{v}\|_1$ and L, we just call $E := \Theta(n^{\gamma + \eta \cdot \|\boldsymbol{v}\|_1 + \nu L})$ the bound above. For each sampling method described below, we choose this bound to be as small as possible under the specific constraints that will arise with the sampling method.

The mildly large element h is sampled so that

$$\|h\| = \Theta(\sqrt{nq}). \tag{7}$$

Remark. In the second variant proposed in [17, Sect. 6.4] to try to prevent averaging attacks, the authors generate h according to a non spherical Gaussian distribution. However, as h is sampled only once, its distribution does not matter for the attack we analyze in this article. This is why we only specify here the size of h, and not its distribution.

We now give a condition on the modulus q to ensure correctness of the GGH13 multilinear map. This condition will depend on the number κ of fresh encodings that we have to multiply in order to obtain a top level encoding. A natural upper bound for κ is ℓ, the number of levels of the multilinear map. However, in the following, we will be interested in cases where we are provided with fresh encodings at a somewhat high level and we only need to multiply a small number of them (much smaller than ℓ) to obtain a top level encoding. Choosing a small degree κ is motivated by the fact that we want to obtain a small modulus q. We will see below that q should be at least exponential in κ. Hence, in order to achieve a polynomial modulus q, it should be that κ is at most logarithmic in the security parameter (while ℓ can be much larger). In the simple setting we describe in Sect. 4.1, we choose $\kappa = 2$, which enables q to be polynomial (if we use the good sampling methods).

Correctness of zero-testing a homogeneous polynomial of degree κ, whose absolute sum of the coefficients is bounded by n^B and evaluated in fresh encodings, is guaranteed if $n^B \cdot \|\frac{h}{g} \prod_{i=1}^{\kappa} c_i\| \leq q^{3/4}$. It is then sufficient to have

$$B + \frac{\kappa + 1}{2} + \frac{Q + 1}{2} + 2 + \kappa(\gamma + \nu L) + \eta \ell \leq \frac{3}{4}Q. \tag{8}$$

The term $\frac{\kappa+1}{2}$ appears from applying inequality (1) $\kappa + 1$ times. One should also note that $\sum_{i=1}^{\kappa} \|\boldsymbol{v}_i\|_1 = \|\boldsymbol{v}^*\|_1 = \ell$, because we can only zero test at level $\boldsymbol{v}^*$ (where $\boldsymbol{v}_i$ is the level of encoding c_i). More compactly, correctness holds if:

$$B + 3 + \kappa(1/2 + \gamma + \nu L) + \eta \ell \leq Q/4. \tag{9}$$

In our simple setting of the GGH multilinear map defined in Sect. 4.1, we will only query the zero-testing procedure on encodings of this form, with $\kappa = 2$

and $B = \log(m)/\log(n)$, for some constant m we will define later. Hence, taking $4 + 2\gamma + 2\nu L + \eta \ell + \log(m)/\log(n) \leq Q/4$ will be sufficient in our setting to ensure correctness of the zero-testing procedure.

Remark. We note that the bound $q^{3/4}$ for positive zero-tests is somewhat arbitrary and could very well be replaced by $q/4$, allowing to square-root the parameter q. Indeed, the probability of a false positive during zero-testing would remain as small as 2^{-n}. This would have a serious impact on concrete efficiency and security.

3 Sampling Methods

We describe in this section different sampling methods that can be used to generate the fresh encodings of the GGH multilinear map and we give the values of γ, η and ν that correspond to these methods. As said above, we will be interested in cases where (at least some of) the fresh encodings have a somewhat high degree and we just have to multiply a constant number of them (say 2) to obtain an encoding at maximal level $\boldsymbol{v}^*$. We denote by $\mathcal{A}$ the set of "atoms", that is the set of levels $\boldsymbol{v} \in \{0,1\}^\ell$ at which we want to encode fresh encodings. In our simple setting of the GGH multilinear map (see Sect. 4.1 for a full description of our setting), we will chose $\mathcal{A}$ to be the set of levels $\boldsymbol{v} \in \{0,1\}^\ell$ that have weight exactly 1 or $\ell - 1$, where the weight of $\boldsymbol{v}$ is the number of its non-zero coefficients. For all $\boldsymbol{v} \in \mathcal{A}$, we denote by $\tilde{\boldsymbol{v}} = \boldsymbol{v}^* - \boldsymbol{v}$ the complement of $\boldsymbol{v}$. We note that $\mathcal{A}$ is closed by complement.

In all the following sampling methods except the first one, one chooses a representative $z_v \in R$ of $[z_v] \in R_q$ for all $\boldsymbol{v} \in \mathcal{A}$. This representative will not necessarily be the canonical one, with coefficients in $[-q/2, q/2]$. Then, we will take $\Sigma_v = \sigma_v^2 z_v \bar{z}_v$, with $\sigma_v = \Theta(n^2 \|1/z_v\|)$. Using Inequalities (3) and (4), we can see that $\|1/\sqrt{\Sigma_v}\| \leq 1/\sigma_v \cdot n^{1/4} \cdot \|1/z_v\|$. Hence, with our choice of σ_v and the fact that $\|g\| = O(n)$, we obtain

$$\left\| \frac{g}{\sqrt{\Sigma_v}} \right\| \leq \sqrt{n} \cdot \|g\| \cdot \left\| \frac{1}{\sqrt{\Sigma_v}} \right\| = O\left(\frac{1}{n^{1/4}} \right) = o\left(\frac{1}{\sqrt{\log n}} \right).$$

We can therefore apply Theorem 2 to sample the numerators of fresh encodings at level $\boldsymbol{v}$, according to a Gaussian distribution of parameter Σ_v. Using tail-cut of Gaussian distributions, we have that if c is the numerator of a fresh encoding, then $\|c\| \leq n\|\sqrt{\Sigma_v}\| \leq n^{1.5}\sigma_v\|z_v\|$ with overwhelming probability. This means that we can take

$$E \leq \Theta(n^{3.5} \cdot \|1/z_v\| \cdot \|z_v\|). \tag{10}$$

Hence, in the following methods (except the simplistic one), we will focus on the size of $\|1/z_v\| \cdot \|z_v\|$ to get a bound on the value of E.

Remark. Inequality (10) above is not tight. We could at least improve it to $E \leq \Theta(n^{3+\varepsilon} \cdot \|1/z_v\| \cdot \|z_v\|)$ for any $\varepsilon > 0$, by taking $\sigma_v = \Theta(n^{1.75+\varepsilon}\|1/z_v\|)$ (it still satisfies the condition of Theorem 2) and by noticing that $\|c\| \leq n\|\sqrt{\Sigma_v}\| \leq n^{1.25}\sigma_v\|z_v\|$ for the numerator of a fresh encoding. This ensures statistical closeness to the desired distribution up to $\exp(-n^{2\varepsilon})$. Considering that there are already classical attacks in time $\exp(\tilde{O}(\sqrt{n}))$ (namely, using [6,14] to recover h from the ideal hR), one may just choose $\varepsilon = 1/4$.

3.1 The Simplistic Method

The simplistic method consists in always choosing $\Sigma_v \sim 1$, independently of v and z_v. This is done by applying Klein's algorithm [27], and requires for correctness [19, Theorem 4.1] that $\Sigma_v = \sigma^2$ for a positive scalar $\sigma \in \mathbb{R}$, where $\sigma \geq \|g\| \cdot \omega(\sqrt{\log n})$. So by taking $\sigma = \Theta(n^{1+\varepsilon})$ with $\varepsilon > 0$, one may have $E = \Theta(\sqrt{n}\sigma) = \Theta(n^{1.5+\varepsilon})$, that is $\gamma = 1.5 + \varepsilon$ and $\eta = \nu = 0$.

This method was deemed subject to averaging attacks and hence less secure than the following one in [17], but the authors claim that their attack attempts failed because all recovered elements were larger that $\sqrt{q}$, and that averaging attacks would need super-polynomially many elements.[7] We make explicit an attack, and will show that this attack is possible even for exponential q, as long as E^κ remains polynomial: in other words, the presence of the mildly large factor h (of size $\sqrt{q}$) can be circumvented.

3.2 The Exponential Method

We present here the countermeasure of [17, Sect. 6.4], generalized to multi-dimensional universe, as done in [15, Sect. 2.1]. For $1 \leq i \leq \ell$, set z_i to be the canonical representative of $[z_i]$ in R (with coefficients in the range $[-q/2, q/2]$). Using rejection sampling when choosing z_i, assume that $\|z_i\| \cdot \|1/z_i\| \leq Z$; this is efficient for Z as small as $n^{5/2}$ using [15], and can even be improved to $Z = n^{3/2}$ using Lemma 3 below and its corollary.

For v in $\mathcal{A}$, set $z_v = \prod z_i^{v_i}$ over R. Recall that Inequality (10) gives us: $E \leq \Theta(n^{3.5}\|1/z_v\| \cdot \|z_v\|)$. But we have $\|z_v\| \leq n^{(\|v\|_1-1)/2}\prod_{i \in v} \|z_i\|$ and $\|1/z_v\| \leq n^{(\|v\|_1-1)/2}\prod_{i \in v} \|1/z_i\|$. Hence we can take

$$E = \Theta(n^{2.5+\|v\|_1} \cdot Z^{\|v\|_1}) = \Theta(n^{2.5+2.5\|v\|_1}).$$

This means that we have $\gamma = 2.5, \eta = 2.5$ and $\nu = 0$.

Correctness is guaranteed for $q \geq n^{\Omega(\ell)}$ (because $\eta \neq 0$), and because ℓ is much larger than the constant degree κ in [15], this is not a satisfying solution, as we aim at decreasing q to polynomial. Two alternatives (conservative and aggressive) are therefore developed in [15].

---

[7] Recall that the original proposal was setting E and therefore q to be superpolynomial even for bounded degree ℓ because of the drowning technique for publicly sampling encodings. Since then, attacks using encodings of zero [13,24,34] have restricted encodings to be private, allowing polynomially large E.

3.3 The Conservative Method [15]

The first alternative suggested is to do as above, but reducing the z_v modulo q, that is, set z_v to be the representative of $[\prod z_i^{v_i}]$ with coefficients in $[-q/2, q/2]$. One then ensures, by rejection of all the z_i's together, that $\|z_v\| \cdot \|1/z_v\| \leq n^{2.5}$ for all $v \in \mathcal{A}$. This leads to $E = \Theta(n^{3.5} \cdot n^{2.5}) = \Theta(n^6)$ (i.e., $\gamma = 6$, $\eta = \nu = 0$) and therefore allows correctness for q as small as $n^{O(\kappa)}$, which is polynomial for constant degree κ.

Using [15, Lemma 8] restated below, the authors conclude that this method is quite inefficient because for the above bound to hold simultaneously for all $v \in \mathcal{A}$ with good probability, n must increase together with ℓ. Indeed, using Lemma 2, we can bound the probability that one of the z_v does not satisfy $\|z_v\| \cdot \|1/z_v\| \leq n^{2.5}$ by $2|\mathcal{A}|/n = 4\ell/n$. So if we want this probability to be small (say less than $1/2$) in order for the sampling procedure to be efficient, we should increase n with ℓ.

Lemma 2 (Lemma 8 from [15]). *Let $[z]$ be chosen uniformly at random in R_q and z be its canonical representative in R (i.e., with coefficients in $[-q/2, q/2]$). Then it holds that*

$$Pr\left[\|1/z\| \geq n^2/q\right] \leq 2/n.$$

In the following section, we revisit the conservative method by generalizing this lemma.

3.4 The Conservative Method Revisited

In the following lemma, we introduce an extra degree of freedom c compared to the lemma of [15], but also improve the upper bound from $O(n^{1-c})$ to $O(n^{1-2c})$.

Lemma 3. *Let $[z]$ be chosen uniformly at random in R_q and z be its representative with coefficients between $-q/2$ and $q/2$. Then, for any $c \geq 1$, it holds that*

$$Pr[z = 0 \vee \|1/z\| \geq n^c/q] \leq 4/n^{2c-1}.$$

Corollary 2. *Let $[z]$ be chosen uniformly at random in $R_q^\times$ and z be its representative with coefficients between $-q/2$ and $q/2$. Then, for any $c \geq 1$, it holds that*

$$Pr[\|1/z\| \geq n^c/q] \leq 8/n^{2c-1}.$$

We can use this corollary to compute the probability that one of the z_v does not satisfy $\|1/z_v\| \leq n^c/q$ when the $[z_i]$'s are independent and chosen uniformly at random in $R_q^\times$. Indeed, the $[z_v]$'s are uniform in $R_q^\times$ because they are a product of uniform invertible elements, and, by union bound, we have

$$\Pr\left[\exists v \in \mathcal{A} \text{ s.t. } \|1/z_v\| > n^c/q\right] \leq \sum_{v \in \mathcal{A}} \Pr\left[\|1/z_v\| > n^c/q\right]$$
$$\leq \frac{8|\mathcal{A}|}{n^{2c-1}}.$$

If we want this probability to be less than $1/2$, in order to re-sample all the z_i's only twice on average, we should take

$$|\mathcal{A}| \leq \frac{n^{2c-1}}{16}. \tag{11}$$

But we also have $\|z_v\| \leq \sqrt{n}\|z_v\|_\infty \leq \sqrt{n}q$, hence $\|1/z_v\| \cdot \|z_v\| \leq n^{c+0.5}$. In order to minimize E, we wish to minimize c, under (11). By taking the minimal value of c that satisfies this constraint, and recalling that $|\mathcal{A}| = 2\ell$, we obtain

$$E = \Theta(n^{4.5+L/2}).$$

This means that $\gamma = 4.5$, $\nu = 0.5$ and $\eta = 0$. This conservative method revisited is the same as the original one, except that we improve on the encodings size bound E.[8] In the following, we will then only focus on the conservative method revisited and not on the original one.

Proof (Proof of Lemma 3). The proof of this lemma uses the same ideas as the one of [36, Lemma 4.1], but here, the element z is sampled uniformly modulo q instead of according to a Gaussian distribution. Let $[z]$ be chosen uniformly at random in R_q and z be its representative with coefficients between $-q/2$ and $q/2$. Recall that we denote $\sigma_j : K \to \mathbb{C}$ the complex embeddings of K in $\mathbb{C}$, with $1 \leq j \leq n$. We know that the size of z is related to the size of its embeddings. Hence, if we have an upper bound on the $|\sigma_j(1/z)|$, we also have an upper bound on $\|1/z\|$. Moreover, the σ_j's are morphisms, so $\sigma_j(1/z) = 1/\sigma_j(z)$, and it suffices to have a lower bound on $|\sigma_j(z)|$.

Let $j \in \{1, \cdots, n\}$, there exists a primitive $2n$-th root of unity ζ such that

$$\sigma_j(z) = \sum_{i=0}^{n-1} a_i \zeta^i,$$

where the a_i's are the coefficients of z, and so are sampled uniformly and independently between $-q/2$ and $q/2$. As ζ is a primitive 2^k-th root of unity for some k, there exists i_0 such that $\zeta^{i_0} = I$, where I is a complex square root of -1. So we can write

$$\sigma_j(z) = a_0 + I a_{i_0} + \tilde{z},$$

for some $\tilde{z} \in \mathbb{C}$ that is independent of a_0 and a_{i_0}. Now, we have that

$$\Pr\left[|\sigma_j(z)| < \frac{q}{n^c}\right] = \Pr\left[a_0 + I a_{i_0} \in B(-\tilde{z}, \frac{q}{n^c})\right]$$
$$\leq \frac{\text{Vol}(B(-\tilde{z}, \frac{q}{n^c}))}{q^2}$$
$$\leq \frac{4}{n^{2c}},$$

---

[8] We also change a bit the point of view by fixing n first and then obtaining an upper bound on ℓ (which will appear because $\nu \neq 0$ in E), while the authors of [15] first fix ℓ and then increase n consequently.

where $B(-\tilde{z}, q/n^c)$ is the ball centered in $-\tilde{z}$ of radius q/n^c. A union bound yields that

$$\Pr\left[\exists j, \ |\sigma_j(z)| < \frac{q}{n^c}\right] \leq n \cdot \frac{4}{n^{2c}} = \frac{4}{n^{2c-1}}.$$

Which in turns implies

$$\Pr\left[\forall j, \ \left|\sigma_j\left(\frac{1}{z}\right)\right| \leq \frac{n^c}{q}\right] \geq 1 - \frac{4}{n^{2c-1}}.$$

To complete the proof, we use the fact that for cyclotomic fields of power-of-two order, we have $\|1/z\| \leq \max_j(|\sigma_j(1/z)|)$. This gives the desired result. $\square$

Proof (Proof of Corollary 2). First, note that sampling $[z]$ uniformly in $R_q^\times$ is the same as sampling $[z]$ uniformly in R_q and re-sampling it until $[z]$ is invertible. We denote by $U(R_q)$ (resp. $U(R_q^\times)$) the uniform distribution in R_q (resp. $R_q^\times$). We then have that

$$\Pr_{[z]\leftarrow U(R_q^\times)}[\|1/z\| \geq n^c/q] = \Pr_{[z]\leftarrow U(R_q)}[\|1/z\| \geq n^c/q \mid [z] \in R_q^\times].$$

But using the definition of conditional probabilities, we can rewrite

$$\Pr_{[z]\leftarrow U(R_q)}[\|1/z\| \geq n^c/q \mid [z] \in R_q^\times] = \frac{\Pr_{[z]\leftarrow U(R_q)}[[z] \in R_q^\times \text{ and } \|1/z\| \geq n^c/q]}{\Pr_{[z]\leftarrow U(R_q)}[[z] \in R_q^\times]}.$$

The numerator of this fraction is less than $\Pr_{[z]\leftarrow U(R_q)}[\|1/z\| \geq n^c/q]$, which is less than $\frac{4}{n^{2c-1}}$ using Lemma 3. And at least half of the elements of R_q are invertible (if q is prime, we can even say that the proportion of non invertible elements is at most n/q, because $q \equiv 1 \mod 2n$). Hence, $\Pr_{[z]\leftarrow U(R_q)}[[z] \in R_q^\times] \geq 1/2$ and we obtain the desired result

$$\Pr_{[z]\leftarrow U(R_q^\times)}[\|1/z\| \geq n^c/q] \leq \frac{8}{n^{2c-1}}.$$

$\square$

3.5   The Aggressive Method

This aggressive method was proposed by Döttling et al. in [15] in order to instantiate the GGH multilinear map for their obfuscator. This method cannot be used for any set of atoms $\mathcal{A}$, as it relies on the fact that the levels at which we encode fresh encodings have a specific structure. Indeed, for each $v \in \mathcal{A}$, we have either $[z_v] = [z_i]$ for some $i \in \{1, \cdots, \ell\}$ or $[z_v] = [z^* \cdot z_i^{-1}]$. Using this remark, the secret $[z_i]$'s are generated in the following way.

For i from 1 to ℓ do:

- *sample a uniformly random invertible element $[z_i]$ in R_q. Let z_i be the representative of $[z_i]$ in R with coefficients between $-q/2$ and $q/2$, and $\widetilde{z}_i$ be the representative of $[z_i^{-1}]$ in R with coefficients between $-q/2$ and $\mathrm{q}/2$.*
- *until both following conditions are satisfied, re-sample $[z_i]$:*

$$\|1/z_i\| \leq n^3/q \tag{12}$$
$$\|1/\widetilde{z}_i\| \leq n/q. \tag{13}$$

- *if $i = \ell$, we also re-sample $[z_i]$ until this third condition is met*

$$\|1/z^*\| \leq n/q, \tag{14}$$

where z^* is the representative of $[\prod_{1 \leq i \leq \ell} z_i]$ with its coefficients between $-q/2$ and $\mathrm{q}/2$.

Remark. As we sample the $[z_i]$'s from $i = 1$ to ℓ, when we generate $[z_\ell]$ all other $[z_i]$'s are already fixed, so we can define $[z^*]$.

Note that with this method, we re-sample each z_i an expected constant number of times, independently of ℓ. Indeed, all $[z_i]$'s for $i \leq \ell - 1$ are sampled independently. And the two conditions we want are satisfied except with probability at most $\frac{8}{n}$ for each condition (using Corollary 2 with $[z_i]$ and $[z_i^{-1}]$ that are uniform in $R_q^\times$ and with $c = 3$ or $c = 1$). So, applying a union bound, the probability that we have to re-sample $[z_i]$ is at most $\frac{16}{n}$, which is less than $1/2$ if $n \geq 32$. The idea is the same for $[z_\ell]$ except that we also want $\|1/z^*\|$ to be small. But all $[z_i]$ for $i < \ell$ are already fixed, so $[z^*]$ only depends on $[z_\ell]$ and is uniform in $R_q^\times$. Hence this last condition is also satisfied except with probability $\frac{8}{n}$ from Corollary 2. And the probability that the three conditions are met for $[z_\ell]$ is at least $1/2$ as long as $n \geq 48$.

To conclude, if $n \geq 48$, the procedure described above will sample each $[z_i]$ at most twice in average, independently of the choice of ℓ. So we can choose ℓ arbitrarily large and the sampling procedure will take time $O(\ell) \cdot \mathrm{poly}(n)$.

It remains to choose our representative $z_v \in R$ of $[z_v] \in R_q$ and to get a bound on $\|1/z_v\| \cdot \|z_v\|$ for all $v \in \mathcal{A}$, in order to get the value of E. We will show that $\|z_v\| \cdot \|1/z_v\| \leq n^4$ for some choice of the representative z_v we detail below.

First case. If v has weight 1, that is $[z_v] = [z_i]$ for some i, then we take $z_v = z_i$. With our choice of $[z_i]$, we have that $\|1/z_v\| \leq n^3/q$. And as $\|z_v\|$ has its coefficients between $-q/2$ and $q/2$ we have that $\|z_v\| \leq \sqrt{n}q$ and hence $\|z_v\| \cdot \|1/z_v\| \leq n^{3.5} \leq n^4$.

Second case. If v has weight $\ell - 1$, then there exists $i \in \{1, \cdots, \ell\}$ such that $[z_v] = [z^* \cdot z_i^{-1}]$. We choose as a representative of $[z_v]$ the element $z_v = z^* \cdot \widetilde{z}_i \in R$, with z^* and $\widetilde{z}_i$ as above (with coefficients between $-q/2$ and $q/2$). We then have

$$\|1/z_v\| = \|1/z^* \cdot 1/\widetilde{z}_i\| \leq \sqrt{n} \cdot \|1/z^*\| \cdot \|1/\widetilde{z}_i\| \leq n^{2.5}/q^2.$$

Further, we have that $\|z_v\| = \|z^* \cdot \tilde{z}_i\| \leq \sqrt{n} \cdot \sqrt{n}q \cdot \sqrt{n}q = n^{1.5}q^2$. This finally gives us

$$\|z_v\| \cdot \|1/z_v\| \leq n^4.$$

To conclude, this method gives us

$$E = \Theta(n^{7.5}).$$

This means that $\gamma = 7.5$ and both η and ν are zero.

Remark. For all methods with $\Sigma_v \sim z_v \bar{z}_v$ (i.e., all methods except the simplistic one), if $c \leftarrow D_{I+a,\sqrt{\Sigma_v}}$ is sampled using a Gaussian distribution of standard deviation $\sqrt{\Sigma_v}$, we can rewrite $c = c^* z_v$ with $c^* \leftarrow D_{\frac{I+a}{z_v},\sigma_v}$ for some $\sigma_v \in \mathbb{R}$. Note that c^* is now a following a spherical Gaussian distribution but its support depends on z_v. In addition to this remark, one can observe that in all the methods described above, there exists a real σ such that $\sigma_v \sigma_{\tilde{v}} = \sigma$ for all $v \in \mathcal{A}$ (in fact, σ_v only depends on the weight of v in all the methods above). This means that for every fresh encodings $[c_v z_v^{-1}]$ and $[c_{\tilde{v}} z_{\tilde{v}}^{-1}]$ at level v and $\tilde{v}$ generated independently, we have an element $c^* \in K$, following an isotropic distribution[9] of variance σ^2 such that $c_v c_{\tilde{v}} = c^* z_v z_{\tilde{v}}$ in R. Again, we note that the support of c^* depends on z_v and $z_{\tilde{v}}$, but as σ is larger than the smoothing parameter, this has no influence on the variance of c^* (by Lemma 1).

A summary of the different values of γ, η and ν for the different sampling methods can be found in Table 1.

4 Averaging Attack

4.1 Our Simple Setting of the GGH Multilinear Map

To study the leakage of the GGH multilinear map, we need to make reasonable assumptions on what is given to the adversary. It has been shown in [24] that knowing low level encodings of zero for the GGH13 multilinear map leads to zeroizing attacks that completely break the scheme. So our setting should not provide any, yet we will provide enough information for some zero-tests to pass. To this end, we will prove our setting to be secure in the weak multilinear map model, which supposedly prevents zeroizing attacks.

This setting is inspired by the use of multilinear maps in current candidate obfuscator constructions, and more precisely the low noise candidate obfuscator of [15]. Yet, for easier analysis, we tailored this setting to the bare minimum. We will assume the degree of the multilinear map to be exactly $\kappa = 2$, and will provide the attacker with elements that pass zero-test under a known polynomial. The restriction $\kappa = 2$ can easily be lifted but it would make the exposition of the model and the analysis of the leakage less readable.

---

[9] c^* is isotropic as it is the product of two independent isotropic Gaussian variables.

More precisely, we fix a number $m > 1$ of monomials, and consider the homogeneous degree-2 polynomial:

$$H(x_1, y_1, \ldots, x_m, y_m) = \sum x_i y_i.$$

Recall that we chose the set of "atoms" $\mathcal{A}$ to be the set of levels $\boldsymbol{v} \in \{0,1\}^\ell$ that have weight exactly 1 or $\ell-1$, where the weight of $\boldsymbol{v}$ is the number of its non-zero coefficients. For all $\boldsymbol{v} \in \mathcal{A}$, we let $\tilde{\boldsymbol{v}} = \boldsymbol{v}^* - \boldsymbol{v}$ (we say that $\tilde{\boldsymbol{v}}$ is the complement of $\boldsymbol{v}$). We assume that for each $\boldsymbol{v} \in \mathcal{A}$ of weight 1, the authority reveals encodings $u_{\boldsymbol{v},1}, \ldots, u_{\boldsymbol{v},m}$ at level $\boldsymbol{v}$ of random values $a_{\boldsymbol{v},1}, \ldots, a_{\boldsymbol{v},m}$ modulo I, and encodings $u_{\tilde{\boldsymbol{v}},1}, \ldots, u_{\tilde{\boldsymbol{v}},m}$ at level $\tilde{\boldsymbol{v}}$ of random values $a_{\tilde{\boldsymbol{v}},1}, \ldots, a_{\tilde{\boldsymbol{v}},m}$ modulo I, under the only constraint that

$$H(a_{\boldsymbol{v},1}, a_{\tilde{\boldsymbol{v}},1}, \ldots, a_{\boldsymbol{v},m}, a_{\tilde{\boldsymbol{v}},m}) = 0 \bmod I.$$

We remark that generating almost uniform values $a_{\cdot,\cdot}$ under the constraint above is easily done, by choosing all but one of them at random, and setting the last one to

$$a_{\tilde{\boldsymbol{v}},m} = -a_{\boldsymbol{v},m}^{-1} \sum_{i=1}^{m-1} a_{\boldsymbol{v},i} a_{\tilde{\boldsymbol{v}},i} \bmod I.$$

In the weak multilinear map model [15,18,34], we can prove that an attacker that has access to this simple setting of the GGH multilinear map cannot recover a multiple of the secret element g, except with negligible probability. The definition of the weak multilinear map model and the proof that an attacker cannot recover a multiple of g can be found in the full version [16].[10] This weak multilinear-map model was used to prove security of candidate obfuscators in [15,18], as it is supposed to capture zeroizing attacks, like the ones of [11,34]. In the weak multilinear map model, recovering a multiple of g is considered to be a successful attack. This is what motivates our proof that no polynomial time adversary can recover a multiple of g in our simple setting, under this model.

4.2   Analysis of the Leaked Value

We describe in this section the information we can recover using averaging attacks, depending on the sampling method. We will see that depending on the sampling method, we can recover an approximation of $A(z^*h/g)$, or an approximation of $A(h/g)$ or even the exact value of $A(h/g)$. In order to unify notation, we introduce the leakage $\mathfrak{L}$, which will refer to $A(z^*h/g)$ or $A(h/g)$ depending the method. We explain below what is the value of $\mathfrak{L}$ for the different methods, and how we can recover an approximation of it. In the case of the simplistic method, we also explain how we can recover the exact value of $\mathfrak{L}$ from its approximation and how to use it to create a zero-testing parameter at level $2\boldsymbol{v}^*$.

---

[10] The idea of the proof is the same as in [15,18], in a much simpler context (this is based on a generalized version of the Schwartz-Zippel lemma from [34]).

Statistical leakage. Let $v \in \mathcal{A}$ be of weight 1. We denote by $[u_v]$ the encoding $[H(u_{v,1}, u_{\tilde{v},1}, \ldots, u_{v,m}, u_{\tilde{v},m})]$. Recall that we have $[u_{i,v}] = [c_{i,v} z_v^{-1}]$, where $c_{i,v} = a_{i,v} + r_{i,v} g$ for some $r_{i,v} \in R$. So using the definition of H and the fact that $[u_v]$ passes the zero test, we can rewrite

$$
\begin{aligned}
[u_v p_{zt}] &= [H(c_{v,1}, c_{\tilde{v},1}, \ldots, c_{v,m}, c_{\tilde{v},m})(z_v z_{\tilde{v}})^{-1} \cdot z^* h g^{-1}] \\
&= [H(c_{v,1}, c_{\tilde{v},1}, \ldots, c_{v,m}, c_{\tilde{v},m}) \cdot h g^{-1}] \\
&= H(c_{v,1}, c_{\tilde{v},1}, \ldots, c_{v,m}, c_{\tilde{v},m}) \cdot h/g.
\end{aligned}
$$

Note that the product of the last line is in R, as it is a product of small elements compared to q. Also, the first term is a small multiple of g so we can divide by g. We denote by $w_v \in R$ the value above (i.e., the representative of $[u_v p_{zt}]$ with coefficients in $[-q/2, q/2]$). The term h/g of the product is fixed, but the first factor $H(c_{v,1}, c_{\tilde{v},1}, \ldots, c_{v,m}, c_{\tilde{v},m})$ depends on v: we can average over it. We now analyze this first factor, depending on the method we choose for generating the fresh encodings of the GGH map. We will denote by Y_v the random variable $H(c_{v,1}, c_{\tilde{v},1}, \ldots, c_{v,m}, c_{\tilde{v},m})$.

By definition of the polynomial H, we know that $Y_v = \sum c_{i,v} c_{i,\tilde{v}}$. Moreover, all the $c_{i,v}$ are independent when i or v vary. So the $c_{i,v} c_{i,\tilde{v}}$ are centered random variables of variance $\Sigma_v \Sigma_{\tilde{v}}$ (observe that the variance of a product of independent centered variables is the product of their variances) and Y_v is a centered random variable of variance $m \Sigma_v \Sigma_{\tilde{v}}$ (recall that H is a sum of m monomials). We now consider several cases, depending on the choice of Σ_v.

Case 1 (the simplistic method). In this case, we have $\Sigma_v = \sigma^2$ for all $v \in \mathcal{A}$, for some $\sigma \in \mathbb{R}$. This means that the Y_v are centered isotropic random variables with the same variance. Let us call $\mu := \mathbb{E}[A(Y_v)] = m\sigma^2 \in \mathbb{R}^+$ this variance. If we compute the empirical mean of the $A(Y_v)$, this will converge to μ and we can bound the speed of convergence using Hoeffding's inequality. Going back to the variables $w_v = Y_v \cdot h/g$, we have that $\mathbb{E}[A(w_v)] = \mu \cdot A(h/g)$ for some μ in $\mathbb{R}^+$. Furthermore, all the $A(w_v)$, with v of weight 1, are independent variables with the same mean, so we can apply Hoeffding's inequality.

Case 2 (the conservative method). In this case, we chose $\Sigma_v \sim z_v z_{\tilde{v}}$. We do not know the variance of the Y_v (because the z_v are secret) but we will be able to circumvent this difficulty, by averaging over the z_v's.

First, using the remark we made at the end of Sect. 3, we have that $Y_v = \sum c_{i,v} c_{i,\tilde{v}} = \sum c_{i,v}^* z_v z_{\tilde{v}}$, with the $c_{i,v}^*$ being independent centered isotropic random variables with the same variance $\sigma^2 \in \mathbb{R}^+$. Hence, we can rewrite $Y_v = X_v z_v z_{\tilde{v}}$ with X_v a centered isotropic variable of variance $m\sigma^2$ (which is independent of v). Unlike the previous case, we now have some $z_v z_{\tilde{v}}$ that contribute in Y_v. However, we will be able to remove them again by averaging. Indeed, even if all the z_v satisfy $[z_v z_{\tilde{v}}] = [z^*]$ in R_q, this is not the case in R, and that individually each z_v is essentially[11] uniform in the hypercube

---

[11] Up to the invertibility condition in R_q.

$[-q/2, q/2]^n$, in particular it is isotropic. For our analysis, let us treat the $z_v z_{\tilde{v}}$ as random variables in R, that are isotropic and independent when v varies. The isotropy follows from the fact that the two factors are isotropic. The independence assumption is technically incorrect, yet as the only dependence are of arithmetic nature over R_q and that the elements in question are large, one does not expect the correlation to be geometrically visible.

We will call $\mu_z := \mathbb{E}[A(z_v z_{\tilde{v}})]$ their variance. Recall that as the $z_v z_{\tilde{v}}$ are isotropic, μ_z is in $\mathbb{R}^+$. While the independence assumption may be technically incorrect, experiments confirm that the empirical mean $\mathbb{E}[A(z_v z_{\tilde{v}})]$ does indeed converge to some $\mu_z \in \mathbb{R}^+$ as the number of sample grows, and more precisely it seems to converge as $\mu_z \cdot (1 + \varepsilon)$ where $\varepsilon \in K_{\mathbb{R}}$ satisfies $\|\varepsilon\|_\infty = \tilde{O}(\sqrt{1/|\mathcal{A}|})$, as predicted by the Hoeffding bound (results of the experiments are given in the full version [16]).

Assuming that the X_v are independent of the $z_v z_{\tilde{v}}$,[12] we finally obtain

$$\mathbb{E}[A(Y_v)] = \mathbb{E}[A(X_v)]\mathbb{E}[A(z_v z_{\tilde{v}})] = m\sigma^2 \mu_z.$$

We denote by $\mu = m\sigma^2 \mu_z$ this value. As in the previous case, the variables $A(w_v)$ are independent (when v has weight 1) and have the same mean

$$\mathbb{E}[A(w_v)] = \mu \cdot A(h/g),$$

with $\mu \in \mathbb{R}^+$.

Case 3 (the exponential and aggressive methods). In these methods, we can again write $Y_v = X_v z_v z_{\tilde{v}}$ with X_v a centered isotropic variable of variance $m\sigma^2$ for some $\sigma \in \mathbb{R}^+$, independent of v. However, unlike the previous case, the $z_v z_{\tilde{v}}$ are not isotropic variables anymore and therefore the z's do not "average-out".

In the exponential method, the identity $z_v z_{\tilde{v}} = z^*$ holds over R (where $z^* = \prod_i z_i \in R$ is a representative of $[z^*]$), hence, $z_v z_{\tilde{v}}$ is constant when v varies, and we have

$$\mathbb{E}[A(w_v)] = \mu \cdot A(hz^*/g),$$

for some scalar $\mu \in \mathbb{R}^+$.

In the aggressive method, we have $z_v z_{\tilde{v}} = z^* \cdot \tilde{z}_i \cdot z_i$ for some $1 \le i \le \ell$, with z^* the representative of $[z^*]$, z_i the representative of $[z_i]$ and $\tilde{z}_i$ the representative of $[z_i^{-1}]$ with coefficients in $[-q/2, q/2]$. The element z^* is fixed, but, as in the conservative case, we can see the $\tilde{z}_i \cdot z_i$ as isotropic variables. Assuming they are independent, we then have $\mathbb{E}[A(z_v z_{\tilde{v}})] = \mu_z A(z^*)$ for some scalar $\mu_z \in \mathbb{R}^+$. And we again have

$$\mathbb{E}[A(w_v)] = \mu \cdot A(hz^*/g),$$

for some scalar $\mu \in \mathbb{R}^+$.

---

[12] We can view the variables $c_{i,v}^*$ as being independent of the variables z_v because the standard deviation of the Gaussian distribution is larger than the smoothing parameter (see Lemma 1).

Conclusion on the average. To conclude, we have argued that in all methods,

$$\mathbb{E}\left[A(w_v)\right] = \mu \cdot \mathfrak{L}$$

for some scalar $\mu \in \mathbb{R}^+$, where the leaked variable $\mathfrak{L}$ depends on the sampling method in the following way:

- $\mathfrak{L} = A(h/g)$ for the simplistic and the conservative methods.
- $\mathfrak{L} = A(hz^*/g)$ for the exponential and the aggressive methods.

Now, using the fact that the random variables $A(w_v)$ are independent for different $v \in \mathcal{A}$ of weight 1, we can compute their empirical mean and Hoeffding's inequality will allow us to bound the distance to the theoretical mean. In the following we assume that we know μ.[13]

Relative error of the leakage. Compute

$$W = \frac{2}{|\mathcal{A}|} \sum_{\substack{v \in \mathcal{A} \\ v \text{ of weight } 1}} A(w_v)$$

the empirical mean of the random variables $A(w_v)$. This is an approximation of $\mu \cdot \mathfrak{L}$. We know that the coefficients of the random variable w_v are less than q, so the coefficients of $A(w_v)$ are less that nq^2. By applying Hoeffding's inequality in R (Corollary 1) with $\varepsilon = 1/n$, $B = nq^2$ and $m = |\mathcal{A}|/2$, we have that $\|W - \mu \cdot \mathfrak{L}\|_\infty < \frac{nq^2\sqrt{8\ln n}}{\sqrt{|\mathcal{A}|}}$ (except with probability at most $2/n$). As the coefficients of $\mu\mathfrak{L}$ are of the order of nq^2, we have a relative error $\delta < \sqrt{8\ln n/|\mathcal{A}|}$ for each coefficient of $\mu\mathfrak{L}$. As μ is known, this means that we know $\mathfrak{L}$ with a relative error at most $\sqrt{8\ln n/|\mathcal{A}|}$.[14]

Unfortunately, we cannot directly recover the exact value of $\mathfrak{L}$ because its coefficients are not integers. When $\mathfrak{L} = A(hz^*/g)$, i.e., for the exponential and aggressive methods, we do not know how to use this approximation of $\mathfrak{L}$ to recover the exact value of $\mathfrak{L}$.[15] When $\mathfrak{L} = A(h/g)$, i.e., for the simplistic and conservatives methods, we can circumvent this difficulty. The idea is to transform our approximation of $\mathfrak{L}$ into an approximation of an element $r \in R$, with coefficients that are integers of logarithmic bit-size. Indeed, if we have an approximation of r with error less that $1/2$ we can round its coefficients and recover the exact value of r. And we can get such an approximation using a polynomial

---

[13] The value of the scalar μ can be obtained from the parameters of the multilinear maps. If we do not want to analyze the multilinear map, we can guess an approximation of μ with a sufficiently small relative error, by an exhaustive search.

[14] Again, if we do not know μ, we can guess an approximation of μ with relative error at most $\sqrt{8\ln n/|\mathcal{A}|}$ (so that it has no influence on our approximation of $\mathfrak{L}$), with an exhaustive search.

[15] Note that if we recover the exact value of $A(hz^*/g)$, then its denominator is a multiple of g and this is considered as a success of the attacker in the weak multilinear map model.

number of samples because the coefficients we want to recover have logarithmic bit-size. This is what we explain in next subsection. Unfortunately, we will see that for the conservative method, the number of samples we need to be able to round r to its exact value is not compatible with the constraint we had on $|\mathcal{A}|$ for being able to generate the z_v.

From the leakage to a complete attack against the GGH map. In this section, we explain how we can recover the exact value of $A(h/g)$, when $\mathfrak{L} = A(h/g)$ and we have enough samples. We then show how we can use this exact value to construct a zero-testing parameter at level $2v^*$.

Recovering $\mathfrak{L}$ exactly when $\mathfrak{L} = A(h/g)$. In the following, we assume that we have an approximation of $A(h/g)$ with relative error $\delta < \sqrt{8 \ln n / |\mathcal{A}|}$ and we want to recover the exact value of $A(h/g)$. Let u be any encoding at level v^* that passes the zero test (we can take u to be one of the $[u_v] = [H(u_{v,1}, u_{\tilde{v},1}, \ldots, u_{v,m}, u_{\tilde{v},m})]$). We have that $[u \cdot p_{zt}] = c \cdot h/g \in R$ for some small multiple c of g. In particular, the coefficients of c are somehow small[16] and are integers. Using our approximation W of $\mu \cdot A(h/g)$ with relative error δ plus the fact that we know μ and $c \cdot h/g$, we can recover an approximation of $A(c)$ with relative error at most $\delta \cdot n^2$ by computing $A(c \cdot h/g) \cdot \mu \cdot W^{-1}$.

The coefficients of $A(c)$ are integers and are less than $m^2 n^2 E^4$. Indeed, $c = H(c_{v,1}, c_{\tilde{v},1}, \ldots, c_{v,m}, c_{\tilde{v},m})$ for some v and we have $\|c_{v,i}\| \le E$ for all v's and i's. So we know that $\|c\| \le m n^{1/2} E^2$ and we get the desired bound on $\|A(c)\|_\infty$. Hence, if we have an approximation of the coefficients of $A(c)$ with relative error at most $\frac{1}{2m^2 n^2 E^4}$, the absolute error is less that $1/2$ and we can round the coefficients to recover $A(c)$ exactly. We can then recover $A(h/g)$ exactly by computing $A(c \cdot h/g)/A(c)$.

Putting together the conditions we got on the parameters, we have $\delta < \sqrt{\frac{8 \ln n}{|\mathcal{A}|}}$ and we want $\delta \cdot n^2 < \frac{1}{2m^2 n^2 E^4}$ to be able to recover $A(c)$. This is satisfied if $\sqrt{\frac{8 \ln n}{|\mathcal{A}|}} < \frac{1}{2m^2 n^4 E^4}$, i.e., $|\mathcal{A}| > 32 E^8 m^4 n^8 \ln n$.

To conclude, if $|\mathcal{A}| > 32 E^8 m^4 n^8 \ln n$, we can recover $A(g/h) \in K$ exactly.[17] In Sect. 4.3, we compare this constraint to the ones we had for the samplings methods. We will see that for the simplistic method, our constraints are compatible, so we can perform the attack. But this is not the case with the conservative method.

Using $A(h/g)$ to create a zero testing parameter at a forbidden level. We present here a possible way of using the recovered value $A(h/g)$. Note that in current obfuscation model (for instance the weak multilinear map model of [18] or [15]), recovering $A(h/g)$ is already considered as a success for the attacker. Indeed, its denominator is a multiple of $A(g) = g\bar{g}$ so in particular we have recovered a

---

[16] Recall that q may be exponentially large but we assumed that the numerator of a top level encoding remains polynomial in n.

[17] Note that this bound does not depends on q but only on E. This is why our attack still works even if q is exponential in n, as long as E remains polynomial in n.

multiple of g, which is considered as a success of the attacker in these models.[18] Moreover, even if we do not consider that recovering a multiple of g is bad news, we present here a way of using $A(h/g)$ to create a zero-testing parameter at a higher level than $\boldsymbol{v}^*$ (here we create a zero-testing parameter at level $2\boldsymbol{v}^*$).

First, note that the complex conjugation ‾ in R is compatible with R_q. Indeed, let $c, r \in R$, we have $\overline{c + qr} = \overline{c} + \overline{qr} = \overline{c} + q\overline{r}$ (because ‾ is $\mathbb{R}$-linear). So $\overline{c + qr} \equiv \overline{c}$ mod q and we can define the operation ‾ in R_q by $\overline{[r]} = [\overline{r}]$. We will use this to construct our zero-testing parameter. Let again $[u]$ be an encoding of zero at level $\boldsymbol{v}^*$ and write $[u] = [c \cdot (z^*)^{-1}]$ where c is a small multiple of g. Compute

$$p'_{zt} = [\overline{u} \cdot p_{zt}^2 \cdot \overline{p_{zt}} \cdot A(h/g)^{-1}]$$

$$= \left[\frac{\overline{c}}{\overline{z}^*} \cdot \frac{(z^*)^2 h^2}{g^2} \cdot \frac{\overline{z}^* \overline{h}}{\overline{g}} \cdot \frac{g\overline{g}}{h\overline{h}} \right]$$

$$= \left[\frac{(z^*)^2 \cdot (h\overline{c})}{g} \right].$$

As $h\overline{c}$ is small compared to q, this is likely to give us a zero-testing parameter at level $2\boldsymbol{v}^*$. To be sure that we can indeed zero-test at level $2\boldsymbol{v}^*$, we should check that the noise obtained at that level, when multiplied by $h\overline{c}$, does not become larger than q.

A sufficient condition for this attack to succeed is that

$$B + 3 + 3\kappa(1/2 + \gamma + \nu L) + \eta\ell \leq Q/4 \tag{15}$$

which is a variation on Inequality (9) where κ has been replaced by 3κ.

Note that the typical choice of q in [15,17] includes quite some extra margin compared to our condition (9). But even if q is chosen tightly following Inequality (9), it is not clear that the attack is prevented. Indeed, these conditions (9) and (15) are derived from the worst case inequality (1) ($\|xy\| \leq \sqrt{n} \cdot \|x\| \cdot \|y\|$), and may therefore be far from tight in the average case. In fact, $\|xy\|/(\|x\| \cdot \|y\|)$ can be arbitrarily small for well chosen x and y.

Determining whether there exist parameters that guarantee that legitimate zero-tests at level $\boldsymbol{v}^*$ almost always succeed while fraudulent zero-tests at level $2\boldsymbol{v}^*$ almost always fail would require a quite refined analysis of the distributions at hand, which is beyond the scope of this work. Indeed, we find it preferable to block this type of attacks by more robust means.

4.3   Noise Analysis of the Leakage

We sum up in this section the leakage that we can obtain and with which precision, depending on the sampling methods presented in Sect. 3.

---

[18] For this to be true, we need h and g to be co-prime. But as the ideal $\langle g \rangle$ is prime, this will be true unless h is a multiple of g. And the case where h is a multiple of g is not a problem, as we can easily recover multiples of h (and so multiples of g).

The simplistic method. In this method, we have $\mathfrak{L} = A(h/g)$. Recall that in this case, we can recover the exact value of $\mathfrak{L}$ if $\ell > 16E^8 m^4 n^8 \ln n$ (using the fact that $|\mathcal{A}| = 2\ell$). But in this method, we had $E = O(n^{1.5+\varepsilon})$, for any $\varepsilon > 0$. Hence, taking $\ell = \Theta(n^{20+8\varepsilon} m^4 \ln n)$ satisfies the conditions for generating the parameters plus our condition $\ell > 16E^8 m^4 n^8 \ln n$. To conclude, when using the simplistic method with some choice of the parameters, we can recover the exact value $A(h/g)$ and use it to construct a forbidden zero-testing parameter at level $2\boldsymbol{v}^*$. Note that recovering $A(h/g)$ also means that we recovered a multiple of g. However, we proved that in the weak multilinear map model, no polynomial time attacker could recover a multiple of g. This proves that the averaging attack described above is not captured by the weak multilinear map model.

Remark. For this sampling method, as $\Sigma_v \sim 1$, we do not need to average over the $\boldsymbol{v}$, so we could also have $\ell = 2$ as long as we have enough samples for each $\boldsymbol{v}$.

The exponential method. In this method, we have $\mathfrak{L} = A(z^* h/g)$. We can recover an approximation of $\mu\mathfrak{L}$ with relative error at most $\sqrt{\frac{8 \ln n}{|\mathcal{A}|}}$. We do not know if it is possible to recover $\mathfrak{L}$ exactly.

The conservative method revisited. In this method, we have $\mathfrak{L} = A(h/g)$, we can recover an approximation of $\mu\mathfrak{L}$ with relative error at most $\sqrt{\frac{8 \ln n}{|\mathcal{A}|}}$ according to our heuristic analysis. While the independence condition between the $A(z_v z_{\tilde{v}})$ for applying Hoeffding's bound may not be satisfied, we show that this rate of convergence seems correct in practice (see the experiments in the full version [16]).

Recall that if $\ell > 16E^8 m^4 n^8 \ln n$, then we can recover $A(h/g)$ exactly. But for the sampling method to work, we need to take $E = \Theta(n^{4.5}\sqrt{\ell})$. Hence, the condition $\ell > 16E^8 m^4 n^8 \ln n$ can be rewritten

$$\ell > \Theta(n^{44} \ell^4 m^4 \ln n).$$

This condition cannot be satisfied, so we cannot have enough samples for our attack when using this sampling method. And all we get is an approximation of $\mu A(h/g)$. Nevertheless, the only thing that prevents the full attack is the size of the parameters we have to choose in order to be able to generate the fresh encodings.

The aggressive method. In this method, we have $\mathfrak{L} = A(z^* h/g)$. We can recover an approximation of $\mu\mathfrak{L}$ with relative error at most $\sqrt{\frac{8 \ln n}{|\mathcal{A}|}}$. We do not know if it is possible to recover $\mathfrak{L}$ exactly.

4.4   Conclusion

We give in Table 1 a summary of the parameters used for the different sampling methods, and of the resulting leakage. The column'constraints' specifies possible constraints on the parameters or on the atoms set $\mathcal{A}$, that arise when using this sampling method. Recall that due to the correctness bound (9), there is always a constraint on the modulus q, so we do not mention it in the column 'constraints'. This constraint on q can be obtained from the columns γ, η and ν, using the formula $\log q \geq 4\log(n)(3 + \kappa/2 + \kappa\gamma + \kappa\nu L + \eta\ell) + 4\log(m)$.

Table 1. Summary of the leakage analysis, depending on the sampling method. This includes our new method, sketched in Sect. 5. We recall that, according to correctness bound (9), the modulus q must satisfy $\log q \geq 4\log(n)(3+\kappa/2+\kappa\gamma+\kappa\nu L+\eta\ell)+4\log(m)$.

Sampling method	γ	η	ν	leakage $\mathcal{L}$	full attack?	constraints
Simplistic [17]	$1.5 + \varepsilon$	0	0	$A(h/g)$	yes	none
Exponential [17]	2.5	2.5	0	$A(z^*h/g)$	no	none
Conservative [15]	6	0	0	$A(h/g)$	no	$n \geq 4\ell$
Conservative (revisited)	4.5	0	0.5	$A(h/g)$	no	none
Aggressive [15]	7.5	0	0	$A(z^*h/g)$	no	structure of $\mathcal{A}$
Compensation (Sec. 5)	$1.5 + 1/\kappa + \varepsilon$	0	0	1	no	none

We have seen that the leakage obtained in the conservative method is the same as the one of the unprotected scheme (the simplistic method). However, in the case of the conservative method, the number of available samples is not sufficient to complete the attack, as it is the case in the simplistic method. This limitation on the number of samples comes from some constraints in the sampling procedure and seems a bit accidental, we do not find this version of the countermeasure fully satisfactory.

We can also question the security of the other methods (exponential and aggressive), which leak an approximation of $A(hz^*/g)$, related to secret values. More precisely, one could wonder whether this noisy leakage could be combined with the knowledge of $p_{zt} = [hz^*g^{-1}]$ to mount an attack. As this problem does not look like any traditional (ideal) lattice problem, we fail to conclude beyond reasonable doubt that it should be intractable. We would find it more rational to make the leakage unrelated to secret parameters. In the following section, we propose such a design, which is simple, and leads to better parameters.

5   The Compensation Method

In this section, we propose a new sampling method which is designed so that the leakage $\mathcal{L}$ that an attacker can recover by using the averaging attack described above, reveals no information about secret parameters of the GGH map. Nevertheless, we note that even if the attack described above does not apply directly to this method, other averaging attacks may be able to leak secret information. An idea could be to fix some encodings and average over the others.

Discussion on design. We have seen that choosing different covariance parameters Σ_v at different levels v can in fact make the leak *worse*, as the attacker can choose to average them out. We also remark that the parameters $[z_v]$ can be *publicly re-randomized* without affecting anything else, in particular without affecting the covariance Σ_v of the numerator of the encodings. Indeed, we can choose random invertible elements $[\hat{z}_i] \in R_q^\times$, and apply the following transformation to all encodings e_v at level v, as well as to the zero-testing parameter $[p_{zt}]$:

$$[e_v] \mapsto \left[\prod_{i \in v} \hat{z}_i^{-1}\right] \cdot [e_v], \quad [p_{zt}] \mapsto \left[\prod_{i \in v^*} \hat{z}_i\right][p_{zt}].$$

This means that the relation between the covariance Σ_v and the denominators z_v can be publicly undone while maintaining functionality.

The compensation method. We therefore proceed to set $\Sigma_v = \Sigma$ for all levels v, and to choose Σ independently of the z_v. Doing so, we observe that the leakage $\mathfrak{L}$ will generically be:

$$\mathfrak{L} \sim \Sigma^\kappa \cdot A(h/g). \tag{16}$$

We then choose $\Sigma \sim A(g/h)^{1/\kappa}$, ensuring $\mathfrak{L} \sim 1$: the leakage is made constant, unrelated to any secret. We insist nevertheless that, as the previous methods, this method comes with no formal security argument. We also warn that we have not thoroughly explored more general leakage attacks, varying the zero-tested polynomials or keeping some encodings fixed.

It remains to see how short one can efficiently sample encodings following this choice. To get tighter bounds, we look at the conditioning number (or distortion) $\delta(\sqrt{\Sigma}) = \frac{\max(\sigma_i(\sqrt{\Sigma}))}{\min(\sigma_i(\sqrt{\Sigma}))}$, where σ_i runs over all embeddings. One easily verifies the following properties:

$$\delta(A(x)) = \delta(x)^2 \tag{17}$$

$$\delta(x^k) = \delta(x)^{|k|} \quad \text{for any } k \in \mathbb{R}, \tag{18}$$

$$\delta(xy) \le \delta(x)\delta(y). \tag{19}$$

If a variable $x \in K_\mathbb{R}$ has independent continuous Gaussian coefficients of parameter 1, then its embeddings are (complex) Gaussian variables of parameter $\Theta(\sqrt{n})$, and it holds with constant probability that

$$\forall i, \quad \Omega(1) \le |\sigma_i(x)| \le O(\sqrt{n \log n}). \tag{20}$$

Indeed, the right inequality follows from classic tail bounds on Gaussian. For the left inequality, consider that $|\sigma_i(x)| \ge \max(|\Re(\sigma_i(x))|, |\Im(\sigma_i(x))|)$, where both the real and imaginary parts are independent Gaussian of parameter $\Theta(\sqrt{n})$: each part will be smaller than $\Theta(1)$ with probability at most $1/\sqrt{2n}$. By independence, $|\sigma_i(x)| \le \Theta(1)$ holds with probability at most $1/2n$ for each i, and one may conclude by the union bound.

By scaling (and plausibly ignoring discreteness issues since g and h are sampled above the smoothing parameter of $\mathbb{Z}^n$) we can therefore assume, using rejection sampling over h and g, that $\delta(g), \delta(h) \leq O(\sqrt{n \log n})$, and therefore

$$\delta(\sqrt{\Sigma}) = \delta(A(g/h))^{1/2\kappa} \leq (\delta(g)\delta(h))^{1/\kappa} \leq O(n \log n)^{1/\kappa}.$$

This allows us to scale Σ so that:

- $\|g/\sqrt{\Sigma}\| \leq o(1/\sqrt{\log n})$, so that we can sample efficiently via Theorem 2.
- $E = \sqrt{n} \cdot \|\sqrt{\Sigma}\| \leq \sqrt{n} \cdot \|g\| \cdot \delta(\sqrt{\Sigma}) \cdot \omega(\sqrt{\log n}) = O(n^{1.5+1/\kappa+\varepsilon})$: the size of the numerators of the encodings is barely worse than in the simplistic method, and significantly better than in all other methods.

Acknowledgments. The authors are grateful to Alex Davidson, Nico Döttling and Damien Stehlé for helpful discussions. The first author was supported by a Veni Innovational Research Grant from NWO under project number 639.021.645. The second author was supported by an ERC Starting Grant ERC-2013-StG-335086-LATTAC.

References

1. Albrecht, M., Bai, S., Ducas, L.: A subfield lattice attack on overstretched NTRU assumptions. In: Robshaw, M., Katz, J. (eds.) CRYPTO 2016, Part I. LNCS, vol. 9814, pp. 153–178. Springer, Heidelberg (2016). https://doi.org/10.1007/978-3-662-53018-4_6
2. Ananth, P., Sahai, A.: Projective arithmetic functional encryption and indistinguishability obfuscation from degree-5 multilinear maps. Cryptology ePrint Archive, Report 2016/1097 (2016). http://eprint.iacr.org/2016/1097
3. Barak, B., Brakerski, Z., Komargodski, I., Kothari, P.K.: Limits on low-degree pseudorandom generators (or: Sum-of-squares meets program obfuscation). Cryptology ePrint Archive, Report 2017/312 (2017). http://eprint.iacr.org/2017/312
4. Barak, B., Garg, S., Kalai, Y.T., Paneth, O., Sahai, A.: Protecting obfuscation against algebraic attacks. In: Nguyen, P.Q., Oswald, E. (eds.) EUROCRYPT 2014. LNCS, vol. 8441, pp. 221–238. Springer, Heidelberg (2014). https://doi.org/10.1007/978-3-642-55220-5_13
5. Barak, B., et al.: On the (Im)possibility of obfuscating programs. In: Kilian, J. (ed.) CRYPTO 2001. LNCS, vol. 2139, pp. 1–18. Springer, Heidelberg (2001). https://doi.org/10.1007/3-540-44647-8_1
6. Biasse, J.-F., Espitau, T., Fouque, P.-A., Gélin, A., Kirchner, P.: Computing generator in cyclotomic integer rings. In: Coron, J.-S., Nielsen, J.B. (eds.) EUROCRYPT 2017. LNCS, vol. 10210, pp. 60–88. Springer, Cham (2017). https://doi.org/10.1007/978-3-319-56620-7_3
7. Biasse, J.-F., Song, F.: Efficient quantum algorithms for computing class groups and solving the principal ideal problem in arbitrary degree number fields. In: Proceedings of the Twenty-Seventh Annual ACM-SIAM Symposium on Discrete Algorithms, pp. 893–902. Society for Industrial and Applied Mathematics (2016)
8. Boneh, D., Franklin, M.: Identity-based encryption from the weil pairing. In: Kilian, J. (ed.) CRYPTO 2001. LNCS, vol. 2139, pp. 213–229. Springer, Heidelberg (2001). https://doi.org/10.1007/3-540-44647-8_13

9. Brakerski, Z., Rothblum, G.N.: Virtual black-box obfuscation for all circuits via generic graded encoding. In: Lindell, Y. (ed.) TCC 2014. LNCS, vol. 8349, pp. 1–25. Springer, Heidelberg (2014). https://doi.org/10.1007/978-3-642-54242-8_1

10. Campbell, P., Groves, M., Shepherd, D.: Soliloquy: a cautionary tale. In: ETSI 2nd Quantum-Safe Crypto Workshop, pp. 1–9 (2014)

11. Chen, Y., Gentry, C., Halevi, S.: Cryptanalyses of candidate branching program obfuscators. In: Coron, J.-S., Nielsen, J.B. (eds.) EUROCRYPT 2017. LNCS, vol. 10212, pp. 278–307. Springer, Cham (2017). https://doi.org/10.1007/978-3-319-56617-7_10

12. Cheon, J.H., Jeong, J., Lee, C.: An algorithm for NTRU problems and cryptanalysis of the GGH multilinear map without a low level encoding of zero. LMS J. Comput. Math. **19**(A), 255–266 (2016)

13. Coron, J.-S., et al.: Zeroizing without low-level zeroes: new MMAP attacks and their limitations. In: Gennaro, R., Robshaw, M. (eds.) CRYPTO 2015, Part I. LNCS, vol. 9215, pp. 247–266. Springer, Heidelberg (2015). https://doi.org/10.1007/978-3-662-47989-6_12

14. Cramer, R., Ducas, L., Peikert, C., Regev, O.: Recovering short generators of principal ideals in cyclotomic rings. In: Fischlin, M., Coron, J.-S. (eds.) EUROCRYPT 2016, Part II. LNCS, vol. 9666, pp. 559–585. Springer, Heidelberg (2016). https://doi.org/10.1007/978-3-662-49896-5_20

15. Döttling, N., Garg, S., Gupta, D., Miao, P., Mukherjee, P.: Obfuscation from low noise multilinear maps. Cryptology ePrint Archive, Report 2016/599 (2016). http://eprint.iacr.org/2016/599

16. Ducas, L., Pellet-Mary, A.: On the statistical leak of the GGH13 multilinear map and some variants. Cryptology ePrint Archive, Report 2017/482 (2017). http://eprint.iacr.org/2017/482

17. Garg, S., Gentry, C., Halevi, S.: Candidate multilinear maps from ideal lattices. In: Johansson, T., Nguyen, P.Q. (eds.) EUROCRYPT 2013. LNCS, vol. 7881, pp. 1–17. Springer, Heidelberg (2013). https://doi.org/10.1007/978-3-642-38348-9_1

18. Garg, S., Miles, E., Mukherjee, P., Sahai, A., Srinivasan, A., Zhandry, M.: Secure obfuscation in a weak multilinear map model. In: Hirt, M., Smith, A. (eds.) TCC 2016, Part II. LNCS, vol. 9986, pp. 241–268. Springer, Heidelberg (2016). https://doi.org/10.1007/978-3-662-53644-5_10

19. Gentry, C., Peikert, C., Vaikuntanathan, V.: Trapdoors for hard lattices and new cryptographic constructions. In: Ladner, R.E., Dwork, C. (eds.) 40th Annual ACM Symposium on Theory of Computing, pp. 197–206. ACM Press, May 2008

20. Gentry, C., Szydlo, M.: Cryptanalysis of the revised NTRU signature scheme. In: Knudsen, L.R. (ed.) EUROCRYPT 2002. LNCS, vol. 2332, pp. 299–320. Springer, Heidelberg (2002). https://doi.org/10.1007/3-540-46035-7_20

21. Goldreich, O., Goldwasser, S., Halevi, S.: Public-key cryptosystems from lattice reduction problems. In: Kaliski, B.S. (ed.) CRYPTO 1997. LNCS, vol. 1294, pp. 112–131. Springer, Heidelberg (1997). https://doi.org/10.1007/BFb0052231

22. Hoffstein, J., Howgrave-Graham, N., Pipher, J., Silverman, J.H., Whyte, W.: NTRUSign: digital signatures using the NTRU lattice. In: Joye, M. (ed.) CT-RSA 2003. LNCS, vol. 2612, pp. 122–140. Springer, Heidelberg (2003). https://doi.org/10.1007/3-540-36563-X_9

23. Hoffstein, J., Pipher, J., Silverman, J.H.: NSS: an NTRU lattice-based signature scheme. In: Pfitzmann, B. (ed.) EUROCRYPT 2001. LNCS, vol. 2045, pp. 211–228. Springer, Heidelberg (2001). https://doi.org/10.1007/3-540-44987-6_14

24. Hu, Y., Jia, H.: Cryptanalysis of GGH map. In: Fischlin, M., Coron, J.-S. (eds.) EUROCRYPT 2016, Part I. LNCS, vol. 9665, pp. 537–565. Springer, Heidelberg (2016). https://doi.org/10.1007/978-3-662-49890-3_21
25. Joux, A.: A one round protocol for tripartite Diffie-Hellman. In: Bosma, W. (ed.) ANTS 2000. LNCS, vol. 1838, pp. 385–393. Springer, Heidelberg (2000). https://doi.org/10.1007/10722028_23
26. Kirchner, P., Fouque, P.-A.: Revisiting lattice attacks on overstretched NTRU parameters. In: Coron, J.-S., Nielsen, J.B. (eds.) EUROCRYPT 2017. LNCS, vol. 10210, pp. 3–26. Springer, Cham (2017). https://doi.org/10.1007/978-3-319-56620-7_1
27. Klein, P.N.: Finding the closest lattice vector when it's unusually close. In: Shmoys, D.B. (ed.) 11th Annual ACM-SIAM Symposium on Discrete Algorithms, pp. 937–941. ACM-SIAM, January 2000
28. Langlois, A., Stehlé, D., Steinfeld, R.: GGHLite: more efficient multilinear maps from ideal lattices. In: Nguyen, P.Q., Oswald, E. (eds.) EUROCRYPT 2014. LNCS, vol. 8441, pp. 239–256. Springer, Heidelberg (2014). https://doi.org/10.1007/978-3-642-55220-5_14
29. Lin, H.: Indistinguishability obfuscation from constant-degree graded encoding schemes. In: Fischlin, M., Coron, J.-S. (eds.) EUROCRYPT 2016. LNCS, vol. 9665, pp. 28–57. Springer, Heidelberg (2016). https://doi.org/10.1007/978-3-662-49890-3_2
30. Lin, H.: Indistinguishability obfuscation from SXDH on 5-linear maps and locality-5 PRGs. In: Katz, J., Shacham, H. (eds.) CRYPTO 2017. LNCS, vol. 10401, pp. 599–629. Springer, Cham (2017). https://doi.org/10.1007/978-3-319-63688-7_20
31. Lin, H., Tessaro, S.: Indistinguishability obfuscation from bilinear maps and block-wise local PRGs. Cryptology ePrint Archive, Report 2017/250 (2017). http://eprint.iacr.org/2017/250
32. Lombardi, A., Vaikuntanathan, V.: On the non-existence of blockwise 2-local PRGs with applications to indistinguishability obfuscation. Cryptology ePrint Archive, Report 2017/301 (2017). http://eprint.iacr.org/2017/301
33. Micciancio, D., Regev, O.: Worst-case to average-case reductions based on Gaussian measures. In: 45th Annual Symposium on Foundations of Computer Science, pp. 372–381. IEEE Computer Society Press, October 2004
34. Miles, E., Sahai, A., Zhandry, M.: Annihilation attacks for multilinear maps: cryptanalysis of indistinguishability obfuscation over GGH13. In: Robshaw, M., Katz, J. (eds.) CRYPTO 2016, Part II. LNCS, vol. 9815, pp. 629–658. Springer, Heidelberg (2016). https://doi.org/10.1007/978-3-662-53008-5_22
35. Nguyen, P.Q., Regev, O.: Learning a parallelepiped: cryptanalysis of GGH and NTRU signatures. In: Vaudenay, S. (ed.) EUROCRYPT 2006. LNCS, vol. 4004, pp. 271–288. Springer, Heidelberg (2006). https://doi.org/10.1007/11761679_17
36. Stehlé, D., Steinfeld, R.: Making NTRUEncrypt and NTRUSign as secure as standard worst-case problems over ideal lattices. Cryptology ePrint Archive, Report 2013/004 (2013). http://eprint.iacr.org/2013/004

LWE Without Modular Reduction and Improved Side-Channel Attacks Against BLISS

Jonathan Bootle[1], Claire Delaplace[2,3], Thomas Espitau[4],
Pierre-Alain Fouque[2], and Mehdi Tibouchi[5(✉)]

[1] University College London, London, UK
jonathan.bootle.14@ucl.ac.uk
[2] Univ Rennes, Rennes, France
{claire.delaplace,pierre-alain.fouque}@univ-rennes1.fr
[3] Univ Lille, Lille, France
[4] Sorbonne Université, Paris, France
thomas.espitau@lip6.fr
[5] NTT Secure Platform Laboratories, Tokyo, Japan
tibouchi.mehdi@lab.ntt.co.jp

Abstract. This paper is devoted to analyzing the variant of Regev's learning with errors (LWE) problem in which modular reduction is omitted: namely, the problem (ILWE) of recovering a vector $\mathbf{s} \in \mathbb{Z}^n$ given polynomially many samples of the form $(\mathbf{a}, \langle \mathbf{a}, \mathbf{s} \rangle + e) \in \mathbb{Z}^{n+1}$ where $\mathbf{a}$ and e follow fixed distributions. Unsurprisingly, this problem is much easier than LWE: under mild conditions on the distributions, we show that the problem can be solved efficiently as long as the variance of e is not superpolynomially larger than that of $\mathbf{a}$. We also provide almost tight bounds on the number of samples needed to recover $\mathbf{s}$.

Our interest in studying this problem stems from the side-channel attack against the BLISS lattice-based signature scheme described by Espitau et al. at CCS 2017. The attack targets a *quadratic* function of the secret that leaks in the rejection sampling step of BLISS. The same part of the algorithm also suffers from a *linear* leakage, but the authors claimed that this leakage could not be exploited due to signature compression: the linear system arising from it turns out to be *noisy*, and hence key recovery amounts to solving a high-dimensional problem analogous to LWE, which seemed infeasible. However, this noisy linear algebra problem does not involve any modular reduction: it is essentially an instance of ILWE, and can therefore be solved efficiently using our techniques. This allows us to obtain an improved side-channel attack on BLISS, which applies to 100% of secret keys (as opposed to ≈7% in the CCS paper), and is also considerably faster.

© International Association for Cryptologic Research 2018
T. Peyrin and S. Galbraith (Eds.): ASIACRYPT 2018, LNCS 11272, pp. 494–524, 2018.
https://doi.org/10.1007/978-3-030-03326-2_17

1   Introduction

Learning with Errors. Regev's *learning with errors* problem (LWE) is the problem of recovering a uniformly random vector $\mathbf{s} \in (\mathbb{Z}/q\mathbb{Z})^n$ given polynomially many samples of the form $(\mathbf{a}, \langle \mathbf{a}, \mathbf{s} \rangle + e \bmod q)$, with $\mathbf{a}$ uniform in $(\mathbb{Z}/q\mathbb{Z})^n$, and e sampled according to a fixed distribution over $\mathbb{Z}/q\mathbb{Z}$ (typically a discrete Gaussian). Regev showed [43] that for suitable parameters, this problem is as hard as worst-case lattice problems, and is polynomial-time equivalent to its decision version, which asks to distinguish the distribution of tuples $(\mathbf{a}, \langle \mathbf{a}, \mathbf{s} \rangle + e \bmod q)$ as above from the uniform distribution over $(\mathbb{Z}/q\mathbb{Z})^{n+1}$. These results are a cornerstone of modern lattice-based cryptography, which is to a large extent based on LWE and related problems.

Many variants of the LWE problem have been introduced in the literature, mostly with the goal of improving the efficiency of lattice-based cryptography. For example, papers have been devoted to the analysis of LWE when the error e has a non-Gaussian distribution and/or is very small [6,16,38], when the secret $\mathbf{s}$ is sampled from a non-uniform distribution [2,3,5,7,12], or when the vectors $\mathbf{a}$ are non-uniform [20,23]. A long line of research has considered variants of LWE in which auxiliary information is provided about the secret $\mathbf{s}$ [12,15,21,31]. Extensions of LWE over more general rings have also been extensively studied, starting from the introduction of the Ring-LWE problem [29,36,37,46]. Yet another notable variant of LWE is the learning with rounding (LWR) problem [4,8,9], in which the scalar product $\langle \mathbf{a}, \mathbf{s} \rangle$ is partly hidden not by adding some noise e, but by disclosing only its most significant bits.

Recently, further exotic variants have emerged in association with schemes submitted to the NIST postquantum cryptography standardization process. One can mention for example Compact-LWE [33,34], which has been broken [11,30, 48]; learning with truncation, considered in pqNTRUSign [24]; and Mersenne variants of Ring-LWE, introduced for ThreeBears [22] and Mersenne–756839 [1].

The ILWE Problem. In this paper, we introduce a simpler variant of LWE in which computations are carried out over $\mathbb{Z}$ rather than $\mathbb{Z}/q\mathbb{Z}$, i.e. without modular reduction. More precisely, we consider the problem which we call ILWE ("integer LWE") of finding a vector $\mathbf{s} \in \mathbb{Z}^n$ given polynomially many samples of the form $(\mathbf{a}, \langle \mathbf{a}, \mathbf{s} \rangle + e) \in \mathbb{Z}^{n+1}$, where $\mathbf{a}$ and e follow fixed distributions on $\mathbb{Z}$.

This problem may occur more naturally in statistical learning theory or numerical analysis than it does in cryptography; indeed, contrary to LWE, it is usually not hard. It can even be solved efficiently when the error e is *much larger* than the inner product $\langle \mathbf{a}, \mathbf{s} \rangle$ (but not superpolynomially larger), under relatively mild conditions on the distributions involved.

The fact that standard learning techniques like least squares regression should apply to this problem can be regarded as folklore, and is occasionally mentioned in special cases in the cryptographic literature (see e.g. [20, Sect. 7.6]). The main purpose of this work is to give a completely rigorous treatment of this question, and in particular to analyze the number of samples needed to solve ILWE both in an information-theoretic sense and using concrete algorithms.

ILWE and Side-Channel Attacks on BLISS. Our main motivation for studying the ILWE problem is a side-channel attack against the BLISS lattice-based signature scheme described by Espitau et al. at CCS 2017 [19].

BLISS [17] is one of the most prominent, efficient and widely implemented lattice-based signature schemes, and it has received significant attention in terms of side-channel analysis. Several papers [13,19,40] have pointed out that, in available implementations, certain parts of the signing algorithm can leak sensitive information about the secret key via various side-channels like cache timing, electromagnetic emanations and secret-dependent branches. They have shown that this leakage can be exploited for key recovery.

We are in particular interested in the leakage that occurs in the rejection sampling step of BLISS signature generation. Rejection sampling is an essential element of the construction of BLISS and other lattice-based signatures following Lyubashevsky's "Fiat–Shamir with aborts" framework [35]. Implementing it efficiently in a scheme using Gaussian distributions, as is the case for BLISS, is not an easy task, however, and as observed by Espitau et al., the optimization used in BLISS turns out to leak two functions of the secret key via side-channels: an *exact, quadratic* function, as well as a *noisy, linear* function.

The attack proposed by Espitau et al. relies only on the quadratic leakage, and as a result uses very complex and computationally costly techniques from algorithmic number theory (a generalization of the Howgrave-Graham–Szydlo algorithm for solving norm equations). In particular, not only does the main, polynomial-time part of their algorithm takes over a CPU month for standard BLISS parameters, technical reasons related to the hardness of factoring make their attack only applicable to a small fraction of BLISS secret key (around 7%; these are keys satisfying a certain smoothness condition). They note that using the *linear* leakage instead would be much simpler if the linear function was exactly known, but cannot be done due to its noisy nature: recovering the key then become a high-dimensional noisy linear algebra problem analogous to LWE, which should therefore be hard.

However, the authors missed an important difference between that linear algebra problem and LWE: the absence of modular reduction. The problem can essentially be seen as an instance of ILWE instead, and our analysis thus shows that it is easy to solve. This results in a much more computationally efficient attack taking advantage of the leakage in BLISS rejection sampling, which moreover applies to *all* secret keys.

Our Contributions. We propose a detailed theoretical analysis of the ILWE problem and show how it can be applied to the side-channel attack on BLISS. We also provide numerical simulations showing that our proposed algorithms behave in a way consistent with the theoretical predictions.

On the theoretical side, our first contribution is to prove that, in an information-theoretic sense, solving the ILWE problem requires at least $m = \Omega\big((\sigma_e/\sigma_a)\big)^2$ samples from the ILWE distribution when the error e has standard deviation σ_e, and the coefficients of the vectors $\mathbf{a}$ in samples have standard deviation σ_a. We show this by estimating the statistical distance between the distributions arising from two distinct secret vectors $\mathbf{s}$ and $\mathbf{s}'$. In particular, the ILWE problem is hard when σ_e is superpolynomially larger than σ_a, but can be easy otherwise, including when σ_e exceeds σ_a by a large polynomial factor.

We then provide and analyze concrete algorithms for solving the problem in that case. Our main focus is least squares regression followed by rounding. Roughly speaking, we show that this approach solves the ILWE problem with m samples when $m \geq C \cdot (\sigma_e/\sigma_a)^2 \log n$ for some constant C (and is also a constant factor larger than n, to ensure that the noise-free version of the corresponding linear algebra problem has a unique solution, and that the covariance matrix of the vectors $\mathbf{a}$ is well-controlled). Our result applies to a very large class of distributions for $\mathbf{a}$ and e including bounded distributions and discrete Gaussians. It relies on subgaussian concentration inequalities.

Interestingly, ILWE can be interpreted as a bounded distance decoding problem in a certain lattice in $\mathbb{Z}^n$ (which is very far from random), and the least squares approach coincides with Babai's rounding algorithm for the approximate closest vector problem (CVP) when seen through that lens. As a side contribution, we also show that even with a much stronger CVP algorithm (including an exact CVP oracle), one cannot improve the number of samples necessary to recover $\mathbf{s}$ by more than a constant factor. And on another side note, we also consider alternate algorithms to least squares when very few samples are available (so that the underlying linear algebra system is not even full-rank), but the secret vector is known to be sparse. In that case, compressed sensing techniques using linear programming [14] can solve the problem efficiently.

After this theoretical analysis, we concretely examine the noisy linear algebra problem arising from the linear part of the BLISS rejection sampling leakage, and show that is strongly resembles an ILWE problem, which allows us to estimate the number of side-channel traces needed to recover the secret key.

Simulation results both for the vanilla ILWE problem and the BLISS attack are consistent with the theoretical predictions (only with better constants). In particular, we obtain a much more efficient attack on BLISS than the one in [19], which moreover applies to 100% of possible secret keys. The only drawback is that our attack requires a larger number of traces (around 20000 compared to 512 in [19] for BLISS–I parameters), and even that is to a large extent counterbalanced by the fact that we can easily handle errors in the values read off from side-channel traces, whereas Espitau et al. need all their leakage values to be exact.

2 Preliminaries

2.1 Notation

For $r \in \mathbb{R}$, we denote by $\lceil r \rfloor$ the nearest integer to r (rounding down for half-integers), and by $\lfloor r \rfloor$ the largest integer less or equal to r. For a vector $\mathbf{x} = (x_1, \ldots, x_n) \in \mathbb{R}^n$, the p-norm $\|\mathbf{x}\|_p$ of $\mathbf{x}$, $p \in [1, \infty)$, is given by $\|\mathbf{x}\|_p = (|x_1|^p +$

$\cdots + |x_n|^p)^{1/p}$, and the infinity norm by $\|\mathbf{x}\|_\infty = \max\left(|x_1|, \ldots, |x_n|\right)$. For a matrix $A \in \mathbb{R}^{m \times n}$, the operator norm $\|A\|_p^{\mathrm{op}}$ of A with respect to the p-norm, $p \in [1, \infty]$, is given by:

$$\|A\|_p^{\mathrm{op}} = \sup_{\mathbf{x} \in \mathbb{R}^n \setminus \{0\}} \frac{\|A\mathbf{x}\|_p}{\|\mathbf{x}\|_p} = \sup_{\|\mathbf{x}\|_p = 1} \|A\mathbf{x}\|_p.$$

For any random variable X, we denote by $\mathbb{E}[X]$ its expectation and by $\mathrm{Var}(X) = \mathbb{E}[X^2] - \mathbb{E}[X]^2$ its variance. We write $X \sim \chi$ to denote that X follows the distribution χ. If χ is a discrete distribution over some set S, then for any $s \in S$, we denote by $\chi(s)$ the probability that a sample from χ is equal to s. In particular, if $f \colon S \to \mathbb{R}$ is any function and $X \sim \chi$, we have:

$$\mathbb{E}[f(s)] = \sum_{s \in S} f(s) \cdot \chi(s).$$

Similarly, the statistical distance $\Delta(\chi, \chi')$ of two distributions χ, χ' over the set S is:

$$\Delta(\chi, \chi') = \frac{1}{2} \sum_{s \in S} |\chi(s) - \chi(s')|.$$

Let $\rho(x) = \exp(-\pi x^2)$ for all $x \in \mathbb{R}$. We define $\rho_{c,\sigma}(x) = \rho((x - c)/\sigma)$ the Gaussian function of parameters c, σ. For any subset $S \subset \mathbb{R}$ such that the sum converges, we let:

$$\rho_{c,\sigma}(S) = \sum_{s \in S} \rho_{c,\sigma}(s).$$

The discrete Gaussian distribution $D_{c,\sigma}$ centered at c and of parameter σ is the distribution on $\mathbb{Z}$ defined by

$$D_{c,\sigma}(x) = \frac{\rho_{c,\sigma}(x)}{\rho_{c,\sigma}(\mathbb{Z})} = \frac{\exp\left(-\pi(x - c)^2/\sigma^2\right)}{\rho_{c,\sigma}(\mathbb{Z})}$$

for all $x \in \mathbb{Z}$. We omit the subscript c in $\rho_{c,\sigma}$ and $D_{c,\sigma}$ when $c = 0$.

2.2 LWE over the Integers

It is possible to define a variant of the LWE problem "over the integers", i.e. without modular reduction. We call this problem ILWE ("integer-LWE"), and define it as follows. The problem arising from the scalar product leakage in the BLISS rejection sampling is essentially of that form.

Definition 2.1 (ILWE Distribution). *For any vector $\mathbf{s} \in \mathbb{Z}^n$ and any two probability distributions χ_a, χ_e over $\mathbb{Z}$, the ILWE distribution $\mathscr{D}_{\mathbf{s},\chi_a,\chi_e}$ associated with those parameters (which we will simply denote $\mathscr{D}_{\mathbf{s}}$ for short when χ_a, χ_e are clear) is the probability distribution over $\mathbb{Z}^n \times \mathbb{Z}$ defined as follows: samples from $\mathscr{D}_{\mathbf{s},\chi_a,\chi_e}$ are of the form*

$$(\mathbf{a}, b) = \left(\mathbf{a}, \langle \mathbf{a}, \mathbf{s} \rangle + e\right) \quad \text{with} \quad \mathbf{a} \leftarrow \chi_a^n \text{ and } e \leftarrow \chi_e.$$

Definition 2.2 (ILWE Problem). *The* ILWE *problem is the computational problem parametrized by* n, m, χ_a, χ_e *in which, given m samples $\{(\mathbf{a}_i, b_i)\}_{1 \leq i \leq m}$ from a distribution of the form $\mathscr{D}_{\mathbf{s}, \chi_a, \chi_e}$ for some $\mathbf{s} \in \mathbb{Z}^n$, one is asked to recover the vector $\mathbf{s}$.*

2.3   Subgaussian Probability Distributions

In this paper, the distributions χ_a, χ_e we will consider will usually be of mean zero and rapidly decreasing. More precisely, we will assume that those distributions are *subgaussian*. The notion of a subgaussian distribution was introduced by Kahane in [27], and can be defined as follows.

Definition 2.3. *A random variable X over $\mathbb{R}$ is said to be τ-subgaussian for some $\tau > 0$ if the following bound holds for all $s \in \mathbb{R}$:*

$$\mathbb{E}\big[\exp(sX)\big] \leq \exp\left(\frac{\tau^2 s^2}{2}\right). \tag{2.1}$$

A τ-subgaussian probability distribution is defined in the same way.

This section collects useful facts about subgaussian random variables; most of them are well-known, and presented mostly in the interest of a self-contained and consistent presentation (as definitions of related notions tend to vary slightly from one reference to the next).

For a subgaussian random variable X, there is a minimal τ such that X is τ-subgaussian. This τ is sometimes called the *subgaussian moment* of the random variable (or of its distribution).

As expressed in the next lemma, subgaussian distributions always have mean zero, and their variance is bounded by τ^2.

Lemma 2.4. *A τ-subgaussian random variable X satisfies:*

$$\mathbb{E}[X] = 0 \quad and \quad \mathbb{E}[X^2] \leq \tau^2.$$

Proof. For s around zero, we have:

$$\mathbb{E}[\exp(sX)] = 1 + s\mathbb{E}[X] + \frac{s^2}{2}\mathbb{E}[X^2] + o(s^2).$$

Since, on the other hand, $\exp(s^2\tau^2/2) = 1 + \frac{s^2}{2}\tau^2 + o(s^2)$, the result follows immediately from (2.1). $\qquad\square$

Many usual distributions over $\mathbb{Z}$ or $\mathbb{R}$ are subgaussian. This is in particular the case for Gaussian and discrete Gaussian distributions, as well as all *bounded* probability distributions with mean zero.

Lemma 2.5. *The following distributions are subgaussian.*

(i) *The centered normal distribution $\mathcal{N}(0, \sigma^2)$ is σ-subgaussian.*
(ii) *The centered discrete Gaussian distribution D_σ of parameter σ is $\frac{\sigma}{\sqrt{2\pi}}$-subgaussian for all $\sigma \geq 0.283$.*
(iii) *The uniform distribution $\mathcal{U}_\alpha$ over the integer interval $[-\alpha, \alpha] \cap \mathbb{Z}$ is $\frac{\alpha}{\sqrt{2}}$-subgaussian for $\alpha \geq 3$.*
(iv) *More generally, any distribution over $\mathbb{R}$ of mean zero and supported over a bounded interval $[a, b]$ is $\left(\frac{b-a}{2}\right)$-subgaussian.*

Moreover, in the cases (i)–(iii) above, the quotient $\tau \geq 1$ between the subgaussian moment and the standard deviation satisfies:

(i) $\tau = 1$;
(ii) $\tau < \sqrt{2}$ *assuming* $\sigma \geq 1.85$;
(iii) $\tau \leq \sqrt{3/2}$

respectively.

Proof. See the full version of this paper [10].   □

The main property of subgaussian distributions is that they satisfy a very strong tail bound.

Lemma 2.6. *Let X be a τ-subgaussian distribution. For all $t > 0$, we have*

$$\Pr[X > t] \leq \exp\left(-\frac{t^2}{2\tau^2}\right). \tag{2.2}$$

Proof. Fix $t > 0$. For all $s \in \mathbb{R}$ we have, by Markov's inequality:

$$\Pr[X > t] = \Pr[\exp(sX) > e^{st}] \leq \frac{\mathbb{E}[\exp(sX)]}{e^{st}}$$

since the exponential is positive. Using the fact that X is τ-subgaussian, we get:

$$\Pr[X > t] \leq \exp\left(\frac{s^2\tau^2}{2} - st\right)$$

and the right-hand side is minimal for $s = t/\tau^2$, which exactly gives (2.2).   □

The following result states that a linear combination of *independent* subgaussian random variables is again subgaussian.

Lemma 2.7. *Let $X_1, \ldots, X_n$ be independent random variables such that X_i is τ_i-subgaussian. For all $\mu_1, \ldots, \mu_n \in \mathbb{R}$, the random variable $X = \mu_1 X_1 + \cdots + \mu_n X_n$ is τ-subgaussian with:*

$$\tau^2 = \mu_1^2 \tau_1^2 + \cdots + \mu_n^2 \tau_n^2.$$

Proof. Since the X_i's are independent, we have, for all $s \in \mathbb{R}$:

$$\mathbb{E}[\exp(sX)] = \mathbb{E}\left[\exp\left(s(\mu_1 X_1 + \cdots + \mu_n X_n)\right)\right]$$

$$= \mathbb{E}\left[\exp(\mu_1 s X_1) \cdots \exp(\mu_n s X_n)\right] = \prod_{i=1}^{n} \mathbb{E}\left[\exp(\mu_i s X_i)\right].$$

Now, since X_i is τ_i-subgaussian, we have

$$\mathbb{E}\left[\exp(\mu_i s X_i)\right] \leq \exp\left(\frac{s^2(\mu_i \tau_i)^2}{2}\right)$$

for all i. Therefore:

$$\mathbb{E}[\exp(sX)] \leq \prod_{i=1}^{n} \exp\left(\frac{s^2(\mu_i \tau_i)^2}{2}\right) = \exp\left(\frac{s^2 \tau^2}{2}\right)$$

with $\tau^2 = \mu_1^2 \tau_1^2 + \cdots + \mu_n^2 \tau_n^2$ as required. $\qquad \square$

The previous result shows that the notion of a subgaussian random variable has a natural extension to higher dimensions.

Definition 2.8. *A random vector $\mathbf{x}$ in $\mathbb{R}^n$ is called a τ-subgaussian random vector if for all vectors $\mathbf{u} \in \mathbb{R}^n$ with $\|\mathbf{u}\|_2 = 1$, the inner product $\langle \mathbf{u}, \mathbf{x} \rangle$ is a τ-subgaussian random variable.*

It clearly follows from Lemma 2.7 that if $X_1, \ldots, X_n$ are independent τ-subgaussian random variables, then the random vector $\mathbf{x} = (X_1, \ldots, X_n)$ is τ-subgaussian. In particular, if χ is a τ-subgaussian distribution, then a random vector $\mathbf{x} \sim \chi^n$ is τ-subgaussian. A nice feature of subgaussian random vectors is that the image of such a random vector under any linear transformation is again subgaussian.

Lemma 2.9. *Let $\mathbf{x}$ be a τ-subgaussian random vector in $\mathbb{R}^n$, and $A \in \mathbb{R}^{m \times n}$. Then the random vector $\mathbf{y} = A\mathbf{x}$ is τ'-subgaussian, with $\tau' = \|A^T\|_2^{\mathrm{op}} \cdot \tau$.*

Proof. Fix a unit vector $\mathbf{u}_0 \in \mathbb{R}^m$. We want to show that the random variable $\langle \mathbf{u}_0, \mathbf{y} \rangle$ is τ'-subgaussian. To do so, first observe that:

$$\langle \mathbf{u}_0, \mathbf{y} \rangle = \langle A^T \mathbf{u}_0, \mathbf{x} \rangle = \mu \langle \mathbf{u}, \mathbf{x} \rangle$$

where $\mu = \|A^T \mathbf{u}_0\|_2$, and $\mathbf{u} = \frac{1}{\mu} A^T \mathbf{u}_0$ is a unit vector of $\mathbb{R}^n$. Since $\mathbf{x}$ is τ-subgaussian, we know that the inner product $\langle \mathbf{u}, \mathbf{x} \rangle$ is a τ-subgaussian random variable. As a result, by Lemma 2.7 in the trivial case of a single variable, we obtain that $\langle \mathbf{u}_0, \mathbf{y} \rangle = \mu \langle \mathbf{u}, \mathbf{x} \rangle$ is $(|\mu|\tau)$-subgaussian. But by definition of the operator norm, $|\mu| \leq \|A^T\|_2^{\mathrm{op}}$, and the result follows. $\qquad \square$

3   Information-Theoretic Analysis

A first natural question one can ask regarding the ILWE problem is how hard it is in an information-theoretic sense. In other words, given two vectors $\mathbf{s}, \mathbf{s}' \in \mathbb{Z}^n$, how close are the ILWE distributions $\mathscr{D}_\mathbf{s}, \mathscr{D}_{\mathbf{s}'}$ associated to $\mathbf{s}$ and $\mathbf{s}'$, or equivalently, how many samples do we need to distinguish between those distributions?

In this section, we show that, at least when the error distribution χ_e is either uniform or Gaussian, the statistical distance between $\mathscr{D}_\mathbf{s}$ and $\mathscr{D}_{\mathbf{s}'}$ admits a bound of the form $O\left(\frac{\sigma_a}{\sigma_e}\|\mathbf{s} - \mathbf{s}'\|\right)$. In particular, distinguishing between those distributions with constant success probability requires

$$\Omega\left(\frac{1}{\|\mathbf{s} - \mathbf{s}'\|^2}\left(\frac{\sigma_e}{\sigma_a}\right)^2\right)$$

samples, and the distributions are statistically indistinguishable when σ_e is superpolynomially larger than σ_a. To see this, we first give a relatively simple expression for the statistical distance.

Lemma 3.1. *The statistical distance between $\mathscr{D}_\mathbf{s}$ and $\mathscr{D}_{\mathbf{s}'}$ is given by:*

$$\Delta(\mathscr{D}_\mathbf{s}, \mathscr{D}_{\mathbf{s}'}) = \mathbb{E}\left[\Delta(\chi_e, \chi_e - \langle \mathbf{a}, \mathbf{s} - \mathbf{s}' \rangle)\right],$$

where $\chi_e + t$ denotes the translation of χ_e by the constant t, and the expectation is taken over $\mathbf{a} \leftarrow \chi_a^n$.

Proof. By definition of the statistical distance, we have:

$$\Delta(\mathscr{D}_\mathbf{s}, \mathscr{D}_{\mathbf{s}'}) = \frac{1}{2}\sum_{(\mathbf{a},b)\in\mathbb{Z}^{n+1}} \left|\Pr\left[(\mathbf{a}, b) \leftarrow \mathscr{D}_\mathbf{s}\right] - \Pr\left[(\mathbf{a}, b) \leftarrow \mathscr{D}_{\mathbf{s}'}\right]\right|.$$

Now to sample from $\mathscr{D}_\mathbf{s}$, one first samples $\mathbf{a}$ according to χ_a^n, independently sample e according to χ_e, and returns $(\mathbf{a}, b)$ with $b = \langle \mathbf{a}, \mathbf{s} \rangle + e$. Therefore:

$$\Pr\left[(\mathbf{a}, b) \leftarrow \mathscr{D}_\mathbf{s}\right] = \chi_a^n(\mathbf{a}) \cdot \chi_e(b - \langle \mathbf{a}, \mathbf{s} \rangle),$$

and similarly for $\mathscr{D}_{\mathbf{s}'}$. Thus, we can write:

$$\begin{aligned}
\Delta(\mathscr{D}_\mathbf{s}, \mathscr{D}_{\mathbf{s}'}) &= \frac{1}{2}\sum_{(\mathbf{a},b)\in\mathbb{Z}^{n+1}} \chi_a^n(\mathbf{a}) \cdot |\chi_e(b - \langle \mathbf{a}, \mathbf{s} \rangle) - \chi_e(b - \langle \mathbf{a}, \mathbf{s}' \rangle)| \\
&= \sum_{\mathbf{a}\in\mathbb{Z}^n} \chi_a^n(\mathbf{a}) \cdot \frac{1}{2}\sum_{b\in\mathbb{Z}} |\chi_e(b - \langle \mathbf{a}, \mathbf{s} \rangle) - \chi_e(b - \langle \mathbf{a}, \mathbf{s}' \rangle)| \\
&= \sum_{\mathbf{a}\in\mathbb{Z}^n} \chi_a^n(\mathbf{a}) \cdot \frac{1}{2}\sum_{x\in\mathbb{Z}} |\chi_e(x) - \chi_e(x + \langle \mathbf{a}, \mathbf{s} - \mathbf{s}' \rangle)|
\end{aligned}$$

where the last equality is obtained with the change of variables $x = b - \langle \mathbf{a}, \mathbf{s} \rangle$. We now observe that the expression

$$\frac{1}{2}\sum_{x\in\mathbb{Z}} |\chi_e(x) - \chi_e(x + \langle \mathbf{a}, \mathbf{s} - \mathbf{s}' \rangle)|$$

is exactly the statistical distance $\Delta(\chi_e, \chi_e - \langle \mathbf{a}, \mathbf{s} - \mathbf{s}' \rangle)$, and therefore we do obtain:

$$\Delta(\mathcal{D}_\mathbf{s}, \mathcal{D}_{\mathbf{s}'}) = \mathbb{E}\big[\Delta(\chi_e, \chi_e - \langle \mathbf{a}, \mathbf{s} - \mathbf{s}' \rangle)\big]$$

as required. □

Thus, we can bound the statistical distance $\Delta(\mathcal{D}_\mathbf{s}, \mathcal{D}_{\mathbf{s}'})$ using a bound on the statistical distance between χ_e and a translated distribution $\chi_e + t$. We provide such a bound when χ_e is either uniform in a centered integer interval, or a discrete Gaussian distribution.

Lemma 3.2. *Suppose that χ_e is either the uniform distribution $\mathcal{U}_\alpha$ in $[-\alpha, \alpha] \cap \mathbb{Z}$ for some positive integer α, or the centered discrete Gaussian distribution D_σ with parameter $\sigma \geq 1.60$. In either case, let $\sigma_e = \sqrt{\mathbb{E}[\chi_e^2]}$ be the standard deviation of χ_e. We then have the following bound for all $t \in \mathbb{Z}$:*

$$\Delta(\chi_e, \chi_e + t) \leq C \cdot |t|/\sigma_e$$

where $C = 1/\sqrt{12}$ in the uniform case and $C = 1/\sqrt{2}$ in the discrete Gaussian case.

Proof. See the full version of this paper [10]. □

Combining Lemmas 3.1 and 3.2, we obtain a bound of the form announced at the beginning of this section.

Theorem 3.3. *Suppose that χ_e is as in the statement of Lemma 3.2. Then, for any two vectors $\mathbf{s}, \mathbf{s}' \in \mathbb{Z}^n$, the statistical distance between $\mathcal{D}_\mathbf{s}$ and $\mathcal{D}_{\mathbf{s}'}$ is bounded as:*

$$\Delta(\mathcal{D}_\mathbf{s}, \mathcal{D}_{\mathbf{s}'}) \leq C \cdot \frac{\sigma_a}{\sigma_e} \|\mathbf{s} - \mathbf{s}'\|_2,$$

where C is the constant appearing in Lemma 3.2.

Proof. Lemma 3.1 gives:

$$\Delta(\mathcal{D}_\mathbf{s}, \mathcal{D}_{\mathbf{s}'}) = \mathbb{E}\big[\Delta(\chi_e, \chi_e - \langle \mathbf{a}, \mathbf{s} - \mathbf{s}' \rangle)\big],$$

and according to Lemma 3.2, the statistical distance on the right-hand side is bounded as:

$$\Delta(\chi_e, \chi_e + \langle \mathbf{a}, \mathbf{s} - \mathbf{s}' \rangle) \leq \frac{C}{\sigma_e} \cdot |\langle \mathbf{a}, \mathbf{s} - \mathbf{s}' \rangle|.$$

It follows that:

$$\Delta(\mathcal{D}_\mathbf{s}, \mathcal{D}_{\mathbf{s}'}) \leq \frac{C}{\sigma_e} \cdot \mathbb{E}\big[|\langle \mathbf{a}, \mathbf{s} - \mathbf{s}' \rangle|\big] \leq \frac{C}{\sigma_e} \sqrt{\mathbb{E}\big[\langle \mathbf{a}, \mathbf{s} - \mathbf{s}' \rangle^2\big]}$$

where the second inequality is a consequence of the Cauchy–Schwarz inequality. Now, for any $\mathbf{u} \in \mathbb{Z}^n$, we can write:

$$\mathbb{E}\big[\langle \mathbf{a}, \mathbf{u} \rangle^2\big] = \mathbb{E}\Big[\sum_{1 \leq i,j \leq n} u_i u_j a_i a_j\Big] = \sum_{1 \leq i,j \leq n} u_i u_j \mathbb{E}[a_i a_j] = \sigma_a^2 \|\mathbf{u}\|_2^2$$

since $\mathbb{E}[a_i a_j] = \sigma_a^2 \delta_{ij}$. As a result:

$$\Delta(\mathscr{D}_{\mathbf{s}}, \mathscr{D}_{\mathbf{s}'}) \leq C \cdot \frac{\sigma_a}{\sigma_e} \|\mathbf{s} - \mathbf{s}'\|_2$$

as required.   □

As discussed in the beginning of this section, this shows that distinguishing between $\mathscr{D}_{\mathbf{s}}$ and $\mathscr{D}_{\mathbf{s}'}$ requires $\Omega\left(\frac{1}{\|\mathbf{s}-\mathbf{s}'\|^2}\left(\frac{\sigma_e}{\sigma_a}\right)^2\right)$ samples. In particular, recovering $\mathbf{s}$ (which implies distinguishing $\mathscr{D}_{\mathbf{s}}$ from all $\mathscr{D}_{\mathbf{s}'}$ for $\mathbf{s}' \neq \mathbf{s}$) requires

$$m = \Omega\big((\sigma_e/\sigma_a)^2\big) \tag{3.1}$$

samples. In what follows, we will describe efficient algorithms that actually recover $\mathbf{s}$ from only slightly more samples than this lower bound.

Remark 3.4. Contrary to the results of the next section, which will apply to arbitrary subgaussian distributions, we cannot establish an analogue of Lemma 3.2 using only a bound on the tail of the distribution χ_e. For example, if χ_e is supported over $2\mathbb{Z}$, then $\Delta(\chi_e, \chi_e + t) = 1$ for any odd t! One would presumably need an assumption of the small-scale regularity of χ_e to extend the result.

4   Solving the ILWE Problem

We now turn to describing efficient algorithms to solve the ILWE problem. We are given m samples $(\mathbf{a}_i, b_i)$ from the ILWE distribution $\mathscr{D}_{\mathbf{s}}$, and try to recover $\mathbf{s} \in \mathbb{Z}^n$. Since $\mathbf{s}$ can a priori be any vector, we, of course, need at least n samples to recover it; indeed, even without any noise, fewer samples can at best reveal an affine subspace on which $\mathbf{s}$ lies, but not its actual value. We are thus interested in the regime when $m \geq n$.

The equation for $\mathbf{s}$ can then be written in matrix form:

$$\mathbf{b} = A\mathbf{s} + \mathbf{e} \tag{4.1}$$

where $A \in \mathbb{Z}^{m \times n}$ is distributed according to $\chi_a^{m \times n}$, $\mathbf{e} \in \mathbb{Z}^m$ is distributed as χ_e^m, $A, \mathbf{b}$ are known and $\mathbf{e}$ is unknown.

The idea to find $\mathbf{s}$ will be to use simple statistical inference techniques to find an approximate solution $\tilde{\mathbf{s}} \in \mathbb{R}^n$ of the noisy linear system (4.1) and to simply round that solution coefficient by coefficient to get a candidate $\lceil \tilde{\mathbf{s}} \rfloor = (\lceil \tilde{s}_1 \rfloor, \ldots, \lceil \tilde{s}_n \rfloor)$ for $\mathbf{s}$. If we can establish the bound:

$$\|\mathbf{s} - \tilde{\mathbf{s}}\|_\infty < 1/2 \tag{4.2}$$

or, a fortiori, the stronger bound $\|\mathbf{s} - \tilde{\mathbf{s}}\|_2 < 1/2$, then it follows that $\lceil \tilde{\mathbf{s}} \rfloor = \mathbf{s}$ and the ILWE problem is solved.

The main technique we propose to use is least squares regression. Under the mild assumption that both χ_a and χ_e are subgaussian distributions, we will show that the corresponding $\tilde{\mathbf{s}}$ satisfies the bound (4.2) in the linear programming setting with high probability when m is sufficiently large. Moreover, the number m of samples necessary to establish those bounds, and hence solve ILWE, is only a $\log n$ factor larger than the information-theoretic minimum given in (3.1) (with the additional constraint that m should be a constant factor larger than n, to ensure that A is invertible and has well-controlled singular values).

We also briefly discuss lattice reduction as well as compressed sensing techniques based on linear programming. We show that even an exact-CVP oracle cannot significantly improve upon the $\log n$ factor of the least squares method. On the other hand, if the secret is known to be very sparse, compressed sensing techniques can recover the secret even in cases when $m < n$, where the least squares method is not applicable.

4.1 Least Squares Method

The first approach we consider to obtain an estimator $\tilde{\mathbf{s}}$ of $\mathbf{s}$ is the linear, unconstrained least squares method: $\tilde{\mathbf{s}}$ is chosen as a vector in $\mathbb{R}^n$ minimizing the squared Euclidean norm $\|\mathbf{b} - A\tilde{\mathbf{s}}\|_2^2$. In particular, the gradient vanishes at $\tilde{\mathbf{s}}$, which means that $\tilde{\mathbf{s}}$ is simply a solution to the linear system:

$$A^T A \tilde{\mathbf{s}} = A^T \mathbf{b}.$$

As a result, we can compute $\tilde{\mathbf{s}}$ in polynomial time (at most $O(mn^2)$) and it is uniquely defined if and only if $A^T A$ is invertible.

It is intuitively clear that $A^T A$ should be invertible when m is large. Indeed, one can write that matrix as:

$$A^T A = \sum_{i=1}^m \mathbf{a}_i \mathbf{a}_i^T$$

where the $\mathbf{a}_i$'s are the independent identically distributed rows of A, so the law of large numbers shows that $\frac{1}{m} A^T A$ converges almost surely to $\mathbb{E}\left[\mathbf{a}\mathbf{a}^T\right]$ as $m \to +\infty$, where $\mathbf{a}$ is a random variable in $\mathbb{Z}^n$ sampled from χ_a^n. We have:

$$\mathbb{E}\left[(\mathbf{a}\mathbf{a}^T)_{ij}\right] = \mathbb{E}[a_i a_j] = \delta_{ij} \sigma_a^2,$$

and therefore we expect $A^T A$ to be close to $m\sigma_a^2 I_n$ for large m.

Making this heuristic argument rigorous is not entirely straightforward, however. Assuming some tail bounds on the distribution χ_a, concentration of measure results can be used to prove that, with high probability, the smallest eigenvalue $\lambda_{\min}(A^T A)$ is not much smaller than $m\sigma_a^2$ (and in particular $A^T A$ is invertible) for m sufficiently large, with a concrete bound on m. This type of bound on the smallest eigenvalue is exactly what we will need in the rest of our analysis.

More precisely, when χ_a is bounded, one can apply a form of the so-called Matrix Chernoff inequality, such as [47, Corollary 5.2]. However, we would prefer a result that applies to e.g. discrete Gaussian distributions as well, so we only assume a subgaussian tail bound for χ_a. Such result can be derived from the following lemma due to Hsu et al. [26, Lemma 2] (for simplicity, we specialize their statement to $\epsilon_0 = 1/4$ and to the case of jointly independent vectors).

Lemma 4.1. *Let χ be a τ-subgaussian distribution of variance 1 over $\mathbb{R}$, and consider m random vectors $\mathbf{x}_1, \ldots, \mathbf{x}_m$ in $\mathbb{R}^n$ sampled independently according to χ^m. For any $\delta \in (0, 1)$, we have:*

$$\Pr\left[\lambda_{\min}\left(\frac{1}{m}\sum_{i=1}^{m}\mathbf{x}_i\mathbf{x}_i^T\right) < 1 - \varepsilon(\delta, m) \text{ or } \lambda_{\max}\left(\frac{1}{m}\sum_{i=1}^{m}\mathbf{x}_i\mathbf{x}_i^T\right) > 1 + \varepsilon(\delta, m)\right] < \delta$$

where the error bound $\varepsilon(\delta, m)$ is given by:

$$\varepsilon(\delta, m) = 4\tau^2\left(\sqrt{\frac{8\log 9 \cdot n + 8\log(2/\delta)}{m}} + \frac{\log 9 \cdot n + \log(2/\delta)}{m}\right).$$

Using this lemma, one can indeed show that for χ_a subgaussian, $\lambda_{\min}(A^T A)$ is within an arbitrarily small factor of $m\sigma_a^2$ with probability $1 - 2^{-\eta}$ for $m = \Omega(n + \eta)$ (and similarly for $\lambda_{\max}$).

Theorem 4.2. *Suppose that χ_a is τ_a-subgaussian, and let $\tau = \tau_a/\sigma_a$. Let A be an $m \times n$ random matrix sampled from $\chi_a^{m \times n}$. There exist constants C_1, C_2 such that for all $\alpha \in (0, 1)$ and $\eta \geq 1$, if $m \geq (C_1 n + C_2 \eta) \cdot (\tau^4/\alpha^2)$ then*

$$\Pr\left[\lambda_{\min}(A^T A) < (1 - \alpha) \cdot m\sigma_a^2 \text{ or } \lambda_{\max}(A^T A) > (1 + \alpha) \cdot m\sigma_a^2\right] < 2^{-\eta}. \quad (4.3)$$

Furthermore, one can choose $C_1 = 2^8 \log 9$ and $C_2 = 2^9 \log 2$.

Proof. Let $\mathbf{a}_i$ be the i-th row of A, and $\mathbf{x}_i = \frac{1}{\sigma_a}\mathbf{a}_i$. Then the coefficients of $\mathbf{x}_i$ follow a τ-subgaussian distribution of variance 1, and every coefficient of any of the $\mathbf{x}_i$ is independent from all the others, so the $\mathbf{x}_i$'s satisfy the hypotheses of Lemma 4.1. Now:

$$\frac{1}{m}\sum_{i=1}^{m}\mathbf{x}_i\mathbf{x}_i^T = \frac{1}{m\sigma_a^2}\sum_{i=1}^{m}\mathbf{a}_i\mathbf{a}_i^T = \frac{1}{m\sigma_a^2}A^T A.$$

Therefore, Lemma 4.1 shows that:

$$\Pr\left[\lambda_{\min}(A^T A) < (1 - \varepsilon(2^{-\eta}, m)) \cdot m\sigma_a^2 \text{ or } \lambda_{\max}(A^T A) > (1 + \varepsilon(2^{-\eta}, m)) \cdot m\sigma_a^2\right] < 2^{-\eta}$$

with $\varepsilon(\delta, m)$ defined as above. Thus, to obtain (4.3), it suffices to take m such that $\varepsilon(2^{-\eta}, m) \leq \alpha$.

The value $\varepsilon(\delta, m)$ can be written as $4\tau^2 \cdot (\sqrt{8\rho} + \rho)$ where $\rho = (\log 9 \cdot n + \log(2/\delta))/m$. For the choice of m in the statement of the theorem, we necessarily have $\rho < 1$ since $\sigma_a \leq \tau_a$, and hence $\tau^4 \geq 1$. As a result, $\varepsilon(\delta, m) \leq 16\tau^2 \cdot \sqrt{\rho}$. Thus, to obtain the announced result, it suffices to choose:

$$m \geq \frac{2^8 \tau^4}{\alpha^2}\left(\log 9 \cdot n + \log 2^{1+\eta}\right),$$

which concludes the proof. $\qquad\qquad\qquad\qquad\qquad\qquad\qquad\qquad\qquad\qquad\qquad\qquad\qquad\qquad\square$

Remark 4.3. The ratio τ between the subgaussian moment τ_a of χ_a and the actual standard deviation σ_a is typically small (e.g. 1 for Gaussians, $\sqrt{3}$ for uniform distributions in a centered interval, etc.), so it isn't the important factor in the theorem.

The asymptotic bound saying that $m = \Omega((n + \eta)/\alpha^2)$ suffices to ensure that $\lambda_{\min}(A^T A)$ is within a factor α of the limit $m\sigma_a^2$ is a satisfactory result, but the implied constant in our theorem is admittedly rather large. This is an artifact of our reliance on Hsu et al.'s lemma. A more refined analysis is carried out by Litvak et al. in [32], and can in principle be used to reduce the constant C_1 in our theorem to $1 + o(1)$ for sufficiently large n. The authors omit concrete constants, however, and making [32, Theorem 3.1] explicit is nontrivial.

From now on, let us suppose that the assumptions of Theorem 4.2 are satisfied for some $\alpha \in (0, 1)$, and η equal to the "security parameter". In particular, $A^T A$ is invertible with overwhelming probability, and we can thus write:

$$\tilde{\mathbf{s}} = (A^T A)^{-1} \cdot A^T \mathbf{b}.$$

As discussed in the beginning of this section, we would like to bound the distance between the estimator $\tilde{\mathbf{s}}$ and the actual solution $\mathbf{s}$ of the ILWE problem in the infinity norm, so as to obtain an inequality of the form (4.2). Since by definition $\mathbf{b} = A\mathbf{s} + \mathbf{e}$, we have:

$$\tilde{\mathbf{s}} - \mathbf{s} = (A^T A)^{-1} \cdot A^T (A\mathbf{s} + \mathbf{e}) - \mathbf{s} = (A^T A)^{-1} \cdot A^T \mathbf{e} = M\mathbf{e},$$

where M is the matrix $(A^T A)^{-1} \cdot A^T$. Now suppose that all the coefficients of $\mathbf{e}$ are τ_e-subgaussian. Since they are also independent, the vector $\mathbf{e}$ is a τ_e-subgaussian random vector in the sense of Definition 2.8. Therefore, it follows from Lemma 2.9 that $\tilde{\mathbf{s}} - \mathbf{s} = M\mathbf{e}$ is $\tilde{\tau}$-subgaussian, where:

$$\tilde{\tau} = \|M^T\|_2^{\mathrm{op}} \cdot \tau_e = \tau_e \sqrt{\lambda_{\max}(MM^T)} = \tau_e \sqrt{\lambda_{\max}((A^T A)^{-1}A^T \cdot A(A^T A)^{-1})}$$
$$= \tau_e \sqrt{\lambda_{\max}((A^T A)^{-1})} = \frac{\tau_e}{\sqrt{\lambda_{\min}(A^T A)}}.$$

As a result, under the hypotheses of Theorem 4.2, $\tilde{\mathbf{s}} - \mathbf{s}$ is a $\frac{\tau_e}{\sigma_a \sqrt{(1-\alpha)m}}$-subgaussian random vector, except with probability at most $2^{-\eta}$ on the randomness of the matrix A.

This bound on the subgaussian moment can be used to derive a bound with high probability on the infinity norm as follows.

Lemma 4.4. *Let $\mathbf{v}$ be a τ-subgaussian random vector in $\mathbb{R}^n$. Then:*

$$\Pr\left[\|\mathbf{v}\|_\infty > t\right] \leq 2n \cdot \exp\left(-\frac{t^2}{2\tau^2}\right).$$

Proof. If we write $\mathbf{v} = (v_1, \ldots, v_n)$, we have $\|\mathbf{v}\|_\infty = \max(v_1, \ldots, v_n, -v_1, \ldots, -v_n)$. Therefore, the union bound shows that:

$$\Pr\left[\|\mathbf{v}\|_\infty > t\right] \leq \sum_{i=1}^n \Pr[v_i > t] + \Pr[-v_i > t]. \tag{4.4}$$

Now each of the random variables $v_1, \ldots, v_n, -v_1, \ldots, -v_n$ can be written as the scalar product of $\mathbf{v}$ with a unit vector of $\mathbb{R}^n$. Therefore, they are all τ-subgaussian. If X is one of them, the subgaussian tail bound of Lemma 2.6 shows that $\Pr[X > t] \leq \exp\left(-\frac{t^2}{2\tau^2}\right)$. Combined with (4.4), this gives the desired result. $\qquad\square$

This is all we need to establish a sufficient condition for the least squares approach to return the correct solution to the ILWE problem with good probability.

Theorem 4.5. *Suppose that χ_a is τ_a-subgaussian and χ_e is τ_e-subgaussian, and let $(A, \mathbf{b} = A\mathbf{s}+\mathbf{e})$ the data constructed from m samples of the ILWE distribution $\mathscr{D}_{\mathbf{s},\chi_a,\chi_e}$, for some $\mathbf{s} \in \mathbb{Z}^n$. There exist constants $C_1, C_2 > 0$ (the same as in the hypotheses of Theorem 4.2) such that for all $\eta \geq 1$, if:*

$$m \geq 4\frac{\tau_a^4}{\sigma_a^4}(C_1 n + C_2\eta) \quad \text{and} \quad m \geq 32\frac{\tau_e^2}{\sigma_a^2}\log(2n)$$

then the least squares estimator $\tilde{\mathbf{s}} = (A^TA)^{-1}A^T\mathbf{b}$ satisfies $\|\mathbf{s}-\tilde{\mathbf{s}}\|_\infty < 1/2$, and hence $\lceil\tilde{\mathbf{s}}\rfloor = \mathbf{s}$, with probability at least $1 - \frac{1}{2n} - 2^{-\eta}$.

Proof. Applying Theorem 4.2 with $\alpha = 1/2$ and the same constants C_1, C_2 as introduced in the statement of that theorem, we obtain that for $m \geq \frac{\tau_a^4}{\sigma_a^4}(4C_1 n + 4C_2\eta)$, we have

$$\Pr\left[\lambda_{\min}(A^TA) < m\sigma_a^2/2\right] < 2^{-\eta}. \tag{4.5}$$

Therefore, except with probability at most $2^{-\eta}$, we have $\lambda_{\min}(A^TA) \geq m\sigma_a^2/2$. We now assume that this condition is satisfied.

We have shown above that $\tilde{\mathbf{s}} - \mathbf{s}$ is a $\tilde{\tau}$-subgaussian random vector with $\tilde{\tau} = \tau_e/\sqrt{\lambda_{\min}(A^TA)}$. Applying Lemma 4.4 with $t = 1/2$, we therefore have:

$$\Pr\left[\|\tilde{\mathbf{s}} - \mathbf{s}\|_\infty > \frac{1}{2}\right] \leq 2n \cdot \exp\left(-\frac{1}{8\tilde{\tau}^2}\right) \leq 2n \cdot \exp\left(-\frac{\lambda_{\min}(A^TA)}{8\tau_e^2}\right)$$
$$\leq \exp\left(\log(2n) - \frac{m\sigma_a^2}{16\tau_e^2}\right).$$

Thus, if we assume that $m \geq 32\frac{\tau_e^2}{\sigma_a^2}\log(2n)$, it follows that:

$$\Pr\left[\|\tilde{\mathbf{s}} - \mathbf{s}\|_\infty > \frac{1}{2}\right] \leq \exp\left(\log(2n) - 2\log(2n)\right) = \frac{1}{2n}.$$

This concludes the proof. $\qquad\square$

In the typical case when τ_a and τ_e are no more than a constant factor larger than σ_a and σ_e, Theorem 4.5 with $\eta = \log(2n)$ says that there are constants C, C' such that whenever

$$m \geq Cn \qquad \text{and} \qquad m \geq C' \cdot \frac{\sigma_e^2}{\sigma_a^2} \log n \qquad (4.6)$$

one can solve the ILWE problem with m samples with probability at least $1 - 1/n$ by rounding the least squares estimator. The first condition ensures that $A^T A$ is invertible and to control its eigenvalues: a condition of that form is clearly unavoidable to have a well-defined least squares estimator. On the other hand, the second condition gives a lower bound of the form (3.1) on the required number of samples; we see that this bound is only a factor $\log n$ worse than the information-theoretic lower bound, which is quite satisfactory.

We also note that the cost of this approach is equal to the complexity of computing $(A^T A)^{-1} A^T \mathbf{b}$, hence at most $O(n^2 \cdot m)$. This is quite efficient in practice (see Sect. 6 for concrete timings). In practice, arithmetic operations can be implemented using standard floating point instructions, since the almost scalar nature of $A^T A$ ensures that the computations are numerically very stable.

4.2   An Exact-CVP Oracle Will Not Help

One can interpret this approach to solving ILWE by computing a least squares estimator and rounding it as an application of Babai's *rounding algorithm* for the closest vector problem (CVP).

More precisely, consider the sublattice $L = A^T A \cdot \mathbb{Z}^n$ of $\mathbb{Z}^n$, which is full-rank when $A^T A$ is invertible (i.e. m large enough). Then, the ILWE problem can be seen as the problem of recovering the lattice vector $\mathbf{v} = A^T A \mathbf{s} \in L$ given the close vector $A^T \mathbf{b} = \mathbf{v} + A^T \mathbf{e}$ (which is essentially an instance of bounded distance decoding in L). Closeness in this setting is best measured in terms of the infinity norm. Now, since for large m, the matrix $A^T A$ is almost scalar, and hence the corresponding lattice basis of L is somehow already reduced, one can try to solve this problem by applying a CVP algorithm like Babai rounding directly on this basis. It is easy to see that this approach is identical to our least squares approach.

One could ask whether applying another CVP algorithm such as Babai's *nearest plane* algorithm could allow solving the problem with asymptotically fewer samples (e.g. reduce the $\log n$ factor in (4.6)). The answer is no. In fact, a much stronger result holds: one cannot improve Condition (4.6) using that strategy even given access to an *exact*-CVP oracle for any p-norm, $p \in [2, \infty]$. Given such an oracle, the secret vector $\mathbf{v}$ can be recovered uniquely if and only if the vector of noise $A^T \mathbf{e}$ lies in a ball centered on $\mathbf{v}$ and of radius half the first minimum of L in the p-norm, $\lambda_1^{(p)}(L) = \min_{x \in L} \|x\|_p$, that is:

$$\|A^T \mathbf{e}\|_p \leq \frac{\lambda_1^{(p)}(L)}{2}. \qquad (4.7)$$

To take advantage of this condition, we need to get sufficiently precise estimates of both sides.

Estimation of the First Minimum. Due to the quasi-scalar shape of the matrix $A^T A$, one can estimate accurately the $\lambda_1^{(p)}(L)$. Indeed, $A^T A$ has a low orthogonality defect, so that it is in a sense already reduced. Hence, the shortest vector of this basis constitutes a very good approximation of the shortest vector of L.

Lemma 4.6. *Suppose that χ_a is τ_a-subgaussian, and let $\tau = \tau_a/\sigma_a$. Let A be an $m \times n$ random matrix sampled from $\chi_a^{m \times n}$. Let L be the lattice generated by the rows of the matrix $A^T A$. There exist constants C_1, C_2 (the same as in Theorem 4.2) such that for all $\alpha \in (0,1)$, $p \geq 2$ and $\eta \geq 1$, if $m \geq (C_1 n + C_2 \eta) \cdot (\tau^4/\alpha^2)$ then*

$$\Pr\left[\lambda_1^{(p)}(L)\left(A^T A\right) > m\sigma_a^2(1+\alpha)\right] \leq 2^{-\eta}. \tag{4.8}$$

Proof. Remark first that by norm equivalence in finite dimension, $\mathbf{x} \in \mathbb{R}^n$ we have $\|\mathbf{x}\|_p \leq \|\mathbf{x}\|_2$ so that $\lambda_1^{(p)}(L) \leq \lambda_1^{(2)}(L)$, this bound being actually sharp. Without loss of generality it then suffices to prove the result in 2-norm. From Theorem 4.2, we can assert that except with probability at most $2^{-\eta}$, $\|A^T A\|_2^{\text{op}} \leq m\sigma_a^2(1 + \alpha)$; for any integral vector $\mathbf{x} \in \mathbb{Z}^n$ we therefore have by definition of the operator norm:

$$\|A^T A \mathbf{x}\|_2 \leq m\sigma_a^2 \|\mathbf{x}\|_2 (1 + \alpha).$$

In particular, for any $\mathbf{x} \in \mathbb{Z}^n$ of unit 2-norm, $\lambda_1^{(2)}(L) \leq \|A^T A \mathbf{x}\|_2 \leq (1+\alpha)m\sigma_a^2$. $\square$

Estimation of the p-norm of $A^T \mathbf{e}$. Suppose that χ_e is a centered Gaussian distribution of standard deviation σ_e. The distribution of $A^T \mathbf{e}$ for $\mathbf{e} \sim \chi_e^n$ is then a Gaussian distribution of covariance matrix $\sigma_e^2 A^T A \approx m\sigma_a^2 \sigma_e^2 I_n$. We deal with the cases $p = \infty$ and $p \leq \infty$ separately.

Case $p < \infty$: The expected p-th power of the p-norm of $A^T \mathbf{e}$ satisfies:

$$\mathbb{E}\left[\|A^T \mathbf{e}\|_p^p\right] = n\mathbb{E}[x^p] = n(2m)^{p/2}\sigma_e^p \sigma_a^p \cdot \frac{\Gamma\left(\frac{p}{2} + \frac{1}{2}\right)}{\sqrt{\pi}},$$

where x is drawn under the centered gaussian distribution of variance $m\sigma_e^2 \sigma_a^2$, and Γ is classically the Euler's Gamma function. But by the partial converse of Jensen's inequality for norms of Stadje [44] we have:

$$\mathbb{E}\left[\|A^T \mathbf{e}\|_p^p\right] \leq 2^p \Gamma\left(\frac{p}{2} + \frac{1}{2}\right) \sqrt{\pi}^{(p-1)} \mathbb{E}\left[\|A^T \mathbf{e}\|_p\right]^p$$

so that:

$$n^{1/p}\sigma_e \sigma_a \sqrt{\frac{m}{2\pi}} \leq \mathbb{E}\left[\|A^T \mathbf{e}\|_p\right]$$

Case $p = \infty$: The estimate is obtained by the order statistic theory of Gaussian distributions (see e.g. [42]):

$$C_\infty \sigma_e \sigma_a \sqrt{m \log n} \leq \mathbb{E}\left[\|A^T\mathbf{e}\|_\infty\right],$$

where $C_\infty = \frac{3}{2}\left(1 - \frac{1}{e}\right) - \frac{1}{\sqrt{2\pi}} \approx 0.23$

Now that we have access to the expected value of the random variable $\|A^T\mathbf{e}\|_p$, we are going to use the concentration of its distribution around its expected value. Explicitly by the random version of Dvoretzky's theorem proven in [39], there exist absolute constants $K, c > 0$ such that for any $0 < \varepsilon < 1$:

$$\Pr\left[\left|\|A^T\mathbf{e}\| - \mathbb{E}\left[\|A^T\mathbf{e}\|_p\right]\right| > \varepsilon\mathbb{E}\left[\|A^T\mathbf{e}\|_p\right]\right] \leq K e^{-c\beta(n,p,\varepsilon)} \qquad (4.9)$$

with

$$\beta(m, p, \varepsilon) = \begin{cases} \varepsilon^2 n & \text{if } 1 < p \leq 2 \\ \max(\min(2^{-p}\varepsilon^2 n, (\varepsilon n)^{2/p}), \varepsilon p n^{2/p}) & \text{if } 2 < p \leq c_0 \log n \\ \varepsilon \log n & \text{if } p > c_0 \log n \end{cases}$$

for $0 < c_0 < 1$ a fixed absolute constant.

Summing Up. Taking $\varepsilon = 1/2$ in (4.9) ensures that, except with probability $K e^{-c\beta(n,p,1/2)}$,

$$\frac{1}{2}\mathbb{E}\left[\|A^T\mathbf{e}\|_p\right] \leq \|A^T\mathbf{e}\|_p \leq \frac{3}{2}\mathbb{E}\left[\|A^T\mathbf{e}\|_p\right]. \qquad (4.10)$$

For any fixed p, the probability can be made as small as desired for large enough n. We can therefore assume that (4.10) occurs with probability at least $1 - \delta$ for some small $\delta > 0$.

In that case, Condition (4.7) asserts that if $\mathbb{E}\left[\|A^T\mathbf{e}\|_p\right] > \lambda_1^{(p)}(L)$ then $\mathbf{s}$ can't be decoded uniquely in L. Now using the result of Lemma 4.6 with $\alpha = 1/2$ and the previous estimates, we know that this is the case when:

$$n^{1/p}\sigma_e\sigma_a\sqrt{\frac{m}{2\pi}} > \frac{3}{2}m\sigma_a^2, \qquad \text{that is, } m < \left(\frac{\sigma_e}{\sigma_a}\right)^2\frac{2n^{2/p}}{9\pi},$$

when $p < \infty$, and

$$0.23\sigma_e\sigma_a\sqrt{m \log n} > \frac{3}{2}m\sigma_a^2, \qquad \text{that is, } m < 0.02\left(\frac{\sigma_e}{\sigma_a}\right)^2 \log n,$$

otherwise. In both cases, it follows that we must have $m = \Omega((\sigma_e/\sigma_a)^2 \log n)$ for the CVP algorithm to output the correct secret with probability $> \delta$. Thus, this approach cannot improve upon the least squares bound 4.5 by more than a constant factor.

4.3 Sparse Secret and Compressed Sensing

Up until this point, we have supposed that the number m of samples we have access to is greater than the dimension n. Indeed, without additional information on the secret $\mathbf{s}$, this condition is necessary to get a well-defined solution to the ILWE problem *even without noise*.

Suppose however that the secret $\mathbf{s}$ is known to be *sparse*, with only a small number $S \ll n$ of non zero coefficients. Even if the positions of these non zero coefficients are not known, knowledge of the sparsity S may help in determining the secret, possibly even with fewer samples than the ambient dimension n with the sole additional knowledge of its sparsity (though of course more than S samples are necessary!). Such a recovery is made possible by compressed sensing techniques, epitomized by the results of Candes and Tao in [14]. The idea is once again to find an estimator $\tilde{\mathbf{s}}$ such that the infinity norm $\|\tilde{\mathbf{s}} - \mathbf{s}\|_\infty$ is small enough to fully recover the secret $\mathbf{s}$ from it. This can be done with the Dantzig selector introduced in [14], and efficiently computable as a solution $\tilde{\mathbf{s}} = (\tilde{s}_1, \ldots, \tilde{s}_n)$ of the following linear program with $2n$ unknowns $\tilde{s}_i, \tilde{u}_i, 1 \le i \le n$:

$$\min \sum_{i=1}^{n} u_i \quad \text{such that} \quad -u_i \le \tilde{s}_i \le u_i \quad \text{and} \tag{4.11}$$
$$-\sigma_e \sigma_a \sqrt{2m \log n} \le \left[A A^T (A^T \mathbf{b} - A^T A \tilde{\mathbf{s}}) \right]_i \le \sigma_e \sigma_a \sqrt{2m \log n}.$$

In the case when the distributions χ_e and χ_a are Gaussian distributions of respective standard deviations σ_e and σ_e, the quality of the output of the program defined by (4.11) is quantified as follows.

Theorem 4.7 (adapted from [14]). *Suppose $\mathbf{s} \in \mathbb{Z}^n$ is any S-sparse vector so that $\log(m\sigma_a^2/n)S \le m$ Then with large probability, $\tilde{\mathbf{s}}$ obeys the relation*

$$\|\tilde{\mathbf{s}} - \mathbf{s}\|_2^2 \le 2C_1^2 S \log n \left(\frac{\sigma_e}{\sqrt{m}\sigma_a} \right)^2 \tag{4.12}$$

for some constant $C_1 \approx 4$.

Hence as before, if $\|\tilde{\mathbf{s}} - \mathbf{s}\|_2^2 \le 1/4$, we have $\|\tilde{\mathbf{s}} - \mathbf{s}\|_\infty \le 1/2$ and one can then decode the coefficients of $\mathbf{s}$ by rounding $\tilde{\mathbf{s}}$. This is satisfied with high probability as soon as:

$$2C_1^2 \frac{S \log n}{m} \left(\frac{\sigma_e}{\sigma_a} \right)^2 \le \frac{1}{4}.$$

Since we aim at solving the ILWE problem in parsimonious sample setting, where $m < n$ we deduce that the compressed sensing methodology can be successfully applied when

$$S \le \frac{n}{8C_1^2 \log n} \left(\frac{\sigma_a}{\sigma_e} \right)^2. \tag{4.13}$$

Table 1. Maximum value of the ratio σ_e/σ_a to recover a S sparse secret in dimension n with the Dantzig selector

n \ (S/n)	0.1	0.3	0.5	0.7	0.9
128	16.2	9.4	7.3	6.1	5.4
256	15.2	8.8	6.8	5.7	5.0
512	14.3	8.3	6.4	5.4	4.8
1024	13.6	7.8	6.0	5.1	4.5
2048	13.0	7.5	5.8	4.9	4.3

Let us discuss the practicality of this approach with regards to the parameters of the ILWE problem. First of all, note that in order to make Condition (4.13) non-vacuous, one needs σ_e and σ_a to satisfy:

$$2C_1\sqrt{\frac{2\log n}{n}} \leq \frac{\sigma_a}{\sigma_e} \leq 2C_1\sqrt{2\log n},$$

where the lower bound follows from the fact that S is a positive integer, and the upper bound from the observation that the right-hand side of (4.13) must be smaller than n to be of any interest compared to the trivial bound $S \leq n$. Practically speaking, this means that this approach is only interesting when the ratio σ_e/σ_a is relatively small; concrete bounds are provided in Table 1 various sparsity levels and dimensions ranging from 128 to 2048.

We note that the required sparsity is much higher than proposed parameters for BLISS, for example. Moreover, the complexity of this linear programming based approach is worse than least squares regression. However, only this method is applicable when only $m < n$ samples are available.

5 Application to the Side-Channel Attack of BLISS

5.1 BLISS Signatures and Rejection Sampling Leakage

The BLISS signature scheme [17] is a lattice-based signature scheme based on the Ring-Learning With Error (RLWE) assumption. Its signing algorithm is recalled in Fig. 1.

The Rejection Sampling. The BLISS signature scheme follows the "Fiat–Shamir with aborts" paradigm of Lyubashevsky [35]. In particular, signature generation involves a *rejection sampling* step (Step 8 of function SIGN in Fig. 1)

```
1: function SIGN(μ, pk = v₁, sk = s = (s₁, s₂))
2:     y₁, y₂ ← D_σ^ñ
3:     u = ζ · v₁ · y₁ + y₂  mod 2q
4:     c ← H(⌈u⌋_d mod p, μ)
5:     choose a random bit b
6:     z₁ ← y₁ + (−1)^b s₁c
7:     z₂ ← y₂ + (−1)^b s₂c
8:     continue with probability 1/(M exp(−‖sc‖²/(2σ²)) cosh(⟨z, sc⟩/σ²)); other-
       wise restart
9:     z₂^† ← (⌈u⌋_d − ⌈u − z₂⌋_d)  mod p
10:    return (z₁, z₂^†, c)
```

Fig. 1. BLISS signing algorithm. The hash function H is modeled as a RO with values in the set of polynomials in $\mathcal{R}$ with 0/1-coefficient and Hamming weight κ. See [17] for details regarding notation like ζ, $\lceil \cdot \rfloor_d$ and p not discussed in this paper.

which is essential for security: in order to ensure that the distribution of signatures is independent of the secret key $s = (s_1, s_2)$, a signature candidate $\big(z = (z_1, z_2), c\big)$ should be kept with probability

$$1 \bigg/ \left(M \exp\left(- \frac{\|sc\|^2}{2\sigma^2} \right) \cosh\left(\frac{\langle z, sc \rangle}{\sigma^2} \right) \right).$$

Since it would be impractical to directly compute this expression involving transcendental functions with sufficient precision, all existing implementations of BLISS [18,41,45] rely instead on the iterated Bernoulli trials technique described in [17, Sect. 6]. A signature (z, c) is kept if the function calls SAMPLEBERNEXP($x_{\exp}$) and SAMPLEBERNCOSH($x_{\cosh}$) both return 1, where functions SAMPLEBERNEXP and SAMPLEBERNCOSH are described in Fig. 2 and the values $x_{\exp}, x_{\cosh}$ are given respectively by $x_{\exp} = \log M - \|sc\|^2$ and $x_{\cosh} = 2 \cdot \langle z, sc \rangle$.

Side-Channel Leakage of the Rejection Sampling. Based on their description in Fig. 2, it is clear that SAMPLEBERNEXP and SAMPLEBERNCOSH do not run in constant time. In fact, they iterate over the bits of their input, and part of the code is executed when the bit is 1 and skipped over when the bit is 0. As a result, as observed by Espitau et al. [19, Sect. 3], the inputs $x_{\exp}, x_{\cosh}$ of these functions can be read off directly on a trace of power consumption or electromagnetic emanations, in much the same way as naive square-and-multiply implementations of RSA leak the secret exponent via simple power analysis [28, Sect. 3.1]. As a result, side-channel analysis allows to reliably recover the squared norm $\|sc\|^2 = \|s_1 c\|^2 + \|s_2 c\|^2$ and the scalar product $\langle z, sc \rangle = \langle z_1, s_1 c \rangle + \langle z_2, s_2 c \rangle$ from generated signatures.

1: **function** SampleBernExp(x)	1: **function** SampleBernCosh(x)
2: **for** $i = 0$ to $\ell - 1$ **do**	2: **if** $x < 0$ **then** $x \leftarrow -x$
3: **if** $x_i = 1$ **then**	3: Sample $a \leftarrow \mathcal{B}_{\exp(-x/f)}$
4: Sample $a \leftarrow \mathcal{B}_{c_i}$	4: **if** $a = 1$ **then return** 1
5: **if** $a = 0$ **then return** 0	5: Sample $b \leftarrow \mathcal{B}_{1/2}$
6: **return** 1	6: **if** $b = 1$ **then restart**
	7: Sample $c \leftarrow \mathcal{B}_{\exp(-x/f)}$
	8: **if** $c = 1$ **then restart**
	9: **return** 0

Fig. 2. Sampling algorithms for the distributions $\mathcal{B}_{\exp(-x/2\sigma^2)}$ and $\mathcal{B}_{1/\cosh(x/\sigma^2)}$. The values $c_i = 2^i/f$ precomputed, and the x_i's are the bits in the binary expansion of $x = \sum_{i=0}^{\ell-1} 2^i x_i$. BLISS uses $x = K - \|\mathbf{sc}\|^2$ for the input to the exponential sampler, and $x = 2\langle \mathbf{z}, \mathbf{sc}\rangle$ for the input to the cosh sampler.

Espitau et al. show that the norm leakage can be leveraged in practice to recover the secret key from a little over $\bar{n}$ signature traces, where $\bar{n}$ is the extension degree of the ring $\mathcal{R}$ ($\bar{n} = 512$ for the most common parameters). However, the recovery technique is mathematically quite involved and computationally costly (it is based on the Howgrave-Graham–Szydlo solution to cyclotomic norm equations [25], and takes over a month of CPU time for typical parameters). More importantly, it has the major drawback of relying on the ability to factor this norm and thus only applying to "weak" signing keys satisfying a certain semismoothness condition (around 7% of BLISS secret keys).

It is natural to think that the scalar product leakage, which is linear rather than quadratic in the secret key, is a more attractive target to attack. And indeed, Espitau et al. point out that in a simplified version of BLISS where $\mathbf{z}_2$ is returned in full as part of signatures, it is very easy to recover the secret key from about $2\bar{n}$ side-channel traces using elementary linear algebra. However, in the actual BLISS scheme, the element $\mathbf{z}_2$ is returned in a compressed form $\mathbf{z}_2^\dagger$, so that the linear system arising from scalar product leakage is noisy. Solving this linear system amounts to solving a problem analogous to LWE [43] in dimension about $2\bar{n}$, which leads Espitau et al. to conclude that this approach is unlikely to be helpful. In doing so, however, they overlook a crucial difference between standard LWE and the problem that actually arises in this way, namely the *lack of modular reduction*.

5.2 Description of the Attack

As we have mentioned already, recovering the secret $\mathbf{s} \in \mathbb{Z}^{2\bar{n}} = \mathbb{Z}^n$ from the linear leakage $\langle \mathbf{z}, \mathbf{sc}\rangle$ essentially amounts to an instance of the ILWE problem. We now describe more precisely in what sense. To do so, we need to write this inner product in terms of the known ring elements $(\mathbf{c}, \mathbf{z}_1, \mathbf{z}_2^\dagger)$ that appear in the signature on the one hand, and unknown elements on the other hand. This can be done as follows:

$$\langle \mathbf{z}, \mathbf{sc} \rangle = \langle \mathbf{z}_1, \mathbf{s}_1\mathbf{c} \rangle + \langle \mathbf{z}_2, \mathbf{s}_2\mathbf{c} \rangle = \langle \mathbf{z}_1\mathbf{c}^*, \mathbf{s}_1 \rangle + \langle 2^d\mathbf{z}_2^\dagger, \mathbf{s}_2\mathbf{c} \rangle + \langle \mathbf{z}_2 - 2^d\mathbf{z}_2^\dagger, \mathbf{s}_2\mathbf{c} \rangle$$
$$= \langle \mathbf{z}_1\mathbf{c}^*, \mathbf{s}_1 \rangle + \langle 2^d\mathbf{z}_2^\dagger\mathbf{c}^*, \mathbf{s}_2 \rangle + e = \langle \mathbf{a}, \mathbf{s} \rangle + e,$$

where we let:

$$\mathbf{a} = (\mathbf{z}_1\mathbf{c}^*, 2^d\mathbf{z}_2^\dagger\mathbf{c}^*) \in \mathbb{Z}^{2\bar{n}} = \mathbb{Z}^n \quad \text{and} \quad e = \langle \mathbf{z}_2 - 2^d\mathbf{z}_2^\dagger, \mathbf{s}_2\mathbf{c} \rangle.$$

The vector $\mathbf{a}$ can be computed from the signature, and is therefore known to the side-channel attacker, whereas e is some unknown value. In these expressions, $\mathbf{c}^*$ is the conjugate of $\mathbf{c}$ with respect to the inner product (i.e. the matrix of multiplication by $\mathbf{c}$ in the polynomial basis of $\mathbb{Z}[x]/(x^{\bar{n}} + 1)$ is the transpose of that of $\mathbf{c}$).

Now the rejection sampling ensures that the coefficients of $\mathbf{z}_1$ are independent and distributed according to a discrete Gaussian D of standard deviation σ. On the other hand, $\mathbf{c}$ is a random vector with coefficients in $\{0,1\}$ and exactly κ non zero coefficients; thus, $\mathbf{c}^*$ has a similar shape possibly up to the sign of coefficients. It follows that the coefficients of $\mathbf{z}_1\mathbf{c}^*$ are all linear combinations with ± 1 coefficients of exactly κ independent samples from D and the signs clearly do not affect the resulting distribution.

Therefore, if we denote by χ_a the distribution $D^{*\kappa}$ obtained by summing κ independent samples from D, the coefficients of $\mathbf{z}_1\mathbf{c}^*$ follow χ_a. It is not exactly correct that $\mathbf{z}_1\mathbf{c}^*$ as a whole follows $\chi_a^{\bar{n}}$ (as its coefficients are not rigorously independent), but we will heuristically ignore that subtlety and pretend it does. Note that χ_a is a distribution of variance:

$$\sigma_a^2 = \mathrm{Var}\left(D^{*\kappa}\right) = \kappa \cdot \mathrm{Var}(D) = \kappa\sigma^2.$$

We have not precisely described how the BLISS signature compression works, but roughly speaking, $\mathbf{z}_2^\dagger$ is essentially obtained by keeping the $(\log q - d)$ most significant bits of $\mathbf{z}_2$, and therefore the distribution of $2^d\mathbf{z}_2^\dagger$ is close to that of $\mathbf{z}_2$. The distributions cannot coincide exactly, since all the coefficients of $2^d\mathbf{z}_2^\dagger$ are multiples of 2^d while this normally does not happen for $\mathbf{z}_2$, but the difference will not matter much for our purposes, and we will therefore heuristically assume that the entire vector $\mathbf{a}$ is distributed as χ_a^n.

We now turn our attention to the noise value e, which we write as $\langle \mathbf{w}, \mathbf{u} \rangle$ with $\mathbf{w} = \mathbf{z}_2 - 2^d\mathbf{z}_2^\dagger$ and $\mathbf{u} = \mathbf{s}_2\mathbf{c}$. Now, $\mathbf{w}$ is obtained as the difference between $\mathbf{z}_2$ and $2^d\mathbf{z}_2^\dagger$, where again the latter is roughly speaking obtained by zeroing out the d least significant bits of $\mathbf{z}_2$ in a centered way. We can therefore heuristically expect that the coefficients of $\mathbf{w}$ are distributed uniformly in $[-2^{d-1}, 2^{d-1}] \cap \mathbb{Z}$, i.e. $\mathbf{w} \sim \mathcal{U}_\alpha^n$ with $\alpha = 2^{d-1}$. In particular, these coefficients have variance $\alpha(\alpha + 1)/3 \approx 2^{2d}/12$.

As for $\mathbf{u}$, its coefficients are obtained as sums of κ coefficients of $\mathbf{s}_2$. Now $\mathbf{s}_2$ itself (ignoring the constant coefficient, which is shifted by 1) is obtained as a random vector with $\delta_1 \bar{n}$ coefficients equal to ± 2, $\delta_2 \bar{n}$ coefficients equal to ± 4 and all its other coefficients equal to zero. This is a somewhat complicated distribution to describe, but we do not make a large approximation by pretending that all the coefficients are sampled independently in the set $\{-4, -2, 0, 2, 4\}$ with probabilities $\delta_2/2, \delta_1/2, (1 - \delta_1 - \delta_2), \delta_1/2$ and $\delta_2/2$ respectively. Making that approximation, it follows that the coefficients of $\mathbf{u}$ have variance $\kappa \cdot (4\delta_1 + 16\delta_2)$.

Write $\mathbf{u} = (u_1, \ldots, u_{\bar{n}})$ and $\mathbf{w} = (w_1, \ldots, w_{\bar{n}})$. Under the heuristic approximations above, since $\mathbf{w}$ and $\mathbf{u}$ are independent and their coefficients have mean zero, the error e follows a certain bounded distribution χ_e of variance σ_e^2 given by:

$$\sigma_e^2 = \mathbb{E}[e^2] = \mathbb{E}\left[\left(\sum_{i=1}^{\bar{n}} w_i u_i\right)^2\right] = \mathbb{E}\left[\sum_{i,j} w_i w_j u_i u_j\right] = \mathbb{E}\left[\sum_{i=1}^{\bar{n}} w_i^2 u_i^2\right]$$

$$= \sum_{i=1}^{\bar{n}} \mathbb{E}[w_i^2] \cdot \mathbb{E}[u_i^2] = \bar{n} \cdot \mathrm{Var}\left(\mathscr{U}_\alpha\right) \cdot \kappa(4\delta_1 + 16\delta_2) \approx \frac{2^{2d}}{3}(\delta_1 + 4\delta_2)\bar{n}\kappa.$$

With these various approximations, recovering $\mathbf{s}$ from the leakage exactly becomes an ILWE problem with distributions χ_a and χ_e, where each side-channel trace provides a sample. It should therefore be feasible to recover the full secret key with least squares regression using $m = O\left((\sigma_e/\sigma_a)^2 \log n\right)$ traces.

5.3 Experimental Distributions

The description of the previous section made a number of heuristic approximations which we know cannot be precisely satisfied in practice. In order to validate those approximations nonetheless, we have carried out numerical simulations comparing in particular our estimates for the standard deviations σ_a and σ_e of the distributions of $\mathbf{a}$ and e with the standard deviations obtained from the actual rejection sampling leakage in BLISS.

These simulations were carried out in Python using the numpy package. We used 10000 ILWE samples arising from side channel leaks for each BLISS parameter set. Results are collected in Table 2; experimental values for σ_a are provided separately for the two halves $(\mathbf{a}_1, \mathbf{a}_2)$ of the vector $\mathbf{a}$, which we have seen are computed differently. As we can see, the experimental values match the heuristic estimates quite closely overall.

6   Numerical Simulations

In this section, we present simulation results for recovering ILWE secrets using linear regression, first for normal ILWE instances, and then for ILWE instances arising from BLISS side-channel leakage, as described in Sect. 5.2, leading to BLISS secret key recovery. These results are based on simulated leakage data

Table 2. Parameter estimation for ILWE instances arising from the side channel attack

	BLISS–0	BLISS–I	BLISS–II	BLISS–III	BLISS–IV
$n = 2\bar{n}$	512	1024	1024	1024	1024
σ_a (theory)	346	1031	513	1369	1692
σ_e (theory)	1553	49695	49695	38073	24535
$\sigma_{\mathbf{a}_1}$ (exp.)	347	1031	513	1370	1691
$\sigma_{\mathbf{a}_2}$ (exp.)	349	2009	1418	1782	1814
σ_e (exp.)	1532	42170	32319	38627	23926

rather than actual side-channel traces. However, we note that the leakage scenario for BLISS is essentially identical to the one described in [19] (namely, a SPA/SEMA setting where each trace reveals the exact value of a certain function of the secret key—in our case, the linear function given by the inner product), and was therefore experimentally validated in that paper.

6.1   Plain ILWE

Recall that the ILWE problem is parametrized by $n, m \in \mathbb{Z}$ and probability distributions χ_a and χ_e. Samples are computed as $\mathbf{b} = A\mathbf{s} + \mathbf{e}$, where $\mathbf{s} \in \mathbb{Z}^n$, $\mathbf{b} \in \mathbb{Z}^m$, $A \in \mathbb{Z}^{m \times n}$ with entries drawn from χ_a, and $e \in \mathbb{Z}^m$ with entries drawn from χ_e. Choosing χ_a and χ_e as discrete gaussian distributions with standard deviations σ_a and σ_e respectively, we investigated the number of samples, m required to recover ILWE secret vectors $\mathbf{s} \in \mathbb{Z}^n$ for various concrete values of n, σ_a and σ_e. We sampled sparse secret vectors $\mathbf{s}$ uniformly at random from the set of vectors with $\lceil 0.15n \rceil$ entries set to ± 1, $\lceil 0.15n \rceil$ entries set to ± 2, and the rest zero.

We present two types of experimental results for plain ILWE. In our first experiment, we began by estimating the number of samples m required to recover the secret perfectly with good probability, for different values of n, σ_a, and σ_e. Then, fixing m, we measured the probability of recovering $\mathbf{s}$ over the random choices of $\mathbf{s}$, A and e. Our results are displayed in Table 3.

In our second experiment, we investigated the distribution of the minimum value of m required to recover the secret perfectly, over the random choices of $\mathbf{s}$, A, and $\mathbf{e}$, when the linear regression method was run to completion. In other words, for fixed n, σ_a, and σ_e, we generated more and more samples until the secret could be perfectly recovered. Our results for $\sigma_e = 2000$ are plotted in Fig. 3. Additional results and some additional notes may be found in the full version of this paper [10]. Each figure plots the dimension n against the mean number of samples m required to recover the secret, for $\sigma_a = 100, 200$, and 500. Here, 'mean' refers to the interquartile mean number of samples. The error bars show the upper and lower quartiles for the number of samples required.

The results of our second experiment are consistent with the theoretical results given in Sect. 4.1. According to (4.6), we require

$$m \geq C' \cdot \frac{\sigma_e^2}{\sigma_a^2} \log n$$

samples in order to recover the secret correctly. The dimension n on the horizontal axis of each graph is plotted on a logarithmic scale. Therefore, theory predicts that we should observe a straight line, which the graphs confirm.

The gradient of the graph corresponds to the constant C' giving the number of samples required for secret-recovery in practice. Note that in this case, where χ_a and χ_e follow the discrete Gaussian distribution, Theorem 4.5 gives $C' = 32$ for a small failure probability of $\frac{1}{2n}$. However, in this experiment, we are likely to succeed much sooner, with a smaller number of samples. For example, in any particular trial, as soon as m is such that the failure probability is at least one half, we are likely to recover the secret. This explains why the gradient is much lower than given by Theorem 4.5. Computing the gradients of the lines of best fit and dividing by $(\sigma_e/\sigma_a)^2$ gives an estimate for the observed value of the constant C'. See the full version of this paper [10] for details.

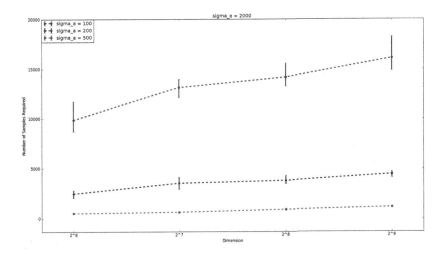

Fig. 3. Results for $\sigma_e = 2000$

6.2 BLISS Side-Channel Attack

Having obtained an instance of the ILWE problem from BLISS side-channel leakage as described in Sect. 5.2, we used linear regression to recover BLISS secret keys. We performed several trials. For each trial, we generated ILWE samples using side-channel leakage until we could recover the secret key. For BLISS–0, we

Table 3. Practical results of the experiments on ILWE

n	σ_a	σ_e	m	Success	n	σ_a	σ_e	m	Success
	100	1000	3300	6/10		400	5000	6000	5/10
	100	2000	11500	6/10	256	500	1000	450	7/10
	100	5000	65000	4/10		500	2000	950	8/10
	200	1000	900	5/10		500	5000	4200	5/10
	200	2000	4000	7/10					
	200	5000	17000	4/10		100	1000	5100	7/10
	300	1000	550	10/10		100	2000	16000	4/10
128	300	2000	1890	8/10		200	1000	1600	9/10
	300	5000	9000	7/10		200	2000	5200	7/10
	400	1000	350	8/10	512	300	1000	1000	8/10
	400	2000	800	5/10		300	2000	2600	8/10
	400	5000	5750	7/10		400	1000	900	10/10
	500	1000	350	10/10		400	2000	1500	4/10
	500	2000	700	6/10		500	1000	800	10/10
	500	5000	3300	4/10		500	2000	1250	8/10
	100	1000	5600	9/10		100	1000	5950	10/10
	100	2000	14500	6/10		100	2000	19000	5/10
	100	5000	95000	7/10		200	1000	2250	6/10
	200	1000	1300	6/10		200	2000	5900	6/10
256	200	2000	4700	8/10	1024	300	1000	1550	7/10
	200	5000	23000	6/10		300	2000	3350	6/10
	300	1000	900	9/10		400	1000	1350	9/10
	300	2000	1800	5/10		400	2000	2300	7/10
	300	5000	12000	8/10		500	1000	1500	10/10
	400	1000	550	10/10		500	2000	1900	8/10

simply used regression to recover the entire secret key. For BLISS–I and BLISS–II, we usually ran into memory issues before being able to successfully recover the entire secret key. However, we noticed that in practice, we could recover the first half of the secret key correctly using far fewer samples. Since the two halves of the secret key are related by the public key, this is sufficient to compute the entire secret key. Therefore, for BLISS–I and BLISS–II, we stopped generating samples as soon as the least-squares estimator correctly recovered the first half of the secret.

For these two different scenarios, we obtain the results displayed on Table 4, which gives information on the range, quartiles, and interquartile mean of the number of samples required. Typical timings for the side-channel attacks, using

Table 4. Number of samples required to recover the secret key (minimum, lower quartile, interquartile mean, upper quartile, maximum)

	# Trials	Min	LQ	IQM	UQ	Max
BLISS–0	12	1203	1254	1359.5	1515	1641
BLISS–I	12	14795	18648	20382.9	21789	24210
BLISS–II	8	19173	20447	22250.3	24482	29800

Table 5. Typical timings for secret key recovery

	Typical ILWE sample gen.	Typical time for regression
BLISS–0	≈2 min	≈5 s
BLISS–I	≈10 min	≈2 min
BLISS–II	≈10 min	≈2 min

SAGEMath, on a laptop with 2.60 GHz processor, are displayed in Table 5. Timings are in the orders of minutes and seconds. By comparison, some of the attacks from [19] may take hours, or even days, of CPU time.

Acknowledgments. This work has been supported in part by the European Union's H2020 Programme under grant agreement number ERC-669891.

References

1. Aggarwal, D., Joux, A., Prakash, A., Santha, M.: A new public-key cryptosystem via Mersenne numbers. Cryptology ePrint Archive, Report 2017/481 (2017). http://eprint.iacr.org/2017/481
2. Albrecht, M.R.: On dual lattice attacks against small-secret LWE and parameter choices in HElib and SEAL. In: Coron, J.-S., Nielsen, J.B. (eds.) EUROCRYPT 2017, part II. LNCS, vol. 10211, pp. 103–129. Springer, Cham (2017). https://doi.org/10.1007/978-3-319-56614-6_4
3. Albrecht, M.R., Faugère, J.-C., Fitzpatrick, R., Perret, L.: Lazy modulus switching for the BKW algorithm on LWE. In: Krawczyk, H. (ed.) PKC 2014. LNCS, vol. 8383, pp. 429–445. Springer, Heidelberg (2014). https://doi.org/10.1007/978-3-642-54631-0_25
4. Alwen, J., Krenn, S., Pietrzak, K., Wichs, D.: Learning with rounding, revisited. In: Canetti, R., Garay, J.A. (eds.) CRYPTO 2013, part I. LNCS, vol. 8042, pp. 57–74. Springer, Heidelberg (2013). https://doi.org/10.1007/978-3-642-40041-4_4
5. Applebaum, B., Cash, D., Peikert, C., Sahai, A.: Fast cryptographic primitives and circular-secure encryption based on hard learning problems. In: Halevi, S. (ed.) CRYPTO 2009. LNCS, vol. 5677, pp. 595–618. Springer, Heidelberg (2009). https://doi.org/10.1007/978-3-642-03356-8_35
6. Arora, S., Ge, R.: New algorithms for learning in presence of errors. In: Aceto, L., Henzinger, M., Sgall, J. (eds.) ICALP 2011, part I. LNCS, vol. 6755, pp. 403–415. Springer, Heidelberg (2011). https://doi.org/10.1007/978-3-642-22006-7_34

7. Bai, S., Galbraith, S.D.: Lattice decoding attacks on binary LWE. In: Susilo, W., Mu, Y. (eds.) ACISP 2014. LNCS, vol. 8544, pp. 322–337. Springer, Cham (2014). https://doi.org/10.1007/978-3-319-08344-5_21

8. Banerjee, A., Peikert, C., Rosen, A.: Pseudorandom functions and lattices. In: Pointcheval, D., Johansson, T. (eds.) EUROCRYPT 2012. LNCS, vol. 7237, pp. 719–737. Springer, Heidelberg (2012). https://doi.org/10.1007/978-3-642-29011-4_42

9. Bogdanov, A., Guo, S., Masny, D., Richelson, S., Rosen, A.: On the hardness of learning with rounding over small modulus. In: Kushilevitz, E., Malkin, T. (eds.) TCC 2016, part I. LNCS, vol. 9562, pp. 209–224. Springer, Heidelberg (2016). https://doi.org/10.1007/978-3-662-49096-9_9

10. Bootle, J., Delaplace, C., Espitau, T., Fouque, P.A., Tibouchi, M.: LWE without modular reduction and improved side-channel attacks against BLISS. Cryptology ePrint Archive, Report 2018/822 (2018). http://eprint.iacr.org/2018/822. Full version of this paper

11. Bootle, J., Tibouchi, M., Xagawa, K.: Cryptanalysis of compact-LWE. In: Smart, N.P. (ed.) CT-RSA 2018. LNCS, vol. 10808, pp. 80–97. Springer, Cham (2018). https://doi.org/10.1007/978-3-319-76953-0_5

12. Brakerski, Z., Langlois, A., Peikert, C., Regev, O., Stehlé, D.: Classical hardness of learning with errors. In: Boneh, D., Roughgarden, T., Feigenbaum, J. (eds.) 45th ACM STOC, pp. 575–584. ACM Press, June 2013

13. Groot Bruinderink, L., Hülsing, A., Lange, T., Yarom, Y.: Flush, gauss, and reload – a cache attack on the BLISS lattice-based signature scheme. In: Gierlichs, B., Poschmann, A.Y. (eds.) CHES 2016. LNCS, vol. 9813, pp. 323–345. Springer, Heidelberg (2016). https://doi.org/10.1007/978-3-662-53140-2_16

14. Candes, E., Tao, T.: The Dantzig selector: statistical estimation when p is much larger than n. Ann. Statist. **35**(6), 2313–2351 (2007)

15. Dodis, Y., Goldwasser, S., Tauman Kalai, Y., Peikert, C., Vaikuntanathan, V.: Public-key encryption schemes with auxiliary inputs. In: Micciancio, D. (ed.) TCC 2010. LNCS, vol. 5978, pp. 361–381. Springer, Heidelberg (2010). https://doi.org/10.1007/978-3-642-11799-2_22

16. Döttling, N., Müller-Quade, J.: Lossy codes and a new variant of the learning-with-errors problem. In: Johansson, T., Nguyen, P.Q. (eds.) EUROCRYPT 2013. LNCS, vol. 7881, pp. 18–34. Springer, Heidelberg (2013). https://doi.org/10.1007/978-3-642-38348-9_2

17. Ducas, L., Durmus, A., Lepoint, T., Lyubashevsky, V.: Lattice signatures and bimodal Gaussians. In: Canetti, R., Garay, J.A. (eds.) CRYPTO 2013, part I. LNCS, vol. 8042, pp. 40–56. Springer, Heidelberg (2013). https://doi.org/10.1007/978-3-642-40041-4_3

18. Ducas, L., Lepoint, T.: BLISS: Bimodal Lattice Signature Schemes, June 2013. http://bliss.di.ens.fr/bliss-06-13-2013.zip. (proof-of-concept implementation)

19. Espitau, T., Fouque, P.A., Gérard, B., Tibouchi, M.: Side-channel attacks on BLISS lattice-based signatures: exploiting branch tracing against strongSwan and electromagnetic emanations in microcontrollers. In: Thuraisingham, B.M., Evans, D., Malkin, T., Xu, D. (eds.) ACM CCS 2017, pp. 1857–1874. ACM Press, October/November 2017

20. Galbraith, S.D.: Space-efficient variants of cryptosystems based on learning with errors. On-Line (2012). https://www.math.auckland.ac.nz/~sgal018/compact-LWE.pdf

21. Goldwasser, S., Kalai, Y.T., Peikert, C., Vaikuntanathan, V.: Robustness of the learning with errors assumption. In: Yao, A.C.C. (ed.) ICS 2010, pp. 230–240. Tsinghua University Press, January 2010

22. Hamburg, M.: Post-Quantum Cryptography Proposal: ThreeBears (2017). https://csrc.nist.gov/projects/post-quantum-cryptography/round-1-submissions

23. Herold, G., May, A.: LP solutions of vectorial integer subset sums – cryptanalysis of galbraith's binary matrix LWE. In: Fehr, S. (ed.) PKC 2017, part I. LNCS, vol. 10174, pp. 3–15. Springer, Heidelberg (2017). https://doi.org/10.1007/978-3-662-54365-8_1

24. Hoffstein, J., Pipher, J., Whyte, W., Zhang, Z.: A signature scheme from learning with truncation. Cryptology ePrint Archive, Report 2017/995 (2017). http://eprint.iacr.org/2017/995

25. Howgrave-Graham, N., Szydlo, M.: A method to solve cyclotomic norm equations $f * \bar{f}$. In: Buell, D. (ed.) ANTS 2004. LNCS, vol. 3076, pp. 272–279. Springer, Heidelberg (2004). https://doi.org/10.1007/978-3-540-24847-7_20

26. Hsu, D., Kakade, S., Zhang, T.: Tail inequalities for sums of random matrices that depend on the intrinsic dimension. Electron. Commun. Probab. **17**(14), 1–13 (2012)

27. Kahane, J.P.: Propriétés locales des fonctions à séries de Fourier aléatoires. Stu. Math. **19**, 1–25 (1960)

28. Kocher, P.C., Jaffe, J., Jun, B., Rohatgi, P.: Introduction to differential power analysis. J. Cryptogr. Eng. **1**(1), 5–27 (2011)

29. Langlois, A., Stehlé, D.: Worst-case to average-case reductions for module lattices. Des. Codes Cryptogr. **75**(3), 565–599 (2015)

30. Li, H., Liu, R., Pan, Y., Xie, T.: Cryptanalysis of Compact-LWE submitted to NIST PQC project. Cryptology ePrint Archive, Report 2018/020 (2018). https://eprint.iacr.org/2018/020

31. Ling, S., Phan, D.H., Stehlé, D., Steinfeld, R.: Hardness of k-LWE and applications in traitor tracing. In: Garay, J.A., Gennaro, R. (eds.) CRYPTO 2014, part I. LNCS, vol. 8616, pp. 315–334. Springer, Heidelberg (2014). https://doi.org/10.1007/978-3-662-44371-2_18

32. Litvak, A., Pajor, A., Rudelson, M., Tomczak-Jaegermann, N.: Smallest singular value of random matrices and geometry of random polytopes. Adv. Math. **195**(2), 491–523 (2005)

33. Liu, D.: Compact-LWE for lightweight public key encryption and leveled IoT authentication. In: Pierpzyk, J., Suriadi, S. (eds.) ACISP 2017, part I. LNCS, vol. 10342, p. XVI. Springer, Heidelberg (2017)

34. Liu, D., Li, N., Kim, J., Nepal, S.: Compact-LWE (2017). https://csrc.nist.gov/projects/post-quantum-cryptography/round-1-submissions

35. Lyubashevsky, V.: Fiat-Shamir with aborts: applications to lattice and factoring-based signatures. In: Matsui, M. (ed.) ASIACRYPT 2009. LNCS, vol. 5912, pp. 598–616. Springer, Heidelberg (2009). https://doi.org/10.1007/978-3-642-10366-7_35

36. Lyubashevsky, V., Peikert, C., Regev, O.: On ideal lattices and learning with errors over rings. In: Gilbert, H. (ed.) EUROCRYPT 2010. LNCS, vol. 6110, pp. 1–23. Springer, Heidelberg (2010). https://doi.org/10.1007/978-3-642-13190-5_1

37. Lyubashevsky, V., Peikert, C., Regev, O.: A toolkit for ring-LWE cryptography. In: Johansson, T., Nguyen, P.Q. (eds.) EUROCRYPT 2013. LNCS, vol. 7881, pp. 35–54. Springer, Heidelberg (2013). https://doi.org/10.1007/978-3-642-38348-9_3

38. Micciancio, D., Peikert, C.: Hardness of SIS and LWE with small parameters. In: Canetti, R., Garay, J.A. (eds.) CRYPTO 2013, part I. LNCS, vol. 8042, pp. 21–39. Springer, Heidelberg (2013). https://doi.org/10.1007/978-3-642-40041-4_2

39. Paouris, G., Valettas, P., Zinn, J.: Random version of Dvoretzky's theorem in ℓ_p^n. Stoch. Process. Their Appl. **127**(10), 3187–3227 (2017)

40. Pessl, P., Bruinderink, L.G., Yarom, Y.: To BLISS-B or not to be: attacking strongSwan's implementation of post-quantum signatures. In: Thuraisingham, B.M., Evans, D., Malkin, T., Xu, D. (eds.) ACM CCS 2017, pp. 1843–1855. ACM Press, October/November 2017

41. Pöppelmann, T., Oder, T., Güneysu, T.: High-performance ideal lattice-based cryptography on 8-bit ATxmega microcontrollers. In: Lauter, K.E., Rodríguez-Henríquez, F. (eds.) LATINCRYPT 2015. LNCS, vol. 9230, pp. 346–365. Springer, Heidelberg (2015). https://doi.org/10.1007/978-3-319-22174-8_19

42. van Handel, R.: Probability in high dimension. Princeton University, Technical report (2014)

43. Regev, O.: On lattices, learning with errors, random linear codes, and cryptography. In: Gabow, H.N., Fagin, R. (eds.) 37th ACM STOC, pp. 84–93. ACM Press, May 2005

44. Stadje, W.: An inequality for ℓ_p-norms with respect to the multivariate normal distribution. J. Math. Anal. Appl. **102**(1), 149–155 (1984)

45. Steffen, A., et al.: strongSwan: the Open Source IPsec-Based VPN Solution (version 5.5.2), March 2017. https://www.strongswan.org/

46. Stehlé, D., Steinfeld, R., Tanaka, K., Xagawa, K.: Efficient public key encryption based on ideal lattices. In: Matsui, M. (ed.) ASIACRYPT 2009. LNCS, vol. 5912, pp. 617–635. Springer, Heidelberg (2009). https://doi.org/10.1007/978-3-642-10366-7_36

47. Tropp, J.A.: User-friendly tail bounds for sums of random matrices. Found. Comput. Math. **12**(4), 389–434 (2012)

48. Xiao, D., Yu, Y.: Cryptanalysis of Compact-LWE and related lightweight public key encryption. In: Security and Communication Networks 2018 (2018)

Quantum Symmetric Cryptanalysis

Quantum Algorithms for the k-xor Problem

Lorenzo Grassi[1]([✉]), María Naya-Plasencia[2], and André Schrottenloher[2]

[1] IAIK, Graz University of Technology, Graz, Austria
`lorenzo.grassi@iaik.tugraz.at`
[2] Inria, Paris, France
{`maria.naya_plasencia,andre.schrottenloher`}`@inria.fr`

Abstract. The k-xor (or generalized birthday) problem is a widely studied question with many applications in cryptography. It aims at finding k elements of n bits, drawn at random, such that the xor of all of them is 0. The algorithms proposed by Wagner more than fifteen years ago remain the best known classical algorithms for solving them, when disregarding logarithmic factors.

In this paper we study these problems in the quantum setting, when considering that the elements are created by querying a random function (or k random functions) $H : \{0,1\}^n \rightarrow \{0,1\}^n$. We consider two scenarios: in one we are able to use a limited amount of quantum memory (i.e. a number $O(n)$ of qubits, the same as the one needed by Grover's search algorithm), and in the other we consider that the algorithm can use an exponential amount of qubits. Our newly proposed algorithms are of general interest. In both settings, they provide the best known quantum time complexities.

In particular, we are able to considerately improve the 3-xor algorithm: with limited qubits, we reach a complexity considerably better than what is currently possible for quantum collision search. Furthermore, when having access to exponential amounts of quantum memory, we can take this complexity below $O(2^{n/3})$, the well-known lower bound of quantum collision search, clearly improving the best known quantum time complexity also in this setting.

We illustrate the importance of these results with some cryptographic applications.

Keywords: Quantum algorithms · Generalized birthday problem Quantum cryptanalysis · 3-xor · k-xor · List-merging algorithms Amplitude amplification

1 Introduction

In this paper we consider a generic algorithmic problem with numerous applications in cryptography: the k-xor problem. We study it when considering elements generated by a random function (or k random functions) $H : \{0,1\}^n \rightarrow \{0,1\}^n$,

© International Association for Cryptologic Research 2018
T. Peyrin and S. Galbraith (Eds.): ASIACRYPT 2018, LNCS 11272, pp. 527–559, 2018.
https://doi.org/10.1007/978-3-030-03326-2_18

and we provide the best known quantum algorithms for solving it, taking into account two possible scenarios regarding quantum memory.

In this section we first introduce the studied problem and provide some examples of applications. Second, we recall the scenario of post-quantum cryptography; and finally, we summarize our contributions, that propose the best known quantum time complexities and, in most of the cases, give considerable quantum speedups over the best classical algorithms.

1.1   Generalized Birthday Problem

The *birthday problem* is a widely used cryptanalytical tool.

Birthday Problem. *Given two lists L_1, L_2 of elements drawn at random from $\{0,1\}^n$, find $x_1 \in L_1$ and $x_2 \in L_2$ such that $x_1 \oplus x_2 = 0$ (where $\oplus$ denotes the bitwise exclusive-or, below xor, operation).*

A solution of this problem exists with high probability once $|L_1| \times |L_2| \gg 2^n$ holds, and it can be found in $\mathcal{O}(2^{n/2})$ time by e.g. sorting and then scanning L_1 and L_2.

The birthday problem has many applications, the most used one being perhaps the research of a collision for a hash function $h(\cdot) : \{0,1\}^* \rightarrow \{0,1\}^n$. The application to this case is simple. First of all, one constructs the list L_i by defining the j−th element of L_i as $h(i|j)$ (where $i|j$ denotes i concatenated with j). Assuming that h behaves like a random function, the lists contain values distributed uniformly and independently at random, so the premises of the problem statement will be met. Consequently, one may expect to find a solution to the corresponding problem, and a collision for the hash function, with $O(2^{n/2})$ work.

A generalization of this problem – called *generalized birthday problem* (GBP) or *k-list problem* – has been introduced by Wagner [54].

Generalized Birthday Problem. *Given k lists $L_1, L_2, \ldots, L_k$ of elements drawn at random from $\{0,1\}^n$, find $x_1 \in L_1$, $x_2 \in L_2$, $\ldots x_k \in L_k$ such that $x_1 \oplus x_2 \oplus \ldots \oplus x_k = \bigoplus_{i=1}^k x_i = 0$.*

Obviously, if $|L_1| \times |L_2| \times \ldots \times |L_k| \geq 2^n$, then with a high probability the solution exists. The real challenge, however, is to find it efficiently. When $k = 2^t$, Wagner's algorithm requires classical time and space $\mathcal{O}(2^{n/(t+1)})$.

Applications. Even if the GBP may not appear very natural at first sight, it has been applied successfully to the cryptanalysis of various systems. In the following, we recall the most relevant applications for symmetric cryptography.

XHASH and the (R)FSB SHA-3 Candidate. XHASH [8] has been introduced as a plausible candidate for an incremental collision-free hash function, defined as

$$H(x) := \bigoplus_{i=1}^k h(i|x_i),$$

where each x_i is a b-bit block and $h(\cdot) : \{0,1\}^l \rightarrow \{0,1\}^n$. The size $l = b + \log_2(k)$ is chosen to be large enough to accommodate the block plus an encoding of its index, by dint of making k larger than the number of blocks in any message to be hashed. As showed e.g. in [8,22], it is possible to set up an attack based on GBP that easily finds collisions in XHASH.

Among other designs, this construction appears in the "fast syndrome-based" hash function (R)FSB [4], a candidate of the SHA-3 competition. It uses a compression function in a Merkle-Damgård construction and it, is based on xoring the columns of a random binary matrix and has the advantages to be fast, incremental and parallelizable. In particular, this candidate can be rewritten as

$$FSB(H,m) := \bigoplus_{i=1}^{k} h_i(m_i).$$

As showed in [12,13,22,35,47], the previous GBP attack applies as well also in this case.

AdHash, NASD Incremental Hashing and the SWIFFT SHA-3 Candidate. One proposal for network-attached secure disks (NASD) [27] uses the following hash function for integrity purposes [8]:

$$H(x) := \sum_{i=1}^{k} h(i|x_i) \mod 2^{256},$$

where $x = \langle x_1, ..., x_k \rangle$ denotes a padded k-block message. By simple observation, inverting this hash corresponds to a k-sum problem over the additive group $(\mathbb{Z}/2^{256}\mathbb{Z}, +)$.

This may be viewed as a special case of a general incremental hashing construction proposed by Bellare *et al.* [8], where the sum is computed modulo m and where the modulus m is public and chosen randomly.

Among other designs, such a construction has been exploited in the SWIFFT hash function [42], one candidate of the SHA-3 competition. SWIFFT is a collection of provably secure hash functions, based on the fast Fourier transform (FFT). The SWIFFT function can be described as a simple algebraic expression over some polynomial ring $R = \mathbb{Z}_p[\alpha]/(\alpha^n + 1)$, that is

$$SWIFFT(a,x) = \sum_{i=1}^{m} f(x_i) \mod (\alpha^n + 1) = \sum_{i=1}^{m} (a_i \cdot x_i) \mod (\alpha^n + 1)$$

where the m fixed elements $a_1, ..., a_m \in R$ – called multipliers – specify the hash function, and each x_i is an element of R. Examples of attacks on the SWIFFT hash function based on the k-sum problem over the additive group $(\mathbb{Z}/2^{256}\mathbb{Z}, +)$ are given in [5,35,47].

The PCIHF Hash. Another hash construction that can be attacked using a similar strategy is the PCIHF hash function [28], proposed for incremental hashing and defined as

$$H(x) := \sum_{i=1}^{k} SHA(x_i|x_{i+1}) \mod 2^{160} + 1.$$

With respect to the previous case, the main difference is that each x_i affects two terms. To overcome this problem and apply an attack based on the GBP, it is sufficient to choose (and fix) $x_{2j} = 0$ for each j. In this case, the hash computations takes the form

$$H(x) := \sum_{j=1}^{\lfloor (k+1)/2 \rfloor} h(x_{2j-1}) \mod 2^{160} + 1 \text{ where } h(x) = SHA(x|0) + SHA(0|x).$$

CAESAR Candidates and the 3-xor Problem. The GBP has been as well applied to the cryptanalysis of authenticated encryption schemes proposed at the ongoing CAESAR competition [18]. To process the final incomplete blocks of messages, some of these schemes use the XLS construction proposed by Ristenpart and Rogaway [49].

Even if XLS was initially proven secure, Nandi [44] pointed out flaws in the security proof and showed a very simple attack that requires three queries to break the construction. Actually, the CAESAR candidates that rely on XLS do not allow this trivial attack as the required decryption queries are not permitted by the schemes. A possible way to overcome this limitation has been proposed by Nandi in [44], whose forgery attack requires only encryption queries. As a result, it is possible the design flaw of XLS can be reduced to the 3-xor problem.

The CAESAR schemes based on XLS are – the COPA modes of – the finalist Deoxys [23], Joltik [32], KIASU [33] and SHELL [55]. As a result, any 3-xor algorithm that goes below the birthday bound results in a slight weakness of some of these candidates. We refer to [45,48] for concrete examples of attacks.

Fast Correlation Attacks. Finally, the k-xor problem (especially for $k \geq 4$) is interesting for searching parity check relations in *fast correlation attacks* [21,51, 52], whose main targets are *synchronous stream ciphers*.

A synchronous stream cipher is a stream cipher where the ciphertext is produced by bitwise adding the plaintext bits to a stream of bits called the keystream, which is independent of the plaintext, only produced from the secret key and the initialization vector. A large number of stream ciphers use Linear Feedback Shift Registers (LFSR) as building blocks, the initial state of these LFSRs being related to the secret key and to the initialization vector. In nonlinear combination generators, the keystream bits are then produced by combining the outputs of these LFSRs through a nonlinear boolean function. Examples – among many others – of stream ciphers based on the previous construction are the hardware oriented finalists of the eSTREAM project [24], e.g. Grain-v0 [31].

A fast correlation attack targets nonlinear combination keystream generators. In particular, it requires the existence of linear correlations between LFSR internal stages and the nonlinear function output. GBP can be used to find such correlations – which is the hardest part of the job.

Remark. Though the GBP could be defined with many operations other than XOR, like modular additions (the k-sum problem then), and the algorithms proposed by Wagner would still apply, *in this paper we concentrate for the sake of simplicity, on solving the k-xorproblem*, i.e. the case of having a XOR operation. In general, our algorithms can be easily adapted to other settings.

1.2   Cryptography in the Quantum World

Post-quantum cryptography (or quantum-resistant cryptography) is a whole new line of research that aims at developing new cryptographic primitives that would (hopefully) withstand attackers equipped with quantum computers. It is now a well-known fact that the existence of sufficiently large quantum computers would severely impact the security of many cryptographic schemes in use today. In particular, the seminal work of Shor [50] showed that such computers would allow to factor numbers and compute discrete logarithms in abelian groups in polynomial time. As almost all public key schemes currently in use are build upon the assumption that those problems are intractable, the advent of quantum computers has motivated the rise of quantum-resistant public-key cryptography.

Post-quantum Symmetric Cryptography. At first sight, the situation seems less critical for symmetric primitives: Grover's algorithm [54] for searching in an unstructured database finds a marked element among 2^n in time $O(2^{n/2})$, providing a quadratic speedup compared to the classical exhaustive search, essentially optimal. Hence doubling the key length of block ciphers seems sufficient to counter that attack, and achieve the same security against quantum attackers.

However, recent works have shown that Grover's algorithm might *not* be the only threat for symmetric cryptography. One of the most relevant works is the one by Kuwakado and Morii [36,37], who first showed that the Even-Mansour construction [25] could be broken in polynomial time in the quantum CPA setting. Briefly, the Even-Mansour construction consists of a public permutation P on n bits and of two secret keys k_1 and k_2 that are used as pre- (resp. post-) whitening keys for the encryption $Enc_{EM}(m) := k_2 \oplus P(m \oplus k_2)$ of some message m. The main idea of [36,37] was to consider the function

$$f(x) := Enc_{EM}(x) \oplus P(x) = P(x \oplus k_1) \oplus k_2 \oplus P(x).$$

Since such a function has period k_1, it is possible to exploit Simon's quantum algorithm [15,53] to compute the (unknown) period in polynomial time.

Many other works have since appeared in the literature – such as attacks on symmetric cryptosystems based on quantum period finding [34], a quantum attack of the FX-construction [38],... – showing that the post-quantum security of some symmetric primitives, depending on the quantum adversary model, could fall largely below the limit provided by the Grover's algorithm.

As we are trying to build quantum-safe primitives, understanding and improving quantum algorithms, as well as designing new quantum attacks is of main importance: only this way can we know what are the needs in order to resist to the mentioned attacks.

1.3   Our Contributions

How can we solve the k-xor problem in the quantum setting? We answer this question by proposing new quantum algorithms. We consider two different settings, of separate interest: *(1st)* the case in which the adversary has access to a big amount of quantum memory and *(2nd)* the case in which she has access to small quantum memory, say $O(n)$. How one should treat classical vs. quantum memory is an open problem (e.g. can quantum memory become as cheap as classical memory?) that we do not attempt to fix here. Instead, we consider separately the two cases and take both *classical* and *quantum memory* into account in the cost of our algorithms.

About the 2-xor problem, Brassard *et al.* [17] provide a quantum algorithm that requires $O(2^{n/3})$ time and $O(2^{n/3})$. When "only" $O(n)$ qubits of memory are allowed, Grover's algorithm provides a solution in time $O(2^{n/2})$. Chailloux *et al.* [19] showed that the problem can be solved in quantum time $O(2^{2n/5})$ and using $O(2^{n/5})$ classical memory.

While the quantum *query* complexity of the k-xor problem is well-known, and can be attained by a modification of the algorithm in [3], there has been - to the best of our knowledge - no previous attempt at systematic time-efficient quantum algorithms (apart from the 2-xor case above).

Parallelized Algorithms. While the k-xor algorithms using $O(n)$ quantum memory that we develop are first intended to be used by "small" quantum computers, we further remark that they can be efficiently parallelized. Even with the most restrictive (and debatable) benchmark on "total cost" (which counts together the number of processors and the memory consumption, and multiplies this "hardware cost" by the time complexity), we show that our parallelized 3-xor algorithm reaches below the classical product $O(2^{n/2})$. We conclude that it attains a range of effectiveness unreached by all collision search algorithm previously known.

Our Results. In this paper, we present the *first* analysis of the k-xor problem in the quantum world for generic $k \geq 3$ *with competitive quantum time* with respect to both algorithms in the classical and in the quantum setting present in the literature. Our results – compared to others in the literature – are provided in Table 1.

Linear – Quantum Memory. For the case in which the adversary can use only $O(n)$ quantum memory, we propose solutions with better time complexity than

Table 1. Complexity of k-xor quantum algorithms (without logarithmic factors). Our results are in bold. When referring to Ambainis' work [3], we hint at our own quantum time complexity analysis from Sect. 3.

k (collision)	Quantum time	Superposition queries	Quantum memory	Classical memory	Reference
2	$2^{n/2}$	$2^{n/2}$	$O(n)$	-	[29]
2	$2^{n/3}$	$2^{n/3}$	$2^{n/3}$	-	[17]
2	$2^{2n/5}$	$2^{2n/5}$	$O(n)$	$2^{n/5}$	[19]
3	$\mathbf{2^{5n/14}}$	$\mathbf{2^{5n/14}}$	$\mathbf{O(n)}$	$\mathbf{2^{n/7}}$	**Theorem 1**
3	$2^{n/2}$	$2^{n/4}$	$2^{n/4}$	-	[3]
3	$\mathbf{2^{3n/10}}$	$\mathbf{2^{3n/10}}$	$\mathbf{2^{n/5}}$	-	**Theorem 2**
4	$\mathbf{2^{n/3}}$	$\mathbf{2^{n/3}}$	$\mathbf{O(n)}$	$\mathbf{2^{n/9}}$	**Theorem 1**
4	$2^{n/2}$	$2^{n/5}$	$2^{3n/10}$	-	[3]
4	$\mathbf{2^{n/4}}$	$\mathbf{2^{n/4}}$	$\mathbf{2^{n/4}}$	-	**Theorem 4**
5	$\mathbf{2^{7n/22}}$	$\mathbf{2^{7n/22}}$	$\mathbf{O(n)}$	$\mathbf{2^{n/11}}$	**Theorem 1**
5	$2^{n/2}$	$2^{n/6}$	$2^{1/3}$	-	[3]
5	$\mathbf{2^{n/4}}$	$\mathbf{2^{n/4}}$	$\mathbf{2^{n/4}}$	-	**Theorem 4**
6	$\mathbf{2^{4n/13}}$	$\mathbf{2^{4n/13}}$	$\mathbf{O(n)}$	$\mathbf{2^{n/13}}$	**Theorem 1**
6	$2^{n/2}$	$2^{n/7}$	$2^{5n/14}$	-	[3]
6	$\mathbf{2^{n/4}}$	$\mathbf{2^{n/4}}$	$\mathbf{2^{n/4}}$	-	**Theorem 4**
7	$\mathbf{2^{3n/10}}$	$\mathbf{2^{3n/10}}$	$\mathbf{O(n)}$	$\mathbf{2^{n/15}}$	**Theorem 1**
7	$2^{n/2}$	$2^{n/8}$	$2^{3n/8}$	-	[3]
7	$\mathbf{2^{n/4}}$	$\mathbf{2^{n/4}}$	$\mathbf{2^{n/4}}$	-	**Theorem 4**
$k \geq 8$	$2^{n/2}$	$2^{n/(k+1)}$	$2^{\frac{n(k+1)}{2(k+1)}}$	-	[3]
$\mathbf{k \geq 8}$	$\mathbf{2^{n/(2+\lfloor \log_2(k) \rfloor)}}$	$\mathbf{2^{n/(2+\lfloor \log_2(k) \rfloor)}}$	$\mathbf{2^{n/(2+\lfloor \log_2(k) \rfloor)}}$	-	**Theorem 4**

classical algorithms up to $k < 8$. We use building blocks from [19] (initially used for collision search) and ideas from [46], inspired for instance from the *parallel matching techniques*.

Exponential – Quantum Memory. When the adversary might use big amounts quantum memory, we propose a strategy that improves k-xor problems for all $k \geq 3$. For $k \geq 4$, we use the well-known quantum walk framework. Our attack requires time $O(2^{n/(2+\lfloor \log_2(k) \rfloor)})$ and memory $O(2^{n/(2+\lfloor \log_2(k) \rfloor)})$, giving an exponential quantum speedup over Wagner's algorithm. For the 3-xor problem, we specially design an algorithm with time $O(2^{3n/10})$ and $O(2^{n/5})$ quantum memory.

We highlight that, in the two cases above, the 3-xor algorithm has an exponential acceleration over collision search, which was not the case classically.

Organization. In the next section, we detail some basic notions of quantum computing and building blocks for our new algorithms. In Sect. 3, we recall the algorithms present in the literature to solve the k-xor problem both in the classical and in the quantum setting. New quantum algorithms for the 3-xor problem – both for the linear and the exponential quantum memory – are proposed in Sect. 4, while in Sect. 5 we describe algorithms for the k-xor problem for $k \geq 4$. We emphasize again that our goal is to set up algorithms with optimal time and memory complexities (rather than query complexity). We give insights on *parallelization* in Sect. 6. We conclude in Sect. 7 with implications of our results and some open problems for future research.

2   Preliminaries

In this section, we recall some definitions and simple quantum algorithmic techniques that will be used throughout the paper. We stress that most of our algorithms, and the design principles thereof, can be understood with only some basic notions of quantum computing, which we provide below.

2.1   Quantum Algorithms

For a comprehensive introduction into quantum algorithms, we suggest the textbooks of Mermin [41] and Lipton, Regan [39].

Quantum Circuit Model. We only work in the standard quantum circuit model. A quantum circuit is an abstract representation of a quantum algorithm running on a universal quantum computer. Given a number of qubits, put in an arbitrary initial state (say $|0\rangle$), we apply a succession of quantum gates, analog to classical boolean gates. After, the state of the qubits is measured. The final measurement should contain the result of the algorithm. The quantum computing literature also often considers that a quantum algorithm can run in a number of successive steps, which we will do below. The sequence of gates of a step can depend on the results of the previous measurements.

Superposition Oracles. When solving k-xor instances, if the elements in the lists are produced by a random function H (or multiple random functions) – which we safely assume below, then instead of mere *classical query access* to H, we require access to a superposition oracle:

$$O_H \ : |x\rangle\,|0\rangle \rightarrow |x\rangle\,|H(x)\rangle$$

which, as a linear operator, acts on superposition of states:

$$O_H \ : \left(\sum \alpha_i\,|x_i\rangle\right)|0\rangle \rightarrow \sum \alpha_i\,|x_i\rangle\,|H(x_i)\rangle \ .$$

This implies that H has been implemented as a quantum circuit.

Quantum Complexities. We adopt the following usual definitions of complexities:

- The quantum *query complexity* is the number of superposition oracle calls performed.
- The *time complexity* is the gate count of the quantum circuit. In all algorithms in this paper, it will turn out to be equal to the circuit depth, up to a logarithmic factor.
- The *memory complexity* is the number of qubits (including ancillas) on which it runs. Our memory complexities hide the constant overhead induced by running an oracle O_H.

Conventions. Hereafter, we count oracle queries and n-qubit register operations such as comparisons between n-bit numbers as a single time unit $O(1)$, in order to make the complexities more readable. We use the notation $\widetilde{O}$ when the time or memory complexity contains additional factors due to the management of quantum data structures, since the details of such implementations remain out of the scope of our work.

2.2   Grover's Algorithm and Amplitude Amplification

Alongside Shor's, Grover's algorithm [29] is one of the most widely known quantum algorithms. While a complete description - for which we refer to the quantum computing literature - would be outside the scope of this work, we recall that this algorithm speeds up quadratically exhaustive search.

More precisely, given a search space, e.g. $\{0,1\}^n$, and a function f : $\{0,1\}^n \rightarrow \{0,1\}$ for which there are 2^t preimages of 1, such a preimage can be found in quantum time $O(2^{(n-t)/2})$, assuming that a superposition oracle O_f can be efficiently implemented. Grover's algorithm first constructs the uniform superposition over the whole search space, then repeatedly applies an operator ($O(2^{(n-t)/2})$ times) which moves the current state towards the superposition of all preimages of 1. There are some errors, which can in turn be corrected if the exact number of preimages is known. Such errors will not impact our algorithms below.

Amplitude Amplification [16] is a generalization of Grover's algorithm where the search space has some structure. If *(1st)* there are 2^t solutions among a search space of size 2^n, *(2nd)* this search space is constructed using a quantum algorithm $\mathcal{A}$ and *(3rd)* the test uses the oracle O_f, then Amplitude Amplification returns (up to some error) the superposition of all preimages of 1 in time:

$$c \cdot 2^{(n-t)/2} \left(|\mathcal{A}| + |O_f| \right)$$

where c is a constant, and $|\mathcal{A}|$ and $|O_f|$ are the respective quantum time complexities of $\mathcal{A}$ and O_f.

More precisely, the procedure starts in an initial state $|s\rangle$, the uniform superposition over the whole search space, and applies $c2^{(n-t)/2}$ iterations. Each iteration contains a reflection through the search space (applying the operator $2|s\rangle\langle s| - I$) and another through the "good" subspace (the uniform superposition over all wanted solutions). The first reflection requires to recompute $|s\rangle$, the second to apply O_f and flip the phase of the good elements. After $c2^{(n-t)/2}$ iterations, the state is the uniform superposition over the good subspace.

2.3   Quantum Algorithms with Small Quantum Space

While constant progress has been made towards quantum fault-tolerant computation, the number of qubits seems to be, to date, a more challenging limitation on the realizability of universal quantum computers. Indeed, a quantum computer acting on S qubits needs to maintain a coherent superposition over this whole system during the computation. In light of this potential caveat, some time-efficient quantum algorithms may reveal themselves costly. This was already argued by Grover and Rudolph regarding collision search in [30].

This is why we are interested in reducing at most the quantum time complexity *while working with a limited number of qubits.* "Limited", in the rest of this paper, means $O(n)$ (the same number as Grover's algorithm).

A technique helping to turn quantum memory requirements into classical ones is used in [19] for collision search: if one is interested in collision search *with few qubits*, the best time complexity manageable is $O(2^{2n/5})$ (instead of the lower bound $O(2^{n/3})$), using distinguished points.

Given a random function $H : \{0,1\}^n \rightarrow \{0,1\}^n$, the query-optimal BHT algorithm for collision search [17] works in two steps:

- Query $2^{n/3}$ arbitrary inputs;
- With Grover, search for a collision on one of these inputs: there are $2^{n/3}$ solutions among 2^n, hence $2^{n/3}$ Grover iterations.

In order to perform each iteration in time $O(1)$, this algorithm needs superposition query access to the memory that holds the $2^{n/3}$ results of the first step. In other terms, this algorithm requires $O(n2^{n/3})$ qubits.

Sequential Membership Testing. To overcome this cost, Chailloux *et al.* first remark that testing membership in a set of size 2^t, without quantum memory, can be done in time $O(2^t)$ (even in superposition). Indeed, given an input x, it suffices to compare sequentially x against all 2^t elements. This replaces the initial need for *quantum* memory by *classical storage*, as performing this test amounts to go through the whole set in a sequential manner.

Now, since this would bring the time complexity of BHT's algorithm to the heights of $2^{2n/3}$, we reduce the size of the list, and we now replace the arbitrary inputs by distinguished points: the list now contains only inputs x such that $H(x)$ is distinguished (say, by a zero-prefix of some size).

Since the collision we are looking for happens on a distinguished point, the search space is more structured: we use amplitude amplification instead of a simple Grover search. Assume that the list has size v and the distinguished points have all the same prefix of length u. The first step costs $2^{v+u/2}$, as each element now needs to be constructed using Grover search. The second step has $2^{(n-u-v)/2}$ iterations, as there are 2^v solutions among all distinguished points (2^{n-u}). Inside each iteration, the set of distinguished points needs to be constructed (time $2^{u/2}$) and membership to the intermediate list needs to be tested (time 2^v). This gives:

$$2^{v+u/2} + 2^{(n-u-v)/2}(2^{u/2} + 2^v)$$

optimized to $O(2^{2n/5})$ by taking $u = 2n/5$ and $v = n/5$.

3   State-of-the-Art: Known Results for the k-xor Problem

3.1   Classical Algorithms for the k-xor Problem

In [54], Wagner analyses the k-xor problem between k lists $L_1, \ldots L_k$ of elements drawn uniformly at random from $\{0,1\}^n$. The goal is to find a k-tuple of elements $x_1 \in L_1, \ldots, x_k \in L_k$ which xor to 0. Alternatively, one may consider a random function $H : \{0,1\}^n \to \{0,1\}^n$; the elements of the lists are created by querying H and the goal is to find $x_1, \ldots x_k$ such that $H(x_1) \oplus \ldots \oplus H(x_k) = 0$.

Problem 1 (k-xor with a random function). Given query access to a random function $H : \{0,1\}^n \to \{0,1\}^n$, find $x_1, \ldots x_k$ such that $H(x_1) \oplus \ldots \oplus H(x_k) = 0$.

Problem 2 (k-xor, with k random functions). Given query access to k random functions $H_1, \ldots, H_k : \{0,1\}^n \to \{0,1\}^n$, find $x_1, \ldots x_k$ such that $H_1(x_1) \oplus \ldots \oplus H_k(x_k) = 0$.

Both problems will remain equivalent throughout this paper. All algorithms studied and developed below have the same time and memory complexities in either formulation.

Wagner gives an algorithm that requires $O\left(k \cdot 2^{n/(\lfloor \log_2(k)\rfloor + 1)}\right)$ time and space. The design principle is to construct a binary tree whose leafs are the k initial lists. We number these levels from 1 (leafs) to $\lfloor \log_2(k)\rfloor + 1$ (root). Level i, for $i \leq \lfloor \log_2(k)\rfloor$, contains lists of 2^i-tuples which xor to 0 on the $\frac{n}{\lceil \log_2(k)\rceil + 1} \times i$ first bits, of size $2^{\frac{n}{\lceil \log_2(k)\rceil + 1}}$ each. The root of the tree contains the expected k-xor instance. We omit constant factors in the analysis.

The base operation of Wagner's k-tree algorithm is *merging* two lists in order to obtain their parent in the tree. Merging two lists at level $i - 1$ costs time $O(2^{\frac{n}{\lceil \log_2(k)\rceil + 1}})$ (the size of the lists). The resulting list at level i contains all pairs of 2^{i-1}-tuples (hence 2^i-tuples) which collide on $\frac{n}{\lceil \log_2(k)\rceil + 1}$ more bits. This explains why the parent list has (up to a constant) the same size as its children.

Remark 1. The information-theoretic query lower bound for the k-xor (alternatively, the k-sum) problem is $O(2^{n/k})$. Using a simple time-memory tradeoff, a trivial algorithm for this problem runs in time and memory $O(2^{n/2})$ if $k \geq 3$. (When $k = 2$, we fall back on collision search).

Wagner's algorithm offers *classically* the best time complexity exponent. In particular, by taking $k = 2^{\sqrt{n}}$, finding a k-xor can be done in time $O(2^{2\sqrt{n}})$.

Various improvements have proposed [12,14,43,48] but, as they target the logarithmic factors in the k-tree algorithm, study specific instances or concern time-memory tradeoffs, they remain out of scope of this paper.

ℓ-xor is easier than k-xor for $\ell \geq k$. Classically and quantumly, an algorithm for the k-xor problem can also be applied to the ℓ-xor problem for $\ell \geq k$, with the same time complexity. This reduction was outlined by Wagner [54]. Using a formulation such as Problem 2, one can remark that given an instance $H_1, \ldots, H_\ell$ it suffices to call the k-xor algorithm with functions $G_1 = H_1, \ldots, G_{k-1} = H_{k-1}$, $G_k = H_k \oplus \ldots \oplus H_\ell$.

3.2   Quantum Algorithms for the k-xor Problem

In this section, we review known quantum algorithms that can be applied to the k-xor problem or some of its instances. As we turn ourselves towards quantum algorithms, instead of considering lists of elements drawn at random (as Wagner does in his work), we consider these lists to be produced by random functions that we can query in superposition (Problem 1 or 2).

Ambainis [3] presented a quantum algorithm for element distinctness and extended it to k-distinctness. With this algorithm, deciding k-distinctness among 2^n elements can be done with $O(2^{nk/(k+1)})$ queries and $\widetilde{O}(2^{nk/(k+1)})$ quantum time, using the same amount of *quantum memory* (i.e., qubits), by a quantum random walk on the Johnson graph. It was later noticed [20] that this algorithm works as well for the k-sum problem, or any k-relation, giving a good *query* complexity. In [9], Belovs and Spalek proved this upper bound to be optimal, using an adversary method.

Lemma 1 ([9,20]). *The quantum query complexity of k-xor for a random function is $O(2^{n/(k+1)})$, the bound is tight.*

A Problem with Time. While no best method is currently known for general k when limited to $O(2^{n/(k+1)})$ superposition queries, the algorithm derived from Ambainis' is highly uncompetitive with respect to time. We estimate that it needs at least $\widetilde{O}(2^{n/2})$ operations, for any k. In a sense, this method can be seen as the quantum equivalent of classically taking the cross-product of k lists of size $2^{n/k}$.

Grover Search. Using Grover's algorithm [29] in a "raw" manner seems also a poor idea. If the search space spans all k-tuples in input to H, looking for one whose images xors to 0, the probability that this happens is 2^{-n}. Hence a k-xor will be found in time $O(2^{n/2})$. This complexity is trivially beaten by classical algorithms for $k > 2$ and does not perform better than classical collision search when $k = 2$. Grover is known to be parallelized on 2^s quantum processors with a $2^{s/2}$ time speedup. Improvements of this speedup have been obtained for some search problems (see [6] for preimage search) but we choose to focus primarily on single-processor algorithms.

Collision Search. As mentioned above, any k-xor instance can be reduced to a ℓ-xor instance for $\ell \leq k$. From the point of view of time complexity alone, the best quantum algorithm for collision search (2-xor) runs in time and queries $O(2^{n/3})$ for an n-bit to n-bit random function [17]. This has been proven to be optimal [1,2,56]. In return, this means that there exists a quantum algorithm for the k-xor problem, for any k, running with the same time complexity. As Wagner's algorithm already obtains time $O(2^{n/3})$ for $k = 4$, this seems only relevant for collision and 3-xor search.

Subset-sum Problem. In the subset-sum problem, one is given a set of elements and looks for a subset which xors (or sums) to zero. The k-xor problem can be seen as a simpler case where the size of the sum is fixed. This problem has been widely studied classically and the quantum walk framework has been successfully applied to it [11], but these works remain, to our knowledge, unrelated to ours.

4   Quantum Algorithms for the 3-xor Problem

We now present our new quantum algorithms for the 3-xor problem. Further results for the k-xor problem for $k \geq 4$ are left to the next section. In Sect. 3, we saw that 3-xor was at least easier than collision search; while there is no exponential gap in the classical setting, we find better quantum algorithms for 3-xor than the current best known algorithms for collision search:

- First with $O(n)$ memory, improving on the time complexity of $O(2^{2n/5})$ [19];
- Second, with an exponential number of qubits, improving on $O(2^{n/3})$ [17], which is optimal for quantum collision search.

4.1   First Approach

We consider a first approach to the 3-xor problem, formulated as Problem 1, with a single random function $H : \{0,1\}^n \rightarrow \{0,1\}^n$, to which we have superposition query access via a quantum oracle O_H. The algorithm obtained below gives an overview of the techniques that enable us to overcome the complexity of collision search. In the rest of this paper, when storing the results of queries of H, we will often omit that we keep track of the antecedents of these queries. We put the focus on outputting a k-xor of *images* $H(x_1), \ldots, H(x_k)$ while disregarding the $x_1, \ldots x_k$.

Algorithm Description. Let S be the set of all $x \in \{0,1\}^n$ such that $H(x)$ has a prefix of u zeroes.

Our algorithm runs in two mains steps:

1. Build two lists L_1 and L_2 of size 2^v, where v is a parameter to be set later, which have the form in Fig. 1. That is, they contain images $H(x) \in \{0,1\}^n$ such that $H(x)$ has a prefix of u zeroes (for example, in the first u bits).[1]
2. Using *Amplitude Amplification* [16], look for an element $x \in S$ (the search space of this subprocedure) such that $H(x) \oplus z_1 \oplus z_2 = 0$ for some $z_1, z_2 \in L_1 \times L_2$.

---

[1] At first sight, the parameters already seem over-restricted: nothing prevents us to use lists L_1 and L_2 of different sizes. We considered this situation and did not find any advantage.

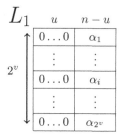 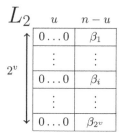

Fig. 1. Structure of the lists L_1 and L_2, of size 2^v. In the rest of this paper, the elements of the lists and their structures refer only to $H(x)$, while we may keep x alongside in order to output the antecedents of our final k-xor tuple.

Algorithm Analysis: First Step. Finding an element of S can be done using Grover's algorithm in $O(2^{u/2})$ iterations, as there is a proportion $\frac{1}{2^u}$ of "good elements" to find, the prefix condition being a u-bit condition. This gives in total $2^v \times 2^{u/2}$ calls to O_H (for simplicity, we dismiss constant factors in the complexity analyses).

Algorithm Analysis: Second Step. The second step is an Amplitude Amplification instance. It starts from the *initial state* $|s\rangle$, which is a uniform superposition over the whole search space S, and applies a sequence of iterations. Inside each iteration, we must recompute the initial state and check (in superposition) whether elements are good or not (see Sect. 2 for more details).

Checking Step. Given $x \in \{0,1\}^n$, checking if there exists $z_1 \in L_1$ and $z_2 \in L_2$ such that $H(x) \oplus z_1 \oplus z_2 = 0$ can be done in time 2^{2v} via sequential testing. More precisely, given a precomputed list L of 2^t elements in $\{0,1\}^n$, it is easy to build a quantum oracle which tests if an input x appears in L. On input $|x\rangle |0\rangle$, the oracle returns $|x\rangle |1\rangle$ if $x \in L$ and $|x\rangle |0\rangle$ otherwise. It runs in quantum time $O(n \cdot 2^t)$, without any quantum memory requirement: this amounts to control a sequence of n-bit comparisons against x (see Sect. 2 for a reminder of [19]).

The fact that L is known beforehand introduces a cost in *classical storage*. This storage is read sequentially (it only instructs which operations to perform) and does not need random-access. In our case, the list L contains the sums of all pairs $z_1 \in L_1, z_2 \in L_2$. It is produced on the fly and does not need to be stored itself. As it has 2^{2v} elements, the checking step costs 2^{2v} comparisons.

Initial State. The initial state of this Amplitude Amplification is the uniform superposition over the search space S (elements whose image has a prefix of u zeroes). It can be produced in $2^{u/2}$ time and queries using Grover's algorithm.

Number of Iterations. The search space S is of size 2^{n-u}. A "good element" in this search space gives a solution to the 3-xor problem. As it must collide with some sum $z_1 \oplus z_2$ in $L_1 \times L_2$ and there are 2^{2v} such sums, the number of good elements is 2^{2v}. Hence the number of iterations is $O\left(\sqrt{2^{n-u}/2^{2v}}\right)$. In each of these iterations, the initial state is computed and uncomputed, and the current superposition goes through the checking step.

All in all, the second step costs a quantum time:

$$2^{(n-u-2v)/2}\left(2^{u/2}+2^{2v}\right)$$

Optimizing both parameters u and v gives $v = \frac{n}{8}$ and $u = 4v$, which yields a time complexity $O(2^{3n/8})$. The classical memory complexity is $O(2^{n/8})$. All of this analysis is average-case. With a random function H, the fluctuations (e.g., in the size of S_u) cannot, with overwhelming probability, yield more than constant variations in the total time complexity.

Remark 2. Although the obtained time complexity is higher than the collision query lower bound $O(2^{n/3})$, it improves on $O(2^{2n/5})$, the current best known collision query and time complexity with $O(n)$ quantum memory.

Another Consequence of this Approach. If we disregard quantum memory consumption, the lists L_1 and L_2 may be stored using qubits. More precisely, to perform the checking step more efficiently, one may store L_1 in a quantum memory and then, given x, try every element y in L_2 sequentially and test whether $x \oplus y \in L_1$ efficiently (even when x is given in superposition). This decreases the cost of this test from 2^{2v} to 2^v. As a consequence, the time complexity becomes:

$$2^{u/2+v}+2^{(n-u-2v)/2}\left(2^{u/2}+2^v\right)$$

which implies $2u = v$ as best parameters and $v = \frac{n}{6}$. We obtain a time complexity of $O(2^{n/3})$ using $O(2^{n/6})$ quantum memory, improving on [17] w.r.t quantum memory.

4.2   Second Approach

In order to improve over the previous algorithm, we modify the structure of the lists (Fig. 2). This new algorithm is inspired from the list-merging ones from [46]. We introduce not two, but three parameters v, u, t such that:

- Both lists[2] have size 2^v;
- The "completely free" part has size t;
- Elements of L_1 take 0 on u bit positions;
- Elements of L_2 take 0 on u *different* bit positions;
- Elements of both L_1 and L_2 take 0 on the $n - 2u - t$ remaining bits (a common prefix, as before).

We first consider the case $v \geq u$.

---

[2] As before, we seem to over-restrict the parameters, since both lists could have different sizes. We found that it gave no improvement: intuitively, we wish to maximize a certain number of "good elements" given by a cross-product of L_1 and L_2, whose size is maximized w.r.t the cost of producing L_1 and L_2 when both have equal size.

L_1

$n-2u-t$	u	u	t
$0\ldots0$	$0\ldots0$	x_1	β_1
$\vdots$	$\vdots$	$\vdots$	$\vdots$
$0\ldots0$	$0\ldots0$	x_i	β_i
$\vdots$	$\vdots$	$\vdots$	$\vdots$
$0\ldots0$	$0\ldots0$	x_{2^v}	β_{2^v}

L_2

$n-2u-t$	u	u	t
$0\ldots0$	y_1	$0\ldots0$	α_1
$\vdots$	$\vdots$	$\vdots$	$\vdots$
$0\ldots0$	y_i	$0\ldots0$	α_i
$\vdots$	$\vdots$	$\vdots$	$\vdots$
$0\ldots0$	y_{2^v}	$0\ldots0$	α_{2^v}

(each list of size 2^v)

Fig. 2. Structure of the lists L_1 and L_2 of size 2^v.

Algorithm Design. As above, we consider the set S of "distinguished" elements x such that $H(x)$ has zeroes in the first $n-2u-t$ bits. We build the lists L_1 and L_2 and look for a 3-xor instance $H(x) \oplus z_1 \oplus z_2 = 0$ with $z_1 \in L_1, z_2 \in L_2$. But the new structure of the lists L_1 and L_2 makes the checking step more efficient: there will be no need to go through the whole product $L_1 \times L_2$.

Our algorithm runs in two main steps:

1. Build the lists L_1 and L_2;
2. Using Amplitude Amplification, look for $x \in S$ (the search space) such that $H(x) \oplus z_1 \oplus z_2 = 0$.

Analysis: First Step. The first step builds two lists of 2^v elements with zeroes in $u + n - 2u - t$ positions. Each of these elements is produced separately using Grover search. The total time complexity, without constant factors, is:

$$2^v \times 2^{\frac{n-u-t}{2}}.$$

Analysis: Second Step. In the second step, the search space is S, and it contains 2^{2u+t} elements among 2^n. The initial state $\sum_{x \in S} |x\rangle$ can be constructed using Grover's algorithm in $2^{\frac{n-2u-t}{2}}$ time and queries. To estimate the number of iterations, we have to find the number of good elements, that is, the number of $x \in S$ such that there exists $z_1 \in L_1, z_2 \in L_2$, $H(x) \oplus z_1 \oplus z_2 = 0$. For $x \in S$, there are on average 2^{v-u} elements z_1 in L_1 that collide with $H(x)$ on the third column and 2^{v-u} elements z_2 in L_2 that collide with $H(x)$ on the second column. Each of these $2^{2(v-u)}$ pairs z_1, z_2 yields a 3-xor to 0 on the three first columns. For each of these pairs, there are t remaining bits to cancel (the last column). Hence the probability that x yields a solution is $\frac{2^{2(v-u)}}{2^t}$, which gives $2^{\frac{t-2(v-u)}{2}}$ iterations.

Checking Step. We now detail how to check quantumly whether $x \in S$ yields a solution or not, in 2^{2v-u} comparisons only (with minor constants). Since $v \geq u$, we can cut the list L_1 in sublists of size 2^u and expect each of these sublists to contain an element z_1 which collides partially with $H(x)$ on the third column. We will simply assume that there is exactly one. If there are more, these additional solutions will be dismissed. If there is none, we will skip this sublist and go directly to the next one.

We can build a unitary that, given x in input, does for each sublist L'_1:

1. Go through L'_1 and retrieve z_1 which yields the partial collision. This requires 2^u comparisons, since this is the size of L'_1, and no additional quantum memory, since these comparisons are performed sequentially as above;
2. After retrieving z_1 and storing it, go through L_2 and find z_2 which yields a 3-xor, if it exists. This requires 2^v comparisons.
3. If a solution is found, return it, if not, return None.

As there are 2^{v-u} sublists to analyze, there are in total $2^{v-u}(2^u + 2^v) = 2^{2v-u}$ comparisons performed (since $v \geq u$). The output gives whether x is a good element or not and if so, the corresponding 3-xor instance.

Reduction of the Solution Space. Keeping only *one* partially colliding z_1 where there could be more has the consequence of reducing the actual set of good elements of the Amplitude Amplification procedure (the test function drops some good elements). We show that this has no asymptotic consequence.

Let x be a fixed element of the search space. There are 2^{v-u} sublists L'_1, from which $(1 - e^{-1})2^{v-u}$ contain at least one solution z_1 (the others yield no solution). We bound probabilistically the total number of z_1 that will be dropped. Let $Z(x)$ be the total number of z_1 over all these sublists, then $Z(x)$ is the sum of $(1 - e^{-1})2^{v-u}$ independent random variables of expectation 1. An additive Chernoff bound applies. For any $0 < \delta \leq 1$:

$$Pr\left(Z(x) \geq (1 + \delta)(1 - e^{-1})2^{v-u}\right) \leq e^{-\delta^2(1-e^{-1})2^{v-u}/3} .$$

Where $\left(Z(x) - (1 - e^{-1})2^{v-u}\right)$ represents the total number of z_1 lost for x.

We can do a union bound with x spanning the whole search space (of size 2^{2u+t}):

$$Pr\left(\exists x, Z(x) \geq (1 + \delta)(1 - e^{-1})2^{v-u}\right) \leq 2^{2u+t}e^{-\delta^2(1-e^{-1})2^{v-u}/3} .$$

By taking an appropriate δ, we find that with high and constant probability, for all x simultaneously, the number of z_1 dropped is negligible w.r.t the total amount. Assume now that x should have been a solution. Some z_1 yields a 3-xor instance: with our test, it may or not be dropped. We see that the probability for it to be dropped is negligible. With high probability, x remains a solution; the same goes for any x. Hence the final solution space is only negligibly smaller than the previous one, with no consequence on the time complexity.

Total Time. The time complexity rewrites:

$$2^{v+\frac{u}{2}+\frac{n-2u-t}{2}} + 2^{\frac{t-2(v-u)}{2}}\left(2^{\frac{n-2u-t}{2}} + 2^{2v-u}\right) = 2^{\frac{n}{2}+v-\frac{u+t}{2}} + 2^{\frac{n}{2}-v} + 2^{\frac{t}{2}+v} .$$

To find the right point of optimization, let us write the partial derivative in v and nullify it:

$$2^{\frac{n}{2}+v-\frac{u+t}{2}} - 2^{\frac{n}{2}-v} + 2^{\frac{t}{2}+v} = 0 .$$

This gives an equality between the exponents: $\frac{n}{2} - v = \frac{t}{2} + v$ i.e. $t = n - 4v$ and $\frac{n}{2} + v - \frac{u+t}{2} = \frac{n}{2} - v$ i.e. $u = 8v - n$.

Optimization. The final complexity is $2^{\frac{n}{2} - v}$ with an (apparently) free parameter v. Let us have a look at the conditions on the range of v: first, we have considered the case $v \geq u$, i.e. $v \geq 8v - n \Rightarrow v \leq \frac{n}{7}$. Second, we must have $t - 2(v - u) \geq 0$ (the Amplification Amplitude procedure needs a positive number of iterations, 1 means that all elements of the initial space are solutions), i.e. $v \geq \frac{n}{10}$. Finally, we must have $u \geq 0$, i.e. $8v - n \geq 0$ i.e. $v \geq \frac{n}{8}$. This means that this technique works only in the range $v \in \left[\frac{n}{8}; \frac{n}{7}\right]$ where it gives a quantum time complexity $2^{\frac{n}{2} - v}$ and a classical memory complexity 2^v.

Case $u > v$. When $u > v$, the probability that an element $x \in S$ in the search space yields a partial collision with $z \in L_1$ is $2^{v-u} < 1$. The checking procedure needs to be reconsidered with this point of view: we now go through the whole list L_1 sequentially (and computationally, by performing comparisons) and find the element z_1, if it exists, which collides with $H(x)$ on the u bits of the third column. If it does not exist, we return 0 immediately (not a good element). Otherwise, we go through L_2 and find the element z_2, if it exists, which collides with $H(x)$ on the u bits of the second column. The number of comparisons performed by this checking step is now 2^v. The other terms in the total time complexity are unchanged. It rewrites:

$$2^{v + \frac{u}{2} + \frac{n - 2u - t}{2}} + 2^{\frac{t - 2(v - u)}{2}} \left(2^{\frac{n - 2u - t}{2}} + 2^{2v - u}\right) = 2^{\frac{n}{2} + v - \frac{u+t}{2}} + 2^{\frac{n}{2} - v} + 2^{\frac{t}{2} + u} .$$

Optimizing gives $t = 10v - n$ and $u = n - 6v$, but $u \geq v$ enforces the condition $n - 6v \geq v$ i.e. $v \leq \frac{n}{7}$, which means that we fall back in the complexity range of above.

This leads to a few remarks:

- When v is minimal in this range, $v = \frac{n}{8}$ leads to $u = 0$: we obtain the first approach as above.
- When v is maximal, $v = \frac{n}{7}$ leads to $u = v$, and the best time complexity, in $O(2^{5n/14})$. This is very close to $2^{n/3}$, but does not yet reach the quantum collision bound (optimal number of queries).

Details of the Best Method. The case $v = \frac{n}{7}$ and $u = v$ - represented in Fig. 3 - gives the best quantum time complexity. Given an element $x \in \{0,1\}^n$ such that $H(x)$ has the according zero-prefix, we expect it to collide on average with one element of L_1 on the third column and with one element of L_2 on the second column. Finding these elements takes time 2×2^v to go through both lists. It remains to verify if $H(x) \oplus z_1 \oplus z_2$ sums to zero in the last t bits.

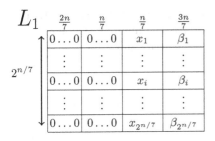

Fig. 3. Structure of the lists L_1 and L_2 of size $2^{n/7}$.

To build the lists L_1 and L_2, one needs time $2^{n/7+n/7+n/14} = 2^{5n/14}$. To find a 3-xor, one needs time:

$$2^{3n/14}\left(2^{n/7} + 2^{n/7}\right)$$

since, given an element of the $2n/7$-zero prefix space, there exists a match on the intermediate $n/7$ bits of L_1 and L_2 with high probability; then the probability that it is the good one only depends on the $3n/7$ remaining degrees of freedom (hence $2^{3n/14}$ iterations are necessary).

Theorem 1 (Quantum 3-xor Algorithm with Small Number of Qubits). *There exists a quantum algorithm for the 3-xor problem running in quantum time $O(2^{5n/14})$, using $O(n)$ qubits and $O(2^{n/7})$ classical memory.*

It is worth to notice that this algorithm, as the others in this paper, is inherently quantum: although we can write a classical counterparts (by replacing Grover search steps with classical exhaustive searches), trying to optimize the classical time complexity gives a time $O(2^{n/2})$ and $O(2^{n/4})$ classical memory (we get $u = v = t = \frac{n}{4}$).

4.3   Using Exponential Quantum Memory

If we allow an exponential amount of qubits to be used, we can also take the time complexity of the 3-xor problem below the best quantum time for collision search. This time, it is more surprising, since we go below the *optimal* query complexity for collision search.

Theorem 2 (Quantum 3-xor Algorithm). *There exists a quantum algorithm for the 3-xor problem running in time $\widetilde{O}(2^{3n/10})$ and using $O(2^{n/5})$ qubits.*

Proof. This procedure is inspired from the low-memory one. Since we authorize quantum memory, the $2n/7$ common prefix of zeroes is not necessary anymore (it has been used to amortize the cost of the membership oracle in the amplitude amplification procedure).

As before, building two lists of different sizes does not give better results, nor does building lists of size 2^v with $v \leq u$, where u is the number of inner zeroes in the intermediate columns. So we take $v \geq u$ and write the time complexity:

$$2^{v+\frac{u}{2}} + 2^{\frac{n-2v}{2}}\left(2^{v-u}\right) = 2^{v+\frac{u}{2}} + 2^{\frac{n-2u}{2}} .$$

Since we store the lists in quantum memory, testing membership now costs a logarithmic overhead which we dismiss. The 2^{v-u} factor stems from the fact that there are approximately 2^{v-u} partial collisions on L_1, each of which yields a membership test to L_2.

Optimization now yields $v + \frac{u}{2} = \frac{n}{2} - u$ i.e. $u = \frac{n}{3} - \frac{2v}{3}$. The complexity is $2^{\frac{2v}{3} + \frac{n}{6}}$. We also need $v \geq u$, hence $v \geq \frac{n}{5}$. $\qquad\square$

We cannot reduce v below $\frac{n}{5}$, but there is also no interest in increasing it, since this would increase both the time and memory complexity. Taking $v = \frac{n}{5}$ also implies $u = v = \frac{n}{5}$.

5 Quantum Algorithms for the k-xor Problem, $k \geq 4$

In this section, we present new algorithms for the k-xor problem, with $k \geq 4$. Again, we propose algorithms in two different models. When using exponential quantum memory, we propose a general quantum algorithm for the k-xor problem which gives a speedup over Wagner's k-tree method for any k. With $O(n)$ qubits, we find quantum speedups for specific values of k.

Table 2 gives a summary of our k-xor quantum algorithms with exponential quantum memory, while Table 3 gives a summary of k-xor quantum algorithms with $O(n)$ quantum memory. In both cases, complexities given are those of the best algorithms available, with respect to the time (in particular, there can be memory-efficient algorithms with higher time complexity).

Table 2. k-xor quantum algorithms with exponential quantum memory. Complexities C are given as $\log_2(C)/n$. The complexities of the classical algorithms are given by Pollard's rho algorithm for collisions, and by [54].

k	Classical time	Classical memory	Quantum time	Quantum memory	Reference
2	1/2	0	1/3	1/3	[17]
3	1/2	0	3/10	1/5	Theorem 2
4	1/3	1/3	1/4	1/4	Theorem 4
5	1/3	1/3	1/4	1/4	Theorem 4
6	1/3	1/3	1/4	1/4	Theorem 4
7	1/3	1/3	1/4	1/4	Theorem 4
8	1/4	1/4	1/5	1/5	Theorem 4
...	...	...	...	...	...
k	$(1 + \lfloor\log_2(k)\rfloor)^{-1}$	$(1 + \lfloor\log_2(k)\rfloor)^{-1}$	$(2 + \lfloor\log_2(k)\rfloor)^{-1}$	$(2 + \lfloor\log_2(k)\rfloor)^{-1}$	Theorem 4
...	...	...	...	...	...

Table 3. k-xor quantum algorithms with *polynomial* quantum memory. Complexities C are given as $\log_2(C)/n$. The complexities of the classical algorithms are given by Pollard's rho algorithm for collisions, and by [54].

k	Classical time	Classical memory	Quantum time	Classical memory	Reference
2	1/2	0	2/5	1/5	[19]
3	1/2	0	5/14	1/7	Theorem 1
4	1/3	1/3	1/3	1/9	Theorem 3
5	1/3	1/3	7/22	1/11	Theorem 3
6	1/3	1/3	4/13	1/13	Theorem 3
7	1/3	1/3	3/10	1/15	Theorem 3

A graphical comparison between these cases is provided in Fig. 4.

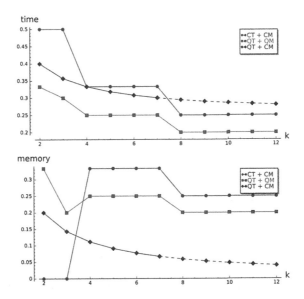

Fig. 4. Time and memory complexities of some k-xor algorithms. *Blue*: algorithm with classical time and classical memory (CT+CM), as provided in Pollard's rho algorithm for collisions, and by [54]. *Red*: algorithm with quantum time and exponential quantum memory (QT+QM), as provided in Theorems 2 and 4. *Green*: algorithm with quantum time and $O(n)$ quantum memory (QT+CM), as provided in Theorems 1 and 3. (Color figure online)

5.1   Quantum k-xor Algorithms With Low Quantum Memory

We propose an algorithm that enables us to find better-than-classical quantum time complexities, when using $O(n)$ qubits only. The result can be applied successfully for $k = 5, 6, 7$. Its complexity is given by the following theorem:

Theorem 3. *For each k, there exists a quantum algorithm for solving the k-xor problem running in time $O\left(2^{\frac{(k+2)n}{2(2k+1)}}\right)$ and using $O\left(2^{n/(2k+1)}\right)$ classical storage.*

L_1	t	u	u	$\ldots$	u	$n-(k-1)u-t$
	$0\ldots0$	x_1	$0\ldots0$	$0\ldots0$	$0\ldots0$	α_1
	$\vdots$	$\vdots$	$\vdots$	$\vdots$	$\vdots$	$\vdots$
	$0\ldots0$	x_i	$0\ldots0$	$0\ldots0$	$0\ldots0$	α_i
	$\vdots$	$\vdots$	$\vdots$	$\vdots$	$\vdots$	$\vdots$
	$0\ldots0$	x_{2^u}	$0\ldots0$	$0\ldots0$	$0\ldots0$	α_{2^u}

Fig. 5. Structure of the list L_1 of size 2^u.

L_j	t	u	$\ldots$	u (column $j+1$)	$\ldots$	u	$n-(k-1)u-t$
	$0\ldots0$	$0\ldots0$	$0\ldots0$	y_1	$0\ldots0$	$0\ldots0$	β_1
	$\vdots$	$\vdots$	$\vdots$	$\vdots$	$\vdots$	$\vdots$	$\vdots$
	$0\ldots0$	$0\ldots0$	$0\ldots0$	y_i	$0\ldots0$	$0\ldots0$	β_i
	$\vdots$	$\vdots$	$\vdots$	$\vdots$	$\vdots$	$\vdots$	$\vdots$
	$0\ldots0$	$0\ldots0$	$0\ldots0$	y_{2^u}	$0\ldots0$	$0\ldots0$	β_{2^u}

Fig. 6. Structure of the list L_j of size 2^u.

Proof. We take $k-1$ lists $L_1, \ldots, L_{k-1}$, each of size 2^u and containing elements with $t+(k-2)u$ zeroes, a prefix of size t and $k-2$ ranges of size u (Figs. 5 and 6). Of these ranges in list L_j, they all contain zeroes, except column $j+1$ (see Figs. 5 and 6).

Given $x \in \{0,1\}^n$, it collides on average with one element in L_1 on its corresponding non-zero column of size u, the same for L_2, etc. It remains to obtain 0 in $n-(k-2)u-t$ bits. The time is:

$$2^{u+(k-2)u/2+t/2} + 2^{\frac{n-(k-1)u-t}{2}}\left(2^{t/2}+2^u\right) \qquad (1)$$

which gives $u = \frac{n}{2k+1}$, $t = 2u$ and a complexity exponent $\frac{(k+2)n}{2(2k+1)}$.   □

When $k = 4$, we fall back on complexity $2^{n/3}$, but the memory complexity is better than Wagner's $2^{n/3}$: it drops to $2^{n/9}$.

When $4 < k < 8$, this gives better-than-classical time complexities in the bounded quantum memory setting[3]. In particular, setting $k = 7$ gives $O(2^{3n/10})$ time.

For $k \geq 8$, the cost of the Grover search step fails to decrease enough to be competitive against Wagner's algorithm, which is why Table 3 stops at $k = 7$. With $k \geq 8$, no quantum speedup for k-xor, with polynomial quantum memory, is known.

5.2 A Quantum Walk 4-xor Algorithm

In this subsection and the next one, we present a quantum walk algorithm for the general k-xor problem. First, we focus on the 4-xor case; a generalization of this method to any power of 2 will be presented later. Our algorithm uses the framework of quantum walks as described in [40]. It is inspired by [3] in that it also walks on the Johnson graph.

We formulate the 4-xor problem as following: given superposition query access to a random function $H : \{0,1\}^n \to \{0,1\}^n$, finding 4 or less distinct elements x_1, x_2, x_3, x_4 such that $H(x_1) \oplus H(x_2) \oplus H(x_3) \oplus H(x_4) = 0$. This algorithm adapts when we consider 4 random functions instead of one, when we consider quantum random memory accesses instead of oracle calls and when we enforce exactly 4 outputs (and refuse "smaller" collisions).

We define the Johnson graph $J(2^n, 2^r)$, where vertices are subsets of 2^r elements in $\{0,1\}^n$. This is the same graph as used by Ambainis' element-distinctness algorithm in [3]; its spectral gap is approximately $\delta = 2^{-r}$.

We add additional information to a vertex in the graph: we maintain the list of all r-collisions (collisions on the first r bits) within this set. There are approximately 2^r such collisions. A vertex in the graph is *marked* if two of these r-collisions collide. Hence, a random vertex in the graph has probability $2^{2r-(n-r)}$ of being marked, as there are approximately 2^{2r} pairs of r-collisions to construct and $n - r$ bit conditions to check.

Remark 3. In the way we mark vertices, we are losing information: indeed, there are vertices which contain a 4-sum to zero, but are not marked. Any method to efficiently mark more vertices would improve the complexity of our quantum walk, but it would also have consequences on the classical complexity of k-xor.

There is actually no need to perform this check on the fly; in the data structure representing a vertex, we store the list of r-collisions in a sorted manner (using e.g. a skip list, as in [3], which adds logarithmic overhead) and keep updated a "flag" bit which indicates whether the vertex is marked.

---

[3] Note that $2^{\frac{(k+2)n}{2(2k+1)}} \geq 2^{\frac{n}{1+\lfloor \log_2 k \rfloor}}$ for each $k \geq 8$, since

$$\frac{k+2}{4k+2} \geq \frac{1}{1 + \lfloor \log_2 k \rfloor} \Leftrightarrow (1 + \lfloor \log_2 k \rfloor)(k+2) \geq 4(k+2) \geq 4k+2.$$

Using this data structure, the cost of an update (constructing the superposition of all neighbors) is constant. Indeed, we only need to perform one query and update the list of r-collisions: on average, a given element appears in 1 of these collisions; we remove this one and add the potential new collision (which is found in constant time, since the list of elements is also sorted).

The time complexity of this quantum walk is, by [40]:

$$S + \frac{1}{\sqrt{\epsilon}} \left(C + \frac{1}{\sqrt{\delta}} U \right)$$

where U is the update cost (constant), C the checking cost (constant), S the setup cost (equal to 2^r, as there are 2^r initial queries to perform), ϵ the proportion of marked vertices and δ the spectral gap. In our case, this gives:

$$2^r + 2^{\frac{n-3r}{2}} \left(2^{r/2} \right) = 2^r + 2^{\frac{n}{2} - r} \ .$$

As it appears, the optimal time complexity is $\widetilde{O}(2^{n/4})$ (there are logarithmic factors to take into account while updating the quantum data structures) with a quantum memory complexity of $\widetilde{O}(2^{n/4})$. Besides, this gives a quantum time-quantum memory trade-off curve $T \times S = 2^{n/2}$ for the 4-xor problem.

Lemma 2. *For any quantum memory size $S \leq 2^{n/4}$, there exists a quantum algorithm for the 4-xor problem running in time $T = 2^{n/2}/S$.*

Remark 4. There are some possible caveats to this method, which we address in the next subsection. First, it is possible that the final 4-xor is a sum of the form $H(x_1) \oplus H(x_2) \oplus H(x_3) \oplus H(x_4) = 0$ where $H(x_1) = H(x_3)$ and $H(x_2) = H(x_4)$, giving a trivial result. This kind of failure happens infrequently. Furthermore, we did not bound precisely the cost of a vertex update: such an update is performed in superposition on all vertices. When we remove and add an element of a vertex, although there would be on average only one r-collision to remove and add, the "average case" is not enough, since we are considering all vertices at the same time. This may incur another quantum time overhead.

5.3   A Quantum Walk 2^k-xor Algorithm

The technique used successfully for the 4-xor problem can be applied for the 2^k-xor, in a similar manner as Wagner's classical k-tree technique. We perform a quantum walk on the Johnson graph $J(2^n, 2^r)$. Marked ("good") vertices contain a 2^k-xor, but most of the vertices with a 2^k-xor are actually not marked: this is where we lose the most against the quantum query lower bound.

Our quantum data structure for vertices stores much additional information, multiplying the quantum memory by a factor k. There are k sorted lists on k levels:

- On the first level, we store the 2^r elements of the vertex (L_1);

- On the second level, we store the 2^r r-collisions expected from these elements (and store, for each collision, a pair of pointers towards the elements which produced it) (L_2);
- On the third level, we store the 2^r $2r$-4-xor (4-xor on $2r$ bits) expected from the collisions above (collisions of collisions) (L_3);
- ...
- On the k-th level, we store the (approximately) 2^r $(k-1)r$-2^{k-1}-xor expected (L_k).

What remains is, from pairs of these 2^r $(k-1)r$-2^{k-1}-xor, to obtain a collision on the $n - (k-1)r$ remaining bits. Such a collision is easy to find, since the list at the k-th level is sorted.

Updating the vertex data structure (i.e., removing an element and adding another) should be done in time $O(k)$, as we have k levels to go through and to update. The time (and memory) complexity of this walk then amounts to:

$$k \times 2^r + 2^{\frac{n-(k-1)r-2r}{2}} \left(2^{r/2} \times k\right)$$

which we optimize using $r = \frac{n}{k+2}$ to $O\left(k2^{\frac{n}{k+2}}\right)$. A number of technicalities remain to be handled.

The Diminution of the Number of Collisions. Suppose that at level i, the 2^r bit-strings corresponding to the non-colliding part of the $(i-1)r$-2^{i-1}-xor of this level take exactly 2^r different values (i.e., $|L_i| = 2^r$). At level $i + 1$, they make take strictly *less* values (i.e., $|L_{i+1}| < |L_i|$). This could make the number of distinct elements stored at level $i + 2$ decrease further, and so on. If we authorize non-distinct elements in the 2^k-xor instance in output, this is not an issue. Indeed, $|L_{i+1}| < |L_i|$ happens only if a pair of elements at level i already *completely collides*. We can check this while computing or updating L_i and immediately mark the vertex: a full collision at level $i + 1$ corresponds to a 2^i-xor instance, which in turn corresponds trivially to a 2^k-xor instance with non-distinct elements. If this is not authorized, then the average size of the lists indeed decreases. We will handle this below.

Increasing the Number of Collisions. On the contrary, there may be too much collisions at level i and L_{i+1} may increase in size. This is an issue for all vertices, since the quantum memory used stores the data structures in superposition for all. We must ensure that L_i is bounded for all i and for *all vertices*. But this is trivially done: if there are too much collisions, we dismiss them. Recall that the goal of our marking procedure is to mark *efficiently some* vertices containing a 2^k-xor, not all of them.

Outputting the 2^k-xor Result. At the end of the quantum walk, we perform a measurement and get the whole data structure of a vertex. We make sure to store, for each partial collision or xor at level i, the two elements of level $i - 1$ which produced it (this introduces only a constant overhead). Hence, outputting the whole 2^k-xor instance amounts to the traversal of a tree of pointers, performed in time $O(2^k)$. This adds to the complexity of our algorithm.

The Real Cost of an Update. Updating the data structure is done when we remove, and then add an element to the vertex (going to one of its neighbors). We then have to go through the k levels. We expect "on average" $O(1)$ computations to be performed at each level, as each element on level i intervenes "on average" in one collision at level $i + 1$ (collision which we have to remove, or to add, depending on the situation). Classically, we may consider such an average case, but quantumly, we are studying all elements in superposition.

Suppose that $x \in \{0,1\}^n$ intervenes in multiple collisions of a random function $H : \{0,1\}^n \to \{0,1\}^n$. This means that $f(x) \oplus f(y_i) = 0$ for multiple values: $y_1, \ldots y_{\ell-1}$. This means, in turn, that x is actually involved in a ℓ-collision for some $\ell > 2$.

The average number of ℓ-collisions in a random n-bit to n-bit function is $\frac{e^{-1}2^n}{\ell!}$ ([26], Theorem 4). At each level, computing the next collisions is done by sorting a list of 2^r values; this enables us to select *only* 2-collisions and avoid any element to appear twice. That way, only *one* update has to be propagated towards the next levels. Besides, some of the branches die out, as the number of collisions is below 2^r: we expect $2^r e^{-1}/2 \simeq 0.184 \times 2^r$.

This seems to be a caveat of our technique: as the number of levels grows higher, the number of collisions at the k-th level is of the order $\frac{2^r}{(2e)^k}$. The number of marked vertices, in turn, is smaller than our first estimation.

Adapted Time Complexity. The remarks above make us rewrite the time complexity by taking k into account more precisely:

$$k \times 2^r + 2^{\frac{n-(k-1)r-2r}{2}}(2e)^k(2^{r/2} \times k) + 2^k = k2^r + k2^{\frac{n-kr}{2}+k(1+1/\ln 2)} + 2^k$$

which optimizes to $(k+2)r = n + 2k\left(1 + \frac{1}{\ln 2}\right)$. Notice that $2^{2k\left(1+\frac{1}{\ln 2}\right)/(k+2)} \le 4e^2$, a constant.

General Case. We studied the case of a power of 2, but generally, the K-xor problem may be solved using a similar quantum walk as the $2^{\lfloor \log_2 K \rfloor}$-xor.

Theorem 4 (Quantum Walk K-xor Algorithm). *For any integer K, there exists a quantum algorithm that, given superposition oracle access to a random function $H : \{0,1\}^n \to \{0,1\}^n$, solves the K-xor problem in quantum time and memory (asymptotic in K and with additional factors in r due to data structure management):*

$$\widetilde{O}\left(K2^{\frac{n}{\lfloor \log_2 K \rfloor+2}}\right) .$$

At first, the time complexity could have been with a factor K^c with $c = 1 + \frac{1}{\ln 2}$ slightly greater than 1, coming from the way we propagate the update in the $\log_2 K$-leveled data structure. We correct this time complexity by slightly increasing the size of the lists stored in the structure, which in turn increases the number of partial collisions we get, and makes the time and memory complexities equal.

When querying K independent oracles instead of one (alternatively, when we have K independent lists), the complexities are the same. Since the lists are independent, we consider K levels instead of $\log_2 K$; level i contains increasing partial collisions between elements from $L_1 \ldots L_i$.

Multiple K-xor. Let $\lfloor \log_2 K \rfloor = k$. Using Wagner's algorithm, [54], one can output 2^c K-xor instances in time $O\left(K2^{\frac{n}{k+1}} \times 2^{\frac{c}{k+1}}\right)$, provided that $c \leq \frac{n}{k}$. Using our quantum walk algorithm, it is possible to obtain a similar result. We use more quantum memory. The initialization step is performed as above. The march is then divided in 2^c steps, each of which corresponds to a new K-xor instance, that we may store until the end. First, we march on the Johnson graph and marked vertices are those which contain at least a K-xor; second, we march on *vertices that contain a* K-xor and marked vertices are those which contain at least *two* K-xors, and so on. The end of each subwalk is the beginning of the next one. The quantum time complexity becomes approximately:

$$K \times 2^r + 2^c \times 2^{\frac{n-(k-1)r-2r}{2}}\left(2^{r/2} \times K\right)$$

with a final $r = \frac{2c+n}{k+2}$ and a time complexity: $\widetilde{O}\left(K2^{\frac{2c+n}{k+2}}\right)$. This is legitimate as long as $n \geq (k+1)r$ (positive number of iterations), i.e. $n \geq \frac{2c+n}{k+2}(k+1)$, i.e. $c \leq \frac{n}{2(k+1)}$.

6   Quantum k-xor Parallel Algorithms

While an involved discussion on all respective parallelization strategies for classical and quantum algorithms for the k-xor problem would be outside the scope of our work, we can make a few remarks on the cost of parallelized versions of our algorithms.

First of all, we consider as "quantum parallel algorithm" a quantum algorithm written in the circuit model, with an adapted definition of *time complexity*: instead of merely counting the number of quantum gates, we authorize up to 2^s of them, if there are 2^s "quantum processors" available, to be applied in a single time step. Such a definition, which puts away possible communication overheads between quantum processors, has been extensively justified in [7].

Parallelization of quantum algorithms seems sometimes to give more negative than positive results: as an example, although Grover's algorithm can be parallelized, it cannot gain more than a factor $2^{s/2}$ in time when using 2^s processors, while classical exhaustive search does not suffer from this issue.

Quantum Parallel 3-xor Algorithm. Consider our 3-xor algorithm of Sect. 4, running on one processor in time $O(2^{5n/14})$ with classical storage of size $O(2^{n/7})$. We distribute it over 2^s quantum processors, in the following way: both the computation of intermediate lists and the final step (amplitude amplification) are shared among these processors; the former more efficiently (a factor 2^{-s}) than the latter ($2^{-s/2}$). Rewriting the time complexity and performing a similar optimization process, we obtain a time $O\left(2^{\frac{n}{2}-v-\frac{s}{2}}\right)$ for $v \leq \frac{n+s}{7}$.

By taking $v = \frac{n+s}{7}$, i.e. increasing the classical resources[4], we get a time $\widetilde{O}\left(2^{\frac{5n}{14}-\frac{9s}{14}}\right)$, with a more significant parallelization speedup compared to Grover's algorithm.

Although trading quantum memory for classical storage seems advantageous, many alternative and debatable benchmarks can be used to quantify the overall cost of running algorithms. One of these benchmarks (used in [10] against the quantum collision algorithm of [19]) binds together the memory and the number of processors used as *hardware resources*. Using this particular benchmark, single-processor Pollard rho costs $O(2^{n/2})$, while 2^s-processor parallelized rho costs $O(2^{n/2-s} \times 2^s) = O(2^{n/2})$, and no quantum collision search (because of their memory usage) outperforms the classical ones.

Even with this benchmark, our new 3-xor algorithm performs efficiently. Suppose that we equalize the number of processors and the memory used (which remains single-access): $s = \frac{n+s}{7}$ gives $s = \frac{n}{6}$. This gives a time $\widetilde{O}\left(2^{n/4}\right)$. The product time-resources is $\widetilde{O}\left(2^{5n/12}\right)$ and improves over the best classical complexity.

7   Conclusion

In this work, we have studied quantum k-xor algorithms, proposing new ones with the lowest known *time complexity*.

The previous best known quantum attacks could only rely on collision search for $k = 3$ and did not outperform Wagner's algorithm for $k \geq 4$. Even though the optimal quantum query complexity could be attained, there was virtually no quantum time-efficient method for the k-xor problem.

We filled this gap in two settings, depending on the status of *quantum memory* (see Fig. 4 for more details).

- If quantum memory is considered as cheap as classical memory, we authorize the adversary to use exponential amounts of it. We obtain an improvement over quantum collision search for the 3-xor problem ($\widetilde{O}(2^{3n/10})$ instead of $\widetilde{O}(2^{n/3})$, with significantly reduced quantum memory). For general k, we also improve Wagner's time and memory complexities of $O(2^{n/(1+\lfloor \log_2(k) \rfloor)})$ towards $O(2^{n/(2+\lfloor \log_2(k) \rfloor)})$ quantum time and memory.
- If quantum memory is reduced to $O(n)$, we obtain quantum speedups for k-xor up to $k = 7$. In particular, 3-xor search can be performed in time $O(2^{5n/14})$, which is better than the current state of the art for low-qubits quantum collision search.

---

[4] Notice also that, although all 2^s processors seem to require concurrent accesses to the classical intermediate storage, we can do better if communication overheads between processors are negligible, as advocated by [7]. All processors perform the sequential membership oracle at the same time and in exactly the same manner. Hence, lists elements need only to be sent to one of them and broadcasted to the others with logarithmic overhead.

In particular, contrary to classical algorithms, we have clearly shown that the quantum 3-xor problem is exponentially easier to solve than the quantum collision finding problem, which was not an intuitive conclusion. In contrast, classical time improvements of the 3-xor problem have concerned only logarithmic factors.

Parallelization. Our algorithms for k-xor running with $O(n)$ qubits give rise to efficient parallel versions. In particular, our quantum parallelized 3-xor algorithm attains, using $2^{n/6}$ processors and the same amount of classical storage, a time-hardware product of $\widetilde{O}(2^{5n/12})$, effectively below classical algorithms.

7.1 Implications of Our Results

Our results, in particular for small k, can be used to improve quantumly cryptanalysis results of particular hash constructions or authenticated encryption schemes.

In the following, we give some practical examples:

XHASH and the (R)FSB SHA-3 Candidate: we are able to improve the best GBP attack on the SHA-3 candidate (R)FSB. Referring to [4], the parameters for FSB_{length} (the SHA-3 proposal contains five versions of FSB, that is FSB_{160}, FSB_{224}, FSB_{256}, FSB_{384} and FSB_{512}) are given by r – i.e. the output size in bits – and n – i.e. the size of the message to be hashed, where the message is split in ω blocks of size $u = 2^a$. Given the FSB hash function

$$FSB(H, m) := \bigoplus_{i=1}^{k} h_i(m_i),$$

to set up the GBP the idea is to construct $l = 2 \log_2(u) - 1$ lists (see [22] for details), where each list is given by the xor-sum of ω/l values $h_i(m_i)$. The complexity of a classical GBP is well estimated $2^{n/(1+\lfloor \log_2(l) \rfloor)}$. A Wagner-type attack (see [4, Table 7]) against FSB_{160} finds a 16-xor between 16 lists which contain elements of size 632. Time and memory, up to smaller constant factors, are given by Wagner's 16×2^{127}. If we are able to query the elements of these lists in superposition, in other words, to produce them quantumly on-the-fly, the quantum time and memory complexities of this operation decrease to 2^{105}. Similar results can be obtained also for the SWIFFT hash function previously recalled.

Authenticated Encryption Schemes - CAESAR: we are able to improve the best forgery attacks on the CAESAR schemes based on XLS. Let us focus on the 128-bit CAESAR candidates Deoxys and KIASU (64 bits of – claimed – security level). The 3-xor problem for XLS in these candidates has the parameter $n = 128$. According to Table 1, the 3-xor can be produced in quantum time $2^{45.7}$ and $2^{18.3}$ classical memory (w.r.t. quantum time $2^{51.2}$ and $2^{25.6}$ classical memory of [19]) or in quantum time $2^{38.4}$ and $2^{25.6}$ quantum memory (w.r.t. quantum time $2^{42.7}$ and $2^{42.7}$ quantum memory of [17]).

Similar results can be obtained for the other applications previously discussed.

7.2   Open Questions

There are still some open questions and further lines of research that would be interesting to investigate. Most of them concern k-xor algorithms with $O(n)$ qubits:

1. Does there exist such a 3-xor algorithm reaching below the quantum collision bound of $O(2^{n/3})$?
2. Is it possible to find a 4-xor quantum algorithm with $O(n)$ quantum memory giving a quantum time speedup over Wagner's method?
3. Still with $O(n)$ quantum memory, can we give a quantum speedup over Wagner's method for a general k?
4. How to adapt our algorithms to the k-sum case? The evolved ones will have a certain overhead that should be computed.

Another question that we believe to be of interest is the fact that classical algorithms for solving the 3-xor problem had a comparable complexity to collision-finding algorithms. With our new quantum algorithm, the 3-xor problem is clearly easier to solve, and might therefore imply that new applications of this problem can appear, as for instance for building bricks of attacks.

Acknowledgements. This project has received funding from the European Research Council (ERC) under the European Union?s Horizon 2020 research and innovation programme (grant agreement no. 714294 - acronym QUASYModo). The results presented here were started during the Flexible Symmetric Cryptography workshop held at the Lorentz Center in Leiden, Netherlands. The authors would like to thank Yunwen Liu and Arnab Roy for preliminary discussions, as well as Elena Kirshanova and Steven Galbraith for all the helpful comments and remarks.

References

1. Aaronson, S.: Quantum lower bound for the collision problem. In: STOC, pp. 635–642. ACM (2002)
2. Aaronson, S., Shi, Y.: Quantum lower bounds for the collision and the element distinctness problems. J. ACM **51**(4), 595–605 (2004)
3. Ambainis, A.: Quantum walk algorithm for element distinctness. SIAM J. Comput. **37**(1), 210–239 (2007)
4. Augot, D., Finiasz, M., Gaborit, P., Manuel, S., Sendrier, N.: SHA-3 proposal: FSB. https://www.rocq.inria.fr/secret/CBCrypto/fsbdoc.pdf
5. Bai, S., Galbraith, S.D., Li, L., Sheffield, D.: Improved exponential-time algorithms for inhomogeneous-sis. Cryptology ePrint Archive, Report 2014/593 (2014). https://eprint.iacr.org/2014/593
6. Banegas, G., Bernstein, D.J.: Low-communication parallel quantum multi-target preimage search. In: Adams, C., Camenisch, J. (eds.) SAC 2017. LNCS, vol. 10719, pp. 325–335. Springer, Cham (2018). https://doi.org/10.1007/978-3-319-72565-9_16
7. Beals, R., et al.: Efficient distributed quantum computing. Proc. R. Soc. A **469**(2153), 20120686 (2013)

8. Bellare, M., Micciancio, D.: A new paradigm for collision-free hashing: incrementality at reduced cost. In: Fumy, W. (ed.) EUROCRYPT 1997. LNCS, vol. 1233, pp. 163–192. Springer, Heidelberg (1997). https://doi.org/10.1007/3-540-69053-0_13

9. Belovs, A., Spalek, R.: Adversary lower bound for the k-sum problem. In: Innovations in Theoretical Computer Science, ITCS 2013, pp. 323–328. ACM (2013)

10. Bernstein, D.J.: 2017.10.17: Quantum algorithms to find collisions. The cr.yp.to blog (2017). https://blog.cr.yp.to/20171017-collisions.html

11. Bernstein, D.J., Jeffery, S., Lange, T., Meurer, A.: Quantum algorithms for the subset-sum problem. In: Gaborit, P. (ed.) PQCrypto 2013. LNCS, vol. 7932, pp. 16–33. Springer, Heidelberg (2013). https://doi.org/10.1007/978-3-642-38616-9_2

12. Bernstein, D.J., Lange, T., Niederhagen, R., Peters, C., Schwabe, P.: FSBday. In: Roy, B., Sendrier, N. (eds.) INDOCRYPT 2009. LNCS, vol. 5922, pp. 18–38. Springer, Heidelberg (2009). https://doi.org/10.1007/978-3-642-10628-6_2

13. Bernstein, D.J., Lange, T., Niederhagen, R., Peters, C., Schwabe, P.: Implementing wagner's generalized birthday attack against the SHA-3 round-1 candidate FSB. Cryptology ePrint Archive, Report 2009/292 (2009). https://eprint.iacr.org/2009/299

14. Bouillaguet, C., Delaplace, C., Fouque, P.: Revisiting and improving algorithms for the 3XOR problem. IACR Trans. Symmetric Cryptol. **2018**(1), 254–276 (2018). https://doi.org/10.13154/tosc.v2018.i1.254-276

15. Brassard, G., Høyer, P.: An exact quantum polynomial-time algorithm for Simon's problem. In: Fifth Israel Symposium on Theory of Computing and Systems, ISTCS 1997, pp. 12–23. IEEE Computer Society (1997). https://doi.org/10.1109/ISTCS.1997.595153

16. Brassard, G., Hoyer, P., Mosca, M., Tapp, A.: Quantum amplitude amplification and estimation. Contemp. Math. **305**, 53–74 (2002)

17. Brassard, G., HØyer, P., Tapp, A.: Quantum cryptanalysis of hash and claw-free functions. In: Lucchesi, C.L., Moura, A.V. (eds.) LATIN 1998. LNCS, vol. 1380, pp. 163–169. Springer, Heidelberg (1998). https://doi.org/10.1007/BFb0054319

18. CAESAR: Competition for Authenticated Encryption: Security, Applicability, and Robustness. http://competitions.cr.yp.to/caesar.html

19. Chailloux, A., Naya-Plasencia, M., Schrottenloher, A.: An efficient quantum collision search algorithm and implications on symmetric cryptography. In: Takagi, T., Peyrin, T. (eds.) ASIACRYPT 2017. LNCS, vol. 10625, pp. 211–240. Springer, Cham (2017). https://doi.org/10.1007/978-3-319-70697-9_8

20. Childs, A.M., Eisenberg, J.M.: Quantum algorithms for subset finding. Quantum Inf. Comput. **5**(7), 593–604 (2005)

21. Chose, P., Joux, A., Mitton, M.: Fast correlation attacks: an algorithmic point of view. In: Knudsen, L.R. (ed.) EUROCRYPT 2002. LNCS, vol. 2332, pp. 209–221. Springer, Heidelberg (2002). https://doi.org/10.1007/3-540-46035-7_14

22. Coron, J.S., Joux, A.: Cryptanalysis of a provably secure cryptographic hash function. Cryptology ePrint Archive, Report 2004/013 (2004). https://eprint.iacr.org/2004/013

23. Datta, N., Nandi, M.: ELmD. https://competitions.cr.yp.to/round1/elmdv10.pdf

24. eSTREAM: the ECRYPT Stream Cipher Project. http://www.ecrypt.eu.org/stream/

25. Even, S., Mansour, Y.: A construction of a cipher from a single pseudorandom permutation. J. Cryptol. **10**(3), 151–161 (1997)

26. Flajolet, P., Odlyzko, A.M.: Random mapping statistics. In: Quisquater, J.-J., Vandewalle, J. (eds.) EUROCRYPT 1989. LNCS, vol. 434, pp. 329–354. Springer, Heidelberg (1990). https://doi.org/10.1007/3-540-46885-4_34

27. Gobioff, H., Nagle, D., Gibson, G.: Integrity and performance in network attached storage. In: Polychronopoulos, C., Fukuda, K.J.A., Tomita, S. (eds.) ISHPC 1999. LNCS, vol. 1615, pp. 244–256. Springer, Heidelberg (1999). https://doi.org/10.1007/BFb0094926

28. Bok-Min, G., Siddiqi, M.U., Hean-Teik, C.: Incremental hash function based on pair chaining & modular arithmetic combining. In: Rangan, C.P., Ding, C. (eds.) INDOCRYPT 2001. LNCS, vol. 2247. Springer, Heidelberg (2001). https://doi.org/10.1007/3-540-45311-3_5

29. Grover, L.K.: A fast quantum mechanical algorithm for database search. In: Proceedings of the Twenty-Eighth Annual ACM Symposium on the Theory of Computing 1996, pp. 212–219. ACM (1996). https://doi.org/10.1145/237814.237866

30. Grover, L.K., Rudolph, T.: How significant are the known collision and element distinctness quantum algorithms? Quantum Inf. Comput. 4(3), 201–206 (2004). http://portal.acm.org/citation.cfm?id=2011622

31. Hell, M., Johansson, T., Meier, W.: Grain - a stream cipher for constrained environments. http://www.ecrypt.eu.org/stream/p3ciphers/grain/Grain_p3.pdf

32. Jean, J., Nikolić, I., Peyrin, T.: ELmD. https://competitions.cr.yp.to/round2/joltikv13.pdf

33. Jean, J., Nikolić, I., Peyrin, T.: KIASU. https://competitions.cr.yp.to/round1/kiasuv1.pdf

34. Kaplan, M., Leurent, G., Leverrier, A., Naya-Plasencia, M.: Breaking symmetric cryptosystems using quantum period finding. In: Robshaw, M., Katz, J. (eds.) CRYPTO 2016. LNCS, vol. 9815, pp. 207–237. Springer, Heidelberg (2016). https://doi.org/10.1007/978-3-662-53008-5_8

35. Kirchner, P.: Improved generalized birthday attack. Cryptology ePrint Archive, Report 2011/377 (2011). https://eprint.iacr.org/2011/377

36. Kuwakado, H., Morii, M.: Quantum distinguisher between the 3-round Feistel cipher and the random permutation. In: IEEE International Symposium on Information Theory, ISIT 2010, pp. 2682–2685. IEEE (2010)

37. Kuwakado, H., Morii, M.: Security on the quantum-type Even-Mansour cipher. In: Proceedings of the International Symposium on Information Theory and its Applications, ISITA 2012. IEEE (2012)

38. Leander, G., May, A.: Grover meets simon – quantumly attacking the FX-construction. In: Takagi, T., Peyrin, T. (eds.) ASIACRYPT 2017. LNCS, vol. 10625, pp. 161–178. Springer, Cham (2017). https://doi.org/10.1007/978-3-319-70697-9_6

39. Lipton, R.J., Regan, K.W.: Quantum Algorithms via Linear Algebra: A Primer. The MIT Press, Cambridge (2014)

40. Magniez, F., Nayak, A., Roland, J., Santha, M.: Search via quantum walk. SIAM J. Comput. 40(1), 142–164 (2011)

41. Mermin, N.D.: Quantum Computer Science: An Introduction. Cambridge University Press, New York (2007)

42. Micciancio, D., Arbitman, Y., Dogon, G., Lyubashevsky, V., Peikert, C., Rosen, A.: SWIFFT. https://www.eecs.harvard.edu/alon/PAPERS/lattices/swifftx.pdf

43. Minder, L., Sinclair, A.: The extended k-tree algorithm. J. Cryptol. 25(2), 349–382 (2012)

44. Nandi, M.: XLS is not a strong pseudorandom permutation. In: Sarkar, P., Iwata, T. (eds.) ASIACRYPT 2014. LNCS, vol. 8873, pp. 478–490. Springer, Heidelberg (2014). https://doi.org/10.1007/978-3-662-45611-8_25

45. Nandi, M.: Revisiting security claims of XLS and COPA. Cryptology ePrint Archive, Report 2015/444 (2015). https://eprint.iacr.org/2015/444

46. Naya-Plasencia, M.: How to improve rebound attacks. In: Rogaway, P. (ed.) CRYPTO 2011. LNCS, vol. 6841, pp. 188–205. Springer, Heidelberg (2011). https://doi.org/10.1007/978-3-642-22792-9_11
47. Niebuhr, R., Cayrel, P.L., Buchmann, J.: Improving the efficiency of Generalized Birthday Attacks against certain structured cryptosystems. In: Workshop on Coding and Cryptography, WCC 2011, pp. 163–172 (2011)
48. Nikolić, I., Sasaki, Y.: Refinements of the k-tree algorithm for the generalized birthday problem. In: Iwata, T., Cheon, J.H. (eds.) ASIACRYPT 2015. LNCS, vol. 9453, pp. 683–703. Springer, Heidelberg (2015). https://doi.org/10.1007/978-3-662-48800-3_28
49. Ristenpart, T., Rogaway, P.: How to enrich the message space of a cipher. In: Biryukov, A. (ed.) FSE 2007. LNCS, vol. 4593, pp. 101–118. Springer, Heidelberg (2007). https://doi.org/10.1007/978-3-540-74619-5_7
50. Shor, P.W.: Algorithms for quantum computation: discrete logarithms and factoring. In: Proceedings of the 35th Annual Symposium on Foundations of Computer Science, SFCS 1994, pp. 124–134. IEEE Computer Society (1994)
51. Siegenthaler, T.: Correlation-immunity of nonlinear combining functions for cryptographic applications. IEEE Trans. Inf. Theory **30**(5), 776–780 (1984)
52. Siegenthaler, T.: Decrypting a class of stream ciphers using ciphertext only. IEEE Trans. Comput. **34**(1), 81–85 (1985)
53. Simon, D.R.: On the power of quantum computation. SIAM J. Comput. **26**(5), 1474–1483 (1997)
54. Wagner, D.: A generalized birthday problem. In: Yung, M. (ed.) CRYPTO 2002. LNCS, vol. 2442, pp. 288–304. Springer, Heidelberg (2002). https://doi.org/10.1007/3-540-45708-9_19
55. Wang, L.: SHELL. https://competitions.cr.yp.to/round2/shellv20.pdf
56. Zhandry, M.: A note on the quantum collision and set equality problems. Quantum Info. Comput. **15**(7–8), 557–567 (2015). http://dl.acm.org/citation.cfm?id=2871411.2871413

Hidden Shift Quantum Cryptanalysis
and Implications

Xavier Bonnetain[1,2]($\boxtimes$) and María Naya-Plasencia[2]

[1] Sorbonne Université, Collège Doctoral, F-75005 Paris, France
[2] Inria, Paris, France
xavier.bonnetain@inria.fr

Abstract. At Eurocrypt 2017 a tweak to counter Simon's quantum attack was proposed: replace the common bitwise addition with other operations, as a modular addition. The starting point of our paper is a follow up of these previous results:

First, we have developed new algorithms that improves and generalizes Kuperberg's algorithm for the hidden shift problem, which is the algorithm that applies instead of Simon when considering modular additions. Thanks to our improved algorithm, we have been able to build a quantum attack in the superposition model on Poly1305, proposed at FSE 2005, widely used and claimed to be quantumly secure. We also answer an open problem by analyzing the effect of the tweak to the FX construction.

We have also generalized the algorithm. We propose for the first time a quantum algorithm for solving the hidden problem with parallel modular additions, with a complexity that matches both Simon and Kuperberg in its extremes.

In order to verify our theoretical analysis, and to get concrete estimates of the cost of the algorithms, we have simulated them, and were able to validate our estimated complexities.

Finally, we analyze the security of some classical symmetric constructions with concrete parameters, to evaluate the impact and practicality of the proposed tweak. We concluded that the tweak does not seem to be efficient.

Keywords: Quantum cryptanalysis · Hidden shift problem Simon-meets-kuperberg · Poly1305 · Symmetric cryptography Modular additions

1 Introduction

As years go by, quantum computers becomes an increasingly concrete threat. The scientific community is already anticipating the changes in the hardness of various problems such a computer would produce. Cryptology is one of the affected disciplines. Indeed, the current state-of-the-art asymmetric primitives

© International Association for Cryptologic Research 2018
T. Peyrin and S. Galbraith (Eds.): ASIACRYPT 2018, LNCS 11272, pp. 560–592, 2018.
https://doi.org/10.1007/978-3-030-03326-2_19

would become insecure, and the NIST has launched a competition for finding new primitives.

Symmetric cryptography, essential for enabling secure communications, seemed much less affected at first sight: for a long time, the greatest known threat was Grover's algorithm, which allows exhaustive key searches in the square root of the normal complexity. Thus, it was believed that doubling the key lengths suffices to maintain an equivalent security in the post-quantum world.

At the same time, the security proofs in symmetric cryptography often need to make unrealistic assumptions. Therefore, the security of concrete symmetric primitives is mainly based on cryptanalysis: we only gain confidence in their security through extensive and continuous scrutiny. Hence, it is not possible to determine if a symmetric primitive is secure in the quantum world without first understanding how a quantum adversary can attack it. New results in this direction have appeared lately, like quantum generic meet-in-the-middle attacks on iterative block ciphers [28], quantum linear and differential attacks [30], or improved algorithms for collisions or multicollisions [17,27].

Using Simon's Algorithm. Some other recent attacks are based on the polynomial-time quantum algorithm of Simon [43]. It began with [34], which presented a distinguisher for 3-round Feistel schemes. It has then been followed among other works by an attack against the classically secure Even-Mansour construction [35], some quantum related-key attacks [41] or a key-recovery attack against the CAESAR candidate AEZ [11].

This algorithm has also been proven efficient against well-known modes of operation for MACs and authenticated encryption at Crypto 2016 [29], where a quantum slide attacks was also demonstrated, with a complexity linear in the block size (see also [42]). An analysis of the FX construct against quantum adversaries was presented at Asiacrypt 2017 [37]. A combination of Grover and Simon showed it was much less secure than expected, and for instance the PRINCE cipher is broken in the quantum setting. These surprising results were the first clearly showing that doubling the key-length of symmetric primitives is not enough – in some cases – to provide an equivalent security against quantum adversaries when considering the superposition scenario, that we discuss next.

The Attack Model. These last mentioned attacks apply in a scenario of superposition quantum queries. It means that the adversary is not only allowed to perform local computations on a quantum computer[1], but is also allowed to perform superposition queries to a remote quantum cryptographic oracle, to obtain the superposition of the outputs. These attacks have been described as *superposition attacks* [20], *quantum chosen message attacks* [10] or *quantum security* [50].

This is a strong model for the attacker, but there are very good arguments for studying the security of symmetric primitives in this setting (see for instance [24] or [25] for more detailed justifications of the model):

---

[1] In [9,15,47,51], it can query a quantum oracle with an arbitrary quantum input.

1. This model is simple. Using another model would imply artificial and hard to respect measures with respect to cryptographic oracles in a world with quantum resources, with complex manipulations of yet uncertain outcome[2].
2. Safety in this model implies safety in any other scenario, even advanced ones (*e.g.* obfuscated algorithms).
3. Though powerful, this model is not trivial: not all primitives are broken in it. Actually, several resistant constructions have been proposed [4,10,20,25,44].

All the attacks proposed in this paper fit in this model.

Countering the Attacks [2]. At Eurocrypt 2017, a proposal for countering the attacks from [29] was presented [2]. The authors propose to replace the common $(\mathbb{Z}/(2))^n$ addition, vulnerable to the Simon algorithm, with other operations that imply a harder problem to solve. The most promising of these operations, because of efficiency and implementations issues, already used in several symmetric schemes (*i.e.* [26,40,49]), is addition over $\mathbb{Z}/(2^n)$, i.e. modular addition. The authors claim the quantum hardness of the hidden shift problem proves the security of their proposal against quantum chosen-plaintext attacks.

This approach is a priori an interesting direction to analyze and study. The authors did not provide a deeper analysis of the impact of various parameters on the security. The attacks are no longer in $O(n)$ (with n the state size) when using the modular addition, as Simon's algorithm does not apply anymore, but we could describe attacks that are still a lot faster than the generic ones by using Kuperberg's algorithm [32], e.g. $2^{O(\sqrt{n})}$ instead of $O\left(\sqrt{2^n}\right)$.

Indeed, classically, a symmetric primitive is considered secure when no attack better than the generic attack exists. While the complexity of the generic exhaustive search is exponential ($2^{n/2}$), the quantum attacks on primitives with modular additions have a sub-exponential complexity. This implies a need for a redefinition of *security*, when building *secure* primitives with these counter measures, as the best generic attacks that define the security of the cipher (based on Kuperberg now) will be better than the exhaustive search. Also, concrete proposals for the size of the primitives needed in order to provide the typical security needs (*i.e.* 128 bits) are missing.

Describing in detail the new best quantum attacks on the proposed constructions is necessary to provide concrete designs for a given wanted security. To evaluate the interest of such constructions, we should compare these designs with concrete parameters to other (quantum-secure) ones, like the Advanced Encryption Standard (AES) [19].

On Kuperberg's Complexity, Improvements, Applications. Studying in detail Kuperberg's algorithm, proposing improvements and simulating the complexity for concrete parameters has not been done before and is of algorithmic general interest. Such an analysis is required to determine suitable parameter sizes for

---

[2] Implementations of theoretically secure quantum cryptography remain yet not fully understood, as shown by the attacks [38,48,52].

a given security level. Hidden shift algorithms have an impact beyond the symmetric variants we just mentioned, and can threaten other primitives, such as Poly1305 [6], which uses modular additions. Hidden shift problems also arise in some other cryptographic areas, such as isogenies. They are for example relevant to assess the security of CSIDH [16].

1.1   Our Contributions

1. Kuperberg's algorithm: improvement, generalization. We studied Kuperberg's quantum algorithm for hidden shifts in the group $\mathbb{Z}/(N)$ [32] and its applications in symmetric cryptography.[3] We focus on the groups $\mathbb{Z}/(2^n)$, which are widely used in symmetric cryptography. The original algorithm retrieves one bit of the secret shift at a time and uses a reducibility property to get the next bit. We propose a variant that performs better by getting all the bits in one step, allowing a drastic cost reduction of the attack on Poly1305. In the extended version of this paper [12], we also propose a generic algorithm to solve the hidden shift problem in non-abelian groups.

2. Simon Meets Kuperberg. We propose a new quantum algorithm that considers a generalization for products of cyclic groups $(\mathbb{Z}/(2^w))^p$ and its subgroups), commonly used in symmetric primitives. The problem is more easily solvable in these groups than in $\mathbb{Z}/(2^{wp})$. Our complexity analysis shows how it meets Simon ($w = 1$) and Kuperberg ($p = 1$) in each extreme.

3. Simulation of the algorithms. We have implemented the classical part of these algorithms (Kuperberg, improved Kuperberg and Simon-meets-Kuperberg) and simulated them in order to estimate the asymptotic query complexity, and to get values for parameters of interest, verifying the expected complexities[4].

4. Attack on Poly1305 in the superposition model. We propose a quantum attack on Poly1305 [6], a MAC that has been standardized for TLS 1.2 [36] and 1.3 [1], and is notably used by OpenSSH, Firefox and Chrome. In [8] a classical and quantum security of 128 bits is claimed for Poly1305: *"'Information-theoretic' MACs such as GMAC and Poly1305 already protect against quantum computers without any modifications: their security analysis already assumes an attacker with unlimited computing power."* Our attack, that works in the superposition model, has a complexity of 2^{38} and uses our improved Kuperberg's algorithm. It recovers half of the 234-bit key, allowing forgeries of authenticator

---

[3] Even if some later algorithms have been developed and are more efficient, we focus on the original algorithm for two main reasons. We focus on quantum query and time complexity and the gain from [39] is in memory and [21] needs an exponential time classical post-processing. Moreover, we want concrete values and not asymptotic exponents and the algorithm in [33] is far harder to estimate precisely.

[4] The code is available at https://who.paris.inria.fr/Xavier.Bonnetain/extra/code.tar.gz.

messages with the same nonce. The attack is not a direct application of the algorithm and requires some additional techniques.

5. Attack on the FX variants. We answer an open question asked in [37], assessing the quantum security of the FX construction with any group law. If the inner key addition is done with a commutative group law, the security gain of the construct is marginal, and the best we can hope to achieve with a non-abelian group is a gain of around $n/3$ bits of security for an n-bit inner key.

6. Evaluate the proposed countermeasures from [2]. The final aim was to determine how to size the symmetric primitives in order to offer a certain desired security, and to decide whether the proposed countermeasure was sufficient, and efficient enough in practice. Using modular additions in vulnerable constructions instead of xors for key addition increases the complexity of the corresponding quantum key-recovery attack, but we show that the proposal from [2] does not seem practical. It would require an internal state size of a few thousand bits, to be compared with the size of the internal state of AES-256, which is 128 bits.

Organization of the Paper. Section 2 introduces some preliminary material. Section 3 presents our study on Kuperberg's algorithm and our improvement, several generalizations, our simulations and the inferred complexities. Section 4 describes our new quantum algorithm for parallel additions. Section 5 presents the first quantum attack on Poly1305 in the superposition model, using Kuperberg's algorithm. Section 6 estimates the strength of the FX construct with new group laws. Section 7 applies our previous results to actual symmetric primitives, deducing the key or internal state size that must be used in those constructs to offer a desired quantum security. The paper ends with a conclusion in Sect. 8.

2 Preliminaries

In this section, we present the quantum symmetric attacks from [29,37], the proposed solution from [2] and our cost model.

2.1 Quantum Attacks Using Simon's Algorithm from [29]

In [29] Simon's quantum algorithm was applied to cryptanalyze several widely used modes of operation and CAESAR candidates. This was possible due to the exponential speedup of Simon's algorithm, that solves the following problem:
    Let $f : \{0,1\}^n \rightarrow \{0,1\}^n$. Given the promise that there exists $s \in \{0,1\}^n$ such that for any $(x,y) \in \{0,1\}^n$, $[f(x) = f(y)] \Leftrightarrow [x \oplus y \in \{0^n, s\}]$, find s.
    The authors applied Simon's algorithm to find a secret information in time linear in the block size ($O(n)$ instead of $O(2^{n/2})$ classically). One implication of the problem was not verified in the attacks: with a small probability, we might have $f(x) = f(y)$ and $x \oplus y \notin \{0^n, s\}$. However, they showed that the algorithm is still efficient with a random function in place of a random permutation.

2.2   Solution Proposed in [2]

In [2], the authors propose to change the group law in the primitives broken by [29], to prevent the use of Simon's algorithm. They also propose a security reduction from the primitives to the corresponding hidden shift problem, and claim that they are safe, as no polynomial algorithm for these problems is known. They notably propose $(\mathbb{Z}/(2^n), +)$ (for which Kuperberg's algorithm is, in a sense, not a threat, as it is superpolynomial), or the symmetric group $\mathcal{S}_n$.

2.3   Cryptanalysis of the FX Construction [37]

The FX construction [31] uses a block cipher E_k and two additional keys k_1, k_2, and is defined as $\mathrm{FX}_{k_0,k_1,k_2}(x) = E_{k_0}(x \oplus k_1) \oplus k_2$. It can be broken by combining Simon's and Grover's algorithms: one can perform an exhaustive search on k_0 and then see the FX construct as an Even-Mansour with the public permutation E_{k_0}, which can be broken with Simon's algorithm. The authors left as an open problem the case where the whitening keys were added with modular addition.

2.4   Cost Model

We're interested in the explicit costs of the algorithms we study. These algorithm have all a similar shape: they use a generation circuit that produces some relevant qubits, a combination circuit that uses the produced qubits, and a control circuit that chooses which qubits are to be combined. The generation circuit is a Quantum Fourier Transform applied to an oracle, whose total cost in time and memory is the number of queries. The combination circuit has a fixed cost, and can only be used once per query. The control circuit can be more complex, but only have to reason about classical values, and hence can be implemented purely classically. Its cost in time and memory will be the cost in query, with a polynomial overhead. As we expect that a classical computer will be far more efficient than a quantum computer to apply the same number of gates, we estimated that the bottleneck of our algorithm will be the quantum part of it, and that the relevant cost unit here is the number of queries.

3   New Results on Kuperberg's Algorithm

In this section, we study Kuperberg's quantum algorithm for solving the hidden shift problem. While the final aim is to be able to accurately estimate the complexities of the cryptanalysis on primitives whose security rely on the hidden shift problem, we have also performed a deeper work that verifies and helps better understanding Kuperberg's algorithm and its performance. We propose a new variant of the algorithm that reduces its cost, and that will allow to build the performant attack from Sect. 5. We've implemented the classical part of these algorithms and made some simulations in order to get concrete estimates of the asymptotic complexity and values for parameters of interest, that match and refine the theoretical expectations. In the extended version of this paper [12], we also propose a generic algorithm to solve the hidden shift problem in non-abelian groups.

3.1   Hidden Shift Problem and Quantum Algorithms

The hidden shift problem (HSP) is defined as follows:

Let f, g be two injective functions, $(\mathbb{G}, \cdot)$ a group. Given the promise that there exists $s \in \mathbb{G}$ such that, for all x, $f(x) = g(x \cdot s)$, retrieve s.

We say that f is a shifted version of g, the shift being s. To estimate the complexity, we consider $n = \log_2 |\mathbb{G}|$. The hardness of the problem depends on the group law. If it is a bitwise xor, Simon's algorithm [43] solves it in polynomial time. If the group law is a modular addition, it can be solved with a linear number of queries [21]. This method requires an exponential-time classical post-processing, and as such, won't be interesting for us. The first sub-exponential (in quantum query and quantum and classical time) algorithms are presented in [32]. They have a time and space complexity in $2^{O(\sqrt{n})}$ for a group of size 2^n. Other variants were developed later, with an algorithm with quantum polynomial space, but slightly worse time complexity, in $2^{O(\sqrt{n \log(n)})}$ [39], and some algorithms in [33], that generalize the previous one, allowing some trade-offs between classical and quantum memory and time.

From this point, we focus on additions modulo a power of 2, as they are very common in symmetric cryptography, due to implementation reasons.

Single Modular Addition. All these algorithms are in two parts: an oracle that calls f and g to produce some labeled qubits $(\ell, |\psi_\ell\rangle)$, with ℓ a classical value that we call a *label*, and a combination circuit that transforms them into more interesting ones. The oracle part uses the quantum oracle

$$O : |b\rangle |x\rangle |y\rangle \mapsto \begin{cases} |0\rangle |x\rangle |y \oplus f(x)\rangle & \text{if } b = 0 \\ |1\rangle |x\rangle |y \oplus g(x)\rangle & \text{if } b = 1 \end{cases}.$$

Generation. The oracle circuit (Fig. 1a) produces the uniform superposition in the registers b and x with Hadamard gates (H), feeds them to the oracle (O), and then measures register y. This measurement gives a result y_0 and collapses the b and x registers in the state $\sum_{f(x)=y_0} |0\rangle |x\rangle + \sum_{g(x)=y_0} |1\rangle |x\rangle$, which is the state $|0\rangle |x_0\rangle + |1\rangle |x_0 + s\rangle$ for a given (unknown) x_0, thanks to the promise. We then apply a quantum Fourier transform (QFT) on the x register and measure the result. This gives us a uniformly distributed ℓ, and collapses the remaining qubit in the state $|\psi_\ell\rangle = |0\rangle + \exp\left(2i\pi \frac{s\ell}{2^n}\right) |1\rangle$.

This qubit depends on s, but is not directly exploitable. The qubit $|\psi_{2^{n-1}}\rangle = |0\rangle + \exp(i\pi s) |1\rangle$ is very interesting, as it is $|+\rangle$ if the lowest bit of s is 0, and else is $|-\rangle$. Hence, if we measure it in the $\{|-\rangle, |+\rangle\}$ basis, we get one bit of s.

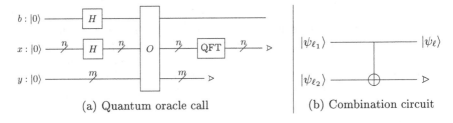

(a) Quantum oracle call   (b) Combination circuit

Fig. 1. Quantum circuits for Kuperberg's algorithm

Combination. We have then a combination part, that uses the produced qubits to generate some more interesting ones. The combination is done with the circuit in Fig. 1b, that consists of one controlled-not and a measurement of the second register. By doing so, we destroy two elements in order to produce one. Before the measurement, the system is in the state CNOT $|\psi_{\ell_1}\rangle |\psi_{\ell_2}\rangle =$

$$|00\rangle + \exp\left(2i\pi \frac{s(\ell_1 + \ell_2)}{2^n}\right)|10\rangle + \exp\left(2i\pi \frac{s\ell_2}{2^n}\right)\left(|01\rangle + \exp\left(2i\pi \frac{s(\ell_1 - \ell_2)}{2^n}\right)|11\rangle\right)$$

If we measure a 0 we'll get the qubit $|\psi_{\ell_1+\ell_2}\rangle$, and if we measure a 1 we'll get $|\psi_{\ell_1-\ell_2}\rangle$. Both outcomes are equiprobable. If we only look at the labels, the combination routine destroys 2 labels and produces a new label, which is either their sum or difference. We want to obtain the label 2^{n-1}. This abstract problem would be a problem of subset-sum modulo 2^n if the operation at each combination was fixed, and not picked randomly in $\{+,-\}$, as we would want to find a tuple satisfying

$$\sum_{i \in I} \ell_i = 2^{n-1} \mod 2^n.$$

However, in our situation, the problem is closer to finding a tuple satisfying

$$\sum_{i \in I} \delta_i \ell_i = 2^{n-1} \mod 2^n,$$

with $\delta_i \in \{-1, 1\}$ unknown before the actual destructive computation.

With these quantum tools, we can produce random elements and combine them, but we need an algorithm to choose which elements to combine.

Choosing the Elements to Combine. As a combination produces either $a + b$ or $a - b$, we need to find a property preserved in both cases, to not lose everything if the wrong outcome occurs. It turns out divisibility by 2 is such a property: if both a and b are multiples of 2^k, $a + b$ and $a - b$ will also be multiples of 2^k. Hence comes naturally the idea of the combination algorithm: from the elements we have, generate elements with a higher divisibility by 2, until we get 2^{n-1}. To achieve this, we can combine elements such that $a + b$ or $a - b$ has a high divisibility by 2 (e.g. have a long trail of 0 in their binary representation).

Hence, an algorithm to find 2^{n-1} is then to separate the elements in pools by their divisibility by 2, and, beginning with the odd numbers, to combine the two elements that can produce a number with the highest possible divisibility by 2. As this property corresponds to the longest partial collision in the binary representation of the elements, they can be efficiently found with a radix tree. There is however one caveat: we don't want the useless 0 element, so we try to not combine two identical elements, or one element and its opposite.

As the interesting a and b collide on their lowest bits, they have the same divisibility by 2, hence $a = 2^k(2a' + 1)$ and $b = 2^k(2b' + 1)$. Then, $a + b = 2^{k+1}(a + b + 1)$ and $a - b = 2^{k+1}(a - b)$. This means that even in the bad case (with a small divisibility by 2), we still get a slightly better divisibility by 2. Then, the algorithm consists in using this heuristic until we get 2^{n-1}.

This is Algorithm 1, which is Algorithm 3 of [32]. The paper also presents a sketch of proof that its complexity is in $\widetilde{O}\left(2^{\sqrt{2\log_2(3)n}}\right)$. As the paper only focuses on the asymptotic exponent complexity, the polynomial part is not well known. We can however deduce from the sketch of proof a complexity in $O\left(n\sqrt{n}2^{\sqrt{2\log_2(3)n}}\right)$ to retrieve the whole hidden shift, which may not be a tight bound (both for the polynomial and the exponent), due to the way the sketch of proof works.

Algorithm 1. Kuperberg's original algorithm [32], without qubits, in base 2

Generate a sufficiently large number N of elements in $\mathbb{Z}/(2^n)$ ▷ Queries
Separate them in pools P_i of elements divisible by 2^i and not 2^{i+1}
for $i := 0$ to $n - 2$ **do**
    while $|P_i| \geq 2$ **do**
        Pop two elements (a, b) of P_i where $a + b$ or $a - b$ has the highest possible divisibility by 2 (and is not 0)
        c is chosen randomly in $\{a + b, a - b\}$ ▷ Combination
        Insert c in the corresponding P_j
        if $P_{n-1} \neq \emptyset$ **then**   ▷ Found $|\psi_{2^{n-1}}\rangle$?
            Perform a measurement on $|\psi_{2^{n-1}}\rangle$
            return s_0
        end if
    end while
end for
return Failure

If this succeeds, we get the value of the lowest significant bit of the hidden shift, s_0. We have then to retrieve the other bits of s. This can be done using a recursive procedure: with the knowledge of $s \mod 2 = s_0$, we can construct the functions $f'(x) = f(2x)$ and $g'(x) = g(2x + s_0)$, that have the hidden shift

$s' = (s - s_0)/2$ in $\mathbb{Z}/(2^{n-1})$. The 2nd bit of s is the lowest bit of s', and we can reapply the routine, and so on until we get all the bits.

Quantum Memory Cost. This algorithm has a cost in quantum memory of one qubit per query, plus the memory cost of the quantum oracle, which depends on the concrete instance. This memory is weakly entangled: after the quantum oracle queries, we will have only pairs of entangled qubits. This notably implies that a corrupted qubit will not disrupt the whole computation, one would only need to erase the corresponding label.

Classical Cost. The classical part needs to search for the best colliding pairs. This can be efficiently implemented using a radix tree. Moreover, as for our purposes, the labels x and $-x$ are equivalent, we can normalize them, for example by forcing, in the binary representation, the most significant bit or the bit after the lowest significant one to be a zero. The time and memory cost will be in $O(N \log(N))$. With $N = O(2^{\sqrt{2 \log_2(3)n}})$, the complexity will be in $O(\sqrt{n} 2^{\sqrt{2 \log_2(3)n}})$. This represents a logarithmic overhead compared to the quantum query cost. This part is purely classical, and we consider here that the relevant cost metric is the quantum cost.

3.2   New Variant with Improved the Time Complexity

In this section we propose an optimization of the previous algorithm that allows to perform the attack in Sect. 5. Previously each bit of the shift was retrieved independently. We have noticed that if some qubits remains once we have found the target qubit, we can reuse them in the rest of the computation. The phase of the element ℓ is $2\pi \frac{\ell s}{2^n} = 2\pi \frac{\ell(s_0 + 2s')}{2^n} = 2\pi \frac{\ell s'}{2^{n-1}} + 2\pi \frac{\ell s_0}{2^n}$. If $s_0 = 0$, we can reuse them directly as elements of $\mathbb{Z}/(2^{n-1})$ to retrieve the next bit (we just have to see the label modulo 2^{n-1}, that is, drop its most significant bit).

If $s_0 = 1$, we have an additional phase of $2\pi \frac{\ell}{2^n}$ that prevents us to do so. We can get rid of it by applying a phase shift gate of angle $-2\pi \frac{\ell}{2^n}$ (which is the identity for $|0\rangle$ and changes the phase of $|1\rangle$ by a given angle) before reusing it. We can apply this trick to reuse the remaining qubits, once we have found 2^{n-1}. Moreover, in the 2nd phase, the interesting elements are $010\ldots0$ and $110\ldots0$, that is, any element of the penultimate pool. Likewise, we can use an element in a pool to retrieve one bit of the shift if we know all the preceding bits.

This strategy leads to the improved Algorithm 2, where we ensure that each pool stays non-empty. If we miss one qubit, won't have the value of the corresponding bit of s, and, as we won't know which rotations to do, on the following bits of s.

Differences in Complexity. The elements we keep to retrieve the whole shift are not used in a combination, hence we can have $n - 1$ combination less. The combination not done will be the least interesting one, hence this will have a negligible impact. Another constraint is that all the pools must be nonempty. As the hardest to fill is the one targeted by the original algorithm, it does not change much the cost. Empirically, we found that the overhead compared to the original algorithm is less than 2, and converges to 1 as n grows. The main difference is that we only need to proceed once and not n times.

The complexity proof of the original algorithm naturally carries to the new one. The core idea is that by combining 2^e elements, we can expect to produce around $2^e/3$ elements whose label is a multiple of 2^e. Applying this principle multiple times leads to needing an initial pool of size $O\left(n2^{\sqrt{2\log_2(3)n}}\right)$ in order produce the wanted qubit with a negligible failure probability. Hence, the complexity is in $O\left(n2^{\sqrt{2\log_2(3)n}}\right)$. As the only difference in both algorithms concerns the use of $2n$ qubits, the same principle is applicable for both algorithms. With these complexity estimates, we obtain that the cost to retrieve the whole secret with our algorithm is in $O\left(n2^{\sqrt{2\log_2(3)n}}\right)$, while the original algorithm would be in $O\left(n\sqrt{n}2^{\sqrt{2\log_2(3)n}}\right)$. We found out that it is better in practice, as developed in Sect. 3.4.

The memory complexity is negligibly increased, as we have slightly more elements to deal with at once.

Algorithm 2. Variant to get all the bits of the secret in one pass

---

Generate N random numbers in $\mathbb{Z}/(2^n)$
Separate them in pools P_i of elements divisible by 2^i and not 2^{i+1}
for $i := 0$ to $n - 2$ **do**
    while $|P_i| \geq 3$ **do**   ▷ Ensures P_i stays non-empty
        Pop two elements (a, b) of P_i where $a + b$ or $a - b$ has the highest possible divisibility by 2 (and is not 0)
            c is chosen randomly in $\{a + b, a - b\}$
            Insert c in the corresponding P_j
            if $\forall i \in [0, n-1], P_i \neq \emptyset$ **then**
                Perform a measurement on a qubit in each pool
                return s
            end if
    end while
end for
return Failure

3.3 Approximated Promise

In concrete attacks, we may want to use this algorithm on functions that respect partially the promise. We study in this section various cases.

Lemma 1 (Unwanted collisions). *Let* $f : \mathbb{Z}/(2^n) \rightarrow \mathbb{Z}/(2^n)$ *be a random function,* $s \in \mathbb{Z}/(2^n)$, g *such that* $g(x) = f(x + s)$. *Given a quantum oracle*

access to f and g, we can retrieve s in Q quantum queries if we can solve the hidden shift problem in $\mathbb{Z}/(2^n)$ with a permutation using Q/e quantum queries.

Proof. This case was studied in Sect. 2.2 of [29] in the context of Simon's algorithm. It corresponds to the hidden subgroup problem with a non-injective function. It then still respect for all x, $f(x) = g(x + s)$ for a secret s.

Let's decompose each step. The measurement of the third register of

$$\sum_x |0\rangle \, |x\rangle \, |f(x)\rangle + |1\rangle \, |x\rangle \, |g(x)\rangle$$

produces

$$|0\rangle \sum_{j=1}^{c} |x_j\rangle + |1\rangle \sum_{j=1}^{c} |x_j + s\rangle$$

and the measurement yields $f(x_j)$ with probability $c/2^n$. After the QFT, the measurement will give us a label ℓ and a qubit

$$\left(\sum_{j=1}^{c} \exp\left(2i\pi \frac{x_j \ell}{2^n} \right) \right) \left(|0\rangle + \exp\left(2i\pi \frac{s\ell}{2^n} \right) |1\rangle \right)$$

As a qubit is invariant by a global phase shift, we still get a valid element. However, it is not uniformly sampled, and the probability of getting a given ℓ is

$$p = \frac{1}{c2^n} \left| \sum_{j=1}^{c} \exp\left(2i\pi \frac{x_j \ell}{2^n} \right) \right|^2.$$

Notably, the case $\ell = 0$, which is useless for us, is the most probable.

It is known [23] that for a random function, the expected number of images with r preimages is $2^n/(er!)$. The first measurement samples on the images, uniformly if it is a bijection, and proportionally to the number of preimages in the general case. That means we'll have a probability of $r/(er!) = 1/(e(r-1)!)$ of getting an image with r preimages. We'll get a unique preimage with probability $1/e$, so that means with e times the number of samples, we'll get enough elements with only one preimage. This is a very rough approximation, as the multiple preimages induces only a bias on the generated elements.

Remark 1. Alternatively, we can consider the function $F(x) = (f(x), f(x + 1), \dots)$, that has the same shifts as f, but has a smaller probability of unwanted collisions, at the cost of having to query f multiple times for one query of F.

Lemma 2 (Multiple shifts). *Let $(s_i)_{i \le m} \in \mathbb{Z}/(2^n)^m$, let f, g two permutations of $\mathbb{Z}/(2^n)$ such that, for all x, i, $f(x) = g(x + s_i)$. The first bits of the s_i can be retrieved if and only if they are all equal. They can be retrieved by solving the HSP in $\mathbb{Z}/(2^k)$ with the same functions, with $2^k = \gcd_{i \ne j}(2^n, s_i - s_j)$.*

Proof. We can study what happens with two shifts, s and t. We have, for all x, $f(x) = g(x + s) = g(x + t)$.

From these equalities, we can deduce that for all x and λ, $f(x) = f(x + \lambda(s - t)) = g(x + s + \lambda(s - t))$. The functions have in fact plenty of shifts: $s + \lambda(s - t)$, the exact number depending on the divisibility by 2 of $s - t$. The bits of x that are above this level have in fact no impact on the value of f, so this problem is degenerate: if $s - t = 2^k \mu$, we have an instance of the problem in $\mathbb{Z}/(2^k)$, with a hidden shift $s' = s \mod 2^k = t \mod 2^k$, and we have $2^k = \gcd(2^n, s - t)$. We cannot get the other bits of s or t, as all the $s + \lambda(s - t)$ are also valid shifts.

For more shifts, we need to consider the difference that have the smallest divisibility by two, that is, the gcd of all the differences with 2^n.

As the divisibility by two of the difference corresponds to an equality in the first bits, the lemma holds.

Remark 2. If we don't know that the functions have multiple shifts, or if the gcd is not known in advance, this is still detectable, as the labels we measure will always divide 2^{n-k}.

Proof of the Remark. The formula of the probability of measuring ℓ is $p(\ell) = \frac{1}{c2^n} \left| \sum_{j=1}^{c} \exp\left(2i\pi \frac{x_j \ell}{2^n}\right) \right|^2$ with c shifts. This reduces to

$$\frac{1}{c2^n} \left| \exp\left(2i\pi \frac{x\ell}{2^n}\right) \sum_{\lambda} \exp\left(2i\pi \frac{\lambda 2^k \ell}{2^n}\right) \right|^2.$$

This is 0 if $\exp\left(2i\pi \frac{2^k \ell}{2^n}\right) \neq 1$, that is, if $2^{n-k} \nmid \ell$. This means we'll only get some ℓs with at least $n - k$ trailing zeros.

The following lemma addresses the problem of functions which respect the shift promise only for a subset of their input, and shows this is still resolvable if the number of wrong inputs is small enough.

Lemma 3 (Partial shift). *Let f, g two permutations of $\mathbb{Z}/(N)$, $s \in \mathbb{Z}/(N)$, $X \subset \mathbb{Z}/(N)$ such that, for all $x \in X$, $f(x) = g(x + s)$. Then if the hidden subgroup problem in $\mathbb{Z}/(N)$ costs Q queries, we can retrieve s given quantum oracle access to f and g in Q queries, with probability $(|X|/N)^Q$.*

Proof. If we measure an $f(x)$ whose x is in X, then we have a valid element. This happens with probability $|X|/N$. If this is not the case, we get a malformed qubit. We can expect the algorithm to succeed only if all the Q queried elements are valid, which happens with probability $(|X|/N)^Q$.

Remark 3. It would also be possible for the algorithm to succeed if we have a way to identify the bad x from the value $f(x)/g(x)$, which is measured, as it would allow us to drop the corrupted qubit when we create it. The problem would then only concern the unidentified bad x.

Lemma 4 (Input restriction). *Let f, g be two permutations of $\mathbb{Z}/(N)$, $s \in \mathbb{Z}/(N)$ such that, for all x, $f(x) = g(x + s)$. Given a quantum oracle access to f and g restricted to the inputs $0 \leq x < 2^n$, if $0 \leq s < 2^{n-1}$ and the hidden subgroup problem in $\mathbb{Z}/(2^{n-1})$ can be solved in Q queries, s can be retrieved in eQ^2 queries.*

Proof. We are only given access to the interval $[0; 2^n)$. We cannot see the hidden shift in $\mathbb{Z}/(N)$ as a hidden shift in $\mathbb{Z}/(2^n)$. However, if s is small enough, we have an instance of a partial hidden shift, the valid elements being the ones such that $0 \leq x < 2^n$ and $0 \leq x + s < 2^n$. The probability to get a bad element is less than $s/2^n$ in this case. If we need Q queries, and $s/2^n \simeq 1/Q$, then the success probability will be greater than $(1 - 1/Q)^Q \simeq 1/e$. This fails for greater s.

However, we can query a subinterval of $[0; 2^n)$ for f and g. For $A \in [0; 2^{n-1})$, if we query $[0; 2^{n-1})$ to $f(x)$ and $g(x + A)$, we will retrieve s with probability $1/e$ if $0 \leq s - A < 2^{n-1}/Q'$, if we need Q' queries to solve the hidden subgroup problem in $\mathbb{Z}/(2^{n-1})$.

To retrieve s, we can sequentially test for all A multiples of $2^{n-1}/Q'$, until we reach 2^{n-1}. We then have Q' intervals to test, and each test costs Q' queries. Moreover, the algorithm will succeed if the test with the right guess of A succeeds, and can be verified with a few classical queries. As the right guess has a success probability greater than $1/e$, we expect to find the shift in eQ'^2 queries.

Remark 4. Here, we do a sequential test of the intervals. We could do a Grover search on it instead, but we would need to choose a slightly higher number of queries, in order to have a success probability very close to one. Moreover, it would force us to implement all the control system that chooses which qubit to collide quantumly and not classically.

Remark 5. We can see this method as trying to solve the HSP in $\mathbb{Z}$. It also shows that considering only the cyclic groups $\mathbb{Z}/(2^n)$ allows to solve the problem in *any* cyclic group in subexponential time, despite a different group structure.

3.4   Simulations

We have simulated the classical part of the algorithm by replacing the quantum measurements by random outcomes. We used this to get an estimate of the query complexity: We generate a certain amount of random numbers, and then combine them in order to get the values we want. We hence get an estimate of the success probability for a given amount of samples (Fig. 2), and deduce from it an asymptotic complexity for a constant success probability. Table 1 shows some results of these simulations for different values of n, for 90% success probability. The code of this implementation is available at https://who.paris.inria.fr/Xavier.Bonnetain/extra/code.tar.gz.

Figure 2 shows the estimated probability of retrieving the whole secret in function of the number of initial queries for a 64-bit secret. We've considered this parameter instead of some finer ones, such as the numbers of bits we retrieved

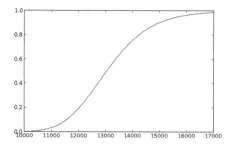

Fig. 2. Estimated success probability in the number of samples, for 64 bits

because of the dependency between the bits we can retrieve: we have to retrieve them in order, and the first ones are the hardest to get. We can try to guess the missing bits, but as we destroy our qubits when we measure them, we can't recover from a wrong guess. It shows a transition from a negligible probability of success to a negligible probability of failure in less than a factor 2. As the algorithm is collision-based, it performs significantly better if it is run once with a bigger initial pool than many times with smaller pools. It also shows that the gap to get an arbitrarily small failure probability is small, which is useful if we want to combine it with another quantum algorithm, like a Grover search.

Table 1. Some results of the simulation of Algorithm 2 for 90% success probability

n	Queries	$\log_2$(queries)	$1.8\sqrt{n} - 0.5$	Number of tests
16	118	6.9	6.7	10^6
32	826	9.7	9.7	10^6
64	14975	13.9	13.9	5×10^5
80	49200	15.6	15.6	10^5
128	9.8×10^5	19.9	19.9	5×10^4

We can then deduce a heuristic complexity in query of $0.7 \times 2^{1.8\sqrt{n}}$ for a 90% success probability for Algorithm 2, which matches the exponent complexity of $\tilde{O}\left(2^{\sqrt{2\log_2(3)n}}\right)$ of the less efficient Algorithm 1, as $\sqrt{2\log_2(3)} \simeq 1.8$. We also performed a few simulations of Algorithm 1, which gave slightly smaller results (the ratio was less than 2, and decreased as n increased). As Algorithm 1 needs to be repeated n times, it performs worse, both asymptotically and for the ranges we were able to simulate. We see that the polynomial part is in fact a constant next to 1 for Algorithm 2, which hints that the bound in [32] for Algorithm 1 of $O\left(n2^{\sqrt{2\log_2(3)n}}\right)$ to retrieve the last bit is probably tight for the exponent part, but not for the polynomial part.

4   New Algorithm: Simon Meets Kuperberg

We describe in this section a new quantum algorithm, that, for the first time, solves efficiently the HSP problem when considering a product of cyclic groups, which often appears in symmetric constructions [5,7,22,45]. We also provide a simulation of the algorithm in Sect. 4.3, showing that our complexity estimations are correct.

4.1   Solving the Hidden Shift Problem for Parallel Modular Additions

An interesting generalization for, inter alia, symmetric cryptography is to consider p termwise additions modulo 2^w, that is, a modular addition in $\mathbb{Z}/(2^w)^p$. The hidden shift in this case is a vector $s = (s_1, \ldots, s_p)$ of p words of w bits each. The aim of this section is to propose a new algorithm that deals efficiently with that group. The first natural approach was to apply an adapted variant of Kuperberg (as suggested in [32, Thm 7.1]), but its complexity of $2^{O(\sqrt{n})}$ significantly differs from optimal: we explain in this section how to considerably improve this. We propose a new algorithm which complexity is close to optimal. It exploits three facts in particular that allow us to consequently improve the complexity. In order to describe our algorithm, we need to previously adapt the first part of Kuperberg's algorithm by considering a quantum Fourier transform compatible with the group law, so the original one is changed to into a termwise variant. The oracle circuit produces the qubits $\left| \psi_{\ell_1, \ldots, \ell_p} \right\rangle = |0\rangle + \exp\left(2i\pi \frac{\sum s_j \ell_j}{2^w} \right) |1\rangle$, the product is replaced by an inner product. The combination circuit also works the same way, and produces a termwise sum or difference.

Better Worst-Case Gain. The first fact that allows to improve the complexity over a basic algorithm is realizing that, though the combination strategy can be quite similar with a research of partial collisions on the lowest significant bits of each term, there is however a difference in the behavior in the disadvantageous case: while we gained only one 0 in the former situation, here, we'll get a 0 in each term in which we have a collision in the lowest 1 (p zeros) while the size of the corresponding list is big enough. We also have more choices in the combinations, and we can have various equivalent and incompatible possibilities, with collisions on different parts of the vector.

With p+1 Equations We Can Always Gain p Zeros. As before, we can separate the elements in pools, depending on the divisibility by 2 of each term. Instead of looking at the position of the first one, we look at the position of the first one in any component of the vector to separate in pools. In each w pool, we can restrict ourselves to the bit slice corresponding to the corresponding level. This slice corresponds to a vector in $(\mathbb{Z}/(2))^p$. Hence, we can produce a vector that will fit in the next pool if we manage to find some linearly dependent vectors, that is, whose sum (or difference, as it is the same in $\mathbb{Z}/(2)$) is 0.

Recovering the Shift. We realized that the elements with $\ell_j \in \{0, 2^{w-1}\}$ are of the form $|\psi_{\ell_1,\ldots,\ell_p}\rangle = |0\rangle + \exp{(i\pi \sum s_j \ell_j)}|1\rangle$, so measuring them in the $\{|-\rangle, |+\rangle\}$ basis will give us the parity of $\sum s_j \ell_j$, that is, a linear equation in the parity bits of the s_j. In the case $w = 1$, we get a variant of Simon's algorithm for hidden shifts.

We describe next how to apply each approach separately, and then describe how our algorithm combines them to obtain an optimized complexity, that will be discussed and analyzed in Sect. 4.2.

First Idea: Kuperberg's Variant with a Better Worst-Case Gain. A simple strategy represented in Algorithm 3 is to mimic the former one: we apply directly the strategy with the first term to zero all its bits except the most significant one, and then process the second term, and so on. We can also apply it the other way around: we can see the vector $(s_1^{w-1} \cdots s_1^0, \ldots, s_p^{w-1} \cdots s_p^0)$ as the number $s_p^{w-1} s_{p-1}^{w-1} \cdots s_1^{w-1} s_p^{w-2} \cdots s_p^0 \cdots s_1^0$, and apply directly the former strategy, until we get enough elements of the form $s_p^{w-1} s_{p-1}^{w-1} \cdots s_1^{w-1} 0 \cdots 0$ that we can measure. Another approach is to weight all the possible combinations with the expected gain in the total number of trailing zeros, and choose the most favorable one. The first two have the advantage of being classically easy to implement, with a radix tree.

Algorithm 3. Variant 1 for termwise additions

Generate N random numbers in $\mathbb{Z}/(2^w)^p$
Separate them in pools P_i of elements with all p terms divisible by 2^i and at least one term not divisible by 2^{i+1}
for $i := 0$ to $w - 1$ **do**
    while $|P_i| \geq 2$ **do**
        Pop two elements (a, b) of P_i where $a + b$ or $a - b$ has the highest possible divisibility by 2 on each term
        c is chosen randomly in $\{a + b, a - b\}$
        Insert c in the corresponding P_j
    end while
end for
if $P_{w-1} \neq \emptyset$ **then return** Found
else return Failure
end if

Second Idea: $p+1$ Dependent Equations Always Gain p Zeros. There is however another way to use the parallel structure of the hidden subgroup: given $p + 1$ random elements, we can find a subset whose sum (or difference) will always be even on all the components: if we look at the parity vector of the elements, this corresponds to a linearly dependent subset of the vectors. This approach can be useful if p is big with respect to the size of the pools: with on average $p/2 + 1$ vectors, we can zero p bits. We can then iterate the technique to set to zero the next row of bits, and so on. This is described in Algorithm 4.

Moreover, seeing the elements in a pool as equations allows us to perform the same optimisation we have proposed for the case $p = 1$, to get all the secret in one pass. Instead of storing one element per pool, we have to store p elements that are linearly independent, that is, a full system of equations. As this optimisation does not depend on what we do to each pool, we can also apply it to improve Algorithm 3.

As, on average, we combine $(p/2 + 1)$ elements, we divide at each w step the pool by $(p/2 + 1)$. This algorithm has a complexity in $O((p/2 + 1)^w)$. If $w = 1$, it matches Simon's complexity (and is, indeed, Simon's algorithm). It is interesting for big p, as it is polynomial in p, but it quickly becomes costly if w rises, as it is exponential in it.

Our New Algorithm: Combining both Ideas. As the two variants merge the elements to progressively create new elements with a greater number of zeros, we can, to be more efficient, combine both methods. Algorithm 4 is more efficient when we have a small number of qubits to deal with, with a large p, but is exponential in w, while Algorithm 3, having the same structure than the original algorithm, is subexponential. Hence, the most efficient way to combine them is to begin with Algorithm 3 until we produce some elements that lies in a subgroup $(\mathbb{Z}/(2^{w'}))^p$ with a sufficiently small w', where we can use Algorithm 4.

Algorithm 4. Variant 2 for termwise additions

Generate N random numbers in $\mathbb{Z}/(2^w)^p$
Separate them in pools P_i of elements with each terms divisible by 2^i and at least one term not divisible by 2^{i+1}
System $= \emptyset$
for $i := 0$ to $w - 1$ **do**
  Pop p elements from P_i linearly independent at the level i, put them in System
  Basis $= \emptyset$
  for $e \in P_i$ **do**
    if $\{x \mod 2^{i+1} | x \in \{e\} \cup \text{Basis}\}$ is linearly independent **then**
      Add e to Basis
    else
      Find a linearly dependent subset J
      Compute $c = \pm \sum_{x \in J} x$
      Insert c in the corresponding P_j
    end if
  end for
end for
if System is full **then return** Found
else return Failure
end if

To estimate the complexity, we reasoned backwards: we estimated how many elements in $(\mathbb{Z}/(2^w))^p$ we needed to obtain a given number of elements in $(\mathbb{Z}/(2^{w'}))^p$, with $w' < w$, for increasing w.

The point at which we change of algorithm is the threshold, τ. The value of this threshold is estimated and studied in the next section. Our new algorithm is described in Algorithm 5, where all the bits are also recovered in one pass thanks to our adapted improvement.

4.2   Complexity Analysis

In this section we provide a complexity analysis of the previously described algorithm, that will depend on the relation between the parameters w and p. A summary can be found in Table 4.

We first estimate the complexity of Algorithms 3 and 4, and then combine these costs to compute the best thresholds, and derive the final complexity.

Complexity Using Partial Collisions. To estimate the complexity of partial collisions, we first need to estimate the cost of the partial collisions with independent bits (in $(\mathbb{Z}/(2))^p$), which is a more favourable situation than the collisions in $\mathbb{Z}/(2^n)$, as we do not have any uncertainty in the outcome of a combination. We had the same approach as for the original algorithm: we performed simulations. An optimistic approach could estimate that the complexity is $2^{\sqrt{2p}}$, which would mean that a pool of 2^e elements produces a pool of 2^{e-1} elements that all have e more zeroes. In practice, this is not what we observed, and we found a complexity of around $2^{\sqrt{2.3p}}$, as presented in Table 2. This algorithm is far from the best method to solve this problem, but it can become relevant if we need a huge number of elements that are zeroed on p bits.

Collision Cost. We have two heuristics for collision cost. When we don't have enough elements to have some collisions, we estimate from our simulations the cost to produce E elements to be around $2^{\sqrt{2.3p+\log_2(E)^2}}$ in this situation.

The minimal cost is around $2E$, as we need to combine every element with another one. Doing simulations, we found that it is $(2E + 2^{p-2})/(1 + 1/2^p)$,

Table 2. Some results of the simulations, for 90% success.

p	Queries	$\log_2$(queries)	$\sqrt{2.3p} - 0.2$	Number of tests
40	642	9.3	9.4	10^6
80	10770	13.4	13.4	10^6
100	33100	15.0	15.0	10^6
128	132600	17.0	17.0	10^5
140	228500	17.8	17.8	10^5
170	808000	19.6	19.6	10^4

Algorithm 5. Combined algorithm for termwise additions

Generate N random numbers in $\mathbb{Z}/(2^w)^p$
Separate them in pools P_i of elements with each terms divisible by 2^i and at least one term not divisible by 2^{i+1}
System $= \emptyset$
for $i := 0$ to $w - \tau - 1$ **do**   ▷ Partial collisions
   Pop p elements from P_i linearly independent at the level i, put them in System
   while $|P_i| \geq 2$ **do**
      Pop two elements (a, b) of P_i where $a + b$ or $a - b$ has the highest possible divisibility by 2 on each term
      c is chosen randomly in $\{a + b, a - b\}$
      Insert c in the corresponding P_j
   end while
end for
for $i := w - \tau$ to $w - 1$ **do**   ▷ Zero-sum
   Pop p elements from P_i linearly independent at the level i, put them in System
   Basis $= \emptyset$
   for $e \in P_i$ **do**
      if $\{x \bmod 2^{i+1} | x \in \{e\} \cup \text{Basis}\}$ is linearly independent **then**
         Add e to Basis
      else
         Find a linearly dependent subset J
         Compute $c = \pm\sum\limits_{x \in J} x$
         Insert c in the corresponding P_j
      end if
   end for
end for
if System is full **then return** Found
else return Failure
end if

---

asymptotically in E. The $2E$ comes from the fact that we do for almost all non-zero elements one combination, the 2^{p-2} corresponds to the small number of elements that don't have a total collision with another element, and the $(1 + 1/2^p)$ corresponds to the zero element that can naturally occur, with probability $1/2^p$.

Alternative Approach. Instead of considering only one row of bits and try to zero it, we can consider a bigger chunk. That is, we want to produce E elements that have a certain amount (greater than p) of zeroes in their firsts bits. In order to estimate this cost, we refer to Kuperberg's original algorithm. In practice, the algorithm will be more efficient, but we can approximate it with the original complexity. We can then estimate the cost of the algorithm to zero q bits to be $2^{\sqrt{2\log_2(3)q + \log_2(E)^2}}$. As before, this will not hold if we have to many elements to produce, as the minimal cost is $3E$. We should never be in this regime, as this would mean that we can obtain what the wanted value in one good combination.

Complexity Using Equations

Lemma 5 (Equation cost). *An iteration of the outer for loop of Algorithm 4 produces on average $N/(p/2 + 1)$ elements with p zeroed bits using N elements, and needs p qubits.*

Proof. A step of Algorithm 4 uses random equations to produce a zeroed element. If we have p elements that form a basis of $\mathbb{Z}/(2)^p$, any other element is a linear combination of $p/2$ elements, on average, in this basis. If we have a basis, we can hence get an equation that has, on average $p/2 + 1$ elements, and that sums to zero on the p bits. We can then construct such a basis by choosing p random elements: if they form a free family, we have a basis, if not, we then have some elements that sums to zero. This allows to perform the algorithm on-the-fly: each time a new element arrives, we can try to form a basis with the previous ones. If we new element is linearly independent, we add it in our memory. If it is not, we combine all the elements that sums to zero. ∎

Theorem 1. *Algorithm 4 has a complexity in quantum queries and time of around $2(p/2 + 1)^w$. It needs $2p(w - 1)$ quantum memory, plus the oracle cost.*

Proof. At each outer for loop iteration, we store p independent elements that will allow us to retrieve p bits, and divide the remaining number of elements by $p/2 + 1$ (Lemma 5). At the end, we want p elements (with only p elements, as they would be random, the success probability is only of $1/e$, but we can get arbitrarily close to 1 with a fixed overhead). The total cost is then of

$$p(p/2 + 1)^{w-1} + p(p/2 + 1)^{w-2} + \cdots + p,$$

which reduces to $2(p/2+1)^w$. The total cost in quantum memory is then $p(w-1)$ qubits for the $w - 1$ steps, and $p(w - 1)$ qubits that will yield an equation in the bits of the shift, but that we cannot measure immediately. This cost in memory is optional, as we could do the algorithm w times, but we would then have to pay the constant overhead at each step and not only at the last one. ∎

Remark 6. We found that the marginal cost of $(p/2 + 1)$ elements to produce one can be beaten if the total number of elements is huge by sorting them before searching for a zero-sum set. As extracting values from a radix tree naturally produces a sorted list, this was observed in our simulations.

Determining the Total Complexity. To determine the complexity, we will run the algorithm backwards : we estimate how many elements we need at a point of the algorithm, and then deduce how many elements we need before to obtain this number of elements. More precisely, we consider a fixed p, and estimate what we have to do to get the elements we want as w grows. We considered four cases. First, when w is small enough to use Algorithm 4. Next, when we have to use Algorithm 3 but the number of queries is small enough to have partial collisions on independent bits, such that we never have bad outcomes in our combination.

For bigger w, we considered another approximation, which is that a combination gains at least one zero in each independent component in the worst case. This is not a relevant model when $p = 1$, as it produces estimates exponential in w, but it is interesting here. Finally, the last approximation model is to neglect the gains due to the parallel additions, and consider Kuperberg's original algorithm complexity estimation.

The Final Steps. The final steps uses Algorithm 4. The complexity to process w rows is then $C_0(p, w) = 2(p/2 + 1)^w$.

Changing to Collision Finding. With collision finding, we can erase one row and produce E elements at a cost of $2^{\sqrt{2.3p + \log_2(E)^2}}$. Hence, if we combine this algorithm, the cost is $C_1(p, w) = 2^{\sqrt{2.3p(w-\tau) + \log_2(C_0(p,\tau))^2}}$, with τ rows handled by the other algorithm.

Threshold. We want to change of algorithm if $C_0(p, w) > 2^{\sqrt{2.3p + \log_2(C_0(p,w-1))^2}}$. This means that $2(p/2 + 1)^w \geq 2^{\sqrt{2.3p + (1 + (w-1)\log_2(p/2+1))^2}}$, which implies

$$\tau = \lfloor 1.15p/\log_2(p/2 + 1)^2 + 1/\log_2(p/2 + 1) - 1/2 \rfloor.$$

This threshold is the number of steps in which we should use Algorithm 4, and the previous steps are solved using Algorithm 3.

Saturated Regime of Collisions. We saw before that the cost of zeroing one row is asymptotically around $2E$, and cannot outperform this bound. We can now estimate when our previous estimate violates this bound. This occurs when $2^{\sqrt{2.3p + \log_2(E)^2}} \leq 2E$, which implies $E \geq 2^{\frac{2.3p-1}{2}} \simeq 2^{1.15p}$. Using this constraint to the previous complexity, we get that w must be lower than

$$w_1 = \lfloor 2.3p/4 + \tau - (1 + \tau \log_2(p/2 + 1))^2/2.3p \rfloor.$$

We can still use the algorithm in this saturated regime, and estimate that one row can be erased if we divide by 2 the number of elements. Then, the complexity is $C_2(p, w) = 2^{w - w_1 + \sqrt{(1 + \tau \log_2(p/2+1))^2 + 2.3p(w_1 - \tau)}}$.

Multiple Steps at Once. The complexity we got at the previous step does not have any constraint. It can however become irrelevant, as we have a better approximation if w is big enough, as it is exponential in w. Indeed, we can consider Kuperberg's original algorithm model and estimate that we can erase pw' zeros and get E elements at a cost of $2^{\sqrt{2\log_2(3)pw' + \log_2(E)^2}}$, as the combinations we are doing here are more favorable than the ones done with a cyclic group. This approximation will become relevant when $2^{\sqrt{2\log_2(3)p + \log_2(C_2(p,w-1))^2}} \leq C_2(p, w)$, which implies

$$w \geq w_2 = \lfloor \log_2(3)p - 1/2 + w_1 - \sqrt{(1 + \tau \log_2(p/2 + 1))^2 + 2.3p(w_1 - \tau)} \rfloor.$$

The total complexity is then $C_3(p, w) = 2^{\sqrt{2\log_2(3)p(w - w_2) + (\log_2(C_2(p,w_2)))^2}}$.

Table 3. Threshold points for Algorithm 5.

Threshold	Value
τ	$= \lceil 1.15p/\log_2(p/2+1)^2 + 1/\log_2(p/2+1) - 1/2 \rceil$
w_1	$= \lfloor 2.3p/4 + \tau - (1 + \tau\log_2(p/2+1))^2/2.3p \rfloor$
w_2	$= \lfloor \log_2(3)p - 1/2 + w_1 - \sqrt{(1 + \tau\log_2(p/2+1))^2 + 2.3p(w_1 - \tau)} \rfloor$

Table 4. Complexity of Algorithm 5.

Constraint	Cost
$(w \leq \tau)$	$C_0(p,w) = 2(p/2+1)^w$
$\tau \leq w \leq w_1$	$C_1(p,w) = 2^{\sqrt{(\log_2(C_0(p,\tau))^2 + 2.3p(w-\tau)}}$
$w_1 \leq w \ (\leq w_2)$	$C_2(p,w) = 2^{w-w_1}C_1(p,w_1)$
$w_2 \leq w$	$C_3(p,w) = 2^{\sqrt{2\log_2(3)p(w-w_2) + \log_2(C_2(p,w_2))^2}}$

Quantum Memory Cost. The quantum memory cost is the same than in the original algorithm, of one qubit per query, plus the oracle cost. Also, as the original algorithm, we only have at most pairs of entangled qubits at a time in the combinations.

Classical Cost. The classical cost for Algorithm 3 is the same as the original algorithm, as the only change to choose the combinations is the computation of a sum and a difference of labels. The other difference is that we take a basis before looking for combinations. This can be done in time linear in the size of the basis, hence it is negligible.

Algorithm 4 is slightly less memory-consuming, as it can look for combinations on-the-fly, hence performing classically in $O(N)$, with N queries (Table 3).

Simon Meets Kuperberg. From Table 4 we can see how Simon's complexity is met in the extreme case where $w = 1$ and Kuperberg's complexity is obtained when $p = 1$, as expected. It also shows that even if asymptotically in w, the complexity becomes closer to the complexity of Kuperberg's algorithm in $\mathbb{Z}/(2^{pw})$, the last w_2 rows of bits of the state do not provide as much security.

4.3   Simulations of the Algorithm

We have performed various simulations of the algorithm, in order to confirm our models and theoretical complexities. For $w = 1$, the obtained complexity corresponds to solving an equation system, hence it needs around p queries, and our model holds. For $p = 1$, the complexity is reduced to $2^{\sqrt{2\log_2(3)p}}$, which corresponds to our previous simulations. We've considered two types of simulations in order to confirm the model of complexity of our algorithm. First, as before, we simulated the success probability of the algorithm for a given input size. Second,

Table 5. Simulations compared with our model, with a success probability of 90%, 1000 tests per estimation, in log scale, for $pw = 100$ and 128.

p/w	2/50	4/25	5/20	10/10	20/5	25/4	50/2	2/64	4/32	8/16	16/8	32/4	64/2
Theoretical model	17.7	17.5	17.3	15.3	14.2	13.7	10.4	20.1	19.9	18.8	16.6	15.2	11.1
Simulations	17.9	17.5	16.9	15.3	14.4	13.9	10.6	20.3	19.7	18.2	16.7	15.4	11.2

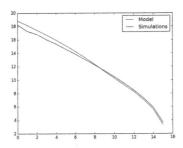

Fig. 3. Comparison between our model and our simulations for the number of elements in each pool at each step for $p, w = 8, 16$, in log scale.

we simulated the number of elements at each step of the algorithm, in order to see more precisely the accuracy of each model.

From Table 5, we see that our estimates correspond to the simulations in the ranges we were able to simulate, with a slightly pessimistic estimation when p is not too small and w is bigger than p. In order to estimate the accuracy of our different models, we also simulated the number of elements in each pool at the beginning of each step, as for example in Fig. 3.

The computed thresholds for Fig. 3 are $(2,3,7)$. As they are in reverse, they correspond to $(13,12,8)$ on the graph. The two curves are converging at around step 9, which suggests that our models 3 and 4 are slightly pessimistic. This is explained by the fact that model 3 neglects the gains of good combinations and model 4 the gains of bad combinations.

5 Cryptanalysis of Poly1305 in the Superposition Model

We propose in this section the first quantum superposition attack on the Poly1305 primitive, with a complexity of about 2^{38} in time and queries, that shows that it is not secure in the superposition model.

5.1 Poly1305 Description

Poly1305 is a MAC designed by Bernstein [6]. It has been standardized for TLS 1.2 [36], is currently a part of a recommended cipher suite in the TLS 1.3 draft [1], and is notably supported by OpenSSH, Firefox and Chrome. The designer announced in [8] a classical and quantum security of Poly1305 of 128 bits. We'll describe Poly1305-AES, but our analysis works with any internal block cipher used.

Poly1305-AES uses two 128-bit keys (r, k) and a 128-bit nonce n, takes as input a variable-length message m considered as an array of 128-bit blocks, and outputs a 128-bit tag. For efficiency purposes, some bits of r are fixed to 0, which means it can only take 2^{106} different values. The function is

$$\text{Poly1305-AES}_{(r,k,n)}\big((m_i)_{i \leq q}\big) = \left(\sum_{i=1}^{q} (m_{q-i+1} + 2^{128}) r^i \mod 2^{130} - 5 \right) + \text{AES}_k(n).$$

5.2   Quantum Attack in the Superposition Setting

For our quantum attack, we consider having access to the oracle

$$Poly_n : |m_1\rangle\, |m_2\rangle\, |0\rangle \mapsto |m_1\rangle\, |m_2\rangle\, |\text{Poly1305-AES}_{(r,k,n)}(m_1, m_2)\rangle\,.$$

The nonce is classical, and changes at each query. As we consider the superposition scenario, we consider that the function can be called in superposition. We aim at retrieving r (and not k), as r is sufficient to retrieve $\text{AES}_k(n)$ for any tag, which allows some forgeries. If one also wants k, one can perform a Grover search on it, with an additional cost of 2^{64}. In the long version of this paper [12] we describe a distinguisher on Poly1305 and a simple key-recovery attack, but in this section we propose a more evolved attack that uses Kuperberg's algorithm.

Poly1305 uses a polynomial structure for hashing, and the commutative algebra $\mathbb{Z}/(2^{130} - 5)[X]$ contains many possible shift structures, both in $\mathbb{Z}/(2^{130} - 5)$ (with addition) and in $\mathbb{Z}/(2^{130} - 6)$ (with multiplication). For example, one can consider the two functions $f(x) = xr + r^2 + 2^{128}(r + r^2)$ and $g(x) = xr + 2^{128}(r + r^2)$, which satisfies $f(x) = g(x+r)$. We cannot call them directly, but we can call $F(x) = \text{Poly1305-AES}_{(r,k,n)}(1, x)$ and $G(x) = \text{Poly1305-AES}_{(r,k,n)}(0, x)$, which also satisfy $F(x) = G(x + r)$ if the nonce is the same.

There are two issues that do not allow the direct application of Kuperberg's algorithm: first, the nonce changes at each query, which means that in order to have $F(x) = G(x+r)$, we must compute F and G in only one query to Poly1305. This is feasible, as both are of the form $\text{Poly1305}(a(x))$, with $a(x)$ a function of x: one can compute $a_F(x) = (1, x)$ and $a_G(x) = (0, x)$ in superposition in an auxiliary register, and then call $Poly_n$ on it. Second, and more annoyingly, the inputs of Poly1305 are restrained to be between 0 and $2^{128} - 1$, which means we cannot sample all group elements.

This can still be solved by using Lemma 4, as we can query $[0; 2^{128})$. Solving the hidden shift in $\mathbb{Z}/(2^{127})$ costs around 2^{20}. We can thus set the interval size at 2^{106}. r can be retrieved if it is below 2^{127}. This is the case, as the bit constraints on r implies $r < 2^{124}$, which means we need only to test 2^{18} intervals. The total cost is then $2^{20} \times 2^{18} = 2^{38}$, for a success probability better than one half. We can check if the found r is the right one by trying to forge some valid messages, or we can use the distinguisher presented in Appendix A of [12].

Quantum Memory Use. This attack needs around 2^{20} qubits, plus the cost of the quantum oracle, which would need at least a few hundred qubits.

Grover Acceleration. As the previous attack involves an exhaustive search on the correct interval among the 2^{18}, one might want to use Grover's algorithm, in order to gain up to 2^9 on the attack. We automatically lose a factor 2 because of the uncomputation of the algorithm. Moreover, we would need to compute all the qubit choices quantumly, and we must have a success probability of the inner function very close to one. All these factors make the attack more efficient in queries (around 2^{31}), with a small time gain.

5.3 Impact of Our Improvements

The total cost of the attack is highly dependent of the precise cost of Kuperberg's algorithm. The original algorithm, with an estimated complexity of around $n\sqrt{n}2^{\sqrt{2\log_3(2^n)}}$, has here a cost of around 2^{31} queries. The total attack is then more costly, around 2^{59}, which is very close to the cost of a simple exhaustive search on the key if AES-128 is used, and exceeds the cost of the simple quantum attack described in [12]. We could also use a Grover search, which would lead to a cost estimate of around 2^{45}, which is higher than both the non-Grover variant of our attack (at 2^{38}) and the Grover variant (at 2^{31}).

6 Attack on the FX Construction

The FX construction, proposed by Killian and Rogaway [31], is a simple way to extend the key-length of a block cipher. It uses a block cipher E_{k_0} and two additional keys k_1, k_2 whose length is the block size of the block cipher, and the new cipher is

$$FX_{k_0,k_1,k_2}(x) = E_{k_0}(x \oplus k_1) \oplus k_2.$$

We can see it as an Even-Mansour construction, with a block cipher taking the role of the random permutation. The quantum security of this scheme has been studied by Leander and May in [37] in the superposition model. Their conclusion is that this construction is essentially as secure as the inner cipher E_{k_0}.

Their approach is close to the quantum attack against the Even-Mansour construction, with the addition that the key of the inner cipher has to be sought. They consider the function $f(k, x) = FX_{k_0,k_1,k_2}(x) \oplus E_k(x)$, which fulfills the promise $f(k_0, x) = f(k_0, x \oplus k_1)$. They then recover k_0 and k_1 by performing a Grover search on k_0, with a test function that is the application of Simon's algorithm to the partial function $x \mapsto f(k_0, x)$. If this function is periodic, then k_0 has a very high probability of being correct, and the period of the function is k_1. It can moreover be efficiently checked, by testing the periodicity for a few values. Once k_0 and k_1 are known, k_2 can be retrieved with one known plaintext/ciphertext pair. The total cost is around $2|k_1|2^{|k_0|/2}$.

This leads to some efficient attacks against the FX-based primitives DESX, PRINCE [14] and PRIDE [3]. For PRINCE and PRIDE, $|k_0| = |k_1| = 64$, the attack costs around 2^{39} queries and time, whereas for DESX, $|k_0| = 56$ and $|k_1| = 64$, the attack costs around 2^{35} queries and time[5].

The authors only considered the original construction, that uses some xors, and left as an open problem the evaluation of the security using another group law. We can here give an answer for the most natural variant, which is to use modular additions instead of xors, with the cipher

$$\text{FX+}_{k_0,k_1,k_2}(x) = E_{k_0}(x + k_1) + k_2.$$

The function is no longer periodic in this situation, but we can find a hidden shift problem with the two functions $f(k,x) = \text{FX+}_{k_0,k_1,k_2}(x) + E_k(-x)$ and $g(k,x) = \text{FX+}_{k_0,k_1,k_2}(-x) + E_k(x)$, which fulfills the promise $f(k_0,x) = g(k_0, x + k_1)$. These two function can efficiently be computed in superposition, for a total cost of one query and one encryption. The attack consists then in a Grover search that uses Kuperberg's algorithm as a test function. The Grover search needs the same number of iterations $(2^{|k_0|/2})$, but Kuperberg's algorithm needs around $2^{1.8\sqrt{|k_1|}}$ samples. The total cost is around $2^{|k_0|/2+1.8\sqrt{|k_1|}} \times 2$ queries (we can factor the query to f and g to only one query to FX+, and we double to uncompute Kuperberg's algorithm).

Other Group Laws. If the group is abelian, the attack can be straightforwardly applied. If the group law is not abelian, we need a slightly different approach which is developed in the extended version of this paper [12].

Quantum Attack on PRINCE+ and PRIDE+. We can directly attack a variant of PRINCE and PRIDE where the key whitening is done through a modular addition. Concretely, we can attack them in around $2^{47.4}$ queries and time, which is smaller than the ideal 64-bits of quantum security. We also attack DESX+ in $2^{43.4}$ queries and time.

7   Concrete Proposals

The most interesting idea from [2] for preventing Simon-based attacks is using modular additions, which is already common in symmetric primitives (see for instance [26,40,49]). Based on the complexities of the new algorithms and attacks from the previous sections, we can now correctly size some of the primitives that were broken using Simon-based algorithms, now patched to use modular additions, in order to provide a certain desired post-quantum security.

Let us point out that we used a slightly unconventional definition of the *security*: we consider a cipher to provide a security of Q bits when no attack of complexity lower than 2^Q exists (the more conventional definition being when no attack better than the generic exhaustive search is known, whose complexity usually is $2^Q = 2^{k/2}$).

---

[5] In [37], they considered the time of a parallelized Simon's algorithm, which can be neglected, leaving a complexity of 2^{32}.

7.1 Concrete Parameters and Security of Some Generic Constructions

If we consider the generic Even-Mansour constructions, with a xor, it will provide a security of 8 or 9 bits for an state size of 128 or 256 bits respectively. When using one or several modular additions, this security is augmented, becoming 20 or 28.5 bits for states of 128 or 256 bits respectively, but all the constructions are far from the ideal 2^{64} security offered by an ideal cipher with a 128-bit key, and even more from the 2^{128} offered quantumly by a classical primitive with a 256-bit key. To the best of our knowledge, the quantum security offered by the AES [19] meets these ideal claims.

In Table 6 we show the needed security parameters of some popular constructions in order to resist their corresponding attacks when using Kuperberg's algorithm. As expected, p modular additions of words of size w provide less security than one modular addition of the state size. We can see that, in all the cases, the size of the state needed to achieve a certain security becomes much bigger than for common symmetric primitives (128 bits for instance), needing to be bigger than 5200 bits in some cases. The problem of a bigger state is not limited to implementation issues: designing a secure permutation for such a big state would be a very challenging task. We considered the needed size when using non-abelian groups in the extended version [12].

Table 6. Examples of parameters for 128-bit security when using modular additions instead of $\oplus$. E-M stands for Even-Mansour and O-M for operation modes.

(p/w)	E-M($1/n$)	O-M/LRW($1/n$)	E-M($2048/13$)	E-M($1024/14$)	E-M($4/1304$)
State	5168	5168	26624	14336	5216
Key	5168	$k \geq 256$	26624	14336	5216

8 Conclusion

Modular Additions Are Not Enough. We have shown that the proposal from [2], even though it is interesting and could provide any wanted security with the right (big) parameters, does not seem practical. Indeed, using modular additions[6] instead of xors, in most constructions vulnerable to Simon's attacks, would increase the complexity of such attacks when using Kuperberg's algorithm, and therefore also the security, but it would need a much larger internal state to provide reasonable security, far beyond the size of typical classical symmetric constructions providing an equivalent degree of security. For instance, a key-alternating cipher with modular addition that provides a 128-bit security would need around 5200 bits of internal state and key size, to be compared with the 128 bits of internal state and 256 key-bits of AES-256. Beyond the obvious efficiency

---

[6] The most realistic counter measure proposed.

drawback, the design of a correspondingly large secure permutation would be a very challenging task. Intuitively, we can see how more bits need to be mixed, which will imperatively imply more rounds and bigger transformations (also slower to mix).

That is why, regarding constructions that are vulnerable to Simon's or Kuperberg's attacks, the substitution of xors by modular additions seems hazardous, as can be seen in the previous section, and we rather recommend the use of some of the resistant constructions (many exist).

Kuperberg's Algorithm Simulation and Verification. We have been able to study, improve and simulate Kuperberg's algorithm: the concrete complexity of our tweaked version is $2^{1.8\sqrt{n}}$, which is small enough for a practical use on typical parameters of n (we have therefore implemented the part that could be simulated and verified this). We also have presented a way to solve the hidden shift problem in various situations (which extends to non-abelian groups), and provided an estimate of the complexity.

New Algorithm Representing Simon-Meets-Kuperberg. We provided a new efficient algorithm that solves the problem when considering parallel modular additions. We have simulated the algorithm and verified that our estimated complexity is met in practice. As in the case of single modular additions, though the security is increased with respect to the same constructions when using xors, the size state is equally increased, and the tweak does not seem more promising.

Cryptanalysis of FX Variants and Poly1305. This paper proposes some new quantum attacks, mainly using our generalized and improved Kuperberg's algorithm, that provide an important speed-up with respect to Grover's quantum generic exhaustive search attack.

Further Applications. Hidden shift algorithms can be applied in other cryptographic fields. They have in particular been successfully applied to ordinary isogenies [18] and are relevant to assess the security of some proposed post-quantum asymetric schemes, such as CSIDH [16]. Indeed, in [13] one of the first concrete quantum cryptanalysis of post-quantum primitives is proposed, suggesting an important re-dimension of parameters in order to propose the wanted security. This result builds upon our work and simulations.

Open Problems

(1) Prove a tighter bound on the complexity of Kuperberg's algorithm, or study the success probability.
(2) Study combinations and alternance of xor and modular additions to increase the complexity of the attacks or counter them.
(3) Find more attacks using the new algorithm, for instance, considering ARX constructions. Also study applications to other post-quantum primitives, like lattice-based ones.

Acknowledgements. The authors would like to thank André Chailloux, Anthony Leverrier and André Schrottenloher for their helpful comments and discussions, as well as our anonymous reviewers, Bo-Yin Yang and Steven Galbraith for all the helpful remarks.

This project has received funding from the European Research Council (ERC) under the European Union's Horizon 2020 research and innovation programme (grant agreement no. 714294 - acronym QUASYModo).

References

1. https://tools.ietf.org/html/draft-ietf-tls-tls13-23#section-9.1
2. Alagic, G., Russell, A.: Quantum-secure symmetric-key cryptography based on hidden shifts. In: Coron, J.-S., Nielsen, J.B. (eds.) EUROCRYPT 2017. LNCS, vol. 10212, pp. 65–93. Springer, Cham (2017). https://doi.org/10.1007/978-3-319-56617-7_3
3. Albrecht, M.R., Driessen, B., Kavun, E.B., Leander, G., Paar, C., Yalçın, T.: Block ciphers – focus on the linear layer (feat. PRIDE). In: Garay, J.A., Gennaro, R. (eds.) CRYPTO 2014. LNCS, vol. 8616, pp. 57–76. Springer, Heidelberg (2014). https://doi.org/10.1007/978-3-662-44371-2_4
4. Anand, M.V., Targhi, E.E., Tabia, G.N., Unruh, D.: Post-quantum security of the CBC, CFB, OFB, CTR, and XTS modes of operation. In: Takagi, T. (ed.) PQCrypto 2016. LNCS, vol. 9606, pp. 44–63. Springer, Cham (2016). https://doi.org/10.1007/978-3-319-29360-8_4
5. Berger, T.P., Francq, J., Minier, M., Thomas, G.: Extended generalized Feistel networks using matrix representation to propose a new lightweight block cipher: LILLIPUT. IEEE Trans. Comput. **65**(7), 2074–2089 (2016)
6. Bernstein, D.J.: The Poly1305-AES message-authentication code. In: Gilbert, H., Handschuh, H. (eds.) FSE 2005. LNCS, vol. 3557, pp. 32–49. Springer, Heidelberg (2005). https://doi.org/10.1007/11502760_3
7. Bernstein, D.J.: The Salsa20 family of stream ciphers. In: Robshaw, M., Billet, O. (eds.) New Stream Cipher Designs. LNCS, vol. 4986, pp. 84–97. Springer, Heidelberg (2008). https://doi.org/10.1007/978-3-540-68351-3_8
8. Bernstein, D.J., Tanja, L.: Post-quantum cryptography. Nature **549**(7671), 188–194 (2017)
9. Boneh, D., Dagdelen, Ö., Fischlin, M., Lehmann, A., Schaffner, C., Zhandry, M.: Random oracles in a quantum world. In: Lee, D.H., Wang, X. (eds.) ASIACRYPT 2011. LNCS, vol. 7073, pp. 41–69. Springer, Heidelberg (2011). https://doi.org/10.1007/978-3-642-25385-0_3
10. Boneh, D., Zhandry, M.: Secure signatures and chosen ciphertext security in a quantum computing world. In: Canetti, R., Garay, J.A. (eds.) CRYPTO 2013. LNCS, vol. 8043, pp. 361–379. Springer, Heidelberg (2013). https://doi.org/10.1007/978-3-642-40084-1_21
11. Bonnetain, X.: Quantum key-recovery on Full AEZ. In: Adams, C., Camenisch, J. (eds.) SAC 2017. LNCS, vol. 10719, pp. 394–406. Springer, Cham (2018). https://doi.org/10.1007/978-3-319-72565-9_20
12. Bonnetain, X., Naya-Plasencia, M.: Hidden shift quantum cryptanalysis and implications. Cryptology ePrint Archive, Report 2018/432 (2018). https://eprint.iacr.org/2018/432

13. Bonnetain, X., Schrottenloher, A.: Quantum security analysis of CSIDH and ordinary isogeny-based schemes. IACR Cryptology ePrint Archive 2018, 537 (2018)
14. Borghoff, J., et al.: PRINCE – a low-latency block cipher for pervasive computing applications. In: Wang, X., Sako, K. (eds.) ASIACRYPT 2012. LNCS, vol. 7658, pp. 208–225. Springer, Heidelberg (2012). https://doi.org/10.1007/978-3-642-34961-4_14
15. Brassard, G., Høyer, P., Kalach, K., Kaplan, M., Laplante, S., Salvail, L.: Merkle puzzles in a quantum world. In: Rogaway, P. (ed.) CRYPTO 2011. LNCS, vol. 6841, pp. 391–410. Springer, Heidelberg (2011). https://doi.org/10.1007/978-3-642-22792-9_22
16. Castryck, W., Lange, T., Martindale, C., Panny, L., Renes, J.: CSIDH: an efficient post-quantum commutative group action. Cryptology ePrint Archive, Report 2018/383 (2018). https://eprint.iacr.org/2018/383
17. Chailloux, A., Naya-Plasencia, M., Schrottenloher, A.: An efficient quantum collision search algorithm and implications on symmetric cryptography. In: Takagi and Peyrin [46], pp. 211–240
18. Childs, A.M., Jao, D., Soukharev, V.: Constructing elliptic curve isogenies in quantum subexponential time. J. Math. Cryptol. 8(1), 1–29 (2014)
19. Daemen, J., Rijmen, V.: The Design of Rijndael: AES - The Advanced Encryption Standard. Information Security and Cryptography. Springer, Heidelberg (2002). https://doi.org/10.1007/978-3-662-04722-4
20. Damgård, I., Funder, J., Nielsen, J.B., Salvail, L.: Superposition attacks on cryptographic protocols. In: Padró, C. (ed.) ICITS 2013. LNCS, vol. 8317, pp. 142–161. Springer, Cham (2014). https://doi.org/10.1007/978-3-319-04268-8_9
21. Ettinger, M., Høyer, P.: On quantum algorithms for noncommutative hidden subgroups. In: Meinel, C., Tison, S. (eds.) STACS 1999. LNCS, vol. 1563, pp. 478–487. Springer, Heidelberg (1999). https://doi.org/10.1007/3-540-49116-3_45
22. Ferguson, N., et al.: The skein hash function family (2010)
23. Flajolet, P., Odlyzko, A.M.: Random mapping statistics. In: Quisquater, J.-J., Vandewalle, J. (eds.) EUROCRYPT 1989. LNCS, vol. 434, pp. 329–354. Springer, Heidelberg (1990). https://doi.org/10.1007/3-540-46885-4_34
24. Gagliardoni, T.: Quantum Security of Cryptographic Primitives. Ph.D. thesis, Darmstadt University of Technology, Germany (2017)
25. Gagliardoni, T., Hülsing, A., Schaffner, C.: Semantic security and indistinguishability in the quantum world. In: Robshaw, M., Katz, J. (eds.) CRYPTO 2016. LNCS, vol. 9816, pp. 60–89. Springer, Heidelberg (2016). https://doi.org/10.1007/978-3-662-53015-3_3
26. Government Committee of the USSR for Standards: Cryptographic protection for data processing system. In: GOST 28147-89, Gosudarstvennyi Standard of USSR (1989)
27. Hosoyamada, A., Sasaki, Y., Xagawa, K.: Quantum multicollision-finding algorithm. In: Takagi, T., Peyrin, T. (eds.) ASIACRYPT 2017. LNCS, vol. 10625, pp. 179–210. Springer, Cham (2017). https://doi.org/10.1007/978-3-319-70697-9_7
28. Kaplan, M.: Quantum attacks against iterated block ciphers. CoRR abs/1410.1434 (2014)
29. Kaplan, M., Leurent, G., Leverrier, A., Naya-Plasencia, M.: Breaking symmetric cryptosystems using quantum period finding. In: Robshaw, M., Katz, J. (eds.) CRYPTO 2016. LNCS, vol. 9815, pp. 207–237. Springer, Heidelberg (2016). https://doi.org/10.1007/978-3-662-53008-5_8
30. Kaplan, M., Leurent, G., Leverrier, A., Naya-Plasencia, M.: Quantum differential and linear cryptanalysis. IACR Trans. Symmetric Cryptol. 2016(1), 71–94 (2016)

31. Kilian, J., Rogaway, P.: How to protect DES against exhaustive key search. In: Koblitz, N. (ed.) CRYPTO 1996. LNCS, vol. 1109, pp. 252–267. Springer, Heidelberg (1996). https://doi.org/10.1007/3-540-68697-5_20

32. Kuperberg, G.: A subexponential-time quantum algorithm for the dihedral hidden subgroup problem. SIAM J. Comput. **35**(1), 170–188 (2005)

33. Kuperberg, G.: Another subexponential-time quantum algorithm for the dihedral hidden subgroup problem. In: Severini, S., Brandão, F.G.S.L. (eds.) 8th Conference on the Theory of Quantum Computation, Communication and Cryptography, TQC 2013, 21–23 May 2013, Guelph, Canada. LIPIcs, vol. 22, pp. 20–34. Schloss Dagstuhl - Leibniz-Zentrum fuer Informatik (2013)

34. Kuwakado, H., Morii, M.: Quantum distinguisher between the 3-round Feistel cipher and the random permutation. In: 2010 IEEE International Symposium on Information Theory Proceedings (ISIT), pp. 2682–2685, June 2010

35. Kuwakado, H., Morii, M.: Security on the quantum-type Even-Mansour cipher. In: 2012 International Symposium on Information Theory and its Applications (ISITA), pp. 312–316, October 2012

36. Langley, A., Chang, W., Mavrogiannopoulos, N., Strombergson, J., Josefsson, S.: chacha20-poly1305 cipher suites for transport layer security (TLs). In: RFC 7905, June 2016. https://doi.org/10.17487/RFC7905

37. Leander, G., May, A.: Grover meets Simon - quantumly attacking the FX-construction. In: Takagi and Peyrin [46], pp. 161–178

38. Lydersen, L., Wiechers, C., Wittmann, C., Elser, D., Skaar, J., Makarov, V.: Hacking commercial quantum cryptography systems by tailored bright illumination. Nat. Photonics **4**(10), 686–689 (2010)

39. Regev, O.: A Subexponential Time Algorithm for the Dihedral Hidden Subgroup Problem with Polynomial Space. CoRR (2004)

40. Rivest, R.L., Robshaw, M.J.B., Yin, Y.L.: RC6 as the AES. In: AES Candidate Conference, pp. 337–342 (2000)

41. Roetteler, M., Steinwandt, R.: A note on quantum related-key attacks. Inf. Process. Lett. **115**(1), 40–44 (2015)

42. Santoli, T., Schaffner, C.: Using Simon's Algorithm to Attack Symmetric-Key Cryptographic Primitives. arXiv preprint arXiv:1603.07856 (2016)

43. Simon, D.R.: On the power of quantum cryptography. In: 35th Annual Symposium on Foundations of Computer Science, Santa Fe, New Mexico, USA, 20–22 November 1994, pp. 116–123. IEEE Computer Society (1994)

44. Song, F., Yun, A.: Quantum security of NMAC and related constructions. In: Katz, J., Shacham, H. (eds.) CRYPTO 2017. LNCS, vol. 10402, pp. 283–309. Springer, Cham (2017). https://doi.org/10.1007/978-3-319-63715-0_10

45. Suzaki, T., Minematsu, K., Morioka, S., Kobayashi, E.: *TWINE*: a lightweight block cipher for multiple platforms. In: Knudsen, L.R., Wu, H. (eds.) SAC 2012. LNCS, vol. 7707, pp. 339–354. Springer, Heidelberg (2013). https://doi.org/10.1007/978-3-642-35999-6_22

46. Takagi, T., Peyrin, T. (eds.): ASIACRYPT 2017. LNCS, vol. 10625. Springer, Cham (2017). https://doi.org/10.1007/978-3-319-70697-9

47. Unruh, D.: Non-interactive zero-knowledge proofs in the quantum random oracle model. In: Oswald, E., Fischlin, M. (eds.) EUROCRYPT 2015. LNCS, vol. 9057, pp. 755–784. Springer, Heidelberg (2015). https://doi.org/10.1007/978-3-662-46803-6_25

48. Xu, F., Qi, B., Lo, H.K.: Experimental demonstration of phase-remapping attack in a practical quantum key distribution system. New J. Phys. **12**(11), 113026 (2010)

49. Yuval, G.: Reinventing the travois: encryption/MAC in 30 ROM bytes. In: Biham, E. (ed.) FSE 1997. LNCS, vol. 1267, pp. 205–209. Springer, Heidelberg (1997). https://doi.org/10.1007/BFb0052347
50. Zhandry, M.: How to construct quantum random functions. In: 53rd Annual IEEE Symposium on Foundations of Computer Science, FOCS 2012, New Brunswick, NJ, USA, 20–23 October 2012, pp. 679–687 (2012)
51. Zhandry, M.: Secure identity-based encryption in the quantum random oracle model. Int. J. Quantum Inf. 13(04), 1550014 (2015)
52. Zhao, Y., Fung, C.H.F., Qi, B., Chen, C., Lo, H.K.: Quantum hacking: experimental demonstration of time-shift attack against practical quantum-key-distribution systems. Phys. Rev. A 78(4), 042333 (2008)

Zero-Knowledge

Arya: Nearly Linear-Time Zero-Knowledge Proofs for Correct Program Execution

Jonathan Bootle[✉], Andrea Cerulli, Jens Groth, Sune Jakobsen, and Mary Maller

University College London, London, UK
{jonathan.bootle.14,andrea.cerulli.13,j.groth,s.jakobsen, mary.maller.15}@ucl.ac.uk

Abstract. There have been tremendous advances in reducing interaction, communication and verification time in zero-knowledge proofs but it remains an important challenge to make the prover efficient. We construct the first zero-knowledge proof of knowledge for the correct execution of a program on public and private inputs where the prover computation is nearly linear time. This saves a polylogarithmic factor in asymptotic performance compared to current state of the art proof systems.

We use the TinyRAM model to capture general purpose processor computation. An instance consists of a TinyRAM program and public inputs. The witness consists of additional private inputs to the program. The prover can use our proof system to convince the verifier that the program terminates with the intended answer within given time and memory bounds. Our proof system has perfect completeness, statistical special honest verifier zero-knowledge, and computational knowledge soundness assuming linear-time computable collision-resistant hash functions exist. The main advantage of our new proof system is asymptotically efficient prover computation. The prover's running time is only a superconstant factor larger than the program's running time in an apples-to-apples comparison where the prover uses the same TinyRAM model. Our proof system is also efficient on the other performance parameters; the verifier's running time and the communication are sublinear in the execution time of the program and we only use a log-logarithmic number of rounds.

Keywords: Zero-knowledge proofs
Succinct arguments of knowledge · TinyRAM
Ideal linear commitments · Post-quantum security

The research leading to these results has received funding from the European Research Council under the European Union's Seventh Framework Programme (FP/2007-2013)/ERC Grant Agreement n. 307937.
M. Maller—Supported by a scholarship from Microsoft Research.

© International Association for Cryptologic Research 2018
T. Peyrin and S. Galbraith (Eds.): ASIACRYPT 2018, LNCS 11272, pp. 595–626, 2018.
https://doi.org/10.1007/978-3-030-03326-2_20

1 Introduction

A zero-knowledge proof system [GMR85] enables a prover to convince a verifier that a statement is true without revealing anything else. We are interested in proving statements of the form $u \in \mathcal{L}$, where $\mathcal{L}$ is a language in NP. A zero-knowledge proof is an interactive protocol between a prover and a verifier, where both hold the same instance u, and the prover also holds a witness w to $u \in \mathcal{L}$. The protocol should satisfy three properties:

Completeness: A prover holding a witness to $u \in \mathcal{L}$ can convince the verifier.
Soundness: A cheating prover cannot convince the verifier when $u \notin \mathcal{L}$.
Zero-knowledge: The interaction only shows the statement $u \in \mathcal{L}$ is true. It
  reveals nothing else, in particular it does not disclose anything of the witness.

Zero-knowledge proofs have numerous applications and are for instance used in constructions of public-key encryption schemes secure against chosen ciphertext attack, digital signatures, voting systems, auction systems, e-cash, secure multi-party computation, and verifiable outsourced computation. The zero-knowledge proofs impact the performance of all these applications, and it is therefore important for them to be as efficient as possible.

There are many zero-knowledge proofs for dealing with arithmetic or boolean circuit satisfiability. However, in applications usually the type of statements we want to prove is that a protocol participant is following the protocol honestly; whatever that protocol may be. This means we want to express statements relating to program execution such as "running program P specified by the protocol on public input x and private input y returns the output z." In principle such a statement can be reduced to circuit satisfiability but the cost of the NP-reduction incurs a prohibitive cost. In this paper, we therefore focus on the important question of getting zero-knowledge proofs for statements relating directly to program execution.

Performance can be measured on a number of parameters including the prover's running time, the verifier's running time, the number of transmitted bits and the number of rounds the prover and verifier interact. Current state of the art zero-knowledge proofs get very good performance on verification time, communication and round complexity, which makes the prover's running time the crucial bottleneck. Indeed, since the other costs are so low, we would happily increase them for even modest savings on the proving time since this is the barrier that make some applications such as verifiable outsourced computation currently unviable. The research challenge we focus on is therefore to get *prover-efficient* zero-knowledge proofs for correct program execution.

1.1 Our Contribution

We use the TinyRAM model [BCG+13,BSCG+13] for computation. TinyRAM specifies a random access machine with a small instruction set working on W-bit words and addresses. The specification of TinyRAM considers a Harvard-architecture processor, which means that the program being executed is stored separately from the data being processed and does not change during execution.[1] Experimental results [BCG+13] show that programs written in C can be compiled efficiently into TinyRAM programs and only have a modest constant overhead compared to optimized compilation to machine code on a modern processor.

In our proof system, an instance consists of a TinyRAM program and public data given to the program, and a witness is private data given as input to the program. The statement is the claim that the TinyRAM program P running on given public and private data will terminate with answer 0 within specific time and memory bounds. When measuring performance we think of the prover and verifier as being TinyRAM programs with the same word size[2].

Our main contribution is an interactive proof system for correct TinyRAM computation, which has perfect completeness, statistical zero-knowledge, and computational knowledge soundness based on collision-resistant hash functions. Knowledge soundness means that not only do we have soundness and it is infeasible to prove a false statement, but it is also a proof of knowledge such that given access to a successful prover it is possible to extract a witness. For maximal asymptotic efficiency we may use linear-time computable hash functions, which yields the performance given in Fig. 1.

Our proof system is highly efficient for computationally intensive programs where the execution time dominates other parameters (see Sect. 6 for a detailed discussion of parameter choices). For a statement about the execution of a TinyRAM program of length L, running with time bound T and memory bound M, the prover runs in $\mathcal{O}(\alpha T)$ steps[3] for an arbitrarily small supercon-stant function $\alpha(\lambda) = \omega(1)$. The proof system is also efficient on other performance parameters: the verifier running time and the communication grows roughly with the square-root of the execution time[4] and we have log-logarithmic round complexity. Figure 1 gives an efficiency comparison with a state of the art zk-SNARK [BCTV14b] for verifying correct program execution on TinyRAM.

---

[1] TinyRAM can with minor changes also be adapted to a von Neumann architecture where program instructions are fetched from memory [BCTV14b]. The performance of our proof systems adapted to a von Neumann architecture would remain the same up to a constant factor.

[2] We stress the choice of comparing the prover and verifier to program execution on the same platform. We do this to get an apples-to-apples comparison; there are many zero-knowledge proofs that are "linear time" because they use different metrics for statement evaluation and the prover time, for instance that the cost of validating the statement given the witness is measured in field multiplications and the prover computation is measured in exponentiations.

[3] The big-O notation hides big constants and we do not recommend implementing the proof system as it is; our contribution is to make significant *asymptotic* gains compared to state-of-the-art zero-knowledge proofs by demonstrating that the prover's computation can be nearly linear.

[4] Disregarding the SHVZK property for a moment, this is also the first proof system for general purpose computation that has both nearly linear computation for the prover and sublinear communication.

Further discussion of other proof systems that can verify correct TinyRAM or other types of program execution can be found in Sect. 1.3. The best of these achieve similar asymptotic prover efficiency as [BCTV14b].

Work	Prover	Verifier	Communication	Rounds	Assumption
[BCTV14b]	$\Omega(T \log^2 T)$	$\omega(L + |v|)$	$\omega(1)$	1	KoE
This work	$\mathcal{O}(\alpha T)$	$\text{poly}(\lambda)(\sqrt{T} + L + |v|)$	$\text{poly}(\lambda)(\sqrt{T} + L)$	$\mathcal{O}(\log \log T)$	LT-CRHF

Fig. 1. Efficiency comparisons between our arguments and the most efficient zero-knowledge argument for the correct execution of TinyRAM programs, both at security level $2^{-\omega(\log \lambda)}$. Computation is measured in TinyRAM steps and communication in words of length $W = \Theta(\log \lambda)$ with λ the security parameter. KoE stands for knowledge of exponent type assumption in pairing-based groups and LT-CRHF stands for linear-time collision resistant hash function. It is worth noting KoE assumptions do not resist quantum computers while a LT-CRHF may be quantum resistant.

Remarks. Our proof system assumes some public parameters to be set up that include a description of a finite field, an error-correcting code, and a collision-resistant hash function. The size of the public parameters is just $\text{poly}(\lambda)(L + M + \sqrt{T})$ bits which can be computed from a small uniformly random string in $\text{poly}(\lambda)(L + M + \sqrt{T})$ TinyRAM steps. This means the public parameters have little effect on the overall efficiency of the proof system. Moreover, there are variants of the parameters where it is efficiently verifiable the public parameters have the correct structure. This means the prover does not need to trust the parameters to get special honest verifier zero-knowledge, so they can be chosen by the verifier making our proof systems work in the plain model without setup. We let the public parameter be generated by a separate setup though because they are independent of the instance and can be used over many separate proofs.

We did not optimize communication and verification time to go below $\sqrt{T}$ but if needed it is possible to compose our proof system with a verifier-efficient proof system and get verification time that grows logarithmically in T. This is done by letting the prover send linear-time computable hashes of her messages to the verifier instead of the full messages. Since our proof system is public coin the prover knows after this interaction exactly how the verifier in our proof system ought to run if given the messages in our proof system. She can therefore give a verifier-efficient proof of knowledge that she knows pre-images to the hashes that would make the verifier in our proof system accept. We outline this procedure in the full paper [BCG+18].

1.2   New Techniques

Ben-Sasson et al. [BCG+13, BCTV14b] offer proof systems for correct TinyRAM program execution where the prover commits to a time-sorted execution trace as well as an address-sorted memory trace. They embed words, addresses and flags that describe the TinyRAM state at a given time into field elements. The correct transition in the execution trace between the state at time t and the state at time $t + 1$ can then be checked by an arithmetic circuit, the correct writing and reading of memory at a particular address in the memory trace can be checked by another arithmetic circuit, and finally the consistency of memory values in the two traces can be checked by a third arithmetic circuit that embeds a permutation network. Importantly, in these proofs the state transitions can be proved with the same arithmetic circuits in each step so many of the proofs can be batched together at low average cost.

Combining their approach with the recent linear-time proofs for arithmetic circuit satisfiability by Bootle et al. [BCG+17] it would be possible to get a zero-knowledge proof system with sublinear communication and efficient verification. The prover time, however, would incur at least a logarithmic overhead compared to the time to execute the TinyRAM program. First, the use of an arithmetic circuit that embeds a permutation network to check consistency between execution and memory traces requires a logarithmic number of linear-size layers to describe an arbitrary permutation which translates into a logarithmic overhead when generating the proof. Second, TinyRAM allows both arithmetic operations such as addition and multiplication of words, and logical operations such as bitwise XOR, AND and OR. To verify logical operations they decompose words into single bits that are handled individually. Bit-decomposition makes it easy to implement the logical operations, but causes an overhead when embedding bits into full size field elements. From a technical perspective our main contribution is to overcome these two obstacles.

To reduce the time required to prove the execution trace is consistent with the memory usage we do not embed a permutation network into an arithmetic circuit. Instead we relate memory consistency to the existence of a permutation that maps one memory access in the execution trace to the next access of the same memory address in the execution trace. Neff [Nef01] proposed permutation proofs in the context of shuffle proofs used in mix-nets. Follow-up works [Gro10b, GI08] have improved efficiency of such proofs with Bayer and Groth [BG12] giving a shuffle argument in the discrete logarithm setting where the prover uses a linear number of exponentiations and communication is sublinear. These shuffle proofs are proposed for the discrete logarithm setting and we do not want to pay the cost of computing exponentiations. The core of the shuffle proofs can be formulated abstractly using homomorphic commitments to vectors though. Since the proofs by Bootle et al. [BCG+17] also rely on an idealization of homomorphic commitments to vectors the ideas are compatible and we get permutation proofs that cost a linear number of field operations.

To remove the overhead of bit-decomposition we invent a less costly decomposition. While additions and multiplications are manageable using a natural embedding of words into field elements, such a representation is not well suited to logical operations though. However, instead of decomposing words into individual bits, we decompose them into interleaved odd-position bits and even-position bits. A nibble (a_3, a_2, a_1, a_0) can for instance be decomposed into $(a_3, 0, a_1, 0) + (0, a_2, 0, a_0)$. The key point of this idea is that adding two interleaved even bit nibbles yields $(0, a_2, 0, a_0) + (0, b_2, 0, b_0) = (a_2 \wedge b_2, a_2 \oplus b_2, a_0 \wedge b_0, a_0 \oplus b_0)$. So using another decomposition into odd-position and even-position bits we can now extract the XORs and the ANDs. Using this core idea, it is possible to represent all logical operations using field additions together with decomposition into odd and even-position bits. This reduces the verification of logical operations to verifying correct decomposition into odd and even bits. This decomposition and its use are described in the full paper [BCG+18].

To enable decomposition proofs into odd and even-position bits, we develop a new lookup proof that makes it possible to check that a field element belongs to a table of permitted values. By creating a lookup table of all words with even-position bits, we make it possible to verify such decompositions. Lookup proofs not only enable decomposition into odd and even-position bits but also turn out to have many other uses such as demonstrating that a field element represents a correct program instruction, or that a field element represents a valid word within the range $\{0, \ldots, 2^W - 1\}$.

Combining arithmetic circuits, permutations and table lookups we get a set of conditions for a TinyRAM execution being correct. The program execution of T steps on the TinyRAM machine can in our system be encoded as $\mathcal{O}(T)$ field elements that satisfy the conditions. Using prime order fields of size $2^{\mathcal{O}(W)}$ would make it possible to represent these field elements as $\mathcal{O}(1)$ words each. However, the soundness of our proof systems depends on the field size and to get negligible soundness error we choose a larger field to get a superconstant ratio $e = \frac{\log |\mathbb{F}|}{W}$. This factors into the efficiency of our proof system giving a prover runtime of $\mathcal{O}(\alpha T)$ TinyRAM steps for an instance requiring time T, where α is a superconstant function which specifies how many steps it takes to compute a field operation, i.e., $\alpha = \mathcal{O}(e^2)$.

Having the inner core of conditions in place: arithmetic circuits for instruction executions, permutations for memory consistency, and look-ups for word decompositions we now deploy the framework of Bootle et al. [BCG+17] to get a zero-knowledge proof system. They use error-correcting codes and linear-time collision-resistant hash functions to give proof systems for arithmetic circuit satisfiability, while we will use their techniques to prove our conditions on the execution trace are satisfied. Their proof system for arithmetic circuit satisfiability requires the prover to use a linear number of field multiplications and the verifier to use a linear number of field additions. However, we can actually get sublinear verification when the program and the input is smaller than the execution time. Technically, the performance difference stems from the type of permutation proof that they use for verifying the correct wiring of the circuit and that we use for memory consistency in the execution trace. In their use, the permutation needs to be linked to the publicly known wiring of the arithmetic circuit and in order for the verifier to check the wiring is correct he must read the entire circuit. We on the other hand do not disclose the memory accesses in the execution trace to the verifier, indeed to get zero-knowledge it is essential the memory accesses remain secret. We therefore need a hidden permutation proof and such proofs can have sublinear verification time.

1.3   Related Work

Interaction. Interaction is measured by the number of rounds the prover and verifier exchange messages. Feige and Shamir [FS90] showed that constant round argument systems exist, and Blum, Feldman and Micali [BFM88] showed that if the prover and verifier have access to an honestly generated common reference string it is possible to have non-interactive zero-knowledge proofs where the prover sends a single message to the verifier.

Communication. A series of works [KR08, IKOS09, Gen09, GGI+15] have constructed proof systems where the number of transmitted bits is proportional to the witness size. It is unlikely that sublinear communication is possible in proof systems with statistical soundness but Kilian [Kil92] constructed an argument system, a computationally sound proof system, with polylogarithmic communication complexity. Kilian's zero-knowledge argument relies on probabilistically checkable proofs [AS98], which are still complex for practical use, but the invention of interactive oracle proofs [BCS16] have made this type of proof system a realistic option. Recent work by Ben-Sasson et al. [BSBTHR18] presents a new PCP-based argument system, known as STARKs, which also has polylogarithmic communication costs, and is optimized for better practicality. Ishai et al. [IKO07] give laconic arguments where the prover's communication is minimal. Groth [Gro10a], working in the common reference string model and using strong assumptions, gave a pairing-based non-interactive zero-knowledge argument consisting of a constant number of group elements. Follow-up works on succinct non-interactive arguments of knowledge (SNARKs) have shown that it is possible to have both a modest size common reference string and proofs as small as 3 group elements [BCCT12, GGPR13, PHGR16, BCCT13, Gro16].

Verifier Computation. In general the verifier has to read the entire instance since even a single deviating bit may render the statement $u \in \mathcal{L}$ false. However, in many cases an instance can be represented more compactly than the witness and the instance may be small compared to the computational effort it takes to verify a witness for the instance. In these cases it is possible to get sublinear verification time compared to the time it takes to check the relation defining the language $\mathcal{L}$. This is for instance the case for the SNARKs mentioned above, where the verification time only depends on the size of the instance but not the complexity of the relation.

Prover Computation. Given the success in reducing interaction, communication and verification time, the important remaining challenge is to get good efficiency for the prover.

Boolean and Arithmetic Circuits. Many classic zero-knowledge proofs rely on cyclic groups and have applications in digital signatures, encryption schemes, etc. The techniques first suggested by Schnorr [Sch91] can be generalized to NP-completel languages such as boolean and arithmetic circuit satisfiability [CD, Gro09, BCC+16]. In these proofs and arguments the prover uses $\mathcal{O}(N)$ group exponentiations, where N is the number of gates in the circuit. For the discrete logarithm assumption to hold, the groups must have superpolynomial size in the security parameter though, so exponentiations incur a significant overhead compared to direct evaluation of the witness in the circuit. The SNARKs mentioned earlier also rely on cyclic groups and likewise require the prover to do $\mathcal{O}(N)$ exponentiations. Recently, Bootle et al. [BCG+17] used the structure of [Gro09] to give constant overhead zero-knowledge proofs for arithmetic circuit satisfiability, where the prover uses $\mathcal{O}(N)$ field multiplications, relying on error-correcting codes and efficient collision-resistant hash functions instead of cyclic groups. STARKs [BSBTHR18] achieve slightly worse, quasilinear prover computation but have lower asymptotic verification costs.

An alternative to these techniques is to use the "MPC in the head" paradigm by Ishai et al. [IKOS09]. Relying on efficient MPC techniques, Damgård, Ishai and Krøigaard gave zero-knowledge arguments with little communication and a prover complexity of polylog(λ)N. Instead of focusing on theoretical performance, ZKBoo [GMO16] and its subsequent optimisation ZKB++ [CDG+17] are practical implementations of a "3PC in the head" style zero-knowledge proof for boolean circuit satisfiability. Communication grows linearly in the circuit size in both proofs, and a superlogarithmic number of repetitions is required to make the soundness error negligible, but the speed of the symmetric key primitives makes practical performance good. Ligero [AHIV17] provides another implementation using techniques related to [BCG+17]. It has excellent practical performance but asymptotically it is not as efficient as [BCG+17] due to the use of more expensive error-correcting codes. Another alternative also inspired by the MPC world is to use garbled circuits to construct zero-knowledge arguments for boolean circuits [BP12, JKO13, FNO15]. The proofs grow linearly in the size of the circuit and there is a polylogarithmic overhead for the prover and verifier due to the cryptographic operations but implementations are practical [JKO13].

There are several proof systems for efficient verification of outsourced computation [GKR08, CMT12, Tha13, WHG+16]. While this line of works mostly focus on verifying deterministic computation and does not require zero-knowledge, recent works add in cryptographic techniques to obtain zero-knowledge [ZGK+17, WJB+17, WTas+17]. Hyrax [WTas+17] offers an implementation with good concrete performance. It has sublinear communication and verification, while the prover computation is dominated by $\mathcal{O}(dN + S \log S)$ field operations for a depth d and width S circuit when the witness is small compared to the circuit size. If in addition the circuit can be parallelized into many identical sub-computations the prover cost can be further reduced to $O(dN)$ field operations. The system vSQL [ZGK+17] is tailored towards verifying database queries and as in this work it avoids the use of permutation networks using permutation proofs based on invariance of roots in polynomials as first suggested by Neff [Nef01].

Correct Program Execution. In practice, most computation does not resemble circuit evaluation but is instead done by computer programs processing one instruction at a time. There has been a sustained effort to construct efficient zero-knowledge proofs that support real-life computation, i.e., proving statements of the form "when executing program P on public input x and private input y we get the output z." In the context of SNARKs there are already several systems for proving correct execution of programs written in C [PHGR16, BFR+13, BCG+13, WSR+15]. These system generally involve a *front-end* which compiles the program into an arithmetic circuit which is then fed into a cryptographic *back-end*. Much work has been dedicated to improving both sides and achieving different trade-offs between efficiency and expressiveness of the computation.

When we want to reason theoretically about zero-knowledge proofs for correct program execution, it is useful to abstract program execution as a random-access machine that in each instruction can address an arbitrary location in memory and do integer operations on it. For closer resemblance to real-life computation, we can bound the integers to a specific word size and specify a more general set of operations the random-access machine can execute. TinyRAM [BSCG+13, BCG+13] is a prominent example of a computational model bridging the gap between theory and real-word computation. It comes with a compiler from C to TinyRAM code and underpins several implementations of zero-knowledge proofs for correct program execution [BCG+13, BCTV14b, BCTV14a, CTV15, BBC+17] where the prover time is $\Omega(T \log^2 \lambda)$ for a program execution that takes time T. Similar efficiency is also achieved, asymptotically, by other proof systems that can compile (restricted) C programs and prove correct execution such as Pinocchio [PHGR16], Pantry [BFR+13] and Buffet [WSR+15]. Our work reduces the prover's overhead from $\Omega(\log^2 \lambda)$ to an arbitrary superconstant $\alpha = \omega(1)$ and is therefore an important step towards optimal prover complexity.

Concurrent Work. Zhang et al. [ZGK+18] have concurrently with our work developed and implemented a scheme for verifying RAM computations. Like us and [ZGK+17], they avoid the use of permutation networks by using permutation proofs based on polynomial invariance by Neff [Nef01]. The idea underlying their technique for proving the correct fetch of an operation is related to the idea underpinning our look-up proofs. There are significant differences between the techniques used in our works; e.g. they rely on techniques from [CMT12] for instantiating proofs where we use techniques based on ideal linear commitments [BCG+17]. The proofs in [ZGK+18] are not zero-knowledge since they leak the number of times each type of instruction is executed, while our proofs are zero-knowledge. In terms of prover efficiency, [ZGK+18] focuses on concrete efficiency and yields impressive concrete performance. Asymptotically speaking, however, we are a polylogarithmic factor more efficient. This may require some explanation because they claim linear complexity for the prover. The reason is that they treat the prover as a TinyRAM machine with logarithmic word size in their performance measurement. Looking under the hood, we see that they use bit-decomposition to handle logical operations, which is constant overhead when you fix a particular word size (e.g. 32 bits) but asymptotically the cost of this is logarithmic since it is linear in the word size. Also, they base commitments on cyclic groups and the use of exponentiations incurs a superlogarithmic overhead for the prover when implemented in TinyRAM.

Setup and Assumptions. Many proof systems, such as SNARKs, require a large and complex common reference string in order to run. The common reference string must be generated correctly, or the security of the proof system is at stake. This leads to concerns over parameter subversion, and efficiency, since the more complex the common reference string, the more costly it is to ensure that it was generated correctly. Recently, alternatives have been investigated. Hyrax [WTas+17] relies on the discrete logarithm assumption, and Ligero [AHIV17] and STARKs [BSBTHR18] rely on collision-resistant hash functions. Our scheme relies only on collision-resistant hash functions for soundness, and pseudorandom generators in order to achieve full zero-knowledge, which means that the setup information required is comparable to existing works, like STARKs, which focus on transparency.

Our proof system benefits from simple setup ingredients, nearly linear prover costs, and sublinear, hence, scalable communication and verification costs, and therefore enjoys many of the same desirable properties as STARKs [BSBTHR18].

In addition, although we do not know how to prove that our scheme is secure in any quantum security model, it is based on post-quantum assumptions and may offer some security against quantum adversaries, since it is not known how to efficiently attack collision-resistant hash functions and pseudorandom generators using quantum algorithms. Note that there are general proof systems, such as ZKB++ [CDG+17], which do have quantum proofs of security, but are asymptotically less efficient as previously discussed.

2 Preliminaries

2.1 Notation

We write $y \leftarrow A(x)$ for an algorithm returning y on input x. When the algorithm is randomized, we write $y \leftarrow A(x; r)$ to explicitly refer to the random coins r picked by the algorithm. We use a security parameter λ to indicate the desired level of security. The higher the security parameter, the smaller the risk of an adversary compromising security should be. For functions $f, g : \mathbb{N} \to [0, 1]$, we write $f(\lambda) \approx g(\lambda)$ if $|f(\lambda) - g(\lambda)| = \frac{1}{\lambda^{\omega(1)}}$. We say a function f is *overwhelming* if $f(\lambda) \approx 1$ and that it is *negligible* if $f(\lambda) \approx 0$. In general we want the adversary's chance of breaking our proof systems to be negligible in λ. As a minimum requirement for an algorithm or adversary to be efficient it has to run in polynomial time in the security parameter. We abbreviate probabilistic (deterministic) polynomial time in the security parameter PPT (DPT). For a positive integer n, $[n]$ denotes the set $\{1, \ldots, n\}$. We use bold letters such as v for row vectors over a finite field $\mathbb{F}$.

2.2   Proofs of Knowledge

We follow [BCG+17] in defining proofs of knowledge over a communication channel and their specification of the ideal linear commitment channel and the standard channel. A *proof system* is defined by stateful PPT algorithms $(\mathcal{K}, \mathcal{P}, \mathcal{V})$. The setup generator $\mathcal{K}$ is only run once to provide public parameters pp that will be used by the prover $\mathcal{P}$ and verifier $\mathcal{V}$. We will in our security definitions just assume $\mathcal{K}$ is honest, which is reasonable since in our constructions the public parameters are publicly verifiable and could even be generated by the verifier.

The prover and verifier communicate with each other through a *communication channel* $\overset{\text{chan}}{\longleftrightarrow}$. When $\mathcal{P}$ and $\mathcal{V}$ interact on inputs s and t through a channel $\overset{\text{chan}}{\longleftrightarrow}$ we let $\text{view}_{\mathcal{V}} \leftarrow \langle \mathcal{P}(s) \overset{\text{chan}}{\longleftrightarrow} \mathcal{V}(t) \rangle$ be the view of the verifier in the execution, i.e., all inputs he gets including random coins, and we let $\text{trans}_{\mathcal{P}} \leftarrow \langle \mathcal{P}(s) \overset{\text{chan}}{\longleftrightarrow} \mathcal{V}(t) \rangle$ denote the transcript of the communication between prover and channel. The protocol ends with the verifier accepting or rejecting the proof. We write $\langle \mathcal{P}(s) \overset{\text{chan}}{\longleftrightarrow} \mathcal{V}(t) \rangle = b$ depending on whether he accepts $(b = 1)$ or rejects $(b = 0)$.

In the *standard channel* $\longleftrightarrow$, all messages are forwarded between prover and verifier. As in [BCG+17], we also consider an *ideal linear commitment* channel, $\overset{\text{ILC}}{\longleftrightarrow}$, described in Fig. 2. When using the ILC channel, the prover can submit a `commit` command to commit to vectors of field elements of some fixed length k, specified in the public parameters. The vectors remain secretly stored in the channel, and will not be forwarded to the verifier. Instead, the verifier only learns how many vectors the prover has committed to. The verifier can submit a `send` command to the ILC channel to send a message to the prover. In addition, the verifier can also submit `open` queries to the ILC channel to obtain openings of linear combinations of the vectors sent by the prover. We stress that the verifier can request several linear combinations of stored vectors within a single `open` query, as depicted in Fig. 2 using matrix notation.

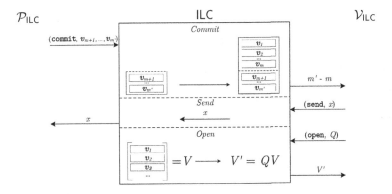

Fig. 2. Description of the ILC channel.

We say a proof system is *public coin* if the verifier's messages to the communication channel are chosen uniformly at random and independently of the actions of the prover, i.e., the verifier's messages to the prover correspond to the verifier's randomness ρ. All our proof systems will be public coin. In a proof system over the ILC channel, sequences of commit, send and open queries can alternate arbitrarily. However, since our proof systems are public coin we can without loss of generality assume the verifier will only make one big open query at the end of the protocol and then decide whether to accept or reject.

Let $\mathcal{R}$ be an efficiently decidable relation of tuples (pp, u, w). We can define a matching language $\mathcal{L} = \{(pp, u) | \exists w : (pp, u, w) \in \mathcal{R}\}$. We refer to u as the *instance* and w as the *witness* to $(pp, u) \in \mathcal{L}$. The public parameter pp will specify the security parameter λ, perhaps implicitly through its length, and may also contain other parameters used for specifying the relation. Typically, pp will also contain parameters that do not influence membership of $\mathcal{R}$ but may aid the prover and verifier, for instance the field and vector size in the ILC channel.

The protocol $(\mathcal{K}, \mathcal{P}, \mathcal{V})$ is called a *proof of knowledge* over a communication channel $\xleftrightarrow{chan}$ for a relation $\mathcal{R}$ if it has perfect completeness and computational knowledge soundness as defined below.

Definition 1 (Perfect Completeness). *A proof system is perfectly complete if for all PPT adversaries $\mathcal{A}$*

$$\Pr\left[\begin{array}{c} pp \leftarrow \mathcal{K}(1^\lambda); (u, w) \leftarrow \mathcal{A}(pp) : \\ (pp, u, w) \notin \mathcal{R} \vee \langle \mathcal{P}(pp, u, w) \xleftrightarrow{chan} \mathcal{V}(pp, u)\rangle = 1 \end{array} \right] = 1.$$

Definition 2 (Knowledge soundness). *A public-coin proof system has computational (strong black-box) knowledge soundness if for all DPT $\mathcal{P}^*$ there exists an expected PPT extractor $\mathcal{E}$ such that for all PPT adversaries $\mathcal{A}$*

$$\Pr\left[\begin{array}{c} pp \leftarrow \mathcal{K}(1^\lambda); (u, s) \leftarrow \mathcal{A}(pp); w \leftarrow \mathcal{E}^{\langle \mathcal{P}^*(s) \xleftrightarrow{chan} \mathcal{V}(pp,u)\rangle}(pp, u) : \\ b = 1 \wedge (pp, u, w) \notin \mathcal{R} \end{array} \right] \approx 0.$$

Here the oracle $\langle \mathcal{P}^*(s) \xleftrightarrow{chan} \mathcal{V}(pp, u)\rangle$ runs a full protocol execution and if the proof is successful it returns the transcript trans$_{\mathcal{P}}$ of the prover's communication with the channel. The extractor $\mathcal{E}$ can ask the oracle to rewind the proof to any point in a previous transcript and execute the proof again from this point on with fresh public-coin challenges from the verifier. We let $b \in \{0, 1\}$ be the verifier's output in the first oracle execution, i.e., whether it accepts or not, and we think of s as the state of the prover. The definition can then be paraphrased as saying that if the prover in state s makes a convincing proof, then $\mathcal{E}$ can extract a witness.

If the definition holds also for unbounded $\mathcal{P}^*$ and $\mathcal{A}$ we say the proof has statistical knowledge soundness.

If the definition holds for a non-rewinding extractor, i.e., $\mathcal{E}$ only requires a single transcript of the prover's communication with the channel, we say the proof system has knowledge soundness with straight-line extraction.

We will construct public-coin proofs of knowledge that have special honest-verifier zero-knowledge. This means that if the verifier's challenges are known in advance then it is possible to simulate the verifier's view without knowing a witness. In our definition, the simulator works even for verifiers who may use adversarial biased coins in choosing their challenges as long as they honestly follow the specification of the protocol.

Definition 3 (Special Honest-Verifier Zero-Knowledge). *A public-coin proof of knowledge is computationally special honest-verifier zero-knowledge (SHVZK) if there exists a PPT simulator S such that for all stateful interactive PPT adversaries A that output randomness ρ for the verifier, and (u, w) such that $(pp, u, w) \in R$,*

$$\Pr\left[\begin{array}{c} pp \leftarrow \mathcal{K}(1^\lambda); (u, w, \rho) \leftarrow \mathcal{A}(pp); \\ \mathsf{view}_{\mathcal{V}} \leftarrow \langle \mathcal{P}(pp, u, w) \xleftrightarrow{chan} \mathcal{V}(pp, u; \rho) \rangle : \mathcal{A}(\mathsf{view}_{\mathcal{V}}) = 1 \end{array}\right]$$
$$\approx \Pr\left[pp \leftarrow \mathcal{K}(1^\lambda); (u, w, \rho) \leftarrow \mathcal{A}(pp); \mathsf{view}_{\mathcal{V}} \leftarrow \mathcal{S}(pp, u, \rho) : \mathcal{A}(\mathsf{view}_{\mathcal{V}}) = 1\right].$$

We say the proof is statistically SHVZK *if the definition holds also against unbounded adversaries, and we say the proof is* perfectly SHVZK *if the probabilities are exactly equal.*

2.3   TinyRAM

TinyRAM is a random-access machine model operating on W-bit words and using K registers. We now describe the key features of TinyRAM but refer the reader to the specification [BSCG+13] for full details. A state of the TinyRAM machine consists of a program P (list of L instructions), a program counter pc (word), K registers $\mathsf{reg}_0, \ldots, \mathsf{reg}_{K-1}$ (words), a condition flag flag (bit), and M words of memory with addresses $0, \ldots, M - 1$.

The TinyRAM specification includes two read-only tapes to retrieve its inputs but with little loss of efficiency we may assume the program starts by reading the tapes into memory[5] We will therefore skip the reading phase and assume the memory is initialized with the inputs (and 0 for the remaining words). Also, we will assume on initialization that pc, the registers and flag are all set to 0.

The program consists of a sequence of L instructions that include bit-wise logical operations, arithmetic operations, shifts, comparisons, jumps, and storing and loading data in memory. The program terminates by using a special command **answer** that returns a word. A description of the allowed operations is given in Table 1. We consider the program to have succeeded if it answers 0, otherwise we consider the answer to be a failure code.

We write reg_i and r_i when referring to register i and to its content, respectively. We write A to refer to either a register or an immediate value specified in a program instruction and write A for the value stored therein. Depending on the

---

[5] The specification [BSCG+13] calls a program *proper* if it first reads all inputs into memory and provides a 7-line TinyRAM program that does this in $\sim 5M$ steps.

instruction a word a may be interpreted as an unsigned value in $\{0, \ldots, 2^W - 1\}$ or as a signed value in $\{-2^{W-1}, \ldots, 2^{W-1} - 1\}$. Signed values are in two's complement, so given a word $a = (a_{w-1}, \ldots, a_0) \in \{0, 1\}^W$ the bit a_{W-1} is the sign and the signed value is $-2^W + a$ if $a_{W-1} = 1$ and a if $a_{W-1} = 0$. We distinguish operations over signed values by using subscript s, e.g. $a \times_s b$ and $a \geq_s b$ are used to denote product and comparison over the signed values.

Correct Program Execution. It is often important to check that a protocol participant supposedly running program P on public input x and private input w provides the correct output z. Without loss of generality, we can formulate the verification as an extended program that takes public input $v = (x, z)$ and answers 0 if and only if z is the output of the computation. We therefore formulate correct program execution as the program just answering 0.

We now give a relation that captures correct TinyRAM program execution. An instance is of the form $u = (P, v, T, M)$, where P is a TinyRAM program, v is a list of words given as input to the program, T is a time bound, and M is the size of the memory. A witness w is another list of words. We assume without loss of generality that the witness is appended by 0's, such that $|v| + |w| = M$ and the program starts with the memory being initialized to these words.

The statement we want to prove is that the program P terminates in T steps using M words of memory on the public input v and private input w with the instruction **answer** 0. We therefore define

$$
\mathcal{R}_{\mathsf{TinyRAM}} = \left\{ \begin{array}{l} (pp, u, w) = ((W, K, *), (P, v, T, M), w) \mid \\ P \text{ is a TinyRAM program with } W\text{-bit words, } K \text{ registers,} \\ \text{and } M \text{ words of addressable memory, which on inputs } v \text{ and } w \\ \text{terminates in } T \text{ steps with the instruction } \mathbf{answer}\ 0. \end{array} \right\}
$$

Our main interest is to prove correct execution of programs that require heavy computation so we will throughout the article assume the number of steps outweigh the other parameters, i.e., $T > L + M$, where L is the number of instructions in the program.

3   Arithmetization of Correct Program Execution

As a first step towards the realization of proofs for the correct execution of TinyRAM programs we translate $\mathcal{R}_{\mathsf{TinyRAM}}$ into a more amenable relation involving elements in a finite field. Given a TinyRAM machine with word-size W and a finite field $\mathbb{F}$, we can in a natural way embed words into field elements by encoding a word $a \in \{0, \ldots, 2^W - 1\}$ as the field element $a \cdot 1_{\mathbb{F}} = 1_{\mathbb{F}} + \cdots + 1_{\mathbb{F}}$ (a times). We will use fields of characteristic $p > 2^{2W} - 2^{W-1}$ because then sums and products of words are less than p and we avoid overflow in the field operations we apply to the embedded words.

We will encode the program, memory and states of a TinyRAM program as tuples of field elements. We then introduce a new relation $\mathcal{R}_{\mathsf{TinyRAM}}^{\mathsf{field}}$ consisting of a set of arithmetic constraints these encodings should satisfy to guarantee the correct program execution. The relation will take instances $u = (P, v, T, M)$, and witnesses w consisting of the encodings as well as a set of auxiliary field elements.

In this section we specify instructions supported by TinyRAM machines and the structure of the witness w and how the relation of correct program execution decomposes into simpler sub-relations. It will be the case that the encoding of the witness can be done alongside an execution of the program in $\mathcal{O}(L + M + T)$ field operations.

Table 1 described the supported operations in TinyRAM. Each line in the program consists of one of these instructions in and up to three operands, e.g. **add** $\text{reg}_i \ \text{reg}_j \ A$. The first operand, reg_i, usually points to the register storing the result of the operation, **add**, computed on the words specified by the next two operands, reg_j, A. The last operand A indicates an immediate value that could be either used directly in the operation or to point to the content of another register. We refer to the value to be used in the operation generically as A, stressing that the selection between either the immediate value or a register value can be handled by using the appropriate selection vector.

Formatting the Witness. Given a correct program execution we encode program, memory and states of the TinyRAM machine as field elements and arrange them in a number of tables as pictured in Table 2. The execution table Exe, contains the field elements encoding of the states of the TinyRAM machine. It consists of T rows, where row t describes the state at the beginning of step t. A row includes field elements that encode the time t, the program counter pc_t, the instruction $\text{inst}_{\text{pc}_t}$ corresponding to pc_t, an immediate value A_t, the values $r_{0,t}, \ldots, r_{K-1,t}$ contained in the registers $\text{reg}_0, \ldots, \text{reg}_{K-1}$ at time t, and the flag flag_t. The next row contains the resulting state of the TinyRAM machine at time $t + 1$. Each row also includes a memory address addr_t, and the value v_{addr_t} stored at this address after the execution of the step, as well as a constant number of auxiliary field elements to be specified later that will be used to check correctness of program execution.

The next table is the program table Prog, which contains the field elements encoding of the TinyRAM program P. Each row contains the description of one line of the program, consisting of one instruction, at most three operands, and possibly an immediate value. Furthermore, we introduce a constant number of auxiliary field elements in each row. These entries can be efficiently computed given the program line stored in the same row and will help verifying its execution, e.g. we encode the position of input and output registers as auxiliary field elements.

The memory table Mem has rows that list the possible memory addresses, their initial values, and an auxiliary field element $\text{usd} \in \{0, 1\}$. For every pair of address and corresponding initial value, the memory table Mem contains a row in which $\text{usd} = 0$ and another row in which $\text{usd} = 1$. Recall that the memory is initialized with input words listed in v, w, i.e., the input words contributing to the instance and witness of the relation $\mathcal{R}_{\text{TinyRAM}}$.

Table 1. TinyRAM instruction set, excluding the **read** command. The flag is set equal to 1 if the condition is met and 0 otherwise. If the pc exceeds the program length, i.e., pc $\geq L$, or we address a non-existing part of memory, i.e., in a **store** or **load** instruction A $\geq M$, the TinyRAM machine halts with answer 1.

Instruction	Operands			Effect	Flag
and	reg_i	reg_j	A	Compute r_i as bitwise AND of r_j and A	Result is 0^W
or	reg_i	reg_j	A	Compute r_i as bitwise OR of r_j and A	Result is 0^W
xor	reg_i	reg_j	A	Compute r_i as bitwise XOR of r_j and A	Result is 0^W
not	reg_i		A	Compute r_i as bitwise NOT of A	Result is 0^W
add	reg_i	reg_j	A	Compute $r_i = r_j + A \bmod 2^W$	Overflow: $r_j + A \geq 2^W$
sub	reg_i	reg_j	A	Compute $r_i = r_j - A \bmod 2^W$	Borrow: $r_j < A$
mull	reg_i	reg_j	A	Compute $r_i = r_j \times A \bmod 2^W$	$\neg$ overflow: $r_j \times A < 2^W$
umulh	reg_i	reg_j	A	Compute r_i as upper W bits of $r_j \times A$	$\neg$ overflow: $r_i = 0$
smulh	reg_i	reg_j	A	Compute r_i as upper W bits of the signed $2W$-bit $r_j \times_s A$ (**mull** gives lower word)	$\neg$ over/underflow: $r_i = 0$
udiv	reg_i	reg_j	A	Compute r_i as quotient of r_j / A	Division by zero: A $= 0$
umod	reg_i	reg_j	A	Compute r_i as remainder of r_j / A	Division by zero: A $= 0$
shl	reg_i	reg_j	A	Compute r_i as r_i shifted left by A bits	MSB of r_j
shr	reg_i	reg_j	A	Compute r_i as r_i shifted right by A bits	LSB of r_j
cmpe	reg_i		A	Compare if equal	Equal: $r_i = A$
cmpa	reg_i		A	Compare if above	Above: $r_i > A$
cmpae	reg_i		A	Compare if above or equal	Above/equal: $r_i \geq A$
cmpg	reg_i		A	Signed compare if greater	Greater: $r_i >_s A$
cmpge	reg_i		A	Signed compare if greater or equal	Greater/equal: $r_i \geq_s A$
mov	reg_i		A	Set $r_i = A$	Flag unchanged
cmov	reg_i		A	if flag $= 1$ set $r_i = A$	Flag unchanged
jmp	A			Set pc $= A$	Flag unchanged
cjmp	A			If flag $= 1$ set pc $= A$	Flag unchanged
cnjmp	A			If flag $= 0$ set pc $= A$	Flag unchanged
store	A	reg_i		Store in memory address A the word r_i	Flag unchanged
load	reg_i		A	Set r_i to the word stored at address A	Flag unchanged
answer	A			Stall or halt returning the word A	Flag unchanged

Table 2. The execution table Exe, the program table Prog, the memory table Mem and the table EvenBits.

Time	pc	Instruction	Immediate	reg_0	...	reg_{K-1}	Flag	Address	Value	$\boldsymbol{aux}_{\mathsf{Exe}}$
1	0	inst_0	A_0	0	...	0	0	0	0	...
					$\vdots$					
t	pc_t	inst_{pc_t}	A_t	$r_{0,t}$	...	$r_{K-1,t}$	flag_t	addr_t	$\mathsf{v}_{\mathsf{addr}_t}$	...
$t+1$	pc_{t+1}	$\mathsf{inst}_{pc_{t+1}}$	A_{t+1}	$r_{0,t+1}$	...	$r_{K-1,t+1}$	flag_{t+1}	addr_{t+1}	$\mathsf{v}_{\mathsf{addr}_{t+1}}$	...
					$\vdots$					
T	pc_T	answer 0	0	$r_{0,T}$	...	$r_{K-1,T}$	flag_T	addr_T	$\mathsf{v}_{\mathsf{addr}_T}$	...

(a) The execution table Exe.

pc	Instruction	Immediate	$\boldsymbol{aux}_{\mathsf{Prog}}$
0	inst_0	A_0	...
	$\vdots$		
$L-1$	inst_{L-1}	A_{L-1}	...

(b) The program table Prog.

Address	Initial value	usd
0	0	0
1	v_1	0
	$\vdots$	
$M-1$	v_{M-1}	0
0	0	1
1	v_1	1
	$\vdots$	
$M-1$	v_{M-1}	1

(c) The memory table Mem.

Values
0
1
4
5
$\vdots$
$\sum_{i=0}^{\frac{W}{2}-1} 2^{2i}$

(d) The table EvenBits.

In addition to these, we also consider an auxiliary lookup table EvenBits containing the encoding of words of length W whose binary expansion has 0 in all odd positions. The table contains $2^{\frac{W}{2}}$ field elements and will be used as part of a check that certain field elements encode a word of length W.

3.1 Decomposition of TinyRAM

Let (Exe, Prog, Mem, EvenBits) be the tables of field elements encoding the program execution and the auxiliary values. We can now reformulate the correct execution of a TinyRAM program defined by $\mathcal{R}_{\mathsf{TinyRAM}}$ as a relation that imposes a number of constraints the field elements included in tables should satisfy:

$$\mathcal{R}_{\mathsf{TinyRAM}}^{\mathsf{field}} = \left\{ \begin{array}{l} (pp, u, w) = ((W, K, \mathbb{F}, *), (P, v, T, M), \mathsf{w}) \mid \\ \mathsf{w} = (\mathsf{Exe}, \mathsf{Prog}, \mathsf{Mem}, \mathsf{EvenBits}, *) \\ (pp, (P, v, T, M), \mathsf{w}) \in \mathcal{R}_{\mathsf{check}} \\ (pp, (T, M), \mathsf{w}) \in \mathcal{R}_{\mathsf{mem}} \\ (pp, \bot, \mathsf{w}) \in \mathcal{R}_{\mathsf{step}} \end{array} \right\}$$

where the relations $\mathcal{R}_{\mathsf{check}}$, $\mathcal{R}_{\mathsf{mem}}$, $\mathcal{R}_{\mathsf{step}}$ jointly guarantee the witness w consists of field elements encoding a correct TinyRAM execution that answers 0 in T steps using M words of memory, public input v, and additional private inputs.

Specifically, the relation $\mathcal{R}_{\mathsf{check}}$ checks the initial values of the memory are correctly included into Mem, the program is correctly encoded in Prog, EvenBits contains the correct encodings of the auxiliary lookup table, the initial state of the TinyRAM machine is correct and that it terminates with answer 0 in step T. The role of $\mathcal{R}_{\mathsf{mem}}$ is to check that memory usage is consistent throughout the execution of the program. That is, if a memory value is loaded at time t then it should match the last stored value at the same address. Finally, $\mathcal{R}_{\mathsf{step}}$ checks that each step of the execution has been performed correctly. In the rest of the section we describe $\mathcal{R}_{\mathsf{check}}$, $\mathcal{R}_{\mathsf{mem}}$ and $\mathcal{R}_{\mathsf{step}}$, gradually decomposing them into smaller and simpler relations. Ultimately, we specify each of these subrelations in terms of some building block: equality, lookup, permutation, and range relations. Figure 3 illustrates the decomposition of $\mathcal{R}^{\mathsf{field}}_{\mathsf{TinyRAM}}$ into progressively smaller relations.

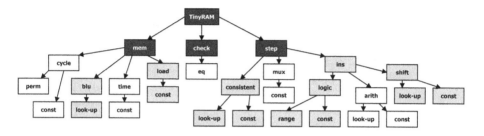

Fig. 3. Diagram of the decomposition of TinyRAM into equality, lookup, permutation, and range relations.

Building Blocks. We give a brief description of the building block relations used in the decomposition of $\mathcal{R}^{\mathsf{field}}_{\mathsf{TinyRAM}}$.

– An equality relation $\mathcal{R}_{\mathsf{eq}}$ checks that rows Tab_i of a table Tab in the witness encode tuples $v_1, \ldots, v_m$ of given W-bit words
– A lookup relation checks the membership of a tuple of field elements w in the set of rows of a table Tab. This differs from the previous relation as both w and Tab are both in the witness. We extend this relation in the natural way for checking the membership of multiple tuples $w_1, w_2, \ldots$ in a table.
– A range relation to check that a field element a can be written as a W-bit word, i.e., a is in the range $\{0, \ldots, 2^W - 1\}$.
– A permutation relation can be used to check that two ordered sets of a given size are permutations of each other. The permutation is in the witness i.e. it is unknown to the verifier.

3.2 Checking the Correctness of Values

The role of $\mathcal{R}_{\mathsf{check}}$ is to check that w consists of the correct number of field elements that can be partitioned into the appropriate tables and also to check that specific entries in these tables are correct.

$$\mathcal{R}_{\mathsf{check}} = \left\{ \begin{array}{l} (pp, u, w) = ((W, K, \mathbb{F}, *), (P, v, T, M), \mathsf{w}) \mid \\ \mathsf{w} = (\mathsf{Exe}, \mathsf{Prog}, \mathsf{Mem}, \mathsf{EvenBits}, *), \\ \mathsf{Exe} = \{\mathsf{Exe}_t\}_{t=1}^{T}, \quad \mathsf{Prog} = \{\mathsf{Prog}_i\}_{i=0}^{L-1} \\ \mathsf{Prog}_0 = (0, \mathsf{inst}_0, A_0, \ldots) \\ (pp, (1, 0, \mathsf{inst}_0, A_0, 0, \ldots, 0, \ldots), \mathsf{Exe}_1) \in \mathcal{R}_{\mathsf{eq}} \\ (pp, (T, \mathbf{answer}, 0, \ldots), \mathsf{Exe}_T) \in \mathcal{R}_{\mathsf{eq}} \\ \left(pp, \left(0, 1, 4, 5, \ldots, \sum_{i=0}^{\frac{W}{2}-1} 2^{2i}\right), \mathsf{EvenBits}\right) \in \mathcal{R}_{\mathsf{eq}} \\ (pp, P, \mathsf{Prog}) \in \mathcal{R}_{\mathsf{eq}} \quad (pp, v, \mathsf{Mem}) \in \mathcal{R}_{\mathsf{eq}} \end{array} \right\}.$$

The relation $\mathcal{R}_{\mathsf{check}}$ checks that: the first and last row of the execution table contains the correct initial values; the auxiliary lookup table $\mathsf{EvenBits}$ contains the embeddings of all W-bit words with 0 in all odd positions; the program table Prog contains the correct field element embedding of the program P as well as the correct auxiliary entries; the memory table Mem contains the correct embedding of the input words listed in v.

3.3   Checking Memory Consistency

The relation $\mathcal{R}_{\mathsf{mem}}$ checks that the memory is used consistently across different steps in the execution. For instance, if at step t a value is loaded from memory, then it should be equal to the last value stored in the same address. If it is the first time a memory address is accessed, we need to ensure consistency with the initial values. If two consecutive memory accesses to the same address were placed into two adjacent rows of Exe it would be easy to check their consistency. However, this is generally not the case since the Exe table is sorted by execution time rather than memory access. Therefore, we need to devise a way to check consistency of memory accesses that could be located in any position of Exe. Overall the memory consistency relation $\mathcal{R}_{\mathsf{mem}}$ decomposes as follows

$$\mathcal{R}_{\mathsf{mem}} = \left\{ \begin{array}{l} (pp, u, w) = ((W, K, \mathbb{F}, *), (T, M), \mathsf{w}) \mid \\ \quad\quad \mathsf{w} = (\mathsf{Exe}, \mathsf{Prog}, \mathsf{Mem}, \mathsf{EvenBits}, \pi, *), \\ \mathsf{Exe} = \{\mathsf{Exe}_t\}_{t=1}^{T} \quad\quad\quad \mathsf{Mem} = \{\mathsf{Mem}_j\}_{j=0}^{2M-2} \\ (pp, T, (\mathsf{Exe}, \pi)) \in \mathcal{R}_{\mathsf{cycle}}, \quad\quad (pp, T, \mathsf{Exe}) \in \mathcal{R}_{\mathsf{time}} \\ (pp, (T, M), (\mathsf{Exe}, \mathsf{Mem})) \in \mathcal{R}_{\mathsf{blookup}}, \quad (pp, T, \mathsf{Exe}) \in \mathcal{R}_{\mathsf{load}} \end{array} \right\}$$

To help with checking the memory consistency, we include in each row of the execution table the following auxiliary entries

$$\boldsymbol{aux}_{\mathsf{Exe}} = \boxed{\eta_{\mathsf{link}}\,|\,\mathsf{v}_{\mathsf{link}}\,|\,\mathsf{v}_{\mathsf{init}}\,|\,\mathsf{usd}\,|\,\mathsf{S}\,|\,\mathsf{L}\,|\,\cdots}$$

where η_{link} contains the previous time-step at which the current address was accessed, unless this is the first time a location is accessed in which case it is set equal to the last time-step this location is accessed. Similarly, $\mathsf{v}_{\mathsf{link}}$ stores the value contained in the address after time η_{link}, unless this is the first time that location is accessed, in which case it stores the last value stored in that location. The value v_{init} is a copy of the initial value assigned to that memory location, which is also stored in the memory table Mem. The value usd is a flag which is set equal to 0 if this is the first time we access the current memory address, and 1 otherwise. The values S, L are flags set equal to 1 in case the current instruction is a **store** or **load** operation, respectively, and 0 otherwise. The values S, L are also stored in the auxiliary entries of the program table $\textbf{\textit{aux}}_{\text{Prog}} = \boxed{S\,L\,\cdots}$.

Memory Accesses Form Cycles. We check memory consistency by specifying cycles of memory accesses, so that consecutive terms in a cycle correspond to two consecutive accesses to the same memory location. By using the above auxiliary entries, we use the relation $\mathcal{R}_{\text{cycle}}$ for the memory access pattern in the rows of Exe being in correspondence with a permutation π defined by such cycles. The relation $\mathcal{R}_{\text{cycle}}$ checks that all memory accesses (i.e. with $S + L = 1$) relative to the same address are connected into cycles and that rows not involving memory operations $(S + L = 0)$ are not included in these cycles. The relation does not include any explicit checks on whether $S + L$ is equal to 0 or 1. It is sufficient to check that $S_t + L_t = S_{t'} + L_{t'}$, $t = \tau_{\text{link}t'}$, $v_{\text{addr}_t} = v_{\text{link}t'}$ and $\text{addr}_t = \text{addr}_{t'}$ for some $t' = \pi(t)$, which ensures that operations which are not memory operations are not part of cycles including memory operations.

$$
\mathcal{R}_{\text{cycle}} = \left\{
\begin{array}{c}
(pp, u, w) = ((W, K, \mathbb{F}, *), T, (\text{Exe}, \pi)) \mid \\
\text{Exe}_t = (t, \ldots, \text{addr}_t, v_{\text{link}t}, \tau_{\text{link}t}, \ldots, S_t, L_t, \ldots) \text{ for } t \in [T] \\
\boldsymbol{a}_t = (t, \text{addr}_t, v_{\text{addr}_t}, S_t + L_t) \text{ for } t \in [T] \\
\boldsymbol{b}_t = (\tau_{\text{link}t}, \text{addr}_t, v_{\text{link}t}, S_t + L_t) \text{ for } t \in [T] \\
((W, K, \mathbb{F}, *), T, (\{\boldsymbol{a}_i, \boldsymbol{b}_i\}_{i=1}^T, \pi)) \in \mathcal{R}_{\text{perm}}
\end{array}
\right\}
$$

Memory Accesses are in the Correct Order. Consecutive terms in a cycle should correspond to the consecutive time-steps in which the memory is accessed. To check that the memory cycles are time-ordered we can simply verify that $t > \tau_{\text{link}t}$ for any given time-step $t \in [T]^6$. Since memory accesses are connected into cycles, the first time we access a new memory location the τ_{link} entry stores the last point in time that location is accessed by the program. In this case (usd = 0), we verify that $t \leq \tau_{\text{link}t}$. The relation $\mathcal{R}_{\text{time}}$ incorporates these conditions

$$
\mathcal{R}_{\text{time}} = \left\{
\begin{array}{c}
(pp, u, w) = ((W, K, \mathbb{F}, *), T, \text{Exe}) \mid \\
\text{Exe}_t = (t, \ldots, \tau_{\text{link}t}, \ldots, \text{usd}_t, \ldots) \text{ for } t \in [T] \\
\forall\, t \in [T] : (\text{usd} = 0 \wedge t \leq \tau_{\text{link}t}) \vee (\text{usd} = 1 \wedge t > \tau_{\text{link}t})
\end{array}
\right\}
$$

Memory Locations are in no more than one Cycle. To ensure that the cycles correspond to sequences of memory addresses we also require that all the

---

[6] For this to be sufficient we also need the time-steps in the execution table to be correct but this is ensured by the $\mathcal{R}_{\text{check}}$ and $\mathcal{R}_{\text{consistent}}$ (appears later) relations.

rows touching the same memory address are included in the *same* cycle. Since the cycles are time-ordered, they require one time-step for which $\mathsf{usd} = 0$ in order to close a cycle. Thus, we can ensure each memory location to be part of at most on cycle by letting usd to be set equal to 0 at most once for each memory address. We introduce a *bounded* lookup relation $\mathcal{R}_{\mathsf{blookup}}$ to address this requirement. The relation checks that for any row in Exe, the tuple $(\mathsf{addr}_t, \mathsf{v}_{\mathsf{init}\,t}, \mathsf{usd})$ is contained in one row of the table Mem and that each row $(j, \mathsf{v}_j, 0)$ of Mem is accessed at most once by the program.

$$
\mathcal{R}_{\mathsf{blookup}} = \left\{
\begin{array}{l}
(pp, u, w) = ((W, K, \mathbb{F}, *), (T, M), (\mathsf{Exe}, \mathsf{Mem})) \mid \\
\mathsf{Exe}_t = (t, \ldots, \mathsf{addr}_t, \ldots, \mathsf{v}_{\mathsf{init}\,t}, \mathsf{usd}_t, \ldots) \text{ for } t \in [T] \\
\forall\, t \in [T]\ (pp, \perp, ((\mathsf{addr}_t, \mathsf{v}_{\mathsf{init}\,t}, \mathsf{usd}_t), \mathsf{Mem})) \in \mathcal{R}_{\mathsf{lookup}} \wedge \\
\forall\, (j, \mathsf{v}_j, 0) \in \mathsf{Mem} : (\ldots, j, \ldots, \mathsf{v}_j, 0, \ldots) \text{ occurs at most once in } \mathsf{Exe}
\end{array}
\right\}
$$

Load Instructions are Consistent. Finally, we are only left to check that if the program executes a **load** instruction the value $\mathsf{v}_{\mathsf{addr}_t}$ loaded from memory is consistent with the value stored at the same address at the previous access. Similarly, if **load** is executed on a new memory location, then the value loaded should match with the initial value $\mathsf{v}_{\mathsf{init}\,t}$. No additional checks are required for **store** instructions. These checks are incorporated in the relation $\mathcal{R}_{\mathsf{load}}$.

$$
\mathcal{R}_{\mathsf{load}} = \left\{
\begin{array}{l}
(pp, u, w) = ((W, K, \mathbb{F}, *), T, \mathsf{Exe}) \mid \\
\mathsf{Exe}_t = (t, \ldots, \mathsf{addr}_t, \mathsf{v}_{\mathsf{addr}_t}, \eta_{\mathsf{link}\,t}, \mathsf{v}_{\mathsf{link}\,t}, \mathsf{v}_{\mathsf{init}\,t}, \mathsf{usd}_t, \ldots) \text{ for } t \in [T] \\
\forall\, t \in [T] : \mathsf{L}_t(\mathsf{v}_{\mathsf{addr}_t} - \mathsf{v}_{\mathsf{init}\,t} + \mathsf{usd}_t(\mathsf{v}_{\mathsf{init}\,t} - \mathsf{v}_{\mathsf{link}\,t})) = 0
\end{array}
\right\}
$$

3.4   Checking Correct Execution of Instructions

We use the relation $\mathcal{R}_{\mathsf{step}}$ to guarantee that each step of the execution has been performed correctly. This involves checking for each row Exe_t of the execution table that the stored words are in the range $\{0, \ldots, 2^W - 1\}$, the flag_t is a bit, the program counter pc_t matches the instruction and the immediate value A_t in the program, and that inst_t is correctly executed. An instruction takes some inputs, e.g., values indicated by the operands reg_j, A or the flag and as a result may change the program counter, a register value, a value stored at a memory address, or the flag. Since we have already checked memory correctness, if the operation is a load or store we may assume the memory value is correct.

$$
\mathcal{R}_{\mathsf{step}} = \left\{
\begin{array}{l}
(pp, u, w) = ((W, K, \mathbb{F}, *), \perp, \mathsf{w}) \mid \\
\mathsf{w} = (\mathsf{Exe}, \mathsf{Prog}, \mathsf{Mem}, \mathsf{EvenBits}, *) \wedge \mathsf{Exe} = \{\mathsf{Exe}_t\}_{t=1}^{T} \\
\forall t \in \{1, \ldots, T-1\} : \\
\quad (pp, \perp, (\mathsf{Exe}_t, \mathsf{Exe}_{t+1})) \in \mathcal{R}_{\mathsf{mux}} \\
\quad (pp, \perp, (\mathsf{Exe}_i, \mathsf{Exe}_{i+1}, \mathsf{Prog})) \in \mathcal{R}_{\mathsf{consistent}} \\
\quad (pp, \perp, (\mathsf{Exe}_i, \mathsf{Exe}_{i+1}, \mathsf{EvenBits}, *)) \in \mathcal{R}_{\mathsf{ins}}
\end{array}
\right\} .
$$

To help checking the consistency of the operations the rows of the execution and program tables include some auxiliary entries. These consist of some *temporary variables*, an output vector, and some *selection vectors* which are also listed in the program table. The temporary variables are used to store a copy of the inputs and outputs of an instruction. The advantage of the temporary variables is that for each addition operation we check, we will always have the inputs and outputs stored, instead of having to handle multiple registers holding inputs and output in arbitrary order.

Ensuring Temporary Values are Correct. A multiplexing relation $\mathcal{R}_{\mathsf{mux}}$ is used to check that the temporary variables are consistent with operands contained in inst_t. Checking operations on temporary values require us to multiplex the corresponding register, immediate, and memory values in and out of the temporary values. We do this using selection vectors that are bit-vectors encoding the operands of an instruction. Each row of the execution table includes multiple variables that may be selected as an operand. A selection vector will have a bit for each of these variables indicating whether it is picked or not. More details about the multiplexing relation are provided in the full version of the paper [BCG+18].

The Execution Table and the Program Table are Consistent. The consistency relation $\mathcal{R}_{\mathsf{consistent}}$ checks that the time is correctly incremented and that the program counter is in the correct range, i.e. $\mathsf{pc}_{t+1} \in \{0, \ldots, L-1\}$ and is incremented unless a jump-instruction is executed. It also checks that the instruction, the immediate value and the selection vectors stored in the execution table are consistent with the program the line indexed pc. Furthermore, it checks that the entries in the output vector relevant to inst_t are all equal to zero and that the contents of the registers do not change, unless specified by the instruction, e.g. the register storing the result of the computation. Verifying that rows of the execution table match with states of a TinyRAM machine involves checking that entries that are not affected by an instruction remain the same in the next state. For this we use another selector vector with entries equal to 0, positioned in correspondence of entries that are changed during the execution, and 1 for entries that do not change in the execution.

Instructions are Executed Correctly. An instruction checker relation $\mathcal{R}_{\mathsf{ins}}$ checking that the temporary values are in the range $\{0, \ldots, 2^W - 1\}$ and are consistent with the output vector. We divide the entries of the output vector into 4 groups: logical $(\mathsf{AND}, \mathsf{XOR}, \mathsf{OR})$, arithmetic $(\mathsf{SUM}, \mathsf{PROD}, \mathsf{SSUM}, \mathsf{SPROD}, \mathsf{MOD})$, shift (SHIFT), and flag $(\mathsf{FLAG}_1, \mathsf{FLAG}_2, \mathsf{FLAG}_3, \mathsf{FLAG}_4)$. By specifying constraints to all these entries, we can directly verify all the logical, arithmetic, and shifts operations after which the variables are named.

The $\mathcal{R}_{\mathsf{ins}}$ can be decomposed into 3 sub-relations: $\mathcal{R}_{\mathsf{logic}}$, $\mathcal{R}_{\mathsf{arith}}$, and $\mathcal{R}_{\mathsf{shift}}$. In the full paper [BCG+18] we show choices of selection vectors which reduce the verification of any other operation to the ones contained in these 3 categories. We also describe the decomposition of $\mathcal{R}_{\mathsf{logic}}$, $\mathcal{R}_{\mathsf{arith}}$, $\mathcal{R}_{\mathsf{shift}}$ into our elementary building blocks.

4   Efficient Bit Decomposition for Logical Relations

In this section we summarise a new decomposition technique which will enable verification of bitwise AND and XOR operations. This allows us to check all boolean operations more efficiently. Let a, b be the inputs of the bit-wise AND or bit-wise XOR operation, and let c be the output. To verify the correctness of the operation, e.g. $a \wedge b = c$, consider the decompositions of the inputs into their odd and even-position bits, namely $a = 2a_o + a_e$ and $b = 2b_o + b_e$. Observe that taking the sum of the integers storing the even-positions of a and b gives

$$a_e + b_e = (0, a_{W-2}, \ldots, 0, a_0) + (0, b_{W-2}, \ldots, 0, b_0)$$
$$= (a_{W-2} \wedge b_{W-2}, a_{W-2} \oplus b_{W-2}, \ldots, a_0 \wedge b_0, a_0 \oplus b_0)$$

The above contains the bit-wise AND of the even bits of a and b placed in odd position and the bit-wise XOR of the even bits of a and b in even position. Therefore we can consider taking again the decomposition of $a_e + b_e$ into its odd and even-position bits, i.e. $a_e + b_e = 2e_o + e_e$ so that half of the bits of $a \wedge b$ are stored in e_o and half of the bits of $a \oplus b$ are stored in e_e. We can repeat the above procedure starting from the odd-position bits of a and b getting the following

$$a_o + b_o = (0, a_{W-1}, \ldots, 0, a_1) + (0, b_{W-1}, \ldots, 0, b_1)$$
$$= (a_{W-1} \wedge b_{W-1}, a_{W-1} \oplus b_{W-1}, \ldots, a_1 \wedge b_1, a_1 \oplus b_1) = 2o_o + o_e$$

where o_o stores half of the bits of $a \wedge b$ and o_e stores and half of the bits of $a \oplus b$. Putting everything together, given the decompositions $a_o, a_e, b_o, b_e, o_o, o_e, e_o, e_e \in \mathsf{EvenBits}$ such that the following hold

$$a = 2a_o + a_e \quad b = 2b_o + b_e \quad a_o + b_o = 2o_o + o_e \quad a_e + b_e = 2e_o + e_e$$

then the bit-wise AND and XOR of a and b is given by the following

$$a \wedge b = 2o_o + e_o \quad a \oplus b = 2o_e + e_e$$

it is then sufficient to check $c = 2o_o + e_o$ for checking $a \wedge b = c$.

5   Proofs for the Correct Program Execution over the ILC Channel

In this section we give an overview of our proof system for correct TinyRAM program execution over the ILC channel by giving a breakdown of it into simpler proofs, which are detailed in the full paper [BCG+18]. Recall that in the idealised linear commitment channel ILC the prover can submit `commit` commands to commit vectors of field elements of length k. The vectors remain secretly stored in the channel. The verifier can do two things: it can use a `send` command to send a message to the prover; and it can submit `open` queries to the ILC channel for obtaining the openings of linear combinations of vectors committed by the prover. The field $\mathbb{F}$ and the vector length k are specified by the public parameter pp_{ILC}. It will later emerge that the best communication and computation complexity for a TinyRAM program terminating in T is achieved when k is approximately $\sqrt{T}$.

In Sect. 3 we broke the relation of correct program execution down to a number of sub-relations defined over a finite field $\mathbb{F}$. Our strategy for proving that they are all satisfied is to commit the extended witness to the ILC channel and then give an sub-proofs for each sub-relation. To begin we describe how we commit to the execution trace to the ILC model and discuss a relation $\mathcal{R}_{\mathsf{format}}$ for checking that the commitments are well formed. We then take a top down approach in order to describe how to check in the ILC model that the program has been executed correctly. In the first layer we describe a proof for correct TinyRAM execution in the ILC model. This proof decomposes into proofs checking that $\mathcal{R}_{\mathsf{check}}$, $\mathcal{R}_{\mathsf{mem}}$, $\mathcal{R}_{\mathsf{step}}$, and $\mathcal{R}_{\mathsf{format}}$ all hold. In the second layer we then decompose proofs for $\mathcal{R}_{\mathsf{format}}$, $\mathcal{R}_{\mathsf{check}}$, $\mathcal{R}_{\mathsf{mem}}$, and $\mathcal{R}_{\mathsf{step}}$ in terms of generic proofs for checking relations $\mathcal{R}_{\mathsf{const}}$, $\mathcal{R}_{\mathsf{perm}}$, $\mathcal{R}_{\mathsf{range}}$, $\mathcal{R}_{\mathsf{eq}}$, $\mathcal{R}_{\mathsf{blookup}}$ and $\mathcal{R}_{\mathsf{lookup}}$. In the third layer we detail how these proofs decompose into proofs in ILC for elemental relations, such as sums, products, shifts, entry-products and grand-sums of committed vectors. Our fourth and final layer will provide proofs in the ILC for these elemental relations.

5.1   Commitments to the Tables

In our proof system, the prover first commits to the extended witness w. The extended witness includes the field elements in the execution table Exe, the memory table Mem, the program table Prog, the range table EvenBits and the exponent table Pow. The prover arranges these tables in multiple matrices and to their rows.

The prover commits to each column of the execution table (such as the T entries containing the time t, the T entries containing the programt counter pc_t, etc.) by arranging it into an ℓ by k matrix, and making a commitment to each row of the resulting matrix. Entries of Exe relative to the same TinyRAM state will be inserted in the same position across the different matrices. Furthermore, in all these matrices the last entry of each column is duplicated in the first entry of the next column. As an example, let consider the first column of Exe which contains field elements representing the time-steps of the execution. Without loss of generality let $T = (\ell - 1)k + 1$, where T is the number of steps executed by the program and k is the vector length of the ILC. The prover organizes the field elements representing time in a matrix $\mathsf{E}_t \in \mathbb{F}^{\ell \times k}$

$$
\mathsf{E}_t = \begin{pmatrix}
1 & \ell & 2\ell - 1 \dots & \\
2 & \ell + 1 & 2\ell & \dots \\
\vdots & & & \ddots \\
\ell - 1 & 2\ell - 2 & 3\ell - 3 \dots & (\ell - 1)k \\
\ell & 2\ell - 1 & 3\ell - 2 \dots & T
\end{pmatrix}
$$

Similarly, the prover organizes the rest of the Exe table into matrices $\mathsf{E}_{\mathsf{pc}}, \mathsf{E}_{\mathsf{inst}}, \mathsf{E}_A, \ldots$ one for each column. Let E be the matrix obtained by stacking all matrices on top of each other and let $\mathsf{E} = \{e_i\}$, for $e_i \in \mathbb{F}^k$. The prover commits to Exe by sending the command $(\texttt{commit}, \{e_i\}_i)$ to the ILC.

Each column of the program table is also committed to the ILC separately. In case $L \leq k$ we can store each column of Prog in one vector, i.e.

$$
\mathsf{P} = \begin{pmatrix} \mathsf{P}_{\mathsf{pc}} \\ \mathsf{P}_{\mathsf{inst}} \\ \mathsf{P}_A \\ \ldots \end{pmatrix} = \begin{pmatrix} 0 & 1 & \ldots & L-1 \\ \mathsf{inst}_0 & \mathsf{inst}_1 & \ldots & \mathsf{inst}_{L-1} \\ A_0 & A_1 & \ldots & A_{L-1} \\ \ldots & & \ldots \end{pmatrix}
$$

otherwise, multiple rows can be used. The prover sends $(\texttt{commit}, \{\mathsf{P}_{\mathsf{pc}}, \mathsf{P}_{\mathsf{inst}}, \ldots\})$ to the ILC channel to commit to P.

The memory table Mem, the auxiliary lookup table EvenBits and the exponent table Pow can be committed in a similar way using matrices M, R and S

$$
\mathsf{M} = \begin{pmatrix} \mathsf{M}_0 \\ \mathsf{M}_1 \end{pmatrix} \quad \mathsf{R} = \begin{pmatrix} 0\ 1\ 4\ 5 \ldots \sum_{i=0}^{\frac{W}{2}-1} k_i 2^{2i} \\ \ddots \\ \sum_{i=0}^{\frac{W}{2}-1} 2^{2i} \end{pmatrix} \quad \mathsf{S} = \begin{pmatrix} 0\ 1\ 2\ 3 \ldots W-1\ W \\ 1\ 2\ 4\ 8\ \ddots\ 2^{W-1}\ 0 \end{pmatrix}
$$

where

$$
\mathsf{M}_0 = \begin{pmatrix} \mathsf{M}_{\mathsf{addr},0} \\ \mathsf{M}_{\mathsf{v},0} \\ \mathsf{M}_{\mathsf{usd},0} \end{pmatrix} = \begin{pmatrix} 0 & 1 & \ldots & M-1 \\ v_0 & v_1 & \ldots & v_{M-1} \\ 0 & 0 & \ldots & 0 \end{pmatrix} \quad \mathsf{M}_1 = \begin{pmatrix} \mathsf{M}_{\mathsf{addr},1} \\ \mathsf{M}_{\mathsf{v},1} \\ \mathsf{M}_{\mathsf{usd},1} \end{pmatrix} = \begin{pmatrix} 0 & 1 & \ldots & M-1 \\ v_0 & v_1 & \ldots & v_{M-1} \\ 1 & 1 & \ldots & 1 \end{pmatrix}
$$

and $(k_{\frac{W}{2}-1}, \ldots, k_0)$ is the binary expansion of k.

In order to show that the tables are committed to in the above manner the prover will show that the first row each of the matrices describing [Exe] is a shift the last row.

$$
\mathcal{R}_{\mathsf{format}} = \left\{ \begin{array}{l} (pp, u, w) = ((W, K, \mathbb{F}, *), [\mathsf{E}], \perp) \mid \\ \text{for } 1 \leq j \leq k-1 : [\mathsf{E}]_{\ell,j} = [\mathsf{E}]_{1,j+1} \end{array} \right\}
$$

5.2   Proof for Correct TinyRAM Execution in the ILC Model

Given the witness for the correct execution of a TinyRAM program, we now describe how a prover can use the ILC channel to convince a verifier that the trace satisfies the relation $\mathcal{R}^{\mathsf{field}}_{TinyRAM}$ corresponding to the correct program execution. The prover and verifier are given in Fig. 4.

Theorem 1. $(\mathcal{K}_{\mathsf{ILC}}, \mathcal{P}_{TinyRAM}, \mathcal{V}_{TinyRAM})$ *is a proof system for* $\mathcal{R}^{\mathsf{field}}_{TinyRAM}$ *over the ILC channel with perfect completeness, statistical knowledge soundness with straight-line extraction, and perfect special honest-verifier zero-knowledge.*

$\mathcal{P}_{\text{TinyRAM}}(pp_{\text{ILC}}, u, w)$	$\mathcal{V}_{\text{TinyRAM}}(pp_{\text{ILC}}, u)$
– Parse $u = (P, v, T, M)$. – Extend w to w and parse it as $\left\{\begin{array}{l} \mathsf{E}_t, \mathsf{E}_{pc}, \mathsf{E}_{\text{inst}}, \mathsf{E}_A, \mathsf{E}_{\text{reg}_0}, \dots, \mathsf{E}_{\text{reg}_{K}-1}, \dots \\ \mathsf{P}_{pc}, \mathsf{P}_{\text{inst}}, \dots, \mathsf{M}_{0,\text{addr}}, \mathsf{M}_{0,\text{val}}, \dots, \mathsf{R} \end{array}\right\}$ as in Section 5.1. Commit w in this form to the ILC channel. – $\mathcal{P}_{\text{check}}(pp_{\text{ILC}}, u, \mathsf{w})$ – $\mathcal{P}_{\text{mem}}(pp_{\text{ILC}}, u, \mathsf{w})$ – $\mathcal{P}_{\text{step}}(pp_{\text{ILC}}, u, \mathsf{w})$ – $\mathcal{P}_{\text{format}}(pp_{\text{ILC}}, u, \mathsf{w})$	– parse $u = \{ [\mathsf{E}], [\mathsf{P}], [\mathsf{M}], [\mathsf{R}] \}$ – $\mathcal{V}_{\text{check}}(pp_{\text{ILC}}, u)$ – $\mathcal{V}_{\text{mem}}(pp_{\text{ILC}}, u)$ – $\mathcal{V}_{\text{step}}(pp_{\text{ILC}}, u)$ – $\mathcal{V}_{\text{format}}(pp_{\text{ILC}}, [\mathsf{E}])$ – Return 1 if all checks pass Return 0 otherwise

Fig. 4. Proof of correct TinyRAM execution in the ILC model

Proof. Perfect completeness follows from the perfect completeness of the subproofs. Perfect SHVZK follows from the perfect SHVZK of the sub-proofs. A simulated transcript is obtained by combining the outputs of the simulators of all the sub-proofs. Statistical knowledge soundness follows from the knowledge soundness of the sub-proofs. Since all sub-proofs have knowledge soundness with straight-line extraction, so does the main proof. □

The efficiency of our TinyRAM proof in the ILC model is given in Fig. 5. The asymptotic results displayed below are obtained when the parameter k specified by pp_{ILC} is approximately $\sqrt{T}$. The query complexity qc is the number of linear combinations the verifier queries from the ILC channel in the opening query. The verifier communication C_{ILC} is the number of messages sent from the verifier to the prover via the ILC channel and in our proof system it is proportional to the number of rounds. Let μ be the number of rounds in the ILC proof and $t_1, \dots, t_\mu$ be the numbers of vectors that the prover sends to the ILC channel in each round, and let $t = \sum_{i=1}^{\mu} t_i$.

Prover computation	$T_{\mathcal{P}_{\text{ILC}}} = \mathcal{O}(T)$ multiplications in $\mathbb{F}$
Verifier computation	$T_{\mathcal{V}_{\text{ILC}}} = \text{poly}(\lambda)(L + \lvert v \rvert + \sqrt{T})$ multiplications in $\mathbb{F}$
Query complexity	qc $= \mathcal{O}(1)$
Verifier communication	$C_{\text{ILC}} = \mathcal{O}(\log \log T)$ field elements
Round complexity	$\mu = \mathcal{O}(\log \log T)$
Total number of committed vectors	$t = \mathcal{O}\left(\sqrt{T}\right)$ vectors in $\mathbb{F}^k$

Fig. 5. Efficiency of our TinyRAM proof in the ILC model for $(pp, u, w) \in \mathcal{R}_{\text{TinyRAM}}$. Here we are assuming that the number of instructions and words of memory $L, M < \sqrt{T}$, and that the number of registers K is constant.

6 Proofs for the Correct Program Execution over the Standard Channel

In the previous section we gave an efficient SHVZK proof of knowledge over the ILC channel for correct TinyRAM program execution. We now want to give a SHVZK proof of knowledge for correct TinyRAM program execution in the standard communication model where messages are exchanged directly between prover and verifier. To do this, we use the compiler from Bootle et al. [BCG+17] who use an error-correcting code and a collision-resistant hash function to compile a zero-knowledge proof over the ILC channel to a zero-knowledge proof over the standard communication channel. We refer to the full paper [BCG+18] for a transformation to turn SHVZK proofs into ones achieving full-zero knowledge, and for a recursive approach for reducing the verification time of our proofs.

From ILC to the Standard Channel. The compiler from Bootle et al. [BCG+17] uses an hash function to instantiate a non-interactive commitment scheme which realizes the commitment functionality of the ILC in the standard model. The compilation relies on a common reference string that specifies an error-correcting code and the hash function. However, the common reference string is instance-independent and can be reused for several proofs. Moreover, it can be generated from uniformly random bits in $\text{poly}(\lambda)(L+M+\sqrt{T})$ TinyRAM steps and has similar size, so it has little effect on the overall performance of the system. The following theorem follows directly from their work.

Theorem 2 (Bootle et al. [BCG+17]). *Using a linear-distance linear error-correcting code and a statistically-hiding commitment scheme, we can compile a public-coin straight-line extractable proof $(\mathcal{K}_{\mathsf{ILC}}, \mathcal{P}_{\mathsf{ILC}}, \mathcal{V}_{\mathsf{ILC}})$ for a relation $\mathcal{R}$ over the ILC channel to a proof $(\mathcal{K}, \mathcal{P}, \mathcal{V})$ for $\mathcal{R}$ over the standard channel. The compilation is computationally knowledge sound, statistically SHVZK, and preserves perfect completeness of the ILC proof.*

Combining the above with Theorem 1 we get our main theorem.

Theorem 3 (Main Theorem). *Compiling the ILC proof system $(\mathcal{K}_{\mathsf{ILC}}, \mathcal{P}_{TinyRAM}, \mathcal{V}_{TinyRAM})$ of Fig. 4, we get a proof system over the standard channel for the relation $\mathcal{R}^{\text{field}}_{\text{TinyRAM}}$ with perfect completeness, statistical SHVZK, and computational knowledge soundness assuming the existence of collision-resistant hash functions.*

In the following section we detail the efficiency of the proof system obtained by compiling the proof system of Fig. 4.

Efficiency of the compiled TinyRAM Proof System. Computation is feasible only when it is polynomial in the security parameter, i.e., $T = \text{poly}(\lambda)$ and $M = \text{poly}(\lambda)$. Assuming $T, M \geq \lambda$, this means $\log T = \Theta(\log \lambda)$ and $\log M = \Theta(\log \lambda)$. To address all memory we therefore need $W = \Omega(\log \lambda)$. To keep the circuit size of a processor modest, it is reasonable to keep the word size low, so we will assume $W = \Theta(\log \lambda)$. Our proof system also works for larger word size but it is less efficient when the word size is superlogarithmic. Note that we can at the cost of a constant factor overhead store register values in memory and therefore without loss of generality assume $K = \mathcal{O}(1)$.

To get negligible knowledge error we need the field to have superpolynomial size $|\mathbb{F}| = \lambda^{\omega(1)}$. This means we need a superconstant ratio $e = \frac{\log|\mathbb{F}|}{W} = \omega(1)$. On a TinyRAM machine, field elements require e words to store and using school book arithmetic field operations can be implemented in $\alpha = \mathcal{O}(e^2)$ steps[7].

Our proof system is designed for a setting where the running time is large, so we will assume $T \gg L + M$. In the ILC proof for correct program execution the prover commits to $\mathcal{O}(T)$ field elements and uses $\mathcal{O}(T)$ field operations. The verifier on the other hand, only uses $\mathcal{O}(L + |v| + \sqrt{T})$ field operations.

To compile the ILC proof into a proof over the standard channel, Bootle et al. use a linear-time collision-resistant hash function and linear error-correcting codes. The collision-resistant hash function by Applebaum et al. [AHI+17] based on the bSVP assumption for sparse matrices is computable in linear time and can be used to instantiate the statistically hiding commitment scheme used in the compilation. As the hash function operates over bit-strings we need to ensure that the efficiency is preserved once implemented in a TinyRAM program. If we stored each bit in a separate word of size $W = \Theta(\log \lambda)$ we would incur a logarithmic overhead. However, the hash function is computable by a linear-size boolean circuit and we can therefore apply a bit-slicing technique. We view the hash of an n-word string as W parallel hashes of n-bit strings. Each of the bit-strings is processed with the same boolean circuit, which means they can computed in parallel in one go by a TinyRAM program using a linear number of steps.

The error-correcting codes by Druk and Ishai [DI14] have constant rate and can be computed with a linear number of field additions. Applying the error-correcting codes therefore only changes the prover and verifier complexities by constant factors during the compilation. This means the compilation preserves the efficiency of the ILC proof up to constant factors. Taking into account the overhead of doing field operations, we summarize the efficiency of our proof system in Fig. 6.

	Field operations	TinyRAM operations
Prover Computation	$\mathcal{O}(T)$ operations in $\mathbb{F}$	$\mathcal{O}(\alpha T)$ TinyRAM steps
Verifier Computation	$\mathrm{poly}(\lambda)(L + |v| + \sqrt{T})$ ops in $\mathbb{F}$	$\mathrm{poly}(\lambda)(L + |v| + \sqrt{T})$ steps
Communication	$\mathrm{poly}(\lambda)\sqrt{T}$ field elements	$\mathrm{poly}(\lambda)\sqrt{T}$ words
Round Complexity	$\mathcal{O}(\log \log T)$	$\mathcal{O}(\log \log T)$

Fig. 6. Efficiency of our proof system for $\mathcal{R}_{\mathsf{TinyRAM}}$ under the assumption $W = \Theta(\log \lambda)$, $K = \mathcal{O}(1)$, $L + M < T \approx 2^W$, $k \approx \sqrt{T}$, and $\log|\mathbb{F}| = \Theta(\sqrt{\alpha}) \log \lambda$ for an arbitrarily small $\alpha = \omega(1)$.

---

[7] More sophisticated techniques such as FFT may reduce the cost of field multiplications to $\mathcal{O}(e \log e)$ steps, but if e is only slightly superconstant it will take a long time before the asymptotics kick in.

References

[AHI+17] Applebaum, B., Haramaty, N., Ishai, Y., Kushilevitz, E., Vaikuntanathan, V.: Low-complexity cryptographic hash functions. Electron. Colloq. Comput. Complex. (ECCC) **24**, 8 (2017)

[AHIV17] Ames, S., Hazay, C., Ishai, Y., Venkitasubramaniam, M.: Ligero: lightweight sublinear arguments without a trusted setup. In: CCS 2017 (2017)

[AS98] Arora, S., Safra, S.: Probabilistic checking of proofs: a new characterization of NP. J. ACM **45**(1), 70–122 (1998)

[BBC+17] Ben-Sasson, E., et al.: Computational integrity with a public random string from quasi-linear PCPs. In: Coron, J.-S., Nielsen, J.B. (eds.) EUROCRYPT 2017. LNCS, vol. 10212, pp. 551–579. Springer, Cham (2017). https://doi.org/10.1007/978-3-319-56617-7_19

[BCC+16] Bootle, J., Cerulli, A., Chaidos, P., Groth, J., Petit, C.: Efficient zero-knowledge arguments for arithmetic circuits in the discrete log setting. In: Fischlin, M., Coron, J.-S. (eds.) EUROCRYPT 2016. LNCS, vol. 9666, pp. 327–357. Springer, Heidelberg (2016). https://doi.org/10.1007/978-3-662-49896-5_12

[BCCT12] Bitansky, N., Canetti, R., Chiesa, A., Tromer, E.: From extractable collision resistance to succinct non-interactive arguments of knowledge, and back again. In: Innovations in Theoretical Computer Science (ITCS), pp. 326–349 (2012)

[BCCT13] Bitansky, N., Canetti, R., Chiesa, A., Tromer, E.: Recursive composition and bootstrapping for SNARKS and proof-carrying data. In: STOC 2013, pp. 111–120 (2013)

[BCG+13] Ben-Sasson, E., Chiesa, A., Genkin, D., Tromer, E., Virza, M.: SNARKs for C: verifying program executions succinctly and in zero knowledge. In: Canetti, R., Garay, J.A. (eds.) CRYPTO 2013. LNCS, vol. 8043, pp. 90–108. Springer, Heidelberg (2013). https://doi.org/10.1007/978-3-642-40084-1_6

[BCG+17] Bootle, J., Cerulli, A., Ghadafi, E., Groth, J., Hajiabadi, M., Jakobsen, S.K.: Linear-time zero-knowledge proofs for arithmetic circuit satisfiability. In: Takagi, T., Peyrin, T. (eds.) ASIACRYPT 2017. LNCS, vol. 10626, pp. 336–365. Springer, Cham (2017). https://doi.org/10.1007/978-3-319-70700-6_12

[BCG+18] Bootle, J., Cerulli, A., Groth, J., Jakobsen, S.K., Maller, M.: Nearly linear-time zero-knowledge proofs for correct program execution. IACR Cryptology ePrint Archive (2018)

[BCS16] Ben-Sasson, E., Chiesa, A., Spooner, N.: Interactive oracle proofs. In: Hirt, M., Smith, A. (eds.) TCC 2016. LNCS, vol. 9986, pp. 31–60. Springer, Heidelberg (2016). https://doi.org/10.1007/978-3-662-53644-5_2

[BCTV14a] Ben-Sasson, E., Chiesa, A., Tromer, E., Virza, M.: Scalable zero knowledge via cycles of elliptic curves. In: Garay, J.A., Gennaro, R. (eds.) CRYPTO 2014. LNCS, vol. 8617, pp. 276–294. Springer, Heidelberg (2014). https://doi.org/10.1007/978-3-662-44381-1_16

[BCTV14b] Ben-Sasson, E., Chiesa, A., Tromer, E., Virza, M.: Succinct non-interactive zero knowledge for a von neumann architecture. In: USENIX Security Symposium, pp. 781–796 (2014)

[BFM88] Blum, M., Feldman, P., Micali, S.: Non-interactive zero-knowledge and its applications (extended abstract). In: ACM Symposium on Theory of Computing, STOC 1998, pp. 103–112 (1988)

[BFR+13] Braun, B., Feldman, A.J., Ren, Z., Setty, S.T.V., Blumberg, A.J., Walfish, M.: Verifying computations with state. In: ACM SOSP, pp. 341–357 (2013)

[BG12] Bayer, S., Groth, J.: Efficient zero-knowledge argument for correctness of a shuffle. In: Pointcheval, D., Johansson, T. (eds.) EUROCRYPT 2012. LNCS, vol. 7237, pp. 263–280. Springer, Heidelberg (2012). https://doi.org/10.1007/978-3-642-29011-4_17

[BP12] Bitansky, N., Paneth, O.: Point obfuscation and 3-round zero-knowledge. In: Cramer, R. (ed.) TCC 2012. LNCS, vol. 7194, pp. 190–208. Springer, Heidelberg (2012). https://doi.org/10.1007/978-3-642-28914-9_11

[BSBTHR18] Ben-Sasson, E., Ben-Tov, I., Horesh, Y., Riabzev, M.: Scalable, transparent, and post-quantum secure computational integrity (2018). https://eprint.iacr.org/2018/046.pdf

[BSCG+13] Ben-Sasson, E., Chiesa, A., Genkin, D., Tromer, E., Virza, M.: Tinyram architecture specification, v0. 991 (2013)

[CD] Cramer, R., Damgård, I.: Zero-knowledge proofs for finite field arithmetic, or: can zero-knowledge be for free? In: Krawczyk, H. (ed.) CRYPTO 1998. LNCS, vol. 1462, pp. 424–441. Springer, Heidelberg (1998). https://doi.org/10.1007/BFb0055745

[CDG+17] Chase, M., et al.: Post-quantum zero-knowledge and signatures from symmetric-key primitives. In: ACM Conference on Computer and Communications Security, CCS 2017, pp. 1825–1842 (2017)

[CMT12] Cormode, G., Mitzenmacher, M., Thaler, J.: Practical verified computation with streaming interactive proofs. In: Innovations in Theoretical Computer Science, ITCS 2012, pp. 90–112 (2012)

[CTV15] Chiesa, A., Tromer, E., Virza, M.: Cluster computing in zero knowledge. In: Oswald, E., Fischlin, M. (eds.) EUROCRYPT 2015. LNCS, vol. 9057, pp. 371–403. Springer, Heidelberg (2015). https://doi.org/10.1007/978-3-662-46803-6_13

[DI14] Druk, E., Ishai, Y.: Linear-time encodable codes meeting the Gilbert-Varshamov bound and their cryptographic applications. In: Innovations in Theoretical Computer Science, ITCS 2014, pp. 169–182 (2014)

[FNO15] Frederiksen, T.K., Nielsen, J.B., Orlandi, C.: Privacy-free garbled circuits with applications to efficient zero-knowledge. In: Oswald, E., Fischlin, M. (eds.) EUROCRYPT 2015. LNCS, vol. 9057, pp. 191–219. Springer, Heidelberg (2015). https://doi.org/10.1007/978-3-662-46803-6_7

[FS90] Feige, U., Shamir, A.: Witness indistinguishable and witness hiding protocols. In: ACM Symposium on Theory of Computing, STOC 1990, pp. 416–426 (1990)

[Gen09] Gentry, C.: Computing on encrypted data. In: Garay, J.A., Miyaji, A., Otsuka, A. (eds.) CANS 2009. LNCS, vol. 5888, pp. 477–477. Springer, Heidelberg (2009). https://doi.org/10.1007/978-3-642-10433-6_32

[GGI+15] Gentry, C., Groth, J., Ishai, Y., Peikert, C., Sahai, A., Smith, A.D.: Using fully homomorphic hybrid encryption to minimize non-interactive zero-knowledge proofs. J. Cryptol. **28**(4), 820–843 (2015)

[GGPR13] Gennaro, R., Gentry, C., Parno, B., Raykova, M.: Quadratic span programs and succinct NIZKs without PCPs. In: Johansson, T., Nguyen, P.Q. (eds.) EUROCRYPT 2013. LNCS, vol. 7881, pp. 626–645. Springer, Heidelberg (2013). https://doi.org/10.1007/978-3-642-38348-9_37

[GI08] Groth, J., Ishai, Y.: Sub-linear zero-knowledge argument for correctness of a shuffle. In: Smart, N. (ed.) EUROCRYPT 2008. LNCS, vol. 4965, pp. 379–396. Springer, Heidelberg (2008). https://doi.org/10.1007/978-3-540-78967-3_22

[GKR08] Goldwasser, S., Kalai, Y.T., Rothblum, G.N.: Delegating computation: interactive proofs for muggles. In: Proceedings of the 40th Annual ACM Symposium on Theory of Computing, Victoria, British Columbia, Canada, 17–20 May 2008, pp. 113–122 (2008)

[GMO16] Giacomelli, I., Madsen, J., Orlandi, C.: Zkboo: faster zero-knowledge for boolean circuits. In: 25th USENIX Security Symposium, pp. 1069–1083 (2016)

[GMR85] Goldwasser, S., Micali, S., Rackoff, C.: The knowledge complexity of interactive proof-systems (extended abstract). In: ACM Symposium on Theory of Computing, STOC 1985, pp. 291–304 (1985)

[Gro09] Groth, J.: Linear algebra with sub-linear zero-knowledge arguments. In: Halevi, S. (ed.) CRYPTO 2009. LNCS, vol. 5677, pp. 192–208. Springer, Heidelberg (2009). https://doi.org/10.1007/978-3-642-03356-8_12

[Gro10a] Groth, J.: Short pairing-based non-interactive zero-knowledge arguments. In: Abe, M. (ed.) ASIACRYPT 2010. LNCS, vol. 6477, pp. 321–340. Springer, Heidelberg (2010). https://doi.org/10.1007/978-3-642-17373-8_19

[Gro10b] Groth, J.: A verifiable secret shuffle of homomorphic encryptions. J. Cryptol. 23(4), 546–579 (2010)

[Gro16] Groth, J.: On the size of pairing-based non-interactive arguments. In: Fischlin, M., Coron, J.-S. (eds.) EUROCRYPT 2016. LNCS, vol. 9666, pp. 305–326. Springer, Heidelberg (2016). https://doi.org/10.1007/978-3-662-49896-5_11

[IKO07] Ishai, Y., Kushilevitz, E., Ostrovsky, R.: Efficient arguments without short PCPs. In: IEEE Conference on Computational Complexity, CCC 2007, pp. 278–291 (2007)

[IKOS09] Ishai, Y., Kushilevitz, E., Ostrovsky, R., Sahai, A.: Zero-knowledge proofs from secure multiparty computation. SIAM J. Comput. 39(3), 1121–1152 (2009)

[JKO13] Jawurek, M., Kerschbaum, F., Orlandi, C.: Zero-knowledge using garbled circuits: how to prove non-algebraic statements efficiently. In: ACM Conference on Computer and Communications Security, CCS 2013, pp. 955–966 (2013)

[Kil92] Kilian, J.: A note on efficient zero-knowledge proofs and arguments (extended abstract). In: ACM Symposium on Theory of Computing, STOC 1992, pp. 723–732 (1992)

[KR08] Kalai, Y.T., Raz, R.: Interactive PCP. In: Aceto, L., Damgård, I., Goldberg, L.A., Halldórsson, M.M., Ingólfsdóttir, A., Walukiewicz, I. (eds.) ICALP 2008. LNCS, vol. 5126, pp. 536–547. Springer, Heidelberg (2008). https://doi.org/10.1007/978-3-540-70583-3_44

[Nef01] Neff, C.A.: A verifiable secret shuffle and its application to e-voting. In: ACM Conference on Computer and Communications Security, CCS 2001, pp. 116–125 (2001)

[PHGR16] Parno, B., Howell, J., Gentry, C., Raykova, M.: Pinocchio: nearly practical verifiable computation. Commun. ACM **59**(2), 103–112 (2016)

[Sch91] Schnorr, C.-P.: Efficient signature generation by smart cards. J. Cryptol. **4**(3), 161–174 (1991)

[Tha13] Thaler, J.: Time-optimal interactive proofs for circuit evaluation. In: Canetti, R., Garay, J.A. (eds.) CRYPTO 2013. LNCS, vol. 8043, pp. 71–89. Springer, Heidelberg (2013). https://doi.org/10.1007/978-3-642-40084-1_5

[WHG+16] Wahby, R.S., Howald, M., Garg, S., Shelat, A., Walfish, M.: Verifiable ASICs. In: IEEE Symposium on Security and Privacy, SP 2016, pp. 759–778 (2016)

[WJB+17] Wahby, R.S., et al.: Full accounting for verifiable outsourcing. In: ACM Conference on Computer and Communications Security, CCS 2017, pp. 2071–2086 (2017)

[WSR+15] Wahby, R.S., Setty, S.T.V., Ren, Z, Blumberg, A.J., Walfish, M.: Efficient RAM and control flow in verifiable outsourced computation. In: Network and Distributed System Security Symposium, NDSS 2015 (2015)

[WTas+17] Wahby, R.S., Tzialla, I., Shelat, A., Thaler, J., Walfish, M.: Doubly-efficient zkSNARKs without trusted setup. Cryptology ePrint Archive, Report 2017/1132 (2017). https://eprint.iacr.org/

[ZGK+17] Zhang, Y., Genkin, D., Katz, J., Papadopoulos, D., Papamanthou, C.: vSQL: verifying arbitrary SQL queries over dynamic outsourced databases. In: IEEE Symposium on Security and Privacy, SP 2017, pp. 863–880 (2017)

[ZGK+18] Zhang, Y., Genkin, D., Katz, J., Papadopoulos, D., Papamanthou, C.: vRAM: faster verifiable ram with program-independent preprocessing (2018)

Improved (Almost) Tightly-Secure Simulation-Sound QA-NIZK with Applications

Masayuki Abe[1]([✉]), Charanjit S. Jutla[2]([✉]), Miyako Ohkubo[3]([✉]),
and Arnab Roy[4]([✉])

[1] NTT Corporation, Tokyo, Japan
abe.masayuki@lab.ntt.co.jp
[2] IBM T. J. Watson Research Center, Yorktown Heights, USA
csjutla@us.ibm.com
[3] Security Fundamentals Laboratories, CSR, NICT, Tokyo, Japan
m.ohkubo@nict.go.jp
[4] Fujitsu Laboratories of America, Sunnyvale, USA
aroy@us.fujitsu.com

Abstract. We construct the first (almost) tightly-secure unbounded-simulation-sound quasi-adaptive non-interactive zero-knowledge arguments (USS-QA-NIZK) for linear-subspace languages with compact (number of group elements independent of the security parameter) common reference string (CRS) and compact proofs under standard assumptions in bilinear-pairings groups. In particular, under the SXDH assumption, the USS-QA-NIZK proof size is only seventeen group elements with a factor $O(\log Q)$ loss in security reduction to SXDH. The USS-QA-NIZK primitive has many applications, including structure-preserving signatures (SPS), CCA2-secure publicly-verifiable public-key encryption (PKE), which in turn have applications to CCA-anonymous group signatures, blind signatures and unbounded simulation-sound Groth-Sahai NIZK proofs. We show that the almost tight security of our USS-QA-NIZK translates into constructions of all of the above applications with (almost) tight-security to standard assumptions such as SXDH and, more generally, $\mathcal{D}_k$-MDDH. Thus, we get the first publicly-verifiable (almost) tightly-secure multi-user/multi-challenge CCA2-secure PKE with practical efficiency under standard bilinear assumptions. Our (almost) tight SPS construction is also improved in the signature size over previously known constructions.

Keywords: QA-NIZK · Simulation-soundness · Tight security
Public-key encryption · CCA · Structure-preserving signatures

1 Introduction

Over the last decade, pairing-based cryptography has facilitated many new cryptographic protocols and applications that are provably-secure under static

© International Association for Cryptologic Research 2018
T. Peyrin and S. Galbraith (Eds.): ASIACRYPT 2018, LNCS 11272, pp. 627–656, 2018.
https://doi.org/10.1007/978-3-030-03326-2_21

assumptions. Some of these static assumptions (SXDH, DLIN, MDDH) are now considered standard, as they generalize decisional-Diffie-Hellman (DDH) assumption to pairings-based groups. Some of the ground-breaking ideas include the Groth-Sahai (GS) non-interactive zero-knowledge (NIZK) proofs [GS12], fully-secure identity-based-encryption (IBE) [Wat09], structure-preserving signatures (SPS) [AFG+10], quasi-adaptive NIZK arguments (QA-NIZK) [JR13], and tightly-secure IBE [CW13]. In particular, structure-preserving signatures use Groth-Sahai NIZK proof structure to enable a wide-range of privacy-preserving applications, such as, group signatures [AHO10], blind signatures [AO09a, AFG+10], group encryption [CLY09], among others. Recent works [JR17, JOR18] have employed QA-NIZK to get more efficient SPS, and tightly-secure unbounded-simulation-sound QA-NIZK (USS-QA-NIZK [LPJY14,KW15]) to get tightly-secure CCA2-secure public-key encryption (PKE) in the multi-user and multi-challenge setting [LPJY15].

In this work we focus on the basic primitive of USS-QA-NIZK for linear-subspaces of vector spaces of bilinear groups, which has important implications as a structure-preserving version of it directly implies structure-preserving signatures. Further, it is already known to imply CCA2-secure PKE [LPJY15], which in turn leads to several new applications such as CCA-anonymous group signatures [AHO10], and UC-commitments [FLM11]. Further, an (almost) tightly-secure USS-QA-NIZK implies (almost) tightly-secure version of all the above applications. While an (almost) tightly-secure USS-QA-NIZK was given in [LPJY15] it required a large common reference string (CRS), which was of the order of the security parameter λ. In this work, we give the first (almost) tightly-secure USS-QA-NIZK for linear-subspaces with compact (number of group elements independent of λ) CRS and compact proofs. Moreover, the earlier construction only worked under the DLIN assumption in symmetric groups, and required non-standard assumptions in the asymmetric pairing-group setting, whereas we give a construction which is tightly-secure under the SXDH assumption in asymmetric groups. Asymmetric groups usually allow leaner constructions, which we validate below. At the same time, we make the CRS compact. Our construction of USS-QA-NIZK is also structure-preserving.

Related Techniques. In [KW15], Kiltz and Wee observed that QA-NIZK can be seen as a generalization of hash proof systems [CS98] to public-verifiability by publishing a "partial commitment" to the secret hash-key **k** in the second group $\mathbb{G}_2$ of a pairings-based groups $(\mathbb{G}_1, \mathbb{G}_2, \mathbb{G}_T, e)$. Simulation of proofs of statements then just requires hash computation using the secret hash-key **k**. Computational-soundness is slightly more tricky to prove than in the hash-proof setting, but essentially an adversary cannot generate hash proofs of false statements given only the "partial commitment" to **k** and the projection-key (of the hash-proof system). In the simulation-soundness setting, the simulation of fake proofs would give additional information to the adversary about secret-hash key **k**, and hence to obtain a USS-QA-NIZK, [KW15] encrypt the hash-proofs and employ a dual-system [Wat09] technique to achieve soundness. This methodology should be contrasted with the "OR" proof methodology of [LPJY15] (for USS-QA-NIZK) and [CCS09] (for unbounded simulation-sound GS-NIZK). While the USS-QA-NIZK of [KW15] leads to compact proofs (of size only $(2k + 2)$ under k-linear assumption), the security reduction to the underlying hardness assumption is not tight. The reason behind this being that the dual-system approach is itself not tight as at its heart it employs one-time simulation-soundness along with two-universal hash-proof systems [JR15], similar to Cramer-Shoup CCA2-encryption [CS98]. A nested-version of dual-system approach does lead to (almost) tight IBE [CW13], but then requires non-compact (master) public keys.

However, the concept of identity-space partitioning introduced in [CW13] is also applicable to signature schemes, and this technique repeatedly splits the message space into two based on the message or a tag. This idea was further enhanced in [Hof17] to adaptive partitioning in which the partitioning is decided dynamically based on an encrypted partitioning-bit. [AHN+17] refined this technique by introducing new ideas using "OR" GS-NIZK systems and made the scheme structure-preserving. Since signature schemes, especially the ones considered in the above works, usually encrypt a secret and prove in zero-knowledge that such a secret is encrypted in the signature, the question arises if this refined adaptive-partitioning methodology can be employed to the USS-QA-NIZK of [KW15] discussed above that encrypted the hash-proofs. One main difference between NIZK proofs embedded in signature schemes is that they need only be "designated-prover" NIZK proofs. In other words, such NIZK proofs while still providing public verifiability, need only give the proving capability to a designated party, namely the CRS (or public-key) generator itself. Hence, such designated-prover NIZK proofs are much easier to devise and it is not immediately clear if such restricted NIZK proofs can be extended to usual NIZK proofs (especially in the tight USS-NIZK setting).

Finally, we argue that the recent constructions of tight CCA2-secure PKE [GHK17,Hof17] (along with [CCS09]) also do not easily imply tight USS-NIZK. [CCS09] requires proving an OR-statement where one of the disjuncts is that a CCA2-PKE ciphertext is well-formed. For [GHK17], this statement is not Groth-Sahai friendly as its own "qualified"-OR proof in the ciphertexts employs a mapping that maps group elements to $\mathbb{Z}_q$ elements. This should be contrasted with Cramer-Shoup CCA2-PKE, which also has such a tag, but that is publicly computable from other elements in the ciphertext. This is not the case for [GHK17] as the mapping is from private elements. As for [Hof17], it uses disjunctive hash-proofs from [ABP15] which require the hash proof to be in the target group; GS-proofs of such statements are only possible in the Witness-Indistinguishable setting.

Our Contributions. We show that a different "OR" system than considered in [AHN+17] (or later works such as [JOR18]) does allow one to give (almost) tight (structure-preserving) USS-QA-NIZK for linear-subspaces with compact proof sizes and compact CRS-es. This "OR" system can be proved in the generic framework of [Råf15], allowing us to obtain USS-QA-NIZKs under the SXDH assumption in asymmetric pairings groups, which was not previously known even for non-compact CRS. We also mention that while our structure-preserving USS-QA-NIZK construction loses a factor of $O(\lambda)$ in the security reduction, we give another variant employing tags (and hence not structure-preserving) that only has a $O(\log Q)$ factor loss in security reduction, where Q is the number of adversarial requests for simulated proofs. In yet another variant, we consider the "designated prover" setting as described above, and give a leaner structure-preserving construction with a tighter reduction as well, i.e. with only a $O(\log Q)$ factor loss.

As a first application, we show that a labeled version of our tight USS-QA-NIZK construction gives us a tight CCA2-secure *publicly-verifiable* labelled PKE in the multi-user multi-challenge setting[1]. In Table 1, we compare our scheme with the state of the art schemes in [GHKW16, Hof17, GHK17] with the smallest possible assumption for each. While being practical by itself, our scheme is not the best one in terms of efficiency. What separates our scheme from other tightly secure schemes is the public verifiability, which allows anyone, without knowing the secret key, to check if a ciphertext decrypts to some plaintext. Feasibility results for publicly-verifiable tight CCA-PKE can be found in [HJ16] and [ADKNO13], but their ciphertext overhead is hundreds or even more than a thousand of group elements. Ours is the first practical publicly-verifiable scheme having only 19 elements of ciphertext overhead. Our scheme is also secure under the SXDH assumption with only a $O(\log Q)$ loss in security reduction, where Q is the total number of (multi-challenge, multi-user) encryption-oracle requests by the adversary. CCA2-secure PKE and its variants that encrypt long messages have further applications, such as UC commitments, and we refer the reader to [LPJY15] for a good introduction.

Table 1. Comparison of tightly-secure public-key encryption schemes when the underlying assumptions are set to minimum ones, SXDH or DDH. Sizes count the number of group elements and (n_1, n_2) denotes n_1 and n_2 elements in $\mathbb{G}_1$ and $\mathbb{G}_2$, respectively. Column 'Pairings?' shows necessity of pairing groups. SAE stands for symmetric authenticated encryption.

	$|pk|$	$|ct| - |m|$	Verifiability	Pairings?	Sec. Loss	Assumption
[GHKW16]	$O(\lambda)$	3	private	no	$O(\lambda)$	DDH
[Hof17]	28	6	private	yes	$O(\lambda)$	DLIN
[GHK17]	6	3	private	no	$O(\lambda)$	DDH+SAE
Ours Sect. 5.1	$(13, 8)$	$(13, 6)$	public	yes	$O(\log Q)$	SXDH

As a second application, we show that our designated-prover variant of structure-preserving USS-QA-NIZK from Sect. 5.2 yields an SPS scheme with

---

[1] This requires adapting our USS-QA-NIZK to the multi-language USS-QA-NIZK described in [LPJY15], but our scheme readily adapts to that.

the shortest signature size in the literature. Recall that unbounded simulation-soundness guarantees that it is hard to create a valid proof for any no-instances taken out of the legitimate subspace even after seeing simulated proofs for (also no-) instances of one's choice. If we look at the simulation trapdoor as a secret-key and the simulated proofs as signatures, the USS-QA-NIZK can be considered as a signature scheme for message space consisting of no-instances, and the notion of unbounded simulation-soundness is exactly the same as existential unforge-ability against adaptive chosen-message attacks. As formally proven in [AAO18], for bringing this idea to reality, we need an efficient mapping from desired mes-sage space to these no-instances. Since our USS-QA-NIZK allows simulation of fake proofs and we present a simple and efficient construction of injective mapping from a sequence of group elements to no-instances, this construction suffers no overhead for unilateral messages. This, along with the more efficient (designated-prover) USS-QA-NIZK gives us the shortest SPS known under the SXDH assumption, and with only a $O(\log Q)$ factor loss in security-reduction (see Table 2).

Table 2. Comparison with existing SPS schemes for unilateral messages when assumptions are set to minimal ones. Columns labeled as $|M|$, $|\sigma|$, and $|pk|$ show number of group elements in a message, a signature and a public key. For [HJ16], the parameter d limits number of signing queries to 2^d.

	$|M|$	$|\sigma|$	$|pk|$	Sec. Loss	Assumption
[HJ16]	1	$10d + 6$	13	8	DLIN
[ACD+12]	$(n_1, 0)$	$(7, 4)$	$(5, n_1 + 12)$	$O(Q)$	SXDH, XDLIN
[LPY15]	$(n_1, 0)$	$(10, 1)$	$(16, 2n_1 + 5)$	$O(Q)$	SXDH, XDLIN
[KPW15]	$(n_1, 0)$	$(6, 1)$	$(0, n_1 + 6)$	$O(Q^2)$	SXDH
[JR17]	$(n_1, 0)$	$(5, 1)$	$(0, n_1 + 6)$	$O(Q \log Q)$	SXDH
[AHN+17]	$(n_1, 0)$	$(13, 12)$	$(18, n_1 + 11)$	$O(\lambda)$	SXDH
[JOR18]	$(n_1, 0)$	$(11, 6)$	$(7, n_1 + 16)$	$O(\lambda)$	SXDH
[GHKP18]	$(n_1, 0)$	$(8, 6)$	$(2, n_1 + 9)$	$O(\log Q)$	SXDH
Ours (Sect. 5.2)	$(n_1, 0)$	$(6, 6)$	$(10, n_1 + 5)$	$O(\log Q)$	SXDH

Finally, we mention some plug-in applications of our tightly-secure PKE and SPS without details. Combining these two applications, we have the first (almost) tightly-secure CCA-anonymous dynamic group signature scheme with compact signature sizes and compact public keys under standard assumptions. Also we can instantiate a generic structure-preserving blind signature scheme of [Fis06] using our SPS to get an (almost) tight round-optimal scheme under $\mathcal{D}_k$-MDDH with compact signature size, whereas previous schemes in standard model were based on non-static assumptions [Fuc09, AO09b]. Finally, our (almost) tight CCA2-secure PKE scheme along with the generic construction of [CCS09], leads to a first (almost) tightly-secure unbounded simulation-sound Groth-Sahai NIZK proof system with compact CRS and proofs.

2 Preliminaries

We will consider cyclic groups $\mathbb{G}_1, \mathbb{G}_2$ and $\mathbb{G}_T$ of prime order q, with an efficient bilinear map $\mathbf{e} : \mathbb{G}_1 \times \mathbb{G}_2 \to \mathbb{G}_T$. Group elements $\mathbf{g}_1$ and $\mathbf{g}_2$ will typically denote generators of the group $\mathbb{G}_1$ and $\mathbb{G}_2$ respectively. Following [EHK+13], we will use the notations $[a]_1, [a]_2$ and $[a]_T$ to denote $a\mathbf{g}_1, a\mathbf{g}_2$, and $a \cdot \mathbf{e}(\mathbf{g}_1, \mathbf{g}_2)$ respectively and use additive notations for group operations. When talking about a general group $\mathbb{G}$ with generator $\mathbf{g}$, we will just use the notation $[a]$ to denote $a\mathbf{g}$. The notation generalizes to vectors and matrices in a natural component-wise way.

For two vector or matrices A and B, we will denote the product $A^\top B$ as $A \cdot B$. The pairing product $\mathbf{e}([A]_1, [B]_2)$ evaluates to the matrix product $[AB]_T$ in the target group with pairing as multiplication and target group operation as addition.

2.1 Matrix-DDH Assumptions and Boosting

We recall the *Matrix Decisional Diffie-Hellman* or MDDH assumptions from [EHK+13]. A matrix distribution $\mathcal{D}_{l,k}$, where $l > k$, is defined to be an efficiently samplable distribution on $\mathbb{Z}_q^{l \times k}$ which is full-ranked with overwhelming probability. The $\mathcal{D}_{l,k}$-*MDDH assumption* in group $\mathbb{G}$ states that with samples $\mathbf{A} \leftarrow \mathcal{D}_{l,k}, \mathbf{s} \leftarrow \mathbb{Z}_q^k$ and $\mathbf{s}' \leftarrow \mathbb{Z}_q^l$, the tuple $([\mathbf{A}], [\mathbf{As}])$ is computationally indistinguishable from $([\mathbf{A}], [\mathbf{s}'])$. A matrix distribution $\mathcal{D}_{k+1,k}$ is simply denoted by $\mathcal{D}_k$.

It was shown in [JR16] that a $\mathcal{D}_k$-MDDH assumption can be *boosted* to generate additional (computationally) independently random elements.

For an $l \times k$ matrix $\mathbf{A}$, we denote $\bar{\mathbf{A}}$ to be the top $k \times k$ square sub-matrix of $\mathbf{A}$ and $\underline{\mathbf{A}}$ to be the bottom $(l - k) \times k$ sub-matrix of $\mathbf{A}$.

Theorem 1 (Boosting [JR16]). *Let $\mathcal{D}_k$ be a matrix distribution on $\mathbb{Z}_q^{(k+1) \times k}$. Define another matrix distribution $\mathcal{D}_{l,k}$ on $\mathbb{Z}_q^{l \times k}$ as follows: First sample matrices $\mathbf{A} \leftarrow \mathcal{D}_k$ and $\mathbf{R} \leftarrow \mathbb{Z}_q^{(l-k) \times k}$ and then output $\begin{pmatrix} \bar{\mathbf{A}} \\ \mathbf{R} \end{pmatrix}$. Then the $\mathcal{D}_k$-MDDH assumption implies the $\mathcal{D}_{l,k}$-MDDH assumption with an $(l - k)$ security reduction.*

They called *boosting* to be the process of stretching $\mathcal{D}_k$ to $\mathcal{D}_{l,k}$ as above. In our construction we will need to boost $\mathcal{D}_k$ to $\mathcal{D}_{2k,k}$.

2.2 Quasi-Adaptive NIZK Proofs

A witness relation is a binary relation on pairs of inputs, the first called a word and the second called a witness. Each witness relation R defines a corresponding language L which is the set of all words x for which there exists a witness w, such that $R(x, w)$ holds.

We will consider Quasi-Adaptive NIZK proofs [JR13] for a probability distribution $\mathcal{D}$ on a collection of (witness-) relations $\mathcal{R} = \{R_\rho\}$ (with corresponding languages L_ρ). Recall that in a quasi-adaptive NIZK, the CRS can be set after the language parameter has been chosen according to $\mathcal{D}$. Please refer to [JR13] for detailed definitions.

For our USS-QA-NIZK construction we will also need a property called true-simulation-soundness. We recall the definitions of these concepts below.

Definition 1 (QA-NIZK [JR13]). *We call a tuple of efficient algorithms* (pargen, crsgen, prover, ver) *a quasi-adaptive non-interactive zero-knowledge (QA-NIZK) proof system for witness-relations $\mathcal{R}_\eta = \{R_\rho\}$ with parameters sampled from a distribution $\mathcal{D}$ over associated parameter language* Lpar, *if there exist simulators* crssim *and* sim *such that for all non-uniform PPT adversaries* $\mathcal{A}_1, \mathcal{A}_2, \mathcal{A}_3$, *we have (in all of the following probabilistic experiments, the experiment starts by setting η as $\eta \leftarrow$ pargen(1^λ), and choosing ρ as $\rho \leftarrow \mathcal{D}_\eta$):*

Quasi-Adaptive Completeness:

$$\Pr \left[\begin{array}{l} \text{CRS} \leftarrow \text{crsgen}(\eta, \rho) \\ (x, w) \leftarrow \mathcal{A}_1(\text{CRS}, \rho) \\ \pi \leftarrow \text{prover}(\text{CRS}, x, w) \end{array} : \begin{array}{l} \text{ver}(\text{CRS}, x, \pi) = 1 \text{ if} \\ R_\rho(x, w) \end{array} \right] = 1$$

Quasi-Adaptive Soundness:

$$\Pr \left[\begin{array}{l} \text{CRS} \leftarrow \text{crsgen}(\eta, \rho) \\ (x, \pi) \leftarrow \mathcal{A}_2(\text{CRS}, \rho) \end{array} : \begin{array}{l} x \notin L_\rho \text{ and} \\ \text{ver}(\text{CRS}, x, \pi) = 1] \end{array} \right] \approx 0$$

Quasi-Adaptive Zero-Knowledge:

$$\Pr \left[\text{CRS} \leftarrow \text{crsgen}(\eta, \rho) : \mathcal{A}_3^{\text{prover}(\text{CRS}, \cdot, \cdot)}(\text{CRS}, \rho) = 1 \right]$$
$$\approx$$
$$\Pr \left[(\text{CRS}, \text{trap}) \leftarrow \text{crssim}(\eta, \rho) : \mathcal{A}_3^{\text{sim}^*(\text{CRS}, \text{trap}, \cdot, \cdot)}(\text{CRS}, \rho) = 1 \right],$$

where $\text{sim}^*(\text{CRS}, \text{trap}, x, w) = \text{sim}(\text{CRS}, \text{trap}, x)$ *for* $(x, w) \in R_\rho$ *and both oracles (i.e.* prover *and* sim^**) output failure if* $(x, w) \notin R_\rho$.

Definition 2 (True-Simulation-Sound [Har11]). *A QA-NIZK is called* **true** **-simulation-sound** *if soundness holds even when an adaptive adversary has access to simulated proofs on language members. More precisely, for all PPT $\mathcal{A}$,*

$$\Pr \left[\begin{array}{l} (\text{CRS}, \text{trap}) \leftarrow \text{crssim}(\eta, \rho) \\ (x, \pi) \leftarrow \mathcal{A}^{\text{sim}(\text{CRS}, \text{trap}, \cdot, \cdot)}(\text{CRS}, \rho) \end{array} : \begin{array}{l} x \notin L_\rho \text{ and} \\ \text{ver}(\text{CRS}, x, \pi) = 1 \end{array} \right] \approx 0,$$

where the experiment aborts if the oracle is called with some $x \notin L_\rho$.

The construction of [JR14] yielded k element proofs of any linear subspace language membership and [KW15] generalized it to any $\mathcal{D}_k$-MDDH assumption. Both constructions are true-simulation-sound.

We now define the unbounded simulation-soundness (USS) property, which we seek to achieve in this paper. The prover and verifier can additionally accept a label which is bound to the proof.

Definition 3 (Unbounded Simulation-Soundness). *A QA-NIZK is called (labeled)* **unbounded simulation sound** *if soundness holds even when an adaptive adversary has access to simulated proofs on arbitrary words of its choice. More precisely, for all PPT $\mathcal{A}$,*

$$\Pr\left[\begin{array}{c}(\text{CRS}, \text{trap}) \leftarrow \text{crssim}(\eta, \rho) \\ (x, \text{lbl}, \pi) \leftarrow \mathcal{A}^{\text{sim}(\text{CRS}, \text{trap}, \cdot, \cdot)}(\text{CRS}, \rho)\end{array} : \begin{array}{c} x \notin L_\rho \wedge (x, \text{lbl}) \notin \mathcal{Q} \\ \text{ver}(\text{CRS}, x, \pi) = 1 \end{array}\right] \approx 0,$$

where the set $\mathcal{Q}$ records (word, label) tuples queried to the simulator.

A stronger notion called *Enhanced Unbounded Simulation-Soundness in the multi-CRS setting* was formalized by [LPJY15], where soundness holds even if the discrete logs of the language are given to the adversary and the adversary has access to multiple CRS-es and corresponding oracles. We note that our construction satisfies this property as well.

Our main construction is also *Structure-Preserving* as the CRS and proof elements are all in the base groups of the bilinear map and verification consists only of pairing product equations.

2.3 Public-Key Encryption Schemes

Let GEN be an algorithm that, on input security parameter λ, outputs par that includes parameters of pairing groups.

Definition 4 (Public-key encryption). *A Public-Key Encryption (PKE) scheme consists of probabilistic polynomial-time algorithms* PKE := (KeyGen, Enc, Dec):

- *Key generation algorithm* KeyGen(par) *takes* par $\leftarrow$ GEN(1^λ) *as input and generates a pair of public and secret keys* (pk, sk). *Message space $\mathcal{M}$ is determined by* pk.
- *Encryption algorithm* Enc(pk, M) *returns a ciphertext* ct.
- *Decryption algorithm* Dec(sk, ct) *is deterministic and returns a message* M.

For correctness, it must hold that, for all par $\leftarrow$ GEN(1^λ), (pk, sk) $\leftarrow$ KeyGen(par), *messages* M $\in \mathcal{M}$, *and* ct $\leftarrow$ Enc(pk, M), Dec(sk, ct) = M.

Definition 5 (IND-mCPA Security [BBM00]). *A PKE scheme* PKE *is indistinguishable against multi-instance chosen-plaintext attack (*IND-mCPA-secure*)* *if for any $q_e \geq 0$ and for all PPT adversaries $\mathcal{A}$ with access to oracle $\mathcal{O}_e$ at most q_e times the following advantage function $\mathsf{Adv}_{\mathsf{PKE}}^{\mathsf{mcpa}}(\mathcal{A})$ is negligible,*

$$\mathsf{Adv}_{\mathsf{PKE}}^{\mathsf{mcpa}}(\mathcal{A}) := \left| \Pr\left[b' = b \left| \begin{array}{l} \mathsf{par} \leftarrow \mathsf{GEN}(1^\lambda); (\mathsf{pk}, \mathsf{sk}) \leftarrow \mathsf{KeyGen}(\mathsf{par}); \\ b \leftarrow \{0,1\}; b' \leftarrow \mathcal{A}^{\mathcal{O}_e(\cdot,\cdot)}(\mathsf{pk}) \end{array} \right. \right] - \frac{1}{2} \right|,$$

where $\mathcal{O}_e(\mathsf{M}_0, \mathsf{M}_1)$ runs $\mathsf{ct}^* \leftarrow \mathsf{Enc}(\mathsf{pk}, \mathsf{M}_b)$, and returns ct^* to $\mathcal{A}$.

There exist public-key encryption schemes that are structure-preserving, IND-mCPA secure, and have tight reductions based on compact assumptions. Examples are ElGamal encryption [ElG84] and Linear encryption [BBS04] based on the DDH assumption and the Decision Linear assumption, respectively. In particular, we will use the scheme of [EHK+13], which is based on the $\mathcal{D}_k$-MDDH assumption. We will use the linear homomorphic property of this PKE in the construction - adding the ciphertexts implicitly adds the underlying plaintexts.

We now recall the definition of IND-CCA2 secure public key encryption scheme in the multi-challenge multi-user setting [BBM00], where the par are shared by multiple users while generating their own keys using KeyGen.

Definition 6 (Multi-CCA [BBM00] (or see [LPJY15])).
A public-key encryption scheme is (μ, q_e)-IND-CCA secure, for integers $\mu, q_e \in poly(\lambda)$, if no PPT adversary has non-negligible advantage in the following game:

1. *The challenger first generates* $\mathsf{par} \leftarrow \mathsf{GEN}(1^\lambda)$ *and runs* $(\mathsf{sk}^{(i)}, \mathsf{pk}^{(i)}) \leftarrow \mathsf{KeyGen}(\mathsf{par})$ *for $i = 1$ to μ. It gives $\{\mathsf{pk}^{(i)}\}_{i=1}^\mu$ to the adversary $\mathcal{A}$ and retains $\{\mathsf{sk}^{(i)}\}_{i=1}^\mu$. In addition, the challenger initializes a set $\mathcal{D} \leftarrow \phi$ and a counter $j_q \leftarrow 0$. Finally, it chooses a random bit $d \leftarrow \{0,1\}$.*

2. *The adversary $\mathcal{A}$ adaptively makes queries to the following oracles on multiple occasions:*
   - *Encryption query: $\mathcal{A}$ chooses an index $i \in [1..\mu]$ and a pair (M_0, M_1) of equal length messages. If $j_q = q_e$, the oracle returns $\perp$. Otherwise, it computes $C \leftarrow \mathsf{Enc}(\mathsf{pk}^{(i)}, M_d)$ and returns C. In addition, it sets $\mathcal{D} := \mathcal{D} \cup \{(i, C)\}$ and $j_q := j_q + 1$.*
   - *Decryption query: $\mathcal{A}$ can also invoke the decryption oracle on arbitrary ciphertexts C and indices $i \in [1..\mu]$. If $(i, C) \in \mathcal{D}$, the oracle returns $\perp$. Otherwise, the oracle returns $M \leftarrow \mathsf{Dec}(\mathsf{sk}^{(i)}, C)$, which may be $\perp$ if C is an invalid ciphertext.*

3. *The adversary $\mathcal{A}$ outputs a bit d' and is deemed successful if $d' = d$. As usual, $\mathcal{A}$'s advantage is measured as the distance $\mathsf{Adv}^{\mathsf{mcca}}(\mathcal{A}) = |2\Pr[d' = d] - 1|$.*

2.4 Structure-Preserving Signatures

Let GEN be a common parameter generation algorithm that outputs par for given security parameter λ.

Definition 7 (Structure-Preserving Signature). *A structure-preserving signature scheme SPS is a triple of probabilistic polynomial time (PPT) algorithms* SPS = (KeyGen, Sign, Verify)*:*

- *Key generation algorithm* KeyGen(par) *takes common parameter* par *and returns a public/secret key,* (pk, sk)*, where* $pk \in \mathbb{G}^{n_{pk}}$ *for some* $n_{pk} \in poly(\lambda)$*. It is assumed that* pk *implicitly defines a message space* $\mathcal{M} := \mathbb{G}^n$ *for some* $n \in poly(\lambda)$*.*
- *Signing algorithm* Sign(sk, M) *takes secret key* sk *and a message* $M \in \mathcal{M}$ *as input and returns a signature* $\sigma \in \mathbb{G}^{n_\sigma}$ *for* $n_\sigma \in poly(\lambda)$*.*
- *Verification algorithm* Verify(pk, M, σ) *takes public key* pk*, message* $M \in \mathcal{M}$*, and signature* σ *and outputs 1 or 0. It only evaluates group membership operations and pairing product equations.*

Perfect correctness holds if for all $(pk, sk) \leftarrow$ KeyGen(par) *and all messages* $M \in \mathcal{M}$ *and all* $\sigma \leftarrow$ Sign(sk, M) *we have* Verify(pk, M, σ) = 1.

Definition 8 (Existential Unforgeability against Chosen Message Attack). *To an adversary A and scheme SPS we associate the advantage function:*

$$\mathsf{Adv}^{cma}_{\mathsf{SPS}}(A) := \Pr \left[\begin{array}{l} \mathsf{par} \leftarrow \mathsf{GEN}(1^\lambda) \\ (pk, sk) \leftarrow \mathsf{KeyGen}(\mathsf{par}) \\ (M^*, \sigma^*) \leftarrow A^{SignO(\cdot)}(pk) \end{array} : \begin{array}{l} M^* \notin Q_{msg} \text{ and} \\ \mathsf{Verify}(pk, M^*, \sigma^*) = 1 \end{array} \right]$$

where $SignO(M)$ *runs* $\sigma \leftarrow$ Sign(sk, M)*, adds M to* Q_{msg} *(initialized with* $\emptyset$*) and returns* σ *to A. An SPS is said to be (unbounded) EUF-CMA-secure if for all PPT adversaries A,* $\mathsf{Adv}^{cma}_{\mathsf{SPS}}(A)$ *is negligible.*

3   The New (Almost) Tightly-Secure USS-QA-NIZK

The new USS-QA-NIZK scheme is formally described in Fig. 1, with the CRS and proof simulators described in Fig. 2. While a brief overview of the new scheme was given in the introduction, we now describe it in more detail.

We essentially combine techniques from the USS-QA-NIZK scheme of Kiltz and Wee [KW15] and the tightly secure SPS scheme of Jutla, Ohkubo and Roy [JOR18]. Following [KW15], we encrypt a basic QA-NIZK proof of the given word $\mathbf{y} = [\mathbf{Mx}]_1$ using an augmented ElGamal encryption scheme:

$$\boldsymbol{\rho} := [\bar{\mathbf{B}}\mathbf{r}]_1^\top, \quad \hat{\boldsymbol{\rho}} := [\underline{\mathbf{B}}\mathbf{r}]_1^\top, \quad \gamma := \mathbf{x}^\top [\mathbf{p}_1]_1 + \mathbf{r}^\top [\mathbf{p}_2]_1$$

Notice that unlike [KW15], we did not use an integer tag in the encryption. This helps us keep the construction structure preserving. We also include a QA-NIZK Π_2 certifying that $(\boldsymbol{\rho}, \hat{\boldsymbol{\rho}}, \gamma)$ is well-formed. Now we extend this tuple with elements which enable adaptive partitioning as in [JOR18]. This includes a double ElGamal encryption of a bit z, along with a QA-NIZK proof of equality of plaintexts. The final piece is an OR-NIZK proof that proves either $(\boldsymbol{\rho}, \hat{\boldsymbol{\rho}})$ is consistent, or that z is same as a bit x which is given encrypted in the public key. Intuitively, in several games in the proof, the OR proof enables us to randomize the ciphertexts in the partitions where the disjunct $z = x$ holds, while restricting the adversary to attempt a win only in the other partitions. Instantiations of OR-NIZKs are given in Sect. 4.

The (almost) tight security of this scheme is proved in the next section. We prove that this construction has an $O(\lambda)$ reduction to $\mathcal{D}_k$-MDDH. In Sect. 3.2, we provide another construction which builds upon this one and enjoys a better $O(\log Q)$ reduction, where Q is the number of simulated proofs given out. Finally, in Sect. 3.3, we describe some optimizations which reduce the size of the proofs even further.

3.1 Security of the USS-QA-NIZK Scheme

In this section we state and prove the security of the USS-QA-NIZK scheme Π described in Fig. 1, with simulators described in Fig. 2.

Theorem 2. *For any efficient adversary $\mathcal{A}$, which makes at most Q simulator queries before attempting a forged proof, its probability of success ($\mathrm{ADV}_{\Pi}^{\mathsf{uss}}(Q)$) in the USS game against the scheme Π is at most*

$$\mathrm{ADV}_{\Pi_2}^{\mathsf{tss}} + 12L \cdot \mathrm{ADV}_{\Pi_1}^{\mathsf{tss}} + 8L \cdot \mathrm{ADV}_{\mathcal{D}_{2k,k}\text{-MDDH}} + (12L + 1)\mathrm{ADV}_{\Pi_0}^{\mathsf{zk}}$$

$$+4L \cdot \mathrm{ADV}_{\mathsf{PKE}}^{\mathsf{mcpa}} + \frac{6L + (Q+1)^2 + 1}{q} + \frac{Q}{2^L}$$

Here L is the least integer greater than the bit size of q and hence is $O(\lambda)$.

Remark 1. $\mathrm{ADV}_{\Pi_i}^{\mathsf{tss}}$ of a QA-NIZK Π_i reduces to $\mathcal{D}_k$-MDDH by a factor of $(n-t)$ where the (affine) linear subspace language is of dimension t within a full space of dimension n. Also, $\mathrm{ADV}_{\Pi_0}^{\mathsf{zk}}$ of the OR-NIZK Π_0 reduces to $\mathcal{D}_k$-MDDH by a factor of 1.

Finally, $\mathcal{D}_{2k,k}$-MDDH reduces to $\mathcal{D}_k$-MDDH by a factor of k by boosting (See Sect. 2.1). Thus the overall reduction in Theorem 2 to $\mathcal{D}_k$-MDDH is $O(\lambda)$.

Proof Intuition. At the highest level, we go through a sequence of games (0–4), starting from Game 0 which is the NIZK simulator of Fig. 2 playing against a USS adversary and ending with Game 4, where the adversary has information theoretically negligible chance of winning. Essentially, in going from Game 2 to Game 3, the γ component is masked with an independently random element which depends on the input word, except for a randomly chosen point τ, where the mask is 0. Then finally in Game 4, the quantity $\mathbf{k}_1$ is shifted by a random vector in the kernel of the language matrix $\mathbf{M}$. This still keeps the CRS unchanged and since the simulated proofs have been masked by independently random elements (except at the point τ which occurs with negligible probability), they are also independent of this random kernel vector. However, the random kernel vector shows up in the winning condition of Game 4 and makes it statistically hard for the adversary to satisfy verification with a non-member word.

---

crsgen $(q, \mathbb{G}_1, \mathbb{G}_2, \mathbb{G}_T, \mathsf{e}, [1]_1, [1]_2, [\mathbf{M}]_1 \in \mathbb{G}_1^{n \times t})$:
Sample $\mathrm{CRS}^0 \leftarrow \Pi_0.\mathsf{crsgen}(q, \mathbb{G}_1, \mathbb{G}_2, \mathbb{G}_T, \mathsf{e}, [1]_1, [1]_2)$.
Boost the given distribution $\mathcal{D}_{k+1,k}$ to $\mathcal{D}_{2k,k}$.
Sample $\mathbf{B} \leftarrow \mathcal{D}_{2k,k}$-MDDH and $(\mathbf{k}_1, \mathbf{k}_2) \leftarrow \mathbb{Z}_q^n \times \mathbb{Z}_q^k$.
Set $\mathbf{p}_1 := \mathbf{M}^\top \mathbf{k}_1$ and $\mathbf{p}_2 := \bar{\mathbf{B}}^\top \mathbf{k}_2$
Sample $(\mathrm{CRS}_p^i, \mathrm{CRS}_v^i) \leftarrow \Pi_i.\mathsf{crsgen}(q, \mathbb{G}_1, \mathbb{G}_2, \mathbb{G}_T, \mathsf{e}, [1]_1, [1]_2, \cdot)$ for $i = 1, 2$, with
parameters described below.

Sample $(\mathsf{pk}_i, \mathsf{sk}_i) \leftarrow \mathsf{PKE.KeyGen}(\mathbb{G}_1)$ for $i = 1, 2$.
Sample $\mathbf{r}_x \leftarrow \mathbb{Z}_q^k$. Set $x := 0$ and $\mathsf{ct}_x := \mathsf{PKE.Enc}(\mathsf{pk}_1, x; \mathbf{r}_x)$.

Set $\mathrm{CRS}_p := (\mathrm{CRS}^0, \mathrm{CRS}_p^1, \mathrm{CRS}_p^2, [\mathbf{B}]_1, [\mathbf{p}_1]_1, [\mathbf{p}_2]_1, \mathsf{pk}_1, \mathsf{pk}_2, \mathsf{ct}_x)$.
Set $\mathrm{CRS}_v := (\mathrm{CRS}^0, \mathrm{CRS}_v^1, \mathrm{CRS}_v^2, [\mathbf{B}]_1, \mathsf{pk}_1, \mathsf{pk}_2, \mathsf{ct}_x)$.

Return $(\mathrm{CRS}_p, \mathrm{CRS}_v)$.

---

prover $(\mathrm{CRS}_p, \mathbf{y} = [\mathbf{Mx}]_1, \mathbf{x})$:
Sample $(\mathbf{r}, \mathbf{r}_z^1, \mathbf{r}_z^2) \leftarrow \mathbb{Z}_q^k \times \mathbb{Z}_q^k \times \mathbb{Z}_q^k$.
Set $\boldsymbol{\rho} := [\bar{\mathbf{B}}\mathbf{r}]_1^\top$, $\hat{\boldsymbol{\rho}} := [\underline{\mathbf{B}}\mathbf{r}]_1^\top$, $\gamma := \mathbf{x}^\top [\mathbf{p}_1]_1 + \mathbf{r}^\top [\mathbf{p}_2]_1$.

Set $z := 0$, $\mathsf{ct}_z^1 := \mathsf{PKE.Enc}(\mathsf{pk}_1, z; \mathbf{r}_z^1)$ and $\mathsf{ct}_z^2 := \mathsf{PKE.Enc}(\mathsf{pk}_2, z; \mathbf{r}_z^2)$.

Set $\pi_0 := \Pi_0.\mathsf{prover}(\mathrm{CRS}^0, (\boldsymbol{\rho}, \hat{\boldsymbol{\rho}}, \mathsf{ct}_z^1 - \mathsf{ct}_x), (\mathbf{r}, 0))$.
Set $\pi_1 := \Pi_1.\mathsf{prover}(\mathrm{CRS}_p^1, (\mathsf{ct}_z^1, \mathsf{ct}_z^2), (0, \mathbf{r}_z^1, \mathbf{r}_z^2))$.
Set $\pi_2 := \Pi_2.\mathsf{prover}(\mathrm{CRS}_p^2, (\mathbf{y}, \boldsymbol{\rho}, \hat{\boldsymbol{\rho}}, \gamma), (\mathbf{x}, \mathbf{r}))$.

Return $\pi := (\boldsymbol{\rho}, \hat{\boldsymbol{\rho}}, \gamma, \mathsf{ct}_z^1, \mathsf{ct}_z^2, \pi_0, \pi_1, \pi_2)$.

---

ver $(\mathrm{CRS}_v, \mathbf{y}, \pi)$:
Check all the NIZK proofs:
$\quad \Pi_0.\mathsf{ver}(\mathrm{CRS}^0, (\boldsymbol{\rho}, \hat{\boldsymbol{\rho}}, \mathsf{ct}_z^1 - \mathsf{ct}_x), \pi_0)$
$\quad$ and $\Pi_1.\mathsf{ver}(\mathrm{CRS}_v^1, (\mathsf{ct}_z^1, \mathsf{ct}_z^2), \pi_1)$
$\quad$ and $\Pi_2.\mathsf{ver}(\mathrm{CRS}_v^2, (\mathbf{y}, \boldsymbol{\rho}, \hat{\boldsymbol{\rho}}, \gamma), \pi_2)$.

Languages:

Π_0 is an OR-NIZK for $L_0 \overset{\text{def}}{=} \{(\boldsymbol{\rho}, \hat{\boldsymbol{\rho}}, \mathsf{ct}) \mid \exists (\mathbf{r}, \mathbf{r}_c) : (\boldsymbol{\rho} = [\bar{\mathbf{B}}\mathbf{r}]_1^\top$ and $\hat{\boldsymbol{\rho}} = [\underline{\mathbf{B}}\mathbf{r}]_1^\top)$ or $\mathsf{ct} = \mathsf{PKE.Enc}(\mathsf{pk}_1, 0; \mathbf{r}_c)\}$. Instantiation is given in Fig. 5.

Π_1 is a QA-NIZK for $L_1 \overset{\text{def}}{=} \{(\mathsf{ct}_z^1, \mathsf{ct}_z^2) \mid \exists (z, \mathbf{r}_z^1, \mathbf{r}_z^2) : \mathsf{ct}_z^1 = \mathsf{PKE.Enc}(\mathsf{pk}_1, z; \mathbf{r}_z^1)$ and $\mathsf{ct}_z^2 = \mathsf{PKE.Enc}(\mathsf{pk}_2, z; \mathbf{r}_z^2)\}$, with parameters $(\mathsf{pk}_1, \mathsf{pk}_2)$. Instantiations as in [JR14,KW15].

Π_2 is a QA-NIZK for $L_2 \overset{\text{def}}{=} \{(\mathbf{y}, \boldsymbol{\rho}, \hat{\boldsymbol{\rho}}, \gamma) \mid \exists (\mathbf{x}, \mathbf{r}) : \mathbf{y} = [\mathbf{Mx}]_1$ and $\boldsymbol{\rho} = [\bar{\mathbf{B}}\mathbf{r}]_1^\top$ and $\hat{\boldsymbol{\rho}} = [\underline{\mathbf{B}}\mathbf{r}]_1^\top$ and $\gamma = \mathbf{x}^\top [\mathbf{p}_1]_1 + \mathbf{r}^\top [\mathbf{p}_2]_1\}$, with parameters $([\mathbf{M}]_1, [\mathbf{B}]_1, [\mathbf{p}_1]_1, [\mathbf{p}_2]_1)$. Instantiations as in [JR14,KW15].

Fig. 1. Tightly-secure USS-QA-NIZK Π.

crssim $(q, \mathbb{G}_1, \mathbb{G}_2, \mathbb{G}_T, \mathsf{e}, [1]_1, [1]_2, [\mathbf{M}]_1 \in \mathbb{G}_1^{n \times t})$:
Sample $\mathrm{CRS}^0 \leftarrow \Pi_0.\mathsf{crsgen}(q, \mathbb{G}_1, \mathbb{G}_2, \mathbb{G}_T, \mathsf{e}, [1]_1, [1]_2)$.
Boost the given distribution $\mathcal{D}_{k+1,k}$ to $\mathcal{D}_{2k,k}$.
Sample $\mathbf{B} \leftarrow \mathcal{D}_{2k,k}$-MDDH and $(\mathbf{k}_1, \mathbf{k}_2) \leftarrow \mathbb{Z}_q^n \times \mathbb{Z}_q^k$.
Set $\mathbf{p}_1 := \mathbf{M}^\top \mathbf{k}_1$ and $\mathbf{p}_2 := \bar{\mathbf{B}}^\top \mathbf{k}_2$
Sample $(\mathrm{CRS}_p^1, \mathrm{CRS}_v^1) \leftarrow \Pi_1.\mathsf{crsgen}(\cdots)$ and $(\mathrm{CRS}_p^2, \mathrm{CRS}_v^2, \mathsf{trap}^2) \leftarrow \Pi_2.\mathsf{crssim}(\cdots)$.

Sample $(\mathsf{pk}_i, \mathsf{sk}_i) \leftarrow \mathsf{PKE.KeyGen}(\mathbb{G}_1)$ for $i = 1, 2$.
Sample $\mathbf{r}_x \leftarrow \mathbb{Z}_q^k$. Set $x := 0$ and $\mathsf{ct}_x := \mathsf{PKE.Enc}(\mathsf{pk}_1, x; \mathbf{r}_x)$.

Set $\mathrm{CRS}_p := (\mathrm{CRS}^0, \mathrm{CRS}_p^1, \mathrm{CRS}_p^2, [\mathbf{B}]_1, [\mathbf{p}_1]_1, [\mathbf{p}_2]_1, \mathsf{pk}_1, \mathsf{pk}_2, \mathsf{ct}_x)$.
Set $\mathrm{CRS}_v := (\mathrm{CRS}^0, \mathrm{CRS}_v^1, \mathrm{CRS}_v^2, [\mathbf{B}]_1, \mathsf{pk}_1, \mathsf{pk}_2, \mathsf{ct}_x)$.
Set $\mathsf{trap} := (\mathbf{k}_1, \mathsf{trap}^2)$

Return $(\mathrm{CRS}_p, \mathrm{CRS}_v, \mathsf{trap})$.

sim $(\mathrm{CRS}_p, \mathsf{trap}, \mathbf{y})$:
Sample $(\mathbf{r}, \mathbf{r}_z^1, \mathbf{r}_z^2) \leftarrow \mathbb{Z}_q^k \times \mathbb{Z}_q^k \times \mathbb{Z}_q^k$.
Set $\boldsymbol{\rho} := [\bar{\mathbf{B}}\mathbf{r}]_1^\top$, $\hat{\boldsymbol{\rho}} := [\underline{\mathbf{B}}\mathbf{r}]_1^\top$, $\gamma := \mathbf{y}^\top \mathbf{k}_1 + \mathbf{r}^\top [\mathbf{p}_2]_1$.

Set $z := 0$, $\mathsf{ct}_z^1 := \mathsf{PKE.Enc}(\mathsf{pk}_1, z; \mathbf{r}_z^1)$ and $\mathsf{ct}_z^2 := \mathsf{PKE.Enc}(\mathsf{pk}_2, z; \mathbf{r}_z^2)$.

Set $\pi_0 := \Pi_0.\mathsf{prover}(\mathrm{CRS}^0, (\boldsymbol{\rho}, \hat{\boldsymbol{\rho}}, \mathsf{ct}_z^1 - \mathsf{ct}_x), (\mathbf{r}, 0))$.
Set $\pi_1 := \Pi_1.\mathsf{prover}(\mathrm{CRS}_p^1, (\mathsf{ct}_z^1, \mathsf{ct}_z^2), (0, \mathbf{r}_z^1, \mathbf{r}_z^2))$.
Set $\pi_2 := \Pi_2.\mathsf{sim}(\mathrm{CRS}_p^2, \mathsf{trap}^2, (\mathbf{y}, \boldsymbol{\rho}, \hat{\boldsymbol{\rho}}, \gamma))$.

Return $\pi := (\boldsymbol{\rho}, \hat{\boldsymbol{\rho}}, \gamma, \mathsf{ct}_z^1, \mathsf{ct}_z^2, \pi_0, \pi_1, \pi_2)$.

Fig. 2. CRS and Proof simulators for Π.

Going from Game 2 to 3 requires another set of hybrid games in which we introduce the mask elements into the γ's. The games proceed bit by bit based on a random bit-string $\mathrm{RP}(\mathbf{y})$ of length L, which is obtained by applying a random injective function RP to the input word $\mathbf{y}$. In every hybrid j, which runs from 0 to L, the mask depends on the first j bits of $\mathrm{RP}(\mathbf{y})$. The mask function is inductively defined as follows:

$$\mathrm{RF}_j(\mathrm{RP}(\mathbf{y})|_j) \stackrel{\text{def}}{=} \begin{cases} \mathrm{RF}_{j-1}(\mathrm{RP}(\mathbf{y})|_{j-1}), & \text{if } (\mathrm{RP}(\mathbf{y}))_j = \tau_j \\ \mathrm{RF}'_{j-1}(\mathrm{RP}(\mathbf{y})|_{j-1}), & \text{if } (\mathrm{RP}(\mathbf{y}))_j \neq \tau_j \end{cases},$$

where RF_j is a random function from $\{0,1\}^j$ to $\mathbb{Z}_q$, except at a point $\tau|_j$, the first j bits of τ, where its value is 0. RF'_{j-1} is another independently random function from $\{0,1\}^{j-1}$ to $\mathbb{Z}_q$. The 0-th hybrids start as Game 2 with the '0' mask, which is the value of $\mathrm{RF}_0(\epsilon)$. The L-th hybrids end in Game 3 with the mask depending on all the bits of $\mathrm{RP}(\mathbf{y})$, hence essentially the whole word.

The adaptive partitioning technique of [Hof17] helps us switching from RF_{j-1} to RF_j with a constant number of MDDH reductions. Essentially, in the j-th hybrid, the j-th bit of $\mathrm{RP}(\mathbf{y})$ induces two partitions of the message space: (1) where the bit is τ_j, soundness is enforced to hold in the winning condition and (2) where the bit is $1 - \tau_j$, all such simulated proofs can be switched in one go with a constant number of MDDH transitions. Formal details follow.

Proof. We go through a sequence of Games $\mathbf{G}_0$ to $\mathbf{G}_4$ which are described below and summarized in Fig. 3. In the following, $\mathrm{Pr}_i[X]$ will denote probability of predicate X holding in probability space defined in game $\mathbf{G}_i$ and WIN_i will denote the winning condition for the adversary in game $\mathbf{G}_i$.

Game $\mathbf{G}_0$: This game exactly replicates the simulator in Fig. 2 to the adversary. So the adversary's advantage in $\mathbf{G}_0$ (defined as WIN_0 below) is the USS advantage we seek to bound.

$$\mathsf{WIN}_0 \stackrel{\triangle}{=} (\mathbf{y}^* \notin \{\mathbf{y}^i\}_i \cup \mathrm{span}([\mathbf{M}]_1)) \text{ and } \mathsf{ver}(\mathrm{CRS}_v, \mathbf{y}^*, \pi^*)$$

Game $\mathbf{G}_0'$: In Game $\mathbf{G}_0'$, the challenger lazily simulates (by maintaining a table) a random function RP from $\mathbb{G}_1^n$ to $\{0,1\}^L$. Define Col to be the predicate which returns true when there is a collision, i.e., when any pair of message vectors from the set of signature queries union the adversarial response message at the end get mapped to the same output L-bit string. In this game, the adversary is allowed to win outright if Col is true at the end:

$$\mathsf{WIN}_0' \stackrel{\triangle}{=} \mathsf{Col} \text{ or } ((\mathbf{y}^* \notin \{\mathbf{y}^i\}_i \cup \mathrm{span}([\mathbf{M}]_1)) \text{ and } \mathsf{ver}(\mathrm{CRS}_v, \mathbf{y}^*, \pi^*))$$

The difference in advantage is at most the collision probability, which is bounded by $(Q+1)^2/q$.

Game $\mathbf{G}_1$: In this game the CRS of Π_2 is generated in the simulation mode and the trapdoor is kept by the challenger to generate simulated proofs. The challenge-response in this game is the same as $\mathbf{G}_0$. The winning condition is now defined as:

$$\mathsf{WIN}_1 \stackrel{\triangle}{=} \mathsf{Col} \text{ or}$$
$$\mathsf{WIN}_0 \text{ and } \pi^* = (\rho^*, \hat{\rho}^*, \gamma^*, \mathsf{ct}_z^{1*}, \mathsf{ct}_z^{2*}, \pi_0^*, \pi_1^*, \pi_2^*) \text{ s.t.}$$
$$(\gamma^* = \mathbf{y}^{*\top}\mathbf{k}_1 + \rho^*\mathbf{k}_2) \text{ and } (\rho^*\|\hat{\rho}^*)^\top \in \mathrm{span}([\mathbf{B}]_1)$$

The difference in advantages of the adversary is upper bounded by the unbounded true-simulation-soundness of Π_2:

$$|\mathrm{Pr}_1[\mathsf{WIN}_1] - \mathrm{Pr}_0[\mathsf{WIN}_0]| \leq \mathrm{ADV}_{\Pi_2}^{\mathsf{tss}} \tag{1}$$

Game $\mathbf{G}_2$: In this game, the OR-NIZK CRS is generated as a simulation CRS and the witness of $(\rho^i, \hat{\rho}^i, \mathsf{ct}_z^{1i} - \mathsf{ct}_x) \in L_0$, is switched to $(\mathbf{0}, \mathbf{r}_z^{1i} - \mathbf{r}_x)$. The winning condition WIN_2 remains the same as WIN_1.

$$|\mathrm{Pr}_2[\mathsf{WIN}_2] - \mathrm{Pr}_1[\mathsf{WIN}_1]| \leq \mathrm{ADV}_{\Pi_0}^{\mathsf{zk}} \tag{2}$$

crssim() : $\cdots$

Games 0-1 $\text{CRS}^0 \leftarrow \Pi_0.\mathsf{crsgen}()$

Games 2-4 $(\text{CRS}^0, \mathsf{trap}^0) \leftarrow \Pi_0.\mathsf{crssim}()$

Game 0 $\text{CRS}^2 \leftarrow \Pi_2.\mathsf{crsgen}()$

Games 1-4 $(\text{CRS}^2, \mathsf{trap}^2) \leftarrow \Pi_2.\mathsf{crssim}()$

Sample $(\mathbf{k}_1', \mathbf{u}) \leftarrow \mathbb{Z}_q^n \times \mathbb{Z}_q^{n-t}$

Games 1-3   Set $\mathbf{k}_1 := \mathbf{k}_1'$

Game 4   Set $\mathbf{k}_1 := \mathbf{k}_1' + \mathbf{M}^\perp \mathbf{u}$

$\cdots$

$\mathsf{sim}(\mathbf{y}^i \in \mathbb{G}_1^n)$:

Set $(\boldsymbol{\rho}^i, \hat{\boldsymbol{\rho}}^i, \gamma^i) :=$

Games 0-2 $([\bar{\mathbf{B}}\mathbf{r}^i]_1^\top, \ [\underline{\mathbf{B}}\mathbf{r}^i]_1^\top, \ \mathbf{y}^{i\top}\mathbf{k}_1 + \boldsymbol{\rho}^i\mathbf{k}_2)$

Game 3 $([\bar{\mathbf{B}}\mathbf{r}^i]_1^\top, \ [\underline{\mathbf{B}}\mathbf{r}^i]_1^\top, \ \mathbf{y}^{i\top}\mathbf{k}_1 + [\mathrm{RF}_L(\nu^i)]_1 + \boldsymbol{\rho}^i\mathbf{k}_2)$

Game 4 $([\bar{\mathbf{B}}\mathbf{r}^i]_1^\top, \ [\underline{\mathbf{B}}\mathbf{r}^i]_1^\top, \ \mathbf{y}^{i\top}\mathbf{k}_1' + \mathbf{y}^{i\top}\mathbf{M}^\perp\mathbf{u} + [\mathrm{RF}_L(\nu^i)]_1 + \boldsymbol{\rho}^i\mathbf{k}_2)$

$\cdots$

$\mathsf{WIN} \overset{\mathrm{def}}{=}$

Games 0'-4   if (CoI) **return true; else**

$\pi^* = (\boldsymbol{\rho}^*, \hat{\boldsymbol{\rho}}^*, \gamma^*, \mathsf{ct}_z^{1*}, \mathsf{ct}_z^{2*}, \pi_0^*, \pi_1^*, \pi_2^*) :$

$(\mathbf{y}^* \notin \{\mathbf{y}^i\}_i \cup \mathrm{span}([\mathbf{M}]_1))$ **and** $\mathsf{ver}(\text{CRS}_v, \mathbf{y}^*, \pi^*)$

Games 1-3   **and** $\gamma^* = \mathbf{y}^{*\top}\mathbf{k}_1 + \boldsymbol{\rho}^*\mathbf{k}_2$

Game 4   **and** $\gamma^* = \mathbf{y}^{*\top}\mathbf{k}_1' + \mathbf{y}^{*\top}\mathbf{M}^\perp\mathbf{u} + \boldsymbol{\rho}^*\mathbf{k}_2$

Games 1-4   **and** $(\boldsymbol{\rho}^*\|\hat{\boldsymbol{\rho}}^*)^\top \in \mathrm{span}([\mathbf{B}]_1)$

Fig. 3. Top level games and winning conditions

Game $\mathbf{G}_3$: In this game, the challenger first chooses a uniformly random string $\tau \in \{0,1\}^L$ and also lazily maintains a function RF_L mapping $\{0,1\}^L$ to $\mathbb{Z}_q$. The function RF_L has the property that it is a random and independent function from $\{0,1\}^L$ to $\mathbb{Z}_q$, except at τ where its value is 0. In $\mathbf{G}_3$, each signature component γ^i is generated as $\mathbf{y}^{i\top}\mathbf{k}_1 + [\mathrm{RF}_L(\mathrm{RP}(\mathbf{y}^i))]_1 + \boldsymbol{\rho}^i\mathbf{k}_2$, instead of $\mathbf{y}^{i\top}\mathbf{k}_1 + \boldsymbol{\rho}^i\mathbf{k}_2$. For ease of exposition, we will denote $\mathrm{RP}(\mathbf{y}^i)$ as ν^i. The winning condition WIN_3 remains the same as WIN_2.

Lemma 1. $|\mathrm{Pr}_3[\mathsf{WIN}_3] - \mathrm{Pr}_2[\mathsf{WIN}_2]| \leq$

$$12L \cdot \mathrm{ADV}^{\mathsf{tss}}_{\Pi_1} + 8L \cdot \mathrm{ADV}_{\mathcal{D}_{2k,k}\text{-MDDH}}$$

$$+12L \cdot \mathrm{ADV}^{\mathsf{zk}}_{\Pi_0} + 4L \cdot \mathrm{ADV}^{\mathsf{mcpa}}_{\mathsf{PKE}} + \frac{6L}{q}$$

We prove this lemma in the full paper by going through a finer set of hybrid games.

Game G_4: In this game, the challenger samples $(\mathbf{k}'_1, \mathbf{u}) \leftarrow \mathbb{Z}^n_q \times \mathbb{Z}^{n-t}_q$, and generates $\mathbf{k}_1$ differently as $\mathbf{k}'_1 + \mathbf{M}^\perp \mathbf{u}$, where $\mathbf{M}^\perp$ is a $\mathbb{Z}^{t \times (n-t)}_q$ matrix such that $\mathbf{M}^\top \mathbf{M}^\perp = \mathbf{0}^{t \times (n-t)}$. Observe that the public key component $[\mathbf{p}]_1$ becomes $[\mathbf{M}^\top \mathbf{k}_1]_1 = [\mathbf{M}^\top \mathbf{k}'_1]_1$. So $\mathbf{u}$ does not show up in the public key.

Consequently, the computations of γ^i's are changed to $\mathbf{y}^{i\top}\mathbf{k}'_1 + \mathbf{y}^{i\top}\mathbf{M}^\perp\mathbf{u} + [\mathrm{RF}_L(\nu^i)]_1 + \rho^i \mathbf{k}_2$. Also, the winning condition check on γ^* is modified accordingly to $\gamma^* = \mathbf{y}^{*\top}\mathbf{k}'_1 + \mathbf{y}^{*\top}\mathbf{M}^\perp\mathbf{u} + \rho^*\mathbf{k}_2$.

We now claim that $\mathrm{Pr}_4[\mathsf{WIN}_4] \leq \frac{1}{q} + \frac{Q}{2^L}$. To see this, recall that RF maps any element of $\{0,1\}^L$ to a uniformly random element of $\mathbb{Z}_q$, except τ, which it maps to 0. Now, if none of the adversary queries is actually mapped to τ by RP, no information about it is leaked to the adversary. The probability that for any i, $\mathrm{RP}(\mathbf{y}^i) = \tau$, is upper bounded by $\frac{Q}{2^L}$.

Now, in the case that $\mathrm{RP}(\mathbf{y}^i)$ is not τ for any i, we have that $\mathrm{RF}(\mathrm{RP}(\mathbf{y}^i))$ is uniformly random and independent of everything else. This means that it completely hides the term $\mathbf{y}^{i\top}\mathbf{M}^\perp\mathbf{u}$ in the γ^i components of the signature responses.

As for the adversary's forged proof, $\mathbf{y}^{*\top}\mathbf{M}^\perp$ is non-zero if $\mathbf{y}^*$ is not in the span of $[\mathbf{M}]_1$. Also, $\mathbf{u}$ is not shown in any public key and as we reasoned in the last paragraph, it doesn't show up (whp) in any signature either. Consequently, $\mathbf{y}^{*\top}\mathbf{M}^\perp\mathbf{u}$ is uniformly random in $\mathbb{Z}_q$ and independent of the adversary's view. Therefore, the probability of satisfying $\gamma^* - \mathbf{y}^{*\top}\mathbf{k}'_1 - \rho^*\mathbf{k}_2 = \mathbf{y}^{*\top}\mathbf{M}^\perp\mathbf{u}$ is upper bounded by $1/q$. This proves the claim.

3.2   USS-QA-NIZK Scheme with $O(\log Q)$ Reduction

The scheme is given in Fig. 4 and the top level proof game table is given in the full paper. Since this scheme is very similar to the one given earlier, we only point out the essential points of difference in the construction and proof.

The scheme uses a similar augmented ElGamal encryption of a basic QA-NIZK proof:

$$\rho := [\bar{\mathbf{B}}\mathbf{r}]^\top_1, \ \hat{\rho} := [\underline{\mathbf{B}}\mathbf{r}]^\top_1, \ \gamma := \mathbf{x}^\top[\mathbf{p}_1]_1 + \mathbf{r}^\top[\mathbf{p}_2 + \tau\mathbf{p}_3]_1$$

The additional part is a tagged component reminiscent of the Cramer-Shoup CCA2 encryption scheme [CS02], where τ is a collision resistant hash on rest of the proof components. Rest of it is fairly similar to the earlier construction. Unfortunately, this construction is no longer structure-preserving due to the tag computation.

To prove $O(\log Q)$ reduction, we follow the partitioning strategy of [GHKP18], where the partition is done on the bits of the query index i, instead of a random function applied to the argument. This strategy did not work for our earlier construction because RF mapped to 0 at one point of it's domain and the proof relied on the fact that such a point is exponentially hard to determine since the domain size is exponential in λ.

In the proof of security of this construction, we take account of the fact that RF could map to 0 at a point which can non-negligibly occur in a query. We instead argue that since the tag of such a query response would be different from the tag of the adversary's output proof, the response can still be randomized due to pairwise independence. A detailed proof will be in the full version of the paper.

Theorem 3. *For any efficient adversary $\mathcal{A}$, which makes at most Q simulator queries before attempting a forged proof, its probability of success ($\mathrm{ADV}^{\mathsf{uss}}_{\Pi'}(Q)$) in the USS game against the scheme Π' is at most (Here L is $\log Q$):*

$$\mathrm{ADV}^{\mathsf{tss}}_{\Pi_2} + 12L \cdot \mathrm{ADV}^{\mathsf{tss}}_{\Pi_1} + 8L \cdot \mathrm{ADV}_{\mathcal{D}_{2k,k}\text{-MDDH}} + (12L+1)\mathrm{ADV}^{\mathsf{zk}}_{\Pi_0}$$

$$+4L \cdot \mathrm{ADV}^{\mathsf{mcpa}}_{\mathsf{PKE}} + \frac{6L + (Q+1)^2 + 1}{q}.$$

3.3 Optimizations

In this section, we describe two optimizations which reduce the size of the proofs further by $2k$ elements under the $\mathcal{D}_k$-MDDH assumption.

ElGamal Encryption with Common Randomness. As described in [AHN+17], the randomnesses $\mathbf{r}^1_z$ and $\mathbf{r}^2_z$ of ciphertexts ct^1_z and ct^2_z can be shared and merged into a single k-element $\mathbf{r}_z$. In more details, let's say $\mathsf{ct}^1_z = ([\bar{\mathbf{A}}_1\mathbf{r}^1_z]_1, [z + \underline{\mathbf{A}}_1\mathbf{r}^1_z]_1)$ and $\mathsf{ct}^2_z = ([\bar{\mathbf{A}}_2\mathbf{r}^2_z]_1, [z + \underline{\mathbf{A}}_2\mathbf{r}^2_z]_1)$, which are encryptions of z under public keys $[\mathbf{A}_1]_1$ and $[\mathbf{A}_2]_1$. Then instead of computing the ciphertexts independently, we can merge them into $([\bar{\mathbf{A}}_1\mathbf{r}_z]_1, [z + \underline{\mathbf{A}}_1\mathbf{r}_z]_1), [z + \underline{\mathbf{A}}_2\mathbf{r}_z]_1)$. This saves us k elements. Importantly, we can still enable transitions where we can hold the decryption key of one system, while switching the plaintext of the other.

Merge QA-NIZKs in the Same Group. The reason we did not combine Π_1 and Π_2 is that we needed to use the true-simulation-soundness of one system, while producing proofs over fake instances with the other. However, we show in the full paper, that we can still merge the proofs into one proof over the combined linear system, and still be independently able to use the true-simulation-soundness of its parts. This saves us k elements from Π.

crsgen $(q, \mathbb{G}_1, \mathbb{G}_2, \mathbb{G}_T, \mathsf{e}, [1]_1, [1]_2, [\mathbf{M}]_1 \in \mathbb{G}_1^{n \times t})$:
   Sample $\text{CRS}^0 \leftarrow \Pi_0.\mathsf{crsgen}()$.
   Boost the given distribution $\mathcal{D}_{k+1,k}$ to $\mathcal{D}_{2k,k}$.
   Sample $\mathbf{B} \leftarrow \mathcal{D}_{2k,k}\text{-MDDH}$ and $(\mathbf{k}_1, \mathbf{k}_2, \mathbf{k}_3) \leftarrow \mathbb{Z}_q^n \times \mathbb{Z}_q^k \times \mathbb{Z}_q^k$.
   Set $\mathbf{p}_1 := \mathbf{M}^\top \mathbf{k}_1$, $\mathbf{p}_2 := \bar{\mathbf{B}}^\top \mathbf{k}_2$ and $\mathbf{p}_3 := \bar{\mathbf{B}}^\top \mathbf{k}_3$.
   Sample $(\text{CRS}_p^i, \text{CRS}_v^i) \leftarrow \Pi_i.\mathsf{crsgen}()$ for $i = 1, 2$.

   Sample $(\mathsf{pk}_i, \mathsf{sk}_i) \leftarrow \mathsf{PKE.KeyGen}(\mathbb{G}_1)$ for $i = 1, 2$.
   Sample $\mathbf{r}_x \leftarrow \mathbb{Z}_q^k$. Set $x := 0$ and $\mathsf{ct}_x := \mathsf{PKE.Enc}(\mathsf{pk}_1, x; \mathbf{r}_x)$.
   Let crh be a collision resistant hash from $\{0, 1\}^*$ to $\mathbb{Z}_q$.

   Set $\text{CRS}_p := (\text{CRS}^0, \text{CRS}_p^1, \text{CRS}_p^2, [\mathbf{B}]_1, [\mathbf{p}_1]_1, [\mathbf{p}_2]_1, \mathsf{pk}_1, \mathsf{pk}_2, \mathsf{ct}_x)$.
   Set $\text{CRS}_v := (\text{CRS}^0, \text{CRS}_v^1, \text{CRS}_v^2, [\mathbf{B}]_1, \mathsf{pk}_1, \mathsf{pk}_2, \mathsf{ct}_x)$.

   Return $(\text{CRS}_p, \text{CRS}_v)$.

prover $(\text{CRS}_p, \mathbf{y} = [\mathbf{Mx}]_1, \mathbf{x}$, label $\mathtt{lbl})$:
   Sample $(\mathbf{r}, \mathbf{r}_z^1, \mathbf{r}_z^2) \leftarrow \mathbb{Z}_q^k \times \mathbb{Z}_q^k \times \mathbb{Z}_q^k$.
   Set $\boldsymbol{\rho} := [\bar{\mathbf{B}}\mathbf{r}]_1^\top$, $\hat{\boldsymbol{\rho}} := [\underline{\mathbf{B}}\mathbf{r}]_1^\top$.

   Set $z := 0$, $\mathsf{ct}_z^1 := \mathsf{PKE.Enc}(\mathsf{pk}_1, z; \mathbf{r}_z^1)$ and $\mathsf{ct}_z^2 := \mathsf{PKE.Enc}(\mathsf{pk}_2, z; \mathbf{r}_z^2)$.

   Set $\pi_0 := \Pi_0.\mathsf{prover}(\text{CRS}^0, (\boldsymbol{\rho}, \hat{\boldsymbol{\rho}}, \mathsf{ct}_z^1 - \mathsf{ct}_x), (\mathbf{r}, 0))$.
   Set $\pi_1 := \Pi_1.\mathsf{prover}(\text{CRS}_p^1, (\mathsf{ct}_z^1, \mathsf{ct}_z^2), (0, \mathbf{r}_z^1, \mathbf{r}_z^2))$.

   Set $\tau := \mathsf{crh}(\boldsymbol{\rho}, \hat{\boldsymbol{\rho}}, \mathsf{ct}_z^1, \mathsf{ct}_z^2, \pi_0, \pi_1, \mathtt{lbl})$.
   Set $\gamma := \mathbf{x}^\top [\mathbf{p}_1]_1 + \mathbf{r}^\top [\mathbf{p}_2 + \tau \mathbf{p}_3]_1$.
   Set $\pi_2 := \Pi_2.\mathsf{prover}(\text{CRS}_p^2, (\mathbf{y}, \boldsymbol{\rho}, \hat{\boldsymbol{\rho}}, \gamma, \mathsf{tag} = \tau), (\mathbf{x}, \mathbf{r}))$.

   Return $\pi := (\boldsymbol{\rho}, \hat{\boldsymbol{\rho}}, \gamma, \mathsf{ct}_z^1, \mathsf{ct}_z^2, \pi_0, \pi_1, \pi_2)$.

ver $(\text{CRS}_v, \mathbf{y}, \pi, \mathtt{lbl})$:
   Set $\tau := \mathsf{crh}(\boldsymbol{\rho}, \hat{\boldsymbol{\rho}}, \mathsf{ct}_z^1, \mathsf{ct}_z^2, \pi_0, \pi_1, \mathtt{lbl})$.
   Check all the NIZK proofs:
       $\Pi_0.\mathsf{ver}(\text{CRS}^0, (\boldsymbol{\rho}, \hat{\boldsymbol{\rho}}, \mathsf{ct}_z^1 - \mathsf{ct}_x), \pi_0)$
       and $\Pi_1.\mathsf{ver}(\text{CRS}_v^1, (\mathsf{ct}_z^1, \mathsf{ct}_z^2), \pi_1)$
       and $\Pi_2.\mathsf{ver}(\text{CRS}_v^2, (\mathbf{y}, \boldsymbol{\rho}, \hat{\boldsymbol{\rho}}, \gamma, \mathsf{tag} = \tau), \pi_2)$.

Languages:

Π_0 is an OR-NIZK for $L_0 \overset{\text{def}}{=} \{(\boldsymbol{\rho}, \hat{\boldsymbol{\rho}}, \mathsf{ct}) \mid \exists (\mathbf{r}, \mathbf{r}_c) : (\boldsymbol{\rho} = [\bar{\mathbf{B}}\mathbf{r}]_1^\top$ and $\hat{\boldsymbol{\rho}} = [\underline{\mathbf{B}}\mathbf{r}]_1^\top)$ or $\mathsf{ct} = \mathsf{PKE.Enc}(\mathsf{pk}_1, 0; \mathbf{r}_c)\}$.

Π_1 is a QA-NIZK for $L_1 \overset{\text{def}}{=} \{(\mathsf{ct}_z^1, \mathsf{ct}_z^2) \mid \exists (z, \mathbf{r}_z^1, \mathbf{r}_z^2) : \mathsf{ct}_z^1 = \mathsf{PKE.Enc}(\mathsf{pk}_1, z; \mathbf{r}_z^1)$ and $\mathsf{ct}_z^2 = \mathsf{PKE.Enc}(\mathsf{pk}_2, z; \mathbf{r}_z^2)\}$, with parameters $(\mathsf{pk}_1, \mathsf{pk}_2)$.

Π_2 is a QA-NIZK for $L_2 \overset{\text{def}}{=} \{(\mathbf{y}, \boldsymbol{\rho}, \hat{\boldsymbol{\rho}}, \gamma, \mathsf{tag} = \tau) \mid \exists (\mathbf{x}, \mathbf{r}) : \mathbf{y} = [\mathbf{Mx}]_1$ and $\boldsymbol{\rho} = [\bar{\mathbf{B}}\mathbf{r}]_1^\top$ and $\hat{\boldsymbol{\rho}} = [\underline{\mathbf{B}}\mathbf{r}]_1$ and $\gamma = \mathbf{x}^\top [\mathbf{p}_1]_1 + \mathbf{r}^\top [\mathbf{p}_2 + \tau \mathbf{p}_3]_1\}$, with parameters $([\mathbf{M}]_1, [\mathbf{B}]_1, [\mathbf{p}_1]_1, [\mathbf{p}_2]_1, [\mathbf{p}]_3)$.

Fig. 4. Labeled Tightly-secure USS-QA-NIZK Π', with $O(\log Q)$ reduction to $\mathcal{D}_k$-MDDH.

In more details, let the combined language be defined by the matrix $\mathbf{M} = \begin{pmatrix} \mathbf{M}_1^{n_1 \times t} \\ \mathbf{M}_2^{n_2 \times t} \end{pmatrix}$, where both n_1 and n_2 are greater than t. What we show is, provided the words corresponding to $[\mathbf{M}_1]_1$ are not faked then even if the words corresponding to $[\mathbf{M}_2]_1$ are faked, true-simulation-soundness holds for the $[\mathbf{M}_1]_1$ components.

4 NIZK for Disjunction of Linear Subspaces

We have critically used an "OR"-NIZK in our USS-QA-NIZK construction. In this section we describe three flavors of OR-NIZKs. The first one is a standard NIZK where both the prover and verifier are public algorithms. The second one is a designated prover system where only the verifier is public - this flavor is useful for signature schemes where the signing key is held private. The final one is a designated verifier system where the prover is public, but the verifier is private - this is useful in public-key encryption schemes where the public encryption algorithm is required to prove consistency, but only the private decryption algorithm needs to check a proof.

4.1 Public CRS Setting

In this section we describe a NIZK proof system for languages of the following type:

$$L^\vee \stackrel{\text{def}}{=} \left\{ \begin{array}{c} ([\mathbf{x}_0]_1, [\mathbf{x}_1]_1) \in \mathbb{G}_1^{n_0} \times \mathbb{G}_1^{n_1} \mid \\ \exists \mathbf{r}_0 \in \mathbb{Z}_q^{t_0} : [\mathbf{x}_0]_1 = [\mathbf{A}_0]_1 \mathbf{r}_0 \text{ or } \exists \mathbf{r}_1 \in \mathbb{Z}_q^{t_1} : [\mathbf{x}_1]_1 = [\mathbf{A}_1]_1 \mathbf{r}_1 \end{array} \right\}$$

The system is described in Fig. 5 and is based on [Ràf15] with syntax based on [GHKP18]. The proofs of completeness, zero-knowledge and soundness are similar to these papers. We only give a sketch below.

The completeness of the system is straightforward. Zero-knowledge is proved by transitioning to a different way of generating the CRS along with a trapdoor. The transition is enabled by the $\mathcal{D}_k$-MDDH assumption on $([\mathbf{D}]_1, [\mathbf{z}]_1)$ and the resulting CRS and proof simulators are also given in the same figure.

We now prove perfect soundness. Since $\mathbf{z}_0 + \mathbf{z}_1 = \mathbf{z} \notin \text{span}(\mathbf{D})$, at least one of $\mathbf{z}_0$ and $\mathbf{z}_1$ should be outside the span of $\mathbf{D}$. WLOG, let this be $\mathbf{z}_0$. Therefore, there should be a vector $\mathbf{d}^\perp \in \mathbb{Z}_q^{k+1}$, such that $\mathbf{D}^\top \mathbf{d}^\perp = \mathbf{0}$ and $\mathbf{z}_0^\top \mathbf{d}^\perp = 1$. Right multiplying this vector to the verification equation $\mathbf{A}_0 \mathbf{C}_0 = \mathbf{P}_0 \mathbf{D}^\top + \mathbf{x}_0 \mathbf{z}_0^\top$ gives us $\mathbf{A}_0 \mathbf{C}_0 \mathbf{d}^\perp = \mathbf{x}_0$. This means $\mathbf{r}_0 \stackrel{\text{def}}{=} \mathbf{C}_0 \mathbf{d}^\perp$ satisfies the disjunct $\mathbf{x}_0 = \mathbf{A}_0 \mathbf{r}_0$.

4.2 Designated Prover Setting

In Fig. 5 we saw an efficient NIZK proof for the "OR" language of Fig. 1, where one of the disjuncts was a predicate on group elements in the CRS of the USS-QA-NIZK, namely that ct_x was a binding commitment to x (using randomness

---

OR Languages :

Let $L^{\vee} \stackrel{\text{def}}{=} \left\{ \begin{array}{c} ([\mathbf{x}_0]_1, [\mathbf{x}_1]_1) \in \mathbb{G}_1^{n_0} \times \mathbb{G}_1^{n_1} \mid \\ \exists \mathbf{r}_0 \in \mathbb{Z}_q^{t_0} : \mathbf{x}_0 = [\mathbf{A}_0 \mathbf{r}_0]_1 \text{ or } \exists \mathbf{r}_1 \in \mathbb{Z}_q^{t_1} : [\mathbf{x}_1]_1 = [\mathbf{A}_1 \mathbf{r}_1]_1 \end{array} \right\}.$

crsgen $(q, \mathbb{G}_1, \mathbb{G}_2, \mathbb{G}_T, e, [1]_1, [1]_2)$:
  Sample $\mathbf{D} \leftarrow \mathcal{D}_k\text{-MDDH}$ and $\mathbf{z} \leftarrow \mathbb{Z}_q^{k+1} \setminus \text{span}(\mathbf{D})$.
  Return CRS $:= ([\mathbf{D}]_2, [\mathbf{z}]_2)$.

prover $(\text{CRS}, ([\mathbf{x}_0]_1, [\mathbf{x}_1]_1), (j, \mathbf{r}_j))$:
  Sample $(\mathbf{v}, \mathbf{S}_0, \mathbf{S}_1) \leftarrow \mathbb{Z}_q^k \times \mathbb{Z}_q^{t_0 \times k} \times \mathbb{Z}_q^{t_1 \times k}$.
  Set $[\mathbf{z}_{1-j}]_2 := [\mathbf{D}]_2 \mathbf{v}$ and $[\mathbf{z}_j]_2 := [\mathbf{z}]_2 - [\mathbf{z}_{1-j}]_2$.
  Set $[\mathbf{C}_j]_2 := \mathbf{S}_j [\mathbf{D}]_2^{\top} + \mathbf{r}_j [\mathbf{z}_j]_2^{\top}$ and $[\mathbf{P}_j]_1 := [\mathbf{A}_j]_1 \mathbf{S}_j$.
  Set $[\mathbf{C}_{1-j}]_2 := \mathbf{S}_{1-j} [\mathbf{D}]_2^{\top}$ and $[\mathbf{P}_{1-j}]_1 := [\mathbf{A}_{1-j}]_1 \mathbf{S}_{1-j} - [\mathbf{x}_j]_1 \mathbf{v}^{\top}$.
  Return $\pi := ([\mathbf{z}_0]_2, [\mathbf{C}_0]_2, [\mathbf{P}_0]_1, [\mathbf{C}_1]_2, [\mathbf{P}_1]_1) \in \mathbb{G}_1^{(n_0+n_1)k} \times \mathbb{G}_2^{(t_0+t_1+1)(k+1)}$.

ver $(\text{CRS}, ([\mathbf{x}_0]_1, [\mathbf{x}_1]_1), \pi)$:
  Set $[\mathbf{z}_1]_2 := [\mathbf{z}]_2 - [\mathbf{z}_0]_2$.
  Check the following equations for all $j \in \{0, 1\}$:
    $e([\mathbf{A}_j]_1, [\mathbf{C}_j]_2) = e([\mathbf{P}_j]_1, [\mathbf{D}]_2^{\top}) \cdot e([\mathbf{x}_j]_1, [\mathbf{z}_j]_2^{\top})$.

crssim $(q, \mathbb{G}_1, \mathbb{G}_2, \mathbb{G}_T, e, [1]_1, [1]_2)$:
  Sample $\mathbf{D} \leftarrow \mathcal{D}_k\text{-MDDH}$ and $\mathbf{u} \leftarrow \mathbb{Z}_q^k$.
  Set $\mathbf{z} := \mathbf{D} \mathbf{u}$
  Return CRS $:= ([\mathbf{D}]_2, [\mathbf{z}]_2)$ and trap $:= \mathbf{u}$.

sim $(\text{CRS}, \text{trap}, ([\mathbf{x}_0]_1, [\mathbf{x}_1]_1))$:
  Sample $(\mathbf{v}, \mathbf{S}_0, \mathbf{S}_1) \leftarrow \mathbb{Z}_q^k \times \mathbb{Z}_q^{t_0 \times k} \times \mathbb{Z}_q^{t_1 \times k}$.
  Set $[\mathbf{z}_0]_2 := [\mathbf{D}]_2 \mathbf{v}$ and $[\mathbf{z}_1]_2 := [\mathbf{z}]_2 - [\mathbf{z}_0]_2$.
  Set $[\mathbf{C}_0]_2 := \mathbf{S}_0 [\mathbf{D}]_2^{\top}$ and $[\mathbf{P}_0]_1 := [\mathbf{A}_0]_1 \mathbf{S}_0 - [\mathbf{x}_0]_1 \mathbf{v}^{\top}$.
  Set $[\mathbf{C}_1]_2 := \mathbf{S}_1 [\mathbf{D}]_2^{\top}$ and $[\mathbf{P}_1]_1 := [\mathbf{A}_1]_1 \mathbf{S}_1 - [\mathbf{x}_1]_1 (\mathbf{u} - \mathbf{v})^{\top}$.
  Return $\pi := ([\mathbf{z}_0]_2, [\mathbf{C}_0]_2, [\mathbf{P}_0]_1, [\mathbf{C}_1]_2, [\mathbf{P}_1]_1)$.

Fig. 5. NIZK for OR languages based on [Ràf15].

r_x). The quantity r_x cannot be made public in this general setting as proving simulation-soundness requires us to hide x from the public. However, in the application of USS-QA-NIZK to build SPS, the quantity r_x can indeed be given to a "designated" prover, i.e. the signer, and the quantity still remains private. In particular, in a forgery attempt, the adversary does not have access to r_x, as the signer is an honest party. In such a situation, i.e. where r_x in the commitment to x is available to the designated prover, we can give an even more efficient

NIZK. For ease of exposition, we will restrict ourselves to the SXDH asymmetric pairings-group setting in this section. The results can easily be generalized to $\mathcal{D}_k$-MDDH setting.

Consider the "OR" language,

$$\mathcal{L} = \left\{ \begin{array}{c} \boldsymbol{\alpha}, \hat{\boldsymbol{\alpha}}, \boldsymbol{x} \mid \exists r, r_x \in \mathbb{Z}_q : \\ (\boldsymbol{\alpha} = r[1]_1 \text{ and } \hat{\boldsymbol{\alpha}} = r[b]_1) \text{ or } \boldsymbol{x} = \text{com}(0; r_x) \end{array} \right\}$$

where $\text{com}(x; r_x)$ is a binding commitment to x using randomness r_x (e.g. a GS-commitment or ElGamal encryption), and $[b]_1$ is public.

It is not difficult to see that the above is implied by the following (i.e. $\mathcal{L}_1 \subseteq \mathcal{L}$)

$$\mathcal{L}_1 = \left\{ \begin{array}{c} \boldsymbol{\alpha}, \hat{\boldsymbol{\alpha}}, \boldsymbol{x} \mid \exists x, r_x, \hat{x} \in \mathbb{Z}_q : \\ \hat{\boldsymbol{\alpha}} \cdot x - [b]_1 \cdot \hat{x} = 0 \text{ and } [1]_1 \cdot \hat{x} - \boldsymbol{\alpha} \cdot x = 0 \text{ and } \boldsymbol{x} = \text{com}(x; r_x) \end{array} \right\}$$

since if $x \neq 0$ in $\mathcal{L}_1$, one can take $r = \hat{x}/x$, and otherwise $\boldsymbol{x}$ is commitment to zero with r_x. Thus soundness of NIZK proof of $\mathcal{L}_1$ implies the tuple is in $\mathcal{L}$.

Now, consider another language $\mathcal{L}_2$,

$$\mathcal{L}_2 = \left\{ \begin{array}{c} \boldsymbol{\alpha}, \hat{\boldsymbol{\alpha}}, \boldsymbol{x} \mid \exists r, x, r_x \in \mathbb{Z}_q : \\ ((\boldsymbol{\alpha} = r[1]_1 \text{ and } \hat{\boldsymbol{\alpha}} = r[b]_1) \text{ or } (x = 0)) \text{ and } \boldsymbol{x} = \text{com}(x; r_x) \end{array} \right\}$$

Thus, in the language the value $\boldsymbol{x}$ is always a commitment to x under r_x. First note that $\mathcal{L}_2$ implies $\mathcal{L}_1$, i.e. $\mathcal{L}_2 \subseteq \mathcal{L}_1$. This is so because if $x = 0$ in $\mathcal{L}_2$, then we just set $\hat{x} = 0$ as well, and if there is a good r, then we set $\hat{x} = r \cdot x$.

Since the "designated" prover always knows x and r_x in the commitment $\boldsymbol{x}$, then if it has an (r, x) which satisfies the "or" part of $\mathcal{L}_2$, it can generate the witnesses required to satisfy membership in $\mathcal{L}_1$ and hence give a valid NIZK proof.

Under the SXDH assumption, $\mathcal{L}_1$ can be proved by using two group elements and in addition two elements for commitment to $\hat{x}$ (and not counting the two for $\boldsymbol{x}$ which is commitment to x) using the technique by Escala and Groth in [EG14]. Namely, the size of π_0 is $(2, 2)$. For this to work, we also need to sample public keys pk_1 of ElGamal encryption (i.e. com) from $\mathbb{G}_2$. Furthermore, pk_1 is taken from CRS^1 (see Fig. 1). We note that this dependency of pk_1 to CRS^1 does not affect the security proof since we can use ciphertext with respect to pk_2 when CRS^1 is set to the simulation mode. We further optimize ct_z^1 and ct_z^2 by applying the common randomness technique from Sect. 3.3. With these modifications, ct_z^1 and ct_z^2 together consist of $(0, 3)$ elements, and proof π_1 is a single element in $\mathbb{G}_2$ (rather than in $\mathbb{G}_1$ in the original construction). Other components, $\rho, \hat{\rho}, \gamma$, and π_2 are unchanged; each of them is represented by a single element in $\mathbb{G}_1$. In total, the proof size will be $(6, 6)$. Under general $\mathcal{D}_k$-MDDH assumption, the optimized proof will consist of $(5k + 1, 4k + 2)$ elements.

Finally we note that in the designated prover setting, the scheme Π_1 can be made $O(\log Q)$-reduction secure, while maintaining its structure-preserving property. Essentially we add an affine constant to γ as done in [JOR18]. In the split-CRS QA-NIZK setting, this constant would only appear in the prover CRS. This still lets the security proof go through as the adversary's view at the final game would be independent of this affine constant.

4.3   Designated Verifier Setting

As the most expensive part (from the size of USS-QA-NIZK perspective and applications) is the size of the "OR"-proof considered in our general construction, we now consider the designated-verifier setting [ES02]. In the designated-verifier setting of a NIZK, the CRS is split into two parts, CRS_p and CRS_v, and only a designated-verifier gets access to CRS_v and the public information is only CRS_p (required by the prover). Alternatively, one can think of designated-verifier NIZKs as hash-proof systems, as the CRS_v is just the secret hash-key, and CRS_p is the projection hash-key – by the fact that hash-proofs can be generated without the witness (but using the secret hash-key), zero-knowledge is automatic; further, soundness is information-theoretic. Since hash-proofs for linear subspace languages are well known [CS98], and we even have hash-proofs for "OR"-languages [ABP15], so we have designated-verifier NIZK proofs for our "OR"-language used in the USS-QA-NIZK construction. Consequently, we have smaller sized (almost) tightly-secure designated-verifier USS-QA-NIZKs.

For this idea to work, we instantiate PKE in $\mathbb{G}_2$ in our construction so that the OR-language consists of relations from both $\mathbb{G}_1$ and $\mathbb{G}_2$. This allows us to use the hash proof system of [ABP15]. The downside of such a construction is that we have more $\mathbb{G}_2$ elements in the proof and the USS-QA-NIZK is itself in the target group $\mathbb{G}_T$, as the construction of [ABP15] generates hashes in the target group. Since these elements require much longer representation we give a more precise estimation. In the original construction of our USS-QA-NIZK with optimizations in Sect. 3.3, a proof consists of $(11, 6)$ elements in the SXDH setting, of which $(3, 6)$ are for proof π_0. In remaining $(8, 0)$ elements, $(4, 0)$ are the ciphertext of PKE and proof π_1. Moving the $(4, 0)$ elements to $\mathbb{G}_2$ and replacing $(3, 6)$ of π_0 with a target group element, the proof size of our designated-verifier USS-QA-NIZK will be $(4, 4)$ source group elements and 1 target group element. Thus it saves $(7, 2)$ elements in exchange of having an extra target group element. Since the target group element is computed from a product of four pairings, it can also be represented by randomized $(4, 4)$ group elements by using the PPE randomization technique of [AFG+16]. However, either representation requires larger space than original $(7, 2)$ elements. Thus, the known approach with [ABP15] does not seem to yield shorter proofs than our original construction in the designated verifier setting.

5   Applications

In this section, we demonstrate that our tightly secure USS-QA-NIZK can be used to develop CCA2-secure public key encryption and structure-preserving signatures (SPS). Besides being (almost) tightly secure under standard matrix assumptions in bilinear groups, these applications have particular advantage over previous constructions. Our CCA2-secure public-key encryption is *publicly verifiable* and our SPS scheme yields the *shortest signatures*. By plugging our CCA2-secure public key encryption and SPS into the generic frameworks of blind signatures [Fis06], group signatures [Gro07], and simulation-sound NIZKs [CCS09] we have blind SPS, group SPS, and simulation-sound Groth-Sahai proofs, all of which have (almost) tight reduction to standard matrix assumptions in bilinear groups and efficiency improvements over known schemes. Details for these plug-in applications are given in the full version of this paper.

5.1   (Almost) Tight CCA2-Secure PKE Scheme

In this section we show that the labelled (enhanced) USS-QANIZK for linearsubspaces can be used to build a publicly verifiable labeled CCA-secure publickey encryption (PKE) scheme (described in Fig. 6) which is (almost) tightlysecure in the multi-user, multi-challenge setting. The security reduction to USS-QANIZK is tight and is independent of the number of decryption-oracle requests of the CCA2 adversary.

KeyGen $(q, \mathbb{G}_1, \mathbb{G}_2, \mathbb{G}_T, \mathsf{e}, [1]_1, [1]_2)$:
  [Boost distribution $\mathcal{D}_{k+1,k}$ to $\mathcal{D}_{2k,k}$.]
  Sample $\mathbf{B} \leftarrow \mathcal{D}_{2k,k}$-MDDH and $\mathbf{k} \leftarrow \mathbb{Z}_q^k$,
  Sample $(\mathrm{CRS}_p, \mathrm{CRS}_v) \leftarrow \Pi'.\mathsf{crsgen}(\langle q, \mathbb{G}_1, \mathbb{G}_2, \mathbb{G}_T, \mathsf{e}, [1]_1, [1]_2 \rangle, [\mathbf{B}]_1)$,
  Set $\mathbf{p} := \bar{\mathbf{B}}^\top \mathbf{k}$, $\mathsf{pk} := (\mathrm{CRS}_p, [\mathbf{B}]_1, [\mathbf{p}]_1)$, $\mathsf{sk} := (\mathrm{CRS}_v, \mathbf{k})$.

  Return $(\mathsf{pk}, \mathsf{sk})$.

Enc $(\mathsf{pk} = (\mathrm{CRS}_p, [\mathbf{B}], [\mathbf{p}]_1), \; M \in \mathbb{G}_1, \; \mathtt{lbl})$:
  Sample $\mathbf{r} \leftarrow \mathbb{Z}_q^k$, and set $\boldsymbol{\rho} := [\bar{\mathbf{B}}\mathbf{r}]_1^\top$, $\hat{\boldsymbol{\rho}} := [\underline{\mathbf{B}}\mathbf{r}]_1^\top$, $\gamma := M + \mathbf{r}^\top [\mathbf{p}]_1$,
  $\pi := \Pi'.\mathsf{prover}(\mathrm{CRS}_p, \langle \boldsymbol{\rho}, \hat{\boldsymbol{\rho}} \rangle, \langle \gamma, \mathtt{lbl} \rangle; \mathbf{r})$.

  Return $\mathtt{ctxt} := (\boldsymbol{\rho}, \hat{\boldsymbol{\rho}}, \gamma, \pi)$.

Dec $(\mathsf{sk} = (\mathrm{CRS}_v, \mathbf{k}), \; \mathtt{ctxt} = (\boldsymbol{\rho}, \hat{\boldsymbol{\rho}}, \gamma, \pi), \; \mathtt{lbl})$:
  If the NIZK proof verification
    $\Pi'.\mathsf{ver}(\mathrm{CRS}_v, \; \langle \boldsymbol{\rho}, \hat{\boldsymbol{\rho}} \rangle, \; \langle \gamma, \mathtt{lbl} \rangle, \; \pi)$
  returns true then return $\gamma - \boldsymbol{\rho}\mathbf{k}$ else return $\bot$.

Language for Π':
  $L \stackrel{\text{def}}{=} \{(\boldsymbol{\rho}, \hat{\boldsymbol{\rho}}) \mid \exists \mathbf{r} : \boldsymbol{\rho} = [\bar{\mathbf{B}}\mathbf{r}]_1^\top \text{ and } \hat{\boldsymbol{\rho}} = [\underline{\mathbf{B}}\mathbf{r}]_1^\top \}$ with parameters $([\mathbf{B}]_1)$.

Fig. 6. CCA2 Public-Key Encryption using labelled (strong) USS-QA-NIZK.

Theorem 4. *Under the $\mathcal{D}_k$-MDDH assumption, and using the labeled USS-QANIZK Π' of Fig. 4, the public-key encryption scheme described in Fig. 6 is (μ, q_e) IND-CCA secure with Adversary's advantage $\mathcal{A}$ upper-bounded by*

$$2 \cdot \mathrm{ADV}_{\Pi'}^{\mathsf{tss}} + 6k \cdot \mathrm{ADV}_{\mathcal{D}_k\text{-MDDH}} + 2 \cdot \mathrm{ADV}_{\Pi'}^{\mathsf{uss}}(q_e) + O(1/q).$$

The proof of this theorem can be found in the full paper.

Remark. The public-key encryption construction in Fig. 6, during encryption, uses randomness $\mathbf{r}$ to construct ρ. Then, it calls USS-QA-NIZK prover in a black-box manner to obtain π. The USS-QANIZK construction itself picks another $\mathbf{s}$ and constructs its own ρ. We remark that in a non-black box construction of tight CCA2-secure public key encryption scheme, i.e. by utilizing the USS-QA-NIZK construction in a non-black fashion, one can use the same $\bar{\mathbf{B}}$ matrix in the PKE construction above and the USS-QANIZK construction, while keeping $\underline{\mathbf{B}}$ matrices sampled randomly and independently. This leads to a savings of k group elements. The proof of the (almost) tight security of this scheme combines the proof given in the full paper with the proof of the USS-QANIZK tight-security (Theorem 2).

5.2   Direct Construction of Tight SPS from Tight USS-QA-NIZK

Recall that unbounded simulation-soundness assures that, after having simulated proofs for any instances of adversary's choice, it is hard for the adversary to find a valid proof for any fresh no-instances. This corresponds to the notion of unforgeability against adaptive chosen message attacks of a signature scheme where no adversary can find a valid signature for any fresh messages after seeing signatures for any chosen messages. Indeed, syntactically, an unbounded simulation-sound NIZK system can be seen as a signature scheme whose key generation, signature generation, and signature verification functions correspond to CRS simulation, proof simulation, and proof verification functions of the NIZK system, respectively. For this translation to work in reality, it is required that the NIZK system allows simulation for any no-instance in a certain set and there exists a collision resistant mapping (ideally injection) from the desired message space for the signature scheme to the set of no-instances. In [AAO18], this intuition is proven formally in a more general setting (allowing errors in correctness, etc). We use the simplest form of their result with adjustment to the syntax of USS-QA-NIZK.

Let $\Pi := (\mathsf{pargen}, \mathsf{crsgen}, \mathsf{prover}, \mathsf{ver}, \mathsf{crssim}, \mathsf{sim})$ be a designated prover USS-QANIZK system for $\mathcal{L} := \mathrm{span}([\mathbf{M}]_1) \subset \mathbb{G}_1^n$ with soundness advantage $\mathsf{Adv}_{\Pi}^{\mathsf{uss}}(A)$. We assume that Π is *perfectly no-instance simulation correct* with respect to $\mathcal{C} := \mathbb{G}_1^n \setminus \mathrm{span}([\mathbf{M}]_1)$ which means that, for any CRS_v and trap generated by $\Pi.\mathsf{crssim}$, $y \in \mathcal{C}$, $\pi \leftarrow \Pi.\mathsf{sim}(\mathsf{trap}, y)$, $1 \leftarrow \Pi.\mathsf{ver}(\mathrm{CRS}_v, y, \pi)$ holds with probability 1.

Let $[\mathbf{M}]_1 \leftarrow \mathbb{G}_1^{n \times t}$ denote a sampling where matrix $\mathbf{M}$ is chosen uniformly with constraint that its upper square sub-matrix is full rank. For message space $\mathcal{M} := \mathbb{G}_1^t$ and $n \geq 2t+1$, we construct a function $H : \mathcal{M} \to \mathcal{C}$ as follows. Choose $\mathbf{c}$ uniformly from $\mathbb{G}_1^{n-t}$. Then define $H(M)$ for $M \in \mathbb{G}_1^t$ as $M||\mathbf{c}$. For any $\mathbf{M}$ and $M \in \mathbb{G}_1^t$, with probability at least $1 - 1/q$ over the choice of $\mathbf{c}$, there exists no x that satisfies $(M||\mathbf{c})^\top = [\mathbf{M}x]_1$. Thus H is an efficiently computable injection from $\mathcal{M}$ to $\mathcal{C}$. Following this idea, we construct a signature scheme as shown in Fig. 7.

Theorem 5. *With the above USS-QA-NIZK system Π, SIG in Fig. 7 is a signature scheme for message space $\mathcal{M} := \mathbb{G}_1^t$. It is tightly unforgeable against*

Common parameters: $\mathsf{par} := (q, \mathbb{G}_1, \mathbb{G}_2, \mathbb{G}_T, \mathsf{e}, [1]_1, [1]_2, [\mathbf{M}]_1 \in \mathbb{G}_1^{n \times t})$.

KeyGen(1^m) :
    $\lambda := (q, \mathbb{G}_1, \mathbb{G}_2, \mathbb{G}_T, \mathsf{e}, [1]_1, [1]_2) \leftarrow \Pi.\mathsf{pargen}(1^m)$
    $[\mathbf{M}]_1 \leftarrow \mathbb{G}_1^{n \times t}$
    $\mathbf{c} \leftarrow \mathbb{G}_1^{n-t}$
    $(\mathrm{CRS}, \mathsf{trap}) \leftarrow \Pi.\mathsf{crssim}(\lambda, [\mathbf{M}]_1)$
    $\mathsf{pk} := (\mathrm{CRS}, \mathbf{c}), \quad \mathsf{sk} := (\mathsf{trap}, \mathbf{c})$
    $\mathsf{return}(\mathsf{pk}, \mathsf{sk})$

Sign(sk, M) :
    $(\mathsf{trap}, \mathbf{c}) \leftarrow \mathsf{sk}$
    $\mathbf{y} := M \| \mathbf{c}$
    $\sigma \leftarrow \Pi.\mathsf{sim}(\mathsf{trap}, y)$
    $\mathsf{return}(\sigma)$

Verify(pk, M, σ) :
    $(\mathrm{CRS}, \mathbf{c}) \leftarrow \mathsf{pk}$
    $\mathbf{y} := M \| \mathbf{c}$
    $b \leftarrow \Pi.\mathsf{ver}(\mathrm{CRS}_v, y, \sigma)$
    $\mathsf{return}(b)$

Fig. 7. Signature scheme SIG for unilateral messages in $\mathbb{G}_1^t$ based on USS-QA-NIZK Π for a linear subspace language.

adaptive chosen message attacks, i.e., for every PPT *adversary* $\mathcal{A}$ *breaking the unforgeability of* SIG *with a chosen message attack with advantage* $\mathsf{Adv}^{\mathsf{cma}}_{\mathsf{SIG}}(\mathcal{A})$, *there exists a* PPT *algorithm* $\mathcal{B}$ *that breaks the unbounded simulation soundness of* Π *with advantage* $\mathsf{Adv}^{\mathsf{uss}}_{\Pi}(\mathcal{B}) \geq \mathsf{Adv}^{\mathsf{cma}}_{\mathsf{SIG}}(\mathcal{A}) - 1/q$ *and almost the same running time as* $\mathcal{A}$. *Furthermore, if* Π *is structure preserving, so is* SIG.

Proof. To show unforgeability, we construct $\mathcal{B}$ using $\mathcal{A}$ as black-box as follows. Given CRS, $[\mathbf{M}]_1$, $\mathcal{B}$ picks $c \leftarrow \mathbb{G}_1^{n-t}$ and send $\mathsf{pk} := (\mathrm{CRS}, \mathbf{c})$ to $\mathcal{A}$. For message M queried from $\mathcal{A}$, $\mathcal{B}$ sends $\mathbf{y} := M \| \mathbf{c}$ to its oracle, receives a simulated proof π, and returns $\sigma := \pi$ to $\mathcal{A}$. Given a forgery M^*, σ_* from $\mathcal{A}$, $\mathcal{B}$ outputs $\mathbf{y}^* := M^* \| \mathbf{c}$ and $\pi^* := \sigma^*$. Since $H(M) := M \| \mathbf{c}$ is an injection to $\mathbb{G}_1^n \backslash \mathsf{span}([\mathbf{M}]_1)$ with probability at least $1 - 1/q$, $\mathbf{y}^*$ is a fresh instance not in $\mathsf{span}([\mathbf{M}]_1)$, and $(\mathbf{y}^*, \pi^*)$ passes the verification whenever $\mathcal{A}$ succeeds. Hence we have $\mathsf{Adv}^{\mathsf{uss}}_{\Pi}(\mathcal{B}) \geq \mathsf{Adv}^{\mathsf{cma}}_{\mathsf{SIG}}(\mathcal{A}) - 1/q$. Running time of $\mathcal{B}$ is the same as $\mathcal{A}$ except for performing concatenation and parsing. Structure-preserving property is obvious from the construction.

We remark that we can remove the negligible $1/q$ term in the above bound in an enhanced model [LPJY15, JR13] where $\mathbf{M}$ is given to the adversary playing the simulation soundness game.

In Fig. 8 we present an instantiation of SIG in Fig. 7 using our optimized designated prover USS-QA-NIZK from Sect. 4.2 under the SXDH assumption. Designated prover is sufficient in this application as the signing key is private. The signature size is exactly the same as the proof size of the underlying USS-QA-NIZK and it retains structure preserving property. Hence the signature scheme in Fig. 8 is an SPS scheme having signatures consisting of $(6, 6)$ elements for unilateral messages. (Under $\mathcal{D}_k$-MDDH assumption, the signature size will be $(5k+1, 4k+2)$). For bilateral messages $(M_1, M_2) \in \mathbb{G}_1^{t_1} \times \mathbb{G}_2^{t_2}$ where $t_1 = t - 1$,

Common parameters: $\mathsf{par} := (q, \mathbb{G}_1, \mathbb{G}_2, \mathbb{G}_T, \mathsf{e}, [1]_1, [1]_2, [\mathbf{M}]_1 \in \mathbb{G}_1^{n \times t})$.

KeyGen(par):
    Sample $\mathrm{CRS}^0 \leftarrow \varPi_0.\mathsf{crsgen}(q, \mathbb{G}_1, \mathbb{G}_2, \mathbb{G}_T, \mathsf{e}, [1]_1, [1]_2)$,
$(\mathrm{CRS}_p^1, \mathrm{CRS}_v^1) \leftarrow \varPi_1.\mathsf{crsgen}(\mathsf{par})$, and $(\mathrm{CRS}_p^2, \mathrm{CRS}_v^2, \mathsf{trap}^2) \leftarrow \varPi_2.\mathsf{crssim}(\mathsf{par})$.
    Let $([u_1]_2, [u_2]_2, [u_3]_2)$ denote elements of $\mathbb{G}_2$ in CRS^0.
    Set $\mathsf{pk}_1 := [u_3]_2$ and $\mathsf{sk}_1 := u_3$.
    Sample $\mathsf{sk}_2 \leftarrow \mathbb{Z}_q$ and set $\mathsf{pk}_2 := [\mathsf{sk}_2]_2$.
    Sample $\mathbf{B} \leftarrow \mathcal{D}_{2,1}\text{-MDDH}$ and $(\mathbf{k}_1, \mathbf{k}_2) \leftarrow \mathbb{Z}_q^n \times \mathbb{Z}_q$.
    Set $\mathbf{p}_1 := \mathbf{M}^\top \mathbf{k}_1$ and $\mathbf{p}_2 := \bar{\mathbf{B}}^\top \mathbf{k}_2$

    Sample $\mathsf{r}_x \leftarrow \mathbb{Z}_q$. Set $x := 0$, $R_x := [\mathsf{r}_x]_2$, and $E_x := [x]_2 + \mathsf{r}_x \, \mathsf{pk}_1$.

    Set $\mathrm{CRS}_p := (\mathrm{CRS}^0, \mathrm{CRS}_p^1, \mathrm{CRS}_p^2, [\mathbf{B}]_1, [\mathbf{p}_1]_1, [\mathbf{p}_2]_1, \mathsf{pk}_1, \mathsf{pk}_2, E_x, R_x)$.
    Set $\mathrm{CRS}_v := (\mathrm{CRS}^0, \mathrm{CRS}_v^1, \mathrm{CRS}_v^2, [\mathbf{B}]_1, \mathsf{pk}_1, \mathsf{pk}_2, E_x, R_x)$.
    Set $\mathsf{trap} := (\mathbf{k}_1, \mathsf{trap}^2)$.

    Set $\mathbf{c} \leftarrow \mathbb{G}_1^{n-t}$.

    Set $\mathsf{pk} := (\mathrm{CRS}_v, \mathbf{c})$, $\mathsf{sk} := (\mathrm{CRS}_p, \mathsf{trap}, \mathbf{c})$.
    Return $(\mathsf{pk}, \mathsf{sk})$.

Sign($\mathsf{sk}, M \in \mathbb{G}_1^t$):
    Parse $(\mathsf{trap}, \mathbf{c}) \leftarrow \mathsf{sk}$, and set $\mathbf{y} := M \| \mathbf{c}$.

    Sample $(\mathsf{r}, \mathsf{r}_z) \leftarrow \mathbb{Z}_q \times \mathbb{Z}_q$.
    Set $\rho := [\bar{\mathbf{B}}\mathsf{r}]_1^\top$, $\hat{\rho} := [\underline{\mathbf{B}}\mathsf{r}]_1^\top$, $\gamma := \mathbf{y}^\top \mathbf{k}_1 + \mathsf{r}^\top [\mathbf{p}_2]_1$.

    Set $z := 0$. Compute $R_z := [\mathsf{r}_z]_2$.
    Compute $E_z^i := [z]_2 + \mathsf{r}_z \, \mathsf{pk}_i$ for $i = 1, 2$.
    Set $E_\delta := E_z^1 - E_x$, $R_\delta := R_z - R_x$, $\mathsf{r}_\delta := \mathsf{r}_x - \mathsf{r}_z$.

    Set $\pi_0 := \varPi_0.\mathsf{prover}(\mathrm{CRS}^0, (\rho, \hat{\rho}, E_\delta, R_\delta), (x, \mathsf{r}_\delta, \hat{x}))$.
    Set $\pi_1 := \varPi_1.\mathsf{prover}(\mathrm{CRS}_p^1, (E_z^1, E_z^2, R_z), (0, \mathsf{r}_z))$.
    Set $\pi_2 := \varPi_2.\mathsf{sim}(\mathrm{CRS}_p^2, \mathsf{trap}^2, (\mathbf{y}, \rho, \hat{\rho}, \gamma))$.

    Return $\sigma := (\rho, \hat{\rho}, \gamma, E_z^1, E_z^2, R_z, \pi_0, \pi_1, \pi_2)$.

Verify(pk, M, σ):
    Parse $(\mathrm{CRS}, \mathbf{c}) \leftarrow \mathsf{pk}$, and set $\mathbf{y} := M \| \mathbf{c}$.
    Parse $(\rho, \hat{\rho}, \gamma, E_z^1, E_z^2, R_z, \pi_0, \pi_1, \pi_2) \leftarrow \sigma$.

    Check all the NIZK proofs:
        $\varPi_0.\mathsf{ver}(\mathrm{CRS}^0, (\rho, \hat{\rho}, E_\delta, R_\delta), \pi_0)$
        and $\varPi_1.\mathsf{ver}(\mathrm{CRS}_v^1, (E_z^1, E_z^2, R_z), \pi_1)$
        and $\varPi_2.\mathsf{ver}(\mathrm{CRS}_v^2, (\mathbf{y}, \rho, \hat{\rho}, \gamma), \pi_2)$.

Languages:

$\varPi_0$ is a NIZK proof for OR-language $L_0 \overset{\text{def}}{=} \{(\rho, \hat{\rho}, E_\delta, R_\delta) \mid \exists x, \mathsf{r}_\delta, \hat{x} \in \mathbb{Z}_q : x \hat{\rho} - \hat{x} [\mathbf{B}]_1 = [0]_1$ **and** $\hat{x} [1]_1 - x \rho = [0]_1$ **and** $(E_\delta, R_\delta) = \mathrm{com}_2(x; \mathsf{r}_\delta)\}$ by Escala-Groth proof system for multi scalar multiplication equations.

$\varPi_1$ is a QA-NIZK for linear language $L_1 \overset{\text{def}}{=} \{(E_z^1, E_z^2, R_z) \mid \exists(z, \mathsf{r}_z) : E_z^1 := [z]_2 + \mathsf{r}_z \, \mathsf{pk}_1$ **and** $E_z^2 := [z]_2 + \mathsf{r}_z \, \mathsf{pk}_2\}$ with parameters $(\mathsf{pk}_1, \mathsf{pk}_2)$.

$\varPi_2$ is a QA-NIZK for linear language $L_2 \overset{\text{def}}{=} \{(\mathbf{y}, \rho, \hat{\rho}, \gamma) \mid \exists(\mathbf{x}, \mathsf{r}) : \mathbf{y} = [\mathbf{M}\mathbf{x}]_1$ **and** $\rho = [\bar{\mathbf{B}}\mathsf{r}]_1^\top$ **and** $\hat{\rho} = [\underline{\mathbf{B}}\mathsf{r}]_1^\top$ **and** $\gamma = \mathbf{x}^\top [\mathbf{p}_1]_1 + \mathsf{r}^\top [\mathbf{p}_2]_1\}$ with parameters $([\mathbf{M}]_1, [\mathbf{B}]_1, [\mathbf{p}_1]_1, [\mathbf{p}_2]_1)$.

Fig. 8. An SPS constructed directly by using the customized USS-QA-NIZK with designated prover (in Sect. 4.2) with optimizations from Sect. 3.3.

we follow a generic construction in [ACD+16, Sect. 6.3] that combines partially one-time signature for a part of messages in $\mathbb{G}_2$. It requires extra $(0, t_2)$ public-key elements, and the signature size increases by $(1, 2)$ elements sacrificing one group element in the message space $\mathbb{G}_1^{t_1}$. A signature thus consists of $(7, 8)$ elements for a bilateral message.

Acknowledgments. We thank the anonymous reviewers for detailed and insightful feedback on the paper. We especially thank Carla Ràfols for her significant effort in helping us revise the paper.

References

[ABP15] Abdalla, M., Benhamouda, F., Pointcheval, D.: Disjunctions for hash proof systems: new constructions and applications. In: Oswald, E., Fischlin, M. (eds.) EUROCRYPT 2015, Part II. LNCS, vol. 9057, pp. 69–100. Springer, Heidelberg (2015). https://doi.org/10.1007/978-3-662-46803-6_3

[ACD+12] Abe, M., Chase, M., David, B., Kohlweiss, M., Nishimaki, R., Ohkubo, M.: Constant-size structure-preserving signatures: generic constructions and simple assumptions. In: Wang, X., Sako, K. (eds.) ASIACRYPT 2012. LNCS, vol. 7658, pp. 4–24. Springer, Heidelberg (2012). https://doi.org/10.1007/978-3-642-34961-4_3

[ADKNO13] Abe, M., David, B., Kohlweiss, M., Nishimaki, R., Ohkubo, M.: Tagged one-time signatures: tight security and optimal tag size. In: Kurosawa, K., Hanaoka, G. (eds.) Public-Key Cryptography – PKC 2013. PKC 2013. LNCS, vol. 7778. Springer, Heidelberg (2013). https://doi.org/10.1007/978-3-642-36362-7_20

[ACD+16] Abe, M., Chase, M., David, B., Kohlweiss, M., Nishimaki, R., Ohkubo, M.: Constant-size structure-preserving signatures: generic constructions and simple assumptions. J. Cryptol. **29**(4), 833–878 (2016)

[AFG+10] Abe, M., Fuchsbauer, G., Groth, J., Haralambiev, K., Ohkubo, M.: Structure-preserving signatures and commitments to group elements. In: Rabin, T. (ed.) CRYPTO 2010. LNCS, vol. 6223, pp. 209–236. Springer, Heidelberg (2010). https://doi.org/10.1007/978-3-642-14623-7_12

[AFG+16] Abe, M., Fuchsbauer, G., Groth, J., Haralambiev, K., Ohkubo, M.: Structure-preserving signatures and commitments to group elements. J. Cryptol. **29**(2), 363–421 (2016)

[AHN+17] Abe, M., Hofheinz, D., Nishimaki, R., Ohkubo, M., Pan, J.: Compact structure-preserving signatures with almost tight security. In: Katz, J., Shacham, H. (eds.) CRYPTO 2017, Part II. LNCS, vol. 10402, pp. 548–580. Springer, Cham (2017). https://doi.org/10.1007/978-3-319-63715-0_19

[AHO10] Abe, M., Haralambiev, K., Ohkubo, M.: Signing on elements in bilinear groups for modular protocol design. Cryptology ePrint Archive, Report 2010/133 (2010). http://eprint.iacr.org/2010/133

[AAO18] Abe, M., Ambrona, M., Ohkubo, M.: Impossibility of Black-Box Language Extension, and Signatures from SS-NIZK for any Language (2018, Unpublished manuscript)

[AO09a] Abe, M., Ohkubo, M.: A framework for universally composable non-committing blind signatures. In: Matsui, M. (ed.) ASIACRYPT 2009. LNCS, vol. 5912, pp. 435–450. Springer, Heidelberg (2009). https://doi.org/10.1007/978-3-642-10366-7_26

[AO09b] Abe, M., Ohkubo, M.: A framework for universally composable non-committing blind signatures. Cryptology ePrint Archive, Report 2009/494 (2009). http://eprint.iacr.org/2009/494

[BBM00] Bellare, M., Boldyreva, A., Micali, S.: Public-key encryption in a multi-user setting: security proofs and improvements. In: Preneel, B. (ed.) EUROCRYPT 2000. LNCS, vol. 1807, pp. 259–274. Springer, Heidelberg (2000). https://doi.org/10.1007/3-540-45539-6_18

[BBS04] Boneh, D., Boyen, X., Shacham, H.: Short group signatures. In: Franklin, M. (ed.) CRYPTO 2004. LNCS, vol. 3152, pp. 41–55. Springer, Heidelberg (2004). https://doi.org/10.1007/978-3-540-28628-8_3

[CCS09] Camenisch, J., Chandran, N., Shoup, V.: A public key encryption scheme secure against key dependent chosen plaintext and adaptive chosen ciphertext attacks. In: Joux, A. (ed.) EUROCRYPT 2009. LNCS, vol. 5479, pp. 351–368. Springer, Heidelberg (2009). https://doi.org/10.1007/978-3-642-01001-9_20

[CLY09] Cathalo, J., Libert, B., Yung, M.: Group encryption: non-interactive realization in the standard model. In: Matsui, M. (ed.) ASIACRYPT 2009. LNCS, vol. 5912, pp. 179–196. Springer, Heidelberg (2009). https://doi.org/10.1007/978-3-642-10366-7_11

[CS98] Cramer, R., Shoup, V.: A practical public key cryptosystem provably secure against adaptive chosen ciphertext attack. In: Krawczyk, H. (ed.) CRYPTO 1998. LNCS, vol. 1462, pp. 13–25. Springer, Heidelberg (1998). https://doi.org/10.1007/BFb0055717

[CS02] Cramer, R., Shoup, V.: Universal hash proofs and a paradigm for adaptive chosen ciphertext secure public-key encryption. In: Knudsen, L.R. (ed.) EUROCRYPT 2002. LNCS, vol. 2332, pp. 45–64. Springer, Heidelberg (2002). https://doi.org/10.1007/3-540-46035-7_4

[CW13] Chen, J., Wee, H.: Fully, (almost) tightly secure IBE and dual system groups. In: Canetti, R., Garay, J.A. (eds.) CRYPTO 2013, Part II. LNCS, vol. 8043, pp. 435–460. Springer, Heidelberg (2013). https://doi.org/10.1007/978-3-642-40084-1_25

[EHK+13] Escala, A., Herold, G., Kiltz, E., Ràfols, C., Villar, J.: An algebraic framework for Diffie-Hellman assumptions. In: Canetti, R., Garay, J.A. (eds.) CRYPTO 2013, Part II. LNCS, vol. 8043, pp. 129–147. Springer, Heidelberg (2013). https://doi.org/10.1007/978-3-642-40084-1_8

[ElG84] ElGamal, T.: A public key cryptosystem and a signature scheme based on discrete logarithms. In: Blakley, G.R., Chaum, D. (eds.) CRYPTO 1984. LNCS, vol. 196, pp. 10–18. Springer, Heidelberg (1985). https://doi.org/10.1007/3-540-39568-7_2

[ES02] Elkind, E., Sahai, A.: A unified methodology for constructing public-key encryption schemes secure against adaptive chosen-ciphertext attack. Cryptology ePrint Archive, Report 2002/042 (2002). http://eprint.iacr.org/2002/042

[Fis06] Fischlin, M.: Round-optimal composable blind signatures in the common reference string model. In: Dwork, C. (ed.) CRYPTO 2006. LNCS, vol. 4117, pp. 60–77. Springer, Heidelberg (2006). https://doi.org/10.1007/11818175_4

[FLM11] Fischlin, M., Libert, B., Manulis, M.: Non-interactive and re-usable universally composable string commitments with adaptive security. In: Lee, D.H., Wang, X. (eds.) ASIACRYPT 2011. LNCS, vol. 7073, pp. 468–485. Springer, Heidelberg (2011). https://doi.org/10.1007/978-3-642-25385-0_25

[Fuc09] Fuchsbauer, G.: Automorphic signatures in bilinear groups and an application to round-optimal blind signatures. Cryptology ePrint Archive, Report 2009/320 (2009). http://eprint.iacr.org/2009/320

[GHKP18] Gay, R., Hofheinz, D., Kohl, L., Pan, J.: More efficient (almost) tightly secure structure-preserving signatures. In: Nielsen, J.B., Rijmen, V. (eds.) EUROCRYPT 2018, Part II. LNCS, vol. 10821, pp. 230–258. Springer, Cham (2018). https://doi.org/10.1007/978-3-319-78375-8_8

[GHKW16] Gay, R., Hofheinz, D., Kiltz, E., Wee, H.: Tightly CCA-secure encryption without pairings. In: Fischlin, M., Coron, J.-S. (eds.) EUROCRYPT 2016, Part I. LNCS, vol. 9665, pp. 1–27. Springer, Heidelberg (2016). https://doi.org/10.1007/978-3-662-49890-3_1

[GHK17] Gay, R., Hofheinz, D., Kohl, L.: Kurosawa-Desmedt meets tight security. In: Katz, J., Shacham, H. (eds.) CRYPTO 2017, Part III. LNCS, vol. 10403, pp. 133–160. Springer, Cham (2017). https://doi.org/10.1007/978-3-319-63697-9_5

[Gro07] Groth, J.: Fully anonymous group signatures without random oracles. In: Kurosawa, K. (ed.) ASIACRYPT 2007. LNCS, vol. 4833, pp. 164–180. Springer, Heidelberg (2007). https://doi.org/10.1007/978-3-540-76900-2_10

[GS12] Groth, J., Sahai, A.: Efficient non-interactive proof systems for bilinear groups. SIAM J. Comput. 41(5), 1193–1232 (2012)

[Har11] Haralambiev, K.: Efficient cryptographic primitives for non-interactive zero-knowledge proofs and applications. Ph.D. thesis, New York University (2011)

[HJ16] Hofheinz, D., Jager, T.: Tightly secure signatures and public-key encryption. Des. Codes Cryptogr. 80(1), 29–61 (2016)

[Hof17] Hofheinz, D.: Adaptive partitioning. In: Coron, J.-S., Nielsen, J.B. (eds.) EUROCRYPT 2017, Part III. LNCS, vol. 10212, pp. 489–518. Springer, Cham (2017). https://doi.org/10.1007/978-3-319-56617-7_17

[JOR18] Jutla, C.S., Ohkubo, M., Roy, A.: Improved (almost) tightly-secure structure-preserving signatures. In: Abdalla, M., Dahab, R. (eds.) PKC 2018, Part II. LNCS, vol. 10770, pp. 123–152. Springer, Cham (2018). https://doi.org/10.1007/978-3-319-76581-5_5

[JR13] Jutla, C.S., Roy, A.: Shorter quasi-adaptive NIZK proofs for linear subspaces. In: Sako, K., Sarkar, P. (eds.) ASIACRYPT 2013, Part I. LNCS, vol. 8269, pp. 1–20. Springer, Heidelberg (2013). https://doi.org/10.1007/978-3-642-42033-7_1

[JR14] Jutla, C.S., Roy, A.: Switching lemma for bilinear tests and constant-size NIZK proofs for linear subspaces. In: Garay, J.A., Gennaro, R. (eds.) CRYPTO 2014, Part II. LNCS, vol. 8617, pp. 295–312. Springer, Heidelberg (2014). https://doi.org/10.1007/978-3-662-44381-1_17

[JR15] Jutla, C.S., Roy, A.: Dual-system simulation-soundness with applications to UC-PAKE and more. In: Iwata, T., Cheon, J.H. (eds.) ASIACRYPT 2015, Part I. LNCS, vol. 9452, pp. 630–655. Springer, Heidelberg (2015). https://doi.org/10.1007/978-3-662-48797-6_26

[JR16] Jutla, C., Roy, A.: Smooth NIZK arguments with applications to asymmetric UC-PAKE. Cryptology ePrint Archive, Report 2016/233 (2016). http://eprint.iacr.org/2016/233

[JR17] Jutla, C.S., Roy, A.: Improved structure preserving signatures under standard bilinear assumptions. In: Fehr, S. (ed.) PKC 2017, Part II. LNCS, vol. 10175, pp. 183–209. Springer, Heidelberg (2017). https://doi.org/10.1007/978-3-662-54388-7_7

[KPW15] Kiltz, E., Pan, J., Wee, H.: Structure-preserving signatures from standard assumptions, revisited. In: Gennaro, R., Robshaw, M. (eds.) CRYPTO 2015, Part II. LNCS, vol. 9216, pp. 275–295. Springer, Heidelberg (2015). https://doi.org/10.1007/978-3-662-48000-7_14

[KW15] Kiltz, E., Wee, H.: Quasi-adaptive NIZK for linear subspaces revisited. In: Oswald, E., Fischlin, M. (eds.) EUROCRYPT 2015, Part II. LNCS, vol. 9057, pp. 101–128. Springer, Heidelberg (2015). https://doi.org/10.1007/978-3-662-46803-6_4

[LPJY14] Libert, B., Peters, T., Joye, M., Yung, M.: Non-malleability from malleability: simulation-sound quasi-adaptive NIZK proofs and CCA2-secure encryption from homomorphic signatures. In: Nguyen, P.Q., Oswald, E. (eds.) EUROCRYPT 2014. LNCS, vol. 8441, pp. 514–532. Springer, Heidelberg (2014). https://doi.org/10.1007/978-3-642-55220-5_29

[LPJY15] Libert, B., Peters, T., Joye, M., Yung, M.: Compactly hiding linear spans. In: Iwata, T., Cheon, J.H. (eds.) ASIACRYPT 2015, Part I. LNCS, vol. 9452, pp. 681–707. Springer, Heidelberg (2015). https://doi.org/10.1007/978-3-662-48797-6_28

[LPY15] Libert, B., Peters, T., Yung, M.: Short group signatures via structure-preserving signatures: standard model security from simple assumptions. In: Gennaro, R., Robshaw, M. (eds.) CRYPTO 2015, Part II. LNCS, vol. 9216, pp. 296–316. Springer, Heidelberg (2015). https://doi.org/10.1007/978-3-662-48000-7_15

[Ràf15] Ràfols, C.: Stretching Groth-Sahai: NIZK proofs of partial satisfiability. In: Dodis, Y., Nielsen, J.B. (eds.) TCC 2015, Part II. LNCS, vol. 9015, pp. 247–276. Springer, Heidelberg (2015). https://doi.org/10.1007/978-3-662-46497-7_10

[Wat09] Waters, B.: Dual system encryption: realizing fully secure IBE and HIBE under simple assumptions. In: Halevi, S. (ed.) CRYPTO 2009. LNCS, vol. 5677, pp. 619–636. Springer, Heidelberg (2009). https://doi.org/10.1007/978-3-642-03356-8_36

[EG14] Escala, A., Groth, J.: Fine-tuning Groth-Sahai proofs. In: Krawczyk, H. (ed.) PKC 2014. LNCS, vol. 8383, pp. 630–649. Springer, Heidelberg (2014). https://doi.org/10.1007/978-3-642-54631-0_36

Author Index